T0414313

The Cambridge Handbook of Anxiety and Related Disorders

This handbook surveys existing descriptive and experimental approaches to the study of anxiety and related disorders, emphasizing the provision of empirically guided suggestions for treatment. Based upon the findings from the Diagnostic and Statistical Manual of Mental Disorders (DSM-5), the chapters collected here highlight contemporary approaches to the classification, presentation, etiology, assessment, and treatment of anxiety and related disorders. The collection also considers a biologically informed framework for the understanding mental disorders proposed by the National Institute of Mental Health's Research Domain Criteria (RDoC). The RDoC has begun to create a new kind of taxonomy for mental disorders by bringing the power of modern research approaches in genetics, neuroscience, and behavioral science to the problem of mental illness. The framework is a key focus for this book as an authoritative reference for researchers and clinicians.

BUNMI O. OLATUNJI, PH.D., is a professor in the Department of Psychology and Psychiatry at Vanderbilt University, USA, where he also serves as the Director of Clinical Training. He is Associate Editor of the *Journal of Consulting and Clinical Psychology*.

The Cambridge Handbook of Anxiety and Related Disorders

Edited by

Bunmi O. Olatunji
Vanderbilt University

CAMBRIDGE
UNIVERSITY PRESS

University Printing House, Cambridge CB2 8BS, United Kingdom

One Liberty Plaza, 20th Floor, New York, NY 10006, USA

477 Williamstown Road, Port Melbourne, VIC 3207, Australia

314–321, 3rd Floor, Plot 3, Splendor Forum, Jasola District Centre,
New Delhi – 110025, India

79 Anson Road, #06–04/06, Singapore 079906

Cambridge University Press is part of the University of Cambridge.

It furthers the University's mission by disseminating knowledge in the pursuit of
education, learning, and research at the highest international levels of excellence.

www.cambridge.org
Information on this title: www.cambridge.org/9781107193062
DOI: 10.1017/9781108140416

First published 2019

Printed in the United Kingdom by TJ International Ltd. Padstow Cornwall

A catalogue record for this publication is available from the British Library.

Library of Congress Cataloging-in-Publication Data
Names: Olatunji, Bunmi O., editor.
Title: The Cambridge handbook of anxiety and related disorders / edited by Bunmi
Olatunji, Vanderbilt University, Tennessee.
Description: Cambridge, United Kingdom ; New York, NY, USA : University Printing
House, 2019. | Includes bibliographical references.
Identifiers: LCCN 2018024059 | ISBN 9781107193062
Subjects: LCSH: Anxiety – Handbooks, manuals, etc. | Anxiety disorders – Handbooks,
manuals, etc.
Classification: LCC RC531 .C355 2019 | DDC 616.85/22–dc23
LC record available at https://lccn.loc.gov/2018024059

ISBN 978-1-107-19306-2 Hardback

To Eun Ha, Aiden, and Mitchell for all the inspiration that I will ever need

Contents

Contributors

JONATHAN S. ABRAMOWITZ, University of North Carolina at Chapel Hill, Department of Psychology and Neuroscience

BRIAN ALBANESE, Florida State University, Department of Psychology

Nicholas Allan, Ohio University, Department of Psychology

Emma Baldock, King's College London, Department of Psychology

MIRANDA L. BELTZER, University of Virginia, Department of Psychology

DAVID M. BENEDEK, Uniformed Services University, Department of Psychiatry

ERIN C. BERENZ, University of Illinois at Chicago, Department of Psychology

YANNICK BODDEZ, University of Groningen, Department of Clinical Psychology and Experimental Psychopathology, Katholieke Univeriteit (KU) Leuven, Center for the Psychology of Learning and Experimental Psychopathology

KATHERINE BUCHHOLZ, National Center for PTSD

SIMONE BUDZYN, University of Pennsylvania, School of Medicine

ERIC BUI, Massachusetts General Hospital, Harvard Medical School

TIMOTHY A. BROWN, Boston University, Department of Psychology

RACHEL M. BUTLER, Temple University, Department of Psychology

R. NICHOLAS CARLETON, University of Regina, Department of Psychology

JOSEPH K. CARPENTER, Boston University, Department of Psychology

PETER J. CASTAGNA, Louisiana State University, Department of Psychology

KRISTINA CONROY, Boston University, Department of Psychology

KELLY CORREA, University of Illinois at Chicago, Department of Psychology

REBECCA COX, Department of Psychology, Vanderbilt University

THOMPSON E. DAVIS III, Louisiana State University, Department of Psychology

RACHELE DILIBERTO, University of Nevada, Las Vegas, Department of Psychology

ANDREW R. EISEN, Fairleigh Dickinson University, School of Psychology

ZOE FEINGOLD, National Center for PTSD

KATYA C. FERNANDEZ, Stanford University, Department of Psychology

MARTIN E. FRANKLIN, University of Pennsylvania, School of Medicine

HOLLY FREEMAN, University of the Sciences in Philadelphia

TARA E. GALOVSKI, National Center for PTSD

ANDREW GERTHOFFER, University of Nevada, Las Vegas, Department of Psychology

FALLON R. GOODMAN, George Mason University, Department of Psychology

JAMES J. GROSS, Stanford University, Department of Psychology

RICHARD G. HEIMBERG, Temple University, Department of Psychology

DIRK HERMANS, Katholieke Univeriteit (KU) Leuven, Center for the Psychology of Learning and Experimental Psychopathology

DEVON HINTON, Massachusetts General Hospital, Harvard Medical School

STEFAN G. HOFMANN, Boston University, Department of Psychology

ARIELLE HORENSTEIN, Temple University, Department of Psychology

AMANDA HOWARD, University of Nevada at Las Vegas, Department of Psychology

TODD B. KASHDAN, George Mason University, Department of Psychology

CHRISTOPHER A. KEARNEY, University of Nevada at Las Vegas, Department of Psychology

ANDREW M. KISELICA, University of South Florida, Department of Psychology

SARAH E. KLEIMAN, VA Boston Healthcare System

KELLY A. KNOWLES, Vanderbilt University, Department of Psychology

ERNST H. W. KOSTER, Ghent University, Department of Experimental Clinical and Health Psychology

LUCAS S. LAFRENIERE, Pennsylvania State University, Department of Psychology

MARIA A. LARRAZABAL, George Mason University, Department of Psychology

DANIEL J. LEE, National Center for PTSD, VA Boston Healthcare System, Boston University School of Medicine

CARL LEJUEZ, University of Kansas, Department of Psychology

WEN LI, Florida State University, Department of Psychology

CHRISTINE LOCHNER, Stellenbosch University, Department of Psychiatry

PETER M. MCEVOY, Curtin University, School of Psychology and Speech Pathology, Centre for Clinical Interventions, Perth

JOSHUA C. MORGANSTEIN, Uniformed Services University, Department of Psychiatry

AMANDA S. MORRISON, California State University at East Bay, Department of Psychology

PETER MURIS, Maastricht University, Department of Clinical Psychological Science

MARIE NEBEL-SCHWALM, Illinois Wesleyan University, Department of Psychology

MICHELLE G. NEWMAN, Pennsylvania State University, Department of Psychology

BUNMI O. OLATUNJI, Vanderbilt University, Department of Psychology

LANCE M. RAPPAPORT, Commonwealth University, Department of Psychology

SHEILA A. M. RAUCH, Emory University, Department of Psychiatry and Behavioral Sciences

KIMBERLY RENK, University of Central Florida, Department of Psychology

LILLIAN REUMAN, University of North Carolina at Chapel Hill, Department of Psychology and Neuroscience

ROXANN ROBERSON-NAY, Commonwealth University, Department of Psychology

ANTHONY J. ROSELLINI, Boston University, Department of Psychological and Brain Sciences

SARA SCHEVENEELS, Katholieke Univeriteit (KU) Leuven, Center for the Psychology of Learning and Experimental Psychopathology

NORMAN B. SCHMIDT, Florida State University, Department of Psychology

STEWART A. SHANKMAN, University of Illinois at Chicago, Department of Psychology

ANDREW M. SHERRILL, Emory University, School of Medicine

SARAH SHIHATA, Curtin University, School of Psychology and Speech Pathology

KI EUN SHIN, Pennsylvania State University, Department of Psychology

NICOLE SHORT, Florida State University, Department of Psychology

KRISTEN S. SPRINGER, The Institute of Living

IAN STANLEY, Florida State University, Department of Psychology

DAN J. STEIN, University of Cape Town, Department of Psychiatry and Mental Health

ERIC A. STORCH, University of South Florida, Department of Psychology, Rogers Behavioral Health – Tampa Bay, Johns Hopkins All Children's Hospital

BETHANY A. TEACHMAN, University of Virginia, Department of Psychology

KRISTIN L. TOFFEY, Fairleigh Dickinson University, School of Psychology

DAVID F. TOLIN, The Institute of Living, Yale University School of Medicine

ESTHER S. TUNG, Boston University, Department of Psychology

ROBERT J. URSANO, Uniformed Services University, Department of Psychiatry

ANOUK VANDEN BOGAERDE, Ghent University, Department of Experimental Clinical and Health Psychology

DAVID VEALE, King's College London, Department of Psychology

DAVID WATSON, University of Notre Dame, Department of Psychology

FRANK W. WEATHERS, Auburn University, Department of Psychology

ALEXANDRA J. WERNTZ, University of Virginia, Department of Psychology

JOHN T. WEST, George Mason University, Department of Psychology

BLAISE L. WORDEN, The Institute of Living

GARY H. WYNN, Uniformed Services University, Department of Psychiatry

SUZANNE YANG, Uniformed Services University, Department of Psychiatry; Henry M. Jackson Foundation for the Advancement of Military Medicine

Research does suggest that treatment for anxiety disorders is often not sought until adulthood (Christiana et al., 2000), indicating several years of untreated symptoms in many individuals with these disorders. This delay between typical age of onset and treatment may contribute to findings that suggest anxiety disorders are generally chronic (Bruce et al., 2005). Prospective research indicates that the majority of anxiety disorders persist over 12 years, with a lower probability of recovery compared to major depressive disorder (Bruce et al., 2005). Recurrence is also highly likely (Scholten et al., 2013), particularly among those with comorbid conditions (Bruce et al., 2005). Further, daily functioning remains diminished in those who remit from an anxiety disorder compared to controls (Iancu et al., 2014). This is notable, given that functional impairment, along with anxiety sensitivity, predicts anxiety disorder recurrence (Scholten et al., 2013).

Anxiety disorders are further complicated by high rates of comorbidity, as approximately 90% of those with an anxiety disorder have a history of additional psychopathology (Kaufman & Charney, 2000. Indeed, half of those with one anxiety disorder meet criteria for another (Kaufman & Charney, 2000). Further, anxiety disorders commonly co-occur with other psychological conditions, including mood disorders, substance use disorders (Kessler et al., 2005a), and eating disorders (Kaye, Bulik, Thornton, Barbarich, & Masters, 2004). Notably, anxiety disorders often precede the development of these disorders (Goodwin & Stein, 2013; Rojo-Moreno et al., 2015; Wittchen, Kessler, Pfister, & Lieb, 2000), suggesting that treating the anxiety disorder may result in improvement in the comorbid condition.

Anxiety disorders also often co-occur with medical conditions. Indeed, anxiety disorders are uniquely associated with medical disorders over and above the effects of mood and substance use disorders (Sareen, Cox, Clara, & Asmundson, 2005a), and this pattern of comorbidity is associated with increased illness severity (Katon, Lin, & Kroenke, 2007). Though anxiety disorders co-occur with a wide range of medical conditions, illnesses characterized by pain are particularly common in those with an anxiety disorder (Harter, Conway, & Merikangas, 2003; Sareen et al., 2005a). Further, reductions in health-related anxiety are associated with improvements in pain conditions (McCracken, Gross, & Eccleston, 2002; Spinhoven, Van der Does, Van Dijk, & Van Rood, 2010), suggesting the utility of targeting anxiety comorbid with medical conditions.

Furthering our understanding of anxiety and related disorders can also save lives, as anxiety disorders are linked to suicidal ideation and attempts, even after adjusting for psychiatric comorbidity, in both cross-sectional (Cougle, Keough, Riccardi, & Sachs-Ericsson, 2008; Nepon, Belik, Bolton, & Sareen, 2010; Sareen et al., 2005b) and longitudinal samples (Sareen et al., 2005b). Further, one study found that among individuals with a history of suicidality, 70% met criteria for an anxiety disorder (Nepon et al., 2010). A similar relationship is also evident among adolescents with anxiety disorders, with increased rates of suicide associated with increased number of anxiety disorders (Boden, Fergusson, & Horwood, 2007). Although the available literature clearly shows that a preexisting anxiety disorder is an independent risk factor for suicidality and that comorbid anxiety amplifies the risk of suicide attempts among those with mood disorders, the psychobiological processes that may explain this effect remain unclear.

Current understanding of the psychobiological processes associated with anxiety has resulted in significant changes in the diagnostic classification of anxiety disorders in recent years. In the modern classification system, the Diagnostic and Statistical Manual of Mental Disorders (DSM), classes of disorders are clustered around shared phenomenological features, with the defining features of anxiety disorders being symptoms of anxiety and avoidance behavior (APA, 1987). Since the introduction of diagnostic classes in DSM-III (APA, 1980), the anxiety disorders class has consistently included panic disorder with/without agoraphobia, specific phobias, social phobia, GAD, obsessive-compulsive disorder (OCD), and posttraumatic stress disorder (PTSD). However, DSM-5 has represented a notable departure from this standard, such that OCD and PTSD have been removed from the anxiety disorders and placed within two newly created classes, obsessive-compulsive and related disorders and trauma- and stressor-related disorders, respectively (APA, 2013).

These changes have proved controversial. The obsessive-compulsive and related disorders class was introduced on the assertion that OCD is phenomenologically and biologically distinct from anxiety disorders (Stein et al., 2010). For example, proponents of the obsessive-compulsive and related disorders class suggest that the distinguishing phenomenon of OCD is not anxiety, but repetitive behaviors and emphasize the unique neural profile of hyperactivity in the fronto-striatal loop in OCD (Stein et al., 2010). In contrast, critics of this approach argue that the one of the primary features of OCD is anxiety in response to obsessions and that efforts to adapt classification systems based on findings from neuroimaging research are premature (Abramowitz & Jacoby, 2014). Likewise, while proponents of the changes to PTSD in DSM-5 have praised the addition of symptoms to the diagnostic criteria (Kilpatrick, 2013), others have argued that the new criteria result in excessive heterogeneity (Galatzer-Levy & Bryant, 2013).

Such controversies highlight the limitations inherent to categorical diagnostic approaches. The utility of the diagnostic criteria defined by the DSM is to guide differential diagnosis and selection of treatment and provide a common language for practitioners (APA, 2013). Though the categorical diagnoses contained in the DSM framework arguably imply true distinctions between disorders that represent unique etiologies, DSM-5 notes that such a classification system may not fully account for the various complexities of mental illness (APA, 2013). Indeed, critics of the categorical approach have argued that the excessive rates of comorbidity suggest shared etiology among multiple disorders that the categorical approach would classify as distinct (Widiger & Samuel, 2005). For example, high comorbidity between GAD and depression may reflect shared genetic diatheses and overlap of core phenotypic processes, such as negative affect (Mineka, Watson, & Clark, 1998).

Likewise, the necessity of "black-and-white" boundaries between disorders in a categorical system has contributed to a proliferation of new disorders designed to bridge the gap between extant disorders, a practice that may reflect artificial cutoffs of dimensional domains (Widiger & Samuel, 2005). This practice is seen in the addition of acute stress disorder to DSM-IV to identify pathological stress responses that surpass adjustment disorder but do not meet the minimum duration required for PTSD (Marshall, Spitzer, & Liebowitz, 1999). In contrast, a dimensional framework is arguably a better representation of complex phenotypes that are unlikely to derive from singular etiologies. In addition to addressing the issues of comorbidity and arbitrary distinctions, a dimensional framework also allows for quantitative descriptions of severity and treatment progress and lends itself to empirical elucidation of physiological underpinnings of observable symptoms (Helzer, Kraemer, & Krueger, 2006).

Research has shown that the severity, duration of anxiety, and disability are able to better identify severe chronic course trajectory as compared with DSM-IV categories (Batelaan, Rhebergen, Spinhoven, Van Balkom, & Penninx, 2014). Findings of this sort suggest that a targeted focus on cross-cutting dimensions may explain more variance in anxiety-related processes than diagnostic categories. The purported benefits of such a dimensional approach to psychopathology has led in part to the development of the National Institute of Mental Health (NIH) Research Domain Criteria (RDoC). The RDoC outlines a framework in which five core domains relevant for psychopathology (Negative Valence Systems, Positive Valence Systems, Cognitive Systems, Social Processes, Arousal and Regulatory Systems) can be measured and described at multiple levels ranging from genes to self-report (Insel et al., 2010). RDoC represents a major departure from the categorical diagnoses of the DSM in a push toward defining mental illness by dysfunction along transdiagnostic dimensions. Importantly, in addition to taking a step toward a dimensional diagnostic system, RDoC also asserts that mental illnesses are "brain disorders" that can be understood and measured in terms of dysfunction at genetic and molecular levels (Insel et al., 2010).

The RDoC perspective has been highly debated, particularly among cognitive and behaviorally oriented psychological scientists (Deacon, 2013). The veracity of this perspective remains to be seen, as clinical neuroscience is in its relative infancy. Likewise, the RDoC's impact on the future of anxiety and related disorders research is unclear. Though neurobiology has been critical for delineating certain mechanisms of anxiety-related pathology, such as fear conditioning (Lissek, 2012), there is concern that behavioral or verbal indices are undervalued in a brain disorders framework. Given that an important goal of the RDoC approach is to inform the development of novel, circuit-based interventions and the personalization of treatments available, it will be vital to examine the extent to which this approach complements existing empirically supported models of anxiety and related disorders.

Treatments of anxiety and related disorders have largely centered on two modalities: psychotropic medications and cognitive behavior therapy (CBT). While a variety of psychotropic medications have been utilized for the treatment of anxiety and related disorders, selective serotonin reuptake inhibitors (SSRIs) and serotonin-norepinephrine reuptake inhibitors (SNRIs) are the current first-line pharmacological agents due to both efficacy and tolerability (Ravindran & Stein, 2010). CBT for anxiety and related disorders generally includes intervention strategies aimed at reducing maladaptive beliefs (e.g., cognitive restructuring) and behavioral avoidance (e.g., exposure) (Hofmann & Smits, 2008). Considerable research has found CBT to be efficacious for the treatment of anxiety and related disorders (Hofmann & Smits, 2008; Olatunji, Cisler, & Deacon, 2010). Extant research comparing CBT to psychotropic medications indicates comparable efficacy, while evidence for an additive effect of combination treatments (i.e., CBT + medication) is mixed (Bandelow, Seidler-Brandler, Becker, Wedekind, & Ruther, 2007). However, CBT treatment gains are generally sustained over one to two years (Butler, Chapman, Forman, & Beck, 2006), whereas medication effects are generally lost upon discontinuation (see Otto, Smits, & Reese, 2005, for a review). Despite the established efficacy of CBT, a substantial proportion of patients do not respond to CBT or relapse, and a paucity of research examines outcomes beyond two years (Arch & Craske, 2009). These findings highlight major areas for improvement to the current "gold standard" of psychotherapy. Paradigm shifts in research, such as the dimensional approach and emphasis on neurobiology espoused by RDoC, may yield novel treatment targets or personalized medicine insights to increase treatment efficacy and decrease nonresponse and relapse.

Overview of This Book

Much remains unknown about the etiology, maintenance, and treatment of anxiety and related disorders. This volume aims to bridge this gap in knowledge with a focus on the divide between current classification systems and approaches to anxiety and related disorders in a rapidly changing field. This book integrates many levels of information to better explain the basic dimensions of functioning underlying anxiety and related disorders. First, Section 1 outlines basic mechanisms of anxiety. Consistent with a dimensional perspective, Section 1 describes the effects of basic processes of learning, perception, and attention on fear and anxiety. For example, how might learning mechanisms that underlie fear conditioning contribute to clinical fear and anxiety? Can the threat processing that underlies anxiety and its disorders be modeled at the level of sensory perception? Consistent with the RDoC research framework, Section 1 examines basic dimensions of functioning that span the full range of human behavior from normal to abnormal. Section 2 then describes various transdiagnostic processes that may confer risk for the development of anxiety and related disorders. Transdiagnostic processes reflect common psychological *processes* that underlie clinical syndromes. Section 2 highlights that rather than focusing on discrete diagnostic entities, the co-occurrence of many diagnoses likely reflects different patterns of symptoms that result from shared risk factors and the same underlying processes.

Section 3 of this volume covers assessment, diagnosis, and cultural manifestations of anxiety and related disorders. DSM-5 represents a significant departure in traditional conceptualizations of disorders that fall in the anxiety disorder category. Section 3 highlights these changes as well as their implications for research and practice. Sections 4–6 discuss the etiology and phenomenology of specific anxiety disorders, OCD spectrum disorders, and trauma- and stressor-related disorders. A common theme for Sections 4–6 is a critical analysis of contemporary models of the development of the various disorders that is informed by basic science. Furthermore, this part of the volume examines the potential implications for the RDoC research framework in advancing current knowledge regarding the etiology of anxiety and related disorders. Last, Section 7 examines the treatment and prevention of anxiety and related disorders. This portion of the volume identifies which treatments are most effective for anxiety and related disorders and why. In addition to a survey of existing descriptive and experimental approaches to the study of anxiety and related disorders, an important goal of this book is empirically guided suggestions for the treatment of anxiety and related disorders.

References

Abramowitz, J. S. & Jacoby, R.J. (2014). Obsessive-compulsive disorder in the *DSM-5*. *Clinical Psychology Science and Practice*, *21*, 221–235.

American Psychiatric Association. (1980). *Diagnostic and statistical manual of mental disorders* (3rd edn). Washington, DC: American Psychiatric Association.

American Psychiatric Association. (1987). *Diagnostic and statistical manual of mental disorders* (3rd edn, rev.). Washington, DC: American Psychiatric Association.

American Psychiatric Association. (2000). *Diagnostic and statistical manual of mental disorders* (4th edn). Washington, DC: American Psychiatric Association.

American Psychiatric Association. (2013). *Diagnostic and statistical manual of mental disorders* (5th edn). Washington, DC: American Psychiatric Association.

Arch, J. J. & Craske, M. G. (2009). First-line treatment: A critical appraisal of cognitive behavioral therapy developments and alternatives. *Psychiatric Clinics of North America*, *32*, 525–547. http://dx.doi.org/10.1016/j.psc.2009.05.001

Bandelow, B., Seidler-Brandler, U., Becker, A., Wedekind, D., & Ruther, E. (2007). Meta-analysis of randomized controlled comparisons of psychopharmacological and psychological treatments for anxiety disorders. *World Journal of Biological Psychiatry*, *8*, 175–187. http://dx.doi.org/10.1080/15622970601110273

Batelaan, N. M., Rhebergen, D., Spinhoven, P., Van Balkom, A. J., & Penninx, B. W. (2014). Two-year course trajectories of anxiety disorders: Do DSM classifications matter? *Journal of Clinical Psychiatry*, *75*, 985–993. http://dx.doi.org/10.4088/JCP .13m08837

Baxter, A. J., Vos, T., Scott, K. M., Ferrari, A. J., & Whiteford, H. A. (2010). The global burden of anxiety disorders in 2010. *Psychological Medicine*, *44*, 2363–2374. http://dx.doi.org/10.1017/S0033291713003243

Boden, J. M., Fergusson, D. M., & Horwood, L. J. (2007). Anxiety disorders and suicidal behaviours in adolescence and young adulthood: Findings from a longitudinal study. *Psychological Medicine*, 37, 431–440. http://dx.doi.org/10.1017/S0033291706009147

Bruce, S. E., Yonkers, K. A., Otto, M. W., Eisen, J. L., Weisberg, R. B., Pagano, M., . . . Keller, M. B. (2005). Influence of psychiatric comorbidity on recovery and recurrence in generalized anxiety disorder, social phobia, and panic disorder: A 12-year prospective study. *American Journal of Psychiatry*, *162*, 1179–1187. http://dx.doi.org/10.1176/appi.ajp.162.6.1179

Butler, A. C., Chapman, J. E., Forman, E. M., & Beck, A. T. (2006). The empirical status of cognitive-behavioral therapy: A review of meta-analyses. *Clinical Psychology Review*, *26*, 17–31. http://dx.doi.org/10.1016/j.cpr.2005.07.003

Christiana, J. M., Gilman, S. E., Guardino, M., Mickelson, K., Morselli, P. L., Olfson, M., & Kessler, R. C. (2000). Duration between onset and time of obtaining initial treatment among people with anxiety and mood disorders: An international survey of members of mental health patient advocate groups. *Psychological Medicine*, *30*, 693–703.

Costello, E. J., Mustillo, S., Erkanli, A., Keeler, G., & Angold, A. (2003). Prevalence and development of psychiatric disorders in childhood and adolescence. *Archives of General Psychiatry*, *60*, 837–844.

Cougle, J. R., Keough, M. E., Riccardi, C. J., & Sachs-Ericsson, N. (2008). Anxiety disorders and suicidality in the National Comorbidity Survey-Replication. *Journal of Psychiatric Research*, *43*, 825–829. http://dx.doi.org/10.1016/j.jpsychires.2008.12.004

Deacon, B. J. (2013). The biomedical model of mental disorder: A critical analysis of its validity, utility, and effects on psychotherapy research. *Clinical Psychology Review*, *33*, 846–861. http://dx.doi.org/10.1016/j.cpr.2012.09.007

Galatzer-Levy, I. R. & Bryant, R. A. (2013). 636,120 ways to have posttraumatic stress disorder. *Perspectives on Psychological Science*, *8*, 651–662. http://dx.doi.org/10.1177/1745691613504115

Greenberg, P. E., Sisitsky, T., Kessler, R. C., Finkelstein, S. N., Berndt, E. R., . . . Fyer, A. J. (1999). The economic burden of anxiety disorders in the 1990s. *Journal of Clinical Psychiatry*, *60*, 427–435.

Goodwin, R. D. & Stein, D. J. (2013). Anxiety disorders and drug dependence: Evidence on sequence and specificity among adults. *Psychiatry and Clinical Neurosciences*, *67*, 167–173. http://dx.doi.org/10.1111/pcn.12030

Harter, M. C., Conway, K. P., & Merikangas, K. R. (2003). Associations between anxiety disorders and physical illness. *European Archives of Psychiatry and Clinical Neuroscience*, *253*, 313–320. http://dx.doi.org/10.1007/s00406-003-0449-y

Helzer, J. E., Kraemer, H. C., & Krueger, R. F. (2006). The feasibility and need for dimensional psychiatric diagnoses. *Psychological Medicine*, *36*, 1671–1680. http://dx.doi.org/10.1017/S003329170600821X

Hendriks, S. M., Spijker, J., Licht, C. M. M., Beekman, A. T. F., Hardeveld, F., de Graaf, R., . . . Penninx, B. W. J. H. (2014). Disability in anxiety disorders.

Journal of Affective Disorders, 166, 227–233. http://dx.doi.org/10.1016/j.jad
.2014.05.006

Hofmann, S. G. & Smits, J. A. J. (2008). Cognitive-behavioral therapy for adult anxiety
disorders: A meta-analysis of randomized placebo-controlled trials. *Journal of
Clinical Psychiatry, 69,* 621–632.

Iancu, S. C., Batelaan, N. M., Zweekhorst, M. B. M., Bunders, J. F. G., Veltman, D. J.,
Penninx, B. W. J. H., & Van Balkom, A. J. L. M. (2014). Trajectories of function-
ing after remission from anxiety disorders: 2-year course and outcome predictors.
Psychological Medicine, 44, 593–605. http://dx.doi.org/10.1017
/S0033291713001050

Insel, T., Cuthbert, B., Garvey, M., Heinssen, R., Pine, D.S., Quinn, K., . . . Wang, P. (2010).
Research Domain Criteria (RDoC): Toward a new classification framework for
research on mental disorders. *American Journal of Psychiatry, 167,* 748–751.
http://dx.doi.org/10.1176/appi.ajp.2010.09091379

Katon, W., Lin, E. H. B., & Kroenke, K. (2007). The association of depression and anxiety
with medical symptom burden in patients with chronic medical illness. *General
Hospital Psychiatry, 29,* 147–155. http://dx.doi.org/10.1016/j.genhosppsych.2006
.11.005

Kaufman, J. & Charney, D. (2000). Comorbidity of mood and anxiety disorders. *Depression
and Anxiety* 12, 69–76.

Kaye, W. H., Bulik, C. M., Thornton, L., Barbarich, N., & Masters, K. (2004). Comorbidity
of anxiety disorders with anorexia and bulimia nervosa. *American Journal of
Psychiatry, 161,* 2215–2221.

Kessler, R. C., Berglund, P., Demler, O., Jin, R., Merikangas, K. R., & Walters, E. E.
(2005b). Lifetime prevalence and age-of-onset distributions of *DSM-IV* disorders
in the National Comorbidity Survey Replication. *Archives of General Psychiatry,
62,* 593–602.

Kessler, R. C., Chiu, W. T., Demler, O., & Walters, E. E. (2005a). Prevalence, severity, and
comorbidity of 12-month *DSM-IV* disorders in the National Comorbidity Survey
Replication. *Archives of General Psychiatry, 62,* 617–627.

Kilpatrick, D. G. (2013). The *DSM-5* got PTSD right: Comment on Friedman (2013).
Journal of Traumatic Stress, 26, 563–566. http://dx.doi.org/10.1002/jts.21844

Lissek, S. (2012). Toward an account of clinical anxiety predicated on basic, neutrally
mapped mechanisms of Pavlovian fear-learning: The case for conditioned
overgeneralization. *Depression and Anxiety, 29,* 257–263. http://dx.doi.org/10
.1002/da.21922

Marshall, R. D., Spitzer, R., & Liebowitz, M. R. (1999). Review and critique of the new
DSM-IV diagnosis of acute stress disorder. *American Journal of Psychiatry, 156,*
1677–1685.

McCracken, L. M., Gross, R. T., & Eccleston, C. (2002). Multimethod assessment of
treatment process in chronic low back pain: Comparison of reported pain-related
anxiety with directly measured physical capacity. *Behaviour Research and
Therapy, 40,* 585–594.

Mendlowicz, M. V. & Stein, M. B. (2000). Quality of life in individuals with anxiety
disorders. *American Journal of Psychiatry, 157,* 669–682.

Mineka, S., Watson, D., & Clark, L. A. (1998). Comorbidity of anxiety and unipolar mood
disorders. *Annual Review of Psychology, 49,* 377–412.

Nail, J. E., Christofferson, J., Ginsburg, G. S., Drake, K., Kendall, P. C., McCracken, J. T., . . . Sakolsky, D. (2015). Academic impairment and impact of treatments among youth with anxiety disorders. *Child Youth Care Forum*, *44*, 327–342. http://dx.doi.org/10.1007/s10566-014-9290-x

Nepon, J., Belik, S. L., Bolton, J., & Sareen, J. (2010). The relationship between anxiety disorders and suicide attempts: Findings from the National Epidemiologic Survey on Alcohol and Related Conditions. *Depression and Anxiety*, *27*, 791–798. http://dx.doi.org/10.1002/da.20674

Olatunji, B. O., Cisler, J. M., & Deacon, B. J. (2010). Efficacy of cognitive behavioral therapy for anxiety disorders: A review of meta-analytic findings. *Psychiatric Clinics of North American*, *33*, 557–577. http://dx.doi.org/10.1016/j.psc.2010.04.002

Otto, M. W., Smits, J. A. J., & Reese, H. E. (2005). Combined psychotherapy and pharmacotherapy for mood and anxiety disorders in adults: Review and analysis. *Clinical Psychology Science and Practice*, *12*, 72–86. http://dx.doi.org/10.1093/clipsy/bpi009

Ravindran, L. N. & Stein, M. B. (2010). The pharmacologic treatment of anxiety disorders: A review of progress. *Journal of Clinical Psychiatry*, *71*, 839–854. http://dx.doi.org/10.4088/JCP.10r06218blu

Rice, D. P. & Miller, L. S. (1998). Health economics and cost implications of anxiety and other mental disorders in the United States. *British Journal of Psychiatry*, *34*, 4–9.

Rojo-Moreno, L., Arribas, P., Plumed, J., Gimeno, N., Garcia-Blanco, A., Vaz-Leal, F., . . . Livianos, L. (2015). Prevalence and comorbidity of eating disorders among a community sample of adolescents: 2-year follow-up. *Psychiatry Research*, *227*, 52–57. http://dx.doi.org/10.1016/j.psychres.2015.02.015

Sareen, J., Cox, B. J., Afifi, T. O., de Graaf, R., Asmundson, G. J. G., ten Have, M., & Stein, M. B. (2005b). Anxiety disorders and risk for suicidal ideation and suicide attempts: A population-based longitudinal study of adults. *Archives of General Psychiatry*, *62*, 1249–1257.

Sareen, J., Cox, B. J., Clara, I., & Asmundson, G. J. G. (2005a). The relationship between anxiety disorders and physical disorders in the U.S. National Comorbidity Survey. *Depression and Anxiety*, *21*, 193–202. http://dx.doi.org/10.1002/da.20072

Scholten, W. D., Batelaan, N. M., Van Balkom, A. J. L. M., Penninx, B. W. J. H., Smit, J. H., & Van Oppen, P. (2013). Recurrence of anxiety disorders and its predictors. *Journal of Affective Disorders*, *147*, 180–185. http://dx.doi.org/10.1016/j.jad.2012.10.031

Spinhoven, P., Van der Does, A. J. W., Van Dijk, E., & Van Rood, Y. R. (2010). Heart-focused anxiety as a mediating variable in the treatment of noncardiac chest pain by cognitive-behavioral therapy and paroxetine. *Journal of Psychosomatic Research*, *69*, 227–235. http://dx.doi.org/10.1016/j.jpsychores.2010.02.005

Stein, D. J., Fineberg, N. A., Bienvenu, O. J., Denys, D., Lochner, C., Nestadt, G., . . . Phillips, K. A. (2010). Should OCD be classified as an anxiety disorder in *DSM-V*? *Depression and Anxiety*, *27*, 495–506. http://dx.doi.org/10.1002/da.20699

Stein, M. B., Roy-Byrne, P. P., Craske, M. G., Bystritsky, A., Sullivan, G., Pyne, J. M., . . . Sherbourne, C. D. (2005). Functional impact and health utility of anxiety disorders in primary care outpatients. *Medical Care*, *43*, 1164–1170.

Widiger, T. A. & Samuel, D. B. (2005). Diagnostic categories or dimensions? A question for the *Diagnostic and Statistical Manual of Mental Disorders: Fifth Edition. Journal of Abnormal Psychology, 114*, 494–504. http://dx.doi.org/10.1037/0021-843X .114.4.494

Wittchen, H. U., Kessler, R. C., Pfister, H., & Lieb, M. (2000). Why do people with anxiety disorders become depressed? A prospective-longitudinal community study. *Acta Psychiatrica Scandinavica, 102*, 14–23.

SECTION 1

Basic Mechanisms in Fear and Anxiety

1 Learning Mechanisms in Fear and Anxiety

It Is Still Not What You Thought It Was

Sara Scheveneels, Yannick Boddez, and Dirk Hermans

Alex is a 24-year-old male who recently dropped out of work because it became difficult to function well in his job as a communication assistant. For example, he avoids making telephone calls in the presence of others and dodges having lunch with his colleagues. When talking to a superior in particular, Alex is extremely self-conscious and aware of certain physical symptoms such as blushing, sweating, and trembling. He is afraid that others will notice these symptoms and would evaluate him as incompetent, stupid, or weird. Alex grew up in a family of lawyers in which the importance of a professional career was stressed. Alex mentions that he has always been timid, but his social anxiety became worse at university, especially after he gave a wrong answer on a question during class. The professor reacted by saying that Alex did not belong at university if he could not answer so obvious a question. Alex responded to this by running out of the classroom. He remembers that his classmates were laughing when he left, but he is not sure whether this memory is accurate or he imagined it. After this incident, Alex started to skip classes and avoided contact with his classmates.

Learning experiences play a crucial role in the etiology of anxiety. An individual with social anxiety, such as Alex, might have learned that (saying something stupid in) the company of others is related to rejection and exclusion, which might have caused his current symptoms of social anxiety and avoidance. Learning theory has not only provided valuable insights into the onset of anxiety disorders, it has also given and still does give a major impetus in the development and optimization of the treatment of anxiety.

In this chapter, we discuss how learning mechanisms as investigated in basic fear conditioning research are at work in clinical fear and anxiety. We mainly examine research in human (healthy and anxious) participants and occasionally address findings from rodent research as well. The first section of this chapter focuses on different procedures and outcomes when modeling fear acquisition in the laboratory. Subsequently, we evaluate whether we can translate the findings from fear conditioning research in the laboratory to clinical anxiety based on three established criteria of external validity: face validity, construct validity, and predictive validity. We demonstrate that recent developments in the field can respond to often-heard critiques on the classical fear conditioning model of anxiety.

A Learning Perspective on the Etiology of Anxiety Disorders

A Classical Conditioning Account of Anxiety

One of the first, and without doubt most famous, case studies illustrating that fear reactions can be acquired by learning experiences is the one of Albert B. as described by Watson and Rayner (1920). A phobic reaction was induced in Albert by pairing a stimulus that initially did not evoke fear (i.e., a white rat) with an aversive outcome (i.e., a loud noise). After repeatedly seeing the rat together with hearing the loud noise, Albert started to react fearfully to the rat. This is one of the first demonstrations of fear conditioning, nowadays an established procedure to induce fear in the laboratory.

Watson and Rayner's early demonstration that anxiety for a stimulus can develop by learning experiences, and in particular by pairing the stimulus with an aversive event, relies on the experimental work of Pavlov (1927). Using dogs as subjects, Pavlov paired stimuli such as sounds with food intake. Pavlov demonstrated that the dogs initially did not show increased saliva production in response to the sound. However, after several pairings of the sound together with the food, the sound started to elicit increased saliva production. This is referred to as *classical or Pavlovian conditioning*. We now use Pavlov's procedure to define the concepts involved in learning. The increased saliva production in response to the sound is called the *conditional response* (CR). A CR can be defined as a change in responding that is conditional upon the relation between the presence of at least two stimuli (De Houwer, Barnes-Holmes, & Moors, 2013). In Pavlov's procedure, one of these two stimuli is the sound, which functions as a *conditional stimulus* (CS). Such CS can be defined as a stimulus to which responding changes conditional upon a relation with another stimulus (i.e., with the food). The food stimulus itself is termed the *unconditional stimulus* (US). In case of successful conditioning, the US changes responding to the stimulus it is related to (i.e., to the CS).[1] Notably, in Pavlov's early experiments, the US was an appetitive stimulus (i.e., food). This is different for fear conditioning research, where the US is an aversive stimulus (e.g., loud noise). However, as becomes clear in the next paragraph, besides this, the procedure is fairly similar.

(Human) Fear Conditioning: Procedures and Outcomes

The fear conditioning model is widely recognized as a model for the pathogenesis of fear and anxiety disorders (e.g., Beckers, Krypotos, Boddez, Effting, & Kindt, 2013). Typically, the CS is paired (repeatedly) with an aversive US until it elicits conditional responding indicative of fear and anxiety.

In human fear conditioning, a variety of stimuli has been used as a *CS*, ranging from fairly neutral stimuli (e.g., geometrical shapes) to fear-relevant stimuli (e.g., spiders, fearful faces). Often the CS is a visual stimulus, but other modalities such as auditory and olfactory stimuli have been used as well. An electrocutaneous stimulus or electric shock is typically used in the laboratory as a *US*, with an intensity set at a level that is perceived as "uncomfortable, but not painful" by the individual participant. However, also auditory stimuli such as human screams or (bursts of a) loud (white) noise (100–105 dB) and aversive pictures or movie clips have been used as a US (e.g., Joos, Vansteenwegen, & Hermans, 2012; Lenaert et al., 2014). For modeling panic symptoms in the laboratory, CO_2-enriched air leading to a sensation of breathing restriction has proven successful (Leibold et al., 2013).

As described earlier, after pairing a CS (repeatedly) with a US, presenting the CS will elicit a *CR* indicative of fear or anxiety. Several dependent variables can be included as indices of fear and anxiety in response to the CS. In line with Lang's bio-informational theory (1979) and emotion theory (Frijda, 1986), dependent variables in fear conditioning research can focus on each of the three response systems: the verbal, psychophysiological, and behavioral levels.

On the *verbal* level, US expectancy ratings are commonly used by asking participants to indicate the extent to which they expect US occurrence (Boddez et al., 2013). In the example of Alex, this could correspond to the extent to which he expects that others will exclude or reject him after saying something (stupid) during lunchbreak. In addition to US expectancy ratings, ratings of subjective fear, CS valence, and subjective units of distress are sometimes included.

As *physiological* indices, skin-conductance response (SCR) and fear-potentiated startle (FPS) have a long history in human fear conditioning research. In SCR (also known as galvanic skin response, electrodermal responding, or sympathetic skin response), changes in the electrical conductance of the skin are measured. This is informative for fear learning because the conductive properties of the skin are influenced by sympathetic autonomic arousal and are reactive to signals of salient events. Notably, SCR is not specific for the anticipation of aversive events, but increases in response to any salient event (e.g., also appetitive ones) (Lipp, 2006). In contrast to SCR, a potential advantage of FPS is that it is modulated by emotional valence (Grillon & Baas, 2003, but see Mallan, Sax, & Lipp, 2009). For measuring FPS in humans, an eye-blink reflex is elicited by the administration of a high-intensity probe of white noise (e.g., Blumenthal et al., 2005). The amplitude of this eye-blink reflex, as measured by the electromyographic activity of the muscles around the eye (orbicularis oculi), is potentiated in anticipation of aversive events. In addition to SCR and FPS, other physiological indices of fear and anxiety, such as heart rate and pupil dilation, have been included in human fear conditioning studies (e.g., Leuchs, Schneider, Czisch, & Spoormaker, 2017). Importantly, these physiological indices correspond to the physical symptoms in clinical anxiety. In the clinical example, Alex started to sweat when he was confronted with a fear-eliciting situation such as when talking to a superior, typically resulting in increased electrical conduction of the skin. In addition, his heart started pounding really fast. He also reported that, while at the office, he had a tendency to startle each time the telephone of a colleague rang.

Construct validity. The evaluation of the construct validity revolves around the question whether the same (etiological) processes are at play in the model and the clinical disorder. Different from face validity, construct validity is not about a first impression, but about underlying mechanisms.

A first indication for similar (neurobiological) processes underlying the fear conditioning model and clinical anxiety can be found in neuroimaging studies that reveal a similar neurocircuitry involved in anxiety patients and in fear conditioning in animals and healthy humans (e.g., Sehlmeyer et al., 2009). In particular, a central role of amygdaloid nuclei has consistently been demonstrated in the acquisition and expression of fear responses and across different anxiety disorders (e.g., Kent & Rauch, 2003; Sehlmeyer et al., 2009; Shin & Liberzon, 2010). In addition, other brain areas such as the hippocampus, insula, anterior cingulate cortex, and ventromedial prefrontal cortex have been identified as regions of interest across anxiety disorders and in fear conditioning research (e.g., Damsa, Kosel, & Moussally, 2009; Etkin & Wager, 2007; Ipser, Singh, & Stein, 2013).[3]

An assumption of the conditioning approach is that learning processes underlie the etiology and treatment of clinical anxiety. Early learning theorists such as Watson used simple acquisition procedures to model the etiology of anxiety disorders. In these procedures, one neutral stimulus (e.g., a white rat) was paired with one aversive outcome (e.g., a loud noise). This simple acquisition procedure has been subject to some important critiques. We discuss some of these earlier shortcomings as well as how they are addressed by more recent developments in learning theory.

A contemporary learning theory approach on the etiology of anxiety disorders. One criticism that has been formulated on the conditioning perspective is *that many anxiety patients are not able to report a CS-US event that can account for the current anxiety symptoms*. A first possibility to nonetheless explain this from a learning account is to simply assume that a CS-US event has occurred, but that people are not accurate in remembering and retrospectively reporting this conditioning experience (Merckelbach, Van den Hout, Hoekstra, & de Ruiter, 1989; Öst & Hugdahl, 1981).

Alternatively and maybe more likely, generalization and higher-order conditioning might obscure learning as the actual cause of the anxiety symptoms. Generalization is discussed in more detail later, but can already be illustrated by an anecdote about Albert from the study by Watson and Rayner (1920). It was said that Albert did not fear only white rats after the conditioning experience but also women wearing fur coats. If Albert would have entered treatment with this complaint, one might have speculated about the sensational (Freudian) origins of this fear. Nonetheless, it can easily be explained by a learning account if one assumes that the fear generalized from the rat to fur coats based on their looking alike. With respect to higher-order conditioning, emetophobia (i.e., fear of vomiting) may serve as an example. Although some dry foods (e.g., cereal without milk) might never have been directly involved in an aversive learning experience, the patient might relate these foods to difficulties to swallow, which in turn is related to vomiting (Bouman & Van Hout, 2006). This allows for an explanation of fear and avoidance of these foods from a learning perspective.

As discussed earlier, conditioning can be defined as a change in responding due to a relation in the presence of stimuli (De Houwer et al., 2013). Importantly, this definition also covers observational learning (e.g., Cameron, Roche, Schlund, & Dymond, 2016). Take the example of a patient who developed dog phobia after observing somebody else get bitten by a dog. Crucially, in such cases, the fear can still be explained by (an observed) relation between the presence of stimuli; more precisely, by a relation between the presence of a dog and a dog bite. In addition, one might develop dog phobia if one is told that dogs cause bite wounds. In such fear learning via instruction, the fear is caused by a verbal description of the relation between the presence of stimuli. Accounting for learning via observation and instruction of course significantly increases the explanatory territory of the learning framework. Olsson and Phelps (2004) compared fear acquisition through direct pairings, instructions, and observational learning in an experimental study with human participants. In the Pavlovian (direct) learning group, a CS was paired with an electric shock. The observational-learning group observed a confederate that was presented with the CS paired with shock. Participants in the instructed-learning group were given verbal instructions about the CS being followed by shock. Interestingly, similar levels of conditional fear responding, as measured by the skin-conductance response, were found for all three pathways. Moreover, in follow-up studies, it has been demonstrated that the neural correlates of direct and indirect pathways to fear acquisition are largely overlapping, with amygdala activation observed in both pathways (Olsson, Nearing, & Phelps, 2007; Phelps, Connor, Gatenby, Gore, & Davis, 2001). These results provide experimental evidence that learning processes can be involved even when no direct conditioning experience is reported by the patient (also see Rachman, 1977).

Another reason why patients may not be able to report a CS-US event that can account for their anxiety symptoms is that USs may be more subtle than the bite of an animal. For example, in patients suffering from chronic fatigue syndrome, something as subtle as experiencing fatigue may function as a US. If such patients learn a relation between stair climbing and fatigue, stair climbing may come to elicit fear (Lenaert, Boddez, Vlaeyen, & Van Heugten, 2018). In the case of such subtle USs, it is easy to overlook that learning is involved. A similar argument holds for other interoceptive USs like panic (Bouton, Mineka, & Barlow, 2001).

Until now, we have discussed how learning theory can handle the observation that many anxiety patients are not able to report a CS-US event that can account for their anxiety symptoms. Another intriguing observation that learning theory has to account for is that *not everyone undergoing a traumatic event will eventually develop an anxiety disorder* (Poulton & Menzies, 2002). Although about 95% of people experience one or more traumatic events during their lifetime, only 10–30% develop an anxiety disorder (Engelhard, Van den Hout, & McNally, 2008). One can make this insightful by assuming that additional variables also moderate the learning process. Such variables include *temperamental/biological vulnerabilities* as well as interindividual differences in *contextual/experiential factors before, during, and following the conditioning experience*. In the following paragraphs, a selection of these variables is discussed. For a more comprehensive overview, we refer the interested reader to Lonsdorf and Baas (2015) and Lonsdorf and Merz (2017).

Given the same conditioning experience, some individuals are more vulnerable to develop an anxiety disorder than others, due to moderation by individual differences in genetic predisposition and temperamental factors. So far, among the most established genetic factors identified as being related to anxiety problems is a polymorphism in the serotonin transporter gene promoter region, 5-HTTLPR[4] (e.g., Lonsdorf & Kalisch, 2011). In particular, carriers of the 5-HTTLPR s-allele have been found to suffer from more severe panic symptoms and social anxiety (Lonsdorf et al., 2009; Miu, Vulturar, Chis, Ungureanu, & Gross, 2013; but see Blaya, Salum, Lima, Leistner-Segal, & Manfro, 2007). The 5-HTTLPR s-allele has been associated with anxiety-related personality traits as well (Munafò et al., 2009). In addition, it has been demonstrated consistently that the low-efficacy 5-HTTLPR s-allele is associated with facilitated fear conditioning (e.g., Bauer, 2015; Lonsdorf et al., 2009; Wendt et al., 2014). Importantly, in line with a diathesis-stress model of psychopathology, the 5-HTTLPR genotype has been found to interact with stressful life events. Klucken et al. (2013), for example, found that carriers of the 5-HTTLPR s-allele showed elevated activity in the neural fear network in response to a CS, but only if they had a history of stressful life events.

In addition, particular *personality traits* might moderate the relation between learning and anxiety. An extensive set of personality traits has been investigated in this context. Among the most commonly studied measures is *intolerance of uncertainty (IU)*. Individuals scoring high on IU react negatively to uncertain situations and consider such situations as threatening (e.g., Carleton, 2016; Lonsdorf & Merz, 2017). Available evidence shows that IU is a transdiagnostic risk factor for the development and maintenance of anxiety disorders (e.g., Gentes & Ruscio, 2011; McEvoy & Mahoney, 2012). In some fear conditioning studies, IU has been positively correlated with fear responding and generalization (e.g., Chin, Nelson, Jackson, & Hajcak, 2016; Morriss, Macdonald, & Van Reekum, 2016; Nelson, Weinberg, Pawluk, Gawlowska, & Proudfit, 2015). Notably, these results were only observed under conditions in which the aversive US (i.e., an electric shock) followed on 50% of the trials (Chin et al., 2016). These results confirm that individuals high on IU show stronger fear responding in ambiguous situations. Other studies, however, have failed to replicate these findings (e.g., Arnaudova et al., 2013).

In addition, contextual factors *before, during*, or *after* the crucial conditioning event can moderate its outcome by either protecting the individual against developing an anxiety disorder or by making the individual more vulnerable. Therefore, it seems important to take into account the entire learning history when trying to explain why some individuals do and some do not develop an anxiety disorder even though experiencing the same trauma. We now demonstrate that these contextual factors fall within the scope of learning theory as well.

If an individual has safe experiences with the CS *prior to* conditioning, this can attenuate the development of a CR. For example, if a tone is first repeatedly presented by itself and in a second phase presented together with electric shock, then fear will develop slower as compared to when pre-exposure to the tone did not happen. In learning theory, this phenomenon is referred to as *latent inhibition* (Lubow & Moore, 1959). Similarly, it has been shown that nontraumatic experiences with the event or stimulus prior to trauma (e.g., visiting the dentist) are protective against the development of psychopathology (e.g., dental phobia) (Kent, 1997). On the other hand, preexisting stress or trauma can make an individual more vulnerable to developing an anxiety disorder following a conditioning event. In a study by Rau, Decola, and Fanselow (2005), rats were exposed to a very mild electric shock in a specific cage (say, cage B). Importantly, the experimental group received 15 heavy shocks in a very different cage in advance (say, cage A), whereas the control group did not undergo this additional treatment. At test, rats in the experimental group behaved very fearful in cage B (more so than rats in the control group), even though they had only received a mild shock in this cage. This might serve to explain why posttraumatic stress disorder (PTSD) patients or individuals with already increased stress levels are more sensitive to develop new anxieties after a mild aversive event. In the example of Alex, having bad experiences in social situations in the past (e.g., being bullied as a child) could have made him more vulnerable to develop social anxiety after the incident with the professor.

During conditioning or the traumatic event, having a sense of control or mastery might be a protective factor. Mineka, Cook, and Miller (1984) presented one group of rats with unsignaled escapable shocks and another group of yoked subjects with the same amount of unsignaled but – crucially – inescapable shocks. The group that could not escape the shocks showed more freezing to both the conditioning context and cue than the group that could escape the shock. Similar results have been found in humans by Meulders et al. (2013). Participants that had control over the offset of the US showed less conditional responding than a group of participants that had no such control. Almost immediately after Alex gave the wrong answer, he realized that he had misunderstood the professor's question. Alex could have felt more control or mastery if he had replied to the professor's nasty remark with a joke or even with a simple statement that he had misunderstood the question. Instead, he panicked and ran out of the room.

Finally, contextual variables *after* conditioning can moderate whether a learning experience results in clinical anxiety. In learning theory, a phenomenon referred to as *US inflation* has been described: the isolated presentation of a strong US after a conditioning experience with a mild US can result in an increase in conditional fear responding (Rescorla, 1974). For example, having a severe panic attack after having experienced mild panic in an elevator might strengthen fear responding to the elevator even if the severe panic attack did not occur in the elevator. Importantly, the inflation effect can also be installed by providing verbal information about the US (e.g., den Hollander, Meulders, Jakobs, & Vlaeyen, 2015). For instance, an individual can initially experience only limited driving anxiety and avoidance after a car accident. However, verbal threat information about the potential consequences of the accident by others afterward might increase fear responding and avoidance. Similarly, Alex's parents, attaching much importance to a professional career, responded to the incident by saying that he will definitely not be able to pursue a career at a university following such a negative remark from the professor.

In addition, repeatedly thinking or ruminating about the traumatic event can make an individual more vulnerable to develop an anxiety disorder. In particular, worrying or ruminating about the conditioning experience might result in repeated activation of the CS-US contingency, which might strengthen and retain the fear memory. Joos, Vansteenwegen, and Hermans (2012) investigated this in a human fear conditioning study. In an acquisition phase, participants learned two CS-US contingencies. Both CSs were pictures of faces; the USs were a human scream and a burst of white noise. Participants were instructed to rehearse one of these contingencies in an experimental session and during the subsequent week. More precisely, they were asked to "think back to the picture (CS), the scream/noise (US) and the relationship between them." When tested with both CSs one week after acquisition, it was found that fear responding was better retained for the contingency that was rehearsed than for the non-rehearsed contingency. Importantly, these results could not be explained by merely rehearsing the CS or by increasing the negative value of the US representation (i.e., US inflation; Davey & Matchett, 1994). In a follow-up study by Joos, Vansteenwegen, Vervliet, and Hermans (2013), rehearsal of the CS alone failed to produce sustained responding. Moreover, in Joos et al. (2013) two CSs were paired with the same US. Whereas changes in the US representation would impact both CSs similarly, it was found that only the CS from the rehearsed CS-US contingency resulted in sustained responding. This indicates that the CS, the US, and the contingency between them have to be rehearsed in order to obtain the effect. Taken together, this set of experiments provides another explanation of why not everyone undergoing a traumatic event will eventually develop an anxiety disorder: rumination moderates the outcome of the learning process in such a way that rumination increases the risk.

More complex procedures to model the acquisition of fear and anxiety. Early learning theorists such as Watson used simple acquisition procedures, in which one neutral stimulus was paired with one aversive outcome, to model the etiology of anxiety disorders. This simple acquisition procedure has been subject to some important critiques. In the previous section, we discussed how a learning theoretical account can overcome this criticism and expand its explanatory territory by including phenomena that moderate the learning process. In this section, we introduce a set of complex learning procedures that further add to the construct validity of the fear conditioning approach. More precisely, we discuss three procedures that mimic important but underappreciated processes underlying anxiety disorders: (1) context conditioning, (2) inhibitory conditioning, and (3) generalization.[5]

In a typical *context conditioning* procedure, a CS is paired with a US (i.e., simple acquisition procedure) in a control group, whereas the experimental group receives USs that are presented explicitly unpaired with the CS (e.g., Grillon & Davis, 1997). As a result of these unpaired CS-US presentations, the context (rather than a discrete CS) indicates that the US might occur somewhere in the not too distant future. Note that context in these experiments is typically operationalized as a background picture or color on the computer screen that stretches out in time before and after CS and US presentation (although other operationalizations have been used as well; Boddez et al., 2014). Context conditioning typically results in a sense of unpredictability and in a generalized and sustained state of arousal, because participants cannot precisely predict when the US will occur (e.g., Grillon, 2002; Grillon, Baas, Lissek, Smith, & Milstein, 2004).

Context conditioning has been proposed as a model for pathological conditions that are characterized by chronic, future-oriented (anticipation) anxiety, such as generalized anxiety disorder (e.g., Luyten, Vansteenwegen, Van Kuyck, & Nuttin, 2011). In addition, context conditioning might also explain agoraphobic avoidance often observed in individuals with panic disorder (e.g., Craske, Glover, & DeCola, 1995; Gorman, Kent, Sullivan, & Coplan, 2000). In particular, un-cued panic attacks might serve as USs that are not predicted by discrete cues but merely occur in a particular context (e.g., a supermarket). As a consequence, people might come to avoid the entire context and related contexts (e.g., crowded places), engaging in generalized avoidance. Therefore, one component in the treatment of panic disorder is to identify discrete exteroceptive and interoceptive cues that are predictive for panic attacks (Craske & Barlow, 2008). Fonteyne, Vervliet, Baeyens, and Vansteenwegen (2009) provided experimental evidence for the importance of this treatment component. They used a context conditioning procedure in which both groups received predictable shocks (i.e., paired with a discrete CS) in context A and shocks that were presented unpaired with a discrete CS in context B. As predicted, higher contextual fear was observed in context B as compared to context A. To investigate whether increasing the predictability of the US would reduce contextual fear, in a subsequent phase the shocks were signaled by a novel discrete CS in context B. Results showed that this intervention led to a reduction of contextual fear and therefore confirmed that increasing predictability can decrease contextual fear.

A second set of complex conditioning procedures relates to discriminating between danger and safety. In real life, the ability to discriminate between stimuli that signal danger and stimuli that indicate the absence of danger can be considered highly adaptive. For instance, the symptoms of a panic attack might resemble a life-threatening heart attack or a stroke, but are in fact innocuous (Haddad, Pritchett, Lissek, & Lau, 2012). Responding to a panic attack as if it is a heart attack or a stroke leads to unnecessary escape and avoidance and an inefficient use of resources. The ability to discriminate between danger and safety cues can be modeled in a *differential inhibition* procedure, in which one stimulus (CS+) is paired with an aversive outcome, whereas another stimulus (CS−) predicts the absence of an aversive outcome. Using this procedure, elevated fear responding to safe stimuli (CS−) and impaired discrimination between danger and safety cues have been found in individuals with subclinical levels of anxiety (e.g., Ganzendam, Kamphuis, & Kindt, 2013; Haddad et al., 2012) and in patients with clinical anxiety (Duits et al., 2015; Lenaert, Boddez, Vervliet, Schruers, & Hermans, 2015; Lissek et al., 2005; Lissek et al., 2009). This suggests that the differential inhibition procedure taps into a process that is relevant to anxiety disorders and therefore has construct validity. Nonetheless, it should also be mentioned that some fear conditioning studies failed to find an effect of trait anxiety or observed an effect in only one of the outcome measures but not in the other(s) (e.g., Kindt & Soeter, 2014; Torrents-Rodas et al., 2013).

Other procedures have been used to examine impairments in safety learning. One of them is the *conditioned inhibition procedure*, a procedure known from the animal literature. In intermixed trials, one stimulus A is paired with the US, but when this stimulus is presented together with another stimulus B, the US is omitted. This procedure corresponds to the use of safety signals in clinical practice. For example, an individual with driving phobia might be fearful of driving on a highway (A), but feel safe when accompanied by a passenger (AB). Here as well, it has been found that high-anxious individuals show higher fear responding to the safe AB stimulus compound than low-anxious individuals (Chan & Lovibond, 1996; Grillon & Ameli, 2001).

A third defining feature of anxiety disorders is *stimulus generalization*. Boddez, Bennett, Van Esch, and Beckers (2017) proposed to speak of generalization when a stimulus elicits a response due to a learning experience in which that stimulus as such was not featured. As an example, consider a child experiencing painful skin burns upon touching the stove in his grandparents' place. Behaving cautious around not just this but any stove will prevent the child from acquiring additional skin burns. In anxiety disorders, however, fear responding typically spreads to a range of stimuli and situations that are not dangerous (Dymond, Dunsmoor, Vervliet, Roche, & Hermans, 2015; Hermans, Baeyens, & Vervliet, 2013). An individual suffering from dog phobia, for instance, will typically not only react with intense fear to the specific dog involved in the biting incident (who has proven dangerous), but to each and every dog.

In *perceptual stimulus generalization*, the fear responding is elicited by stimuli that share perceptual similarity with the original CS+ (Kalish, 1969; Lissek et al., 2010). The person suffering from dog phobia can be considered an example of perceptual generalization. In a fear conditioning paradigm, Lissek et al. (2008)

investigated perceptual generalization by presenting small- and large-sized circles as CS+ and CS−, respectively, counterbalanced across participants. Subsequently, perceptual generalization of fear responding was tested by presenting participants with circles that ranged in size between the CS+ and CS− (i.e., generalization stimuli). This generated a generalization gradient, with stronger fear responses to stimuli that resemble the CS+ and decreasing responding with decreasing similarity. Using this procedure, stronger responding to the generalization stimuli (GSs) has been observed in patients with panic disorder (Lissek et al., 2010), generalized anxiety disorder (Lissek et al., 2014), and posttraumatic stress disorder (Lissek & Grillon, 2012) compared to healthy controls. Taken together, this suggests that the generalization procedure seizes a mechanism that is relevant to anxiety disorders and therefore is construct valid.

It is important to note that perceptual generalization can also involve interoceptive CSs (Dymond et al., 2015; Lissek et al., 2010; Schroijen & Pappens, 2015). In a patient suffering from panic disorder, fear responding might be elicited not only by the interoceptive symptoms that directly preceded and accompanied the first panic attack (e.g., tight chest), but also by other physical symptoms (e.g., full stomach after overeating).

In addition to these different forms of perceptual generalization, fear responses can also generalize across stimuli that diverge greatly in perceptual features, based on non-perceptual grounds such as categories and conceptual knowledge (e.g., Dunsmoor & Murphy, 2015). Alex not only avoided going to the class of the specific professor that was involved in the incident, he also skipped other classes and started to avoid all kinds of (social) situations, including going to activities of the student club and meeting new people. Although these situations might clearly differ from the original learning experience with regard to their physical characteristics, they can be considered part of an idiosyncratic category of situations in which Alex considers himself at risk of saying something stupid and being rejected by others. This type of generalization is called *non-perceptual-based generalization* (Dymond et al., 2015).

As an experimental illustration, Dunsmoor, Martin, and LaBar (2012) presented participants with a heterogeneous collection of images of animals and tools. Images of one of these categories (e.g., animals) served as the CS+ category and were paired with an electric shock; the other stimulus category (e.g., tools) was never reinforced (i.e., CS− category). Subsequently, they tested for the generalization of fear to new stimuli stemming from the CS+ and CS− category. Results indicated higher fear responding, as measured by shock expectancy and skin-conductance response, to stimuli stemming from the CS+ category compared to stimuli from the CS− category. These results suggest that fear can generalize based on categorical and conceptual knowledge. However, this paradigm using stimuli from preexisting categories does not allow ruling out the potential influence of perceptual similarity on the generalization of fear. It can indeed be argued that all stimuli of one category (e.g., animals) share more perceptual similarity with each other than with stimuli from the other category (e.g., tools).

To completely rule out the potential influence of perceptual overlap, research has been conducted using de novo categories by inducing concept-like relations between arbitrary stimuli in an experimental way. Vervoort, Vervliet, Bennett, and Baeyens (2014) investigated the generalization of fear acquisition within novel arbitrary categories by first creating two four-member stimulus equivalence categories (i.e., A1-B1-C1-D1 and A2-B2-C2-D2). This was done using a matching-to-sample task. Stimuli were arbitrary line drawings. In the matching-to-sample task, a sample stimulus was presented together with two comparison figures and participants were instructed to choose the comparison figure that matched the sample stimulus. After every trial participants received feedback on whether their response was correct. Next, one member of the first category (B1) was presented repeatedly with an electric shock, whereas the member of the second category (B2) was never paired with a shock. In a subsequent test for generalization in which C1, D1, C2, and D2 were presented, it was found that conditional fear responses generalized to other members of the arbitrary category (i.e., C1, D1). These results confirm that fears can generalize across conceptually related stimuli in addition to perceptually related stimuli.

Finally, Boddez et al. (2012) used a blocking procedure to assess fear generalization. In the first stage of the experiment, a CS was paired with a US. In a subsequent phase, a second CS was presented in compound with the first CS. This compound was paired with the same US as in the first phase. The newly added second CS therefore did not provide any information about the onset of the US over and above the information provided by the first CS. Interestingly, high trait anxious participants showed higher fear responding when this second CS was presented by itself at test. Such deficit in blocking might explain why certain individuals are more prone to develop clinical anxiety. A soldier might, for example, have experienced a bomb attack preceded by different cues such as a screaming colleague warning of the attack, a sandy surface, and the fire of the bombing raid. A deficit in blocking would imply that the soldier, after his mission, does not only experience anxiety when a colleague is warning of another bomb attack (i.e., the most informative cue), but also when he is invited to a barbecue (fire) or when visiting the beach (sand).

In summary, we discussed complex learning procedures that allow the mimicking of specific processes at play in anxiety disorders. As such, these procedures add to the construct validity of the fear conditioning approach.

Predictive validity. Arguments about theoretical processes notwithstanding, an important question remains whether the fear conditioning model allows for translation to real-life situations that pertain to clinical anxiety. This concerns the predictive validity of the fear conditioning model and is discussed now. Two aspects of predictive validity can be distinguished (Scheveneels et al., 2016). A first aspect refers to whether environmental variables exert a similar influence in the fear conditioning model and in real-life situations. A second aspect concerns testing whether a factor at the level of the individual exerts a similar influence as well. Both aspects are about the question of whether a factor, be it an environmental intervention or at the level of the individual, moderates the relation between learning experiences and fear in the lab in the same way as the relation between aversive experiences and anxiety symptoms in real life.

Do interventions have a similar effect in the fear conditioning model and in real life? With regard to the first aspect of predictive validity, presenting the CS without US following fear conditioning is known to result in a decrease in fear responding (e.g., Hermans, Craske, Mineka, & Lovibond, 2006). This procedure is termed *fear extinction.* Interestingly, in real life, a similar intervention also results in a decrease in fear responding, thus adding to the predictive validity of the fear conditioning account. Indeed, exposure therapy or repeated and systematic confrontation with the feared stimulus or situation without occurrence of the expected aversive outcome is the (psychological) treatment of choice in anxiety (e.g., Cusack et al., 2016; Öst, Havnen, Hansen, & Kvale, 2015, Wolitzky-Taylor, Horowitz, Powers, & Telch, 2008). During treatment, Alex was exposed to those social situations in which he expected to be rejected by others, such as making telephone calls when his colleagues are in the same room, meeting new people at parties, and returning things to shops After repeated confrontation with these situations, Alex reported experiencing less anxiety.

In addition, experimental research has demonstrated that fear responding can return after (partial or complete) fear extinction (Rachman, 1989; Vervliet, Craske, & Hermans, 2013). In clinical practice, a return in fear responding is unfortunately not uncommon either. It is estimated that 19–62% of clients experience at least some return of fear after exposure-based treatment (Craske & Mystkowski, 2006). Interesting for our present purposes, the interventions that cause a return of fear after extinction in experimental conditioning studies correspond to pathways to return of fear in real life. This again confirms the predictive validity of the model (Vervliet et al., 2013). We now discuss the most well-studied pathways to return of fear: spontaneous recovery, (context) renewal, and reinstatement.

In the laboratory, return of fear can occur when a time interval is introduced after extinction. Pavlov (1927) described this phenomenon as *spontaneous recovery,* and it has been established in multiple laboratory studies (e.g., Huff, Hernandez, Blanding, & LaBar, 2009; Norrholm et al., 2008). Spontaneous recovery in the lab corresponds to the clinical observation that due to the mere passage of time after exposure treatment, a client can show a reappearance of fearful responding (e.g., Mystkowski, Craske, Echiverri, & Labus, 2006; Vasey, Harbaugh, Buffington, Jones, & Fazio, 2012).

A second manipulation that causes return of fear and that has been investigated in fear conditioning research is a change in (background) context between extinction and a subsequent test phase. This is referred to as (contextual) *renewal* (e.g., Bouton, 2002; Effting & Kindt, 2007; Vervliet, Baeyens, Van den

In particular, the simple fear acquisition model, as proposed by Watson, might be insufficient to explain why some individuals develop anxiety disorders and others do not. We discussed how modern learning approaches have addressed these criticisms by, among other things, taking into account contextual variables before, during, or after the conditioning experience. Furthermore, the use of more complex conditioning procedures might add to the construct validity of the fear conditioning model by mimicking additional processes at play in anxiety disorders. In the section on predictive validity, we discussed that environmental and individual-level factors that decrease and increase fear after aversive experiences in the lab also do so in real life. In conclusion, the fear conditioning approach allows the investigation of the acquisition of fear under highly controlled circumstances and makes it possible to identify the exact (learning) mechanisms involved in the etiology of anxiety disorders. This knowledge can provide meaningful directions in how to prevent and treat (clinical) anxiety.

This work was supported by KU Leuven Program Funding Grant PF/10/005 awarded to Dirk Hermans and by the Belgian Science Policy Office Grant P7/33.

Notes

1. Changes in responding to the US, as caused by its relation with the CS, are possible but are typically left uninvestigated in conditioning research.
2. The reader may note that the subtitle of our chapter ("It is still not what you thought it was") is similar to the subtitle used in Mineka and Zinbarg's (2006) article.
3. Results regarding these areas are less univocal and their role remains a subject of discussion (e.g., Maren, 2008; Sehlmeyer et al., 2009).
4. Importantly, the field of genetics in psychopathology is characterized by several pitfalls and limitations such as small effects, post hoc testing, underpowered studies, and failed replications. We refer the interested reader to Dick et al. (2015), Duncan and Keller (2011), and Tabor, Risch, and Myers (2002) for a more elaborate discussion of this topic.
5. For a more elaborate review of complex conditioning procedures, we refer the interested reader to Boddez, Baeyens, Hermans, and Beckers (2014).

References

Acheson, D. T., Geyer, M. A., Baker, D. G., Nievergelt, C. M., Yurgil, K., & Risbrough, V. B. (2015). Conditioned fear and extinction learning performance and its association with psychiatric symptoms in active duty Marines. *Psychoneuroendocrinology, 51,* 495–505.

American Psychiatric Association (2013). *Diagnostic and Statistical Manual of Mental Disorders: DSM-5.* Washington, DC: American Psychiatric Association.

Arnaudova, I., Krypotos, A.-M., Effting, M., Boddez, Y., Kindt, M., & Beckers, T. (2013). Individual differences in discriminatory fear learning under conditions of ambiguity: A vulnerability factor for anxiety disorders. *Frontiers in Psychology, 4,* 298. doi: 10.3389/fpsyg.2013.00298

Baas, J. M., Grillon, C., Böcker, K. B., Brack, A. A., Morgan, C. A., Kenemans, L. J., & Verbaten, M. N. (2002). Benzodiazepines have no effect on fear-potentiated startle in humans. *Psychopharmacology, 161*, 233–247. doi: 10.1007/s00213-002-1011-8

Baas, J. M., Nugent, M., Lissek, S., Pine, D. S., & Grillon, C. (2004). Fear conditioning in virtual reality contexts: A new tool for the study of anxiety. *Biological Psychiatry, 55*, 1056–1060. doi: 10.1016/j.biopsych.2004.02.024

Bandarian-Balooch, S., Neumann, D. L., & Boschen, M. J. (2012). Extinction treatment in multiple contexts attenuates return ABC renewal in humans. *Behaviour Research and Therapy, 50*, 604–609. doi: 10.1016/j.brat.2012.06.003

Bauer, E. P. (2015). Serotonin in fear conditioning processes. *Behavioural Brain Research, 277*, 68–77. doi: 10.1016/j.bbr.2014.07.028

Beckers, T., Krypotos, A.-M., Boddez, Y., Effting, M., & Kindt, M. (2013). What's wrong with fear conditioning? *Biological Psychology, 92*, 90–96. doi: 10.1016/j.biopsycho.2011.12.015

Blaya, C., Salum, G. A., Lima, M. S., Leistner-Segal, S., & Manfro, G. G. (2007). Lack of association between the serotonin transporter promotor polymorphism (5-HTTLPR) and panic disorder: A systematic review and meta-analysis. *Behavioral and Brain Functions, 41*. doi: 10.1186/1744-9081-3-41

Blumenthal, T. D., Cuthbert, B. N., Filion, D. L., Hackley, S., Lipp, O. V., & Van Boxtel, A. (2005). Committee report: Guidelines for human startle eyeblink electromyographic studies. *Psychophysiology, 42*, 1–15.

Boddez, Y., Baeyens, F., Hermans, D., & Beckers, T. (2014). A fear conditioning approach to anxiety disorders: The added value of complex acquisition procedures. In P. Emmelkamp & T. Ehring (eds.), *The Wiley Handbook of Anxiety Disorder* (pp. 85–103). New York, NY: Wiley-Blackwell.

Boddez, Y., Baeyens, F., Luyten, L., Vansteenwegen, D., Hermans, D., & Beckers, T. (2013). Rating data are underrated: Validity of US expectancy in human fear conditioning. *Journal of Behavior Therapy and Experimental Psychiatry, 44*, 201–206. doi: 10.1016/j.jbtrp.2012.08.003

Boddez, Y., Bennett, M., Van Esch, S., & Beckers, T. (2017). Bending rules: The shape of the perceptual generalization gradient is sensitive to inference rules. *Cognition & Emotion, 31*, 1444–1452.

Boddez, Y., Vervliet, B., Baeyens, F., Lauwers, S., Hermans, D., & Beckers, T. (2012). Expectancy bias in a selective conditioning procedure: Trait anxiety increases the threat value of a blocked stimulus. *Journal of Behavior Therapy and Experimental Psychiatry, 43*, 832–837. doi: 10.1016/j.jbtep.2011.11.005

Bouman, T. K. & Van Hout, W. J. P. J. (2006). CS-exposure werkt bij emetofobie. *Gedragstherapie, 39*, 127–138.

Bouton, M. E. (2002). Context, ambiguity, and unlearning: Sources of relapse after behavioral extinction. *Biological Psychiatry, 52*, 976–986.

Bouton, M. E. & Bolles, R. C. (1979). Contextual control of the extinction of conditioned fear. *Learning and Motivation, 10*, 445–466.

Bouton, M. E., Mineka, S., & Barlow, D. H. (2001). A modern learning theory perspective on the etiology of panic disorders. *Psychological Review, 108*, 4–32.

Cameron, G., Roche, B., Schlund, M. W., & Dymond, S. (2016). Learned, instructed and observed pathways to fear and avoidance. *Journal of Behavior Therapy and Experimental Psychiatry, 50*, 106–112. doi: 10.1016/j.jbtep.2015.06.003

Carleton, R. N. (2016). Into the unknown: A review and synthesis of contemporary models involving uncertainty. *Journal of Anxiety Disorders, 39*, 30–43. doi: 10.1016/j.anxdis.2016.02.007

Chan, C. K. & Lovibond, P. F. (1996). Expectancy bias in trait anxiety. *Journal of Abnormal Psychology, 105*, 637–647.

Chin, B., Nelson, B. D., Jackson, F., & Hajcak, G. (2016). Intolerance of uncertainty and startle potentiation in relation to different threat reinforcement rates. *International Journal of Psychophysiology, 99*, 79–84. doi: 10.1016/j.ijpsycho.2015.11.006

Craske, M. G. & Barlow, D. H. (2008). Panic disorder and agoraphobia. In D. H. Barlow (ed.), *Clinical Handbook of Psychological Disorders* (pp. 1–64). New York, NY: Guilford Press.

Craske, M. G., Glover, D., & DeCola, J. (1995). Predicted versus unpredicted panic attacks: Acute versus general stress. *Journal of Abnormal Psychology, 104*, 214–223.

Craske, M. G. & Mystkowski, J. L. (2006). Exposure therapy and extinction: Clinical studies. In M. G. Craske, D. Hermans, & D. Vansteenwegen (eds.), *Fear and Learning: From Basic Processes to Clinical Implications* (pp. 217–233). Washington, DC: American Psychiatric Association.

Cusack, K., Jonas, D. E., Fomeris, C. A., Wines, C., Sonis, J., Middleton, J. C., . . ., Gaynes, B. N. (2016). Psychological treatments for adults with posttraumatic stress disorder: A systematic review and meta-analysis. *Clinical Psychology Review, 43*, 128–141. doi: 10.1016/j.cpr.2015.10.003

Damsa, C., Kosel, M., & Moussally, J. (2009). Current status of brain imaging in anxiety disorders. *Current Opinion in Psychiatry, 22*, 96–110. doi: 10.1097/YCO.0b013e328319bd10

Davey, G. C. (2017). A research pathway for experimental psychopathology: The role of external validity criteria. *Psychopathology Review, 4*, 129–140.

Davey, G. C. L. & Matchett, G. (1994). Unconditioned stimulus rehearsal and the retention and enhancement of differential "fear" conditioning: Effects of trait and state anxiety. *Journal of Abnormal Psychology, 103*(4), 708–718.

De Houwer, J., Barnes-Holmes, D., & Moors, A. (2013). What is learning? On the nature and merits of a functional definition of learning. *Psychonomic Bulletin & Review, 20*, 631–642. doi: 10.3758/s13423-013-0386-3

den Hollander, M., Meulders, A., Jakobs, M., & Vlaeyen, J. W. S. (2015). The effect of threat information on acquisition, extinction and reinstatement of experimentally conditioned fear of movement-related pain. *Pain Medicine, 16*, 2302–2315. doi: 10.1111/pme.12839

Dick, D. M., Agrawal, A., Keller, M. C., Adkins, A., Aliev, F., Monroe, S., . . ., Sher, K. J. (2015). Candidate gene–environment interaction research reflections and recommendations. *Perspectives on Psychological Science, 10*, 37–59. doi: 10.1177/1745691614556682

Duits, P., Cath, D. C., Lissek, S., Hox, J. J., Hamm, A. O., Engelhard, I. M., . . ., Baas, J. M. P. (2015). Updated meta-analysis of classical fear conditioning in the anxiety disorders. *Depression and Anxiety, 32*, 239–253. doi: 10.1002/da.22353

Duncan, L. E. & Keller, M. C. (2011). A critical review of the first 10 years of candidate gene-by-environment interaction research in psychiatry. *American Journal of Psychiatry, 168*, 1041–1049. doi: 10.1176/appi.ajp.2011.11020191

Dunsmoor, J. E., Martin, A., & LaBar, K. S. (2012). Role of conceptual knowledge in learning and retention of conditioned fear. *Biological Psychology, 89*, 300–305. doi: 10.1016/j.biopsycho.2011.11.002

Dunsmoor, J. E. & Murphy, G. L. (2015). Categories, concepts, and conditioning: How humans generalize fear. *Trends in Cognitive Sciences, 19*, 73–75. doi: 10.1016/j.tics.2014.12.003

Dymond, S., Dunsmoor, J. E., Vervliet, B., Roche, B., & Hermans, D. (2015). Fear generalization in humans: Systematic review and implications for anxiety disorder research. *Behavior Therapy, 46*, 561–582.

Effting, M. & Kindt, M. (2007). Contextual control of human fear associations in a renewal paradigm. *Behaviour Research and Therapy, 45*, 2002–2018. doi: 10.1016/j.brat.2007.02.011

Engelhard, I. M., Van den Hout, M. A., & McNally, R. J. (2008). Memory consistency for traumatic events in Dutch soldiers deployed to Iraq. *Memory, 16*, 3–9.

Etkin, A. & Wager, T. D. (2007). Functional neuroimaging of anxiety: A meta-analysis of emotional processing in PTSD, social anxiety disorder, and specific phobia. *American Journal of Psychiatry, 164*, 1476–1488. doi: 10.1176/appi.ajp.2007.07030504

Fonteyne, R., Vervliet, B., Hermans, D., Baeyens, F., & Vansteenwegen, D. (2009). Reducing chronic anxiety by making the threatening event predictable: An experimental approach. *Behaviour Research and Therapy, 47*, 830–839. doi: 10.1016/j.brat.2009.06.011

Frijda, N. H. (1986). *The Emotions*. Cambridge: Cambridge University Press.

Ganzendam, F. J., Kamphuis, J. H., & Kindt, M. (2013). Deficient safety learning characterizes high trait anxious individuals. *Biological Psychology, 92*, 342–352. doi: 10.1016/j.biopsycho.2012.11.006

Gentes, E. L. & Ruscio, A. M. (2011). A meta-analysis of the relation of intolerance of uncertainty to symptoms of generalized anxiety disorder, major depressive disorder, and obsessive-compulsive disorder. *Clinical Psychology Review, 31*, 923–933. doi: 10.1016/j.cpr.2011.05.001

Gorman, J. M., Kent, J. M., Sullivan, G. M., & Coplan, J. D. (2000). Neuroanatomical hypothesis of panic disorder, revised. *American Journal of Psychiatry, 157*, 493–505.

Grillon, C. (2002). Startle reactivity and anxiety disorders: Aversive conditioning, context, and neurobiology. *Biological Psychiatry, 52*, 958–975.

Grillon, C. & Ameli, R. (2001). Conditioned inhibition of fear-potentiated startle and skin conductance in humans. *Psychophysiology, 38*, 807–815.

Grillon, C. & Baas, J. (2003). A review of the modulation of the startle reflex by affective states and its application in psychiatry. *Clinical Neurophysiology, 114*, 1557–1579.

Grillon, C., Baas, J., Lissek, S., Smith, K., & Milstein, J. (2004). Anxious responses to predictable and unpredictable aversive events. *Behavioral Neuroscience, 118*, 916–924. doi: 10.1037/0735-7044.118.5.916

Grillon, C., Baas, J., Pine, D. S., Lissek, S., Lawley, M., Ellis, V., & Levine, J. (2006). The benzodiazepine alprazolam dissociates contextual fear from cued fear in humans as assessed by fear-potentiated startle. *Biological Psychiatry, 60,* 760–766. doi: 10.1016/biopsych.2005.11.027

Grillon, C. & Davis, M. (1997). Fear-potentiated startle conditioning in humans: Explicit and contextual cue conditioning following paired versus unpaired training. *Psychophysiology, 34,* 451–458. doi: 10.1111/j.1469-8986.1997.tb02389.x

Guthrie, R. M. & Bryant, R. A. (2006). Extinction learning before trauma and subsequent posttraumatic stress. *Psychosomatic Medicine, 68,* 307–311.

Haaker, J., Golkar, A., Hermans, D., & Lonsdorf, T. B. (2014). A review on human reinstatement studies: An overview and methodological challenges. *Learning and Memory, 21,* 424–440. doi: 10.1101/lm.036053.114

Haddad, A. D. M., Pritchett, D., Lissek, S., & Lau, J. Y. F. (2012). Trait anxiety and fear responses to safety cues: Stimulus generalization of sensitization? *Journal of Psychopathology and Behavioral Assessment, 34,* 323–331. doi: 10.1007/s10862-012-9284-7

Hedge, C., Powell, G., & Sumner, P., (2017). The reliability paradox: Why robust cognitive tasks do produce reliable individual differences. *Behavior Research Methods, 50* (3), 1166–1186. doi: 10.3758/s13428-017-0935-1

Hermans, D., Baeyens, F., & Vervliet, B. (2013). Generalization of acquired emotional responses. In M. D. Robinson, E. R. Watkins, & E. Harmon-Jones (eds.), *Handbook of Cognition and Emotion* (pp. 117–134). New York, NY: Guilford Press.

Hermans, D., Craske, M. G., Mineka, S., & Lovibond, P. F. (2006). Extinction in human fear conditioning. *Biological Psychiatry, 60,* 361–368. doi: 10.1016/j.biopsych.2005.10.006

Hermans, D., Dirickx, T., Vansteenwegen, D., Baeyens, F., Van den Bergh, O., & Eelen, P. (2005). Reinstatement of fear responses in human aversive conditioning. *Behavior Research and Therapy, 43,* 533–551. doi: 10.1016/j.brat.2004.03.013

Hodgson, R., & Rachman, S. (1974). Desynchrony in measures of fear. *Behaviour Research and Therapy, 12,* 319–326.

Huff, N. C., Hernandez, J. A., Blanding, N. Q., & LaBar, K. S. (2009). Delayed extinction attenuates conditioned fear renewal and spontaneous recovery in humans. *Behavioral Neuroscience, 123,* 834–843. doi: 10.1037/a0016511

Ipser, J. C., Singh, L., & Stein, D. J. (2013). Meta-analysis of functional brain imaging in specific phobia. *Psychiatry and Clinical Neurosciences, 67,* 311–322. doi: 10.1111/pcn.12055

Joos, E., Vansteenwegen, D., & Hermans, D. (2012). Post-acquisition repetitive thought in fear conditioning: An experimental investigation of the effect of CS-US rehearsal. *Journal of Behavior Therapy and Experimental Psychiatry, 43,* 737–744. doi: 10.1016/j.btep.2011.10.011

Joos, E., Vansteenwegen, D., Vervliet, B., & Hermans, D. (2013). Repeated activation of a CS-US-contingency results in sustained conditioned responding. *Frontiers in Psychology, 4.* doi: 10.3389/fpsyg.2013.00305

Kalish, H. (1969). Stimulus generalization. In M. Marx (ed.), *Learning: Processes* (pp. 205–297). Oxford: Macmillan.

Kent, G. (1997). Dental phobias. In G. C. Davey (ed.), *Phobias: A Handbook of Theory, Research and Treatment* (pp. 107–127). Chichester: Wiley.

Kent, J. M. & Rauch, S. L. (2003). Neurocircuitry of anxiety disorders. *Current Psychiatry Reports, 5,* 266–273.

Kindt, M., & Soeter, M. (2014). Fear inhibition in high trait anxiety. *PLoS ONE*, *9*, e86462. doi: 10.1371/journal.pone.0086462

Klucken, T., Alexander, N., Schweckendiek, J., et al. (2013) Individual differences in neural correlates of fear conditioning as a function of 5-HTTLPR and stressful life events. *Social, Cognitive and Affective Neuroscience*, *8*, 318–325.

Krypotos, A.-M., Arnaudova, I., Effting, M., Kindt, M., & Beckers, T. (2015). Effects of approach-avoidance training on the extinction and return of fear responses. *PLoS ONE*, *10*, e0131581. doi: 10.1371/journal.pone.0131581

Krypotos, A.-M., Effting, M., Arnaudova, I., Kindt, M., & Beckers, T. (2014). Avoided by association: Acquisition, extinction, and renewal of avoidance tendencies towards conditioned fear stimuli. *Clinical Psychological Science*, *2*, 336–343. doi: 10.1177/2167702613503139

Lang, P. J. (1979). A bio-informational theory of emotional imagery. *Psychophysiology*, *16*, 495–512.

Leibold, N. K., Viechtbauer, W., Goossens, L., De Cort, K., Griez, E. J., Myin-Germeys, I., & Steinbusch, H. W. M. (2013). Carbon dioxide inhalation as a human experimental model of panic: The relationship between emotions and cardiovascular physiology. *Biological Psychology*, *94*, 331–340. doi: 10.1016/j.biopsycho.2013.06.004

Lenaert, B., Boddez, Y., Griffith, J. W., Vervliet, B., Schruers, K., & Hermans, D. (2014). Aversive learning and generalization predict subclinical levels of anxiety: A six-month longitudinal study. *Journal of Anxiety Disorders*, *28*, 747–753. doi: 10.1016/j.anxdis.2014

Lenaert, B., Boddez, Y., Vervliet, B., Schruers, K., & Hermans, D. (2015). Reduced autobiographical memory specificity is associated with impaired discrimination learning in anxiety disorder patients. *Frontiers in Psychology*, *6*, 889. doi: 10.3389/fpsyg.2015.00889

Lenaert B., Boddez Y., Vlaeyen J., & Van Heugten C. (2018). Learning to feel tired: A learning trajectory towards chronic fatigue. *Behaviour Research and Therapy*, *100*, 54–66.

Leuchs, L., Schneider, M., Czisch, M., & Spoormaker, V. I. (2017). Neural correlated of pupil dilation during human fear learning. *NeuroImage*, *147*, 186–197. doi: 10.1016/j.neuroimage.2016.11.072

Lipp, O. V. (2006). Human fear learning: Contemporary procedures and measurement. In M. G. Craske, D. Hermans, & D. Vansteenwegen (eds.), *Fear and Learning: From Basic Processes to Clinical Implications* (pp. 37–52). Washington, DC: American Psychological Association.

Lissek, S., Biggs, A. L., Rabin, S. J., Cornwell, B. R., Alvarez, R. P., Pine, D. S., & Grillon, C. (2008). Generalization of conditioned fear-potentiated startle in humans: Experimental validation and clinical relevance. *Behaviour Research and Therapy*, *46*, 678–687. doi: 10.1016/j.brat.2008.02.005

Lissek, S., & Grillon, C. (2012). Learning models of PTSD. In J. G. Beck, & D. M. Sloan (eds.), *The Oxford Handbook of Traumatic Stress Disorders*. New York, NY: Oxford University Press.

Lissek, S., Kaczkurkin, A. N., Rabin, S., Geraci, M., Pine, D. S., & Grillon, C. (2014). Generalized anxiety disorder is associated with overgeneralization of classically conditioned fear. *Biological Psychiatry*, *75*, 909–956. doi: 10.1016/j. biopsych.2013.07.025

Lissek, S., Powers, A. S., McClure, E. B., Phelps, E. A., Woldehawariat, G., Grillon, C., & Pine, D. S. (2005). Classical fear conditioning in the anxiety disorders: A meta-analysis. *Behaviour Research and Therapy*, *43*, 1391–1424.

Lissek, S., Rabin, S., Heller, R. E., Lukenbaugh, D., Geraci, M., Pine, D. S., & Grillon, C. (2010). Overgeneralization of conditioned fear as a pathogenic marker of panic disorder. *American Journal of Psychiatry*, *167*, 47–55. doi: 10.1176/appi. ajp.2009.09030410

Lissek, S., Rabin, S. J., McDowell, D. J., Dvir, S., Bradford, D. E., Geraci, M., . . ., & Grillon, C. (2009). Impaired discriminative fear-conditioning resulting from elevated fear responding to learned safety cues among individuals with panic disorder. *Behaviour Research and Therapy*, *47*, 111–118. doi: 10.1016/j. brat.2008.10.017

Lommen, M. J., Engelhard, I. M., Sijbrandij, M., Van den Hout, M. A., & Hermans, D. (2013). Pre-trauma individual differences in extinction learning predict posttraumatic stress. *Behaviour Research and Therapy*, *51*, 63–67.

Lonsdorf, T. B. & Baas, J. M P. (2015). Genetics in experimental psychopathology: From laboratory models to therapygenetics. Where do we go from here? *Psychopathology Review*, 4(2), 169–188.

Lonsdorf, T. B. & Kalisch, R. (2011).A review on experimental and clinical genetic association studies on fear conditioning, extinction and cognitive-behavioral treatment. *Translational Psychiatry*, *1*, e41. doi: 10.1038/tp.2011.36

Lonsdorf, T. B. & Merz, C. J. (2017). More than just noise: Inter-individual differences in fear acquisition, extinction and return of fear in humans – biological, experiential, temperamental factors, and methodological pitfalls. *Neuroscience & Biobehavioral Reviews*. doi: 10.1016/j.neubiorev.2017.07.007

Lonsdorf, T. B., Rück, C., Bergström, J., Andersson, G., Öhman, A., Schalling, M., & Lindefors, N. (2009). The symptomatic profile of panic disorder is shaped by the 5-HTTLPR polymorphism. *Progress in Neuro-Psychopharmacology and Biological Psychiatry*, *33*, 1479–1483. doi: 10.1016/j.pnpbp.2009.08.004

Lonsdorf, T., Weike, A., Nikamo, P., Schalling, M., Hamm, A., & Öhman, A. (2009). Genetic gating of human fear learning and extinction: Possible implication for gene-environment interaction in anxiety disorder. *Psychological Science*, *20*, 198–206. doi: 10.1111/j.1467-9280.2009.02280.x

Lovibond, P. F., Mitchell, C. J., Minard, E., Brady, A., & Menzies, R. G. (2009). Safety behaviours preserve threat beliefs: Protection from extinction of human fear conditioning by an avoidance response. *Behaviour Research and Therapy*, *47*, 716–720. doi: 10.1080/17470210701503229

Lubow, R. E. & Moore, A. U. (1959). Latent inhibition: The effect of nonreinforced pre-exposure to the conditional stimulus. *Journal of Comparative and Physiological Psychology*, *52*, 415–419. doi: 10.1037/h0046700

Luyten, L., Vansteenwegen, D., Van Kuyck, K., & Nuttin, B. (2011). Contextual conditioning in rats as an animal model for generalized anxiety disorder. *Cognitive, Affective, & Behavioral Neuroscience*, *11*, 228–244. doi: 10.3758/s13415-011-0021-6

Mallan, K. M., Sax, J., & Lipp, O. V. (2009). Verbal instruction abolishes fear conditioned to racial out-group faces. *Journal of Experimental Social Psychology, 45,* 1303–1307. doi: 10.1016/j.jesp.2009.08.001

Manufò, M. R., Freimer, N. B., Ng, W., Ophoff, R., Veijola, J., Miettunen, J., . . . Flint, J. (2009). 5-HTTLPR genotype and anxiety-related personality traits: A meta-analysis and new data. *American Journal of Medical Genetics. Part B, Neuropsychiatric Genetics: The Official Publication of the International Society of Psychiatric Genetics, 150B,* 271–281. doi: 10.1002/ajmg.b.30808

Maren, S. (2008). Pavlovian fear conditioning as a behavioral assay for hippocampus and amygdala function: Caution and caveats. *European Journal of Neuroscience, 28,* 1661–1666. doi: 10.1111/j.1460-9568.2008.06485.x

McEvoy, P. M. & Mahoney, A. E. J. (2012). To be sure, to be sure: Intolerance of uncertainty mediates symptoms of various anxiety disorders and depression. *Behavior Therapy, 43,* 533–545. doi: 10.1016/j.beth.2011.02.007

Merckelbach, H., Van den Hout, M. A., Hoekstra, R., & de Ruiter, C. (1989). Conditioning experiences and phobias. *Behaviour Research and Therapy, 27,* 657–662. doi: 10.1016/0005-7967(89)90149-6

Meulders, A., Mampaey, J., Boddez, Y., Blanco, F., Vansteenwegen, D., & Baeyens, F. (2013). Offset-control attenuates context conditioning induced by US-unpredictability in a human conditioned suppression paradigm. *Psychologica Belgica, 53,* 39–56. doi: 10.5334/pb-53-1-39

Mineka, S., Cook, M., & Miller, S. (1984). Fear conditioned with escapable and inescapable shock: Effects of a feedback stimulus. *Journal of Experimental Psychology: Animal Behavior Processes, 10,* 307–323.

Mineka, S. & Zinbarg, R. (2006). A contemporary learning theory perspective on the etiology of anxiety disorders. *American Psychologist, 61,* 10–26. doi: 10.1037/0003-066X.61.1.10

Miu, A. C., Vulturar, R., Chis, A., Ungureanu, L., & Gross, J. J. (2013). Reappraisal as a mediator in the link between 5-HTTLPR and social anxiety symptoms. *Emotion, 13,* 1012–1022. doi: 10.1037/a0033383

Mystkowski, J. L., Craske, M. G., & Echiverri, A. M. (2002). Treatment context and return of fear in spider phobia. *Behavior Therapy, 33,* 399–416.

Mystkowski, J. L., Craske, M. G., Echiverri, A. M., & Labus, J. S. (2006). Mental reinstatement of context and return of fear in spider-fearful participants. *Behavior Therapy, 37,* 49–60. doi: 10.1016/j.beth.2005.04.001

Nelson, B. D., Weinberg, A., Pawluk, J., Gawlowska, M., & Proudfit, G. H. (2015). An event-related potential investigation of fear generalization and intolerance of uncertainty. *Behavior Therapy, 46,* 661–670. doi: 10.1016/j.beth.2014.09.010

Norrholm, S. D., Vervliet, B., Jovanovic, T., Boshoven, W., Myers, K. M., Davis, M., . . ., & Duncan, E. J. (2008). Timing of extinction relative to acquisition: A parametric analysis of fear extinction in humans. *Behavioral Neuroscience, 122,* 1016–1030. doi: 10.1037/a0012604

Offidani, E., Guidi, J., Tomba, E., & Fava, G. A. (2013). Efficacy and tolerability of benzodiazepines versus antidepressants in anxiety disorders: A systematic review and meta-analysis. *Psychotherapy and Psychosomatics, 82,* 355–362. doi: 10.1159/000353198

Olatunji, B. O., Tomarken, A., Wentworth, B., & Fritzsche, L. (2017). Effects of exposure in single and multiple contexts on fear renewal: The moderating role of threat-specific and nonspecific emotionality. *Journal of Behavior Therapy and Experimental Psychiatry, 54*, 270–277. doi: 10.1016/j.jbtep.2016.09.004

Olsson, A., Nearing, K. I., & Phelps, E. A. (2007). Learning fear by observing other: The neural systems of social fear transmission. *Social Cognitive and Affective Neuroscience, 2*, 3–11. doi: 10.1093/scan/nsm005

Olsson, A. & Phelps, E. A. (2004). Learned fear of "unseen" faces after Pavlovian, observational, and instructed fear. *Psychological Science, 15*, 822–828. doi: 10.1111/j.0956-7976.2004.00762.x

Öst, L.-G., Havnen, A., Hansen, B., & Kvale, G. (2015). Cognitive behavioral treatment of obsessive-compulsive disorder: A systematic review and meta-analysis of studies published 1993–2014. *Clinical Psychology Review, 40*, 156–169. doi: 10.1016/j.cpr.2015.06.003

Öst, L.-G. & Hugdahl, K. (1981). Acquisition of phobias and anxiety response patterns in clinical patients. *Behaviour Research and Therapy, 19*, 439–447.

Pavlov, I. P. (1927). *Conditioned Reflexes: An Investigation of the Physiological Activity of the Cerebral Cortex*. London: Oxford University Press.

Phelps, E. A., Connor, K. J. O., Gatenby, J. C., Gore, J. C., & Davis, M. (2001). Activation of the left amygdala to a cognitive representation of fear. *Nature Neuroscience, 4*, 437–441. doi: 10.1038/86110

Pittig, A., Brand, M., Pawlikowski, M., & Alpers, G. W. (2014). The cost of fear: Avoidant decision making in a spider gambling task. *Journal of Anxiety Disorders, 28*, 326–334. doi: 10.1016/j.anxdis.2014.03.001

Poulton, R. & Menzies, R. (2002). Non-associative fear acquisition: A review of the evidence from retrospective and longitudinal research. *Behaviour Research and Therapy, 40*, 127–149.

Rachman, S. J. (1977). The conditioning theory of fear acquisition: A critical examination. *Behaviour Research and Therapy, 15*, 375–387. doi: 10.1016/0005-7967(77)90041-9

Rachman, S. J. (1989). The return of fear: Review and prospect. *Clinical Psychology Review, 9*, 147–168. doi: 10.1016/0272-7358(89)90025-1

Rau, V., DeCola, J. P., & Fanselow, M. S. (2005). Stress-induced enhancement of fear learning: An animal model of posttraumatic stress disorder. *Neuroscience and Biobehavioral Reviews, 29*, 1207–1223. doi: 10.1016/j.neubiorev.2005.04.010

Rescorla, R. A. (1974). Effect of inflation of the unconditioned stimulus value following conditioning. *Journal of Comparative and Physiological Psychology, 86*, 101–106.

Rinck, M. & Becker, E. S. (2006). Spider fearful individuals attend to threat, then quickly avoid it: Evidence from eye movements. *Journal of Abnormal Psychology, 115*, 231–238. doi: 10.1037/0021-843X.115.2.231

Rodriguez, B. I., Craske, M. G., Mineka, S., & Hladek, D. (1999). Context-specificity of relapse: Effects of therapist and environmental context on return of fear. *Behaviour Research and Therapy, 37*, 845–862.

Scheveneels, S., Boddez, Y., Vervliet, B., & Hermans, D. (2016). The validity of laboratory-based treatment research: Bridging the gap between fear extinction and exposure treatment. *Behaviour Research and Therapy*, *86*, 87–94. doi: 10.1016/j.brat.2016.08.015

Schroijen, M. & Pappens, M. (2015). Generalization of fear to respiratory sensations. *Behavior Therapy*, *46*, 611–626. doi: 10.1016/j.beth.2015.05.004

Sehlmeyer, C., Schöning, S., Zwitserlood, P., Pfleiderer, B., Kircher, T., Arolt, V., & Konrad, C. (2009). Human fear conditioning and extinction in neuroimaging: A systematic review. *PLoS ONE*, *4*, e5865. doi: 10.1371/journal.pone.0005865

Shin, L. M. & Liberzon, I. (2010). The neurocircuitry of fear, stress, and anxiety disorders. *Neuropsychopharmacology Reviews*, *35*, 169–191. doi: 10.1038/npp.2009.83

Sijbrandij, M., Engelhard, I. M., Lommen, M. J., Leer, A., & Baas, J. M. (2013). Impaired fear inhibition learning predicts the persistence of symptoms of posttraumatic stress disorder (PTSD). *Journal of Psychiatric Research*, *47*, 1991–1997.

Tabor, H. K., Risch, N. J., & Myers, R. M. (2002). Candidate-gene approaches for studying complex genetic traits: Practical considerations. *Nature Reviews. Genetics*, *3*, 391–397. doi: 10.1038/nrg796

Torrents-Rodas, D., Fullana, M. A., Bonillo, A., Caseras, X., Andión, O., & Torrubia, R. (2013). No effect of trait anxiety on differential fear conditioning or fear generalization. *Biological Psychology*, *92*, 185–190. doi: 10.1016/j.biopsycho.2012.10.006

Van Gucht, D., Vansteenwegen, D., Van den Bergh, O., & Beckers, T. (2008). Conditioned craving cues elicit an automatic approach tendency. *Behaviour Research and Therapy*, *46*, 1160–1169.

Van Meurs, B., Wiggert, N., Wicker, I., & Lissek, S. (2014). Maladaptive behavioral consequences of conditioned fear generalization: A pronounced, yet sparsely studied feature of anxiety pathology. *Behaviour Research and Therapy*, *57*, 29–37. doi: 10.1016/j.brat.2014.03.009

Vansteenwegen, D., Vervliet, B., Hermans, D., Thewissen, R., & Eelen, P. (2007). Verbal, behavioural and physiological assessment of the generalization of exposure-based fear reduction in a spider-anxious population. *Behavioural Research and Therapy*, *45*, 291–300. doi: 10.1016/j.brat.2006.03.008

Vasey, M. W., Harbaugh, C. N., Buffington, A. G., Jones, C. R., & Fazio, R. H. (2012). Predicting return of fear following exposure therapy with an implicit measure of attitudes. *Behaviour Research and Therapy*, *50*, 767–774. doi: 10.1016/j.brat.2012.08.007

Vervliet, B., Baeyens, F., Van den Bergh, O., & Hermans, D. (2013). Extinction, generalization, and return of fear: A critical review of renewal research in humans. *Biological Psychology*, *92*, 51–58. doi: 10.1016/j.biopsycho.2012.01.006

Vervliet, B., Craske, M. G., & Hermans, D. (2013). Fear extinction and relapse: State of the art. *Annual Review of Clinical Psychology*, *9*, 215–248. doi: 10.1146/annurev-clinpsy-050212-185542

Vervliet, B. & Indekeu, E. (2015). Low-cost avoidance behaviors are resistant to fear extinction in humans. *Frontiers in Behavioral Neuroscience*, *9*. doi: 10.3389/fnbeh.2015.00351

Vervliet, B. & Raes, F. (2013). Criteria of validity in experimental psychopathology: Application to models of anxiety and depression. *Psychological Medicine*, *43*, 2241–2244. doi: 10.1017/S0033291712002267

Vervoort, E., Vervliet, B., Bennett, M., & Baeyens, F. (2014). Generalization of human fear acquisition and extinction within a novel arbitrary stimulus category. *PLoS ONE*, *9*(5): e96569. https://doi.org/10.1371/journal.pone.0096569

Waters, A., LeBeau, R., & Craske, M. (2017). Experimental psychopathology and clinical psychology: An integrative model. *Psychopathology Review*, *4*, 112–128. doi: 10.5127/pr.038015

Watson, J. B. & Rayner, R. (1920). Conditioned emotional reactions. *Journal of Experimental Psychology*, *3*, 1–14.

Wendt, J., Neubert, J., Lindner, K., Ernst, F. D., Homuth, G., Weike, A. I., Hamm, A. O. (2014). Genetic influences on the acquisition and inhibition of fear. *International Journal of Psychophysiology*, *98*, 499–505. doi: 10.1016/j.ijpsycho.2014.10.007

Wolitzky-Taylor, K. B., Horowitz, J. D., Powers, M. B., & Telch, M. J. (2008). Psychological approaches in the treatment of specific phobias: A meta-analysis. *Clinical Psychology Review*, *28*, 1021–1037. doi: 10.1016/j.cpr.2008.02.007

2 Attentional Bias and the Anxiety Disorders

Ernst H. W. Koster and Anouk Vanden Bogaerde

In understanding anxiety and its related disorders several distinctive questions have been raised that are considered crucial in developing a mechanistic understanding of how anxiety develops and persists. One initial question pertains to why some individuals are more prone to experience anxiety than others. Another key question is why in some individuals encountering threatening events is associated with the persistence of anxiety. Cognitive behavioral accounts of anxiety have typically integrated behavioral mechanisms derived from learning theory (e.g., classical conditions, see Chapter 1, this volume) and cognitive processes at the level of attention, interpretation, and memory (e.g., Beck, Emery, & Greenberg, 1985). In anxiety especially, attentional mechanisms have received huge research interest in the past 40 years. The current chapter provides an overview of the progress in this research area.

Initial research in this domain was strongly influenced by the cognitive model of Beck (Beck et al., 1985) and the associative network model by Bower (1981, 1987). Beck's cognitive model of anxiety argues that, based on previous experiences, individuals develop cognitive schemas: memory representations of situations in relation to the self and emotions. Based on threatening experiences, individuals develop so-called danger schemas that subsequently guide information processing. For instance, if a child has experienced bullying by a group of kids at a playground, upon entering the playground at another moment the child will be more vigilant for novel signs of potential bullying (e.g., groups of kids). These notions led Beck to propose that anxious individuals were characterized by overactive danger schemas. Through the influence of these danger schemas, attention is mainly focused on information that is schema-congruent, which leads to the confirmation of existing negative beliefs.

Bower (1981) developed an associative network model of memory that proposed that through the process of co-activation, concepts become associated in memory with specific concepts being stored as nodes. Importantly, emotions are also stored as nodes in these representational networks, where, based on individual experiences, emotions are linked to a plethora of other concepts. Within this framework it becomes clear that once emotions are active, processing of information is mood-dependent and frequently mood-congruent. These latter ideas have strongly influenced the focus on disorder-relevant information in the study of attentional mechanisms.

These initial models instigated a dearth of empirical research into the association between anxiety and attentional bias to threat. Within this research attentional bias was conceptualized as the excessive processing of threat at the expense of other information. Recently, within the Research Domain Criteria (RDoC) initiative within the Negative Valence Systems Domain, the construct of sustained threat has been related to attention to threat (Cuthbert, 2014). One of the key advantages of the RDoC matrix is that constructs can be defined within multiple units of analysis, including genes, molecules, cells, neural circuits, physiology, behavior, and self-report. Attentional biases can be assessed at several of these levels, including behavioral (e.g., reaction times or eye tracking), physiological (e.g., event-related potentials), and neural units of analysis. We briefly consider the main empirical designs that have been used to establish the link between anxiety and attentional bias to threat, where most studies have used behavioral designs.

Measuring Attentional Bias

A wide range of tasks has been developed to measure attentional bias to threat. Most of these tasks are modifications of well-known cognitive-experimental tasks. The majority of research uses tasks where reaction times are the main dependent variable.

Emotional Stroop task. This task is based on the traditional Stroop color-word task (Stroop, 1935) where individuals need to name the print color of words while ignoring their semantic content (e.g., participants have to identify "green" as the print color of the word "red"). In the emotional version, reaction times to name the color of threat-related versus neutral words are compared to index to what extent the threatening meaning of a word interferes with the main task. The typical pattern of findings is that individuals with high trait anxiety or an anxiety disorder require more time to name the color of threatening, disorder-related words compared to low-anxious individuals (see Williams, Mathews, & MacLeod, 1996).

Although very widely used, the emotional Stroop task has been criticized as a measure of attentional bias since the color-naming interference observed for threatening words could be due to other non-attentional processing, such as behavioral interference or avoidance (Algom, Chajut, & Lev, 2004; Brosschot & De Ruiter, 1994).

Dichotic listening task. In a number of early studies, researchers used the dichotic listening paradigm where individuals are presented with auditory information that they have to shadow verbally. Occasionally in the other ear they are presented with threatening or neutral words at low volume. Participants are then probed about the target words they heard in the other ear. In several experiments it was demonstrated that individuals with elevated anxiety states were more likely to identify target words with a threatening meaning as compared to target words with a neutral meaning (Mathews & MacLeod, 1985). Moreover, in an elegant experiment, Parkinson and Rachman (1981) provided evidence for the notion of mood congruency. They presented illness-related and neutral words to either mothers with a child who was in the hospital or a mother without a sick child. Results showed that illness-related words were more likely perceived by the mothers with a child in the hospital.

Problems with this task have also been noted. One particularly difficult issue is to present auditory information close to awareness. Here it has been argued that awareness is influenced by a host of different processes where it is difficult to assure that stimuli cannot be perceived consciously (Holender, 1986).

Dot probe task. Another very commonly used task to assess spatial attention is the visual dot probe task. The dot probe task (MacLeod et al., 1986) displays two words on a computer screen with one at the top and one at the bottom (alternatively, the words may appear on the left and right sides of the screen). Following a brief stimulus presentation duration (e.g., 500 ms), the stimuli disappear and a probe appears in a location previously occupied by one of the stimuli. The participant is asked to press a button indicating whether the top or bottom stimulus had been replaced by the probe. Attentional biases are inferred from different response times to probes that replace threatening stimuli (i.e., congruent trials) compared to probes that replace neutral stimuli (i.e., incongruent trials). If an individual's attention is systematically drawn to the threat stimulus, response times will be shorter for probes that replace threatening stimuli compared to probes that replace neutral stimuli. A wealth of research has demonstrated attentional biases in the dot probe task (e.g., Bar-Haim et al., 2007; Mogg & Bradley, 1998).

It is noteworthy that compared with the original dot probe task of MacLeod et al. (1986), there have been several methodological variations and improvements, which include the removal of the instruction to read aloud one of the words, the use of a probe classification task instead of a detection task, and the comparison between stimulus categories, including all neutral trials as baseline comparison.

Visual search task. The visual search task (e.g., Öhman, Flykt, & Lundqvist, 2000) also allows for the assessment of spatial attentional allocation. Participants are directed to detect a target stimulus that is embedded in a matrix of distracting stimuli. For example, the target word "spider" might be displayed in a matrix (e.g., a three-row by three-column pattern of stimulus presentation) of neutral distracter words. Conversely, a neutral target word may be embedded in a matrix of spider-related words. Attentional biases are inferred from faster response times to detect a threatening stimulus in a matrix of neutral stimuli relative to response times to detect neutral stimuli in neutral matrices (i.e., the individual's attention is drawn to the threat stimulus). Attentional biases can also be inferred from slower response times to detect neutral stimuli in a matrix of threatening stimuli relative to response times to detect neutral stimuli in a matrix of neutral stimuli (i.e., the individual's attention is captured by the threat stimulus).

One of the important advantages of the visual search task over the other attentional tasks is that many stimuli are presented simultaneously, which requires an active search process of participants. Moreover, the speed of the target search in relation to the number of distracting stimuli allows examining whether threatening information "pops out," with search slopes being unaffected by the number of distracters. Some initial studies suggested that threatening information is indeed associated with flat search slopes, suggesting that threatening information automatically attracts attention (Öhman et al., 2000). However, more recent research suggests that threatening information can be detected faster than neutral information but still is affected by the amount of distracting information and does not meet the criteria for pop-out (Horstmann, 2007).

Spatial cueing task. The spatial cueing task (Fox, Russo, Bowles, & Dutton, 2001; Posner, 1980) also allows for the assessment of spatial attention allocation. Participants focus on a fixation point located between two rectangles. A cue is then presented (in the emotional variant of the cueing task, typically an emotional word or picture), followed by the appearance of a target in one of the two rectangles. Participants are asked to press a key indicating the rectangle in which the target is located. Some of the trials are valid cues (the cue draws attention to the rectangle in which the target is located); some of the trials are invalid cues (the cue draws attention away from the rectangle in which the target is located). Facilitated attentional engagement with threat is indicated by faster responses on valid threat-cued trials relative to neutral-cued trials. Impaired attentional disengagement from threat is indicated by slower responses on invalidly threat-cued trials relative to neutral-cued trials. The spatial cueing task has been used in a considerable number of studies and has proven useful in studying different components (attentional engagement and disengagement) of attentional bias to threat (Fox et al., 2001). However, there is debate over the validity of distinguishing between these two components of attentional bias using the spatial cueing task (see Mogg, Holmes, Garner, & Bradley, 2008).

Other paradigms. In addition to these very commonly used measures there now are a number of paradigms that have been used in multiple studies that have specific advantages over the paradigms discussed previously in investigating specific research questions. One important research in the domain of attentional bias to threat is whether attentional bias emerges automatically. Specific paradigms that are well suited to investigate this question are *rapid serial visual presentation* (e.g., Anderson, 2005) and *binocular rivalry* (Bannerman, Milders, De Gelder, & Sahraie, 2008).

Eye tracking. Eye tracking is an interesting ecologically valid measure of spatial attention as there is a close relation between covert and overt shifts of attention (see Weierich, Treat, & Hollingworth, 2008). Eye tracking is often combined with the spatial attention paradigms discussed earlier. Under normal circumstances, visual information is gathered by making rapid eye movements, known as saccades.

Saccadic eye movements are crucial to visual perception as they bring objects of interest onto the fovea, the central region of the retina, which is required for high-resolution processing of visual information. In studies using eye tracking, several components of visual attention can be studied, including the speed of initial saccades, the number of fixations made to specific stimuli, and the fixation duration on stimuli. Although there are a number of studies where correspondence is shown between manual response data and eye movements (e.g., Bradley, Mogg, & Millar, 2000), other studies indicate that eye tracking (speed of saccades) may under some circumstances provide a more sensitive measure of early attentional bias for emotional information (e.g., Bannerman, Milders, & Sahraie, 2009).

Several early studies have used eye tracking to obtain a more comprehensive picture of the temporal unfolding of attentional bias to threat. For instance, Hermans, Vansteenwegen, and Eelen (1999) presented spider-anxious and non-spider-anxious individuals with pictures of a spider and a flower for three seconds. Results showed that spider-anxious participants initially looked more to spiders than to flowers, yet subsequently their viewing pattern shifted more and more away from the spiders. Interestingly, eye tracking can also be used outside of the context of well-controlled laboratory tasks to study free viewing in more naturalistic environments. In this context, researchers have combined eye tracking with virtual reality environments to study the deployment of attention to potentially threatening information (e.g., Rinck et al., 2010). Importantly, meta-analytic evidence from eye-tracking studies indicates that anxiety is characterized by attentional bias to threat (Armstrong & Olatunji, 2012).

Main Research Findings

What are the main findings based on the large empirical literature on attentional bias? Meta-analytic evidence indicates that there is empirical evidence for an attentional bias across the different anxiety disorders, obtained through a variety of different tasks (Bar-Haim et al., 2007). Importantly, attentional bias is also observed in individuals with high trait anxiety scores, which suggests that attentional bias is not a mere correlate of clinical anxiety but may also be involved in the development of anxiety disorders. Although the observed effect size of attentional bias in high-anxious versus low-anxious individuals is moderate, subsequent research has indicated that there is strong heterogeneity in the results obtained in individual studies (Van Bockstaele et al., 2014). Within this broad literature, several more specific issues emerged that are important to discuss here.

Nature of Attentional Bias

Despite the large number of studies, there is ongoing debate about the nature of attentional bias. The general notion of preferential processing of threatening, disorder-relevant information over more neutral information does not seem to provide a sufficiently clear description of the phenomenon. A topic that received ample attention is the question with regard to the *automaticity of attentional bias*. Based on the observation that attentional bias could be observed at very early stages of processing, with very brief stimulus presentation and interfering with top-down goals, early theories suggested that attentional bias is an automatic process that is based on a very fast evaluation mechanism that operates at a preconscious level (Williams, Watts, MacLeod, & Mathews, 1988). Indeed, there is some empirical evidence showing that attentional bias to threat can occur very fast (Öhman et al., 2000). However, other theorists (Wells & Matthews, 1994) have refuted this claim by highlighting that attentional bias to threat occurs because of the link between specific stimuli (e.g., angry faces) and individuals' goals (e.g., avoiding rejection). Interestingly, recent studies suggest, in line with findings from basic attention studies, that goals are highly relevant in the deployment of attention. In an interesting study, Vogt and colleagues (Vogt, Houwer, Crombez, & Van Damme, 2013) showed that the presence of goal-relevant stimuli can override attentional bias to threat, even in high trait anxious individuals.

Another debate entails the *time course of attentional bias to threat*. There is a broad distinction between early and later stages of processing where at early stages most research seems to suggest that attention is oriented more toward threat in high-anxious individuals. At later processing stages, especially in certain types of anxiety disorders, attention is oriented away from threat. This pattern of deployment of attention has been labeled the *vigilance-avoidance pattern of attentional bias*, which is argued to explain how initial attentional bias to threat causes elevated anxiety with the attentional avoidance interfering with subsequent habituation (Mogg, Mathews, & Weinman, 1987). Other theorists have proposed somewhat different patterns of temporal unfolding of attentional bias to threat. For instance, Eysenck (1992) suggested that high-anxious individuals initially show broad scanning of the environment for threat, followed by a narrowed focus of attention to threat upon detection, combined with difficulties to disengage attention away from threat.

A recent contribution to this topic is the idea that maybe previous research has ignored the temporal dynamics of attentional bias to threat through the way traditional attentional bias scores have been used. Several groups have argued that the typical approach to aggregate attentional bias scores from more than 100 trials in standard attentional tasks may not be the appropriate way to capture the dynamic nature of attentional bias (Iacoviello et al., 2014; Zvielli, Bernstein, & Koster, 2015). These authors argued that analyses based on shorter bouts of trials could help to express attentional bias in a more dynamic way. In several studies, it now has been shown that more dynamic expressions seem to be more closely linked to psychopathology. Moreover, the psychometrics of attentional bias indexes, where traditional bias scores typically have low split-half and test-retest reliability (see Rodebaugh et al., 2016 for an extensive discussion), are much more acceptable. Here it is noteworthy that some of the novel bias scores may be susceptible to false positive findings, Type I error (Kruit, Field, & Fox, 2016). Hence, further research is needed to develop better operationalization of the dynamic aspects of attentional bias.

Attentional Bias and the Development and Maintenance of Anxiety Disorders

Whether attentional bias to threat is a mere correlate of anxiety disorders or has an important causal role in the development or maintenance of anxiety disorders is a topic of intense research interest (for an extensive discussion, see Van Bockstaele et al., 2014). One could argue that there is a bidirectional link with anxiety influencing attentional processes and attentional processes influencing anxiety. With regard to the first notion, some empirical research shows that the presence of anxiety disorders influences the presence of attentional bias. For instance, there is a wealth of research showing that after treatment of anxiety disorders, attentional bias to threat is reduced to levels similar to non-anxious individuals (e.g., Tobon, Ouimet, & Dozois, 2011). Still, this observation does not rule out the possibility that attentional bias plays a role in the development and maintenance of anxiety disorders. We now discuss the research approaches used to assess whether attentional biases play a causal role in anxiety disorders.

Given the well-documented association between anxiety and attentional bias (which is a prerequisite to studying the nature of the association), several research lines have been developed to provide more information about the potential causal role of attentional bias to threat in developing anxiety disorders. Key research lines are: (1) developmental studies; (2) prospective studies; (3) experimental studies. Note that none of the research lines by itself is sufficient to conclude that attentional bias to threat has a causal influence on the development and maintenance of anxiety disorders: a comprehensive understanding can only emerge through assessment of the data available on all three research lines.

Developmental Studies

Provided that many anxiety disorders have their origin in childhood, there has been a fair amount of research on the presence of attentional bias to threat in anxious youth, yet oftentimes with variable results. This could be due to many different reasons, where (1) compared to adults there is more variability in response times, which makes reaction times as outcome variable difficult; (2) maturational processes in executive functions may influence the expression of attentional bias where it is difficult to include many age ranges in a single study; and finally (3) many studies use slightly different task parameters, which makes studies difficult to compare.

A recent, highly relevant study (Abend et al., 2018) reported on a large participant pool (N = 1,291) comprised of a mixed, heterogeneous sample of children and adolescents with an age range of 6–18 years with a wide range in anxiety symptoms. This sample was collected over a number of different sites where they completed an identical variant of a dot probe task. In this dot probe task, emotional and neutral faces were presented for 500 ms. In this study, a positive correlation was found between attentional bias to threat and severity of overall anxiety symptoms. Although significant, this correlation was small (r < 0.1), where associations appeared most pronounced for social anxiety and school phobia symptoms. Interestingly, no support was found for strong influences of age or gender on the expression of attentional bias.

Next to establishing an association between attentional bias to threat and anxiety disorders in youth, research has also examined possible developmental trajectories between well-known temperamental factors that are associated with anxiety disorders and attentional bias. One of these factors is *behavioral inhibition*, which is considered a highly robust temperamental factor predicting anxiety disorders (Biederman et al., 1993). A wide body of studies has examined whether behavioral inhibition and anxiety in interaction predict anxiety disorders later on (Pérez-Edgar, Bar-Haim, McDermott, Chronis-Tuscano, Pine, & Fox, 2010). Here, several studies find a prospective relationship (Pérez-Edgar et al., 2010) whereas other studies fail to find a prospective association between behavioral inhibition and attentional bias on later-stage anxiety disorders (White et al., 2017).

Another factor considered in empirical research is effortful control in relation to attentional bias and anxiety. Effortful control is the ability to activate or inhibit behavior and voluntarily deploy attention as required to better adaptively fit the context (i.e., being able to refocus on a task after being distracted; Rothbart & Bates, 2006). The idea within this context is that children who are able to efficiently and flexibly shift their attention can more readily disengage their attention from threat. This could help them to counteract or override attentional bias to threat (Lonigan, Vasey, Phillips, & Hazen, 2004; White et al., 2017). Some empirical evidence supports this assertion (Cole, Zapp, Fettig, & Pérez-Edgar, 2016).

Prospective Studies

The approach adopted in the initial prospective studies is to examine whether attentional bias measured at an initial time point can predict subsequent emotional reactivity and state anxiety, with the latter variable serving as a proxy for the vulnerability to develop anxiety disorders. In this context, Macleod and Hagan (1992) examined whether attentional bias to threat influenced emotional reactivity in individuals confronted with stressful life events. For this purpose, women awaiting a colonoscopy (an endoscopic examination of the bowels) were screened with an emotional Stroop task containing masked and unmasked presentations of emotional words. The results showed that trait anxiety was associated with an automatic Stroop interference, indicating selective attention to threat. In the women diagnosed with cervical pathology, automatic Stroop interference predicted the intensity of emotional distress. The Stroop interference effect also predicted the emotional response better than any of the explicit questionnaire measures (such as trait anxiety).

These effects were replicated in normal volunteers who were, at the time of administration of the emotional Stroop task, not in a stressful state. Trait anxiety correlated with responding to interference at a subliminal version of the emotional Stroop, and the subliminal Stroop effect correlated with questionnaire scores on emotional vulnerability (Van den Hout, Tenney, Huygens, Merckelbach, & Kindt, 1995). Moreover, a more recent, larger prospective study examined whether conscious or nonconscious threat bias predicted emotional reactivity using salivary cortisol and state anxiety measures (Fox, Cahill, & Zougkou, 2010). This study found that a preconscious negative processing bias predicted cortisol responding to stressful events, again to a larger degree than self-report measures of neuroticism, trait anxiety, and extraversion.

Despite these interesting studies suggesting that attentional bias to threat is prospectively associated with stress reactivity, note that at present not many large-scale prospective studies are examining whether attentional bias predicts anxiety disorders. Hence, the current data are in line with the idea that attentional bias to threat may increase the vulnerability to anxiety, yet this link needs to be established more definitively in larger-scale studies.

Experimental Manipulation

Experimental designs are undoubtedly crucial in establishing the causal influence of one variable on another variable. MacLeod and colleagues (2001) conducted several seminal experiments manipulating attentional bias and examining the causal impact on emotional reactivity. Using a modified dot probe task, they manipulated attentional bias either toward or away from threat by consistently placing the task-relevant probe at the location of a threatening word (attention toward threat) or at the location opposite from a threat word (reducing attentional bias). They found that such a single session of attention training (consisting of close to 600 trials) was sufficient to influence emotional reactivity in a subsequent stressful task: the group trained to orient toward threatening information responded with more distress than the group trained to orient attention away from threat.

The procedure to retrain attentional bias to threat received wide research interest and was subsequently termed *attentional bias modification* (ABM) (Koster, MacLeod, & Fox, 2009). A number of initial studies were able to demonstrate that ABM could also be applied in clinical populations (e.g., in social phobia and generalized anxiety disorder) and had interesting effects on anxiety symptoms (Amir, Beard, Burns, & Bomyea, 2009). These results seem to suggest that attentional bias plays a causal role in the maintenance of anxiety disorders. However, no conclusions can be drawn with regard to attentional bias as an etiological factor since it is not clear whether an induced attentional bias operates in the same way as a naturally occurring attentional bias. In recent years a number of non-replications and null results were published and current meta-analyses indicate that the effects of ABM are highly limited (Cristea, Kok, & Cuijpers, 2015; Hallion & Ruscio, 2011; Mogoase, David, & Koster, 2014). One main reason for the mixed findings seems to be the varying efficacy of the dot probe training in manipulating attentional bias. There are both theoretical and empirical reasons to doubt whether the current dominant procedure to induce or reduce attentional bias to threat is the most optimal procedure (see Koster & Bernstein, 2015). It is noteworthy that more novel, gamified training procedures have been developed recently that could provide promising avenues. These procedures include Attention Feedback and Awareness Training (A-FACT) (Bernstein & Zvielli, 2014) and the Eye-gaze Contingent Attentional Training (ECAT) (Sanchez et al., 2016). In A-FACT, individuals are made aware when their attention is biased and are instructed to allocate attention in a more balanced way to threatening as well as neutral information. In ECAT, individuals' reading behavior is monitored through eye tracking and individuals receive online feedback about their deployment of attention to negative and positive information. Initial findings suggest that such novel attentional training procedures can influence emotional reactivity. In another novel approach, individuals are reinforced for allocating attention away from negative toward positive information (Lazarov et al., 2017; Price et al., 2016). The paper by Lazarov et al. showed that such innovative attention training had beneficial effects in individuals with social anxiety disorder.

In sum, there is some evidence that experimental manipulation of attentional bias has a causal influence on emotional reactivity and anxiety symptoms, suggesting a causal relationship. However, given the problems with current methodology to experimentally manipulate attentional bias, novel methodologies are needed to more firmly establish the strength of this association.

Major Theoretical Models

Based on the extensive research, a number of different models have been developed to account for attentional bias in anxiety. Here we do not aim to provide a detailed and exhaustive overview of the many different models that have been proposed throughout the past decades (for such overviews, see Cisler & Koster, 2010; Mogg & Bradley, 2016). In this section, we describe some of the most influential models that provide important conceptual ideas with regard to the interplay between attentional bias and anxiety. This model was in line with observations that high-anxious individuals allocated more attention to threat than low-anxious individuals and was instrumental in providing detailed models of attentional bias to threat that could be investigated empirically.

Biased attentional direction account (Williams et al., 1988). One of the earliest detailed specifications of the mechanisms governing attentional bias to threat is the model by Williams et al. (1988). They propose that stimulus input is initially appraised (automatically) as threatening or nonthreatening through an affective decision mechanism. The outcome of the affective decision process feeds into a resource allocation mechanism where the direction of attention to threat is determined. The resource allocation mechanism is influenced by trait anxiety, where high trait anxiety individuals have the tendency to attend to threat, whereas low trait anxiety individuals have the tendency to avoid threat.

Cognitive-motivational model (Mogg & Bradley, 1998). Based on the initial work of Williams et al. (1988), Mogg and Bradley argued that from an evolutionary perspective, a stable tendency to orient attention away from threat in low-anxious individuals would make little sense. That is, attention to highly threatening stimuli is crucial for survival in all individuals. Therefore, they reconsidered the mechanisms involved in attentional bias to threat. They proposed that incoming information is appraised with a valence-evaluation system where there is a crude evaluation of stimuli being either low or highly threatening. This evaluation is influenced by several contextual variables such as state anxiety and learning history with certain stimuli. If stimuli are appraised, this information feeds into a goal engagement system where current attention to ongoing task and behavior is maintained if a stimulus is tagged as low threatening. If a stimulus is appraised as highly threatening, ongoing behavior is interrupted and attention is allocated to threat in order to further process this information. Individual differences in trait anxiety are proposed to influence the sensitivity of the valence-evaluation system. Anxious individuals have a lower threshold before stimuli are appraised as highly threatening.

Empirical support for these ideas has come from studies where attentional bias was studied for stimuli with varying degrees of threat. This allows researchers to test the prediction from the cognitive-motivational model that all individuals will allocate attentional bias to threat and only high-anxious individuals will allocate attention to more mildly threatening information. Several studies indeed found that attentional bias to threat was observed more strongly in high-anxious individuals even for only moderately threatening information (Mogg et al., 2000; Wilson & MacLeod, 2003).

Self-regulatory executive function model (Wells & Matthews,1994). Wells and Matthews (1994) developed a markedly different view in their self-regulatory executive function (S-REF) model. In this model, the authors lend more weight to the influence of top-down beliefs in guiding attentional bias to threat where they argue that attentional biases are linked to top-down processes instead of the more automatic processes that play a central role in the aforementioned models. Trait anxiety is linked to negative beliefs and problems at the level of executive control. These authors argue that the evidence for unconscious, fully automatic threat bias is very limited.

Attentional control theory (Eysenck et al., 2007). A more recent theory that has been highly influential is the attentional control theory. In this theory, the authors rely on the distinction by Corbetta and Schulman (2002) with regard to stimulus-driven, bottom-up and goal-driven, top-down processing to argue that anxiety changes this balance in favor of stimulus-driven processing when threat is present. This hampers several of the top-down functions related to executive control. This theory also uses the distinction between processing efficiency and effectiveness (Eysenck & Calvo, 1992) to argue that under conditions of low stress, individuals can counteract the effects of attentional bias to threat on performance effectiveness. Unfortunately, this requires compensatory efforts, which reduces processing efficiency.

In summary, a host of different models have been proposed to account for attentional bias to threat in anxiety. It is noteworthy that many of the different theories have focused on different aspects of attentional bias to threat where some of the tenets of different models are not mutually exclusive. Consequently, in some newer models authors have tried to integrate key ideas of different models to provide a more encompassing picture of attentional bias in anxiety (e.g., Mogg & Bradley, 2016).

Conclusions and Future Challenges

Attentional bias to threat is considered one of the key cognitive vulnerability factors for the development and maintenance of anxiety disorders. The past decades have seen important advances in the study of the nature as well as the influence of attentional bias in anxiety. The overview attests to the wide range of different research strategies that have addressed these questions from a number of different angles. Importantly, the current available data are suggestive of a causal role of attentional bias in both the vulnerability to anxiety disorders (emotional reactivity) as well as the maintenance of anxiety disorders (see Van Bockstaele et al., 2014). Within the RDoC framework, attentional bias to threat could be a key mechanism linking temperament and life experiences to cognitive and neural mechanisms of information processing, which can be linked to key elements of anxiety, including a stronger initial anxiety response and anxiety perseveration. Interestingly, initial work shows that different patterns of attentional bias to threat are related to these different components of anxiety (Rudaizky, Basanovic, & Macleod, 2014).

However, it is important to realize that currently the empirical evidence is suggestive rather than conclusive for a causal relation. The latter state of affairs seems to be related to key conceptual and methodological limitations. At the conceptual level, recent years have seen novel developments and discussion about the nature of attentional bias. In much research, anxiety-related attentional bias is implicitly treated as a stable phenomenon that can be captured across several hundred trials, with phasic fluctuation in attentional bias ignored or considered noise. Zvielli and colleagues (2015) have argued that this conceptualization seems to fit poorly with empirical data stemming from reaction time paradigms to assess attentional bias to threat. Based on a reconceptualization of attentional bias as a more dynamic phenomenon that can be expressed in phasic bursts of attentional bias toward as well as away from threatening information, novel ways to quantify attentional bias were developed. This type of reconceptualization also holds interesting promise for the field of attentional bias modification. This latter field holds great promise theoretically as well as clinically, but progress has been hampered by suboptimal ways to change attentional bias (see Koster & Bernstein, 2015). Here, improving on the conceptualization of attentional bias as well as developing more engaging ways to retrain attentional bias may provide major steps forward.

These innovations may be crucial to take the next step in clinical applications of attentional bias modification procedures. Theorists have quite early on argued that attentional bias modification is unlikely to serve as a stand-alone intervention in anxiety disorders (Baert, Koster, & De Raedt, 2011). Instead, there might be merit in combining attentional bias modification with current first-line treatments of anxiety disorders to facilitate the processing of anxiety-disconfirming information. The past years, several studies have tried to combine attentional bias modification with cognitive behavioral therapy techniques, with some studies finding beneficial effects of attentional bias modification as augmentation strategy (Lazarov, Marom, Yahalom, Pine, Haggai, & Bar-Haim, 2017), yet with other studies not observing beneficial effects of combining cognitive behavioral therapy and attentional bias modification on treatment outcomes (Rapee et al., 2013). In order for this research endeavor to succeed, it may be crucial to examine whether further individual assessment on the presence of attentional bias and subsequent tailoring of interventions is beneficial.

References

Abend, R., de Voogd, L., Salemink, E., Wiers, R.W., Pérez-Edgar, K., Fitzgerald, A., White, L. K., Salum, G. A., He, J., Silverman, W. K., Pettit, J. W., Pine, D.S., & Bar-Haim, Y. (2018). Association between attention bias to threat and anxiety symptoms in children and adolescents. *Depression and Anxiety, 35*(3), 229–238.

Algom, D., Chajut, E., & Lev, S. (2004). A rational look at the emotional Stroop phenomenon: A generic slowdown, not a Stroop effect. *Journal of Experimental Psychology: General, 133*, 323–338.

Amir, N., Beard, C., Burns, M., & Bomyea, J. (2009). Attention modification program in individuals with generalized anxiety disorder. *Journal of Abnormal Psychology, 118*, 28–33.

Anderson, A. K. (2005). Affective influences on the attentional dynamics supporting awareness. *Journal of Experimental Psychology: General, 134*, 258–281.

Armstrong, T. & Olatunji, B. O. (2012). Eye tracking of attention in the affective disorders: A metaanalytic review and synthesis. *Clinical Psychology Review, 32*, 704–723.

Baert, S., Koster, E. H. W., & De Raedt, R. (2011). Modification of information-processing biases in emotional disorders: Clinically relevant developments in experimental psychopathology. *International Journal of Cognitive Therapy, 4*, 205–219.

Bannerman, R. L., Milders, M., De Gelder, B., & Sahraie, A. (2008). Influence of emotional facial expressions on binocular rivalry. *Ophthalmic and Physiological Optics, 28* (4), 317–326.

Bannerman, R. L., Milders, M., & Sahraie, A. (2009). Processing emotional stimuli: Comparison of saccadic and manual choice-reaction times. *Cognition & Emotion, 23*, 930–954.

Bar-Haim, Y., Lamy, D., Pergamin, L., Bakermans-Kranenburg, M. J., & Van IJzendoorn, M. H. (2007). Threat-related attentional bias in anxious and nonanxious individuals: A meta-analytic study. *Psychological Bulletin, 133*(1), 1–24.

Beck, A. T., Emery, G., & Greenberg, R. L. (1985). *Anxiety Disorders and Phobias: A Cognitive Perspective.* New York, NY: Basic Books.

Bernstein, A. & Zvielli, A. (2014). Attention feedback awareness and control training (A-FACT): Experimental test of a novel intervention paradigm targeting attentional bias. *Behaviour Research and Therapy, 55*, 18–26.

Biederman, J., Rosenbaum, J. F., Bolducmurphy, E. A., Faraone, S. V., Chaloff, J., Hirshfeld, D. R., & Kagan, J. (1993). A 3-year follow-up of children with and without behavioural-inhibition. *Journal of the American Academy of Child and Adolescent Psychiatry, 32*, 814–821.

Bower, G. H. (1981). Mood and memory. *American Psychologist, 36*, 129–148.

Bower, G. H. (1987). Commentary on mood and memory. *Behaviour Research and Therapy, 25*, 443–455.

Bradley, B. P., Mogg, K., & Millar, N. H. (2000). Covert and overt orienting of attention to emotional faces in anxiety. *Cognition & Emotion, 14*(6), 789–808.

Cisler, J. M. & Koster, E. H. W. (2010). Mechanisms underlying attentional biases towards threat: An integrative review. *Clinical Psychology Review, 30*, 203–216.

Clark, D. M. (1999). Anxiety disorders: Why they persist and how to treat them. *Behaviour Research and Therapy, 37*, S5–S27.

Cole, C., Zapp, D. J., Fettig, N. B., & Pérez-Edgar, K. (2016). Impact of attention biases to threat and effortful control on individual variations in negative affect and social withdrawal in very young children. *Journal of Experimental Child Psychology, 141*, 210–221.

Corbetta, M. & Shulman, G. L. (2002). Control of goal-directed and stimulus-driven attention in the brain. *Nature Reviews Neuroscience, 3*, 201–215.

Cristea, I. A., Kok, R. N., & Cuijpers, P. (2015) Efficacy of cognitive bias modification interventions in anxiety and depression: Meta-analysis. *British Journal of Psychiatry, 206*, 7–16.

Cuthbert, B. N. (2014). The RDoC framework: Facilitating transition from ICD/DSM to dimensional approaches that integrate neuroscience and psychopathology. *World Psychiatry, 13*, 28–35.

De Ruiter, C. & Brosschot, J. F. (1994). The emotional Stroop interference effect in anxiety: Attentional bias or cognitive avoidance?*Behaviour Research and Therapy, 32*, 315–319.

Derryberry, D. & Reed, M. A. (2002). Anxiety-related attentional biases and their regulation by attentional control. *Journal of Abnormal Psychology, 111*, 225–236.

Eysenck, M. W. (1992). *Anxiety: The Cognitive Perspective*. Hove, UK: Erlbaum Ltd.

Eysenck, M. W. (1997). *Anxiety and Cognition: A Unified Theory*. Hove, UK: Erlbaum Ltd.

Eysenck, M. W. & Calvo, M. G. (1992). Anxiety and performance: The processing efficiency theory. *Cognition & Emotion, 6*, 409–434.

Eysenck, M. W., Derakshan, N., Santos, R., & Calvo, M. G. (2007). Anxiety and cognitive performance: Attentional control theory. *Emotion, 7*(2), 336–353.

Fox, E., Cahill, S., & Zougkou, K. (2010). Preconscious processing biases predict emotional reactivity to stress. *Biological Psychiatry, 67*, 371–377.

Fox, E., Russo, R., Bowles, R., & Dutton, K. (2001). Do threatening stimuli draw or hold visual attention in subclinical anxiety? *Journal of Experimental Psychology: General, 130*(4), 681–700.

Hallion, L. S., & Ruscio, A. M. (2011). A meta-analysis of the effect of cognitive bias modification on anxiety and depression. *Psychological Bulletin, 137*, 940–958.

Hermans, D., Vansteenwegen, D., & Eelen, P. (1999). Eye movement registration as a continuous index of attention deployment: Data from a group of spider anxious students. *Cognition & Emotion, 13*, 419–434.

Holender, D. (1986). Semantic activation without conscious identification in dichotic listening, parafoveal vision, and visual masking: A survey and appraisal. *Behavioral and Brain Sciences, 9*, 1–23.

Horstmann, G. (2007). Preattentive face processing: What do visual search experiments with schematic faces tell us? *Visual Cognition, 15*, 799–833.

Iacoviello, B. M., Wu, G., Abend, R., Murrough, J. W., Feder, A., Fruchter, E., Levinstein, Y., Wald, I., Bailey, C. R., Pine, D. S., Neumeister, A., Bar-Haim , Y., & Charney, D. S. (2014). Attention bias variability and symptoms of post-traumatic stress disorder. *Journal of Traumatic Stress, 27*, 1–8.

Koster, E. H. W. & Bernstein, A. (2015). Introduction to the special issue on cognitive bias modification: Taking a step back to move forward? *Journal of Behavior Therapy and Experimental Psychiatry, 49*, 1–4.

Koster, E. H. W., Fox, E., & MacLeod, C. (2009). Introduction of the special section on cognitive bias modification. *Journal of Abnormal Psychology, 118*, 1–4.

Kruijt, A. W., Field, A. P., & Fox, E. (2016). Capturing dynamics of biased attention: Are new attention variability measures the way forward? *PLOS One*, 11, e0166600.

Lazarov, A., Marom, S., Yahalom, N., Pine, D. S., Hermesh, H., & Bar-Haim, Y. (2017). Attention bias modification augments cognitive-behavioral group therapy for social anxiety disorder: A randomized controlled trial. *Psychological Medicine*, 1–9. doi: 10.1017/S003329171700366X.

Lazarov, A., Pine, D. S., & Bar-Haim, Y. (2017). Gaze-contingent music reward treatment for social anxiety disorder: A randomized controlled trial. *American Journal of Psychiatry, 174*, 649–656.

Lonigan, C. J., Vasey, M. W., Phillips, B. M., & Hazen, R. A. (2004). Temperament, anxiety, and the processing of threat-relevant stimuli. *Journal of Clinical Child and Adolescent Psychology, 33*, 8–20.

Macleod, C., & Hagan, R. (1992). Individual differences in the selective processing of threatening information, and emotional responses to a stressful life event. *Behaviour Research and Therapy, 30*, 151–161.

MacLeod, C. & Mathews, A. (1988). Anxiety and the allocation of attention to threat. *Quarterly Journal of Experimental Psychology, 40A*, 653–670.

MacLeod, C., Mathews, A., & Tata, P. (1986). Attentional bias in emotional disorders. *Journal of Abnormal Psychology, 95*, 15–20.

MacLeod, C. & Rutherford, E. M. (1992). Anxiety and the selective processing of emotional information: Mediating roles of awareness, trait and state variables, and personal relevance of stimulus materials. *Behaviour Research and Therapy, 30*, 479–491.

MacLeod, C., Rutherford, E., Campbell, L., Ebsworthy, G., & Holker, L. (2001). Selective attention and emotional vulnerability: Assessing the causal basis of their association through the experimental manipulation of attentional bias. *Journal of Abnormal Psychology, 111*, 107–123.

Mathews, A. & MacLeod, C. (1985). Selective processing of threat cues in anxiety states. *Behaviour Research and Therapy, 23*, 563–569.

Mathews, A. & MacLeod, C. (1994). Cognitive approaches to emotion and emotional disorders. *Annual Review of Psychology, 45*, 25–50.

Mogg, K. & Bradley, B. P. (1998). A cognitive-motivational analysis of anxiety. *Behaviour Research and Therapy, 36*, 809–848.

Mogg, K., & Bradley, B. P. (2016). Anxiety and attention to threat: Cognitive mechanisms and treatment with attention bias modification. *Behaviour Research and Therapy, 87*, 76–108.

Mogg, K., Bradley, B. P., Dixon, C., Fisher, S., Twelftree, H., & McWilliams, A. (2000). Trait anxiety, defensiveness and selective processing of threat: An investigation using two measures of attentional bias. *Personality and Individual Differences, 28*, 1063–1077.

Mogg, K., Holmes, A., Garner, M., & Bradley, B. P. (2008). Effects of threat cues on attentional shifting, disengagement and response slowing in anxious individuals. *Behaviour Research and Therapy, 46*, 656–667.

Mogg, K., Mathews, A., & Weinman, J. (1987). Memory bias in clinical anxiety. *Journal of Abnormal Psychology, 96*, 94–98.

Mogoase, C., David, D., & Koster, E. H. W. (2014). Clinical efficacy of attentional bias modification procedures: An updated meta-analysis. *Journal of Clinical Psychology, 70*, 1133–1157.

Öhman, A., Flykt, A., & Lundqvist, D. (2000). Unconscious emotion: Evolutionary perspectives, psychophysiological data, and neuropsychological mechanisms. In R. D. Lane & L. Nadel (eds.), *Cognitive Neuroscience of Emotion* (pp. 296–327). New York, NY: Oxford University Press.

Parkinson, L. & Rachman, S. (1981). Intrusive thoughts: The effects of an uncontrived stress. *Advances in Behaviour Research and Therapy, 3*, 111–118.

Pérez-Edgar, K., Bar-Haim, Y., McDermott, J. M., Chronis-Tuscano, A., Pine, D. S., & Fox, N. A. (2010). Attention biases to threat and behavioral inhibition in early childhood shape adolescent social withdrawal. *Emotion, 10*, 349–357.

Posner, M. I. (1980). Orienting of attention. *Quarterly Journal of Experimental Psychology, 32*(1), 3–25.

Price, R. B., Greven, I. M., Koster, E. H. W., Siegle, G. J., & De Raedt, R. (2016). A novel attention training paradigm based on operant conditioning of eye gaze: Preliminary findings. *Emotion, 16*, 110–116.

Rapee, R., Macleod, C., Carpenter, L., Gaston, J., Frei, J., Peters, L., & Baillie, A. (2013). Integrating cognitive bias modification into a standard cognitive behavioural treatment package for social phobia: A randomized controlled trial. *Behaviour Research and Therapy, 51*, 207–215.

Rinck, M., Kwakkenbos, L., Dotsch, R., Wigboldus, D., & Becker, E. S. (2010). Attentional and behavioral responses of spider fearfuls to virtual spiders. *Cognition & Emotion, 24*, 1199–1206.

Rodebaugh, T. L., Sculin, R. B., Langer, J. K., Dixon, D. J., Huppert, J. D., Bernstein, A., Zvielli, A., & Lenze, E. J. (2016). Unreliability as a threat to understanding psychopathology: The dot-probe task as cautionary tale. *Journal of Abnormal Psychology*, 125(6). 840–851.

Rothbart, M. K. & Bates, J. E. (2006). Temperament. In W. Damon, R. Lerner, & N. Eisenberg (eds.), *Handbook of Child Psychology: vol. 3. Social, Emotional, and Personality Development* (6th edn, pp. 99–166). New York, NY: Wiley.

Rudaizky, D., Basanovic, J., & Macleod, C. (2014). Biased attentional engagement with, and disengagement from, negative information: Independent cognitive pathways to anxiety vulnerability? *Cognition & Emotion, 28*, 245–259.

Sanchez, A., Everaert, J., & Koster, E. H. W. (2016). Attention training through gaze-contingent feedback: Effects on reappraisal and negative emotions. *Emotion, 16*.

Stroop, J. R. (1935). Studies of interference in serial verbal reactions. *Journal of Experimental Psychology, 18*(6), 643–662.

Tobon, J. I., Ouimet, A. J., & Dozois, D. J. A. (2011). Attentional bias in anxiety disorders following cognitive behavioral treatment. *Journal of Cognitive Psychotherapy, 25*, 114–129.

Van Bockstaele, B., Verschuere, B., Crombez, G., De Houwer, J., Tibboel, H., & Koster, E. H. W. (2014). A review of current evidence for the causal impact of attentional bias on fear and anxiety. *Psychological Bulletin, 140*, 682–721.

Van den Hout, M., Tenney, N., Huygens, K., Merckelbach, H., & Kindt, M. (1995). Responding to subliminal threat cues is related to trait anxiety and emotional vulnerability: S successful replication of MacLeod and Hagan (1992). *Behaviour Research and Therapy, 33*, 451–454.

Vogt, J., Houwer, J., Crombez, G., & Van Damme, S. (2013) Competing for attentional priority: Temporary goals versus threats. *Emotion, 13*, 587–598.

Weierich, M. R., Treat, T. A., & Hollingworth, A. (2008). Theories and measurement of visual attentional processing in anxiety. *Cognition & Emotion, 22*(6), 985–1018.

Wells, A. & Matthews, G. (1994). *Attention and Emotion: A Clinical Perspective*. Hove, UK: Erlbaum Ltd.

White, L. K., Henderson, H. A., Walker, O. L., Leibenluft, E., Pine, D.S., Degnan, K. A., Pérez-Edgar, K., Shechner, T., Bar-Haim, Y., Fox, N. A. (2017). Developmental relations among behavioral inhibition, anxiety, and attention bias to threat and positive information. *Child Development, 88*, 141–155.

Williams, J. M. G., Watts, F. N., MacLeod, C., & Mathews, A. (1988). *Cognitive Psychology and Emotional Disorders*. Chichester, UK: Wiley.

Williams, J. M. G., Mathews, A., & MacLeod, C. (1996). The emotional Stroop task and psychopathology. *Psychological Bulletin, 120*, 3–24.

Wilson, E. & Macleod, C. (2003). Contrasting two accounts of anxiety-linked attentional bias: Selective attention to varying levels of stimulus threat intensity. *Journal of Abnormal Psychology, 112*, 212–218.

Zvielli, A., Bernstein, A., & Koster, E. H. W. (2015). Temporal dynamics of attentional bias. *Clinical Psychological Science, 3*, 772–788.

3 Perceptual Mechanisms of Anxiety and Its Disorders

Wen Li

The ability to minimize contact with aversive events is a hallmark of adaptive behavior, among which the ability to quickly detect danger and initiate an immediate response can mean life or death. Anxiety, characterized by an overactive defense system, often exaggerates threat processing to the extent that significant functional impairment occurs (Barlow, 2002; Gray & McNaughton, 2000; Lang et al., 2000). Research in the past few decades has characterized an array of cognitive biases to threat in anxiety, in domains of attention, memory, interpretation, emotional association, and inhibitory control (Mathews & Macleod, 1994, 2005). However, biases in sensory perception, a fundamental cognitive operation, have not been well recognized in anxiety research. From an evolutionary perspective, it is conceivable that the sensory system, where an environmental cue first registers with an organism, is endowed with the capacity to categorize motivational significance of the stimulus, optimizing the animal's response with no delay (Li, 2014; Weinberger, 2007). Given that sensory perception constitutes one of the first operations in the cognitive stream, biased sensory perception of threat would influence downstream processes, directly or indirectly contributing to a variety of cognitive and emotional anomalies observed in anxiety. This chapter is thus dedicated to sensory perceptual mechanisms of anxiety with the hope to shed light on this crucial but so far overlooked aspect of anxiety pathology.

As reviewed in what follows, dominant theories of anxiety have conceptualized threat processing into a framework of three primary stages and systems. Importantly, the first stage of this framework is characterized by basic, sensory processing of environmental stimuli, "tagging" the stimuli with "threat codes" and triggering elaborate threat analysis in the later stages. In essence, this first stage represents sensory perception of threat, but presumably, the early and brief nature of this sensory stage has rendered it obscure from behavioral observations, leaving sensory perception of threat still poorly understood. Toward that end, this chapter garners evidence from neuroscience research that has gained remarkable access to this otherwise elusive stage.

In clinical conceptualization, the term *perception*, or *threat perception* specifically, can describe abstract ideas or views such as perception of health risks or perception of social tension, which heavily engages higher-order processes such as appraisal and reasoning. Here, in reference to basic mechanisms of fear and anxiety, in particular sensory perception of threat, the term *perception* pertains specifically to the processes that organize and translate sensory input (e.g., light, sound, odor) from the environment into concrete sensory experiences (i.e., percepts) such as the perception of an angry face or a frightened and screaming crowd.

This chapter starts with a survey and synthesis of dominant, influential theories of information-processing biases in anxiety. As these theories were largely constructed on behavioral data, neuroscience findings are then discussed to furnish empirical support to these models. This chapter then proceeds with neural data providing mechanistic insights into sensory perception of threat and related anomalies in anxiety, and ends with a proposal of a neurosensory model of anxiety pathology.

Summary and Synthesis of Dominant Information-Processing Models of Anxiety

Experimental psychopathology research in the past few decades has generated a voluminous literature on information processing in anxiety. Phenomena of anxiety-related biases to threat in various cognitive domains, such as detection, attention, interpretation, and expectation, have been ably summarized and synthesized in excellent reviews and meta-analyses (Armstrong & Olatunji, 2012; Beard & Amir, 2010; Cisler & Koster, 2010; McNally, 1995; Ouimet et al., 2009; Staugaard, 2010; Sussman et al., 2016; Van Bockstaele et al., 2014; Williams et al., 1996). Based on this literature, several influential theoretical models of anxiety have been proposed to isolate and describe critical cognitive systems underlying vulnerability to and pathology of anxiety. In spite of certain disparaging terminology and nuances, these models, some older and classical, some newer and integrative, largely converge on a sequence of automatic and strategic processes unfolding over time (as reviewed later in this chapter and also in Bar-Haim et al., 2007; Mathews & Mackintosh, 1998; Van Bockstaele et al., 2014). Building on their consensus, we synthesized these models into an integrative information-processing account of anxiety, where the relevant cognitive processes were organized and streamlined into three primary stages (Figure 3.1A).

The Schema-Based Theory of Beck and Colleagues (1985, 1997)

Beck and colleagues proposed a three-stage, schema-based information-processing model, where the first and third stages are biased in anxiety, resulting in "erroneous or biased interpretation of stimuli as dangerous or threatening" as a core feature of anxiety disorders (Beck & Clark, 1997; Beck et al., 1985). Stage I – initial registration – involves rapid, automatic stimulus processing. By automaticity, this stage is characterized by low-level parallel processing that operates outside consciousness and volition and is capacity-free.

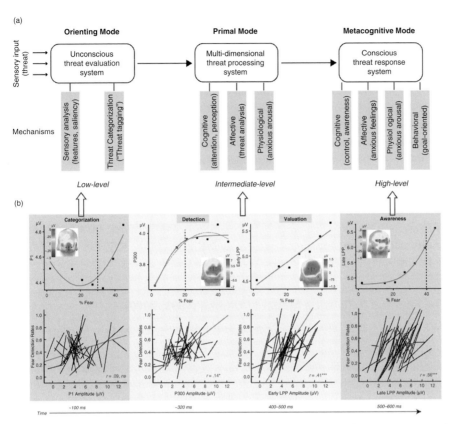

Figure 3.1 *A synthesized psychological model of anxiety. (A). A synthesis across several dominant cognitive models of anxiety yields a three-stage model, composed of an early "orienting mode," an intermediate "primal mode," and a late "metacognitive mode." (B). Psychometric and neurometric modeling of fear detection performance and ERPs in a fear detection task maps out four key operations unfolding in sequence, which align nicely with the three-stage model of anxiety. The open arrows point the key operations to the three stages in (A).*

These processes are more "perceptually" than "conceptually" driven. The first stage is also referred to as the "orienting mode." Anxious orienting would facilitate threat detection, which triggers Stage II – immediate preparation, also known as the "primal mode." This second stage is characterized by a rigid, reflexive set of affective, cognitive, behavioral, and physiological responses that constitute a state of anxiety, including (a) autonomic arousal, (b) negative thoughts, (c) avoidance behavior, (d) fearful emotions and feelings, and (e) hypervigilance for threat cues. Stage III – secondary elaboration, also known as the "metacognitive mode" – is represented by strategic, higher-order information processing. Anxiogenic schemas would bias this processing to generate anxious interpretations and maladaptive coping behavior.

The Information-Processing Model of Williams et al. (1988, 1997)

Williams and colleagues postulated that two distinct pre-attentive processing stages are relevant to anxiety (Williams et al., 1988, 1997). The first stage involves the evaluation of threat value of a stimulus through an "affective decision mechanism" (ADM). Similar to Beck and colleagues' orienting mode, this ADM engages parallel processing over a distributed network and is automatic ("pre-attentive"). High levels of *state anxiety* can amplify threat value output from this stage. If the threat value output is sufficiently high, the second stage will be activated, which involves the "resource allocation mechanism" (RAM) regulating cognitive resources, especially attention. This stage resembles the primal mode in Beck and colleagues' model. The RAM is subject to the influence of *trait anxiety*, prompting high trait-anxious individuals to show vigilance to threat and low trait-anxious individuals to display avoidance of threat. Furthermore, stressful contexts or elevated state anxiety would exacerbate the biases of the RAM in trait-anxious individuals.

The Emotion Activation Model of Ohman (1993, 2000)

Ohman's emotion activation model consists of three main stages – feature detection, significance evaluation, and conscious threat perception (Ohman, 1993, 2000). Similar to Beck and colleagues' first stage of initial registration, an external stimulus first registers with the "feature detectors" in a nonconscious, automatic fashion. These detectors isolate signal features of biologically significant stimuli, which then triggers the unconscious "significance evaluator." Confirmation from the significance evaluator turns on the third stage: controlled, strategic processing of the stimulus, generating conscious threat perception. Notably, Ohman's model also emphasizes that autonomic arousal is directly activated by feature detectors, which provides input to facilitate significance evaluation and conscious threat perception. A central and somewhat unique concept of this model is that preliminary, unconscious analysis of basic stimulus features is enhanced in anxiety, which shifts subsequent cognitive processes such as attention to favor threat information.

The Cognitive-Motivation Model of Mogg and Bradley (1998)

Mogg and Bradley proposed a cognitive-motivation model consisting of two stages – a valence evaluation system (VES) and a goal engagement system (GES) (Mogg & Bradley, 1998). The VES resembles the ADM in Williams and colleagues' model, although the VES is susceptible to *trait anxiety* in contrast to the ADM, which is susceptible to *state anxiety*. Mogg and Bradley argued that trait-anxious individuals are prone to tag relatively innocuous stimuli as threat. Threat output is then fed into the GES, similar to the RAM in Williams et al. (1988, 1997), which interrupts ongoing (non-threat-relevant) goals and prioritizes threat processing. Therefore, the hypersensitive VES in anxiety can lead to the hyper-reactivity of the GES, resulting in affective, cognitive, and behavioral anomalies. This model emphasizes a lowered threshold in anxiety for identifying *minute* environmental threat and argues that attentional biases to threat in anxiety are rather a passive consequence of the former.

The Selective Processing Model of Mathews and Mackintosh (1998)

This model concerns primarily how threat intervenes with the processing of nonemotional stimuli, as observed in the emotional Stroop task, which is especially salient in anxious individuals (Williams et al., 1996). Mathews and Mackintosh posited that stimuli are first evaluated via a threat evaluation system (TES), and threat output from this system turns on threat-relevant "distractor representation," which disrupts non-threat "target representation" (Mathews & Mackintosh, 1998). Here, Mathews and Mackintosh further introduced the idea of "voluntary task-related effort," such that higher-level cognitive control is triggered by the TES output to inhibit and override interference due to the distractor. The extent of biases in information processing and behavioral output lies in the balance of the TES and the voluntary control system. Similar to the notions of ADM (Williams et al., 1988, 1997), significance detectors (Ohman 1993, 2000), and VES (Mogg & Bradley, 1998), anxiety enhances threat analysis by the TES and intensifies its activation of distractor representation.

The Integrative Attention Model of Bar-Haim et al. (2007)

Building on previous models, primarily Williams et al. (1988, 1997) and Mogg and Bradley (1998), Bar-Haim and colleagues proposed a four-stage integrative model of attentional biases. The model starts off with a pre-attentive threat evaluation system (PTES), which tags a potential threat stimulus with high threat value (Bar-Haim et al., 2007). In consequence, the PTES transitions into a resource allocation system (RAS), which sets off an anxious state of physiological arousal, attentional biases, and anxious feelings. With that, a guided threat evaluation system (GTES) ensues, turning on a set of strategic operations, including context- and memory-based cognitive appraisal and coping assessment. Finally, the entire process concludes with a GES, prompting goal-oriented behavior. If the GTES evaluates the threat to be low, the GTES will provide inhibitory feedback to the PTES and RAS. In contrast, if the GTES confirms the threat alert by the PTES, a full-blown state of anxiety is likely to follow. As Bar-Haim and colleagues emphasize, anxiety could intensify threat processing at all four stages.

A Synthesis of Dominant Models

As has probably become evident to the reader, these dominant models of information processing in anxiety overlap substantially. Although the numbers of main stages differ somewhat, ranging from two to four, these six models agree on two primary systems: a *threat evaluation system* that is largely pre-attentive or uncon-scious, and a delayed *goal-oriented processing system* that is largely conscious and voluntary. In between these two stages, some models postulate additional stages, concerning intermediate processes in multiple dimensions (i.e., affective, cogni-tive, and physiological). This middle stage is characterized by resource allocation processes, which distribute cognitive resources to threat information, often at the cost of disrupting task-related or ongoing processes that are not threat-relevant.

In order to organize and streamline the processes implicated in these dominant models, especially along the time course delineated by brain electrophysiological evidence (reviewed later in this chapter), we provide a synthesis of these models. An effort is also made to apply relatively standard terms in cognitive psychology and neuroscience to the implicated mechanisms and processes. Our synthesis results in three main stages and systems of threat processing (Figure 3.1A). We borrowed the terms used by Beck and colleagues (Beck & Clark, 1997; Beck et al., 1985) for the succinct abstraction of the stages, ensuing the onset of a threat stimulus: (1) the orienting mode, (2) the primal mode, and (3) the metacognitive mode.

In terms of cognitive operations, the orienting mode is characterized by low-level, unconscious threat evaluation, involving specific mechanisms of basic sen-sory analysis of stimulus features, such as features signaling threat (Ohman 1993, 2000) and coarse, broad categorization of threat (vs. non-threat), such as threat tagging proposed in multiple models. Anxiety can bias the orienting mode to threat by increasing signal detection sensitivity or lowering threat threshold such that minute threat will be detected. The orienting mode is brief, and once threat is tagged, the primal mode starts to unfold. The primal mode, the main stage of information processing, is characterized by preconscious, intermediate-level, mul-tidimensional threat processing, evoking interactive cognitive, affective, and psy-chological processes. Processes in different domains work in concert to efficiently allocate resources to prioritize threat processing. Mechanisms in this stage include selective attention, intermediate-level perception, progressively elaborate threat evaluation, and autonomic arousal. Anxiety can bias the primal mode by allocating cognitive resources heavily to threat information. For example, anxiety can heighten selective attention to threat and amplify autonomic arousal, which further fuels threat prioritization. Finally, the primal mode gives rise to the third stage, the metacognitive mode. Characterized by conscious threat responses, this mode involves high-level, voluntary, goal-guided, and motivationally meaningful responses. Mechanisms engaged in this stage include conscious perception, stra-tegic deployment of attention, conscious experience of feelings, and sustained arousal. Goal-oriented behavior will occur (e.g., avoidance) in this stage. Anxiety can bias the metacognitive mode by negatively altering interpretation and apprai-sal, disrupting top-down effortful control, and exaggerating defensive behavior.

In summary, several influential models were generated from a voluminous body of work. However, this body of work comprises almost exclusively behavioral observations (besides relatively simple physiological measures such as eye tracking and skin conductance responses), and many of the models were proposed prior to the "neuroscientific revolution" of emotion and anxiety research. It thus begs the question as to how these models fare in comparison to findings from the neuroscience field.

Threat Processing in the Brain

Neural Mapping of the Threat-Processing Stages

A remarkable fact, as reviewed in what follows, is that these brilliant and, to some extent, intuitive models have closely mapped onto empirical, neuro-electrophysiological delineations of the different processes and stages of threat processing. Starting from the two-stage model of early "quick-and-dirty" and delayed elaborate processing of threat information (LeDoux, 1995), this literature has expanded to support a complex system involving multiple stages and processes, mediated by distributed, parallel neural pathways (Adolphs, 2002b; Pessoa & Adolphs, 2010; Vuilleumier & Pourtois, 2007).

Akin to these neural models of emotion processing, brain electrophysiological (mainly event-related potential [ERP]) research has leveraged its precise temporal resolution to delineate the time course of information processing of emotional stimuli on the scale of milliseconds. Findings from this research implicate three temporal stages of emotion processing (cf. Adolphs, 2002b; Miskovic & Keil, 2012; Olofsson & Polich, 2007; Vuilleumier & Pourtois, 2007). The first stage, indexed by the P1 component (a visual ERP that appears at ~100 ms), represents sensory processing of emotional stimuli in the low-level, occipital visual cortex. The second stage, indexed by the N1/N170 components (onset ~170 ms), entails intermediate-level, configural perceptual analysis in the temporal visual cortex. The third stage, indexed by the P3/P300 and late positive potential (LPP) components (~300 ms and beyond), reflects high-level, cognitive, and motivational processes. During this stage, emotion processing engages memory-based, goal-oriented operations, often culminating in conscious perception of the stimuli and volitional behavioral response. Broadly speaking, this sequence of electrophysiological events corresponds really closely to the three main stages of the cognitive models presented earlier in this chapter.

Pertinent to the perception of threat specifically, a recent study in our lab acquired fear detection rates and ERPs to parametrically varied levels of fearful expressions along a morphing continuum (Forscher et al., 2016). To provide further insights into the specific cognitive mechanisms involved at different stages in threat perception, we decomposed threat processing by combining psychometric and neurometric modeling. Building on the psychometric curve marking fear perception thresholds (e.g., detection, sub- and suprathreshold perception), neurometric model fitting identified four key operations along the information-processing stream (Figure 3.1B). Unfolding in sequence following face presentation, these four psychological processes are: (1) swift, coarse categorization of fear versus neutral stimuli (~100 ms, indexed by the P1); (2) detection of fear by picking up minute but psychologically meaningful signals of fear (~320 ms, indexed by the P3); (3) valuation of fear signal by tracking small distances in fear intensity, including subthreshold fear (400–500 ms, indexed by an early subcomponent of the LPP); and, lastly, (4) conscious awareness of fear, supporting the visibility of suprathreshold fear (500–600 ms, indexed by a late subcomponent of the LPP). Furthermore, as the processes became progressively refined over time, they were also increasingly linked to behavioral performance (i.e., fear detection rates; Figure 3.1B, bottom row). Specifically, from the first to the last operations, within-subject brain–behavior association grew from no association, to weak, then moderate, and finally strong, respectively.

Overall, these findings provide specific descriptions and temporal profiling of threat processing stages. The first operation – broad threat-non-threat categorization – would correspond to the orienting mode in threat processing, which automatically tags the stimuli as threat or non-threat. Such gross categorization (at the P1 window) concurs with standard object categorization (e.g., natural vs. domestic scenes) (Thorpe, 2009). This finding also aligns with the notion that emotional stimuli can elicit rapid emotion categorization based on automatic, bottom-up sensory input (Brosch et al., 2010; Young et al., 1997), coinciding with Ohman's idea of "feature detectors" that isolate threat-relevant signal features (Ohman 1993, 2000). This significance detection then activates salience-driven, bottom-up attention and the brain's salience network, which switches on other networks to start resource allocation (via attention and working memory) and goal-driven processes in the subsequent stages (Corbetta & Shulman, 2002; Menon & Uddin, 2010; Seeley et al., 2007).

The second and third operations – threat detection and valuation – would largely fall into the primal mode as the intermediate-level threat analysis. As illustrated in Figure 3.1B, the neural detection threshold aligns with the inflection point (25% fear) of the psychometric function, and the strength of this neural response was significantly (though only weakly) predictive of fear detection rates, suggesting somewhat reliable threat detection at this stage. The third operation is more sophisticated and advanced, linearly tracking the intensity of fearful expressions and directly predicting behavior performance ($r = 0.41$). The last operation brings about conscious awareness, corresponding closely to the metacognitive mode, where consciousness of threat emerges and conscious processes ensue. In keeping with that, this last operation accounts for a remarkable 31% of the total variance of the behavioral output.

Compared to the later operations (especially threat valuation and awareness), the first operation (threat tagging) does not show a relation with the behavior. This finding underscores the notion made earlier in this chapter that the orienting mode is likely to be elusive to behavioral observation. Many creative paradigms (e.g., emotional Stroop, dot-probe, visual cueing, and visual search) have been used to isolate early operations in threat processing, but as pointed out early in the chapter, behavioral measures from these tasks are inevitably confounded by operations from multiple stages (McNally, 1995). By virtue of rapid development of neuroscientific methods, especially brain electrophysiology technologies, relatively pure measures of the orienting mode have become viable.

Early Neural Response to Threat

Neuroimaging (fMRI and PET) studies and meta-analyses have provided compelling evidence that threat (relative to neutral) information leads to greater activation in the visual system, including primary (V1) and associative (e.g., fusiform, lateral occipital) visual cortices (Adolphs, 2008; Lang et al., 1998; Lindquist et al., 2012; Phan et al., 2002; Phelps, 2006; Sabatinelli et al., 2013; Trautmann et al., 2009; Vuilleumier et al., 2003; Vuilleumier & Pourtois 2007). Whereas attention strongly modulates activity in visual cortices, potentially mediating the threat-related augmentation of visual activity (Pessoa et al., 2002, 2003), preferential threat perception can also operate independently of attention (Phelps, 2006; Vuilleumier et al., 2001) and outside of conscious awareness (Morris et al., 1998, 2001; Pessoa et al., 2005). Nevertheless, in terms of disentangling the multiple processes and stages in threat processing, neuroimaging research appears to be facing a similar conundrum that has confronted behavioral research. That is, as late processing also activates low-level sensory cortices (Foxe & Simpson, 2002), it is unclear whether these effects reflect early basic sensory perception or the complex end stage where multiple information streams bind to form a final percept of threat.

By contrast, with its superior temporal resolution, brain electrophysiological research has a unique technical advantage in this regard. In particular, the P1, arising from the extrastriate cortex around 100 ms post stimulus, has proven very useful in indexing early visual perception (Gomez Gonzalez et al., 1994; Mangun et al., 1993; Morris & Dolan, 2001). Work from our laboratory and others' has demonstrated enlarged P1 in response to threat than non-threat stimuli, and intracranial source estimation has confirmed the sources of P1 threat response in the occipital cortex, including the extrastriate and occipital fusiform cortices (Eimer & Holmes, 2007; Holmes et al., 2008; Krusemark & Li, 2011, 2013; Li et al., 2008b; Li et al., 2007; Pizzagalli et al., 1999; Pourtois et al., 2004, 2005; Wieser et al., 2012; You & Li, 2016).

Recently, a series of studies examining ERPs to fear and disgust (vs. neutral) stimuli (scenes or faces) have indicated divergent processing of fear and disgust during early sensory perception: relative to neutral stimuli, fear stimuli enhance whereas disgust stimuli suppress the P1 response (Krusemark & Li, 2011, 2013; Liu et al., 2015; You & Li, 2016). These intriguing P1 response patterns were consistent across various tasks and contexts, and importantly, they were incompatible with the arousal levels of these emotions (i.e., fear > disgust > neutral), thereby excluding confounds of arousal and arousal-related attention and emphasizing basic sensory encoding of these threat stimuli. In addition, this differentiation of fear and disgust in early sensory processing also raises the question whether the coarse significance detection during early sensory processing operates along the dimension of threat-versus-non-threat or the dimension of approach-versus-avoidance (as fear elicits immediate approach while disgust immediate avoidance (Adolphs, 2002a). Or, this significance detection process is "smarter" than we think. At any rate, future research is needed to shed more light on this process.

Furthermore, the P1 component precedes the onset of the N170 component, which arises around 170 ms and reflects feature configuration and object identity (e.g., face) categorization (Bentin et al., 1996; Eimer, 2000; Vlamings et al., 2009). The fact that the P1 occurs before configural object representation helps to isolate these P1 effects to low-level sensory processes (e.g., "feature detectors") that define the orienting mode. In keeping with that, single-unit recording data in the macaque temporal cortex demonstrated rapid emotion discrimination prior to face identification (Sugase et al., 1999). Strikingly, recent work has demonstrated that threat can enhance the C1 component, one of the first visual evoked potentials arising ~50–70 ms in the primary visual (V1) cortex (cf. Miskovic & Keil, 2012), pushing threat processing even earlier and lower-level in the information-processing stream. In sum, electrophysiological data provide support that threat processing takes place as early as the initial sweep of sensory processing (Vuilleumier & Pourtois, 2007), underlying the orienting mode characterized by fast, automatic, low-level sensory processing of threat stimuli.

Early Neural Response to Threat in Anxiety

How does anxiety influence this early sensory processing of threat? fMRI data have revealed enhanced visual (Åhs et al., 2009; Etkin & Wager, 2007; Lipka et al., 2011; Paquette et al., 2003; Straube et al., 2005) and olfactory cortical activity (Krusemark & Li, 2012; Krusemark et al., 2013) in response to threat in anxious patients and individuals. Again, as mentioned earlier, the sluggish fMRI response does not permit the disentanglement of early, low-level activity from later, higher-order activity in the sensory cortex. Nevertheless, ERP evidence, especially based on early visual ERPs such as the P1 and C1, has amassed to address this question.

Reflecting enhanced early visual processing of threat in anxiety, threat (vs. neutral or positive) stimuli (e.g., faces, words, and pictures) elicit augmented P1 and C1 responses in anxious individuals, including both clinical and nonclinical groups (Eldar et al., 2010; Holmes et al., 2008; Krusemark & Li, 2011; Lee et al., 2017; Li et al., 2008b; Li et al., 2007; Mueller et al., 2009; Rossignol et al., 2013; Sass et al., 2010; Venetacci et al., 2017; Weinberg & Hajcak, 2011). Using bimodal (visual and olfactory) threat presentation, a study further demonstrated that trait-anxious individuals are particularly adept at integrating bimodal threat cues to improve early visual processing of micro-fear expressions (12% fear) (Forscher & Li, 2012). Administering cortisol one hour before the test, van Peer and colleagues observed enhanced P1 to angry (vs. happy) faces in both high trait-avoidant individuals (van Peer et al., 2007) and patients with social anxiety disorder (van

Peer et al., 2009), highlighting a close relationship between this heightened early threat processing and stressful arousal in anxiety.

That said, an intriguing finding from this literature is that in other studies, anxious individuals exhibit a broad, nonspecific (vs. threat-specific) enhancement of early visual processing. Spider phobics show elevated P1 and C1 responses to images of spiders and non-phobic objects (e.g., flowers and butterflies), relative to the control group (Michalowski et al., 2009, 2014, 2015). In addition, socially anxious individuals exhibit enhanced P1 and C1 responses to all faces, regardless of their expressions (Helfinstein et al., 2008; Kolassa & Miltner, 2006; Kolassa et al., 2007, 2009; Mühlberger et al., 2009; Peschard et al., 2013; Rossignol et al., 2012a, 2012b; Wieser & Moscovitch, 2015). Similarly, individuals with high trait anxiety also show a general P1 augmentation to all faces relative to non-face images (Walentowska & Wronka, 2012).

Faces are probably inherently salient, emotion-relevant stimuli such that even "neutral" faces would be emotionally charged due to its race, gender, or eye gaze, thereby attaining preferential perception compared to other objects (cf. Farah et al., 1998) and reliably activating the amygdala regardless of emotion (Johnson, 2005). It is thus plausible that in early sensory analysis, anxious individuals are particularly tuned to faces, even "neutral" ones, due to the inherent emotional salience. Another explanation for the general P1 enhancement to faces is that a threat-relevant context is elicited by threatening faces (e.g., fearful or angry) among socially anxious individuals, which generates a broad amplification of early sensory processing of all images presented in that context. Consistently, the presence of spider images amidst other images (even positive images) sets up a threatening context among spider phobics, which in turn exaggerates early sensory processing. A third possible explanation holds that there is a general, threat-neutral exaggeration of basic sensory processing, akin to the notion of hypervigilance. This idea is explicated in depth later in this chapter.

Mechanisms Underlying Early Threat Processing

How does such fast threat processing arise in the sensory cortex? Traditional theories of cortical organization hold that the primary sensory cortex (e.g., the V1 cortex) deals rather exclusively with sensory analysis of environmental inputs, and association cortices (e.g., the extrastriate cortex) interpret the primary cortical output into object percepts (i.e., "visual psychic," e.g., color and shape) (Campbell, 1905; Leipsic, 1901). In parallel to this sensory modular view or the "sensory module," a "threat/fear module" exists, according to traditional views (Fodor, 1983; Tooby & Cosmides, 1992). As promoted by the influential review by (Ohman & Mineka, 2001) and echoed by (LeDoux, 2012), threat processing arises from a selective, automatic, and encapsulated module, which is underpinned by a specialized neural circuitry. This fear circuitry centers around the amygdala and extends onto other limbic regions such as the hypothalamus and hippocampus (see reviews by Davis,

1992; Fanselow, 1994; Kapp et al., 1992; Lang et al., 2000; LeDoux, 2000; Panksepp, 1982). According to this view, environmental input from midbrain and thalamic nuclei can directly turn on this fear circuitry and the entire encapsulated fear system. Output from the amygdala then relays emotionally charged information of the stimulus to the sensory cortex via reentrant projections to these areas (Phelps, 2006; Phelps & LeDoux, 2005; Vuilleumier & Pourtois, 2007), thereby activating sensory cortical processing of emotion. In addition, a magnocellular subcortical pathway subserves the rapid transmission of environmental input from peripheral sensors through the pulvinar thalamus to the amygdala (Leventhal et al., 1985; Schiller & Tehovnik, 2001) to allow for fast threat processing.

However, electrophysiology studies with depth electrodes in the amygdala have reported threat-induced responses well over 100 ms post stimulus (Kreiman et al., 2000; Kuraoka & Nakamura, 2007; Leonard et al., 1985; Oya et al., 2002; Wang et al., 2014), but also see Méndez-Bértolo et al. (2016) for a fast latency of 74 ms. Obviously, such responses are not faster but even slower than activity in the extrastriate cortex as indexed by the P1, let alone the V1 cortical activity as indexed by the C1, implying that the amygdala's reentrant influence is not swift enough to contribute to early threat perception (Adolphs, 2008). Posing further challenge to amygdala dependence in early threat perception, patient SM with complete bilateral amygdala lesions exhibited normal rapid detection and nonconscious perception of fearful faces (Tsuchiya et al., 2009). In addition, a group of 18 participants with unilateral amygdala resections showed intact response to threat in the ventral visual cortex (both ipsilateral and contralateral to the lesion site (Edmiston et al., 2013). Furthermore, two other patients with complete amygdala lesions (Bach et al., 2011) and another group of 26 patients with unilateral amygdala lesions (Piech et al., 2011) displayed comparable enhancement in detecting emotional (vs. neutral) words (relative to healthy controls) in an attentional blink task.

Therefore, extant evidence suggests that early processing of threat could recruit multiple parallel pathways, some of which are located outside the amygdala (Chikazoe et al., 2014; Pessoa & Adolphs, 2010). While the amygdala can modulate later high-level perceptual processing, it may play a relatively small role in initial low-level sensory analysis (Tsuchiya et al., 2009). Challenging the "sensory module" idea, the electrophysiological evidence reviewed earlier raises the possibility that beyond standard sensory analysis, the sensory cortex participates in threat processing, particularly, early threat encoding. Indeed, recent computational modeling of fMRI data support sensory cortical *feedforward input* to the amygdala (instead of the widely assumed amygdala feedback input to the sensory cortex) as an essential mechanism underlying threat processing (Krusemark et al., 2013; Kumar et al., 2012).

A Sensory Cortical Account of Threat Processing

How does the sensory cortex support threat encoding during initial sensory processing? Using Pavlovian conditioning paradigms, early animal electrophysiological studies, dated to the 1950s, demonstrated conditioning-related plasticity in the primary and associative auditory cortex (Diamond & Weinberger, 1984; Galambos et al., 1955; Kraus & Disterhoft, 1982; Weinberger et al., 1984). As summarized in excellent reviews (Dunsmoor & Paz, 2015; McGann, 2015; Miskovic & Keil, 2012; Ohl & Scheich, 2005), recent years have witnessed a resurgence of interest in this topic, corroborating and extending the early findings to all sensory modalities in both humans and animals. For instance, a recent fMRI study in our lab demonstrated that newly acquired negative value via aversive conditioning can be represented in the olfactory (piriform) cortex (an associative sensory cortex), which updates the encoding of the conditioned odor, allowing discrimination of this odor from its initially indistinguishable counterpart (Li et al., 2008a).

Animal evidence further suggests that this associative plasticity in the sensory cortex not only emerges immediately after conditioning but also shows long-term retention with growing specificity to the CS (Weinberger, 2004). Importantly, new evidence indicates that this lasting associative plasticity in the associative sensory cortex supports long-term associative emotional memory (Cambiaghi et al., 2016; Grosso et al., 2015a, 2015b, 2016; Kwon et al., 2012). Moreover, this associative sensory cortical plasticity plays a *necessary* role in the long-term retrieval of fear memory (Sacco & Sacchetti, 2010) as sensory cortical efferents to the amygdala activate the basolateral amygdala to trigger fear memory (Cambiaghi et al., 2016). Conceivably, these long-term memory traces can support threat representation in the sensory cortex. Hopefully, this growing body of work would start to dismantle the dichotomy of "sensory module" and "threat module," which has been deeply woven into the fabric of emotion research and theorization. The former, a century-old modularity conceptualization of the sensory cortex, has remained unchallenged to date. Consequently, such efforts will compel sensory cortical accounts of threat processing.

Recently, we have proposed a sensory cortical account of threat processing, which holds that the sensory cortex stores threat codes/representations and independently supports threat encoding as incoming stimuli activate these codes/representations (Li, 2014). As James (1890) asserted, "every perception is an acquired perception"; human perception is largely learned and depends on long-term memory (Goldstone, 1998; Stevenson & Boakes, 2003). Animals and humans are especially adept at developing associative fear learning for biologically prepared objects, sometimes with as few as a single trial (Ohman & Mineka, 2001; Seligman, 1970). In keeping with that, our account takes a learning perspective, building on mnemonically based threat codes/representations acquired through life experiences. Given the associative nature of the olfactory cortex and olfactory perception that is deeply ingrained in associative memory (Gluck & Granger, 1993; Haberly, 1998; Stevenson & Boakes, 2003; Wilson & Stevenson, 2006; Wilson & Sullivan, 2011), we chose olfaction as a model system for this sensory account.

As illustrated in Figure 3.2, this account consists of two key elements: (1) contingency between an odor and an aversive experience induces acquisition/consolidation of aversive associative learning in the amygdala, thereby attaching threat

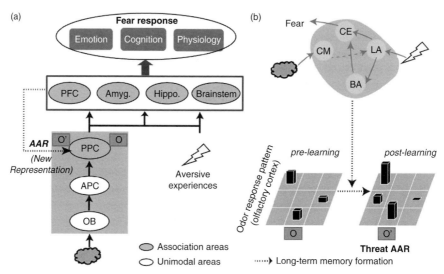

Figure 3.2 *A sensory cortical model of olfactory threat encoding. (A). Associative learning occurs when an odor is co-experienced with an aversive event. Conditioning-related long-term plasticity results in long-lasting changes in the olfactory (piriform) cortex, updating cortical response pattern to the CS odor. As such, original representation of the odor (O) turns into acquired associative representation/AAR (O'). Such threat AARs constitute the basis of sensory cortical encoding of threat. Later encounters of the same odor will activate O' to directly support threat encoding and trigger emotion responding. (B). Neural mechanisms. Initial association between the odor and aversive experience is formed in the lateral amygdala (LA), which projects directly or indirectly (via the basal nucleus of amygdala/BA) to the central nucleus (CE) to initiate and control fear responses. Over time, the acquired association is converted into a long-term memory trace stored in the piriform cortex supporting the threat AAR. APC = anterior piriform cortex; OB = olfactory bulb; PFC = prefrontal cortex; Amyg. = amygdala; Hippo = hippocampus; CM = corticomedial nucleus of amygdala. Adapted from Li (2014)*

meanings to innocuous odors; and (2) over time, the initial amygdala-based learning gives rise to long-term plasticity in the associative sensory cortex (the piriform cortex), resulting in updated neural response patterns to the conditioned odors. Accordingly, subsequent encounters of these odors will activate the acquired threat representations in the olfactory cortex, supporting olfactory cortical encoding of threat. Finally, out-puts from this sensory process (i.e., threat-laden sensory impulses) trigger a constellation of fear responses via projections to a wide range of associative neural networks (especially the amygdala, prefrontal cortex, and brain stem structures).

A Neurosensory Account of Anxiety

Linking the cognitive model of anxiety (Figure 3.1) and the sensory cortical model (Figure 3.2) of threat processing, here we propose a neurosensory model of anxiety

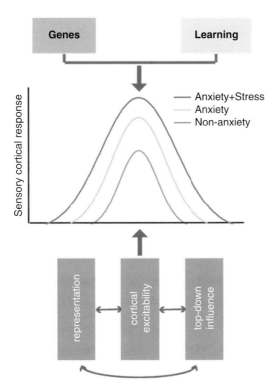

Figure 3.3 *A neurosensory model of anxiety. The three curves represent sensory cortical activity in individuals with low anxiety, high anxiety, and high anxiety and high stress (e.g., stressful, anxiety-provoking contexts, chronic or acute life stress), respectively. The three boxes in the bottom refer to the three key mechanisms underlying sensory cortical hyperactivity, which often interact with each other to generate synergistic effects.*

(Figure 3.3). We propose that three mechanisms can underlie enhanced sensory cortical response to threat in anxiety, which, in turn, feeds into the second and third stages of threat processing (i.e., the primal mode and the metacognitive mode), triggering a cascade of threat responses to induce and perpetuate anxiety. Specifically, consequent to a combination of genetic predispositions and negative environmental exposures and experiences (i.e., aversive learning), three pathological processes emerge in sensory cortical encoding of threat among anxious individuals: (1) intensified activation of threat representation, which consequently tunes up sensory cortical sensitivity and responsivity to threat stimuli; (2) broad enhancement in sensory cortical excitability, resulting in broad sensory hypersensitivity and hyper-responsivity to all incoming stimuli; and (3) biased top-down influence in favor of threat-related predictive coding of upcoming stimuli. Importantly, these three mechanisms can interact with each other to generate synergistic effects.

Concerning the first mechanism, animal electrophysiological data of associative learning via Pavlovian conditioning have revealed preferential sensory tuning of the conditioned stimuli (CS) (Weinberger, 2007). Conditioning can shift the sensory cortical turning curve to optimally respond to the CS. For example, a neuron in the A1 (primary auditory cortex) of the guinea pig shifted its preconditioning best frequency of 0.75 KHz to the CS frequency of 2.5 KHz after tone-shock conditioning (Bakin & Weinberger, 1990). Conditioning can also expand the receptive field of the CS such that more neurons become responsive to the CS cue. Both CS-specific tuning shifts and CS-specific receptive field enlargement can heighten the activation of threat representation in the sensory cortex such that only minimal sensory input is required to activate threat response. Although such low-level tuning plasticity remains difficult to assess in humans, these animal findings provide useful explanations for the heightened threat response in early sensory processing, which could be especially exaggerated in anxiety.

In line with the second mechanism, besides this threat-specific sensory hyper-activity, many studies reviewed earlier show that anxious individuals display a broad enhancement in early sensory processing, regardless of the emotional content of the stimuli. In that section, we alluded to a possible explanation of hypervigilance, which is general, threat-neutral exaggeration of basic sensory processing. This means that in order to maintain a high level of alertness to readily detect environmental threat, the sensory cortex in anxious individuals would have adapted to a high level of excitability such that it can be activated with minimal sensory input. Such broad sensory cortical excitability is highly susceptible to fluctuations in levels of brain monoamines, including norepinephrine, dopamine, and serotonin (Hurley et al., 2004). It is known that anxiety can lead to chronic, tonic increases of noradrenergic and dopaminergic levels, which would result in suppressed sensory gating and heightened postsynaptic activity in the sensory cortex (i.e., increased sensory cortical excitability) (Adler et al., 1988; Aston-Jones et al., 1994; Baisley et al., 2012; Berridge & Waterhouse, 2003; Sherin & Nemeroff, 2011; Southwick et al., 1997).

In an fMRI study, we induced an anxious state in participants and examined their basic olfactory cortical responses to neutral odors before and after anxiety induction (Krusemark et al., 2013). Our data indicate significant increases in information relay from the low-level, primary to a higher-level (associative) olfactory cortex as a result of induced anxiety, highlighting decreased sensory gating in anxiety (Figure 3.4A). Importantly, paralleling this neural change, participants perceived the initially neutral odors as somewhat negative post anxiety induction, suggesting that anxiety-related sensory gating reduction can contribute to biased threat perception. In keeping with these findings, an early ERP study using a standard paired-click paradigm demonstrated a lack of repetition suppression such that the P1 potential failed to show a dampened response to the second click, suggesting reduced sensory gating in patients with PTSD (Skinner et al., 1999).

A new study from our lab further revealed that even during an idling state with no sensory stimulation (also known as a resting state), patients with PTSD exhibited

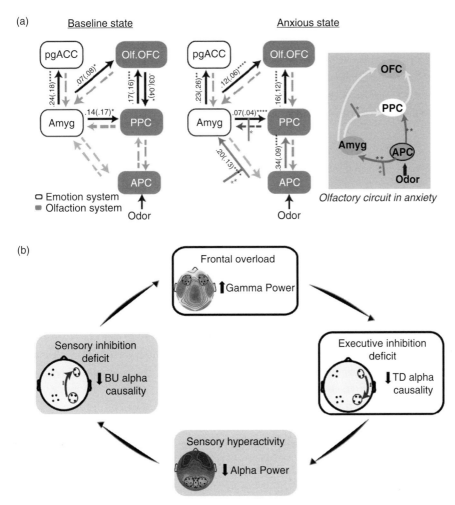

Figure 3.4 *Deficient sensory gating in anxiety. (A). The olfactory sensory pathway adapts readily with induced anxiety, characterized by strengthened APC efferents to the amygdala and PPC and amplified amygdala efferents to the PPC. This olfactory circuitry reorganization is accompanied by a significant negative shift in perceived pleasantness of odors (not shown here). Yellow lines represent intrinsic connections initially significant, green lines those that become significant in anxiety, and red intercepting lines modulation by odors in anxiety. (B). A vicious cycle in PTSD, rooted in sensory hyperactivity at resting: (1) sensory hyperactivity, (2) deficient bottom-up (BU) sensory inhibition, (3) frontal overload (due to sensory overflow), and (4) deficient top-down (TD), executive inhibition and regulation. OFC = orbitofrontal cortex; PPC = posterior piriform cortex; pgACC = pregenual anterior cingulate cortex; Amyg. = amygdala; olf. = olfactory; APC = anterior piriform cortex. Panel A adapted from Krusemark et al., 2013, and Panel B from Clancy et al., 2017.*

markedly suppressed alpha oscillatory activity in the visual cortex (Clancy et al., 2017). Alpha oscillations represent a primary mechanism of sensory gating, with greater alpha power associated with greater sensory gating and lower sensory cortical excitability (Bollimunta et al., 2008; Foxe & Snyder, 2011; Klimesch, 2012; Palva & Palva, 2007; Shaw, 2003; Worden et al., 2000). The severely depressed alpha activity in patients with PTSD, during a resting state, underscores the severity of sensory hyperactivity such that the sensory cortex remains active even in the absence of any sensory input. Accompanying this alpha deficit, patients with PTSD also exhibited deficient bottom-up inhibitory influence along with heighted frontal gamma activity. These aberrations together form a vicious cycle in PTSD that is in action even at rest, where intrinsic sensory hyperactivity and disinhibition give rise to frontal overload and disrupt executive control, fueling and perpetuating PTSD symptoms (Figure 3.4B).

Notably, absent in generalized anxiety disorder, these aberrations highlight a unique sensory pathology of PTSD (ruling out effects of mere anxious hyperarousal), suggesting that in extremely severe anxious conditions, sensory hyperactivity can be constant and pervasive. In fact, such broad sensory anomalies in PTSD draw an interesting parallel to more severe mental illnesses such as psychosis, where sensory anomalies have been recognized as part of the pathology (Geyer et al., 2001; Park et al., 2015; Thoma et al., 2003). Such broad sensory hyperactivity and gating deficits would allow irrelevant sensory input to inundate the entire information-processing stream, proliferating brain-wide dysfunctions and causing significant cognitive and executive dysfunctions (Javitt, 2009).

Concerning the third mechanism, the "New Look" movement in the middle of the past century made a strong argument for higher-order cognitive processes (prediction, expectation) and motivation to influence perception (Bruner, 1957; Bruner et al., 1951). This concept fits Beck's cognitive schema model in that information processing is performed according to a person's view of the world and the self (Beck, 1967), and has inspired emotion theorists to promote the idea of "seeing it with feelings" (Barrett & Bar, 2009), namely, standard object perception being influenced by affective predictions. The "New Look" theory has received a resurgence of interest in the past few years, owing to recent discoveries in cognitive and computational neuroscience (Clark, 2013; Friston, 2012). Simply put, this view holds that the brain regularly generates predictions about an upcoming stimulus based on prior knowledge. In keeping with that, multiple groups have observed that expectation and prediction shifts responses in both visual (Kastner et al., 1999; Puri et al., 2009; Stokes et al., 2009) and olfactory (Zelano et al., 2011) cortices to otherwise invariant visual or olfactory stimuli.

Anxiety has long been characterized by heightened prediction and anticipation of negative future events. For instance, anxious individuals tend to overestimate the probability and cost of negative events (Butler & Mathews, 1983; Grupe & Nitschke, 2013; Mitte, 2007). Conceivably, this negative world view would bias their prediction of upcoming events negatively. By this token, the sensory cortex of anxious individuals would receive threat-laden, top-down input (from the prefrontal cortex) before stimulus onset such that sensory cortical activity will prioritize threat encoding and impede neutral encoding.

In sum, we propose three mechanisms that can be at play synergistically in the sensory cortex to facilitate sensory threat processing. Current neural models of anxiety and related disorders have concentrated on the prefrontal-cortex-amygdala circuit pathology in response to threat; namely, anxiety disorders are associated with hypoactivity in the ventromedial prefrontal and anterior cingulate cortices (especially in PTSD) and hyperactivity in the amygdala in response to threat (Etkin & Wager, 2007; Patel et al., 2012; Rauch et al., 2006; Shin & Liberzon, 2010). The inclusion of these sensory mechanisms would expand our conceptualization of anxiety pathophysiology to a tripartite sensory-prefrontal-cortex-amygdala circuit that has gone awry in anxiety. Manifested in information processing, the tripartite neural circuit pathology in anxiety can exaggerate sensory cortical threat "tagging" and intensify subsequent processes such as attention and interpretation. Furthermore, these sensory mechanisms are likely to interact with downstream mechanisms such as selective attention to threat and negative interpretations, engendering compounded, supra-additive impacts on information processing to underpin a host of anxiety-related symptoms. Last but most important, the identification of attentional and interpretational biases in anxiety has motivated new anxiety treatments using inventive protocols to rectify these biases. We hope that the knowledge of sensory mechanisms underlying anxiety pathology can encourage more research in this area and, more important, inspire novel interventions targeting sensory processing and the sensory brain in anxious patients.

References

Adler, L. E., Pang, K., Gerhardt, G., & Rose, G. M. (1988). Modulation of the gating of auditory evoked potentials by norepinephrine: Pharmacological evidence obtained using a selective neurotoxin. *Biological Psychiatry, 24,* 179–190.

Adolphs, R. (2002a). Neural systems for recognizing emotion. *Current Opinion in Neurobiology, 12,* 169–177.

Adolphs, R. (2002b). Recognizing emotion from facial expressions: Psychological and neurological mechanisms. *Behavioral and Cognitive Neuroscience Reviews, 1,* 21–62.

Adolphs, R. (2008). Fear, faces, and the human amygdala. *Current Opinion in Neurobiology, 18,* 166–172,

Åhs, F., Pissiota, A., Michelgård, Å., Frans, Ö., Furmark, T., Appel, L., & Fredrikson, M. (2009). Disentangling the web of fear: Amygdala reactivity and functional connectivity in spider and snake phobia. *Psychiatry Research: Neuroimaging 172,* 103–108.

Armstrong, T. & Olatunji, B. O. (2012). Eye tracking of attention in the affective disorders: A meta-analytic review and synthesis. *Clinical Psychology Review, 32,* 704–723.

Aston-Jones, G., Rajkowski, J., Kubiak, P., & Alexinsky, T. (1994). Locus coeruleus neurons in monkey are selectively activated by attended cues in a vigilance task. *Journal of Neuroscience, 14,* 4467–4480.

Bach, D. R., Talmi, D., Hurlemann, R., Patin, A., & Dolan, R. J. (2011). Automatic relevance detection in the absence of a functional amygdala. *Neuropsychologia*, *49*, 1302–1305.

Baisley, S. K., Fallace, K. L., Rajbhandari, A. K., & Bakshi, V. P. (2012). Mutual independence of 5-HT(2) and alpha1 noradrenergic receptors in mediating deficits in sensorimotor gating. *Psychopharmacology (Berl)*, *220*, 465–479.

Bakin, J. S. & Weinberger, N. M. (1990). Classical conditioning induces CS-specific receptive field plasticity in the auditory cortex of the guinea pig. *Brain Research*, *536*, 271–286.

Bar-Haim, Y., Lamy, D., Pergamin, L., Bakermans-Kranenburg, M. J., & van Ijzendoorn, M. H. (2007). Threat-related attentional bias in anxious and nonanxious individuals: A meta-analytic study. *Psychological Bulletin*, *133*, 1.

Barlow, D. H. (2002). *Anxiety and Its Disorders*. New York, NY: Guilford Press.

Barrett, L. F. & Bar, M. (2009). See it with feeling: Affective predictions during object perception. *Philosophical Transactions of the Royal Society of London B Biological Science*, *364*, 1325–1334.

Beard, C. & Amir, N. (2010). Negative interpretation bias mediates the effect of social anxiety on state anxiety. *Cognitive Therapy and Research*, *34*, 292–296.

Beck, A. T. (1967). *Depression: Clinical, Experimental, and Theoretical Aspects*. Philadelphia, PA: University of Pennsylvania Press.

Beck, A. T. & Clark, D. A. (1997). An information processing model of anxiety: Automatic and strategic processes. *Behaviour Research and Therapy*, *35*, 49–58.

Beck, A. T., Emery, G., & Greenberg, R. (1985). *Anxiety Disorders and Phobias: A Cognitive Approach*. New York, NY: Basic Books, b58.

Bentin, S., Allison, T., Puce, A., Perez, A., & McCarthy G. (1996). Electrophysiological studies of face perception in humans. *Journal of Cognitive Neuroscience*, *8*, 551–565.

Berridge, C. W. & Waterhouse, B. D. (2003). The locus coeruleus-noradrenergic system: Modulation of behavioral state and state-dependent cognitive processes. *Brain Research. Brain Research Reviews*, *42*, 33–84.

Bollimunta, A., Chen, Y., Schroeder, C. E., & Ding, M. (2008). Neuronal mechanisms of cortical alpha oscillations in awake-behaving macaques. *Journal of Neuroscience*, *28*, 9976–9988.

Brosch, T., Pourtois, G., & Sander, D. (2010). The perception and categorisation of emotional stimuli: A review. *Cognition Emotion*, *24*, 377–400.

Bruner, J. S. (1957). On perceptual readiness. *Psychological Review*, *64*, 123.

Bruner, J. S., Postman, L., & Rodrigues, J. (1951). Expectation and the perception of color. *American Journal of Psychology*, *64*, 216–227.

Butler, G. & Mathews, A. (1983). Cognitive processes in anxiety. *Advances in Behaviour Research and Therapy*, *5*, 51–62.

Cambiaghi, M., Grosso, A., Likhtik, E., Mazziotti, R., Concina, G., Renna, A., Sacco, T., Gordon, J. A., & Sacchetti, B. (2016). Higher-order sensory cortex drives basolateral amygdala activity during the recall of remote, but not recently learned fearful memories. *Journal of Neuroscience*, *36*, 1647–1659.

Campbell, A. W. (1905). *Histological Studies on the Localisation of Cerebral Function*. University Press. https://archive.org/details/histologicalstu00campgoog

Chikazoe, J., Lee, D. H., Kriegeskorte, N., & Anderson, A. K. (2014). Population coding of affect across stimuli, modalities and individuals. *Nature Neuroscience*, *17*, 1114–1122.

Cisler, J. M. & Koster, E. H. (2010). Mechanisms of attentional biases towards threat in anxiety disorders: An integrative review. *Clinical Psychology Review*, *30*, 203–216.

Clancy, K., Ding, M., Bernat, E., Schmidt, N. B., & Li, W. (2017). Restless "rest": Intrinsic sensory hyperactivity and disinhibition in posttraumatic stress disorder. *Brain*, 140(7), 2041–2050.

Clark, A. (2013). Whatever next? Predictive brains, situated agents, and the future of cognitive science. *Behavioral and Brain Sciences*, *36*, 181–204.

Corbetta, M. & Shulman, G. L. (2002). Control of goal-directed and stimulus-driven attention in the brain. *Nature Reviews Neuroscience*, *3*, 201–215.

Davis, M. (1992). The role of the amygdala in fear and anxiety. *Annual Review of Neuroscience*, *15*, 353–375.

Diamond, D. M. & Weinberger, N. M. (1984). Physiological plasticity of single neurons in auditory cortex of the cat during acquisition of the pupillary conditioned response: II. Secondary field (AII). *Behavioral Neuroscience*, *98*, 189.

Dunsmoor, J. E. & Paz, R. (2015). Fear generalization and anxiety: Behavioral and neural mechanisms. *Biological Psychiatry*, *78*, 336–343.

Edmiston, E. K., McHugo, M., Dukic, M. S., Smith, S. D., Abou-Khalil, B., Eggers, E., & Zald, D. H. (2013). Enhanced visual cortical activation for emotional stimuli is preserved in patients with unilateral amygdala resection. *Journal of Neuroscience*, *33*, 11023–11031.

Eimer, M. (2000). The face-specific N170 component reflects late stages in the structural encoding of faces. *Neuroreport*, *11*, 2319–2324.

Eimer, M. & Holmes, A. (2007). Event-related brain potential correlates of emotional face processing. *Neuropsychologia*, *45*, 15–31.

Eldar, S., Yankelevitch, R., Lamy, D., & Bar-Haim, Y. (2010). Enhanced neural reactivity and selective attention to threat in anxiety. *Biological Psychology*, *85*, 252–257.

Etkin, A. & Wager, T. D. (2007). Functional neuroimaging of anxiety: A meta-analysis of emotional processing in PTSD, social anxiety disorder, and specific phobia. *American Journal of Psychiatry*, *164*, 1476–1488.

Fanselow, M. S. (1994). Neural organization of the defensive behavior system responsible for fear. *Psychonomic Bulletin & Review*, *1*, 429–438.

Farah, M. J., Wilson, K. D., Drain, M., & Tanaka, J. N. (1998). What is "special" about face perception? *Psychological Review*, *105*, 482.

Fodor, J. A. (1983). *The Modularity of Mind: An Essay on Faculty Psychology*. Cambridge, MA: MIT Press.

Forscher, E. C. & Li, W. (2012). Hemispheric asymmetry and visuo-olfactory integration in perceiving subthreshold (micro) fearful expressions. *Journal of Neuroscience*, *32*, 2159–2165.

Forscher, E. C., Zheng, Y., Ke, Z., Folstein, J., & Li, W. (2016). Decomposing fear perception: A combination of psychophysics and neurometric modeling of fear perception. *Neuropsychologia*, *91*, 254–261.

Foxe, J. J. & Simpson, G. V. (2002). Flow of activation from V1 to frontal cortex in humans: A framework for defining "early" visual processing. *Experimental Brain Research*, *142*, 139–150.

Foxe, J. J. & Snyder, A. C. (2011). The role of alpha-band brain oscillations as a sensory suppression mechanism during selective attention. *Frontiers in Psychology, 2,* 154.

Friston, K. (2012). Prediction, perception and agency. *International Journal of Psychophysiology, 83,* 248–252.

Galambos, R., Sheatz, G., & Vernier, V. G. (1955). Electrophysiological correlates of a conditioned response in cats. *Science, 123,* 376–377.

Geyer, M. A., Krebs-Thomson, K., Braff, D. L., & Swerdlow, N. R. (2001). Pharmacological studies of prepulse inhibition models of sensorimotor gating deficits in schizophrenia: A decade in review. *Psychopharmacology (Berl), 156,* 117–154.

Gluck, M. A. & Granger, R. (1993). Computational models of the neural bases of learning and memory. *Annual Review of Neuroscience, 16,* 667–706.

Goldstone, R. L. (1998). Perceptual learning. *Annual Review of Psychology, 49,* 585–612.

Gomez Gonzalez, C. M., Clark, V. P., Fan, S., Luck, S. J., & Hillyard, S. A. (1994). Sources of attention-sensitive visual event-related potentials. *Brain Topography, 7,* 41–51.

Gray, J. A. & McNaughton, N. (2000). *The Neuropsychology of Anxiety: An Enquiry into the Functions of the Septo-Hippocampal System.* Oxford: Oxford University Press.

Grosso, A., Cambiaghi, M., Concina, G., Sacco, T., & Sacchetti B. (2015a). Auditory cortex involvement in emotional learning and memory. *Neuroscience, 299,* 45–55.

Grosso, A., Cambiaghi, M., Milano, L., Renna, A., Sacco, T., & Sacchetti, B. (2016). Region-and layer-specific activation of the higher order auditory cortex Te2 after remote retrieval of fear or appetitive memories. *Cerebral Cortex, 27*(6), 3140–3151. bhw159

Grosso, A., Cambiaghi, M., Renna, A., Milano, L., Merlo, G. R., Sacco, T., & Sacchetti, B. (2015b). The higher order auditory cortex is involved in the assignment of affective value to sensory stimuli. *Nature Communications, 6.*

Grupe, D. W. & Nitschke, J. B. (2013). Uncertainty and anticipation in anxiety: An integrated neurobiological and psychological perspective. *Nature Reviews Neuroscience, 14,* 488–501.

Haberly, L. B. (1998). *Olfactory Cortex.* New York, NY: Oxford University Press.

Helfinstein, S. M., White, L. K., Bar-Haim, Y., & Fox, N. A. (2008). Affective primes suppress attention bias to threat in socially anxious individuals. *Behaviour Research and Therapy, 46,* 799–810.

Holmes, A., Nielsen, M. K, & Green, S. (2008). Effects of anxiety on the processing of fearful and happy faces: An event-related potential study. *Biological Psychology, 77,* 159–173.

Hurley, L. M., Devilbiss, D. M., & Waterhouse, B. D. (2004.) A matter of focus: Monoaminergic modulation of stimulus coding in mammalian sensory networks. *Current Opinion in Neurobiology, 14,* 488–495.

James, W. (1890). *Principles of Psychology.* New York, NY: Holt.

Javitt, D. C. (2009). When doors of perception close: Bottom-up models of disrupted cognition in schizophrenia. *Annual Review of Clinical Psychology, 5,* 249–275.

Johnson, M. H. (2005). Subcortical face processing. *Nature Reviews Neuroscience, 6,* 766–774.

Kapp, B. S., Whalen, P. J., Supple, W. F., & Pascoe, J. P. (1992). Amygdaloid contributions to conditioned arousal and sensory information processing. In J. P. Appleton (ed.),

The Amygdala: Neurobiological Aspects of Emotion, Memory, and Mental Dysfunction (pp. 229–254). New York, NY: Wiley-Liss.

Kastner, S., Pinsk, M. A., De Weerd, P., Desimone, R., & Ungerleider, L. G. (1999). Increased activity in human visual cortex during directed attention in the absence of visual stimulation. *Neuron, 22,* 751–761.

Klimesch, W. (2012). Alpha-band oscillations, attention, and controlled access to stored information. *Trends in Cognitive Science, 16,* 606–617.

Kolassa, I.-T., Kolassa, S., Bergmann, S., Lauche, R., Dilger, S., Miltner, W. H. R., & Musial, F. (2009). Interpretive bias in social phobia: An ERP study with morphed emotional schematic faces. *Cognition and Emotion, 23,* 69–95.

Kolassa, I.-T., Kolassa, S., Musial, F., & Miltner, W. H. (2007). Event-related potentials to schematic faces in social phobia. *Cognition and Emotion, 21,* 1721–1744.

Kolassa, I.-T. & Miltner, W. H. (2006). Psychophysiological correlates of face processing in social phobia. *Brain Research, 1118,* 130–141.

Kraus, N. & Disterhoft, J. F. (1982). Response plasticity of single neurons in rabbit auditory association cortex during tone-signalled learning. *Brain Research, 246,* 205–215.

Kreiman, G., Koch, C., & Fried, I. (2000). Category-specific visual responses of single neurons in the human medial temporal lobe. *Nature Neuroscience, 3,* 946–953.

Krusemark, E. A. & Li, W. (2011). Do all threats work the same way? Divergent effects of fear and disgust on sensory perception and attention. *Journal of Neuroscience, 31,* 3429–3434.

Krusemark, E. A. & Li, W. (2012). Enhanced olfactory sensory perception of threat in anxiety: An event-related fMRI study. *Chemosensory Perception, 5,* 37–45.

Krusemark, E. A. & Li, W. (2013). From early sensory specialization to later perceptual generalization: Dynamic temporal progression in perceiving individual threats. *Journal of Neuroscience, 33,* 587–594.

Krusemark, E. A., Novak, L. R., Gitelman, D. R., & Li, W. (2013). When the sense of smell meets emotion: Anxiety-state-dependent olfactory processing and neural circuitry adaptation. *Journal of Neuroscience, 33,* 15324–15332.

Kumar, S., von Kriegstein, K., Friston, K., & Griffiths, T. D. (2012). Features versus feelings: Dissociable representations of the acoustic features and valence of aversive sounds. *Journal of Neuroscience, 32,* 14184–14192.

Kuraoka, K. & Nakamura, K. (2007). Responses of single neurons in monkey amygdala to facial and vocal emotions. *Journal of Neurophysiology, 97,* 1379–1387.

Kwon, J.-T., Jhang, J., Kim, H.-S., Lee, S., & Han, J.-H. (2012). Brain region-specific activity patterns after recent or remote memory retrieval of auditory conditioned fear. *Learning & Memory, 19,* 487–494.

Lang, P. J., Bradley, M. M., Fitzsimmons, J. R., Cuthbert, B. N, Scott, J. D., Moulder, B., & Nangia, V. (1998). Emotional arousal and activation of the visual cortex: An fMRI analysis. *Psychophysiology, 35,* 199–210.

Lang, P. J., Davis, M., & Ohman, A. (2000). Fear and anxiety: Animal models and human cognitive psychophysiology. *Journal of Affective Disorders, 61,* 137–159.

LeDoux, J. (2012). Rethinking the emotional brain. *Neuron, 73,* 653–676.

LeDoux, J. E. (1995). Emotion: Clues from the Brain. *Annual Review of Psychology, 46,* 209–235.

LeDoux, J. E. (2000). Emotion circuits in the brain. *Annual Review of Neuroscience, 23,* 155–184.

Lee, S. A., Kim, C.-Y., Shim, M., & Lee, S.-H. (2017). Gender differences in neural responses to perceptually invisible fearful face: An ERP study. *Frontiers in Behavioral Neuroscience, 11*.

Leipsic, P. F. O. (1901). Developmental (myelogenetic) localisation of the cerebral cortex in the human subject. *Lancet, 158*, 1027–1030.

Leonard, C. M., Rolls, E. T., Wilson, F. A., & Baylis, G. C. (1985). Neurons in the amygdala of the monkey with responses selective for faces. *Behavioural Brain Research, 15*, 159–176.

Leventhal, A. G., Rodieck, R. W., & Dreher, B. (1985). Central projections of cat retinal ganglion cells. *Journal of Comparative Neurology, 237*, 216–226.

Li, W. (2014). Learning to smell danger: Acquired associative representation of threat in the olfactory cortex. *Frontiers in Behavioral Neuroscience, 8*, 98.

Li, W., Howard, J. D., Parrish, T. B., & Gottfried, J. A. (2008a). Aversive learning enhances perceptual and cortical discrimination of indiscriminable odor cues. *Science, 319*, 1842–1845.

Li, W., Zinbarg, R. E., Boehm, S. G., & Paller, K. A. (2008b). Neural and behavioral evidence for affective priming from unconsciously perceived emotional facial expressions and the influence of trait anxiety. *Journal of Cognitive Neuroscience, 20*, 95–107.

Li, W., Zinbarg, R. E., & Paller, K. A. (2007). Trait anxiety modulates supraliminal and subliminal threat: Brain potential evidence for early and late processing influences. *Cognitive, Affective, & Behavioral Neuroscience, 7*, 25–36.

Lindquist, K. A., Wager, T. D., Kober, H., Bliss-Moreau, E., & Barrett, L. F. (2012). The brain basis of emotion: A meta-analytic review. *Behavioral and Brain Sciences, 35*, 121–143.

Lipka, J., Miltner, W. H., & Straube, T. (2011). Vigilance for threat interacts with amygdala responses to subliminal threat cues in specific phobia. *Biological Psychiatry, 70*, 472–478.

Liu, Y., Lin, W., Xu, P., Zhang, D., & Luo, Y. (2015). Neural basis of disgust perception in racial prejudice. *Human Brain Mapping, 36*, 5275–5286.

Mangun, G. R., Hillyard, S. A., & Luck, S. L. (1993). *Electrocortical Substrates of Visual Selective Attention*. Cambridge, MA: MIT Press.

Mathews, A. & Mackintosh, B. (1998). A cognitive model of selective processing in anxiety. *Cognitive Therapy and Research, 22*, 539–560.

Mathews, A. & Macleod, C. (1994). Cognitive approaches to emotion and emotional disorders. *Annual Review of Psychology, 45*, 25–50.

Mathews, A. & MacLeod, C. (2005). Cognitive vulnerability to emotional disorders. *Annual Review of Clinical Psychology, 1*, 167–195.

McGann, J. P. (2015). Associative learning and sensory neuroplasticity: How does it happen and what is it good for? *Learning & Memory, 22*, 567–576.

McNally, R. J. (1995). Automaticity and the anxiety disorders. *Behaviour Research and Therapy, 33*, 747–754.

Méndez-Bértolo, C., Moratti, S., Toledano, R., Lopez-Sosa, F., Martínez-Alvarez, R., Mah, Y. H., Vuilleumier, P., Gil-Nagel, A., & Strange, B. A. (2016). A fast pathway for fear in human amygdala. *Nature Neuroscience, 19*, 1041–1049.

Menon, V. & Uddin, L. Q. (2010). Saliency, switching, attention and control: A network model of insula function. *Brain Structure and Function, 214*, 655–667.

Michalowski, J. M., Melzig, C. A., Weike, A. I., Stockburger, J., Schupp, H. T., & Hamm, A. O. (2009). Brain dynamics in spider-phobic individuals exposed to phobia-relevant and other emotional stimuli. *Emotion*, *9*, 306.

Michalowski, J. M., Pané-Farré, C. A., Löw, A., & Hamm, A. O. (2015). Brain dynamics of visual attention during anticipation and encoding of threat-and safe-cues in spider-phobic individuals. *Social, Cognitive, & Affective Neuroscience*, *10*(9), 1177–1186. pnsv002

Michalowski, J. M., Weymar, M., & Hamm, A. O. (2014). Remembering the object you fear: Brain potentials during recognition of spiders in spider-fearful individuals. *PloS One*, *9*, e109537.

Miskovic, V. & Keil, A. (2012). Acquired fears reflected in cortical sensory processing: A review of electrophysiological studies of human classical conditioning. *Psychophysiology*, *49*, 1230–1241.

Mitte, K. (2007). Anxiety and risky decision-making: The role of subjective probability and subjective costs of negative events. *Personality and Individual Differences*, *43*, 243–253.

Mogg, K. & Bradley, B. P. (1998). A cognitive-motivational analysis of anxiety. *Behaviour Research and Therapy*, *36*, 809–848.

Morris, J. S., DeGelder, B., Weiskrantz, L., & Dolan, R. J. (2001). Differential extrageniculostriate and amygdala responses to presentation of emotional faces in a cortically blind field. *Brain*, *124*, 1241–1252.

Morris, J. S. & Dolan, R. J. (2001). *The Amygdale and Unconscious Fear Processing*. Oxford: Oxford University Press.

Morris, J. S., Ohman, A., & Dolan, R. J. (1998). Conscious and unconscious emotional learning in the human amygdala. *Nature*, *393*, 467–470.

Mueller, E. M., Hofmann, S. G., Santesso, D. L., Meuret, A. E., Bitran, S., & Pizzagalli, D. A. (2009). Electrophysiological evidence of attentional biases in social anxiety disorder. *Psychological Medicine*, *39*, 1141–1152.

Mühlberger, A., Wieser, M. J., Herrmann, M. J., Weyers, P., Tröger, C., & Pauli, P. (2009). Early cortical processing of natural and artificial emotional faces differs between lower and higher socially anxious persons. *Journal of Neural Transmission*, *116*, 735–746.

Ohl, F. W. & Scheich, H. (2005). Learning-induced plasticity in animal and human auditory cortex. *Current Opinion in Neurobiology*, *15*, 470–477.

Ohman, A. (1993). Fear and anxiety as emotional phenomena: Clinical phenomenology, evolutionary perspectives, and information-processing mechanisms. In M. Lewis & J. M. Haviland (eds.), *Handbook of Emotions* (pp. 511–536). New York, NY: Guilford Press.

Ohman, A. (2000). Fear and anxiety: Evolutionary cognitive and clinical perspectives. In M. Lewis & J. M. Haviland (eds.), *Handbook of Emotions* (2nd edn) (pp. 573–593). New York, NY: Guilford Press.

Ohman, A. & Mineka, S. (2001). Fears, phobias, and preparedness: Toward an evolved module of fear and fear learning. *Psychological Review*, *108*, 483.

Olofsson, J. K. & Polich, J. (2007). Affective visual event-related potentials: Arousal, repetition, and time-on-task. *Biological Psychology*, *75*, 101–108.

Ouimet, A. J., Gawronski, B., & Dozois, D. J. (2009). Cognitive vulnerability to anxiety: A review and an integrative model. *Clinical Psychology Review*, *29*, 459–470.

Oya, H., Kawasaki, H., Howard, M. A., 3rd, & Adolphs, R. (2002). Electrophysiological responses in the human amygdala discriminate emotion categories of complex visual stimuli. *Journal of Neuroscience*, *22*, 9502–9512.

Palva, S. & Palva, J. M. (2007). New vistas for alpha-frequency band oscillations. *Trends in Neuroscience*, *30*, 150–158.

Panksepp, J. (1982). Toward a general psychobiological theory of emotions. *Behavioral and Brain Sciences*, *5*, 407–422.

Paquette, V., Lévesque, J., Mensour, B., Leroux, J.-M., Beaudoin, G., Bourgouin, P., & Beauregard, M. (2003). "Change the mind and you change the brain": Effects of cognitive-behavioral therapy on the neural correlates of spider phobia. *Neuroimage*, *18*, 401–409.

Park, H. R. P., Lim, V. K., Kirk, I. J., & Waldie, K. E. (2015). P50 sensory gating deficits in schizotypy. *Personality and Individual Differences*, *82*, 142–147.

Patel, R., Spreng, R. N., Shin, L. M., & Girard, T. A. (2012). Neurocircuitry models of posttraumatic stress disorder and beyond: A meta-analysis of functional neuroimaging studies. *Neuroscience and Biobehavioral Review*, *36*, 2130–2142.

Peschard, V., Philippot, P., Joassin, F., & Rossignol, M. (2013). The impact of the stimulus features and task instructions on facial processing in social anxiety: An ERP investigation. *Biological Psychology*, *93*, 88–96.

Pessoa, L. & Adolphs, R. (2010). Emotion processing and the amygdala: From a "low road" to "many roads" of evaluating biological significance. *Nature Reviews Neuroscience*, *11*, 773–783.

Pessoa, L., Japee, S., & Ungerleider, L. G. (2005). Visual awareness and the detection of fearful faces. *Emotion*, *5*, 243–247.

Pessoa, L., Kastner, S., & Ungerleider, L. G. (2003). Neuroimaging studies of attention: From modulation of sensory processing to top-down control. *Journal of Neuroscience*, *23*, 3990–3998.

Pessoa, L., McKenna, M., Gutierrez, E., & Ungerleider, L. G. (2002). Neural processing of emotional faces requires attention. *Proceedings of the National Academy of Science USA*, *99*, 11458–11463.

Phan, K. L., Wager, T., Taylor, S. F., & Liberzon, I. (2002). Functional neuroanatomy of emotion: A meta-analysis of emotion activation studies in PET and fMRI. *Neuroimage*, *16*, 331–348.

Phelps, E. A. (2006). Emotion and cognition: Insights from studies of the human amygdala. *Annual Review of Psychology*, *57*, 27–53.

Phelps, E. A. & LeDoux, J. E. (2005). Contributions of the amygdala to emotion processing: From animal models to human behavior. *Neuron*, *48*, 175–187.

Piech, R. M., McHugo, M., Smith, S. D., Dukic, M. S., van der Meer, J., Abou-Khalil, B., Most, S. B., & Zald, D. H. (2011). Attentional capture by emotional stimuli is preserved in patients with amygdala lesions. *Neuropsychologia*, *49*, 3314–3319.

Pizzagalli, D., Regard, M., & Lehmann, D. (1999). Rapid emotional face processing in the human right and left brain hemisphere: An ERP study. *Neuroreport*, 2691–2698.

Pourtois, G., Dan, E. S., Grandjean, D., Sander, D., & Vuilleumier, P. (2005). Enhanced extrastriate visual response to bandpass spatial frequency filtered fearful faces: Time course and topographic evoked-potentials mapping. *Human Brain Mapping*, *26*, 65–79.

Pourtois, G., Grandjean, D., Sander, D., & Vuilleumier, P. (2004). Electrophysiological correlates of rapid spatial orienting towards fearful faces. *Cerebral Cortex, 14,* 619–633.

Puri, A. M., Wojciulik, E., & Ranganath, C. (2009). Category expectation modulates baseline and stimulus-evoked activity in human inferotemporal cortex. *Brain Research, 1301,* 89–99.

Rauch, S. L., Shin, L. M., & Phelps, E. A. (2006). Neurocircuitry models of posttraumatic stress disorder and extinction: Human neuroimaging research – past, present, and future. *Biological Psychiatry, 60,* 376–382.

Rossignol, M., Campanella, S., Bissot, C., & Philippot, P. (2013). Fear of negative evaluation and attentional bias for facial expressions: An event-related study. *Brain and Cognition, 82,* 344–352.

Rossignol, M., Campanella, S., Maurage, P., Heeren, A., Falbo, L., & Philippot, P. (2012a). Enhanced perceptual responses during visual processing of facial stimuli in young socially anxious individuals. *Neuroscience Letters, 526,* 68–73.

Rossignol, M., Philippot, P., Bissot, C., Rigoulot, S., & Campanella, S. (2012b). Electrophysiological correlates of enhanced perceptual processes and attentional capture by emotional faces in social anxiety. *Brain Research, 1460,* 50–62.

Sabatinelli, D., Keil, A., Frank, D. W., & Lang, P. J. (2013). Emotional perception: Correspondence of early and late event-related potentials with cortical and subcortical functional MRI. *Biological Psychology, 92,* 513–519.

Sacco, T. & Sacchetti, B. (2010). Role of secondary sensory cortices in emotional memory storage and retrieval in rats. *Science, 329,* 649–656.

Sass, S. M., Heller, W., Stewart, J. L., Silton, R. L., Edgar, J. C., Fisher, J. E., & Miller, G. A. (2010). Time course of attentional bias in anxiety: Emotion and gender specificity. *Psychophysiology, 47,* 247–259.

Schiller, P. H. & Tehovnik, E. J. (2001). Look and see: How the brain moves your eyes about. *Progress in Brain Research, 134,* 127–142.

Seeley, W. W., Menon, V., Schatzberg, A. F., Keller, J., Glover, G. H., Kenna, H., Reiss, A. L., & Greicius, M. D. (2007). Dissociable intrinsic connectivity networks for salience processing and executive control. *Journal of Neuroscience, 27,* 2349–2356.

Seligman, M. E. (1970). On the generality of the laws of learning. *Psychological Review, 77,* 406.

Shaw, J. C. (2003). *The Brain's Alpha Rhythms and the Mind.* Amsterdam: Elsevier.

Sherin, J. E. & Nemeroff, C. B. (2011). Posttraumatic stress disorder: The neurobiological impact of psychological trauma. *Dialogues in Clinical Neuroscience, 13,* 263–278.

Shin, L. M. & Liberzon, I. (2010). The neurocircuitry of fear, stress, and anxiety disorders. *Neuropsychopharmacology, 35,* 169–191.

Skinner, R., Rasco, L., Fitzgerald, J., Karson, C., Mathew, M., Williams, D. K., & Garcia-Rill, E. (1999). Reduced sensory gating of the P1 potential in rape victims and combat veterans with posttraumatic stress disorder. *Depression and Anxiety, 9,* 122–130.

Southwick, S. M., Krystal, J. H., Bremner, J. D., Morgan, C. A., 3rd, Nicolaou, A. L., Nagy, L. M., Johnson, D. R., Heninger, G. R., & Charney, D. S. (1997). Noradrenergic and serotonergic function in posttraumatic stress disorder. *Archives of General Psychiatry, 54,* 749–758.

Staugaard, S. R. (2010). Threatening faces and social anxiety: A literature review. *Clinical Psychology Review, 30*, 669–690.

Stevenson, R. J. & Boakes, R. A. (2003). A mnemonic theory of odor perception. *Psychological Review, 110*, 340–364.

Stokes, M., Thompson, R., Nobre, A. C., & Duncan, J. (2009). Shape-specific preparatory activity mediates attention to targets in human visual cortex. *Proceedings of the National Academy of Sciences, 106*, 19569–19574.

Straube, T., Mentzel, H. J., & Miltner, W. H. (2005). Common and distinct brain activation to threat and safety signals in social phobia. *Neuropsychobiology, 52*, 163–168.

Sugase, Y., Yamane, S., Ueno, S., & Kawano, K. (1999). Global and fine information coded by single neurons in the temporal visual cortex. *Nature, 400*, 869–873.

Sussman, T. J., Jin, J., & Mohanty, A. (2016). Top-down and bottom-up factors in threat-related perception and attention in anxiety. *Biological Psychology, 121*, 160–172.

Thoma, R. J., Hanlon, F. M., Moses, S. N., Edgar, J. C., Huang, M., Weisend, M. P., Irwin, J., Sherwood, A., Paulson, K., Bustillo, J., Adler, L. E., Miller, G. A., & Cañive, J. M. (2003). Lateralization of auditory sensory gating and neuropsychological dysfunction in schizophrenia. *American Journal of Psychiatry, 160*, 1595–1605.

Thorpe, S. J. (2009). The speed of categorization in the human visual system. *Neuron, 62*, 168–170.

Tooby, J. & Cosmides, L. (1992). The psychological foundations of culture. In J. Barkow, L. Cosmides, & J. Tooby (eds.), *The Adapted Mind: Evolutionary Psychology and the Generation of Culture* (pp. 19–136). New York, NY: Oxford University Press.

Trautmann, S. A., Fehr, T., & Herrmann, M. (2009). Emotions in motion: Dynamic compared to static facial expressions of disgust and happiness reveal more widespread emotion-specific activations. *Brain Research, 1284*, 100–115.

Tsuchiya, N., Moradi, F., Felsen, C., Yamazaki, M., & Adolphs, R. (2009). Intact rapid detection of fearful faces in the absence of the amygdala. *Nature Neuroscience, 12*, 1224–1225.

van Bockstaele, B., Verschuere, B., Tibboel, H., De Houwer, J., Crombez, G., & Koster, E. H. (2014). A review of current evidence for the causal impact of attentional bias on fear and anxiety. *Psychological Bulletin*, 140, 682–721.

van Peer, J. M., Roelofs, K., Rotteveel, M., van Dijk, J. G., Spinhoven, P., & Ridderinkhof, K. R. (2007). The effects of cortisol administration on approach-avoidance behavior: An event-related potential study. *Biological Psychology, 76*, 135–146.

van Peer, J. M., Spinhoven, P., van Dijk, J. G., & Roelofs, K. (2009). Cortisol-induced enhancement of emotional face processing in social phobia depends on symptom severity and motivational context. *Biological Psychology, 81*, 123–130.

Venetacci, R., Johnstone, A., Kirkby, K. C., & Matthews, A. (2018). ERP correlates of attentional processing in spider fear: Evidence of threat-specific hypervigilance. *Cognition and Emotion, 32*(3), 437–449.

Vlamings, P. H., Goffaux, V., & Kemner, C. (2009). Is the early modulation of brain activity by fearful facial expressions primarily mediated by coarse low spatial frequency information? *Journal of Vision, 9*(12), 1–13.

Vuilleumier, P., Armony, J. L., Driver, J., & Dolan, R. J. (2001). Effects of attention and emotion on face processing in the human brain: An event-related fMRI study. *Neuron*, *30*, 829–841.

Vuilleumier, P., Armony, J. L., Driver, J., & Dolan, R. J. (2003). Distinct spatial frequency sensitivities for processing faces and emotional expressions. *Nature Neuroscience*, *6*, 624–631.

Vuilleumier, P. & Pourtois, G. (2007). Distributed and interactive brain mechanisms during emotion face perception: Evidence from functional neuroimaging. *Neuropsychologia*, *45*, 174–194.

Walentowska, W. & Wronka, E. (2012). Trait anxiety and involuntary processing of facial emotions. *International Journal of Psychophysiology*, *85*, 27–36.

Wang, S., Tudusciuc, O., Mamelak, A. N., Ross, I. B., Adolphs, R., & Rutishauser, U. (2014). Neurons in the human amygdala selective for perceived emotion. *Proceedings of the National Academy of Sciences*, *111*, E3110–E19.

Weinberg, A. & Hajcak, G. (2011). Electrocortical evidence for vigilance-avoidance in generalized anxiety disorder. *Psychophysiology*, *48*, 842–851.

Weinberger, N. M. (2004). Specific long-term memory traces in primary auditory cortex. *Nature Reviews Neuroscience*, *5*, 279–290.

Weinberger, N. M. (2007). Associative representational plasticity in the auditory cortex: A synthesis of two disciplines. *Learning and Memory*, *14*, 1–16.

Weinberger, N. M., Hopkins, W., & Diamond, D. M. (1984). Physiological plasticity of single neurons in auditory cortex of the cat during acquisition of the pupillary conditioned response: I. Primary field (AI). *Behavioral Neuroscience*, *98*, 171–188.

Wieser, M. J., McTeague, L. M., & Keil, A. (2012). Competition effects of threatening faces in social anxiety. *Emotion*, *12*, 1050.

Wieser, M. J. & Moscovitch, D. A. (2015). The effect of affective context on visuocortical processing of neutral faces in social anxiety. *Frontiers in Psychology*, *6*, 1824.

Williams, J. M. G., Mathews, A., & MacLeod, C. (1996). The emotional Stroop task and psychopathology. *Psychological Bulletin*, *120*, 3.

Williams, J. M. G, Watts, F. N., MacLeod, C., & Mathews, A. (1988). *Cognitive Psychology and Emotional Disorders*. Oxford: John Wiley & Sons.

Williams, J. M. G., Watts, F. N., MacLeod, C., & Mathews, A. (1997). *Cognitive Psychology and Emotional Disorders* (2nd edn). Oxford: John Wiley & Sons.

Wilson, D. A. & Stevenson, R. J. (2006). *Learning to Smell: Olfactory Perception from Neurobiology to Behavior*. Baltimore, MD: Johns Hopkins University Press.

Wilson, D. A. & Sullivan, R. M. (2011). Cortical processing of odor objects. *Neuron*, *72*, 506–519.

Worden, M. S., Foxe, J. J., Wang, N., & Simpson, G. V. (2000). Anticipatory biasing of visuospatial attention indexed by retinotopically specific alpha-band electroence-phalography increases over occipital cortex. *Journal of Neuroscience*, *20*, RC63.

You, Y. & Li, W. (2016). Parallel processing of general and specific threat during early stages of perception. *Social, Cognitive, & Affective Neuroscience*, *11*, 395–404.

Young, A. W., Rowland, D., Calder, A. J., Etcoff, N. L., Seth, A., & Perrett, D. I. (1997). Facial expression megamix: Tests of dimensional and category accounts of emotion recognition. *Cognition*, *63*, 271–313.

Zelano, C., Mohanty, A., & Gottfried, J. A. (2011). Olfactory predictive codes and stimulus templates in piriform cortex. *Neuron*, 72, 178–187.

SECTION 2

Transdiagnostic Processes

4 Neuroticism/Negative Affectivity

David Watson

Multiple disorders tend to co-occur within the same individual, such that comorbidity is a pervasive feature of psychopathology (Kotov et al., 2017; Watson, 2005, 2009). This has led to intense interest in transdiagnostic processes that (a) are common to different disorders and (b) help to explain the substantial associations between them. This chapter focuses on individual differences in neuroticism and its core components. Neuroticism is the most widely studied and best-established transdiagnostic personality factor in psychopathology. It has been described as "an almost ubiquitously elevated trait within clinical populations" (Widiger & Costa, 1994, p. 81). Elevated levels of neuroticism have been reported in virtually all major forms of psychopathology, including the psychotic disorders, bipolar disorders, depressive disorders, anxiety disorders, obsessive-compulsive and related disorders, trauma- and stressor-related disorders, dissociative disorders, somatic symptom disorders, substance use disorders, feeding and eating disorders, and personality and conduct disorders (e.g., Koffel & Watson, 2009; Kotov, Gamez, Schmidt, & Watson, 2010; Samuel & Widiger, 2008).

In this chapter, I examine associations between neuroticism and anxiety and related disorders. Specifically, I consider symptoms and diagnoses that fell within the anxiety disorders in the fourth edition of the *Diagnostic and Statistical Manual of Mental Disorders* (*DSM-IV*) (American Psychiatric Association, 2000). In the revised framework of *DSM-5* (American Psychiatric Association, 2013), these conditions now fall into three adjacent diagnostic classes: anxiety disorders, obsessive-compulsive and related disorders, and trauma- and stressor-related disorders.

I begin by providing a brief review of the basic features of neuroticism. I then examine how broad individual differences in neuroticism are linked to anxiety-related psychopathology, looking first at its associations with diagnoses, and then considering relations with the specific symptom dimensions subsumed within various disorders. Next, I explicate the nature of these associations further by examining links between anxiety-related psychopathology and the core component traits – or *facets* – within neuroticism. In the final sections of the chapter, I (a) highlight the complex causal mechanisms underlying these relations, (b) examine associations between neuroticism and other transdiagnostic traits that have been linked to the anxiety and related disorders (e.g., anxiety sensitivity, experiential avoidance), and (c) discuss key methodological issues and directions for future research.

Basic Features of Neuroticism

Relations with Negative Affect

Neuroticism reflects broad individual differences in subjective distress and dissatisfaction. In particular, it has been shown to be the strongest and broadest predictor of negative emotional experience. For example, Watson, Wiese, Vaidya, and Tellegen (1999) reported a 0.58 correlation between neuroticism and the trait Negative Affect scale from the Positive and Negative Affect Schedule (PANAS) (Watson, Clark, & Tellegen, 1988). Similarly, Beer, Watson, and McDade-Montez (2013) found that neuroticism was strongly correlated with scores on the PANAS Negative Affect scale in both self-ratings (weighted mean $r = 0.59$) and other-ratings (weighted mean $r = 0.69$). Watson (2000a) examined relations between neuroticism and four specific types of negative affectivity, which were assessed using the Expanded Form of the PANAS (PANAS-X) (Watson & Clark, 1999): Fear (e.g., *afraid, nervous*), Sadness (e.g., *blue, lonely*), Guilt (e.g., *ashamed, dissatisfied with self*), and Hostility (e.g., *angry, disgusted*). Watson (2000a) reported that neuroticism was strongly related to individual differences in Sadness ($r = 0.59$), Guilt ($r = 0.57$), and Fear ($r = 0.52$), and more moderately linked to Hostility ($r = 0.41$). In light of these associations, neuroticism often is called *negative emotionality* or *negative affectivity* in the personality literature (e.g., Soto & John, 2017; Watson, 2000a).

Genetic and Biological Basis

Heritability of neuroticism. All major personality traits have a strong genetic basis, with heritability estimates from twin studies generally falling in the 0.40 to 0.60 range. In a review of the behavior genetics literature that drew primarily from twin studies, Bouchard (2004) reported a 0.48 heritability estimate for neuroticism, noting that it displays evidence of both additive and nonadditive genetic effects. In a subsequent meta-analysis that included a broader range of both twin and adoption studies, Vukasović and Bratko (2015) reported lower – but still substantial – heritability estimates ranging from 0.37 to 0.47 across various models and measures (see their Table 4.4).

    Biological basis of neuroticism. In terms of its underlying biology, neuroticism reflects individual differences in the withdrawal-oriented behavioral inhibition system (BIS) (Fowles, 1994; Gray, 1982, 1987; Watson et al., 1999). The essential purpose of the BIS is to inhibit behavior that might lead to pain, punishment, or some other aversive consequence. Gray (1987) called the BIS a "stop, look, and listen system" to emphasize how it redirects attention toward the environment. According to Gray, BIS activity focuses maximum attention on analyzing environmental stimuli, especially novel stimuli that potentially signal danger. The BIS also has a strongly anticipatory quality: it promotes a vigilant scanning of the environment for potential threats and motivates the organism to proceed cautiously until safety is indicated. Finally, elevated BIS activity is associated with a heightened sensitivity to punishment (e.g., Aluja & Blanch, 2011; Corr & Cooper, 2016; Torrubia, Ávila, Moltó, & Caseras, 2001). Extensive evidence has established strong associations between neuroticism and various indicators of the BIS and punishment sensitivity (Aluja & Blanch, 2011; Carver & White, 1994; Corr & Cooper, 2016; Torrubia et al., 2001; Watson et al., 1999).

Given this link to the BIS – which is an ancient biobehavioral system – it is interesting to note that reliable individual differences in neuroticism also have been identified in numerous other species. For example, in an early review of the animal personality literature, Gosling and John (1999) identified neuroticism-like factors in a broad range of species, including chimpanzees, gorillas, rhesus and vervet monkeys, hyenas, dogs, cats, rats, guppies, and octopi. Gartner, Powell, and Weiss (2014) subsequently found robust individual differences in neuroticism among snow leopards, clouded leopards, and lions.

Stability versus Change

Rank-order stability. Similar to other personality traits, neuroticism shows only modest to moderate rank-order stability during childhood and adolescence. Starting in the 20s, however, it begins to display strong levels of stability, eventually reaching correlations > 0.70 over periods of six to seven years (Roberts & DelVecchio, 2000). Collapsed across all age ranges, Roberts and DelVecchio reported an overall stability coefficient of 0.50 for neuroticism, a value very similar to those obtained for other general traits (see their Table 4.5).

Mean-level change. Average levels of neuroticism vary systematically over the life span. Specifically, neuroticism scores tend to increase during adolescence (especially in females), and then show a consistent decline during early and middle adulthood (Roberts, Walton, & Viechtbauer, 2006; Soto, John, Gosling, & Potter, 2011). It is noteworthy that this decline in neuroticism during adulthood has been shown to be quite robust cross-culturally, although the timing of these age-related changes differs substantially across countries (Bleidorn, 2015).

Cohort effects. Average levels of neuroticism have increased over time. From the 1950s through the early 1990s, there is evidence of birth cohort increases in neuroticism that is consistent across samples and nationalities (Twenge, Gentile, & Campbell, 2015). Since the early 1990s, however, trait levels have remained relatively stable or even declined slightly. Nevertheless, Twenge et al. (2015) conclude their review by stating that neuroticism remains "at historically high levels" (p. 543).

The Hierarchical Structure of Personality

Personality traits are ordered hierarchically at different levels of abstraction or breadth (Markon, Krueger, & Watson, 2005; Watson, Nus, & Wu, 2017). Neuroticism is a key component in all of the major structural models of personality, including both the prominent Big Three and Big Five schemes (Markon et al., 2005). It is one of the "Big" traits in these models, which means that it is a broad, higher-order dimension that can be decomposed into more specific lower-order facets.

We currently lack consensus regarding the specific facets that fall within the higher-order domain of neuroticism. For instance, the NEO Personality Inventory-3 (NEO-PI-3) (McCrae, Costa, & Martin, 2005) contains six neuroticism facets; in contrast, the Faceted Inventory of the Five-Factor Model (FI-FFM) (Watson et al., 2017) has only five neuroticism facets, whereas the Big Five Inventory-2 (BFI-2) (Soto & John, 2017) includes only three. To create a consensually defined facet structure of neuroticism, Naragon-Gainey and Watson (2014) conducted a structural analysis using specific trait scales from five hierarchical instruments: the Revised NEO Personality Inventory (NEO PI-R) (Costa & McCrae, 1992), the Multidimensional Personality Questionnaire (MPQ) (Tellegen & Waller, 2008), the Sixteen Personality Factor Questionnaire (16PF) (Cattell, Eber, & Tatsuoka, 1970), the Hogan Personality Inventory (HPI) (Hogan & Hogan, 1992), and the Jackson Personality Inventory-Revised (JPI-R) (Jackson, 1994). These analyses revealed three consensual facets that represent specific types of negative affectivity: Anxiety (defined by scales such as NEO PI-R Anxiety, 16 PF Apprehension, JPI-R Anxiety, and MPQ Stress Reaction), Anger (marked on one end by NEO PI-R Angry Hostility, and on the other by scales such as HPI Even-Temperedness), and Depression (defined on one end by NEO PI-R Depression, and on the other by scales such as HPI No Depression and HPI No Guilt). I use this consensual three-facet structure to model relations with psychopathology at the lower-order level.

Methods

Overview

I examine four types of data to explicate the associations between neuroticism and anxiety-related psychopathology: (a) domain scores and anxiety diagnoses, (b) domain scores and anxiety symptoms, (c) facet scores and anxiety diagnoses, and (d) facet scores and anxiety symptoms. In the initial set of analyses, I summarize the meta-analytic findings of Kotov et al. (2010). For the other three sets of analyses, I use data collected from three samples. In the following sections, I describe these participants and the measures that are examined in subsequent analyses.

Participants and Procedure

Sample 1. This sample (N = 669) included 296 psychiatric outpatients and 373 college students (for more details, see Watson & Naragon-Gainey, 2014; Watson et al., 2012). These participants completed multiple self-report measures of various types of anxiety symptoms (e.g., several social anxiety scales). I first standardized the scores on these highly correlated indicators – so they would be equally weighted – and then averaged them to produce an overall composite score for each type of symptom; these self-report composites are described later. To eliminate mean-level differences across populations, I standardized all of the symptom and trait scores on a within-population basis (i.e., the patient and student responses were standardized separately) so that they could be combined in a single overall analysis.

These participants also were interviewed using the Clinician Rating version of the Inventory of Depression and Anxiety Symptoms (IDAS-CR) (Koffel, 2011; Watson, 2009; Watson et al., 2008, 2012) and a companion instrument, the Personality, Cognitions, Consciousness, and Perceptions Interview (PCCP) (Koffel, 2011; Watson et al., 2012). The IDAS-CR and PCCP both consist of a series of single-item ratings representing specific types of symptoms. Each rating is made on a three-point scale (*absent, subthreshold, present*). To rate each symptom, the clinicians asked a standard initial probe question, as well as several standard follow up questions.

IDAS-CR ratings were available for six specific anxiety symptoms: the assessed variables included Generalized Anxiety, Social Anxiety, and Panic, as well as three types of posttraumatic stress disorder (PTSD) symptoms (Hyperarousal, Intrusions, Avoidance), which also were summed to create an overall PTSD composite. In addition, the PCCP was used to assess five specific types of obsessive-compulsive disorder (OCD) symptoms: Checking, Cleaning, Ordering, Hoarding, and Obsessions; these ratings also were summed to create a general OCD composite. Across the two instruments, I report data on 13 interview-based symptom ratings; this includes five overall scores (Generalized Anxiety, Social Anxiety, Panic, PTSD, OCD), three specific types of PTSD symptoms, and five types of OCD symptoms.

IDAS-CR/PCCP data were available on 625 participants (252 patients, 373 students). As before, I standardized the scores on a within-population basis and then examined them in a single overall analysis.

Finally, the outpatients (N = 252) also were interviewed using the Structured Clinical Interview for *DSM-IV* (SCID-IV) (First, Spitzer, Gibbon, & Williams, 1997). I report associations between specific neuroticism facets and five *DSM-IV* anxiety disorder diagnoses: generalized anxiety disorder (GAD), PTSD, panic disorder, social phobia, and OCD.

Sample 2. The participants were 406 community adults who completed an extensive battery of self-report symptom measures (see Watson et al., 2017; Watson, Stasik, Ellickson-Larew, & Stanton, 2015). Although this sample was not fully clinical in nature, roughly half of the participants (46.3%) were either currently receiving treatment for mental health issues or had received it in the past. Consequently, these participants exhibited a relatively high level of psychopathology. As in Sample 1, multiple measures were available for most types of symptoms; these indicators were standardized and then combined to yield an overall composite for each symptom dimension.

In addition, the participants were interviewed using an adapted version (with the authorization of the author) of the Mini-International Neuropsychiatric Interview (M.I.N.I) (Sheehan et al., 1998) that incorporated diagnostic changes for *DSM-5* (see Watson et al., 2015). I examine associations between neuroticism facets and six *DSM-5* diagnoses: GAD, PTSD, panic disorder, agoraphobia, social phobia, and OCD.[1]

Sample 3. This sample consisted of 268 outpatients (see Watson & Naragon-Gainey, 2014; Watson et al., 2012) who were interviewed using the revised version of the Interview for Mood and Anxiety Symptoms (IMAS) (Gamez, Kotov, & Watson, 2010; Waszczuk, Kotov, Ruggero, Gamez, & Watson, 2017). The IMAS provides multi-item measures of current (i.e., past month) symptoms; each item is scored on a three-point rating scale (*absent, subthreshold, above threshold*). Its items were designed to cover all *DSM-IV* Mood and Anxiety Disorder symptom criteria.

Based on data from prior studies (Watson et al., 2007; Gamez et al., 2010), the IMAS was revised to improve its symptom coverage. I examine 18 anxiety symptom scores derived from this revised version (see Waszczuk et al., 2017): GAD (12 items), Social Phobia (15 items), Panic (23 items), four types of PTSD symptoms (overall PTSD [25 items], Hyperarousal [6 items], Intrusions [4 items], Avoidance [3 items]), Agoraphobia (15 items), Claustrophobia [6 items], four indicators of specific phobia (overall Specific Phobia [13 items], Animal Phobia [3 items], Situational Phobia [3 items], Blood-Injection-Injury Phobia [4 items]), and five measures of OCD symptoms (overall OCD [18 items], Obsessions [6 items], Checking [4 items], Ordering [6 items], Cleaning [5 items]).

Neuroticism Measures

Sample 1. The Sample 1 participants completed three overall measures of neuroticism: (a) an eight-item version of the Big Five Inventory (BFI) (John & Srivastava, 1999) Neuroticism scale; (b) the sum of the Anxiety, Depression, and Angry Hostility facet scales from the NEO PI-R (Costa & McCrae; 1992); and (c) the sum of the Anxiety, Depression, and Anger Proneness facet scales from the FI-FFM (Watson et al., 2017). Correlations between these measures ranged from 0.79 to 0.90, with a mean coefficient of 0.85. These indicators were standardized and then averaged to form an overall domain score for neuroticism.

I also used the individual NEO PI-R and FI-FFM scales to create three standardized facet scores. Thus, NEO PI-R Anxiety and FI-FFM Anxiety ($r = 0.81$) were averaged to assess Anxiety; NEO PI-R Depression and FI-FFM Depression ($r =$ 0.85) were used to model Depression; and NEO PI-R Angry Hostility and FI-FFM Anger Proneness ($r = 0.84$) were combined to measure Anger.

Sample 2. These participants completed the full NEO-PI-3 (McCrae et al., 2005) and FI-FFM (Watson et al. 2017). The Neuroticism domain scores from these instruments correlated 0.84 with each other; they were standardized and then combined into a composite. In addition, I again created standardized facet scores by averaging NEO-PI-3 Anxiety and FI-FFM Anxiety ($r = 0.81$), NEO-PI-3 Depression and FI-FFM Depression ($r = 0.81$), and NEO-PI-3 Angry Hostility and FI-FFM Anger Proneness ($r = 0.79$).

Sample 3. These participants completed a nine-item version of the BFI Neuroticism scale (John & Srivastava, 1999).

Self-Rated Symptoms

GAD symptoms. The participants in Samples 1 and 2 completed three GAD symptom measures that were combined into composites: (1) the 7-item Anxious Mood scale from the Inventory of Depression and Anxiety Symptoms (IDAS) (Watson et al., 2007); (2) the 9-item Generalized Anxiety Disorder Questionnaire-IV (GADQ-IV) (Newman et al., 2002); and (3) the 10-item Worry Domains Questionnaire-Short Form (Stöber & Joormann, 2001).

PTSD symptoms. The Sample 1 participants were assessed on two PTSD symptom measures: (1) the 17-item PTSD Checklist-Civilian Version (PCL) (Weathers, Litz, Herman, Huska, & Keane, 1993); and (2) an aggregate score based on the Traumatic Intrusions (4 items) and Traumatic Avoidance (4 items) scales of the Expanded Version of the IDAS (IDAS-II) (Watson et al., 2012). In addition to creating an overall PTSD score, I also examined four specific types of PTSD symptoms (for discussions of PTSD symptom structure, see Watson, 2009; Watson et al., 2012; Yufik & Simms, 2010). The Sample 1 battery included two measures of Intrusions (PCL Intrusions, IDAS-II Traumatic Intrusions), two indicators of Avoidance (PCL Avoidance, IDAS-II Traumatic Avoidance), and single markers of both Dysphoria (PCL Dysphoria) and Hyperarousal (PCL Hyperarousal).

The Sample 2 participants completed (1) the five intrusions items and two avoidance items from the PCL and (2) the IDAS-II Traumatic Intrusions and Traumatic Avoidance scales. These measures were used to create three composites: overall PTSD, Intrusions, and Avoidance.

Social anxiety. The Sample 1 participants completed three indicators of social anxiety: (1) the 5-item Social Phobia scale from the Fear Questionnaire (FQ) (Marks & Mathews, 1979); (2) the 10-item Social Phobia scale from the Albany Panic and Phobia Questionnaire (APPQ) (Rapee, Craske, & Barlow, 1994/1995); and (3) the 6-item IDAS-II Social Anxiety scale (Watson et al., 2012). The Sample

2 participants were assessed on these same three measures, plus a factor analytically derived 10-item Social Anxiety scale from the Schizotypal Personality Questionnaire (Chmielewski & Watson, 2008).

Panic. The Sample 1 battery contained two measures of panic symptoms: (1) the 17-item Anxious Arousal scale from the Mood and Anxiety Symptom Questionnaire (MASQ) (Watson et al., 1995) and (2) the 13-item Panic Attack Symptom Questionnaire (PASQ) (Watson, 2000b). The Sample 2 participants completed three indicators of panic: (1) a reduced, 9-item version of the MASQ Anxious Arousal scale (Watson et al., 1995), (2) an abbreviated, 6-item version of the PASQ (Watson, 2000b), and (3) the 8-item IDAS-II Panic scale (Watson et al., 2012).

OCD. Participants in both samples completed three OCD measures: (1) the 18-item Obsessive-Compulsive Inventory-Revised (OCI-R) (Foa et al., 2002); (2) a total score based on the Obsessive Checking (14 items), Obsessive Cleanliness (12 items), Compulsive Rituals (8 items), and Hoarding (5 items) scales from the Schedule of Compulsions, Obsessions, and Pathological Impulses (SCOPI) (Watson & Wu, 2005); and (3) a combined score based on the IDAS-II Checking (3 items), Ordering (5 items), and Cleaning (7 items) scales. In addition to creating an overall OCD score, I constructed five specific OCD symptom composites in each sample (for reviews of OCD symptom structure, see Watson, 2009; Watson et al., 2012): Obsessions (OCI-R Obsessions), Checking (OCI-R Checking, SCOPI Obsessive Checking, IDAS-II Checking), Ordering (OCI-R Ordering, SCOPI Compulsive Rituals, IDAS-II Ordering), Cleaning (OCI-R Washing, SCOPI Obsessive Cleanliness, IDAS-II Cleaning), and Hoarding (OCI-R Hoarding, SCOPI Hoarding).

Agoraphobia. The Sample 2 battery included two measures of agoraphobia: (1) the nine-item APPQ Agoraphobia scale and the five-item FQ Agoraphobia scale.

Claustrophobia. The Sample 2 participants completed the five-item IDAS-II Claustrophobia scale, which assesses experienced fear and behavioral avoidance related to crowded public settings (e.g., afraid of getting trapped in a crowd); small, tight spaces (e.g., avoided small spaces); and dark, confined places (e.g., afraid of tunnels).

Specific phobia. Participants in Sample 2 were assessed on two types of specific phobia. First, they completed three measures of blood-injection-injury (BII) phobia: (1) the 5-item FQ Blood-Injection scale; (2) the 10-item Blood-Injection scale from the Phobic Stimuli Response Scales (PSRS) (Cutshall & Watson, 2004); and (3) a 5-item BII scale created from the Fear Survey Schedule (FSS) (Wolpe & Lang, 1964). Second, they were assessed on three measures of animal phobia: (1) the 8-item PSRS Animal fear scale (Cutshall & Watson, 2004); (2) a 5-item Animal Phobia scale constructed from the FSS (Wolpe & Lang, 1964); and the provisional 9-item Animal Phobia scale of the IDAS-II (Watson et al., 2012). These scores were used to create three composite measures: Blood-Injection Phobia, Animal Phobia, and overall Specific Phobia.

Neuroticism and Anxiety Disorder Diagnoses

Kotov et al. (2010) conducted a meta-analysis in which they compared the mean trait scores of individuals with and without 14 *DSM-IV* diagnoses (e.g., the mean neuroticism scores of individuals with and without GAD). Specifically, they examined three *DSM-IV* mood disorder (major depression, dysthymic disorder, unspecified unipolar depression), seven anxiety disorder (GAD, PTSD, panic disorder, agoraphobia, social phobia, specific phobia, OCD), and four substance use disorder (overall substance use, primarily alcohol, primarily drugs, mixed use) diagnoses. The mean differences between diagnostic cases and non-cases were divided by their pooled standard deviations to yield effect sizes expressed as Cohen's *d* (Cohen, 1992; see their Table 4.4); positive *d* values indicate that the diagnostic cases scored higher on the trait.

Kotov et al. (2010) examined relations with six broad traits: the higher-order Big Five domains, plus disinhibition from the Big Three model. Neuroticism easily was the strongest predictor of psychopathology in these analyses. It was significantly – and substantially – related to every diagnosis. In fact, it produced large effect sizes (Cohen, 1992) with 13 of the 14 analyzed disorders (the exception was alcohol use) and displayed very little diagnostic specificity overall (*d*s ranged from 0.77 to 2.25, mean *d* = 1.65). Table 4.1 presents Kotov et al.'s (2010) meta-analytic results for the seven anxiety disorder diagnoses. It is noteworthy that six of the *d* values exceeded 1.60; the *d* for specific phobia was substantially smaller (0.92), but still represented a large effect size. These findings clearly establish neuroticism as a strong transdiagnostic factor in the *DSM-IV* anxiety disorders (as well as in the depressive and substance use disorders).

Table 4.1 *Meta-analytic associations between neuroticism and anxiety disorder diagnoses*

Diagnosis	K	N_C	N_{NC}	d
Posttraumatic stress disorder	16	1,714	22,174	2.25
Obsessive-compulsive disorder	18	905	25,152	2.07
Generalized anxiety disorder	14	1,674	44,570	1.96
Panic disorder	24	2,556	32,227	1.92
Social phobia	18	3,188	36,165	1.63
Agoraphobia	15	1,451	24,902	1.61
Specific phobia	10	2,800	21,367	0.92
Mean effect size				**1.77**

Note. K = number of studies. N_C = number of cases (patients). N_{NC} = number of non-cases. Adapted from Kotov, Gamez, Schmidt, and Watson (2010), Tables 4.3 and 4.4.

Neuroticism and Anxiety Symptoms

The Problem of Heterogeneity

Disorder-based analyses are limited in several important ways (see Watson, 2005, 2009). One particularly important problem is that diagnosis-based analyses fail to capture the marked heterogeneity of many *DSM* disorders. As already noted, structural analyses have identified replicable symptom dimensions within several of the *DSM-IV* anxiety disorders, including PTSD, OCD, and specific phobia (Watson, 2005, 2009; Watson et al., 2007, 2012; Watson & Wu, 2005); moreover, these symptom dimensions are highly distinctive and often correlate quite differently with other variables. Consequently, symptom-based analyses provide a clearer, more nuanced view of the associations between neuroticism and psychopathology; they also show much greater evidence of specificity.

Associations with Anxiety Symptoms

Overall symptom composites. Neuroticism shows substantial specificity at the symptom level (Watson, Gamez, & Simms, 2005; Watson & Naragon-Gainey, 2014). It correlates most strongly with indicators of subjective distress (e.g., the anxious, apprehensive mood that is the core feature of GAD), more moderately with symptoms associated with more limited forms of distress (e.g., panic, social anxiety), and weakly with symptoms characterized primarily by behavioral avoidance of specific stimuli (e.g., phobias).

Table 4.2 presents correlations between neuroticism domain scores and self-rated (Samples 1 and 2) and interview-based (IDAS-CR in Sample 1, IMAS in Sample 3) anxiety symptoms in the three current samples. Consistent with previous studies (Watson et al., 2005; Watson & Naragon-Gainey, 2014), neuroticism was significantly related to every type of anxiety symptom, which again establishes it as a strong transdiagnostic factor in the *DSM-IV* anxiety disorders. Nevertheless, the magnitude of these relations varied dramatically, ranging from a high of 0.81 (self-rated GAD symptoms in Sample 1) to a low of only 0.15 (IMAS Blood-Injection Phobia in Sample 3). Replicating previous findings (Watson et al., 2005; Watson & Naragon-Gainey, 2014), neuroticism was most strongly linked to GAD symptoms: across the four sets of analyses, these correlations ranged from 0.47 to 0.81, with a weighted mean value (after r-to-z transformation) of 0.70. Neuroticism also was strongly related to overall symptoms of PTSD (weighted mean $r = 0.59$), Panic ($r = 0.55$), and Social Anxiety ($r = 0.53$). It was more moderately related to Agoraphobia ($r = 0.45$), OCD ($r = 0.42$), and Claustrophobia ($r = 0.38$), and only modestly linked to Specific Phobia ($r = 0.28$). These data again demonstrate that neuroticism shows substantial specificity at the symptom level: it is most strongly related to core indicators of subjective distress/negative mood and exhibits more moderate associations with other types of anxiety symptoms.

Table 4.2 *Correlations between neuroticism and anxiety symptoms*

	Self-Report		Interview	
Symptom Score	Sample 1	Sample 2	IDAS-CR	IMAS
Generalized anxiety	**0.81**	**0.74**	**0.47**	**0.73**
PTSD	**0.62**	**0.60**	**0.42**	**0.71**
Dysphoria	**0.71**	.—	**0.41**	.—
Hyperarousal	**0.55**	.—	0.29	**0.58**
Intrusions	**0.50**	**0.60**	0.30	0.39
Avoidance	**0.47**	**0.52**	0.31	**0.42**
Social anxiety	**0.57**	**0.64**	**0.43**	**0.47**
Panic	**0.57**	**0.64**	0.34	**0.64**
OCD	**0.42**	**0.45**	**0.40**	**0.40**
Obsessions	**0.53**	**0.55**	**0.41**	**0.43**
Checking	**0.43**	**0.44**	0.24	0.33
Ordering	0.34	0.34	0.21	0.30
Hoarding	0.29	0.35	0.21	.—
Cleaning	0.26	0.25	0.11	0.36
Agoraphobia	.—	**0.44**	.—	**0.46**
Claustrophobia	.—	0.39	.—	0.36
Specific Phobia	.—	0.26	.—	0.31
Situational	.—	.—	.—	0.30
Blood-Injection	.—	0.24	.—	0.15
Animal	.—	0.22	.—	0.23

Note. $N = 669$ (Sample 1), 406 (Sample 2), 625 (IDAS-CR), 268 (IMAS). Correlations ≥ 0.40 are highlighted. IDAS-CR = Clinician Rating Version of the IDAS. IMAS = Interview of Mood and Anxiety Symptoms. PTSD = posttraumatic stress disorder. OCD = obsessive-compulsive disorder.

PTSD symptoms. PTSD symptoms differ markedly in their specificity and in their associations with neuroticism/negative affectivity. In particular, Dysphoria symptoms (e.g., feeling numb, feeling irritable, difficulty concentrating) show much greater non-specificity, correlating more strongly with indicators of depression (Gootzeit & Markon, 2011; Watson, 2009), anxiety (Gootzeit & Markon, 2011), and neuroticism (Watson et al., 2005; Watson & Naragon-Gainey, 2014) than other types of PTSD symptoms. Table 4.2 demonstrates that the current participants exhibited the same basic pattern. Thus, neuroticism correlated more strongly with Dysphoria (weighted $r = 0.58$) than with Hyperarousal ($r = 0.46$), Intrusions ($r = 0.45$), and Avoidance ($r = 0.43$). Follow-up significance tests (Kenny, 1987) indicated that neuroticism correlated significantly more strongly with Dysphoria than with other types of PTSD symptoms in all six comparisons (all $ps < 0.05$, two-tailed). These results illustrate the heterogeneity of the PTSD diagnosis and establish the importance of examining specific types of symptoms separately.

OCD symptoms. OCD symptoms also display different levels of specificity, although the observed pattern varies somewhat across instruments (Watson, 2009; Watson & Naragon-Gainey, 2014). The most robust finding is that obsessive intrusions correlate more strongly with indicators of depression, anxiety, and neuroticism than other types of OCD symptoms. Consistent with these previous data, Table 4.2 establishes that neuroticism was more strongly related to Obsessions (weighted mean $r = 0.48$) than to Checking ($r = 0.36$), Ordering ($r = 0.30$), Hoarding (0.28), and Cleaning (0.25). Follow-up tests indicated that neuroticism correlated significantly more strongly ($p < 0.01$, 2-tailed) with Obsessions than with other types of OCD symptoms in 13 of 15 comparisons; the only exceptions were that it did not correlate more strongly with IMAS Obsessions ($r = 0.43$) than with IMAS Checking ($r = 0.33$, $z = 1.53$) and IMAS Cleaning ($r = 0.36$, $z = 1.14$) in Sample 3. Paralleling the PTSD analyses, these findings demonstrate the value of examining specific types of OCD symptoms separately.

Specific phobia symptoms. All of the specific phobia measures displayed relatively weak associations with neuroticism. In fact, the strongest individual coefficient was only 0.30 (with IMAS Situational Phobia in Sample 3). These results are consistent with previous findings indicating that neuroticism is weakly linked to symptoms characterized primarily by behavioral avoidance (Watson et al., 2005; Watson & Naragon-Gainey, 2014).

Neuroticism Facets and Anxiety Disorder Diagnoses

PANAS-X Analyses

I now examine how specific types of neuroticism/negative affectivity relate to anxiety disorder diagnoses. Watson, Clark, and Stasik (2011) reported associations between the specific affect scales of the PANAS-X and five *DSM-IV* anxiety disorder diagnoses – GAD, PTSD, panic disorder, social phobia, and OCD. Data were obtained from two samples of outpatients who completed the PANAS-X using either general trait instructions ($N = 331$) or "past week" instructions ($N = 253$).

Watson et al. (2011) conducted logistic regression analyses to identify the unique, incremental predictive power of the individual affect scales. PANAS-X Fear clearly emerged as the strongest individual predictor of the anxiety disorders. It produced significant positive effects in 8 of 10 analyses (80%), showing robust associations with GAD, PTSD, and panic disorder that replicated across samples. In contrast, the Sadness and Guilt scales had consistent associations with major depression, but failed to contribute significantly to any of the anxiety disorder diagnoses. Finally, PANAS-X Hostility had a significant positive effect in only one analysis (involving GAD). These results suggest that individual differences in fear and nervousness primarily are responsible for observed associations between neuroticism and *DSM-IV* anxiety diagnoses.

Neuroticism Facet Analyses

Bivariate analyses. We can test the generalizability of these findings across measures (viz., the PANAS-X scales vs. the neuroticism facet scales from the NEO-PI-3 and FI-FFM) and diagnostic systems (i.e., *DSM-IV* vs. *DSM-5*). Table 4.3 presents polyserial correlations between the neuroticism facet scales and anxiety disorder diagnoses in Samples 1 and 2, as well as weighted mean coefficients computed across both samples. Polyserial correlations estimate the linear association between two normally distributed latent continuous variables when one of the observed variables is ordinal and the other is continuous (Flora & Curran, 2004; Olsson, Drasgow, & Dorans, 1982). They retain the relative rank order information provided by Pearson correlations but are unaffected by differences in prevalence rates, thereby facilitating comparisons across dichotomous diagnoses. The interview variables were scored as 0 = *absent*, 1 = *present*, so that positive correlations indicate that higher scores on a facet were associated with an increased likelihood of receiving that rating.

Consistent with the findings of Watson et al. (2011), the Anxiety facet displayed the strongest and broadest associations with anxiety disorder diagnoses in these data.

Table 4.3 *Polyserial correlations between neuroticism facet scales and anxiety disorder diagnoses*

Facet/Sample	GAD	PTSD	Panic	Agora	Social Phobia	OCD
Anxiety						
Sample 1	**0.55**	**0.42**	**0.52**	.—	0.35	0.39
Sample 2	**0.57**	**0.54**	**0.50**	**0.43**	**0.53**	**0.61**
Weighted *M*	**0.56**	**0.49**	**0.51**	**0.43**	**0.46**	**0.52**
Depression						
Sample 1	**0.44**	**0.44**	0.31	.—	0.36	0.22
Sample 2	**0.60**	**0.53**	**0.40**	0.37	**0.49**	**0.48**
Weighted *M*	**0.54**	**0.50**	0.36	0.37	**0.44**	0.38
Anger						
Sample 1	0.28	0.29	0.21	.—	0.18	0.25
Sample 2	**0.42**	**0.46**	0.36	0.36	0.27	**0.40**
Weighted *M*	0.36	0.39	0.31	0.36	0.24	0.35

Note. $N = 252$ (Sample 1), 402 (Sample 2). Correlations ≥ 0.40 are highlighted. GAD = generalized anxiety disorder. PTSD = posttraumatic stress disorder. Agora = agoraphobia. OCD = obsessive-compulsive disorder.

Across the six assessed diagnoses, it had weighted mean correlations ranging from 0.43 (agoraphobia) to 0.56 (GAD), with a grand mean value of 0.50. The Depression facet also showed moderate to strong associations with these disorders. It had weighted mean correlations ranging from 0.36 (panic disorder) to 0.54 (GAD), with a grand mean value of 0.43. Finally, the Anger facet clearly had the weakest links to anxiety diagnoses: It had weighted mean correlations ranging from only 0.24 (social phobia) to 0.39 (PTSD), with a grand mean value of 0.33.

Multivariate analyses. To determine the unique incremental information provided by each trait, I conducted logistic regression analyses in which the three facets were included as predictors of each diagnosis. Table 4.4 presents the odds ratios (ORs) from these logistic regressions. Note that an OR significantly greater than 1.00 indicates that the facet was associated with an increased likelihood of receiving that diagnosis (i.e., greater psychopathology). In contrast, an OR significantly less than 1.00 indicates that higher scores on the trait were associated with a *reduced* likelihood of receiving that diagnosis (i.e., lower levels of psychopathology). The latter represent suppressor effects (Watson, Clark, Chmielewski, & Kotov, 2013), wherein positive bivariate relations (see Table 4.3) are transformed into significant *negative* associations at the multivariate level.

Replicating the findings of Watson et al. (2011), the Anxiety facet clearly was the strongest and broadest predictor of anxiety disorder diagnoses in these samples. It produced significant positive effects in 8 of 11 analyses (72.7%) and showed consistent associations with three diagnoses – GAD, panic disorder, and OCD – that replicated across samples. It also had two additional associations that approached significance: PTSD in Sample 2 (OR = 2.04, $p < 0.06$) and social

Table 4.4 *Odds ratios from logistic regression analyses predicting DSM anxiety disorder diagnoses from the neuroticism facet scales*

Facet/Sample	GAD	PTSD	Panic	Agora	Social Phobia	OCD
Anxiety						
Sample 1	**2.86**	1.57	**3.45**	.—	1.48	**2.35**
Sample 2	**1.96**	2.04	**2.81**	**2.34**	**3.33**	**3.68**
Depression						
Sample 1	1.28	1.77	0.92	.—	**1.59**	0.79
Sample 2	**2.64**	1.67	1.10	1.03	**2.05**	1.19
Anger						
Sample 1	0.89	1.13	0.93	.—	0.91	1.33
Sample 2	0.89	1.43	1.16	1.34	**0.57**	1.22

Note. $N = 252$ (Sample 1), 402 (Sample 2). Significant effects ($p < 0.05$) are highlighted. GAD = generalized anxiety disorder. PTSD = posttraumatic stress disorder. Agora = agoraphobia. OCD = obsessive-compulsive disorder.

phobia in Sample 1 (OR = 1.48, p < 0.08). In contrast, the Depression facet contributed positively in only three cases (27.3%), although it was a consistent predictor of social phobia. Finally, the Anger facet yielded only a single suppressor effect (OR = 0.57 with social phobia in Sample 2).

Summary

Taken together with the findings of Watson et al. (2011), the current results establish that individual differences in fear/anxiety have the strongest and broadest links to anxiety disorder diagnoses. Overall, the fear/anxiety scales produced significant positive associations in 16 of 21 analyses (76.2%). Moreover, these scales had highly robust associations with both (a) GAD and (b) panic disorder that replicated across four different samples. In marked contrast, indicators of sadness/depression displayed a significant positive effect in only three (14.3%) analyses, whereas the anger/hostility scales contributed positively in only one case (4.8%); furthermore, neither facet produced an association that consistently replicated across samples. Consequently, it seems reasonable to conclude that individual differences in fear and nervousness primarily are responsible for observed associations between neuroticism and *DSM-IV/DSM-5* anxiety disorder diagnoses.

Neuroticism Facets and Anxiety Symptoms

Overview

Finally, I examine relations between these three neuroticism facets and anxiety symptoms. These associations are presented in Tables 4.5 (self-rated symptoms in Sample 1), 4.6 (self-rated symptoms in Sample 2), and 4.7 (IDAS-CR ratings in Sample 1). Each table reports both (a) simple Pearson correlations and (b) standardized β weights from multiple regression analyses in which the three facets were entered as joint predictors of each symptom dimension. Overall, 45 sets of analyses are reported across the three tables.

Anxiety

Bivariate relations. Consistent with the diagnostic data, the Anxiety facet was the strongest and broadest predictor of these symptom dimensions. Across the three sets of analyses, it correlated most strongly with GAD symptoms (weighted mean r = 0.66), but also displayed substantial associations with Social Anxiety (r = 0.49), overall PTSD (r = 0.48), Panic (r = 0.47), Dysphoria (r = 0.45), Agoraphobia (r = 0.45), Obsessions (r = 0.43), Intrusions (r = 0.41), and Hyperarousal (r = 0.40). Its weakest associations were with various indicators of specific phobia (mean r = 0.27 with overall Specific Phobia, 0.25 with Blood-Injection Phobia, and 0.23 with

Table 4.5 *Associations between neuroticism facets and self-rated anxiety symptoms (Sample 1)*

Symptom Score	Correlations			Regressions		
	Anxiety	Depression	Anger	Anxiety	Depression	Anger
Generalized anxiety	**0.77**	**0.76**	**0.52**	0.47[*]	0.44[*]	0.01
PTSD	**0.53**	**0.63**	**0.43**	0.18[*]	0.47[*]	0.06
Dysphoria	**0.56**	**0.74**	**0.51**	0.07	0.64[*]	0.10[*]
Hyperarousal	**0.51**	**0.48**	**0.42**	0.31[*]	0.19[*]	0.14[*]
Intrusions	**0.45**	**0.50**	0.35	0.20[*]	0.34[*]	0.04
Avoidance	**0.41**	**0.49**	0.31	0.14[*]	0.40[*]	−0.00
Social anxiety	**0.53**	**0.56**	0.35	0.30[*]	0.38[*]	−0.04
Panic	**0.53**	**0.53**	0.39	0.31[*]	0.29[*]	0.05
OCD	0.39	0.34	0.33	0.26[*]	0.09	0.13[*]
Obsessions	**0.47**	**0.51**	0.36	0.22[*]	0.34[*]	0.04
Checking	**0.44**	0.32	0.33	0.37[*]	−0.01	0.12[*]
Ordering	0.33	0.24	0.29	0.26[*]	−0.02	0.16[*]
Hoarding	0.24	0.26	0.27	0.08	0.12[*]	0.16[*]
Cleaning	0.29	0.16	0.21	0.30[*]	−0.10	0.11[*]

Note. $N = 669$. Correlations ≥ 0.40 are highlighted. Depress = Depression. PTSD = posttraumatic stress disorder. OCD = obsessive-compulsive disorder.
[*] Standardized β weight is significant at $p < 0.05$.

Table 4.6 *Associations between neuroticism facets and self-rated anxiety symptoms (Sample 2)*

Symptom Score	Correlations			Regressions		
	Anxiety	Depression	Anger	Anxiety	Depression	Anger
Generalized anxiety	**0.71**	**0.73**	**0.53**	0.39[*]	0.45[*]	−0.02
PTSD	**0.57**	**0.56**	**0.49**	0.29[*]	0.26[*]	0.13[*]
Intrusions	**0.55**	**0.57**	**0.48**	0.24[*]	0.30[*]	0.12[*]
Avoidance	**0.51**	**0.48**	**0.43**	0.31[*]	0.17[*]	0.11
Social anxiety	**0.59**	**0.61**	**0.42**	0.33[*]	0.42[*]	−0.08
Panic	**0.56**	**0.60**	**0.52**	0.20[*]	0.34[*]	0.17[*]
OCD	**0.41**	0.38	**0.42**	0.20[*]	0.07	0.24[*]
Obsessions	**0.48**	**0.51**	**0.47**	0.17[*]	0.26[*]	0.18[*]
Checking	**0.43**	0.39	0.36	0.27[*]	0.12	0.11
Ordering	0.31	0.28	0.33	0.16[*]	0.01	0.22[*]
Hoarding	0.29	0.31	0.31	0.07	0.15	0.17[*]
Cleaning	0.24	0.19	0.28	0.14	−0.08	0.25[*]
Agoraphobia	**0.45**	0.35	0.31	0.44[*]	−0.00	0.03
Claustrophobia	0.32	0.33	0.39	0.07	0.09	0.28[*]
Specific phobia	0.27	0.19	0.23	0.24[*]	−0.07	0.12
Blood-injection	0.25	0.19	0.18	0.23[*]	−0.01	0.04
Animal	0.23	0.16	0.23	0.21[*]	−0.11	0.17[*]

Note. $N = 406$. Correlations ≥ 0.40 are highlighted. Depress = Depression. PTSD = posttraumatic stress disorder. OCD = obsessive-compulsive disorder.
[*] Standardized β weight is significant at $p < 0.05$

Table 4.7 *Associations between neuroticism facets and clinician-rated anxiety symptoms (Sample 1)*

Symptom Score	Correlations			Regressions		
	Anxiety	Depress	Anger	Anxiety	Depress	Anger
Generalized anxiety	**0.45**	**0.40**	0.32	0.31*	0.15*	0.05
PTSD	0.36	**0.44**	0.29	0.11*	0.36*	0.02
Dysphoria	0.32	**0.48**	0.26	−0.00	0.51*	−0.04
Hyperarousal	0.26	0.27	0.23	0.12*	0.15*	0.07
Intrusions	0.27	0.30	0.20	0.11*	0.23*	0.00
Avoidance	0.29	0.32	0.24	0.12*	0.21*	0.05
Social anxiety	0.36	**0.43**	0.29	0.11*	0.33*	0.03
Panic	0.34	0.31	0.21	0.24*	0.14*	−0.01
OCD	0.36	0.36	0.33	0.18*	0.15*	0.15*
Obsessions	0.35	**0.44**	0.25	0.09	0.40*	−0.03
Checking	0.24	0.17	0.19	0.21*	−0.03	0.09
Ordering	0.20	0.14	0.23	0.14*	−0.07	0.19*
Hoarding	0.14	0.21	0.23	−0.05	0.14*	0.18*
Cleaning	0.14	0.07	0.08	0.17*	−0.06	0.02

Note. $N = 625$. Correlations ≥ 0.40 are highlighted. Depress = Depression. PTSD = posttraumatic stress disorder. OCD = obsessive-compulsive disorder.
* Standardized β weight is significant at $p < 0.05$.

Animal Phobia) and with certain types of OCD symptoms ($r = 0.28$ with Ordering, 0.22 with Hoarding, 0.22 with Cleaning).

Multivariate relations. At the multivariate level, Anxiety made a significant incremental contribution in 37 analyses (82.2%). It is noteworthy that it had robust associations with several types of symptoms that replicated across multiple samples; these included GAD, overall PTSD, Hyperarousal, Intrusions, Avoidance, Social Anxiety, Panic, overall OCD, Checking, and Ordering. In contrast, it failed to predict Dysphoria and Hoarding in any analysis. Overall, however, Anxiety emerged as a consistent predictor across a very broad range of symptoms.

Depression

Bivariate relations. The Depression facet was a stronger predictor of anxiety symptoms than anxiety diagnoses. It showed several substantial associations at the bivariate level. Across the three sets of analyses, its strongest links were with GAD symptoms (weighted mean $r = 0.65$), Dysphoria ($r = 0.63$), overall PTSD ($r = 0.55$), Social Anxiety ($r = 0.53$), Obsessions ($r = 0.49$), Panic ($r = 0.47$), Intrusions

factors (such as genetic diatheses), whereas the *spectrum* or *continuum* model argues that they represent different locations on the same underlying dimension.

Neuroticism as a Cause

We now have ample evidence establishing that neuroticism is a prospective predictor of psychopathology; moreover, it is significantly related to the subsequent development of internalizing problems, even after controlling for baseline symptoms and psychiatric history (for a meta-analytic review, see Jeronimus, Kotov, Riese, & Ormel, 2016). At the symptom level, for example, Levenson, Aldwin, & Bossé (1988) reported that neuroticism was substantially related to levels of internalizing psychopathology (including anxiety) assessed 10 years later. Watson and Walker (1996) found that negative emotionality scores predicted anxious mood and panic symptoms assessed six to seven years later. Kopala-Sibley et al. (2016) reported that individual differences in fearfulness at age three predicted anxiety symptoms at age 11, even after controlling for symptom levels at age nine.

Neuroticism also has been shown to predict the future onset of diagnoses. Krueger (1999) found that elevated levels of negative emotionality assessed at age 18 were associated with an increased likelihood of anxiety disorder diagnoses at age 21. Zinbarg et al. (2016) reported that neuroticism (assessed when participants were high school juniors) predicted first onsets of anxiety disorders over a subsequent three-year period. Conway, Craske, Zinbarg, and Mineka (2016) found that individual differences in negative emotionality predicted both first onsets and recurrences of internalizing disorders across a four-year follow-up period. Goldstein, Kotov, Perlman, Watson, and Klein (2017) examined both neuroticism domain and facet scores in adolescent females; these trait scores (assessed when the participants were 13 to 15 years old) were used to predict first onset of disorders over an 18-month follow-up period. Neuroticism domain scores predicted first onsets of GAD, social phobia, and specific phobia in these data. At the lower-order level, the Anxiety facet predicted first onsets of all three anxiety disorders. In contrast, the Depression facet predicted the first onsets of GAD and specific phobia, but not social phobia, whereas the Anger facet was significantly linked only to the initial onset of specific phobia.

Neuroticism as an Effect

The scar model has received mixed support to date, with studies finding evidence both consistent (e.g., Kendler, Neale, Kessler, Heath, & Eaves, 1993; Rohde, Lewinsohn, & Seeley, 1994) and inconsistent (e.g., Ormel, Oldehinkel, & Vollebergh, 2004; Shea et al., 1996) with it. Moreover, the supportive evidence essentially is limited to major depression, such that there currently is very little evidence indicating that anxiety-related psychopathology can produce permanent increases in neuroticism (see Klein et al., 2011; Ormel et al., 2013).

In contrast, the state model has received much stronger support (see Klein et al., 2011; Ormel et al., 2013), as multiple studies have reported that neuroticism scores show transient elevations during episodes of internalizing psychopathology (e.g., De Fruyt, van Leeuwen, Bagby, Rolland, & Rouillon, 2006; Morey et al., 2010; Ormel, Oldehinkel et al., 2004). Again, the supportive evidence is confined largely to episodes of major depression, although Spinhoven, Penelo, de Rooij, Penninx, and Ormel (2014) found that neuroticism scores fluctuated concomitantly with both distress disorders (which included GAD) and fear disorders (which included panic disorder, agoraphobia, and social phobia). Furthermore, the state model is consistent with extensive data demonstrating that general trait measures – including neuroticism – are influenced by *transient error*, such that they reflect the respondents' current affective state to a significant extent (Chmielewski & Watson, 2009; Gnambs, 2014). Finally, in a recent meta-analysis, Roberts et al. (2017) reported that clinical interventions were associated with marked reductions in neuroticism trait scores. Thus, it now is clearly established that trait neuroticism scores are sensitive to respondents' current clinical and affective state.

Third Variable Models

Several studies have obtained support for the common cause model (see Middeldorp, Cath, van Dyck, & Boomsma, 2005). For instance, Hettema, Prescott, and Kendler (2004) found a very strong genetic correlation ($r = 0.80$) between neuroticism and GAD. Hettema, Neale, Myers, Prescott, and Kendler (2006) reported genetic correlations ranging from 0.58 (animal phobia) to 0.82 (social phobia) with six different anxiety disorders. In an examination of OCD symptom dimensions, Bergin et al. (2014) found that neuroticism had strong genetic correlations with both aggressive obsessions ($r = 0.89$) and checking ($r = 0.66$), and a more moderate association with contamination concerns ($r = 0.40$). Consequently, it is clear that shared genetic factors are at least partly responsible for observed associations between neuroticism and anxiety-related psychopathology.

With regard to the spectrum model, several authors have highlighted the significant content overlap between neuroticism items and anxiety symptoms (e.g., Ormel, Rosmalen, & Farmer, 2004; Uliaszek et al., 2009). GAD provides the most obvious case of content overlap. The *DSM-5* diagnostic criteria for GAD include "excessive anxiety and worry (apprehensive expectation), occurring more days than not for at least 6 months" (American Psychiatric Association, 2013, p. 222). Similarly, the FI-FFM Anxiety facet scale contains items such as "I constantly worry about things that might have gone wrong" and "I find myself worrying a lot." Based on this content overlap, it seems reasonable to argue that GAD and the anxiety facet of neuroticism essentially represent alternative indicators of the same underlying dimension.

Relations with Other Transdiagnostic Traits

Many other transdiagnostic traits have been studied in relation to internalizing psychopathology. It is important to note that neuroticism is strongly linked to many of these so-called *clinical traits* (see Mahaffey, Watson, Clark, & Kotov, 2016; Naragon-Gainey & Watson, 2018). For example, Stanton, Rozek, Stasik-O'Brien, Ellickson-Larew, and Watson (2016) reported moderate to strong associations between neuroticism and factors identified within the Difficulties in Emotion Regulation Scale (Gratz & Roemer, 2004). Zinbarg et al. (2016) obtained support for a model in which anxiety sensitivity, negative inferential style, sociotropy, and autonomy were specified as distinct facets within the broader neuroticism domain. Mahaffey et al. (2016) examined six clinical traits – ruminative response style, self-criticism, perfectionism, anxiety sensitivity, fear of negative evaluation, and thought suppression – in student and patient samples. All six clinical traits were strong and clear markers of a neuroticism factor in both samples, with loadings ranging from 0.59 to 0.75 (mean loading = 0.68) in the patients, and from 0.56 to 0.77 (mean loading = 0.69) in the students. Naragon-Gainey and Watson (2018) found that four clinical traits – anxiety sensitivity, intolerance of uncertainty, maladaptive perfectionism, and experiential avoidance were strongly related to neuroticism. Moreover, structural analyses revealed that all four traits were moderate to strong markers of its Anxiety facet, with loadings ranging from 0.32 to 0.76 (mean loading = 0.55).

This raises the crucial question of whether these clinical traits provide significant incremental information beyond neuroticism – and each other. The answer is a qualified "Yes," although the results are inconsistent and the incremental gains vary widely in magnitude. For example, Mahaffey et al. (2016) reported that the six assessed clinical traits jointly provided modest but significant incremental validity beyond a comprehensive set of higher-order and lower-order personality scales, accounting for an additional 2% to 8% of the variance in patients (mean = 6%), and an additional 3% to 7% in students (mean = 4%). Naragon-Gainey and Watson (2018) examined the incremental validity of four clinical traits vis-à-vis six types of internalizing symptoms: depression, PTSD, GAD, social anxiety, panic, and OCD. The clinical traits jointly contributed an additional 9.1% to 20.6% of the variance (mean = 14.3%) beyond neuroticism in five of the six analyses, but showed no incremental validity in the prediction of GAD. Anxiety sensitivity demonstrated the greatest incremental power, as it contributed significantly to the prediction of panic, depression, PTSD, and social anxiety. Perfectionism added significantly to the prediction of OCD, whereas intolerance of uncertainty contributed unique variance only in the prediction of depression. Finally, experiential avoidance showed only a single suppressor effect, displaying a weak inverse association with panic symptoms.

The key point is that one cannot assume that a given trait has incremental validity in predicting psychopathology; rather, this must be established empirically. These results again highlight the importance of examining multiple traits together in a single integrated framework.

Directions for Future Research

I conclude by discussing three important methodological issues that should direct future work in this area. First, as I noted at the beginning of this chapter, recent interest in transdiagnostic traits has been stimulated by the increasing recognition of the pervasive comorbidity within psychopathology: virtually all symptoms and disorders are positively related to each other, thereby giving rising to an overarching general factor (Caspi et al., 2014; Lahey et al., 2012). As I have shown, however, many of these transdiagnostic traits are substantially related to each other. Accordingly, it is crucial to study multiple traits together in joint analyses that allow one to identify their unique incremental effects. For example, Table 4.3 indicates that the Anger facet of neuroticism had mean correlations ranging from 0.24 to 0.39 with various anxiety disorder diagnoses. Viewed in isolation, these results might be taken to suggest that Anger is a significant transdiagnostic factor in these disorders. However, once its shared variance with the Anxiety and Depression facets was removed, Anger failed to show any significant incremental validity across 12 logistic regression analyses (see Table 4.4). These results clearly demonstrate that transdiagnostic traits cannot be studied in isolation.

Second, although I replicated many key findings across methods, measures, and samples, the data I presented are based heavily on self-report, either directly or indirectly through the filter of clinical interviews. As such, these relations are inflated to some extent by mono-method bias (Johnson, Rosen & Djurdjevic, 2011; Podsakoff, MacKenzie, Lee, & Podsakoff, 2003). Future work should examine the generality of these findings across a broader range of methods. It would be particularly valuable to include non-self-report indicators of personality, such as informant ratings. Given that neuroticism-related traits tend to be subjective and internal in nature and, therefore, are low in visibility (Connelly & Ones, 2010), it will be important to use well-acquainted informants in these studies.

Third, most of the existing evidence is cross-sectional in nature (Kotov et al., 2010). Longitudinal data are needed to clarify the etiological basis of these relations. Longitudinal studies begun relatively early in life – more specifically, before the first onsets of diagnosable disorders – will be particularly helpful in explicating the nature of the relations between traits and anxiety-related psychopathology (see Goldstein et al., 2017; Zinbarg et al., 2016).

Note

1. This study was ongoing when *DSM-5* was finalized. It used a version of the M.I.N.I. that included the proposed changes for GAD that later were rejected by the American Psychiatric Association. Thus, this version of the GAD diagnosis differs slightly from that in *DSM-5*.

References

Aluja, A., & Blanch, A. (2011). Neuropsychological behavioral inhibition system (BIS) and behavioral approach system (BAS) assessment: A shortened Sensitivity to Punishment and Sensitivity to Reward Questionnaire version (SPSRQ-20). *Journal of Personality Assessment*, *93*, 628–636.

American Psychiatric Association. (2000). *Diagnostic and Statistical Manual of Mental Disorders* (4th edn, text rev.). Washington, DC: American Psychiatric Association.

American Psychiatric Association. (2013). *Diagnostic and Statistical Manual of Mental Disorders* (5th edn). Washington, DC: American Psychiatric Association.

Beer, A., Watson, D., & McDade-Montez, E. (2013). Self-other agreement and assumed similarity in neuroticism, extraversion, and trait affect: Distinguishing the effects of form and content. *Assessment*, *20*, 723–737.

Bergin, J., Verhulst, B., Aggen, S. H., Neale, M. C., Kendler, K. S., Bienvenu, O. J., & Hettema, J. M. (2014). Obsessive compulsive symptom dimensions and neuroticism: An examination of shared genetic and environmental risk. *American Journal of Medical Genetics Part B: Neuropsychiatric Genetics*, *165*, 647–653.

Bleidorn, W. (2015). What accounts for personality maturation in early adulthood? *Current Directions in Psychological Science*, *24*, 245–252.

Bouchard, T. J., Jr. (2004). Genetic influence on human psychological traits: A survey. *Current Directions in Psychological Science*, *13*, 148–151.

Carver, C. S. & White, T. L. (1994). Behavioral inhibition, behavioral activation, and affective responses to impending reward and punishment: The BIS/BAS Scales. *Journal of Personality and Social Psychology*, *67*, 319–333.

Caspi, A., Houts, R. M., Belsky, D. W., Goldman-Mellor, S. J. Harrington, H., Israel, S., . . . Moffitt, T. E. (2014). The p factor: One general psychopathology factor in the structure of psychiatric disorders? *Clinical Psychological Science*, *2*, 119–137.

Cattell, R. B., Eber, H. W., & Tatsuoka, M. M. (1970). *Handbook for the Sixteen Personality Factor Questionnaire (16PF)*. Champaign, IL: Institute for Personality and Ability Testing.

Chmielewski, M. & Watson, D. (2008). The heterogeneous structure of schizotypal personality disorder: Item-level factors of the Schizotypal Personality Questionnaire and their associations with obsessive-compulsive disorder symptoms, dissociative tendencies, and normal personality. *Journal of Abnormal Psychology*, *117*, 364–376.

Chmielewski, M. & Watson, D. (2009). What is being assessed and why it matters: The impact of transient error on trait research. *Journal of Personality and Social Psychology*, *97*, 186–202.

Clark, L. A., Watson, D., & Mineka, S. (1994). Temperament, personality, and the mood and anxiety disorders. *Journal of Abnormal Psychology*, *103*, 103–116.

Cohen, J. (1992). A power primer. *Psychological Bulletin*, *112*, 155–159.

Connelly, B. S. & Ones, D. S. (2010). An other perspective on personality: Meta-analytic integration of observers' accuracy and predictive validity. *Psychological Bulletin*, *136*, 1092–1122.

Conway, C. C., Craske, M. G., Zinbarg, R. E., & Mineka, S. (2016). Pathological personality traits and the naturalistic course of internalizing disorders among high-risk young adults. *Depression and Anxiety*, *33*, 84–93.

Corr, P. J. & Cooper, A. J. (2016). The Reinforcement Sensitivity Theory of Personality Questionnaire (RST-PQ): Development and validation. *Psychological Assessment, 28,* 1427–1440.

Costa, P. T., Jr. & McCrae, R. R. (1992). *Revised NEO Personality Inventory (NEO-PI-R) and NEO Five-Factor Inventory (NEO-FFI) Professional Manual.* Odessa, FL: Psychological Assessment Resources.

Cutshall, C. & Watson, D. (2004). The Phobic Stimuli Response Scales: A new self-report measure of fear. *Behaviour Research and Therapy, 42,* 1193–1201.

De Fruyt, F., van Leeuwen, K., Bagby, R. M., Rolland, J.-P., & Rouillon, F. (2006). Assessing and interpreting personality change and continuity in patients treated for major depression. *Psychological Assessment, 18,* 71–80.

First, M. B., Spitzer, R. L., Gibbon, M., & Williams, J. B. W. (1997). *Structured Clinical Interview for DSM-IV Axis I Disorders – Patient Edition (SCID-I/P).* New York, NY: Biometrics Research, New York State Psychiatric Institute.

Flora, D. B. & Curran, P. J. (2004). An empirical evaluation of alternative methods of estimation for confirmatory factor analysis with ordinal data. *Psychological Methods, 9,* 466–491.

Foa, E. B., Huppert, J. D., Leiberg, S., Langner, R., Kichic, R., Hajcak, G., & Salkovskis, P. M. (2002). The Obsessive-Compulsive Inventory: Development and validation of a short version. *Psychological Assessment, 14,* 485–496.

Fowles, D. C. (1994). A motivational theory of psychopathology. In W. Spaulding (ed.), *Nebraska Symposium on Motivation: Integrated Views of Motivation, Cognition, and Emotion* (Vol.41, pp. 181–238). Lincoln, NE: University of Nebraska Press.

Gamez, W., Kotov, R., & Watson, D. (2010). The validity of self-report assessment of avoidance and distress. *Anxiety, Stress & Coping: An International Journal, 23,* 87–99.

Gartner, M. C., Powell, D. M., & Weiss, A. (2014). Personality structure in the domestic cat (*Felis silvestris catus*), Scottish wildcat (*Felis silvestris grampia*), clouded leopard (*Neofelis nebulosa*), snow leopard (*Panthera uncial*), and African lion (*Panthera leo*): A comparative study. *Journal of Comparative Psychology, 128,* 414–426.

Gnambs, T. (2014). A meta-analysis of dependability coefficients (test-retest reliabilities) for measures of the Big Five. *Journal of Research in Personality, 52,* 20–28.

Goldstein, B. L., Kotov, R., Perlman, G., Watson, D., & Klein, D. N. (2017). Trait and facet-level predictors of first-onset depressive and anxiety disorders in a community sample of adolescent girls. *Psychological Medicine.* Advance online publication.

Gootzeit, J. & Markon, K. (2011). Factors of PTSD: Differential specificity and external correlates. *Clinical Psychology Review, 31,* 993–1003.

Gosling, S. D. & John, O. P. (1999). Personality dimensions in non-human animals: A cross-species review. *Current Directions in Psychological Science, 8,* 69–75.

Gratz, K. L. & Roemer, L. (2004). Multidimensional assessment of emotion regulation and dysregulation: Development, factor structure, and initial validation of the Difficulties in Emotion Regulation Scale. *Journal of Psychopathology and Behavioral Assessment, 26,* 41–54.

Gray, J. A. (1982). *The Neuropsychology of Anxiety: An Enquiry into the Functions of the Septo-Hippocampal System.* New York, NY: Oxford University Press.

Gray, J. A. (1987). Perspectives on anxiety and impulsivity: A commentary. *Journal of Research in Personality, 21,* 493–509.

Hettema, J. M., Neale, M. C., Myers, J. M., Prescott, C. A., & Kendler, K. S. (2006). A population-based twin study of the relationship between neuroticism and internalizing disorders. *American Journal of Psychiatry, 163*, 857–864.

Hettema, J. M., Prescott, C. A., & Kendler, K. S. (2004). Genetic and environmental sources of covariation between generalized anxiety disorder and neuroticism. *American Journal of Psychiatry, 161*, 1581–1587.

Hogan, R. & Hogan, J. (1992). *Hogan Personality Inventory Manual*. Tulsa, OK: Hogan Assessment Systems.

Jackson, D. N. (1994). *Jackson Personality Inventory – Revised Manual*. Port Huron, MI: Sigma Assessment Systems.

Jeronimus, B. F., Kotov, R., Riese, H., & Ormel, J. (2016). Neuroticism's prospective association with mental disorders halves after adjustment for baseline symptoms and psychiatric history, but the adjusted association hardly decays with time: A meta-analysis of 59 longitudinal/prospective studies with 443,313 participants. *Psychological Medicine, 46*, 2883–2906.

John, O. P. & Srivastava, S. (1999). The Big Five trait taxonomy: History, measurement, and theoretical perspectives. In L. A Pervin & O. P. John (eds.), *Handbook of Personality* (2nd. edn) (pp. 102–138). New York, NY: Guilford.

Johnson, R. E., Rosen, C. C., & Djurdjevic, E. (2011). Assessing the impact of common method variance on higher order multidimensional constructs. *Journal of Applied Psychology, 96*, 744–761.

Kendler, K. S., Neale, M. C., Kessler, R. C., Heath, A. C., & Eaves, L. J. (1993). A longitudinal twin study of personality and major depression in women. *Archives of General Psychiatry, 50*, 853–862.

Kenny, D. A. (1987). *Statistics for the Social and Behavioral Sciences*. Boston, MA: Little, Brown and Company.

Klein, D. N., Kotov, R., & Bufferd, S. J. (2011). Personality and depression: Explanatory models and review of the evidence. *Annual Review of Clinical Psychology, 7*, 269–295.

Koffel, E. (2011). Further validation of the Iowa Sleep Disturbances Inventory. *Psychological Assessment, 23*, 587–598.

Koffel, E. & Watson, D. (2009). The two-factor structure of sleep complaints and its relation to depression and anxiety. *Journal of Abnormal Psychology, 118*, 183–194.

Kopala-Sibley, D. C., Danzig, A. P., Kotov, R., Bromet, E. J., Carlson, G. A., Olino, T. M., ... & Klein, D. N. (2016). Negative emotionality and its facets moderate the effects of exposure to Hurricane Sandy on children's postdisaster depression and anxiety symptoms. *Journal of Abnormal Psychology, 125*, 471–481.

Kotov, R., Gamez, W., Schmidt, F., & Watson, D. (2010). Linking "big" personality traits to anxiety, depressive, and substance use disorders: A meta-analysis. *Psychological Bulletin, 136*, 768–821.

Kotov, R., Krueger, R. F., Watson, D., Achenbach, T. M., Althoff, R. R., Bagby, M., ... & Zimmerman, M. (2017). The Hierarchical Taxonomy Of Psychopathology (HiTOP): A dimensional alternative to traditional nosologies. *Journal of Abnormal Psychology*, 126, 454–477.

Krueger, R. F. (1999). Personality traits in late adolescence predict mental disorders in early adulthood: A prospective-epidemiological study. *Journal of Personality, 67*, 39–65.

Lahey, B. B. Applegate, B., Hakes, J. K., Zald, D. H., Hariri, A. R., & Rathouz, P. J. (2012). Is there a general factor of prevalent psychopathology during adulthood? *Journal of Abnormal Psychology, 121*, 971–977.

Levenson, M. R., Aldwin, C. M., Bossé, R., & Spiro, A., III. (1988). Emotionality and mental health: Longitudinal findings from the Normative Aging Study. *Journal of Abnormal Psychology, 97*, 94–96.

Mahaffey, B. L., Watson, D., Clark, L. A., & Kotov, R. (2016). Clinical and personality traits in emotional disorders: Evidence of a common framework. *Journal of Abnormal Psychology, 125*, 758–767.

Markon, K. E., Krueger, R. F., & Watson, D. (2005). Delineating the structure of normal and abnormal personality: An integrative hierarchical approach. *Journal of Personality and Social Psychology, 88*, 139–157.

Marks, I. M. & Mathews, A. M. (1979). Brief standard self-rating for phobic patients. *Behaviour Research and Therapy, 23*, 563–569.

McCrae, R. R., Costa, P. T., Jr., & Martin, T. A. (2005). The NEO-PI-3: A more readable Revised NEO Personality Inventory. *Journal of Personality Assessment, 84*, 261–270.

Middeldorp, C. M., Cath, D. C., van Dyck, R., & Boomsma, D. I. (2005). The co-morbidity of anxiety and depression in the perspective of genetic epidemiology: A review of twin and family studies. *Psychological Medicine, 35*, 611–624.

Morey, L. C., Shea, M. T., Markowitz, J. C., Stout, R. L., Hopwood, C. J., Gunderson, J. G., . . . & Skodol, A. E. (2010). State effects of major depression on the assessment of personality and personality disorder. *American Journal of Psychiatry, 167*, 528–535.

Naragon-Gainey, K. & Watson, D. (2014). Consensually-defined facets of personality as prospective predictors of change in depression symptoms. *Assessment, 21*, 387–403.

Naragon-Gainey, K. & Watson, D. (2016, July 13). What lies beyond neuroticism? An examination of the unique contributions of social-cognitive vulnerabilities to internalizing disorders. *Assessment, 25*, 143–158.

Newman, M. G., Zuellig, A. R., Kachin, K. E., Constantino, M. J., Przeworski, A., Erickson, T., & Cashman-McGrath, L. (2002). Preliminary reliability and validity of the GADQ-IV: A revised self-report diagnostic measure of generalized anxiety disorder. *Behavior Therapy, 33*, 215–233.

Olsson, U., Drasgow, F., & Dorans, N. J. (1982). The polyserial correlation coefficient. *Psychometrika, 47*, 337–347.

Ormel, J., Jeronimus, B. F., Kotov, R., Riese, H., Bos, E. H., Hankin, B., . . . Oldehinkel, A. J. (2013). Neuroticism and common mental disorders: Meaning and utility of a complex relationship. *Clinical Psychology Review, 33*, 686–697.

Ormel, J. Oldehinkel, A. J., & Vollebergh, W. (2004). Vulnerability before, during, and after a major depressive episode. *Archives of General Psychiatry, 61*, 990–996.

Ormel, J., Rosmalen, J., & Farmer, A. (2004). Neuroticism: A non-informative marker of vulnerability to psychopathology. *Social Psychiatry and Psychiatric Epidemiology, 39*, 906–912.

Podsakoff, P. M., MacKenzie, S. B., Lee, J., & Podsakoff, N. P. (2003). Common method biases in behavioral research: A critical review of the literature and recommended remedies. *Journal of Applied Psychology, 88*, 879–903.

Rapee, R. M., Craske, M. G., & Barlow, D. H. (1994/1995). Assessment instrument for panic disorder that includes fear of sensation-producing activities: The Albany Panic and Phobia Questionnaire. *Anxiety, 1*, 114–122.

Roberts, B. W. & DelVecchio, W. F. (2000). The rank-order consistency of personality traits from childhood to old age: A quantitative review of longitudinal studies. *Psychological Bulletin, 126*, 3–25.

Roberts, B. W., Luo, J., Briley, D. A., Chow, P. I., Su, R., & Hill, P. L. (2017). A systematic review of personality trait change through intervention. *Psychological Bulletin, 143*, 117–141.

Roberts, B. W., Walton, K. E., & Viechtbauer, W. (2006). Patterns of mean-level change in personality traits across the life course: A meta-analysis of longitudinal studies. *Psychological Bulletin, 132*, 1–25.

Rohde, P., Lewinsohn, P. M., & Seeley, J. R. (1994). Are adolescents changed by an episode of major depression? *Journal of the American Academy of Child & Adolescent Psychiatry, 33*, 1289–1298.

Samuel, D. B. & Widiger, T. A. (2008). A meta-analytic review of the relationships between the five-factor model and *DSM-IV-TR* personality disorders: A facet level analysis. *Clinical Psychology Review, 28*, 1326–1342.

Shea, M. T., Leon, A. C., Mueller, T. I., Solomon, D. A., Warshaw, M. G., & Keller, M. B. (1996). Does major depression result in lasting personality change? *American Journal of Psychiatry, 153*, 1404–1410.

Sheehan, D. V., Lecrubier, Y., Sheehan, K. H., Amorim, P., Janavas, J., Weiller, E., ... Dunbar, G. C. (1998). The Mini-International Neuropsychiatric Interview (M.I.N.I.): The development and validation of a structured diagnostic psychiatric interview for DSM-IV and ICD-10. *Journal of Clinical Psychiatry, 59*, 34–57.

Soto, C. J. & John, O. P. (2017). The next Big Five Inventory (BFI-2): Developing and assessing a hierarchical model with 15 facets to enhance bandwidth, fidelity, and predictive power. *Journal of Personality and Social Psychology, 113*, 117–143.

Soto, C. J., John, O. P., Gosling, S. D., & Potter, J. (2011). Age differences in personality traits from 10 to 65: Big Five domains and facets in a large cross-sectional sample. *Journal of Personality and Social Psychology, 100*, 330–348.

Spinhoven, P., Penelo, E., de Rooij, M., Penninx, B. W., & Ormel, J. (2014). Reciprocal effects of stable and temporary components of neuroticism and affective disorders: Results of a longitudinal cohort study. *Psychological Medicine, 44*, 337–348.

Stanton, K., Rozek, D. C., Stasik-O'Brien, S. M., Ellickson-Larew, S., & Watson, D. (2016). A transdiagnostic approach to examining the incremental predictive power of emotion regulation and basic personality dimensions. *Journal of Abnormal Psychology, 125*, 960–975.

Stöber, J. & Joormann, J. (2001). A short form of the Worry Domains Questionnaire: Construction and factorial validation. *Personality and Individual Differences, 31*, 591–598.

Tellegen, A. & Waller, N. G. (2008). Exploring personality through test construction: Development of the Multidimensional Personality Questionnaire. In G. J. Boyle, G. Matthews, & D. H. Saklofske (eds.), *The SAGE Handbook of Personality Theory and Assessment, Vol. 2: Personality Measurement and Testing* (pp. 261–292). Thousand Oaks, CA: Sage Publications.

Torrubia, R., Ávila, C., Moltó, J., & Caseras, X. (2001). The Sensitivity to Punishment and Sensitivity to Reward Questionnaire (SPSRQ) as a measure of Gray's anxiety and impulsivity dimensions. *Personality and Individual Differences, 31*, 837–862.

Twenge, J. M., Gentile, B., & Campbell, W. K. (2015). Birth cohort differences in personality. In M. Mikulincer, P. R. Shaver, M. L. Cooper, & R. J. Larsen (eds.), *APA Handbook of Personality and Social Psychology, Vol. 4: Personality Processes and Individual Differences* (pp. 535–551). Washington, DC: American Psychological Association.

Uliaszek, A. A., Hauner, K. K. Y., Zinbarg, R. E., Craske, M. G., Mineka, S., Griffith, J. W., & Rose, R. D. (2009). An examination of content overlap and disorder-specific predictions in the associations of neuroticism with anxiety and depression. *Journal of Research in Personality, 43*, 785–794.

Vukasović, T. & Bratko, D. (2015). Heritability of personality: A meta-analysis of behavior genetic studies. *Psychological Bulletin, 141*, 769–785.

Waszczuk, M. A., Kotov, R., Ruggero, C., Gamez, W., & Watson, D. (2017). Hierarchical structure of emotional disorders: From individual symptoms to the spectrum. *Journal of Abnormal Psychology., 126*, 613–634.

Watson, D. (2000a). *Mood and Temperament*. New York, NY: Guilford Press.

Watson, D. (2000b). Panic Attack Symptom Questionnaire. Unpublished physiological hyperarousal measure.

Watson, D. (2005). Rethinking the mood and anxiety disorders: A quantitative hierarchical model for *DSM-V. Journal of Abnormal Psychology, 114*, 522–536.

Watson, D. (2009). Differentiating the mood and anxiety disorders: A quadripartite model. *Annual Review of Clinical Psychology, 5*, 221–247.

Watson, D. & Clark, L. A. (1999). *The PANAS-X: Manual for the Positive and Negative Affect Schedule – Expanded Form*. Retrieved from University of Iowa, Department of Psychology Web site: www.psychology.uiowa.edu/Faculty/Watson/Watson.html.

Watson, D., Clark, L. A., Chmielewski, M., & Kotov, R. (2013). The value of suppressor effects in explicating the construct validity of symptom measures. *Psychological Assessment, 25*, 929–941.

Watson, D., Clark, L. A., & Stasik, S. M. (2011). Emotions and the emotional disorders: A quantitative hierarchical perspective. *International Journal of Clinical and Health Psychology, 11*, 429–442.

Watson, D., Clark, L. A., & Tellegen, A. (1988). Development and validation of brief measures of positive and negative affect: The PANAS scales. *Journal of Personality and Social Psychology, 54*, 1063–1070.

Watson, D., Gamez, W., & Simms, L. J. (2005). Basic dimensions of temperament and their relation to anxiety and depression: A symptom-based perspective. *Journal of Research in Personality, 39*, 46–66.

Watson, D. & Naragon-Gainey, K. (2014). Personality, emotions, and the emotional disorders. *Clinical Psychological Science, 2*, 422–442.

Watson, D., Nus, E., & Wu, K. D. (2017). Development and validation of the Faceted Inventory of the Five-Factor Model (FI-FFM). *Assessment*.

Watson, D., O'Hara, M. W., Chmielewski, M., McDade-Montez, E. A., Koffel, E., Naragon, K., & Stuart, S. (2008). Further validation of the IDAS: Evidence of

must be correlated. The second criterion of this framework requires that the risk factor (e.g., AS) precedes an outcome (e.g., anxiety diagnosis). At this point, Kraemer makes a distinction in the conception of risk in terms of fixed versus malleable factors. A fixed risk factor is one that is relatively unchangeable, such as demographic factors. On the other hand, malleable risk factors are those that can change and are critical to identify because of this property since it is informative regarding the possibility of intervention. Finally, criterion four of the framework indicates that changes in the factor must yield changes in the outcome. If we can identify a factor (e.g., AS) that affects outcomes when changed, then the construct is considered a causal risk factor within the Kraemer framework.

In the context of the Kraemer framework, these meta-analyses have essentially focused on only the first criterion and are therefore insufficient to determine whether AS is a causal risk factor. While these reviews are consistent with the idea that AS is a risk factor, we need to also consider the other criteria before we are able to make conclusive statements about the causal risk status of AS. Therefore, we attempt to summarize the more recent literature in terms of the broader Kraemer framework.

Anxiety Sensitivity and Anxiety Psychopathology

As we noted earlier, AS has been extensively evaluated in the context of anxiety disorders with a particularly robust relationship with panic attacks and panic disorder. Since the meta-analytic papers appeared in 2009–2011, reports continue to show these associations, but they have tended to focus on providing more specificity with respect to AS and other mechanistic risk variables as well as AS subcomponents and psychopathology. The interest in AS subcomponents can be considered in light of our knowledge of the structure of AS, so it is worth considering a few more recent papers that have refined our ideas about the structure of AS.

The structure of AS. To most effectively use AS from both a research and a clinical perspective, knowledge of the manifest structure of AS should closely match its underlying latent structure. As Allan, Albanese, Short, Raines, and Schmidt (2015) note, "[t]o best utilize AS as a transdiagnostic risk factor, it is important to fully understand the underlying structure of this construct" (p. 78). Considerable research efforts have been dedicated to investigating the latent structure of AS over the past two decades, and while an in-depth exploration of this literature is beyond the scope of this chapter, it is worth summarizing some interesting findings in this area, since they speak to the transdiagnostic nature of the construct.

Anxiety sensitivity has been conceptualized as a hierarchical construct, comprising three lower-order dimensions. Recent findings (Allan, Albanese, et al., 2015), however, suggest that AS may be better conceptualized as a general dimension and *unrelated* physical, cognitive, and social concerns dimensions, that is, a bi-factor model. Bi-factor modeling approaches appear to better account for the structure of AS relative to more traditional factor-analytic techniques, and the bi-factor structures that emerge tell a somewhat different story. For example, Allan et al. (2015) found of all the AS factors, the general factor was most associated with negative affect. After accounting for this general AS factor, cognitive concerns was related to worry and depression and social concerns was related to worry, depression, and social anxiety. Interestingly, the physical concerns factor was not related to emotional distress. These findings are consistent with the idea that AS consists of a general facet that primarily taps into concerns about physical symptoms of anxiety, which is associated with emotional distress generally, and several facets more specifically associated with components of emotional distress. As work continues to tease apart the unique contributions of AS subscales to various conditions, our understanding of the structure of AS will be increasingly important.

AS and childhood anxiety psychopathology. To begin our review, it is important to note the work with AS in children. Studies following the meta-analytic review by Noël and Francis (2011) continue to suggest that AS may play a role in many anxiety problems in children. For example, a behavior genetic analysis suggested that AS at age eight was broadly associated with most anxiety subtypes at age 10 (Waszczuk, Zavos, & Eley, 2013). The exact risk trajectories and contributors are not well researched, though AS is partially heritable (Waszczuk et al., 2013), and some reports indicate that parental AS is moderately associated with child AS (Francis, 2014).

AS and phobic anxiety disorders. Following the meta-analytic reviews, a variety of reports have confirmed that AS is associated with panic, panic disorder, and social anxiety disorder. Since these findings are not particularly novel with respect to the goals of this chapter, we simply state that the literature has continued to confirm an association between AS and phobic anxiety disorders (see, for example, Kang et al., 2015; Kemper, Lutz, Bähr, Rüddel, & Hock, 2012; Sandin, Sánchez-Arribas, Chorot, & Valiente, 2015; Teale Sapach, Carleton, Mulvogue, Weeks, & Heimberg, 2015; Wheaton, Deacon, McGrath, Berman, & Abramowitz, 2012).

AS and generalized anxiety disorder. Relative to the phobic anxiety disorders, the association between AS and generalized anxiety disorder (GAD) is less well established, but several additional studies suggest that this association exists (Holmes & Bourne, 2008). K. M. Kraemer, Luberto, and McLeish (2013) showed that AS was associated with worry, GAD symptoms, and GAD diagnoses in adolescents. Given the high correspondence between depression and worry symptoms, it is notable that at least some studies have found that AS can discriminate between patients with GAD and major depressive disorder (MDD) (Hendriks et al., 2014). When considering AS subscales, some work indicates that it is the cognitive

AS component that is most strongly associated with GAD (Allan, Capron, Raines, & Schmidt, 2014).

AS and obsessive compulsive disorder. Similar to GAD, relations between AS and OCD are less well established, but a number of reports indicate an association (see Robinson & Freeston, 2014, for a review). Moreover, AS appears to be related to functional impairment (Storch et al., 2014), as well as OC symptom severity (Raines, Capron, Bontempo, Dane, & Schmidt, 2014) among treatment-seeking patients with OCD diagnoses. There have been some efforts to tease apart OCD and AS subdimensions, but the pattern of findings at this time doesn't seem particularly compelling or clear (Poli, Melli, Ghisi, Bottesi, & Sica, 2017; Wheaton et al., 2012).

AS and other mechanisms. A fair number of studies have begun to explore the more complex situation of AS as it relates to other risk mechanisms such as emotion regulation, distress tolerance, intolerance of uncertainty, and the relations between multiple risk factor constructs and psychopathology. These papers are generally consistent in showing associations between AS and anxiety psychopathology and occasionally find that the effects are moderated by other variables. For example, Lebowitz, Shic, Campbell, Basile, and Silverman (2015) showed that AS moderated behavioral avoidance in anxious youth. A series of studies from the Zvolensky group (Zvolensky, Bakhshaie, Garza, Paulus et al., 2015; Zvolensky, Bakhshaie, Garza, Valdivieso, Ortiz, Bogiaizian, Robles, Schmidt et al., 2015; Zvolensky, Bakhshaie, Garza, Valdivieso, Ortiz, Bogiaizian, Robles, & Vujanovic, 2015; Zvolensky et al., 2016) has similarly suggested a complex interplay between AS and other variables in predicting symptoms.

Longitudinal studies of AS. Because prospective studies of AS are relatively rare, it's worth highlighting these. We have already noted the Waszczuk et al. (2013) study showing that AS at age eight was related to a broad range of anxiety symptoms two years later. Allan, Felton, Lejuez, MacPherson, and Schmidt (2016) showed that AS at age 11 was associated with later anxiety at age 16. Finally, Spinhoven et al. (2016) showed in a clinical sample that AS was related to the trajectory and maintenance of anxiety symptoms. These important prospective studies support earlier work suggesting that AS is associated with a range of anxiety psychopathology over time.

Treatment and AS. There are two areas to consider in regard to AS and treatment. First, it is important to consider the treatment of AS since this is relevant to conclusions we can make about the etiology of AS. Second, it is clinically important to consider the role of AS in the treatment of phobic anxiety conditions. In terms of interventions for AS, there is a considerable literature that has explored whether AS can be reduced in the context of a variety of CBT interventions. In a meta-analysis, Smits, Berry, Tart, and Powers (2008) showed that CBT can substantially reduce AS. Our group has been interested in developing interventions designed to directly target AS and we have shown in a number of clinical trials that relatively brief interventions (usually one to three hours) can effectively reduce AS, that these reductions are quite durable up to two years, and that such reductions mediate later symptom change (Keough & Schmidt, 2012; Schmidt, Capron, Raines, & Allan, 2014) as well as reduce the incidence of later psychopathology (Schmidt et al., 2007). Other groups have also shown that interventions specifically designed to address AS can reduce anxiety symptoms. For example, Olthuis, Watt, Mackinnon, and Stewart (2014) used a telephone-delivered AS intervention to community participants and found the intervention reduced panic and social anxiety symptoms, though it was not effective for depression and GAD symptoms.

What about the role of AS in the treatment of anxiety psychopathology? Relevant to this chapter, Boswell et al. (2013) conceptualized AS as a transdiagnostic treatment target for Barlow's Unified Protocol, which is designed for use across anxiety conditions. In this particular study, the authors were interested in AS change during treatment and speculated that interoceptive exposure, repeated exposure designed to extinguish fear responding to bodily cues, would be particularly effective in reducing AS. Consistent with prediction, changes in AS were associated with the utilization of interoceptive exposure in a mixed group of patients having panic disorder, social phobia, GAD, and OCD. Interestingly, Collimore and Asmundson (2014) found that level of AS was not associated with fearful responding to a variety of interoceptive exercises among those with social phobia. Consistent with the idea that AS reflects over-reactivity to bodily perturbations, these studies suggest that interventions such as interoceptive exposure designed to mitigate fearful responding to such perturbations may be particularly relevant to normalizing AS. Importantly, work has found that changes in AS during cognitive behavioral therapy (CBT) for panic disorder precede the reductions in later symptoms (Gallagher et al., 2013). While a number of studies attest to the malleability of AS in treatment, at least one report suggests that elevated AS may interfere with CBT. Blakey, Abramowitz, Reuman, Leonard, and Riemann (2017) showed that elevated AS predicted a poorer response to treatment for OCD.

Summary. So what does the literature tell us in regard to the role of AS in the etiology, maintenance, and treatment of anxiety psychopathology? In terms of etiology, using H. C. Kraemer et al.'s (1997) framework, a variable must first demonstrate correlation with the outcome of interest. As we have noted, myriad studies have linked AS and anxiety as correlates, including two meta-analyses (Naragon-Gainey, 2010; Olatunji & Wolitzky-Taylor, 2009). Next, the risk factor must precede the outcome. Here, there is a much more limited literature, but the prospective studies reviewed are consistent with the idea that AS predicts the later development of anxiety problems. Kraemer's next criterion focuses on the idea that the risk factor must be malleable, and a number of studies indicate that AS can be rapidly ameliorated (Schmidt et al., 2014, 2007; Schmidt, Norr, Allan, Raines, & Capron, 2017). Critically, the last piece of the puzzle in Kraemer's framework is that manipulating the risk factor must lead to changes in the outcome. Indeed, several studies have demonstrated that reductions in AS are associated with reductions in anxiety symptoms (Schmidt et al., 2014, 2017). However, this literature is limited in that we do not have compelling studies suggesting that reductions in AS lead to reductions in specific anxiety diagnoses. Schmidt et al. (2014, 2017), for example, showed that reductions in AS lead to reductions in anxiety symptoms, and Schmidt, Raines, Allan, and Zvolensky (2016) found that reducing AS led to later reductions in panic attacks. Finally, Schmidt et al. (2007) showed that reductions in AS were associated with a lower incidence of all diagnoses during the following two years; the relatively low incidence of diagnoses does not allow us to conclusively say that reductions in AS will lead to later reductions in phobic anxiety diagnoses. By and large, the data are consistent with the idea that AS is a causal risk factor for anxiety psychopathology.

Anxiety Sensitivity and Trauma Disorders

Anxiety sensitivity is also thought to play a role in the development and maintenance of posttraumatic stress symptoms (PTSS). Indeed, there is a burgeoning line of research in this area. Beginning with the two meta-analyses, Olatunji and Wolitzky-Taylor (2009) revealed the relationship between AS and anxiety symptoms was large, but the strongest association was for panic disorder and posttraumatic stress disorder (PTSD) in comparison to other anxiety disorders ($d = 2.58$ for the comparison of AS levels in PTSD vs. nonclinical controls). Naragon-Gainey (2010) also suggested AS was most closely tied to panic disorder and PTSD, as well as GAD. Furthermore, when examining symptom clusters of PTSD, AS was associated with each symptom cluster. Hyperarousal symptoms demonstrated the strongest association with AS compared to reexperiencing and avoidance/numbing ($\rho s = 0.42\text{–}0.54$). Findings also indicated that among AS subfactors, physical and cognitive concerns were more closely related to reexperiencing ($\rho s = 0.42$ and 0.41, respectively) and hyperarousal ($\rho s = 0.55$ and 0.52, respectively) compared to social concerns, while numbing/avoidance symptoms were weakly associated with all AS dimensions. Finally, PTSD was included within the distress disorders, which demonstrated higher levels of AS in comparison to the fear-based disorders.

Since the publication of these meta-analyses, the literature on AS and PTSD has continued to grow, with 20 studies directly focused on trauma or PTSS and AS. Furthermore, an additional 20 studies have investigated the role of AS as a moderator or mediator of associations between PTSS and other variables. We review these articles in terms of the role of AS in PTSD's etiology, mainte-nance, and treatment.

Etiology. More recent studies have moved beyond cross-sectional associations between AS and PTSS and have begun to examine prospectively and experimen-tally whether AS actually acts as an etiological factor in PTSD. Olatunji and Fan

(2015) utilized the trauma film paradigm (Holmes & Bourne, 2008) to prospectively examine associations between AS and PTSS among a sample of undergraduate students ($N = 45$). Participants viewed a graphic film of fatal traffic accidents while undergoing psychophysiological assessment, and were then followed up over one week to assess intrusions. Results indicated AS, in particular physical and cognitive concerns, predicted greater PTSS a week after film viewing. This association was mediated by post-film intrusions. Finally, physiological arousal during film exposure moderated the association between AS and subsequent intrusions. This study was one of the first to identify that pre-analog trauma AS is associated with later PTSS-like symptoms, and to examine mediators and moderators of this relationship.

Zerach and Magal (2016) studied AS and PTSS among a sample of first-time fathers ($N = 171$). The authors found that higher levels of prenatal paternal AS interacted with subjective exposure to stress during birth to predict increased PTSS one month following birth. Again, this study suggests AS prospectively predicts PTSS in response to a potentially traumatic event. More recently, Boffa et al. (2016) conducted a prospective investigation of pre-trauma AS as a predictor of post-trauma PTSS among a sample of undergraduates exposed to a campus shooting ($N = 71$). Results indicated that all three subfactors of AS were associated with PTSS, but that physical concerns significantly interacted with severity of trauma exposure to predict PTSS. This study was the first to our knowledge to identify that pre-trauma AS predicts PTSS in response to a DSM-5 criterion event.

Maintenance. Few studies have longitudinally examined the role of AS as a maintenance factor in PTSD. Marshall, Miles, and Stewart (2010) used cross-lagged panel analysis to examine temporal associations between AS and PTSS among traumatic physical injury survivors ($N = 677$). Results indicated that AS and PTSS reciprocally influenced one another over time, potentially indicating a more complex, bidirectional relationship than cross-sectional research suggests. In addition, Gutner, Nillni, Suvak, Wiltsey-Stirman, and Resick (2013) examined changes in AS during cognitive processing therapy (CPT) among a sample of 70 women with PTSD undergoing various forms of CPT. Results revealed that AS reduces throughout CPT, and these reductions were associated with reductions in PTSS. In sum, the limited research in this area indicates that AS may act as a maintenance factor in PTSD.

More studies, however, have attempted to better understand associations between lower-order AS and PTSD dimensions among trauma-exposed individuals with ongoing PTSS. For example, Zvielli, Bernstein, and Berenz (2012) used factor mixture modeling to evaluate cross-sectional taxonic-dimensional relationships between AS and psychiatric symptoms among young adults exposed to traumatic stress ($N = 103$). Results indicated that the high AS group had higher levels of PTSD symptoms, and that the high AS group accounted for nearly all cases of past-month PTSD. Furthermore, AS physical and cognitive concerns were significantly related to PTSS only among the high AS group. Allan et al. (2014)

examined cross-sectional associations between AS dimensions and psychiatric symptoms using structural equation modeling among a treatment-seeking sample ($N = 256$). Results indicated that AS cognitive concerns were uniquely associated with PTSD diagnoses when taking into account associations between PTSD and other dimensions of AS. Finally, Raines, Walton et al. (2017) investigated cross-sectional associations between AS subfactors and DSM-5 symptoms of PTSD among veterans presenting for outpatient psychological services ($N = 50$). Results revealed that AS cognitive concerns were associated with higher levels of all four PTSD symptom clusters (i.e., reexperiencing, avoidance, alterations in cognition and mood, alterations in arousal). In sum, studies have continued to demonstrate associations between elevated AS and increased PTSS in various samples, but have also begun to suggest a potentially unique role of AS cognitive concerns in the etiology of PTSD. However, studies have also shown AS physical concerns are associated with PTSS.

In addition to examining finer-grained associations between AS and PTSD, other studies have examined moderators affecting the relationship between AS and PTSD. Two studies have found that distress intolerance cross-sectionally moderates the association between AS and PTSD, such that individuals with high self-reported and behaviorally assessed distress intolerance and high AS had the highest level of PTSD symptoms among trauma-exposed adults (N = 88) (Holmes & Bourne, 2008), and trauma-exposed tobacco smokers (N = 137) (Olatunji & Wolitzky-Taylor, 2009). However, this effect was not replicated in a sample of nonclinical undergraduate students ($N = 416$) (Kraemer et al., 2013). Other studies have found AS moderates associations between similar affective risk factors and PTSS. For example, Bardeen (2015) found that AS interacts with experiential avoidance to predict increased PTSS following an emotional task among undergraduates ($N = 199$). Finally, Sippel and colleagues (2015) reported that AS interacts with emotion regulation difficulties to predict PTSS among individuals with PTSD participating in a residential substance use treatment program. In sum, it may be that cognitive-affect risk factors interact with AS to promote risk for PTSS. However, many of these studies are limited by their cross-sectional nature and there are mixed findings, suggesting a need for further research.

Studies have also examined the role of physical symptoms in moderating the association between AS and PTSS. For example, Babson et al. (2013) explored the cross-sectional moderating role of sleep quality in the relationship between AS and PTSD among a sample of male military veterans seeking treatment for PTSD ($N = 187$). Results indicated that individuals with good sleep quality and high AS had the lowest level of PTSD symptoms, potentially indicating that good sleep quality may be a protective factor for those with high levels of AS. Nillni, Pineles, Rohan, Zvolensky, and Rasmusson (2017) found a synergistic effect of premenstrual symptoms and AS on PTSS among a sample of 63 trauma-exposed women, suggesting premenstrual symptoms may exacerbate PTSS only among individuals with high AS. Studies have also indicated that nicotine withdrawal may interact with AS to cross-sectionally predict elevated PTSS among treatment-seeking smokers with PTSD (N = 117) (Horowitz, 1986). Finally, Lies, Lau, Jones, Jensen, and Tan (2017) found that trauma history and AS acted in a synergistic fashion to predict higher levels of PTSS among individuals with chronic pain (N = 100). Collectively, these studies suggest AS may interact with physical or environmental vulnerabilities to predict heightened PTSD symptoms.

Work on AS and PTSS has raised the question as to what mechanism accounts for this association. Only one study to our knowledge has examined this question empirically (as well as Olatunji & Fan, 2015, reviewed earlier). Many researchers suggest that AS may heighten avoidance among individuals with PTSS by causing individuals to fear not only trauma reminders, but also their own reactions to them. Indeed, Naifeh, Tull, and Gratz (2012) found that experiential avoidance cross-sectionally mediated the association between AS and PTSS among trauma-exposed substance-dependent patients in residential treatment (N = 62). However, analyses indicated that results were also significant in the opposite direction, with AS mediating the association between experiential avoidance and PTSS, raising the question of the specificity of this mediation model.

Treatment. Work regarding whether reducing AS results in reductions in PTSS has recently accumulated. To our knowledge, the first study testing whether AS treatments affect PTSS was a case series of five trauma-exposed adults who underwent a brief AS intervention (Vujanovic, Bernstein, Berenz, & Zvolensky, 2012). Results indicated that targeting AS was a feasible and potentially efficacious approach to reducing PTSS, but raised the need for randomized controlled trials (RCTs). Olthuis et al. (2014) tested whether an eight-week protocol of telephone-delivered CBT for AS would result in reductions in PTSS among community individuals with high AS. Indeed, results revealed that CBT for AS resulted in reductions in PTSS compared to a waitlist control at up to eight weeks later.

Our lab has also investigated whether AS treatments affect PTSS across three studies. First, Mitchell, Capron, Raines, and Schmidt (2014) examined the effects of a computerized AS intervention focusing on AS cognitive concerns vs. a physical health control on PTSS in a matched sample of civilians and veterans with high AS (N = 56). Results indicated that reductions in AS were associated with reductions in PTSS over a one-month follow-up. Second, we examined the effects of a one-session, therapist-led AS intervention vs. a physical health control on PTSS among trauma-exposed undergraduates with high AS (N = 82; Allan, Short, Albanese, Keough, & Schmidt, 2015). Results indicated that the AS intervention led to reductions in PTSS at a one-month follow-up, which was mediated by reductions in AS. Finally, we tested the effects of a computerized AS intervention focusing on cognitive concerns vs. a repeated contact control among 63 trauma-exposed individuals, a third of whom met criteria for PTSD (Short, Boffa, et al., 2017). Findings again found that the AS intervention led to reductions in PTSS and PTSD diagnoses at a one-month follow-up, which were accounted for by reductions in AS post treatment. In sum, increasing evidence suggests that targeting AS may be an efficacious and efficient way to reduce PTSS.

However, further studies are needed among clinical samples and with longer-term follow-ups.

AS as a mediator between PTSS and related difficulties. In recent years, many studies have suggested that AS may account for associations between PTSS and negative outcomes. First, cross-sectional studies have suggested that AS may account for associations between PTSS and factors related to smoking maintenance and cessation difficulties (Bakhshaie, Zvolensky, Salazar, Vujanovic, & Schmidt, 2016; Farris, Zvolensky, & Schmidt, 2015). Second, AS may account for relationships between PTSS and physical health problems, such as elevated body mass index (BMI) (Farris et al., 2015), respiratory problems (Mahaffey et al., 2017), and quality of life and physical health (Kugler, Phares, Salloum, & Storch, 2016). Third, AS may play a role in linking other cognitive-affective risk factors to PTSS, such as emotional non-acceptance (Bakhshaie, Zvolensky, Allan, Vujanovic, & Schmidt, 2015; Viana et al., 2017), and avoidant coping (Brandt et al., 2015). Fourth and finally, one study suggests that AS cognitive concerns could account for associations between PTSS and suicidality among treatment-seeking male veterans (N = 60) (Raines, Capron, et al., 2017). Overall, these studies coalesce to suggest AS may account for associations between PTSS and smoking, physical health problems, other risk factors, and suicidality; however, the majority of these studies are cross-sectional, suggesting a need for future prospective research.

AS as a moderator of associations between PTSS and related difficulties. In addition, a limited number of studies have examined whether AS acts as a moderator of associations between PTSS and other mental health-related problems. Again, some of these focused on substance use-related difficulties. For example, Berenz et al. (2016) noted that AS interacts with PTSS to predict maladaptive drinking motives. Similarly, Gillihan, Farris, and Foa (2011) found that AS and PTSD symptoms have a synergistic effect promoting increased drinking frequency. Finally, one study examined the effects of AS and PTSS on deliberate self-harm (DSH) and reported that youth with high AS evidenced a stronger association between PTSS and DSH than those with low AS.

Role of trauma in the development of high AS. Finally, a select few studies have examined the role of traumatic event exposure in the development of AS. This area is interesting as the origin of AS is relatively unexplored. Specifically, Martin, Steinley, Vergés, and Sher (2011) found a cross-sectional association between childhood trauma and high levels of AS among adolescents (*N* = 1149). Furthermore, Klauke et al. (2011) identified a cross-sectional gene by environmental interaction on AS among healthy adults (*N* = 363), such that those with certain genotypes (i.e., LL) for the 5-HTT gene and childhood maltreatment had higher levels of physical AS concerns. Similarly, another study by Baumann et al. (2013) examined an interaction between genes coding for catechol-O-methyltransferase (COMT) and monoamine oxidase with traumatic life events among healthy adults ($N = 782$). Individuals with the low-active met allele and higher levels of childhood trauma had the highest levels of AS. These studies raise the idea that trauma exposure itself may increase AS, which then may exacerbate PTSS, corresponding with previously reviewed studies noting a bidirectional relationship between AS and PTSS.

Summary. To integrate the reviewed studies, we consider each of the areas in which AS may be relevant to PTSD: etiology, maintenance, and treatment. Using the Kraemer et al. (1997) framework described earlier, many studies have linked AS and PTSD as correlates, including two meta-analyses (Naragon-Gainey, 2010; Olatunji & Wolitzky-Taylor, 2009). Second, one study shows that AS precedes PTSS after a trauma (Boffa et al., 2016), while two show that AS precedes PTSS prior to a trauma-analogous experience (Olatunji & Fan, 2015; Ong, Kuo, & Manber, 2008). Another study suggests AS immediately post trauma predicts later PTSS, but that the relationship is reciprocal (Marshall et al., 2010). Due to the dearth of prospective studies examining pre-trauma AS and its association with PTSS, it is difficult to determine whether AS precedes PTSS. However, the available literature suggests it may.

Third, the malleability of AS has been reviewed earlier, and finally, several studies have demonstrated that reductions in AS are associated with reductions in PTSS (e.g., Allan et al., 2015; Short, Boffa, et al., 2017; Vujanovic et al., 2012). However, these trials have all been among individuals who have *already* developed PTSS. Thus, it is unclear whether targeting AS would actually prevent PTSS among an at-risk sample. Despite the need for more prospective research and intervention trials, the available evidence suggests that AS may be a causal risk factor for PTSD.

Conceivably, AS may act as a risk factor for PTSS through the amplification of normative emotional and physiological peri- and posttraumatic reactions (Elwood, Hahn, Olatunji, & Williams, 2009; Wald & Taylor, 2008). During traumatic event exposure, a wide range of physiological sensations will occur. Those with high AS may interpret these as threatening, and thus become more reactive to the trauma itself, and develop greater fear around the event (Olatunji & Wolitzky-Taylor, 2009). Following traumatic event exposure, the vast majority of survivors will experience at least some symptoms of posttraumatic stress, which typically subside over the subsequent weeks. However, high AS could interfere with the normative recovery process. For example, most survivors of trauma experience reexperiencing and hyperarousal symptoms immediately after trauma (Horowitz, 1986). Those with high AS may interpret these reactions as catastrophic. For example, intrusive memories may be interpreted as evidence that one is "going crazy," and physiological sensations of anxiety may be seen as signs that something is very wrong. These interpretations would escalate the distress associated with the trauma, and memories of it, potentially motivating increased avoidance of trauma memories and trauma-related cues. Indeed, it is thought that avoidance is what leads to the development of PTSD as individuals are prevented from learning they are not in ongoing danger, and that they can handle the distress associated with their trauma (Foa, Hembree, & Rothbaum, 2007). Unfortunately, few empirical studies have actually tested these hypotheses, raising the need for further investigations of mechanisms accounting for associations between AS and PTSD.

In terms of maintenance of PTSD, it is likely that AS plays an ongoing role in exacerbating the distress and avoidance associated with various PTSD symptoms, including intrusive memories, emotional or physiological reminders of the event, sleep disturbance, difficulties concentrating, hypervigilance, etc. Indeed, considering research indicating the relationship between AS and PTSD may be reciprocal (Marshall et al., 2010), it is possible that this relationship reflects an escalating cycle of symptoms. For example, AS may increase PTSD symptoms, which would increase physiological arousal and sensations associated with anxiety, potentially resulting in increased sensitivity toward those sensations.

Finally, regarding the role of AS in PTSD treatment, many have noted the naturally occurring role of interoceptive exposure in treatments like prolonged exposure (PE) (Foa et al., 2007), which would theoretically decrease PTSS. Some have also recommended integrating separate interoceptive exercises into PTSD treatment to target AS, and thus reduce PTSS (Wald & Taylor, 2007). Thus, targeting AS may be a complementary approach to evidence-based treatment for PTSD, such as PE. However, as the studies reviewed suggest, there may also be a role of AS interventions as stand-alone treatments for PTSD, as they lead to reductions in PTSD symptoms on their own. It would also be interesting to investigate whether AS interventions prior to PE could improve treatment outcomes for individuals with PTSD.

In sum, AS is a promising risk factor for PTSS that has recently begun to garner even greater empirical support. There are many interesting avenues for further research, including prospective studies, and those designed to better understand the mechanism of how AS leads to increased PTSS. Perhaps most intriguing is discovering how to best to integrate available interventions for AS into treatments for PTSD to reduce the burden associated with often difficult to treat disorder.

Anxiety Sensitivity and Mood/Suicide

Mood disorders. Among adults in the United States, the lifetime prevalence rate of mood disorders is approximately 20.8% (Kessler et al., 2005). The comorbidity between mood and anxiety disorders is high, with more than 50% of individuals with MDD reporting a lifetime occurrence of one or more anxiety disorders (Kaufman & Charney, 2000). These findings have led researchers to advocate for the understanding of psychopathological traits and processes that may underlie both mood and anxiety disorders (Krueger, 1999). Although AS was initially conceptualized with regard to anxiety disorders, namely panic disorder (Reiss & McNally, 1985; Reiss, Peterson, Gursky, & McNally, 1986), later research has revealed that elevated AS is found across psychiatric disorders, including among mood disorders (Cox, Borger, & Enns, 1999; Taylor, 2014; Taylor, Koch, Woody, & McLean, 1996). In this regard, AS represents one prominent psychopathological trait that underlies both classes of disorders (Naragon-Gainey, 2010; Rector, Szacun-Shimizu, & Leybman, 2007). In this section, we briefly review a meta-analysis conducted by Naragon-Gainey (2010) examining AS across depressive disorders, discuss research on other mood disorders (e.g., bipolar disorder) in this domain, highlight research that has occurred since the Naragon-Gainey (2010) meta-analysis, and outline areas of future inquiry.

Naragon-Gainey (2010) identified 42 studies (aggregated $N = 10,193$) that examined correlations between the higher-order AS factor and depression symptoms. The association of AS with depression symptoms was found to be robust (mean $r = 0.41$), although the effect was weaker than for panic disorder and GAD. Studies were additionally identified that examined correlations between the lower-order AS factors and depression symptoms: AS cognitive ($k = 33$, $N = 8,815$), AS physical ($k = 35$, $N = 9,205$), and AS social ($k = 31$, $N = 7,871$). The AS cognitive subfactor (mean $r = 0.43$) was more strongly related to depression symptoms than the AS physical (mean $r = 0.33$) and AS social (mean $r = 0.28$) subfactors. Additionally, depression symptoms can be divided into heterogeneous symptom domains. Naragon-Gainey (2010) found that the higher-order AS factor demonstrated the strongest link with dysphoria symptoms (mean $r = 0.54$), followed by symptoms of suicidality (mean $r = 0.41$), lassitude (mean $r = 0.39$), and insomnia (mean $r = 0.34$); symptoms of appetite loss (mean $r = 0.26$) and gain (mean $r = 0.23$) as well as overall well-being (mean $r = -0.20$) evinced the weakest correlations to AS. When examining the AS subfactors, the AS cognitive subfactor demonstrated robust associations with dysphoria (mean $r = 0.52$) and suicidality (mean $r = 0.42$). The other dimensions of depression symptoms did not appear to differ regarding the AS subfactors. Together, this meta-analysis demonstrated that AS is strongly linked to depression symptoms; that suicidality, dysphoria, and insomnia may be most implicated in this link; and that the AS cognitive concerns subfactor may be most relevant.

We emphasize that the meta-analysis conducted by Naragon-Gainey (2010) was focused on depressive disorders, because few studies at the time of publication had examined AS regarding the broader spectrum of mood disorders, including the manic phase of bipolar disorder. Among 122 individuals with bipolar disorder and 114 individuals with MDD, Simon, Smoller, Fava, Sachs, and Racette (2003) found that mean AS levels were higher in the patients with bipolar disorder. However, when controlling for the effects of a current mood state, there were no longer any statistically significant differences, suggesting that research examining AS among individuals with bipolar disorder should consider whether the individual is in a depressed, hypomanic, manic, or mixed state. Further underscoring this point, one study of 202 individuals (n = 110 with bipolar disorder, n = 92 with MDD) found that AS is elevated in states of hypomania and mania, even after controlling for comorbid anxiety disorders (Simon, Otto, Fischmann, Racette, Nierenberg, &

Pollack, 2005). Given that AS was found to be elevated in manic states and that previous research has also linked AS to panic disorder (McNally, 2002; Schmidt, Lerew, & Jackson, 1997), the researchers concluded that AS may be the underlying mechanism contributing to the high comorbidity of panic disorder with bipolar disorder. Additionally, among a sample of 114 psychiatric outpatients with bipolar disorder, AS was found to be a significant predictor of impulsivity at nine-month follow-up (Taylor, Hirshfeld-Becker, Ostacher, Chow, & LeBeau, 2008), suggesting that AS may confer worse outcomes for individuals with bipolar disorder. To our knowledge, there remains a dearth of data examining AS in bipolar disorder. This gap in the literature is intriguing, as hypomanic and manic states, as well as AS, are characterized by overarousal; thus, future research may benefit from disentangling the role of AS in bipolar disorder.

Although research examining AS and bipolar disorder has been stagnant, since the publication of the Naragon-Gainey (2010) meta-analysis a robust body of literature has continued examining different facets of the role of AS in depressive disorders. For example, recent research has endeavored to investigate the contribution of each AS subfactor to mood disorders. Olthuis et al. (2014) investigated the unique contributions of the AS subfactors to a range of psychopathology among a sample of 85 treatment-seeking adults with elevated AS scores. The researchers found that only the AS cognitive concerns subfactor predicted unique variance in depressive symptoms. Similarly, among a sample of 256 psychiatric outpatients, Allan et al. (2014) found that both AS cognitive and AS social concerns were uniquely associated with MDD. Moreover, as is discussed in detail later in this chapter, the researchers found that the AS cognitive concerns subfactor was uniquely related to a core symptom of MDD: suicidal ideation. That independent investigations have found different results regarding the unique relation of subfactors to MDD (i.e., cognitive versus physical and social) may speak to the heterogeneity of MDD as a disorder. Indeed, there are 227 ways by which an individual can meet diagnostic criteria for MDD (Zimmerman, Ellison, Young, Chelminski, & Dalrymple, 2015). Together, these findings underscore the import of considering the multidimensional nature of AS and its concomitant psychopathology (e.g., MDD) in both research and practice.

This approach dovetails with the National Institute of Mental Health's Research Domain Criteria (RDoC) (Insel et al., 2010). An overarching goal of RDoC is to identify transdiagnostic factors at multiple levels of analysis (see also Cacioppo & Berntson, 1992; Cuthbert & Insel, 2013). One emerging area of research regarding AS and mood disorders that is couched in the RDoC framework is sleep disturbances. Sleep disturbances, such as insomnia, are cardinal features of mood pathology (American Psychiatric Association, 2013). Importantly, whereas sleep disturbances were once considered an epiphenomenon, there is clear and convincing evidence that sleep disturbances play a causal and maintenance role in mood pathology broadly (see Harvey, 2011, for review). Among a sample of individuals with panic disorder, Hoge et al. (2011) found that higher levels of AS were associated with greater sleep disturbances, particularly regarding increased sleep latency (cf. initial insomnia). These findings were replicated among a nonclinical sample of 149 undergraduate students – that is, anxiety sensitivity was a significant predictor of sleep dysfunction (Calkins, Hearon, Capozzoli, & Otto, 2013). Interestingly, the researchers found that of the AS subfactors, AS cognitive concerns appeared to be the most robust predictor of sleep problems. Baker et al. (2017) demonstrated that AS has transdiagnostic relevance with regard to sleep disturbances. They found that AS and a primary anxiety disorder diagnosis were each independently associated with greater sleep disturbances; however, when the effects of AS were accounted for, a primary anxiety disorder diagnosis no longer demonstrated significant associations with sleep disturbances. Notably, Short, Allan, Raines, and Schmidt (2015) demonstrated that an intervention composed of psychoeducation and interoceptive exposures that specifically targets AS concerns demonstrates measurable reductions in insomnia symptoms from baseline to one-month follow-up. Taken together, these findings suggest that AS may confer potent risk for a core symptom of depression – sleep disturbances – and that sleep disturbances are a promising AS-related construct within the RDoC framework (see Baker et al., 2017).

The aforementioned research has several notable gaps, which serve as a springboard for future research. First, as alluded to, there is a paucity of studies examining AS in its relation to bipolar disorder. Given that the hypomanic or manic phase of a bipolar disorder is characterized in part by overarousal and that AS too is characterized in part by overarousal, it would be interesting to test how AS may be implicated in the etiology or maintenance of hypomanic or manic states – or, perhaps, in the switching of polarities. Further, only limited research has examined the differential impact of AS on specific components of depressive symptoms, such as vegetative, reversed vegetative, or non-vegetative. Parsing apart these relationships may serve to enhance the understanding of the transdiagnostic relevance of the AS construct. Interestingly, there are gender differences in depression, such that women appear to be at elevated risk compared to men (Nolen-Hoeksema, 1987). Recently, Norr, Albanese, Allan, and Schmidt (2015) proposed that gender differences in the experience of AS may account for gender differences in the rate of depression. Among a sample of 106 individuals at baseline prior to randomization for a clinical trial, the researchers found that overall AS statistically mediated the association between gender and psychiatric symptoms such that women experience greater levels of AS and this, in turn, may lead to increased psychiatric symptoms. Moreover, Norr et al. (2015) found that AS cognitive concerns specifically accounted for the link between gender and depression symptoms. Thus, moving forward, AS may additionally be a useful sex-linked, variable risk factor that may explain the higher prevalence of mood disorders, namely depression, among women.

Suicidality. Whereas the majority of the literature regarding AS and mood disorders has been previously synthesized (Naragon-Gainey, 2010; Olatunji &

Wolitzky-Taylor, 2009), to our knowledge, there are no reviews of the literature with regard to a related burgeoning area of research: the role of AS in the etiology and maintenance of suicidal thoughts and behaviors.

Across the globe, more than 800,000 individuals die by suicide each year (World Health Organization [WHO], 2002), leaving in their wake profound suffering for the bereaved (Cerel, Jordan, & Duberstein, 2008). In the United States, 9.8 million adults seriously think about suicide, 1.4 million adults make a nonfatal suicide attempt, and more than 40,000 individuals die by suicide annually (Centers for Disease Control and Prevention [CDC], 2017; Piscopo, Lipari, Cooney, & Glasheen, 2016). Despite a corpus of research aimed at identifying risk and protective factors for suicide (see Franklin et al., 2017, for review), no appreciable changes in the rates of suicide fatalities have been observed (CDC, 2017). Moreover, the degree to which research has led to clinically actionable tangibles has been stagnant (Franklin et al., 2017). This constellation of findings underscores the need to identify novel vulnerability and maintenance factors for suicidal ideation. Indeed, emerging evidence suggests that AS – particularly the AS cognitive concerns subfactor – may serve to fill this gap.

The identification of a transdiagnostic vulnerability factor is important because suicide does not discriminate by psychiatric diagnoses; indeed, the presence of a psychiatric diagnosis itself increases risk for suicide, although some are more potent risk factors than others (Franklin et al., 2017; Harris & Barraclough, 1997). Rigorous psychological autopsy studies have revealed that the vast majority of individuals who die by suicide had a diagnosable psychiatric disorder at the time of their death (see Cavanagh, Carson, Sharpe, & Lawrie, 2003, for review). Thus, it follows that the identification of a transdiagnostic risk factor has broad implications for the prevention and treatment of suicide risk.

In what follows, we outline the state of the science on research examining AS and suicide risk in both cross-sectional and longitudinal studies; describe AS-focused treatment studies that have a demonstrated impact on suicidality outcomes; delineate theoretical models that may explain why AS is related to suicide risk; and identify future research that may illuminate the relevance of AS to suicide prevention and intervention initiatives.

One of the earliest references that AS may be implicated in the pathogenesis of suicidality was by Schmidt, Woolaway-Bickel, and Bates (2001). Among a sample of 146 psychiatric outpatients with panic disorder, the researchers found that AS cognitive concerns (referred to as *phrenophobia* by the researchers, that is, the fear of cognitive incapacitation) was a significant predictor of suicidal ideation in analyses that controlled for the possible effects of a comorbid mood disorder as well as depression symptoms. To our knowledge, research in this area then remained stagnant over the next decade with one exception. That is, among a sample of 98 psychiatric outpatients with bipolar disorder, Simon, Pollack, Ostacher, Zalta, and Chow (2007) found that global AS concerns predicted suicide risk. More recently, research linking AS and suicidality has occurred across diverse populations, including adolescents (Capron, Allan, Ialongo, Leen-

Feldner, & Schmidt, 2015), undergraduate students (Rogers et al., 2016), military cadets in basic training (Capron, Cougle, Ribeiro, Joiner, & Schmidt, 2012), veterans (Raines, Capron et al., 2017), firefighters (Stanley, Hom, Spencer-Thomas, & Joiner, 2017), primary care patients (Zvolensky et al., 2016), and psychiatric outpatients (Allan et al., 2014). This research has examined AS as both a cross-sectional and longitudinal predictor of suicidal ideation (see Capron, Cougle et al., 2012).

The role of anxiety sensitivity in prospectively predicting suicide attempts is less clear, in part due to the difficulties of collecting data on a low base rate event such as suicide attempts. Nevertheless, past research has found that AS cognitive concerns predict past suicide attempts at low levels of AS physical concerns (Capron, Cougle et al., 2012). This finding has relevance to a prominent theory of suicide – the interpersonal theory (Joiner, 2005; Van Orden et al., 2010) – which proposes that individuals will only attempt suicide if they have the desire to do so as well as the capability. In this model, the capability for suicide manifests, in part, as lowered physical pain tolerance. Thus, it follows that low levels of AS physical concerns are analogous, albeit an imperfect proxy, to lowered physical pain tolerance, creating conditions under which suicidal behaviors may emerge.

Interestingly, of the AS subfactors (i.e., cognitive, physical, social), the link between AS and suicidality may be specific to the AS cognitive subfactor (Allan, Norr et al., 2015; Capron, Blumenthal et al., 2012; Capron et al., 2012; Oglesby, Capron, Raines, & Schmidt, 2015). The AS cognitive concerns subfactor is characterized by fears of loss of cognitive control. That AS cognitive concerns appear to be most consistently linked to suicidality is important as specific interventions with demonstrated efficacy in reducing AS cognitive concerns.

To our knowledge, three randomized trials of AS-focused interventions have reported on suicidality outcomes. Among a sample of 169 smokers randomized to either a standard CBT intervention or a CBT intervention with a component specifically addressing AS concerns, Capron, Norr, Zvolensky, and Schmidt (2014) found lower levels of suicidality at follow-up for those in the AS-augmented intervention. Underscoring the potency of the AS-focused intervention on suicidality outcomes, these effects persisted even after controlling for baseline suicidality; current mood, anxiety, and substance use; and current smoking status. It is important to note that this intervention focused on AS broadly, and given the robust associations between AS cognitive concerns and suicidality, it is essential to test interventions that specifically target AS cognitive concerns. Achieving this, Schmidt et al. (2014) randomly assigned 108 individuals with elevated AS scores to a single session of either (1) psychoeducation and interoceptive exposure techniques specifically targeting AS cognitive concerns (i.e., Cognitive Anxiety Sensitivity Treatment [CAST]); or (2) a health information control condition. Importantly, the researchers found that, at one-month follow-up, changes in AS cognitive concerns mediated suicidality outcomes. This study laid the foundation to examine intervention effects among a more clinically severe sample. Schmidt et al. (2017) randomized 74 individuals with co-occurring anxiety pathology and active suicidal ideation to a single session of either: (1) CAST plus a computerized cognitive bias modification for interpretation bias (CBM-I) paradigm; or (2) a health information plus sham CBM control condition. Here too the researchers found that reductions in AS cognitive concerns mediated suicidality outcomes. Together, these three studies provide compelling evidence that AS may operate as a causal and/or maintaining risk factor for suicidality, consistent with the criteria outline by Kraemer et al. (1997). Of note, these interventions are brief (i.e., a single session) and computerized; coupled with the high levels of participant acceptability (Short, Fuller, Norr, & Schmidt, 2017), the scalability of these interventions focused on AS cognitive concerns for suicide prevention efforts is notable.

Regarding theoretical models of the link between AS and suicidality, the most widely tested is the depression-distress amplification model proposed by Capron, Norr, Macatee, and Schmidt (2013). The model makes the following observations: (1) uncomfortable sensations (e.g., concentration difficulties) occur during depression; (2) these uncomfortable sensations are amplified by AS cognitive concerns, which are characterized as extreme reactions to the sensations such as fears of "going crazy"; and (3) as depression symptoms worsen, suicidal ideation emerges. The model posits that insofar as AS cognitive concerns amplify depression symptoms, AS cognitive concerns are related to suicide risk. Support for this model has been found among diverse samples, including middle school students (Capron et al., 2015), undergraduate students with suicidal ideation (Capron, Lamis, & Schmidt, 2014), and psychiatric outpatients (Capron et al., 2013). By contrast, Norr, Allan, Macatee, Capron, and Schmidt (2016) did not find full support for the model, although the researchers concluded that suicidal ideation may be an insufficient criterion to study the model, given robust links between anxiety disorders, which themselves are characterized by high levels of AS, and suicide attempts (Cougle, Keough, Riccardi, & Sachs-Ericsson, 2009; Klonsky, May, & Saffer, 2016; Nock et al., 2009).

Beyond this model, several other theories of suicide may be illuminative (for reviews, see Selby, Joiner, & Ribeiro, 2014; Stanley, Hom, Rogers, Hagan, & Joiner, 2016). For example, as posited by Allan and colleagues (2015), Shneidman's (1993) psychache theory of suicide may explain, in part, the link between AS and suicidality. The psychache theory states that suicide is the result of intense psychological pain that is perceived as intractable. AS cognitive concerns too are characterized by intolerability of psychological symptoms, and thus suicidal behaviors may occur, in part, due to a desire to escape from these symptoms (see also Baumeister, 1990). Moreover, as referenced earlier, Joiner's (2005) interpersonal theory of suicide (see also Van Orden et al., 2010) may help explain the interplay between the AS subfactors and suicidality, given that the theory proposes distinct pathways to suicidal ideation versus suicidal behaviors and the AS subfactors have also demonstrated differential relations to each of these constructs (e.g., Capron, Cougle et al., 2012).

As future research endeavors to examine the relationship between AS and suicidality, it will be important to test these theoretical models. It will also be important to position studies within the ideation-to-action framework. The ideation-to-action framework notes that the vast majority of individuals who think about suicide do not go on to make a suicide attempt (e.g., Piscopo et al., 2016), and thus, it is imperative to understand factors implicated in the transition from thinking about suicide to engaging in suicidal behavior (Klonsky & May, 2014; Klonsky et al., 2016; Nock, Kessler, & Franklin, 2016). To wit, instead of a focus on simple main effects in relation to the broad construct of suicidality, it is important to study moderators and mediators in their relation to clearly defined suicide-related outcomes. Given that manifestations of overarousal are implicated in this transition from ideation to action (Klonsky et al., 2016; see also Joiner & Stanley, 2016), it may be that AS is uniquely positioned within the ideation-to-action framework. To test this, future studies should evaluate the effects of AS and its subfactors on suicidal behaviors among a sample of suicide ideators. On this point, it may also be useful to understand how AS interacts with other levels of analysis to confer risk for suicidality; the RDoC framework may be illuminative in this regard. For an overview of considerations of conducting suicide-related research within the RDoC framework, the reader is referred to Glenn, Cha, Kleiman, and Nock (2017).

Future research is also needed in the following domains. First, although logistically difficult given that suicide (and to an extent, suicide attempts) is a low base rate event, it will be important to examine the effects of AS on suicide attempts and fatalities. Studies would also benefit from examining AS in samples with no current or lifetime suicidal symptoms and prospectively following these individuals to determine whether AS predicts the onset of suicidality. This type of work would certainly help to establish AS as a causal risk factor within Kraemer and colleagues' (1997) framework. Finally, it will be important to continue to refine and test the degree to which AS-focused interventions can inoculate against suicidality (Schmidt et al., 2017). Scalable preventive interventions may be particularly relevant to certain segments of the population that are at increased risk for suicide, such as first responders (see Stanley, Hom, & Joiner, 2016, for review) and military service members (see Nock et al., 2013, for review). Given the tragically high rates of suicide across the globe, we welcome future research that attempts to understand the ways by which AS may confer risk – and, importantly, the ways by which treating AS may contribute to decrements in the suicide rate.

Summary. Consistent with the previous sections, we conclude by synthesizing the literature on AS and mood/suicidality across three domains: etiology, maintenance, and treatment. Criterion one of Kraemer and colleagues' (1997) framework for what constitutes a risk factor (cf. etiology) is that two variables must be correlated. Indeed, robust evidence suggests that AS and depressive disorders are linked (see Naragon-Gainey, 2010, for review). Fewer data are available regarding bipolar disorder, but the existing evidence suggests that

AS and bipolar disorder/mania are linked as well (Simon et al., 2003, 2005). An emerging line of research has also linked AS – specifically, AS cognitive concerns – to suicidal thoughts and behaviors (Allan et al., 2015; Allan, Capron, Raines, & Schmidt, 2014; Capron et al., 2012; Oglesby, Capron, Raines, & Schmidt, 2015; Stanley et al., 2017). These data indicate that, at the least, AS serves as a risk marker for mood disorders and suicidality. However, criterion two of Kraemer and colleagues' (1997) framework requires that one variable (i.e., AS) precedes an outcome (i.e., mood disorders, suicidality) to be considered a risk factor. Most studies reviewed were cross-sectional, especially regarding suicidality, precluding definitive statements regarding the role of AS in the etiology of mood disorders and suicidality. There is some evidence, however, that AS precedes the onset of mood pathology, namely depressive disorders. For example, Grant, Beck, and Davila (2007) found that among a sample of undergraduates, AS physical concerns (but not AS cognitive or AS social concerns) predicted increases in depression symptoms at one-year follow-up. Further, among a sample of 1,401 individuals undergoing military basic training, Schmidt, Lerew, and Jackson (1997) found that baseline AS predicted greater depression symptoms at five-week follow-up. Thus, the available evidence suggests AS may, in some cases, precede depression symptoms.

Criterion three of Kraemer and colleagues' (1997) framework for what constitutes a risk factor underscores that the factor must be malleable. As has been reviewed earlier, AS is malleable (Capron and Schmidt, 2016; Norr et al., 2017; Schmidt et al., 2017, 2014; see Smits et al., 2008, for review). In turn, criterion four of Kraemer and colleagues' (1997) framework indicates that changes in the factor must yield changes in the outcome. Regarding mood disorders, Smits and colleagues (2008) demonstrated that within the context of an exercise intervention, reductions in AS mediated reductions in depression symptoms. Regarding suicidality, as we have reviewed, at least three randomized trials have demonstrated that interventions focused on ameliorating AS successfully yield reductions in AS and, moreover, these reductions mediate changes in suicidal ideation at follow-up (Capron, Norr, Zvolensky, & Schmidt, 2014; Schmidt et al., 2014, 2017). Of note, Schmidt and colleagues (2017) specifically recruited for individuals with suicidal ideation. In this sense, while the existing evidence suggests that AS may serve as a risk factor for suicidality, more robust evidence suggests that AS may operate as a maintaining factor for mood disorders and suicidality.

Regarding the maintenance of mood disorders and suicidality, it is likely that these symptom domains interact bidirectionally. For example, cognitive distortions are a maintaining factor in mood disorders such as MDD (Beck, 2011). AS concerns are, in a sense, an amplification of cognitive distortions, and thus may themselves represent maintaining factors. Further, as noted in a previous section, AS and PTSD are reciprocally linked (Marshall, Miles, & Stewart, 2010). PTSD is characterized in part by symptoms that closely resemble mood pathologies, such as anhedonia and social disconnectedness (cf. numbing symptoms). Insofar as mood disorders overlap to a degree with PTSD symptoms, it is reasonable to assume that AS and mood symptoms too may interact bidirectionally. However, we emphasize that this is speculative and must undergo empirical testing. Moreover, the degree to which AS serves as a maintenance factor for suicidal thoughts and behavior is even less clear.

Regarding treatment, in the context of a meta-analysis demonstrating the strength with which CBT-focused interventions reduce AS (Smits, Berry, Tart et al., 2008), the promise of AS treatments for reducing mood pathology is considerable. In terms of suicidality, findings suggest that specifically targeting AS cognitive concerns may yield reductions in suicidal ideation (Schmidt et al., 2014, 2017). Although research has not yet examined whether treating AS yields reductions in suicide attempts, that reductions are observed regarding suicidal ideation is promising, as suicidal ideation is conceptualized as a precursor to suicide attempts.

Anxiety Sensitivity and Substance Use Disorders

Although AS has been regarded primarily as a risk factor for mood and anxiety disorders, AS has also been implicated in the development and maintenance of alcohol and substance use disorders. Specifically, high AS has been posited as a catalyst for problems with substances that possess anxiolytic or arousal-dampening effects (McNally, 1996; Stewart, Samoluk, & MacDonald, 1999). The effects of AS on these substances is thought to arise, at least partially, through negative reinforcement-motivated substance use behaviors such as using substances to cope with negative affect or anxiety as well as expectations that these substances will have arousal-dampening effects (DeMartini & Carey, 2011; Stewart et al., 1999).

As of yet, no meta-analyses have been conducted exploring the relations between AS and substance use. Stewart et al. (1999) provided the most comprehensive review of the literature to date, with the bulk of the research presented concerning alcohol use. Stewart et al. (1999) highlighted studies demonstrating that people with an alcohol use disorder (AUD) have higher levels of AS than do people without an AUD. As Stewart and colleagues note, these findings are not informative regarding the role of AS in the etiology of AUDs. In studies of nonalcoholic young adults, those with high AS were more likely to drink in negatively reinforcing contexts, such as to cope with negative affect or to conform as well as to drink because of the expected relaxation and tension-reduction effects of alcohol (i.e., arousal-dampening effects; e.g., Stewart & Zeitlin, 1995). Studies conducted after the review by Stewart et al. have also found significant associations between AS and similar negative reinforcement drinking motives and tension-reduction expectations (e.g., Allan, Albanese, Norr, Zvolensky, & Schmidt, 2015; Comeau, Stewart, & Loba, 2001; Paulus et al., 2017; Stewart, Zvolensky, & Eifert, 2001).

This pattern of findings is especially problematic in regard to risk for alcohol problems given that these drinking motives and expectancies are riskier than positively reinforcing reasons for drinking (Cooper, Russell, Skinner, & Windle, 1992).

In their review, Stewart et al. (1999) indicated that self-report studies examining the relations between AS and drinking behaviors were equivocal. Several studies found higher rates of drinking in people with high AS than in people with low AS (Stewart et al., 1995; Cox, Swinson, Shulman, Kuch, & Reichman, 1993); however, at least one study, by Novak et al. (2003), failed to replicate these findings. A more recent review focused on the mechanisms from AS to problematic alcohol use (DeMartini & Carey, 2011) expanded on the review of Stewart et al. (1999) by positing a model to explain the relations between AS and alcohol use. Based on self-report and lab studies of alcohol use, DeMartini and Carey (2011) suggested that the relations between AS and problematic alcohol use are mediated by several variables, including anxiety symptoms and negative reinforcement drinking motives (i.e., coping and conformity). They also suggest that gender and social context likely moderate these relations. Allan et al. (2015) provided support for this model in a study using chained mediation to examine AS and alcohol. This study found a direct relationship between AS and alcohol problems. However, this pathway was mediated first through worry and then through coping motives, as well as through conformity motives. When depression was included as a possible mediator instead of worry, a chained mediation effect was also found from AS to alcohol problems through depression and then coping motives. Several other studies have found indirect pathways from AS to problematic drinking behavior, through various anxiety- and depression-related variables, including emotion dysregulation (Chandley, Luebbe, Messman-Moore, & Ward, 2014; Lechner et al., 2014; Paulus et al., 2017; Paulus, Vujanovic, & Wardle, 2016; Torres & Matagreve, 2016). Thus, the equivocal findings between AS and problematic alcohol use might be because the relations between AS and alcohol use are not always direct, but rather indirect, through several intervening variables, including negative reinforcement drinking motives, increased anxiety and depression, and emotion dysregulation.

Stewart et al. (1999) also discussed lab-based studies exploring alcohol as negatively reinforcing for high AS people (e.g., distress or tension reducing). Alcohol administration studies indicate that people with high AS appear more sensitive to negatively reinforcing drinking outcomes, especially at high alcohol dosages (Kushner et al., 1996; Stewart & Pihl, 1994). Summarizing findings from several laboratory task studies, Stewart et al. (1999) state that there is clear support for the hypothesis that alcohol aids in tension reduction for people with high AS, although they also note that there is less support from lab-based studies that alcohol-induced tension reduction leads to an increase in alcohol consumption.

At the time of the Stewart et al. (1999) review, there was little research exploring high AS as a risk factor for other substances. AS should, in theory, be positively associated with other anxiolytic substances and negatively associated with anxiogenic substances (McNally, 1996). Studies reviewed by Stewart et al. (1999) provide support for positive relations between AS and medications for stress, including benzodiazepines (Telch, Lucas, & Nelson, 1989), analgesics for pain (Asmundson & Norton, 1995), and heroin (McNally & Lorenz, 1987). There was little evidence, and findings were mixed, regarding the relations between AS and anxiogenics. Norton et al. (1997) reported that high AS substance users were less likely than moderate AS substance users to report stimulants as their preferred drug. However, Stewart, Karp, Pihl, and Peterson (1997) found that high AS young adults were no less likely to use caffeine than were low AS young adults.

Several studies have focused on the relations between AS and marijuana after the review article by Stewart and colleagues (1999). These studies provide preliminary evidence that the relations between AS and marijuana use mirror the relations between AS and alcohol use. That is, several studies have confirmed that AS is not necessarily directly associated with elevated marijuana use, but rather is associated with problematic marijuana use through elevated coping and conformity motives for marijuana use (e.g., Chowdhury, Kevorkian, Sheerin, Zvolensky, & Berenz, 2016; Comeau et al., 2001; Johnson, Mullin, Marshall, & Bonn-miller, 2011; Zvolensky et al., 2009).

Note that a comprehensive theoretical model focused on explicating the relations between vulnerability factors and substance use has emerged that incorporates AS and several other vulnerability factors (hopelessness, impulsivity, and sensation seeking (Brunelle et al., 2004; Woicik, Stewart, Pihl, & Conrod, 2009). Within this model, people with high AS and high hopelessness are posited to be susceptible to negative reinforcement substance use motives whereas people with high impulsivity and sensation seeking are posited to be susceptible to positive reinforcement substance use motives (e.g., Jurk et al., 2015; Woicik et al., 2009). Several studies that evaluated this model have provided support for the combined influences of AS and alcohol and drug use and motives in predicting substance use outcomes (e.g., Jurk et al., 2015; Loxton, Bunker, Dingle, & Wong, 2015; Woicik et al., 2009).

Etiology

Although the literature has tended to confirm an association between AS and substance use disorders, few studies have more directly examined whether AS is implicated in the development of a substance use disorder (SUD). We are aware of four longitudinal studies that are informative regarding whether AS is predictive of later substance use. In one of the first studies to do so, Schmidt et al. (2007) examined the impact of AS on SUDs in a sample of 404 young adults with high AS (M age = 19.3, SD = 3.9) but no current or recent (past 12 months) psychopathology. AS at baseline significantly predicted the likelihood of receiving an SUD diagnosis approximately 20 months later. A total of 11 people met for an SUD. All met for AUD, which was the primary diagnosis for 10 of 11 people, providing preliminary evidence that high AS may contribute to the development of an AUD. Mackie, Castellanos-Ryan, and Conrod (2011) examined the unique impact of baseline AS, hopelessness, impulsivity, and sensation seeking on growth in alcohol use over an 18-month period in a sample of 393 adolescents (M age = 13 years, SD = 9 months). AS was associated with alcohol use at baseline. However, AS only predicted rates of change in alcohol use when adolescents also had high levels of trait anxiety. Jurk et al. (2015) examined the unique predictive relations between AS and the other substance use vulnerability factors at baseline and the onset of drinking, binge drinking, smoking, and cannabis use within 18 months of baseline in samples ranging from 975 to 1,854 adolescents. In this study, only impulsivity and sensation seeking predicted the onset of alcohol and substance use. Finally, Loxton and colleagues (2015) examined the impact of baseline substance use profile risk factors on drinking motives and alcohol consumption rates during orientation week as well as rates of change over six months in a sample of incoming university students (M age = 18.09 years, SD = 1.21). Controlling for the other substance use risk factors, no effects were found for AS. At this point in time, the evidence for AS as a clear premorbid contributor to the development of substance use is weak. There is some support for this, and it may be that AS is only a contributor under certain conditions (such as for those with high trait anxiety).

Maintenance

To date, we could find no studies that have directly attempted to examine the role of AS in maintaining SUD diagnoses. However, associations between AS and other variables that may maintain substance use have been examined. In a sample of 77 people meeting for current AUD and PTSD, Simpson, Jakupcak, and Luterek (2006) found no significant relationship between AS and the alcohol use and craving variables. In another report focused on those with comorbid AUD and PTSD, Gillihan, Farris, and Foa (2011) found that AS was significantly associated with percent days drinking alcohol (r = 0.20), though this finding indicates only a 4% overlap between AS and percent days drinking. The authors also examined whether AS and PTSD symptom clusters interacted in predicting percent days drinking and found that AS significantly moderated the relation between avoidance symptoms and percent days drinking such that there was a stronger association between avoidance symptoms and percent days drinking at low levels of AS as compared to high levels of AS. Finally, McCaul, Hutton, Stephens, Xu, and Wand (2017) examined the relations that AS, anxiety, and stress shared with the frequency and intensity of recent drinking, as well as laboratory measures of alcohol craving and stress reactivity among a sample of people diagnosed with an AUD. Whereas 87 participants (M age = 33.3, SD = 10.4) completed measures of current drinking behavior, only 30 (M age = 35.1, SD = 11.0) were selected to complete the laboratory procedures. Controlling for anxiety and stress, AS was significantly associated with number of drinking days and binge drinking days over the preceding 90 days.

Few studies have examined the role of AS in maintaining substances other than alcohol. McHugh et al. (2010) examined the relations between AS and past-month nonmedical use of benzodiazepines in a sample of 257 people (*M* age = 28.4, *SD* = 10) receiving treatment for opiate use disorder. A gender-moderated relation between AS and past-month use of benzodiazepines was found, such that higher AS scores were associated with an increased use of benzodiazepines in females but not in males. Lejuez, Paulson, Daughters, Bornovalova, and Zvolensky (2006) reported on levels of AS in a sample of 172 inner-city treatment-seeking drug users, using heroin, crack/cocaine, both, or neither two to three times per week over the past year. AS scores were significantly elevated in the heroin group compared to the other groups. To our knowledge, no other studies have examined whether AS maintains problematic substance use in people diagnosed with other SUDs. In summary, we would suggest that it is currently unclear whether AS helps to maintain substance use problems, but research designed to answer such relationships is sorely lacking.

Treatment

Few studies have examined whether AS-focused treatments result in reductions of substance use and most of these studies have focused on alcohol use. To our knowledge, the first study focusing on the effect of an AS-focused treatment to reduce substance use problems was conducted by Watt, Stewart, Birch, and Bernier (2006). In this study, the effect of a small group CBT-based intervention (lasting for three one-hour sessions) targeting AS was compared to a control group seminar in a sample of 221 undergraduate females (*M* age = 19.0 years, *SD* = 1.8), selected to have either high or low AS. At follow-up, 10 weeks after treatment, women with high AS in the treatment group had greater reductions in conformity-motivated drinking and in emotional relief expectancies about drinking. There was also a 50% reduction in proportion of women with high AS meeting criteria for hazardous drinking in the treatment group. More recently, Olthuis, Watt, Mackinnon, and Stewart (2015) examined drinking motives and problematic drinking behavior in a sample of 80 people with high AS (*M* age = 36.3 years, *SD* = 11.3; 79% female) assigned to receive an eight-week CBT-based telephone intervention or to a wait-list control. AS was significantly reduced in the active condition compared to the control condition. When researchers examined the rate of change at post intervention through 12-week follow-up, they found significant reductions in alcohol-related physical problems, as well as marginally significant reductions in intrapersonal alcohol-related problems. Mediation models were conducted to determine whether the effect of the intervention reduced alcohol-related variables through reductions in AS. Coping with anxiety motives were reduced indirectly through AS reductions. Although alcohol-related physical problems were not indirectly reduced through reductions in AS, alcohol-related physical problems were reduced through reductions in coping with anxiety drinking motives. Finally, Worden, Davis, Genova, and Tolin (2015) developed and pilot tested a brief intervention aimed at reducing AS and substance use in a sample of 21 patients (*M* age = 42.6 years, *SD* = 12.1) who primarily were in treatment for alcohol use disorders. The intervention comprised six one-and-a-half-hour sessions targeting AS but also integrating psychoeducation about the relations between AS and substance use. This uncontrolled study was carried out following an outpatient day treatment program with all participants receiving treatment in either a group or a one-on-one setting. The majority of participants (78.7%) in this study reported alcohol as the primary substance of use in the three months prior to study entry. Cannabis (21.7%), cocaine (17.4%), opiates (4.3%), and sedatives (4.3%) were other primary substances used. Significant declines in AS scores were reported following the intervention, with scores below clinical range for the 15 participants who remained in the study at the three-month follow-up. Regarding substance use outcomes, percent days abstinent increased from 51.6% ($SD = 31.9$) at baseline to 91.4% ($SD = 16.6$) post intervention. These improvements were maintained through three-month follow-up. Though limited, these studies support the idea that reductions in AS could mitigate alcohol use problems.

Few treatment studies have focused on substance use outcomes other than alcohol. Tull, Barrett, McMillan, and Roemer (2007) evaluated a development of a brief (six-session) behavioral treatment for heightened AS among heroin users. Preliminary data on this treatment were provided in the form of a case study with one patient in an inner-city residential substance use treatment facility. Results indicate reductions in AS (especially physical concerns), as well as decreases in heroin cravings and improvements in emotion regulation. Of note, Lejuez et al. (2008) examined AS as a predictor of treatment dropout in a sample of crack/cocaine and/or heroin-using patients in a residential substance use treatment facility. They found that high AS uniquely predicted treatment dropout, controlling for demographics, drug use variables, legal obligation to treatment, alcohol use frequency, and depressive symptoms.

Discussion

Consistent with our review of other forms of psychopathology, we briefly consider each of the areas in which AS may be relevant to SUDs: etiology, maintenance, and treatment. In terms of etiology, there is limited evidence that AS serves as a risk factor using Kraemer's (1997) framework. Whereas numerous studies have demonstrated that AS is associated with problematic alcohol and substance use, the majority of these studies are cross-sectional. To date, a single study by Schmidt et al. (2007) provides evidence that AS precedes the development of SUDs. Thus, although available evidence suggests that high AS can predict the development of an SUD, more research is needed to firmly establish this link.

As detailed elsewhere in this review, AS is malleable. Further, there is some evidence that reducing AS leads to subsequent reductions in substance use. Several studies have demonstrated that treatments targeting AS lead to reductions in negative reinforcement motives for alcohol use, expectancies about the effects of alcohol, and problematic drinking behavior, and that this mechanism appears to be through reductions in AS (Olthuis et al., 2015; Watt et al., 2006).

Finally, Worden et al. (2015) provided preliminary evidence that interventions targeting AS and substance use can lead to significant increases in days abstinent for participants using alcohol as well as other substances. Whereas more work is needed to establish that reductions in AS lead to reductions in substances beyond alcohol, there is at least preliminary evidence that AS is a causal risk factor for SUDs.

To summarize, there is ample evidence establishing a link between AS and anxiolytic substances. Most likely, this association occurs through people with high AS using substances for negative reinforcement motives and because of expectations that substance use will reduce arousal levels. However, there are many interesting pathways for future research, including a need for additional longitudinal studies and for treatment studies focused on anxiolytic substances other than alcohol.

The Neurobiology of Anxiety Sensitivity: Evidence for a Potential Circuit That May Contribute to Its Transdiagnostic Impact

Taken together, the self-report and behavioral literature clearly indicates that AS is characterized by the evaluation of interoceptive events that are potentially harmful or dangerous, greater vigilance toward bodily perturbations, and accuracy in detecting interoceptive events. Therefore, we would expect that AS would be characterized by hyperactivity in two brain structures that form a neural circuit that is critical to, among other functions, the detection and evaluation of interoceptive threats similar to what is observed among those with elevated AS: the anterior insula and anterior cingulate cortex (ACC). Importantly, insula and ACC each have major afferent and efferent connections with other brain structures, including the amygdala and prefrontal cortex, and are believed to contribute to a variety of emotional and cognitive processes. Hence, it is not surprising that aberrations in insula and ACC structure and/or activity have been implicated in a number of psychopathologies – including anxiety (e.g., Paulus & Stein, 2006), posttraumatic stress disorder (Garfinkel & Liberzon, 2009), mood disorders (Beauregard, Vincent, & Le'vesque, 2006), suicidality (Oquendo et al., 2016), and substance use (Naqvi & Bechara, 2010) – and may offer an explanation for the transdiagnostic nature of AS.

Review of Literature Evaluating AS and Neurocognitive Mechanisms of Interoception

As predicted, AS has been linked to structural and functional aberrations in the anterior insula and ACC. For instance, self-reported AS predicts structural differences in the right anterior insula, such that those with elevated AS have greater right anterior insula thickness and volume (Rosso et al., 2010). Prior research suggests that reductions in insular thickness and volume occur with age as a result of the refinement of insula reactivity to specific body states (i.e., via learned experiences the insula thickness reduces as it refines what is necessary to react to; Chechik et al., 1998; Huttenlocher & Dabholkar, 1997). Thus, it is plausible that the greater anterior insular thickness observed among those with AS reflects deficiency in learning associations between harmful and benign interoceptive states.

Several studies have also found anterior insula and ACC hyperactivity among those with high AS. For instance, Holtz and colleagues (2012) found that individuals with high AS exhibited greater activation in the anterior insula and ACC when shown cues previously paired with hyperventilation, and slower extinction to these cues when they were no longer paired with hyperventilation. Interestingly, those with high AS also showed hyperactive anterior insula and ACC activity in response to safety cues (i.e., cues never paired with hyperventilation) throughout the task. In concert with Rosso et al.'s (2010) finding that those with high AS have greater anterior insula thickness and volume, it is plausible that those with high AS have difficulty distinguishing between cues indicating interoceptive threat and safety. Moreover, the relationship between anterior insula/ACC driven interoception and AS appears to be specific to the detection of anxiety-related sensations. For instance, Ochsner and colleagues (2006) collected fMRI data during the delivery of painful and neutral thermal stimuli to compare the relationships between the ASI and Fear of Pain Questionnaire-III (FPQ-III) (McNeil & Rainwater, 1998) to activation of ACC, insula, and other brain regions. Results indicated that the fear of pain, but not the fear of anxiety-related sensations (i.e., AS), predicted ACC activation during the experience of painful relative to non-painful sensations. This finding suggests that, although this circuitry is involved in the detection and evaluation of all bodily sensations, AS is unrelated to activations when the stimuli are not arousal-related.

Several studies further demonstrate that AS is specific to circuits involved in interoceptive threat, and not associated with amygdala activation, a closely related area involved broadly in emotional reactivity, particularly to external stimuli. Stein and colleagues (2007) used fMRI imaging in combination with an emotional face-matching task and found that although state anxiety and neuroticism were associated with both insula and amygdala activity, AS was only associated with insula activation. Ball et al. (2012) similarly found that, when controlling for trait and social anxiety, AS significantly predicted ACC but not amygdala activation while viewing emotional faces. Two other studies in which participants were shown masked (Killgore et al., 2011) and unmasked (Poletti et al., 2015) emotional faces demonstrated that AS was associated with insula (Killgore et al., 2011; Poletti et al., 2015) and ACC (Poletti et al., 2015) hyperactivity but not amygdala activation. Last, Yang et al. (2016) demonstrated that high AS individuals display greater anterior insula activation and no difference in amygdala activation while reading anxiety-related symptom words (e.g., "dizziness") relative to individuals with low AS. Taken together, these findings lend further support to the idea that AS is marked by anterior insula and ACC activation, specifically.

Neurobiological Model of AS as an Explanatory Platform for Transdiagnostic Risk

Anterior insula and ACC hyperactivity observed among those with high AS may provide an explanation for why AS behaves as a transdiagnostic risk factor. The anterior insula and ACC are core components of what is referred to as the *salience network*; a cluster of distinct and interconnected structures that also includes the amygdala, ventral striatum, and ventral tegmental area (Menon, 2015). The salience network is believed to play an integral role in guiding our emotional and behavioral experiences, and disruptions of the salience network (or key components of it) have been associated with transdiagnostic risk for psychopathology, including anxiety, mood/suicide, posttraumatic stress disorder, and substance abuse (see Menon, 2015, for a review). Thus, it is certainly plausible, if not probable, that the AS construct reflects the expression of hyperactivity in two integral pieces of the salience network: the anterior insula and the ACC. It is also reasonable to suggest that these disruptions may influence a delicate balance of connectivity among other structures in the salience (e.g., amygdala) related (e.g., executive control; Critchley, 2005) networks. Although speculative, the available data lead us to suggest that AS represents a specific disruption of anterior insula- and ACC-driven interoceptive processing, which may initiate or maintain a cascade of dysfunction in related but distinct neural networks, thereby yielding an array of psychopathological phenotypes.

References

Allan, N. P., Albanese, B. J., Short, N. A., Raines, A. M., & Schmidt, N. B. (2015). Support for the general and specific bifactor model factors of anxiety sensitivity. *Personality and Individual Differences*, *74*, 78–83.

Allan, N. P., Capron, D. W., Raines, A. M., & Schmidt, N. B. (2014). Unique relations among anxiety sensitivity factors and anxiety, depression, and suicidal ideation. *Journal of Anxiety Disorders*, *28*(2), 266–275.

Allan, N. P., Felton, J. W., Lejuez, C. W., MacPherson, L., & Schmidt, N. B. (2016). Longitudinal investigation of anxiety sensitivity growth trajectories and relations with anxiety and depression symptoms in adolescence. *Development and Psychopathology*, *28*(2), 459–469.

Allan, N. P., Norr, A. M., Boffa, J. W., Durmaz, D., Raines, A. M., & Schmidt, N. B. (2015). Examining the unique relations between anxiety sensitivity factors and suicidal ideation and past suicide attempts. *Psychiatry Research*, *228*(3), 441–447.

Allan, N. P., Short, N. A., Albanese, B. J., Keough, M. E., & Schmidt, N. B. (2015). Direct and mediating effects of an anxiety sensitivity intervention on posttraumatic stress disorder symptoms in trauma-exposed individuals. *Cognitive Behaviour Therapy*, *44*(6), 512–524.

American Psychiatric Association. (2013). *DSM 5*. Washington, DC: American Psychiatric Association.

Asmundson, G. J. G. & Norton, G. R. (1995). Anxiety sensitivity in patients with physically unexplained chronic back pain: A preliminary report. *Behaviour Research and Therapy*, *33*(7), 771–777. https://doi.org/10.1016/0005–7967(95)00012-M

Babson, K. A., Boden, M. T., Woodward, S., Alvarez, J., & Bonn-Miller, M. (2013). Anxiety sensitivity and sleep quality: Independent and interactive predictors of posttraumatic stress disorder symptoms. *Journal of Nervous and Mental Disease*, *201*(1), 48–51.

Babson, K. A., Heinz, A. J., Ramirez, G., Puckett, M., Irons, J. G., Bonn-Miller, M. O., & Woodward, S. H. (2015). The interactive role of exercise and sleep on veteran recovery from symptoms of PTSD. *Mental Health and Physical Activity*, *8*, 15–20.

Baker, A. W., Keshaviah, A., Goetter, E. M., Bui, E., Swee, M., Rosencrans, P. L., & Simon, N. M. (2017). Examining the role of anxiety sensitivity in sleep dysfunction across anxiety disorders. *Behavioral Sleep Medicine*, *15*(3), 216–227.

Bakhshaie, J., Zvolensky, M. J., Allan, N., Vujanovic, A. A., & Schmidt, N. B. (2015). Differential effects of anxiety sensitivity components in the relation between emotional non-acceptance and posttraumatic stress symptoms among trauma-exposed treatment-seeking smokers. *Cognitive Behaviour Therapy*, *44*(3), 175–189.

Bakhshaie, J., Zvolensky, M. J., Salazar, A., Vujanovic, A. A., & Schmidt, N. B. (2016). Anxiety sensitivity and smoking behavior among trauma-exposed daily smokers: The explanatory role of smoking-related avoidance and inflexibility. *Behavior Modification*, *40*(1–2), 218–238.

Ball, T. M., Sullivan, S., Flagan, T., Hitchcock, C. A., Simmons, A., Paulus, M. P., & Stein, M. B. (2012). Selective effects of social anxiety, anxiety sensitivity, and negative affectivity on the neural bases of emotional face processing. *Neuroimage*, *59*(2), 1879–1887.

Bardeen, J. R. (2015). Short-term pain for long-term gain: The role of experiential avoidance in the relation between anxiety sensitivity and emotional distress. *Journal of Anxiety Disorders*, *30*, 113–119.

Baumann, C., Klauke, B., Weber, H., Domschke, K., Zwanzger, P., Pauli, P., . . . Reif, A. (2013). The interaction of early life experiences with COMT val158 met affects anxiety sensitivity. *Genes, Brain and Behavior*, *12*(8), 821–829.

Baumeister, R. F. (1990). Suicide as escape from self. *Psychological Review*, *97*(1), 90–113. https://doi.org/10.1037/0033-295X.97.1.90

Beauregard, M., Paquette, V., & Levesque, J. (2006). Dysfunction in the neural circuitry of emotional self-regulation in major depressive disorder. *Neuroreport*, *17*(8), 843–846.

Berenz, E. C., Kevorkian, S., Chowdhury, N., Dick, D. M., Kendler, K. S., & Amstadter, A. B. (2016). Posttraumatic stress disorder symptoms, anxiety sensitivity, and alcohol-use motives in college students with a history of interpersonal trauma. *Psychology of Addictive Behaviors*, *30*(7), 755.

Blakey, S. M., Abramowitz, J. S., Reuman, L., Leonard, R. C., & Riemann, B. C. (2017). Anxiety sensitivity as a predictor of outcome in the treatment of obsessive-compulsive disorder. *Journal of Behavior Therapy and Experimental Psychiatry*, *57*, 113–117.

Boffa, J. W., Norr, A. M., Raines, A. M., Albanese, B. J., Short, N. A., & Schmidt, N. B. (2016). Anxiety sensitivity prospectively predicts posttraumatic stress symptoms following a campus shooting. *Behavior Therapy*, *47*(3), 367–376.

Boswell, J. F., Farchione, T. J., Sauer-Zavala, S., Murray, H. W., Fortune, M. R., & Barlow, D. H. (2013). Anxiety sensitivity and interoceptive exposure: A transdiagnostic construct and change strategy. *Behavior Therapy*, *44*(3), 417–431.

Brandt, C. P., Zvolensky, M. J., Vujanovic, A. A., Grover, K. W., Hogan, J., Bakhshaie, J., & Gonzalez, A. (2015). The mediating role of anxiety sensitivity in the relation between avoidant coping and posttraumatic stress among trauma-exposed HIV+ individuals. *Psychological Trauma: Theory, Research, Practice, and Policy*, *7*(2), 146.

Brunelle, C., Assaad, J.-M., Barrett, S. P., Avila, C., Conrod, P. J., Tremblay, R. E., & Pihl, R. O. (2004). Heightened heart rate response to alcohol intoxication is associated with a reward-seeking personality profile. *Alcoholism, Clinical and Experimental Research*, *28*(3), 394–401. https://doi.org/10.1097/01.ALC .0000117859.23567.2E

Cacioppo, J. T. & Berntson, G. G. (1992). Social psychological contributions to the decade of the brain: Doctrine of multilevel analysis. *American Psychologist*, *47*(8), 1019.

Calkins, A. W., Hearon, B. A., Capozzoli, M. C., & Otto, M. W. (2013). Psychosocial predictors of sleep dysfunction: The role of anxiety sensitivity, dysfunctional beliefs, and neuroticism. *Behavioral Sleep Medicine*, *11*(2), 133–143.

Capron, D. W., Allan, N. P., Ialongo, N. S., Leen-Feldner, E., & Schmidt, N. B. (2015). The depression distress amplification model in adolescents: A longitudinal examination of anxiety sensitivity cognitive concerns, depression and suicidal ideation. *Journal of Adolescence*, *41*, 17–24.

Capron, D. W., Blumenthal, H., Medley, A. N., Lewis, S., Feldner, M. T., Zvolensky, M. J., & Schmidt, N. B. (2012). Anxiety sensitivity cognitive concerns predict suicidality among smokers. *Journal of Affective Disorders*, *138*(3), 239–246.

Capron, D. W., Cougle, J. R., Ribeiro, J. D., Joiner, T. E., & Schmidt, N. B. (2012). An interactive model of anxiety sensitivity relevant to suicide attempt history and future suicidal ideation. *Journal of Psychiatric Research*, *46*(2), 174–180.

Capron, D. W., Fitch, K., Medley, A., Blagg, C., Mallott, M., & Joiner, T. E. (2012). Role of anxiety sensitivity subfactors in suicidal ideation and suicide attempt history. *Depression and Anxiety*, *29*(3), 195–201.

Capron, D. W., Lamis, D. A., & Schmidt, N. B. (2014). Test of the depression distress amplification model in young adults with elevated risk of current suicidality. *Psychiatry Research*, *219*(3), 531–535.

Capron, D. W., Norr, A. M., Macatee, R. J., & Schmidt, N. B. (2013). Distress tolerance and anxiety sensitivity cognitive concerns: Testing the incremental contributions of affect dysregulation constructs on suicidal ideation and suicide attempt. *Behavior Therapy*, *44*(3), 349–358.

Capron, D. W., Norr, A. M., Zvolensky, M. J., & Schmidt, N. B. (2014). Prospective evaluation of the effect of an anxiety sensitivity intervention on suicidality among smokers. *Cognitive Behaviour Therapy*, *43*(1), 72–82.

Cavanagh, J. T., Carson, A. J., Sharpe, M., & Lawrie, S. M. (2003). Psychological autopsy studies of suicide: A systematic review. *Psychological Medicine, 33*(3), 395–405.

Centers for Disease Control and Prevention (CDC). (2017). *WISQARS: Web-Based Injury Statistics Query and Reporting System.* Retrieved from www.cdc.gov/injury/wis qars/index.html.

Cerel, J., Jordan, J. R., & Duberstein, P. R. (2008). The impact of suicide on the family. *Crisis, 29*(1), 38–44.

Chandley, R. B., Luebbe, A. M., Messman-Moore, T. L., & Ward, R. M. (2014). Anxiety sensitivity, coping motives, emotion dysregulation, and alcohol-related outcomes in college women: A moderated-mediation model. *Journal of Studies on Alcohol and Drugs, 75*(1), 83–92. https://doi.org/10.15288/JSAD.2014.75.83

Chechik, G., Meilijson, I., & Ruppin, E. (1998). Synaptic pruning in development: A computational account. *Neural Computation, 10*(7), 1759–1777.

Chowdhury, N., Kevorkian, S., Sheerin, C. M., Zvolensky, M. J., & Berenz, E. C. (2016). Examination of the association among personality traits, anxiety sensitivity, and cannabis use motives in a community sample. *Journal of Psychopathology and Behavioral Assessment, 38*(3), 373–380. https://doi.org/10.1007/s10862-015-9526-6

Collimore, K. C. & Asmundson, G. J. (2014). Fearful responding to interoceptive exposure in social anxiety disorder. *Journal of Anxiety Disorders, 28*(2), 195–202.

Comeau, N., Stewart, S. H., & Loba, P. (2001). The relations of trait anxiety, anxiety sensitivity, and sensation seeking to adolescents' motivations for alcohol, cigarette, and marijuana use. *Addictive Behaviors, 26*(6), 803–825. https://doi.org/10.1016/S0306-4603(01)00238-6

Cooper, M. L., Russell, M., Skinner, J. B., & Windle, M. (1992). Development and validation of a three-dimensional measure of drinking motives. *Psychological Assessment, 4*(2), 123–132. https://doi.org/10.1037/1040–3590.4.2.123

Cougle, J. R., Keough, M. E., Riccardi, C. J., & Sachs-Ericsson, N. (2009). Anxiety disorders and suicidality in the National Comorbidity Survey-Replication. *Journal of Psychiatric Research, 43*(9), 825–829.

Cox, B. J., Borger, S. C., & Enns, M. W. (1999). Anxiety sensitivity and emotional disorders: Psychometric studies and their theoretical implications. In S. Taylor (ed.), *Anxiety Sensitivity: Theory, Research, and Treatment of the Fear of Anxiety* (pp. 115–148). The LEA Series in Personality and Clinical Psychology. Mahwah, NJ: Lawrence Erlbaum Associates.

Cox, B. J., Swinson, R. P., Shulman, I. D., Kuch, K., & Reichman, J. T. (1993). Gender effects and alcohol use in panic disorder with agoraphobia. *Behaviour Research and Therapy, 31*(4), 413–416.

Critchley, H. D. (2005). Neural mechanisms of autonomic, affective, and cognitive integration. *Journal of Comparative Neurology, 493*(1), 154–166.

Cuthbert, B. N. & Insel, T. R. (2013). Toward the future of psychiatric diagnosis: The seven pillars of RDoC. *BMC Medicine, 11*(1), 126.

DeMartini, K. S. & Carey, K. B. (2011). The role of anxiety sensitivity and drinking motives in predicting alcohol use: A critical review. *Clinical Psychology Review, 31*(1), 169–177. https://doi.org/10.1016/j.cpr.2010.10.001

Elwood, L. S., Hahn, K. S., Olatunji, B. O., & Williams, N. L. (2009). Cognitive vulnerabilities to the development of PTSD: A review of four vulnerabilities and the proposal of an integrative vulnerability model. *Clinical Psychology Review*, *29*(1), 87–100. doi: 10.1016/j.cpr.2008.10.002

Farris, S. G., Zvolensky, M. J., & Schmidt, N. B. (2015). Difficulties with emotion regulation and psychopathology interact to predict early smoking cessation lapse. *Cognitive Therapy and Research*, 1–11. doi: 10.1007/s10608-015-9705-5

Foa, E. B., Hembree, E., & Rothbaum, B. O. (2007). *Prolonged Exposure Therapy for PTSD: Emotional Processing of Traumatic Experiences Therapist Guide*. Oxford: Oxford University Press.

Francis, S. E. (2014). The role of parental anxiety sensitivity in parent reports of child anxiety in treatment seeking families. *Clinical Child Psychology and Psychiatry*, *19*(1), 111–124.

Franklin, J. C., Ribeiro, J. D., Fox, K. R., Bentley, K. H., Kleiman, E. M., Huang, X., . . . Nock, M. K. (2017). Risk factors for suicidal thoughts and behaviors: A meta-analysis of 50 years of research. *Psychological Bulletin*, *143*(2), 187.

Gallagher, M. W., Payne, L. A., White, K. S., Shear, K. M., Woods, S. W., Gorman, J. M., & Barlow, D. H. (2013). Mechanisms of change in cognitive behavioral therapy for panic disorder: The unique effects of self-efficacy and anxiety sensitivity. *Behaviour Research and Therapy*, *51*(11), 767–777.

Garfinkel, S. N. & Liberzon, I. (2009). Neurobiology of PTSD: A review of neuroimaging findings. *Psychiatric Annals*, *39*(6), 370.

Gillihan, S. J., Farris, S. G., & Foa, E. B. (2011). The effect of anxiety sensitivity on alcohol consumption among individuals with comorbid alcohol dependence and posttraumatic stress disorder. *Psychology of Addictive Behaviors*, *25*(4), 721.

Glenn, C. R., Cha, C. B., Kleiman, E. M., & Nock, M. K. (2017). Understanding suicide risk within the Research Domain Criteria (RDoC) framework: Insights, challenges, and future research considerations. *Clinical Psychological Science*, *5*(3), 568–592. https://doi.org/10.1177/2167702616686854

Grant, D. M., Beck, J. G., & Davila, J. (2007). Does anxiety sensitivity predict symptoms of panic, depression, and social anxiety? *Behaviour Research and Therapy*, *45*(9), 2247–2255. https://doi.org/10.1016/j.brat.2007.02.008

Gutner, C. A., Nillni, Y. I., Suvak, M., Wiltsey-Stirman, S., & Resick, P. A. (2013). Longitudinal course of anxiety sensitivity and PTSD symptoms in cognitive-behavioral therapies for PTSD. *Journal of Anxiety Disorders*, *27*(7), 728–734.

Harris, E. C. & Barraclough, B. (1997). Suicide as an outcome for mental disorders: A meta-analysis. *British Journal of Psychiatry*, *170*(3), 205–228.

Harvey, A. G. (2011). Sleep and circadian functioning: Critical mechanisms in the mood disorders? *Annual Review of Clinical Psychology*, *7*, 297–319.

Hendriks, S. M., Licht, C. M., Spijker, J., Beekman, A. T., Hardeveld, F., de Graaf, R., & Penninx, B. W. (2014). Disorder-specific cognitive profiles in major depressive disorder and generalized anxiety disorder. *BMC Psychiatry*, *14*(1), 96.

Hoge, E. A., Marques, L., Wechsler, R. S., Lasky, A. K., Delong, H. R., Jacoby, R. J., & Worthington, J. J. (2011). The role of anxiety sensitivity in sleep disturbance in panic disorder. *Journal of Anxiety Disorders*, *25*, 536–538.

Holmes, E. A. & Bourne, C. (2008). Inducing and modulating intrusive emotional memories: A review of the trauma film paradigm. *Acta Psychologica*, *127*(3), 553–566.

Holtz, K., Pané-Farré, C. A., Wendt, J., Lotze, M., & Hamm, A. O. (2012). Brain activation during anticipation of interoceptive threat. *Neuroimage*, *61*(4), 857–865.

Horowitz, M. J. (1986). Stress-response syndromes: A review of posttraumatic and adjustment disorders. *Psychiatric Services*, *37*(3), 241–249.

Huttenlocher, P. R. & Dabholkar, A. S. (1997). Regional differences in synaptogenesis in human cerebral cortex. *Journal of Comparative Neurology*, *387*(2), 167–178.

Insel, T., Cuthbert, B., Garvey, M., Heinssen, R., Pine, D. S., Quinn, K., . . . Wang, P. (2010). *Research Domain Criteria (RDoC): Toward a New Classification Framework for Research on Mental Disorders* Washington, DC: American Psychiatric Association.

Johnson, K., Mullin, J. L., Marshall, E. C., & Bonn-miller, M. O. (2011). *NIH Public Access*, *19*(3), 277–282. https://doi.org/10.1111/j.1521–0391.2010.00041.x.Exploring

Joiner, T. E. (2005). *Why People Die by Suicide*. Cambridge, MA: Harvard University Press.

Jurk, S., Kuitunen-Paul, S., Kroemer, N. B., Artiges, E., Banaschewski, T., Bokde, A. L. W., . . . Smolka, M. N. (2015). Personality and substance use: Psychometric evaluation and validation of the Substance Use Risk Profile Scale (SURPS) in English, Irish, French, and German Adolescents. *Alcoholism: Clinical and Experimental Research*, *39*(11), 2234–2248. https://doi.org/10.1111/acer.12886

Kang, E.-H., Kim, B., Choe, A. Y., Lee, J.-Y., Choi, T. K., & Lee, S.-H. (2015). Panic disorder and health-related quality of life: The predictive roles of anxiety sensitivity and trait anxiety. *Psychiatry Research*, *225*(1), 157–163.

Kaufman, J. & Charney, D. (2000). Comorbidity of mood and anxiety disorders. *Depression and Anxiety*, *12*(S1), 69–76.

Kemper, C. J., Lutz, J., Bähr, T., Rüddel, H., & Hock, M. (2012). Construct validity of the anxiety sensitivity index–3 in clinical samples. *Assessment*, *19*(1), 89–100.

Keough, M. E. & Schmidt, N. B. (2012). Refinement of a brief anxiety sensitivity reduction intervention. *Journal of Consulting and Clinical Psychology*, *80*(5), 766–772.

Kessler, R. C., Berglund, P., Delmer, O., Jin, R., Merikangas, K. R., & Walters, E. E. (2005). Lifetime prevalence and age-of-onset distributions of DSM-IV disorders in the National Comorbidity Survey Replication. *Archives of General Psychiatry*, *62*(6), 593–602.

Killgore, W. D., Britton, J. C., Price, L. M., Gold, A. L., Deckersbach, T., & Rauch, S. L. (2011). Neural correlates of anxiety sensitivity during masked presentation of affective faces. *Depression and Anxiety*, *28*(3), 243–249.

Klauke, B., Deckert, J., Reif, A., Pauli, P., Zwanzger, P., Baumann, C., . . . Domschke, K. (2011). Serotonin transporter gene and childhood trauma: A G× E effect on anxiety sensitivity. *Depression and Anxiety*, *28*(12), 1048–1057.

Klonsky, E. D. & May, A. M. (2014). Differentiating suicide attempters from suicide ideators: A critical frontier for suicidology research. *Suicide and Life-Threatening Behavior*, *44*(1), 1–5. https://doi.org/10.1111/sltb.12068

Klonsky, E. D., May, A. M., & Saffer, B. Y. (2016). Suicide, suicide attempts, and suicidal ideation. *Annual Review of Clinical Psychology*, *12*, 307–330.

Kraemer, H. C., Kazdin, A. E., Offord, D. R., Kessler, R. C., Jensen, P. S., & Kupfer, D. J. (1997). Coming to terms with the terms of risk. *Archives of General Psychiatry*, *54*(4), 337–343. doi: 10.1001/archpsyc.1997.01830160065009

Kraemer, K. M., Luberto, C. M., & McLeish, A. C. (2013). The moderating role of distress tolerance in the association between anxiety sensitivity physical concerns and panic and PTSD-related re-experiencing symptoms. *Anxiety, Stress & Coping, 26* (3), 330–342.

Krueger, R. F. (1999). The structure of common mental disorders. *Archives of General Psychiatry, 56*(10), 921–926. doi: 10.1001/archpsyc.56.10.921

Kugler, B. B., Phares, V., Salloum, A., & Storch, E. A. (2016). The role of anxiety sensitivity in the relationship between posttraumatic stress symptoms and negative outcomes in trauma-exposed adults. *Anxiety, Stress, & Coping, 29*(2), 187–201.

Kushner, M. G., Mackenzie, T. B., Fiszdon, J., Valentiner, D. P., Foa, E., Anderson, N., & Wangensteen, D. (1996). The effects of alcohol consumption on laboratory-induced panic and state anxiety. *Archives of General Psychiatry, 53* (3), 264.

Lebowitz, E. R., Shic, F., Campbell, D., Basile, K., & Silverman, W. K. (2015). Anxiety sensitivity moderates behavioral avoidance in anxious youth. *Behaviour Research and Therapy, 74*, 11–17.

Lechner, W. V., Shadur, J. M., Banducci, A. N., Grant, D. M., Morse, M., & Lejuez, C. W. (2014). The mediating role of depression in the relationship between anxiety sensitivity and alcohol dependence. *Addictive Behaviors, 39*(8), 1243–1248. https://doi.org/10.1016/j.addbeh.2014.04.002

Lejuez, C. W., Paulson, A., Daughters, S. B., Bornovalova, M. A., & Zvolensky, M. J. (2006). The association between heroin use and anxiety sensitivity among inner-city individuals in residential drug use treatment. *Behaviour Research and Therapy, 44*(5), 667–677. https://doi.org/10.1016/j.brat.2005.04.006

Lejuez, C. W., Zvolensky, M. J., Daughters, S. B., Bornovalova, M. A., Paulson, A., Tull, M. T., . . . Otto, M. W. (2008). Anxiety sensitivity: A unique predictor of dropout among inner-city heroin and crack/cocaine users in residential substance use treatment. *Behaviour Research and Therapy, 46*(7), 811–818. https://doi.org /10.1016/j.brat.2008.03.010

Lies, J., Lau, S. T., Jones, L. E., Jensen, M. P., & Tan, G. (2017). Predictors and moderators of posttraumatic stress disorder: An investigation of anxiety sensitivity and resilience in individuals with chronic pain. *Annals of the Academy of Medicine, Singapore, 46*(3), 102.

Loxton, N. J., Bunker, R. J., Dingle, G. A., & Wong, V. (2015). Drinking not thinking: A prospective study of personality traits and drinking motives on alcohol consumption across the first year of university. *Personality and Individual Differences, 79*, 134–139. https://doi.org/10.1016/j.paid.2015.02.010

Mackie, C. J., Castellanos-Ryan, N., & Conrod, P. J. (2011). Personality moderates the longitudinal relationship between psychological symptoms and alcohol use in adolescents. *Alcoholism: Clinical and Experimental Research, 35*(4), 703–716. https://doi.org/10.1111/j.1530–0277.2010.01388.x

Mahaffey, B. L., Gonzalez, A., Farris, S. G., Zvolensky, M. J., Bromet, E. J., Luft, B. J., & Kotov, R. (2017). Understanding the connection between posttraumatic stress symptoms and respiratory problems: Contributions of anxiety sensitivity. *Journal of Traumatic Stress, 30*(1), 71–79.

Marshall, G. N., Miles, J. N., & Stewart, S. H. (2010). Anxiety sensitivity and PTSD symptom severity are reciprocally related: Evidence from a longitudinal study of physical trauma survivors. *Journal of Abnormal Psychology, 119*(1), 143–150.

Martin, C. S., Steinley, D. L., Vergés, A., & Sher, K. J. (2011). Letter to the editor: The proposed 2/11 symptom algorithm for DSM-5 substance-use disorders is too lenient. *Psychological Medicine, 41*(9), 2008–2010. doi: 10.1017/ S0033291711000717.Letter.

McCaul, M. E., Hutton, H. E., Stephens, M. A. C., Xu, X., & Wand, G. S. (2017). Anxiety, anxiety sensitivity, and perceived stress as predictors of recent drinking, alcohol craving, and social stress response in heavy drinkers. *Alcoholism: Clinical and Experimental Research, 41*(4), 836–845. https://doi.org/10.1111/acer.13350

McHugh, R. K., Daughters, S. B., Lejuez, C. W., Murray, H. W., Hearon, B. A., Gorka, S. M., & Otto, M. W. (2010). Shared variance among self-report and behavioral measures of distress intolerance. *Cognitive Therapy and Research, 35*, 266–275. doi: 10.1007/s10608-010–9295-1

McNally, R. J. (2002). Anxiety sensitivity and panic disorder. *Biological Psychiatry, 52*(10), 938–946.

McNally, R. J. & Eke, M. (1996). Anxiety sensitivity, suffocation fear, and breath-holding duration as predictors of response to carbon dioxide challenge. *Journal of Abnormal Psychology, 105*(1), 146–153.

McNally, R. J. & Lorenz, M. (1987). Anxiety sensitivity in agoraphobics. *Journal of Behavior Therapy and Experimental Psychology, 18*, 3–11.

McNeil, D. W. & Rainwater, A. J. (1998). Development of the fear of pain questionnaire-III. *Journal of Behavioral Medicine, 21*(4), 389–410.

Menon, V. (2015). Salience network. *Brain Mapping: An Encyclopedic Reference, 2*, 597–611.

Mitchell, M. A., Capron, D. W., Raines, A. M., & Schmidt, N. B. (2014). Reduction of cognitive concerns of anxiety sensitivity is uniquely associated with reduction of PTSD and depressive symptoms: A comparison of civilians and veterans. *Journal of Psychiatric Research, 48*(1), 25–31.

Naifeh, J. A., Tull, M. T., & Gratz, K. L. (2012). Anxiety sensitivity, emotional avoidance, and PTSD symptom severity among crack/cocaine dependent patients in residential treatment. *Cognitive Therapy and Research, 36*(3), 247–257.

Naqvi, N. H. & Bechara, A. (2010). The insula and drug addiction: An interoceptive view of pleasure, urges, and decision-making. *Brain Structure and Function, 214*(5–6), 435–450.

Naragon-Gainey, K. (2010). Meta-analysis of the relations of anxiety sensitivity to the depressive and anxiety disorders. *Psychological Bulletin, 136*(1), 128.

Nillni, Y. I., Pineles, S. L., Rohan, K. J., Zvolensky, M. J., & Rasmusson, A. M. (2017). The influence of the menstrual cycle on reactivity to a CO_2 challenge among women with and without premenstrual symptoms. *Cognitive Behaviour Therapy, 46*(3), 239–249.

Nock, M. K., Deming, C. A., Fullerton, C. S., Gilman, S. E., Goldenberg, M., Kessler, R. C., . . . Ursano, R. J. (2013). Suicide among soldiers: A review of psychosocial risk and protective factors. *Psychiatry: Interpersonal and Biological Processes, 76*(2), 97–125. https://doi.org/10.1521/psyc.2013.76.2.97

Nock, M. K., Hwang, I., Sampson, N., Kessler, R. C., Angermeyer, M., Beautrais, A., . . . De Girolamo, G. (2009). Cross-national analysis of the associations among mental disorders and suicidal behavior: Findings from the WHO World Mental Health Surveys. *PLoS Medicine, 6*(8), e1000123.

Nock, M. K., Kessler, R. C., & Franklin, J. C. (2016). Risk factors for suicide ideation differ from those for the transition to suicide attempt: The importance of creativity, rigor, and urgency in suicide research. *Clinical Psychology: Science and Practice, 23* (1), 31–34. https://doi.org/10.1111/cpsp.12133

Noël, V. A. & Francis, S. E. (2011). A meta-analytic review of the role of child anxiety sensitivity in child anxiety. *Journal of Abnormal Child Psychology, 39*(5), 721–733.

Nolen-Hoeksema, S. (1987). Sex differences in unipolar depression: Evidence and theory. *Psychological Bulletin, 101*(2), 259.

Norr, A. M., Albanese, B. J., Allan, N. P., & Schmidt, N. B. (2015). Anxiety sensitivity as a mechanism for gender discrepancies in anxiety and mood symptoms. *Journal of Psychiatric Research, 62,* 101–107.

Norr, A. M., Allan, N. P., Macatee, R. J., Capron, D. W., & Schmidt, N. B. (2016). The role of anxiety sensitivity cognitive concerns in suicidal ideation: A test of the Depression-Distress Amplification Model in clinical outpatients. *Psychiatry Research, 238,* 74–80.

Norton, G. R., Rockman, G. E., Ediger, J., Pepe, C., Goldberg, S., Cox, B. J., & Asmundson, G. J. G. (1997). Anxiety sensitivity and drug choice in individuals seeking treatment for substance abuse. *Behaviour Research and Therapy, 35*(9), 859–862. https://doi.org/10.1016/S0005-7967(97)00037-5

Novak, A., Burgess, E. S., Clark, M., Zvolensky, M. J., & Brown, R. A. (2003). Anxiety sensitivity, self-reported motives for alcohol and nicotine use, and level of consumption. *Journal of Anxiety Disorders, 17*(2), 165–180. https://doi.org/10.1016/S0887-6185(02)00175-5

Ochsner, K. N., Ludlow, D. H., Knierim, K., Hanelin, J., Ramachandran, T., Glover, G. C., & Mackey, S. C. (2006). Neural correlates of individual differences in pain-related fear and anxiety. *Pain, 120*(1), 69–77.

Oglesby, M. E., Capron, D. W., Raines, A. M., & Schmidt, N. B. (2015). Anxiety sensitivity cognitive concerns predict suicide risk. *Psychiatry Research, 226*(1), 252–256.

Olatunji, B. & Wolitzky-Taylor, K. B. (2009). Anxiety sensitivity and the anxiety disorders: A meta-analytic review and synthesis. *Psychological Bulletin, 135*(6), 974–999. doi: 10.1037/a0017428

Olatunji, B. O. & Fan, Q. (2015). Anxiety sensitivity and posttraumatic stress reactions: Evidence for intrusions and physiological arousal as mediating and moderating mechanisms. *Journal of Anxiety Disorders, 34,* 76–85.

Olthuis, J. V., Watt, M. C., Mackinnon, S. P., & Stewart, S. H. (2014). Telephone-delivered cognitive behavioral therapy for high anxiety sensitivity: A randomized controlled trial. *Journal of Consulting and Clinical Psychology, 82*(6), 1005.

Olthuis, J. V., Watt, M. C., Mackinnon, S. P., & Stewart, S. H. (2015). CBT for high anxiety sensitivity: Alcohol outcomes. *Addictive Behaviors, 46,* 19–24. https://doi.org/10.1016/j.addbeh.2015.02.018

Olthuis, J. V., Watt, M. C., & Stewart, S. H. (2014). Anxiety Sensitivity Index (ASI-3) subscales predict unique variance in anxiety and depressive symptoms. *Journal of Anxiety Disorders, 28*(2), 115–124. https://doi.org/10.1016/j.janxdis.2013.04.009

Ong, J. C., Kuo, T. F., & Manber, R. (2008). Who is at risk for dropout from group cognitive-behavior therapy for insomnia? *Journal of Psychosomatic Research, 64*(4), 419–425.

Oquendo, M. A., Currier, D., & Mann, J. J. (2006). Prospective studies of suicidal behavior in major depressive and bipolar disorders: What is the evidence for predictive risk factors?. *Acta Psychiatrica Scandinavica*, *114*(3), 151–158.

Paulus, M. P. & Stein, M. B. (2006). An insular view of anxiety. *Biological Psychiatry*, *60*(4), 383–387.

Paulus, D. J., Valadka, J., Businelle, M. S., Gallagher, M. W., Viana, A. G., Schmidt, N. B., & Zvolensky, M. J. (2017). Emotion dysregulation explains associations between anxiety sensitivity and hazardous drinking and drinking motives among adult treatment-seeking smokers. *Psychology of Addictive Behaviors*, *31*(2), 189–199. https://doi.org/10.1037/adb0000252

Paulus, D. J., Vujanovic, A. A., & Wardle, M. C. (2016). Anxiety sensitivity and alcohol use among acute-care psychiatric inpatients: The mediating role of emotion regulation difficulties. *Cognitive Therapy and Research*, *40*(6), 813–823. https://doi.org/10.1007/s10608-016–9792-y

Piscopo, K., Lipari, R., Cooney, J., & Glasheen, C. (2016). Suicidal thoughts and behavior among adults: Results from the 2015 National Survey on Drug Use and Health. NSDUH Data Review.

Poletti, S., Radaelli, D., Cucchi, M., Ricci, L., Vai, B., Smeraldi, E., & Benedetti, F. (2015). Neural correlates of anxiety sensitivity in panic disorder: A functional magnetic resonance imaging study. *Psychiatry Research: Neuroimaging*, *233*(2), 95–101.

Poli, A., Melli, G., Ghisi, M., Bottesi, G., & Sica, C. (2017). Anxiety sensitivity and obsessive-compulsive symptom dimensions: Further evidence of specific relationships in a clinical sample. *Personality and Individual Differences*, *109*, 130–136.

Raines, A. M., Capron, D. W., Bontempo, A. C., Dane, B. F., & Schmidt, N. B. (2014). Obsessive compulsive symptom dimensions and suicide: The moderating role of anxiety sensitivity cognitive concerns. *Cognitive Therapy and Research*, *38*(6), 660–669.

Raines, A. M., Capron, D. W., Stentz, L. A., Walton, J. L., Allan, N. P., McManus, E. S., ... Franklin, C. L. (2017). Posttraumatic stress disorder and suicidal ideation, plans, and impulses: The mediating role of anxiety sensitivity cognitive concerns among veterans. *Journal of Affective Disorders*, *222*, 57–62.

Raines, A. M., Walton, J. L., McManus, E. S., Cuccurullo, L.-A. J., Chambliss, J., Uddo, M., & Franklin, C. L. (2017). Associations between lower order anxiety sensitivity dimensions and DSM-5 posttraumatic stress disorder symptoms. *Cognitive Behaviour Therapy*, *46*(2), 162–173.

Rector, N. A., Szacun-Shimizu, K., & Leybman, M. (2007). Anxiety sensitivity within the anxiety disorders: Disorder-specific sensitivities and depression comorbidity. *Behaviour Research and Therapy*, *45*(8), 1967–1975.

Reiss, S. & McNally, R. (1985). Expectancy model of fear. In S. Reiss & R. R. Bootzin (eds.), *Theoretical Issues in Behavior Therapy* (pp. 107–121). San Diego, CA: Academic Press.

Reiss, S., Peterson, R. A., Gursky, D. M., & McNally, R. J. (1986). Anxiety sensitivity, anxiety frequency and the prediction of fearfulness. *Behavior Research and Therapy*, *24*(1), 1–8.

Robinson, L. J. & Freeston, M. H. (2014). Emotion and internal experience in obsessive compulsive disorder: Reviewing the role of alexithymia, anxiety sensitivity and distress tolerance. *Clinical Psychology Review*, *34*(3), 256–271.

Rogers, M. L., Tucker, R. P., Law, K. C., Michaels, M. S., Anestis, M. D., & Joiner, T. E. (2016). Manifestations of overarousal account for the association between cognitive anxiety sensitivity and suicidal ideation. *Journal of Affective Disorders, 192*, 116–124.

Rosso, I. M., Makris, N., Britton, J. C., Price, L. M., Gold, A. L., Zai, D., . . . & Rauch, S. L. (2010). Anxiety sensitivity correlates with two indices of right anterior insula structure in specific animal phobia. *Depression and Anxiety, 27*(12), 1104–1110.

Sandin, B., Sánchez-Arribas, C., Chorot, P., & Valiente, R. M. (2015). Anxiety sensitivity, catastrophic misinterpretations and panic self-efficacy in the prediction of panic disorder severity: Towards a tripartite cognitive model of panic disorder. *Behaviour Research and Therapy, 67*, 30–40.

Schmidt, N. B., Capron, D. W., Raines, A. M., & Allan, N. P. (2014). Randomized clinical trial evaluating the efficacy of a brief intervention targeting anxiety sensitivity cognitive concerns. *Journal of Consulting and Clinical Psychology, 82*(6), 1023–1033.

Schmidt, N. B., Eggleston, A. M., Woolaway-Bickel, K., Fitzpatrick, K. K., Vasey, M. W., & Richey, J. A. (2007). Anxiety Sensitivity Amelioration Training (ASAT): A longitudinal primary prevention program targeting cognitive vulnerability. *Journal of Anxiety Disorders, 21*(3), 302–319.

Schmidt, N. B., Lerew, D. R., & Jackson, R. J. (1997). The role of anxiety sensitivity in the pathogenesis of Panic: prospective evaluation of spontaneous panic attacks during acute stress. *Journal of Abnormal Psychology, 106*(3), 355.

Schmidt, N. B., Norr, A. M., Allan, N. P., Raines, A. M., & Capron, D. W. (2017). A randomized clinical trial targeting anxiety sensitivity for patients with suicidal ideation. *Journal of Consulting and Clinical Psychology, 85*(6), 596.

Schmidt, N. B., Raines, A. M., Allan, N. P., & Zvolensky, M. J. (2016). Anxiety sensitivity risk reduction in smokers: A randomized control trial examining effects on panic. *Behaviour Research and Therapy, 77*, 138–146.

Schmidt, N. B., Woolaway-Bickel, K., & Bates, M. (2001). Evaluating panic-specific factors in the relationship between suicide and panic disorder. *Behaviour Research and Therapy, 39*(6), 635–649.

Selby, E. A., Joiner, T. E., & Ribeiro, J. D. (2014). Comprehensive theories of suicidal behaviors. In M. K. Nock (ed.), *The Oxford Handbook of Suicide and Self-Injury.* (pp. 286–307). New York, NY: Oxford University Press.

Shneidman, E. S. (1993). Suicide as psychache. *Journal of Nervous and Mental Disease, 181*(3), 145–147.

Short, N. A., Allan, N. P., Raines, A. M., & Schmidt, N. B. (2015). The effects of an anxiety sensitivity intervention on insomnia symptoms. *Sleep Medicine, 16*(1), 152–159.

Short, N. A., Boffa, J. W., Norr, A. M., Albanese, B. J., Allan, N. P., & Schmidt, N. B. (2017). Randomized clinical trial investigating the effects of an anxiety sensitivity intervention on posttraumatic stress symptoms: A replication and extension. *Journal of Traumatic Stress, 30*(3), 296–303.

Short, N. A., Fuller, K., Norr, A. M., & Schmidt, N. B. (2017). Acceptability of a brief computerized intervention targeting anxiety sensitivity. *Cognitive Behaviour Therapy, 46*(3), 250–264.

Simon, N. M., Otto, M. W., Fischmann, D., Racette, S., Nierenberg, A. A., Pollack, M. H., & Smoller, J. W. (2005). Panic disorder and bipolar disorder: Anxiety sensitivity as a potential mediator of panic during manic states. *Journal of Affective Disorders, 87*(1), 101–105.

Simon, N. M., Pollack, M. H., Ostacher, M. J., Zalta, A. K., Chow, C. W., Fischmann, D., ... Otto, M. W. (2007). Understanding the link between anxiety symptoms and suicidal ideation and behaviors in outpatients with bipolar disorder. *Journal of Affective Disorders*, *97*(1), 91–99.

Simon, N. M., Smoller, J. W., Fava, M., Sachs, G., Racette, S. R., Perlis, R., ... Rosenbaum, J. F. (2003). Comparing anxiety disorders and anxiety-related traits in bipolar disorder and unipolar depression. *Journal of Psychiatric Research*, *37*(3), 187–192.

Simpson, T., Jakupcak, M., & Luterek, J. A. (2006). Fear and avoidance of internal experiences among patients with substance use disorders and PTSD: The centrality of anxiety sensitivity. *Journal of Traumatic Stress*, *19*(4), 481–491. https://doi.org/10.1002/jts.20128

Sippel, L. M., Jones, R. E., Bordieri, M. J., Dixon, L. J., May, A. C., Malkin, M. L., ... Coffey, S. F. (2015). Interactive effects of anxiety sensitivity and difficulties in emotion regulation: An examination among individuals in residential substance use treatment with comorbid posttraumatic stress disorder. *Cognitive Therapy and Research*, *39*(2), 245–252.

Smits, J. A., Berry, A. C., Tart, C. D., & Powers, M. B. (2008). The efficacy of cognitive-behavioral interventions for reducing anxiety sensitivity: A meta-analytic review. *Behaviour Research and Therapy*, *46*(9), 1047–1054.

Spinhoven, P., Batelaan, N., Rhebergen, D., van Balkom, A., Schoevers, R., & Penninx, B. W. (2016). Prediction of 6-yr symptom course trajectories of anxiety disorders by diagnostic, clinical and psychological variables. *Journal of Anxiety Disorders*, *44*, 92–101.

Stanley, I. H., Hom, M. A., & Joiner, T. E. (2016). A systematic review of suicidal thoughts and behaviors among police officers, firefighters, EMTs, and paramedics. *Clinical Psychology Review*, *44*, 25–44. https://doi.org/10.1016/j.cpr.2015.12.002

Stanley, I. H., Hom, M. A., Spencer-Thomas, S., & Joiner, T. E. (2017). Examining anxiety sensitivity as a mediator of the association between PTSD symptoms and suicide risk among women firefighters. *Journal of Anxiety Disorders*, *50*, 94–102.

Stein, M. B., Simmons, A. N., Feinstein, J. S., & Paulus, M. P. (2007). Increased amygdala and insula activation during emotion processing in anxiety-prone subjects. *American Journal of Psychiatry*, *164*(2), 318–327.

Stewart, S. H., Karp, J., Pihl, R. O., & Peterson, R. A. (1997). Anxiety sensitivity and self-reported reasons for drug use. *Journal of Substance Abuse*, *9*(1), 223–240. https://doi.org/10.1016/S0899-3289(97)90018-3

Stewart, S. H. & Pihl, R. O. (1994). Effects of alcohol administration on psychophysiological and subjective-emotional responses to aversive stimulation in anxiety-sensitive women. *Psychology of Addictive Behaviors*, *8*, 29–42.

Stewart, S. H., Samoluk, S. B., & MacDonald, A. B. (1999). Anxiety sensitivity and substance use and abuse. In S. Taylor (ed.), *Anxiety Sensitivity: Theory, Research, and Treatment of Fear of Anxiety* (pp. 287–320). Mahwah, NJ: Lawrence Erlbaum Associates.

Stewart, S. H., & Zeitlin, S. B. (1995). Anxiety sensitivity and alcohol use motives. *Journal of Anxiety Disorders*, *9*(3), 229–240. https://doi.org/10.1016/0887–6185(95)00004–8

Stewart, S. H., Zvolensky, M. J., & Eifert, G. H. (2001). Negative-reinforcement drinking motives mediate the relation between anxiety sensitivity and increased drinking behavior. *Personality and Individual Differences, 31*(2), 157–171. https://doi.org /10.1016/S0191-8869(00)00213-0

Storch, E. A., Wu, M. S., Small, B. J., Crawford, E. A., Lewin, A. B., Horng, B., & Murphy, T. K. (2014). Mediators and moderators of functional impairment in adults with obsessive-compulsive disorder. *Comprehensive Psychiatry, 55*(3), 489–496.

Taylor, C. T., Hirshfeld-Becker, D. R., Ostacher, M. J., Chow, C. W., LeBeau, R. T., Pollack, M. H., . . . Simon, N. M. (2008). Anxiety is associated with impulsivity in bipolar disorder. *Journal of Anxiety Disorders, 22*(5), 868–876.

Taylor, S. (2014). *Anxiety Sensitivity: Theory, Research, and Treatment of the Fear of Anxiety*: New York, NY: Routledge.

Taylor, S., Koch, W. J., Woody, S., & McLean, P. (1996). Anxiety sensitivity and depression: How are they related? *Journal of Abnormal Psychology, 105*(3), 474–479. https:// doi.org/10.1037/0021-843X.105.3.474

Teale Sapach, M. J., Carleton, R. N., Mulvogue, M. K., Weeks, J. W., & Heimberg, R. G. (2015). Cognitive constructs and social anxiety disorder: Beyond fearing negative evaluation. *Cognitive Behaviour Therapy, 44*(1), 63–73.

Telch, M. J., Lucas, J. A., & Nelson, P. (1989). Nonclinical panic in college students: An investigation of prevalence and symptomatology. *Journal of Abnormal Psychology, 98*(3), 300–306.

Torres, L. & Mata-greve, F. (2016). Anxiety sensitivity as a predictor of Latino alcohol use: A moderated mediational model. *Journal of Latina/o Psychology, 5*(2), 61–75.

Tull, M. T., Barrett, H. M., McMillan, E. S., & Roemer, L. (2007). A preliminary investigation of the relationship between emotion regulation difficulties and posttraumatic stress symptoms. *Behavior Therapy, 38*(3), 303–313.

Van Orden, K. A., Witte, T. K., Cukrowicz, K. C., Braithwaite, S. R., Selby, E. A., & Joiner, T. E., Jr. (2010). The interpersonal theory of suicide. *Psychology Review, 117*(2), 575–600.

Viana, A. G., Paulus, D. J., Bakhshaie, J., Garza, M., Valdivieso, J., Ochoa-Perez, M., . . . Zvolensky, M. J. (2017). Emotional nonacceptance within the context of traumatic event exposure: The explanatory role of anxiety sensitivity for traumatic stress symptoms and disability among Latinos in a primary care setting. *General Hospital Psychiatry, 44*, 30–37.

Vujanovic, A. A., Bernstein, A., Berenz, E. C., & Zvolensky, M. J. (2012). Single-session anxiety sensitivity reduction program for trauma-exposed adults: A case series documenting feasibility and initial efficacy. *Behavior Therapy, 43*(3), 482–491.

Wald, J. & Taylor, S. (2007). Efficacy of interoceptive exposure therapy combined with trauma-related exposure therapy for posttraumatic stress disorder: A pilot study. *Journal of Anxiety Disorders, 21*(8), 1050–1060.

Wald, J. & Taylor, S. (2008). Responses to interoceptive exposure in people with posttraumatic stress disorder (PTSD): A preliminary analysis of induced anxiety reactions and trauma memories and their relationship to anxiety sensitivity and PTSD symptom severity. *Cognitive Behaviour Therapy, 37*(2), 90–100.

Waszczuk, M., Zavos, H., & Eley, T. (2013). Genetic and environmental influences on relationship between anxiety sensitivity and anxiety subscales in children. *Journal of Anxiety Disorders, 27*(5), 475–484.

Watt, M., Stewart, S., Birch, C., & Bernier, D. (2006). Brief CBT for high anxiety sensitivity decreases drinking problems, relief alcohol outcome expectancies, and conformity drinking motives: Evidence from a randomized controlled trial. *Journal of Mental Health*, *15*(6), 683–695. https://doi.org/10.1080/09638230600998938

Wheaton, M. G., Deacon, B. J., McGrath, P. B., Berman, N. C., & Abramowitz, J. S. (2012). Dimensions of anxiety sensitivity in the anxiety disorders: Evaluation of the ASI-3. *Journal of Anxiety Disorders*, *26*(3), 401–408.

Woicik, P. A., Stewart, S. H., Pihl, R. O., & Conrod, P. J. (2009). The substance use risk profile scale: A scale measuring traits linked to reinforcement-specific substance use profiles. *Addictive Behaviors*, *34*(12), 1042–1055. https://doi.org/10.1016/j.addbeh.2009.07.001

Worden, B. L., Davis, E., Genova, M., & Tolin, D. F. (2015). Development of an anxiety sensitivity (AS) intervention for high-AS individuals in substance use disorders treatment. *Cognitive Therapy and Research*, *39*(3), 343–355. https://doi.org/10.1007/s10608-014-9666-0

World Health Organization (WHO). (2002). Revised global burden of disease (GBD) 2002 estimates. *Estimates by WHO Region and Sub-region. Disability adjusted life years (DALY).*

Yang, Y., Lueken, U., Wittmann, A., Holtz, K., Kleint, N. I., Herrmann, M. J., . . . Straube, B. (2016). Neural correlates of individual differences in anxiety sensitivity: An fMRI study using semantic priming. *Social Cognitive and Affective Neuroscience*, *11*(8), 1245–1254. http://doi.org/10.1093/scan/nsw024

Zerach, G. & Magal, O. (2016). Anxiety sensitivity among first-time fathers moderates the relationship between exposure to stress during birth and posttraumatic stress symptoms. *Journal of Nervous and Mental Disease*, *204*(5), 381–387.

Zimmerman, M., Ellison, W., Young, D., Chelminski, I., & Dalrymple, K. (2015). How many different ways do patients meet the diagnostic criteria for major depressive disorder? *Comprehensive Psychiatry*, *56*, 29–34.

Zvielli, A., Bernstein, A., & Berenz, E. C. (2012). Exploration of a factor mixture-based taxonic-dimensional model of anxiety sensitivity and transdiagnostic psychopathology vulnerability among trauma-exposed adults. *Cognitive Behaviour Therapy*, *41*(1), 63–78.

Zvolensky, M. J., Bakhshaie, J., Garza, M., Paulus, D. J., Valdivieso, J., Lam, H., . . . Vujanovic, A. (2015). Anxiety sensitivity and mindful attention in terms of anxiety and depressive symptoms and disorders among Latinos in primary care. *Psychiatry Research*, *229*(1–2), 245–251.

Zvolensky, M. J., Bakhshaie, J., Garza, M., Valdivieso, J., Ortiz, M., Bogiaizian, D., . . . Vujanovic, A. (2015). The role of anxiety sensitivity in the relation between experiential avoidance and anxious arousal, depressive, and suicidal symptoms among Latinos in primary care. *Cognitive Therapy and Research*, 39(5), 688–669.

Zvolensky, M. J., Bakhshaie, J., Garza, M., Valdivieso, J., Ortiz, M., Bogiaizian, D., . . . Vujanovic, A. (2015). Anxiety sensitivity and subjective social status in relation to anxiety and depressive symptoms and disorders among Latinos in primary care. *Journal of Anxiety Disorders*, *32*, 38–45.

Zvolensky, M. J., Paulus, D. J., Bakhshaie, J., Garza, M., Ochoa-Perez, M., Medvedeva, A., . . . Schmidt, N. B. (2016). Interactive effect of negative affectivity and anxiety sensitivity in terms of mental health among Latinos in primary care. *Psychiatry Research*, *243*, 35–42.

6 Disgust Proneness

Kelly A. Knowles and Bunmi O. Olatunji

Wrinkling one's nose, furrowing one's brows, and turning away: these are easily recognizable signals that an individual is feeling disgusted. Disgust is a visceral emotion that occurs in a variety of situations, but at its center disgust serves to prevent contamination and the transmission of disease, especially through the oral route (Matchett & Davey, 1991; Rozin & Fallon, 1987). Therefore, at its most basic level, the experience of disgust informs what we eat and touch. Disgust in this domain is commonly referred to as *core disgust* and is elicited by stimuli such as rotting food, waste products, and small animals that may carry disease. However, disgust can be experienced in reaction to a variety of stimuli that are not avoided due to disease concerns. For example, *animal-reminder disgust* stimuli consist of those that remind us that we are no different from animals. Seeing exposed intestines and contact with a dead body or cremated ashes can evoke animal-reminder disgust, as they serve as reminders of human mortality. However, recent research does suggest that not all unpleasant animal reminders are disgusting. Some disgusting things may remind us of our animal nature, but they may not necessarily be disgusting because they do so (Kollareth & Russell, 2017). Contamination disgust focuses on the concern of contracting a disease, especially from another person; after all, can we be sure that the man handing out newspapers washed his hands after relieving himself? Each of these domains of disgust may have distinct personality, behavioral, and physiological correlates (Olatunji, Haidt, McKay, & David, 2008, but see van Overveld, de Jong, & Peters, 2009. for evidence of similar physiological responses across domains).

Other disgust domains, including interpersonal disgust and socio-moral disgust, are often referred to as *complex* types of disgusts due to their relationship with other negative emotions such as fear and anger and their theoretical distance from the disease-avoidance underpinnings of "primary" or core and animal-reminder disgust (Marzillier & Davey, 2004). Interpersonal disgust leads to the avoidance of other people, especially strangers, who may spread disease. For example, individuals with HIV/AIDS may be ostracized even though their illness cannot be spread by casual contact. Socio-moral disgust includes responses to immoral behavior, including deviations from sexual norms, but also less tangible concepts such as racism or hypocrisy. Although overt disease concerns are not evident in all situations that elicit disgust (Rozin, Haidt, & McCauley, 2008), the motivation to avoid does appear to be common across these situations.

Although disgust is universally experienced (Angyal, 1941; Curtis & Biran, 2001), there are cultural differences in what people find disgusting and how they react to disgusting situations. Despite the formal abolishment of the caste system in India, touching someone of a lower class is still considered taboo and has disgust-based overtones. Many Americans would be revolted by the idea of eating dog meat, but it is a perfectly ordinary food choice in some cultures. Individual differences in disgust reactions may also be readily observed. Indeed, preliminary evidence suggests that greater variability in disgust responses may be observed at the individual level compared to that which may be observed at the cultural level (Curtis, de Barra, & Aunger, 2011). For example, some individuals may be disgusted by the prospect of getting an injection or a dental cleaning, while others consider these normal health behaviors. One woman thinks nothing of having to change her child's diaper, while another couldn't bear to have children because she might have to come into close contact with feces and other body products that children readily produce. These individual differences in disgust experiences are referred to broadly as *disgust proneness*.

Although the developmental origins of disgust proneness have not been clearly delineated, the personality trait may emerge by interactions between various environmental factors, including social transmission during formative stages of development (Kim, Ebesutani, Young, & Olatunji, 2013; Rozin, Haidt, & McCauley, 2008). Socially acquired information shared by a particular culture may also contribute to variation in disgust proneness through social learning and prescribed group hygiene behavior (Curtis et al., 2011). Individual differences in disgust proneness may also be partly heritable. In an initial test of this assumption, Rozin and Millman (1987) examined the similarity of food contamination disgust proneness between identical and nonidentical twins. The findings showed that the correlation between identical twins' food contamination disgust was not significantly different from that of nonidentical twins. Although this initial study suggests that variability in disgust proneness does not have a strong genetic component, two important limitations of this study prevent such a conclusion. First, the study was conducted with fewer than 40 identical and nonidentical twin pairs. Contemporary statistical approaches would recommend a larger sample size for adequate power. Therefore, definitive conclusions cannot be made from these data regarding the relative magnitude of genetic and environmental effects from such a small sample size. Second, the assessment of individual differences in disgust was limited to contaminated foods, and therefore cannot be generalized to other disgust domains.

Recent research has attempted to more precisely delineate the genetic and environmental contributions to the development of disgust proneness. Sherlock, Zietsch, Tybur, and Jern (2016) recently estimated the proportion of variation due to genetic effects, the shared environment, and other (residual) sources across multiple domains (pathogen, sex, moral) of disgust proneness in a large sample of female identical and nonidentical twins ($N = 1,041$ individuals) and their siblings

($N = 170$). Twin modeling of these data revealed that approximately half of the variation in disgust proneness is due to genetic effects. Preliminary research has also begun to examine which specific genes may be implicated. For example, the dopamine receptor D4 (DRD4) and catechol-O-methyltransferase (COMT) genes have been associated with heightened disgust proneness (Kang, Kim, Namkoong, & An, 2010). These findings suggest that individual differences in disgust proneness may arise from the combination of genetics and environmental factors, including childhood socializing experiences where disgust responses are modeled excessively (Stevenson, Oaten, Case, Repacholi, & Wagland, 2010).

Measuring Disgust Proneness

Disgust proneness can be measured using a number of different methods. There are several validated self-report measures of disgust proneness, which can provide information about how an individual responds to disgust situations across a variety of domains of disgust. However, self-report measures can be affected by demand characteristics. Other objective measures of disgust proneness include measures of behavioral and physiological response. Additionally, implicit cognitive tasks can be useful to determine attitudes toward disgust. Finally, neuroimaging methods have revealed neural correlates of disgust proneness that may be useful in characterizing the biological origins of the personality trait. Each method is associated with different strengths and weaknesses, and using a combination of these methods produces a reliable assessment of individual differences in disgust proneness.

Self-Reports

The first self-report measure of trait disgust, the Disgust Questionnaire (DQ) (Rozin, Fallon, & Mandell, 1984), was created in an attempt to examine contamination sensitivity in relation to food. Participants are asked to imagine pleasurable food items, including a bowl of soup and a cookie, and then asked to imagine various scenarios that involve contamination in relation to those food items. Participants rate how likely they are to eat the food after various levels of contamination on a nine-point hedonic scale. For example, a participant might say that they would "dislike moderately (3/9)" to eat a bowl of soup that has been stirred with a washed but previously used fly swatter. The sum of the scores of all 24 items is used as a measure of disgust proneness. This scale has also been adapted for use in spider-fearful samples, in which participants are asked how much they would like to eat a candy bar after a spider has walked across the bar when wrapped and unwrapped (de Jong, Andrea, & Muris, 1997; de Jong, Vorage, & van den Hout, 2000). However, the DQ is limited in its applicability due to its exclusive focus on food items. With this in mind, additional questionnaires were developed to examine reactions to a broader range of disgust stimuli.

The Disgust Scale (DS) (Haidt, McCauley, & Rozin, 1994) was specifically created as a reliable measure of individual differences in disgust proneness across multiple domains of disgust elicitors. These domains were developed ad hoc by asking individuals to list disgusting experiences. The domains of disgust that were the most well-represented included disgust in reaction to certain foods, body products (i.e., feces), and sex (sexual behavior and immorality, such as incest or pedophilia). Another domain, body envelope violations, involved situations in which the normal exterior of the body is violated, such as gore or surgical procedures. The remaining domains consisted of disgusting animals (roaches, fleas), death (contact with dead bodies), and hygiene (dirt, germs). Finally, an eighth domain of sympathetic magic involved benign things that resemble disgusting objects (for example, candy shaped like dog feces). The DS includes 32 items with two different item formats: Personal Reactions assessing avoidance behavior and affective reactions (true/false) and Disgust Ratings ("not disgusting at all," "slightly disgusting," or "very disgusting"). The Disgust Scale has been validated through the use of behavioral tests, which found that scores on the scale were moderately correlated with avoidance behavior across a series of disgust tasks (Rozin, Haidt, McCauley, Dunlop, & Ashmore, 1999).

A thorough investigation of the factor structure and psychometric properties of the DS was conducted more than a decade later (Olatunji, Williams, Tolin et al., 2007). The authors suggested several items for removal due to poor factor loading, low item-to-scale correlations, extreme skew, and/or redundancy. Removing these items led to the Disgust-Scale-Revised (DS-R), a 25-item scale with a three-factor solution: Core Disgust, Animal-Reminder Disgust, and Contamination-Based Disgust. The authors also suggested revised scoring for these items; true-false questions are now rated on a scale from 0 (strongly disagree/very untrue about me) to 4 (strongly agree/very true about me), and the remaining questions ask respondents to rate how disgusting they would find the situations described from 0 (not disgusting at all) to 4 (extremely disgusting). The DS-R is now widely used in disgust research and has been validated in multiple countries with different cultural backgrounds (Olatunji et al., 2009). Recognizing the need for a disgust scale that could be used in children, Viar-Paxton and colleagues created the Child Disgust Scale (CDS) (Viar-Paxton et al., 2015). Items considered irrelevant or inappropriate for children were removed, and thematically similar but age-appropriate new items were added. A factor analysis of the items revealed a two-factor solution, labeled Disgust Avoidance and Disgust Affect. The CDS contains 14 items, has a lower reading level, uses a simplified three-point rating scale, and has acceptable psychometric properties.

The Disgust Emotion Scale (DES) (Walls & Kleinknecht, 1996) is another measure often used to assess disgust proneness. The DES assesses reactions to five domains of disgust elicitors: animals, injections and blood draws, mutilation and death, rotting foods, and odors. Although not as widely utilized as the other measures of disgust, the DES does have strong psychometric properties, including internal consistency and convergent validity (Kleinknecht, Kleinknecht, &

Thorndike, 1997; Olatunji, Sawchuk, de Jong, & Lohr, 2007). The Three-Domain Disgust Scale (TDDS) (Tybur, Lieberman, & Griskevicius, 2009) was developed to further broaden the scope of disgust elicitors that are assessed from a functional perspective. The TDDS emphasizes the evolutionary function of disgust in three areas: avoiding pathogens, choosing a mate, and interacting in other social relationships. Accordingly, the TDDS contains 21 items that assess pathogen, sexual, and moral disgust. Although concerns have been raised regarding the limited convergent validity of the moral disgust subscale (Olatunji et al., 2012), the TDDS may be useful for researchers who are particularly interested in how evolutionary processes influence disgust and related constructs.

Behavioral Measures

Experiencing disgust is associated with a behavioral tendency to avoid or withdraw (Rozin & Fallon, 1987); thus, behavioral measures of avoidance of disgusting stimuli can be used to measure individual differences in disgust proneness. Disgust facial expressions are one form of avoidance. Individuals who are disgusted typically wrinkle their nose and raise their upper lip, which serves to reduce the inhalation of foul odors (Darwin, 1872/2009; Rozin, Lowery, & Ebert, 1994). Disgusted individuals may also open their mouth and protrude their tongue, as if they were expelling a bad-tasting food (Rozin et al., 1994). Researchers can measure these forms of passive avoidance by coding participants' facial expressions using the Facial Action Coding System (FACS) (Ekman & Friesen, 1978) or by using facial electromyogram (EMG), a physiological measure of muscle movements in the face. For example, disgust is associated with activation of the levator labii, the muscle that raises the upper lip and wrinkles the nose (Vrana, 1993). Studies of spider-fearful individuals have found greater levator labii activation compared to controls when viewing pictures of spiders (de Jong, Peters, & Vanderhallen, 2002; Leutgeb, Schäfer, Köchel, Scharmüller, & Schienle, 2010).

The behavioral tasks used in research typically measure active avoidance. In fact, the first published measurements of individual differences in disgust proneness were based on behavioral tasks. Children were asked if they would eat or drink a pleasant food after varying degrees of contamination had occurred; for example, the experimenter would place a dead grasshopper in a glass of milk and ask the child if they would take a sip with the grasshopper in the milk, once the grasshopper had been removed, once the milk had been poured out and replaced, and once the glass had been thoroughly washed and new milk was poured into the same glass (Fallon, Rozin, & Pliner, 1984; Rozin, Fallon, & Augustoni-Ziskind, 1985). The resulting behavioral differences in milk consumption reflected children's differences in contamination sensitivity.

Behavioral approach tasks (BATs) are commonly used as a measure of individual disgust proneness. BATs can be useful in determining the convergent and predictive validity of self-report measures of disgust proneness (Rozin et al., 1999). For example, one study used both the DS and three disgust-relevant BATs to compare individuals with high and low contamination fear (Deacon & Olatunji, 2007). Individuals were asked to follow a series of steps involving increased levels of exposure to a used comb, a cookie on the floor, and a bedpan of toilet water. Although differences between the two groups for the amount of anxiety experienced during the BATs and the number of steps completed did not reach significance, a mediation model demonstrated that disgust proneness, as measured by the DS, fully mediated the relationship between contamination-related cognitions and the emotional and behavioral responses to the BATs. This finding suggests that disgust proneness is a specific vulnerability factor for contamination-related anxiety and avoidance, and that it is unique in its ability to predict this relationship compared to other factors, such as overall anxiety and depressive symptoms.

BATs have also been used to examine the extent to which disgust proneness may differentiate one group from another. For example, Tsao and McKay (2004) used a set of six BATs from different disgust domains to determine if there were individual differences between contamination-fearful individuals and individuals with high and low trait anxiety. Two of the BATs differentiated between the contamination fear group and the high-anxiety group: the animal BAT, in which researchers measured how long a participant was willing to hold a live earthworm and the latency until contact with the earthworm (i.e., hesitation); and the sympathetic magic BAT, in which participants were asked to drink water from a cup labeled "Saliva" and the amount of water consumed and latency to drinking was measured. In both of these tasks, the highly trait-anxious individuals displayed greater approach behavior, suggesting that disgust plays a stronger role in contamination fear compared to generalized anxiety. In another study comparing individuals with blood-injection-injury (BII) phobia to controls, two sets of BATs were used. Individuals were exposed to (fake) bloodied gauze and a severed deer leg, representing BII concerns, as well as a cockroach and a worm, representing more general disgust. While there were predicted group differences in approach to BII stimuli, there were no differences in the number of steps completed or in the disgust ratings for the insect stimuli (Koch, Neill, Sawchuk, & Connolly, 2002). Thus, those with BII phobia are disgusted by items from the mutilation domain specifically and may not have higher general disgust proneness compared to the rest of the population.

BATs may be viewed as more objective measures of disgust proneness that offer a level of adaptability that may not be available with self-report measures. That is, researchers have the flexibility to choose the specific disgust elicitors to use in their BATs depending on the nature of the research. However, an important limitation of BATs is that it can be difficult to determine the emotional process that is driving the avoidance response. For example, consider the BAT where the experimenter places a dead grasshopper in a glass of milk and asks you to take a sip with the grasshopper in the milk or even once the grasshopper had been removed. Although the emotion of disgust may be predicted to drive avoidance of the milk, the emotion of fear may also play a role. Accordingly, the collection of verbal reports of disgust and other emotions during the BAT can be useful for identifying the affective process that drives behavioral avoidance.

Physiological Aspects of Disgust Proneness

Psychophysiological measures can be used in conjunction with behavioral and self-report measures of disgust proneness to provide insight into the specific emotion driving behavioral avoidance, for example. Although both fear and disgust motivate individuals to avoid, these emotions have different psychophysiological profiles (Levenson, 1992; Vrana, 1993). Fear usually involves a greater increase in heart rate than disgust, while both involve increases in electrodermal activity. During disgust, heart rate may decelerate as the parasympathetic nervous system is activated, which does not typically occur during fear. Increased parasympathetic activity during disgust has been measured in the laboratory, with researchers noting increased saliva production, evidence of digestive parasympathetic activity, as well as increased heart rate variability, which indicates a parasympathetic cardiac response, during the video of disgust film clips (de Jong, van Overveld, & Peters, 2011).

Empirical studies have examined sympathetic and parasympathetic responses to stimuli from different disgust domains, with mixed results. Higher core disgust and higher contamination disgust were associated with greater facial muscle tension during a vomit video, while animal-reminder disgust was associated with greater facial muscle tension and a lower heart rate during a blood draw video (Olatunji et al., 2008). However, both core disgust and animal-reminder disgust were found to lead to increased digestive activity (salivary excretion), decreased sympathetic cardiac activity, and increased skin conductance when the disgust stimuli were guided imagery scripts of different disgust-evoking scenarios (van Overveld et al., 2009). The addition of physiological measurement in disgust research can inform researchers of the underlying emotional processes motivating participant behavior. However, best practices require concordance of physiological measures with self-report and behavioral outcomes.

Cognitive Aspects of Disgust Proneness

Cognitive indicators of disgust proneness may be observed in domains of attention, memory, and appraisals, including magical thinking and the ability to cope with disgust (Teachman, 2006). Attentional bias to disgust may involve orienting toward disgust stimuli or an inability to shift attention away from these stimuli relative to other stimuli. Memory biases include having a strong recall of disgusting events or outcomes while failing to retrieve memories of similar situations that did not involve a disgust-related outcome. Cognitive appraisals might include thoughts such as "I cannot cope with being disgusted" or thoughts that follow the laws of sympathetic magic, such as "Now that my shoe has touched the dog poop, it is forever contaminated" (Rozin & Nemeroff, 1990).

Direct measurement of disgust-related cognitions. Some disgust-related cognitions can be measured directly. The Contamination Cognitions Scale (CCS) asks participants to give ratings of the likelihood and severity of being contaminated by a given object presented in a BAT on a scale of 0–100. The CCS thus provides a measure of threat estimation, and has been specifically used to examine overestimations of threat in response to disgust. In one study, scores on the CCS were significantly positively associated with performance on a BAT, and this relationship was fully accounted for by scores on the DS (Deacon & Olatunji, 2007). In another study, individuals who performed clinically representative safety behaviors for one week had significant increases in threat overestimation in addition to increased symptoms of contamination fear, although disgust proneness was not specifically measured (Deacon & Maack, 2008). The CCS can be used in conjunction with a behavioral assessment of disgust proneness in order to get a sense of inflated threat estimation, which is an important cognitive component of obsessive-compulsive disorder (OCD), a disorder in which disgust proneness is specifically implicated (Olatunji, Cisler, McKay, & Phillips, 2010).

Another self-reported measure of cognitive biases associated with disgust is the Looming of Disgust Questionnaire (LODQ) (Williams, Olatunji, Elwood, Connolly, & Lohr, 2006). Riskind and Williams (2006) define looming vulnerability to threat as the tendency to construct mental scenarios that involve increased risk or danger in response to a variety of potentially threatening stimuli and suggest that this looming vulnerability style is common across anxiety disorders. Looming vulnerability to disgust is conceptualized as an important cognitive component of threat or danger that elicits anxiety, sensitizes the individual to signs of movement and threat, biases cognitive processing, and makes the anxiety more persistent and less likely to habituate. Accordingly, the looming vulnerability model proposes that individuals with anxiety generate dynamic mental scenarios of disgust-relevant stimuli as intensifying and approaching faster than they can cope or respond. The LODQ specifically measures differences in appraisals that individuals make in response to disgust-relevant scenarios (e.g., a drunk person vomiting on your feet at a party). Individuals answer six questions about eight different scenarios; the questions address changes in the level of disgust throughout the imagined scenario, the likelihood of something bad happening, and one's ability to cope with the situation. The authors suggest that this questionnaire can be used in research to assess an individual's propensity to develop disgust-related psychopathology. Indeed, research has demonstrated that having a general looming cognitive style and having a specific looming vulnerability to contamination contributes significantly to contamination-related anxiety symptoms (Elwood, Riskind, & Olatunji, 2011).

Implicit measures of disgust-related cognitions. Although explicit self-report measures of disgust-related cognitions can be useful, assessment of such cognitions outside of conscious awareness may have incremental utility. Thus, researchers use a variety of methods to measure implicit reactions toward disgust. One widely used method is a variant of the Implicit Association Test (IAT) (Greenwald, McGhee, & Schwartz, 1998). The IAT is a task in which participants match target concepts to attributes while response time is measured. The same set of response keys are used simultaneously; if the concept and attribute are highly associated and share a response key, reaction time will be quicker compared to concepts and attributes that share a response key but are less easily associated. For example, one study asked individuals with either a spider or snake phobia to label pictures and words into the categories snake, spider, disgusting, or appealing. In one trial, the participants saw the response options as "snake/disgusting" and "spider/appealing" for each key, with the inverse pairings ("snake/appealing," "spider/disgusting") used in the next trial. Participants with snake phobias made faster responses to images when the option was "snake/disgusting," while participants with spider phobias made faster responses when the option was "spider/disgusting," supporting the idea that participants with spider and snake phobias implicitly associate threat-relevant stimuli with spiders or snakes, respectively (Teachman, Gregg, & Woody, 2001). Another study of spider phobia found implicit associations between spiders and contamination using the IAT (Huijding & de Jong, 2007). A single-block version of the IAT was also developed to specifically measure disgust proneness, and found that performance on the IAT was related to disgust facial expressions and avoidance behavior during a BAT with a worm (Zinkernagel, Hofmann, Dislich, Gschwendner, & Schmitt, 2011), though it did not significantly correlate with self-reported disgust proneness.

The Implicit Relational Assessment Procedure (IRAP) (Barnes-Holmes et al., 2006) was developed to address the shortcomings of the IAT. The IAT does not reveal anything about the nature of the relationship between two concepts and only shows the strength of their association; it also cannot reflect conditional beliefs, such as appraisals about disgust ("If I touch something disgusting, I cannot tolerate it"; De Houwer, 2002; Nicholson & Barnes-Holmes, 2012). The IRAP was designed to allow for the discovery of more complex associations and to provide a direct measure of an association, rather than a relative association. For example, for individuals without a snake phobia, snakes may be viewed as more disgusting than appealing on a dichotomous scale, but might actually be considered more neutral or interesting instead of disgusting or appealing. In one study, disgust-relevant IRAPs were created to examine differences in primary reactions and secondary appraisals to disgust stimuli. Participants viewed either a disgusting image or a pleasant image along with a phrase that was either consistent or inconsistent with the content of the image. Phrases could be primary appraisals ("I am disgusted"; "I like this") or secondary appraisals ("I cannot tolerate this"; I know I won't get sick"). As in the IAT, the key variable of interest is the difference in participant reaction time on consistent and inconsistent trials. This study found that performance on the disgust IRAPs predicted overall obsessive-compulsive tendencies and specific obsessing and washing concerns (Nicholson & Barnes-Holmes, 2012).

The Stroop task is another cognitive task used to measure disgust-related attentional biases. In this task, disgust, threat, and neutral words are presented in different colors and participants are asked to report the color of each word when it appears. Disgust proneness has been found to be correlated with longer response latencies for disgust words for participants who were primed with a disgust-related story (Charash & McKay, 2002). However, a study that used an implicit Stroop task found the opposite effect; participants with higher disgust proneness demonstrated a faster reaction time in response to disgust words that were presented for very short periods below conscious awareness (Charash, McKay, & Dipaolo, 2006). These findings, along with evidence from other studies, provide evidence for two different types of attentional biases in disgust. Individuals high in disgust proneness orient more quickly toward and demonstrate difficulty in disengaging from disgusting stimuli compared to neutral and fearful stimuli (Cisler, Olatunji, Lohr, & Williams, 2009; van Hooff, Devue, Vieweg, & Theeuwes, 2013).

Although improved reaction time measures have been developed to better differentiate components of attention (e.g., Posner's 1980 cuing paradigm), many researchers have turned to eye-tracking technology to overcome the limitations inherent in manual reaction time measures. The measurement of eye movements has been pursued for more than a century; however, only in the past 30 years have accurate, noninvasive methods been developed (Duchowski, 2002). Today, the most popular methods involve directing a camera and infrared light source at the participant's eye(s). By recording the surface of the eye with a video camera, one can detect the pupil by its lack of reflectance (dark pupil tracking) (Richardson & Spivey, 2004); alternatively, with a bright light aimed at the eye, the pupil can be identified by the light reflecting through the pupil, off of the retina (light pupil tracking) (Richardson & Spivey, 2004). While locating the pupillary reflection provides the primary indicator of eye movement, a second corneal reflection is often used to control for head movement (Duchowski, 2002). An alternative method of eye tracking involves electro-oculography, the use of electrodes placed near the eye to record changes in electrical potentials produced by eye movements (e.g., Rohner, 2002). The eye movements measured by these methods are more closely linked to attention than key press behavior, which occurs downstream of intervening response selection and skeletal muscle movement (Weierich, Treat, & Hollingworth, 2008). Research using eye-tracking methodology has demonstrated that individuals high in contamination fear (and disgust proneness) orient their gaze toward disgust stimuli more than individuals low in contamination fear, with no differences in maintenance of gaze toward these stimuli (Armstrong, Sarawgi, & Olatunji, 2012), supporting the finding that orienting bias may be especially strong in those with high disgust proneness. Additionally, evidence from a study employing eye tracking in a basic conditioning paradigm has pointed to increased attentional avoidance of disgusting images in individuals high in disgust proneness, as well as greater resistance to extinction (Mason & Richardson, 2010).

A memory bias for disgust-related information has also been found. Participants demonstrated enhanced memory for disgusting images compared to fearful and neutral images (Chapman, Johannes, Poppenk, Moscovitch, & Anderson, 2013), and disgust words were recalled with greater accuracy than neutral and fear words (Ferré, Haro, & Hinojosa, 2017). Individual differences in disgust proneness also affect the magnitude of the memory bias for disgust. Disgust proneness predicts the number of disgust words recalled following a Stroop task for individuals primed with disgust stories (Charash & McKay, 2002). Additionally, individuals high in contamination concerns recalled more disgust words in an implicit memory task compared to non-anxious controls (Charash & McKay, 2009).

Neural Correlates

Functional magnetic resonance imaging (fMRI) research has revealed important neural correlates of disgust proneness. While no one brain region is specific to a given emotion, the insula has been consistently demonstrated to play a role in the experience and recognition of disgust (Calder, Lawrence, & Young, 2001; Wright, He, Shapira, & Goodman, 2004). Additionally, the anterior insula and anterior cingulate cortex were found to activate both during the individual experience of disgust (i.e., while smelling a foul odor), and while observing videos of others smelling presumably disgusting odors and making disgust faces (Wicker et al., 2003). In a sample of healthy adults, Mataix-Cols and colleagues (2008) found that scores on the DS were correlated with activation in brain regions associated with disgust, including the anterior insula and putamen, when viewing disgusting images. These findings were not attributable to differences in state anxiety and depression or biological sex. Thus, evidence suggests that the key neural architecture involved in disgust is activated to a greater degree for those who report being more sensitive to disgust when faced with disgust stimuli. Additionally, high disgust proneness was related to difficulty in down-regulating negative emotional experience, as measured by activation in various prefrontal regions associated with emotion regulation (Mataix-Cols et al., 2008). This related finding reveals one possible treatment target for individuals with anxiety disorders characterized by high disgust proneness, suggesting that improving emotion regulation skills may help these individuals.

Electroencephalography (EEG) has also been used to measure electrical activity in the brain during disgust processing. Event-related potentials (ERPs), or electrical responses associated with specific neural events, can be used as an indicator of attentional allocation. Such studies have found evidence for an attentional pattern where disgusting stimuli capture and hold attention, similar to the pattern found for other threatening emotional stimuli such as fear and anger (Liu, Zhang, & Luo, 2015; Zhang, Liu, Zhou, Chen, & Luo, 2014). Differences between disgust and other threatening information are mixed. One study found greater ERP amplitudes in the cuneus, a visual area, for disgust distractors compared to fear distractors during a digit categorization task (Carretié, Ruiz-Padial, López-Martín, & Albert, 2011), while another found the weakest ERP amplitudes in associate visual areas for disgust images compared to fear and neutral images (Krusemark & Li, 2011). Krusemark and Li suggest that their findings are evidence of suppressed neural processing of disgust-related threatening information, especially in individuals with higher self-reported anxiety.

Finally, EEG has been used in phobic populations to study neural activity in response to phobic stimuli. In a study of young girls with spider phobia, ERPs in the parietal region of the brain were examined during the viewing of fearful, disgusting, neutral, and spider images. For those with spider phobia, spider images were rated as the most fearful and equivalently disgusting as disgust images. Girls with spider phobia also had ERP amplitudes during spider image viewing compared to controls, suggesting a higher allocation of attentional resources to these stimuli; these girls also had higher disgust proneness. The authors suggest that these results provide psychophysiological evidence of the role of disgust in spider phobia in children (Leutgeb et al., 2010).

Correlates of Disgust Proneness

Demographic Correlates. Available research suggests that disgust proneness can be reliably assessed across multiple levels of analysis. Researchers have applied additional statistical methods to assess the construct of disgust proneness and consider it a personality trait that is present to a greater or lesser extent in all individuals (Olatunji & Broman-Fulks, 2007). Gender differences in disgust proneness have also been consistently found in the literature, with women typically experiencing greater disgust proneness than men (Druschel & Sherman, 1999; Kraines, Kelberer, & Wells, 2016). Gender is one potential link between the disgust and anxiety-related disorders, as women also report more symptoms of anxiety disorders than men (Craske, 2003). However, in a recent meta-analysis, the magnitude of the association between disgust proneness and symptoms of anxiety-related disorders was not moderated by gender (Olatunji, Armstrong, & Elwood, 2017).

Age-related differences in disgust have also been noted. For instance, Rozin and colleagues have suggested that children under the age of eight may not be able to experience disgust on a cognitive level, although they can learn to avoid and reject disgust stimuli through observation (Rozin & Fallon, 1987). Fallon and Rozin have suggested that children demonstrate increasing disgust proneness as they get older, as measured through behavioral tasks (Fallon, Rozin, & Pliner, 1984; Rozin, Fallon, & Augustoni-Ziskind, 1985). Stevenson and colleagues tested this theory in a cross-sectional study using a mixture of parental report and behavioral tests with children between the ages of 2 and 16. They found a general developmental trajectory, where disgust reactions to core disgust elicitors emerged before animal and socio-moral elicitors (Stevenson et al., 2010). This finding suggests that reactivity to distinct disgust elicitors varies across development.

Disgust proneness has also been examined in children using self-report measures (de Jong, Andrea, & Muris, 1997; Knowles, Viar-Paxton, Riemann, Jacobi, & Olatunji, 2016; Muris, Merckelbach, Schmidt, & Tierney, 1999; Viar-Paxton et al., 2015), but specific relationships between age and disgust proneness were not reported in these studies. Age was significantly linked to disgust proneness in a sample of college students, where individuals under age 18 had higher disgust proneness than individuals 18 years and older, but the age range for the sample was restricted (Quigley, Sherman, & Sherman, 1997). No longitudinal studies have examined change in disgust proneness over a significant period of time (i.e., through childhood) in order to examine developmental changes within individuals.

Personality Correlates. Disgust proneness is also related to other personality traits. A significant positive relationship has been found between disgust proneness and neuroticism in multiple samples (Druschel & Sherman, 1999; Haidt, McCauley, & Rozin, 1994). Research examining the relationship of disgust proneness to other "Big Five" personality dimensions has found positive correlations between disgust proneness and agreeableness and conscientiousness, and negative correlations between disgust proneness and openness to experience (Druschel & Sherman, 1999), though these relationships have not been found in other samples (Olatunji et al., 2008). Other personality traits that confer risk for the development of anxiety-related disorders, such as anxiety sensitivity, have also been examined. In a sample of undergraduates, disgust proneness was significantly correlated with the physical domain of anxiety sensitivity, but not with the social or cognitive domains (Wheaton, Abramowitz, Berman, Fabricant, & Olatunji, 2012). Another study examined the structure of disgust proneness and anxiety sensitivity and their association with OCD symptoms in a structural equation model and found a significant relationship between disgust proneness and anxiety sensitivity (Olatunji, Ebesutani, & Kim, 2016). Both disgust proneness and anxiety sensitivity may serve as vulnerability factors for the development of anxiety-related psychopathology, although specific comparisons between the two are limited, especially in the prospective designs needed to predict future psychopathology. Importantly, though disgust proneness, neuroticism, and anxiety sensitivity are all emotional factors that predict psychopathology, these concepts are theoretically distinct forms of negative affect and share only small portions of variance in structural equation and regression models (Olatunji et al., 2008, 2016).

Disgust Proneness and Psychopathology

The role of disgust proneness as a vulnerability and maintenance factor for psychopathology is a key research area. Available studies have implicated disgust proneness in OCD, health anxiety, and a variety of specific phobias, including BII, spider, and other small animal phobias (Olatunji, Cisler, McKay, & Phillips, 2010). A recent meta-analysis of 126 studies demonstrated moderate associations between disgust proneness and symptoms of anxiety-related psychopathology, even after controlling for negative affect (Olatunji, Armstrong, & Elwood, 2017). Though a complete review of the literature investigating the relationship between disgust proneness and specific disorders is beyond the scope of this chapter, we offer a summary of the research in the major anxiety-related disorders with which disgust proneness has been implicated.

Specific Phobias

The disease-avoidance model of phobias suggests that phobic avoidance of specific animals may develop due to concerns of contamination, dirt, and the spreading of disease (Matchett & Davey, 1991). This includes small animals such as flies, cockroaches, and maggots that are commonly found in dirty kitchens and near piles of waste and rats that are known to spread diseases such as rabies and even the bubonic plague (McEvedy, 1988). Though typically harmless to humans, spiders, snakes, insects, and other small animals are common targets of phobias. Other small-animal phobias include animals that have physical characteristics that are considered disgusting; for example, frogs and worms are slimy in appearance, snakes slither in an unfamiliar way, and spiders have eight legs and can be hairy, all of which may evoke disgust in some individuals. In a non-selected sample, disgust proneness was significantly positively correlated with level of fear for animals such as rats, spiders, and snakes, but not for large, predatory animals such as sharks, bears, or tigers (Ware, Jain, Burgess, & Davey, 1994).

Much of the research on small-animal phobias and disgust focuses on spider phobia. Spider phobia is commonly observed in the general population and can easily be studied in analog samples of individuals with spider fear, whose fear may not reach clinical significance but who still exhibit significant fear and avoidance of spiders. In a number of studies, disgust proneness has been consistently associated with spider fear in both children (Mulkens, de Jong, & Merckelbach, 1996; Muris, van der Heiden, & Rassin, 2008) and adults (de Jong & Merckelbach, 1998; Olatunji, Williams, Lohr et al., 2007). Spider avoidance is also associated with self-reported state disgust during spider BATs, though not necessarily with trait disgust proneness (Woody, McLean, & Klassen, 2005; Woody & Tolin, 2002). Importantly, disgust proneness remains significantly associated with spider phobia even when controlling for trait anxiety (Olatunji, Williams, Lohr et al., 2007).

Disgust proneness has also been implicated in BII phobia. BII phobia is commonly associated with a vasovagal response (i.e., fainting), which is mediated through the parasympathetic nervous system. The physiological and psychological processes underlying the vasovagal response are similar to those underlying disgust, including a decrease in blood pressure and heart rate. The vasovagal response (syncope) occurs after a strong parasympathetic response due to the rapid change in blood pressure (Page, 1994). Despite these theoretical links, empirical research has not shown a consistent relationship between disgust proneness and a history of fainting in individuals with BII, and disgust does not always elicit a parasympathetic reaction in these individuals (Vossbeck-Elsebusch & Gerlach, 2012; Vossbeck-Elsebusch, Steinigeweg, Vögele, & Gerlach, 2012). Thus, although fainting is sometimes found in individuals with BII phobia, the once theorized link between disgust proneness and fainting has not been consistently supported.

Although a unique relationship between fainting and disgust proneness is not substantiated, a relationship has been found between disgust proneness and general symptoms of BII phobia. Self-reported disgust proneness is significantly correlated with BII phobia (Sawchuk, Lohr, Tolin, Lee, & Kleinknecht, 2000), and individuals with BII demonstrate a memory bias for medical and disgust words (Sawchuk et al., 1999). BII phobia is also significantly correlated with disgust proneness after controlling for trait anxiety (Olatunji, Williams, Lohr et al., 2007). In studies directly comparing BII and spider phobia, individuals with BII phobia had higher levels of contamination fear (Sawchuk et al., 2000) and higher disgust sensitivity than those with spider phobia (Sawchuk, Lohr, Westendorf, Meunier, & Tolin, 2002). When examining these phobias with respect to specific domains of disgust, differences between these two phobias emerge. BII phobia is associated with animal-reminder disgust, but not core disgust (de Jong & Merckelbach, 1998; Olatunji, Sawchuk, de Jong, & Lohr, 2006). Specifically, body envelope violations are uniquely associated with BII fear, while spider fear is uniquely associated with animal disgust elicitors (de Jong & Merckelbach, 1998).

Obsessive-Compulsive Disorder

Contamination fear is observed in approximately half of those with OCD (Rachman, 2004). Individuals with contamination-focused OCD have primary obsessions about dirt and disease, as well as washing and cleaning compulsions in direct response to these obsessional fears. Research on disgust proneness in contamination-focused OCD has been conducted across a wide variety of methods. Self-report measures consistently demonstrate a relationship between elevated disgust proneness and OCD symptoms. In a nonclinical sample, increased obsessive-compulsive symptoms was positively correlated with self-reported disgust proneness even after controlling for symptoms of depression and anxiety (Tolin, Woods, & Abramowitz, 2006). These results were replicated in a clinical OCD sample, demonstrating a significant relationship between disgust proneness and OCD symptoms when controlling for negative affect (Olatunji, Ebesutani, David, Fan, & McGrath, 2011). Additionally, in a prospective study of disgust proneness and OCD symptoms in a clinical sample, changes in disgust proneness were associated with changes in self-reported OCD symptoms over a six-month period (Berle et al., 2012).

Studies utilizing multimodal assessment of OCD have found links with disgust proneness beyond those measured by self-report. Individuals with high OCD contamination symptoms reported more disgust when viewing a disgusting video than individuals with low OCD contamination symptoms, and they also demonstrated more avoidance in disgust BATs (Olatunji, Lohr, Sawchuk, & Tolin, 2007). During treatment, individuals with contamination OCD symptoms habituated more slowly to disgust stimuli than individuals with other forms of OCD (McKay, 2006). Neuroimaging studies have also found that patients with OCD have greater insula activation when viewing disgusting images compared to healthy controls (Husted,

Shapira, & Goodman, 2006; Shapira et al., 2003). This pattern of findings is consistent with previous research that has shown that individuals with high disgust proneness have greater insula activity than individuals with lower disgust proneness (Mataix-Cols et al., 2008). Stein and colleagues have suggested that contamination-focused OCD is the neurobiological result of dysfunction in the cortico-striatal-thalamic-cortical circuits during the experience of disgust (Stein & Bouwer, 1997; Stein, Liu, Shapira, & Goodman, 2001). In other words, individuals with OCD may have a higher tendency to experience disgust and thus receive many false alarm signals that can be reliably tracked at the neural level of analysis. These false alarms may then manifest as obsessions about being contaminated, which leads to washing compulsions that attempt to alleviate the obsessions.

Health Anxiety

The latest version of the Diagnostic and Statistical Manual of Mental Disorders, Fifth Edition (DSM-5) has redefined preoccupation with the idea that one has or will develop a serious illness as illness anxiety disorder, formerly called hypochondriasis (American Psychiatric Association, 2013). In multiple samples, self-reported health anxiety has been found to be significantly correlated with disgust proneness as measured by the Disgust Scale (Thorpe, Patel, & Simonds, 2003), a relationship that remained significant after controlling for trait anxiety (Davey & Bond, 2006). In another study, disgust proneness mediated the relationship between health anxiety and washing compulsions in a nonclinical sample (Thorpe, Barnett, Friend, & Nottingham, 2011). In a clinical sample, while there was a significant relationship between disgust proneness and health anxiety, there were no differences between individuals with hypochondriasis and those with another anxiety disorder, suggesting less specificity than previously asserted (Weck, Esch, & Rohrmann, 2014). However, behavioral measures continue to demonstrate a strong link between health anxiety and disgust proneness. Using a series of health-related behavioral tasks, Fan and Olatunji (2013) found that disgust proneness was related to anxious and avoidant responding during the tasks, even after controlling for gender and symptoms of anxiety and depression. Evidence of a bidirectional relationship between behavior and changes in disgust proneness is evident as well. In a nonclinical sample, individuals who were instructed to increase the number of health behaviors they performed in their daily life (e.g., handwashing, disinfecting surfaces) exhibited a greater increase in disgust proneness compared to individuals who were simply asked to monitor their health behaviors without changing them (Olatunji, 2015).

Recent research has examined how media coverage of health-related events influences the relationship between disgust proneness and health anxiety symptoms. For instance, multiple studies have been published establishing a relationship between disgust proneness and anxiety about swine flu during the H1N1 influenza pandemic of 2009–2010, which was particularly prevalent on college campuses (Brand, McKay, Wheaton, & Abramowitz, 2013; Wheaton, Abramowitz, Berman,

Fabricant, & Olatunji, 2012). Similarly, a relationship between fears of contracting the Ebola virus and disgust proneness was found in a study conducted in late 2014, around the peak of media coverage of Ebola (Blakey, Reuman, Jacoby, & Abramowitz, 2015). Disgust proneness also uniquely predicted safety behaviors in response to Ebola (Blakey et al., 2015). These findings suggest that those high in disgust proneness may be especially influenced by media coverage of pandemics and other significant health-related events, which may lead to exacerbated health anxiety. Such individuals may create a further burden on the health system by frequently visiting doctors' offices and emergency rooms (Barsky, Ettner, Horsky, & Bates, 2001). Specifically addressing disgust during the treatment of health anxiety may lead to more successful treatment outcomes and help reduce future health care costs.

Posttraumatic Stress Disorder

Disgust reactions are also noted in response to traumatic events. In a study of veterans of the war in Afghanistan, veterans who reported greater disgust in response to a traumatic experience during their deployment had greater post-traumatic stress six months later, independent of their reported levels of fear in response to the event (Engelhard, Olatunji, & de Jong, 2011). In a sample of female victims of sexual assault, self-focused disgust reactions in response to sexual trauma predicted feelings of mental contamination (Badour, Ojserkis, McKay, & Feldner, 2014). A study of veterans who had experienced interpersonal trauma found that posttraumatic disgust and guilt mediated the relationship between peri-traumatic disgust and PTSD symptoms. This finding suggests that the experience of disgust may be an important mechanism in the development of PTSD. Additionally, the study also found that the relationship between peritraumatic and posttraumatic disgust was stronger for men than for women (Bomyea & Allard, 2017). This may highlight an important gender-specific mechanism for PTSD that should be examined in future research.

Research has now shown that disgust proneness (measured before deployment) moderates the effect of peritraumatic disgust reactions on PTSD symptoms in a veteran sample, and predicts mental contamination in a sample of sexual assault victims (Badour et al., 2014; Engelhard et al., 2011). In addition to a diathesis-stress model in which the interaction of high trait disgust proneness and exposure to a traumatic stressor leads to increased symptoms of PTSD, other potential mechanisms of disgust proneness have been explored. For instance, high disgust proneness may serve to increase intrusive memories of traumatic events, although thus far evidence is limited to a nonclinical sample of students exposed to a distressing film (Bomyea & Amir, 2012). Conversely, low disgust proneness may instead be considered a protective factor in response to trauma. In a study of veterans with PTSD, trauma-exposed veterans without PTSD, and healthy non-veteran controls, veterans who did not develop PTSD in response to trauma had lower self-reported disgust proneness compared to veterans with PTSD and non-veterans (Olatunji,

Armstrong, Fan, & Zhao, 2014). Further research into the specific mechanisms of disgust proneness that lead to different traumatic outcomes may advance understanding of reactions to trauma and reveal potential treatment targets.

Distinct Effects of Disgust Propensity and Disgust Sensitivity

Programmatic research on the etiology of anxiety disorders has found that it is not just the frequency and intensity of the experience of anxiety, but how an individual appraises the feeling of anxiety that confers risk (Schmidt, Zvolensky, & Maner, 2006). The same distinction may be true with regard to individual differences in disgust. The majority of available measures of disgust appear to assess disgust propensity, or how easily someone is disgusted. However, these measures fail to capture a person's disgust sensitivity, or how unpleasant experiencing disgust is appraised to be for the individual (van Overveld, de Jong, Peters, Cavanagh, & Davey, 2006). Kim might feel disgusted in a variety of situations but not see this as anything harmful or particularly disruptive in her life; Alex may only feel strong disgust in situations involving insects, but he may also be afraid of the negative consequences associated with disgust, such as fainting or vomiting. Olatunji and Sawchuk (2005) suggest that it is this disgust sensitivity that may be more strongly associated with the development of psychopathology. Preliminary data support this assertion, as an implicit measure of these two components of disgust proneness demonstrated that disgust sensitivity, but not disgust propensity, predicted avoidance behavior in multiple disgust-relevant BATs (Nicholson & Barnes-Holmes, 2012).

In order to better differentiate disgust propensity and sensitivity with self-report, the Disgust Propensity and Sensitivity Scale was developed (Cavanagh & Davey, 2000) and subsequently revised by removal of a few ill-fitting items to create the Disgust Propensity and Sensitivity Scale-Revised (DPSS-R). The DPSS-R consists of 16 items that load onto the two factors of Disgust Propensity and Disgust Sensitivity. Research has shown that the subscales differentially explained unique variance in spider fear, spider avoidance, and injection fear and avoidance in a nonclinical sample (Olatunji, Cisler, Deacon, Connolly, & Lohr, 2007). The DPSS-R also significantly predicts behavior. Using a series of behavioral tasks, van Overveld and colleagues found that participants with higher scores on the DPSS-R completed fewer actions across 17 tasks from four domains of disgust: core, animal-reminder, interpersonal, and socio-moral disgust. The DPSS-R disgust propensity subscale also had greater predictive validity for behavioral avoidance in core disgust BATs compared to the Disgust Scale, Disgust Questionnaire, and Disgust Emotion Scale, although the disgust sensitivity subscale of the DPSS-R did not further improve the measure's predictive validity (van Overveld, de Jong, & Peters, 2010). Another study found that disgust propensity predicted washing symptoms and was associated with greater avoidance in behavioral tasks, while disgust sensitivity did not (Goetz, Lee, Cougle, & Turkel, 2013). However, other studies suggest that disgust sensitivity may play an important role in some cases. For example, disgust sensitivity predicts difficulties in emotion regulation and is associated with blood-injection-injury fears and contamination fear (Cisler, Olatunji, & Lohr, 2009; Olatunji, Moretz et al., 2010). Disgust sensitivity also differentially predicted elevated health anxiety in a nonclinical sample, although the relationship was no longer significant after including anxiety sensitivity in the model (Brady, Cisler, & Lohr, 2014). There is also evidence of a significant relationship between disgust sensitivity and OCD symptoms beyond negative affect and anxiety sensitivity (David et al., 2009), and changes in disgust sensitivity predicted changes in symptoms of contamination-based OCD (Olatunji, 2010) in nonclinical samples.

Although disgust propensity and disgust sensitivity may be differentially related to different forms of psychopathological symptoms, it is important to note that only a few studies have examined the distinct forms of disgust vulnerabilities in clinical samples. In a study comparing clients with OCD and GAD to nonclinical controls, individuals with OCD more strongly endorsed disgust propensity than those with GAD and nonclinical controls, but individuals with OCD and GAD did not differ on disgust sensitivity (though both endorsed disgust sensitivity more strongly than nonclinical controls; Olatunji, Tart, Ciesielski, McGrath, & Smits, 2011). A subsequent study found that individuals with OCD had higher mean disgust propensity than individuals with other anxiety disorders and non-anxious controls, but the three groups did not differ on disgust sensitivity (Whitton, Henry, & Grisham, 2014). Last, another study found that individuals with self-diagnosed emetophobia had higher disgust propensity and disgust sensitivity than controls, with disgust sensitivity being the stronger predictor of emetophobic complaints (van Overveld, de Jong, Peters, van Hout, & Bouman, 2008). While disgust propensity seems to be the most useful construct to predict general disgust-related avoidance behavior, disgust sensitivity may predict difficulties in emotion regulation and subsequent psychopathology. Current evidence does not suggest that disgust sensitivity can differentiate between different manifestations of psychopathology, but this construct does appear to meaningfully distinguish individuals with and without anxiety-related psychopathology.

Treating Disgust Proneness

Given the demonstrated role of disgust proneness in the development of various forms of psychopathology, some researchers have begun to consider the treatment implications of the personality trait (Olatunji, Cisler et al., 2010). Despite not being directly addressed in treatment, disgust has been found to decrease over the course of treatment for individuals with spider phobia (de Jong, Andrea, & Muris, 1997; Olatunji, Huijding, de Jong, & Smits, 2011). While changes in disgust proneness were not measured in the study by Olatunji and colleagues, no changes in disgust proneness were found over the course of treatment of young girls with spider phobia (de Jong et al., 1997). However, this study used an older measure of disgust proneness, the DQ, which may not have adequately captured changes in disgust proneness. Additionally, differentiating between disgust sensitivity and disgust propensity may help clarify if and how disgust proneness changes over time.

The role of disgust proneness in the treatment of OCD has also been examined. Disgust reactions can change over the course of treatment, even in contamination-fearful individuals with OCD (McKay, 2006). Evidence for changes in disgust proneness has also been found. In a study of adults with OCD, changes in disgust propensity mediated changes in OCD symptoms from pre to post treatment after controlling for negative affect, while changes in disgust sensitivity did not (Olatunji, Tart et al., 2011). Decreases in disgust propensity also predicted improvement in washing symptoms in a clinical adult sample with OCD, although disgust sensitivity was not assessed (Athey et al., 2015). Changes in disgust proneness also predicted changes in anxiety symptoms during treatment for children with anxiety disorders, with the strongest relationship present for children with a diagnosis of OCD (Knowles, Viar-Paxton, Riemann, Jacobi, & Olatunji, 2016; Taboas, Ojserkis, & McKay, 2014). These two studies demonstrate that although some change in disgust proneness may occur over the course of treatment for individuals with anxiety and depression, those with more disgust-specific disorders may see a greater benefit.

Experimental psychopathology research also highlights the potential implications of the treatment of disgust in PTSD. More specifically, one study examined women with a history of sexual victimization who underwent a single session of imaginal exposure in which they generated a disgust-focused and a fear-focused script based on their sexual trauma. Participants reported higher disgust compared to anxiety during the first exposure trial, but the slopes of change for disgust and anxiety were not significantly different from one another. Additionally, change in disgust significantly predicted improvement in PTSD symptoms during the exposure session for individuals who also had a significant decline in anxiety (Badour & Feldner, 2016). These findings suggest that disgust can change over the course of exposure, and that changes in disgust are predictive of symptom improvement for some individuals with PTSD.

Although currently available studies suggest that disgust proneness may play a role in the treatment of various disorders, it is important to note that the majority of these studies do not directly target disgust. One study that isolated the role of disgust in treatment used contamination-focused exposure in the treatment of women with spider phobia. Women with high disgust proneness who completed contamination exposures without spiders had lower spider fear and perceived danger compared to women in a wait-list control condition, although treatment did not affect disgust proneness or spider-related disgust (Cougle, Summers, Harvey, Dillon, & Allan, 2016). For individuals high in disgust proneness, addressing both disgust and fear in treatment may lead to better outcomes.

Although interventions directly targeting disgust proneness have not been developed, emerging research on the treatment of anxiety sensitivity may be useful for developing brief interventions that can effectively target disgust proneness. Participants with elevated anxiety sensitivity who participated in a single-session anxiety sensitivity intervention saw greater reductions in anxiety sensitivity compared to participants in a health information control group (Schmidt, Eggleston, Woolaway-Bickel, Fitzpatrick, Vasey, & Richey, 2007). Similar interventions have led to improvements in anxiety sensitivity one month post-intervention (Capron & Schmidt, 2016; Keough & Schmidt, 2012). In similar intervention trials, reductions in anxiety sensitivity also reduced anxiety-related symptoms (Allan, Short, Albanese, Keough, & Schmidt, 2015; Timpano, Raines, Shaw, Keough, & Schmidt, 2016). Interoceptive exposure is a procedure that is used to treat anxiety sensitivity by reducing catastrophic misinterpretations of benign arousal-related body sensations via repeated confrontation with physical sensations (e.g., breathlessness, dizziness, racing heart). Individuals with high disgust proneness may be more likely to attend to bodily sensations that are specifically associated with disgust, such as nausea, and to misinterpret these symptoms as dangerous or catastrophic. These individuals may also benefit from interoceptive exposures that are tailored to target disgust tolerance.

Future Directions in Disgust Proneness Research and Treatment

Our understanding of the role of disgust proneness in anxiety-related disorders has improved dramatically over the past few decades. However, assessing the specific mechanisms by which disgust proneness develops and is maintained is essential to improving treatment outcomes for the disorders in which disgust is implicated. Research examining disgust and disgust proneness may benefit from the National Institute of Mental Health's Research Domain Criteria (RDoC) framework to study mechanisms of change. RDoC is a system of dimensional psychological constructs, which are measured across multiple units of analysis, that guide research on human behavior and psychological disorders ("Definitions of the RDoC Domains and Constructs"). Though disgust is not specifically referenced in the RDoC framework, it fits the criteria as a construct that can be studied using multiple methodologies across different units of analysis, from basic biological components (genetic influences, physiological and neural circuits) to observable behavior, in the context of development and the environment. Other emotional constructs, such as fear (acute threat), anxiety (potential threat), and sadness (loss) are included in the current RDoC matrix under the negative valence system. Disgust is a natural candidate for future inclusion in the RDoC framework given that it is defined by measurable verbal, behavioral, physiological, and neural correlates that have been observed in anxiety and related disorders.

Future studies of disgust proneness will also need to expand research in clinical populations and translate these findings into clear treatment recommendations. Studies that examine changes in disgust proneness at multiple time points throughout treatment are needed to determine if a change in disgust proneness has a causal effect on symptoms. If so, specific treatment modules that address disgust proneness could be developed and added into exposure and response prevention protocols. Finally, clarifying the roles of disgust propensity and sensitivity can help further current understanding of therapeutic targets.

Although we have focused on the relationship between disgust proneness and anxiety-related disorders, high disgust proneness is not limited to individuals with anxiety. Disgust proneness is also associated with eating disorders (Davey, Buckland, Tantow, & Dallos, 1998; Troop, Treasure, & Serpell, 2002) and obesity (Watkins et al., 2015); the close association between disgust and the avoidance of potential contaminants through oral incorporation could influence theoretical perspectives on eating behaviors. High disgust proneness has also been found in patients with sexual dysfunctions, and understanding the role of disgust in sexual inhibition may help in the treatment of these individuals. Clearly, research opportunities abound. Disgust is no longer the forgotten emotion (Phillips, Fahy, David, & Senior, 1998), but more needs to be done to translate research on disgust proneness into effective treatment strategies that can improve the lives of individuals with anxiety-related and other psychological disorders.

References

Adams, T. G. & Lohr, J. M. (2012). Disgust mediates the relation between attentional shifting and contamination aversion. *Journal of Behavior Therapy and Experimental Psychiatry*, *43*(4), 975–980. doi: 10.1016/j.jbtep.2012.03.002

Allan, N. P., Short, N. A., Albanese, B. J., Keough, M. E., & Schmidt, N. B. (2015). Direct and mediating effects of an anxiety sensitivity intervention on posttraumatic stress disorder symptoms in trauma-exposed individuals. *Cognitive Behaviour Therapy*, *44*(6), 512–524. doi: 10.1080/16506073.2015.1075227

American Psychiatric Association. (2013). *Diagnostic and Statistical Manual of Mental Disorders* (5th ed.). Washington, DC: American Psychiatric Association.

Angyal, A. (1941). Disgust and related aversions. *Journal of Abnormal and Social Psychology*, *36*(3), 393–412.

Armstrong, T., Sarawgi, S., & Olatunji, B. O. (2012). Attentional bias toward threat in contamination fear: Overt components and behavioral correlates. *Journal of Abnormal Psychology*, *121*(1), 232–237. doi: 10.1037/a0024453

Athey, A. J., Elias, J. A., Crosby, J. M., Jenike, M. A., Pope, H. G., Hudson, J. I., & Brennan, B. P. (2015). Reduced disgust propensity is associated with improvement in contamination/washing symptoms in obsessive-compulsive disorder. *Journal of Obsessive-Compulsive and Related Disorders*, *4*, 20–24. doi: 10.1016/j.jocrd.2014.11.001

Badour, C. L. & Feldner, M. T. (2016). Disgust and imaginal exposure to memories of sexual trauma: Implications for the treatment of posttraumatic stress. *Psychological Trauma: Theory, Research, Practice, and Policy*, *8*(3), 267–275. doi: 10.1037/tra0000079

Badour, C. L., Ojserkis, R., McKay, D., & Feldner, M. T. (2014). Disgust as a unique affective predictor of mental contamination following sexual trauma. *Journal of Anxiety Disorders, 28*(7), 704–711. doi: 10.1016/j.janxdis.2014.07.007

Barnes-Holmes, D., Barnes-Holmes, Y., Power, P., Hayden, E., Milne, R., & Stewart, I. (2006). Do you really know what you believe? Developing the Implicit Relational Assessment Procedure (IRAP) as a direct measure of implicit beliefs. *Irish Psychologist, 32*, 169–177.

Barsky, A. J., Ettner, S. L., Horsky, J., & Bates, D. W. (2001). Resource utilization of patients with hypochondriacal health anxiety and somatization. *Medical Care, 39*(7).

Berle, D., Starcevic, V., Brakoulias, V., Sammut, P., Milicevic, D., Hannan, A., & Moses, K. (2012). Disgust propensity in obsessive-compulsive disorder: Cross-sectional and prospective relationships. *Journal of Behavior Therapy and Experimental Psychiatry, 43*(1), 656–663. doi: 10.1016/j.jbtep.2011.09.002

Blakey, S. M., Reuman, L., Jacoby, R. J., & Abramowitz, J. S. (2015). Tracing "Fearbola": Psychological predictors of anxious responding to the threat of Ebola. *Cognitive Therapy and Research, 39*(6), 816–825. doi: 10.1007/s10608-015–9701-9

Bomyea, J. & Allard, C. B. (2017). Trauma-related disgust in veterans with interpersonal trauma. *Journal of Traumatic Stress, 30*(2), 149–156. doi: 10.1002/jts.22169

Bomyea, J. & Amir, N. (2012). Disgust propensity as a predictor of intrusive cognitions following a distressing film. *Cognitive Therapy and Research, 36*(3), 190–198. doi: 10.1007/s10608-010–9331-1

Borg, C., de Jong, P. J., Renken, R. J., & Georgiadis, J. R. (2013). Disgust trait modulates frontal-posterior coupling as a function of disgust domain. *Social Cognitive and Affective Neuroscience, 8*(3), 351–358. doi: 10.1093/scan/nss006

Brady, R. E., Cisler, J. M., & Lohr, J. M. (2014). Specific and differential prediction of health anxiety by disgust sensitivity and propensity. *Anxiety, Stress & Coping, 27*(1), 90–99. doi: 10.1080/10615806.2013.772588

Brand, J., McKay, D., Wheaton, M. G., & Abramowitz, J. S. (2013). The relationship between obsessive compulsive beliefs and symptoms, anxiety and disgust sensitivity, and swine flu fears. *Journal of Obsessive-Compulsive and Related Disorders, 2*(2), 200–206. doi: 10.1016/j.jocrd.2013.01.007

Calder, A. J., Lawrence, A. D., & Young, A. W. (2001). Neuropsychology of fear and loathing. *Nature Reviews Neuroscience, 2*, 352–363. doi: 10.1038/35072584

Capron, D. W. & Schmidt, N. B. (2016). Development and randomized trial evaluation of a novel computer-delivered anxiety sensitivity intervention. *Behaviour Research and Therapy, 81*, 47–55. doi: 10.1016/j.brat.2016.04.001

Carretié, L., Ruiz-Padial, E., López-Martín, S., & Albert, J. (2011). Decomposing unpleasantness: Differential exogenous attention to disgusting and fearful stimuli. *Biological Psychology, 86*, 247–253. doi: 10.1016/j.biopsycho.2010.12.005

Cavanagh, K. & Davey, G. C. L. (2000). The development of a measure of individual differences in disgust. Paper presented to the British Psychological Society.

Chapman, H. A., Johannes, K., Poppenk, J. L., Moscovitch, M., & Anderson, A. K. (2013). Evidence for the differential salience of disgust and fear in episodic memory. *Journal of Experimental Psychology: General, 142*(4), 1100–1112. doi: 10.1037/a0030503

Charash, M. & McKay, D. (2002). Attention bias for disgust. *Journal of Anxiety Disorders, 16*(5), 529–541. doi: 10.1016/S0887-6185(02)00171–8

Charash, M. & McKay, D. (2009). Disgust and contamination fear: Attention, memory, and judgment of stimulus situations. *International Journal of Cognitive Therapy*, *2*(1), 53–65. doi: 10.1521/ijct.2009.2.1.53

Charash, M., McKay, D., & Dipaolo, N. (2006). Implicit attention bias for disgust. *Anxiety, Stress & Coping*, *19*(4), 353–364. doi: 10.1080/10615800601055915

Cisler, J. M., Olatunji, B. O., & Lohr, J. M. (2009). Disgust sensitivity and emotion regulation potentiate the effect of disgust propensity on spider fear, blood-injection-injury fear, and contamination fear. *Journal of Behavior Therapy and Experimental Psychiatry*, *40*(2), 219–229. doi: 10.1016/j.jbtep.2008.10.002

Cisler, J. M., Olatunji, B. O., Lohr, J. M., & Williams, N. L. (2009). Attentional bias differences between fear and disgust: Implications for the role of disgust in disgust-related anxiety disorders. *Cognition and Emotion*, *23*(4), 675–687. doi: 10.1080/02699930802051599

Cougle, J. R., Summers, B. J., Harvey, A. M., Dillon, K. H., & Allan, N. P. (2016). Contamination-focused exposure as a treatment for disgust-based fears: A preliminary test in spider-fearful women. *Behavioural and Cognitive Psychotherapy*, *44*, 640–651. doi: 10.1017/S1352465816000333

Craske, M. G. (2003). *The Origins of Phobias and Anxiety Disorders: Why More Women Than Men?* Oxford: Elsevier Science.

Curtis, V. & Biran, A. (2001). Dirt, disgust, and disease. *Perspectives in Biology and Medicine*, *44*(1), 17–31.

Curtis, V., de Barra, M., & Aunger, R. (2011). Disgust as an adaptive system for disease avoidance behaviour. *Philosophical Transactions of the Royal Society B: Biological Sciences*, *366*, 389–401. doi: 10.1098/rstb.2010.0117

Darwin, C., Ekman, P., & Prodger, P. (2009). *The Expression of the Emotions in Man and Animals (200th Anniversary Edition)*. New York, NY: Oxford University Press. (Original work published 1872).

Davey, G. C. L. & Bond, N. (2006). Using controlled comparisons in disgust psychopathology research: The case of disgust, hypochondriasis and health anxiety. *Journal of Behavior Therapy and Experimental Psychiatry*, *37*, 4–15. doi: 10.1016/j.jbtep.2005.09.001

Davey, G. C., Buckland, G., Tantow, B., & Dallos, R. (1998). Disgust and eating disorders. *European Eating Disorders Review*, *6*(3), 201–211. doi: 10.1002/(SICI)1099-0968(199809)6:3<201::AID-ERV224>3.0.CO;2-E

David, B., Olatunji, B. O., Armstrong, T., Ciesielski, B. G., Bondy, C. L., & Broman-Fulks, J. (2009). Incremental specificity of disgust sensitivity in the prediction of obsessive-compulsive disorder symptoms: Cross-sectional and prospective approaches. *Journal of Behavior Therapy and Experimental Psychiatry*, *40*(4), 533–543. doi: 10.1016/j.jbtep.2009.07.004

Deacon, B. J. & Maack, D. J. (2008). The effects of safety behaviors on the fear of contamination: An experimental investigation. *Behaviour Research and Therapy*, *46*(4), 537–547. doi: 10.1016/j.brat.2008.01.010

Deacon, B. J. & Olatunji, B. O. (2007). Specificity of disgust sensitivity in the prediction of behavioral avoidance in contamination fear. *Behaviour Research and Therapy*, *45*(9), 2110–2120. doi: 10.1016/j.brat.2007.03.008

De Houwer, J. (2002). The Implicit Association Test as a tool for studying dysfunctional associations in psychopathology: Strengths and limitations. *Journal of Behavior Therapy and Experimental Psychiatry, 33*, 115–133.

de Jong, P. J., Andrea, H., & Muris, P. (1997). Spider phobia in children: Disgust and fear before and after treatment. *Behaviour Research and Therapy, 35*(6), 559–562. doi: 10.1016/S0005-7967(97)00002-8

de Jong, P. J. & Merckelbach, H. (1998). Blood-injection-injury phobia and fear of spiders: Domain specific individual differences in disgust sensitivity. *Personality and Individual Differences, 24*(2), 153–158. doi: 10.1016/S0191-8869(97)00178-5

de Jong, P. J., Peters, M., & Vanderhallen, I. (2002). Disgust and disgust sensitivity in spider phobia: Facial EMG in response to spider and oral disgust imagery. *Journal of Anxiety Disorders, 16*, 477–493.

de Jong, P. J., van Overveld, M., & Peters, M. L. (2011). Sympathetic and parasympathetic responses to a core disgust video clip as a function of disgust propensity and disgust sensitivity. *Biological Psychology, 88*(2–3), 174–179. doi: 10.1016/j.biopsycho.2011.07.009

de Jong, P. J., Vorage, I., & van den Hout, M. A. (2000). Counterconditioning in the treatment of spider phobia: Effects on disgust, fear and valence. *Behaviour Research and Therapy, 38*(11), 1055–1069. doi: 10.1016/S0005-7967(99)00135-7

Definitions of the RDoC Domains and Constructs. (n.d.). Retrieved October 23, 2017, from www.nimh.nih.gov/research-priorities/rdoc/definitions-of-the-rdoc-domains-and-constructs.shtml.

Druschel, B. A. & Sherman, M. F. (1999). Disgust sensitivity as a function of the Big Five and gender. *Personality and Individual Differences, 26*, 739–748.

Duchowski, A. T. (2002). A breadth-first survey of eye-tracking applications. *Behavior Research Methods, Instruments, & Computers, 34*(4), 455–470. doi: 10.3758/BF03195475

Ekman, P. & Friesen, W. V. (1978). *Facial Action Coding System (FACS): A Technique for the Measurement of Facial Action*. Palo Alto, CA: Consulting Psychologists Press.

Elwood, L. S., Riskind, J. H., & Olatunji, B. O. (2011). Looming vulnerability: Incremental validity of a fearful cognitive distortion in contamination fears. *Cognitive Therapy and Research, 35*, 40–47. doi: 10.1007/s10608-009-9277-3

Engelhard, I. M., Olatunji, B. O., & de Jong, P. J. (2011). Disgust and the development of posttraumatic stress among soldiers deployed to Afghanistan. *Journal of Anxiety Disorders, 25*(1), 58–63. doi: 10.1016/j.janxdis.2010.08.003

Fallon, A. E., Rozin, P., & Pliner, P. (1984). The child's conception of food: The development of food rejections with special reference to disgust and contamination sensitivity. *Child Development, 55*(2), 566–575.

Fan, Q. & Olatunji, B. O. (2013). Individual differences in disgust sensitivity and health-related avoidance: Examination of specific associations. *Personality and Individual Differences, 55*(5), 454–458. doi: 10.1016/j.paid.2013.04.007

Fergus, T. A. & Valentiner, D. P. (2009). The Disgust Propensity and Sensitivity Scale – Revised: An examination of a reduced-item version. *Journal of Anxiety Disorders, 23*, 703–710. doi: 10.1016/j.janxdis.2009.02.009

Ferré, P., Haro, J., & Hinojosa, J. A. (2017). Be aware of the rifle but do not forget the stench: Differential effects of fear and disgust on lexical processing and memory. *Cognition and Emotion*, 1–16. doi: 10.1080/02699931.2017.1356700

Goetz, A. R., Lee, H. J., Cougle, J. R., & Turkel, J. E. (2013). Disgust propensity and sensitivity: Differential relationships with obsessive-compulsive symptoms and behavioral approach task performance. *Journal of Obsessive-Compulsive and Related Disorders*, *2*(4), 412–419. doi: 10.1016/j.jocrd.2013.07.006

Greenwald, A. G., McGhee, D. E., & Schwartz, J. L. K. (1998). Measuring individual differences in implicit cognition: The Implicit Association Test. *Journal of Personality and Social Psychology*, *74*(6), 1464–1480.

Haidt, J., McCauley, C. R., & Rozin, P. (1994). Individual differences in sensitivity to disgust: A scale sampling seven domains of disgust elicitors. *Personality and Individual Differences*, *16*(5), 701–713. doi: 10.1016/0191–8869(94)90212–7

Huijding, J. & de Jong, P. J. (2007). Beyond fear and disgust: The role of (automatic) contamination-related associations in spider phobia. *Journal of Behavior Therapy and Experimental Psychiatry*, *38*, 200–211. doi: 10.1016/j.jbtep.2006.10.009

Husted, D. S., Shapira, N. A., & Goodman, W. K. (2006). The neurocircuitry of obsessive-compulsive disorder and disgust. *Progress in Neuro-Psychopharmacology and Biological Psychiatry*, *30*(3), 389–399. doi: 10.1016/j.pnpbp.2005.11.024

Kang, J. I., Kim, S. J., Namkoong, K., & An, S. K. (2010). Association of DRD4 and COMT polymorphisms with disgust sensitivity in healthy volunteers. *Neuropsychobiology*, *61*, 105–112. doi: 10.1159/000275822

Keough, M. E. & Schmidt, N. B. (2012). Refinement of a brief anxiety sensitivity reduction intervention. *Journal of Consulting and Clinical Psychology*, *80*(5), 766–772. doi: 10.1037/a0027961

Kim, E. H., Ebesutani, C., Young, J., & Olatunji, B. O. (2013). Factor structure of the Disgust Scale-Revised in an adolescent sample. *Assessment*, *20*(5), 620–631. doi: 10.1177/1073191111434200

Kleinknecht, R. A., Kleinknecht, E. E., & Thorndike, R. M. (1997). The role of disgust and fear in blood and injection-related fainting symptoms: A structural equation model. *Behaviour Research and Therapy*, *35*(12), 1075–1087.

Knowles, K. A., Viar-Paxton, M. A., Riemann, B. C., Jacobi, D. M., & Olatunji, B. O. (2016). Is disgust proneness sensitive to treatment for OCD among youth? Examination of diagnostic specificity and symptom correlates. *Journal of Anxiety Disorders*, *44*, 47–54. doi: 10.1016/j.janxdis.2016.09.011

Koch, M. D., Neill, H. K. O., Sawchuk, C. N., & Connolly, K. (2002). Domain-specific and generalized disgust sensitivity in blood-injection-injury phobia: The application of behavioral approach/avoidance tasks. *Journal of Anxiety Disorders*, *16*, 511–527. doi: 10.1016/S0887-6185(02)00170–6

Kollareth, D. & Russell, J. A. (2017). The English word *disgust* has no exact translation in Hindi or Malayalam. *Cognition and Emotion*, *31*(6), 1169–1180. doi: 10.1080/02699931.2016.1202200

Kraines, M. A., Kelberer, L. J. A., & Wells, T. T. (2016). Sex differences in attention to disgust facial expressions. *Cognition and Emotion*, 1–6. doi: 10.1080/02699931.2016.1244044

Krusemark, E. A. & Li, W. (2011). Do all threats work the same way? Divergent effects of fear and disgust on sensory perception and attention. *Journal of Neuroscience, 31* (9), 3429–3434. doi: 10.1523/JNEUROSCI.4394–10.2011

Leutgeb, V., Schäfer, A., Köchel, A., Scharmüller, W., & Schienle, A. (2010). Psychophysiology of spider phobia in 8- to 12-year-old girls. *Biological Psychology, 85*(3), 424–431. doi: 10.1016/j.biopsycho.2010.09.004

Levenson, R. W. (1992). Autonomic nervous system differences among emotions. *Psychological Science, 3*(1), 23–27. doi: 10.1111/j.1467–9280.1992.tb00251.x

Liu, Y., Zhang, D., & Luo, Y. (2015). How disgust facilitates avoidance: An ERP study on attention modulation by threats. *Social Cognitive and Affective Neuroscience, 10*, 598–604. doi: 10.1093/scan/nsu094

Ludvik, D., Boschen, M. J., & Neumann, D. L. (2015). Effective behavioural strategies for reducing disgust in contamination-related OCD: A review. *Clinical Psychology Review, 42*, 116–129. doi: 10.1016/j.cpr.2015.07.001

Marzillier, S. & Davey, G. C. L. (2004). The emotional profiling of disgust-eliciting stimuli: Evidence for primary and complex disgusts. *Cognition and Emotion, 18*(3), 313–336. doi: 10.1080/02699930341000130

Mason, E. C. & Richardson, R. (2010). Looking beyond fear: The extinction of other emotions implicated in anxiety disorders. *Journal of Anxiety Disorders, 24*(1), 63–70. doi: 10.1016/j.janxdis.2009.08.007

Mataix-Cols, D., An, S. K., Lawrence, N. S., Caseras, X., Speckens, A., Giampietro, V., ... Phillips, M. L. (2008). Individual differences in disgust sensitivity modulate neural responses to aversive/disgusting stimuli. *European Journal of Neuroscience, 27*(11), 3050–3058. doi: 10.1111/j.1460–9568.2008.06311.x

Matchett, G. & Davey, G. C. L. (1991). A test of a disease-avoidance model of animal phobias. *Behaviour Research and Therapy, 29*(1), 91–94. doi: 10.1016/S0005-7967(09)80011–9

McEvedy, C. (1988). The bubonic plague. *Scientific American, 258*(2), 118–123. www.jstor.org/stable/24988987

McKay, D. (2006). Treating disgust reactions in contamination-based obsessive-compulsive disorder. *Journal of Behavior Therapy and Experimental Psychiatry, 37*(1), 53–59. doi: 10.1016/j.jbtep.2005.09.005

Mulkens, S. A. N., de Jong, P. J., & Merckelbach, H. (1996). Disgust and spider phobia. *Journal of Abnormal Psychology, 105*(3), 464–468. doi: 10.1037/0021-843X.105.3.464

Muris, P., Merckelbach, H., Schmidt, H., & Tierney, S. (1999). Disgust sensitivity, trait anxiety and anxiety disorders symptoms in normal children. *Behaviour Research and Therapy, 37*, 953–961. doi: 10.1016/S0005-7967(99)00045–5

Muris, P., van der Heiden, S., & Rassin, E. (2008). Disgust sensitivity and psychopathological symptoms in non-clinical children. *Journal of Behavior Therapy and Experimental Psychiatry, 39*(2), 133–146. doi: 10.1016/j.jbtep.2007.02.001

Nicholson, E. & Barnes-Holmes, D. (2012). Developing an implicit measure of disgust propensity and disgust sensitivity: Examining the role of implicit disgust propensity and sensitivity in obsessive-compulsive tendencies. *Journal of Behavior Therapy and Experimental Psychiatry, 43*(3), 922–930. doi: 10.1016/j.jbtep.2012.02.001

Olatunji, B. O. (2010). Changes in disgust correspond with changes in symptoms of contamination-based OCD: A prospective examination of specificity. *Journal of Anxiety Disorders, 24*(3), 313–317. doi: 10.1016/j.janxdis.2010.01.003

Olatunji, B. O. (2015). Selective effects of excessive engagement in health-related behaviours on disgust propensity. *Cognition and Emotion, 29*(5), 37–41. doi: 10.1080/02699931.2014.951314

Olatunji, B. O., Adams, T., Ciesielski, B., David, B., Sarawgi, S., & Broman-Fulks, J. (2012). The Three Domains of Disgust Scale: Factor structure, psychometric properties, and conceptual limitations. *Assessment, 19*(2), 205–225. doi: 10.1177/1073191111432881

Olatunji, B. O., Armstrong, T., & Elwood, L. (2017). Is disgust proneness associated with anxiety and related disorders? A qualitative review and meta-analysis of group comparison and correlational studies. *Perspectives on Psychological Science, 12*(4), 613–648. doi: 10.1177/1745691616688879

Olatunji, B. O., Armstrong, T., Fan, Q., & Zhao, M. (2014). Risk and resiliency in posttraumatic stress disorder: Distinct roles of anxiety and disgust sensitivity. *Psychological Trauma: Theory, Research, Practice, and Policy, 6*(1), 50–55.

Olatunji, B. O. & Broman-Fulks, J. J. (2007). A taxometric study of the latent structure of disgust sensitivity: Converging evidence for dimensionality. *Psychological Assessment, 19*(4), 437–448. doi: 10.1037/1040–3590.19.4.437

Olatunji, B. O., Cisler, J. M., Deacon, B. J., Connolly, K. M., & Lohr, J. M. (2007). The Disgust Propensity and Sensitivity Scale-Revised: Psychometric properties and specificity in relation to anxiety disorder symptoms. *Journal of Anxiety Disorders, 21*(7), 918–930. doi: 10.1016/j.janxdis.2006.12.005

Olatunji, B. O., Cisler, J. M., McKay, D., & Phillips, M. L. (2010). Is disgust associated with psychopathology? Emerging research in the anxiety disorders. *Psychiatry Research, 175*(1–2), 1–10. doi: 10.1016/j.psychres.2009.04.007

Olatunji, B. O., Ebesutani, C., David, B., Fan, Q., & McGrath, P. B. (2011). Disgust proneness and obsessive-compulsive symptoms in a clinical sample: Structural differentiation from negative affect. *Journal of Anxiety Disorders, 25*(7), 932–938. doi: 10.1016/j.janxdis.2011.05.006

Olatunji, B. O., Ebesutani, C., & Kim, E. H. (2016). Does the measure matter? On the association between disgust proneness and OCD symptoms. *Journal of Anxiety Disorders, 44*, 63–72. doi: 10.1016/j.janxdis.2016.10.010

Olatunji, B. O., Haidt, J., McKay, D., & David, B. (2008). Core, animal reminder, and contamination disgust: Three kinds of disgust with distinct personality, behavioral, physiological, and clinical correlates. *Journal of Research in Personality, 42*, 1243–1259. doi: 10.1016/j.jrp.2008.03.009

Olatunji, B. O., Huijding, J., de Jong, P. J., & Smits, J. A. J. (2011). The relative contributions of fear and disgust reductions to improvements in spider phobia following exposure-based treatment. *Journal of Behavior Therapy and Experimental Psychiatry, 42*(1), 117–121. doi: 10.1016/j.jbtep.2010.07.007

Olatunji, B. O., Lohr, J. M., Sawchuk, C. N., & Tolin, D. F. (2007). Multimodal assessment of disgust in contamination-related obsessive-compulsive disorder. *Behaviour Research and Therapy, 45*(2), 263–276. doi: 10.1016/j.brat.2006.03.004

Olatunji, B. O., Moretz, M. W., McKay, D., Bjorklund, F., de Jong, P. J., Haidt, J., . . . Schienle, A. (2009). Confirming the three-factor structure of the Disgust Scale-Revised in eight countries. *Journal of Cross-Cultural Psychology, 40*(2), 234–255.

Olatunji, B. O., Moretz, M. W., Wolitzky-Taylor, K. B., McKay, D., McGrath, P. B., & Ciesielski, B. G. (2010). Disgust vulnerability and symptoms of contamination-based OCD: Descriptive tests of incremental specificity. *Behavior Therapy, 41*(4), 475–490. doi: 10.1016/j.beth.2009.11.005

Olatunji, B. O., Sawchuk, C. N., de Jong, P. J., & Lohr, J. M. (2006). The structural relation between disgust sensitivity and blood-injection-injury fears: A cross-cultural comparison of US and Dutch data. *Journal of Behavior Therapy and Experimental Psychiatry, 37*(1), 16–29. doi: 10.1016/j.jbtep.2005.09.002

Olatunji, B. O., Sawchuk, C. N., de Jong, P. J., & Lohr, J. M. (2007). Disgust sensitivity and anxiety disorder symptoms: Psychometric properties of the Disgust Emotion Scale. *Journal of Psychopathology and Behavioral Assessment, 29*, 115–124. doi: 10.1007/s10862-006–9027-8

Olatunji, B. O., Sawchuk, C. N., Lohr, J. M., & de Jong, P. J. (2004). Disgust domains in the prediction of contamination fear. *Behaviour Research and Therapy, 42*, 93–104. doi: 10.1016/S0005-7967(03)00102–5

Olatunji, B. O., Tart, C. D., Ciesielski, B. G., McGrath, P. B., & Smits, J. A. J. (2011). Specificity of disgust vulnerability in the distinction and treatment of OCD. *Journal of Psychiatric Research, 45*(9), 1236–1242. doi: 10.1016/j .jpsychires.2011.01.018

Olatunji, B. O., Williams, N. L., Lohr, J. M., Connolly, K. M., Cisler, J. M., & Meunier, S. A. (2007). Structural differentiation of disgust from trait anxiety in the prediction of specific anxiety disorder symptoms. *Behaviour Research and Therapy, 45*(12), 3002–3017. doi: 10.1016/j.brat.2007.08.011

Olatunji, B. O., Williams, N. L., Tolin, D. F., Abramowitz, J. S., Sawchuk, C. N., Lohr, J. M., & Elwood, L. S. (2007). The Disgust Scale: Item analysis, factor structure, and suggestions for refinement. *Psychological Assessment, 19*(3), 281–297. doi: 10.1037/1040–3590.19.3.281

Page, A. C. (1994). Blood-injury phobia. *Clinical Psychology Review, 14*(5), 443–461. doi: 10.1016/0272–7358(94)90036–1

Phillips, M. L., Fahy, T., David, A. S., & Senior, C. (1998). Disgust: The forgotten emotion of psychiatry. *British Journal of Psychiatry, 172*, 373–375. doi: 10.1192/ bjp.172.5.373

Posner, M. I. (1980). Orienting of attention. *Quarterly Journal of Experimental Psychology, 32*(1), 3–25. doi: 10.1080/00335558008248231

Quigley, J. F., Sherman, M. F., & Sherman, N. C. (1997). Personality disorder symptoms, gender, and age as predictors of adolescent disgust sensitivity. *Personality & Individual Differences, 22*(5), 661–667.

Rachman, S. (2004). Fear of contamination. *Behaviour Research and Therapy, 42*(11), 1227–1255. doi: 10.1016/j.brat.2003.10.009

Richardson, D. C. & Spivey, M. J. (2004). Eye tracking: Characteristics and methods. *Encyclopedia of Biomaterials and Biomedical Engineering, 3*, 1028–1042.

Riskind, J. H. & Williams, N. L. (2006). A unique vulnerability common to all anxiety disorders: The looming maladaptive style. In L. B. Alloy & J. H. Riskind (eds.),

Cognitive Vulnerability to Emotional Disorders (pp. 175–206). Mahwah, NJ: Lawrence Erlbaum Associates. doi: 10.4324/9781410615787

Rohner, J.-C. (2002). The time-course of visual threat processing: High trait anxious individuals eventually avert their gaze from angry faces. *Cognition and Emotion, 16*(6), 837–844. doi: 10.1080/02699930143000572

Rozin, P. & Fallon, A. E. (1987). A perspective on disgust. *Psychological Review, 94*(1), 23–41. doi: 10.1037/0033-295X.94.1.23

Rozin, P., Fallon, A. E., & Augustoni-Ziskind, M. (1985). The child's conception of food: The development of contamination sensitivity to "disgusting" substances. *Developmental Psychology, 21*(6), 1075–1079. doi: 10.1037/0012-1649.21.6.1075

Rozin, P., Fallon, A. E., & Mandell, R. (1984). Family resemblance in attitudes to foods. *Developmental Psychology, 20*(2), 309–314. doi: 10.1037/0012-1649.20.2.309

Rozin, P., Haidt, J., & McCauley, C. R. (2008). Disgust. In M. Lewis, J. M. Haviland-Jones, & L. F. Barrett (eds.), *Handbook of Emotions* (3rd edn) (pp. 757–776). New York, NY: Guilford Press.

Rozin, P., Haidt, J., McCauley, C. R., Dunlop, L., & Ashmore, M. (1999). Individual differences in disgust sensitivity: Comparisons and evaluations of paper-and-pencil versus behavioral measures. *Journal of Research in Personality, 33*(3), 330–351. doi: 10.1006/jrpe.1999.2251

Rozin, P., Lowery, L., & Ebert, R. (1994). Varieties of disgust faces and the structure of disgust. *Journal of Personality and Social Psychology, 66*(5), 870–881. doi: 10.1037/0022-3514.66.5.870

Rozin, P. & Millman, L. (1987). Family environment, not heredity, accounts for family resemblances in food preferences and attitudes: A twin study. *Appetite, 8*, 125–134.

Rozin, P. & Nemeroff, C. (1990). The laws of sympathetic magic: A psychological analysis of similarity and contagion. In J. W. Stigler, R. A. Shweder, & G. Herdt (eds.), *Cultural Psychology: Essays on Comparative Human Development* (pp. 205–232). New York, NY: Cambridge University Press.

Sawchuk, C. N., Lohr, J. M., Lee, T. C., & Tolin, D. F. (1999). Exposure to disgust-evoking imagery and information processing biases in blood-injection-injury phobia. *Behaviour Research and Therapy, 37*(3), 249–257. doi: 10.1016/S0005-7967(98)00127-2

Sawchuk, C. N., Lohr, M., Tolin, D. F., Lee, T. C., & Kleinknecht, R. A. (2000). Disgust sensitivity and contamination fears in spider and blood-injection-injury phobias. *Behaviour Research and Therapy, 38*, 753–762. doi: 10.1016/S0005-7967(99)00093-5

Sawchuk, C. N., Lohr, J. M., Westendorf, D. H., Meunier, S. A., & Tolin, D. F. (2002). Emotional responding to fearful and disgusting stimuli in specific phobics. *Behaviour Research and Therapy, 40*(9), 1031–1046. doi: 10.1016/S0005-7967(01)00093-6

Schmidt, N. B., Eggleston, A. M., Woolaway-Bickel, K., Fitzpatrick, K. K., Vasey, M. W., & Richey, J. A. (2007). Anxiety Sensitivity Amelioration Training (ASAT): A long-itudinal primary prevention program targeting cognitive vulnerability. *Journal of Anxiety Disorders, 21*(3), 302–319. doi: 10.1016/j.janxdis.2006.06.002

Schmidt, N. B., Zvolensky, M. J., & Maner, J. K. (2006). Anxiety sensitivity: Prospective prediction of panic attacks and Axis I pathology. *Journal of Psychiatric Research, 40*(8), 691–699. doi: 10.1016/j.jpsychires.2006.07.009

Shapira, N. A., Liu, Y., He, A. G., Bradley, M. M., Lessig, M. C., James, G. A., ... Goodman, W. K. (2003). Brain activation by disgust-inducing pictures in obsessive-compulsive disorder. *Biological Psychiatry*, *54*(7), 751–756. doi: 10.1016/S0006-3223(03)00003-9

Sherlock, J. M., Zietsch, B. P., Tybur, J. M., & Jern, P. (2016). The quantitative genetics of disgust sensitivity. *Emotion*, *16*(1), 43–51. doi: 10.1037/emo0000101

Stein, D. J. & Bouwer, C. (1997). A neuro-evolutionary approach to the anxiety disorders. *Journal of Anxiety Disorders*, *11*(4), 409–429. doi: 10.1016/S0887-6185(97)00019-4

Stein, D. J., Liu, Y., Shapira, N. A., & Goodman, W. K. (2001). The psychobiology of obsessive-compulsive disorder: How important is the role of disgust? *Current Psychiatry Reports*, *3*(4), 281–287. doi: 10.1007/s11920-001–0020-3

Stevenson, R. J., Oaten, M. J., Case, T. I., Repacholi, B. M., & Wagland, P. (2010). Children's response to adult disgust elicitors: Development and acquisition. *Developmental Psychology*, *46*(1), 165–177. doi: 10.1037/a0016692

Taboas, W., Ojserkis, R., & McKay, D. (2014). Change in disgust reactions following cognitive-behavioral therapy for childhood anxiety disorders. *International Journal of Clinical and Health Psychology*, *15*(1), 1–7. doi: 10.1016/j.ijchp.2014.06.002

Teachman, B. A. (2006). Pathological disgust: In the thoughts, not the eye, of the beholder. *Anxiety, Stress, and Coping*, *19*(4), 335–351. doi: 10.1080/10615800601055923

Teachman, B. A., Gregg, A. P., & Woody, S. R. (2001). Implicit processing of fear-relevant stimuli among individuals with snake and spider fears. *Journal of Abnormal Psychology*, *110*(2), 226–235. doi: 10.1037//0021-843X.110.2.226

Timpano, K. R., Raines, A. M., Shaw, A. M., Keough, M. E., & Schmidt, N. B. (2016). Effects of a brief anxiety sensitivity reduction intervention on obsessive compulsive spectrum symptoms in a young adult sample. *Journal of Psychiatric Research*, *83*, 8–15. doi: 10.1016/j.jpsychires.2016.07.022

Thorpe, S. J., Barnett, J., Friend, K., & Nottingham, K. (2011). The mediating roles of disgust sensitivity and danger expectancy in relation to hand washing behaviour. *Behavioural and Cognitive Psychotherapy*, *39*(2), 175–190. doi: 10.1017/S1352465810000676

Thorpe, S. J., Patel, S. P., & Simonds, L. M. (2003). The relationship between disgust sensitivity, anxiety and obsessions. *Behaviour Research and Therapy*, *41*, 1397–1409. doi: 10.1016/S0005-7967(03)00058-5

Tolin, D. F., Woods, C. M., & Abramowitz, J. S. (2006). Disgust sensitivity and obsessive-compulsive symptoms in a non-clinical sample. *Journal of Behavior Therapy and Experimental Psychiatry*, *37*(1), 30–40. doi: 10.1016/j.jbtep.2005.09.003

Troop, N. A., Treasure, J. L., & Serpell, L. (2002). A further exploration of disgust in eating disorders. *European Eating Disorders Review*, *10*(3), 218–226.

Tsao, S. D. & McKay, D. (2004). Behavioral avoidance tests and disgust in contamination fears: Distinctions from trait anxiety. *Behaviour Research and Therapy*, *42*(2), 207–216. doi: 10.1016/S0005-7967(03)00119–0

Tybur, J. M., Lieberman, D., & Griskevicius, V. (2009). Microbes, mating, and morality: Individual differences in three functional domains of disgust. *Journal of Personality and Social Psychology*, *97*(1), 103–122. doi: 10.1037/a0015474 van Hooff, J. C., Devue, C., Vieweg, P. E., & Theeuwes, J. (2013). Disgust- and not fear-evoking images hold our attention. *Acta Psychologica*, *143*, 1–6. doi: 10.1016/j.actpsy.2013.02.001

van Overveld, W. J. M., de Jong, P. J., & Peters, M. L. (2009). Digestive and cardiovascular responses to core and animal-reminder disgust. *Biological Psychology*, *80*, 149–157. doi: 10.1016/j.biopsycho.2008.08.002

van Overveld, W. J. M., de Jong, P. J., & Peters, M. L. (2010). The Disgust Propensity and Sensitivity Scale – Revised: Its predictive value for avoidance behavior. *Personality and Individual Differences*, *49*(7), 706–711. doi: 10.1016/j.paid.2010.06.008

van Overveld, W. J. M., de Jong, P. J., Peters, M. L., Cavanagh, K., & Davey, G. C. L. (2006). Disgust propensity and disgust sensitivity: Separate constructs that are differentially related to specific fears. *Personality and Individual Differences*, *41*, 1241–1252. doi: 10.1016/j.paid.2006.04.021

van Overveld, W. J. M., de Jong, P. J., Peters, M. L., van Hout, W. J. P. J., & Bouman, T. K. (2008). An Internet-based study on the relation between disgust sensitivity and emetophobia. *Journal of Anxiety Disorders*, *22*(3), 524–531. doi: 10.1016/j.janxdis.2007.04.001

Viar-Paxton, M. A., Ebesutani, C., Kim, E. H., Ollendick, T. H., Young, J., & Olatunji, B. O. (2015). Development and initial validation of the Child Disgust Scale. *Psychological Assessment*, *27*(3), 1–15. doi: 10.1037/a0038925

Vossbeck-Elsebusch, A. N. & Gerlach, A. L. (2012). The relation between disgust-sensitivity, blood-injection-injury fears and vasovagal symptoms in blood donors: Disgust sensitivity cannot explain fainting or blood donation-related symptoms. *Journal of Behavior Therapy and Experimental Psychiatry*, *43*, 607–613. doi: 10.1016/j.jbtep.2011.08.005

Vossbeck-Elsebusch, A. N., Steinigeweg, K., Vögele, C., & Gerlach, A. L. (2012). Does disgust increase parasympathetic activation in individuals with a history of fainting? A psychophysiological analysis of disgust stimuli with and without blood-injection-injury association. *Journal of Anxiety Disorders*, *26*(8), 849–858. doi: 10.1016/j.janxdis.2012.07.003

Vrana, S. R. (1993). The psychophysiology of disgust: Differentiating negative emotional contexts with facial EMG. *Psychophysiology*, *30*(3), 279–286. doi: 10.1111/j.1469–8986.1993.tb03354.x

Walls, M. M. & Kleinknecht, R. A. (1996). Disgust factors as predictors of blood-injury fear and fainting. Paper presented at the annual meeting of the Western Psychological Association, San Jose, CA.

Ware, J., Jain, K., Burgess, I., & Davey, G. C. L. (1994). Disease-avoidance model: Factor analysis of common animal fears. *Behaviour Research and Therapy*, *32*(1), 57–63. doi: 10.1016/0005–7967(94)90084–1

Watkins, T. J., Di Iorio, C. R., Olatunji, B. O., Benningfield, M. M., Blackford, J. U., Dietrich, M. S., . . . Cowan, R. L. (2015). Disgust proneness and associated neural substrates in obesity. *Social Cognitive and Affective Neuroscience*, *11*(3), 458–465. doi: 10.1093/scan/nsv129

Weck, F., Esch, S., & Rohrmann, S. (2014). The role of disgust in patients with hypochondriasis. *Anxiety, Stress, & Coping*, *27*(5), 576–586. doi: 10.1080/10615806.2013.873793

Weierich, M. R., Treat, T. A., & Hollingworth, A. (2008). Theories and measurement of visual attentional processing in anxiety. *Cognition and Emotion*, 22. doi: 10.1080/02699930701597601

Wheaton, M. G., Abramowitz, J. S., Berman, N. C., Fabricant, L. E., & Olatunji, B. O. (2012). Psychological predictors of anxiety in response to the H1N1 (swine flu) pandemic. *Cognitive Therapy and Research*, *36*, 210–218. doi: 10.1007/s10608-011–9353-3

Whitton, A. E., Henry, J. D., & Grisham, J. R. (2014). Moral rigidity in obsessive-compulsive disorder: Do abnormalities in inhibitory control, cognitive flexibility and disgust play a role? *Journal of Behavior Therapy and Experimental Psychiatry*, *45*(1), 152–159. doi: 10.1016/j.jbtep.2013.10.001

Wicker, B., Keysers, C., Plailly, J., Royet, J.-P., Gallese, V., & Rizzolatti, G. (2003). Both of us disgusted in my insula: The common neural basis of seeing and feeling disgust. *Neuron*, *40*, 655–664. doi: 10.1016/S0896-6273(03)00679–2

Williams, N. L., Olatunji, B. O., Elwood, L. S., Connolly, K. M., & Lohr, J. M. (2006). Cognitive vulnerability to disgust: Development and validation of the Looming of Disgust Questionnaire. *Anxiety, Stress & Coping*, *19*(4), 365–382. doi: 10.1080/10615800601053910

Woody, S. R., McLean, C., & Klassen, T. (2005). Disgust as a motivator of avoidance of spiders. *Journal of Anxiety Disorders*, *19*, 461–475. doi: 10.1016/j.janxdis.2004.04.002

Woody, S. R. & Tolin, D. F. (2002). The relationship between disgust sensitivity and avoidant behavior: Studies of clinical and nonclinical samples. *Journal of Anxiety Disorders*, *16*(5),543–559. doi: 10.1016/S0887-6185(02)00173–1

Wright, P., He, G., Shapira, N. A., Goodman, W. K., & Liu, Y. (2004). Disgust and the insula: fMRI responses to pictures of mutilation and contamination. *Neuroreport*, *15*(15), 2347–2351. doi: 10.1097/00001756–200410250-00009

Zhang, D., Liu, Y., Zhou, C., Chen, Y., & Luo, Y. (2014). Spatial attention effects of disgusted and fearful faces. *PloS One*, *9*(7). doi: 10.1371/journal.pone.0101608

Zinkernagel, A., Hofmann, W., Dislich, F. X. R., Gschwendner, T., & Schmitt, M. (2011). Indirect assessment of implicit disgust sensitivity. *European Journal of Psychological Assessment*, *27*(4), 237–243. doi: 10.1027/1015–5759/a000078

7 Intolerance of Uncertainty

Peter M. McEvoy, R. Nicholas Carleton, Kelly Correa, Stewart A. Shankman, and Sarah Shihata

> [I]nstead of something acquired during life, intolerance of uncertainty is a crucial property of all living organisms, only to be alleviated when safety is perceived.
>
> Brosschot, Verkuil, and Thayer (2016, p. 31)

Why are unpredictability and uncertainty at times coveted and experienced as pleasurable, while at other times they are feared and avoided? How do individual differences in the capacity to tolerate unknowns contribute to the etiology and maintenance of anxiety and anxiety-related disorders? And how can we understand (in)tolerance of uncertainty within the context of established nosologies and emerging frameworks of psychopathology? The current chapter is designed to provide some answers to these intriguing questions.

We first review contemporary definitions of fear of the unknown and intolerance of uncertainty (IU). We then briefly evaluate the large body of evidence suggesting that IU is associated with symptoms and symptom change for a range of emotional disorders, thereby supporting its status as a transdiagnostic construct. Finally, we discuss how IU theory and research could fit within the Research Domain Criteria (RDoC) from the National Institute of Mental Health (NIMH), an initiative that attempts to move beyond categorical diagnostic entities toward dimensional constructs that can be studied with multiple units of analysis. We hope our attempt to integrate IU into the RDoC framework will inspire future integrative research.

What Are Fear of the Unknown and Intolerance of Uncertainty?

Fear of the Unknown

Fear of the unknown (FOTU) is "an individual's propensity to experience fear caused by the perceived absence of information at any level of consciousness or point of processing" (Carleton, 2016b, p. 39). The definition can be broken into several components. First, the definition explicitly includes a focus on individual propensity, which requires the existence of dynamic individual differences best described along a continuum. Second, the definition takes into account Barlow's (2000) distinction between fear and anxiety. In Barlow's model, fear is an emotion elicited by a present or imminent stimulus perceived as threatening, whereas anxiety is an emotion elicited by uncontrollable or unpredictable potential threats that may occur in the future. FOTU is therefore on the border between fear and anxiety (Carleton, 2016b) as the unknown can produce a fear response (Carleton, 2016a), but the "stimulus" is an absence of information, which necessarily means potential harm rather than certain harm (i.e., anxiety) (Barlow, 2000; Carleton, 2016b). Importantly, FOTU was defined within a context that required fear to be understood as describing a "range of physiological changes, emotional intensities, and associated adjectives" (e.g., from bothered to paralyzing terror producing tonic immobility; Carleton, 2016b, p. 31), rather than as an absolute state (i.e., fear or no fear). Contextualizing fear intensity as continuous along such a range also allows for a variable intensity of fearful responses to unknowns.

Third, the definition includes a causal mechanism, the perceived absence of information, which begins the activation of the defensive motivational system. The absent information must be perceived, but in line with contemporary appraisal theories of emotion (Scherer, 2013), that perception need not be at the conscious level (Carleton, 2016b); instead, the perception likely begins preconsciously as a series of "checks" (Scherer, 2013). The checks involve low-level neural substrates engaged with pattern-matching, rapid schematic memory traces, automatic cortical-level associations, and propositional cortical-level associations (Scherer, 2009). The checks function reflexively as perceptions are processed (Scherer, 2013). The aggregate of such checks and perceptions is the foundation for the appraisal processes that ultimately become experienced as emotions (Sacharin, Sander, & Scherer, 2012; Scherer, 2009). In short, perceived stimuli are compared against information stored in a priori memory. If the stimuli are not found in a priori memory, the stimuli are recognized as unknown (Carleton, 2016b). The relative proportion of unknowns perceived in any given moment is necessarily dynamic; however, incremental increases in the proportion of unknowns will incrementally activate the defensive motivational system of the brain (Carleton, 2016b), increasing the intensity of the fear response, because unknowns are unconditioned threat stimuli (Carleton, 2016a). Alternative theoretical frameworks for emotion (e.g., basic, psychological construction, social construction) still appear to accommodate unknowns as triggering fear responses (Gross & Barrett, 2011); however, at the present time, the appraisal theories do so most explicitly.

Carleton (2016a, 2016b) argued that individual levels of FOTU appear to have specific biological underpinnings described in the behavioral inhibition system (BIS) (Gray & McNaughton, 2003), and those ultimately determine the diversity observed in emotion (Moors, 2009; Moors, Ellsworth, Scherer, & Frijda, 2013; Scherer, 2013), temperament (Kagan & Snidman, 2004), attachment (Bowlby, 1973), and neuroticism (Barlow, Ellard, Sauer-Zavala, Bullis, & Carl, 2014; Clark & Beck, 2010). The BIS describes the neurobiological mechanisms underlying the inhibited or avoidant behavior, increased vigilance, and increased arousal typically associated with fear and anxiety (Gray, 1976). The BIS is activated "by stimuli associated with pain, punishment, failure, loss of reward, novelty, or uncertainty" (Gray & McNaughton, 2003, p. 4). BIS theory suggests that, all things being equal, unknowns "should be treated as sources of potential danger" and therein activate the BIS (Gray & McNaughton, 2003, p. 53). Children categorized as having behaviorally inhibited temperaments, which would be comparable to describing difficulties with neuroticism or negative affect (Carleton, 2016b; Clark & Beck, 2010), can be argued as having a BIS that is more likely to be activated when unknowns are perceived (Kagan & Snidman, 2004). Accordingly, FOTU appears to serve as an individual's propensity for BIS activation when initially encountering unknowns, with IU describing an individual's capacity to tolerate BIS activation subsequent to the initial encounter. Behaviorally inhibited temperament describes an observable response to the FOTU-driven BIS activation and subsequent IU. While there is conceptual overlap between FOTU, BIS, and neuroticism, neuroticism and negative affect describe broader personality traits and emotional propensities of persons with behaviorally inhibited temperament, which reflects difficulties with increased BIS activation, which reflects higher levels of IU and greater FOTU. Despite the seemingly neurobiological underpinnings of FOTU and IU, responses to unknowns appear modifiable (e.g., Mahoney & McEvoy, 2012a; McEvoy & Erceg-Hurn, 2016); accordingly, clarifying the role of FOTU and IU, as well as increasing our understanding of both and how the constructs relate with psychopathology and other associated personality constructs, appears critical.

Intolerance of Uncertainty

Intolerance of uncertainty is "an individual's dispositional incapacity to endure the aversive response triggered by the perceived absence of salient, key, or sufficient information, and sustained by the associated perception of uncertainty" (Carleton, 2016b, p. 31). In short, IU describes an individual's capacity to tolerate their consciously perceived FOTU and the associated activation of the defensive motivational system (Carleton, 2016b, Figure 2, p. 35). The definition can again be broken into several components. First, the definition again requires the existence of dynamic individual differences best described along a continuum. Second, the aversive response allows for a continuum of diverse emotional responses ranging from dislike, to intolerant, to extreme avoidance, which will be driven by the experienced intensity of FOTU. Third, the definition includes distinctions based on information relevance and sufficiency. Not all absent information will be treated equally at any given time because propositional networks provide differential conditional values based on existing knowns. A person may perceive an absent piece of information (e.g., the exact number of hairs on their body; the parachute function as they begin a skydive) that is then contextualized by their perceived knowns (e.g., the absent information is currently irrelevant; the absent information determines life or death). If a person perceives sufficient knowns regarding safety, skydiving could be associated with a significantly positive valence; however, some threshold for sufficiency must be met or the activity will be associated with a significantly negative valence. In the absence of a context-independent known, the notion of sufficiency is critical because the threshold for proportion of knowns to mitigate the activation of the defensive motivational system is subjective, dynamic, and likely underlies continua for personality and psychopathology (Carleton, 2016a, 2016b); accordingly, FOTU and IU are fundamental for understanding psychopathology and effective psychotherapy (Carleton, 2012, 2016a, 2016b).

There have also been several attempts to differentiate IU from other related constructs (e.g., [un]certainty, novelty, ambiguity, [un]familiarity, [un]predictability, strange), all of which might best be understood as variations of responses to perceiving one or more unknowns (Carleton, 2016b). For example, for something to be novel, some part must have been previously unknown. Perhaps the most commonly related construct has been intolerance of ambiguity. The two constructs have been used interchangeably (Carleton, 2012), but they are distinguishable. Intolerance of ambiguity has been suggested as difficulties *with* a current situation because of ambiguous or equivocal features, whereas IU has been suggested as difficulties because the *consequences* of a current situation remain unknown and potentially negative (Grenier, Barrette, & Ladouceur, 2005). Subsequent efforts have extended that polarization of intolerance of ambiguity by highlighting the role of features perceived as equivocal (e.g., the Rubin Vase; Carleton, 2012, 2016b); nevertheless, the core difficulty with FOTU remains.

Increasing FOTU and IU also appear inversely associated with predictability, control, and self-efficacy (Carleton, 2016a). Control requires the ability to predict causal event chains with sufficient certainty that agential actions can influence outcomes (Armfield, 2006; Carleton, 2016b; Grupe & Nitschke, 2013; Thompson, 1981). Perceptions of predictability and control, and therein self-efficacy, all appear founded on perceptions of certainty (Bandura, 1977, 1989, 1997). Persons with high levels of FOTU and IU will likely have higher needs for predictability and control, as well as more limited perceptions of self-efficacy (Carleton, 2016a), all of which can facilitate psychopathology (Carleton, 2016a, 2016b). Overall, the many related constructs can be argued as extensions, elements, dimensions, or manifestations of FOTU and IU.

Facets of IU

Efforts to describe the diverse aspects of IU began with the first definition of IU, which described "a relatively broad construct representing cognitive, emotional, and behavioral reactions to uncertainty in everyday life situations" (Freeston, Rhéaume, Letarte, Dugas, & Ladouceur, 1994, p. 792). The clinically driven definition provided the basis for the first self-report measure to explicitly assess IU, the Intolerance of Uncertainty Scale (IUS) (Freeston et al., 1994). The measure includes 27 items assessing a diverse range of reactions to uncertainty, including attempts to control the future, avoidance of uncertainty, inhibited behaviors, frustration, stress, and self-criticism. Initial factor-analytic efforts were largely unsuccessful in disentangling IU reactions (Hong & Lee, 2015), likely because the absence of information would have pervasive influence across domains of reaction (Carleton, 2016b; Hong & Lee, 2015). A 12-item short form was derived (IUS-12) (Carleton, Norton, & Asmundson, 2007) that produced a two-factor structure, the labels for which were Prospective IU and Inhibitory IU (McEvoy & Mahoney, 2011). The two-factor structure was successfully replicated using all 27 items from the IUS (Birrell, Meares, Wilkinson, & Freeston, 2011) and the labels have become part of common parlance in the area (Hong & Lee, 2015).

Prospective IU describes cognitive manifestations of IU, such as a focus on future events and desires for predictability. Inhibitory IU describes behavioral manifestations of IU, such as present-oriented impaired function, in action, or paralysis (Carleton, Norton et al., 2007; McEvoy & Mahoney, 2011). The two factors appear sufficiently replicable and independent to be meaningful (Hong & Cheung, 2015), but can be represented by a single general factor (Hale et al., 2016) that appears to retain FOTU as a common core (Hong & Cheung, 2015). Despite the psychometric convergence and the common core, there is also evidence of differential relationship patterns between prospective IU, inhibitory IU, and different psychopathological symptom clusters (e.g., Boelen, Reijntjes, & Smid, 2016; Carleton, Collimore, & Asmundson, 2010; Fetzner, Horswill, Boelen, & Carleton, 2013; Mahoney & McEvoy, 2012a, 2012b, 2012c; McEvoy & Mahoney, 2011); indeed, the exploration of different relationship patterns for diverse manifestations of FOTU and IU appears to be an important next step in the area (Shihata, McEvoy, Mullan, & Carleton, 2016).

Although self-reported IU has been historically assessed as a trait, where respondents are asked to indicate what is typical of them, these measures are sensitive to change during relatively brief interventions (McEvoy & Erceg-Hurn, 2016). Similar to previous clinical research investigating other traits such as neuroticism, negative affectivity, and the BIS (e.g., Carl et al., 2014), such findings suggest that "trait IU" is modifiable. Researchers have also begun to emphasize the potential importance of differentiating trait responses to uncertainty from state responses, with a focus on individual differences in the contexts within which IU is particularly elevated (e.g., Mahoney & McEvoy, 2012a). Specifically, whereas all individuals with emotional disorders are likely to be elevated in trait IU, uncertainty in diagnosis-congruent situations (e.g., social evaluative context for someone with social anxiety disorder) is likely to differentially elevate IU depending upon an individual's diagnostic profile. Early speculation about differences in manifestations of IU across symptom clusters were proposed by Mahoney and McEvoy (2012c), who suggested that in addition to a general IU factor, some people could have elevated IU specific to a given context. For example, a person could be generally tolerant of uncertainty, except with respect to cardiovascular sensations wherein they have a particularly low level of tolerance for uncertainty. The pattern is analogous to subscales of anxiety sensitivity indices wherein specific symptoms and consequences of the latent fear can be differentially assessed (Taylor et al., 2007). The intolerance could become extremely specific, such that manifestations depend entirely on the perceived absence of sufficient certainty. For example, the same person may only be intolerant of cardiovascular sensations when a readily identifiable explanation perceived as safe is not available, such as exercise (Carleton, Sharpe, & Asmundson, 2007). The focusing of IU on a specific set of circumstances may help to explain the simultaneously similar and distinctive nature of several psychopathologies. Several researchers have already provided evidence for the concurrence of general IU and situation-specific or disorder-specific IU (e.g., Jensen & Heimberg, 2015; Mahoney & McEvoy, 2012a, 2012b, 2012c; Shihata, McEvoy, & Mullan, 2017; Thibodeau et al., 2015).

IU as a Transdiagnostic Construct

IU and Generalized Anxiety Disorder

Dugas and colleagues initially proposed the intolerance of uncertainty model (IUM) to explain the cognitive and behavioral factors that maintain generalized anxiety disorder (GAD) (Dugas, Gagnon, Ladouceur, & Freeston, 1998), for which the core feature is uncontrollable worry (American Psychiatric Association [APA], 2013). Within the IUM, individuals with intrinsically high IU are vulnerable to an escalation of worry in the face of unknowns. Experiencing "what if" questions within uncertain contexts is common; however, three additional core components of the model are considered to exacerbate the distress of high-IU individuals. The first of these processes is positive beliefs about the helpfulness of worry. Recent research has identified five positive belief domains of worry: (1) facilitates problem-solving, (2) enhances motivation, (3) protects against emotions, (4) prevents negative outcomes, and (5) reflects a positive personality trait (Hebert, Dugas, Tulloch, & Holowka, 2014). The more an individual believes that worry is functionally beneficial, the more likely worry will be used as a coping strategy. Most worries are low-probability events, meaning that the usual absence of negative outcomes (and the associated relief) negatively reinforces worry as a coping strategy, as individuals credit worry with preventing feared outcomes.

The second process that serves to maintain worry is labeled poor problem orientation (Dugas et al., 1998), which includes awareness of problems, appraisals of problems, and perceived efficacy for coping with problems. Interestingly, high-IU individuals tend to have comparable problem-solving skills to low-IU individuals, but do not believe their skills to be comparable (Koerner & Dugas, 2006; Ladouceur, Blais, Freeston, & Dugas, 1998). Within the model, poor problem-solving is considered both a cause and a consequence of worry. The third process that serves to maintain worry is cognitive avoidance (Dugas et al., 1998). There is substantial evidence that mental imagery is associated with more intense positive and negative emotions than verbal thoughts (Holmes, Lang, & Deeprose, 2009; Holmes & Mathews, 2005). Consistent with other avoidance models of worry (Borkovec, Alcaine, & Behar, 2004), the IUM therefore posits the verbal-linguistic process as a strategy to suppress more intense and aversive physiological arousal than would ensue from imagery-based cognitive content. Suppression prevents emotional processing of the distressing cognitive content and negatively reinforces further worry. An alternative theory is that rather than reducing the frequency of images, worry reduces the vividness of mental images, resulting in them being less emotionally evocative and distressing (Borkovec, Ray, & Stöber, 1998).

A considerable body of evidence supports the associations between IU and the other constructs within the model (Carleton, 2012; Dugas, Marchand, & Ladouceur, 2005), and IU is a strong and consistent predictor of worry after controlling for a range of related temperamental, affective, cognitive, and behavioral constructs (Buhr & Dugas, 2006; Koerner, Mejia, & Kusec, 2017). There is evidence that IU is a risk factor for worry as changes in IU are associated with prospective changes in the frequency of worry, IU appears to be stable over time, and other constructs, such as appraisals, appear to mediate the relationship between IU and worry (Koerner & Dugas, 2008).

Since the IUM was proposed, research has demonstrated that worry and IU are in fact associated with a broad array of emotional disorders beyond GAD. IU may therefore serve as a vulnerability factor for multiple emotional disorders, and in this respect the current nosology may be inadequate for reflecting nature's joints. We now briefly review evidence that IU is transdiagnostic, before outlining how IU may be better conceptualized within more recent dimensional approaches to psychopathology.

IU and Emotional Disorders

Diagnostic frameworks such as the Diagnostic and Statistical Manual of Mental Disorders (APA, 2013) describe covarying constellations of self-reported symptoms and assume that they reflect discrete underlying disorders. However, clinicians and researchers are increasingly concerned that the categorical-polythetic approach used to define psychopathology may not be valid (Helzer, Kraemer, & Krueger, 2006), as evidenced by the high rate of comorbidity among disorders, lack of taxonicity, and the large number of individuals who fall below cutoffs but nonetheless have significant impairment (Goldberg, Krueger, Andrews, & Hobbs, 2009; Lewinsohn, Shankman, Gau, & Klein, 2004). Additionally, common mechanistic factors are deemphasized when we assume that symptoms of different disorders represent distinct diseases, whereas substantial evidence supports considerably more commonalities than differences in psychopathology (Harvey, Watkins, Mansell, & Shafran, 2004). IU appears to be one such mechanism, as a large body of research has found relationships between self-reported IU and symptoms of a range of emotional experiences and disorders, including:

- Social anxiety disorder (Boelen & Reijntjes, 2009; Teale Sapach, Carleton, Mulvogue, Weeks, & Heimberg, 2015),
- Panic disorder with or without agoraphobia (Buhr & Dugas, 2009; Carleton, Fetzner, Hackl, & McEvoy, 2013),

- Generalized anxiety disorder (Behar, DiMarco, Hekler, Mohlman, & Staples, 2009; Zlomke & Jeter, 2014) and worry (Koerner & Dugas, 2008),
- Health anxiety (Fergus & Bardeen, 2013; Wright, Adams Lebell, & Carleton, 2016),
- Depression (Gentes & Ruscio, 2011; Nelson, Shankman, & Proudfit, 2014),
- Obsessive-compulsive disorder (Holaway, Heimberg, & Coles, 2006; Jacoby, Fabricant, Leonard, Riemann, & Abramowitz, 2013) and hoarding (Mathes et al., 2017),
- Posttraumatic stress disorder (Boelen, 2010; Oglesby, Gibby, Mathes, Short, & Schmidt, 2017),
- Eating disorders (Brown et al., 2017).

Studies that have simultaneously investigated relationships between IU and symptoms of multiple emotional disorders have also demonstrated robust unique relationships (McEvoy & Mahoney, 2011; Shihata et al., 2017). IU also explains unique variance in emotional disorder symptoms after controlling for a range of common and disorder-specific theoretically related variables, including neuroticism, negative affectivity, fear of anxiety, meta-beliefs, fear of negative evaluation, metacognitive beliefs, over-responsibility, distress tolerance, anxiety sensitivity, negative risk orientation, trait curiosity, indecisiveness, perceived constraints, self-oriented and socially prescribed perfectionism, intolerance of ambiguity, need for predictability, and need for order and structure (see Carleton, 2016; Koerner et al., 2017; Shihata et al., 2016; Shihata et al., 2017).

IU and Treatment Outcome

Dugas and colleagues developed Intolerance of Uncertainty Therapy (IUT) (Ladouceur et al., 2000) to target the mechanisms described in the IUM (Dugas et al., 1998). IUT was designed to increase acceptance of uncertainty by providing a rationale for recognizing, accepting, and developing adaptive coping strategies when encountering or anticipating uncertainty. Several randomized controlled trials in GAD have found IUT to be efficacious (Dugas et al., 2003; Ladouceur et al., 2000), but other trials suggest that IUT may not be superior to relaxation at 24-month follow-up (Dugas et al., 2010) and may be less effective than metacognitive therapy at reducing worry and IU (van der Heiden, Muris, & van der Molen, 2012).

Other studies have investigated changes in IU and symptoms following treatments that were not derived from the IUM. For example, Mahoney and McEvoy (2012a) reported on outcomes from group cognitive behavior therapy (CBT) for social anxiety disorder. Participants were encouraged to evaluate their threat expectancies via cognitive restructuring and behavioral experiments, and to test their tolerance for any residual emotional discomfort related to remaining uncertainty. Group CBT was associated with a significant reduction in IU, and these changes were associated with reductions in social anxiety symptoms.

McEvoy and Erceg-Hurn (2016) recently investigated changes in IU across three different group CBT approaches to three different problems to determine whether reducing IU could be considered a universal change process (i.e., both transdiagnostic and trans-therapeutic). The treatments were targeting either social anxiety disorder, repetitive negative thinking (RNT) (worry and/or rumination), or depression. The approaches were CBT with integrated imagery-based techniques, metacognitive therapy, or cognitive therapy (i.e., behavioral activation plus cognitive restructuring), respectively. All three group treatments were associated with significant reductions in IU, which were associated with reductions in RNT. Changes in IU were also associated with changes in social anxiety in the social anxiety disorder group receiving imagery-enhanced group CBT, but not with changes in depression symptoms for group CBT. The authors argued that each treatment, despite not explicitly mentioning IU, inherently involved exposure to uncertainty, which may have increased tolerance and acceptance for uncertainty. Overall, the extant literature suggests that changes in IU are associated with changes in anxiety disorder symptoms and RNT during exposure-based treatments. Further clinical and experimental research identifying the precise mechanisms that most effectively and efficiently reduce IU is required.

Where to from Here?

The past three decades of research on the relationship between IU and emotional disorders have provided substantial knowledge. On the one hand, the results suggest that IU is likely relevant to a broad range of clinical problems, and increasing our understanding of IU will likely improve our capacity to ameliorate vulnerability to emotional disorders. On the other hand, if IU is associated with most clinical disorders, this brings into question the value of drawing boundaries between disorders for understanding vulnerability and maintenance of psychopathology. Perhaps a more helpful approach is to examine risk factors and symptoms dimensionally, where relative exposures to (or "doses of") risk factors titrates the likelihood and severity of displaying symptoms of psychopathology. The RDoC initiative offers a promising framework within which to move the field forward in precisely this way.

Dimensions: IU and RDoC

RDoC Aims

The RDoC initiative was proposed by the NIMH (Insel et al., 2010; Sanislow et al., 2010) to address the limitations of categorical nosologies, which derived from clinical consensus as much as from empirical evidence. The RDoC encourages multidisciplinary approaches so that psychology, genetics, and neuroscience can be integrated (Kozak & Cuthbert, 2016), with the ultimate goal being the development of a classification system based on dimensions of observable behavioral and neurobiological measures, rather than heterogeneous clusters of symptoms. In the meantime, the NIMH in promoting RDoC intends to "elaborate a set of psychological constructs linked to behavioral dimensions for which strong evidence exists for circuits that implement these functions, and relate the extremes of functioning along these dimensions to specified symptoms (i.e., impairment)" (Kozak & Cuthbert, 2016, p. 288). The focus is on increasing our understanding of dimensions of functioning and identifying symptoms and impairments that result from variations along these dimensions.

Kozak and Cuthbert (2016) described three key aims of the RDoC initiative that are compatible with existing IU research. First, RDoC promotes the development and validation of dimensional constructs. IU is frequently treated as a dimensional construct that is normally distributed with a slight positive skew (Carleton, 2016a; Carleton, Weeks et al., 2012), having similar associations with symptoms of psychopathology across community, analog, and clinical samples (Carleton, 2016a; Carleton, Mulvogue et al., 2012; Shihata et al., 2016). A taxometric analysis of the IUS-12 (Carleton, Norton et al., 2007) also supported a dimensional, continuously distributed structure rather than a taxonic structure (Carleton, Weeks et al., 2012). Second, RDoC encourages an integration of psychology and biology. There is now an extensive body of IU research demonstrating associations between psychological and biological units of analysis, which is reviewed later in this chapter. Third, RDoC advocates for identifying psychological and biological associations that are theoretically linked to narrowly defined and clinically relevant impairments. Growing evidence indicates links between uncertainty, high levels of IU, and more severe self-reported, behavioral, cognitive, and physiological indices of psychopathology and associated distress. Accordingly, the remainder of this chapter provides the first attempt to review existing IU theory and research within the RDoC framework.

RDoC Matrix: Domains and Units of Analysis

The RDoC does not currently provide a definitive, alternative classification system; however, the RDoC does provide a *suggested* matrix of constructs and units of analysis. The constructs are listed as matrix rows organized in five domains: (1) Arousal/Regulatory, (2) Cognition, (3) Negative Valence, (4) Positive Valence, and (5) Social Processes. The matrix columns are units of analysis to measure the constructs (e.g., gene, molecule, cell, neural circuits, physiology [e.g., heart rate, cortisol], behavior and self-report). The units of analysis are intended to promote multidisciplinary research into constructs associated with psychopathology. Importantly, the different measures are considered "units" and not "levels" of analysis; indeed, several papers by NIMH staff on RDoC have emphasized that no one unit of analysis is more prominent (and at a higher "level") than any other (Kozak & Cuthbert, 2016). Research paradigms relevant to particular systems are also described. The RDoC aims to promote investigations of multiple units to improve our understanding of how the components interact, how each system interacts with others, and ultimately how they work in concert to yield clinical problems.

Relationship of IU to Acute (Fear) and Potential (Anxiety) Threat in the RDoC Matrix

Only a few studies of IU have been conducted with the RDoC criteria explicitly in mind (e.g., Gorka, Lieberman, Shankman, & Phan, 2017a, 2017b), though much of the existing research has implications for multiple systems. The negative valence domain within the RDoC framework is primarily responsible for responses to aversive situations or contexts, and includes acute threat (i.e., fear), potential threat (i.e., anxiety), sustained threat, loss, and frustrative non-reward. Carleton (2016a, p. 31) argued that because they are internal percepts, unknowns could "induce fear (i.e., the absence of information is perceived as dangerous, present, and imminent) and anxiety (i.e., the perceived absence is expected to continue and alludes to one or more potential events that are uncertain, possibly positive, but potentially negative)." Therefore, our focus is on how IU theory and research reflect RDoC units of analysis for fear and anxiety within the negative valence system. The section is designed to provide a guide for how existing theory and evidence could be integrated into the RDoC framework, rather than a comprehensive integrative review of all IU research with respect to the entire RDoC matrix. We hope this initial effort is helpful for guiding future research endeavors and reviews.

As mentioned earlier, a key distinction between acute threat (i.e., fear) and potential threat (i.e., anxiety) is how much certainty there is regarding the likelihood, timing, or nature of a future threat (Barlow, 2000; Grupe & Nitschke, 2013); as such, IU encompasses both RDoC constructs. *Acute* threat is when the defensive motivation system becomes activated to promote behaviors designed to protect an individual from perceived danger (NIMH, 2016). State uncertainty (e.g., walking through a spider web and not knowing whether a spider was "home" at the time) often elicits acute threat ("fear"), as an individual is exposed to an uncertain or ambiguous threat in the present. *Potential* threat is activated in response to future, distant, ambiguous, or low and uncertain threat (NIMH, 2016), leading to hypervigilance for threat and increased risk assessment. IU describes difficulty enduring the aversive response caused by absent information associated with a potential threat (Carleton, 2016a), which appears intrinsic for anxiety (Carleton, 2012).

Much of the research related to IU and acute threat is likely to be relevant to IU and potential threat, with the latter reflecting more sustained activation of the pathways associated with the former. Moreover, some components of intolerance (e.g., physiological arousal, neural circuitry) in response to unknowns are likely to be comparable to responses to other threatening stimuli. Therefore, many units of analysis related to IU will be identical to those associated with most fears, phobias, and anxiety and related disorders, or to negative affective responses more generally. The unifying principle for the research discussed in this chapter is that salient unknowns in any domain can be associated with intolerance or fear. We now review IU theory and evidence as they relate to the RDoC units of analysis.

Genes

The genetic origins of personality traits, like IU, have been widely studied through linkage and association analyses (de Moor et al., 2012; Fullerton et al., 2003; Hettema et al., 2006; Kuo et al., 2007; Lo et al., 2017; Nash et al., 2004). Linkage studies utilize the known location of a genetic marker that is thought to be located on the same chromosome as the gene associated with the trait of interest. If the marker gene and gene of interest are transmitted together, the genes are considered "linked" and therefore causally related to the passage of the trait of interest within a family. Association studies assess whether the gene thought to be related to the trait of interest is more common in populations that display the trait than in healthy controls. There are two types of association studies – candidate gene(s) studies, in which specific and theoretically relevant genes or polymorphisms in genes are examined, and genome-wide association studies (GWAS) in which associations are examined between a trait and genetic variants across the whole genome. Although not specifically examining IU, a recent GWAS study conducted by Lo et al. (2017) found six genetic loci associated with personality traits in general and that variants on chromosome 8p23.1 and in L3MBTL2 were associated with neuroticism, a broad, emergent, aggregated personality construct that is fundamentally determined by FOTU and IU (Carleton 2016a). The Lo et al. (2017) study and other candidate gene studies (e.g., Hettema et al., 2006) also found a genetic link between neuroticism and internalizing psychopathology. Since IU is a personality trait that is associated with both neuroticism (Berenbaum, Bredemeier, & Thompson, 2008; Carleton 2016a) and internalizing psychopathology (Carleton, Mulvogue et al., 2012; Gentes & Ruscio, 2011), there may also be a genetic link between IU and internalizing psychopathology.

Assessing whether IU is associated with potential genetic loci, genes, or polymorphisms of genes is not the only method for investigating the genetic heritability of IU. Other approaches to examining genetic origins of IU are behavioral genetics studies, which include twin, adoption, and family study designs. These genetic study designs cannot implicate specific genetic variants involved in IU; nevertheless, twin and adoption studies can elucidate the extent to which IU is due to genetic versus environmental factors in general, and family studies can elucidate whether IU is familial more broadly. Several studies have employed the use of twin, adoption, and family designs to investigate the heritability of personality traits in general. Vukasovic and Bratko (2015) conducted a meta-analysis of family, adoption, and twin studies and found 40% of individual differences in personality traits to have genetic origins. This estimate ranged from 22% in studies utilizing family and adoption designs to 47% in twin studies. Estimates of personality heritability have also investigated the heritability of specific personality traits. Neuroticism appears to be 39% genetically heritable (Kendler, Aggen, Jacobson, & Neale, 2003;

Vukasovic & Bratko, 2015). As IU is associated with neuroticism and both personality traits are implicated in internalizing psychopathology, IU may also show a similar rate of genetic heritability.

Studies have not directly investigated the heritability of, or specific genetic mechanisms leading to, IU; however, Eley et al. (2008) examined the genetic heritability of a bias toward interpreting ambiguous situations as threatening among 300 twin pairs who completed a homophone-words task and an ambiguous scenarios task. In the homophone-words task, participants were presented with a word (three-fourths of the words were homophones) and told to write a sentence using that word. The sentences were then coded as threat, non-threat, or other depending on the meaning of the homophone used by the participant. In the ambiguous scenarios task, participants were read scenarios that could be inter-preted as either neutral or threatening. Participants then selected one of four possible scenario interpretations, of which two were threatening and two were neutral. Eley et al. (2008) found the bias toward interpreting ambiguous situations as threatening to be 24% heritable when assessed using the ambiguous scenarios task and 30% heritable as measured by the homophone-words task. Most of the variance in interpretative biases (68–69%) was attributed to non-shared environ-mental influences. The analyses did not directly test the genetic basis of IU, but the biases could reflect negative cognitive reactions resulting from high-IU individuals encountering uncertainty or ambiguity. If so, the results implicate a genetic mechanism for IU as pathogenic. Additionally, given the large role of non-shared environmental influences, it is possible that genetic factors may only predispose one to develop IU and that these genes may also interact with environmental factors such as stressful life events, parenting styles, and epigenetic factors. Therefore, discussing the genetic *correlates*, and not *origins*, of IU may be more appropriate as genetics alone likely do not determine whether one will become intolerant of uncertainty.

Individual differences in responses to unknowns may be reflected by BIS reactivity, which manifests as emotional and behavioral responses to unknowns along a dimension from inhibited to uninhibited to the unfamiliar (Kagan & Snidman, 2004). There is evidence that neonate rats initially respond to unknowns with fear, but that this response attenuates after repeated exposures to unknowns, particularly when mothers provide reliable care to their offspring (Akers et al., 2008; Tang, Akers, Reep, Romeo, & McEwen, 2006; Tang, Reeb-Sutherland, Romeo, & McEwen, 2012). Moehler et al. (2008) found that fearful responses to unknowns in human infants at 4 months of age can predict behavioral inhibition at 14 months of age, therefore demonstrating stability of very early temperamental factors that are likely genetically determined. The concept of an inhibited temperament reflecting trait BIS activation over-laps with the concepts of neuroticism, negative affect, behavioral inhibition, and trait anxiety (Barlow, Sauer-Zavala, Carl, Bullis, & Ellard, 2014). There is abundant evidence that early social experiences such as parental neglect and abusive parenting can impact the anatomical brain regions and circuitry associated with anxiety and anxiety disorders, but also that environmental factors such as maternal caregiving impact the regulation of gene transcription and DNA structure (see Drury, Sánchez, & Gonzalez, 2016). The available results provide critical information about the role that genes may play in determining the bandwidth of fear an individual is vulnerable to experiencing from uncertainty, but also about how individual reactivity can vary within this bandwidth due to environmental influences.

Molecules and Cells

Indicators of IU may be measured at the molecular and cellular levels. Corticotropin-releasing factor receptors appear necessary for anxiety responses to uncertain/potential threat (Smith et al., 1998; Timpl et al., 1998). Corticotropin-releasing factor itself, as well as cytokines and cortisol, appears related to internalizing psychopathologies (Arborelius, Owens, Plotsky, & Nemeroff, 1999; Burke, Davis, Otte, & Mohr, 2005; Capuron & Miller, 2011; Merswolken, Deter, Siebenhuener, Orth-Gomer, & Weber, 2013; Walker, O'Connor, Schaefer, Talbot, & Hendrickx, 2011). Several genetic polymorphisms associated with neurotransmitters have also been implicated in internalizing psychopathologies (Hettema et al., 2006; Lawford, Young, Noble, Kann, & Ritchie, 2006; Nash et al., 2005; Pan, Cheng, Shan, & Yan, 2015; Ryu et al., 2004; Southwick, Vythilingam, & Charney, 2005). Additionally, research implicates epigenetic changes in anxiety (Murphy et al., 2015; Yehuda et al., 2014). IU is related to internalizing psychopathology (see Carleton, 2016a, for review) and threat-responding (Nelson, Liu, Sarapas, & Shankman, 2016; Nelson & Shankman, 2011); accordingly, IU may also relate to cellular, genetic, and molecular factors associated with internalizing psychopathology and threat responding. The specificity of these indicators for responding to uncertain threat is currently unclear because most (if not all) of these indicators have also been associated with constructs other than IU (e.g., harm avoidance, neuroticism; DeYoung, Cicchetti, & Rogosch, 2011; Tyrka et al., 2008).

Bach and Dolan (2012) extensively reviewed evidence for the neural organization of uncertainty estimates and, although several limitations were identified, some conclusions could be supported. First, outcome uncertainty appears to manifest as phasic prediction error signals in dopaminergic neurons, and sustained firing of these neurons may provide a mechanism for coding outcome uncertainty. Second, the firing rate of orbitofrontal cortex (OFC) neurons appears to signal outcome uncertainty. Third, functional magnetic resonance imaging (fMRI) studies implicate 10 distinct brain regions in outcome uncertainty in different circumstances. Bach and Dolan (2012) concluded that the coding of outcome uncertainty is not unitary, but represented based on contextual factors.

Neurocircuitry

Uncertainty about the nature, probability, or timing of threat results in common patterns of physiological responding across species (Grupe & Nitschke, 2013). Recent reviews have extensively summarized the neuroanatomical structures involved in response to uncertain contexts and IU (Brosschot et al., 2016, 2017; Einstein, 2014; Grupe & Nitschke, 2013; Singer, Critchley, & Preuschoff, 2009; Wever, Smeets, & Sternheim, 2015). We therefore only briefly review the roles of key neuroanatomical structures associated with IU, including the insula, amygdala, and several regions in the prefrontal cortex – dorsomedial prefrontal cortex (dmPFC), ventromedial prefrontal cortex (vmPFC), and dorsolateral prefrontal cortex (dlPFC).

The insula plays a role in guiding predictions about subjective feelings that might be experienced within the context of future events. Within the context of uncertainty, Wever et al. (2015) suggest that insula activation can therefore be understood as the brain attempting to predict how an individual will feel in response to possible future outcomes (i.e., subjective probability, cost estimates). The amygdala is made up of numerous nuclei that each play a different role in affective responding and behavior. Grupe and Nitschke (2013) suggest that indiscriminate activation of the amygdala results in a reduced capacity to discriminate between cues, inefficient deployment of attention to the most relevant stimuli in the environment, and therefore impaired learning of stimulus-outcome associations. Interestingly, hyperactivity in brain regions, including the insula and amygdala, reduces after exposure therapy in persons with spider phobia (Goosens, Sunaert, Peeters, Griez, & Schruers, 2007), which suggests activation of such structures is malleable via behavioral techniques and that the structures are correlates of, if not causally associated with, reduced psychopathology.

Regarding the prefrontal cortex, the dlPFC may play a role in hypervigilance toward threatening information as it responds to new information in an attempt to predict outcomes. Over-activation of the dlPFC may lead to checking behavior in an effort to ensure all available relevant information has been integrated to optimize decision-making within the context of uncertainty. The dmPFC appears to play a role in the evaluation of uncertain stimuli (probability estimation), whereas the vmPFC is implicated in emotional regulation following uncertainty. The vmPFC uses contextual information to retrieve safety context memories and facilitate threat reappraisal, thereby downregulating the threat response by inhibiting the amygdala and insula. Accordingly, the vmPFC prevents the amygdala and insula from becoming hyperactive by activating coping mechanisms and facilitating learning of safety cues. Individuals with anxiety disorders display less discriminant activity in the vmPFC in response to cues that are visually similar to conditioned stimuli, which is suggestive of overgeneralization of conditioned fear (Grupe & Nitscke, 2013; Morriss, Macdonald, & van Reekum, 2016). Connections between the amygdala and vmPFC therefore appear to play an important regulatory function in the response to uncertain threat.

Human imaging studies implicate the amygdala and associated connections to regions associated with decision-making and subsequent action (i.e., OFC, lateral PFC, ventral and dorsal striatum, anterior midcingulate cortex) in active avoidance. The medial central nucleus of the amygdala integrates rapid, phasic fear responses to imminent and relatively certain threats (fear). The bed nucleus of the stria terminalis (BNST) (a key region in the extended amygdala) is activated under sustained and unpredictable threat (i.e., anxiety and threat monitoring). With input from the OFC, the BNST promotes behavioral inhibition in response to novel or unfamiliar stimuli, but not in response to known fears (Davis, Walker, Miles, & Grillon, 2010).

The generalized unsafety theory of stress (GUTS) (Brosschot et al., 2016, 2017; Thayer, Åhs, Fredrikson, Sollers, & Wager, 2012) model presents a novel perspective on the relationship between uncertainty and chronic threat responses in particular. Thayer et al. (2012) argue that, from an evolutionary perspective, because natural selection favors an initial cautionary approach, sympathoexcitatory preparation for action (i.e., the fight-or-flight response) is the default response to uncertainty, novelty, and threat (see also Brosschot et al., 2016, 2017; Carleton, 2012, 2016b). According to GUTS, the amygdala is under continuous inhibition by the vmPFC until safety is in doubt. When safety is uncertain, the inhibition of the amygdala by the vmPFC is decreased, thereby increasing amygdala activity (Brosschot et al., 2017). In this sense, Brosschot et al. (2017) state that "organisms are intolerant for uncertainty by default" (p. 291), and thus stress responses occur in between rather than during unpredictable stressors. Research in rodent models has shown that individuals prefer predictable shocks and that their predictability reduces the negative effects of stress (Imada & Nageishi, 1982). These results and GUTS are consistent with clinical reports of patients with anxiety disorders stating that they often prefer knowing to not, even when the known result is negative. Uncertainty makes preparing for future events, or balancing the need to preemptively prepare while minimizing unnecessary effort, difficult. The main problem is when safety signals are not recognized so that stress responses can be inhibited.

Physiology

Several laboratories have investigated physiological symptoms associated with IU using the no (N), predictable (P), and unpredictable (U) threat task paradigm (NPU-threat task) (Schmitz & Grillon, 2012). The three conditions in the NPU-threat task vary in terms of aversive stimuli predictability (e.g., electric shock). Participants are informed that aversive stimuli will never be administered during the N condition, shortly after the presentation of a cue in the P condition, and at any time (whether the cue is presented or not) during the U condition. The P and U conditions distinguish between physiological responding to acute threat (fear) and potential threat (anxiety), respectively (Grillon et al., 2006; Grillon, Chavis, Covington, & Pine, 2009).

A pervasive variant of the NPU-threat task includes startle probe administrations across all conditions to examine differences in defensive responding. For example, Nelson and Shankman (2011) evidenced self-reported IU as specifically and inversely associated with the startle probe-elicited eye-blink reflex in the U condition. Participants with higher IU had smaller startle responses during the U condition, but IU was not related to startle in the P condition. In persons with panic disorder, the IU subscales had divergent correlations with the startle reflex in the U condition, but not the P condition (Nelson et al., 2016). Inhibitory IU was associated with attenuated startle potentiation, whereas prospective IU was related to heightened startle potentiation. Taken together, these studies evidence the startle probe-elicited eye-blink response during the U condition of the NPU-threat task as a key physiological indicator of IU.

The NPU-threat task can also elicit event-related potentials (ERPs) to examine how neural responses become modulated by the different threat conditions – specifically, ERPs to the startle probes, such as the P300 and N100 ERP components. The startle probe-elicited P300 is a positive going deflection in the EEG signal that occurs around 300 ms after the startle probe and is maximal in centro-parietal sites. The startle-probe elicited N100 occurs around 100 ms after the startle probe in frontocentral sites and is a negative going deflection. Nelson, Hajcak, and Shankman (2015) recently showed that the startle probe-elicited P300 is attenuated during both the P and U conditions when compared to the N condition. In contrast, the N100 is enhanced only during the U condition and did not differ between the P and N conditions. The results suggest the startle probe-elicited P300 may generally indicate cognitive processing of threat and the startle probe-elicited N100 may be uniquely associated with responses to uncertainty and another potential physiological indicator of IU.

Uncertainty also appears to be associated with increased heart rate variability (HRV) (Thayer et al., 2012) and higher blood pressure (Greco & Roger, 2003). For individuals with chronic stress, however, the GUTS model argues that reduced HRV is a symptom of the default stress response that, in the absence of detectable safety signals, has failed to be inhibited by the vmPFC (Brosschot et al., 2016, 2017). Brosschot et al. (2017) reviewed evidence that the vagus nerve is important in regulating physiological systems (e.g., HRV, inflammation, glucose, cholesterol) and is closely related to self-rated health. Low HRV, as a measure of vagal (parasympathetic) withdrawal, is linked to prefrontal cortex inhibition of subcortical structures (Brosschot et al., 2017) and higher startle to unpredictable (but not predictable) threat (Gorka et al., 2013). High vagal activity is reflected in high HRV, while low resting HRV (vagal withdrawal) is considered an index of the chronically disinhibited default stress response. Brosschot et al. (2017) argue that humans' general anxiety following birth, as indicated by the default stress response, becomes more specific as the individual learns about the predictability and controllability of threats. Animal models have found that experiencing controllable stressors in adolescence is important for developing self-efficacy and learning safety, with individuals experiencing controllable stressors faring better than individuals who experience no stressors at all. Conversely, failures to learn safety and inhibit the stress response can be facilitated by individual differences in trait anxiety and chronic early life stressors. Brosschot et al. (2016) argue that uncertainty is critical in the initiation and maintenance of the anxiety and stress response, but more specifically they argue that uncertainty about safety is more important than uncertainty about threat in maintaining the stress response. High resting HRV is indicative of inhibition of the amygdala by the prefrontal cortex, and "since the default stress response is only inhibited when there is certainty about safety, uncertainty always implies unsafety" (Brosschot et al., 2016, p. 31). Within the GUTS model, uncertainty and unsafety are considered to be virtually synonymous across species.

Behavior

Studies investigating behavioral principles (e.g., Pavlovian conditioning) or overt behaviors (e.g., decision-making tasks) are considered within the behavior unit of analysis. Studies using conditioning paradigms have improved our understanding of the role that IU may play in distorting contingency beliefs, such that threat expectancies may be disproportionate to safety expectancies, which, in turn, may result in over-generalization of threat expectancies to ambiguous, neutral, or positive cues (Dugas, Buhr, & Ladouceur, 2004; Morriss, Christakou, & van Reekum, 2016). Specifically, behavioral studies have examined relationships between IU and facilitated fear acquisition, generalization, and resistance to extinction. Morriss, Macdonald et al. (2016) investigated the role that IU may play in generalizing learned threat to perceptually similar stimuli. Using an associative learning paradigm, participants were repeatedly presented with a range of yellow squares that differed in size. During acquisition, either the largest or smallest square was paired with a female scream at a 50% reinforcement schedule, while the other squares were presented alone. During extinction, all of the squares were presented alone. After each block of trials, participants were asked to rate how uneasy they felt when viewing each stimulus and skin conductance was recorded throughout the experiment. The results indicated that higher IU was associated with greater threat generalization to safety cues during associative learning, and lower IU individuals demonstrated superior discrimination between threat and safety cues. During extinction, higher IU was also associated with maintenance of fear responding. The effects remained significant even after controlling for trait anxiety and worry. Morriss, McDonald et al. concluded that "high IU individuals take longer to discriminate between threat and safety cues because of threat generalization proneness" (p. 9). They further speculate that threat generalization may be a marker for IU-based maintenance of fear and anxiety in a range of anxiety disorders.

Morriss, Christakou, and van Reekum (2015) investigated the relationship between IU and compromised fear extinction. During acquisition, a square (blue or yellow) was paired with an aversive scream 100% of the time, while the other square (yellow or blue) was presented alone. In extinction both squares were presented alone. In a third partial reacquisition phase, the squares that had previously been paired with screams 100% of the time were now paired only 25% of the time. Higher IU was associated with larger skin conductance responses to threat stimuli relative to safety cues; however, higher IU individuals responded more similarly to threat and safety cues during early extinction than did lower IU individuals. The results are consistent with higher IU individuals failing to quickly discriminate between threat and non-threat cues, and being slower to learn to discriminate between these cues over time. Morriss, Christakou, and van Reekum (2016) followed up this result and found that during early extinction learning, only low IU scores were associated with larger pupil dilation, skin conductance, and right amygdala activation to threat relative to safety cues. In late extinction learning, lower IU was associated with better inhibition of previously learned threat associations, such that responses to threat and safety cues were similar; in contrast, higher IU continued to be associated with fearful responses to safety cues. Higher IU scores were also associated with greater activation of the vmPFC in threat versus safety cues in late extinction, which was particular to IU and not trait anxiety or worry. The researchers concluded that high IU is associated with slower discrimination of threat from safety cues, and that this process results in resistance to extinction.

Researchers have also investigated the impact of uncertainty on decision-making tasks (e.g., the Beads Task; Jacoby, Abramowitz, Buck, & Fabricant, 2014; Jacoby, Abramowitz, Reuman, & Blakey, 2016; Ladouceur, Talbot, & Dugas, 1997). The Beads Task requires individuals to nominate which of two or three jars beads are being drawn from, with dependent variables being number of draws to decision, time taken, accuracy, and degree of certainty, distress, and importance of correct decision assessed on visual analog scales. Jars differ in difficulty based on proportions of bead colors, from easy (two colors across two jars; 85:15 versus 15:85), to intermediate (two colors across two jars; 60:40 versus 40:60), to hard (three colors across three jars; 28:28:44 versus 28:44:28 versus 44:28:28). Other behavioral responses to uncertainty have also been assessed. For instance, Thibodeau, Carleton, Gómez-Pérez, and Asmundson (2013) examined relationships between IU and a typing task, finding that IU positively correlated with typing speed but not accuracy. Overall, the results indicate higher IU is associated with a greater preference for immediate rewards over more probable and valuable delayed rewards, less confidence about decisions, reluctance to change decisions even when presented with additional information, more information seeking, slower decision-making, and more distress during decision-making (see Shihata et al., 2016). IU is associated with behaviors that are designed to seek and achieve certainty and predictability, avoid threat, and thereby reduce adverse emotions associated with unknowns.

Conclusions

After reviewing IU theory and research with respect to diagnoses and then dimensions, we have come closer to answering the question that opened the chapter: why are unpredictability and uncertainty at times coveted and experienced as pleasurable, while at other times they are feared and avoided? Human and nonhuman species appear hard-wired to fear unknowns and therein be intolerant of uncertainty, but we are all born with varying capacities to learn to discriminate threat from safety cues in the face of uncertainty. Subcortical regions such as the amygdala and insula play important roles in signaling and attending to fear, with prefrontal cortical regions being critical for inhibiting activity within these structures so that adaptive behavioral responses can be generated. Unpredictability and uncertainty appear appetitive when safety cues are sufficiently associated with salient contextual factors so that remaining uncertainty is perceived as tolerable.

A parachutist can interpret plummeting to the ground as pleasurable only once the prefrontal cortex is convinced that the preparation process is sufficiently safe, and the perception of certainty therein likely strengthens with each non-injurious jump. Without sufficient perceptions of certain safety, the default threat response is likely to be activated in response to uncertainty between threats (i.e., anxiety about potential catastrophes in between the first, second, and subsequent jumps), or when an imminent threat is uncertain (i.e., panic when primary chute fails and the reliability of the back-up chute is uncertain).

Future research investigating uncertainty within the context of the positive valence system would improve our understanding of processes involved in positive appraisals within the context of sufficient safety. There is evidence that uncertainty serves as an intensifier of both negative and positive affect, possibly by increasing curiosity toward emotional stimuli (Bar-Anan, Wilson, & Gilbert, 2009), which warrants further research. We also need to know more about why individuals vary in their capacity to learn safety associations across different contexts (divergent trajectories). Understanding variables that influence these processes across multiple units of analysis may help to bridge the gap between categorical nosologies and more dimensional approaches to conceptualizing psychopathology.

How do individual differences in the capacity to tolerate unknowns contribute to the etiology and maintenance of anxiety and anxiety-related disorders? Capacity to tolerate unknowns is likely to be determined and maintained by a complex interplay of many factors, including genetics, neurocircuitry, temperament, cognitive processes, and behavioral processes, which have all served us well in the process of natural selection interacting with environmental experiences. Emerging multidimensional frameworks such as the RDoC offer a useful heuristic for integrating existing research and guiding future investigations into these processes. The transdiagnostic and non-taxonic nature of IU suggests that categorical nosologies are unlikely to fully capture the boundaries of psychopathology. Considering manifestations of IU across multiple units of analysis holds promise for increasing our understanding of how multiple systems interact to maintain anxiety and anxiety disorders, which will hopefully improve the short- and long-term effectiveness of treatments targeting these processes. The benefits of such outcomes would be certain.

References

Akers, K. G., Yang, Z., DelVecchio, D. P., Reeb, B. C., Romeo, R. D., McEwen, B. S., & Tang, A. C. (2008). Social competitiveness and plasticity of neuroendocrine function in old age: Influence of neonatal novelty exposure and maternal care reliability. *PLoS ONE*, *3*, e2840. doi: 10.1371/journal.pone.0002840

American Psychiatric Association. (2013). *Diagnostic and Statistical Manual of Mental Disorders: DSM-5*. Washington, DC: American Psychiatric Association.

Arborelius, L., Owens, M. J., Plotsky, P. M., & Nemeroff, C. B. (1999). The role of corticotropin-releasing factor in depression and anxiety disorders. *Journal of Endocrinology*, *160*, 1–12. doi: 10.1677/joe.0.1600001

Armfield, J. M. (2006). Cognitive vulnerability: A model of the etiology of fear. *Clinical Psychology Review*, *26*, 746–768. doi: 10.1016/j.cpr.2006.03.007

Bach, D. R. & Dolan, R. J. (2012). Knowing how much you don't know: A neural organization of uncertainty estimates. *Nature Reviews Neuroscience*, *13*, 572–586. doi: 10.1038/nrn3289

Bandura, A. (1977). Self-efficacy: Toward a unifying theory of behavioral change. *Psychological Review*, *84*, 191–215. doi: 10.1037/0033-295x.84.2.191

Bandura, A. (1989). Human agency in social cognitive theory. *American Psychologist*, *44*, 1175–1184. doi: 10.1037/0003-066x.44.9.1175

Bandura, A. (1997). *Self-Efficacy: The Exercise of Control*. New York, NY: W. H. Freeman.

Bar-Anan, Y., Wilson, T. D., & Gilbert, D. T. (2009). The feeling of uncertainty intensifies affective reactions. *Emotion*, *9*, 123–127. doi: 10.1037/a0014607

Barlow, D. H. (2000). Unraveling the mysteries of anxiety and its disorders from the perspective of emotion theory. *American Psychologist*, *55*, 1247–1263. doi: 10.1037/0003-066x.55.11.1247

Barlow, D. H., Ellard, K. K., Sauer-Zavala, S., Bullis, J. R., & Carl, J. R. (2014). The origins of neuroticism. *Perspectives on Psychological Science*, *9*, 481–496. doi: 10.1177/1745691614544528

Barlow, D. H., Sauer-Zavala, S., Carl, J. R., Bullis, J. R., & Ellard, K. K. (2014). The nature, diagnosis, and treatment of neuroticism: Back to the future. *Clinical Psychological Science*, *2*(3), 344–365. doi: 10.1177/2167702613505532

Behar, E., DiMarco, I. D., Hekler, E. B., Mohlman, J., & Staples, A. M. (2009). Current theoretical models of generalized anxiety disorder (GAD): Conceptual review and treatment implications. *Journal of Anxiety Disorders*, *23*, 1011–1023. doi: 10.1016/j.janxdis.2009.07.006

Berenbaum, H., Bredemeier, K., & Thompson, R. J. (2008). Intolerance of uncertainty: Exploring its dimensionality and associations with need for cognitive closure, psychopathology, and personality. *Journal of Anxiety Disorders*, *22*, 117–125. doi: 10.1016/j.janxdis.2007.01.004

Birrell, J., Meares, K., Wilkinson, A., & Freeston, M. (2011). Toward a definition of intolerance of uncertainty: A review of factor analytical studies of the Intolerance of Uncertainty Scale. *Clinical Psychology Review, 31*, 1198–1208. doi: 10.1016/j.cpr.2011.07.009

Boelen, P. A. & Reijntjes, A. (2009). Intolerance of uncertainty and social anxiety. *Journal of Anxiety Disorders, 23*, 130–135. doi: 10.1016/j.janxdis.2008.04.007

Boelen, P. A., Reijntjes, A., & Smid, G. (2016). Concurrent and prospective associations of intolerance of uncertainty with symptoms of prolonged grief, posttraumatic stress, and depression after bereavement. *Journal of Anxiety Disorders, 41*, 65–72. doi: 10.1016/j.janxdis.2016.03.004

Borkovec, T. D., Alcaine, O. M., & Behar, E. (2004). Avoidance theory of worry and generalized anxiety disorder. In R. Heimberg, C. Turk, & D. Mennin (eds.), *Generalized Anxiety Disorder: Advances in Research and Practice* (pp. 77–108). New York, NY: Guilford Press.

Borkovec, T. D., Ray, W. J., & Stöber, J. (1998). Worry: A cognitive phenomenon intimately linked to affective, physiological, and interpersonal behavioral processes. *Cognitive Therapy and Research, 22*, 561–576. doi: 10.1023/A:1018790003416

Bowlby, J. (1973). *Separation: Anxiety and Anger.* New York, NY: Basic Books.

Brosschot, J. F., Verkuil, B., & Thayer, J. B. (2016). The default response to uncertainty and the importance of perceived safety in anxiety and stress: An evolution-theoretical perspective. *Journal of Anxiety Disorders, 41*, 22–34. doi: 10.1016/j.janxdis.2016.04.012

Brosschot, J. F., Verkuil, B., & Thayer, J. B. (2017). Exposed to events that never happen: Generalized unsafety, the default stress response, and prolonged autonomic activity. *Neuroscience and Biobehavioral Reviews, 74*, 287–296. doi: 10.1016/j.neubiorev.2016.07.019

Brown, M., Roginson, L., Campione, G. C., Wuensch, K., Hildebrandt, T., & Micali, N. (2017). Intolerance of uncertainty in eating disorders: A systematic review and meta-analysis. *European Eating Disorders Review.* doi: 10.1002/erv.2523

Buhr, K. & Dugas, M. J. (2006). Investigating the construct validity of intolerance of uncertainty and its unique relationship with worry. *Journal of Anxiety Disorders, 20*, 222–236. doi: 10.1016/j.janxdis.2004.12.004

Buhr, K. & Dugas, M. J. (2009). The role of fear of anxiety and intolerance of uncertainty in worry: An experimental manipulation. *Behaviour Research and Therapy, 47*, 215–223. doi: 10.1016/j.brat.2008.12.004

Burke, H. M., Davis, M. C., Otte, C., & Mohr, D. C. (2005). Depression and cortisol responses to psychological stress: A meta-analysis. *Psychoneuroendocrinology, 30*, 846–856. doi: 10.1016/j.psyneune.2005.02.010

Capuron, L. & Miller, A. H. (2011). Immune system to brain signaling: Neuropsychopharmacological implications. *Pharmacology & Therapeutics, 130*, 226–238. doi: 10.1016/j.pharmthera.2011.01.014

Carl, J. R., Gallagher, M. W., Sauer-Zavala, S. E., Bentley, K. H., & Barlow, D. H. (2014). A preliminary investigation of the effects of the unified protocol on temperament. *Comprehensive Psychiatry, 55*, 1426–1434.

Carleton, R. N. (2012). The intolerance of uncertainty construct in the context of anxiety disorders: Theoretical and practical perspectives. *Expert Review of Neurotherapeutics, 12*, 937–947. doi: 10.1586/ERN.12.82

Carleton, R. N. (2013). Intolerance of uncertainty and PTSD symptoms: Exploring the construct relationship in a community sample with a heterogeneous trauma history. *Cognitive Therapy and Research, 37*, 725–734. doi: 10.1007/s10608-013-9531-6

Carleton, R. N. (2016a). Fear of the unknown: One fear to rule them all? *Journal of Anxiety Disorders, 41*, 5–21. doi: 10.1016/j.janxdis.2016.03.011

Carleton, R. N. (2016b). Into the unknown: A review and synthesis of contemporary models involving uncertainty. *Journal of Anxiety Disorders, 39*, 30–43. doi: 10.1016/j.janxdis.2016.02.007

Carleton, R. N., Collimore, K. C., & Asmundson, G. J. G. (2010). "It's not just the judgements – it's that I don't know": Intolerance of uncertainty as a predictor of social anxiety. *Journal of Anxiety Disorders, 24*, 189–195. doi: 10.1016/j.janxdis.2009.10.007

Carleton, R. N., Fetzner, M. G., Hackl, J. L., & McEvoy, P. (2013). Intolerance of uncertainty as a contributor to fear and avoidance symptoms of panic attacks. *Cognitive Behaviour Therapy, 42*, 328–341. doi: 10.1080/16506073.2013.792100

Carleton, R. N., Mulvogue, M. K., Thibodeau, M. A., McCabe, R. E., Antony, M. M., & Asmundson, G. J. G. (2012). Increasingly certain about uncertainty: Intolerance of uncertainty across anxiety and depression. *Journal of Anxiety Disorders, 26*, 468–479. doi: 10.1016/j.janxdis.2012.01.011

Carleton, R. N., Norton, P. J., & Asmundson, G. J. G. (2007). Fearing the unknown: A short version of the Intolerance of Uncertainty Scale. *Journal of Anxiety Disorders, 21*, 105–117. doi: 10.1016/j.janxdis.2006.03.014

Carleton, R. N., Sharpe, D., & Asmundson, G. J. G. (2007). Anxiety sensitivity and intolerance of uncertainty: Requisites of the fundamental fears? *Behavior Research and Therapy, 45*, 2307–2316. doi: 10.1016/j.brat.2007.04.006

Carleton, R. N., Weeks, J. W., Howell, A. N., Asmundson, G. J. G., Antony, M. M., & McCabe, R. E. (2012). Assessing the latent structure of the intolerance of uncertainty construct: An initial taxometric analysis. *Journal of Anxiety Disorders, 26*, 150–157. doi: 10.1016/j.janxdis.2011.10.006

Clark, D. A. & Beck, A. T. (2010). *Cognitive Therapy of Anxiety Disorders: Science and Practice*. New York, NY: Guilford Press.

Davis, M., Walker, D. L., Miles, L., & Grillon, C. (2009). Phasic vs sustained fear in rats and humans: Role of the extended amygdala in fear vs anxiety. *Neuropsychopharmacology, 35*, 105–135. doi: 10.1038/npp.2009.109

de Moor, M. H. M., Costa, P. T., Terracciano, A., Krueger, R. F., de Geus, E. J. C., Toshiko, T., ... Boomsma, D. I. (2012). Meta-analysis of genome-wide association studies for personality. *Molecular Psychiatry, 17*, 337–349. doi: 10.1038/mp.2010.128

DeYoung, C. G., Cicchetti, D., & Rogosch, F. A. (2011). Moderation of the association between childhood maltreatment and neuroticism by the corticotropin-releasing hormone receptor 1 gene. *Journal of Child Psychology and Psychiatry, 52*, 898–906. doi: 10.1111/j.1469–7610.2011.02404.x

Drury, S. S., Sánchez, M. M., & Gonzalez, A. (2016). When mothering goes awry: Challenges and opportunities for utilizing evidence across rodent, nonhuman primate and human studies to better define the biological consequences of negative early caregiving. *Hormones and Behavior*, *77*, 182–192. doi: 10.1016/j .yhbeh.2015.10.007

Dugas, M. J., Brillon, P., Savard, P., Turcotte, J., Gaudet, A., Ladouceur, R., … Gervais, N. J. (2010). A randomized clinical trial of cognitive-behavioral therapy and applied relaxation for adults with generalized anxiety disorder. *Behavior Therapy*, *41*, 46–58. doi: 10.1016/j.beth.2008.12.004

Dugas, M. J., Buhr, K., & Ladouceur, R. (2004). The role of intolerance of uncertainty in etiology and maintenance. In R. G. Heimberg, C. L. Turk, & D. S. Mennin (eds.), *Generalized Anxiety Disorder: Advances in Research and Practice*. New York, NY: Guilford Press.

Dugas, M. J., Gagnon, F., Ladouceur, R., & Freeston, M. H. (1998). Generalized anxiety disorder: A preliminary test of a conceptual model. *Behaviour Research and Therapy*, *36*, 215–226. doi: 10.1016/S0005-7967(97)00070–3

Dugas, M. J., Ladouceur, R., Léger, E., Freeston, M. H., Langolis, F., Provencher, M. D., & Boisvert, J. M. (2003). Group cognitive-behavioral therapy for generalized anxiety disorder: Treatment outcome and long-term follow-up. *Journal of Consulting and Clinical Psychology*, *71*, 821–825. doi: 10.1037/0022-006x.71.4.821

Dugas, M. J., Marchand, A., & Ladouceur, R. (2005). Further validation of a cognitive-behavioral model of generalized anxiety disorder: Diagnostic and symptom specificity. *Journal of Anxiety Disorders*, *19*, 329–343. doi: 10.1016/j .janxdis.2004.02.002

Einstein, D. A. (2014). Extension of the transdiagnostic model to focus on intolerance of uncertainty: A review of the literature and implications for treatment. *Clinical Psychology: Science and Practice*, *21*, 280–300. doi: 10.1111/cpsp.12077

Eley, T. C., Gregory, A. M., Lau, J. Y. F., McGuffin, P., Napolitano, M., Rijsdijk, F. V., & Clark, D. M. (2008). In the face of uncertainty: A twin study of ambiguous information, anxiety and depression in children. *Journal of Abnormal Child Psychology*, *36*, 55–65. doi: 10.1007/s10802-007–9159-7

Fergus, T. A. & Bardeen, J. R. (2013). Anxiety sensitivity and intolerance of uncertainty: Evidence of incremental specificity in relation to health anxiety. *Personality and Individual Differences*, *55*, 640–644. doi: 10.1016/j.paid.2013.05.016

Fetzner MG, Horswill SC, Boelen PA, Carleton RN. Intolerance of uncertainty and PTSD symptoms: Exploring the construct relationship in a community sample with a heterogeneous trauma history. *Cognitive Therapy and Research*. 2013;37:725–734. doi: 10.1007/s10608-013-9531-6.

Freeston, M., Rhéaume, J., Letarte, H., Dugas, M. J., & Ladouceur, R. (1994). Why do people worry? *Personality and Individual Differences*, *17*, 791–802. doi: 10.1016/ 0191–8869(94)90048–5

Fullerton, J., Cubin, M., Tiwari, H., Wang, C., Bomhra, A., Davidson, S., … Flint, J. (2003). Linkage analysis of extremely discordant and concordant sibling pairs identifies quantitative-trait loci that influence variation in the human personality trait neuroticism. *American Journal of Human Genetics*, *72*, 879–890. doi: 10.1086/ 374178

Gentes, E. L. & Ruscio, A. M. (2011). A meta-analysis of the relation of intolerance of uncertainty to symptoms of generalized anxiety disorder, major depressive disorder, and obsessive-compulsive disorder. *Clinical Psychology Review*, *31*, 923–933. doi: 10.1016/j.cpr.2011.05.001

Goldberg, D. P., Krueger, R. F., Andrews, G., & Hobbs, M. J. (2009). Emotional disorders: Cluster 4 of the proposed meta-structure for DSM-V and ICD-11. *Psychological Medicine, 39*, 2043–2059. doi: 10.1017/s0033291709990298

Goosens, L., Sunaert, S., Peeters, R., Griez, E., & Schruers, K. (2007). Amygdala hyper function in phobic fear normalizes after exposure. *Biological Psychiatry, 62*, 1119–1125. doi: 10.1016/j.biopsych.2007.04.024

Gorka, S. M., Lieberman, L., Shankman, S. A., & Phan, K. L. (2017a). Association between neural reactivity and startle reactivity to uncertain threat in two independent samples. *Psychophysiology, 54*, 652–662. doi: 10.1111/psyp.12829

Gorka, S. M., Lieberman, L., Shankman, S. A., & Phan, K. L. (2017b). Startle potentiation to uncertain threat as a psychophysiological indicator of fear-based psychopathology: An examination across multiple internalizing disorders. *Journal of Abnormal Psychology, 126*, 8–18. doi: 10.1037/abn0000233

Gorka, S. M., Nelson, B. D., Sarapas, C., Campbell, M., Lewis, G. F., Bishop, J. R., . . . Shankman, S. A. (2013). Relation between respiratory sinus arrhythmia and startle response during predictable and unpredictable threat. *Journal of Psychophysiology, 27*, 95–104. doi: 10.1027/0269–8803/a000091

Gray, J. A. (1976). The behavioural inhibition system: A possible substrate for anxiety. In M. P. Feldman & A. M. Broadhurst (eds.), *Theoretical and Experimental Bases of Behaviour Modification* (pp. 3–41). London: Wiley.

Gray, J. A. & McNaughton, N. (2003). *The Neuropsychology of Anxiety: An Enquiry into the Functions of the Septo-Hippocampal System, Second Edition.* New York, NY: Oxford University Press.

Greco, V. & Roger, D. (2003). Uncertainty, stress, and health. *Personality and Individual Differences, 34*, 1057–1068. doi: 10.1016/S0191-8869(02)00091–0

Grenier, S., Barrette, A. M., & Ladouceur, R. (2005). Intolerance of uncertainty and intolerance of ambiguity: Similarities and differences. *Personality and Individual Differences, 39*, 593–600. doi: 10.1016/j.paid.2005.02.014

Grillon, C., Baas, J. M. P., Pine, D. S., Lissek, S., Lawley, M., Ellis, V., & Levine, J. (2006). The benzodiazepine alprazolam dissociates contextual fear from cued fear in humans as assessed by fear-potentiated startle. *Biological Psychiatry, 60*, 760–766. doi: 10.1016/j.biopsych.2005.11.027

Grillon, C., Chavis, C., Covington, M. F., & Pine, D. S. (2009). Two-week treatment with the selective serotonin reuptake inhibitor citalopram reduces contextual anxiety but not cued fear in healthy volunteers: A fear-potentiated startle study. *Neuropsychopharmacology, 34*, 964–971. doi: 10.1038/npp.2008.141

Gross, J. & Barrett, L. F. (2011). Emotion generation and emotion regulation: One or two depends on your point of view. *Emotion Review, 3*, 8–16. doi: 10.1177/1754073910380974

Grupe, D. W. & Nitschke, J. B. (2013). Uncertainty and anticipation in anxiety: An integrated neurobiological and psychological perspective. *Nature Reviews. Neuroscience, 14*, 488–501. doi: 10.1038/nrn3524

Hale, W., Richmond, M., Bennett, J., Berzins, T., Fields, A., Weber, D., . . . Osman, A. (2016). Resolving uncertainty about the Intolerance of Uncertainty Scale–12: Application of modern psychometric strategies. *Journal of Personality Assessment, 98*, 200–208. doi: 10.1080/00223891.2015.1070355

Harvey, A., Watkins, E., Mansell, W., & Shafran, R. (2004). *Cognitive Behavioural Processes across Psychological Disorders: A Transdiagnostic Approach to Research and Treatment*. Oxford: Oxford University Press.

Hebert, E. A., Dugas, M. J., Tulloch, T. G., & Holowka, D. W. (2014). Positive beliefs about worry: A psychometric evaluation of the Why Worry-II. *Personality and Individual Differences, 56*, 3–8. doi: 10.1016/j.paid.2013.08.009

Helzer, J. E., Kraemer, H. C., & Krueger, R. F. (2006). The feasibility and need for dimensional psychiatric diagnoses. *Psychological Medicine, 36*, 1671. doi: 10.1017/s003329170600821x

Hettema, J. M., An, S. S., Neale, M. C., Bukszar, J., van den Oord, E. J. C. G., Kendler, K. S., & Chen, X. (2006). Association between glutamic acid decarboxylase genes and anxiety disorders, major depression, and neuroticism. *Molecular Psychiatry, 11*, 752–762. doi: 10.1038/sj.mp.4001845

Holaway, R. M., Heimberg, R. G., & Coles, M. E. (2006). A comparison of intolerance of uncertainty in analogue obsessive-compulsive disorder and generalized anxiety disorder. *Journal of Anxiety Disorders, 20*, 158–174. doi: 10.1016/j.janxdis.2005.01.002

Holmes, E. A., Lang, T. J., & Deeprose, C. (2009). Mental imagery and emotion in treatment across disorders: Using the example of depression. *Cognitive Behaviour Therapy, 38*(S1), 21–28. doi: 10.1080/16506070902980729

Holmes, E. A. & Mathews, A. (2005). Mental imagery and emotion: A special relationship? *Emotion, 5*, 489–497. doi: 10.1037/1528–3542.5.4.489

Hong, R. Y. & Cheung, M. W. L. (2015). The structure of cognitive vulnerabilities to depression and anxiety: Evidence for a common core etiologic process based on a meta-analytic review. *Clinical Psychological Science, 3*, 892–912. doi: 10.1177/2167702614553789

Hong, R. Y. & Lee, S. S. (2015). Further clarifying prospective and inhibitory intolerance of uncertainty: Factorial and construct validity of test scores from the Intolerance of Uncertainty Scale. *Psychological Assessment, 27*, 605–620. doi: 10.1037/pas0000074

Imada, H. & Nageishi, Y. (1982). The concept of uncertainty in animal experiments using aversive stimulation. *Psychological Bulletin, 91*, 573–588. doi: 10.1037/0033–2909.91.3.573

Insel, T., Cuthbert, B., Garvey, M., Heinssen, R., Pine, D. S., Quinn, K., . . . Wang, P. (2010). Research domain criteria (RDoC): Toward a new classification framework for research on mental disorders. *American Journal of Psychiatry, 167*, 748–751. doi: 10.1176/appi.ajp.2010.09091379

Jacoby, R. J., Abramowitz, J. S., Buck, B. E., & Fabricant, L. E. (2014). How is the beads task related to intolerance of uncertainty in anxiety disorders? *Journal of Anxiety Disorders, 28*, 495–503. doi: 10.1016/j.janxdis.2014.05.005

Jacoby, R. J., Abramowitz, J. S., Reuman, L., & Blakey, S. M. (2016). Enhancing the ecological validity of the beads task as a behavioral measure of intolerance of uncertainty. *Journal of Anxiety Disorders, 41*, 43–49. doi: 10.1016/j.janxdis.2016.02.003

Jacoby, R. J., Fabricant, L. E., Leonard, R. C., Riemann, B. C., & Abramowitz, J. S. (2013). Just to be certain: Confirming the factor structure of the Intolerance of Uncertainty

Scale in patients with obsessive-compulsive disorder. *Journal of Anxiety Disorders*, *27*, 535–542. doi: 10.1016/j.janxdis.2013.07.008

Jensen, D. & Heimberg, R. G. (2015). Domain-specific intolerance of uncertainty in socially anxious and contamination-focused obsessive-compulsive individuals. *Cognitive Behaviour Therapy*, *44*, 54–62. doi: 10.1080/16506073.2014.959039

Kagan, J. & Snidman, N. (2004). *The Long Shadow of Temperament*. Boston, MA: Harvard College.

Kendler, K. S., Aggen, S. H., Jacobson, K. C., & Neale, M. C. (2003). Does the level of family dysfunction moderate the impact of genetic factors on the personality trait of neuroticism? *Psychological Medicine*, *33*, 817–825. doi: 10.1017/S0033291703007840

Koerner, N. & Dugas, M. J. (2006). A cognitive model of generalized anxiety disorder: The role of intolerance of uncertainty. In G. C. L. Davey & A. Wells (eds.), *Worry and Its Psychological Disorders: Theory, Assessment and Treatment* (pp. 201–216). Hoboken, NJ: Wiley Publishing. doi: 10.1002/9780470713143.ch12

Koerner, N. & Dugas, M. J. (2008). An investigation of appraisals in individuals vulnerable to excessive worry: The role of intolerance of uncertainty. *Cognitive Therapy and Research*, *32*, 619–638. doi: 10.1007/s10608-007-9125-2

Koerner, N., Mejia, T., & Kusec, A. (2017). What's in a name? Intolerance of uncertainty, other uncertainty-relevant constructs, and their differential relations to worry and generalized anxiety disorder. *Cognitive Behaviour Therapy*, *46*, 141–161. doi: 10.1080/16506073.2016.1211172

Kozak, M. J. & Cuthbert, B. N. (2016). The NIMH research domain criteria initiative: background, issues, and pragmatics. *Psychophysiology*, *53*, 286–297. doi: 10.1111/psyp.12518

Kuo, P.-H., Neale, M. C., Riley, B. P., Patterson, D. G., Walsh, D., Prescott, C. A., & Kendler, K. S. (2007). A genome-wide linkage analysis for the personality trait neuroticism in the Irish affected sib-pair study of alcohol dependence. *American Journal of Medical Genetics Part B-NeuroPsychiatric Genetics*, *144B*, 463–468. doi: 10.1002/ajmg.b.30478

Ladouceur, R., Blais, F., Freeston, M. H., & Dugas, M. J. (1998). Problem solving and problem orientation in generalized anxiety disorder. *Journal of Anxiety Disorders*, *12*, 139–152. doi: 10.1016/S0887-6185(98)00002-4

Ladouceur, R., Dugas, M., Freeston, M., Léger, É., Gagnon, F., & Thibodeau, N. (2000). Efficacy of a cognitive-behavioural treatment for generalized anxiety disorder: Evaluation in a controlled clinical trial. *Journal of Consulting and Clinical Psychology*, *68*, 957–964. doi: 10.1037/0022-006X.68.6.957

Ladouceur, R., Talbot, F., & Dugas, M. J. (1997). Behavioral expressions of intolerance of uncertainty in worry: Experimental findings. *Behavior Modification*, *21*, 355–371. doi: 10.1177/01454455970213006

Lawford, B. R., Young, R., Noble, E. P., Kann, B., & Ritchie, T. (2006). The D-2 dopamine receptor (DRD2) gene is associated with co-morbid depression, anxiety and social dysfunction in untreated veterans with posttraumatic stress disorder. *European Psychiatry*, *21*, 180–185. doi: 10.1016/j.eurpsy.2005.01.006

Lewinsohn, P. M., Shankman, S. A., Gau, J. M., & Klein, D. N. (2004). The prevalence and co-morbidity of subthreshold psychiatric conditions. *Psychological Medicine*, *34*, 613–622. doi: 10.1017/s0033291703001466

Lo, M.-T., Hinds, D. A., Tung, J. Y., Franz, C., Fan, C.-C., Wang, Y., . . . Chen, C.-H. (2017). Genome-wide analyses for personality traits identify six genomic loci and show correlations with psychiatric disorders. *Nature Genetics*, *49*, 152–156. doi: 10.1038/ng.3736

Mahoney, A. E. & McEvoy, P. M. (2012a). Changes in intolerance of uncertainty during cognitive behavior group therapy for social phobia. *Journal of Behavior Therapy and Experimental Psychiatry*, *43*, 849–854. doi: 10.1016/j.jbtep.2011.12.004

Mahoney, A. E. & McEvoy, P. M. (2012b). Trait versus situation-specific intolerance of uncertainty in a clinical sample with anxiety and depressive disorders. *Cognitive Behaviour Therapy*, *41*, 26–39. doi: 10.1080/16506073.2011.622131

Mahoney, A. E. & McEvoy, P. M. (2012c). A transdiagnostic examination of intolerance of uncertainty across anxiety and depressive disorders. *Cognitive Behaviour Therapy*, *41*, 212–222. doi: 10.1080/16506073.2011.622130

Mathes, B. M., Oglesby, M. E., Short, N. A., Portero, A. K., Raines, A. M., & Schmidt, N. B. (2017). An examination of the role of intolerance of distress and uncertainty in hoarding symptoms. *Comprehensive Psychiatry*, *72*, 121–129. doi: 10.1016/j.comppsych.2016.10.007

McEvoy, P. M. & Erceg-Hurn, D. M. (2016). The search for universal transdiagnostic and trans-therapy change processes: Evidence for intolerance of uncertainty. *Journal of Anxiety Disorders*, *41*, 96–107. doi: 10.1016/j.janxdis.2016.02.002

McEvoy, P. M. & Mahoney, A. E. (2011). Achieving certainty about the structure of intolerance of uncertainty in a treatment-seeking sample with anxiety and depression. *Journal of Anxiety Disorders*, *25*, 112–122. doi: 10.1016/j.janxdis.2010.08.010

Merswolken, M., Deter, H.-C., Siebenhuener, S., Orth-Gomer, K., & Weber, C. S. (2013). Anxiety as predictor of the cortisol awakening response in patients with coronary heart disease. *International Journal of Behavioral Medicine*, *20*, 461–467. doi: 10.1007/s12529-012–9233-6

Moehler, E., Kagan, J., Oelkers-Ax, R., Brunner, R., Poustka, L., Haffner, J., & Resch, F. (2008). Infant predictors of behavioural inhibition. *British Journal of Developmental Psychology*, *26*, 145–150. doi: 10.1348/026151007X206767

Moors, A. (2009). Theories of emotion causation: A review. *Cognition and Emotion*, *23*, 625–662. doi: 10.1080/02699930802645739

Moors, A., Ellsworth, P. C., Scherer, K. R., & Frijda, N. H. (2013). Appraisal theories of emotion: State of the art and future development. *Emotion Review*, *5*, 119–124. doi: 10.1177/1754073912468165

Morriss, J., Christakou, A., & van Reekum, C. M. (2015). Intolerance of uncertainty predicts fear extinction in amygdala-ventromedial prefrontal cortical circuitry. *Biology of Mood & Anxiety Disorders*, *5*, 1–13. doi: 10.1186/s13587-015–0019-8

Morriss, J., Christakou, A., & van Reekum, C. M. (2016). Nothing is safe: Intolerance of uncertainty is associated with compromised fear extinction learning. *Biological Psychology*, *121*, 187–193. doi: 10.1016/j.biopsycho.2016.05.001

Morriss, J., Macdonald, B., & van Reekum, C. M. (2016). What is going on around here? Intolerance of uncertainty predicts threat generalization. *PLoS ONE*, *11*, e0154494. doi: 10.1371/journal.pone.0154494

Murphy, T. M., O'Donovan, A., Mullins, N., O'Farrelly, C., McCann, A., & Malone, K. (2015). Anxiety is associated with higher levels of global DNA methylation and altered expression of epigenetic and interleukin-6 genes. *Psychiatric Genetics, 25,* 71–78. doi: 10.1097/YPG.0000000000000055

Nash, M. W., Huezo-Diaz, P., Sterne, A., Purcell, S., Hoda, F., Cherny, S. S., . . . Sham, P. C. (2004). Genome-wide linkage analysis of a composite index of neuroticism and mood-related scales in extreme selected sibships. *Human Molecular Genetics, 13,* 2173–2182. doi: 10.1093/hmg/ddh239

Nash, M. W., Sugden, K., Huezo-Diaz, P., Williamson, R., Sterne, A., Purcell, S., . . . Craig, I. W. (2005). Association analysis of monoamine genes with measures of depression and anxiety in a selected community sample of siblings. *American Journal of Medical Genetics Part B-Neuropsychiatric Genetics, 135B,* 33–37. doi: 10.1002/ajmg.b.30063

National Institute of Mental Health (NIMH). (2016). Behavioral Assessment Methods for RDoC Constructs: A report by the National Advisory Mental Health Council Workgroup on Tasks and Measures for Research Domain Criteria (RDoC). Retrieved from www.nimh.nih.gov/about/advisory-boards-and-groups/namhc/reports/rdoc_council_workgroup_report_153440.pdf.

Nelson, B. D., Hajcak, G., & Shankman, S. A. (2015). Event-related potentials to acoustic startle probes during the anticipation of predictable and unpredictable threat. *Psychophysiology, 52,* 887–894. doi: 10.1111/psyp.12418

Nelson, B. D., Liu, H., Sarapas, C., & Shankman, S. A. (2016). Intolerance of uncertainty mediates the relationship between panic and the startle reflex in anticipation of unpredictable threat. *Journal of Experimental Psychopathology, 7,* 172–189. doi: 10.5127/jep.048115

Nelson, B. D. & Shankman, S. A. (2011). Does intolerance of uncertainty predict anticipatory startle responses to uncertain threat? *International Journal of Psychophysiology, 81,* 107–115. doi: 10.1016/j.ijpsycho.2011.05.003

Nelson, B. D., Shankman, S. A., & Proudfit, G. H. (2014). Intolerance of uncertainty mediates reduced reward anticipation in major depressive disorder. *Journal of Affective Disorders, 158,* 108–113. doi: 10.1016/j.jad.2014.02.014

Oglesby, M. E., Gibby, B. A., Mathes, B. M., Short, N. A., & Schmidt, N. B. (2017). Intolerance of uncertainty and posttraumatic stress symptoms: An investigation within a treatment seeking trauma-exposed sample. *Comprehensive Psychiatry, 72,* 34–40. doi: 10.1016/j.comppsych.2016.08.011

Olatunji, B. O. & Sawchuk, C. N. (2005). Disgust: Characteristic features, social manifestations, and clinical implications. *Journal of Social and Clinical Psychology, 27,* 932–962.

Pan, Y., Cheng, Q., Shan, M.-S., & Yan, J. (2015). Association between polymorphism of the norepinephrine transporter gene rs2242446 and rs5669 loci and depression disorders. *International Journal of Clinical and Experimental Medicine, 8,* 18837–18842. Retrieved from www.ncbi.nlm.nih.gov/pmc/articles/PMC4694404/

Ryu, S. H., Lee, S. H., Lee, H. J., Cha, J. H., Ham, B. J., Han, C. S., . . . Lee, M. S. (2004). Association between norepinephrine transporter gene polymorphism and major depression. *Neuropsychobiology, 49,* 174–177. doi: 10.1159/000077361

Sacharin, V., Sander, D., & Scherer, K. R. (2012). The perception of changing emotion expressions. *Cognition and Emotion, 26,* 1273–1300. doi: 10.1080/02699931.2012.656583

Sanislow, C. A., Pine, D. S., Quinn, K. J., Kozak, M. J., Garvey, M. A., Heinssen, R. K., . . . Cuthbert, B. N. (2010). Developing constructs for psychopathology research: Research domain criteria. *Journal of Abnormal Psychology*, *119*, 631–639. doi: 10.1037/a0020909

Scherer, K. R. (2009). The dynamic architecture of emotion: Evidence for the component process model. *Cognition and Emotion*, *23*, 1307–1351. doi: 10.1080/02699930902928969

Scherer, K. R. (2013). The nature and dynamics of relevance and valence appraisals: Theoretical advances and recent evidence. *Emotion Review*, *5*, 150–162. doi: 10.1177/1754073912468166

Schmitz, A. & Grillon, C. (2012). Assessing fear and anxiety in humans using the threat of predictable and unpredictable aversive events (the NPU-threat test). *Nature Protocols*, *7*, 527–532. doi: 10.1038/nprot.2012.001

Shihata, S., McEvoy, P. M., & Mullan, B. A. (2017). Pathways from uncertainty to anxiety: An evaluation of a hierarchical model of trait and disorder-specific intolerance of uncertainty on anxiety disorder symptoms. *Journal of Anxiety Disorders*, *45*, 72–79. doi: 10.1016/j.janxdis.2016.12.001

Shihata, S., McEvoy, P., Mullan, B. A., & Carleton, R. N. (2016). Intolerance of uncertainty in emotional disorders: What uncertainties remain? *Journal of Anxiety Disorders*, *41*, 115–124. doi: 10.1016/j.janxdis.2016.05.001

Singer, T., Critchley, H. D., & Preuschoff, K. (2009). A common role of insula in feelings, empathy and uncertainty. *Trends in Cognitive Sciences*, *13*, 334–340. doi: 10.1016/j.tics.2009.05.001

Smith, G. W., Aubry, J. M., Dellu, F., Contarino, A., Bilezikjian, L. M., Gold, L. H., . . . Lee, K. F. (1998). Corticotropin releasing factor receptor 1-deficient mice display decreased anxiety, impaired stress response, and aberrant neuroendocrine development. *Neuron*, *20*, 1093–1102. doi: 10.1016/S0896-6273(00)80491–2

Southwick, S. M., Vythilingam, M., & Charney, D. S. (2005). The psychobiology of depression and resilience to stress: Implications for prevention and treatment. *Annual Review of Clinical Psychology*, *1*, 255–291. doi: 10.1146/annurev. clinpsy.1.102803.143948

Tang, A. C., Akers, K. G., Reeb, B. C., Romeo, R. D., & McEwen, B. S. (2006). Programming social, cognitive, and neuroendocrine development by early exposure to novelty. *Proceedings of the National Academy of Sciences of the United States of America*, 103, 15716–15721. doi: 10.1073/pnas. 0607374103

Tang, A. C., Reeb-Sutherland, B. C., Romeo, R. D., & McEwen, B. S. (2012). Reducing behavioral inhibition to novelty via systematic neonatal novelty exposure: The influence of maternal hypothalamic-pituitary-adrenal regulation. *Biological Psychiatry*, *72*, 150–156. doi: 10.1016/j.biopsych.2012.03.021

Taylor, S., Zvolensky, M. J., Cox, B. J., Deacon, B., Heimberg, R. G., Ledley, D. R., . . . Cardenas, S. J. (2007). Robust dimensions of anxiety sensitivity: Development and initial validation of the Anxiety Sensitivity Index-3. *Psychological Assessment*, *19*, 176–188. doi: 10.1037/1040–3590.19.2.176

Teale Sapach, M. J. N., Carleton, R. N., Mulvogue, M. K., Weeks, J. W., & Heimberg, R. G. (2015). Cognitive constructs and social anxiety disorder: Beyond fearing negative evaluation. *Cognitive Behaviour Therapy*, *44*, 63–73. doi: 10.1080/16506073.2014.961539

Thayer, J. F., Åhs, F., Fredrikson, M., Sollers, J. J., & Wager, T. D. (2012). A meta-analysis of heart rate variability and neuroimaging studies: Implications for heart rate variability as a marker of stress and health. *Neuroscience and Biobehavioral Reviews*, *36*, 747–756. doi: 10.1016/j.neubiorev.2011.11.009

Thibodeau, M. A., Carleton, R. N., Gómez-Pérez, L., & Asmundson, G. J. (2013). "What if I make a mistake?": Intolerance of uncertainty is associated with poor behavioral performance. *Journal of Nervous and Mental Disease*, *201*, 760–766. doi: 10.1097/NMD.0b013e3182a21298

Thibodeau, M. A., Carleton, R. N., McEvoy, P., Zvolensky, M. J., Brandt, C. P., Boelen, P. A., . . . Asmundson, G. J. G. (2015). Developing scales measuring disorder-specific intolerance of uncertainty (DSIU): A new perspective on transdiagnostic. *Journal of Anxiety Disorders*, *31*, 49–57. doi: 10.1016/j.janxdis.2015.01.006

Thompson, S. C. (1981). Will it hurt less if I can control it? A complex answer to a simple question. *Psychological Bulletin*, *90*, 89–101. doi: 10.1037/0033–2909.90.1.89

Timpl, P., Spanagel, R., Sillaber, I., Kresse, A., Reul, J., Stalla, G. K., . . . Wurst, W. (1998). Impaired stress response and reduced anxiety in mice lacking a functional corticotropin-releasing hormone receptor 1. *Nature Genetics*, *19*, 162–166. doi: 10.1038/520

Tyrka, A. R., Wier, L. M., Price, L. H., Rikhye, K., Ross, N. S., Anderson, G. M., . . . Carpenter, L. L. (2008). Cortisol and ACTH responses to the Dex/CRH test: Influence of temperament. *Hormones and Behavior*, *53*, 518–525. doi: 10.1016/j.yhbeh.2007.12.004

van der Heiden, C., Muris, P., & van der Molen, H. T. (2012). Randomized controlled trial on the effectiveness of metacognitive therapy and intolerance-of-uncertainty therapy for generalized anxiety disorder. *Behaviour Research and Therapy*, *50*, 100. doi: 10.1016/j.brat.2011.12.005

Vukasovic, T. & Bratko, D. (2015). Heritability of personality: A meta-analysis of behavior genetic studies. *Psychological Bulletin*, *141*, 769–785. doi: 10.1037/bul0000017

Walker, S., O'Connor, D. B., Schaefer, A., Talbot, D., & Hendrickx, H. (2011). The cortisol awakening response: Associations with trait anxiety and stress reactivity. *Personality and Individual Differences*, *51*, 123–127. doi: 10.1016/j.paid.2011.03.026

Wever, M., Smeets, P., & Sternheim, L. (2015). Neural correlates of intolerance of uncertainty in clinical disorders. *Journal of Neuropsychiatry and Clinical Neurosciences*, *27*, 345–353. doi: 10.1176/appi.neuropsych.14120387

Wright, K. D., Lebell, M. A. N. A., & Carleton, R. N. (2016). Intolerance of uncertainty, anxiety sensitivity, health anxiety, and anxiety disorder symptoms in youth. *Journal of Anxiety Disorders*, *41*, 35–42. doi: 10.1016/j.janxdis.2016.04.011

Yehuda, R., Daskalakis, N. P., Lehrner, A., Desarnaud, F., Bader, H. N., Makotkine, I., . . . Meaney, M. J. (2014). Influences of maternal and paternal PTSD on epigenetic regulation of the glucocorticoid receptor gene in Holocaust survivor offspring. *American Journal of Psychiatry*, *171*, 872–880. doi: 10.1176/appi.ajp.2014.13121571

Zlomke, K. R. & Jeter, K. M. (2014). Stress and worry: Examining intolerance of uncertainty's moderating effect. *Anxiety, Stress & Coping*, *27*, 202–215. doi: 10.1080/10615806.2013.835400

8 Distress Tolerance

Lance M. Rappaport, Erin C. Berenz, Carl Lejuez, and
Roxann Roberson-Nay

Defined as an individual's perceived or actual ability to withstand negative emotional or physical states (Brown, Lejuez, Kahler, Strong, & Zvolensky, 2005; Linehan, 1993), distress tolerance (DT) has been implicated in a range of internalizing and externalizing psychiatric disorders (e.g., Daughters et al., 2005; Marshall-Berenz et al., 2010). While DT is theoretically and empirically related to components of emotion regulation, it is conceptually distinct. For example, whereas *emotional dysregulation* refers to difficulty downregulating negative affect, or upregulating positive affect (Gross & Thompson, 2007), *DT* has been distinguished as the ability to withstand (viz., tolerate) negative emotion states without altering them. Hence, seeking to quickly terminate an adversive state (i.e., low DT) is implicated in experiential avoidance (e.g., Vujanovic, Litz, & Farris, 2015) and subsequent negative reinforcement of avoidance (see Trafton & Gifford, 2011, for an expanded discussion). As reviewed in what follows, DT has been implicated in anxiety disorders and related conditions. Similar to emotional dysregulation, evidence implicating DT in multiple psychiatric disorders suggests that it may play a transdiagnostic role and supports recent efforts to consider clinical implications.

This chapter is meant to address several key issues related to the construct of DT. Following from the definition of DT provided earlier, the chapter begins with a review and discussion of assessment approaches. Second, it outlines documented associations between DT and various anxiety and related disorders. Third, the chapter contextualizes DT within a transdiagnostic framework. Finally, the chapter closes with considerations for future research and potential clinical applications.

Historical Context and Definition

Although clinical formulation of DT dates back several decades (e.g., Frenkel-Brunswik, 1948; Leyro, Zvolensky, & Bernstein, 2010), modern interest in DT stems from research into smoking cessation and self-harm in the late 1980s and early 1990s. For example, Hajek and colleagues demonstrated that individuals who could hold their breath for a longer period of time were more successful in maintaining abstinence from cigarette smoking (Hajek, Belcher, & Stapelton, 1987). Several years later, DT emerged as a key component and module in

Marsha Linehan's Dialectical Behavior Therapy (DBT) manual for the treatment of suicidality and borderline personality disorder (Linehan, 1993). Within the DBT formulation, increasing an individual's ability to tolerate distress is thought to reduce self-harming and suicidal behaviors. Finally, as interest in emotion regulation grew, applications of DT broadened to other psychiatric disorders, including anxiety, trauma, and substance use disorders.

DT Assessment Approaches

Similar to other transdiagnostic constructs, such as impulsivity, the DT field has undergone challenges related to the concordance of various measures purported to measure DT. Since the concept of DT emerged from both the human laboratory and clinical intervention literatures, the definition of DT broadly encompasses both perceived (i.e., self-report) and behaviorally observed tolerance of physical and psychological distress (Brandon et al., 2003; Brown et al., 2005). The primary distinction between various measures of DT is assessment modality (i.e., behavioral versus self-report). However, while multimodal assessment complicates research on DT, the ability to examine converging evidence from research in two distinct methodologies is a strength of this literature.

Behavioral measures of DT typically involve the presentation of a distress-inducing task followed by assessment of participants' latency to terminating exposure to the task (see Leyro et al., 2010, for review). The distress-inducing task may be designed to elicit physical discomfort or psychological distress, such as anxiety or frustration. Two influential examples of behavioral tasks are the Mirror Tracing Persistence Task 6 (MTPT) and the Paced Auditory Serial Addition Test (PASAT) (Lejeuz, Kahler, & Brown, 2003). The MTPT requires participants to trace objects while observing the mirror image of their movements, either manually or on a computer screen, as if viewing the objects through a mirror (Brandon et al., 2003; Matthews & Stoney, 1988; Tutoo, 1971). When participants make an error, they hear a loud buzzer. The PASAT requires participants to sum a series of numbers, with the interval between number presentations decreasing over time, making the task increasingly difficult.

Unlike the PASAT and MTPT, which focus on stressors of a more psychological nature, other tasks focus on physical or somatic stressors, such as the Cold-Pressor Task (Hines & Brown, 1932) and the breath-holding task (Hajek et al., 1987). The breath-holding task requires participants to hold their breath as long as they can; DT is defined as the mean number of seconds participants hold their breath across two trials. The Cold-Pressor Task requires participants to place their hand in ice water for as long as possible. Studies have typically observed moderate correlations among behavioral DT tasks (e.g., Marshall-Berenz, Vujanovic, Bonn-Miller, Bernstein, & Zvolensky, 2010; McHugh et al., 2011), indicating that the underlying constructs assessed with these tasks are related, but that the tasks are distinct from one another.

In contrast to laboratory-based behavioral assessment, self-report measures of DT ask individuals to rate their own ability to withstand either physical or affective distress (for a comprehensive review of self-report measures, see Leyro et al., 2010). However, similar to laboratory-based behavioral assessment, self-report measures assess tolerance of either physical or psychological distress. The most commonly administered measure of DT is the Distress Tolerance Scale (DTS) (Simons & Gaher, 2005), a 15-item measure that assesses individuals' perceptions of their ability to tolerate emotional distress on a five-point Likert-type scale (e.g., "I can't handle feeling distressed or upset"). Past studies have identified theoretically relevant associations between self-report DT measures and related cognitive-affective risk factors, namely anxiety sensitivity (a fear of anxiety and its consequences; Reiss, Peterson, Gursky, & McNally, 1986). Most notably, past studies have found that self-report measures of DT and anxiety sensitivity share a common higher-order "affect sensitivity and tolerance" factor (Bernstein, Zvolensky, Vujanovic, & Moos, 2009), with some research suggesting that affect sensitivity and affect tolerance may not be distinct constructs (McHugh & Otto, 2012). As such McHugh and Otto (2012) developed the empirically derived 10-item Distress Intolerance Index (DII), which is comprised of the best-performing items from the DTS, the Anxiety Sensitivity Index (ASI) (Peterson & Reiss, 1992), and the Frustration Discomfort Scale (FDS) (Harrington, 2005). The DII has evidenced significant moderate correlations with behavioral measures of DT (McHugh & Otto, 2011).

However, most research suggests little correlation between self-report and behavioral measures (e.g., Anestis, Tull, Bagge, & Gratz, 2012), although self-report measures tend to be significantly related to one another (Bernstein et al., 2009; McHugh & Otto, 2012), and behavioral measures tend to be significantly related to one another (Marshall-Berenz et al., 2010; McHugh et al., 2011). Therefore, significant effort has been made to understand the nature of DT and to refine DT measurement to facilitate future research. For example, additional research indicates that although behavioral measures of psychological DT (e.g., PASAT, MTPT) are significantly correlated, these measures may not be associated with behavioral measures of somatic DT (e.g., Cold-Pressor Task; McHugh et al., 2011). McHugh and Otto (2011) suggest that specific domain measures may be useful in cases where clinical specificity is desired, whereas general domain measures may be useful for assessing DT more broadly. Few studies have explicitly evaluated differences in clinical phenotypes as a function of the DT domain. One study found that anxiety sensitivity is significantly correlated with behavioral measures of somatic, but not psychological, DT (McHugh et al., 2011), which makes intuitive sense given that individuals high in anxiety sensitivity are expressly concerned with the experience of physiological arousal.

Anxiety Disorders

Much of the existing research on distress tolerance has examined its relevance as a correlate of substance use (e.g., Buckner, Keough, & Schmidt, 2007;

Daughters, Lejuez, Kahler, Strong, & Brown, 2005) and psychopathology (e.g., Michel, Rowa, Young, & McCabe, 2016). Broadly, prior research on the role of distress tolerance as a risk factor for, and correlate of, anxiety disorders, has either examined distress tolerance within a specific disorder or attempted to distinguish between sets of anxiety, and internalizing, disorders. While substance use is frequently comorbid with anxiety disorders (Grant et al., 2006; Kessler, Chiu, Demler, & Walters, 2005), a comprehensive review of the literature regarding distress tolerance and substance use is outside the scope of this chapter (see Leyro et al., 2010, for review).

In the largest comparative study to date, DT was measured in a sample of outpatients (n > 600 persons) with panic disorder (PD), social anxiety disorder (SAD), generalized anxiety disorder (GAD), or obsessive-compulsive disorder (OCD) (Michel et al., 2016). Correlation and regression analyses indicated that DT was associated with symptom severity and impairment; however, it did not account for unique variance over the effect of negative affect, stress, intolerance of uncertainty, and anxiety sensitivity. In fact, intolerance of uncertainty and anxiety sensitivity had a stronger relationship with overall symptom severity and impairment in all regression models. This finding suggests that although DT may be transdiagnostic, intolerance of uncertainty and anxiety sensitivity are more relevant to our understanding of anxiety disorders. These study outcomes also are consistent with a study where DT was measured in a treatment-seeking sample and found to significantly predict symptoms associated with OCD, GAD, and SAD, but not PD, with or without agoraphobia (Laposa, Collimore, Hawley, & Rector, 2015). However, the bivariate association of DT with these anxiety symptom domains was non-significant once intolerance of uncertainty and anxiety sensitivity were included as covariates and suggests that, among persons with anxiety disorders, anxiety sensitivity and intolerance of uncertainty are more closely associated with impairment and symptom severity than DT. Taken together, results generally suggest that individuals with anxiety and OCD and elevated symptomatology express difficulty tolerating emotional distress relative to individuals without these emotional difficulties, and DT scores are generally comparable across anxiety disorder symptom domains (Keough, Riccardi, Timpano, Mitchell, & Schmidt, 2010).

Posttraumatic Stress Disorder

A growing body of research has evaluated the relevance of DT to trauma exposure and posttraumatic stress disorder (PTSD). Community-based studies of adults typically have not identified a significant correlation between trauma load (i.e., number of lifetime potentially traumatic events) and DT (e.g., Marshall-Berenz et al., 2010; Vujanovic, Bonn-Miller, Potter, Marshall, & Zvolensky, 2011). However, a recent study of adults in an acute-care psychiatric inpatient study reported that low DT was significantly associated with greater lifetime trauma load (Vujanovic, Dutcher, & Berenz, 2016). Two retrospective studies of childhood trauma and DT, one conducted in college students with a history of interpersonal trauma (e.g., physical or sexual assault) and one conducted in acute-care psychiatric inpatients, also have documented significant associations between certain forms of childhood abuse, namely physical abuse, and *higher* levels of self-reported DT on the DTS (Berenz et al., in press), highlighting the complexity and importance of understanding DT from a developmental perspective.

A number of studies have identified significant associations between lower levels of self-reported DT and greater PTSD symptom severity in a variety of trauma-exposed samples. For example, lower levels of DT on the DTS are associated with greater PTSD symptoms in community members (Marshall-Berenz et al., 2010; Vujanovic et al., 2013; Vujanovic, Bonn-Miller, et al., 2011), veterans (Banducci, Bujarski, Bonn-Miller, Patel, & Connolly, 2016), adults with substance dependence (Vujanovic, Rathnayaka, Amador, & Schmitz, 2016), and adults in an acute-care psychiatric inpatient unit (Vujanovic, Dutcher, et al., 2016), above and beyond demographic variables and lifetime trauma load.

Several studies have failed to detect significant associations between behavioral DT measures and global PTSD symptoms (e.g., Farris, Vujanovic, Hogan, Schmidt, & Zvolensky, 2014; Marshall-Berenz et al., 2010). However, other studies have found support for a role of behavioral DT in PTSD risk. In a sample of tornado-exposed adolescents, low DT as measured by the Behavioral Indicator of Resiliency to Distress task (BIRD) (Lejeuz, Daughters, Danielson, & Ruggiero, 2006) was significantly prospectively associated with greater risk for PTSD and depression symptoms, particularly in the context of low perceived social support (Cohen, Danielson, Adams, & Ruggiero, 2016). Behaviorally observed physical DT may also modify an association between other cognitive-affective risk factors and PTSD symptoms. For example, breath-holding duration has been found to moderate an association between anxiety sensitivity and PTSD avoidance symptoms (Berenz, Vujanovic, Coffey, & Zvolensky, 2012) and hyperarousal symptoms (Farris et al., 2014).

Finally, a few studies have evaluated DT and PTSD with respect to clinically relevant outcomes. One emerging pattern of findings is that DT may modify an association between PTSD and markers of clinical complexity. For example, preliminary research has found evidence for a potentially mediating role of self-reported DT in the association between PTSD symptoms and suicidality (Anestis et al., 2012; Vujanovic, Bakhshaie, Martin, Reddy, & Anestis, 2017). Additionally, self-reported DT may mediate an association between PTSD symptoms and coping-oriented alcohol (Vujanovic, Marshall-Berenz, & Zvolensky, 2011) and marijuana use (Potter, Vujanovic, Marshall-Berenz, Bernstein, & Bonn-Miller, 2011).

Another promising line of clinical study is the utility of DT in predicting treatment success and response among individuals with PTSD. For example, Tull and colleagues showed that PTSD was predictive of substance use treatment dropout among men who were low in behaviorally observed DT (Tull, Gratz, Coffey, Weiss, & McDermott, 2013). Banducci and colleagues found that increases in DT over the course of a PTSD treatment program were associated with greater improvements in PTSD symptoms in a veteran sample (Banducci, Connolly,

Vujanovic, Alvarez, & Bonn-Miller, 2017). However, while previous work is encouraging, further research is needed to clarify the relevance of DT for comorbidity, impairment, and prognosis of individuals with PTSD.

Panic Attacks and Panic Disorder

Individuals attempting to quit smoking who lapse early in their quit attempt have difficulty maintaining abstinence (Brown, Kahler, Zvolensky, Lejuez, & Ramsey, 2001; Cook, Gerkovich, O'Connell, & Potocky, 1995; Doherty, Kinnunen, Militello, & Garvey, 1995; Zvolensky et al., 2007). Increased understanding of psychological processes underlying failure early and throughout smoking cessation as well as long-term abstinence success is needed. One promising line of inquiry on sustained abstinence has focused on the role of DT. Conceptual models concerning people who lapse early during a quit attempt posit that persons with low DT may be distinguished by an inability to tolerate negative affect, bodily sensations associated with nicotine withdrawal symptoms, and other aversive interoceptive cues (Brown et al., 2005). One possible outcome associated with lowered DT among smokers may be a tendency to experience panic or panic-like reactions when faced with uncomfortable, aversive interoceptive cues. For this reason, panic pathophysiology may be relevant to better understanding DT where panic responsivity to internal bodily states may represent a key explanatory construct. In one such study, a panic-like response following a voluntary hyperventilation challenge was significantly associated with DT above and beyond conceptually related constructs including anxiety sensitivity, negative affectivity, and discomfort intolerance as well as smoking rate (Marshall et al., 2008). In a sample of adult smokers, DT (measured behaviorally as breath-holding duration) was significantly related to interoceptive fear and agoraphobia (Brandt, Johnson, Schmidt, & Zvolensky, 2012). In a related study of smokers where half were randomly assigned to 12-hour nicotine deprivation and the other half smoked as usual, lower DT was significantly associated with elevated anxious responding to a 10% CO_2 breathing challenge and negatively associated with post-breathing challenge increases in nicotine withdrawal symptoms (Farris, Zvolensky, Otto, & Leyro, 2015).

In all, while studies regarding DT in the context of panic have yielded mixed findings, DT shows a more promising association with panic anxiety in people who are regular smokers and, therefore, may have treatment implications for smoking cessation programs. Thus, DT represents a promising construct of increasing clinical interest at the intersection of anxious psychopathology and nicotine use.

Obsessive-Compulsive Disorder

Obsessive-compulsive disorder is characterized by distressing, unwanted, or intrusive thoughts, images, or impulses (obsessions) and behaviors performed to prevent feared consequences and/or reduce anxiety. The Obsessive-Compulsive Cognitions Working Group (2005) proposed a number of maladaptive beliefs associated with OCD such as inflated responsibility, overestimated threat and consequences of the obsession, exaggerated importance and control of thoughts, thought–action fusion, perfectionism, intolerance of uncertainty, and misinterpretation of personal significance; all were proposed as key elements of the cognitive core of OCD.

Generally, intolerance of internal experiences concerns difficulty managing unwanted thoughts, emotions, and other internal states, a difficulty often endorsed by persons suffering with obsessions and compulsions (e.g., Forsyth, Eifert, & Barrios, 2006; Robinson & Freeston, 2014; Twohig, 2009). Intolerance of internal experiences comprises two psychological constructs including experiential avoidance and DT. *Experiential avoidance* refers to the unwillingness to experience unpleasant emotions, thoughts, or memories (Hayes, Wilson, Gifford, Follette, & Strosahl, 1996). Experiential avoidance and DT are though to contribute to the maintenance of obsessive-compulsive symptoms (Robinson & Freeston, 2014).

Findings regarding the role of DT in obsessive compulsive symptom expression are somewhat mixed. Although individuals with OCD exhibit lower DT than nonclinical individuals, other relevant covariates (e.g., anxiety sensitivity, intolerance of uncertainty) were not included in models (Ricciardi & McNally, 1995). Thus, the unique contribution of DT to obsessive compulsive symptomatology could not be determined. In a related manner, two additional studies with nonclinical samples found that lower DT was associated with obsessional symptoms, but not with compulsive behaviors (e.g., checking, washing) (Cougle, Timpano, Fitch, & Hawkins, 2011; Cougle, Timpano, & Goetz, 2012).

Low DT was associated with greater severity of obsessions in both clinical and nonclinical samples, but only in the context of greater life stress (i.e., life stressors moderated the DT–OC symptom relationship) (Macatee, Capron, Schmidt, & Cougle, 2013). A recent study sought to estimate the contributions of experiential avoidance and DT in the prediction of obsessive-compulsive symptoms given that no study had examined the unique effects of these two constructs simultaneously after accounting for general distress levels. Results indicated that lower DT was associated with higher obsessive-compulsive symptom severity for all symptom dimensions measured (Blakey, Jacoby, Reuman, & Abramowitz, 2016). However, only experiential avoidance (not DT) predicted obsessional symptoms, but not other obsessive-compulsive symptom dimensions, suggesting that an individual's willingness to endure (i.e., experiential avoidance), rather than their ability to tolerate (i.e., DT) unpleasant internal experiences best predicts obsessional symptoms above and beyond general distress. These varied findings underscore the need for additional studies clarifying the relation of DT to the obsessive-compulsive symptom domains.

Generalized Anxiety Disorder

Research into the association of DT with GAD is sparse. However, recent investigations suggest that examining DT in GAD may clarify the role of DT as a risk factor for other anxiety and internalizing disorders. Similarly, related constructs in cognition (i.e., intolerance of uncertainty, anxiety sensitivity) and emotion regulation (e.g., tolerance of negative emotions) are well described within GAD. Therefore, further examining the association of DT with GAD may clarify the conceptualization of DT. For example, understanding distinctions between DT and intolerance of uncertainty may provide a useful illustration of how DT acts as a risk factor for related anxiety disorders (e.g., PTSD).

Research specific to GAD has, so far, generally focused on associated symptoms in community or college samples. Across two undergraduate samples, students who self-reported lower DT also self-reported elevated symptoms of GAD (MacDonald, Pawluk, Koerner, & Goodwill, 2015; Pawluk & Koerner, 2016) (though see Macatee & Cougle, 2013). Moreover, in both samples, students who endorsed more GAD symptoms also reported greater intolerance of uncertainty. Finally, one study suggests that lower DT, and elevated intolerance of uncertainty, may not be specific to GAD compared to other internalizing disorders; students who reported only elevated depression symptoms reported similar levels of DT and intolerance of uncertainty (MacDonald et al., 2015). However, the other study clarifies unique associations of DT and intolerance of uncertainty with elevated GAD symptoms; both associations remained when DT and intolerance of uncertainty were included in the same model (Pawluk & Koerner, 2016).

Evidence of an association between DT and GAD agrees with recent research in adolescent, clinical, and nonclinical community adult samples. Across two adolescent samples, lower DT was associated with elevated GAD symptoms (Wolitzky-Taylor et al., 2015, 2016). Similarly, adults receiving outpatient psychotherapy for GAD reported lower DT than community adults (Laposa et al., 2015), including following adjustment for concurrent depression, which also was associated with lower DT (Macatee, Capron, Guthrie, Schmidt, & Cougle, 2015). Finally, among community adults, baseline DT was associated with baseline worry (Laposa et al., 2015) as well as elevated worry one month later and higher average worry over eight assessments taken during the intervening month (Macatee et al., 2015) or six assessments over two weeks (Macatee, Albanese, Allan, Schmidt, & Cougle, 2016).

Additionally, considerable theory (Clark & Watson, 1991; Watson et al., 1995) and empirical evidence (e.g., Kendler, Neale, Kessler, Heath, & Eaves, 1992; Kessler et al., 2008) suggest an overlap between GAD and major depressive disorder. However, extant research on the manifestation of DT in major depressive disorder may clarify the association between DT and components of GAD. Research in a variety of samples suggests lower DT among individuals with major depressive disorder or with elevated depression symptoms (Brandt, Zvolensky, & Bonn-Miller, 2013; Buckner et al., 2007; Capron, Norr, Macatee, & Schmidt, 2013; Dennhardt & Murphy, 2011; Ellis, Vanderlind, & Beevers, 2013; Gorka, Ali, & Daughters, 2012; Koball et al., 2016; Magidson et al., 2013; Michel et al., 2016; Starr & Davila, 2012), including daily depressive symptoms (Macatee et al., 2016) and prospective internalizing symptoms (Felton et al., 2017; Hashoul-

Andary et al., 2016). However, the association is somewhat inconsistent (Brown et al., 2009; Cummings et al., 2013). Such inconsistency may arise when DT is associated with a component of depression that is inconsistently present in samples of individuals with major depressive disorder. Specifically, DT may be associated with rumination, which has been well documented within major depressive disorder (Nolen-Hoeksema, 2000) and likened to worry in GAD (Starr & Davila, 2012). In support of this hypothesis, Magidson and colleagues suggest that the association of DT with depression symptoms may be mediated by the degree to which participants engaged in depressive rumination (Magidson et al., 2013).

Meanwhile, while worry may not be sufficient to describe GAD, recent psychological conceptualizations of GAD have emphasized the centrality of worry to the diagnosis (Newman, Llera, Erickson, Przeworski, & Castonguay, 2013). To this end, worry may clarify the transdiagnostic nature of DT. For example, worry is moderately correlated with distress intolerance and intolerance of uncertainty in undergraduate (Norr et al., 2013) and clinical samples (Kertz, Stevens, McHugh, & Björgvinsson, 2015; Michel et al., 2016). Moreover, DT may be associated with worry more strongly than symptoms of other anxiety disorders (e.g., symptoms of SAD) after adjustment for depression and broad anxiety symptoms (Keough et al., 2010). Similarly, among adults seeking outpatient psychotherapy, low DT was associated with worry and diagnosis of GAD though not with depression symptoms or major depressive disorder when adjusting for concurrent worry or GAD (Allan, Macatee, Norr, & Schmidt, 2014).

DT as a Transdiagnostic Process

While highly influential diagnostic systems have refined the categorization of psychiatric syndromes (cf. American Psychiatric Association, 2013), evidence from genetic epidemiology, neuroscience, and developmental psychology indicates a complexity of psychiatric disorders that is not captured by the existing system. For example, evidence implicating distress tolerance in multiple anxiety disorders suggests that distress tolerance may cut across traditional diagnostic boundaries. Similarly, funding initiatives are beginning to further examine such *transdiagnostic* processes. For example, the Research Domain Criteria (RDoC) initiative is part of the National Institute of Mental Health's strategic plan to develop novel ways of organizing and classifying psychiatric disorders based on dimensions of observable behaviors and brain functions (Cuthbert & Insel, 2010; Insel et al., 2010; Insel & Cuthbert, 2009; Sanislow et al., 2010). Transdiagnostic risk factors associated with symptom severity and impairment reduction have clear clinical relevance and are potentially well suited to bridge the gap between psychopathology and its biological roots. DT has potential as a transdiagnostic risk factor that has particular relevance to anxious psychopathology. For this reason, the research base has witnessed growth in the number of studies examining DT's relations to anxiety and obsessive-compulsive symptoms and its potential as a treatment target.

Anxiety and obsessive-compulsive-related disorders, including PTSD, GAD, PD, agoraphobia, SAD, and OCD (American Psychiatric Association, 2013), represent the most prevalent form of psychopathology and are associated with substantial disability and economic burden (Greenberg et al., 1999; Kessler et al., 2005). Additionally, anxiety disorders are highly comorbid with each other as well as with mood disorders and often follow a chronic or recurrent course if not treated (American Psychiatric Association, 2013). Although there are many well-established psychological and pharmacological treatments for anxiety and obsessive-compulsive-related disorders (Chambless & Ollendick, 2001; Mitte, 2005), a significant number of affected individuals do not demonstrate a positive response to treatment (Slaap & den Boer, 2001). Moreover, to demonstrate DT's transdiagnostic utility across anxiety and obsessive-compulsive disorders and symptom domains, DT must be similarly impaired among individuals manifesting different forms of anxious psychopathology (e.g., Michel et al., 2016). The literature addressing this topic is somewhat scant, but enough data exist to estimate the clinical utility of the DT construct.

As described earlier, DT manifests across anxiety disorders and related conditions (e.g., depression). However, results are mixed and generally focused on participant self-reported DT, which may index perceived DT as contrasted with tolerance of acute distress during laboratory tasks (Leyro et al., 2010). Evidence that DT may be associated with components of anxiety disorders (e.g., worry) may clarify the role that DT plays as a risk factor or in the maintenance of internalizing disorders. However, a complete description of these associations requires distinguishing between DT and other, related constructs.

In his seminal work on validity and reliability in psychological and psychiatric research, Paul Meehl developed the notion of a *nomological net* (Waller, Yonce, Grove, Faust, & Lenzenweger, 2006). In this framework, the validity of a new construct is determined based on hypothesized associations with theoretically associated (i.e., convergent validity) or not associated (i.e., divergent validity) constructs (Cronbach & Meehl, 1955). Hence, the new construct is delineated from existing psychological phenomena but is also placed in a context where it can be shown to operate as theoretically expected. DT is primarily defined as distinct from, but related to, other potential transdiagnostic risk factors, specifically intolerance of uncertainty, anxiety sensitivity, and emotion regulation. These are described in turn.

Intolerance of Uncertainty

Much of the research on DT within GAD adjusts for concurrent intolerance of uncertainty. A review of the literature regarding intolerance of uncertainty is described elsewhere in this volume (see Chapter 7). These investigations consistently find an expected negative correlation, suggesting that individuals who report greater tolerance of distress also report less intolerance of uncertainty (Kertz et al., 2015; MacDonald et al., 2015; Michel et al., 2016; Norr et al., 2013; Pawluk &

Koerner, 2016). However, recent attempts to clarify the interrelation of DT and intolerance of uncertainty have produced mixed results. For example, within research on GAD, there is (i) evidence of unique associations of DT and intolerance of uncertainty with GAD symptoms (Pawluk & Koerner, 2016); (ii) evidence that DT alone discriminates between students who report high or low symptom severity (MacDonald et al., 2015); and (iii) evidence that intolerance of uncertainty may mediate (i.e., explain) the association of DT with worry (Kertz et al., 2015).

Carleton previously clarified a historical perspective of the definition of intolerance of uncertainty that emphasizes the perceived threat of future distress (Carleton, 2012). In recent theoretical work, he provides a synthesis of research on intolerance of uncertainty, which provides a theoretical framework to guide future research (Carleton, 2016). In this framework, *intolerance of uncertainty* refers to tolerance of a specific, lower-order form of distress, i.e., that generated by an ambiguous situation (Zvolensky, Vujanovic, Bernstein, & Leyro, 2010). As such, intolerance of uncertainty is defined as a largely cognitive process associated with related cognitive processes such as agency (Bandura, 1989), controllability (Thompson, 1981), and self-efficacy (Bandura, 1977). In contrast, DT refers to an individual's perceived or actual ability to tolerate emotional or physical distress rather than the perceived ability to act on a situation (Leyro et al., 2010). In summary, whereas DT describes the actual or perceived ability to tolerate distress, intolerance of uncertainty is defined as the ability to tolerate ambiguity regarding future potential distress.

Therefore, the conceptual distinction between DT and intolerance of uncertainty clarifies empirical findings on their interrelation with respect to anxiety disorders, specifically GAD. Both DT and intolerance of uncertainty represent correlated yet distinct psychological constructs that may relate to, respectively, global and specific cognitive aspects of anxiety disorders. The extant literature supports this theoretical assertion: DT and intolerance of uncertainty demonstrate distinct associations with GAD symptoms (Pawluk & Koerner, 2016), which may be stronger for DT (MacDonald et al., 2015), despite a potentially stronger association of intolerance of uncertainty with worry, a central cognitive symptom (Kertz et al., 2015; Laposa et al., 2015; Norr et al., 2013).

Anxiety Sensitivity

The definition of DT emphasizes tolerance over sensitivity to distress. For example, a common laboratory-based measure of DT, the mirror-tracing task (Matthews & Stoney, 1988; Strong et al., 2003), includes pre- and post-task assessment of negative affect to gauge the severity of distress or discomfort generated by the task. This is then entered as a covariate in subsequent analyses so that persistence on the task (i.e., tolerance) is not confounded with the overall unpleasantness of the task itself (Leyro et al., 2010; Matthews & Stoney, 1988). Similarly, anxiety sensitivity, an individual difference in distress due to anxiotypic interoceptive experiences (e.g., tachycardia), may be correlated yet conceptually distinct from

DT. For example, two individuals may be sensitive to increased dryness of the mouth yet differ in their ability to tolerate this noxious state. A more detailed description of the literature regarding anxiety sensitivity is provided elsewhere in this volume (see Chapter 5).

As theoretically expected, DT and anxiety sensitivity are consistently, negatively correlated (Bernstein et al., 2009; Capron et al., 2013; Hashoul-Andary et al., 2016; MacDonald et al., 2015; Mitchell, Riccardi, Keough, Timpano, & Schmidt, 2013; Wolitzky-Taylor et al., 2015, 2016). Research into the role of DT in anxiety disorders frequently, appropriately adjusts for concurrent anxiety sensitivity. However, there is not yet consensus on the interplay of the two phenomena regarding different anxiety disorders. For example, in some cases, DT and anxiety sensitivity, while correlated, show unique associations with worry (Keough et al., 2010). However, in other research, anxiety sensitivity and related constructs fully account for the association of DT with symptoms of SAD, OCD, or worry (Michel et al., 2016; Norr et al., 2013; Starr & Davila, 2012). Finally, in yet other research, DT, but not anxiety sensitivity, is associated with symptoms of SAD, OCD, and worry (Laposa et al., 2015) whereas one additional study suggests an interaction between DT and anxiety sensitivity in predicting worry and GAD (Allan et al., 2014).

Emotion Regulation

Considerable prior work has demonstrated emotion regulatory deficits in a wide range of psychiatric conditions (Aldao, Nolen-Hoeksema, & Schweizer, 2010), including anxiety disorders (Cisler, Olatunji, Feldner, & Forsyth, 2010). Moreover, each disorder may be associated with characteristic emotion regulatory deficits that clarify points of comorbidity and distinction between disorders. For example, neuroticism has been associated with greater affective and behavioral variability over time (Moskowitz & Zuroff, 2005) and reduced reactivity to socioemotional information (Tracey & Rohlfing, 2010). However, subsequent investigation clarifies that elevated behavioral variability may be specific to anxiety symptoms (Creed & Funder, 1998; Rappaport, Moskowitz, & D'Antono, 2014) whereas depression symptoms may be associated with blunted reactivity to socioemotional cues (Berking, Wirtz, Svaldi, & Hofmann, 2014; Radkovsky, McArdle, Bockting, & Berking, 2014; Rappaport, Moskowitz, & D'Antono, 2017; Zuroff, Fournier, & Moskowitz, 2007).

A review of the literature regarding emotion regulation in anxiety disorders is presented elsewhere in this volume (see Chapter 10). However, several aspects of the emotion regulatory process clarify the broader context of DT. For example, maladaptive behaviors (e.g., risk-taking behavior) may result when individuals with emotion regulatory difficulties encounter acute distress (Auerbach, Abela, & Ho, 2007; Bibb & Chambless, 1986; Mennin, Heimberg, Turk, & Fresco, 2002). There is emerging evidence of distinctions between anxiety disorders regarding associated emotion regulatory deficits (Cisler et al.,

2010). For example, GAD has been associated with heightened affective intensity and impaired management (Mennin, Heimberg, Turk, & Fresco, 2005; Salters-Pedneault, Roemer, Tull, Rucker, & Mennin, 2006) whereas SAD may be associated with reduced affective clarity and negative expectations about experiencing strong emotions (Mennin, Holaway, Fresco, Moore, & Heimberg, 2007; Mennin, McLaughlin, & Flanagan, 2009). Separately, panic attacks have been associated with greater emotional avoidance and emotional suppression (Tull, Rodman, & Roemer, 2008; Tull & Roemer, 2007). However, further research is needed to integrate DT into existing models of emotion regulation and attendant deficits. For example, an individual's ability to tolerate distress may moderate the association of emotion regulatory deficits and maladaptive, risk-taking behavior (e.g., Linehan, 1993).

Discussion

DT contributes to a variety of anxiety disorders and related internalizing disorders (e.g., major depressive disorder), which indicates that it may function as a transdiagnostic process. Additionally, DT is distinct from related transdiagnostic processes (i.e., intolerance of uncertainty, anxiety sensitivity, and emotion regulation). Distinctions between DT and related transdiagnostic processes may refine the conceptualization of DT and help to distinguish between related conditions. For example, DT and intolerance of uncertainty may distinguish between low tolerance of global and cognitive distress, respectively, which is supported by evidence of distinct associations of DT and intolerance of uncertainty with GAD symptoms (MacDonald et al., 2015; Pawluk & Koerner, 2016) despite an association of worry with only intolerance of uncertainty (Kertz et al., 2015; Laposa et al., 2015; Norr et al., 2013).

Limitations and Recommended Future Research

However, while extant research has indicated a contribution of DT to anxiety disorders, several limitations in prior research suggest promising avenues for future investigation. Initially, with several noteworthy exceptions (e.g., Cummings et al., 2013; Felton et al., 2017; Wolitzky-Taylor et al., 2015), much of the prior research has documented the role of DT in psychopathology among adult samples. Undergraduate, community, and adult clinical samples clarify the construct and develop tools for its assessment. However, the prevalence and phenomenology of anxiety disorders change during development (Merikangas et al., 2010; Pine & Fox, 2015). Similarly, evident multi- and equifinality in anxiety disorders suggests that the manifestation of DT in childhood may differ from its manifestation in adulthood (Nelemans et al., 2014). As such, further research is needed to characterize the manifestation of DT during childhood and adolescence and its role as a risk factor or correlate of psychopathology.

Furthermore, several prior studies attempt to assess mediation hypotheses, such as whether rumination may act as a mechanism by which DT influences depressive symptoms (Magidson et al., 2013). Cross-sectional research may clarify the association of DT with psychopathology; however, Maxwell and colleagues have raised important concerns regarding the interpretation of mediation analyses in cross-sectional data (Maxwell & Cole, 2007; Maxwell, Cole, & Mitchell, 2011). In summary, they suggest that cross-sectional data largely preclude assessing the temporal order of variables, which is necessary to test the causal hypotheses implied by a biopsychological process (Shrout, Keyes, & Ornstein, 2011). Both limitations regarding developmental and mediational models could be addressed by the longitudinal assessment of DT during the transition from childhood to adulthood (Cole & Maxwell, 2003). For example, one such longitudinal study suggests that low DT may predict only later externalizing symptoms despite a cross-sectional association with internalizing symptoms as well (Cummings et al., 2013). Additionally, Felton and colleagues (2017) demonstrate the utility of longitudinal data to examine mediation via modeling change over time.

Considerable evidence highlights the importance of stressful and traumatic life experiences in the development of DT (e.g., Berenz et al., in press). An overview of this literature is outside the purview of the present chapter. However, future research might examine the role of common etiological factors to explain the association between DT and psychopathology, specifically anxiety disorders. For example, cross-disorder research in psychiatric genetics has indicated common genetic and environmental pathways that influence sets of psychiatric conditions (Kendler et al., 2011), including anxiety disorders (Hettema, Prescott, Myers, Neale, & Kendler, 2005). Similar research has examined the role of related psychological processes in anxiety disorders (Battaglia et al., 2009). Preliminary evidence suggests genetic influences on DT (Amstadter et al., 2012). However, candidate gene studies limit identifying points of convergence across the genome (Hindorff et al., 2009). Recent statistical and genetic developments (e.g., Yang, Lee, Goddard, & Visscher, 2011) provide a framework to understand the contribution of shared genetic risk between psychopathology and putative psychological processes. Similarly, traditional analytic approaches can be leveraged to understand the role of common environmental factors in the correlation of DT and psychopathology (Neale & Cardon, 1992). Specifically, mono- and dizygotic twins shared 100% and 50% of their segregating genes, respectively, and 100% of their shared environmental experiences. Thus, family data (e.g., of twins) permit decomposing the variance in DT, and covariance with psychopathology, into that associated with genetic, shared environmental, and unique environmental contributions. Additionally, data on siblings, relatives, or anyone who shares a known proportion of relevant genes can be leveraged to inform the etiology of DT.

Additionally, further investigation is warranted into the neural substrates of DT. Specifically, preliminary research of adult regular cocaine and nicotine users implicates reduced activity in the right insula, anterior cingulate cortex, bilateral medial frontal gyrus, right inferior frontal gyrus, and right ventrome-dial prefrontal cortex in persons with low DT (Daughters et al., 2017). Of these areas, several may be hyperactive in multiple anxiety disorders (see Etkin & Wager, 2007, for review). This suggests that further research is necessary to identify the neural correlates of DT in anxiety disorders and to clarify the role of affective neural regions (e.g., the right insula) to DT, anxiety disorders, and substance use given evidence that individuals with anxiety and substance use disorders show reduced DT.

Finally, given its role in multiple anxiety disorders, DT may represent a promising target for the development of novel treatments. While emotional tolerance has a long tradition in psychiatry and psychology (Henderson, 1973), contemporary treatment approaches have demonstrated the efficacy of forma-lized DT components to broad treatments (Linehan, 1993; Linehan et al., 2002; see Lynch, Trost, Salsman, & Linehan, 2007, for review). As might be expected, early support for treatments including DT focused on efficacy and effectiveness for conditions associated with emotional dysregulation (Linehan, Bohus, & Lynch, 2007; Safer, Telch, & Agras, 2001), which suggests potential utility in treating comorbid anxiety (Harned, Korslund, Foa, & Linehan, 2012). Initial investigations suggest that DT may increase during cognitive behavioral therapy (McHugh et al., 2014; Williams, Thompson, & Andrews, 2013) and a novel anxiety sensitivity reduction treatment (i.e., Anxiety Sensitivity Education and Reduction Training; Norr, Allan, Macatee, Keough, & Schmidt, 2014). Moreover, improvement in DT during psychotherapy may correlate with (McHugh et al., 2016) and predict improved clinical symptoma-tology (Williams et al., 2013).

Recent treatment developments are now examining whether brief DT-focused treatments may augment existing treatments for conditions in which DT may be limited (e.g., nicotine dependence; Brown et al., 2008). While this is consistent with calls for translational research based on known risk factors (Zvolensky, Schmidt, Bernstein, & Keough, 2006), novel treatments that target DT benefit from a clear conceptual framework and well-defined treatment targets with known clinical importance. For example, Bornovalov et al. (2012) report greater clinical improvement during residential substance abuse treatment among patients who received an adjunctive DT-focused treatment as compared against treatment as usual and patients who received supportive counseling. Moreover, patients who received the adjunctive DT treatment demonstrated greater improvement on the MTPT and PASAT, both laboratory-based assessments of DT, which was not evident among patients in both comparisons groups. Potentially, further research and treatment refinement may yield adjunctive treatments to increase DT. If so, these brief interventions could be added to existing disorder-specific (see Butler, Chapman, Forman, & Beck, 2006, for review) and transdiagnostic (Barlow et al., 2017) psychother-apeutic and psychopharmacological treatments to address comorbid substance use, non-suicidal self-injury, and other sequelae of low DT.

Conclusion

DT shows a general association with most anxiety disorders. At present, extant research has documented and replicated a role of DT in several anxiety and related disorders, specifically PTSD, PD, OCD, and GAD. DT is defined and operationalized based on both individuals' self-reported perception and demonstrated performance during standardized laboratory-based assessment. However, these modalities may assess different aspects of the construct. Therefore, multimodal research provides unique opportunities to clarify areas of convergence and divergence between anxiety disorders and related conditions (e.g., mood and affective disorders). Finally, recent evidence indicates that DT is both malleable and associated with clinical improvement during existing psychotherapy treatments. However, several limitations of extant clinical studies indicate promising areas for further research. For example, synthesis of existing research is complicated by wide heterogeneity regarding sample demographics, conceptualization and assessment of DT, and inconsistent adjustment for related constructs (e.g., anxiety sensitivity, intolerance of uncertainty). Recommendations for future directions, proposed here, suggest leveraging longitudinal and genetic methodologies to clarify the development of DT and timing in the association of DT with anxiety disorders. Finally, preliminary evidence suggests that novel, brief treatments may specifically target DT as an adjunctive treatment goal for a range of conditions characterized by low DT. This further suggests that DT may serve as a novel, transdiagnostic treatment associated with anxiety disorders and encourages future inquiry.

Dr. Rappaport is supported by NIH T32MH020030.

References

Aldao, A., Nolen-Hoeksema, S., & Schweizer, S. (2010). Emotion-regulation strategies across psychopathology: A meta-analytic review. *Clinical Psychology Review, 30* (2), 217–237. https://doi.org/10.1016/j.cpr.2009.11.004

Allan, N. P., Macatee, R. J., Norr, A. M., & Schmidt, N. B. (2014). Direct and interactive effects of distress tolerance and anxiety sensitivity on generalized anxiety and depression. *Cognitive Therapy and Research, 38*(5), 530–540. https://doi.org/10.1007/s10608-014–9623-y

American Psychiatric Association. (2013). *Diagnostic and Statistical Manual of Mental Disorders* (5th edn). Washington, DC: American Psychiatric Association.

Amstadter, A. B., Daughters, S. B., MacPherson, L., Reynolds, E. K., Danielson, C. K., Wang, F., . . . Lejuez, C. W. (2012). Genetic associations with performance on a behavioral measure of distress intolerance. *Journal of Psychiatric Research, 46* (1), 87–94. https://doi.org/10.1016/j.jpsychires.2011.09.017

Anestis, M. D., Tull, M. T., Bagge, C. L., & Gratz, K. L. (2012). The moderating role of distress tolerance in the relationship between posttraumatic stress disorder symptom clusters and suicidal behavior among trauma exposed substance users in

residential treatment. *Archives of Suicide Research*, *16*(3), 198–211. https://doi
.org/10.1080/13811118.2012.695269

Auerbach, R. P., Abela, J. R. Z., & Ho, M. R. (2007). Responding to symptoms of depression
and anxiety: Emotion regulation, neuroticism, and engagement in risky behaviors.
Behaviour Research and Therapy, *45*, 2182–2191.

Banducci, A. N., Bujarski, S. J., Bonn-Miller, M. O., Patel, A., & Connolly, K. M. (2016).
The impact of intolerance of emotional distress and uncertainty on veterans with
co-occurring PTSD and substance use disorders. *Journal of Anxiety Disorders*, *41*,
73–81. https://doi.org/10.1016/j.janxdis.2016.03.003

Banducci, A. N., Connolly, K. M., Vujanovic, A. A., Alvarez, J., & Bonn-Miller, M. O.
(2017). The impact of changes in distress tolerance on PTSD symptom severity
post-treatment among veterans in residential trauma treatment. *Journal of Anxiety
Disorders*, *47*, 99–105. https://doi.org/10.1016/j.janxdis.2017.01.004

Bandura, A. (1977). Self-efficacy: Toward a unifying theory of behavioral change.
Psychological Review, *84*(2), 191.

Bandura, A. (1989). Human agency in social cognitive theory. *American Psychologist*, *44*
(9), 1175.

Barlow, D. H., Farchione, T. J., Bullis, J. R., Gallagher, M. W., Murray-Latin, H., Sauer-
Zavala, S., . . . Cassiello-Robbins, C. (2017). The unified protocol for transdiagnostic treatment of emotional disorders compared with diagnosis-specific protocols for anxiety disorders: A randomized clinical trial. *JAMA Psychiatry*. https://
doi.org/10.1001/jamapsychiatry.2017.2164

Battaglia, M., Pesenti-Gritti, P., Medland, S. E., Ogliari, A., Tambs, K., & Spatola, C. A.
(2009). A genetically informed study of the association between childhood
separation anxiety, sensitivity to CO2, panic disorder, and the effect of childhood
parental loss. *Archives of General Psychiatry*, *66*, 64–71.

Berenz, E. C., Vujanovic, A. A., Coffey, S. F., & Zvolensky, M. J. (2012). Anxiety
sensitivity and breath-holding duration in relation to PTSD symptom severity
among trauma exposed adults. *Journal of Anxiety Disorders*, *26*(1), 134–139.
https://doi.org/10.1016/j.janxdis.2011.10.004

Berenz, E. C., Vujanovic, A. A., Rappaport, L., Kevorkian, S., Gonzalez, R. E.,
Chowdhury, N., . . . Amstadter, A. B. (in press). Multimodal study of childhood
trauma and distress tolerance in young adulthood. Journal of Aggression,
Maltreatment & Trauma

Berenz, E. C., Vujanovic, A. A., Rappaport, L., Kevorkian, S., Gonzalez, R. E.,
Chowdhury, N., . . . Amstadter, A. B. (2018). Childhood trauma and distress
tolerance in a trauma-exposed acute-care psychiatric inpatient sample.
Psychological Trauma: Theory, Research, Practice, and Policy, 10, 368–375.
https://doi.org/10.1037/tra0000300

Berking, M., Wirtz, C. M., Svaldi, J., & Hofmann, S. G. (2014). Emotion regulation predicts
symptoms of depression over five years. *Behaviour Research and Therapy*, *57*,
13–20. https://doi.org/10.1016/j.brat.2014.03.003

Bernstein, A., Zvolensky, M. J., Vujanovic, A. A., & Moos, R. (2009). Integrating anxiety
sensitivity, distress tolerance, and discomfort intolerance: A hierarchical model of
affect sensitivity and tolerance. *Behavior Therapy*, *40*, 291–301.

Bibb, J. L. & Chambless, D. L. (1986). Alcohol use and abuse among diagnosed
agoraphobics. *Behaviour Research and Therapy*, *24*, 49–58.

Blakey, S. M., Jacoby, R. J., Reuman, L., & Abramowitz, J. S. (2016). The relative contributions of experiential avoidance and distress tolerance to OC symptoms. *Behavioural and Cognitive Psychotherapy*, *44*(04), 460–471. https://doi.org/10.1017/S1352465815000703

Bornovalova, M. A., Gratz, K. L., Daughters, S. B., Hunt, E. D., & Lejuez, C. W. (2012). Initial RCT of a distress tolerance treatment for individuals with substance use disorders. *Drug and Alcohol Dependence*, *122*(1–2), 70–76. https://doi.org/10.1016/j.drugalcdep.2011.09.012

Brandon, T. H., Herzog, T. A., Juliano, L. M., Irvin, J. E., Lazev, A. B., & Simmons, V. N. (2003). Pretreatment task persistence predicts smoking cessation outcome. *Journal of Abnormal Psychology*, *112*(3), 448–456. https://doi.org/10.1037/0021-843X.112.3.448

Brandt, C. P., Johnson, K. A., Schmidt, N. B., & Zvolensky, M. J. (2012). Main and interactive effects of emotion dysregulation and breath-holding duration in relation to panic-relevant fear and expectancies about anxiety-related sensations among adult daily smokers. *Journal of Anxiety Disorders*, *26*(1), 173–181. https://doi.org/10.1016/j.janxdis.2011.10.007

Brandt, C. P., Zvolensky, M. J., & Bonn-Miller, M. O. (2013). Distress tolerance, emotion dysregulation, and anxiety and depressive symptoms among HIV+ individuals. *Cognitive Therapy and Research*, *37*(3), 446–455. https://doi.org/10.1007/s10608-012-9497-9

Brown, R. A., Kahler, C. W., Zvolensky, M. J., Lejuez, C. W., & Ramsey, S. E. (2001). Anxiety sensitivity: Relationship to negative affect smoking and smoking cessation in smokers with past major depressive disorder. *Addictive Behaviors*, *26*(6), 887–899.

Brown, R. A., Lejuez, C. W., Kahler, C. W., Strong, D. R., & Zvolensky, M. J. (2005). Distress tolerance and early smoking lapse. *Clinical Psychology Review*, *25*(6), 713–733. https://doi.org/10.1016/j.cpr.2005.05.003

Brown, R. A., Lejuez, C. W., Strong, D. R., Kahler, C. W., Zvolensky, M. J., Carpenter, L. L., . . . Price, L. H. (2009). A prospective examination of distress tolerance and early smoking lapse in adult self-quitters. *Nicotine & Tobacco Research*, *11*(5), 493–502. https://doi.org/10.1093/ntr/ntp041

Brown, R. A., Palm, K. M., Strong, D. R., Lejuez, C. W., Kahler, C. W., Zvolensky, M. J., . . . Gifford, E. V. (2008). Distress tolerance treatment for early-lapse smokers. *Behavior Modification*, *32*(3), 302–332. https://doi.org/10.1177/0145445507309024

Buckner, J. D., Keough, M. E., & Schmidt, N. B. (2007). Problematic alcohol and cannabis use among young adults: The roles of depression and discomfort and distress tolerance. *Addictive Behaviors*, *32*(9), 1957–1963. https://doi.org/10.1016/j.addbeh.2006.12.019

Butler, A., Chapman, J., Forman, E., & Beck, A. (2006). The empirical status of cognitive-behavioral therapy: A review of meta-analyses. *Clinical Psychology Review*, *26*(1), 17–31. https://doi.org/10.1016/j.cpr.2005.07.003

Capron, D. W., Norr, A. M., Macatee, R. J., & Schmidt, N. B. (2013). Distress tolerance and anxiety sensitivity cognitive concerns: Testing the incremental contributions of affect dysregulation constructs on suicidal ideation and suicide attempt. *Behavior Therapy*, *44*(3), 349–358.

Carleton, R. N. (2012). The intolerance of uncertainty construct in the context of anxiety disorders: Theoretical and practical perspectives. *Expert Review of Neurotherapeutics*, *12*(8), 937–947. https://doi.org/10.1586/ern.12.82

Carleton, R. N. (2016). Into the unknown: A review and synthesis of contemporary models involving uncertainty. *Journal of Anxiety Disorders*, *39*, 30–43. https://doi.org/10.1016/j.janxdis.2016.02.007

Chambless, D. L. & Ollendick, T. H. (2001). Empirically supported psychological interventions: Controversies and evidence. *Annual Review of Psychology*, *52*, 685–716.

Cisler, J. M., Olatunji, B. O., Feldner, M. T., & Forsyth, J. P. (2010). Emotion regulation and the anxiety disorders: An integrative review. *Journal of Psychopathology and Behavioral Assessment*, *32*, 68–82.

Clark, L. A. & Watson, D. (1991). Tripartite model of anxiety and depression: Psychometric evidence and taxonomic implications. *Journal of Abnormal Psychology*, *100*, 316–336.

Cohen, J. R., Danielson, C. K., Adams, Z. W., & Ruggiero, K. J. (2016). Distress tolerance and social support in adolescence: Predicting risk for internalizing and externalizing symptoms following a natural disaster. *Journal of Psychopathology and Behavioral Assessment*, *38*(4), 538–546. https://doi.org/10.1007/s10862-016–9545-y

Cole, D. A. & Maxwell, S. E. (2003). Testing mediational models with longitudinal data: Questions and tips in the use of structural equation modeling. *Journal of Abnormal Psychology*, *112*(4), 558–577. https://doi.org/10.1037/0021-843X.112.4.558

Cook, M. R., Gerkovich, M. M., O'Connell, K. A., & Potocky, M. (1995). Reversal theory constructs and cigarette availability predict lapse early in smoking cessation. *Research in Nursing & Health*, *18*(3), 217–224.

Cougle, J. R., Timpano, K. R., Fitch, K. E., & Hawkins, K. A. (2011). Distress tolerance and obsessions: An integrative analysis. *Depression and Anxiety*, *28*(10), 906–914. https://doi.org/10.1002/da.20846

Cougle, J. R., Timpano, K. R., & Goetz, A. R. (2012). Exploring the unique and interactive roles of distress tolerance and negative urgency in obsessions. *Personality and Individual Differences*, *52*(4), 515–520. https://doi.org/10.1016/j.paid.2011.11.017

Creed, A. T. & Funder, D. C. (1998). Social anxiety: From the inside and outside. *Personality and Individual Differences*, *25*, 19–33.

Cronbach, L. J. & Meehl, P. E. (1955). Construct validity in psychological tests. *Psychological Bulletin*, *52*(4), 281.

Cummings, J. R., Bornovalova, M. A., Ojanen, T., Hunt, E., MacPherson, L., & Lejuez, C. (2013). Time doesn't change everything: The longitudinal course of distress tolerance and its relationship with externalizing and internalizing symptoms during early adolescence. *Journal of Abnormal Child Psychology*, *41*(5), 735–748. https://doi.org/10.1007/s10802-012–9704-x

Cuthbert, B. N. & Insel, T. R. (2010). Toward new approaches to psychotic disorders: The NIMH Research Domain Criteria Project. *Schizophrenia Bulletin*, *36*(6), 1061–1062. https://doi.org/10.1093/schbul/sbq108

Daughters, S. B., Lejuez, C. W., Kahler, C. W., Strong, D. R., & Brown, R. A. (2005). Psychological distress tolerance and duration of most recent abstinence attempt among residential treatment-seeking substance abusers. *Psychology of Addictive Behaviors*, *19*(2), 208–211. https://doi.org/10.1037/0893-164X.19.2.208

Daughters, S. B., Ross, T. J., Bell, R. P., Yi, J. Y., Ryan, J., & Stein, E. A. (2017). Distress tolerance among substance users is associated with functional connectivity between prefrontal regions during a distress tolerance task: Neural indices of DT. *Addiction Biology*, *22*(5), 1378–1390. https://doi.org/10.1111/adb.12396

Dennhardt, A. A. & Murphy, J. G. (2011). Associations between depression, distress tolerance, delay discounting, and alcohol-related problems in European American and African American college students. *Psychology of Addictive Behaviors*, *25*(4), 595–604. https://doi.org/10.1037/a0025807

Doherty, K., Kinnunen, T., Militello, F. S., & Garvey, A. J. (1995). Urges to smoke during the first month of abstinence: Relationship to relapse and predictors. *Psychopharmacology*, *119*(2), 171–178.

Ellis, A. J., Vanderlind, W. M., & Beevers, C. G. (2013). Enhanced anger reactivity and reduced distress tolerance in major depressive disorder. *Cognitive Therapy and Research*, *37*(3), 498–509. https://doi.org/10.1007/s10608-012-9494-z

Etkin, A. & Wager, T. D. (2007). Functional neuroimaging of anxiety: A meta-analysis of emotional processing in PTSD, social anxiety disorder, and specific phobia. *American Journal of Psychiatry*, *164*(10), 1476–1488.

Farris, S. G., Vujanovic, A. A., Hogan, J., Schmidt, N. B., & Zvolensky, M. J. (2014). Main and interactive effects of anxiety sensitivity and physical distress intolerance with regard to PTSD symptoms among trauma-exposed smokers. *Journal of Trauma & Dissociation*, *15*(3), 254–270. https://doi.org/10.1080/15299732.2013.834862

Farris, S. G., Zvolensky, M. J., Otto, M. W., & Leyro, T. M. (2015). The role of distress intolerance for panic and nicotine withdrawal symptoms during a biological challenge. *Journal of Psychopharmacology*, 0269881115575536.

Felton, J. W., Banducci, A. N., Shadur, J. M., Stadnik, R., MacPherson, L., & Lejuez, C. W. (2017).The developmental trajectory of perceived stress mediates the relations between distress tolerance and internalizing symptoms among youth. *Development and Psychopathology*, 1–11. https://doi.org/10.1017/S0954579417000335

Forsyth, J. P., Eifert, G. H., & Barrios, V. (2006). Fear conditioning in an emotion regulation context: A fresh perspective on the origins of anxiety disorders. In M. G. Craske, D. Hermans, & D. Vansteenwegen (eds.), *Fear and Learning: From Basic Processes to Clinical Implications* (pp. 133–153). Washington, DC: American Psychological Association.

Frenkel-Brunswik, E. (1948). Review of Personality: A biosocial approach to origins and structure. Retrieved from http://psycnet.apa.org/journals/bul/45/4/348/.

Gorka, S. M., Ali, B., & Daughters, S. B. (2012). The role of distress tolerance in the relationship between depressive symptoms and problematic alcohol use. *Psychology of Addictive Behaviors*, *26*(3), 621–626. https://doi.org/10.1037/a0026386

Grant, B. F., Stinson, F. S., Dawson, D. A., Chou, S. P., Dufour, M. C., Compton, W., … Kaplan, K. (2006). Prevalence and co-occurrence of substance use disorders and independent mood and anxiety disorders: Results from the National Epidemiologic Survey on Alcohol and Related Conditions. *Alcohol Research & Health*, *29*(2), 107–121.

Greenberg, P. E., Sisitsky, T., Kessler, R. C., Finkelstein, S. N., Berndt, E. R., Davidson, J. R. T., ... Fyer, A. J. (1999). The economic burden of anxiety disorders in the 1990s. *Journal of Clinical Psychiatry, 60*, 427–435.

Gross, J. J. & Thompson, R. A. (2007). Emotion regulation: Conceptual foundations. In J. J. Gross (ed.), *Handbook of Emotion Regulation*. New York, NY: Guilford Press.

Hajek, P., Belcher, M., & Stapelton, J. (1987). Breath-holding endurance as a predictor of success in smoking cessation. *Addictive Behaviors, 12*, 285–288.

Harned, M. S., Korslund, K. E., Foa, E. B., & Linehan, M. M. (2012). Treating PTSD in suicidal and self-injuring women with borderline personality disorder: Development and preliminary evaluation of a dialectical behavior therapy prolonged exposure protocol. *Behaviour Research and Therapy, 50*(6), 381–386. https://doi.org/10.1016/j.brat.2012.02.011

Harrington, N. (2005). The Frustration Discomfort Scale: Development and psychometric properties. *Clinical Psychology & Psychotherapy, 12*(5), 374–387. https://doi.org/10.1002/cpp.465

Hashoul-Andary, R., Assayag-Nitzan, Y., Yuval, K., Aderka, I. M., Litz, B., & Bernstein, A. (2016). A longitudinal study of emotional distress intolerance and psychopathology following exposure to a potentially traumatic event in a community sample. *Cognitive Therapy and Research, 40*(1), 1–13. https://doi.org/10.1007/s10608-015-9730-4

Hayes, S. C., Wilson, K. G., Gifford, E. V., Follette, V. M., & Strosahl, K. (1996). Experiential avoidance and behavioral disorders: A functional dimensional approach to diagnosis and treatment. *Journal of Consulting and Clinical Psychology, 64*, 1152–1168.

Henderson, J. (1973). A multiprofessional outpatient psychotherapy clinic: (An open letter to government). *Canadian Journal of Public Health [Revue Canadienne de Santé Publique], 64*, 455–464.

Hettema, J. M., Prescott, C. A., Myers, J. M., Neale, M. C., & Kendler, K. S. (2005). The structure of genetic and environmental risk factors for anxiety disorders in men and women. *Archives of General Psychiatry, 62*(2), 182–189.

Hindorff, L. A., Sethupathy, P., Junkins, H. A., Ramos, E. M., Mehta, J. P., Collins, F. S., & Manolio, T. A. (2009). Potential etiologic and functional implications of genome-wide association loci for human diseases and traits. *Proceedings of the National Academy of Sciences, 106*(23), 9362–9367.

Hines, E. A. & Brown, G. E. (1932). A standard stimulus for measuring vasomotor reactions: its application in the study of hypertension. *Mayo Clinic Proceedings*, 7.

Insel, T. R. & Cuthbert, B. N. (2009). Endophenotypes: Bridging genomic complexity and disorder heterogeneity. *Biological Psychiatry, 66*(11), 988–989. https://doi.org/10.1016/j.biopsych.2009.10.008

Insel, T., Cuthbert, B., Garvey, M., Heinssen, R., Pine, D. S., Quinn, K., ... Wang, P. (2010). Research domain criteria (RDoC): Toward a new classification framework for research on mental disorders. *American Journal of Psychiatry, 167*, 748–751.

Kendler, K. S., Aggen, S. H., Knudsen, G. P., Røysamb, E., Neale, M. C., & Reichborn-Kjennerud, T. (2011). The structure of genetic and environmental risk factors for syndromal and subsydromal common DSM-IV axis I and axis II disorders. *American Journal of Psychiatry, 168*, 29–39.

Kendler, K. S., Neale, M. C., Kessler, R. C., Heath, A. C., & Eaves, L. J. (1992). Major depression and generalized anxiety disorder: Same genes,(partly) different environments? *Archives of General Psychiatry, 49*(9), 716–722.

Keough, M. E., Riccardi, C. J., Timpano, K. R., Mitchell, M. A., & Schmidt, N. B. (2010). Anxiety symptomatology: The association with distress tolerance and anxiety sensitivity. *Behavior Therapy, 41*, 567–574.

Kertz, S. J., Stevens, K. T., McHugh, R. K., & Björgvinsson, T. (2015). Distress intolerance and worry: The mediating role of cognitive variables. *Anxiety, Stress, & Coping, 28*(4), 408–424. https://doi.org/10.1080/10615806.2014.974571

Kessler, R. C., Chiu, W. T., Demler, O., & Walters, E. E. (2005). Prevalence, severity, and comorbidity of 12-month DSM-IV disorders in the National Comorbidity Survey Replication. *Archives of General Psychiatry, 62*(6), 617–627.

Kessler, R. C., Gruber, M., Hettema, J. M., Hwang, I., Sampson, N., & Yonkers, K. A. (2008). Co-morbid major depression and generalized anxiety disorders in the National Comorbidity Survey follow-up. *Psychological Medicine, 38*(3).

Koball, A. M., Himes, S. M., Sim, L., Clark, M. M., Collazo-Clavell, M. L., Mundi, M., . . . Grothe, K. B. (2016). Distress tolerance and psychological comorbidity in patients seeking bariatric surgery. *Obesity Surgery, 26*(7), 1559–1564. https://doi.org/10.1007/s11695-015-1926-x

Laposa, J. M., Collimore, K. C., Hawley, L. L., & Rector, N. A. (2015). Distress tolerance in OCD and anxiety disorders, and its relationship with anxiety sensitivity and intolerance of uncertainty. *Journal of Anxiety Disorders, 33*, 8–14. https://doi.org/10.1016/j.janxdis.2015.04.003

Lejeuz, C. W., Daughters, S. B., Danielson, C. W., & Ruggiero, K. (2006). *The Behavioral Indicator of Resiliency to Distress (BIRD)*.

Lejeuz, C. W., Kahler, C. W., & Brown, R. A. (2003). A modified computer version of the Paced Auditory Serial Addition Task (PASAT) as a laboratory-based stressor. *The Behavior Therapist, 26*, 290–293.

Leyro, T. M., Zvolensky, M. J., & Bernstein, A. (2010). Distress tolerance and psycho-pathological symptoms and disorders: A review of the empirical literature among adults. *Psychological Bulletin, 136*(4), 576–600. https://doi.org/10.1037/a0019712

Linehan, M. M. (1993). *Cognitive-Behavioral Treatment of Borderline Personality Disorder*. New York, NY: Guilford Press.

Linehan, M. M., Bohus, M., & Lynch, T. R. (2007). Dialectical behavior therapy for pervasive emotion dysregulation. In J. J. Gross (ed.), *Handbook of Emotion Regulation* (1st edn) (pp. 581–605). New York, NY: Guildford Press.

Linehan, M. M., Dimeff, L. A., Reynolds, S. K., Comtois, K. A., Welch, S. S., Heagerty, P., & Kivlahan, D. R. (2002). Dialectical behavior therapy versus comprehensive validation therapy plus 12-step for the treatment of opioid dependent women meeting criteria for borderline personality disorder. *Drug and Alcohol Dependence, 67*(1), 13–26.

Lynch, T. R., Trost, W. T., Salsman, N., & Linehan, M. M. (2007). Dialectical behavior therapy for borderline personality disorder. *Annual Review of Clinical Psychology, 3*, 181–205. https://doi.org/10.1146/annurev.clinpsy.2.022305.095229

Macatee, R. J., Albanese, B. J., Allan, N. P., Schmidt, N. B., & Cougle, J. R. (2016). Distress intolerance as a moderator of the relationship between daily stressors and affective symptoms: Tests of incremental and prospective relationships. *Journal of Affective Disorders*, *206*, 125–132. https://doi.org/10.1016/j.jad.2016.07.035

Macatee, R. J., Capron, D. W., Guthrie, W., Schmidt, N. B., & Cougle, J. R. (2015). Distress tolerance and pathological worry: Tests of incremental and prospective relationships. *Behavior Therapy*, *46*(4), 449–462. https://doi.org/10.1016/j.beth.2015.03.003

Macatee, R. J., Capron, D. W., Schmidt, N. B., & Cougle, J. R. (2013). An examination of low distress tolerance and life stressors as factors underlying obsessions. *Journal of Psychiatric Research*, *47*(10), 1462–1468. https://doi.org/10.1016/j.jpsychires.2013.06.019

Macatee, R. J. & Cougle, J. R. (2013). The roles of emotional reactivity and tolerance in generalized, social, and health anxiety: A multimethod exploration. *Behavior Therapy*, *44*(1), 39–50.

MacDonald, E. M., Pawluk, E. J., Koerner, N., & Goodwill, A. M. (2015). An examination of distress intolerance in undergraduate students high in symptoms of generalized anxiety disorder. *Cognitive Behaviour Therapy*, *44*(1), 74–84. https://doi.org/10.1080/16506073.2014.964303

Magidson, J. F., Listhaus, A. R., Seitz-Brown, C. J., Anderson, K. E., Lindberg, B., Wilson, A., & Daughters, S. B. (2013). Rumination mediates the relationship between distress tolerance and depressive symptoms among substance users. *Cognitive Therapy and Research*, *37*(3), 456–465. https://doi.org/10.1007/s10608-012-9488-x

Marshall, E. C., Zvolensky, M. J., Vujanovic, A. A., Gregor, K., Gibson, L. E., & Leyro, T. M. (2008). Panic reactivity to voluntary hyperventilation challenge predicts distress tolerance to bodily sensations among daily cigarette smokers. *Experimental and Clinical Psychopharmacology*, *16*(4), 313–321. https://doi.org/10.1037/a0012752

Marshall-Berenz, E. C., Vujanovic, A. A., Bonn-Miller, M. O., Bernstein, A., & Zvolensky, M. J. (2010). Multimethod study of distress tolerance and PTSD symptom severity in a trauma-exposed community sample. *Journal of Traumatic Stress*, *23*(5), 623–630. https://doi.org/10.1002/jts.20568

Matthews, K. A. & Stoney, C. M. (1988). Influences of sex and age on cardiovascular responses during stress. *Psychosomatic Medicine*, *50*(1), 46–56.

Maxwell, S. E. & Cole, D. A. (2007). Bias in cross-sectional analyses of longitudinal mediation. *Psychological Methods*, *12*, 23–44.

Maxwell, S. E., Cole, D. A., & Mitchell, M. A. (2011). Bias in cross-sectional analyses of longitudinal mediation: Partial and complete mediation under an autoregressive model. *Multivariate Behavioral Research*, *46*(5), 816–841. https://doi.org/10.1080/00273171.2011.606716

McHugh, R. K., Daughters, S. B., Lejuez, C. W., Murray, H. W., Hearon, B. A., Gorka, S. M., & Otto, M. W. (2011). Shared variance among self-report and behavioral measures of distress intolerance. *Cognitive Therapy and Research*, *35*(3), 266–275. https://doi.org/10.1007/s10608-010-9295-1

McHugh, R. K., Kertz, S. J., Weiss, R. B., Baskin-Sommers, A. R., Hearon, B. A., & Björgvinsson, T. (2014). Changes in distress intolerance and treatment outcome in a partial hospital setting. *Behavior Therapy*, *45*(2), 232–240.

McHugh, R. K. & Otto, M. W. (2011). Domain-general and domain-specific strategies for the assessment of distress intolerance. *Psychology of Addictive Behaviors*, *25*(4), 745–749. https://doi.org/10.1037/a0025094

McHugh, R. K. & Otto, M. W. (2012). Refining the measurement of distress intolerance. *Behavior Therapy*, *43*(3), 641–651.

McHugh, R. K., Weiss, R. D., Cornelius, M., Martel, M. O., Jamison, R. N., & Edwards, R. R. (2016). Distress intolerance and prescription opioid misuse among patients with chronic pain. *Journal of Pain*, *17*(7), 806–814. https://doi .org/10.1016/j.jpain.2016.03.004

Mennin, D. S., Heimberg, R. G., Turk, C. L., & Fresco, D. M. (2002). Applying an emotion regulation framework to integrative approaches to generalized anxiety disorder. *Clinical Psychology: Science and Practice*, *9*, 85–90.

Mennin, D. S., Heimberg, R. G., Turk, C. L., & Fresco, D. M. (2005). Preliminary evidence for an emotion dysregulation model of generalized anxiety disorder. *Behaviour Research and Therapy*, *43*, 1281–1310.

Mennin, D. S., Holaway, R. M., Fresco, D. M., Moore, M. T., & Heimberg, R. G. (2007). Delineating components of emotion and its dysregulation in anxiety and mood pathology. *Behavior Therapy*, *38*, 284–302.

Mennin, D. S., McLaughlin, K. A., & Flanagan, T. J. (2009). Emotion regulation deficits in generalized anxiety disorders, social anxiety disorder, and their co-occurrence. *Journal of Anxiety Disorders*, *23*, 866–871.

Merikangas, K. R., He, J., Burstein, M., Swanson, S. A., Avenevoli, S., Cui, L., … Swendsen, J. (2010). Lifetime prevalence of mental disorders in U.S. adolescents: Results from the National Comorbidity Survey Replication–Adolescent Supplement (NCS-A). *Journal of the American Academy of Child & Adolescent Psychiatry*, *49*(10), 980–989. https://doi.org/10.1016/j.jaac.2010.05.017

Michel, N. M., Rowa, K., Young, L., & McCabe, R. E. (2016). Emotional distress tolerance across anxiety disorders. *Journal of Anxiety Disorders*, *40*, 94–103. https://doi.org /10.1016/j.janxdis.2016.04.009

Mitchell, M. A., Riccardi, C. J., Keough, M. E., Timpano, K. R., & Schmidt, N. B. (2013). Understanding the associations among anxiety sensitivity, distress tolerance, and discomfort intolerance: A comparison of three models. *Journal of Anxiety Disorders*, *27*(1), 147–154. https://doi.org/10.1016/j.janxdis.2012.12.003

Mitte, K. (2005). Meta-analysis of cognitive-behavioral treatments for generalized anxiety disorder: A comparison with pharmacotherapy. *Psychological Bulletin*, *131*(5), 785–795. https://doi.org/10.1037/0033–2909.131.5.785

Moskowitz, D. S. & Zuroff, D. C. (2005). Robust predictors of flux, pulse, and spin. *Journal of Research in Personality*, *39*, 130–147.

Neale, M. C. & Cardon, L. (1992). *Methodology for Genetic Studies of Twins and Families* (Vol. 67). Springer Science & Business Media.

Nelemans, S. A., Hale, W. W., Branje, S. J. T., Raaijmakers, Q. A. W., Frijns, T., van Lier, P. A. C., & Meeus, W. H. J. (2014). Heterogeneity in development of adolescent anxiety disorder symptoms in an 8-year longitudinal community study. *Development and Psychopathology*, *26*(1), 181–202. https://doi.org/10 .1017/S0954579413000503

Newman, M. G., Llera, S. J., Erickson, T. M., Przeworski, A., & Castonguay, L. G. (2013). Worry and generalized anxiety disorder: A review and theoretical synthesis of evidence on nature, etiology, mechanisms, and treatment. *Annual Review of Clinical Psychology, 9*(1), 275–297. https://doi.org/10.1146/annurev-clinpsy-050212-185544

Nolen-Hoeksema, S. (2000). The role of rumination in depressive disorders and mixed anxiety/depressive symptoms. *Journal of Abnormal Psychology, 109*(3), 504.

Norr, A. M., Allan, N. P., Macatee, R. J., Keough, M. E., & Schmidt, N. B. (2014). The effects of an anxiety sensitivity intervention on anxiety, depression, and worry: Mediation through affect tolerances. *Behaviour Research and Therapy, 59*, 12–19. https://doi.org/10.1016/j.brat.2014.05.011

Norr, A. M., Oglesby, M. E., Capron, D. W., Raines, A. M., Korte, K. J., & Schmidt, N. B. (2013). Evaluating the unique contribution of intolerance of uncertainty relative to other cognitive vulnerability factors in anxiety psychopathology. *Journal of Affective Disorders, 151*(1), 136–142. https://doi.org/10.1016/j.jad.2013.05.063

Obsessive Compulsive Cognitions Working Group. (2005). Psychometric validation of the obsessive belief questionnaire and interpretation of intrusions inventory: Part 2: Factor analyses and testing of a brief version. *Behaviour Research and Therapy, 43*(11), 1527–1542. https://doi.org/10.1016/j.brat.2004.07.010

Pawluk, E. J. & Koerner, N. (2016). The relationship between negative urgency and generalized anxiety disorder symptoms: The role of intolerance of negative emotions and intolerance of uncertainty. *Anxiety, Stress, & Coping, 29*(6), 606–615. https://doi.org/10.1080/10615806.2015.1134786

Peterson, R. A. & Reiss, S. (1992). *Anxiety Sensitivity Index Manual* (2nd edn). Worthington, OH: International Diagnostic Systems.

Pine, D. S. & Fox, N. A. (2015). Childhood antecedents and risk for adult mental disorders. *Annual Review of Psychology, 66*, 459–485.

Potter, C. M., Vujanovic, A. A., Marshall-Berenz, E. C., Bernstein, A., & Bonn-Miller, M. O. (2011). Posttraumatic stress and marijuana use coping motives: The mediating role of distress tolerance. *Journal of Anxiety Disorders, 25*(3), 437–443. https://doi.org/10.1016/j.janxdis.2010.11.007

Quinn, E. P., Brandon, T. H., & Copeland, A. L. (1996). Is task persistence related to smoking and substance abuse? The application of learned industriousness theory to addictive behaviors. *Experimental and Clinical Psychopharmacology, 4*(2), 186.

Radkovsky, A., McArdle, J. J., Bockting, C. L. H., & Berking, M. (2014). Successful emotion regulation skills application predicts subsequent reduction of symptom severity during treatment of major depressive disorder. *Journal of Consulting and Clinical Psychology, 82*(2), 248–262. https://doi.org/10.1037/a0035828

Rappaport, L. M., Moskowitz, D. S., & D'Antono, B. (2014). Naturalistic interpersonal behavior patterns differentiate depression and anxiety symptoms in the community. *Journal of Counseling Psychology, 61*(2), 253–263. https://doi.org/10.1037/a0035625

Rappaport, L. M., Moskowitz, D. S., & D'Antono, B. (2017). Depression symptoms moderate the association between emotion and communal behavior. *Journal of Counseling Psychology, 64*, 269–279.

Reiss, S., Peterson, R. A., Gursky, D. M., & McNally, R. J. (1986). Anxiety sensitivity, anxiety frequency and the prediction of fearfulness. *Behaviour Research and Therapy, 24*, 1–8.

Ricciardi, J. N. & McNally, R. J. (1995). Depressed mood is related to obsessions, but not to compulsions, in obsessive-compulsive disorder. *Journal of Anxiety Disorders, 9*(3), 249–256.

Robinson, L. J. & Freeston, M. H. (2014). Emotion and internal experience in obsessive compulsive disorder: Reviewing the role of alexithymia, anxiety sensitivity and distress tolerance. *Clinical Psychology Review, 34*(3), 256–271. https://doi.org/10.1016/j.cpr.2014.03.003

Safer, D. L., Telch, C. F., & Agras, W. S. (2001). Dialectical behavior therapy for bulimia nervosa. *American Journal of Psychiatry, 158*(4), 632–634.

Salters-Pedneault, K., Roemer, J., Tull, M. T., Rucker, L., & Mennin, D. S. (2006). Evidence of broad deficits in emotion regulation associated with chronic worry and generalized anxiety disorder. *Cognitive Therapy and Research, 30,* 469–480.

Sanislow, C. A., Pine, D. S., Quinn, K. J., Kozak, M. J., Garvey, M. A., Heinssen, R. K., . . . Cuthbert, B. N. (2010). Developing constructs for psychopathology research: Research domain criteria. *Journal of Abnormal Psychology, 119*(4), 631–639. https://doi.org/10.1037/a0020909

Shrout, P. E., Keyes, K., & Ornstein, K. (eds.). (2011). *Causality and Psychopathology: Finding the Determinants of Disorders and Their Cures.* New York, NY: Oxford University Press.

Simons, J. S. & Gaher, R. M. (2005). The Distress Tolerance Scale: Development and validation of a self-report measure. *Motivation and Emotion, 29*(2), 83–102. https://doi.org/10.1007/s11031-005–7955-3

Slaap, B. R. & den Boer, J. A. (2001). The prediction of nonresponse to pharmacotherapy in panic disorder: A review. *Depression and Anxiety, 14,* 112–122.

Starr, L. R. & Davila, J. (2012). Responding to anxiety with rumination and hopelessness: Mechanism of anxiety-depression symptom co-occurrence? *Cognitive Therapy and Research, 36*(4), 321–337. https://doi.org/10.1007/s10608-011–9363-1

Strong, D. R., Lejeuz, C. W., Daughters, S., Marinello, M., Kahler, C. W., & Brown, R. A. (2003). The computerized mirror tracing task. unpublished manual.

Thompson, S. C. (1981). Will it hurt less if I can control it? A complex answer to a simple question. *Psychological Bulletin, 90*(1), 89.

Tracey, T. J. G. & Rohlfing, J. E. (2010). Variations in the understanding of interpersonal behavior: Adherence to the interpersonal circle as a moderator of the rigidity–psychological well-being relation. *Journal of Personality, 78*(2), 711–746. https://doi.org/10.1111/j.1467–6494.2010.00631.x

Trafton, J. A. & Gifford, E. V. (2011). Biological bases of distress tolerance. In M. J. Zvolensky, A. Bernstein, & A. A. Vujanovic (eds.), *Distress Tolerance: Theory, Research, and Clinical Applications.* New York, NY: Guilford Press.

Tull, M. T., Gratz, K. L., Coffey, S. F., Weiss, N. H., & McDermott, M. J. (2013). Examining the interactive effect of posttraumatic stress disorder, distress tolerance, and gender on residential substance use disorder treatment retention. *Psychology of Addictive Behaviors, 27*(3), 763–773. https://doi.org/10.1037/a0029911

Tull, M. T., Rodman, S. A., & Roemer, L. (2008). An examination of the fear of bodily sensations and body hypervigilance as predictors of emotion regulation difficulties among individuals with a recent history of uncued panic attacks. *Journal of Anxiety Disorders, 22*(4), 750–760. https://doi.org/10.1016/j.janxdis.2007.08.001

Tull, M. T. & Roemer, L. (2007). Emotion regulation difficulties associated with the experience of uncued panic attacks: Evidence of experiential avoidance, emotional nonacceptance, and decreased emotional clarity. *Behavior Therapy, 38*(4), 378–391.

Tutoo, D. N. (1971). Psychodiagnostic applications of the mirror tracing test. *Indian Educational Review, 6*, 293–303.

Twohig, M. P. (2009). The application of acceptance and commitment therapy to obsessive-compulsive disorder. *Cognitive and Behavioral Practice, 16*(1), 18–28.

Vujanovic, A. A., Bakhshaie, J., Martin, C., Reddy, M. K., & Anestis, M. D. (2017). Posttraumatic stress and distress tolerance: Associations with suicidality in acute-care psychiatric inpatients. *Journal of Nervous and Mental Disease, 205*(7), 531–541. https://doi.org/10.1097/NMD.0000000000000690

Vujanovic, A. A., Bonn-Miller, M. O., Potter, C. M., Marshall, E. C., & Zvolensky, M. J. (2011). An evaluation of the relation between distress tolerance and posttraumatic stress within a trauma-exposed sample. *Journal of Psychopathology and Behavioral Assessment, 33*(1), 129–135. https://doi.org/10.1007/s10862-010–9209-2

Vujanovic, A. A., Dutcher, C. D., & Berenz, E. C. (2016). Multimodal examination of distress tolerance and posttraumatic stress disorder symptoms in acute-care psychiatric inpatients. *Journal of Anxiety Disorders.* https://doi.org/10.1016/j.janxdis.2016.08.005

Vujanovic, A. A., Hart, A. S., Potter, C. M., Berenz, E. C., Niles, B., & Bernstein, A. (2013). Main and interactive effects of distress tolerance and negative affect intensity in relation to PTSD symptoms among trauma-exposed adults. *Journal of Psychopathology and Behavioral Assessment, 35*(2), 235–243. https://doi.org/10.1007/s10862-012–9325-2

Vujanovic, A. A., Litz, B. T., & Farris, S. G. (2015). Distress tolerance as risk and maintenance factor for PTSD: Empirical and clinical implications. In C. R. Martin, V. R. Preedy, & V. B. Patel (eds.), *Comprehensive Guide to Posttraumatic Stress Disorder* (pp. 1–13). Cham: Springer International Publishing. Retrieved from http://link.springer.com/10.1007/978-3-319–08613-2_66–1

Vujanovic, A. A., Marshall-Berenz, E. C., & Zvolensky, M. J. (2011). Posttraumatic stress and alcohol use motives: A test of the incremental and mediating role of distress tolerance. *Journal of Cognitive Psychotherapy, 25*(2), 130–141. https://doi.org/10.1891/0889-8391.25.2.130

Vujanovic, A. A., Rathnayaka, N., Amador, C. D., & Schmitz, J. M. (2016). Distress tolerance: Associations with posttraumatic stress disorder symptoms among trauma-exposed, cocaine-dependent adults. *Behavior Modification, 40*(1–2), 120–143.

Waller, N. G., Yonce, L. J., Grove, W. M., Faust, D., & Lenzenweger, M. F. (eds.). (2006). *A Paul Meehl Reader: Essays on the Practice of Scientific Psychology.* Mahwah, NJ: Erlbaum.

Watson, D., Weber, K., Assenheimer, J. S., Clark, L. A., Strauss, M. E., & McCormick, R. A. (1995). Testing a tripartite model: I. Evaluating the convergent and discriminant validity of anxiety and depression symptom scales. *Journal of Abnormal Psychology, 104*, 3–14.

Williams, A. D., Thompson, J., & Andrews, G. (2013). The impact of psychological distress tolerance in the treatment of depression. *Behaviour Research and Therapy, 51*(8), 469–475. https://doi.org/10.1016/j.brat.2013.05.005

Wolitzky-Taylor, K., Guillot, C. R., Pang, R. D., Kirkpatrick, M. G., Zvolensky, M. J., Buckner, J. D., & Leventhal, A. M. (2015). Examination of anxiety sensitivity and distress tolerance as transdiagnostic mechanisms linking multiple anxiety pathologies to alcohol use problems in adolescents. *Alcoholism: Clinical and Experimental Research, 39*(3), 532–539. https://doi.org/10.1111/acer.12638

Wolitzky-Taylor, K., McBeth, J., Guillot, C. R., Stone, M. D., Kirkpatrick, M. G., Zvolensky, M. J., . . . Leventhal, A. M. (2016). Transdiagnostic processes linking anxiety symptoms and substance use problems among adolescents. *Journal of Addictive Diseases, 35*(4), 266–277. https://doi.org/10.1080/10550887.2016.1207969

Yang, J., Lee, S. H., Goddard, M. E., & Visscher, P. M. (2011). GCTA: A tool for Genome-wide Complex Trait Analysis. *American Journal of Human Genetics, 88*(1), 76–82. https://doi.org/10.1016/j.ajhg.2010.11.011

Zuroff, D. C., Fournier, M. A., & Moskowitz, D. S. (2007). Depression, perceived inferiority, and interpersonal behavior: Evidence for the involuntary defeat strategy. *Journal of Social and Clinical Psychology, 26*, 751–778.

Zvolensky, M. J., Bernstein, A., Cardenas, S. J., Colotla, V., Marshall, E., & Feldner, M. (2007). Anxiety sensitivity and early relapse to smoking: A test among Mexican daily, low-level smokers. *Nicotine & Tobacco Research, 9*(4), 483–491. https://doi.org/10.1080/14622200701239621

Zvolensky, M. J., Schmidt, N. B., Bernstein, A., & Keough, M. E. (2006). Risk-factor research and prevention programs for anxiety disorders: A translational research framework. *Behaviour Research and Therapy, 44*(9), 1219–1239. https://doi.org/10.1016/j.brat.2006.06.001

Zvolensky, M. J., Vujanovic, A. A., Bernstein, A., & Leyro, T. (2010). Distress tolerance: Theory, measurement, and relations to psychopathology. *Current Directions in Psychological Science, 19*(6), 406–410. https://doi.org/10.1177/0963721410388642

9 Experiential Avoidance

Fallon R. Goodman, Maria A. Larrazabal,
John T. West, and Todd B. Kashdan

Part of being human means experiencing pain and discomfort. At some point in their lives, most people will experience uncertainty of whether one's ideas are worthy of being shared, anxiety prior to disagreeing with someone else, bouts of loneliness, and the heartbreak of a relationship ending. Negative emotional experiences range from mundane to profound, weak to intensely disturbing. From an evolutionary perspective, these (often) uncomfortable thoughts and feelings are expected and even necessary. Anger can help us confront goal-related obstacles. Envy can motivate us to improve our knowledge and skills. Guilt and embarrassment can help us become caring and cooperative. Making progress on important goals often requires working through setbacks, adversity, and discomfort. The presence of negative thoughts and feelings in itself is not problematic. Rather, the way in which a person *evaluates* and *responds* determines whether negative experiences are helpful or unhelpful on the journey toward a successful, fulfilling life.

In this chapter, we explore one response style that is particularly problematic – experiential avoidance. We review research on the role of experiential avoidance in anxiety disorders. We first provide an overview of how experiential avoidance functions as a nearly universal vulnerability in the development and maintenance of anxiety disorders. Next, we detail how experiential avoidance operates in the context of specific anxiety disorders: generalized anxiety disorder, social anxiety disorder, panic disorder, obsessive-compulsive disorder, and posttraumatic stress disorder. We conclude by offering insights into new directions for understanding and altering the unhelpful influence of experiential avoidance.

Experiential Avoidance and Links with Anxiety

Experiential avoidance is defined as the unwillingness to experience unwanted internal thoughts, feelings, and sensations (Hayes, Luoma, Bond, Masuda, & Lillis, 2006; Hayes, Wilson, Gifford, Follette, & Strosahl, 1996). Individuals evaluate these private events negatively and deliberately try to avoid, control, and escape the subjective experience and accompanying physiological arousal. Efforts to escape include overt behavioral strategies such as watching television as a distraction from stressful thoughts, or refusing to give speeches in front of groups. There is evidence to suggest that unwanted bodily sensations and emotions feel even more threatening when people lack confidence in their ability to regulate emotions, increasing the probability of engaging in experiential avoidance (Feldner, Zvolensky, Eifert, & Spira, 2003).

Over the past four decades, a large body of terminology has been coined to describe avoidant-related coping and emotion regulation strategies such as denial, repression, numbing, and blaming. Kashdan and colleagues describe experiential avoidance as an overarching construct that subsumes several specific strategies:

> To some extent, strategic attempts to escape stressful experiences (avoidant coping), to become independent from aversive events and accompanying emotions (detached coping), or to inhibit the expression of emotions (emotion suppression) can be considered component processes of experiential avoidance. Another component is the belief that personal control over threatening events rests outside oneself (uncontrollability). Experiential avoidance is a broader construct that entails tendencies to be cognitively entangled with internal experiences and general psychological inflexibility. (Kashdan, Barrios, Forsyth, & Steger, 2006, p. 1303)

Other researchers adopt similar conceptualizations; Pickett and Kurby (2010) refer to experiential avoidance as "a functional class of maladaptive strategies that contribute to the development and maintenance of psychopathology" (p. 493). Chawla and Ostafin (2007) state that related emotion regulation strategies "can be labeled as [experiential avoidance] in that they represent specific methods by which action is taken to alter aversive private experience" (p. 872). Experiential avoidance is a strategy that a person strategically employs to control the subjective experience, behavioral expression, or subjective arousal of an unwanted internal experience.

Frequent use of experiential avoidance is exhausting. According to the limited self-control model, people possess a finite capacity of mental resources at their disposal to regulate any aspect of the self (Muraven & Baumeister, 2000). Whether a person is trying to patiently wait for an elevator door to open, resist the temptation to use their smartphone, or avoid thinking about an argumentative meeting with their boss, the energy required to self-regulate draws from a single mental reservoir. Individuals drain their resource pool when they engage in any type of self-regulatory behavior. This self-regulatory depletion means fewer resources are available for subsequent tasks. Exhausting one's self-regulatory resources has spillover effects, including hindering performance, interpersonal relationships, and well-being (Baumeister, Gailliot, DeWall, & Oaten, 2006; Tangney, Baumeister, & Boone, 2004; Vohs, Baumeister, & Ciarocco, 2005). People who rely on experiential avoidance devote considerable time, attention, and energy to managing anxiety. When someone's primary focus is on managing and controlling anxiety, they exhaust limited self-regulatory resources and end up less able to attend to the present and potentially rewarding experiences.

Avoiding unpleasant private events can provide temporary relief. For example, during around-the-room introductions at a meeting with a new group, a person might use experiential avoidance to hide their anxiety to appear more self-assured. In this context, employing experiential avoidance is adaptive, helping a person achieve their goal of presenting themselves positively. Relied on too often, these benefits (e.g., tranquil moments, successful impression management) occur at the expense of long-term problems. If this same individual is hyper-focused on concealing their anxiety during subsequent social encounters, the ability to extract joy and meaning and build opportunities for intimacy, social support, shared laughter, and appreciation will be stunted.

The paradox of experiential avoidance is that trying to get rid of internal experiences serves to increase those unwanted experiences (Wegner, 1994). A vicious cycle is incurred whereby consistent use of experiential avoidance over time serves to exacerbate distress, increasing the risk for a range of anxiety and mood disorders (Hayes, Strosahl, & Wilson, 1999; Hayes et al., 2004; Kashdan et al., 2006; Kashdan & Rottenberg, 2010).

For anxiety disorders in particular, there is a robust body of literature to suggest that a rigid pattern of avoiding negative affect is maladaptive. Hayes and colleagues (1996) offer four pathways for how experiential avoidance might functionally contribute to anxiety pathology (see also Chawla & Ostafin, 2007). First, internal verbalizations made about avoided stimuli (e.g., "I won't think about my upcoming date today") increase mental accessibility. If a person suppresses a thought in a particular context, when they return to that context, they are not only more likely to reexperience the thought they tried to suppress, but they are also more likely to experience it at an even greater intensity than in the prior situation. Second, internal experiences may be resistant to verbal control strategies because they are classically conditioned. If painful emotional experiences have been associated with a particular event, it is likely that future encounters with this event will facilitate the same pain. Using verbal control strategies such as experiential avoidance will be ineffective because of an underlying nonverbal, conditioned association between the event and the negative emotional experience. Third, even if successful, avoidance strategies occur at the expense of constricted behavioral activity. A focus on anxiety management means that at times, people give up other personally meaningful activities. Avoidance strategies evoke an opportunity cost. Fourth, sometimes people use experiential avoidance to manage emotional responses that are an appropriate, helpful match for a challenging situation. A slight boost in anxiety prior to giving a presentation can be energizing and help a person better prepare their message delivery; an additional benefit is the anticipation of possible problems during the presentation, preparation of solutions, and readiness to deploy those solutions as needed. When anxiety is perceived as bad or unwanted, the focus shifts from delivering an effective presentation to getting rid of anxiety.

Just how central is experiential avoidance to anxiety disorders? One study examined the use of 14 different coping strategies among people diagnosed with generalized anxiety disorder, social anxiety disorder, and panic disorder (Panayiotou, Karekla, & Mete, 2014). Coping strategies included behavioral strategies (self-distraction, active coping, substance use, emotional support, behavioral disengagement, and venting) and cognitive strategies (denial, positive reframing, self-blame, and planning). Experiential avoidance had stronger associations, compared with other coping strategies, with anxiety-related symptoms. To illustrate the magnitude of this effect, the correlation between experiential avoidance and social anxiety disorder symptoms was $r = 0.40$ whereas the other 13 coping strategies correlated between -0.09 and 0.24 with social anxiety symptoms. For generalized anxiety disorder symptoms, the correlation with experiential avoidance was $r = 0.51$, which was much stronger than the other coping strategies (-0.07 to 0.37). For panic disorder symptoms, the correlation with experiential avoidance was $r = 0.42$, compared to the other coping strategies (-0.06 to 0.35). These findings suggest that experiential avoidance is a transdiagnostic vulnerability factor for anxiety disorders, an empirical finding that has been found in other investigations (Berman, Wheaton, McGrath, & Abramowitz, 2010; Kashdan et al., 2006; Kashdan, Morina, & Priebe, 2009; Spinhoven, Drost, de Rooji, van Hemert, & Pennix, 2014; Venta, Sharp, & Hart, 2012).

Taken together, people who frequently use experiential avoidance are at heightened risk for developing one or more anxiety disorders. In subsequent sections, we review evidence on the contribution of experiential avoidance to five specific anxiety disorders. We provide an overview of each disorder and summarize research on how experiential avoidance contributes to their onset and maintenance.

Generalized Anxiety Disorder

Generalized anxiety disorder (GAD) is characterized by constant and excessive worry about events and activities across life domains. People with GAD tend to overestimate the risk to their safety or well-being in a given situation. They often perceive stressful events as uncontrollable and have difficulty managing worrisome thoughts. Worry is usually paired with physical symptoms such as difficulty sleeping, restlessness, and muscle tension.

Two variables, in combination, can distinguish individuals diagnosed with GAD from individuals without GAD with 98.5% accuracy – a heightened fear of intense emotions and excessive use of experiential avoidance (Lee, Orsillo, Roemer, & Allen, 2010; also see Buhr & Dugas, 2012). Individuals who are unwilling to experience the full range of human emotions are more likely to exert effort to avoid uncomfortable emotions. This creates a restrictive cycle in which fear of emotions leads to avoidance, which leads to greater fear.

In contrast to other anxiety disorders in which there is typically one core fear (e.g., fear of evaluation in social anxiety disorder), GAD is characterized by a range of feared outcomes (Brown, Barlow, & Liebowitz, 1994; Roemer, Molina, & Borkovec, 1997). Theorists have proposed that people with GAD often believe that worrying is adaptive. Contemplating catastrophic outcomes allows for the generation of problem-solving strategies that can be deployed as needed. By thinking through multiple scenarios, people experience a greater sense of certainty, control, and confidence if negative events occur. In this framework, worrying serves to distance individuals from the physiological and subjective experience of feared outcomes, and the belief that this verbal-linguistic act (worrying) can reduce the probability of these feared outcomes (Borkovec, Alcaine, & Behar, 2004). Among individuals diagnosed with GAD, experiential avoidance predicts worry; individuals endorsing greater use of experiential avoidance endorse more frequent worry (Lee et al., 2010). This relationship remains after accounting for the effects of other important predictors of worry (e.g., fear of uncertainty). These results suggest that worry is associated with the tendency to avoid distressing internal events.

Questionnaire research has provided support for the notion that individuals with GAD worry in order to avoid emotional distress. In one study, undergraduate participants were given six different reasons that people worry: motivational energy that increases productivity, an enhancer of problem-solving, preparation for catastrophes, strategy to avoid catastrophes, strategy to avoid negative emotion, or superstitious power (i.e., worrying will reduce the likelihood of something bad happening) (Borkovec & Roemer, 1995). They rated the extent to which they were motivated by these reasons to worry. Clinically anxious individuals worried to avoid negative emotions more often than controls. These findings are congruent with research suggesting a positive relationship between avoidance strategies and worry (e.g., Dugas, Gagnon, Ladouceur, & Freeston, 1998; Dugas, Marchand, & Ladouceur, 2005).

Worrying is reinforced when individuals believe that they have successfully averted the feared situation or outcome. Physiological data suggest that worry suppresses emotional processing. In one study, healthy participants created two-minute audio recordings of themselves worrying out loud (Hoehn-Saric, Lee, McLeod, & Wong, 2005). They were asked to identify their principal worry and speak in the first person to share their internal dialogue. Several days later, their neural activity was measured while exposed to several stimuli. For the first two neural assessments, participants listened to a recording about a neutral topic and were instructed to think about the recording until the scan ended. For the second two neural assessments, participants listened to a recording of their own personal worries and were instructed to worry as much as they could. When participants worried, they showed evidence of decreased emotional processing in the limbic system compared to when they were thinking about a neutral topic. By inhibiting brain regions associated with emotional processing, worry may allow individuals to avoid experiencing distress.

In more recent work, researchers have found that individuals with GAD use worry to avoid a *negative emotional contrast*, which is defined as a sharp shift from a positive emotional state to a negative emotional state (Newman & Llera, 2011). Worrying helps people with GAD anticipate and prepare for worst-case scenarios and prevent major disappointments following unexpected negative events. By keeping themselves in a constant state of worry-induced negative affect, people with GAD avoid experiencing the jarring switch from a positive to negative emotion in the presence of life difficulties. They remain in a heightened negative emotional state that shields them from sharp increases in distress and arousal when confronted with feared stimuli.

Methodologies that allow for repeated measurements over time can capture the broad range of topics individuals with GAD worry about in daily life. In one study, undergraduate students described their most negative event each week for seven consecutive weeks (Crouch, Lewis, Erickson, & Newman, 2017). Participants with high baseline GAD symptoms were more likely to report that their worst event of the week involved a drop off from a positive to a negative emotional state. For instance, an individual might have said their worst event of the week was when they felt proud on a work project but then received a poor performance review, which made them feel anxious and frustrated. Although these negative emotional contrasts increased general distress, weekly worry and baseline GAD symptoms moderated this effect such that negative emotional contrasts led to less of an increase in distress in individuals high in weekly worry and GAD symptoms. Although only one study, results suggest that individuals with GAD are more bothered by negative emotional contrasts than controls and are therefore motivated to rely on worry as a means of preemptively lessening increases in negative emotion.

Experimental studies have yielded similar findings. In one study, upon entering the lab, participants were informed that they had to give an impromptu speech (Skodzik, Zettler, Topper, Blechert, & Ehring, 2016). Participants were then randomly assigned to either a worry or a distraction condition. In the worry condition, participants were instructed to think about details of their upcoming speech, including the possibility of a social failure and the downstream consequences. In the distraction condition, participants were instructed to think about a series of mundane topics. Following the initial induction, participants were given 30 seconds to prepare their speech. Participants in the worry condition reported greater negative affect immediately after the initial induction compared with those in the distraction condition. Since participants in the worry condition had higher negative affect when they began preparing their speech, they experienced less of an increase in negative affect relative to participants in the distraction condition; their worry protected them from experiencing a sharper emotional contrast.

Similar effects are found when participants are shown emotionally laden stimuli. After being instructed to think about their most worrisome topic (worry condition), to think about what they did last weekend (neutral control), or to breathe slowly (relaxation condition), participants then watched films designed to induce one of four emotions: fear, sadness, happiness, or calmness (Llera & Newman, 2010). As expected, worrying led to greater negative affect prior to watching the film. After watching the film, participants in the worry condition demonstrated less physiological and subjective reactivity to the fear-inducing film. Because they were already worried prior to watching the film, they did not experience an abrupt spike in distress.

In a follow-up study, Llera and Newman (2014) again assigned participants to worry, relaxation, or neutral inductions before viewing emotionally laden film clips. Participants assigned to worry demonstrated increased negative affect, which they sustained throughout negative film exposures. In contrast, participants in the relaxation and neutral conditions demonstrated sharp increases in negative emotion from baseline after watching negative films. Interestingly, participants with GAD reported that their worry helped them cope with the negative movies whereas those without GAD felt that worry interfered with self-regulation attempts. These results offer further evidence that worry helps mitigate negative emotional contrasts, and that people with GAD rely on worry because they believe worry is beneficial in coping with aversive events.

We offer three suggestions for future research on experiential avoidance and GAD. First, people with GAD worry because this verbal act is reinforcing, reducing physiological reactions to perceived stressors. Additional studies are needed to test the possibility that experiential avoidance is the mediating mechanism that motivates people to worry. For example, one might predict that individuals who regularly use experiential avoidance are particularly distressed by emotional contrasts and in turn, develop an overreliance on worry to reduce the impact of these contrasts. This particular style of coping with emotions might be a pathway in the development of GAD. Alternatively, those low in experiential avoidance and distressed by emotional contrasts may not be at risk for developing GAD; after all, without the motivation to avoid feared internal experience (emotional contrasts), individuals would find worry to be superfluous. To date, such predictions remain untested. Second, more rigorous tests are needed on the role of experiential avoidance as a vulnerability factor for GAD. Existing empirical work generally supports experiential avoidance as a meaningful predictor of worry, the defining feature of GAD, as well as the severity of GAD symptoms. However, any causal inferences about the role of experiential avoidance within GAD are limited by cross-sectional methodologies. Longitudinal designs are needed to explore the association between experiential avoidance and pathological worry as it occurs over time. Third, we know little about what precedes experiential avoidance that then leads to conditions such as GAD. For instance, it has been suggested that aversive early attachment experiences such as the relative absence of maternal love and maternal rejection may make individuals more likely to rely on avoidant regulatory strategies and, as a result, develop GAD (Cassidy, Lichtenstein-Phelps, Sibrava, Thomas, & Borkovec, 2009; Viana & Rabian, 2008). Other work suggests that children who are forced to adopt the role of caregiver at too early of a developmental stage, taking care of younger siblings of negligent parents (i.e., parentification), are more likely to engage in excessive worry (Haxhe, 2016). When children experience an inflated sense of responsibility while lacking the knowledge and skills to cope, worrying and experiential avoidance appear to be natural, unfortunate by-products. The trajectory and directionality of parentification, distressing thoughts and emotions, experiential avoidance, and GAD await scientific study. Future research should examine whether this sort of early stressful experience increases individuals' propensity to rely on experiential avoidance.

Social Anxiety Disorder

Social anxiety disorder (SAD) is characterized by beliefs that perceived flaws in character exist, will be visible and scrutinized by other people, and will be the cause of rejection (Moscovitch, 2009). These fears stimulate an avoidance of social situations in which there is potential for evaluation and rejection. When SAD is present, the motivation to avoid failure and rejection trumps the motivation to pursue rewards and valued goals. When people with SAD do enter a social situation, they endure it with significant distress. Rather than enjoying the company of others, they are hyper-focused on managing their anxiety. Most often, this anxiety management is in the form of experiential avoidance.

More than the occurrence anxiety, a reliance on experiential avoidance might be the tipping point from normative to pathological social anxiety. In one daily diary study, community adults answered surveys for 14 consecutive days about their mood, emotion regulation strategies, and social experiences (Kashdan et al., 2013). When comparing patterns of response from individuals diagnosed with SAD with healthy controls, only two differences emerged. Individuals with SAD reported highly frequent reliance on experiential avoidance and attenuated positive emotions in daily social interactions. These effects remained even after controlling for levels of social anxiety and negative emotions when socializing. These findings suggest that negative emotions alone, including anxiety, do not distinguish individuals with SAD from healthy adults; rather, frequent reliance on experiential avoidance in everyday life appears unique to SAD.

Consistent with findings suggesting that experiential avoidance paradoxically increases distress, this emotion regulation strategy appears to exacerbate social anxiety. Across two studies, researchers examined the effect of experiential avoidance on anxiety within real-world situations (Kashdan et al., 2014). In the first study, individuals diagnosed with SAD and healthy adults completed surveys each day for two consecutive weeks. Across both groups, experiential avoidance was associated with increased social anxiety during social interactions. This relationship was stronger for individuals with SAD, such that use of experiential avoidance heightened anxiety to a greater degree than for healthy adults. These results were replicated in a second study. Upon entering the research laboratory, college students were randomly paired up into opposite-sex dyads, then each dyad was randomly assigned to one of two experimentally created social situations. The small-talk conversation condition was limited to conversation about mundane topics, whereas the self-disclosure condition had explicit opportunities for intimacy. Results suggest that during the self-disclosure, experiential avoidance (measured in the middle of the conversation) predicted an increase in social anxiety (measured after the social situation concluded); no effect was found in the small-talk condition. No evidence was found for reverse direction – social anxiety did not predict an increase in experiential avoidance. These results offer support for experiential avoidance as a risk factor for generating emotional distress, as experiential avoidance did not merely co-occur with social anxiety and it was not a consequence; it preceded the development of social anxiety.

One explanation for why experiential avoidance is especially problematic in situations that pull for intimate self-disclosure is that individuals high in social anxiety are closer to their feared outcome: rejection. By offering other people access to their vulnerability, they open themselves up to further evaluation and scrutiny. Individuals with SAD fear that by doing so, they are likely to be judged poorly and rejected. One study experimentally created scenarios in which individuals imagined this rejection fear coming true (Breen & Kashdan, 2011). Participants listened to three hypothetical vignettes and were instructed to imagine themselves in each situation as they listened. The vignettes described three different everyday social situations. All participants first listened to a vignette that described a social situation with an ambiguous ending. They were then randomly assigned to listen to a vignette with an alternative ending to the social situation that either ended in rejection or no rejection. In response to imagined rejection, individuals higher in social anxiety reported significantly greater use of experiential avoidance (and greater anger) than those lower in social anxiety. These results suggest that individuals high in social anxiety are likely to respond to upsetting events, especially those involving perceived rejection, by trying to suppress or avoid the resulting negative thoughts and feelings.

Experiential avoidance is also deployed after social events occur. Following stressful social events, individuals high in social anxiety tend to spend time ruminating about the event (Rodebaugh & Heimberg, 2008). Rather than approaching memories of social events constructively, such as trying to uncover a lesson learned or adopt a different perspective, individuals high in social anxiety evaluate social events negatively and persist with these judgments long after interaction partners are physically present.

Theorists have proposed that rigid reliance on experiential avoidance contributes to positivity deficits that are characteristic of SAD (Kashdan, Weeks, & Savostyanova, 2011). Individuals with SAD spend large amounts of time focused on regulating and managing their emotions. During a social situation, they are likely to be more concerned about giving off a favorable impression than enjoying the company around them. They turn inward to manage their anxiety rather than attending to and enjoying the ongoing situation around them. They rely on safety behaviors, in which they take some sort of action to suppress or conceal visible emotions (Moscovitch et al., 2013; Plasencia, Alden, & Taylor, 2011). For example, they may wear certain clothing or makeup to hide blushing so that they do not convey they are anxious. They quickly exhaust internal, self-regulatory resources on managing their anxiety, which comes at the expense of enjoying the social situation they are in. As a result, they have relatively few opportunities to obtain social benefits from others and tend to have less enjoyable social interactions (Kashdan & Steger, 2006).

This research suggests that before, during, and after social situations, individuals with SAD exert considerable effort to control, avoid, and manage negative emotions. By doing so, individuals with SAD constrain their social and emotional experiences. They increasingly constrain their social world, leading to fewer opportunities to enter situations in which they can pursue rewards and extract pleasure and meaning from them. Given this link between positivity deficits and experiential avoidance, more research is needed to understand the precursors that contribute to maladaptive emotion regulation patterns. One promising area of research is related to implicit beliefs about emotions. All individuals make judgments about the extent to which they believe they can or should alter the experience, expression, and/or regulation of emotions (Tamir, John, Srivastava, & Gross, 2007). Preliminary work suggests that individuals with SAD hold fixed beliefs about emotions, in that they believe they cannot be changed (De Castella et al., 2014). This is potentially problematic, as this rigid belief system has been associated with reliance on avoidant emotion regulation strategies and worse emotional experiences (Tamir et al., 2007). Moreover, individuals who judge anxiety as bad across all contexts are at greater risk for heightened experiential avoidance and feelings of social anxiety compared with individuals who hold more flexible valuation of the utility of anxiety (Levin, Haeger, & Smith, 2017). These results suggest that individuals with SAD who frequently rely on experiential avoidance may do so because of rigid, maladaptive beliefs they hold about emotions.

Panic Disorder

A panic attack is characterized by the sudden onset of physical symptoms of anxiety such as sweating, shortness of breath, chest pain, shaking, and nausea. Panic attacks are often accompanied by a sense of derealization (the feeling that one's surroundings are not real), fear of dying, fear of losing control, and depersonalization (the feeling of being a detached, outside observer of oneself). Following panic attacks, individuals with panic disorder persistently worry that they will experience panic attacks in the future and develop intense fear of the situation(s) that might cause a panic attack. They avoid situations (e.g., a location in which they once had a panic attack) or behaviors (e.g., exercise) that they worry might trigger another panic attack. Besides behavioral avoidance, individuals with panic disorder try to control, reduce, or eliminate unwanted internal sensations associated with panic attacks. These include physical sensations such as the feeling that one's heart is racing, intrusive thoughts such as "I am going to die," and emotions such as helplessness.

Preliminary findings, though limited, suggest that experiential avoidance is a risk factor for the development and maintenance of panic disorder. Individuals with a history of panic attacks endorse higher levels of experiential avoidance than individuals without a history of panic attacks (Tull & Roemer, 2007). Because individuals with panic disorder try to avoid uncomfortable feelings, they have more difficulty linking physical symptoms with emotional states (Baker, Holloway, Thomas, Thomas, & Owens, 2004). They have trouble differentiating emotions and tend to view aversive experiences as a more globular negative arousal rather than a more granular differentiation of discrete emotions. Compared with healthy adults, individuals with panic disorder exert considerable effort to control the experience and expression of emotion.

One way to examine predictors of panic is to experimentally induce a panic attack. In a commonly used paradigm, participants are informed that they will receive inhalations of carbon dioxide (CO_2)-enriched air – which might induce physical arousal in the form of racing heartbeat, sweaty palms, dizziness, and difficulty breathing. In one study, undergraduate participants high and low in experiential avoidance (i.e., one standard deviation above and below the mean for healthy undergraduates, respectively) underwent a series of CO_2-enriched air administrations (Karekla, Forsyth, & Kelly, 2004). Participants endorsing greater use of experiential avoidance reported more physical and cognitive symptoms characteristic of panic disorder and rated their cognitive symptoms as more severe. Arousal is perceived as more threatening or dangerous, and fear of having a panic attack becomes more activated.

Researchers have also experimentally manipulated avoidant responses to physiological arousal. Participants are instructed to either do everything possible to maintain control of their feelings (suppression condition) or to observe and simply notice the physical sensations they feel and let them occur naturally (observation condition). All participants then receive CO_2-enriched air administrations and record their emotions afterward. In a study using this paradigm, individuals in the suppression condition endorsing greater use of experiential avoidance reported greater anxiety and displeasure (Feldner et al., 2003). Interestingly, people differing in the use of experiential avoidance did not differ in physiological arousal. A similar response pattern was found among a clinical sample, in which participants diagnosed with panic disorder experienced increased subjective anxiety in response to suppressing response to CO_2 administrations but similar levels of physiological arousal to participants accepting their emotional reactions (Levitt, Brown, Orsillo, & Barlow, 2004). Thus, experiential avoidance facilitates a more maladaptive response pattern whereby individuals perceive events as especially distressing regardless of objective physiological arousal (Bouton, Mineka & Barlow, 2001).

Another way to experimentally examine risk factors for panic is to show individuals fear-provoking films and record their responses (e.g., Kelly & Forsyth, 2007a, 2007b). In these paradigms, participants are told that they will be shown a video of an actual subject participating in the procedure they are about to do. In reality, they are shown a film of a confederate having a mock panic attack. The actor displays facial expressions of distress, rapid breathing, and verbal expressions of anxiety while wearing a respiratory mask. Participants are told that the mask is connected to a machine that is pumping CO_2-enriched air. Physiological arousal and subjective measures of anxiety are recorded while they watch the films. In one study using this methodology, researchers examined how experiential avoidance predicted panic responses to the videos (Kelly & Forsyth,

2009). As expected, experiential avoidance was associated with more severe panic symptoms and greater self-reported fear while watching the film. Similar findings have been reported in clinical samples, such that individuals with panic disorder report greater use of experiential avoidance to manage their responses to negative films compared with healthy adults (Tull & Roemer, 2007). Moreover, avoidance begets avoidance. Following CO_2-enriched air administrations, individuals instructed to suppress their reactions were less willing to participate in future CO_2 administrations (Eifert & Heffner, 2003; Levitt et al., 2004). These findings suggest that individuals high in experiential avoidance are at increased risk of developing symptoms of anxiety and panic following experiences that induce the fear of physiological arousal. Given that individuals who suffer from panic disorder tend to be fearful of their own bodily sensations (Kämpfe et al., 2012), these findings suggest that overreliance on experiential avoidance may contribute to the development and maintenance of panic attacks and panic disorder.

In sum, preliminary evidence suggests that experiential avoidance is a risk factor for the development and maintenance of panic disorder. Experimental research, primarily using CO_2 administrations, suggests that experiential avoidance contributes to heightened sensitivity following uncomfortable physical sensations. We offer three future directions. First, research is needed to clarify the unique role of experiential avoidance beyond other known predictors of panic disorder. For example, there is a large body of work on panic disorder and anxiety sensitivity, and some research suggests that anxiety sensitivity is a stronger predictor of panic symptoms than experiential avoidance (Kämpfe et al., 2012; Kelly & Forsyth, 2009). Future research ought to measure experiential avoidance alongside related constructs to determine its unique contributions above and beyond known predictors. Second, there is a need for ecologically valid methodology to build on experimental and cross-sectional research. Most research in this area has been conducted by measuring responses to experimentally induced panic. Although there is evidence for the validity of this experimental approach (e.g., Rapee, Brown, Antony, & Barlow, 1992; Antony, Brown, & Barlow, 1997), panic attacks that are induced in a laboratory may not adequately capture a person's typical response pattern. Research using experience sampling methodology, for example, may offer additional insight into how and under what conditions experiential avoidance contributes to panic symptoms. Third, little is known about factors that motivate individuals to rely on experiential avoidance. There is evidence that people with panic disorder tend to interpret ambiguous bodily sensations (e.g., rapid heartbeat) as signs of impending harm (e.g., having a heart attack) to a greater extent than non-anxious individuals (Austin & Kiropoulos, 2008). This catastrophic interpretation of bodily sensations is associated with more severe panic disorder symptoms (Sandin, Sánchez-Arribas, Chorot, & Valiente, 2015). Further, these aversive interpretations of bodily sensations, along with a lack of confidence in one's ability to effectively cope with panic attacks, have been described as risk factors for developing panic disorder (Casey, Oei, & Newcombe, 2004). Both perceptions, independently or in combination, may motivate people to deploy experiential avoidance as they attempt to cope with panic attacks and their feared recurrence. Future research should investigate objective and subjective physiological experiences to clarify whether people's beliefs fuel experiential avoidance and consequently contribute to the development and maintenance of panic disorder.

Obsessive-Compulsive Disorder

Obsessions are persistent thoughts, images, or urges that induce an unwanted emotional state, such as anxiety or disgust. To reduce the negative emotions associated with obsessions, individuals with obsessive-compulsive disorder (OCD) often engage in compulsions. Such compulsions typically take the form of repetitive behaviors (e.g., handwashing) or mental acts (e.g., counting) and are performed according to self-imposed rules. In an effort to reduce distress, people with OCD try to avoid situations or stimuli that they believe will facilitate obsessive thoughts or compulsions. When obsessive thoughts arise, they try to ward them off with avoidant strategies. Whether an individual attempts to reduce their distress by avoiding triggers, suppressing their thoughts, or performing compulsive behaviors, such strategies may be conceptualized as attempts to avoid negative internal experiences. As such, experiential avoidance may be a relevant mechanism in OCD symptomatology.

Because individuals with OCD have difficulty managing their negative internal experiences, the distress caused by internal experiences associated with OCD, such as intrusive thoughts, may be exacerbated (Robinson & Freeston, 2014). This difficulty in managing internal experiences may result from an unwillingness to remain in contact with these internal experiences (i.e., experiential avoidance). Alternatively, such difficulties may arise because individuals are less able to endure these aversive states; they are low in distress tolerance (Robinson & Freeston, 2014). When controlling for anxiety and depression, distress tolerance failed to predict OCD symptoms above experiential avoidance (Blakey, Jacoby, Reuman, & Abramowitz, 2016). While greater experiential avoidance predicted increased obsessions when controlling for distress tolerance, experiential avoidance failed to predict compulsions. Thus, it appears that when controlling for distress tolerance, experiential avoidance is uniquely associated with the obsessive but not the compulsive symptoms of OCD. Because attempting to control or change negative internal experiences is thought to amplify OCD symptom severity (Abramowitz & Arch, 2014), the extent to which one relies on experiential avoidance should be a more robust risk factor for developing OCD than the inability to tolerate aversive states.

According to cognitive behavioral models, individuals with OCD possess dysfunctional beliefs about the thoughts and actions that maintain their symptoms. For example, individuals with OCD might believe that thinking about doing something immoral makes them a bad person, or that they bear an unrealistic amount of responsibility for preventing harm (Hezel & McNally, 2015). While one study found that individuals with greater use of experiential avoidance endorsed greater OCD symptoms, this effect disappeared after controlling dysfunctional beliefs and depression (Abramowitz, Lackey, & Wheaton, 2009). Conversely, beliefs that thoughts reflect one's true nature were associated with obsessions, and increased perfectionism/intolerance of uncertainty was associated with checking symptoms above depression and experiential avoidance. Another study found that following treatment, and when controlling for anxiety and depression, greater use of experiential avoidance failed to predict symptom reduction above dysfunctional beliefs, whereas decreased perfectionism/uncertainty predicted treatment gains above experiential avoidance (Manos et al., 2010). Thus, experiential avoidance may be too broad to predict OCD symptoms above dysfunctional beliefs, which are more specific to OCD symptoms.

Taken together, the small body of research on experiential avoidance in OCD thus far has yielded mixed findings. Some research suggests that greater use of experiential avoidance increases an individual's risk for developing OCD (Blakey et al., 2016; Briggs & Price, 2009). Other research suggests that greater use of experiential avoidance is unrelated to OCD symptoms (Abramowitz et al., 2009; Manos et al., 2010). Additional research is needed before substantive conclusions can be drawn. We offer two suggestions for future research in this area. First, past research has suggested that people with OCD are not interchangeable with respect to symptom profiles, but instead belong to various subtypes. Whereas some people with OCD have obsessions and compulsions pertaining to cleanliness and washing, others suffer from obsessions and compulsions related to symmetry concerns (McKay et al., 2004). It is possible that people belonging to different subtypes vary in their use of experiential avoidance. Additionally, if members of these subtypes vary in their reliance on experiential avoidance and this is a symptom maintenance factor, certain subtypes of OCD may respond differently to treatments that aim to reduce experiential avoidance. To date, the possibility that acceptance and commitment therapy (ACT) works better than traditional forms of cognitive behavioral therapy (CBT) for specific subgroups remains untested. Second, it is possible that the efficacy of exposure and ritual prevention, one of the most robust OCD treatments (Abramowitz, 1997), depends on the frequency/intensity/duration that experiential avoidance is used. In exposure and ritual prevention, people with OCD are exposed to anxiety-provoking stimuli and prevented from engaging in compulsions. It may be that the success of this treatment is dependent on whether patients are able to remain in contact with the anxiety-provoking situations and thoughts used in exposure. One might expect greater use of experiential avoidance during treatment to reduce treatment gains by inhibiting successful habituation to threat. Further, the use of experiential avoidance may be more detrimental to the success of particularly intense exposure and ritual prevention treatments, such as daily compared to biweekly treatments (Abramowitz, Foa, & Franklin, 2003).

Posttraumatic Stress Disorder

Posttraumatic stress disorder (PTSD) is characterized by the presence of trauma-related intrusive thoughts and flashbacks, avoidance of trauma-related stimuli, and changes in mood and arousal following a traumatic event. Many of these symptoms are negative internal experiences. As such, experiential avoidance may serve as a risk factor for developing PTSD if individuals habitually avoid trauma-related internal experiences. This avoidance could derive from one of two modes of thinking – fast, instinctive, and emotional, or slower, more deliberative, and logical (e.g., Metcalfe & Mischel, 1999). For example, individuals with PTSD often have distressing flashbacks and intrusive thoughts about their traumatic event. They often try to avoid reminders that may trigger uncomfortable memories or emotions about the event. Over time, triggers become widespread, in that an increasing number of stimuli trigger trauma-related responses. This further exacerbates avoidance and perpetuates the maladaptive belief that negative thoughts and feelings must be avoided to prevent distress.

In a meta-analysis of 57 studies, experiential avoidance was strongly and positively associated with PTSD symptom severity ($r = 0.40$). Experiential avoidance was more strongly related to PTSD symptoms than coping strategies such as suppression, worry, acceptance, and reappraisal (Seligowski, Lee, Bardeen, & Orcutt, 2015). In addition to overall PTSD symptom severity, experiential avoidance also uniquely predicts symptom clusters. In a study of undergraduate students with a history of trauma exposure, experiential avoidance was associated with a greater number of symptom clusters than suppression, acceptance, or reappraisal (Lee, Witte, Weathers, & Davis, 2015). Even after controlling for negative affect, experiential avoidance was positively associated with reexperiencing, emotional numbing, and anxious arousal symptom clusters. Similar results were found in a study of American veterans; experiential avoidance was positively associated with PTSD symptoms, and this relationship remained after controlling for trauma severity, perceived life threat, and negative emotionality (Meyer, Morissette, Kimbrel, Kruse, & Gulliver, 2013). This research offers strong evidence that experiential avoidance is positively associated with PTSD symptom severity, and that it captures unique variance in symptom severity and symptom clusters after taking into consideration other established predictors of PTSD.

Experiential avoidance makes it especially difficult for soldiers to reintegrate into civilian life. One study of combat veterans examined the effects of experiential avoidance on veterans' interactions with their spouses and children (Brockman et al., 2016). Veterans and their families came into the laboratory to participate in three structured tasks: problem-solving with their child, conversations with their child about redeployment, and problem-solving with their spouse about co-parenting. Researchers blind to study hypotheses watched each interaction and rated the degree to which veterans displayed responses characteristic of positive engagement (e.g., supportive, attentive), withdrawal (e.g., disinterested, passive), distress avoidance (e.g., fearful, wary), and reactivity or coercion (e.g., irritable, critical). When interacting with their spouses, veterans high in experiential avoidance demonstrated less positive engagement and more social withdrawal compared with veterans low in experiential avoidance. These relationships remained significant even when controlling for spouses' negative affect and behavior. When interacting with their children, veterans high in experiential avoidance demonstrated less positive engagement and more stress avoidance. Similar to interactions with their spouses, these relationships remained even after controlling for the children's negative affect and behavior. Constructive engagement with other people requires one to be attentive to the ongoing environment. When attention is focused on attempting to avoid or control thoughts, less cognitive resources remain to be actively engaged. Experiential avoidance, therefore, may serve as a risk factor for poor family reengagement after deployment.

A smaller, yet growing body of literature has examined the role of experiential avoidance in the development and course of PTSD following non-combat trauma. Across several types of trauma, cross-sectional research has found that experiential avoidance mediates the association between a history of trauma and the presence of trauma-related symptoms and distress. Among females with a history of sexual abuse (Marx & Sloan, 2002; Merwin, Rosenthal, & Coffey, 2009; Rosenthal, Hall, Palm, Batten, & Follette, 2005), as well as young adults with a history of childhood psychological abuse (Reddy, Pickett, & Orcutt, 2006), experiential avoidance mediated the effect of trauma on psychological distress. Among young adults with a history of interpersonal trauma, experiential avoidance mediated the effect of interpersonal trauma on PTSD symptoms (Orcutt, Pickett, & Pope, 2005). Among individuals with a history of interpersonal violence (i.e., physical assault, sexual assault, and/or assault with a weapon), experiential avoidance mediated the effect of trauma on aggressive behavior (Tull, Jakupcak, Paulson, & Gratz, 2007). These data provide converging support that experiential avoidance is a maladaptive process that accounts for the relationship between traumatic exposure and negative psychosocial outcomes.

Some studies have tested the directional relationship between experiential avoidance and maladaptive responses to trauma – with participants providing data before and after an event occurred. One study examined how students responded to a campus shooting (Reddy, Seligowski, Rabenhorst, & Orcutt, 2015). Experiential avoidance was measured shortly after the shooting and post-traumatic stress symptoms were measured approximately six months later. As expected, experiential avoidance was positively associated with subsequent symptoms. In a study of another campus shooting, experiential avoidance before the campus shooting predicted greater peri-traumatic dissociation (dissociative experiences such as an altered sense of time, disorientation, feeling that one's surroundings are not real), greater dysphoria (sleep disturbance, difficulties concentrating and remembering details of trauma, irritability, loss of interest, restricted affect, detachment, sense of foreshortened future), and more intrusive thoughts about the shooting after it occurred (Kumpula, Orcutt, Bardeen, & Varkovitzky,

2011). Eight months later, pre-trauma experiential avoidance still predicted greater dysphoria and hyperarousal.

Traumatic events can be extremely difficult to work through and make sense of. They often involve threat to one's life or safety. And yet, not all people develop PTSD afterward. Experiential avoidance appears to be one maladaptive response style that increases risk for developing PTSD following traumatic events. This effect appears to generalize to several types of trauma. The tendency to avoid aversive internal experiences following trauma may be a stronger determinant of subsequent PTSD symptoms than the characteristics of the trauma itself. We offer three suggestions for future research. First, research should continue to examine the interactive effects of experiential avoidance and known risk factors for PTSD. There is evidence suggesting experiential avoidance and other maladaptive response styles create toxic combinations, such that their co-occurrence is associated with greater impairment than either condition alone (e.g., behavioral inhibition sensitivity – Pickett, Bardeen, & Orcutt, 2011). Research that examines risk factors simultaneously (rather than studying constructs in isolation) offers a more accurate picture of how response styles exacerbate or attenuate one another. Second, research should examine the relationship between experiential avoidance and PTSD symptoms as they occur in real time. For example, daily diary methodology has been used to examine relationships between veterans' PTSD symptoms and everyday strivings (Kashdan, Breen, & Julian, 2010) and the effects of gratitude on their daily well-being (Kashdan, Uswatte, & Julian, 2006). Employing this sort of methodology in the context of experiential avoidance will clarify the conditions in which experiential avoidance influences PTSD symptoms and well-being. Third, to make a strong case for a causal effect of experiential avoidance on the development of PTSD, research is needed that capitalizes on pre-traumatic event data. The occurrence of traumatic events is unpredictable, but longitudinal researchers may be able to capitalize on existing data and planned follow-up data if large-scale traumatic events occur during the course of their data collection (e.g., death of a loved one – Bonanno et al., 2002; terrorist attack – Fredrickson, Tugade, Waugh, & Larkin, 2003).

Challenges and Future Directions for Experiential Avoidance Research: A Note on Measurement

Research thus far offers promise that understanding the complexities of experiential avoidance will help inform greater scientific knowledge on anxiety disorders. In this chapter, we offered specific suggestions for each disorder, ranging from exploring related content areas to designing experiments that assess the effects of experiential avoidance in situations specific to the disorder. We conclude this chapter by expanding on one future direction that can be applied to all anxiety disorders: measurement.

Experiential avoidance is most commonly measured with the Acceptance and Action Questionnaire (AAQ) (Hayes et al., 2004). This measure captures various aspects of experiential avoidance, including the negative evaluation of unwanted private events, attempts to control or get rid of unwanted private events, and behavioral responses to difficult thoughts. The AAQ has predicted a range of mental health and quality of life outcomes, even after controlling for other known risk factors of compromised well-being such as depression and negative affect (Bond & Bunce, 2003; Chawla & Ostafin, 2007; Hayes et al., 2006). Nonetheless, the AAQ has been criticized for unstable psychometric properties – namely low internal and test-retest reliability—and the complexity of item wording (Bond et al., 2011). Individuals unfamiliar with psychological terminology may have difficulty responding to items such as: "When I evaluate something negatively, I usually recognize that this is just a reaction, not an objective fact." Given these concerns, Bond and colleagues developed an updated version, the Acceptance and Action Questionnaire Version 2 (AAQ-II) (Bond et al., 2011), resulting in an improved seven-item measure with robust psychometric properties.

However, there has been confusion about what the AAQ-II actually measures. The AAQ-II has been criticized for having large overlap with broader trait-like constructs, namely negative affect and neuroticism. Correlations have been as high as 0.74 and 0.71, respectively (Gámez, Chmielewski, Kotov, Ruggero, & Watson, 2011). This lack of independence is problematic because conceptualizations of experiential avoidance are distinguishable from negative emotionality and neuroticism. Experiential avoidance describes a person's *relationship* with distress; it captures how they evaluate and respond to uncomfortable thoughts and feelings, rather than capturing actual thoughts and feelings. Thus, while we expect experiential avoidance to be positively correlated with distress, measurements of experiential avoidance should offer incremental predictive value.

Given the broad nature of experiential avoidance, it might be helpful for researchers to use measures that are specific to the context in which experiential avoidance is being studied. For example, variations of the AAQ have been created for contexts such as diabetes (Gregg, Callaghan, Hayes, & Glenn-Lawson, 2007), epilepsy (Lundgren, Dahl, & Hayes, 2008), cancer (Arch & Mitchell, 2016), body image (Sandoz, Wilson, Merwin, & Kellum, 2013), weight (Lillis & Hayes, 2008), food craving (Juarascio, Forman, Timko, Butryn, & Goodwin, 2011), auditory hallucinations (Shawyer et al., 2007), substance abuse (Luoma, Drake, Kohlenberg, & Hayes, 2011), social anxiety (MacKenzie & Kocovski, 2010), and work (Bond, Lloyd, & Guenole, 2013). Experiential avoidance can also be measured at the daily or momentary level. Kashdan and colleagues (2013) created a brief state measure of experiential avoidance (see also O'Toole, Jenson, Fentz, Zachariae, & Hougaard, 2014; Shahar & Herr, 2011). This four-item measure assesses how bothered individuals were by anxiety-related thoughts and feelings, how much they tried to hide, conceal, or control anxiety-related thoughts and feelings, and the extent to which they gave up valued activities in order to manage their anxiety. Importantly, factor analyses suggest that this measure is related to but distinct from state anxiety (Kashdan et al., 2014). This state measure has been used in daily diary studies, ecological momentary assessments, and experimental paradigms (Kashdan et al., 2013, 2014; Machell, Goodman, & Kashdan, 2015).

Researchers and practitioners might wonder where this risk factor underlying multiple anxiety disorders fits within the Research Domain Criteria (RDoC) framework. From genomics to self-reported mood, the RDoC integrates several levels of analysis to understand human behavior. Experiential avoidance is best conceptualized as a component of the Negative Valence system, which entails distressing experiences and reactions (e.g., anxiety, fear) to aversive situations. Within the Negative Valence system, experiential avoidance is most relevant to the Potential Threat construct (in which harm is viewed as highly probable and hypervigilance is instigated) and the Sustained Threat construct (in which people anticipate or are exposed to threatening stimuli for prolonged periods of time and have difficulty disengaging from the threat). Research thus far has primarily measured experiential avoidance with self-report questionnaires. Researchers can build on this empirical foundation to include behavioral measures and manipulations of experiential avoidance (e.g., Karekla et al., 2004; Feldner et al., 2003). It would also be helpful to compare experiential avoidance and similar constructs (e.g., anxiety sensitivity) on different response modalities (e.g., physiological) to determine if and how related constructs differentiate from one another. Studying experiential avoidance at multiple levels of analyses using frameworks like RDoC offers a broader understanding of the pathways to pathology.

Rigorous longitudinal studies are needed to examine what precedes the onset of experiential avoidance. Most research begins with experiential avoidance as an etiological factor. This leaves little information about what precedes experiential avoidance. Given that experiential avoidance is a transdiagnostic risk factor for anxiety disorders (and other mental illnesses), there is a need to identify experiences and vulnerabilities that lead to frequent and problematic use. How do aversive childhood experiences contribute to rigid patterns of avoidance? Which type of temperament and parenting styles interact to lead to the most problematic coping trajectories? Which genetic combinations confer greater risk? These questions can be answered with comprehensive analyses that examine temporal sequences of life events, individual dispositions, and underlying vulnerabilities. There appears little doubt that regular, intensive use of experiential avoidance amplifies the presence of anxiety and contributes to the development and severity of various conditions. The next stage of research will require the positioning of this risk factor among the network of rich, conceptual models of vulnerabilities and resiliencies in human development.

References

Abramowitz, J. S. (1997). Effectiveness of psychological and pharmacological treatments for obsessive-compulsive disorder: A quantitative review. *Journal of Consulting and Clinical Psychology, 65*, 44–52.

Abramowitz, J. S. & Arch, J. J. (2014). Strategies for improving long-term outcomes in cognitive behavioral therapy for obsessive-compulsive disorder: Insights from learning theory. *Cognitive and Behavioral Practice, 21*, 20–31.

Abramowitz, J. S., Foa, E. B., & Franklin, M. E. (2003). Exposure and ritual prevention for obsessive-compulsive disorder: Effects of intensive versus twice-weekly sessions. *Journal of Consulting and Clinical Psychology, 71*, 394–398.

Abramowitz, J. S., Lackey, G. R., & Wheaton, M. G. (2009). Obsessive-compulsive symptoms: The contribution of obsessional beliefs and experiential avoidance. *Journal of Anxiety Disorders, 23*, 160–166.

Antony, M. M., Brown, T. A., & Barlow, D. H. (1997). Response to hyperventilation and 5.5% CO_2 inhalation of subjects with types of specific phobia, panic disorder, or no mental disorder. *American Journal of Psychiatry, 154*, 1089–1095.

Arch, J. & Mitchell, J. (2016). An acceptance and commitment therapy (ACT) group intervention for cancer survivors experiencing anxiety at re-entry. *Psycho-Oncology, 25*, 610–615.

Austin, D. & Kiropoulos, L. (2008). An Internet-based investigation of the catastrophic misinterpretation model of panic disorder. *Journal of Anxiety Disorders, 22*, 233–242.

Baker, R., Holloway, J., Thomas, P. W., Thomas, S., & Owens, M. (2004). Emotional processing and panic. *Behaviour Research and Therapy, 42*, 1271–1287.

Baumeister, R. F., Gailliot, M., DeWall, C. N., & Oaten, M. (2006). Self-regulation and personality: How interventions increase regulatory success, and how depletion moderates the effects of traits on behavior. *Journal of Personality, 74*, 1773–1802.

Berman, N. C., Wheaton, M. G., McGrath, P., & Abramowitz, J. S. (2010). Predicting anxiety: The role of experiential avoidance and anxiety sensitivity. *Journal of Anxiety Disorders, 24*, 109–113.

Blakey, S. M., Jacoby, R. J., Reuman, L., & Abramowitz, J. S. (2016). The relative contributions of experiential avoidance and distress tolerance to OC symptoms. *Behavioural and Cognitive Psychotherapy, 44*, 460–471.

Bonanno, G. A., Wortman, C. B., Lehman, D. R., Tweed, R. G., Haring, M., Sonnega, J., . . . & Nesse, R. M. (2002). Resilience to loss and chronic grief: A prospective study from preloss to 18-months postloss. *Journal of Personality and Social Psychology, 83*, 1150–1164.

Bond, F. W. & Bunce, D. (2003). The role of acceptance and job control in mental health, job satisfaction, and work performance. *Journal of Applied Psychology, 88*, 1057–1067.

Bond, F. W., Hayes, S. C., Baer, R. A., Carpenter, K. M., Guenole, N., Orcutt, H. K., Waltz, T., & Zettle, R. D. (2011). Preliminary psychometric properties of the Acceptance and Action Questionnaire – II: A revised measure of psychological flexibility and experiential avoidance. *Behavior Therapy, 42*, 676–688.

Bond, F. W., Lloyd, J., & Guenole, N. (2013). The work-related acceptance and action questionnaire: Initial psychometric findings and their implications for measuring psychological flexibility in specific contexts. *Journal of Occupational and Organizational Psychology, 86*, 331–347.

Borkovec, T. D., Alcaine, O., & Behar, E. (2004). Avoidance theory of worry and generalized anxiety disorder. In R. G. Heimberg, C. L. Turk, & D. S. Mennin (eds.), *Generalized Anxiety Disorder: Advances in Research and Practice* (77–108). New York, NY: Guilford Press.

Borkovec, T. D. & Roemer, L. (1995). Perceived functions of worry among generalized anxiety disorder subjects: Distraction from more emotionally distressing topics?. *Journal of Behavior Therapy and Experimental Psychiatry, 26*, 25–30.

Bouton, M. E., Mineka, S., & Barlow, D. H. (2001). A modern learning theory perspective on the etiology of panic disorder. *Psychological Review, 108*, 4–32.

Breen, W. E. & Kashdan, T. B. (2011). Anger suppression after imagined rejection among individuals with social anxiety. *Journal of Anxiety Disorders, 25*, 879–887.

Briggs, E. S. & Price, I. R. (2009). The relationship between adverse childhood experience and obsessive-compulsive symptoms and beliefs: The role of anxiety, depression, and experiential avoidance. *Journal of Anxiety Disorders, 23*, 1037–1046.

Brockman, C., Snyder, J., Gewirtz, A., Gird, S. R., Quattlebaum, J., Schmidt, N., ... & Zettle, R. (2016). Relationship of service members' deployment trauma, PTSD symptoms, and experiential avoidance to postdeployment family reengagement. *Journal of Family Psychology, 30*, 52–62.

Brown, T. A., Barlow, D. H., & Liebowitz, M. R. (1994). The empirical basis of generalized anxiety disorder. *American Journal of Psychiatry, 151*, 1272–1280.

Buhr, K. & Dugas, M. J. (2012). Fear of emotions, experiential avoidance, and intolerance of uncertainty in worry and generalized anxiety disorder. *International Journal of Cognitive Therapy, 5*, 1–17.

Casey, L. M., Oei, T. P., & Newcombe, P. A. (2004). An integrated cognitive model of panic disorder: The role of positive and negative cognitions. *Clinical Psychology Review, 24*, 529–555.

Cassidy, J., Lichtenstein-Phelps, J., Sibrava, N. J., Thomas, C. L., & Borkovec, T. D. (2009). Generalized anxiety disorder: Connections with self-reported attachment. *Behavior Therapy, 40*, 23–38.

Chawla, N. & Ostafin, B. (2007). Experiential avoidance as a functional dimensional approach to psychopathology: An empirical review. *Journal of Clinical Psychology, 63*, 871–890.

Crouch, T. A., Lewis, J. A., Erickson, T. M., & Newman, M. G. (2017). Prospective investigation of the contrast avoidance model of generalized anxiety and worry. *Behavior Therapy, 48*, 544–556.

De Castella, K., Goldin, P., Jazaieri, H., Ziv, M., Heimberg, R. G., & Gross, J. J. (2014). Emotion beliefs in social anxiety disorder: Associations with stress, anxiety, and well-being. *Australian Journal of Psychology, 66*, 139–148.

Dugas, M. J., Gagnon, F., Ladouceur, R., & Freeston, M. H. (1998). Generalized anxiety disorder: A preliminary test of a conceptual model. *Behaviour Research and Therapy, 36*, 215–226.

Dugas, M. J., Marchand, A., & Ladouceur, R. (2005). Further validation of a cognitive-behavioral model of generalized anxiety disorder: Diagnostic and symptom specificity. *Journal of Anxiety Disorders, 19*, 329–343.

Eifert, G. H. & Heffner, M. (2003). The effects of acceptance versus control contexts on avoidance of panic-related symptoms. *Journal of Behavior Therapy and Experimental Psychiatry*, *34*, 293–312.

Feldner, M. T., Zvolensky, M. J., Eifert, G. H., & Spira, A. P. (2003). Emotional avoidance: An experimental test of individual differences and response suppression using biological challenge. *Behaviour Research and Therapy*, *41*, 403–411.

Fredrickson, B. L., Tugade, M. M., Waugh, C. E., & Larkin, G. R. (2003). What good are positive emotions in crisis? A prospective study of resilience and emotions following the terrorist attacks on the United States on September 11th, 2001. *Journal of Personality and Social Psychology*, *84*, 365–376.

Gámez, W., Chmielewski, M., Kotov, R., Ruggero, C., & Watson, D. (2011). Development of a measure of experiential avoidance: The Multidimensional Experiential Avoidance Questionnaire. *Psychological Assessment*, *23*, 692–713.

Gregg, J. A., Callaghan, G. M., Hayes, S. C., & Glenn-Lawson, J. L. (2007). Improving diabetes self-management through acceptance, mindfulness, and values: A randomized controlled trial. *Journal of Consulting and Clinical Psychology*, *75*, 336–343.

Haxhe, S. (2016). Parentification and related processes: Distinction and implications for clinical practice. *Journal of Family Psychotherapy*, *27*, 185–199.

Hayes, S. C., Luoma, J. B., Bond F. W., Masuda, A., & Lillis, J. (2006). Acceptance and commitment therapy: Model, processes and outcomes. *Behaviour Research and Therapy*, *44*, 1–25.

Hayes, S. C., Strosahl, K. D., & Wilson, K. G. (1999). *Acceptance and Commitment Therapy: An Experiential Approach to Behavior Change*. New York, NY: Guilford Press.

Hayes, S. C., Strosahl, K., Wilson, K. G., Bissett, R. T., Pistorello, J., Toarmino, D., ... Stewart, S. H. (2004). Measuring experiential avoidance: A preliminary test of a working model. *Psychological Record*, *54*, 553–578.

Hayes, S. C., Wilson, K. G., Gifford, E. V., Follette, V. M., & Strosahl, K. (1996). Experiential avoidance and behavioral disorders: A functional dimensional approach to diagnosis and treatment. *Journal of Consulting and Clinical Psychology*, *64*, 1152–1168.

Hezel, D. M. & McNally, R. J. (2015). A theoretical review of cognitive biases and deficits in obsessive-compulsive disorder. *Biological Psychology*, *121*, 221–232.

Hoehn-Saric, R., Lee, J. S., McLeod, D. R., & Wong, D. F. (2005). Effect of worry on regional cerebral blood flow in nonanxious subjects. *Psychiatry Research: Neuroimaging*, *140*, 259–269.

Juarascio, A., Forman, E., Timko, C. A., Butryn, M., & Goodwin, C. (2011). The development and validation of the food craving acceptance and action questionnaire (FAAQ). *Eating Behaviors*, *12*, 182–187.

Kämpfe, C. K., Gloster, A. T., Wittchen, H. U., Helbig-Lang, S., Lang, T., Gerlach, A. L., ... Hamm, A. O. (2012). Experiential avoidance and anxiety sensitivity in patients with panic disorder and agoraphobia: Do both constructs measure the same? *International Journal of Clinical and Health Psychology*, *12*, 5–22.

Kashdan, T. B., Barrios, V., Forsyth, J. P., & Steger, M. F. (2006). Experiential avoidance as a generalized psychological vulnerability: Comparisons with coping and emotion regulation strategies. *Behaviour Research and Therapy*, *44*, 1301–1320.

Kashdan, T. B., Breen, W. E., & Julian, T. (2010). Everyday strivings in war veterans with posttraumatic stress disorder: Suffering from a hyper-focus on avoidance and emotion regulation. *Behavior Therapy, 41*, 350–363.

Kashdan, T. B., Farmer, A. S., Adams, L. M., Ferssizidis, P., McKnight, P. E., & Nezlek, J. B. (2013). Distinguishing healthy adults from people with social anxiety disorder: Evidence for the value of experiential avoidance and positive emotions in everyday social interactions. *Journal of Abnormal Psychology, 122*, 645–655.

Kashdan, T. B., Goodman, F. R., Machell, K. A., Kleiman, E. M., Monfort, S. S., Ciarrochi, J., & Nezlek, J. B. (2014). A contextual approach to experiential avoidance and social anxiety: Evidence from an experimental interaction and daily interactions of people with social anxiety disorder. *Emotion, 14*, 769–781.

Kashdan, T. B., Morina, N., & Priebe, S. (2009). Posttraumatic stress disorder, social anxiety disorder, and depression in survivors of the Kosovo war: Experiential avoidance as a contributor to distress and quality of life. *Journal of Anxiety Disorders, 23*, 185–196.

Kashdan, T. B. & Rottenberg, J. (2010). Psychological flexibility as a fundamental aspect of health. *Clinical Psychology Review, 30*, 865–878.

Kashdan, T. B. & Steger, M. F. (2006). Expanding the topography of social anxiety: An experience-sampling assessment of positive emotions, positive events, and emotion suppression. *Psychological Science, 17*, 120–128.

Kashdan, T. B., Uswatte, G., & Julian, T. (2006). Gratitude and hedonic and eudaimonic well-being in Vietnam war veterans. *Behaviour Research and Therapy, 44*, 177–199.

Kashdan, T. B., Weeks, J. W., & Savostyanova, A. A. (2011). Whether, how, and when social anxiety shapes positive experiences and events: A self-regulatory framework and treatment implications. *Clinical Psychology Review, 31*, 786–799.

Karekla, M., Forsyth, J. P., & Kelly, M. M. (2004). Emotional avoidance and panicogenic responding to a biological challenge procedure. *Behavior Therapy, 35*, 725–746.

Kelly, M. M. & Forsyth, J. P. (2007a). Observational fear conditioning in the acquisition and extinction of attentional bias for threat: An experimental evaluation. *Emotion, 7*, 324–335.

Kelly, M. M. & Forsyth, J. P. (2007b). Sex differences in response to an observational fear conditioning procedure. *Behavior Therapy, 38*, 340–349.

Kelly, M. M. & Forsyth, J. P. (2009). Associations between emotional avoidance, anxiety sensitivity, and reactions to an observational fear challenge procedure. *Behaviour Research and Therapy, 47*, 331–338.

Kumpula, M. J., Orcutt, H. K., Bardeen, J. R., & Varkovitzky, R. L. (2011). Peritraumatic dissociation and experiential avoidance as prospective predictors of posttraumatic stress symptoms. *Journal of Abnormal Psychology, 120*, 617–627.

Lee, J. K., Orsillo, S. M., Roemer, L., & Allen, L. B. (2010). Distress and avoidance in generalized anxiety disorder: Exploring the relationships with intolerance of uncertainty and worry. *Cognitive Behaviour Therapy, 39*, 126–136.

Lee, D. J., Witte, T. K., Weathers, F. W., & Davis, M. T. (2015). Emotion regulation strategy use and posttraumatic stress disorder: Associations between multiple strategies and specific symptom clusters. *Journal of Psychopathology and Behavioral Assessment, 37*, 533–544.

Levin, M. E., Haeger, J., & Smith, G. S. (2017). Examining the role of implicit emotional judgments in social anxiety and experiential avoidance. *Journal of Psychopathology and Behavioral Assessment, 39*, 264–278.

Levitt, J. T., Brown, T. A., Orsillo, S. M., & Barlow, D. H. (2004). The effects of acceptance versus suppression of emotion on subjective and psychophysiological response to carbon dioxide challenge in patients with panic disorder. *Behavior Therapy, 35*, 747–766.

Lillis, J. & Hayes, S. C. (2008). Measuring avoidance and inflexibility in weight related problems. *International Journal of Behavioral Consultation and Therapy, 4*, 348–354.

Llera, S. J. & Newman, M. G. (2010). Effects of worry on physiological and subjective reactivity to emotional stimuli in generalized anxiety disorder and nonanxious control participants. *Emotion, 10*, 640–650.

Llera, S. J. & Newman, M. G. (2014). Rethinking the role of worry in generalized anxiety disorder: Evidence supporting a model of emotional contrast avoidance. *Behavior Therapy, 45*, 283–299.

Lundgren, T., Dahl, J., & Hayes, S. C. (2008). Evaluation of mediators of change in the treatment of epilepsy with acceptance and commitment therapy. *Journal of Behavioral Medicine, 31*, 225–235.

Luoma, J., Drake, C. E., Kohlenberg, B. S., & Hayes, S. C. (2011). Substance abuse and psychological flexibility: The development of a new measure. *Addiction Research & Theory, 19*, 3–13.

Machell, K. A., Goodman, F. R., & Kashdan, T. B. (2015). Experiential avoidance and well-being: A daily diary analysis. *Cognition and Emotion, 29*, 351–359.

MacKenzie, M. B. & Kocovski, N. L. (2010). Self-reported acceptance of social anxiety symptoms: Development and validation of the Social Anxiety – Acceptance and Action Questionnaire. *International Journal of Behavioral Consultation and Therapy, 6*, 214–232.

Manos, R. C., Cahill, S. P., Wetterneck, C. T., Conelea, C. A., Ross, A. R., & Riemann, B. C. (2010). The impact of experiential avoidance and obsessive beliefs on obsessive-compulsive symptoms in a severe clinical sample. *Journal of Anxiety Disorders, 24*, 700–708.

Marx, B. P. & Sloan, D. M. (2002). The role of emotion in the psychological functioning of adult survivors of childhood sexual abuse. *Behavior Therapy, 33*, 563–577.

McKay, D., Abramowitz, J. S., Calamari, J. E., Kyrios, M., Radomsky, A., Sookman, D., Taylor, S., & Wilhelm, S. (2004). A critical evaluation of obsessive-compulsive disorder subtypes: Symptoms versus mechanisms. *Clinical Psychology Review, 24*, 283–313.

Merwin, R. M., Rosenthal, M. Z., & Coffey, K. A. (2009). Experiential avoidance mediates the relationship between sexual victimization and psychological symptoms: Replicating findings with an ethnically diverse sample. *Cognitive Therapy and Research, 33*, 537–542.

Metcalfe, J. & Mischel, W. (1999). A hot/cool-system analysis of delay of gratification: Dynamics of willpower. *Psychological Review, 106*, 3–19.

Meyer, E. C., Morissette, S. B., Kimbrel, N. A., Kruse, M. I., & Gulliver, S. B. (2013). Acceptance and Action Questionnaire – II scores as a predictor of posttraumatic stress disorder symptoms among war veterans. *Psychological Trauma: Theory, Research, Practice, and Policy, 5*, 521–528.

Moscovitch, D. A. (2009). What is the core fear in social phobia? A new model to facilitate individualized case conceptualization and treatment. *Cognitive and Behavioral Practice*, *16*, 123–134.

Moscovitch, D. A., Rowa, K., Paulitzki, J. R., Ierullo, M. D., Chiang, B., Antony, M. M., & McCabe, R. E. (2013). Self-portrayal concerns and their relation to safety behaviors and negative affect in social anxiety disorder. *Behaviour Research and Therapy*, *51*, 476–486.

Muraven, M. & Baumeister, R. F. (2000). Self-regulation and depletion of limited resources: Does self-control resemble a muscle? *Psychological Bulletin*, *126*, 247–259.

Newman, M. G. & Llera, S. J. (2011). A novel theory of experiential avoidance in generalized anxiety disorder: A review and synthesis of research supporting a contrast avoidance model of worry. *Clinical Psychology Review*, *31*, 371–382.

Orcutt, H. K., Pickett, S. M., & Pope, E. B. (2005). Experiential avoidance and forgiveness as mediators in the relation between traumatic interpersonal events and posttraumatic stress disorder symptoms. *Journal of Social and Clinical Psychology*, *24*, 1003–1029.

O'Toole, M. S., Jensen, M. B., Fentz, H. N., Zachariae, R., & Hougaard, E. (2014). Emotion differentiation and emotion regulation in high and low socially anxious individuals: An experience-sampling study. *Cognitive Therapy and Research*, *38*, 428–438.

Panayiotou, G., Karekla, M., & Mete, I. (2014). Dispositional coping in individuals with anxiety disorder symptomatology: Avoidance predicts distress. *Journal of Contextual Behavioral Science*, *3*, 314–321.

Pickett, S. M., Bardeen, J. R., & Orcutt, H. K. (2011). Experiential avoidance as a moderator of the relationship between behavioral inhibition system sensitivity and posttraumatic stress symptoms. *Journal of Anxiety Disorders*, *25*, 1038–1045.

Pickett, S. M. & Kurby, C. A. (2010). The impact of experiential avoidance on the inference of characters' emotions: Evidence for an emotional processing bias. *Cognitive Therapy and Research*, *34*, 493–500.

Plasencia, M. L., Alden, L. E., & Taylor, C. T. (2011). Differential effects of safety behaviour subtypes in social anxiety disorder. *Behaviour Research and Therapy*, *49*, 665–675.

Rapee, R. M., Brown, T. A., Antony, M. M., & Barlow, D. H. (1992). Response to hyperventilation and inhalation of 5.5% carbon dioxide-enriched air across the DSM-III – R anxiety disorders. *Journal of Abnormal Psychology*, *101*, 538–552.

Reddy, M. K., Pickett, S. M., & Orcutt, H. K. (2006). Experiential avoidance as a mediator in the relationship between childhood psychological abuse and current mental health symptoms in college students. *Journal of Emotional Abuse*, *6*, 67–85.

Reddy, M. K., Seligowski, A. V., Rabenhorst, M. M., & Orcutt, H. K. (2015). Predictors of expressive writing content and posttraumatic stress following a mass shooting. *Psychological Trauma: Theory, Research, Practice, and Policy*, *7*, 286–294.

Robinson, L. J. & Freeston, M. H. (2014). Emotion and internal experience in obsessive compulsive disorder: Reviewing the role of alexithymia, anxiety sensitivity and distress tolerance. *Clinical Psychology Review*, *34*, 256–271.

Rodebaugh, T. L. & Heimberg, R. G. (2008). Measurement of ambivalent and purposeful engagement after aversive social experiences. *Journal of Anxiety Disorders*, *22*, 693–706.

Roemer, L., Molina, S., & Borkovec, T. D. (1997). An investigation of worry content among generally anxious individuals. *Journal of Nervous and Mental Disease, 185,* 314–319.

Rosenthal, M. Z., Hall, M. L. R., Palm, K. M., Batten, S. V., & Follette, V. M. (2005). Chronic avoidance helps explain the relationship between severity of childhood sexual abuse and psychological distress in adulthood. *Journal of Child Sexual Abuse, 14,* 25–41.

Sandin, B., Sánchez-Arribas, C., Chorot, P., & Valiente, R. M. (2015). Anxiety sensitivity, catastrophic misinterpretations and panic self-efficacy in the prediction of panic disorder severity: Towards a tripartite cognitive model of panic disorder. *Behaviour Research and Therapy, 67,* 30–40.

Sandoz, E. K., Wilson, K. G., Merwin, R. M., & Kellum, K. K. (2013). Assessment of body image flexibility: The body image-acceptance and action questionnaire. *Journal of Contextual Behavioral Science, 2,* 39–48.

Seligowski, A. V., Lee, D. J., Bardeen, J. R., & Orcutt, H. K. (2015). Emotion regulation and posttraumatic stress symptoms: A meta-analysis. *Cognitive Behaviour Therapy, 44,* 87–102.

Shahar, B. & Herr, N. R. (2011). Depressive symptoms predict inflexibly high levels of experiential avoidance in response to daily negative affect: A daily diary study. *Behaviour Research and Therapy, 49,* 676–681.

Shawyer, F., Ratcliff, K., Mackinnon, A., Farhall, J., Hayes, S. C., & Copolov, D. (2007). The voices acceptance and action scale (VAAS): Pilot data. *Journal of Clinical Psychology, 63,* 593–606.

Skodzik, T., Zettler, T., Topper, M., Blechert, J., & Ehring, T. (2016). The effect of verbal and imagery-based worry versus distraction on the emotional response to a stressful in-vivo situation. *Journal of Behavior Therapy and Experimental Psychiatry, 52,* 51–58.

Spinhoven, P., Drost, J., de Rooij, M., van Hemert, A. M., & Penninx, B. W. (2014). A longitudinal study of experiential avoidance in emotional disorders. *Behavior Therapy, 45,* 840–850.

Tamir, M., John, O. P., Srivastava, S., & Gross, J. J. (2007). Implicit theories of emotion: Affective and social outcomes across a major life transition. *Journal of Personality and Social Psychology, 92,* 731–744.

Tangney, J. P., Baumeister, R. F., & Boone, A. L. (2004). High self-control predicts good adjustment, less pathology, better grades, and interpersonal success. *Journal of Personality, 72,* 271–324.

Tull, M. T., Jakupcak, M., Paulson, A., & Gratz, K. L. (2007). The role of emotional inexpressivity and experiential avoidance in the relationship between posttraumatic stress disorder symptom severity and aggressive behavior among men exposed to interpersonal violence. *Anxiety, Stress, and Coping, 20,* 337–351.

Tull, M. T. & Roemer, L. (2007). Emotion regulation difficulties associated with the experience of uncued panic attacks: Evidence of experiential avoidance, emotional non-acceptance, and decreased emotional clarity. *Behavior Therapy, 38,* 378–391.

Venta, A., Sharp, C., & Hart, J. (2012). The relation between anxiety disorder and experiential avoidance in inpatient adolescents. *Psychological Assessment, 24,* 240–248.

Viana, A. G. & Rabian, B. (2008). Perceived attachment: Relations to anxiety sensitivity, worry, and GAD symptoms. *Behaviour Research and Therapy, 46,* 737–747.

Vohs, K. D., Baumeister, R. F., & Ciarocco, N. J. (2005). Self-regulation and self-presentation: Regulatory resource depletion impairs impression management and effortful self-presentation depletes regulatory resources. *Journal of Personality and Social Psychology, 88*, 632–657.

Wegner, D. M. (1994). Ironic processes of mental control. *Psychological Review, 101*, 34–52.

10 Emotion Regulation

Katya C. Fernandez, Amanda S. Morrison,
and James J. Gross

Historically, psychopathology has been conceptualized in categorical terms. The underlying assumption has been that psychopathology naturally manifests as distinct clusters of signs and symptoms. Relatively recently, however, a growing body of research has brought to the fore the notion that many of these clusters of signs and symptoms are in fact correlated, and that common factors may underlie various forms of psychopathology. This has given rise to transdiagnostic theory, which aims to elucidate *transdiagnostic factors*, or processes and constructs that play a role in the onset and/or maintenance of various forms of psychopathology.

Transdiagnostic theory has sought to identify specific constructs relevant to certain families of disorders (e.g., transdiagnostic factors across the anxiety disorders). Constructs such as negative and positive affect (e.g., Brown, Chorpita, & Barlow, 1998; Clark & Watson, 1991), neuroticism (e.g., Barlow, Sauer-Zavala, Carl, Bullis, & Ellard, 2014; Rosellini & Brown, 2011), and experiential avoidance (e.g., Chawla & Ostafin, 2007; Spinhoven, Drost, de Rooij, van Hemert, & Penninx, 2014) are examples that have emerged as part of this theory and that have been studied within the anxiety disorders. However, this search for transdiagnostic constructs relevant to different families of disorders has resulted in a relatively unorganized list of constructs and processes that span disorders both within diagnostic clusters (e.g., anxiety disorders) and across clusters (e.g., anxiety and depressive disorders). One important element lacking in transdiagnostic theory is a unifying framework for understanding how all of these constructs and processes interact with each other to give rise to psychopathology.

To provide such a unifying framework, the National Institute of Mental Health (NIMH) created the Research Domain Criteria (RDoC) (Insel et al., 2010). The RDoC is grounded in a matrix that includes five overarching domains: negative valence systems (e.g., threat, loss), positive valence systems (e.g., approach motivation, reward learning), cognitive systems (e.g., attention, perception, memory), systems for social processes (e.g., social communication, perception and understanding of self and others), and arousal and regulatory systems (e.g., sleep-wake, cardiac activity). Unfortunately, RDoC's domain structure does not specify how these constructs interact to produce different types of psychopathology. To address this limitation, we have argued that it may be useful to supplement the five RDoC domains with additional domains that represent the dynamic interactions among the existing domains. More specifically, we have suggested that the construct of emotion regulation – a transdiagnostic process – might be a sixth RDoC domain that emerges as the result of patterns of interaction among the five existing RDoC domains (Fernandez, Jazaieri, & Gross, 2016). In the current chapter, we apply this unifying framework to a specific cluster of disorders as a preliminary step in exploring its implementation. We begin by considering emotion generation processes and problems, then turn to emotion regulation processes and problems. Next, we consider emotion regulation as a transdiagnostic process that involves interactions among RDoC domains, and examine the role of emotion regulation in anxiety disorders. We conclude by considering the broader clinical implications of this view.

Emotion Generation Processes and Problems

Emotions are responses to important challenges and opportunities, and they involve loosely coordinated changes in subjective experience, behavior, and physiological responding (Mauss, Levenson, McCarter, Wilhelm, & Gross, 2005). When characterizing emotions, it's important to note that they can differ on a number of dimensions, including their intensity, duration, frequency, and type. Understanding variation within and across these dimensions is necessary for understanding the role of affective processes in psychopathology. Notably, variation within and across these dimensions may be attributable to problems with either the emotion generation process or the emotion regulation process.

Emotion Generation Processes

One conceptualization proposes that emotion generation is a four-step process, whereby the following occur: (1) encountering an emotionally relevant situation, (2) directing attention toward the situation, (3) evaluating and interpreting the situation, and (4) manifesting a loosely coupled set of experiential, behavioral, and physiological responses (Gross & Jazaieri, 2014; Figure 10.1A). An often-overlooked point when discussing emotion problems is that difficulties with the emotion generation process do not necessarily mean that there are difficulties with emotion regulation. For example, an individual may report intense and problematic negative emotions, such as anger, but this emotion problem may be the result of high levels of reactivity rather than any deficit with emotion regulation.

Emotion Generation Problems

In the sections that follow, we begin by reviewing ways in which individuals can experience problematic emotional responding. More specifically, we review problems in emotion generation, including problems in emotion intensity, emotion duration, emotion frequency, and emotion quality. We then more formally introduce the construct of emotion regulation and discuss the ways in which

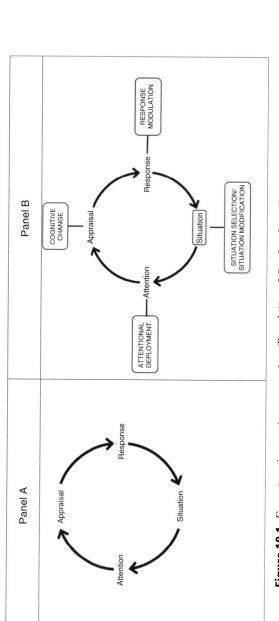

Figure 10.1 *Four steps in emotion generation (Panel A) and five families of emotion-regulatory processes that are defined by their primary impact on the emotion-generative process (Panel B). Taken from (Gross, 2015a).*

emotion regulation can serve as a framework for understanding transdiagnostic processes, with a focus on anxiety disorders.

Problems with emotion intensity. Problematic emotion intensity can take the form of either hyperreactivity (i.e., overreaction) or hyporeactivity (i.e., under-reaction) to a situation. In the case of hyperreactivity, an individual may experience greater intensity of a given emotion than desired, whereas in the case of hyporeactivity, an individual may experience a less-than-appropriate emotion intensity.

In the case of anxiety disorders, problems with emotion intensity often take the form of hyperreactivity. For example, Mennin and colleagues (2009) found that individuals with generalized anxiety disorder (GAD) had greater intensity negative emotions than individuals with social anxiety disorder (SAD) and non-anxious controls (individuals with SAD also differed from non-anxious controls). Hyperreactivity of fear and panic is evident in panic disorder (PD) and is exemplified in the Diagnostic and Statistical Manual of Mental Disorder's (American Psychiatric Association, 2013) definition of a panic attack as "an abrupt surge of intense fear or intense discomfort that reaches a peak within minutes" (p. 208). In addition to panic, which often includes feelings of unreality coupled with distressing physical sensations such as palpitations, sweating, and trembling, individuals with PD may report fearing extreme negative outcomes, such as losing control or going crazy, having a serious medical condition, or dying.

Problems with emotion duration. As with emotion intensity, problems with emotion duration can take the form of emotions occurring for either too long or not long enough for a given situation. For example, the key feature of GAD is the experience of excessive, uncontrollable anxiety about a variety of issues, typically uncertain or potentially negative future outcomes. One study found that individuals with GAD report a lower ability to repair mood, as assessed by the mood repair subscale of the Trait Meta-Mood Scale (Salovey, Mayer, Goldman, Turvey, & Palfai, 1995), than controls; more specifically, they were less able to return to baseline in terms of emotion state once they were experiencing a negative mood (Mennin, Heimberg, Turk, & Fresco, 2005). Problems with emotion duration also can take the form of experiencing emotions too briefly. A relevant construct to the anxiety disorders is the concept of dampening of positive affect, or the tendency to diminish a positive emotion experience. In terms of emotion duration, this suggests that individuals who tend to dampen positive affect will experience positive affect for a shorter duration than those who do not dampen. Eisner and colleagues (2009) examined the presence of dampening across the anxiety disorders in an undergraduate sample and found that, even after controlling for lifetime depressive symptoms, dampening of positive affect was related to PD, SAD, and GAD symptoms.

Problems with emotion frequency. Problems with emotion frequency can take the form of emotions occurring too frequently or too infrequently. Variations in these two characterizations of emotions can be assessed at the trait level (e.g., an individual reports greater frequencies of emotion on average) or at the state level (e. g., an individual may report average levels of trait emotion frequency overall but then show greater frequency when the emotion is assessed at the state level). An example of problematic emotion frequency is PD, where a part of the diagnostic criteria is that an individual experiences panic attacks recurrently. For example, one study found that reported panic attacks ranged from 1 to 12 panic attacks during a two-week period in individuals meeting criteria for PD with agoraphobia (De Beurs, Chambless, & Goldstein, 1997).

Problems with emotion quality. Finally, problematic emotion quality refers to the experience of a type of emotion that is inappropriate for the given context. For example, within the context of SAD, a phenomenon known as fear of positive evaluation (Weeks, Heimberg, Rodebaugh, & Norton, 2008) may serve as an example of a problem with emotion quality. This phenomenon describes the process whereby individuals with SAD tend to respond to praise or compliments with fear and anxiety, possibly because such praise may seem to create an expectation for future performance that the individual fears he or she may not meet. Though perhaps not detrimental in isolation, a chronic pattern of responding to positive stimuli negatively may help explain the increasing body of literature highlighting the relationship between social anxiety and diminished positive experiences (Kashdan, 2007). Within the context of PD, a core feature of panic attacks is that they occur unexpectedly (i.e., in situations where a panic response would normally not be warranted). Individuals with PD may experience panic attacks when confronting a neutral or even positive stimulus (e.g., when feeling relaxed). This asynchronous panic response to a non-panic stimulus could, in a sense, also be considered a problem with emotion quality.

Emotion Regulation Processes and Problems

Emotion regulation refers to efforts to influence which emotions one has, when one has them, or how these emotions are experienced or expressed (Gross, 1998, 2015a, 2015b; Gross & Jazaieri, 2014; Gross, Sheppes, & Urry, 2011). According to the process model (Gross, 1998), five families of emotion regulation processes may be distinguished based on where they have their primary impact on emotion generation (see Figure 10.1B): situation selection, situation modification, attentional deployment, cognitive change, and response modulation.

Emotion Regulation Strategies and Stages

Situation selection refers to the process of selecting a situation with the goal of modifying the type or intensity of emotion one will likely have (e.g., an individual with SAD may choose to avoid going to a party based on a desire to avoid the anxiety that is expected to be aroused by attending the party). *Situation modification* refers to efforts to modify specific aspects of a situation in order to influence the emotions that are experienced (e.g., an individual may choose to attend a party, but then isolate himself rather than interact due to fear of rejection). *Attentional deployment* refers to the selection of a specific aspect of a situation to which an individual will attend, with a view to modifying his emotions (e.g., an anxious individual may elect to focus his attention on the movie being played on the TV at the party so as to not focus attention on other people at the party). *Cognitive change* refers to changing the way one thinks about one's situation with a view to altering one's emotional response (e.g., instead of thinking that others' lack of engagement with him at the party is a sign that other people don't want to talk to him, he might interpret the lack of conversation as the result of his own isolation). The last regulation family, *response modulation*, refers to efforts to influence one or more aspects of the emotional response (e.g., in response to increased anxiety, an individual may try to hide feelings of anxiety or may choose to begin consuming alcohol to help alleviate his feelings of anxiety).

One important question is what leads an individual to decide to regulate an emotion, and then to select one rather than another emotion regulation strategy. According to the process model of emotion regulation (Gross, 2015b), emotion regulation is conceptualized as involving four stages: (1) identifying emotions that need regulation, (2) selecting an emotion regulation strategy, (3) implementing the selected strategy, and (4) monitoring the implemented strategy over time to determine if further modification is necessary. Within the selection stage, an individual can choose from the five families of emotion regulation strategies mentioned earlier. Once a regulation strategy is selected and then implemented, this may result in changes in the emotion targeted for regulation. These changes are monitored, and regulation strategies may also be changed if needed.

Emotion Regulation Problems Difficulties with emotion regulation can arise at any of the four stages in the emotion regulation process. For example, an individual may experience difficulty identifying an emotion that needs regulation (e.g., lacking emotional awareness), selecting an appropriate emotion regulation strategy (e.g., selecting a strategy with low odds of successfully achieving the emotion regulation goal), implementing a selection strategy (e.g., poor or inadequate implementation), and/or monitoring the implemented strategy (e.g., not monitoring an implemented strategy).

In terms of the emotion regulation strategies themselves, researchers generally have found that strategies that intervene earlier in the emotion-generative process tend to be more successful at changing the emotion trajectory than strategies that intervene later in the emotion-generative process (Gross, 1998). However, it is important to note that none of these emotion regulation strategies is inherently adaptive or maladaptive; rather, the adaptiveness of a given approach is determined by whether it allows the individual to meet his or her emotion regulation goals. Importantly, whether a particular emotion regulation goal is adaptive or maladaptive is another question, and can also serve as a point of intervention. For example, an individual with SAD may set the goal of feeling less anxious, and select the strategy of turning down a desired job that would require some public speaking. Whether the goal of decreasing anxiety in the foregoing example is adaptive or maladaptive is orthogonal to whether the emotion regulation attempt was success-ful. Furthermore, a distinction can be made between *emotion regulation failure*, or not engaging in emotion regulation when it would be helpful to do so, and *emotion misregulation*, or using a form of emotion regulation that is poorly matched to the situation (Gross & Jazaieri, 2014).

Emotion Regulation as a Transdiagnostic Factor

Emotion regulation problems have been documented across a variety of forms of psychopathology and, for this reason, emotion regulation has come to be considered an important transdiagnostic factor to consider in clinical research. However, much of the research on emotion regulation is somewhat disjointed, and there are a number of potential reasons for this.

First, there are many definitions of emotion regulation in the literature, and the way key emotion regulation constructs are labeled and operationalized varies according to the context. For example, when studied in the context of affective science, the strategy of avoiding a distressing situation may be termed "situation selection," whereas when studied in the context of psychopathology, this strategy may be termed "avoidance." Second, many studies have assessed the presence of one or more specific emotion regulation strategies (e.g., experiential avoidance) across disorders without considering how those strategies are selected or imple-mented (Aldao, Nolen-Hoeksema, & Schweizer, 2010). Third, heavy reliance on trait approaches has made it difficult to detect process-level commonalities across disorders. For example, Gratz and Roemer's (2004) Difficulties in Emotion Regulation Scale (DERS) is a widely used general measure of difficulties in responding to negative emotions. Though of clear utility, this measure does not examine the mechanism underlying these difficulties, and includes traits that could affect an individual's ability to regulate emotions (e.g., emotional awareness) in addition to constructs directly involved in the emotion regulation process (e.g., limited access to emotion regulation strategies). Taken together, these factors suggest the need for a common overarching framework from which to discuss emotion regulation processes and emotion regulation difficulties. One such frame-work is the process model of emotion regulation.

This framework makes it possible to examine the relationship between emotion regulation and psychopathology in terms of stage-specific difficulties. Indeed, Sheppes and colleagues (2015) use this framework to present a summary of how a broad range of clinical constructs and disorders can be mapped onto each of the stages of the process model of emotion regulation. For example, in certain contexts, the role of worry in GAD might be conceptualized as difficulty implementing an emotion regulation goal. In this case, the individual may have identified the goal of reducing anxiety surrounding uncertain future outcomes, and the individual may have selected thinking (or worrying) about the event as the emotion regulation strategy, but when implementing the strategy, he or she is unable to implement it effectively (e.g., worries for too long, worries without focus or structure to worrisome thoughts).

From the vantage point of the process model of emotion regulation, one important question is how to conceptualize the relationship between emotion regulation and transdiagnostic theory as defined by RDoC. Because the different RDoC domains span many areas of psychological processing, no single domain clearly encompasses all aspects of emotion regulation. Even when examining a single emotion regulation strategy, it becomes clear that emotion regulation is inherently a multi-domain process within the RDoC framework. In an attempt to further clarify how emotion regulation can be conceptualized within RDoC, in prior work we have proposed that emotion regulation be considered a new, sixth RDoC domain (Fernandez et al., 2016). However, rather than conceptualizing it as a new domain that sits apart from the other domains, we have proposed that emotion regulation is the functional consequence of patterns of interaction among the five existing RDoC domains – an emergent construct. In other words, rather than attempt to include all constructs relevant to the experience of emotion regulation into a single domain, the domain itself is defined as the interactive, emergent consequence of constructs from other domains interacting with each other. For any given instance or attempt to regulate emotions, it is likely that constructs from multiple domains are being recruited and are interacting with each other; as a result, changes or interventions with any one construct will likely affect the trajectory of the emotion regulation attempt.

For example, consider the emotion regulation strategy of rumination. Rumination can be defined as a thinking style characterized by repetitive negative thinking about the causes and consequences of distress (Nolen-Hoeksema, Wisco, & Lyubomirsky, 2008). Although originally largely studied within the context of depression, rumination has recently been thought to relate more to anxiety than previously thought, particularly in anxiety disorders characterized by persistent and excessive worry such as GAD (Ruscio et al., 2015). To consider how rumination could be conceptualized within an RDoC framework, one would have to select which domains are relevant to the process of rumination. Two domains that are relevant are negative valence systems, which includes negatively valenced experiences such as loss and potential threat (e.g., thinking about potential threats, as is often the case when worrying), and the cognitive systems domain, which includes constructs such as attention and cognitive control (e.g., inability to shift attention away from the topic of rumination, as is often the case when worrying). However, depending on the nature of the rumination, the other three RDoC domains may come into play. For example, a socially anxious individual may find herself ruminating about all of the positive experiences she is missing because of her anxiety in social situations, such as parties and social gatherings; it is likely in this case that constructs related to the positive valence systems domain (e.g., approach motivation) may be relevant. Likewise, constructs related to the systems for social processes (e.g., perception and understanding of others) may come into play if a socially anxious individual is ruminating about a social interaction that just occurred. Finally, if an anxious individual is ruminating about anxiety-provoking situations, the rumination may include physiological symptoms, such as increasing heart rate or sweating, which are included in the arousal and regulatory systems domain.

As illustrated earlier, constructs relevant to multiple domains may be interacting with each other to give rise to emotion regulation. In this way, emotion regulation is a higher-order domain that is the result of these multiple interactions. It's worth noting that emotion regulation may not be the only such higher-order domain – indeed, other complex cognitive-affective processes may likely be best conceptualized as domains comprised of many inter-domain interactions. Conceptualizing emotion regulation as an emergent, higher-order domain may set the stage for better understanding emotion regulation difficulties. More specifically, identifying RDoC domains and constructs relevant to a given emotion regulation process can be helpful in not only identifying why certain emotion regulation difficulties are occurring but also perhaps how to best intervene when such difficulties become maladaptive. In the following section, we illustrate how emotion regulation as a sixth domain may be helpful in organizing emotion regulation findings relevant to the anxiety disorders.

Emotion Regulation in the Anxiety Disorders

Anxiety disorders are the most common class of mental disorders, and tend to be highly comorbid among themselves and with other disorders, such as depressive disorders (Bandelow & Michaelis, 2015; Kessler, Chiu, Demler, & Walters, 2005). Here, we focus on three major anxiety disorders: GAD, SAD, and PD. GAD is a chronic and disabling disorder, and is associated with substantial costs in terms of disability and quality of life (Henning, Turk, Mennin, Fresco, & Heimberg, 2007). SAD is the second most prevalent anxiety disorder (Kessler, Berglund, Demler, Jin, & Walters, 2005; Kessler, Chiu et al., 2005), and similarly causes impairment across a variety of domains, including interpersonal relationships and occupational functioning, and is associated with decreased overall quality of life (Schneier et al., 1994). As with GAD and SAD, PD is associated with significant functional impairment (Hollifield, Katon, Skipper, & Chapman, 1997), and greater utilization of emergency room and medical provider visits (Roy-Byrne et al., 1999). Interestingly, one study found that quality of life impairment is similar across GAD, SAD, and PD (Barrera & Norton, 2009). Although these three disorders differ in important ways, they have at their core problems with anxiety.

Anxiety can be defined as an emotion that has physical (e.g., increased heart rate), cognitive (e.g., catastrophizing), behavioral (e.g., jitteriness), and subjective (e.g., feeling afraid) components and that is typically associated with apprehension about the future (Barlow, 2002). Anxiety, by itself, is neither inherently adaptive nor maladaptive; indeed, anxiety can serve as a motivating force for preparing for uncertain future outcomes, such as studying for an upcoming exam. However, as with many emotions, the experience of anxiety can become problematic. Examining anxiety through the lens of the process model of emotion regulation can help provide a clearer understanding of how problematic anxiety is developed and maintained over time.

The process model of emotion regulation becomes relevant once an individual activates a goal to influence anxiety – in the case of many anxiety disorders, this goal is typically to reduce anxiety. However, many other emotions are relevant to the experience of anxiety disorders, including embarrassment, shame, irritability, and anger. At this point, the individual must then select an emotion regulation strategy, implement the strategy, and then monitor the implementation of the strategy to determine if additional modifications to the implementation are necessary. In what follows, we illustrate how the process model can be used to better understand the emotion regulation processes that occur in GAD, SAD, and PD.

Generalized Anxiety Disorder and Emotion Regulation

The core features of GAD are (1) excessive anxiety; (2) associated, uncontrollable worry about a variety of topics; and (3) physical and cognitive symptoms, such as restlessness, fatigue, difficulty concentrating, irritability, muscle tension, and sleep disturbances (American Psychiatric Association, 2013). As such, anxiety and irritability are the two emotions considered central to the conceptualization of GAD. In terms of research on the experience of emotions in GAD, some studies have noted that GAD is associated with experiencing emotions quickly and with high intensity (Mennin, Turk, Heimberg, & Carmin, 2004), and at heightened levels (see Brosschot, Gerin, & Thayer, 2006 for a complete review). As noted earlier, the anxiety and worry typically experienced in the context of GAD are difficult to control. Another interpretation of "difficult to control" is "difficult to regulate." Using the process model to help us better understand the process of emotion regulation in GAD, let us begin with the Identification stage.

In the Identification stage, a common emotion regulation goal is to reduce anxiety, broadly speaking. More specifically, an individual feels a sense of apprehension about an unknown future outcome and wants to reduce that feeling. However, the adaptiveness and utility of this goal should be examined. For example, theories highlight that individuals with GAD may have a lower threshold for the maximum experience of emotions (Mennin et al., 2005), implying that they may be more likely to want to downregulate anxiety earlier in the emotion generation and regulation processes than individuals without GAD, even when such downregulation may be counterproductive in the long run.

In the Selection stage, the individual selects a strategy for reducing the apprehension and unease; in the context of GAD, the individual will typically select the strategy of worry, which can be conceptualized as persistent awareness of and thinking about possible future dangers or negative outcomes (Mathews, 1990). Additionally, research using the DERS has found an association between GAD symptoms and emotion regulation difficulties such as lower access to effective regulation strategies (Salters-Pedneault, Roemer, Tull, Rucker, & Mennin, 2006). Taken together, these findings suggest that individuals with GAD view worry as their primary strategy and fail to consider using other strategies, such as mindfulness. Or, perhaps individuals with GAD have access to only relatively unhelpful strategies (e.g., excessive reassurance seeking). Though this hypothesis makes theoretical sense, some studies have failed to find that individuals with GAD use fewer strategies than those without GAD (Decker, Turk, Hess, & Murray, 2008). Another potential explanation for why individuals with GAD prefer the strategy of worry to other strategies is suggested by the Contrast Avoidance Model of Worry, which suggests that individuals engage in prolonged worry because they prefer the negative experience of prolonged worry to the sudden shift from a positive to a negative state of emotion that would be caused by a negative outcome occurring (Newman & Llera, 2011).

In the Implementation stage, the emotion regulation strategy that has been selected in the Selection stage is implemented. In the context of GAD, typically individuals worry for a prolonged period of time, to the extent that the worry will no longer help them achieve their goal of reduction of apprehension or unease; in fact, worry may actually serve the function of prolonging and maintaining a negative emotion state, which in turn can have negative consequences for the individual (Newman & Llera, 2011). Though the worry may seem initially as though it is an attempt to plan for potential negative future outcomes to be better prepared for such outcomes, once at excessive levels it may transform from a problem-solving approach to a future-oriented ruminative-like approach in which the individual unproductively considers various aspects of the potential negative future outcomes.

Finally, the individual will enter the Monitoring stage, and decide whether the worry is helping to attain the goal of anxiety reduction. If the individual notices that worrying is not helping, he or she might switch to a different strategy. However, this switch depends on whether the individual is monitoring the implementation of the worry strategy and whether the individual has access to other regulation strategies. Effective execution of monitoring would alert these individuals that they should either modify some aspect of their worrying or shift to a different strategy, and yet many of them continue to worry. An example of modifying an aspect of worry is limiting its duration; indeed, asking patients to set aside a relatively brief (e.g., 15 minutes) "worry time" during the later part of the day is part of treatment for GAD in certain cognitive approaches such as metacognitive therapy (Wells, 2007). In this case, rather than let a given period of worry extend for a long duration, patients are asked to postpone worrying as soon as they notice it and to instead choose to worry about that given topic during the worry time, which is restricted in its length. An example of shifting to a different strategy might be to mindfully observe one's thoughts and feelings rather than to perseverate on anxiety-provoking thoughts.

Social Anxiety Disorder and Emotion Regulation

SAD is characterized by persistent fear of evaluation/scrutiny and avoidance of social situations. The core emotion present in the conceptualization of SAD is fear of embarrassment and/or humiliation, and the situations most likely to create this fear are those that involve evaluation (American Psychiatric Association, 2013). To meet criteria for SAD, the situations that provoke this fear and anxiety must be either avoided or endured with intense distress, indicating that a core emotional feature of SAD is heightened intensity of fear and anxiety that is disproportionate to the situation. Several researchers have provided overviews of the emotion regulation process in SAD (Goldin, Jazaieri, & Gross, 2014; Jazaieri, Morrison, Goldin, & Gross, 2014), particularly in terms of the specific emotion regulation strategies that individuals with SAD typically select. Later in this chapter, we again use the process model to help us better understand the process of emotion regulation in SAD.

In the Identification stage, a main emotion regulation goal in SAD is to reduce the fear of embarrassment or humiliation (or reduce the experience of these emotions once they are activated). Like GAD, the presumed goal in SAD is reduction of anxiety-related distress, but unlike GAD, the focus of the distress in SAD is typically interpersonal in nature, and reflects beliefs about how other people are viewing the individual or how the individual is viewing himself (Voncken, Dijk, de Jong, & Roelofs, 2010). Again, the utility of a goal focused on anxiety reduction (versus others such as learning to tolerate embarrassment) should be explored. Also relevant to the Identification stage is emotion clarity. There is evidence that individuals with SAD have deficits in identifying and describing their own emotions (Turk, Heimberg, Luterek, Mennin, & Fresco, 2005), which may present difficulties when establishing a goal for the emotion regulation process.

In terms of the Selection stage, prior research suggests that individuals with SAD tend to select and over-rely on avoidance and suppression strategies. In terms of avoidance, two very basic forms of avoidance are situational and experiential avoidance. Additionally, researchers have highlighted the important role of safety behaviors in SAD (McManus, Sacadura, & Clark, 2008; Piccirillo, Dryman, & Heimberg, 2016; Taylor & Alden, 2010). Safety behaviors are behaviors (which may be either overt behaviors or more cognitive in nature) that serve the function of decreasing anxiety in the moment, but oftentimes may reinforce the perception of social situations as dangerous (Wells et al., 1995). For example, an individual with SAD may be more likely to direct attention to nonsocial cues, such as playing on her cell phone while surrounded by individuals or avoiding making direct eye contact, especially with individuals who may be more likely to evaluate her (Langer & Rodebaugh, 2013). In addition to overt behaviors, these subtle avoidance strategies can take a more cognitive form, such as mentally rehearsing what one plans to say in an interaction. In terms of suppression, when assessed at both the trait and state levels, research suggests that individuals with SAD tend to select certain emotion regulation strategies more than others, including being more likely to select emotion suppression (O'Toole, Jensen, Fentz, Zachariae, & Hougaard, 2014) and less likely to select cognitive reappraisal (Blalock, Kashdan, & Farmer, 2017).

In terms of the Implementation stage, research is needed to examine whether individuals with SAD experience difficulties implementing selected regulation strategies. However, one consistent finding is that individuals with SAD report lower self-efficacy in implementing strategies such as cognitive reappraisal and expressive suppression (Werner, Goldin, Ball, Heimberg, & Gross, 2011). This lower self-efficacy is consistent with findings that highlight negative self-views in SAD, such that these individuals are more likely to rate themselves less favorably on a number of self-relevant dimensions (Moscovitch, Orr, Rowa, Reimer, & Antony, 2009). Whether this lower self-efficacy directly influences the Identification, Selection, Implementation, and Monitoring stages should be considered when exploring emotion regulation in SAD. When avoidance is selected as the emotion regulation strategy, implementation will likely yield a temporary decrease in anxiety, but a long-term reinforcement of the anxiety.

In the Monitoring stage, the individual with SAD would ideally monitor the implemented strategy and determine whether any modifications are needed. In the case of situational or experiential avoidance, because the individual experiences immediate anxiety reduction, he or she may not be motivated to modify the strategy or shift to another one, despite the long-term disadvantages of continued avoidance. This pattern would suggest it might be beneficial to take a longer-term view of emotion regulation attempts to notice that although reduction of anxiety is achieved in the short term, it is maintained in the long term; indeed, this is one of the major assumptions driving cognitive behavioral therapy. Another difficulty emerges with avoidance that takes a more cognitive form (e.g., telling yourself that the other person's opinion of you doesn't matter), in that the avoidance itself may inhibit successful monitoring of the emotion regulation attempt (e.g., because one's cognitive resources are already taxed with implementing the cognitive avoidance strategy). For example, if an individual with SAD has decided to avert his or her gaze during a conversation and focus on thoughts not relevant to the conversation partner's impression of him or her, he or she may also not be able to mindfully notice whether such avoidance is indeed helpful in reducing anxiety (if that is the emotion regulation goal).

Panic Disorder and Emotion Regulation

PD is characterized by recurrent, unexpected panic attacks, with at least four of the following symptoms: palpitations or racing heart, sweating, shaking, shortness of breath, choking sensations, chest pain or discomfort, gastrointestinal distress, dizziness or lightheadedness, derealization or depersonalization, fear of losing control or going crazy, fear of dying, numbness or tingling sensations, and chills or hot flushes (American Psychiatric Association, 2013). These panic attacks are typically followed by worry about the possibility of experiencing additional attacks, and efforts to avoid the possibility of experiencing additional attacks (e. g., avoiding crowded places if an individual's most recent panic attack occurred in a crowded place). As with GAD and SAD, the core emotions present in the conceptualization of PD are fear, worry, and panic, defined as "sudden, overwhelming terror or fright" (Barlow, 2004, p. 105). Inherent in this definition is the notion that panic is characterized by high-intensity fear and is out of proportion to the situation (in fact, by definition the panic attack is unexpected).

In terms of the Identification stage, though most anxiety disorders likely target reduction of anxiety, it is particularly understandable in the context of PD given the alarming nature of panic and its strong physiological correlates (e.g., racing heart, trembling/shaking, gastrointestinal distress). Similar to those with GAD and SAD, individuals with PD experience a lack of emotional clarity. They also report greater levels of emotional nonacceptance (Tull, Rodman, & Roemer, 2008), which may help explain how they approach goal-setting in terms of emotion regulation – that is, to not want to experience distressing emotions. An interesting consideration for PD, specifically, is the motivating forces that may be driving the goal to down-regulate panic; the individual may experience thoughts that he or she is going crazy, losing control, or dying, which in turn lead to the goal to reduce panic.

In the Implementation stage, the nature of the difficulties experienced will likely vary depending on the selected strategy. For example, there is some evidence that acceptance as an emotion regulation strategy may be helpful for individuals with PD (Levitt, Brown, Orsillo, & Barlow, 2004). However, acceptance of only part of the panic experience may be problematic. For example, if the individual accepts and tolerates the experience of physiological sensations, but not of beliefs about going crazy or dying, this may result in difficulties with implementing acceptance as a strategy. When implementing situational avoidance, individuals may generalize the avoidance too much (e.g., start by avoiding crowded places and then eventually the avoidance may extend to the workplace or to any area with a moderate-sized crowd of people). Essentially, the individual is employing too much avoidance. This latter difficulty in particular reinforces the idea that asking patients about the functional consequences of their emotion regulation attempt may be helpful in determining specific emotion regulation problems.

Finally, as with GAD and SAD, the Monitoring stage involves monitoring the implemented emotion regulation strategy to determine if any modifications or changes are needed. Two constructs that might be worth considering when exploring the Monitoring stage in individuals with PD are interceptive accuracy (how accurately an individual perceives his or her internal bodily experiences) and interoceptive awareness (how aware an individual is of his or her internal experiences). Whereas some studies suggest that individuals who experience panic attacks report increased awareness of their somatic sensations (Richards, Cooper, & Winkelman, 2003; Schmidt, Lerew, & Trakowski, 1997), and some studies suggest that individuals with PD may be also more accurate than their non-PD counterparts at detecting certain internal sensations (Limmer, Kornhuber, &

Martin, 2015), these findings are generally mixed (Rapee, 1994; Zoellner & Craske, 1999) and may vary depending on the exact measure being used. Regardless, it may be worth noting whether an individual with PD tends toward higher levels of interoceptive awareness/sensitivity, as this may influence the Monitoring stage of emotion regulation.

Clinical Implications

The transdiagnostic emotion regulation perspective we have developed here has clinical implications both for assessment and for intervention. In the following sections, we review how a stage-specific approach to emotion regulation processes may help yield more precise information about emotion regulation difficulties in psychopathology. We also review how this stage-specific approach may better help inform treatment approaches to psychopathology.

Assessment

One key implication of using a transdiagnostic emotion regulation framework is the need for assessment to be based on the process model. While it might be helpful to note a patient's trait level of various constructs relevant to the experience of emotion – such as emotion awareness and, emotion clarity – it is arguably even more important to understand processes relevant to the identification of emotions, selection of strategies to modify the emotions, implementation of strategies, and monitoring of strategies. The Emotion Regulation Interview (ERI) (Werner et al., 2011) is one such promising step in the direction of assessing the process of emotion regulation as it unfolds in real time; however, the ERI in its current form focuses on social anxiety and on the specific strategies that an individual selects without exploring (1) *how* or *why* the individual chose that strategy over other strategies (in the case that other strategies were available), or (2) whether the individual monitored the selected strategy once it was implemented. Clinicians could consider expanding their assessment of emotion regulation (such as the ERI) to include elements relevant to the process model of emotion regulation.

After utilizing a more stage-specific approach to the assessment of emotion regulation difficulties, we encourage clinicians to be specific in conceptualizing the exact emotion regulation difficulty or difficulties occurring in an individual. Rather than to note that an individual may tend to use emotional suppression more than a less-anxious individual, ask whether the individual selects emotional suppression above and beyond other strategies and, if so, whether he or she is successful in emotionally suppressing the experience. Perhaps equally important, ask whether such suppression carries any notable functional consequences. Similarly, ask what the person does if he or she is unsuccessful in deploying emotional suppression. If the individual can generate alternate strategies he or she employs in the event of unsuccessful implementation (e.g., talking through the emotional experience with a friend), the point of intervention may be different than if the individual is unable to generate alternate strategies (e.g., continues to try suppression). Questions such as these may provide more clarity on the stage-specific difficulties the individual is experiencing.

Finally, once a process-based understanding of how the individual approaches emotion regulation has been gathered, it may be worth exploring relevant constructs that may be influencing the emotion regulation attempt. It is here that turning to the RDoC matrix may be helpful. For example, when a socially anxious individual attempts to mindfully engage in a social interaction, does he or she struggle with keeping attention on the conversation (cognitive systems domain)? Or does he or she struggle with interpreting the nonverbal cues of the conversation partner (systems for social processes domain)? Or does he or she struggle to find positive aspects of a social interaction because of the hyperfocus on negative aspects (positive and negative valence systems domains)? Questions such as these may help to explain what is maintaining the emotion regulation attempt, particularly if it is unsuccessful.

Treatment

After utilizing this approach to better understand the specific emotion regulation difficulties a person is experiencing, a clinician could then follow up with a more targeted approach to treatment with explicit skills training modules for the emotion regulatory deficits. For example, if the individual is struggling to identify what emotion he is feeling, or whether it should be altered (Identification stage), a point of intervention could be to help the patient better understand his emotional responses as he experiences them. If, however, the individual is struggling with generating alternative emotion regulation strategies (Selection stage), the intervention could focus on introducing new emotion regulation strategies. In the case where the individual is only aware of avoidance as a viable strategy, the clinician could introduce strategies such as mindfulness, acceptance, and gradated exposure. If the individual has a range of strategies from which to select, but typically only selects maladaptive strategies (or ones that do not allow for the emotion regulation goal to be met), the intervention could instead focus on helping the individual explore how to increase the likelihood that a better strategy will be selected in a given situation.

If an individual has selected an adaptive regulation strategy but struggles to implement it effectively (Implementation stage), treatment may focus on how to help the individual learn to more effectively implement the strategy. For example, if the individual tries to engage in cognitive reappraisal while in a situation, but struggles with generating more balanced and rational interpretations of the situation, the clinician can help the individual practice generating these alternate appraisals. If, instead, the individual struggles with employing mindfulness, the intervention could focus on practicing mindfulness and exploring ways in which the individual could implement it more successfully (e.g., using anchoring techniques). Finally, if the individual struggles with monitoring the implemented strategy (Monitoring stage), the clinician might focus instead on helping the individual be more mindful about monitoring the emotion regulation process and encouraging the individual to consider changing or modifying strategies rather than to simply accept the outcome of the emotion regulation attempt, particularly if it is distressing. Ultimately, this approach to treatment can help nurture interventions that are grounded in a more complete understanding of the emotion regulation process.

Future Research Directions

The process model of emotion regulation suggests a number of directions for future research. Here we consider three of these research directions: extending the emotion regulation framework beyond the anxiety disorders, further expanding the emotion regulation RDoC domain, and considering the role that other psychological constructs may play in the emotion regulation process.

Extend the Emotion Regulation Framework beyond the Anxiety Disorders

A first step in terms of future research is to extend the emotion regulation framework we have presented beyond the anxiety disorders. Of all mental disorder diagnoses, approximately 40% are thought to include some form of affective disturbance (Jazaieri, Urry, & Gross, 2013); therefore, it is likely that the proposed framework would be relevant to many disorders and forms of psychopathology. Additionally, given the high comorbidity between anxiety disorders and other types of disorders such as depressive disorders, eating disorders, and substance use disorders, it is likely that processes relevant to the experience of anxiety would also be relevant to processes of related disorders.

Expand the Emotion Regulation RDoC Domain

We have described emotion regulation as an emergent construct that is the result of interactions of domain constructs with each other, and used clinical examples to articulate how constructs from all five currently existing RDoC domains are relevant to and interact with each other in the emotion regulation process. As part of this proposal, we also highlighted how emotion regulation has been studied across all of the units of analysis proposed within the RDoC matrix (Fernandez et al., 2016). However, more work is needed to further expand emotion regulation as an RDoC domain. For example, constructs relevant to the process of emotion regulation, but not yet present in any of the RDoC domains, should be considered for addition to the RDoC matrix. For example, emotional awareness (i.e., how aware an individual is of his or her internal emotional experiences) is a particularly important construct in terms of the emotion regulation process – degree of awareness can determine whether the individual is able to activate an emotion regulation goal and monitor the emotion regulation process to determine whether that goal has been achieved. Another potentially important construct is distress tolerance (i.e., how tolerant an individual is of distressing emotional experiences). We might expect that an individual's level of distress tolerance would likely determine the nature of the emotion regulation goal and subsequent selection, implementation, and monitoring of the stated goal.

In addition to specifying additional constructs to be added to the RDoC matrix, a clearer delineation of how constructs from the domains interact with each other to give rise to emotion regulation would be helpful for researchers and clinicians aiming to better understand the role of emotion regulation in psychopathology. It's possible that certain domains are more relevant to certain stages in the process model; for example, it's possible that the Monitoring stage relies heavily upon constructs from the cognitive systems domain, as it involves attention to the implemented emotion regulation strategy, memory of the selected strategy and potential alternative strategies, and perceptual abilities to determine relative success of the implemented strategy. Knowledge of the specific constructs and domains that are most relevant to stage-specific difficulties would likely help inform stage-specific interventions. For example, given the Monitoring stage constructs, it's likely that a form of intervention embodying mindful awareness would be helpful for an individual who is struggling with the monitoring process. Finally, additional knowledge about the neural bases of emotion regulation would also be helpful in further examining emotion regulation as an RDoC domain, especially given the relatively strong focus of the RDoC framework on the biological and neurological underpinnings of psychopathology (Etkin, Büchel, & Gross, 2015; Gross, 2015a).

The Role of Other Transdiagnostic Factors in the Emotion Regulation Process

Another future direction is exploring how other transdiagnostic factors interact with emotion regulation to maintain psychopathology. Thus far, we have focused exclusively on the construct of emotion regulation; however, related transdiagnostic constructs likely impact an individual's ability to engage with and carry out the emotion regulation process. A notable example is that of sleep disturbances. Sleep disturbances are highly comorbid with many forms of psychopathology (Benca, Obermeyer, Thisted, & Gillin, 1992). Palmer and Alfano (2017) nicely illustrate how sleep disturbances can impact the different stages within the process model.

For example, sleep disturbances such as insomnia may contribute to an individual's cognitive resources at the Selection stage, such that an individual is more likely to select strategies that require fewer cognitive resources (e.g., avoidance) versus those that require more cognitive resources (e.g., cognitive reappraisal). Identification of these constructs when determining an individual's stage-specific difficulties would likely allow for more effective stage-specific interventions. For example, knowing that an individual suffers from insomnia may prompt an assessor to ask about the individual's emotion regulation difficulties when sleep-deprived vs. not sleep-deprived. If the individual endorses difficulty implementing emotion regulation strategies while sleep-deprived, a potential intervention may be to increase the individual's emotion regulation flexibility, or ability to implement different strategies that require different amounts of cognitive resources flexibly (Aldao, Sheppes, & Gross, 2015) so that the individual can utilize different strategies when sleep-deprived.

Conclusion

Our goals in this chapter were to review transdiagnostic emotion generation and emotion regulation processes using anxiety disorders as an example. More specifically, we aimed to illustrate how stage-specific difficulties in emotion regulation may help provide a clearer understanding of the initiating and maintaining factors of excessive anxiety present across the anxiety disorders. Using the examples of GAD, SAD, and PD, we have provided conceptualizations of how stage-specific difficulties may be maintaining anxiety processes, and proposed ways in which these conceptualizations can better inform assessment and treatment of anxiety disorders. We are excited about novel transdiagnostic conceptualizations of psychopathology, and believe that these conceptualizations carry great promise for better understanding the development and maintenance of psychopathology. Given the core role of emotions in many forms of psychopathology, we especially encourage researchers and clinicians to consider how the emotion generation and emotion regulation processes we have discussed might be affecting an individual's psychological functioning. In line with this, we have provided a framework for doing so, and included specific ways in which these processes can be better assessed. In considering future endeavors with this framework, we hope that this framework will be expanded beyond the anxiety disorders and into other areas of psychopathology. We also encourage researchers and clinicians to consider how other transdiagnostic factors may impact the emotion generation and emotion regulation processes. Finally, we encourage further consideration of the role of emotion regulation within the RDoC framework; more specifically, we encourage consideration of the structure and content of emotion regulation as a sixth domain, and how the other domains interact with each other to give rise to emotion regulation.

References

Aldao, A., Nolen-Hoeksema, S., & Schweizer, S. (2010). Emotion-regulation strategies across psychopathology: A meta-analytic review. *Clinical Psychology Review, 30*, 217–237. doi: 10.1016/j.cpr.2009.11.004

Aldao, A., Sheppes, G., & Gross, J. J. (2015). Emotion regulation flexibility. *Cognitive Therapy and Research, 39*, 263–278. doi: 10.1007/s10608-014–9662-4

American Psychiatric Association. (2013). *Diagnostic and Statistical Manual of Mental Disorders*. Washington, DC: American Psychiatric Association.

Bandelow, B. & Michaelis, S. (2015). Epidemiology of anxiety disorders in the 21st century. *Dialogues in Clinical Neuroscience*, *17*(3), 327–335.

Barlow, D. H. (2002). *Anxiety and Its Disorders: The Nature and Treatment of Anxiety and Panic* (2nd edn). New York, NY: Guilford Press.

Barlow, D. H. (2004). Anxiety and Its Disorders: The Nature and Treatment of Anxiety and Panic. New York, NY: Guilford Press.

Barlow, D. H., Sauer-Zavala, S., Carl, J. R., Bullis, J. R., & Ellard, K. K. (2014). The nature, diagnosis, and treatment of neuroticism: Back to the future. *Clinical Psychological Science*, *2*, 344–365. doi: 10.1177/2167702613505532

Barrera, T. L. & Norton, P. J. (2009). Quality of life impairment in generalized anxiety disorder, social phobia, and panic disorder. *Journal of Anxiety Disorders*, *23*(8), 1086–1090. doi: 10.1016/j.janxdis.2009.07.011

Benca, R. M., Obermeyer, W. H., Thisted, R. A., & Gillin, J. C. (1992). Sleep and psychiatric disorders: A meta-analysis. *Archives of General Psychiatry*, *49*(8), 651–668.

Blalock, D. V., Kashdan, T. B., & Farmer, A. S. (2017). Trait and daily emotion regulation in social anxiety disorder. *Cognitive Therapy and Research*, *40*(3), 416–425. doi: 10.1007/s10608-015–9739-8

Brosschot, J. F., Gerin, W., & Thayer, J. F. (2006). The perseverative cognition hypothesis: A review of worry, prolonged stress-related physiological activation, and health. *Journal of Psychosomatic Research*, *60*(2), 113–124. doi: 10.1016/j.jpsychores.2005.06.074

Brown, T. A., Chorpita, B. F., & Barlow, D. H. (1998). Structural relationships among dimensions of the DSM-IV anxiety and mood disorders and dimensions of negative affect, positive affect, and autonomic arousal. *Journal of Abnormal Psychology*, *107*, 179–192. doi: 10.1037/0021-843X.107.2.179

Chawla, N. & Ostafin, B. (2007). Experiential avoidance as a functional dimensional approach to psychopathology: An empirical review. *Journal of Clinical Psychology*, *63*, 871–890. doi: 10.1002/jclp.20400

Clark, L. A. & Watson, D. (1991). Tripartite model of anxiety and depression: Psychometric evidence and taxonomic implications. *Journal of Abnormal Psychology*, *100*, 316–336.

De Beurs, E., Chambless, D. L., & Goldstein, A. J. (1997). Measurement of panic disorder by a modified panic diary. *Depression and Anxiety*, *6*(4), 133–139. doi: 10.1002/(SICI)1520–6394(1997)6:4<133::AID-DA1>3.0.CO;2-D

Decker, M. L., Turk, C. L., Hess, B., & Murray, C. E. (2008). Emotion regulation among individuals classified with and without generalized anxiety disorder. *Journal of Anxiety Disorders*, *22*(3), 485–494. doi: https://doi.org/10.1016/j.janxdis.2007.04.002

Eisner, L. R., Johnson, S. L., & Carver, C. S. (2009). Positive affect regulation in anxiety disorders. *Journal of Anxiety Disorders*, *23*(5), 645–649. doi: 10.1016/j.janxdis.2009.02.001

Etkin, A., Büchel, C., & Gross, J. J. (2015). The neural bases of emotion regulation. *Nature Reviews Neuroscience*, *16*, 693–700. doi: 10.1038/nrn4044

Fernandez, K. C., Jazaieri, H., & Gross, J. J. (2016). Emotion regulation: A transdiagnostic perspective on a new RDoC domain. *Cognitive Therapy and Research*, *40*(3), 426–440. doi: 10.1007/s10608-016–9772-2

Goldin, P. R., Jazaieri, H., & Gross, J. J. (2014). Emotion regulation in social anxiety disorder. In S. Hofmann & P. DiBartolo (eds.), *Social Anxiety* (3rd edn) (pp. 511–529). San Diego, CA: Academic Press.

Gratz, K. L. & Roemer, L. (2004). Multidimensional assessment of emotion regulation and dysregulation: Development, factor structure, and initial validation of the Difficulties in Emotion Regulation Scale. *Journal of Psychopathology and Behavioral Assessment*, *26*, 41–54. doi: 10.1023/b:joba.0000007455.08539.94

Gross, J. J. (1998). The emerging field of emotion regulation: An integrative review. *Review of General Psychology*, *2*, 271.

Gross, J. J. (2015a). Emotion regulation: Current status and future prospects. *Psychological Inquiry*, *26*(1), 1–26. doi: 10.1080/1047840X.2014.940781

Gross, J. J. (2015b). The extended process model of emotion regulation: Elaborations, applications, and future directions. *Psychological Inquiry*, *26*, 130–137. doi: 10.1080/1047840X.2015.989751

Gross, J. J. & Jazaieri, H. (2014). Emotion, emotion regulation, and psychopathology: An affective science perspective. *Clinical Psychological Science*, *2*, 387–401. doi: 10.1177/2167702614536164

Gross, J. J., Sheppes, G., & Urry, H. L. (2011). Emotion generation and emotion regulation: A distinction we should make (carefully). *Cognition and Emotion*, *25*, 765–781. doi: 10.1080/02699931.2011.555753

Henning, E. R., Turk, C. L., Mennin, D. S., Fresco, D. M., & Heimberg, R. G. (2007). Impairment and quality of life in individuals with generalized anxiety disorder. *Depress Anxiety*, *24*(5), 342–349. doi: 10.1002/da.20249

Hollifield, M., Katon, W., Skipper, B., & Chapman, T. (1997). Panic disorder and quality of life: Variables predictive of functional impairment. *American Journal of Psychiatry*, *154*(6), 766–772.

Insel, T., Cuthbert, B., Garvey, M., Heinssen, R., Kozak, M., Pine, D. S., . . . Wang, P. (2010). Research Domain Criteria (RDoC): Toward a new classification framework for research on mental disorders. *American Journal of Psychiatry*, 167. doi: 10.1176/appi.ajp.2010.09091379

Jazaieri, H., Morrison, A. S., Goldin, P. R., & Gross, J. J. (2014). The role of emotion and emotion regulation in social anxiety disorder. *Current Psychiatry Reports*, *17*(1), 531. doi: 10.1007/s11920-014–0531-3

Jazaieri, H., Urry, H. L., & Gross, J. J. (2013). Affective disturbance and psychopathology: An emotion regulation perspective. *Journal of Experimental Psychopathology*, *4*, 584–599.

Kashdan, T. B. (2007). Social anxiety spectrum and diminished positive experiences: Theoretical synthesis and meta-analysis. *Clinical Psychology Review*, *27*(3), 348–365. doi: 10.1016/j.cpr.2006.12.003

Kessler, R. C., Berglund, P., Demler, O., Jin, R., & Walters, E. E. (2005). Lifetime prevalence and age-of-onset distributions of DSM-IV disorders in the national comorbidity survey replication. *Archives of General Psychiatry*, *62*(6), 593–602.

Kessler, R. C., Chiu, W. T., Demler, O., & Walters, E. E. (2005). Prevalence, severity, and comorbidity of 12-month DSM-IV disorders in the national comorbidity survey replication. *Archives of General Psychiatry*, *62*(6), 617–627.

Langer, J. K. & Rodebaugh, T. L. (2013). Social anxiety and gaze avoidance: Averting gaze but not anxiety. *Cognitive Therapy and Research*, *37*(6), 1110–1120. doi: 10.1007/s10608-013–9546-z

Levitt, J. T., Brown, T. A., Orsillo, S. M., & Barlow, D. H. (2004). The effects of acceptance versus suppression of emotion on subjective and psychophysiological response to carbon dioxide challenge in patients with panic disorder. *Behavior Therapy, 35,* 747–766. doi: 10.1016/S0005-7894(04)80018-2

Limmer, J., Kornhuber, J., & Martin, A. (2015). Panic and comorbid depression and their associations with stress reactivity, interoceptive awareness and interoceptive accuracy of various bioparameters. *Journal of Affective Disorders, 185,* 170–179. doi: https://doi.org/10.1016/j.jad.2015.07.010

Mathews, A. (1990). Why worry? The cognitive function of anxiety. *Behaviour Research and Therapy, 28*(6), 455–468. doi: https://doi.org/10.1016/0005–7967(90)90132–3

Mauss, I. B., Levenson, R. W., McCarter, L., Wilhelm, F. H., & Gross, J. J. (2005). The tie that binds? Coherence among emotion experience, behavior, and physiology. *Emotion, 5,* 175–190. doi: 10.1037/1528–3542.5.2.175

McManus, F., Sacadura, C., & Clark, D. M. (2008). Why social anxiety persists: An experimental investigation of the role of safety behaviours as a maintaining factor. *Journal of Behavior Therapy and Experimental Psychiatry, 39*(2), 147–161. doi: http://dx.doi.org/10.1016/j.jbtep.2006.12.002

Mennin, D. S., Heimberg, R. G., Turk, C. L., & Fresco, D. M. (2005a). Preliminary evidence for an emotion dysregulation model of generalized anxiety disorder. *Behaviour Research and Therapy, 43*(10), 1281–1310.

Mennin, D. S., McLaughlin, K. A., & Flanagan, T. J. (2009). Emotion regulation deficits in generalized anxiety disorder, social anxiety disorder, and their co-occurrence. *Journal of Anxiety Disorders, 23*(7), 866–871. doi: 10.1016/j.janxdis.2009.04.006

Mennin, D., Turk, C., Heimberg, R., & Carmin, C. (2004). *Focusing on the Regulation of Emotion: A New Direction for Conceptualizing and Treating Generalized Anxiety Disorder.* New York, NY: Wiley.

Moscovitch, D. A., Orr, E., Rowa, K., Reimer, S. G., & Antony, M. M. (2009). In the absence of rose-colored glasses: ratings of self-attributes and their differential certainty and importance across multiple dimensions in social phobia. *Behaviour Research and Therapy, 47*(1), 66–70. doi: 10.1016/j.brat.2008.10.007

Newman, M. G. & Llera, S. J. (2011). A novel theory of experiential avoidance in generalized anxiety disorder: A review and synthesis of research supporting a contrast avoidance model of worry. *Clinical Psychology Review, 31*(3), 371–382. doi: 10.1016/j.cpr.2011.01.008

Nolen-Hoeksema, S., Wisco, B. E., & Lyubomirsky, S. (2008). Rethinking rumination. *Perspectives on Psychological Science, 3*(5), 400–424. doi: 10.1111/j.1745–6924.2008.00088.x

O'Toole, M. S., Jensen, M. B., Fentz, H. N., Zachariae, R., & Hougaard, E. (2014). Emotion differentiation and emotion regulation in high and low socially anxious individuals: An experience-sampling study. *Cognitive Therapy and Research, 38*(4), 428–438. doi: http://dx.doi.org/10.1007/s10608-014–9611-2

Palmer, C. A. & Alfano, C. A. (2017). Sleep and emotion regulation: An organizing, integrative review. *Sleep Medicine Reviews, 31,* 6–16. doi: http://dx.doi.org/10.1016/j.smrv.2015.12.006

Piccirillo, M. L., Dryman, M. T., & Heimberg, R. G. (2016). Safety behaviors in adults with social anxiety: Review and future directions. *Behavior Therapy, 47*(5), 675.

Rapee, R. M. (1994). Detection of somatic sensations in panic disorder. *Behaviour Research and Therapy, 32*(8), 825–831. doi: http://dx.doi.org/10.1016/0005–7967(94)90162-7

Richards, J. C., Cooper, A. J., & Winkelman, J. H. (2003). Interoceptive accuracy in nonclinical panic. *Cognitive Therapy and Research, 27*(4), 447–461. doi: http://dx.doi.org/10.1023/A:1025476514714

Rosellini, A. J. & Brown, T. A. (2011). The NEO Five-Factor Inventory: Latent structure and relationships with dimensions of anxiety and depressive disorders in a large clinical sample. *Assessment, 18,* 27–38. doi: 10.1177/1073191110382848

Roy-Byrne, P. P., Stein, M. B., Russo, J., Mercier, E., Thomas, R., McQuaid, J., ... Sherbourne, C. D. (1999). Panic disorder in the primary care setting: Comorbidity, disability, service utilization, and treatment. *Journal of Clinical Psychiatry; Journal of Clinical Psychiatry.*

Ruscio, A. M., Gentes, E. L., Jones, J. D., Hallion, L. S., Coleman, E. S., & Swendsen, J. (2015). Rumination predicts heightened responding to stressful life events in major depressive disorder and generalized anxiety disorder. *Journal of Abnormal Psychology, 124*(1), 17–26. doi: 10.1037/abn0000025

Salovey, P., Mayer, J. D., Goldman, S. L., Turvey, C., & Palfai, T. P. (1995). Emotional attention, clarity, and repair: Exploring emotional intelligence using the Trait Meta-Mood Scale. In J. W. Pennebaker (ed.), *Emotion, Disclosure, & Health* (pp. 125–154). Washington, DC:American Psychological Association.

Salters-Pedneault, K., Roemer, L., Tull, M. T., Rucker, L., & Mennin, D. S. (2006). Evidence of broad deficits in emotion regulation associated with chronic worry and generalized anxiety disorder. *Cognitive Therapy and Research, 30,* 469–480.

Schmidt, N. B., Lerew, D. R., & Trakowski, J. H. (1997). Body vigilance in panic disorder: Evaluating attention to bodily perturbations. *Journal of Consulting and Clinical Psychology, 65*(2), 214–220.

Schneier, F. R., Heckelman, L. R., Garfinkel, R., Campeas, R., Fallon, B. A., Gitow, A., ... Liebowitz, M. R. (1994). Functional impairment in social phobia. *Journal of Clinical Psychiatry, 55*(8), 322–331.

Sheppes, G., Suri, G., & Gross, J. J. (2015). Emotion regulation and psychopathology. *Annual Review of Clinical Psychology, 11,* 379–405. doi: 10.1146/annurev-clinpsy-032814–112739

Spinhoven, P., Drost, J., de Rooij, M., van Hemert, A. M., & Penninx, B. W. (2014). A longitudinal study of experiential avoidance in emotional disorders. *Behavior Therapy, 45,* 840–850. doi: 10.1016/j.beth.2014.07.001

Taylor, C. T. & Alden, L. E. (2010). Safety behaviors and judgmental biases in social anxiety disorder. *Behaviour Research and Therapy, 48*(3), 226–237. doi: http://dx.doi.org/10.1016/j.brat.2009.11.005

Tull, M. T., Rodman, S. A., & Roemer, L. (2008). An examination of the fear of bodily sensations and body hypervigilance as predictors of emotion regulation difficulties among individuals with a recent history of uncued panic attacks. *Journal of Anxiety Disorders, 22*(4), 750–760. doi: https://doi.org/10.1016/j.janxdis.2007.08.001

Turk, C. L., Heimberg, R. G., Luterek, J. A., Mennin, D. S., & Fresco, D. M. (2005). Emotion dysregulation in generalized anxiety disorder: A comparison with social anxiety disorder. *Cognitive Therapy and Research, 5*(1), 89–106.

Voncken, M. J., Dijk, C., de Jong, P. J., & Roelofs, J. (2010). Not self-focused attention but negative beliefs affect poor social performance in social anxiety: An investigation of pathways in the social anxiety-social rejection relationship. *Behaviour Research and Therapy, 48*(10), 984.

Weeks, J. W., Heimberg, R. G., Rodebaugh, T. L., & Norton, P. J. (2008). Exploring the relationship between fear of positive evaluation and social anxiety. *Journal of Anxiety Disorders*, *22*(3), 386–400. doi: http://dx.doi.org/10.1016/j.janxdis.2007.04.009

Wells, A. (2007). Cognition about cognition: Metacognitive therapy and change in generalized anxiety disorder and social phobia. *Cognitive and Behavioral Practice*, *14*(1), 18–25. doi: https://doi.org/10.1016/j.cbpra.2006.01.005

Wells, A., Clark, D. M., Salkovskis, P., Ludgate, J., Hackmann, A., & Gelder, M. (1995). Social phobia: The role of in-situation safety behaviors in maintaining anxiety and negative beliefs. *Behavior Therapy*, *26*(1), 153–161. doi: https://doi.org/10.1016/S0005-7894(05)80088-7

Werner, K. H., Goldin, P. R., Ball, T. M., Heimberg, R. G., & Gross, J. J. (2011). Assessing emotion regulation in social anxiety disorder: The emotion regulation interview. *Journal of Psychopathology and Behavioral Assessment*, *33*, 346–354. doi: 10.1007/s10862-011–9225-x

Zoellner, L. A. & Craske, M. G. (1999). Interoceptive accuracy and panic. *Behaviour Research and Therapy*, *37*(12), 1141–1158. doi: https://doi.org/10.1016/S0005-7967(98)00202-2

Assessment, Diagnosis, and Cultural Manifestations of Anxiety and Related Disorders

11 Anxiety Disorders

Anthony J. Rosellini, Esther S. Tung,
and Timothy A. Brown

The anxiety disorders have changed throughout the various iterations of the *Diagnostic and Statistical Manual of Mental Disorders* (*DSM*), with the most substantial revision occurring when polythetic criteria sets were adopted in *DSM-III* (American Psychiatric Association [APA], 1980). Since *DSM-III*, changes to the anxiety disorders have been predominately organizational (e.g., rearranging disorders into different sections of the *DSM*) and criteria-focused (e.g., adding, deleting, or rewording criteria) rather than substantive (e.g., adopting a dimensional approach to diagnosis). However, there is much debate about the validity of the *DSM*'s diagnostic categories, leading to the creation of alternate approaches to diagnostic classification. One such example is the National Institute of Health (NIMH) Research Domain Criteria (RDoC) (Insel et al., 2010), which seeks to "transform diagnosis by incorporating genetics, imaging, cognitive science, and other levels of information to lay the foundation for a new classification system" (Insel, 2013).

This chapter reviews the current state of assessing and diagnosing anxiety disorders. We discuss the diagnostic changes from *DSM-IV* (APA, 1994) to *DSM-5* (APA, 2013a) and offer a critical review of these revisions. Next, measures that are currently used to assess anxiety disorders are discussed, including the new self-report measures included in *DSM-5* Section III (*Emerging Measures and Models*). The remainder of the chapter focuses on the reliability and validity of *DSM* disorders, and reviews leading alternate approaches to assessing and diagnosing anxiety. Specifically, we critically discuss (a) the biomarker-based classification promoted by RDoC, (b) hierarchical dimensional conceptualizations of disorders, and (c) using person-centered statistical methods to identify empirically based diagnostic categories.

DSM-5 versus DSM-IV Anxiety Disorders

DSM-5 included a few large-scale organizational changes in the anxiety disorders. The anxiety disorders section no longer includes obsessive-compulsive disorder (OCD), posttraumatic stress disorder (PTSD), and acute stress disorder. Instead, these disorders have been split off to form the Obsessive-Compulsive and Related Disorders and Trauma- and Stressor-Related Disorders chapters. Leading up to the release of *DSM-5*, there was much discussion about whether OCD should be considered an anxiety disorder and whether there should be a separate obsessive-compulsive spectrum grouping of disorders (e.g., Hollander, Braun, & Simeon, 2008; Phillips et al., 2010; Stein et al., 2010). The separation was ultimately justified based on findings that OCD and other disorders with obsessional features (e.g., body dysmorphic disorder, trichotillomania) commonly co-occur, and have similar phenomenology, neurocircuitry, and genetic influences (Hollander et al., 2008). Likewise, research demonstrating that individuals with PTSD experience a range of emotions (e.g., guilt, shame, anger, *and* fear/anxiety) led to its separation from the anxiety disorders (Friedman, Resick, Bryant, & Brewin, 2011; Friedman, Resick, Bryant, Strain et al., 2011; Pai, Suris, & North, 2017; Resick & Miller, 2009). The assessment and diagnosis of disorders within these new diagnostic sections is discussed in subsequent chapters of this handbook.

Separation anxiety disorder and selective mutism, which were categorized as "Other Disorders of Infancy, Childhood, or Adolescence" in *DSM-IV*, have been added to the anxiety disorders section. Findings from epidemiological research (e.g., Shear, Jin, Ruscio, Walters, & Kessler, 2006) indicated that separation anxiety had an unexpectedly high prevalence in adults (Baldwin, Gordon, Abelli, & Pini, 2016), which led to this change. Likewise, research on the etiology and treatment of selective mutism demonstrated that it should be conceptualized as an anxiety disorder (e.g., Muris & Ollendick, 2015; Sharp, Sherman, & Gross, 2007). These changes eliminate the arbitrary separation of child and adult anxiety disorders, unifying anxiety-related disorders across the life span into one category.

Other specified anxiety disorder (OSAD) and unspecified anxiety disorder are two new anxiety disorder categories in *DSM-5*, replacing *DSM-IV* anxiety disorder not otherwise specified (NOS). The OSAD diagnosis offers an improvement over anxiety disorder NOS because it allows clinicians to attach a descriptive label that specifies why an individual does not meet full criteria for any of the other anxiety disorders. For instance, one can assign "OSAD – limited-symptom attacks," when a patient does not endorse attacks with four panic symptoms, and "OSAD – generalized anxiety not occurring more days than not," when a patient does not report anxiety and worry occurring more days than not for at least six months. This flexibility allows for increased specificity in diagnosing patients who report most (but not all) criteria required for a diagnosis. Ideally, this change will increase research investigating whether such "subthreshold" patients are substantively different (e.g., in impairment or distress) from those meeting full criteria. In other words, this change may help expand knowledge on dimensional characterizations of anxiety disorders (e.g., whether OSAD – limited symptoms attacks are a less severe version of panic disorder). In comparison, the unspecified anxiety disorder designation can be used when anxiety symptoms are causing significant distress or impairment but it is not clear how the symptoms should be labeled. Unspecified anxiety disorder may be used when it is not possible to fully assess diagnostic criteria (e.g., in emergency room settings), or for atypical manifestations of anxiety that are not consistent with any of the existing anxiety disorder categories.

Overall, the changes to the specific diagnostic criteria for each anxiety disorder were limited in *DSM-5*. Changes include separating agoraphobia from panic disorder, splitting one criterion into two, new specifiers, and other minor wording changes. These next few sections discuss important changes for each anxiety disorder, starting with the disorders that changed most substantively in *DSM-5*.

Panic Disorder, Agoraphobia, and Panic Attacks

Arguably, the anxiety disorders that saw the greatest change in *DSM-5* are panic disorder and agoraphobia. First and foremost, panic disorder and agoraphobia have been separated into two different disorders in *DSM-5*. Major changes were also made to the agoraphobia criteria, primarily with the goal of clarifying differential diagnosis with specific phobia. Finally, a panic attack specifier was created and can be attached to *any* diagnosis.

Separation of panic and agoraphobia. In *DSM-IV*, an individual could be diagnosed with panic disorder with or without agoraphobia, or with agoraphobia without a history of panic disorder. In *DSM-5*, these three disorders were replaced with two: panic disorder and agoraphobia. In other words, the panic disorder diagnosis no longer requires specification of the presence or absence of agoraphobia, and the agoraphobia diagnosis no longer embeds information pertaining to panic attack history. Wittchen, Gloster, Beesdo-Baum, Fava, and Craske's (2010) review of the state of agoraphobia classification served as a catalyst for the separation. Numerous reasons for separating the disorders were presented. For example, epidemiological research found that the majority of individuals with agoraphobia do not have panic attacks, and that agoraphobia can occur prior to the onset of panic symptoms. Research also shows that agoraphobia without panic symptoms is associated with significant functional impairment, persistent course, and infrequent spontaneous remission. Further, there is evidence that panic attacks, panic disorder, and agoraphobia have differences in incidence, gender distribution, and treatment response.

Despite this evidence, there are reasons to be skeptical of the decision to separate panic disorder and agoraphobia in *DSM-5*. For example, most of the evidence supporting the separation has not been confirmed in clinical samples (Wittchen et al., 2010). In fact, the diagnosis of agoraphobia without panic is very rare in clinical samples (Faravelli et al., 2009). The prevalence discrepancies between community and clinical samples may be because individuals who experience agoraphobia without panic are unlikely to seek treatment (Wittchen et al., 2010). Alternatively, the complicated differential diagnosis between *DSM-IV* agoraphobia and specific phobia, which resulted in substantial criteria changes to *DSM-5* agoraphobia (discussed later in this chapter), may have led to inflated rates of agoraphobia in community and population-based studies. Specifically, it is possible the lay diagnostic interviewers used in *DSM-IV* epidemiological research were prone to diagnose pervasive specific phobias (occurring in multiple situations, e.g., claustrophobia in crowds, elevators, tunnels, public transportation) as agoraphobia without panic attacks.

Another complication of the separation of panic disorder and agoraphobia is that these disorders still have overlapping criteria in *DSM-5* (Asmundson, Taylor, & Smits, 2014). Whereas a *DSM-5* agoraphobia diagnosis can satisfy criterion B2 of panic disorder (examples of criterion B2 include "avoiding agoraphobia-type situations," p. 209, APA, 2013a), fear of panic attacks (panic disorder criterion B2) can satisfy criterion B of agoraphobia (fear of developing panic like symptoms; see Tables 11.1 and 11.2). These overlapping criteria may confuse clinicians and compromise diagnostic reliability. Imagine, for instance, a patient who has a history of unexpected panic attacks but who does not currently experience attacks because they avoid all situations where attacks previously occurred (i.e., agoraphobia due to fear of panic attacks). Technically, such a patient does not meet criterion A of *DSM-5* panic disorder because they are not currently experiencing panic attacks. However, clinicians may still be prone to assign panic disorder to capture the core fear of having a panic attack (not just "panic-like" symptoms, cf. agoraphobia criterion B), especially if the patient reports they would have an attack if they entered any of the avoided situations (e.g., as part of an exposure-based treatment).

Agoraphobia criteria. *DSM-IV* does not clearly define how many or what kinds of situations must be feared to give a diagnosis of agoraphobia. Instead, the manual states that agoraphobia criterion A fears involve "clusters" of situations such as being outside the home, being in a crowd, or standing in line. In comparison, *DSM-5* substantially revised criterion A by delineating five specific types of agoraphobic situations: using public transportation, being in open spaces, being in enclosed places, standing in line or being in a crowd, and being outside of the home alone. To assign *DSM-5* agoraphobia, an individual must have fear or avoidance in at least two of these five categories.

The increased specificity of agoraphobia criterion A should enhance diagnostic reliability by clarifying how to differentiate agoraphobia from specific phobia (Asmundson et al., 2014). Although *DSM-IV* encouraged clinicians to consider a diagnosis of specific phobia "if the avoidance is limited to one or only a few specific situations" (p. 433), this recommendation did not clearly define what constitutes "a few" agoraphobic situations. Using the *DSM-IV* differential diagnosis guidelines, for example, a patient who fears buses, trains, airplanes, boats, and cars could be conceptualized as having either agoraphobia (i.e., fear of "a few" different situations) or specific phobia (i.e., fear of one situation – public transportation). According to *DSM-5*, these fears would all be conceptualized within one of the five agoraphobia situations. Thus, a *DSM-5* diagnosis of specific phobia of public transportation would be assigned.

Minor changes were also made to the other agoraphobia criteria. For example, *DSM-5* agoraphobia must now "almost always" provoke fear or anxiety (criterion C).

Table 11.1 *Panic disorder changes*

DSM-IV Criteria	*DSM-5* Criteria

(A) Presence of recurrent, unexpected Panic Attacks followed by at least 1 month of persistent concern about having another Panic Attack, worry about the possible implications or consequences of the Panic Attacks (e.g., losing control, having a heart attack, "going crazy"), or a significant behavioral change related to the attacks.
  • *Like Criterion B for DSM-5.*
(B) Absence of Agoraphobia.
  • *Agoraphobia is a specifier for Panic Disorder, Criterion B for **Panic Disorder with Agoraphobia** is "the presence of Agoraphobia."*
(C) The Panic Attacks are not due to the direct physiological effects of a substance (e.g., a drug of abuse, a medication) or a general medical condition (e.g., hyperthyroidism).
(D) The Panic Attacks are not better accounted for by another mental disorder, such as Social Phobia (e.g., occurring on exposure to feared social situations), Specific Phobia (e.g., on exposure to a specific phobic situation), Obsessive-Compulsive Disorder (e.g., on exposure to dirt in someone with an obsession about contamination), Posttraumatic Stress Disorder (e.g., in response to stimuli associated with a severe stressor), or Separation Anxiety Disorder (e.g., in response to being away from home or close relatives).
	(A) Recurrent unexpected panic attacks. A panic attack is an abrupt surge of intense fear or intense discomfort that reaches a peak within minutes, and during which time four (or more) of the [panic attack] symptoms occur.
	(B) At least one of the attacks has been followed by 1 month (or more) of one or both of the following:
	  (1) Persistent concern or worry about additional panic attacks or their consequences (e.g., losing control, having a heart attack, "going crazy").
	(2) A significant maladaptive change in behavior related to the attacks (e.g., behaviors designed to avoid having panic attacks, such as avoidance of exercise or unfamiliar situations).
	  • *Like Criterion A for DSM-IV.*
	(C) The disturbance is not attributable to the physiological effects of a substance (e.g., a drug of abuse, a medication) or another medical condition (e.g., hyperthyroidism, cardiopulmonary disorders).
	(D) The disturbance is not better explained by another mental disorder (e.g., the panic attacks do not occur only in response to feared social situations, as in social anxiety disorder; in response to circumscribed phobic objects or situations, as in specific phobia; in response to obsessions, as in obsessive-compulsive disorder; in response to reminders of traumatic events, as in posttraumatic stress disorder; or in response to separation from attachment figures, as in separation anxiety disorder).

Note. DSM-IV Criteria for Panic Disorder with Agoraphobia and Panic Disorder without Agoraphobia are the same except for Criterion B. The main criteria listed are those for Panic Disorder without Agoraphobia.

Table 11.2 *Agoraphobia changes*

DSM-IV Criteria	*DSM-5* Criteria
Agoraphobia (A) Anxiety about being in places or situations from which escape might be difficult (or embarrassing) or in which help may not be available in the event of having an unexpected or situationally predisposed Panic Attack or panic-like symptoms. Agoraphobic fears typically involve characteristic clusters of situations that include being outside the home alone; being in a crowd or standing in a line; being on a bridge; and traveling in a bus, train, or automobile. 　• *Stated in list form in the DSM-5* (B) The situations are avoided (e.g., travel is restricted) or else are endured with marked distress or with anxiety about having a Panic Attack or panic-like symptoms, or require the presence of a companion. 　• *Like Criterion D and B in DSM-5* (C) The anxiety or phobic avoidance is not better accounted for by another mental disorder, such as Social Phobia (e.g., avoidance limited to social situations because of fear of embarrassment), Specific Phobia (e.g., avoidance limited to a single situation like elevators), Obsessive-Compulsive Disorder (e.g., avoidance of dirt in someone with an obsession about contamination), Posttraumatic Stress Disorder (e.g., avoidance of stimuli associated with a severe stressor), or Separation Anxiety Disorder (e.g., avoidance of leaving home or relatives). 　• *Like Criterion I in DSM-5* **Agoraphobia without History of Panic Disorder** (A) The presence of Agoraphobia related to fear of developing panic-like symptoms (e.g., dizziness or diarrhea).	(A) Marked fear or anxiety about two (or more) of the following five situations: 　(1) Using public transportation (e.g., automobiles, buses, trains, ships, planes) 　(2) Being in open spaces (e.g., parking lots, marketplaces, bridges). 　(3) Being in enclosed places (e.g., shops, theaters, cinemas). 　(4) Standing in line or being in a crowd. 　(5) Being outside of the home alone. (B) The individual fears or avoids these situations because of thoughts that escape might be difficult or help might not be available in the event of developing panic-like symptoms or other incapacitating or embarrassing symptoms (e.g., fear of falling in the elderly; fear of incontinence). (C) The agoraphobic situations almost always provoke fear or anxiety. 　• *Not stated in DSM-IV* (D) The agoraphobic situations are actively avoided, require the presence of a companion, or are endured with intense fear or anxiety. (E) The fear or anxiety is out of proportion to the actual danger posed by the agoraphobic situations and to the sociocultural context. (F) The fear, anxiety, or avoidance is persistent, typically lasting for 6 months or more. (G) The fear, anxiety, or avoidance causes clinically significant distress or impairment in social, occupational, or other important areas of functioning. 　• *Criteria F and G are not stated in DSM-IV* (H) If another medical condition (e.g., inflammatory bowel disease, Parkinson's disease) is present, the fear, anxiety, or avoidance is clearly excessive.

Table 11.2 (*cont.*)

DSM-IV Criteria	*DSM-5* Criteria
(B) Criteria have never been met for Panic Disorder. (C) The disturbance is not due to the direct physiological effects of a substance (e.g., a drug of abuse, a medication) or a general medical condition. (D) If an associated general medical condition is present the fear described in Criterion A is clearly in excess of that usually associated with the condition. • *Like Criterion H in DSM-5*	(I) The fear, anxiety, or avoidance is not better explained by the symptoms of another mental disorder – for example, the symptoms are not confined to specific phobia, situational type; do not involve only social situations (as in social anxiety disorder); and are not related exclusively to obsessions (as in obsessive-compulsive disorder), perceived defects or flaws in physical appearance (as in body dysmorphic disorder), reminders of traumatic events (as in posttraumatic stress disorder), or fear of separation (as in separation anxiety disorder).

Note. In the *DSM-IV*, Agoraphobia is not a codable disorder, but rather a specifier for Panic Disorder (discussed later in this chapter). Two separate classifications exist for Agoraphobia as shown in the table. *DSM-5* criteria are a combination of *DSM-IV* criteria for both classifications.

The fear, anxiety, or avoidance must now persist for at least six months (criterion F). Although these new frequency and duration requirements are consistent with those used for the other anxiety disorders, there is little research on their validity (Asmundson et al., 2014).

Panic attacks specifier. Another notable change in *DSM-5* is a panic attack specifier that can be attached to *any* diagnosis. Whereas *DSM-IV* distinguished situationally bound/cued, situationally predisposed, and unexpected/uncued panic attacks, *DSM-5* defines panic attacks as either unexpected (e.g., due to panic disorder) or expected (e.g., due to another diagnosis, assigned with the panic attack specifier). As reviewed by Craske and colleagues (2010), research suggests that panic attacks occur in many other disorders besides panic disorder, including other anxiety disorders (cf. *DSM-IV* social and specific phobia) as well as mood, substance use, and psychotic disorders. There is also evidence that the presence of panic attacks is associated with higher overall symptom severity, suicidal behavior and ideation, and poor treatment response. Given that it provides descriptive information about a common and clinically important transdiagnostic symptom presentation, this new specifier is a welcome addition to the *DSM-5*.

Social Anxiety Disorder

Social anxiety disorder (SAD) also underwent some noteworthy changes in *DSM-5* (cf. Heimberg et al., 2014). The most obvious change is that the disorder has been renamed *social anxiety disorder* instead of *social phobia*. This change has long been encouraged given concerns that the name "social phobia" gave the incorrect impression that the disorder is infrequent or not impairing (Liebowitz, Heimberg, Fresco, Travers, & Stein, 2000). This new name helps differentiate SAD from specific phobia, and better conveys the pervasiveness of social anxiety (Bögels et al., 2010; Liebowitz et al., 2000). Along these lines, research demonstrated that community residents were more likely to recommend a person to seek treatment if their symptoms were labeled as SAD rather than social phobia (Bruce, Heimberg, & Coles, 2012).

Criteria changes. SAD also underwent several criteria-level changes in *DSM-5* (Heimberg et al., 2014). Previously, criterion A of *DSM-IV* social phobia described fear of social situations *and* fear that one will act in a way that is humiliating or embarrassing. This criterion was too narrow, as fear of rejection and offending others are also common in SAD (Heimberg et al., 2014). Accordingly, in *DSM-5*, fear of negative evaluation has been given its own expanded criterion. Specifically, criterion B states that "[t]he individual fears that he or she will act in a way or show anxiety symptoms that will be negatively evaluated (i.e., will be humiliating or embarrassing; will lead to rejection or offend others)" (APA, 2013a, p. 202).

Another change is that *DSM-IV*'s criterion C, which stated that individuals must recognize their fear as excessive and unreasonable, was removed. Instead, a new criterion E in *DSM-5* specifies that the "fear or anxiety is out of proportion to the actual threat posed by the social situation and to the sociocultural context" (APA, 2013a, p. 203). The sociocultural aspect of criterion E is important given that certain symptom presentations can appear consistent with SAD, but actually may be culturally appropriate (e.g., avoiding eye contact due to cultural expectations about displaying respect). Finally, similar to the changes made to agoraphobia, the duration criterion (F) now states that SAD must be present for at least six months. In *DSM-IV*, the six-month duration was only required when diagnosing SAD in individuals younger than 18.

Performance-only specifier. *DSM-5* removed the "generalized" specifier for SAD, replacing it with a "performance only" specifier to use when fear is limited to speaking or performing in public. The generalized specifier was introduced in *DSM-III-R* (APA, 1987), and in *DSM-IV* was defined as having fears in *most* social situations. However, there was a lack of specificity regarding what types of situations or how many situations were necessary for the generalized specifier to be assigned. As a result, there was inconsistency across research groups in how generalized social phobia was defined and diagnosed (e.g., Heimberg, Holt, Schneier, Spitzer, & Liebowitz, 1993; Stemberger, Turner, Beidel, & Calhoun, 1995). For *DSM-5*, it was decided that clinicians could more reliably diagnose a more circumscribed SAD subtype (Heimberg et al., 2014). However, the performance-only specifier was also justified empirically. For example, individuals with performance-only SAD are more likely than individuals with broader SAD manifestations (e.g., generalized SAD) to experience increased physiological response (Boone et al., 1999; Heimberg, Hope, Dodge, & Becker, 1990; Levin et al., 1993)

Table 11.3 *Social anxiety disorder changes*

DSM-IV Criteria	DSM-5 Criteria
(A) A marked and persistent fear of one or more social or performance situations in which the person is exposed to unfamiliar people or to possible scrutiny by others. The individual fears that he or she will act in a way (or show anxiety symptoms) that will be humiliating or embarrassing. **Note:** In children, there must be evidence of the capacity for age-appropriate social relationships with familiar people and the anxiety must occur in peer settings, not just in interactions with adults.	(A) Marked fear or anxiety about one or more social situations in which the individual is exposed to possible scrutiny by others. Examples include social interactions (e.g., having a conversation, meeting unfamiliar people), being observed (e.g., eating or drinking), and performing in front of others (e.g., giving a speech). **Note:** In children, the anxiety must occur in peer settings and not just during interactions with adults. • *More specific for situation types*
(B) Exposure to the feared social situation almost invariably provokes anxiety, which may take the form of a situationally bound or situationally predisposed Panic Attack. **Note:** In children, the anxiety may be expressed by crying, tantrums, freezing, or shrinking from social situations with unfamiliar people. • *Like Criterion C in DSM-5*	(B) The individual fears that he or she will act in a way or show anxiety symptoms that will be negatively evaluated (i.e., will be humiliating or embarrassing; will lead to rejection or offend others). • *Included in Criterion A in DSM-IV*
(C) The person recognizes that the fear is excessive or unreasonable. **Note:** In children, this feature may be absent. • *Not stated in DSM-5*	(C) The social situations almost always provoke fear or anxiety. **Note:** In children, the fear or anxiety may be expressed by crying, tantrums, freezing, clinging, shrinking, or failing to speak in social situations.
(D) The feared social or performance situations are avoided or else are endured with intense anxiety or distress.	(D) The social situations are avoided or endured with intense fear or anxiety.
(E) The avoidance, anxious anticipation, or distress in the feared social or performance situation(s) interferes significantly with the person's normal routine, occupational (academic) functioning, or social activities or relationships, or there is marked distress about having the phobia. • *Like Criterion G in DSM-5*	(E) The fear or anxiety is out of proportion to the actual threat posed by the social situation and to the sociocultural context. • *Not stated in DSM-IV*
	(F) The fear, anxiety, or avoidance is persistent, typically lasting for 6 months or more. • *Does not mention adulthood specifier*

Table 11.3 (*cont.*)

DSM-IV Criteria	*DSM-5* Criteria
(F) In individuals under age 18 years, the duration is at least 6 months.	(G) The fear, anxiety, or avoidance causes clinically significant distress or impairment in social, occupational, or other important areas of functioning. • *Like Criterion E in DSM-IV*
(G) The fear or avoidance is not due to the direct physiological effects of a substance (e.g., a drug of abuse, a medication) or a general medical condition and is not better accounted for by another mental disorder (e.g., Panic Disorder with or without Agoraphobia, Separation Anxiety Disorder, Body Dysmorphic Disorder, a Pervasive Developmental Disorder, or Schizoid Personality Disorder).	(H) The fear, anxiety, or avoidance is not attributable to the physiological effects of a substance (e.g., a drug of abuse, a medication) or another medical condition.
(H) If a general medical condition or another mental disorder is present, the fear in Criterion A is unrelated to it, e.g., the fear is not of stuttering, trembling in Parkinson's disease, or exhibiting abnormal eating behavior in Anorexia Nervosa or Bulimia Nervosa. • *Like Criterion J in DSM-5*	(I) The fear, anxiety, or avoidance is not better explained by the symptoms of another mental disorder, such as panic disorder, body dysmorphic disorder, or autism spectrum disorder. • *Criteria H and J form Criterion G in DSM-IV*
	(J) If another medical condition (e.g., Parkinson's disease, obesity, disfigurement from burns or injury) is present, the fear, anxiety, or avoidance is clearly unrelated or is excessive. • *Like Criterion H in DSM-IV*
Specifiers:	**Specifiers:**
1) **Generalized:** if the fears include most social situations (also consider the additional diagnosis of Avoidant Personality Disorder).	1) **Performance Only:** if the fear is restricted to speaking or performing in public.

and to respond to beta-adrenergic blocking agents (Blöte, Kint, Miers, & Westenberg, 2009; Bögels et al., 2010). A large proportion of individuals diagnosed with SAD in epidemiological studies report circumscribed performance-related fears (Stein, Torgrud, & Walker, 2000; Stein, Walker, & Forde, 1996), although this finding has not been replicated in clinical samples (Kerns, Comer, Pincus, & Hofmann, 2013).

Generalized Anxiety Disorder

For the most part, only minor wording changes were made to the generalized anxiety disorder (GAD) criteria. The one exception was removal of text from criteria D and F stating that GAD could not be diagnosed if it occurred exclusively during the course of PTSD or a mood, psychotic, or a pervasive developmental disorder. Research on this "hierarchy rule" found patients with comorbid major depressive disorder (MDD) and GAD (i.e., GAD onset prior to MDD) to have a similar clinical presentation as patients experiencing GAD within the course of MDD (Lawrence, Liverant, Rosellini, & Brown, 2009; Zimmerman & Chelminski, 2003). In addition, both of these diagnostic subgroups reported more severe psychopathology, negative affect, and functional impairment than patients experiencing MDD without GAD. This research suggests that the hierarchy rule obscured important clinical information, which is one reason it was removed in *DSM-5*.

GAD has historically struggled with diagnostic reliability (Rutter & Brown, 2015). In one study, 55% of all GAD diagnosis disagreements were due to the patient describing their symptoms differently across two independent diagnostic interviews (i.e., difference in patient report, Brown, Di Nardo, Lehman, & Campbell, 2001a). Relying on patients to be consistent in reporting the onset and course of worry in relation to mood and other disorders likely played a role in these diagnostic disagreements. Along these lines, mood disorders were involved in 47% of cases where there was GAD diagnostic disagreements (Brown et al., 2001a). Accordingly, removal of the hierarchy rule in *DSM-5* may increase the diagnostic reliability of GAD. Of note, however, other proposed changes to increase GAD reliability were not adopted in *DSM-5* (e.g., adding a criterion for observable worry-related behaviors such as procrastination and over-preparation; Andrews et al., 2010).

Other Disorders

Consistent with agoraphobia and SAD, the diagnosis of *DSM-5* specific phobia now requires the fear to be "out of proportion" to the actual danger (criterion D). In addition, the six-month duration requirement (criterion E) is now applied to all ages, not just individuals under 18. Otherwise, the specific phobia criteria were revised with very minor wording changes. Likewise, very minor wording changes were made to the criteria for substance/medication-induced anxiety disorder and anxiety disorder due to another medical condition.

Finally, as mentioned earlier, separation anxiety disorder and selective mutism were added to the anxiety disorders category in *DSM-5*. Selective mutism's criteria were not revised aside from very minor wording changes. The separation anxiety disorder criteria now mentions "going to work" as a separation example for adult patients (criterion A), requires a six-month duration for adults and four weeks for children and adolescents (criterion B), and removes the early onset specifier (before age six) that had been in *DSM-IV*. Given that this disorder can now be given to adults, these were necessary changes.

Critical Review of Measures for Assessing Anxiety Disorders in Adults

Clinical Interviews

Several well-validated semi-structured *DSM-IV* diagnostic interviews were updated with the release of *DSM-5*, although data are not yet available on their reliability or validity. The Structured Clinical Interview for *DSM-5* (SCID-5) (First, Williams, Karg, & Spitzer, 2015; see Lobbestael, Leurgans, & Arntz, 2011, for *DSM-IV*/SCID-IV reliability information) can be used to assess a wide range of disorders, providing coverage of virtually all *DSM-5* diagnostic sections (including all anxiety disorders except selective mutism). The SCID-5 directs clinicians to rate *DSM-5* criteria for each disorder using an ordinal (0–2) scale of "absent," "sub-threshold," or "present." Several example questions are provided to help assess each criterion. However, the SCID-5 does not include ratings for specific examples of how *DSM-5* criteria may manifest for an individual. For instance, although a single 0–2 rating is made for SAD criterion A (marked fear or anxiety about social situations), ratings are not made for the types of social situations in which fear or anxiety may occur (e.g., participating in meetings, presentations, talking on the phone, initiating conversations). As a result, the SCID has limited utility in planning psychological treatments (e.g., creating a fear and avoidance hierarchy in cognitive behavioral therapy).

The Mini International Neuropsychiatric Interview for *DSM-5* (MINI-5) (Sheehan, 2015; see Sheehan et al., 1998, for *DSM-IV*/MINI-IV reliability information) is similar to the SCID-5 in that it is criteria-focused. However, the MINI-5 provides fewer example questions than the SCID-5 to assist in assessing criteria (e.g., the MINI-5 includes one example question to assess GAD criterion A, the SCID-5 includes eight questions to assess the same criterion). Another difference is that criteria are only rated as present versus absent using the MINI-5 (i.e., no subthreshold designation). The MINI-5 covers a narrower range of disorders than the SCID-5; there is no assessment of specific phobia, separation anxiety disorder, persistent depressive disorder, or body dysmorphic disorder. Collectively, these factors contribute to the MINI-5 having a briefer administration time than the

SCID-5. However, they also limit the MINI-5's clinical and research utility in ways similar to the SCID-5 (e.g., lack of functional analysis).

The Anxiety and Related Disorders Interview Schedule for *DSM-5* (ADIS-5) (Brown & Barlow, 2013; see Brown et al., 2001a, for *DSM-IV*/ADIS-IV reliability information) can be used to assess all *DSM-5* anxiety disorders as well as most mood (e.g., major and persistent depressive disorder, bipolar disorder), obsessive-compulsive (e.g., OCD, body dysmorphic disorder), trauma and stress (e.g., PTSD), somatic symptom (e.g., somatic symptom disorder, illness anxiety disorder), and substance-related disorders (all major drug classes are assessed). The ADIS-5 is unique in that it requires clinicians to make dimensional severity/distress ratings (0–8) for several key (e.g., *DSM-5* criteria) and associated features of each disorder. In the SAD section, for example, separate fear/anxiety and avoidance ratings are made for 16 social situations that could be associated with concerns about negative evaluation (e.g., participating in meetings, presentations, talking on the phone, introducing oneself to groups, initiating conversation, being assertive). Further, *DSM-5* diagnoses are assigned an overall clinical severity rating (CSR) using a 0 (none) to 8 (very severely disturbing/disabling) scale, with a CSR of 4 (definitely disturbing/disabling) or higher representing a formal *DSM-5* diagnosis. Use of the diagnostic CSRs allows clear identification of the "principal" diagnosis (i.e., most interfering disorder) as well as comorbid and subthreshold disorders. The ADIS-5 provides a more thorough assessment of the emotional disorders than the SCID-5 or MINI-5, but takes longer to administer because of the time demands associated with making numerous dimensional ratings.

A new interview developed after the release of *DSM-5* is the Diagnostic Interview for Anxiety, Mood, and Obsessive-Compulsive and Related Neuropsychiatric Disorders (DIAMOND) (Tolin et al., in press). The DIAMOND is intended to provide a detailed assessment of the anxiety, mood, and obsessive-compulsive disorders, although key diagnostic criteria are also included for trauma and stress, schizophrenia spectrum disorders, feeding and eating disorders, somatic symptom disorders, and substance-related disorders. The DIAMOND is similar to the ADIS-5 in that it can be used to assess *DSM-5* criteria *and* associated disorder features. Diagnoses are also assigned an overall severity rating between 0 (normal) and 7 (extreme). The main difference between the DIAMOND and ADIS-5 is that the DIAMOND primarily relies on a checklist-based approach to assess associated features of a disorder, rather than asking clinicians to make dimensional ratings. Continuing with the example of SAD, the DIAMOND provides clinicians with a checklist to indicate the types of social situations where social fear/anxiety occurs (e.g., public speaking, starting or maintaining conversations, assertiveness). This results in a shorter administration time than the ADIS-5, but at the loss of information about symptom severity. One limitation of the DIAMOND is that, unlike the ADIS-IV (Brown et al., 2001a), the diagnostic severity ratings have poor interrater reliability (Tolin et al., in press).

Self-report measures. Over the past 50 years, hundreds of self-report questionnaires have been developed to assess the severity of core features of *DSM* anxiety disorders. These measures typically have been developed to assess dimensions of one or two key *DSM* criteria for the disorder of interest (i.e., severity of fear, anxiety, worry, or avoidance associated with the disorder). As reviewed in Antony, Orsillo, and Roemer's (2001) handbook of empirically supported measures for anxiety disorders, many well-validated measures can be used to assess each disorder. We focus our review on: (a) the most popular measures for the core adult anxiety disorders (i.e., excluding selective mutism, substance/medical induced anxiety, other/unspecified anxiety), and (b) the dimensional measures included in Section III of *DSM-5* (*Emerging Measures and Models*).

We initially identified questionnaires for each anxiety disorder using Antony et al.'s (2001) handbook. As this handbook was published more than 15 years ago, we searched for newer disorder-specific measures using Google Scholar (e.g., using the search terms "panic disorder" AND ["self-report" OR "questionnaire"]). We then determined the relative popularity of each measure based on the number of search results obtained by Google Scholar when using the questionnaire name as the search term (e.g., "Liebowitz Social Anxiety Scale" produced roughly 4,100 results). In Table 11.4, we describe some of the most popular measures found in our review. With the exception of adult separation anxiety disorder, at least two self-report questionnaires (developed prior to *DSM-5*) were identified for each disorder.

Table 11.4 describes the *DSM-5* disorder-specific severity measures for the six core anxiety disorders. These questionnaires are available on the APA website (APA, 2017) but are not included in the printed version of *DSM-5*. The six severity measures are very similar. Each consists of 10 items (0–4 scale) with instructions that direct individuals to answer the questions with a specific disorder in mind. For example, whereas the separation anxiety measure asks individuals to report on symptoms in response to being separated from home or the people who are important to them, the social anxiety measure directs individuals to report on symptoms in response to social situations (example social situations are provided). However, the 10 questions are worded quite similarly across the six measures, assessing common anxiety disorder symptom manifestations in response to the example situation(s) described in the questionnaire instructions. For each disorder, the 10 questions assess: feelings of terror/fear, anxiety/worry/ nervousness, negative thoughts, panic symptoms (e.g., racing heart), tension, avoidance behaviors, escape behaviors, over preparation/procrastination, distraction, and safety behaviors (e.g., using alcohol or carrying medication). Preliminary research in small samples (e.g., *n*s < 100) supports the reliability and convergent/discriminant validity of the disorder-specific severity measures (e.g., LeBeau, Mesri, & Craske, 2016), although most of these studies have been conducted outside the United States using translated versions of the questionnaires (Knappe et al., 2013, 2014; Möller & Bögels, 2016).

Notably, *DSM-5* also includes *cross-cutting* symptom measures in the text (pp. 733–741). Whereas the disorder-specific severity measures correspond closely to

Table 11.4 *Descriptions of popular questionnaires to assess severity of DSM anxiety disorders In adults*

Disorder	Citation	Coverage/focus
Separation anxiety disorder	In adults	
Adult Separation Anxiety Questionnaire (Items: 27; Scale: 0–3)	Manicavasagar, Silove, Wagner, & Drobny (2003)	Multiple manifestations of separation anxiety (e.g., confidence, discomfort, relationship preoccupation)
DSM-5 severity measure (Items: 10; Scale: 0–4)	APA (2013a)	Symptoms in response to separation (panic, anxiety, negative thoughts, avoidance/escape behaviors)
Specific phobia		
Fear Survey Schedule (II-Items: 51; Scale: 0–6; III-Items: 108; Scale 0–4)	II: Geer (1965) III: Wolpe & Lang (1969)	Wide range of common phobias (within all five DSM-5 subtypes), social phobia, and uncommon fears (e.g., vacuums)
Fear Questionnaire (Items: 24; Scale: 0–8)	Marks & Mathews (1979)	Situational fears, blood/injury fears, social phobia, and general distress
DSM-5 severity measure (Items: 10; Scale: 0–4)	APA (2013a)	Symptoms in response to one of the five phobia subtypes (panic, anxiety, negative thoughts, avoidance/escape behaviors)
Social anxiety disorder		
Social Phobia and Anxiety Inventory (Items: 45; Scale: 0–6)	Turner, Beidel, Dancu, & Stanley (1989)	Somatic, cognitive, and behavioral aspects of social phobia across a variety of situations and settings
Liebowitz Social Anxiety Scale (Items: 24; Scale: 0–3)	Liebowitz (1987)	Fear and avoidance of situations involving performance and social interaction
Social Phobia Scale (Items: 20; Scale: 0–4)	Mattick & Clark (1998)	Fear in performance situations involving being observed by others while engaged in activities (e.g., eating or writing)

Measure	Citation	Description
Social Interaction Anxiety Scale (Items: 20; Scale: 0–4)	Mattick & Clark (1998)	Cognitive, affective, and behavioral reactions to interactional social situations
DSM-5 severity measure (Items: 10; Scale: 0–4)	APA (2013)	Symptoms surrounding social situations like public speaking, attending social events, having conversations (panic, anxiety, negative thoughts, avoidance/escape behaviors)
Panic disorder		
Panic Disorder Severity Scale (Items: 7; Scale: 0–4)	Houck, Spiegel, Shear, & Rucci (2002)	Panic attack frequency and associated distress, anticipatory anxiety, avoidance behaviors, impairment
Panic and Agoraphobia Scale (Items: 13; Scale: 0–4)	Bandelow (1999)	Panic attack frequency, checklist of agoraphobic avoidance, impairment
DSM-5 severity measure (Items: 10; Scale: 0–4)	APA (2013)	Unexpected panic attacks and symptoms in response to them (anxiety, negative thoughts, avoidance/escape behaviors)
Agoraphobia		
Albany Panic and Phobia Questionnaire-Agoraphobia (Items: 27; Subscale: 9; Scale: 0–8)	Rapee, Craske, & Barlow (1994/1995)	Fear in common agoraphobic situations
Mobility Inventory for Agoraphobia (Items: 26; Scale: 1–5)	Chambless, Caputo, Jasin, Gracely, & Williams (1985)	Avoidance of common agoraphobic situations when alone and when traveling with a companion (separate questions); brief assessment of panic attacks
DSM-5 severity measure (Items: 10; Scale: 0–4)	APA (2013)	Symptoms surrounding being in crowds, public places, transportation, being away from home (panic, anxiety, negative thoughts, avoidance/escape behaviors)

Generalized anxiety disorder

Measure	Citation	Description
GAD-7 (Items: 7; Scale: 0–3)	Spitzer et al. (2006)	Excessiveness and controllability of worry and associated GAD symptoms
Penn State Worry Questionnaire (Items: 16; Scale: 1–5)	Meyer, Miller, Metzger, & Borkovec (1990)	Tendency to worry excessively in response to various situations
DSM-5 severity measure (Items: 10; Scale: 0–4)	APA (2013a)	Symptoms in response to worry about family, health finances, school, work (panic, anxiety, negative thoughts, avoidance/escape behaviors)

Note. APA = American Psychiatric Association; *DSM* = Diagnostic and Statistical Manual for Mental Disorders; *DSM-5* = Diagnostic and Statistical Manual for Mental Disorders, 5th edition; GAD = generalized anxiety disorder

DSM-5 criteria and are intended to assess the severity of clinical or subclinical diagnoses, the cross-cutting measures are broad and intended to coarsely assess a range of presenting symptoms and problems (i.e., across all *DSM-5* chapters). The "Level 1" cross-cutting measure for adults consists of 23 questions that assess 13 symptom domains (0–4 scale), each of which broadly corresponds to a specific *DSM-5* diagnostic section. Three questions are included for the anxiety disorders to assess (a) nervousness, anxiety, and worry; (b) panic; and (c) avoidance of situations that cause anxiety. If an individual endorses any of the three items at a mild intensity or greater (i.e., 2, 3, or 4 on the response scale), administration of the more detailed "Level 2" cross-cutting anxiety measure is recommended. The Level 2 measure consists of seven questions (1–5 scale) assessing feelings of fear, anxiety, worry, difficulty focusing, nervousness, uneasiness, and tension. Field Trial data indicate the cross-cutting scales for anxiety are reliable (Narrow et al., 2013). Whereas the three Level 1 questions for adult anxiety each had good test-retest reliability (intra-class correlations = 0.64 to 0.70), an analysis combining the Level 1 and Level 2 anxiety scales also indicated good overall test-retest reliability (intra-class correlation = 0.73).

Reliability and Validity of DSM-5 Anxiety Disorders

Reliability of DSM-5 Anxiety Disorders

DSM anxiety disorders have undergone vast revision over the past 40 years with the goals of improving diagnostic reliability and validity. *DSM-5* was no different. Undeniable progress was made prior to *DSM-5*, with a noteworthy leap forward occurring after the adoption of polythetic criteria sets starting in *DSM-III* (APA, 1980). The "splitting" of specific criteria/symptoms into different categories prompted the development of semi-structured diagnostic interviews (e.g., Structured Clinical Interview for *DSM*, Spitzer & Williams, 1983; Anxiety Disorders Interview Schedule, Di Nardo, O'Brien, Barlow, Waddell, & Blanchard, 1983), which inherently improved diagnostic reliability by allowing clinicians to uniformly and systematically assess symptoms within *DSM*'s diagnostic categories.

Diagnostic and symptom-level revisions post *DSM-III* continued to improve reliability. In a sample of 362 outpatients, for example, Brown et al. (2001a) examined the interrater reliability of current *DSM-IV* anxiety (and mood) disorders and compared kappas to those estimated in a similarly designed *DSM-III-R* reliability study (Di Nardo, Moras, Barlow, Rapee, & Brown, 1993). In both studies, individuals presenting for assessment and treatment at an outpatient clinic underwent two independent administrations of the ADIS (ADIS-R, Di Nardo & Barlow, 1988; ADIS-IV, Di Nardo, Brown, & Barlow, 1994). For several disorders that underwent significant revision in *DSM-IV* (e.g., panic disorder, GAD), higher kappas were estimated in the *DSM-IV*/ADIS-IV study than in the earlier *DSM-III-R*/ADIS-R study. In contrast, no diagnosis had a notable decrease in reliability.

Given the nature of the revisions (e.g., minor wording changes), there is little reason to expect *DSM-5* anxiety disorders will be less reliable than *DSM-IV*. Nevertheless, the interrater reliability of *all DSM-5* disorders was criticized shortly after completion of the Field Trials because several disorders had higher kappas in the *DSM-IV* Field Trials (e.g., Frances, 2012; Spitzer, William, & Endicott, 2012). The kappa for GAD, the only anxiety disorder included in the *DSM-5* Field Trials, was 0.20 (Regier et al., 2013). However, there are two methodological, rather than substantive, explanations as to why low kappas were obtained for GAD and other disorders in the *DSM-5* Field Trials. First, the objective of the Field Trial analysis was to examine interrater reliability among two independent clinicians "using their *usual* clinical interviews" (Regier et al., 2013, p. 61), not a preselected semi-structured interview (cf. *DSM-IV* Field Trials). Second, the *DSM-5* Field Trials examined interrater reliability using the *test-retest* method, whereby two clinicians independently conducted assessments (e.g., within a seven-day period) and separately assigned diagnoses. In comparison, the *DSM-IV* Field Trials examined diagnostic agreement using the *audio-recording* method; one clinician conducted the assessment while a second clinician listened to an audio recording of the assessment and independently assigned diagnoses.

Chmielewski, Clark, Bagby, and Watson (2015) recently demonstrated that, even when requiring clinicians to use a single semi-structured interview, the test-retest approach results in much lower reliability estimates than the audio-recording approach. In this study, a sample of 339 outpatients was independently diagnosed by two clinicians with the SCID for *DSM-IV* (First, Spitzer, Gibbon, & Williams, 2002) using either the test-retest (within a seven-day period; $n = 218$) or audio-recording method ($n = 49$). Across the four anxiety disorders examined, average reliability was much lower using the test-retest method (mean $\kappa = 0.46$) than the audio-recording method (mean $\kappa = 0.76$). Social phobia was the most reliable anxiety disorder using the audio-recording method ($\kappa = 0.91$) but *least* reliable using the test-retest method ($\kappa = 0.25$). GAD was otherwise the least reliable anxiety diagnosis (audio recording $\kappa = 0.55$, test-retest $\kappa = 0.45$). These test-retest estimates for GAD are still much higher than obtained in the *DSM-5* Field Trials ($\kappa = 0.20$), presumably because all interviewers used the SCID rather than a personally preferred interview.

To date, only Tolin and colleagues (in press) have examined the interrater reliability of *DSM-5* anxiety disorders using a semi-structured interview. A total of 121 adult outpatients were independently assessed by two interviewers using the DIAMOND (i.e., test-retest method). It is noteworthy that the two assessments occurred within a 48-hour period rather than the 7–14-day period commonly used in prior test-retest studies (cf. Brown et al., 2001a; Chmielewski et al., 2015). Excellent reliability was achieved for panic disorder ($\kappa = 0.88$) and agoraphobia ($\kappa = 0.87$), the two disorders with the most significant revisions in *DSM-5*. Good reliability was also found for GAD ($\kappa = 0.71$), SAD ($\kappa = 0.70$), and specific phobia ($\kappa = 0.66$). These results support the interrater reliability of *DSM-5* anxiety disorders when using a structured assessment protocol. Unfortunately, it is not appropriate to compare interrater reliability of *DSM-5* anxiety disorders based on the DIAMOND to interrater reliability of *DSM-IV* disorders based on the SCID-IV (Chmielewski et al., 2015) or ADIS-IV (Brown et al., 2001a). To determine if the changes to the *DSM-5* anxiety disorders improve diagnostic reliability, research would need to compare the ADIS-IV to ADIS-5 and SCID-IV to SCID-5 using the test-retest method. However, such comparisons would need to be made cautiously (e.g., with consideration of differences in patient samples and the training level of diagnosticians).

Validity of DSM-5 Anxiety Disorders

Although there are several potential sources of diagnostic unreliability (e.g., differences in patient report, changes in clinical status, Brown et al., 2001a), two forms of diagnostic unreliability are particularly noteworthy because they may be the direct consequence of limitations in *DSM-5*'s construct validity. First, threshold disagreements occur when clinicians disagree on whether a symptom or disorder is causing clinically significant interference or distress (i.e., disagreeing if a disorder is present versus absent). Threshold disagreements are a direct result of *DSM*'s ongoing reliance on a categorical approach to conceptualizing psychopathology. Second, conceptualization disagreements occur when clinicians attribute a symptom (or symptoms) to different disorders (e.g., worry about health due to panic disorder, GAD, or illness anxiety disorder). This is a consequence of the vast number of *DSM* diagnoses with overlapping core processes and diagnostic criteria (e.g., panic, worry, avoidance, sleep difficulties). If psychopathology is dimensional in nature, and there are more similarities than differences across *DSM*'s diagnostic categories, then making dichotomous judgments about symptoms and disorders will substantially increase measurement error (Markon, Chmielewski, & Miller, 2011).

Categories versus dimensions. There is evidence that most types of anxiety and fear manifest along a continuum of severity from normal/adaptive to abnormal/interfering. Taxometric research has found social anxiety (Kollman, Brown, Liverant, & Hofmann, 2006), worry (Olatunji, Broman-Fulks, & Bergman, 2010), agoraphobia (Slade & Grisham, 2009), and separation anxiety (Silove et al., 2007) to be dimensional rather than categorical constructs. A dimensional conceptualization of the anxiety disorders is also supported by the frequent use of anxiety disorder not otherwise specified (*DSM-IV*) to capture clinically significant subthreshold symptom presentations in clinical settings (Zimmerman, McDermut, & Mattia, 2000). It is unlikely that these individuals, who often fall "one symptom short" of a non-residual anxiety diagnosis, meaningfully differ from individuals with the minimum number of criteria needed to assign the disorder (Pincus, McQueen, & Elinson, 2003). Despite these findings, *DSM-5* did not fully integrate a dimensional approach to anxiety disorder diagnosis.

Comorbidity and diagnostic boundaries. The validity of *DSM* anxiety disorders has been questioned in the comorbidity literature, which has consistently found the majority of individuals meet criteria for multiple *DSM* disorders. For example, in Brown, Campbell, Lehman, Grisham, and Mancill's (2001) examination of 1,127 outpatients with *DSM-IV* anxiety and mood disorders, rates of current and lifetime comorbidity were 55% and 76%, respectively. Having a current principal diagnosis of panic disorder with agoraphobia was associated with significantly increased risk of having current comorbid GAD (relative risk [RR] = 1.50), whereas a principal diagnosis of GAD was associated with increased risk of comorbid panic disorder with agoraphobia (RR = 2.09) and comorbid social phobia (RR = 2.33). Significant associations were also found between several principal anxiety diagnoses and comorbid unipolar depressive disorders. Similar patterns of comorbidity have been observed in community samples (e.g., Kessler et al., 2005). Given the nature of the changes made to the anxiety disorders in *DSM-5*, there is little reason to expect decreased rates of comorbidity. In fact, based on the continued splitting (e.g., separation of panic disorder and agoraphobia; other specific and unspecified anxiety disorder) and removal of the GAD hierarchy, it is reasonable to hypothesize *increased* rates of comorbidity under *DSM-5*.

The high rates of comorbidity may suggest poor discriminant validity (Andrews, 1996; Brown, 1996). Indeed, it has long been suggested that the vast number of *DSM* disorders may be leading clinicians to erroneously separate disorders that actually reflect negligible variations of broader underlying features (Frances, Widiger, & Fyer, 1990). For example, a large literature has amassed on the relevance of neurotic temperament, a transdiagnostic dimension broadly defined as the tendency to respond to stress with negative emotions and avoidant behaviors. Different facets of temperament/personality have been used to describe neurotic temperament, including the interrelated constructs of neuroticism, behavioral inhibition, and negative affectivity (Campbell-Sills, Liverant, & Brown, 2004). Numerous studies have found elevated levels of neuroticism in most *DSM-IV* disorders, including the anxiety disorders (see Kotov, Gamez, Schmidt, & Watson, 2010, for a meta-analysis). Further, Griffith and colleagues (2010) found that neurotic temperament displayed a near tautological relationship ($r = 0.98$) with a higher-order internalizing disorder factor defined primarily by *DSM-IV* anxiety disorders. Importantly, several other lower-order anxiety phenotype dimensions are also transdiagnostic in nature (see Current Trends and Future Directions of Anxiety Classification section later in this chapter). For instance, individuals with panic disorder (Clark, 1986; Otto, Pollack, Sachs, & Rosenbaum, 1992) *or* GAD (Lee, Lam, Kwok, & Leung, 2014; Lee & Tsang, 2011) may experience anxiety focused on health/physical symptoms (i.e., somatic anxiety). Of course, somatic anxiety is also a defining feature of *DSM-5* illness anxiety and other somatic symptom disorders.

DSM-5 did not take any major steps to reduce diagnostic comorbidity or integrate transdiagnostic features. However, *DSM-5* acknowledges these issues in two ways. First, similar to prior editions of the *DSM*, each disorder chapter includes a differential diagnosis subsection that describes differences between disorders with potential boundary issues. A handbook of differential diagnosis, which includes step-by-step guidelines and decision trees, has also been published with online library access (First, 2013). Second, as mentioned earlier, Section III of *DSM-5* includes new cross-cutting (i.e., transdiagnostic) measures that broadly assess 13 psychopathological dimensions, including anxiety. Early data indicate these scales are reliable (Narrow et al., 2013), but their validity and clinical utility (e.g., feasibility of widespread implementation) have yet to be established.

Current Trends and Future Directions of Anxiety Classification

It might be possible to use a combination of *DSM-5*'s cross-cutting *and* disorder-specific measures for a hybrid dimensional-categorical approach to anxiety disorder classification. This approach could be similar to that of the aforementioned *Alternate DSM-5 Model for Personality Disorders* included in Section III. For example, three criteria could be used to establish an "anxiety disorder" diagnosis: (a) elevations on the anxiety subscale of the cross-cutting measure, (b) elevations on one or more disorder-specific measures, (c) clinically significant impairment or distress. Unfortunately, *DSM-5* did not systematically outline any dimensional approach to diagnosing and classifying the anxiety disorders. It thus seems unlikely that research will evaluate how the *DSM-5* scales could be used to develop a hybrid approach. Instead, the *DSM*'s ongoing reliance on a categorical approach to classification has served as a catalyst for the development of alternative dimensional approaches.

Research Domain Criteria

Shortly prior to the release of *DSM-5*, Thomas Insel, the former NIMH director, issued a statement saying that the "modest" changes in the new edition failed to provide a needed transition away from categorical symptom-based classification (Insel, April 29, 2013). According to Insel, the *DSM*'s categories had serious limitations in validity. The NIMH has consequently distanced itself from *DSM-5* in favor of the RDoC initiative (Cuthbert & Insel, 2013). RDoC is a transdiagnostic framework used to study and classify various impairments in mental health functioning. It is based on five dimensional domains of psychological processes (negative valence system, positive valence systems, cognitive systems, social processes, arousal and regulatory systems) that underlie normal-to-abnormal functioning and are measurable across eight units of analysis (e.g., genetic, neurocircuits, physiology, self-report behavior). Numerous constructs and sub-constructs are defined within each of the five domains. Within the negative valence system, the constructs of acute threat ("fear") and potential threat ("anxiety") have broad face validity with *DSM-5* anxiety disorders. Along these lines, some efforts have been made to conceptualize *DSM-5* anxiety disorders within the RDoC framework (e.g., panic disorder, Hamm et al., 2016).

RDoC might ultimately lead to the development of a dimensional approach to anxiety disorder classification that is more valid than the *DSM*. However, in its current form, it is difficult to envision how RDoC could evolve into an approach that clinicians would accept and adopt. RDoC has prioritized understanding basic biological processes that occur across species rather than clinical phenomena that are observable in humans. In fact, David Kupfer, the chair of the *DSM-5* Task Force, responded to Insel's critique by stating that the field has been awaiting biological and genetic markers for decades, with few promising discoveries (APA, 2013b). He argued that RDoC was not yet ready to replace the *DSM*, and that use of *DSM-5* was necessary in the meantime. Further, given the complexity and costs associated with assessing and understanding the dimensions and units of analysis prioritized by RDoC, it would be very challenging for community mental health providers to use such a biomarker-focused approach to diagnosis (e.g., interpreting results of genetic tests, brain scans). Accordingly, if it ever occurs at all, the translation of RDoC into a valid and practical approach to anxiety disorder assessment and classification is decades away.

Hierarchical Taxonomy of Psychopathology

The *DSM*'s limitations have also led to proposals to classify mental disorders based on dimensions assessed primarily by self-report, interview, or clinical observation (i.e., phenotype-based diagnosis). For example, Kotov and colleagues (2017) forwarded a dimensional-phenotype approach to classification described as the "Hierarchical Taxonomy of Psychopathology" (HiTOP). HiTOP promotes a multi-level approach to organizing and assessing psychopathology symptom dimensions that is rooted in decades of quantitative research on the structure of psychopathology.

At the lowest level of the hierarchy are narrow "homogeneous components" (closely related symptom manifestations, e.g., avoidance, performance anxiety) and personality traits (e.g., trait anxiousness, emotional lability). Components and traits are posited to co-occur to form "syndrome" dimensions, many of which likely represent dimensions underlying current *DSM* categories. To illustrate, a composite of trait anxiousness, interactive anxiety, and performance anxiety might be a "social anxiety syndrome" (i.e., *DSM-5* SAD). Correlated syndrome dimensions form "subfactors" (e.g., social anxiety, phobias, and panic forming a "fear" sub-factor), which in term form "spectra" (e.g., fear, distress, and eating disorder subfactors forming the "internalizing spectrum"). At the top of the hierarchy are "super-spectra," or broad dimensions reflecting general psychopathology and distress. Several well-validated self-report and interview measures are available to assess many (but not all) of the dimensions positioned at varying levels of HiTOP. For anxiety syndromes, the Inventory of Depression and Anxiety Symptoms (self-report; Watson et al., 2007, 2012) and accompanying Interview for Mood and Anxiety Symptoms (clinical interview; Kotov et al., 2015) can be used to assess most of the relevant homogeneous components (Weinberg, Kotov, & Proudfit, 2015).

The HiTOP approach addresses many of the *DSM*'s limitations. First, the dimensional approach acknowledges empirical evidence that psychopathology constructs are best characterized by a continuum of severity. Along these lines, abandonment of diagnostic categories precludes the occurrence of threshold dis-agreements. Second, components and traits are grouped together based on an empirically based (quantitative) bottom-up approach. In comparison, virtually all *DSM-5* disorders were defined (in earlier editions) using an expert consensus (non-quantitative) approach. As a result, HiTOP dimensions inherently have more valid boundaries (i.e., between syndromes and subfactors) than existing *DSM*-5 cate-gories. Third, syndrome comorbidity is integrated into HiTOP using subfactor and spectra dimensions. This would permit clinicians to assess the relative severity of broad comorbidity (e.g., spectra) versus lower-order syndrome dimensions, and to use this information for treatment planning and outcome tracking (e.g., transdiag-nostic versus syndrome-specific approach).

One potential limitation of HiTOP (and RDoC) is the omission of *any* diagnostic categories. In its current form, HiTOP-based assessment and diagnosis would only provide clinicians with a (potentially very long) list of dimensions and associated scores. An alternate approach would be to develop a hybrid system that integrates dimensions *and* categories. Indeed, hybrid approaches to classification are com-mon throughout other areas of medicine (e.g., hypertension diagnosis based on dimensions of systolic and diastolic blood pressure, Kraemer, 2007). HiTOP promoters justify the omission of categories based on findings that dimensional conceptualizations of psychopathology (e.g., confirmatory factor models) provide better model fit than hybrid conceptualizations (e.g., factor mixture models, Eaton et al., 2013; Wright et al., 2013). However, there are several reasons why it would be useful to define empirically based diagnostic categories based on an array of transdiagnostic dimensions (i.e., a "diagnostic profile"). For instance, clinicians are already trained to use categorical labels to describe psychopathology, and may thus be more likely to accept and utilize a hybrid approach to diagnosis over a purely dimensional approach (First, 2005). One cannot ignore the practical advantages of using categorical labels (e.g., ease of communication). In addition, the use of categorical labels is a necessity for managed care organizations (e.g., reimbursing treatment costs only when a disorder is "present").

Hybrid Dimensional-Categorical Classification

Many psychopathology researchers have emphasized the potential utility of a hybrid approach to classification (Maser et al., 2009; Morey et al., 2012; Trull, 2012). Regarding anxiety and related emotional disorders, Brown and Barlow (2009) proposed a hybrid approach in which an array of transdiagnostic phenotype dimensions are assessed via self-report, plotted, and subsequently classified in a diagnostic profile using statistically identified cut-points (e.g., via person-centered methods such as mixture modeling). Several transdiagnostic dimensions are included in this proposal, beginning with two genetically based dimensions of temperament: neurotic temperament (NT) (e.g., neuroticism, behavioral inhibition) and positive temperament (PT) (e.g., extraversion, behavioral activation). Research has documented the importance of NT and PT constructs in predicting the onset (Conway, Craske, Zinbarg, & Mineka, 2016; Zinbarg et al., 2016), severity (Brown, Chorpita, & Barlow, 1998), and course (Naragon-Gainey, Gallagher, & Brown, 2013) of anxiety and other emotional disorders. Whereas high NT is associated with all the anxiety disorders but especially GAD (Brown et al., 1998; Rosellini & Brown, 2011), low PT is associated with SAD and possibly agoraphobia (as well as unipolar depression; Brown et al., 1998; Rosellini, Lawrence, Meyer, & Brown, 2010). NT and PT are also discussed in the *Risk and Prognostic Factors* sections of *DSM-5* anxiety disorders, and overlap with HiTOP (e.g., negative affectivity) and RDoC dimensions (e.g., negative and positive valence systems).

Brown and Barlow's (2009) profile approach includes several additional transdiagnostic anxiety phenotypes, selected with the goal of balancing parsimony (for ease of use) and specificity (to inform treatment planning). The *depressed mood* and *mania* dimensions respectively capture excessive sadness and positive affect. Consideration of mood is important when assessing anxiety because of the high co-occurrence of anxiety and depressive disorders (Brown et al., 2001b; Kessler et al., 2005). The *autonomic arousal* dimension is defined by the experience of physiological symptoms of sympathetic nervous system activation (i.e., panic symptoms). The assessment of autonomic arousal would be necessary because, as now recognized by *DSM-5*, panic attacks and their symptoms "can occur in the context of any mental disorder" (p. 215). *Somatic anxiety* reflects anxiety focused on one's experience of somatic symptoms (i.e., including but not limited to symptoms of autonomic arousal). Assessing somatic anxiety would be helpful as, in addition to being a defining feature of somatic symptom disorders, several studies have documented health-related concerns across the anxiety disorders (e.g., GAD, Lee & Tsang, 2011; panic disorder, Clark, 1986) and obsessive-compulsive disorders (Abramowitz, Brigidi, & Foa, 1999). *DSM-5* also acknowledges the transdiagnostic nature of somatic anxiety in its differential diagnosis guidelines for many anxiety disorders (e.g., pp. 314, 317, 321).

Social evaluation concerns represent the dimension of anxiety focused on performance situations and social interactions. Knowledge of social evaluation concerns is important because it has been observed across the spectrum of anxiety disorders, particularly generalized anxiety disorder (e.g., Rapee, Sanderson, & Barlow, 1988). *DSM-5* also underscores the role of embarrassment fears in trauma and stress disorders (pp. 206–207). *Intrusive cognitions* reflect the experience of uncontrollable thoughts, images, and impulses. Although this is the defining feature of obsessive-compulsive and related disorders, research suggests that assessment of intrusive cognitions is important because this phenotype is also related to GAD (intrusive worry images, Tallis, 1999). Likewise, *DSM-5* discusses the experience of intrusive thoughts in several differential diagnosis sections, particularly for the trauma and stress disorders (e.g., pp. 202, 225, 241). The *traumatic reexperiencing and distress* dimension represents the experience of negative affect, dissociation, and flashback experiences focused on past traumatic events. This dimension captures the defining features of trauma and stress disorders, which commonly co-occur with anxiety disorder (Brown et al., 2001b). Further, there is some evidence of traumatic reexperiencing symptoms among individuals with panic attacks (i.e., focused on past panic attacks, Hagenaars, van Minnen, & Hoogduin, 2009; McNally & Lukach, 1992) and SAD (focused on past negative social events, Carleton, Peluso, Collimore, & Asmundson, 2011).

Finally, the *avoidance* dimension can be defined as behavioral and cognitive strategies to prevent or reduce the intensity of acute states of negative affect. Avoidance is underscored as a key criterion for most *DSM-5* anxiety disorders: separation anxiety disorder (criterion B), panic disorder (criterion B2), agoraphobia (criteria B, D), specific phobia (criterion G), and SAD (criterion D). As mentioned earlier, there were proposals to add an avoidance (i.e., worry behavior) criterion to *DSM-5* GAD (Andrews et al., 2010). There are numerous transdiagnostic forms of avoidance. *DSM-5* panic disorder, agoraphobia, SAD, and specific phobias are all characterized by avoidance of, or escape from, environmental situations that cue feelings of anxiety or panic (e.g., crowds, parties, elevators). Likewise, GAD and SAD may both manifest in the form of excessive preparation *or* procrastination of upcoming events (e.g., work assignment, presentation, or conversation). Clinicians have also extensively recognized avoidance as a transdiagnostic feature of anxiety disorders, and it is inarguably the core treatment target of leading transdiagnostic cognitive behavioral treatments (e.g., Hayes, 2004; Wilamowska et al., 2010).

Of course, this list of constructs is not exhaustive; several other transdiagnostic phenotypes are also likely relevant for the broad spectrum of emotional disorders (e.g., body image concerns within eating disorders and body dysmorphic disorder). Nonetheless, the limited set of aforementioned dimensions could serve as a starting point in the development of a profile approach to anxiety disorder classification. Use of dimensions with empirically identified cut-points could eliminate diagnostic unreliability. Information pertaining to indicator severity could always be included in an individual's profile, and clinician judgment would not be needed to decide if a dimension or profile was clinically significant. Likewise, the focus on cross-cutting transdiagnostic constructs could also address high rates of comorbidity. To illustrate, rather than deciding between a diagnosis of panic disorder, somatic symptom disorder, or both, a patient reporting recent out-of-the-blue panic attacks, lifelong worry about heart disease that triggers panic attacks, and reassurance-seeking behaviors (e.g., going to the ER when having cued or uncued attacks) could be characterized by a single profile with elevations on the neurotic temperament, autonomic arousal, and somatic anxiety dimensions.

Rosellini and Brown (2014) conducted a preliminary evaluation of a profile approach to classification by attempting to develop and validate diagnostic profiles in a sample of 1,218 outpatients seeking treatment for anxiety and related emotional disorders. Questionnaires were used to assess a subset of the aforementioned transdiagnostic phenotype dimensions: neurotic temperament, positive temperament, depressed mood, autonomic arousal, somatic anxiety, social evaluation concerns, and intrusive cognitions. Latent class analysis, a form of mixture modeling, was then used to identify subgroups of individuals who shared similar profiles across the self-report phenotype dimensions.

A six-class (i.e., profile) solution provided the best model fit and was the most conceptually interpretable. The profiles, which are shown in Figure 11.1, were labeled (1) Negligible-Mild (non-pathological scores across all indicators), (2) Panic-Somatic (large elevations on autonomic arousal and somatic anxiety), (3) Social-Depressed (elevations on neurotic temperament, depression mood, and social anxiety concerns, low positive temperament), (4) Mildly-Neurotic (average neurotic temperament and below-average scores on the other dimensions), (5) Severe-Comorbid (pathological levels across all indicators), and (6) Obsessed-Worried (large elevation on intrusive cognitions). These profiles demonstrated strong convergent validity with *DSM-IV* disorders assessed using the ADIS-IV (Di Nardo et al., 1994). Among individuals in the Social-Depressed class, for instance, 76% had a current social phobia diagnosis, and 59% had current unipolar depression (major depression or dysthymia). More importantly, hierarchical regression models were used to test the incremental validity of the profiles over and above *DSM-IV* diagnoses in predicting severity of panic, agoraphobia, social anxiety, obsessions/compulsions, worry, and depression. Controlling for *DSM-IV* disorders, the profiles significantly predicted virtually all of the outcomes of interest (i.e., demonstrating incremental validity). For example, the Panic-Somatic profile predicted clinician-rated panic severity *and* agoraphobia severity while controlling for *DSM-IV* diagnoses of panic disorder with or without agoraphobia and agoraphobia without panic.

These findings suggest that it may be possible to use mixture modeling to develop a hybrid dimensional-categorical approach to anxiety classification with improved clinical utility. In particular, the incremental validity analyses suggest that knowledge of a patient's profile might provide clinicians with important information about symptom severity that is not captured by *DSM* diagnoses alone. In addition to a profile label being easy to communicate (e.g., "John Doe has a profile consistent with the Panic-Somatic type"), scores on the individual transdiagnostic dimensions would provide information pertaining to overall and specific phenotype severities that could be particularly useful in treatment planning (e.g., developing a hierarchy of treatment targets). Knowledge of elevations on the phenotype dimensions along with item-level information from the avoidance dimension could greatly inform cognitive behavioral treatment planning (e.g., the type and foci of exposures). In addition,

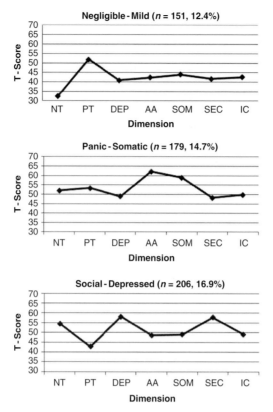

Figure 11.1 *Plotted latent profiles from the six-class solution. Indicator means within each profile type were converted to T-Scores for presentational clarity (i.e., self-report questionnaires scaled in different metrics). NT = neurotic tempera-ment; PT = positive temperament; DEP = depression; AA = autonomic arousal; SOM = somatic anxiety; SEC = social evaluation concerns; IC = intrusive cognitions. Figure reproduced from Rosellini, A. J. & Brown, T. A. (2014). Initial interpretation and evaluation of a profile-based classification system for the anxiety and mood disorders: Incremental validity compared to* DSM-IV *cate-gories.* Psychological Assessment, 26, 1212–1224.

information pertaining to neurotic and positive temperament could give clinicians a sense of who is at greatest risk of developing and maintaining anxiety psychopathol-ogy in the future (i.e., prognostic indicators).

Given that the dimensional assessment of transdiagnostic anxiety phenotypes would require a time-intensive interview (e.g., ADIS-5) that would not be feasible to use in most clinical settings, assessment would ideally occur using a relatively brief questionnaire. One noteworthy limitation of the preliminary validation study of the profile approach was the reliance on several lengthy questionnaires to assess the range of phenotypes of interest. If any dimensional approach to anxiety classification is to be seriously considered, it would need to be accompanied by

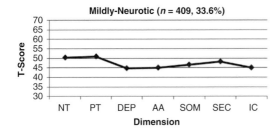

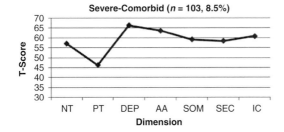

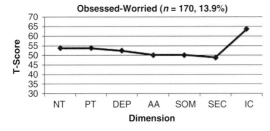

Figure 11.1 (*cont.*)

standardized assessment tools. With these issues in mind, our team has developed the Multidimensional Emotional Disorder Inventory (MEDI), a 50-item self-report questionnaire intended to assess the full range of transdiagnostic phenotypes included in the Brown and Barlow (2009) profile approach to emotional disorder classification. Although the MEDI is currently still under development, a pilot study found promising initial support for its latent structure and convergent/discriminant validity with other well-validated self-report questionnaires (Rosellini, 2013).

Nevertheless, additional research is needed before a profile approach to anxiety classification could be widely adopted. Mixture modeling would need to be applied to a broader range of emotional disorder dimensions (e.g., trauma, mania, and avoidance), both in other clinical samples and in epidemiological samples. Assessing additional dimensions in other samples could also allow the profile approach to be expanded to other classes of disorders (e.g., externalizing disorder profiles characterized by dimensions of disinhibited temperament, anger, substance use). One way to develop a hybrid approach to classifying the gamut of psychopathology would be to apply mixture modeling to the full range of HiTOP dimensions (i.e., regardless if confirmatory factor models provide a better fit than hybrid models). This type of effort would likely require the development of a single self-report assessment of *all* HiTOP components and traits.

Summary and Conclusions

It is commendable that many of the changes made to the anxiety disorders in *DSM-5* were supported by empirical evidence. Overall, the revision was minor, making it possible to seamlessly update and use popular clinical interviews and questionnaires that were validated prior to *DSM-5*. At the same time, it is disappointing that *DSM-5* opted against more substantive changes based on the vast literatures questioning the validity of its diagnostic categories. As a result, empirically based alternatives to classification have been forwarded by NIMH (RDoC) and by leading quantitative psychopathology researchers. It is difficult to predict how anxiety disorder classification will evolve in the future. Researchers will likely continue to prioritize RDoC and quantitative approaches to classification. Although it is possible that a more valid (dimensional) approach to anxiety disorder classification will be developed through these efforts, practicing clinicians will continue to be required by managed care organizations to use *DSM-5*. These competing interests (i.e., researching RDoC versus requiring *DSM-5* in clinical practice) may impede dissemination of any newly developed empirically based approach to anxiety disorder classification. That is, it could be very difficult for clinicians to justify abandoning or supplementing *DSM-5* with a new approach to classification that is not recognized by managed care organizations. Accordingly, the widespread dissemination and adoption of a dimensional approach to anxiety disorder classification in clinical practice likely lies on the shoulders of the *DSM*.

References

Abramowitz, J. S., Brigidi, B. D., & Foa, E. B. (1999). Health concerns in patients with obsessive-compulsive disorder. *Journal of Anxiety Disorders*, *13*, 529–539. doi: 10.1016/s0887-6185(99)00022–5

American Psychiatric Association (APA). (1980). *Diagnostic and Statistical Manual of Mental Disorders* (3rd edn). Washington, DC: American Psychiatric Association.

American Psychiatric Association (APA). (1987). *Diagnostic and Statistical Manual of Mental Disorders: DSM-III-R* (3rd edn). Washington, DC: American Psychiatric Association.

American Psychiatric Association (APA). (1994). *Diagnostic and Statistical Manual of Mental Disorders: DSM-IV* (4th edn). Washington, DC: American Psychiatric Association.

American Psychiatric Association (APA). (2013a). *Diagnostic and Statistical Manual of Mental Disorders: DSM-5* (5th edn). Washington, DC: American Psychiatric Association.

American Psychiatric Association (APA). (2013b). *Statement by David Kupfer, MD: Chair of DSM-5 task force discusses future of mental health research.* [Press release]. Retrieved from www.sardaa.org/wp-content/uploads/2013/05/13–33-statement-from-dsm-chair-david-kupfer-md.pdf.

American Psychiatric Association (APA). (2017). *Online assessment measures.* Retrieved from www.psychiatry.org/psychiatrists/practice/dsm/educational-resources/assessment-measures.

Andrews, G. (1996). Comorbidity in neurotic disorders: The similarities are more important than the differences. In R. M. Rapee (ed.), *Current Controversies in the Anxiety Disorders* (pp. 3–20). New York, NY: Guilford Press.

Andrews, G., Hobbs, M. J., Borkovec, T. D., Beesdo, K., Craske, M. G., Heimberg, R. G., ... Stanley, M. A. (2010). Generalized worry disorder: A review of DSM-IV generalized anxiety disorder and options for DSM-V. *Depression and Anxiety, 27,* 134–147. doi: 10.1002/da.20658

Antony, M. M., Orsillo, S. M., & Roemer, L. (2001). *Practitioner's Guide to Empirically Based Measures of Anxiety.* New York, NY: Springer Publishing.

Asmundson, G. J. G., Taylor, S., & Smits, J. A. J. (2014). Panic disorder and agoraphobia: An overview and commentary on *DSM-5* changes. *Depression and Anxiety, 31,* 480–486. doi: 10.1002/da.22277

Baldwin, D. S., Gordon, R., Abelli, M., & Pini, S. (2016). The separation of adult separation anxiety disorder. *CNS Spectrums, 21,* 289–294. doi: 10.1017/S1092852916000080

Bandelow, B. (1999). *Panic and Agoraphobia Scale (PAS).* Seattle, WA: Hogrefe & Huber Publishers.

Barlow, D. H. (2002). *Anxiety and Its Disorders: The Nature and Treatment of Anxiety and Panic* (2nd edn). New York, NY: Guilford Press.

Beck, A. T. & Steer, R. A. (1990). *Manual for the Beck Anxiety Inventory.* San Antonio, TX: Psychological Corporation.

Blöte, A. W., Kint, M. J. W., Miers, A. C., & Westenberg, P. M. (2009). The relation between public speaking anxiety and social anxiety: A review. *Journal of Anxiety Disorders, 23,* 305–313. doi: 10.1016/j.janxdis.2008.11.007

Bögels, S. M., Alden, L., Beidel, D. C., Clark, L. A., Pine, D. S., Stein, M. B., & Voncken, M. (2010). Social anxiety disorder: Questions and answers for the DSM-V. *Depression and Anxiety, 27,* 168–189. doi: 10.1002/da.20670

Boone, M. L., McNeil, D. W., Masia, C. L., Turk, C. L., Carter, L. E., Ries, B. J., & Lewin, M. R. (1999). Multimodal comparisons of social phobia subtypes and avoidant personality disorder. *Journal of Anxiety Disorders, 13,* 271–292. doi: 10.1016/s0887-6185(99)00004–3

Brown, T. A. (1996). Validity of the *DSM-III-R* and *DSM-IV* classification systems for anxiety disorders. In R. M. Rapee (ed.), *Current Controversies in the Anxiety Disorders* (pp. 21–45). New York, NY: Guilford Press.

Brown, T. A. (2007). Temporal course and structural relationships among dimensions of temperament and *DSM-IV* anxiety and mood disorder constructs. *Journal of Abnormal Psychology, 116,* 313–328. doi: 10.1037/0021-843X.116.2.313

Brown, T. A. & Barlow, D. H. (2005). Dimensional versus categorical classification of mental disorders in the fifth edition of the *Diagnostic and Statistical Manual of Mental Disorders* and beyond: Comment on the special section. *Journal of Abnormal Psychology, 114,* 551–556. doi: 10.1037/0021-843x.114.4.551

Brown, T. A. & Barlow, D. H. (2009). A proposal for a dimensional classification system based on the shared features of the *DSM-IV* anxiety and mood disorders: Implications for assessment and treatment. *Psychological Assessment, 21,*256–271. doi: 10.1037/a0016608

Brown, T. A. & Barlow, D. H. (2013). *Anxiety and Related Disorders Interview Schedule for DSM-5, Adult and Lifetime Version: Clinician Manual.* New York, NY: Oxford University Press.

Brown, T. A., Campbell, L. A., Lehman, C. L., Grisham, J. R., & Mancill, R. B. (2001). Current and lifetime comorbidity of the *DSM-IV* anxiety and mood disorders in a large clinical sample. *Journal of Abnormal Psychology, 110,* 585–599. doi: 10.1037//0021-843x.110.4.585

Brown, T. A., Chorpita, B. F., & Barlow, D. H. (1998). Structural relationships among dimensions of the *DSM-IV* anxiety and mood disorders and dimensions of negative affect, positive affect, and autonomic arousal. *Journal of Abnormal Psychology, 107,*179–192. doi: 10.1037//0021-843x.107.2.179

Brown, T. A., Di Nardo, P. A., Lehman, C. L., & Campbell, L. A. (2001a). Reliability of *DSM-IV* anxiety and mood disorders: Implications for the classification of emotional disorders. *Journal of Abnormal Psychology, 110,* 49–58. doi: 10.1037/0021-843X.110.1.49

Bruce, L. C., Heimberg, R. G., & Coles, M. E. (2012). Social phobia and social anxiety disorder: Effect of disorder name on recommendation for treatment. *American Journal of Psychiatry, 169,* 538. doi: 10.1176/appi.ajp.2012.11121808

Campbell-Sills, L., Liverant, G. I., & Brown, T. A. (2004). Psychometric evaluation of the Behavioral Inhibition/Behavioral Activation Scales in a large sample of outpatients with anxiety and mood disorders. *Psychological Assessment, 16,* 244–254. doi: 10.1037/1040–3590.16.3.244

Carleton, R. N., Peluso, D. L., Collimore, K. C., & Asmundson, G. J. (2011). Social anxiety and posttraumatic stress symptoms: The impact of distressing social events. *Journal of Anxiety Disorders, 25,* 49–57. doi: 10.1016/j.janxdis.2010.08.002

Chambless, D. L., Caputo, G. C., Jasin, S. E., Gracely, E. J., & Williams, C. (1985). The Mobility Inventory for Agoraphobia. *Behaviour Research and Therapy, 23,* 35–44. doi: 10.1037/t10566-000

Chmielewski, M., Clark, L. A., Bagby, R. M., & Watson, D. (2015). Method matters: Understanding diagnostic reliability in *DSM-IV* and *DSM-5. Journal of Abnormal Psychology, 124,* 764–769. doi: 10.1037/abn0000069

Clark, D. M. (1986). A cognitive approach to panic. *Behaviour Research and Therapy, 24,* 461–470. doi: 10.1016/0005–7967(86)90011–2

Conway, C. C., Craske, M. G., Zinbarg, R. E., & Mineka, S. (2015). Pathological personality traits and the naturalistic course of internalizing disorders among high-risk young adults. *Depression and Anxiety,33,* 84–93. doi: 10.1002/da.22404

Craske, M. G., Kircanski, K., Epstein, A., Wittchen, H.-U., Pine, D. S., Lewis-Fernández, R., ... Posttraumatic and Dissociative Disorder Work Group. (2010). Panic disorder: A review of *DSM-IV* panic disorder and proposals for DSM-V. *Depression and Anxiety, 27*,93–112. doi: 10.1002/da.20654

Cuthbert, B. N. & Insel, T. R. (2013). Toward the future of psychiatric diagnosis: The seven pillars of RDoC. *BMC Medicine,11*. doi: 10.1186/1741–7015-11–126

Di Nardo, P. A. & Barlow, D. H. (1988). *Anxiety Disorders Interview Schedule – Revised (ADIS-R)*. Albany, NY: Graywind.

Di Nardo, P. A., Brown, T. A., & Barlow, D. H. (1994). *Anxiety Disorders Interview Schedule for DSM-IV: Lifetime Version (ADIS-1 V-L)*. San Antonio, TX: Psychological Corporation.

Di Nardo, P. A., Moras, K., Barlow, D. H., Rapee, R. M., & Brown, T. A. (1993). Reliability of DSM-III-R anxiety disorder categories: Using the Anxiety Disorders Interview Schedule-Revised (ADIS-R). *Archives of General Psychiatry, 50*(4), 251–256.

Di Nardo, P. A., O'Brien, G. T., Barlow, D. H., Waddell, M. T., & Blanchard, E. B. (1983). Reliability of *DSM-III* anxiety disorder categories using a new structured interview. *Archives of General Psychiatry, 40*, 1070–1074. doi: 10.1001/archpsyc.1983.01790090032005

Eaton, N. R., Krueger, R. F., Markon, K. E., Keyes, K. M., Skodol, A. E., Wall, M., . . . Grant, B. F. (2013). The structure and predictive validity of the internalizing disorders. *Journal of Abnormal Psychology, 122*, 86–92. doi: 10.1037/a0029598

Faravelli, C., Furukawa, T. A., & Truglia, E. (2009). Panic disorder. In G. Andrews, D. S. Charney, P. J. Sirovatka, & D. A. Regier (eds.), *Stress-Induced and Fear Circuitry Disorders* (pp. 31–58). Arlington, VA: American Psychiatric Association.

First, M. B. (2005). Clinical utility: A prerequisite for the adoption of a dimensional approach in DSM. *Journal of Abnormal Psychology, 114*, 560–564. doi: 10.1037/0021-843x.114.4.560

First, M. B. (2013). *DSM-5 Handbook of Differential Diagnosis*. Washington, DC: American Psychiatric Association. Retrieved May 12, 2017, from http://dsm.psychiatryonline.org/doi/book/10.1176/appi.books.9780890425596.

First, M. B., Spitzer, R. L., Gibbon, M., & Williams, J. (2002). *Structured Clinical Interview for DSM-IV-TR Axis I Disorders, Research Version*. New York, NY: Biometrics Research, New York State Psychiatric Institute.

First, M. B., Williams, J. B. W., Karg, R. S., & Spitzer,R. L. (2015). *Structured Clinical Interview for DSM-5 Disorders, Clinician Version (SCID-5-CV)*. Arlington, VA: American Psychiatric Association.

Frances, A. (2012, May 8). *Newsflash from APA Meeting: DSM-5 has flunked its reliability tests*. Retrieved May 12, 2017, from www.huffingtonpost.com/allen-frances/dsm5-reliability-tests_b_1490857.html.

Frances, A., Widiger, T., & Fyer, M. R. (1990). The influence of classification methods on comorbidity. In J. D. Maser & C. R. Cloninger (eds.), *Comorbidity of Mood and Anxiety Disorders* (pp. 41–59). Washington, DC: American Psychiatric Press.

Friedman, M. J., Resick, P. A., Bryant, R. A., & Brewin, C. R. (2011). Considering PTSD for *DSM-5. Depression and Anxiety, 28*, 750–769. doi: 10.1002/da.20767

Friedman, M. J., Resick, P. A., Bryant, R. A., Strain, J., Horowitz, M., & Spiegel, D. (2011). Classification of trauma and stressor-related disorders in *DSM-5. Depression and Anxiety, 28*, 737–749. doi: 10.1002/da.20845

Geer, J. H. (1965). The development of a scale to measure fear. *Behaviour Research and Therapy, 3*, 45–53. doi: 10.1016/0005–7967(65)90040–9

Griffith, J. W., Zinbarg, R. E., Craske, M. G., Mineka, S., Rose, R. D., Waters, A. M., & Sutton, J. M. (2010). Neuroticism as a common dimension in the internalizing disorders. *Psychological Medicine, 40*, 1125–1136. doi: 10.1017/s0033291709991449

Hagenaars, J. A., & McCutcheon, A. L. (eds.). (2002). *Applied Latent Class Analysis.* Cambridge: Cambridge University Press.

Hagenaars, M. A., van Minnen, A., & Hoogduin, K. A. (2009). Reliving and disorganization in posttraumatic stress disorder and panic disorder memories. *Journal of Nervous and Mental Disease, 197*, 627–630. doi: 10.1097/nmd.0b013e3181b08bdf

Hamm, A. O., Richter, J., Pané-Farré, C., Westphal, D., Wittchen, H., Vossbeck-Elsebusch, A. N., . . . Deckert, J. (2016). Panic disorder with agoraphobia from a behavioral neuroscience perspective: Applying the research principles formulated by the Research Domain Criteria (RDoC) initiative. *Psychophysiology, 53*, 312–322. doi: 10.1111/psyp.12553

Hayes, S. C. (2004). Acceptance and commitment therapy, relational frame theory, and the third wave of behavioral and cognitive therapies. *Behavior Therapy, 35*, 639–665. doi: 10.1016/s0005-7894(04)80013-3

Heimberg, R. G., Hofmann, S. G., Liebowitz, M. R., Schneier, F. R., Smits, J. A. J., Stein, M. B., . . . Craske, M. G. (2014). Social anxiety disorder in *DSM-5. Depression and Anxiety, 31*, 472–479. doi: 10.1002/da.22231

Heimberg, R. G., Holt, C. S., Schneier, F. R., Spitzer, R. L., & Liebowitz, M. R. (1993). The issue of subtypes in the diagnosis of social phobia. *Journal of Anxiety Disorders, 7*, 249–269. doi: 10.1016/0887-6185(93)90006-7

Heimberg, R. G., Hope, D. A., Dodge, C. S., & Becker, R. E. (1990). *DSM-III-R* subtypes of social phobia. Comparison of generalized social phobics and public speaking phobics. *Journal of Nervous and Mental Disease, 178*, 172–179.

Hollander, E., Braun, A., & Simeon, D. (2008). Should OCD leave the anxiety disorders in *DSM-V*? The case for obsessive compulsive-related disorders. *Depression and Anxiety, 25*, 317–329. doi: 10.1002/da.20500

Houck, P. R., Spiegel, D. A., Shear, M. K., & Rucci, P. (2002). Reliability of the self-report version of the Panic Disorder Severity Scale. *Depression and Anxiety, 15*, 183–185. doi: 10.1002/da.10049

Insel, T., Cuthbert, B., Garvey, M., Heinssen, R., Pine, D. S., Quinn, K., . . . Wang, P. (2010). Research Domain Criteria (RDoC): Toward a new classification framework for research on mental disorders. *American Journal of Psychiatry, 167*, 748–751. doi: 10.1176/appi.ajp.2010.09091379

Insel, T. R. (2013, April 9). Transforming diagnosis [Blog post]. Retrieved from www.nimh .nih.gov/about/directors/thomas-insel/blog/2013/transforming-diagnosis.shtml.

Kerns, C. E., Comer, J. S., Pincus, D. B., & Hofmann, S. G. (2013). Evaluation of the proposed social anxiety disorder specifier change for *DSM-5* in a treatment-seeking sample of anxious youth. *Depression and Anxiety, 30*, 709–715. doi: 10.1002/da.22067

Kessler, R. C., Chiu, W. T., Demler, O., & Walters, E. E. (2005). Prevalence, severity, and comorbidity of 12-month *DSM-IV* disorders in the national comorbidity survey replication. *Archives of General Psychiatry, 62*, 617–627.

Knappe, S., Klotsche, J., Heyde, F., Hiob, S., Siegert, J., Hoyer, J., . . . Beesdo-Baum, K. (2014). Test–retest reliability and sensitivity to change of the dimensional anxiety scales for *DSM-5. CNS Spectrums, 19*, 256–267. doi: 10.1017/s1092852913000710

Knappe, S., Klotsche, J., Strobel, A., LeBeau, R. T., Craske, M. G., Wittchen, H. U., & Beesdo-Baum, K. (2013). Dimensional Anxiety Scales for *DSM-5*: Sensitivity to clinical severity. *European Psychiatry*, *28*, 448–456. doi: 10.1016/j.eurpsy.2013.02.001

Kollman, D. M., Brown, T. A., Liverant, G. I., & Hofmann, S. G. (2006). A taxometric investigation of the latent structure of social anxiety disorder in outpatients with anxiety and mood disorders. *Depression and Anxiety*, *23*, 190–199. doi: 10.1002/da.20158

Kotov, R., Gamez, W., Schmidt, F., & Watson, D. (2010). Linking "big" personality traits to anxiety, depressive, and substance use disorders: A meta-analysis. *Psychological Bulletin*, *136*, 768–821. doi: 10.1037/a0020327

Kotov, R., Krueger, R. F., Watson, D., Achenbach, T. M., Althoff, R. R., Bagby, R. M., . . . Zimmerman, M. (2017). The Hierarchical Taxonomy of Psychopathology (HiTOP): A dimensional alternative to traditional nosologies. *Journal of Abnormal Psychology*, *126*, 454–477. doi: 10.1037/abn0000258

Kotov, R., Perlman, G., Gámez, W., & Watson, D. (2015). The structure and short-term stability of the emotional disorders: A dimensional approach. *Psychological Medicine*, *45*, 1687–1698. doi: 10.1017/s0033291714002815

Kraemer, H. C. (2007). *DSM* categories and dimensions in clinical and research contexts. *International Journal of Methods in Psychiatric Research,16*, S8–S15. doi: 10.1002/mpr.211

Kraemer, H. C., Kupfer, D. J., Clarke, D. E., Narrow, W. E., & Regier, D. A. (2012). *DSM-5*: How reliable is reliable enough? *American Journal of Psychiatry*, *169*, 13–15. doi: 10.1176/appi.ajp.2011.11010050

Lawrence, A. E., Liverant, G. I., Rosellini, A. J., & Brown, T. A. (2009). Generalized anxiety disorder within the course of major depressive disorder: Examining the utility of the DSM-IV hierarchy rule. *Depression and Anxiety*, *26*, 909–916. https://doi.org/10.1002/da.20607

Lebeau, R. T., Mesri, B., & Craske, M. G. (2016). The *DSM-5* social anxiety disorder severity scale: Evidence of validity and reliability in a clinical sample. *Psychiatry Research*, *244*, 94–96. doi: 10.1016/j.psychres.2016.07.024

Lee, S., Lam, I. M., Kwok, K. P., & Leung, C. M. (2014). A community-based epidemiological study of health anxiety and generalized anxiety disorder. *Journal of Anxiety Disorders*, *28*, 187–194. doi: 10.1016/j.janxdis.2013.10.002

Lee, S., Ma, Y. L., & Tsang, A. (2011). A community study of generalized anxiety disorder with vs. without health anxiety in Hong Kong. *Journal of Anxiety Disorders*, *25*, 376–380. doi: 10.1016/j.janxdis.2010.10.012

Levin, A. P., Saoud, J. B., Strauman, T., Gorman, J. M., Fyer, A. J., Crawford, R., & Liebowitz, M. R. (1993). Responses of "generalized" and "discrete" social phobics during public speaking. *Journal of Anxiety Disorders*, *7*, 207–221. doi: 10.1016/0887–6185(93)90003-4

Liebowitz, M. R. (1987). Social phobia. In D. F. Klein (ed.), *Modern Problems in Pharmacopsychiatry* (pp. 141–173). New York, NY: Karger. doi: 0.1159/000414022

Liebowitz, M. R., Heimberg, R. G., Fresco, D. M., Travers, J., & Stein, M. B. (2000). Social phobia or social anxiety disorder: What's in a name? *Archives of General Psychiatry*, *57*, 191–192.

Lobbestael, J., Leurgans, M., & Arntz, A. (2011). Inter-rater reliability of the Structured Clinical Interview for *DSM-IV* Axis I disorders (SCID I) and Axis II disorders (SCID II). *Clinical Psychology and Psychotherapy*, *18*, 75–79. doi: 10.1002/cpp.693

Lovibond, P. F. & Lovibond, S. H. (1995). The structure of negative emotional states: Comparison of the Depression Anxiety Stress Scales (DASS) with the Beck Depression and Anxiety Inventories. *Behaviour Research and Therapy*, *33*, 335–343. doi: 10.1016/0005–7967(94)00075-u

MacCallum, R. C., Zhang, S., Preacher, K. J., & Rucker, D. D. (2002). On the practice of dichotomization of quantitative variables. *Psychological Methods*, *7*, 19–40. doi: 10.1037//1082-989x.7.1.19

Manicavasagar, V., Silove, D., Wagner, R., & Drobny, J. (2003). A self-report questionnaire for measuring separation anxiety in adulthood. *Comprehensive Psychiatry*, *44*, 146–153.

Markon, K. E., Chmielewski, M., & Miller, C. J. (2011). The reliability and validity of discrete and continuous measures of psychopathology: A quantitative review. *Psychological Bulletin*, *137*, 856–879. doi: 10.1037/a0023678

Marks, I. M. & Mathews, A. M. (1979). Brief standard self-rating for phobic patients. *Behaviour Research and Therapy*, *17*, 263–267. doi: 10.1016/0005–7967(79) 90041-x

Maser, J. D., Norman, S. B., Zisook, S., Everall, I. P., Stein, M. B., Schettler, P. J., & Judd, L. L. (2009). Psychiatric nosology is ready for a paradigm shift in *DSM-V*. *Clinical Psychology: Science and Practice*, *16*, 24–40. doi: 10.1111/j.1468–2850.2009.01140.x

Mattick, R. P. & Clarke, J. C. (1998). Development and validation of measures of social phobia scrutiny fear and social interaction anxiety. *Behaviour Research and Therapy*, *36*, 455–470.

McNally, R. J. & Lukach, B. M. (1992). Are panic attacks traumatic stressors?. *American Journal of Psychiatry*, 149, 824–826. doi: 10.1176/ajp.149.6.824

Meyer, T. J., Miller, M. L., Metzger, R. L., & Borkovec, T. D. (1990). Development and validation of the Penn State Worry Questionnaire. *Behaviour Research and Therapy*, *28*, 487–495. doi: 10.1016/0005–7967(90)90135–6

Möller, E. L. & Bögels, S. M. (2016). The *DSM-5* Dimensional Anxiety Scales in a Dutch non-clinical sample: Psychometric properties including the adult separation anxiety disorder scale. *International Journal of Methods in Psychiatric Research*, *25*, 232–239. doi: 10.1002/mpr.1515

Morey, L. C., Hopwood, C. J., Markowitz, J. C., Gunderson, J. G., Grilo, C. M., Mcglashan, T. H., . . . Skodol, A. E. (2012). Comparison of alternative models for personality disorders, II: 6-, 8- and 10-year follow-up. *Psychological Medicine*, *42*, 1705–1713. doi: 10.1017/s0033291711002601

Muris, P. & Ollendick, T. H. (2015). Children who are anxious in silence: A review on selective mutism, the new anxiety disorder in *DSM-5*. *Clinical Child and Family Psychology Review*, *18*, 151–169. doi: 10.1007/s10567-015–0181-y

Naragon-Gainey, K., Gallagher, M. W., & Brown, T. A. (2013).Stable "trait" variance of temperament as a predictor of the temporal course of depression and social phobia. *Journal of Abnormal Psychology*, *122*, 611–623.

Narrow, W. E., Clarke, D. E., Kuramoto, S. J., Kraemer, H. C., Kupfer, D. J., Greiner, L., & Regier, D. A. (2013). *DSM-5* field trials in the United States and Canada, part III: Development and reliability testing of a crosscutting symptom assessment for *DSM-5*. *Am J Psychiatry, 170*, 71–82.

Olatunji, B. O., Broman-Fulks, J. J., Bergman, S. M., Green, B. A., & Zlomke, K. R. (2010). A taxometric investigation of the latent structure of worry: Dimensionality and associations with depression, anxiety, and stress. *Behavior Therapy, 41*, 212–228. doi: 10.1016/j.beth.2009.03.001

Otto, M. W., Pollack, M. H., Sachs, G. S., & Rosenbaum, J. F. (1992).Hypochondriacal concerns, anxiety sensitivity, and panic disorder. *Journal of Anxiety Disorders, 6*, 93–104. doi: 10.1016/0887–6185(92)90008-u

Page, A. C., Bennett, K. S., Carter, O., Smith, J., & Woodmore, K. (1997). The Blood-Injection Symptom Scale (BISS): Assessing a structure of phobic symptoms elicited by blood and injections. *Behaviour Research and Therapy, 35*, 457–464. doi: 10.1016/s0005-7967(96)00120–9

Pai, A., Suris, A. M., & North, C. S. (2017). Posttraumatic stress disorder in the *DSM-5*: Controversy, change, and conceptual considerations. *Behavioral Sciences, 7*. doi: 10.3390/bs7010007

Peterson, R. A. & Reiss, S. (1992). *Anxiety Sensitivity Index Revised Test Manual*. Worthington, OH: International Diagnostic Services.

Phillips, K. A., First, M. B., & Pincus, H. A. (2003). *Advancing DSM: Dilemmas in Psychiatric Diagnosis*. Washington, DC: American Psychiatric Association.

Phillips, K. A., Stein, D. J., Rauch, S. L., Hollander, E., Fallon, B. A., Barsky, A., … Leckman, J. (2010). Should an obsessive-compulsive spectrum grouping of disorders be included in *DSM-V*? *Depression and Anxiety, 27*, 528–555. doi: 10.1002/da.20705

Pincus, H. A., McQueen, L. E., & Elinson, L. (2003). Subthreshold mental disorders: Nosological and research recommendations. In K. A. Phillips, M. B. First, & H. A. Pincus (eds.), *Advancing DSM: Dilemmas in Psychiatric Diagnosis* (pp. 129–144). Arlington, VA: American Psychiatric Association.

Rapee, R. M., Craske, M. G., & Barlow, D. H. (1994). Assessment instrument for panic disorder that includes fear of sensation-producing activities: The Albany Panic and Phobia Questionnaire. *Anxiety, 1*, 114–122. doi: 10.1002/anxi.3070010303

Rapee, R. M., Sanderson, W. C., & Barlow, D. H. (1988). Social phobia features across the *DSM-III-R* anxiety disorders. *Journal of Psychopathology and Behavioral Assessment, 10*, 287–299. doi: 10.1007/bf00962552

Regier, D. A., Narrow, W. E., Clarke, D. E., Kraemer, H. C., Kuramoto, S. J., Kuhl, E. A., & Kupfer, D. J. (2013). *DSM-5* field trials in the United States and Canada, part II: Test-retest reliability of selected categorical diagnoses. *American Journal of Psychiatry, 170*, 59–70. doi: 10.1176/appi.ajp.2012.12070999

Resick, P. A. & Miller, M. W. (2009). Posttraumatic stress disorder: Anxiety or traumatic stress disorder? *Journal of Traumatic Stress, 22*, 384–390. doi: 10.1002/jts.20437

Rosellini, A. J. (2013). Initial Development and Validation of a Dimensional Classification System for the Emotional Disorders (Doctoral dissertation). Retrieved from https://open.bu.edu/handle/2144/14112.

Rosellini, A. J., & Brown, T. A. (2014). Initial interpretation and evaluation of a profile-based classification system for the anxiety and mood disorders: Incremental validity compared to *DSM-IV* categories. *Psychological Assessment, 26,* 1212–1224. doi: 10.1037/pas0000023

Rosellini, A. J. & Brown, T. A. (2011). The NEO Five-Factor Inventory: Latent structure and relationships with dimensions of anxiety and depressive disorders in a large clinical sample. *Assessment, 18,* 27–38. doi: 10.1177/1073191110382848

Rosellini, A. J., Lawrence, A. E., Meyer, J. F., & Brown, T. A. (2010). The effects of extraverted temperament on agoraphobia in panic disorder. *Journal of Abnormal Psychology, 119,* 420–426. doi: 10.1037/a0018614

Rutter, L. A. & Brown, T. A. (2015). Reliability and validity of the dimensional features of generalized anxiety disorder. *Journal of Anxiety Disorders, 29,* 1–6. doi: 10.1016/j.janxdis.2014.10.003

Sharp, W. G., Sherman, C., & Gross, A. M. (2007). Selective mutism and anxiety: A review of the current conceptualization of the disorder. *Journal of Anxiety Disorders, 21,* 568–579. doi: 10.1016/j.janxdis.2006.07.002

Shear, K., Jin, R., Ruscio, A. M., Walters, E. E., & Kessler, R. C. (2006). Prevalence and correlates of estimated *DSM-IV* child and adult separation anxiety disorder in the National Comorbidity Survey Replication. *American Journal of Psychiatry, 163,* 1074–1083. doi: 10.1176/ajp.2006.163.6.1074

Sheehan, D. V. (2015). *Mini International Neuropsychiatric Interview 7.0.* Jacksonville, FL: Medical Outcomes Systems.

Sheehan, D. V., Lecrubier, Y., Sheehan, K. H., Amorim, P., Janavas, J., Weiller, E., Hergueta, T., Baker, R., Dunbar, G. C. et al. (1998). The Mini-International Interview (M.I.N.I.): The development and validation of a structured diagnostic psychiatric interview for *DSM-IV* and *ICD-10. Journal of Clinical Psychiatry, 59*(S20), 22–33.

Silove, D., Slade, T., Marnane, C., Wagner, R., Brooks, R., & Manicavasagar, V. (2007). Separation anxiety in adulthood: Dimensional or categorical? *Comprehensive Psychiatry, 48,* 546–553. doi: 10.1016/j.comppsych.2007.05.011

Slade, T. & Grisham, J. R. (2009). A taxometric investigation of agoraphobia in a clinical and a community sample. *Journal of Anxiety Disorders, 23,* 799–805. doi: 10.1016/j.janxdis.2009.03.004

Spitzer, R. L., Kroenke, K., Williams, J. B., & Löwe, B. (2006). A brief measure for assessing generalized anxiety disorder: The GAD-7. *Archives of Internal Medicine, 166,* 1092–1097. doi: 10.1001/archinte.166.10.1092

Spitzer, R. L. & Williams, J. B. W. (1983). *Instruction Manual for the Structured Clinical Interview for* DSM-III (SCID). New York, NY: Biometrics Research Department, New York State Psychiatric Institute.

Spitzer, R. L., Williams, J. B., & Endicott, J. (2012). Standards for *DSM-5* reliability. *American Journal of Psychiatry, 169,* 537–537. doi: 10.1176/appi.ajp.2012.12010083

Stein, D. J., Fineberg, N. A., Bienvenu, O. J., Denys, D., Lochner, C., Nestadt, G., ... Phillips, K. A. (2010). Should OCD be classified as an anxiety disorder in *DSM-V? Depression and Anxiety, 27,* 495–506. doi: 10.1002/da.20699

Stein, M. B., Torgrud, L. J., & Walker, J. R. (2000). Social phobia symptoms, subtypes, and severity: Findings from a community survey. *Archives of General Psychiatry, 57,* 1046–1052. doi: 10.1001/archpsyc.57.11.1046

Stein, M. B., Walker, J. R., & Forde, D. R. (1996). Public-speaking fears in a community sample: Prevalence, impact on functioning, and diagnostic classification. *Archives of General Psychiatry, 53*, 169–174. doi: 10.1001/archpsyc.1996.01830020087010

Stemberger, R. T., Turner, S. M., Beidel, D. C., & Calhoun, K. S. (1995). Social phobia: An analysis of possible developmental factors. *Journal of Abnormal Psychology, 104*, 526–531. doi: 10.1037//0021-843x.104.3.526

Stouthard, M. E., Mellenbergh, G. J., & Hoogstraten, J. (1993). Assessment of dental anxiety: A facet approach. *Anxiety, Stress and Coping, 6*, 89–105. doi: 10.1080/10615809308248372

Szymanski, J., & O'Donohue, W. (1995). Fear of Spiders Questionnaire. *Journal of Behavior Therapy and Experimental Psychiatry, 26*, 31–34. doi: 10.1016/0005–7916(94)00072-t

Tallis, F. (1999). Unintended thoughts and images. In T. Dalgleish & M. Power (eds.), *Handbook of Cognition and Emotion* (pp. 281–300). Chicago, IL:John Wiley & Sons. doi: 10.1002/0470013494.ch15

Taylor, S. & Cox, B. J. (1998). An expanded Anxiety Sensitivity Index: Evidence for a hierarchic structure in a clinical sample. *Journal of Anxiety Disorders, 12*, 463–483. doi: 10.1016/s0887-6185(98)00028–0

Tolin, D., Gilliam, C., Wootton, B., Bowe, W., Bragdon, L., Davis, E., Hannan, S., Steinman, S., Worden, B., & Hallion, L. (2016). Psychometric properties of a structured diagnostic interview for DSM-5 anxiety, mood, and obsessive-compulsive and related disorders. *Assessment, 25*. 10.1177/1073191116638410.

Trull, T. J. (2012). The Five-Factor Model of Personality Disorder and *DSM-5*. *Journal of Personality*,80, 1697–1720. doi: 10.1111/j.1467–6494.2012.00771.x

Turner, S. M., Beidel, D. C., Dancu, C. V., & Stanley, M. A. (1989). An empirically derived inventory to measure social fears and anxiety: The Social Phobia and Anxiety Inventory. *Psychological Assessment, 1*, 35–40. doi: 10.1037//1040–3590.1.1.35

Uebelacker, L. A., Strong, D., Weinstock, L. M., & Miller, I. W. (2010). Likelihood of suicidality at varying levels of depression severity: A re-analysis of NESARC data. *Suicide and Life-Threatening Behavior, 40*, 620–627. doi: 10.1521/suli.2010.40.6.620

Watson, D., O'Hara, M. W., Naragon-Gainey, K., Koffel, E., Chmielewski, M., Kotov, R., . . . Ruggero, C. (2012). Development and validation of new anxiety and bipolar symptom scales for an expanded version of the IDAS (the IDAS-II). *Assessment, 19*, 399–420. doi: 10.1177/1073191112449857

Watson, D., O'Hara, M. W., Simms, L. J., Kotov, R., Chmielewski, M., McDade-Montez, E. A., . . . Stuart, S. (2007). Development and validation of the Inventory of Depression and Anxiety Symptoms (IDAS). *Psychological Assessment, 19*, 253–268. doi: 10.1037/1040–3590.19.3.253

Weinberg, A., Kotov, R., & Proudfit, G. H. (2015). Neural indicators of error processing in generalized anxiety disorder, obsessive-compulsive disorder, and major depressive disorder. *Journal of Abnormal Psychology, 124*, 172–185. doi: 10.1037/abn0000019

Wilamowska, Z. A., Thompson-Hollands, J., Fairholme, C. P., Ellard, K. K., Farchione, T. J., & Barlow, D. H. (2010). Conceptual background, development, and preliminary data from the Unified Protocol for Transdiagnostic Treatment of Emotional Disorders. *Depression and Anxiety, 27*, 882–890. doi: 10.1002/da.20735

Wittchen, H.-U., Gloster, A. T., Beesdo-Baum, K., Fava, G. A., & Craske, M. G. (2010). Agoraphobia: A review of the diagnostic classificatory position and criteria. *Depression and Anxiety, 27*, 113–133. doi: 10.1002/da.20646

Wolpe, J. & Lang, P. J. (1964). A fear survey schedule for use in behaviour therapy. *Behaviour Research and Therapy, 2*, 27–30.

Wolpe, J. & Lang, P. J. (1969). *Manual for the Fear Survey Schedule*. San Diego, CA: Educational and Industrial Testing Service.

Wright, A. G., Krueger, R. F., Hobbs, M. J., Markon, K. E., Eaton, N. R., & Slade, T. (2013). The structure of psychopathology: Toward an expanded quantitative empirical model. *Journal of Abnormal Psychology, 122*, 281–294. doi: 10.1037/a0030133

Zimmerman, M. & Chelminski, I. (2003). Generalized anxiety disorder in patients with major depression: Is *DSM-IV*'s hierarchy correct? *American Journal of Psychiatry, 160*, 504–512. https://doi.org/10.1176/appi.ajp.160.3.504

Zimmerman, M., McDermut, W., & Mattia, J. I. (2000). Frequency of anxiety disorders in psychiatric outpatients with major depressive disorder. *American Journal of Psychiatry, 157*, 1337–1340. doi: 10.1176/appi.ajp.157.8.1337

Zinbarg, R. E., Mineka, S., Bobova, L., Craske, M. G., Vrshek-Schallhorn, S., Griffith, J. W., . . . Anand, D. (2016). Testing a hierarchical model of neuroticism and its cognitive facets. *Clinical Psychological Science, 4*, 805–824. doi: 10.1177/2167702615618162

12 Obsessive-Compulsive and Related Disorders

Andrew M. Kiselica and Eric A. Storch

Obsessive-Compulsive Disorder: The Current Debate

Obsessive-compulsive disorder (OCD) diagnostic caseness requires obsessions and/or compulsions that are time-consuming and/or cause clinically significant distress or impairment (APA, 2013). Despite its clear definition, classification and diagnosis of OCD is complicated by high rates of comorbidity (90%), heterogeneous presentations, and large numbers of individuals with subclinical symptoms (Bloch et al., 2008; Ruscio, Stein, Chiu, & Kessler, 2010). Correct classification and diagnosis of OCD is important, given its prevalence and associated impairment. Approximately, 2.3% of individuals in the United States meet criteria for a clinical OCD diagnosis at some point in their lifetimes (Ruscio et al., 2010). Furthermore, a recent review concluded "that those with OCD had diminished quality of life across all domains relative to normative comparison subjects," including mental health, physical health, and social relationships (Subramaniam, Soh, Vaingankar, Picco, & Chong, 2013, p. 367). This impact on quality of life extends to family members of individuals with OCD, who have substantially reduced quality of life relative to controls (Cicek, Cicek, Kayhan, Uguz, & Kaya, 2013; Vikas, Avasthi, & Sharan, 2011). Moreover, health care utilization costs for OCD are comparable to depression and amount to about $11,000 per patient per year (Hankin et al., 2011).

To mitigate the effects of OCD, proper classification, diagnosis, and treatment are needed. However, there is a lack of consensus about how OCD should be classified. In previous versions of the *DSM*, OCD was placed in the Anxiety Disorders category (APA, 2000). However, in the most recent edition (APA, 2013), OCD was moved to the Obsessive-Compulsive Spectrum Disorders (OCSDs) category that also includes Body Dysmorphic Disorder, Hoarding Disorder, Trichotillomania, and Excoriation Disorder. There has been considerable debate regarding this change.

Proponents of the OCSD category argue that compulsivity, or poorly controlled repetitive behavior, is a defining feature of OCD that is common across OCSDs (Fineberg, Menchon, Zohar, & Veltman, 2016; Hollander et al., 2016). Their arguments in favor of moving OCD from the Anxiety Disorders to the OCSD category can be summarized as follows (Bartz & Hollander, 2006; Hollander, Braun, & Simeon, 2008; Hollander & Zohar, 2004; Stein & Lochner, 2006):

- Anxiety is a nonspecific symptom that does not tell us much about etiology and treatment of OCD (Bartz & Hollander, 2006). Therefore, classifying OCD under Anxiety Disorders is not useful.
- OCD is similar to other OCSDs because it couples distressing thoughts with distress-reducing rituals (Bartz & Hollander, 2006). For example, individuals with hoarding disorder have distressing thoughts about throwing away subjectively valued items, leading to collection of large amounts of largely useless objects. Similarly, individuals with OCD engage in checking and rechecking locks on doors to reduce the distress associated with thoughts of harm coming to them or their families.
- OCD has high rates of comorbidity with other compulsive disorders, suggesting that they should be grouped together (e.g., LaSalle et al., 2004).
- Studies suggest similar genetic etiologies of OCD and OCSDs (e.g., Bienvenu et al., 2000).
- OCD shares more biological similarity with OCSDs than anxiety disorders (Bartz & Hollander, 2006). Specifically, OCD and OCSDs are driven by dysfunction in orbitofrontal-subcortical circuitry and serotonergic and dopaminergic dysfunction, whereas anxiety is driven by overactive fear circuitry centering on the amygdala and serotonergic dysfunction.

Opponents of moving OCD to the OCSD category responded to these arguments. They asserted that OCD is more similar to Anxiety than Impulse Control Disorders, citing numerous pieces of evidence. Their point of view is summarized as follows (Abramowitz, Storch, McKay, Taylor, & Asmundson, 2009; Starcevic & Janca, 2011; Storch, Abramowitz, & Goodman, 2008):

- Repetitive behaviors are a nonspecific means of grouping OCSDs together or distinguishing them from other disorders (Starcevic & Janca, 2011).
- OCD cannot be characterized solely by repetitive behaviors; rather, it consists of compulsive behaviors tied to distress-producing obsessions (Foa & Kozak, 1995). Other OCSDs, such as Trichotillomania and Excoriation Disorder, do not share this feature of specific obsessive thoughts.
- Repetitive behaviors are not specific to the OCSDs (Storch et al., 2008); rather, they are characteristic of a host of disorders (e.g., addiction, autism spectrum disorder). Consequently, repetitive behaviors cannot delineate a diagnostic category.
- There is a dearth of evidence to suggest biological similarities between OCD and other disorders, making groupings based on biological evidence premature (Abramowitz, Taylor, & McKay, 2009; Hyman, 2007).
- OCD shares higher comorbidities with Anxiety Disorders than with impulse control/repetitive behavior disorders, suggesting that OCD should be grouped with Anxiety Disorders (Bienvenu et al., 2000).

- OCD shows higher familial similarity with Anxiety Disorders than with impulse control/repetitive behavior disorders (Bienvenu et al., 2000; Nestadt et al., 2001), suggesting that OCD and Anxiety Disorders should be clustered together.
- OCD shows an excellent treatment response to exposure-response prevention therapy (e.g., Abramowitz, Whiteside, & Deacon, 2006; McGuire et al., 2015), the evidence-based psychotherapeutic treatment for Anxiety Disorders. Such findings suggest that OCD is in part caused/maintained by anxiety. Other impulse control/repetitive behavior disorders do not show this treatment response to exposure-based therapies, although they do respond well to other behavioral forms of psychotherapy (McGuire et al., 2014).

This debate makes clear that further consideration of the best means of classifying OCD is necessary. One method of shedding light on the most appropriate way of classifying OCD is to review current assessment instruments for this disorder. Analysis of assessment instruments gives insight into the currently prevailing evidence-based conceptualization of disorders. Consequently, they can provide us with justification for placing OCD into a particular class. In the following chapter, we provide a review of current evidence-based assessments for adult OCD and OCSDs. The chapter does not include a review of the psychometric properties of different instruments in detail, where recent reviews already exist (Duke, Keeley, Geffken, & Storch, 2010; Frost & Hristova, 2011; Grant & Odlaug, 2015; Keuthen, Siev, & Reese, 2012; Overduin & Furnham, 2012; Siev, Reese, Timpano, & Wilhelm, 2012; Snorrason, Houghton, & Woods, 2015); rather, in each section, we focus on assessing the extent to which current assessment instruments suggest that OCD should be grouped alongside OCSDs or Anxiety Disorders. From this evidence, we conclude that OCD assessment instruments share more similarities with assessments of Anxiety Disorders than OCSDs.

Assessment of OCD

Self-report instruments. Overduin and Furnham (2012) completed a review of the literature on self-report measures of OCD. They examined 10 questionnaires that assessed primary OCD. These measures included the Padua Inventory-Washington State University Revision (PI-WSUR) (Burns, 1995), the Padua Inventory-Revised (PI-R) (van Oppen, Hoekstra, & Emmelkamp, 1995), the Padua Inventory-Palatine Revision (PI-PR) (Gönner, Ecker, & Leonhart, 2010), the Obsessive-Compulsive Inventory-Revised (OCI-R) (Foa et al., 2002), the Vancouver Obsessional Compulsive Inventory (Thordarson et al., 2004), the Vancouver Obsessional Compulsive Inventory-Revised (VOCI-R) (Gönner, Ecker, Leonhart, & Limbacher, 2010), the Schedule of Compulsions, Obsessions, and Pathological Impulses (SCOPI) (Watson & Wu, 2005), the Clark–Beck Obsessive-Compulsive Inventory (CBOCI) (Clark, Antony, Beck, Swinson, & Steer, 2005), the Florida Obsessive-Compulsive Inventory (FOCI) (Storch et al.,

2007), and the Dimensional Obsessive-Compulsive Scale (DOCS) (Abramowitz et al., 2010).

The development articles for these measures have all been published in peer-reviewed journals. Each meets minimum standards of internal consistency and convergent validity with other OCD measures. Furthermore, Overduin and Furnham (2012) could not find particular reasons to suggest the choice of one self-report indicator of OCD over the others. Instead, they concluded:

> Selecting an OCD measure for clinical or research purposes will always include a trade-off between obtaining detailed and conceptually nuanced information with a time-intensive method and screening for OCD tendencies more efficiently in large mixed samples. (p. 322)

Though the authors were unable to definitively suggest one measure over the others, they did provide a useful synopsis of the characteristics of a good OCD measure.

Their conclusions clearly support the conceptualization of OCD as an Anxiety Disorder. First, Overduin and Furnham (2012) concluded that quality self-report instruments of OCD should assess both obsessions and compulsions as interconnected phenomena. This stance reinforces the view of Storch and colleagues (2008) that obsessions and compulsions are inextricably linked and that OCD cannot be classified on the basis of compulsions alone. Second, the reviewers noted that self-report instruments should conceptualize OCD severity as multidimensional, and included assessments of distress, functional impairment, length of symptoms, and avoidance to reduce anxiety. Third, Overduin and Furnham emphasized that instruments should examine the function of obsessions and rituals. These next two points dovetail well with the argument that an OCD nosology that does not account for anxiety and its functional significance in causing and maintaining symptoms is incorrect. Finally, Overduin and Furnham point out the importance of having measures of OCD that discriminate between OCD patients and individuals with other disorders (e.g., depression and anxiety). Importantly, the authors do not highlight the need to distinguish OCD from OCSDs, such as Trichotillomania, which have dramatic phenomenological differences. Differences between OCD and these other disorders are so clear on their face that an assessment of divergent validity is unnecessary. However, because OCD overlaps considerably with anxiety, it is important that measures of OCD be empirically established as distinct.

Clinician-rated measures. An upcoming book chapter reviewed available clinician-rated scales for OCD (McGuire et al., in press). Commonly used clinical interviews include the Yale-Brown Obsessive Compulsive Scale (Y-BOCS) (Goodman et al., 1989) and the Yale-Brown Obsessive Compulsive Scale-Second Edition (Y-BOCS-II) (Storch, Rasmussen et al., 2010). The Y-BOCS and Y-BOCS-II are considered the gold standards in OCD assessment and provide a wealth of information about how to best classify OCD.

The Y-BOCS consists of a 54-item symptom checklist and a 10-item severity scale. The clinician inquires with the patient about the presence/absence of 54 obsessions/compulsions. Following completion of the symptom checklist, the clinician rates the severity of obsessions and compulsions on a separate five-point scale. Ratings are made in the following areas: interference, distress, time/frequency, resistance, and degree of control. These ratings result in three scores: a Compulsion Severity score, an Obsession Severity score, and a Total Severity score.

It is important to note that the Total Severity score includes *both* obsessions and compulsions, highlighting the importance of combining these core components in framing OCD. This conceptualization supports the view that OCD cannot be classified based on compulsive behaviors alone. Despite its long-standing use in clinical settings and strong psychometric properties, the Y-BOCS has been criticized on several grounds. The most prominent of these criticisms concerns the modest divergent validity evidence for Y-BOCS scores and their shared overlap with depression and anxiety (McGuire et al., in press). This problem brings to mind Bartz and Hollander's (2006) criticism of the poor specificity of anxiety as a means of classifying OCD. Note, however, that this lack of discrimination could be a measurement issue; the Y-BOCS may indirectly assess symptoms of depression and anxiety (e.g., rumination, avoidance), such that the total score does not represent an independent assay of OCD. Storch and colleagues (2010) addressed this possibility in creating the Y-BOCS-II. Herein, they attempted to overcome the divergent validity problem and include the concept of avoidance of symptom-provoking stimuli. Storch and colleagues succeeded in creating an OCD total score that demonstrates very high correlations with scores on other clinician-rated measures of OCD ($r \geq 0.85$) and only moderate associations ($r \leq 0.38$) with scores on indices of depression and anxiety symptoms.

The overlap of Y-BOCS-II scores with scores for depression and anxiety is still significant, despite the authors' best attempts to create a "clean" assessment of OCD. Clearly, OCD symptoms are difficult to completely separate from anxiety/depression, given naturally occurring rates of comorbidity (Bienvenu et al., 2000; Ruscio et al., 2010; Storch, Lewin, et al., 2010) and the extent to which OCD may contribute to both internalizing symptoms (Zitterl et al., 2000). On the other hand, the magnitude for the associations of the Y-BOCS-II scores with other OCD measure scores is quite a bit higher than their associations with scores on anxiety and depression. Thus, the Y-BOCS-II appears to accurately reflect OCD symptomology and discriminate adequately between OCD and depression/anxiety. And, though some may continue to criticize the continued association of Y-BOCS-II scores with scores on depression/anxiety metrics, others may see it as a strength. Indeed, the nomological network for OCD would logically include significant, moderate associations with depression/anxiety if we believe that OCD is a true anxiety disorder.

Assessment of Body Dysmorphic Disorder (BDD)

The *DSM-5* criteria for BDD require a preoccupation with at least one perceived flaw in physical appearance and repetitive behaviors in response to appearance concerns (APA, 2013). On its face, the definition of BDD has great overlap with that of OCD – there are obsessive thoughts and repeated rituals in response to those thoughts. For instance, an individual may have frequent intrusive thoughts about the size of his nose and repeatedly check his face in the mirror or ask friends for reassurance about his appearance. Though a variety of measures exist for assessing body image disturbance, there are fewer measures specific to BDD.

Self-report measures. There are three self-report measures of BDD symptoms. The most recently developed is the Body Dysmorphic Disorder Symptom Scale (BDDSS) (Wilhelm, Greenberg, Rosenfield, Kasarskis, & Blashill, 2016). This measure includes a checklist of 54 symptoms, divided into seven symptom sub-groups: checking rituals, grooming rituals, shape/weight-related rituals, hair-pulling/skin-picking rituals, surgery/dermatology-seeking rituals, avoidance, and BDD-related cognitions. Respondents state whether they have experienced each symptom in the past week. In subgroups where at least one symptom is endorsed, patients rate the overall severity of symptoms from that group on a 0–10 scale (0 = no problem; 10 = very severe).

The BDDSS provides two summary scores, one indexing severity (sum of all severity ratings, ranging from 0 to 70), and another indexing the total number of symptoms endorsed (0–54). Internal consistencies (KR-20) for the subscale scores ranged from poor to good (0.29 to 0.82); the summary score internal consistencies were not reported. BDDSS scores demonstrated convergent validity with the scores on Body Dysmorphic Disorder Modification of the Y-BOCS (BDD-Y-BOCS) (Phillips, Hollander, Rasmussen, & Aronowitz, 1997), a clinician-rated measure. Correlations for severity and symptoms were 0.46 and 0.64, respectively. Weaker relationships were observed with indices of depression (0.26 and 0.32, respectively). Thus, preliminary evidence for the psychometric properties of BDDSS is mixed. Reliability is variable or unclear, convergent validity evidence is good, and discriminant validity evidence is fair. Independent studies of the BDDSS are necessary as a next step.

The next self-report measure of BDD is the Body Dysmorphic Disorder Questionnaire (BDDQ) (Brohede, Wingren, Wijma, & Wijma, 2013). It is a brief questionnaire derived from the *DSM-IV* criteria that consists of four questions assessing concern with appearance and associated preoccupation, distress, interference, and avoidance. Each positive response is scored as 1 (i.e., presence of symptom), whereas each negative response is scored as 0. Summed scores of 4 indicate the likely presence of clinical BDD. A BDDQ score of 4 was shown to yield excellent sensitivity (94%) and specificity (90%) in a sample of 88 women. However, reliability data for this measure were not reported. Replication of criterion validity results and publication of reliability data are needed for the BDDQ.

The third self-report index of BDD symptoms is the Dysmorphic Concern Questionnaire (DCQ) (Oosthuizen, Lambert, & Castle, 1998), which is a seven-item measure assessing concerns with physical appearance and attempts to deal with these concerns. Respondents rate their dysmorphic concerns on the following scale: 0-no concern; 1-the same as most people; 2-more than most people; 3-much more than most people. Item scores are summed to create a total score, with higher scores indicating greater dysmorphic concern. Reported Cronbach's alphas have been good: 0.80–0.88 (Jorgensen, Castle, Roberts, & Groth-Marnat, 2001; Oosthuizen et al., 1998). Evidence for construct validity has been shown by high correlations of DCQ scores with scores on indices of impairment ($r \geq 0.55$). Moreover, criterion validity is well established, as individuals with BDD score higher on the DCQ than controls and sensitivity (96.4%) and specificity (90.6%) are in the excellent range for a cutoff score of 9 (Jorgensen et al., 2001; Mancuso, Knoesen, & Castle, 2010). Discriminant validity of DCQ scores is fair to poor for depression (r ranged from 0.23 to 0.49) and good for psychotic symptoms ($r \leq 0.17$) (Oosthuizen et al., 1998). Evidence demonstrates solid psychometric properties for this measure in terms of internal consistency, construct validity, and criterion validity, though discrimination from depression could be improved (note that some overlap between BDD and depression scores is expected, given the distress caused by BDD).

The BDD questionnaires diverge in the depth of coverage of symptoms, with the BDDQ and DCQ serving as screening instruments and the BDDSS serving as a full symptom inventory and severity measure. Herein, measure selection may be directed by the purpose of the professional. If selecting a screening measure, the DCQ may be preferred, until the BDDQ has been further evaluated.

Despite their differences, the self-report measures of BDD converge greatly in terms of content/purpose. They all assess obsessions with appearance and efforts to respond to obsessions. Thus, they exhibit definite conceptual overlap with OCD measures, which assess OCD-related obsessions and compulsions. Greater examination of these measures in relation to indices of anxiety is needed to further explore BDD's relationship with Anxiety Disorders and allow comparison to other repetitive-behavior disorders.

Clinician-rated measures. There are two clinician-rated assessment instruments for BDD, the Body Dysmorphic Disorder Examination (BDDE) (Rosen & Reiter, 1996) and the BDD-Y-BOCS. The BDDE consists of one item assessing the presence of a dysmorphic concern and 28 items assessing the severity of related BDD symptoms in the past four weeks. Symptoms are rated by the clinician on a scale of 0 (absent) to 6 (extreme). The measure indexes preoccupation with and negative evaluation of appearance, self-consciousness and embarrassment, excessive importance given to appearance in self-evaluation, avoidance of activities, body camouflaging, and body checking. The total score consists of a sum of the 28 symptom items, with higher scores indicating increased disorder severity.

Rosen and Reiter (1996) conducted an extensive psychometric evaluation of the BDDE in four separate samples. Internal consistencies for the severity score of the BDDE were reported to be good to excellent ($\alpha = 0.81$–0.93). Two-week test-retest reliability was high ($r = 0.87$–0.94) and interrater reliability was strong ($r =0.86$–0.99). In addition to this reliability evidence, the authors presented a wealth of data on validity. Construct validity was exhibited by moderate to strong correlations of BDDE scores with scores on measures of body shape concerns (0.60–0.77), appearance evaluation (0.20–0.58), body area satisfaction (0.25–0.58), appearance orientation (0.23–0.44), and self-esteem (0.33–0.50). Moreover, BDD severity on the BDDE predicted BDD clinical status, even after controlling for body image concerns, self-esteem, and age. Importantly, individuals with BDD scored higher on the BDDE than those without. Finally, BDDE scores changed significantly from baseline to post assessment in a randomized controlled trial with an exposure-based cognitive behavioral intervention. No discriminant validity evidence for the BDDE was reported.

The BDD-Y-BOCS was created around the same time as the BDDE. It follows a similar format as the original Y-BOCS and consists of 12-items designed to rate the severity of BDD (Phillips et al., 1997). Items are rated on a scale of 0 to 4 with higher numbers indicating greater symptom severity. Items are summed to create a total severity scale. The scale indexes intrusive thoughts about body defects and related repetitive behaviors, as well as associated interference, distress, resistance, degree of control, and time spent due to symptoms.

The BDD-Y-BOCS total score exhibits good to excellent reliability in terms of internal consistency (0.80), interrater agreement ($ICC = 0.88$–0.97), and test-retest reliability ($r = 0.93$) over a one-week period (Phillips, Hart, & Menard, 2014). Convergent validity evidence for the BDD-Y-BOCS severity score is demonstrated by high positive correlation with the BDDE severity score ($r = 0.82$), a high positive correlation with the Clinician Global Impression of severity score ($r = 0.55$), and a high negative correlation with clinician-rated Global Assessment of Functioning ($r = -0.63$–0.53; Phillips et al., 2014). Evidence for discriminant validity is fair, as the BDD-Y-BOCS severity score is highly correlated with scores on indices of depression ($r = 0.47$–0.53) and moderately correlated with scores on indices of social anxiety ($r = 0.24$; Phillips et al., 2014). Several studies using the BDD-Y-BOCS show it is sensitive to treatment changes associated with exposure-based therapy and selective serotonin reuptake inhibits/serotonin and norepinephrine reuptake inhibitors (SSRI/SNRI) pharmacotherapies (Allen et al., 2008; Greenberg, Mothi, & Wilhelm, 2016; Phillips et al., 2014; Phillips et al., 1997). Importantly, these treatment changes on the BDD-Y-BOCS are correlated with improvements in quality of life (Phillips & Rasmussen, 2004). The BDD-Y-BOCS is already seeing widespread use, as Dutch (van Rood & Bouman, 2007) and Farsi (Rabiee, Khorramdel, Kalantari, & Molavi, 2010) versions are available.

The BDDE and BDD-Y-BOCS both appear to yield scores with good to excellent psychometric properties in terms of reliability, convergent validity, and construct validity. It is clear that either of these measures represents the best available means of accurately diagnosing and assessing the severity of BDD. Nonetheless, continued research on these measures is needed to firmly establish discriminant validity.

Evidence from clinician-rated measures of BDD suggests a number of similarities between BDD and OCD. Like self-report measures, they highlight the importance of measuring obsessive thoughts about a perceived disfigurement and related compulsions. Unlike self-report measures, though, the clinician-rated measures have a wealth of evidence on changes associated with treatment. Specifically, both the BDDE and BDD-Y-BOCS scores are sensitive to treatment with exposure therapy. Exposure therapy was originally designed to treat anxiety and is the best-supported treatment of OCD in the empirical literature (Öst, Havnen, Hansen, & Kvale, 2015; Skapinakis et al., 2016). These results suggest that the same mechanisms underlying symptoms of OCD and Anxiety are underlying symptoms of BDD. A similar conclusion regarding the overlap of BDD, OCD, and Anxiety can be drawn from the literature on pharmacologic treatments. Indeed, the BDD-Y-BOCS is sensitive to treatment changes with SSRIs. SSRIs are the leading pharmacologic treatment choice for OCD and Anxiety Disorders more generally (Koen & Stein, 2011; Skapinakis et al., 2016). Such studies provide evidence for similar underlying neurochemical mechanisms for OCD, Anxiety, and BDD. Thus, it may be that BDD is best conceptualized as an Anxiety Disorder, alongside OCD.

Assessment of Hoarding Disorder

According to *DSM-5* criteria, Hoarding Disorder is defined by difficulty discarding possessions, regardless of their value, that is due to a perceived need to save items and is associated with congestion and clutter in active living areas. Frost and Hristova (2011) provided a comprehensive review of clinician-rated and self-report measurements of hoarding.

Self-report measures. Frost and Hristova (2011) listed the Saving Inventory-Revised (SI-R) (Frost, Steketee, & Grisham, 2004) and the Hoarding Assessment Scale (HAS) (Schneider, Storch, Geffken, Lack, & Shytle, 2008) as the main self-report measures of hoarding symptoms and cognitions. The HAS had poor evidence of convergent validity and a lack of reliability. Consequently, the authors recommend the SI-R for self-report assessment in their conclusions.

The SI-R is a 23-item measure with three subscales: Clutter, Difficulty Discarding, and Excessive Acquisition. Items are scored on a 0 to 4 scale and total scores range from 0 to 92. The total score exhibits convergence with interview and self-report measures of hoarding, divergence from scores on assessments of OCD symptoms, criterion-related validity, and sensitivity to treatment with cognitive-behavioral therapy.

Clinician-rated measures. Frost and Hristova indicated the UCLA Hoarding Severity Scale (UCLA-HSS) (Saxena, Ayers, Dozier, & Maidment, 2015; Saxena, Brody, Maidment, & Baxter, 2007) and the Hoarding Rating Scale-Interview (HRS-I) (Tolin, Frost, & Steketee, 2010) as the main interview-based measures of Hoarding Disorder. The UCLA–HSS total score has adequate internal consistency ($\alpha = 0.70$), distinguishes individuals with Hoarding Disorder from controls, and exhibits strong correlations with scores from the SI-R (Frost et al., 2004). Nonetheless, the UCLA-HSS lacks evidence on test-retest and interrater reliability, discriminant validity, and construct validity. The HRS-I has more robust evidence for its scores on psychometric properties; therefore, it was recommended in Frost and Hristova's (2011) conclusions.

The HRS-I is a five-question semi-structured interview. Items are rated on a scale of 0 (not at all) to 8 (extreme). Items assess clutter, difficulty discarding items, excessive acquisition of items, and related distress and impairment. Items are summed to create a total score (range = 0–40). This total score exhibits convergent associations with other measures of Hoarding Disorder, but lower correlations with scores on measures of OCD, anxiety, and depression. Furthermore, scores on the HRS-I discriminate Hoarding Disorder patients from OCD patients and are sensitive to treatment changes with a hoarding-specific cognitive behavioral intervention(Steketee, Frost, Tolin, Rasmussen, & Brown, 2010).

Classification of Hoarding Disorder and OCD. The literature on assessment of Hoarding Disorder suggests that it should be classified separately from OCD. First, unlike OCD measures that include obsession items, the hoarding instruments do not assess intrusive thoughts associated with hoarding behavior. Rather, they index specific hoarding behaviors (excessive acquisition of objects and difficulty throwing them away) and related functional consequences (e.g., clutter in the home). Second, scores on hoarding instruments show only low to moderate correlations with scores on measures of OCD. Third, hoarding instruments are sensitive to treatment change with a hoarding-specific cognitive behavioral intervention, which include several elements not characteristic of standard exposure-response prevention for OCD. Because hoarding is frequently ego syntonic (unlike OCD, which tends to be ego dystonic), treatment for hoarding includes motivational enhancement to promote engagement in treatment (Clark & O'Connor, 2005; Frost, Tolin, & Maltby, 2010). Furthermore, cognitive behavioral therapy for hoarding includes skills training for organizing, problem-solving, and decision-making to overcome poor organization and clutter in the home (Muroff et al., 2009; Steketee et al., 2010) Such a step is unnecessary in OCD treatment because OCD is maintained by conditioned associations between obsessions and compulsions and not by a lack of problem-solving skills (Shafran, 2005). In summary, extant literature on hoarding and OCD assessment suggests that these disorders should be classified separately.

Assessment of Excoriation Disorder

Excoriation Disorder is characterized by pathological skin picking (APA, 2013). To meet formal criteria, skin picking must result in lesions, be characterized by attempts to stop or decrease skin picking, and include related distress or impairment. Several recent reviews of assessment instruments available for excoriation disorder exist (Grant & Odlaug, 2015; Keuthen et al., 2012; Siev et al., 2012).

Self-report measures. There is a variety of self-report instruments for Excoriation Disorder. These measures include the Skin Picking Scale-Revised (SPS-R) (Keuthen, Wilhelm et al., 2001; Snorrason et al., 2012), the Skin Picking Impact Scale (SPIS) (Keuthen, Deckersbach et al., 2001), the Skin Picking Symptom Assessment Scale (SP-SAS) (Grant, Odlaugh, & Kim, 2007), and the Milwaukee Inventory for the Dimensions of Adult Skin Picking (MIDAS) (Walther, Flessner, Conelea, & Woods, 2009).

The SPS-R and SP-SAS are similar in that they assess urges to pick skin, skin-picking behavior, and related impairment. The MIDAS differs from these other measures in that it distinguishes between automatic picking (picking behaviors of which the patient is not consciously aware) and focused picking (intentional picking). Psychometric properties for these measures' scores are adequate, but not excellent. In contrast, the SPIS only assesses the burden of skin picking to the individual and yields scores with superior psychometric properties. The SPS, SPIS, and SP-SAS have all shown sensitivity to treatment. Specifically, the SP-SAS is responsive to treatment changes with an antiepileptic (Keuthen et al., 2007), while the SPS and SPIS are sensitive to treatment changes with an SSRI (Grant et al., 2007).

Clinician-rated measures. There are two clinician-rated measures of Excoriation Disorder: the Yale-Brown Obsessive Compulsive Scale Modified for Neurotic Excoriation (NE-Y-BOCS) (Grant, Odlaug, Chamberlain, & Kim, 2010) and the Skin Picking Treatment Scale (SPTS) (Simeon, Stein, Gross, Islam, & Hollander, 1997). The Y-BOCS-NE is modeled from the Y-BOCS and contains five items assessing urges (as opposed to obsessions) to pick skin and five items assessing picking behavior. Each item is rated on a 0–4 severity scale, with items being summed to create a total scale, wherein higher scores indicate greater disorder severity. The SPTS is similarly modeled off of the Y-BOCS, but only contains five items assessing urges to pick, time spent picking, picking severity, degree of control over picking, and interference due to picking. Unfortunately, psychometric data on these measures are limited. The NE-Y-BOCS score converges with scores on other skin-picking measures, shows good test-retest reliability, and demonstrates treatment response to an antiepileptic. The SPTS has not been formally evaluated; nonetheless, it has been shown to be sensitive to treatment changes with an SSRI. Clearly, more research is needed on these measures to establish that they yield reliable and valid scores of skin-picking severity before firm conclusions can be drawn from them.

Classification of Excoriation Disorder and OCD. The extant evidence offers mixed indications on the best means of classifying Excoriation Disorder and OCD. Clearly, most measures of skin picking diverge from OCD measures in their concentration on urges instead of obsessions. Furthermore, the literature on treatment sensitivity suggests different conclusions. Some measures have shown treatment sensitivity to antiepileptics; such drugs are sometimes used to treat OCD, but they are far from the first-line treatments. Typically, SSRIs, SNRIs, and antipsychotics are attempted before antiepileptics. Consequently, this finding suggests a different underlying mechanism for OCD and Excoriation Disorder. On the other hand, some skin-picking instrument scores were sensitive to treatment changes with an SSRI, which is more consistent with a similarity to OCD. Thus, most evidence to date from measures of Excoriation Disorder suggests that it is distinct from OCD, but more research is clearly needed.

Assessment of Trichotillomania

Trichotillomania is characterized by repeated hair pulling and is defined very similarly to Excoriation Disorder (APA, 2013). To meet diagnostic criteria, an individual must pull out hair, resulting in hair loss, have repeated attempts to decrease or stop hair pulling, and experience related distress or impairment. We refer readers to reviews of hair-pulling assessment instruments (Duke et al., 2010; Keuthen et al., 2012; Snorrason et al., 2015).

Self-report measures. Commonly used self-report measures of Trichotillomania include the Massachusetts General Hospital Hairpulling Scale (MGH-HPS) (Keuthen et al., 1995) and the Milwaukee Inventory for Subtypes of Trichotillomania-Adult Version (MIST-A) (Flessner, Woods, Franklin, Cashin, & Keuthen, 2008; Keuthen et al., 2015). The MGH-HPS is a seven-item measure indexing urges to pull hair and hair-pulling behaviors. Items are rated on a 1–4-point scale, with higher numbers indicating greater frequency/severity of symptoms. Item scores are summed to yield a total score. Research has demonstrated strong evidence for this score's reliability and validity. The MIST-A consists of two scores indexing automatic and focused pulling, similar to the MIDAS. Scores from this instrument have shown adequate reliability, convergent validity with scores from other measures of hair pulling, and divergent validity from scores on measures of depression, anxiety, and stress.

Clinician-rated measures. There are several clinician-rated measures of Trichotillomania. They include the Trichotillomania Diagnostic Interview (TDI) (Rothbaum & Ninan, 1994), the National Institute of Mental Health Trichotillomania Impairment Scale (NIMH-TIS) and Severity Scale (NIMH-TSS) (Swedo et al., 1989), the Psychiatric Institute Trichotillomania Scale (PITS)

(Winchel et al., 1992), and the Yale-Brown Obsessive Compulsive Scale – Trichotillomania (Y-BOCS-TTM) (Stanley, Prather, Wagner, Davis, & Swann, 1993).

The TDI is a diagnostic interview, amounting to a checklist of symptoms. Consequently, it is difficult to draw conclusions from this measure beyond what is revealed in the *DSM-5*. The other measures index severity of urges, pulling behaviors, and related impairments, providing more information on how researchers are conceptualizing Trichotillomania. However, each instrument's score exhibits issues with reliability, impinging on validity; thus, we are hesitant to make inferences based on research with these measures.

Classification of Trichotillomania and OCD. Existing data suggest that, as in Excoriation Disorder, urges, and not obsessive thoughts, are a core feature of Trichotillomania. This conceptualization diverges from the evidence on OCD, which suggests the primary importance of obsessions. Moreover, the literature on construct validity demonstrates that Trichotillomania measures are responsive to a number of different types of medications, including tricyclic antidepressants, SSRIs, and antipsychotics (Bloch et al., 2007). However, they have only been found to be responsive to one behavioral treatment, habit-reversal training (Bloch et al., 2007). These findings suggest a lack of a clear connection between OCD and Trichotillomania.

Future Directions

Current OCSD assessment instruments examine phenotypes of these disorders; that is, the behavioral, cognitive, and emotional clusters of symptoms that characterize the dysfunction associated with a particular mental health problem. This approach is likely to change with the rollout of the National Institutes of Health's (NIH) Research Domain Criteria (RDoC) framework (Morris & Cuthbert, 2012). RDoC appears to have two overarching goals: 1) Identification of transdiagnostic factors that can explain commonalities across disorders; and 2) Identification of clear pathognomonic signs that can distinguish across disorders. These efforts are focused on using findings from multiple disciplines, especially genetics, neuroscience, and endocrinology, to inform our understanding of psychological disorders, including OCD (Fineberg et al., 2016; Kendler, 2017).

Consequently, there is likely to be a shift in future research of OCD and related disorders from studying and assessing phenotypes to studying and assessing endophenotypes and genetic markers. As discussed earlier, current research in this area may be inadequate for establishing a nosology for the OCSDs. However, with increased funding from the NIH and the development of new technologies, understanding the biological underpinnings of disorders is likely to progress. In the coming years, evidence may suggest that the genetic or neurological underpinnings of OCD resemble those of OCSDs, Anxiety Disorders, or a separate class altogether (see Gillan, Fineberg, & Robbins, 2017, for an example of a current discussion of this topic). Thus, future research can be used to confirm or modify the conclusions drawn in the current chapter.

Conclusion

This review provided a summary and analysis of existing adult assessment instruments for OCSDs. Data on current OCD measures suggest that obsessions and compulsions are inextricably linked in OCD. Consequently, OCD is poorly classified using only the criterion of repetitive behaviors. Furthermore, the literature emphasizes that OCD cannot be properly classified without reference to the functional significance of anxiety and its role in maintaining OCD symptoms and functional impairment. Finally, OCD researchers point out the importance for OCD measures to distinguish between OCD and anxiety/depression, acknowledging that OCD is similar to these conditions. Taken together, these findings provide evidence against the obsessive-compulsive spectrum of disorders and point to a nosology, wherein OCD is seen as similar to other Anxiety Disorders.

A similar conclusion can be reached from a review of the literature on assessment instruments for a number of the OCSDs. There is little evidence to suggest a connection between Trichotillomania or Excoriation Disorder and OCD. Indeed, these body-focused disorders are reliability distinguished from OCD in their focus on urges to pull/pick, instead of obsessions. Hoarding Disorder also appears to be readily distinguished from OCD, as hoarding measures concentrate on compulsive behaviors and their functional consequences without reference to obsessions. Furthermore, scores from OCD and hoarding measures show responses to different types of treatment. Treatment results indicate that individuals with OCD may be distinguished from individuals with hoarding by ego dystonia and increased problem-solving abilities. This conclusion is supported by empirical research suggesting reduced insight and executive functioning abilities in hoarders (McMillan, Rees, & Pestell, 2013; Tolin & Villavicencio, 2011; Torres et al., 2012). Thus, Excoriation Disorder, Trichotillomania, and Hoarding Disorder all appear to be best classified separately from OCD.

BDD, on the other hand, exhibited several areas of commonality with OCD in the literature on assessment instruments. Similar to OCD measures, BDD indices conceptualized BDD as compulsive behaviors tied to specific obsessive thoughts about a physical deformity. Furthermore, their scores showed a treatment response to exposure therapy and SSRIs, the leading behavioral and pharmacological treatments for OCD. Consequently, evidence from assessment measures suggests that BDD and OCD may be fruitfully classified together. However, research has yet to identify a clear shared etiology for these disorders (Frías, Palma, Farriols, & González, 2015), suggesting that further biologically informed developmental research is needed to inform classification of BDD and OCD.

In summary, OCD appears to share more similarities with Anxiety Disorders than OCSDs. Existing evidence from OCSD assessment instruments suggests that OCD is best classified separately from Excoriation Disorder, Trichotillomania, and Hoarding Disorder. OCD may fruitfully be classified alongside BDD, but more physiological and longitudinal research is necessary to support such a classification.

References

Abramowitz, J. S., Deacon, B. J., Olatunji, B. O., Wheaton, M. G., Berman, N. C., Losardo, D., . . . Adams, T. (2010). Assessment of obsessive-compulsive symptom dimensions: Development and evaluation of the Dimensional Obsessive-Compulsive Scale. *Psychological Assessment, 22*(1), 180.

Abramowitz, J. S., Storch, E. A., McKay, D., Taylor, S., & Asmundson, G. J. G. (2009). The obsessive-compulsive spectrum: A critical review. In D. McKay, J. S. Abramowitz, S. Taylor, & G. J. G. Asmundson (eds.), *Current Perspectives on the Anxiety Disorders: Implications for DSM-V and Beyond.* (pp. 329–352). New York, NY: Springer Publishing.

Abramowitz, J. S., Taylor, S., & McKay, D. (2009). Obsessive-compulsive disorder. *Lancet, 374*(9688), 491–499.

Abramowitz, J. S., Whiteside, S. P., & Deacon, B. J. (2006). The effectiveness of treatment for pediatric obsessive-compulsive disorder: A meta-analysis. *Behavior Therapy, 36*(1), 55–63.

Allen, A., Hadley, S. J., Kaplan, A., Simeon, D., Friedberg, J., Priday, L., . . . Hollander, E. (2008). An open-label trial of venlafaxine in body dysmorphic disorder. *CNS Spectrums, 13*(2), 138–144.

American Psychiatric Association (APA). (2000). *Diagnostic and Statistical Manual of Mental Disorders DSM-IV-TR Fourth Edition* (text revision). Washington, DC: American Psychiatric Association.

American Psychiatric Association (APA). (2013). *Diagnostic and Statistical Manual of Mental Disorders.* Washington, DC: American Psychiatric Association.

Bartz, J. A. & Hollander, E. (2006). Is obsessive-compulsive disorder an anxiety disorder? *Progress in Neuro-Psychopharmacology & Biological Psychiatry, 30*(3), 338–352. doi: 10.1016/j.pnpbp.2005.11.003

Bienvenu, O. J., Samuels, J. F., Riddle, M. A., Hoehn-Saric, R., Liang, K.-Y., Cullen, B. A., . . . Nestadt, G. (2000). The relationship of obsessive-compulsive disorder to possible spectrum disorders: Results from a family study. *Biological Psychiatry, 48*(4), 287–293.

Bloch, M. H., Landeros-Weisenberger, A., Dombrowski, P., Kelmendi, B., Wegner, R., Nudel, J., . . . Coric, V. (2007). Systematic review: Pharmacological and behavioral treatment for trichotillomania. *Biological Psychiatry, 62*(8), 839–846. doi: 10.1016/j.biopsych.2007.05.019

Bloch, M. H., Landeros-Weisenberger, A., Rosario, M. C., Pittenger, C., & Leckman, J. F. (2008). Meta-analysis of the symptom structure of obsessive-compulsive disorder. *American Journal of Psychiatry, 165*(12), 1532–1542.

Brohede, S., Wingren, G., Wijma, B., & Wijma, K. (2013). Validation of the Body Dysmorphic Disorder Questionnaire in a community sample of Swedish women. *Psychiatry Research, 210*(2), 647–652. doi: 10.1016/j.psychres.2013.07.019

Burns, G. (1995). *Padua Inventory-Washington State University Revision.* Pullman, WA: Author.

Cicek, E., Cicek, I. E., Kayhan, F., Uguz, F., & Kaya, N. (2013). Quality of life, family burden and associated factors in relatives with obsessive-compulsive disorder. *General Hospital Psychiatry, 35*(3), 253–258.

Clark, D. A., Antony, M. M., Beck, A. T., Swinson, R. P., & Steer, R. A. (2005). Screening for obsessive and compulsive symptoms: validation of the Clark-Beck Obsessive-Compulsive Inventory. *Psychological Assessment, 17*(2), 132.

Clark, D. A. & O'Connor, K. (2005). Thinking is believing: Ego-dystonic intrusive thoughts in obsessive-compulsive disorder. In D. A. Clark (ed.), *Intrusive Thoughts in Clinical Disorders: Theory, Research, and Treatment.* (pp. 145–174). New York, NY: Guilford Press.

Duke, D. C., Keeley, M. L., Geffken, G. R., & Storch, E. A. (2010). Trichotillomania: A current review. *Clinical Psychology Review, 30*(2), 181–193. doi: 10.1016/j.cpr.2009.10.008

Fineberg, N. A., Menchon, J. M., Zohar, J., & Veltman, D. J. (2016). Compulsivity: A new trans-diagnostic research domain for the Roadmap for Mental Health Research in Europe (ROAMER) and Research Domain Criteria (RDoC) initiatives. *European Neuropsychopharmacology, 26*(5), 797–799. doi: 10.1016/j.euroneuro.2016.04.001

Flessner, C. A., Woods, D. W., Franklin, M. E., Cashin, S. E., & Keuthen, N. J. (2008). The Milwaukee Inventory for Subtypes of Trichotillomania-Adult Version (MIST-A): Development of an instrument for the assessment of "focused" and "automatic" hair pulling. *Journal of Psychopathology and Behavioral Assessment, 30*(1), 20–30. doi: 10.1007/s10862-007-9073-x

Foa, E. B., Huppert, J. D., Leiberg, S., Langner, R., Kichic, R., Hajcak, G., & Salkovskis, P. M. (2002). The Obsessive-Compulsive Inventory: Development and validation of a short version. *Psychological Assessment, 14*(4), 485.

Foa, E. B. & Kozak, M. J. (1995). *DSM-IV* field trial: Obsessive-compulsive disorder. *American Journal of Psychiatry, 152*(1), 90–96.

Frías, Á., Palma, C., Farriols, N., & González, L. (2015). Comorbidity between obsessive-compulsive disorder and body dysmorphic disorder: Prevalence, explanatory theories, and clinical characterization. *Neuropsychiatric Disease and Treatment,* 11.

Frost, R. O. & Hristova, V. (2011). Assessment of hoarding. *Journal of Clinical Psychology, 67*(5), 456–466. doi: 10.1002/jclp.20790

Frost, R. O., Steketee, G., & Grisham, J. (2004). Measurement of compulsive hoarding: Saving inventory-revised. *Behaviour Research and Therapy, 42*(10), 1163–1182. doi: 10.1016/j.brat.2003.07.006

Frost, R. O., Tolin, D. F., & Maltby, N. (2010). Insight-related challenges in the treatment of hoarding. *Cognitive and Behavioral Practice, 17*(4), 404–413. doi: 10.1016/j.cbpra.2009.07.004

Gillan, C. M., Fineberg, N. A., & Robbins, T. W. (2017). A trans-diagnostic perspective on obsessive-compulsive disorder. *Psychological Medicine.* doi: 10.1017/S0033291716002786

Gönner, S., Ecker, W., & Leonhart, R. (2010). The Padua Inventory: Do revisions need revision? *Assessment, 17*(1), 89–106.

Gönner, S., Ecker, W., Leonhart, R., & Limbacher, K. (2010). Multidimensional assessment of OCD: Integration and revision of the Vancouver obsessional-compulsive inventory and the symmetry ordering and arranging questionnaire. *Journal of Clinical Psychology, 66*(7), 739–757.

Goodman, W. K., Price, L. H., Rasmussen, S. A., Mazure, C., Fleischmann, R. L., Hill, C. L., ... Charney, D. S. (1989). The Yale-Brown obsessive compulsive scale: I. Development, use, and reliability. *Archives of General Psychiatry, 46*(11), 1006–1011.

Grant, J. E. & Odlaug, B. L. (2015). Excoriation (skin picking) disorder. In K. A. Phillips & D. J. Stein (eds.), *Handbook on Obsessive-Compulsive and Related Disorders.* (pp. 161–180). Arlington, VA: American Psychiatric Publishing, Inc.

Grant, J. E., Odlaug, B. L., Chamberlain, S. R., & Kim, S. W. (2010). A double-blind, placebo-controlled trial of lamotrigine for pathological skin picking: Treatment efficacy and neurocognitive predictors of response. *Journal of Clinical Psychopharmacology, 30*(4), 396–403. doi: 10.1097/JCP.0b013e3181e617a1

Grant, J. E., Odlaugh, B. L., & Kim, S. W. (2007). Lamotrigine treatment of pathological skin-picking: An open-label study. *Journal of Clinical Psychiatry, 62,* 349–356.

Greenberg, J. L., Mothi, S. S., & Wilhelm, S. (2016). Cognitive-behavioral therapy for adolescent body dysmorphic disorder: A pilot study. *Behavior Therapy, 47*(2), 213–224. doi: 10.1016/j.beth.2015.10.009

Hankin, C. S., Koran, L., Sheehan, D., Hollander, E., Culpepper, L., Black, D. W., ... Wang, Z. (2011). Patients with obsession-compulsive disorder vs depression on comparable health care costs: A retrospective claims analysis of Florida Medicaid enrollees. *Annals of Clinical Psychiatry, 23*(4), 285–596.

Hollander, E., Braun, A., & Simeon, D. (2008). Should OCD leave the anxiety disorders in *DSM-V?* The case for obsessive compulsive-related disorders. *Depression and Anxiety, 25*(4), 317–329. doi: 10.1002/da.20500

Hollander, E., Doernberg, E., Shavitt, R., Waterman, R. J., Soreni, N., Veltman, D. J., ... Fineberg, N. A. (2016). The cost and impact of compulsivity: A research perspective. *European Neuropsychopharmacology, 26*(5), 800–809.

Hollander, E. & Zohar, J. (2004). Introduction – Beyond refractory obsessions and anxiety states: Toward remission. *Journal of Clinical Psychiatry, 65,* 3–5.

Hyman, S. E. (2007). Can neuroscience be integrated into the *DSM-V? Nature Reviews Neuroscience, 8*(9), 725–732. doi: 10.1038/nrn2218

Jorgensen, L., Castle, D., Roberts, C., & Groth-Marnat, G. (2001). A clinical validation of the Dysmorphic Concern Questionnaire. *Australian and New Zealand Journal of Psychiatry, 35*(1), 124–128. doi: 10.1046/j.1440–1614.2001.00860.x

Kendler, K. S. (2017). Introduction to "Obsessive-compulsive and related disorders in *DSM-5, ICD-11,* and RDoC: Conceptual questions and practical solutions." In K. S. Kendler & J. Parnas (eds.), *Philosophical Issues in Psychiatry IV: Classification of Psychiatric Illness* (pp. 53–54). New York, NY: Oxford University Press.

Keuthen, N. J., Deckersbach, T., Wilhelm, S., Engelhard, I., Forker, A., O'Sullivan, R. L., ... Baer, L. (2001). The Skin Picking Impact Scale (SPIS): Scale development and psychometric analyses. *Psychosomatics: Journal of Consultation and Liaison Psychiatry, 42*(5), 397–403. doi: 10.1176/appi.psy.42.5.397

Keuthen, N. J., Jameson, M., Loh, R., Deckersbach, T., Wilhelm, S., & Dougherty, D. D. (2007). Open-label escitalopram treatment for pathological skin picking. *International Clinical Psychopharmacology*, *22*(5), 268–274. doi: 10.1097/YIC.0b013e32809913b6

Keuthen, N. J., O'Sullivan, R. L., Ricciardi, J. N., Shera, D., Savage, C. R., Borgmann, A. S., ... Baer, L. (1995). The Massachusetts General Hospital (MGH) Hairpulling Scale: I. Development and factor analyses. *Psychotherapy and Psychosomatics*, *64*(3–4), 141–145. doi: 10.1159/000289003

Keuthen, N. J., Siev, J., & Reese, H. (2012). Assessment of trichotillomania, pathological skin picking, and stereotypic movement disorder. In J. E. Grant, D. J. Stein, D. W. Woods, & N. J. Keuthen (eds.), *Trichotillomania, Skin Picking, and Other Body-Focused Repetitive Behaviors* (pp. 129–150). Arlington, VA: American Psychiatric Publishing, Inc.

Keuthen, N. J., Tung, E. S., Woods, D. W., Franklin, M. E., Altenburger, E. M., Pauls, D. L., & Flessner, C. A. (2015). Replication study of the Milwaukee Inventory for Subtypes of Trichotillomania–Adult Version in a clinically characterized sample. *Behavior Modification*, *39*(4), 580–599. doi: 10.1177/0145445515580533

Keuthen, N. J., Wilhelm, S., Deckersbach, T., Engelhard, I. M., Forker, A. E., Baer, L., & Jenike, M. A. (2001). The Skin Picking Scale: Scale construction and psychometric analyses. *Journal of Psychosomatic Research*, *50*(6), 337–341. doi: 10.1016/S0022-3999(01)00215-X

Koen, N. & Stein, D. J. (2011). Pharmacotherapy of anxiety disorders: A critical review. *Dialogues in Clinical Neuroscience*, *13*(4), 423–437.

LaSalle, V. H., Cromer, K. R., Nelson, K. N., Kazuba, D., Justement, L., & Murphy, D. L. (2004). Diagnostic interview assessed neuropsychiatric disorder comorbidity in 334 individuals with obsessive-compulsive disorder. *Depression and Anxiety*, *19*(3), 163–173. doi: 10.1002/da.20009

Mancuso, S. G., Knoesen, N. P., & Castle, D. J. (2010). The Dysmorphic Concern Questionnaire: A screening measure for body dysmorphic disorder. *Australian and New Zealand Journal of Psychiatry*, *44*(6), 535–542.

McGuire, J. F., Piacentini, J., Lewin, A. B., Brennan, E. A., Murphy, T. K., & Storch, E. A. (2015). A meta-analysis of cognitive behavior therapy and medication for child obsessive–compulsive disorder: Moderators of treatment efficacy, response, and remission. *Depression and Anxiety*, *32*(8), 580–593. doi: 10.1002/da.22389

McGuire, J. F., Ung, D., Selles, R. R., Rahman, O., Lewin, A. B., Murphy, T. K., & Storch, E. A. (2014). Treating trichotillomania: A meta-analysis of treatment effects and moderators for behavior therapy and serotonin reuptake inhibitors. *Journal of Psychiatric Research*, *58*, 76–83.

McMillan, S. G., Rees, C. S., & Pestell, C. (2013). An investigation of executive functioning, attention and working memory in compulsive hoarding. *Behavioural and Cognitive Psychotherapy*, *41*(5), 610–625. doi: 10.1017/S1352465812000835

Morris, S. E. & Cuthbert, B. N. (2012). Research Domain Criteria: Cognitive systems, neural circuits, and dimensions of behavior. *Dialogues in Clinical Neuroscience*, *14*(1), 29–37.

Muroff, J., Steketee, G., Rasmussen, J., Gibson, A., Bratiotis, C., & Sorrentino, C. (2009). Group cognitive and behavioral treatment for compulsive hoarding: A preliminary trial. *Depression and Anxiety*, *26*(7), 634–640. doi: 10.1002/da.20591

Nestadt, G., Samuels, J., Riddle, M. A., Liang, K. Y., Bienvenu, O. J., Hoehn-Saric, R., ...
    Cullen, B. (2001). The relationship between obsessive-compulsive disorder and
    anxiety and affective disorders: Results from the Johns Hopkins OCD Family Study.
    Psychological Medicine, 31(3), 481–487. doi: 10.1017/S0033291701003579

Oosthuizen, P., Lambert, T., & Castle, D. J. (1998). Dysmorphic concern: Prevalence and
    associations with clinical variables. *Australian and New Zealand Journal of
    Psychiatry, 32*(1), 129–132. doi: 10.3109/00048679809062719

Öst, L.-G., Havnen, A., Hansen, B., & Kvale, G. (2015). Cognitive behavioral treatments of
    obsessive-compulsive disorder. A systematic review and meta-analysis of studies
    published 1993–2014. *Clinical Psychology Review, 40*, 156–169. doi: 10.1016/j
    .cpr.2015.06.003

Overduin, M. K. & Furnham, A. (2012). Assessing obsessive-compulsive disorder (OCD):
    A review of self-report measures. *Journal of Obsessive-Compulsive and Related
    Disorders, 1*(4), 312–324.

Phillips, K. A., Hart, A. S., & Menard, W. (2014). Psychometric evaluation of the
    Yale–Brown Obsessive-Compulsive Scale Modified for Body Dysmorphic
    Disorder (BDD-YBOCS). *Journal of Obsessive-Compulsive and Related
    Disorders, 3*(3), 205–208. doi: 10.1016/j.jocrd.2014.04.004

Phillips, K. A., Hollander, E., Rasmussen, S. A., & Aronowitz, B. R. (1997). A severity
    rating scale for body dysmorphic disorder: Development, reliability, and validity
    of a modified version of the Yale-Brown Obsessive Compulsive Scale.
    Psychopharmacology Bulletin, 33(1), 17–22.

Phillips, K. A., & Rasmussen, S. A. (2004). Change in psychosocial functioning and quality
    of life of patients with body dysmorphic disorder treated with fluoxetine:
    A placebo-controlled study. *Psychosomatics: Journal of Consultation and
    Liaison Psychiatry, 45*(5), 438–444. doi: 10.1176/appi.psy.45.5.438

Rabiee, M., Khorramdel, K., Kalantari, M., & Molavi, H. (2010). Factor structure, validity
    and reliability of the Modified Yale-Brown Obsessive Compulsive Scale for body
    dysmorphic disorder in students. *Iranian Journal of Psychiatry and Clinical
    Psychology, 15*(4), 343–350.

Rosen, J. C. & Reiter, J. (1996). Development of the Body Dysmorphic Disorder
    Examination. *Behaviour Research and Therapy, 34*(9), 755–766. doi: 10.1016/
    0005-7967(96)00024-1

Rothbaum, B. O. & Ninan, P. T. (1994). The assessment of trichotillomania. *Behaviour
    Research and Therapy, 32*(6), 651–662. doi: 10.1016/0005-7967(94)90022-1

Ruscio, A., Stein, D., Chiu, W., & Kessler, R. (2010). The epidemiology of
    obsessive-compulsive disorder in the National Comorbidity Survey Replication.
    Molecular Psychiatry, 15(1), 53–63.

Saxena, S., Ayers, C. R., Dozier, M. E., & Maidment, K. M. (2015). The UCLA Hoarding
    Severity Scale: Development and validation. *Journal of Affective Disorders, 175*,
    488–493. doi: 10.1016/j.jad.2015.01.030

Saxena, S., Brody, A. L., Maidment, K. M., & Baxter, L. R., Jr. (2007). Paroxetine treatment
    of compulsive hoarding. *Journal of Psychiatric Research, 41*(6), 481–487. doi:
    10.1016/j.jpsychires.2006.05.001

Schneider, A. F., Storch, E. A., Geffken, G. R., Lack, C. W., & Shytle, R. D. (2008).
    Psychometric properties of the Hoarding Assessment Scale in college students.
    Illness, Crisis, & Loss, 16(3), 227–236. doi: 10.2190/IL.16.3.c

Shafran, R. (2005). Cognitive-behavioral models of OCD. In J. S. Abramowitz & A. C. Houts (eds.), *Concepts and Controversies in Obsessive-Compulsive Disorder* (pp. 229–252). New York, NY: Springer Science + Business Media.

Siev, J., Reese, H. E., Timpano, K., & Wilhelm, S. (2012). Assessment and treatment of pathological skin picking. In J. E. Grant & M. N. Potenza (eds.), *The Oxford Handbook of Impulse Control Disorders* (pp. 360–374). New York, NY: Oxford University Press.

Simeon, D., Stein, D. J., Gross, S., Islam, N., & Hollander, E. (1997). A double-blind trial of fluoxetine in pathologic skin picking. *Journal of Clinical Psychiatry*, *58*(8), 341–347.

Skapinakis, P., Caldwell, D. M., Hollingworth, W., Bryden, P., Fineberg, N. A., Salkovskis, P., . . . Lewis, G. (2016). Pharmacological and psychotherapeutic interventions for management of obsessive-compulsive disorder in adults: A systematic review and network meta-analysis. *Lancet Psychiatry*, *3*(8), 730–739. doi: 10.1016/s2215-0366(16)30069–4

Snorrason, I., Houghton, D. C., & Woods, D. W. (2015). Trichotillomania (hair-pulling disorder). In K. A. Phillips & D. J. Stein (eds.), *Handbook on Obsessive-Compulsive and Related Disorders* (pp. 135–160). Arlington, VA: American Psychiatric Publishing, Inc.

Snorrason, I., Ólafsson, R. P., Flessner, C. A., Keuthen, N. J., Franklin, M. E., & Woods, D. W. (2012). The Skin Picking Scale-Revised: Factor structure and psychometric properties. *Journal of Obsessive-Compulsive and Related Disorders*, *1*(2), 133–137. doi: 10.1016/j.jocrd.2012.03.001

Stanley, M. A., Prather, R. C., Wagner, A. L., Davis, M. L., & Swann, A. C. (1993). Can the Yale-Brown Obsessive Compulsive Scale be used to assess trichotillomania? A preliminary report. *Behaviour Research and Therapy*, *31*(2), 171–177.

Starcevic, V. & Janca, A. (2011). Obsessive-compulsive spectrum disorders: Still in search of the concept-affirming boundaries. *Current Opinion in Psychiatry*, *24*(1), 55–60. doi: 10.1097/YCO.0b013e32833f3b58

Stein, D. J. & Lochner, C. (2006). Obsessive-Compulsive Spectrum Disorders: A multidimensional approach. *Psychiatric Clinics of North America*, *29*(2), 343–351. doi: 10.1016/j.psc.2006.02.015

Steketee, G., Frost, R. O., Tolin, D. F., Rasmussen, J., & Brown, T. A. (2010). Waitlist-controlled trial of cognitive behavior therapy for hoarding disorder. *Depression and Anxiety*, *27*(5), 476–484.

Storch, E. A., Abramowitz, J., & Goodman, W. K. (2008). Where does obsessive-compulsive disorder belong in *DSM-V*? *Depression and Anxiety*, *25*(4), 336–347. doi: 10.1002/da.20488

Storch, E. A., Bagner, D., Merlo, L. J., Shapira, N. A., Geffken, G. R., Murphy, T. K., & Goodman, W. K. (2007). Florida obsessive-compulsive inventory: Development, reliability, and validity. *Journal of Clinical Psychology*, *63*(9), 851–859.

Storch, E. A., Larson, M. J., Price, L. H., Rasmussen, S. A., Murphy, T. K., & Goodman, W. K. (2010). Psychometric analysis of the Yale–Brown Obsessive-Compulsive Scale Second Edition Symptom Checklist. *Journal of Anxiety Disorders*, *24*(6), 650–656. doi: 10.1016/j.janxdis.2010.04.010

Storch, E. A., Lewin, A. B., Farrell, L., Aldea, M. A., Reid, J., Geffken, G. R., & Murphy, T. K. (2010). Does cognitive-behavioral therapy response among adults with obsessive-compulsive disorder differ as a function of certain comorbidities? *Journal of Anxiety Disorders, 24*(6), 547–552. doi: 10.1016/j.janxdis.2010.03.013

Storch, E. A., Rasmussen, S. A., Price, L. H., Larson, M. J., Murphy, T. K., & Goodman, W. K. (2010). Development and psychometric evaluation of the Yale–Brown Obsessive-Compulsive Scale – Second Edition. *Psychological Assessment, 22*(2), 223.

Subramaniam, M., Soh, P., Vaingankar, J. A., Picco, L., & Chong, S. A. (2013). Quality of life in obsessive-compulsive disorder: Impact of the disorder and of treatment. *CNS Drugs, 27*(5), 367–383.

Swedo, S. E., Leonard, H. L., Rapoport, J. L., Lenane, M. C., Goldberger, E. L., & Cheslow, D. L. (1989). A double-blind comparison of clomipramine and desipramine in the treatment of trichotillomania (hair pulling). *New England Journal of Medicine, 321*(8), 497–501.

Thordarson, D. S., Radomsky, A. S., Rachman, S., Shafran, R., Sawchuk, C. N., & Hakstian, A. R. (2004). The Vancouver Obsessional Compulsive Inventory (VOCI). *Behaviour Research and Therapy, 42*(11), 1289–1314. doi: 10.1016/j.brat.2003.08.007

Tolin, D. F., Frost, R. O., & Steketee, G. (2010). A brief interview for assessing compulsive hoarding: The Hoarding Rating Scale-Interview. *Psychiatry Research, 178*(1), 147–152. doi: 10.1016/j.psychres.2009.05.001

Tolin, D. F. & Villavicencio, A. (2011). Inattention, but not OCD, predicts the core features of Hoarding Disorder. *Behaviour Research and Therapy, 49*(2), 120–125. doi: 10.1016/j.brat.2010.12.002

Torres, A. R., Fontenelle, L. F., Ferrão, Y. A., do Rosário,M. C., Torresan,R. C., Miguel, E. C., & Shavitt, R. G. (2012). Clinical features of obsessive-compulsive disorder with hoarding symptoms: A multicenter study. *Journal of Psychiatric Research, 46*(6), 724–732. doi: 10.1016/j.jpsychires.2012.03.005

Van Oppen, P., Hoekstra, R. J., & Emmelkamp, P. M. (1995). The structure of obsessive-compulsive symptoms. *Behaviour Research and Therapy, 33*(1), 15–23.

van Rood, Y. R. & Bouman, T. K. (2007). De Nederlandstalige versie van de "Yale-Brown Obsessive Compulsive Scale for Body Dysmorphic Disorder" (BDD-YBOCS NL). = The Dutch version of the "Yale-Brown Obsessive Compulsive Scale for Body Dysmorphic Disorder" (BDD-YBOCS ML). *Gedragstherapie, 40*(3), 217–227.

Vikas, A., Avasthi, A., & Sharan, P. (2011). Psychosocial impact of obsessive-compulsive disorder on patients and their caregivers: A comparative study with depressive disorder. *International Journal of Social Psychiatry, 57*(1), 45–56. doi: 10.1177/0020764010347333

Walther, M. R., Flessner, C. A., Conelea, C. A., & Woods, D. W. (2009). The Milwaukee Inventory for the Dimensions of Adult Skin Picking (MIDAS): Initial development and psychometric properties. *Journal of Behavior Therapy and Experimental Psychiatry, 40*(1), 127–135. doi: 10.1016/j.jbtep.2008.07.002

Watson, D. & Wu, K. D. (2005). Development and validation of the Schedule of Compulsions, Obsessions, and Pathological Impulses (SCOPI). *Assessment, 12*(1), 50–65.

Wilhelm, S., Greenberg, J. L., Rosenfield, E., Kasarskis, I., & Blashill, A. J. (2016). The Body Dysmorphic Disorder Symptom Scale: Development and preliminary validation of a self-report scale of symptom specific dysfunction. *Body Image*, *17*, 82–87. doi: 10.1016/j.bodyim.2016.02.006

Winchel, R. M., Jones, J. S., Molcho, A., Parsons, B., Stanley, B., & Stanley, M. (1992). The Psychiatric Institute Trichotillomania Scale (PITS). *Psychopharmacology Bulletin*, *28*(4), 463–476.

Zitterl, W., Demal, U., Aigner, M., Lenz, G., Urban, C., Zapotoczky, H.-G., & Zitterl-Eglseer, K. (2000). Naturalistic course of obsessive compulsive disorder and comorbid depression: Longitudinal results of a prospective follow-up study of 74 actively treated patients. *Psychopathology*, *33*(2), 75–80. doi: 10.1159/000029124

13 Trauma- and Stressor-Related Disorders

Daniel J. Lee, Sarah E. Kleiman,
and Frank W. Weathers

Trauma- and stressor-related disorders (TSRDs) are highly prevalent, often debilitating mental disorders that develop following exposure to an identifiable stressor. TSRDs are characterized by complex clinical presentations and thus present considerable challenges for assessment. This chapter provides an overview of the most widely used evidence-based assessment measures for these disorders. The aim of this chapter is to provide readers with an introduction to valid instruments that can be used to facilitate screening, diagnosis, case formulation, treatment planning, and evaluation of treatment progress with TSRDs.

The TSRD category represents a substantial reorganization of trauma- and stressor-related psychopathology. In the fourth edition of the *Diagnostic and Statistical Manual of Mental Disorders* (*DSM-IV*) (American Psychiatric Association [APA], 2000), posttraumatic stress disorder (PTSD) and acute stress disorder (ASD) were categorized as anxiety disorders; adjustment disorder was its own category; reactive attachment disorder (RAD) was categorized under disorders usually first diagnosed in infancy, childhood, or adolescence; and disinhibited social engagement disorder was categorized as a subtype of RAD. The fifth edition of the *DSM* (*DSM-5*) (APA, 2013) grouped these disorders together under the newly created TSRD chapter. The rationale was that all of these disorders are conceptualized as syndromes that develop in response to an explicit stressor, and all include exposure to a traumatic event or other significant stressor as a diagnostic criterion.

Posttraumatic Stress Disorder

PTSD is a chronic, complex disorder that can develop following exposure to traumatic events such as combat, interpersonal violence, life-threatening accidents, and natural or human-made disasters. Affecting more than 8% of the population (Kilpatrick et al., 2013) and costing upward of $3 billion annually (Tanielian, 2009), PTSD has a substantial public health impact. This portion of the chapter briefly reviews changes in PTSD diagnostic criteria from *DSM-IV* to *DSM-5* and then describes the wide range of measures available to assess PTSD.

Changes to the PTSD Criteria for DSM-5

As described in a series of papers by Friedman and colleagues (Friedman, 2013a, 2013b; Friedman, Resick, Bryant, & Brewin, 2011; Friedman et al., 2011), the revision of the PTSD criteria for *DSM-5* was undertaken in 2008 by the Trauma/Stress-Related and Dissociative Disorders Sub-Work Group (SWG), one of three sub-work groups of the *DSM-5* Anxiety and Dissociative Disorders Work Group. The revision process was based on extensive literature reviews, consultation with a wide range of trauma experts, and public review and commentary. In addition, all proposed revisions were reviewed by several APA committees. The SWG adopted what it described as a conservative approach to the revision process, meaning that any changes to the criteria had to be supported by substantial scientific evidence and the weight of expert opinion. The main aims of the revision process were to maintain continuity with previous PTSD criteria while incorporating accumulated empirical findings and addressing various criticisms of PTSD. Ultimately, few aspects of the *DSM-IV* PTSD criteria were removed; most revisions involved adding new criteria or modifying existing ones.

Major changes for the final *DSM-5* PTSD criteria included (a) moving PTSD from the anxiety disorders to the new TSRD chapter, as noted earlier; (b) eliminating Criterion A2, which required that the individual experience intense fear, helplessness, or horror at the time of the trauma; (c) expanding from three symptom clusters to four by splitting the avoidance and numbing cluster into separate clusters of avoidance and negative alterations in cognition and mood (NACM); (d) adding three new symptoms and substantially revising several others; (e) adding a dissociative subtype, in part to recognize and integrate the clinical picture of complex PTSD; and (f) creating separate criteria for preschool children.

Other important changes include narrowing and clarifying the types of indirect exposure to a stressor that would qualify as a traumatic event under Criterion A; clarifying that the traumatic "event" might not be a single, relatively circumscribed event but instead might consist of multiple similar events; and highlighting the functional link between symptoms and the traumatic event with the phrase "beginning or worsening after the traumatic event(s)," which emphasizes that the trauma may either trigger new symptoms or exacerbate existing ones.

Classification of PTSD

The decision to move PTSD out of the anxiety disorders and into the new TSRD chapter was made primarily to acknowledge substantial heterogeneity in the clinical presentations of trauma survivors. Since it was introduced in *DSM-III* (APA, 1980), PTSD was categorized as an anxiety disorder based on its prominent symptoms of conditioned fear and avoidance. However, it has long been recognized that the clinical picture following trauma exposure often involves prominent dysphoria, anger, guilt, shame, and dissociation (Davidson & Foa, 1991; Lanius, Brand, Vermetten, Frewen, & Spiegel, 2012; Resick & Miller, 2009).

Criterion A

Changes to Criterion A were made partly in response to the criticism that the definition of a traumatic event had become too broad, allowing too many stressors to satisfy Criterion A, and thus allowing too many individuals to qualify for a PTSD diagnosis (see Weathers & Keane, 2007, for a full discussion of the evolution of Criterion A). This issue, labeled "conceptual bracket creep" by McNally (2003) and "criterion creep" by Rosen (2004), is significant because an overly broad definition of trauma could increase heterogeneity of PTSD samples, lead to misuse of PTSD in forensic applications, and pathologize normal stress reactions (McNally, 2004, 2009). McNally (2009) and Spitzer et al. (2007) recommended eliminating indirect exposure and only allowing direct experiencing or witnessing to count for Criterion A. Further, McNally (2009) also recommended eliminating A2, arguing that "[i]n the language of behaviorism it confounds the stimulus with the response. In the language of medicine, it confounds the host with the pathogen" (p. 598).

Several aspects of *DSM-IV* Criterion A did, in fact, represent a broadening of the original *DSM-III* definition of trauma, including (a) use of vague phrases such as "confronted with" and "threat to physical integrity"; (b) allowing indirect exposure to qualify, i.e., learning about an event rather than directly experiencing or witnessing it; and (c) addition of new examples of qualifying events such as "being diagnosed with a life-threatening illness," "developmentally inappropriate sexual experiences without threatened or actual violence or injury," "learning about the sudden, unexpected death of a family member or close friend," and "learning that one's child has a life-threatening disease." To address the concern about an overly broad definition of trauma, the SWG clarified and narrowed several aspects of Criterion A. First, "confronted with" was replaced with "learning that the traumatic event(s) occurred to a close family member or close friend," and "threat to physical integrity" was replaced with the more explicit "sexual violence." Second, although indirect exposure was retained, learning about the actual or threatened death of a loved one was substantially restricted by limiting it to only accidental or violent events, and thus not counting death due to natural causes.

Third, a new type of indirect exposure was identified, involving "repeated or extreme exposure to aversive details of the traumatic event(s)," which was intended to cover, for example, the experiences of first responders or emergency personnel. Although this could be seen as potentially broadening Criterion A, it actually involves much more direct exposure than just learning about the event, and arguably can be considered a form of witnessing. Further, this type of exposure was restricted by the explicit requirement that it not be through visual media unless it is work-related. Last, a restriction was added that life-threatening illnesses or medical conditions qualify as Criterion A events only if they are sudden and catastrophic.

Symptom Criteria

As noted earlier, the most significant changes to the PTSD symptom criteria were splitting the *DSM-IV* avoidance and numbing symptom cluster into avoidance (Criterion C) and NACM (Criterion D); adding three new items, including blame of self or others and negative emotional state to NACM, and reckless or self-destructive behavior to the hyperarousal cluster (Criterion E); and revising a number of other symptoms. Splitting avoidance and numbing into separate clusters was based on consistent evidence from a large number of confirmatory factor analytic studies (for a review, see Elhai & Palmieri, 2011) and other construct validation research (e.g., Asmundson, Stapleton, & Taylor, 2004) indicating that avoidance and numbing are distinct constructs.

The reexperiencing symptoms (Criterion B), now referred to as *intrusion symptoms*, were only slightly revised from *DSM-IV.* All five symptoms (intrusive memories, nightmares, flashbacks, cued distress, and cued arousal) were retained. The most notable change was for B1, which was revised from "recurrent and intrusive distressing recollections of the event" to "recurrent, involuntary, and intrusive distressing memories of the traumatic event(s)," to make an important conceptual distinction between memories and ruminations. Other changes were minor. B2 now indicates that nightmares do not have to replay the event as long as they are thematically related to the event in content or affect. B3 emphasizes that flashbacks are dissociative reexperiencing episodes, and that dissociation occurs on a continuum. B4 was revised from "intense psychological distress" in response to trauma cues to "intense or prolonged psychological distress," and B5 was revised from "physiological reactivity" to "marked physiological reactions."

The two effortful avoidance symptoms, C1 and C2, now constitute their own symptom cluster, with C1 focused on avoidance of thoughts and feelings related to the trauma, and C2 focused on avoidance of external reminders of the trauma, such as people, places, or situations. Revisions were minor. One change addressed a problematic overlap between these two symptoms in *DSM-IV*, in which C1 specified avoidance of "thoughts, feelings, and conversations" and C2 specified avoidance of "activities, places, or people." This was fixed in *DSM-5* by including conversations and people in C2 with other external reminders. In addition, C1 and C2 now specify that avoidance centers on "distressing memories, thoughts, or feelings." This is consistent with the conceptual focus on memories in B1, and also emphasizes that these are effortful avoidance strategies intended to reduce distress.

The new NACM cluster (Criterion D) is the most extensively revised of the four *DSM-5* clusters. Only two symptoms were carried over unchanged from *DSM-IV*: D5 (diminished interest) and D6 (detachment or estrangement), although the only change to D1 (amnesia) was the addition of a specifier that the memory loss is due to dissociative amnesia and not head injury or substance use. Of the other four symptoms, two are new for *DSM-5* (D3 – distorted cognitions leading to blame of self or others, and D4 – negative emotional state); one was broadened considerably, to the point that it almost represents a new symptom (D2 – exaggerated negative beliefs about the self, others or the world, which is a greatly expanded version of *DSM-IV* foreshortened future); and one was significantly narrowed (D7 – inability to experience positive emotions, which is a curtailed version of restricted range of affect in *DSM-IV*).

The last core symptom cluster, alterations in arousal and reactivity (Criterion E), includes four symptoms that are little changed from *DSM-IV* (E3 – hypervigilance, E4 – exaggerated startle, E5 – problems with concentration, and E6 – sleep disturbance). It also includes one symptom revised for a different emphasis (E1 – irritable behavior and angry outbursts, which now focuses specifically on behavioral manifestations of irritability and anger through verbal or physical aggression), and one new symptom (E2 – reckless or self-destructive behavior).

Other Criteria and Specifiers

Of the remaining three criteria, two are unchanged, including Criterion F, which requires that symptoms have lasted at least one month, and Criterion G, which requires that symptoms result in clinically significant distress or functional impairment. The last criterion is the usual *DSM* requirement that the disorder is not due to substance use or other medical condition, which for some reason had not been included in previous versions of the PTSD criteria. Other changes include eliminating the acute vs. chronic specifier (i.e., duration of less than three months vs. three months or more), and recasting the delayed onset specifier (i.e., onset of symptoms is at least six months after the event) as delayed expression by adding the qualifier "although the onset and expression of symptoms may be immediate" to indicate that typically at least some of the symptoms are present soon after the event.

Also, a dissociative subtype was added, which requires the presence of persistent or recurrent depersonalization or derealization, not attributable to substance use or other medical condition. This was based on extensive evidence that individuals with prominent dissociation have more severe and chronic symptoms, emerge as a distinctive group in latent class and taxometric studies, have distinctive neurobiological response profiles, and respond differently to treatment (Friedman, 2013a; Lanius et al., 2012). Another reason for including the dissociative subtype was to improve coverage of the clinical presentation of complex PTSD within the PTSD criteria until sufficient research can determine whether complex PTSD should recognized as a distinct diagnostic entity with its own criteria (Friedman, 2013a).

Finally, *DSM-5* provides separate diagnostic criteria for children six years and younger, partly in an effort to recognize developmental variations in symptom expression and thereby potentially increase the surprisingly low prevalence of PTSD observed among preschool children assessed with *DSM-IV* criteria (Friedman, 2013a). These preschool criteria generally follow the primary criteria for adults, adolescents, and children over six, but include age-appropriate modifications to various criteria, such as the recognition of posttraumatic play as a variant of intrusive memories. In addition, avoidance and numbing are not separated into distinct clusters, and three of the seven symptoms from the NACM cluster (amnesia, exaggerated negative beliefs, and distorted cognitions leading to blame) were excluded because they require a high degree of introspection and do not have overt behavioral referents to facilitate their assessment.

PTSD Assessment Overview

In order to fully assess PTSD diagnostic criteria, several domains should be examined. These include identification of an index (i.e., worst or most impactful) traumatic event (Criterion A), severity of intrusion (Cluster/Criterion B), avoidance (Cluster/Criterion C), negative alterations in cognition and mood (Cluster/ Criterion D), and alterations in arousal and reactivity (Cluster/Criterion E) symptoms, symptom duration (Criterion F), associated distress and impairment in social and occupational functioning (Criterion G), and related dissociation symptoms. Measures reviewed in this chapter cover these domains to varying degrees. Readers are encouraged to consider these important differences relative to assessment needs.

Trauma Exposure

A number of clinician-administered and self-report measures have been developed to assess trauma history. These measures vary in their coverage of different categories of traumatic events and exposure thereto. Many of these measures can be useful in reviewing trauma exposure history as well as facilitating identification of an index trauma. For assessing PTSD diagnostic status, care should be taken to determine that the selected index event satisfies the *DSM-5* Criterion A definition of a traumatic event.

The Life Events Checklist for *DSM-5* (LEC-5) (Weathers et al., 2013b) is a brief self-report measure of exposure to potentially traumatic events. The LEC-5 is a *DSM-5* updated version of the original, *DSM-IV* correspondent LEC (Gray, Litz, Hsu, & Lombardo, 2004). Respondents indicate if they have experienced a range of traumatic events (e.g., natural disaster, physical assault, sexual assault, combat) and the degree to which they were exposed (Happened to me; Witnessed it; Learned about it; Part of my job; Not sure; Doesn't apply). Sixteen categories of events are assessed and an additional category is provided to capture any other potentially traumatic events that do not fall cleanly into the other categories. This measure is also available in an interview format: the LEC-5 Interview (LEC-5-I).

The Traumatic Life Events Questionnaire (TLEQ) (Kubany et al., 2000) is another commonly used self-report measure of exposure to potentially traumatic events. Respondents identify the number of times they were exposed to 22 categories of potentially traumatic events ranging from natural disasters and assault to combat and accidents on a seven-item scale ranging from *never* to *more than five times*. The TLEQ includes several features that may be of interest, including assessment of injury resulting from the event for some events, peri-traumatic emotional responding for some events, and questions related to relationship with the perpetrator (e.g., stranger, friend/acquaintance, relative, intimate partner). Additionally, this measure asks respondents to identify an index trauma. While this measure provides a wide-ranging assessment of trauma history, caution should be used in ensuring that the selected index event satisfies *DSM-5* Criterion A as traumatic as the TLEQ includes assessment of several experiences that may or may not meet this criterion (e.g., being physically punished while growing up, sexual harassment, being stalked). The TLEQ has demonstrated adequate test-retest reliability and criterion-related validity with an interview measure (Kubany et al., 2000).

The Stressful Life Events Screening Questionnaire (SLESQ) (Goodman, Corcoran, Turner, Yuan, & Green, 1998) is a 13-item self-report measure of life-time trauma exposure. Respondents indicate if they have ever been exposed to different potentially traumatic events (e.g., physical assault, life-threatening accident) on dichotomous ("yes" or "no") prompts. Sub-prompts provide additional information for events endorsed (e.g., types of injuries sustained during physical assault, relationship to the perpetrator of sexual assault). In addition to 11 specific categories of events, two general questions screen for other potentially traumatic events not captured by the other categories. The SLESQ has demonstrated adequate test-retest reliability and criterion-related validity with an interview measure (Goodman et al., 1998).

Clinician-Administered Measures

A number of clinician-administered measures are available for assessing PTSD. Two measures, the Clinician-Administered PTSD Scale for *DSM-5* (CAPS-5) (Weathers et al., 2013a) and PTSD Symptom Scale Interview for *DSM-5* (PSSI-5) (Foa et al., 2016), focus specifically on assessment of PTSD. Other clinician-administered measures, such as the Structured Clinical Interview of *DSM-5* Diagnoses (SCID-5) (First, Williams, Karg, & Spitzer, 2015), MINI International Neuropsychiatric Interview (MINI) (Sheehan et al., 1997), and Anxiety Disorders Interview Schedule for *DSM-5* (ADIS-5) (Brown & Barlow, 2014) provide assessment of a wider range of disorders, but include assessment of PTSD. Important features and utility of each measure are described later in this chapter.

Generally regarded as the gold standard for PTSD assessment, the CAPS is a comprehensive measure of all PTSD criteria that has been extensively validated (Weathers, Keane, & Davidson, 2001) and is widely used in research, clinical, and forensic applications (Elhai, Gray, Kashdan, & Franklin, 2005). The CAPS-5 includes behaviorally anchored prompts and rating scales, separate assessment of symptom frequency and intensity, and assessment of trauma relatedness for symptoms not inherently linked to the trauma (e.g., estrangement, sleep disturbance) to provide a detailed assessment of each symptom. After combining information about symptom frequency and intensity, clinicians rate each of the 20 core *DSM-5* symptoms and the two dissociation symptoms on a five-point ordinal rating scale ranging from *0 = absent* to *4 = extreme/incapacitating*. These ratings can be used to provide both dichotomous (present/absent) and continuous ratings for individual symptoms and overall disorder severity. Additional ratings are made for distress, impairment, response validity, symptom severity, and improvement since a previous assessment. The CAPS-5 can be used to establish PTSD diagnostic status, obtain a continuous score reflecting PTSD symptom severity, and determine the dissociative subtype. In initial psychometric research, the CAPS-5 demonstrated strong criterion and construct validity as well as strong agreement with a self-report measure of PTSD (Weathers et al., 2018).

The PSSI-5 (Foa et al., 2016) is a semi-structured clinical interview focused exclusively on PTSD assessment. Like the CAPS-5, the PSSI-5 provides both categorical and continuous ratings for each item and for the overall disorder. Although the PSSI-5 requires less administration time than the CAPS-5, it provides a less detailed assessment of each symptom (e.g., no separate assessment of symptom frequency and intensity), and does not provide additional ratings for response validity, symptom severity, improvement since a previous assessment, or assessment of the dissociative subtype. In initial psychometric research, the PSSI-5 demonstrated strong test-retest reliability, internal consistency, and construct validity, including good agreement with the CAPS-5 (Foa et al., 2016).

The SCID-5 (First et al., 2015) is a widely used structured clinical interview that provides assessment of *DSM-5* disorders, including PTSD. The SCID-5 PTSD module provides a brief assessment of exposure to several categories of potentially traumatic events and identification of an index trauma. Interviewers rate each of the 20 *DSM-5* PTSD symptoms on a three-point rating scale: 1 = absent or false, 2 = subthreshold, 3 = threshold or true. Symptoms rated as threshold or true are counted toward diagnosis. Additionally, ratings are provided for related distress and impairment. Previous versions of the SCID have generally been regarded as gold-standard diagnostic instruments and have been widely used in major clinical trials. Further, past versions of the SCID have been used as the criterion measure for evaluating the validity of self-report measures (e.g., Foa, Cashman, Jaycox, & Perry, 1997).

The ADIS-5 (Brown & Barlow, 2014) is a semi-structured clinical interview of anxiety, mood, somatoform, and substance use disorders as well as a screener for other conditions (e.g., psychotic disorders). Interviewers provide a continuous rating for the severity of the index trauma on a nine-point scale ranging from *none* to *very severe* and degree of exposure is categorized into experienced, witnessed, or involving death, serious injury, and/or sexual violation. Once an index trauma is identified, each of the 20 *DSM-5* PTSD symptoms and two dissociation symptoms are rated using a nine-point clinical severity rating scale ranging from *never/no distress* to *constantly/extreme distress*. Likewise, associated distress and impairment are rated on a nine-point scale ranging from *none* to *very severe*. The *DSM-IV* version of the ADIS demonstrated strong test-retest reliability in large clinical samples (Di Nardo, Brown, Lawton, & Barlow, 1995; Di Nardo, Moras, Barlow, Rapee, & Brown, 1993).

The MINI (Sheehan et al., 1997) is a widely used semi-structured clinical interview that provides assessment of many *DSM-5* disorders, including PTSD. After a brief screen for trauma history and selection of an index trauma, clinicians provide a dichotomous rating (i.e., absent/threshold) for symptoms. The MINI was developed to provide a brief diagnostic interview that sacrifices detail for brevity. For example, unlike other measures described earlier, the MINI uses a single dichotomous rating for all five Criterion B symptoms. The MINI has demonstrated adequate test-retest reliability and criterion-related validity compared against the SCID (Sheehan et al., 1997).

DSM-5-Correspondent Self-Report Measures

The PTSD Checklist for *DSM-5* (PCL-5) (Weathers et al., 2013c) is a 20-item self-report measure of PTSD symptoms. Respondents rate the degree to which they have been bothered by each of the 20 *DSM-5* symptoms during the past month in reference to a specified event on a five-point scale ranging from *not at all* to *extremely*. Three versions of the PCL-5 provide different degrees of detailed assessment of trauma exposure; one without Criterion A assessment (trauma exposures should be established using another measure for this version), a second with a brief Criterion A assessment, and a third with the LEC-5 to provide detailed Criterion A assessment. Several different methods can be used to score the PCL-5. Continuous scores can be obtained for total symptom severity by summing all 20 items or for *DSM-5* symptom cluster severity by summing scores within each cluster (e.g., items 1–5 for Cluster B). Additionally, provisional PTSD diagnosis can be obtained by transforming each item rated as 2 = "Moderately" or higher as threshold and using the *DSM-5* diagnostic algorithm (at least 1 B item, 1 C item, 2 D items, and 2 E items). Alternatively, initial psychometric research suggests a PCL-5 total score cut-point score of 33 can be used to provide a provisional PTSD diagnosis (Bovin et al., 2015). The PCL-5 demonstrated strong psychometric properties among undergraduate (Blevins, Weathers, Davis, Witte, & Domino, 2015), veteran (Bovin et al., 2015), and active duty samples (Wortmann et al., 2016), including test-retest reliability and convergent and discriminant validity, structural validity, and diagnostic utility against the CAPS-5. In addition to the full measure, a brief, five-item screening version has been designed for use in primary care settings; the Primary Care PTSD Screen for *DSM-5* (PC-PTSD-5) (Prins et al., 2016).

The Posttraumatic Diagnostic Scale for *DSM-5* (PDS–5) (Foa et al., 2016) is a 24-item self-report measure of PTSD symptom severity. Two initial items are used to assess for trauma exposure; the first assesses lifetime exposure to several categories of traumatic events (e.g., military combat, child abuse), the second item is used to identify the index event. Respondents then rate how often and how bothersome each of the 20 *DSM-5* PTSD symptoms has been during the past month on a five-item scale ranging from *not at all* to *six or more times a week/severe*. Respondents then rate related distress and impairment on two subsequent items using the scale described earlier. Finally, two additional items are used to establish symptom onset and duration. Initial psychometric research suggests a cutoff score of 28 can be used to provide a provisional PTSD diagnosis (Foa et al., 2016). The PDS-5 demonstrated strong psychometric properties among separate urban community, veteran, and undergraduate samples (Foa et al., 2016), including good test-retest reliability, convergent and discriminant validity, and criterion-related validity compared to the PSSI-5.

Other PTSD Measures

In addition to the *DSM-5*-correspondent measures now available, several other PTSD measures are widely used. These include the Detailed Assessment of Posttraumatic Stress (DAPS) (Briere, 2001), Impact of Event Scale – Revised (IES-R) (Weiss & Marmar, 1996), and Mississippi Scale for Combat-Related PTSD (M-PTSD) (Keane, Caddell, & Taylor, 1988). Although not correspondent to *DSM-5*, these measures each have substantial psychometric evidence supporting their use.

The DAPS (Briere, 2001) is a 104-item self-report measure of trauma exposure, *DSM-IV* PTSD symptoms, and selected related domains. The DAPS begins with an assessment of lifetime exposure to a range of potentially traumatic events. Respondents indicate whether they have ever been exposed to different potentially traumatic events (e.g., natural disaster, combat) on dichotomous ("yes" or "no") prompts, and then identify an index trauma. Peri-traumatic distress and dissociation are assessed in the next section. Respondents rate the degree to which they experienced these reactions on a five-point scale ranging from *none at all* to *very much*. *DSM–IV* PTSD symptoms and related dissociation and impairment are assessed in the second portion. Respondents rate how often they have experienced each symptom during the past month on a five-item scale ranging from *never* to *four or more times a week*. Finally, substance use and suicidality are assessed in the third portion. Respondents rate each of these items using the same rating scale described earlier. In addition to symptom severity, the DAPS also includes two response validity scales to evaluate positive and negative response bias, a unique feature among dedicated PTSD assessment instruments. The DAPS has demonstrated strong psychometric properties among a variety of samples, including internal consistency, construct validity, and diagnostic utility (Briere, 2001).

The IES-R (Weiss & Marmar, 1996) is a 22-item self-report measure of trauma-related intrusion, avoidance, and hyperarousal symptoms. Respondents identify the degree to which they have been bothered by each symptom during the past seven days on a five-point scale ranging from *not at all* to *extremely*. Mean scores can be calculated to reflect overall symptom severity or specific symptom clusters. Unlike some of the other self-report measures described in this chapter, the IES-R lacks data supporting its use in determining provisional diagnostic criteria. However, the

IES-R has demonstrated strong test-retest reliability and adequate construct validity.

The M-PTSD (Keane et al., 1988) is a 35-item self-report measure of PTSD symptoms related to combat. Respondents rate how they feel about each statement on a five-point scale ranging from *not at all true* to *extremely true*. In addition to PTSD symptoms, the M-PTSD includes items related to associated features such as depression, suicide risk, and substance use. After recoding several reverse-scored items, all items are summed into a total score reflecting overall PTSD symptom severity. Cutoff scores have been proposed for provision diagnosis, but may vary across populations. The M-PTSD has demonstrated strong reliability and validity (Keane et al., 1998; Sloan, Arsenault, Hilsenroth, & Harvill, 1995). Additionally, a civilian version of the M-PTSD was developed for use in assessing PTSD in relation to traumatic events other than combat (Lauterbach, Vrana, King, & King, 1997).

Related Measures

In addition to measures of PTSD symptoms, a number of other measures of related domains are widely used in clinical and research applications. Several of the most widely used measures are described in what follows. The Posttraumatic Cognitions Inventory (PTCI) (Foa, Ehlers, Clark, Tolin, & Orsillo, 1999) is a 36-item self-report measure of negative trauma-related beliefs. Respondents rate the degree to which they agree with each statement on a seven-point scale ranging from *totally disagree* to *totally agree*. Factor-analytic research supports a three-factor model; items are scored into negative cognitions about self, negative cognitions about the world, and self-blame subscales. These subscale scores have demonstrated strong test-retest reliability and construct validity in multiple samples (Beck et al., 2004; Foa et al., 1999). Additionally, a brief nine-item version of the measure was recently developed that also demonstrated strong psychometric properties (Wells et al., 2017).

The Posttraumatic Maladaptive Beliefs Scale (PMBS) (Vogt, Shipherd, & Resick, 2012) is a 12-item self-report measure of negative trauma-related beliefs. Respondents rate the degree to which they identify with each statement on a seven-point scale ranging from *not at all true for you* to *completely true for you*. Items are scored into three subscales: threat of harm, self-worth and judgment, and reliability and trustworthiness of others. In the initial psychometric study, the PMBS demonstrated strong reliability and construct validity (Vogt et al., 2012).

The Trauma-Related Guilt Inventory (TRGI) (Kubany et al., 1996) is a 32-item self-report measure of multiple dimensions of guilt related to a traumatic event. Respondents select a rating for each item on a five-point rating scale. Of note, the rating scale varies by item, including those ranging from *not at all true* to *extremely true, never true* to *always true, never* to *always, none* to *extreme*, and *not guilty at all* to *extremely guilty*. Items are scored into four subscales: general distress (e.g., "What happened causes me emotional pain"), hindsight bias/responsibility (e.g.,

"I was responsible for causing what happened"), wrongdoing/violation of personal standards (e.g., "I did something that went against my values"), and lack of justification (e.g., "I had good reasons for doing what I did"). The TRGI has demonstrated strong internal consistency and construct validity.

The Dissociative Subtype of PTSD Scale (DSPS) (Wolf et al., in press) is a 15-item self-report measure of three dimensions of dissociative symptoms: derealization/depersonalization, loss of awareness, and psychogenic amnesia. Using a branching format, respondents are asked if they have ever experienced each symptom and, for those who endorse, if symptoms have been experienced in the past month. Past month frequency and severity ratings are made for each symptom on a five-point rating scales ranging from *never* to *daily* and *not very strong* to *extremely strong*, respectively. The DSPS has demonstrated strong psychometric properties in initial research, including construct validity.

Other DSM-5 Trauma- and Stressor-Related Disorders

Acute Stress Disorder

Several changes were made to the acute stress disorder (ASD) criteria in the transition from *DSM-IV* to *DSM-5*. Revisions to Criterion A (trauma exposure) were identical to that of PTSD (e.g., removal of Criterion A2). Additionally, the *DSM-IV* diagnostic algorithm required endorsement of a particular number of symptoms from each of the dissociation, reexperiencing, avoidance, and arousal symptom clusters. The *DSM-5* criteria require endorsement of nine symptoms, regardless of symptom cluster. Accordingly, existing *DSM-IV* measures may be used to assess *DSM-5* ASD, as long as assessment of Criterion A and the diagnostic rule are updated appropriately.

As with PTSD, several clinician-administered and self-report measures of ASD exist. One of the most widely used clinician-administered measures is the Acute Stress Disorder Interview (ASDI) (Bryant, Harvey, Dang, & Sackville, 1998). The ASDI is a structured clinical interview that includes 19 items corresponding to *DSM-IV* ASD symptoms as well as items covering symptom duration and related impairment. Clinicians rate each symptom as *0 – Absent/1 – Present*; items are summed to a total score to reflect overall ASD symptom severity. The *DSM-5* diagnostic algorithm can be applied to these symptoms to determine diagnostic status. The ASDI has demonstrated strong content validity, internal consistency, test-retest reliability, and criterion-related validity (Bryant et al., 1998).

The SCID-5 (First et al., 2015) and ADIS-5 (Brown & Barlow, 2014) include ASD modules. Both of these measures were described in detail earlier in this chapter. For both the SCID-5 and ADIS-5, each symptom is separately assessed in reference to a Criterion A event. For the SCID-5, clinicians rate each symptom on a three-point rating scale: 1 = absent or false, 2 = subthreshold, 3 = threshold or true. For the ADIS-5, each symptom is rated using a nine-point clinical severity rating scale ranging from *never/no distress* to *constantly/extreme distress*. Both the SCID-5 and ADIS-5 can be used to determine diagnostic status.

The Acute Stress Disorder Scale (ASDS) (Bryant, Moulds, & Guthrie, 2000) is a 19-item self-report measure of ASD. Respondents rate the degree to which they have been bothered by each of the 19 items since the index trauma on a five-item scale ranging from *not at all* to *very much*. Items are summed to a total score reflecting overall symptom severity. The ASDS has demonstrated strong content validity, criterion-related validity compared to the ASDI, test-retest validity, and convergent validity (Bryant et al., 2000). A *DSM-IV* diagnostic algorithm showed good sensitivity and specificity (Bryant et al., 2000). However, findings have yet to be presented showing a cutoff for a provisional *DSM-5* diagnosis.

The Stanford Acute Stress Reaction Questionnaire (SASRQ) (Cardeña, Koopman, Classen, Waelde, & Spiegel, 2000) is a 30-item self-report measure of ASD symptoms. Respondents rate how often they have experienced each symptom in reference to the index traumatic event on a six-point scale ranging from *not experienced* to *very often experienced*. Items are summed to a total score reflecting overall symptom severity. The SASRQ has demonstrated strong internal consistency and convergent validity. One limitation of the SASRQ appears to be lack of criterion-related validity (see Bryant et al., 2000, for a discussion).

Reactive Attachment Disorder (RAD) and Disinhibited Social Engagement Disorder (DSED)

The transition from *DSM-IV* to *DSM-5* resulted in several significant changes to RAD. No longer categorized within the Disorders of Childhood, RAD is now housed with the Trauma- and Stressor-Related Disorders. Additionally, the two *DSM-IV* RAD subtypes (emotionally withdrawn/inhibited type and indiscriminately social/disinhibited type) are now defined as two separate and distinct disorders within *DSM-5*: Reactive Attachment Disorder and Disinhibited Social Engagement Disorder. While these two disorders both result from inadequate caregiving during infancy and early childhood, they have distinct phenomenology and unique assessment considerations for differential diagnoses.

The core feature of *DSM-5* RAD is the insufficient development of appropriate attachment to caregivers among children of at least nine months of age. When distressed, children with RAD rarely or minimally seek out comfort, support, protection, or nurturance from appropriate attachment figures and respond to comforting behaviors from caregivers with indifference. This pattern of disinterested, emotionally withdrawn behavior toward attachment figures (Criterion A), and accompanying social and emotional disturbance (Criterion B), stems from a history of social neglect, deprivation, or frequent changes in caregivers (such as in institutional settings with high child-to-caregiver ratios), which limits a child's ability to form appropriate selective attachments (Criterion C). While *DSM-5* does not specify an age cutoff, it urges caution in diagnosing RAD in children older than five, and indeed the majority of research on RAD has been conducted with children between the ages of one and five (Zeanah et al., 2016).

Care should be taken to differentiate RAD from other disorders, particularly autism spectrum disorder (ASD). While RAD and ASD are both marked by social withdrawal and reduced social reciprocity, the two disorders differ with regard to etiology: a history of social neglect is a required criterion of RAD, but not ASD. Additionally, the presence of restricted interest or ritualized behaviors is a hallmark feature of ASD, but not RAD. Although *DSM-5* explicitly prohibits the simultaneous diagnosis of RAD and ASD, Mayes et al. (2016) argue that while RAD and ASD can be differentiated by the presence of specific autism symptoms, the disorders can also co-occur. The reduced positive affect and emotion regulation difficulties characteristic of RAD share similarities with childhood depression as well, though children with depression do not typically exhibit the attachment behavior deficits characteristic of RAD. Though efforts should be made to determine which diagnosis best accounts for a child's symptoms, RAD is commonly comorbid with mood disorders, anxiety disorders, and PTSD (Zeanah et al., 2016). The clinical presentation of RAD is also commonly marked by co-occurring developmental delays, especially in cognition and language, due to their shared etiology in social neglect.

DSED shares with RAD the diagnostic requirement and etiological basis of extreme social neglect and inadequate caregiving during childhood and similarly is generally thought to occur among children between the ages of nine months and five years old. However, DSED is uniquely characterized by disinhibition and externalizing behavior in contrast to RAD, which is conceptualized as an internalizing disorder with depressive and withdrawn symptoms. As a result of limited opportunities to form selective attachments (Criterion C), children with DSED lack appropriate reticence around unfamiliar adults and instead unhesitatingly approach and engage in overly familiar verbal or physical behavior with strangers (Criterion A). Thus, the socially disinhibited behavioral interactions with strangers that are characteristic of DSED are quite opposite to the clinical presentation of children with RAD; while RAD reflects a lack of attachment behaviors, DSED reflects excessive and indiscriminant attachment behaviors. Diagnosis of both RAD and DSED in children over age five, adolescents, and adults continues to be controversial (Zeanah et al., 2016).

DSM-5 explicitly distinguishes DSED from attention deficit/hyperactivity disorder (ADHD) by clarifying that the impulsivity characteristic of DSED is specific to socially disinhibited behavior, rather than spanning into broader behavioral and cognitive domains (Criterion B). DSED can, however, be comorbidly diagnosed with ADHD. Additionally, while socially inappropriate behaviors consistent with DSED overlap with common presentations in ASD, children with DSED have more flexible communication skills than usually seen in ASD (Zeanah et al., 2016).

Unfortunately, no formal, validated screening instruments are widely used for RAD and DSED. Instead, the *Practice parameter for the assessment and treatment of children and adolescents with Reactive Attachment Disorder and*

Disinhibited Social Engagement Disorder recently published by the American Academy of Child and Adolescent Psychiatry (AACAP) recommends asking caregivers about inappropriate attachment behaviors and directly observing the child's interactions with caregivers and other adults (Zeanah et al., 2016). When signs of potential inappropriate attachment behaviors are noted during screening, the AACAP recommends a more thorough diagnostic assessment. This generally involves gathering historical records and verbal histories of early caregiving environments, observational data of the child's behaviors when in the presence of primary caregivers and strangers, informant reports of the child's behavior in childcare settings or schools, and a comprehensive psychiatric assessment to determine the presence of both comorbid and differentially diagnosed disorders.

Assessment practices for observing children's attachment behaviors with caregivers vary widely. The Strange Situation Procedure is a well-known 25-minute structured observational paradigm that involves brief episodes of parent–child separation and reunions (Ainsworth, Blehar, Waters, & Wall, 1978). It is primarily used for research purposes and has been extensively validated, along with several complimentary behavior classification systems (e.g., Britner, Marvin, & Pianta, 2005). Other structured observational approaches generally involve a careful examination of children's behaviors with their primary attachment figures and unfamiliar adults during a sequence of episodes of separation, reunion, and playtime. Attention is particularly given to the presence, absence, and extent of behaviors such as comfort-seeking when distressed, separation protest, and displaying warmth and affection toward primary caregivers.

The Observational Schedule for RAD (OSR) is a 10-item structured observation designed for use with school-age children in a clinic waiting room setting and has shown adequate initial reliability and validity (McLaughlin, Espie, & Minnis, 2010). Additional research is needed to determine its discriminant validity, and a recent study found the OSR was not able to adequately differentiate between RAD and ASD (e.g., Davidson et al., 2015). Additionally, the AACAP proposed an alternative model of a structured observational assessment, though it does not yet appear to be validated (Zeanah et al., 2016).

For a complete assessment of RAD and DSED, empirically based interview and caregiver-report measures are needed as an adjunct to structured behavioral observations. The RAD module of the Child and Adolescent Psychiatric Assessment (CAPA-RAD) (Angold & Costello, 2000) is a 30-item semi-structured parent-report interview of RAD symptoms. Although the CAPA has been well validated and is commonly used in large epidemiological studies, its current utility is limited given that the CAPA-RAD corresponds to *DSM-IV-TR* and *ICD-10*, and has not been updated to correspond to *DSM-5* RAD and DSED symptoms. Recent studies using the CAPA-RAD have also found that while it could reliably differentiate children with RAD from children who did not have psychiatric disorders (Minnis et al., 2009), the CAPA-RAD was not able to effectively differentiate RAD from ASD (e.g., Davidson et al., 2015). There is a clear need for additional measurement development and validation studies, especially given that a gold-standard instrument for the assessment of RAD and DSED has yet to be developed.

Adjustment Disorder

Adjustment Disorder (AD) has been even more neglected by research than RAD and DSED, which poses challenges for the conceptualization, diagnosis, and assessment of the disorder. Previously located between the V codes and Axis I disorders of *DSM-IV*, AD has been classified within a diagnostic chapter for the first time, with its inclusion in the *DSM-5* TSRD chapter. Despite this elevation in nosological status, there have been no major changes in the diagnostic criteria with the move to *DSM-5* and AD continues to have a "second-class" status as a subthreshold disorder in the sense that it cannot be diagnosed when the threshold for another disorder has been reached. AD is unlike most *DSM-5* disorders in that it continues to lack specific symptom criteria. Instead, *DSM-5* prescribes that symptoms of AD must develop within three months of exposure to a stressful event (Criterion A), must involve clinically significant distress or impairment (Criterion B), cannot be diagnosed if another disorder is present (Criterion C), cannot reflect a normative bereavement response (Criterion D), and symptoms must remit within six months of the conclusion of the stressful event (APA, 2013). *DSM-5* provides classification for several subtypes of AD based on dominant symptoms (depressed mood, anxiety, disturbance of conduct, mixed anxiety and depressed mood, mixed disturbance of emotions and conduct), though these subtypes have been criticized for their lack of research support (O'Donnell et al., 2016).

The vagueness of the diagnostic criteria for AD partially explains the lack of AD measurement development. Many commonly used structured diagnostic interviews of psychiatric disorders exclude AD. Those that include AD, such as the SCID-5 (First et al., 2015) and the MINI (Sheehan et al., 1997), assess for AD using only optional questions to ensure rule-out criteria are absent (e.g., another Axis I disorder), stating "information obtained from overview of present illness will usually be sufficient to rate the criteria."

In the absence of a recognized gold-standard diagnostic instrument, researchers have operationalized the diagnostic criteria in varying ways, such as drawing from items within several existing assessment instruments, including the CAPS-5, MINI, and the World Health Organization Quality of Life-BREF (O'Donnell et al., 2016). The Diagnostic Interview for Adjustment Disorder (DIAD) (Cornelius et al., 2014) is a semi-structured interview designed to be administered by lay interviewers. It was developed based on expert consensus and operationalizes AD using designated cutoff scores on the distress subscale of the Four-Dimensional Symptom Questionnaire (4DSQ) (Terluin et al., 2006) and the Sheehan Disability Scale (SDS) (Leon et al., 1997). Alternatively, the Adjustment Disorder New Module (ADNM) (Einsle et al., 2010) is based on specific proposed diagnostic criteria. The ADNM is a 29-item self-report measure based on Maercker and colleague's (2007) theory that conceptualizes AD as being similar to PTSD, with symptoms falling within three clusters: intrusive symptoms/ruminations associated with reminders of the stressor, avoidance behaviors, and failure to adapt. Although this questionnaire has been used in several studies, its lack of widespread usage may be due to the lack of consensus about whether the conceptualization of AD is a PTSD-like construct. Further research is needed to better understand and reach consensus on the phenomenology of AD. The establishment of a clear delineation of AD symptoms would aid in the development of standardized measures, and further fuel research on the diagnosis.

Research Domain Criteria (RDoC)

The National Institute of Mental Health (NIMH) Research Domain Criteria (RDoC) (Insel & Cuthbert, 2009) is a framework for research to examine psychological disorders at multiple levels of information (e.g., genetics, cellular, physiology, self-report). Specifically, the RDoC framework was developed in an effort "to define for research purposes promising domains of study that are not constrained by traditional diagnostic categories. The aim is to develop measures that might serve as endophenotypes to better relate to emerging data in genetics and clinical neuroscience" (Lang & McTeague, 2011, p. 207). Much of the early research examining RDoC domains relevant to PTSD have focused on fear conditioning and exaggerated startle (e.g., Norrholm et al., 2011). However, PTSD includes features of other domains (e.g., deficits in positive valence systems; e.g., Liu et al., 2014). All of the measures reviewed in this chapter are classified under the self-report units of analysis as they are based on information provided by respondents rather than objective indices (e.g., physiology, behavioral tasks). This is consistent with the RDoC critique that "unlike for most medical disease entities, we currently do not have good quantitative, biological symptom measures that can help the clinician define the pathology of PTSD and assure reliable diagnosis, serve as efficient prognostic tools, and provide better targets for treatment" (Lang & McTeague, 2011, p. 207). Indeed, substantial efforts have been undertaken to identify biomarkers of PTSD (e.g., Keane et al., 1998). Although a comprehensive review of this literature is beyond the scope of the present chapter, the psychological and physiological complexities and heterogeneity of the disorder have made such efforts challenging (see Yehuda & LeDoux, 2007, for a review). Identification of biomarkers of PTSD could hold considerable value for both research and clinical practice.

Summary and Conclusions

DSM-5 introduced the TSRD chapter to aggregate the various mental disorders that require exposure to a traumatic or stressful event as one of their diagnostic criteria, including PTSD, acute stress disorder, adjustment disorder, reactive attachment disorder, and disinhibited social engagement disorder. This new chapter was placed just after the anxiety disorders and obsessive-compulsive and related disorders chapters and just before the dissociative disorders chapter to signify the close conceptual relatedness among all of these disorders. Each of the disorders in the TSRD chapter poses unique challenges for assessment. Variable progress has been made across these disorders in developing reliable and valid measures, but there are at least some evidence-based measures for each disorder.

Of these disorders, PTSD is the most widely studied and has the most extensive array of assessment tools, including a variety of self-report scales and structured diagnostic interviews for assessing trauma exposure, core PTSD criteria, and associated phenomena. Most of the leading PTSD measures have been updated for *DSM-5* and at least in initial validation work appear to be psychometrically sound. Clearly additional validation is needed to replicate the early findings and extend them to diverse trauma populations. Nonetheless, ample measures are now available for evidence-based assessment of PTSD in a wide range of clinical and research contexts.

References

Ainsworth, M., Blehar, M., Waters, E., & Wall, S. (1978). *Patterns of Attachment: A Psychological Study of the Strange Situation*. Hillsdale, NJ: Erlbaum.

American Psychiatric Association (1980). *Diagnostic and Statistical Manual of Mental Disorders* (3rd edn). Washington, DC: American Psychiatric Association.

American Psychiatric Association. (2000). *Diagnostic and Statistical Manual of Mental Disorders* (4th edn, text rev.). Washington, DC: American Psychiatric Association.

American Psychiatric Association. (2013). *Diagnostic and Statistical Manual of Mental Disorders* (5th edn). Washington, DC: American Psychiatric Association.

Angold, A. & Costello, E. J. (2000). The Child and Adolescent Psychiatric Assessment (CAPA). *Journal of the American Academy of Child & Adolescent Psychiatry, 39*, 39–48.

Asmundson, G. G., Stapleton, J. A., & Taylor, S. (2004). Are avoidance and numbing distinct PTSD symptom clusters? *Journal of Traumatic Stress, 17*, 467–475.

Beck, J. G., Coffey, S. F., Palyo, S. A., Gudmundsdottir, B., Miller, L. M., & Colder, C. R. (2004). Psychometric properties of the Posttraumatic Cognitions Inventory (PTCI): A replication with motor vehicle accident survivors. *Psychological Assessment, 16*, 289–298.

Blevins, C. A., Weathers, F. W., Davis, M. T., Witte, T. K., & Domino, J. L. (2015). The Posttraumatic Stress Disorder Checklist for *DSM-5* (PCL-5): Development and initial psychometric evaluation. *Journal of Traumatic Stress, 28*, 489–498.

Bovin, M. J., Marx, B. P., Weathers, F. W., Gallagher, M. W., Rodriguez, P., Schnurr, P. P., & Keane, T. M. (2015). Psychometric properties of the PTSD Checklist for *Diagnostic and Statistical Manual of Mental Disorders-Fifth Edition* (PCL-5) in Veterans. *Psychological Assessment, 28*, 1379–1391.

Briere, J. (2001). *Detailed Assessment of Posttraumatic Stress*. Odessa, FL: Psychological Assessment Resources.

Britner, P. A., Marvin, R. S., & Pianta, R. C. (2005). Development and preliminary validation of the caregiver behavior system: Association with child attachment classification in the preschool Strange Situation. *Attachment and Human Development, 7*, 83–102.

Brown, T. A. & Barlow, D. H. (2014). *Anxiety Disorders Interview Schedule for DSM-5 (ADIS-5)*. New York, NY: Oxford University Press.

Bryant, R. A., Harvey, A. G., Dang, S., & Sackville, T. (1998). Assessing acute stress disorder: Psychometric properties of a structured clinical interview. *Psychological Assessment, 10*, 215–220.

Bryant, R. A., Moulds, M., & Guthrie, R. (2000). Acute Stress Disorder Scale: A self-report measure of acute stress disorder. *Psychological Assessment, 12*, 61–68.

Cardeña, E., Koopman, C., Classen, C., Waelde, L. C., & Spiegel, D. (2000). Psychometric properties of the Stanford Acute Stress Reaction Questionnaire (SASRQ): A valid and reliable measure of acute stress. *Journal of Traumatic Stress, 13*, 719–734.

Casey, P. (2014). Adjustment disorder: New developments. *Current Psychiatry Reports, 16*, 451.

Cornelius, L. R., Brouwer, S., De Boer, M. R., Groothoff, J. W., & van der Klink, J. J. L. (2014). Development and validation of the Diagnostic Interview Adjustment (DIAD). *International Journal of Methods in Psychiatric Research, 23*, 192–207.

Davidson, J. R. T. & Foa, E. B. (1991). Diagnostic issues in posttraumatic stress disorder: Considerations for the *DSM-IV. Journal of Abnormal Psychology, 100*, 346–355.

Davidson, C., O'Hare, A., Mactaggart, F., Green, J., Young, D., Gillberg, C., & Minnis, H. (2015). Social relationship difficulties in autism and reactive attachment disorder: Improving diagnostic validity through structured assessment. *Research in Developmental Disabilities, 40*, 63–72.

Di Nardo, P. A., Brown, T. A., Lawton, J. K., & Barlow, D. H. (1995, November). The Anxiety Disorders Interview Schedule-for *DSM-IV* Lifetime Version: Description and initial evidence for diagnostic reliability. Paper presented at the meeting of the annual meeting of the Association for Advancement of Behavior Therapy, Washington, DC.

Di Nardo, P. A., Moras, K., Barlow, D. H., Rapee, R. M., & Brown, T. A. (1993). Reliability of *DSM-III-R* anxiety disorder categories using the Anxiety Disorders Interview Schedule-Revised (ADIS-R). *Archives of General Psychiatry, 50*, 251–256.

Einsle, F., Köllner, V., Dannemann, S. & Maercker, A. (2010). Development and validation of a self-report for the assessment of adjustment disorders. *Psychology, Health & Medicine*, 15, 584–595.

Elhai, J. D. & Palmieri, P. A. (2011). The factor structure of posttraumatic stress disorder: A literature update, critique of methodology, and agenda for future research. *Journal of Anxiety Disorders, 25*, 849–854.

Elhai, J. D., Gray, M. J., Kashdan, T. B., & Franklin, C. L. (2005). Which instruments are most commonly used to assess traumatic event exposure and posttraumatic effects? A survey of traumatic stress professionals. *Journal of Traumatic Stress, 18*, 541–545.

First, M. B., Williams, J. B. W., Karg, R. S., & Spitzer, R. L. (2015) *Structured Clinical Interview for DSM-5 Disorders, Clinician Version (SCID-5-CV)*. Arlington, VA: American Psychiatric Association.

Foa, E. B., Cashman, L., Jaycox, L., & Perry, K. (1997). The validation of a self-report measure of posttraumatic stress disorder: The Posttraumatic Diagnostic Scale. *Psychological Assessment, 9*, 445–451.

Foa, E. B., Ehlers, A., Clark, D. M., Tolin, D. F., & Orsillo, S. M. (1999). The posttraumatic cognitions inventory (PTCI): Development and validation. *Psychological Assessment, 11*, 303–314.

Foa, E. B., McLean, C. P., Zang, Y., Zhong, J., Powers, M. B., Kauffman, B. Y., ... Knowles, K. (2016). Psychometric properties of the posttraumatic diagnostic scale for *DSM-5* (PDS-5). *Psychological Assessment, 28*, 1166–1171.

Foa, E. B., McLean, C. P., Zang, Y., Zhong, J., Rauch, S., Porter, K., ... Kauffman, B. Y. (2016). Psychometric properties of the Posttraumatic Stress Disorder Symptom Scale Interview for *DSM–5* (PSSI–5). *Psychological Assessment, 28*, 1159–1165.

Friedman, M. J. (2013a). Finalizing PTSD in *DSM-5*: Getting here from there and where to go next. *Journal of Traumatic Stress, 26*, 548–556.

Friedman, M. J. (2013b). PTSD in the *DSM-5*: Reply to Brewin (2013), Kilpatrick (2013), and Maercker and Perkonigg (2013). *Journal of Traumatic Stress, 26*, 567–569.

Friedman, M. J., Resick, P. A., Bryant, R. A., & Brewin, C. R. (2011). Considering PTSD for *DSM-5. Depression and Anxiety, 28*, 750–769.

Friedman, M. J., Resick, P. A., Bryant, R. A., Strain, J., Horowitz, M., & Spiegel, D. (2011). Classification of trauma and stressor-related disorders in DSM-5. *Depression and Anxiety*,28, 737–749.

Goodman, L., Corcoran, C., Turner, K., Yuan, N., & Green, B. (1998). Assessing traumatic event exposure: General issues and preliminary findings for the Stressful Life Events Screening Questionnaire. *Journal of Traumatic Stress, 11*, 521–542.

Gray, M., Litz, B., Hsu, J., & Lombardo, T. (2004). Psychometric properties of the Life Events Checklist. *Assessment, 11*, 330–341.

Insel, T. R. & Cuthbert, B. (2009). Endophenotypes: Bridging genomic complexity and disorder heterogeneity. *Biological Psychiatry, 66*, 988–989.

Keane, T. M., Caddell, J. M., & Taylor, K. L. (1988) Mississippi Scale for Combat-Related Posttraumatic Stress Disorder: Three studies in reliability and validity. *Journal of Consulting and Clinical Psychology, 56*, 85–90.

Keane, T. M., Kolb, L. C., Kaloupek, D. G., Orr, S. P., Blanchard, E. B., Thomas, R. G., ... Lavori, P. W. (1998). Utility of psychophysiology measurement in the diagnosis of posttraumatic stress disorder: Results from a department of Veteran's Affairs cooperative study. *Journal of Consulting and Clinical Psychology, 66*, 914–923.

Kilpatrick, D. G., Resnick, H., Milanak, M. E., Miller, M. W., Keyes, K. M., & Friedman, M. J. (2013). National estimates of exposure to traumatic events and PTSD prevalence using *DSM-IV* and *DSM-5* criteria. *Journal of Traumatic Stress, 26*, 537–547.

Kubany, E. S., Haynes, S. N., Abueg, F. R., Manke, F. P., Brennan, J. M., & Stahura, C. (1996). Development and validation of the Trauma-Related Guilt Inventory (TRGI). *Psychological Assessment, 8*, 428–444.

Kubany, E. S., Leisen, M. B., Kaplan, A. S., Watson, S. B., Haynes, S. N., Owens, J. A., & Burns, K. (2000). Development and preliminary validation of a brief broad-spectrum measure of trauma exposure: The Traumatic Life Events Questionnaire. *Psychological Assessment, 12*, 210–224.

Lang, P. J. & McTeague, L. M. (2011). Discrete and recurrent traumatization in PTSD: Fear vs. anxious misery. *Journal of Clinical Psychology in Medical Settings, 18*, 207–209.

Lanius, R. A., Brand, B. B., Vermetten, E., Frewen, P. A., & Spiegel, D. (2012). The dissociative subtype of posttraumatic stress disorder: Rationale, clinical and neurobiological evidence, and implications. *Depression and Anxiety, 29*, 701–708.

Lauterbach, D., Vrana, S. R., King, D. W., & King, L. A. (1997). Psychometric properties of the civilian version of the Mississippi PTSD Scale. *Journal of Traumatic Stress, 10*, 499–513.

Leon A. C., Olfson M., Portera L., Farber L., & Sheehan D. V. (1997). Assessing psychiatric impairment in primary care with the Sheehan Disability Scale. *International Journal of Psychiatry in Medicine, 27*, 93–105.

Liu, P., Wang, L., Cao,C., Wang, R., Zhang, J., Zhang, B., ... Elhai, J. D. (2014). The underlying dimensions of *DSM-5* posttraumatic stress disorder symptoms in an epidemiological sample of Chinese earthquake survivors. *Journal of Anxiety Disorders, 28*, 345–351.

Maercker, A., Einsle, F., & Köllner, V. (2007). Adjustment disorders as stress response syndromes: A new diagnostic concept and its exploration in a medical sample. *Psychopathology, 40*, 135–146.

Mayes, D. S., Calhoun, S. L., Waschbusch, D. A., & Baweja, R. (2016). Autism and reactive attachment/disinhibited social engagement disorders: Co-occurrence and differentiation. *Clinical Child Psychology and Psychiatry, 22*, 1–12.

McLaughlin, A., Espie, C., & Minis, H. (2010). Development of a brief waiting room observation for behaviors typical of Reactive Attachment Disorder. *Child and Adolescent Mental Health, 15*, 73–79.

McNally, R. J. (2003). Progress and controversy in the study of posttraumatic stress disorder. *Annual Review of Psychology, 54*, 229–252.

McNally, R. J. (2004). Conceptual problems with the *DSM-IV* criteria for posttraumatic stress disorder. In G. M. Rosen (ed.), *Posttraumatic Stress Disorder: Issues and Controversies* (pp.1–14). Chichester, England: Wiley.

McNally, R. J. (2009). Can we fix PTSD in *DSM-V*? *Depression and Anxiety, 26*, 597–600.

Minnis, H., Green, J., O'Connor, T., Liew, A., Glaser, D., Taylor, E., Follan, M., Young, D., Barnes, J., Gillberg, C., Pelosi, A., Arthur, J., Burston, A., Connolly, B., & Sadiq, F. (2009). An exploratory study of the association between reactive attachment disorder and attachment narratives in early school-age children. *Journal of Child Psychology and Psychiatry, and Allied Disciplines, 50*, 931–942.

Norrholm, S. D., Jovanovic, T., Olin, I. W., Sands, L. A., Bradley, B., & Ressler, K. J. (2011). Fear extinction in traumatized civilians with posttraumatic stress disorder: Relation to symptom severity. *Biological Psychiatry, 69*, 556–563.

O'Donnell, M. L., Alkemade, N., Creamer, M., McFarlane, A. C., Silove, D., Bryant, R. A., ... Forbes, D. (2016). A longitudinal study of adjustment disorder after trauma exposure. *American Journal of Psychiatry, 173*, 1231–1238.

Prins, A., Bovin, M. J., Smolenski, D. J., Mark, B. P., Kimerling, R., Jenkins-Guarnieri, M. A., ... Tiet, Q. Q. (2016). The Primary Care PTSD Screen for *DSM-5* (PC-PTSD-5): Development and evaluation within a veteran primary care sample. *Journal of General Internal Medicine, 31*, 1206–1211.

Resick, P. A. & Miller, M. W. (2009). Posttraumatic stress disorder: Anxiety or traumatic stress disorder? *Journal of Traumatic Stress, 22*, 384–390.

Rosen, G. M. (2004). Traumatic events, criterion creep, and the creation of pretraumatic stress disorder. *Scientific Review of Mental Health Practice, 3*, 39–42.

Sheehan, D. V., Lecrubier, Y., Sheehan, K. H., Janavs, J., Weiller, E., Keskiner, A., . . . Dunbar, G. C. (1997). The validity of the Mini International Neuropsychiatric Interview (MINI) according to the SCID-P and its reliability. *European Psychiatry, 12,* 232–241.

Sloan, P., Arsenault, L., Hilsenroth, M., & Harvill, L. (1995) Use of the Mississippi Scale for Combat-Related PTSD in detecting war-related, non-combat stress symptomatology. *Journal of Clinical Psychology, 51,* 799–801.

Spitzer, R. L., First, M. B., & Wakefield, J. C. (2007). Saving PTSD from itself in DSM-V. *Journal of Anxiety Disorders, 21,* 233–241.

Tanielian, T. (2009). *Assessing Combat Exposure and Post-Traumatic Stress Disorder in Troops and Estimating the Costs to Society: Implications from the RAND Invisible Wounds of War Study.* Santa Monica, CA: RAND Corporation.

Terluin B., van Marwijk H. W., Ader H. J., de Vet H. C., Penninx B. W., & Hermens M. L. (2006). The Four-Dimensional Symptom Questionnaire (4DSQ): A validation study of a multidimensional self-report questionnaire to assess distress, depression, anxiety and somatization. *BMC Psychiatry, 6,* 34–54.

Vogt, D. S., Shipherd, J. C., & Resick, P. A. (2012). Posttraumatic maladaptive beliefs scale: Evolution of the personal beliefs and reactions scale. *Assessment, 19,* 308–317.

Weathers, F. W., Blake, D. D., Schnurr, P. P., Kaloupek, D. G., Marx, B. P., & Keane, T. M. (2013a). The Clinician-Administered PTSD Scale for *DSM-5* (CAPS-5). Interview available from the National Center for PTSD at www.ptsd.va.gov.

Weathers, F. W., Blake, D. D., Schnurr, P. P., Kaloupek, D. G., Marx, B. P., & Keane, T. M. (2013b). The Life Events Checklist for *DSM-5* (LEC-5). Instrument available from the National Center for PTSD at www.ptsd.va.gov.

Weathers, F. W., Bovin, M. J., Lee, D. J., Sloan, D. M., Schnurr, P. P., Kaloupek, D. G., . . . Marx, B. P. (2018). The Clinician-Administered PTSD Scale for *DSM-5* (CAPS-5): Development and initial psychometric evaluation in military veterans. *Psychological Assessment, 30*(3), 383–395.

Weathers, F. W. & Keane, T. M. (2007). The Criterion A problem revisited: Controversies and challenges in defining and measuring psychological trauma. *Journal of Traumatic Stress, 20,* 107–121.

Weathers, F. W., Keane, T. M., & Davidson, J. R. T. (2001). Clinician administered PTSD scale: A review of the first ten years of research. *Depression and Anxiety, 13,* 132–156.

Weathers, F. W., Litz, B. T., Keane, T. M., Palmieri, P. A., Marx, B. P., & Schnurr, P. P. (2013c). The PTSD Checklist for *DSM-5* (PCL-5). Scale available from the National Center for PTSD at www.ptsd.va.gov.

Weiss, D. S. & Marmar, C. R. (1996). The Impact of Event Scale – Revised. In J. Wilson & T. M. Keane (eds.), *Assessing Psychological Trauma and PTSD* (pp. 399–411). New York, NY: Guilford Press.

Wells, S. Y., Morland, L. A., Torres, E. M., Kloezeman, K., Mackintosh, M. A., & Aarons, G. A. (2017). The development of a brief version of the Posttraumatic Cognitions Inventory (PTCI-9). *Assessment,* online advance publication.

Wolf, E. J., Mitchell, K. S., Sadeh, N., Hein, C., Fuhrman, I., Pietrzak, R. H., & Miller, M. W. (in press). The Dissociative Subtype of PTSD Scale (DSPS): Initial evaluation in a national sample of trauma-exposed Veterans. *Assessment.*

Wortmann, J. H., Jordan, A. H., Weathers, F. W., Resick, P. A., Dondanville, K. A., Hall-Clark, B., . . . Litz, B. T. (2016). Psychometric analysis of the PTSD Checklist-5 (PCL-5) among treatment-seeking military service members. *Psychological Assessment*, *28*, 1392–1403.

Yehuda, R. & LeDoux, J. (2007). Response variation following trauma: A translational neuroscience approach to understanding PTSD. *Neuron*, *56*(1), 19–32.

Zeanah, C. H., Chesher, T., Boris, N.W., & the American Academy of Child and Adolescent Psychiatry Committee on Quality Issues. (2016). Practice parameter for the assessment and treatment of children and adolescents with Reactive Attachment Disorder and Disinhibited Social Engagement Disorder. *Journal of the American Academic of Child and Adolescent Psychiatry*, 55, 990–1003.

14 Cultural Considerations in Anxiety and Related Disorders

Devon Hinton and Eric Bui

There has been a call to move beyond the *DSM* categorical system, with a disorder defined by a cluster of symptoms, to a dimensional approach, with a disorder described as involving multiple dimensions (Casey et al., 2013; Morris & Cuthbert, 2012; Sanislow et al., 2010). The Research Domain Criteria (RDoC) framework proposed by the National Institute of Mental Health aims to specifically support this shift. One RDoC dimension, namely, cognitive systems, includes catastrophic cognitions, suggesting that how a person cognizes about symptoms – what causes them, what disorders the symptoms indicate, what catastrophic events may occur – are key aspects to assess (e.g., such cognitions will lead to hypervigilance for certain symptoms, scanning for certain triggers, catastrophic cognitions about certain symptoms). In addition, RDoC endorses a comorbidity approach, so that, for instance, multiple dimensions may simultaneously occur in a disorder.

Another key shift in theory has been network theory, in which disorders are conceptualized as an interaction of symptoms that are mutually reinforcing: worry causing poor sleep, poor sleep causing poor concentration, poor sleep leading to irritability, and so on. In these network models, disorders are seen as dynamic interaction of symptoms, as causal sequences (Borsboom & Cramer, 2013; Bui & Fava, 2017; Hofmann, Curtiss, & McNally, 2016; McNally, 2012, 2016). Here we examine anxiety disorders in cross-cultural perspective, considering disorders as complex, dynamic systems of interacting symptoms (network theory) in which catastrophic cognitions play a key role and in which comorbidity is common (RDoC). In our models we take a cognitive-causative view, that is, the position that what a person thinks about a symptom has causal importance, as in catastrophic cognitions in panic (Beck, 1988; Clark, 1986; Clark & Ehlers, 2004; Foa, Ehlers, Clark, Tolin, & Orsillo, 1999; Wells, 2009).

The current chapter examines the *DSM*-defined anxiety disorders from a cultural perspective, trying to determine their applicability to other cultural groups and how findings in other cultural groups might be used to better understand how anxiety disorders are produced and classified. In this review, we focus on three anxiety disorders: panic disorder (PD), generalized anxiety disorder (GAD), and post-traumatic stress disorder (PTSD). In our analysis, we present models of disorder based on current psychological theories of how those disorders are generated in order to explore possible cross-cultural variation, using primarily Cambodian examples. (For other cultural examples, see Hinton & Good, 2009, 2015.) These models can be used for evaluation and treatment.

Panic Disorder in Cross-Cultural Perspective

According to many psychological theories of PD, catastrophic cognitions about symptoms, particularly somatic sensations, play a key role in the generation of the disorder. Cognitive theorists have argued that the *DSM*'s "out-of-the-blue" criterion – that true panic attacks are unprovoked – should be eliminated (for reviews, see Beck, 1988; Khawaja & Oei, 1998; McNally, 1994; Rapee, Craske, & Barlow, 1994). Instead, they contend that catastrophic cognitions about bodily sensations constitute a core process in provoking panic attacks, and that the feared bodily sensations that provoke panic may be induced by a wide range of "triggers."

Clark (1986) summarized this "catastrophic cognitions" theory of panic as follows:

> The trigger for an attack often seems to be the perception of a bodily sensation which itself is caused by a different emotional state (excitement, anger) or by some quite innocuous event such as suddenly getting up from the sitting position (dizziness), exercise (breathlessness, palpitations) or drinking coffee (palpitations). Once perceived, the bodily sensation is interpreted in a catastrophic fashion and then a panic attack results. (p. 462)

Other common ways in which sensations might be induced, and which then trigger panic attacks, were also identified: hyperventilation that produces a host of bodily sensations, including blurry vision and hand numbness, or shifts in temperature and humidity – for example, those resulting from entering a sauna or moving from a warm to a cold space – that cause somatic symptoms such as sweating or cold extremities (Beck, 1988; Rapee et al., 1994).

The catastrophic cognitions theory of panic has important implications in respect to the nature of PD and its cross-cultural variability. In Figure 14.1 we present our modification of Clark's model to show how PD-type panic attacks are generated in different cultural groups, "The Cross-Cultural Panic Model." In what follows, we describe some of the cross-cultural variation of PD that would be expected from the "catastrophic cognitions theory of the generation of PD," and show the evidence that it is the case (on these issues, see Hinton & Good, 2009; Hinton, Park, Hsia, Hofmann, & Pollack, 2009).

The Rate and Severity of Panic Disorder Will Vary across Cultural Groups Depending on the Extent of Catastrophic Cognitions about Anxiety-Related Sensations

According to the catastrophic cognitions theory of panic, the more severe a person's catastrophic cognitions about sensations, particularly anxiety-related sensations (e.g., dizziness, palpitations, chest tightness), the greater the frequency and severity of panic attacks. In support of this hypothesis, multiple studies demonstrate that the severity of catastrophic cognitions about panic sensations is strongly related to the severity and frequency of PD panic attacks (for a review, see Hinton et al., 2006a). This suggests a close relationship between cultural

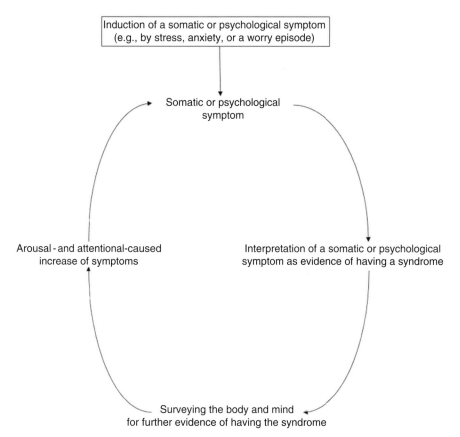

Figure 14.1 *The Cross-Cultural Panic Model. The role of cultural syndromes and ethnophysiology in generating catastrophic cognitions and starting a vicious cycle of worsening.*

interpretations of the danger of particular sensations and whether panic is induced by those sensations. It does appear that certain cultural groups with extensive catastrophic cognitions about anxiety symptoms, such as Cambodian refugees, have very high rates of PD-type panic attacks, and that culturally specific catastrophic cognitions about somatic sensations generate panic (Hinton et al., 2006a; Hinton, Ba, Peou, & Um, 2000; Hinton, Chhean, Fama, Pollack, & McNally, 2007a; Hinton, Um, & Ba, 2001a, 2001b, 2001c).

Catastrophic Cognitions in Panic Disorder Will Vary across Cultural Groups

According to the catastrophic cognitions theory of panic, the catastrophic cognitions about the somatic and psychological symptoms that generate panic attacks would be expected to vary depending on local ideas about the dangers those symptoms pose (Hinton & Good, 2009). Owing to cultural variations in syndromes and ethnophysiology, catastrophic cognitions will vary significantly across culture, cultural subgroup, and even time period.

In the United States, fear of heart attack is a frequent catastrophic cognition during panic (Katon, 1984). In this case, we would refer to the current layperson understanding of the heart and heart attacks, and the symptoms of and risk factors for heart attack, in a particular social and cultural group in the United States, as a cultural syndrome, or a layperson-type cultural syndrome. This may simply be the knowledge that "fatty foods" and cigarettes predispose to heart attack, the idea that chest tightness means a heart attack, and the concern that "stress" may predispose to the disorder. Cambodians have multiple anxiety-related fears owing to an attribution of these symptoms to disturbed flow of *khyâl* (an air-like substance) and blood, called a *khyâl* attack. "*Khyâl* attack" is one of the syndromes listed in the *DSM-5* glossary of cultural explanations of disorders (American Psychiatric Association, 2013). For an overview of "*khyâl* attack," see Figure 14.2. *Khyâl* attack gives rise to extensive catastrophic cognitions about anxiety-generated somatic sensations. Let us examine how *khyâl* attacks create unique catastrophic cognitions that generate panic in the Cambodian case, showing how the catastrophic cognitions in panic vary across cultures.

The "*khyâl* attack" syndrome causes fear of limb sensations. Cambodians consider that tightness and soreness in the limbs result from blockage of "tubes" (*sâsai*) that carry blood and *khyâl* along the limbs, and that coldness in the limbs, for example, the feet and hands, indicates poor blood perfusion (Hinton, Pich, Marques, Nickerson, & Pollack, 2010). It is thought that blockage of the flow of *khyâl* and blood may result in the "death" of the limb, owing to the lack of blood flow, what a Westerner would call a "stroke." The *khyâl* and blood may also rush up into the body: into the trunk of the body, possibly causing asphyxia and cardiac arrest; into the neck, possibly causing rupture of the vessels; and into the cranium, possibly causing multiple adverse events such as syncope, blindness, or death. For these reasons, Cambodian patients greatly fear cold extremities.

Cambodians have a "sore neck" syndrome, which is again related to the "*khyâl* attack" syndrome. Catastrophic cognitions about neck sensations often lead to panic attacks, that is, to neck-focused panic attacks. In a neck-focused panic attack (Hinton, Chhean, et al., 2006; Hinton et al., 2001c), a Cambodian fears death from rupture of the neck vessels, with prominent symptoms including a sore neck (*rooy kâ*), head symptoms (e.g., headache, tinnitus, blurry vision, and dizziness), and general symptoms of autonomic arousal (e.g., cold extremities, palpitations, and shortness of breath). Cambodians attribute neck soreness to excessive *khyâl* and blood pressure in the neck that may rupture vessels at that location, and attribute other symptoms present in a "sore neck" episode, such as tinnitus and blurry vision, to an upward rising of *khyâl* and blood. For these reasons, Cambodian patients greatly fear neck soreness.

The "*khyâl* attack" syndrome causes fear of abdominal sensations (Hinton, Chhean, Fama, Pollack, & McNally, 2007b). The syndrome gives rise to catastrophic

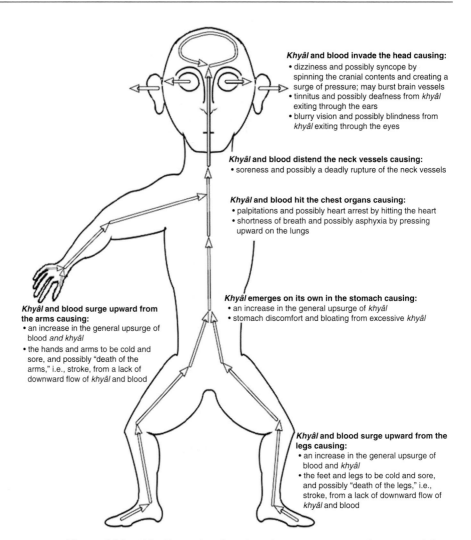

Figure 14.2 *A* khyâl *attack: ethnophysiology, symptoms, and associated disasters. The arrows represent the flow of* khyâl *and blood upward in the body during a* khyâl *attack. During the healthy state,* khyâl *and blood flow downward in the direction opposite the arrows, with* khyâl *exiting the body through the hands and feet, through bodily pores, and down through the gastrointestinal tract, but during a* khyâl *attack,* khyâl *and blood surge upward in the body to cause the disasters outlined earlier in this chapter.*

cognitions about gastrointestinal (GI) sensations that often lead to a GI-focused panic attack. In a GI-focused panic attack, Cambodians worry that *khyâl* will move upward into the body and cause various bodily disasters. Whereas North Americans often complain of "butterflies in the stomach" or of a "sinking sensation in the stomach" when anxious (Chambless, Caputo, Bright, & Gallagher, 1984; Noyes & Hoehn-Saric, 1998), Cambodians worry that abdominal sensations indicate the occurrence of an "upward-hitting *khyâl*" (*khyâl theau laeung leu*). As noted earlier, the rising *khyâl* is believed to potentially cause catastrophic consequences (e.g., syncope, cardiac arrest, or bursting of the neck vessels), with fear of *khyâl* ascent being heightened if additional symptoms indicative of increased *khyâl* pressure occur such as tinnitus, dizziness, or a sore neck. And so, like with cold extremities and neck soreness, Cambodian patients also fear stomach distention and sensations.

The "*khyâl* attack" syndrome gives rise to fear of fainting upon standing. It produces catastrophic cognitions about any sensations felt upon standing, for example, dizziness, palpitations, and cold extremities, and results in orthostatic panic, that is, panic upon rising from lying or sitting to standing (Hinton et al., 2001a, 2001b, 2010). It is thought that a surge of *khyâl* and blood upward in the body toward the head may occur upon standing, a condition called "*khyâl* overload." For this reason, upon standing, Cambodians anxiously assess the bodily state for symptoms that would indicate a pressurized rise of *khyâl* and blood upward in the body and toward and into the head: shortness of breath (from *khyâl* and blood pushing on the lungs), a sore neck (from *khyâl* and blood distending the neck vessels), dizziness (from excessive *khyâl* and blood entering the head), blurry vision (from *khyâl* exiting the eyes), or tinnitus (from *khyâl* escaping from the auditory canals, analogous to the sound made by steam exiting the spout of a tea kettle).

The Triggers of the Sensations That Cause PD-Type Panic Attacks Will Vary across Cultural Groups

According to the catastrophic cognitions theory of panic, what induces the feared sensations and triggers PD-type panic attacks may vary across different individuals and cultural groups. Given local illness concepts and syndromes, specific bodily sensations will be viewed with more fear in certain situations. For example, owing to syndrome-generated catastrophic cognitions, dizziness upon standing causes much greater fear for a Cambodian (e.g., "I having an episode of *khyâl* overload" [which evokes fears of multiple catastrophes: fatal syncope, stroke, bursting of the neck vessels]) than for an American (e.g., "I'm very dizzy, and if I do not sit down I will fall"). The frequency with which certain sensation inducers bring about panic varies by culture: common triggers of panic among Cambodian refugees include standing up and feeling dizzy, seeing a spinning object, smelling car exhaust fumes, or getting neck tightness (Hinton, Chea, Ba, & Pollack, 2004; Hinton, Pich, Chhean, Pollack, & Barlow, 2004; Hinton et al., 2000); or among Vietnamese refugees, common panic triggers include standing up and feeling dizzy, a cold wind hitting the body, or urination (Hinton et al., 2001, 2007; Hinton, Hinton et al., 2006).

The Emphasized Symptoms of PD-Type Panic Attacks Will Vary across Cultural Groups

According to the catastrophic cognitions theory of panic, the sensations most prominent in PD panic attacks will vary, depending on which sensations are viewed as potentially catastrophic by members of a society or social group. Given local illness concepts and syndromes, certain bodily sensations will be viewed with more fear, and those symptoms will form the critical symptoms associated with panic in those contexts. The main symptoms focused on by persons suffering PD panic attacks should vary by cultural group; the catastrophic cognitions about a somatic symptom will often be generated by a cultural syndrome specific to that group. Catastrophic cognitions will be produced by a group's understanding of the physiology of anxiety symptoms, its ethnophysiology.[1] The hypothesis that the catastrophic cognitions in a particular group will lead to certain symptoms being emphasized in panic attacks is clearly supported by the fact that certain somatic symptoms not of concern to Westerners give rise to catastrophic cognitions among Cambodian refugees and that those somatic symptoms are prominent in the panic attacks of Cambodian refugees. Examples of this include neck sensations (see earlier in this chapter for a description of neck-related catastrophic cognitions) and tinnitus, which is referred to as "*khyâl* shooting from the ears" and is greatly feared as an indicator of *khyâl* and blood surging into the head (Hinton, Pich et al., 2010). The degree of fear about each of the anxiety-related somatic symptoms will depend on that culture's catastrophic cognitions about a symptom: the conceptualization of how that symptom is generated, its associated physiology, and the "cultural syndromes" that it indicates (on cultural syndromes, see Hinton, Lewis-Fernández, Kirmayer, & Weiss, 2016; Kirmayer & Sartorius, 2007). We showed in the previous section how *khyâl* attacks generate fear of certain sensations that then give rise to panic.

Hybrid Panic Attacks Combining PD and PTSD Characteristics Should Occur

According to the catastrophic cognitions theory of panic, PD-type panic attacks should frequently co-occur with trauma-related panic. Such a comorbidity approach is endorsed by RDoC. Thinking about a trauma or encountering a trauma-evocative stimulus (the location of the event) may trigger various sensations. Those sensations may, in turn, be interpreted as potentially catastrophic: palpitations may recall a trauma event in which the person had experienced strong palpitations, and palpitations may concurrently evoke catastrophic cognitions (e.g., of a heart attack). Or a somatic symptom that is experienced for some reason other than trauma recall, for example, chest tightness owing to hyperventilation, may trigger both catastrophic cognitions and trauma associations.

Such hybrid panic attacks are common in the Cambodian populations, and within the various panic subtypes – neck-focused panic, gastrointestinal-focused panic, orthostatic-triggered panic – the severity of panic is predicted by both catastrophic cognitions and trauma associations that occur during the panic episodes (Hinton, Chhean et al., 2006, 2007; Hinton, Hofmann et al., 2010; Hinton, Hofmann, Pitman, Pollack, & Barlow, 2008; Hinton, So, Pollack, Pitman, & Orr, 2004). Among Cambodian refugees, neck sensations often both induce catastrophic cognitions, for example, of the neck vessel's bursting, and trigger flashbacks: of slave labor experienced during the Pol Pot regime, during which Cambodians were forced to carry dirt-filled buckets suspended at either end of a pole balanced across a shoulder, resulting in extreme neck and shoulder discomfort (Hinton, Chhean et al., 2006; Hinton, Um et al., 2001c). Among Cambodian refugees, stomach sensations result in both catastrophic cognitions (e.g., of "rising *khyâl*") and trauma associations: of starvation-related experiences during the Pol Pot regime – episodes of hunger-induced peristalsis that caused severe abdominal pain (Hinton, Chhean et al., 2007). Orthostasis-induced dizziness among Cambodian refugees may trigger both catastrophic cognitions (e.g., of "*khyâl* overload") and flashbacks of syncopal and near-syncopal episodes during the Pol Pot regime resulting from overwork and starvation (Hinton et al., 2004; Hinton, Hofmann, et al., 2008, 2010).

In fact, as is further shown in the next section, a further hybridity may occur. For example, a worry episode may trigger somatic sensations, which trigger catastrophic cognitions and great fear, and the somatic sensations and great fear trigger trauma recall. Hence, here we have the dynamic interaction of four RDoC dimensions: worry, somatic symptoms, catastrophic cognitions, and trauma recall.

Generalized Anxiety Disorder in Cross-Cultural Perspective

In our work we have found a modified version of Wells's model (see Figure 14.3) useful to explain the workings of generalized anxiety disorder (GAD) in cross-cultural perspective, such as why GAD rates are very high among Southeast Asian refugees and why their GAD-type worry episodes often escalate to panic (Wells, 2009). Key aspects of Wells's (2000, 2005) model include the following: that

(1) catastrophic cognitions about the negative consequences of worry will worsen GAD (i.e., the application of Clark's "fear of fear" model to GAD);
(2) somatic and psychological symptoms form a key aspect of worry episodes;
(3) attempts at self-treatment influence worry perpetuation; and
(4) worry episodes may escalate to panic.

Let us now use a modified version of Wells's model, "The Cross-Cultural Model of Worry" (Figure 14.3), to explore how GAD may vary cross-culturally, using Cambodian examples.

Worry Domains: Cross-Cultural Differences

Individuals from a particular sociocultural group may, first, differ in the types of worry they have (e.g., Cambodians having prominent spiritual concerns), and second, may differ in the amount of worry (e.g., owing to poverty, health concerns, or spiritual concerns). Cambodian refugees have multiple worry domains that include the following areas (Hinton, Nickerson, & Bryant, 2011):

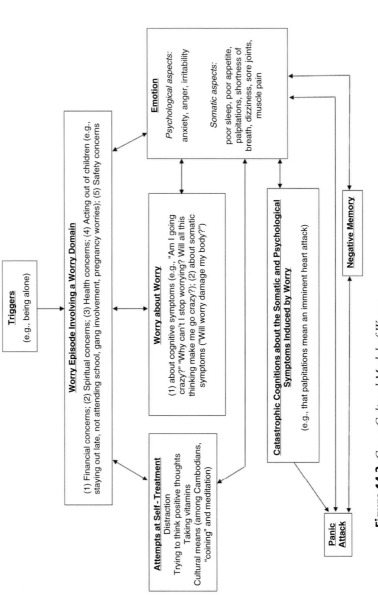

Figure 14.3 *Cross-Cultural Model of Worry*

- *Finances*: concerns about paying the rent, paying for food, paying for dental and health care (often many concerns about the financial status of poor relatives in Cambodia);
- *Spiritual status*: concerns about the spiritual status of relatives who died during the Cambodian genocide, for example, concerns that a relative has not yet been reborn, owing to the manner of death (e.g., the deceased not receiving cremation, which was the case for most who died in the Pol Pot period);
- *Acting-out behaviors of children*: living in impoverished urban environments, Cambodian patients worry often that children will skip school, fail to complete schoolwork, and/or become gang members;
- *Safety*: living in poor urban areas, Cambodians worry about violence, including threat of assaults, observing fights and gunfire in the streets, and frequent house fires; and
- *Health*: owing to (1) Cambodians having elevated rates of diabetes and high blood pressure; (2) Cambodians having multiple somatic symptoms that are generated by high rates of anxiety disorders, including PD and PTSD (the panic-associated somatic symptoms, like dizziness, are often thought to indicate bodily disorder), with those symptoms giving rise to fears of having health problems; and (3) Cambodians having multiple catastrophic cognitions about anxiety-caused somatic and mental symptoms, attributing them to a disturbance of ethnophysiology, to the occurrence of dangerous cultural syndromes such as "weak heart," "*khyâl* attacks," and "hot inside." (Often patients worry about not only their own health but that of others, particularly that of relatives who live in Cambodia and have minimal access to care.)

Catastrophic Cognitions about the Somatic and Psychological Consequences of Worry: Cross-Cultural Differences

Cultural groups may vary in respect to the type and total severity of catastrophic cognitions about the psychological and somatic consequences of worry. For example, many cultures have been shown to have the syndrome "thinking a lot," which produces multiple catastrophic cognitions about the dangers of worry (Hinton, Reis, & de Jong, 2016; Kaiser et al., 2015). Let us examine some Cambodian examples of catastrophic cognitions about the psychological and somatic consequences of worry (Hinton et al., 2011). Cambodians fear that worry will:

- cause mental agitation, permanent deficits in concentration and memory, and ultimately insanity (being Buddhists, Cambodians place great value on a centered and tranquil state of mind, as exemplified by meditation, and consider the agitated cognitions of a worry episode to be the antithesis of that cultural ideal);
- damage the brain by overheating it – analogous to an overworked machine – and so result in (1) poor memory and (2) insanity;
- weaken the mind, which will predispose to worry, creating a vicious cycle of worsening, as worry weakens the mind, which then worsens worry[2];

• weaken the body, possibly leading to (1) poor sleep, leading to depletion; (2) poor appetite, leading to depletion; (3) death from depletion; (4) dizziness, especially on standing; (5) a predisposition to "*khyâl* attacks" and "fever attacks"; (6) poor circulation that may cause stroke; (7) cardiac arrest owing to "heart weakness"; and (8) stroke, which is thought to be caused by poor perfusion of the limbs, resulting from a "weakened heart."

Symptoms Induced by the Worry Episode: Cross-Cultural Differences

The symptoms induced by a worry episode would be expected to vary across cultures for several reasons. In what follows, we explore the processes that may result in such cross-cultural differences, and how each of those processes may explain the frequency – and prominence – of dizziness during the worry episodes of Cambodian refugees.

Inherited biology. Asian individuals appear more predisposed to motion sickness than European Americans, as demonstrated by experimental paradigms (using rotating drums; for a review, see Hinton & Hinton, 2002). Studies indicate that motion sickness is associated with a more general conditionability to dizziness (for a review, as well as an alternative cultural explanation of the motion sickness sensitivity of Asian populations, see Hinton & Hinton, 2002).

Arousal-caused inducibility. High levels of stresses and traumas in a group will cause worry to tend to induce somatic symptoms by purely biological effects (Bouton, Mineka, & Barlow, 2001). Earlier, we indicated that Cambodians have elevated arousal owing to living in high-stress urban environments and having a history of severe trauma (Hinton et al., 2011). Dizziness as well as other symptoms may be induced.

Arousal-caused attentional amplification. As another mechanism, high arousal may lead to a hypervigilant state not only for external threats but also for interior ones, and thus lead to an examination of the body for evidence of dangerous symptoms, for example, dizziness. Cambodian refugees have elevated arousal, as described earlier. As we have documented, Cambodians are hypervigilant to dizziness as an indicator of disorder.

Arousal-caused catastrophizing. High arousal (from past trauma, anxiety disorders, and current stresses) may cause catastrophic-cognitions-type schemas about somatic symptoms – for example, dizziness – to be more prominent. This is because high arousal causes negative interpretive bias, an increased salience of threat schemas (Barlow, 2002; Craske, 2003; Gorman, 2004).

Trauma-network activation. If a symptom is part of trauma memory, then that sensation may tend to be triggered during states of stress or upon encountering other kinds of trauma cues, a kind of somatic flashback (for a review, see Hinton, Howes, & Kirmayer, 2008). Cambodians experienced severe dizziness in the Pol Pot period as a result of starvation, malarial episodes, and other traumas, which may explain in part the salience of dizziness during worry episodes. (Also, there may be a kind of kindling effect so that arousal tends to include the sensation owing to arousal being so often experienced with dizziness.)

Metaphor-guided somatization. Somatic symptoms may be caused by metaphor-induced somatization. The words and phrases used to describe worry and distress may emphasize certain somatic-symptom-related metaphors, leading to the experiencing of that sensation during those emotional states. Multiple Cambodian metaphors configure worry and distress in dizziness-type imagery, which would be expected to result in worry and distress being somaticized as dizziness. In the Cambodian language, if someone causes you to worry – for instance, a child who skips school – one may well say that the child "shakes me like a pill that is shaken in a bottle" (*greulok ok lok khnyom*). In Cambodian, worry is configured as a sort of turning of the head ("think here, think there"; *kut pii nih pii nuh*) or as mental agitation ("think a lot"; *kut caraeun*). In addition, if one is exasperated by many problems, one may say that "my brain is spinning" (*wul khue*), which is sometimes meant in a literal sense.

Cultural-syndrome-caused attentional amplification. If members of a cultural group believe that a certain somatic symptom, such as dizziness, may be induced by worry, and that the symptom indicates a dangerous disorder of physiology, the person will be hypervigilant to that symptom upon engaging in worry. And if even slight dizziness is noted, it will cause fear, and that fear will result in autonomic arousal and increased attentional scrutiny of that symptom, creating a vicious cycle of worsening. As described earlier, Cambodians consider dizziness to be commonly induced by worry, and that it is a symptom indicating a dangerous dysregulation of physiology.

Self-Treatment of Worry Episodes: Cross-Cultural Differences

How others in the family view the worry episode, and how affected individuals treat the worry episode, will have important effects on the course of GAD (Hinton et al., 2011). Cambodians may use Buddhist practices such as meditation to reduce worry. They may also use various tonics to directly increase bodily energy, or may use medicines to increase energy-restorative processes such as sleep and appetite. If the worry episode causes any anxiety-type symptoms (e.g., dizziness, palpitations, cold extremities, muscle soreness), which is usually the case, they will consider the worry episode to indicate a dysregulation of *khyâl* and blood flow – a dysregulation that Cambodians often refer to as a "*khyâl* attack," their term for the sudden onset of anxiety-type somatic symptoms – and will implement culturally indicated treatments. To restore *khyâl* and blood flow, many methods may be used, most commonly "coining," a practice that is common to several East and Southeast Asian medical traditions. To "coin," after first dipping a coin in "*khyâl* oil," a substance thought to promote the release of *khyâl* from the skin pores and to provide heat that dissolves blockages, the edge of the coin is pressed down on the skin and dragged along a limb or along the chest or back, resulting in linear marks. Frequently, family members will perform the coining. Various tonics may be used to directly strengthen the body, or various medications will be taken to promote sleep and appetite, which will in turn increase energy levels in the body. In some cases, the patient may consider the cause to be "bad luck," a condition thought to result in multiple problems and an inability to resolve them, and the patient may consult with priests and other ritual experts who may recommend Buddhist ceremonies to remove "bad luck" (*krueh*).

Worry Episodes Escalating to Panic: Cross-Cultural Differences

As described earlier in this chapter, Cambodian refugees have many catastrophic cognitions about somatic symptoms. These cognitions may cause a worry episode to escalate to panic. For example, if a Cambodian refugee worries about a problem (such as a child skipping school), that anxiety may cause muscular tension that produces neck sensations. These neck sensations will be amplified by the mechanism outlined earlier – attentional amplification – because the patient expects to have neck tension upon worrying. The patient will then worry that the neck sensations indicate that *khyâl* and blood are rising upward in the body, and that this upward surge may cause the neck vessels to burst, or may produce dizziness, tinnitus, and syncope. In addition, the patient will scan the body for other symptoms considered to produce – or indicate – a surge of *khyâl* and blood. One example is cold hands, believed to indicate that *khyâl* and blood are not moving along the limbs, which may cause the "death" of the arms and legs and an upsurge of *khyâl* and blood.

Hybrid Worry Attacks

As described earlier, and as shown in Figure 14.3, the Cross-Cultural Model of Worry, worry events may combine many processes: rumination, arousal, panic, catastrophic cognitions, and negative memory.

Trauma-Related Disorder and PTSD in Cross-Cultural Perspectives

In this section, we argue that trauma results in a broad set of symptoms beyond those outlined in the *DSM*'s PTSD criteria, and that the PTSD symptoms and these other symptoms are locally interpreted (Hinton & Good, 2016). Our model of trauma-related disorder among different cultural groups is based on current cognitive behavioral theories of the generation of PTSD. It is a network model as advocated by trauma theorists, and it is a comorbidity model, and one that includes multiple RDoC dimensions. Our model is based on current theories about the structure of PTSD and its comorbidity with other disorders (Frewen, Schmittmann, Bringmann, & Borsboom, 2013; McNally, 2016; Watson, 2005),

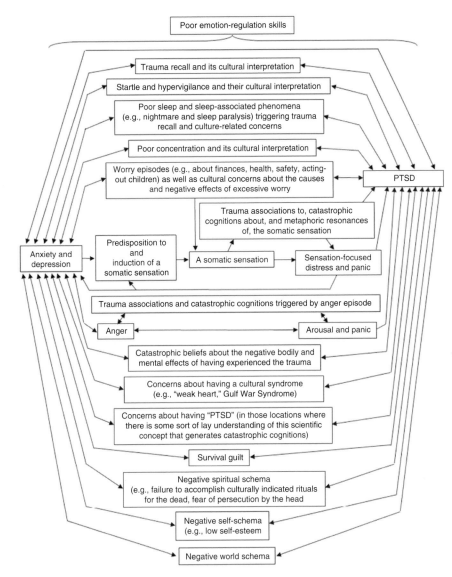

Figure 14.4 *Cross-cultural model of trauma-related disorder: Emphasis on somatic symptoms (in the model, "somatic symptom" could be replaced by "mental symptom")*

and it emphasizes two aspects of current theories of PTSD production and perpetuation: the key role of the catastrophic interpretation of trauma symptoms (another iteration of the "fear of fear" model, but here "fear of trauma-related symptoms") and of dysfunctional "self" and "world" schemas – to which we add "spiritual schema" (Clark & Ehlers, 2004; Dunmore, Clark, & Ehlers, 2001; Foa & Rothbaum, 1998; Halligan, Michael, Clark, & Ehlers, 2003). In our model (see Figure 14.4), several psychopathological processes form feedback loops that produce distress and maintain PTSD. In what follows, we outline those psycho-pathological processes and illustrate their cultural variability by using Cambodian examples.

Unwanted recall of trauma events and its cultural interpretation. Cambodian refugees often have trauma recall: in a nightmare itself; upon awakening from the nightmare owing to trauma associations to the content or to the arousal; upon encountering exteroceptive cues related to the trauma such as seeing someone resembling a perpetrator; upon experiencing interoceptive cues such as dizziness evoking a trauma involving that sensation; upon having an emotion such as anger owing to arousal or similarity of the emotion to that experienced in the trauma. Cambodians often interpret trauma recall catastrophically such as indicating imminent insanity and a kind of mental weakness, the mind floating back to think of the past rather than attending to the present. Cambodians also fear that the trauma recall is caused by a ghost, who forces the dreamer to relive the trauma event.

Startle and hypervigilance and their cultural interpretation. Cambodian patients fear that startle indicates a "weakened heart" that may cause cardiac arrest, and that startle may dislodge the soul and so cause illness and possibly death or insanity, a soul loss syndrome (Hinton, Hinton, Um, Chea, & Sak, 2002).

Poor sleep and its cultural interpretation. Cambodian patients commonly present for psychiatric treatment with the complaint of sleeping only a few hours each night. They fear that poor sleep will increase "weakness," and that the weakness may cause cardiac arrest, "*khyâl* attacks," and other disasters, resulting in a state of hypervigilance for these syndromes and the related symptoms.

Sleep-related disturbances – e.g., nightmares, sleep paralysis (with hypnagogic or hypnopompic hallucinations), and nocturnal panic – and their cultural interpretation. Cambodians have frequent nightmares as well as sleep paralysis that is often accompanied by hypnagogic/hypnopomic hallucinations. These sleep events may recall traumas.[3] Also, Cambodians have catastrophic cognitions about these events. They fear that arousal symptoms may give rise to bodily disaster: a deadly "*khyâl* attack." They fear that nightmares are the actual experiencing of the wandering soul, which may be captured and tortured, and that sleep paralysis is caused by dangerous spirit assault, a pressing down on the body of a ghost (Hinton et al., 2009; Hinton, Pich, Chhean, & Pollack, 2005; Hinton, Pich, Chhean, Pollack, & McNally, 2005).

Poor concentration and its cultural interpretation. As described in the section on worry, Cambodians, who are mainly Buddhists, greatly value a centered and focused mind that attends to events in the current moment. Poor concentration is feared to be a sign of insanity, of a dangerous inner weakness, and of a damaged brain: a brain that is too "loose" in the skull owing to blows sustained in the past (*rolung khue khabaal*) or a brain that has been overheated and damaged from excessive cogitation (*roulieuk khue khabaal*).

Distressful worry episodes and the cultural interpretation of the worry episodes and associated symptoms. Among Cambodian refugees, this worry – for example, about financial problems and poverty – may trigger somatic and psychological symptoms that lead to panic owing to catastrophic cognitions and trauma associations. (See the section in this chapter for a description using Cambodian examples of the cultural variation in worry and GAD.)

Panic attacks that combine PD characteristics (viz., catastrophic cognitions) and PTSD characteristics (viz., trauma recall). The panic attacks are often triggered by somatic sensations among Cambodian refugees, by somatic symptoms that are induced by multiple processes such as exertion, orthostasis, and trauma recall (Hinton, Hofmann et al., 2008). The resulting somatic symptoms give rise to catastrophic cognitions and trauma associations. (The commonality of these panic attacks among Cambodian refugees was described in the earlier sections.)

Anger, including trauma recall triggered by anger and catastrophic cognitions, about anger-induced arousal. Cambodians have prominent anger, and culturally specific interpretations of it, with the anger episode triggering both catastrophic cognitions, for example, that anger-associated heat in the body means a dangerous inner boiling. Anger also often triggers trauma recall, for example, when a child's talking disrespectfully evokes memories of abuse in the Pol Pot period (Hinton, Hsia, Um, & Otto, 2003; Hinton, Rasmussen, Nou, Pollack, & Good, 2009; Nickerson & Hinton, 2011).

The attribution of trauma-related symptoms to a cultural syndrome. In the case of Western military populations, for example, there was the Gulf War Syndrome, leading to catastrophic cognitions about somatic and psychological symptoms and increased anxiety and distress. Cambodians attribute trauma symptoms to multiple syndromes, including "weak heart," "upward hitting *khyâl*," and "*khyâl* attacks"; anxious Cambodians often have motion-type sickness when traveling or when in complex sensory environments such as a large shopping mall, labeling these conditions as "car sickness" (*pul laan*) and "people sickness" (*pul menuh*), respectively, syndromes thought to result from weakness. Also, as described in what follows, trauma symptoms are often attributed to spiritual causes, such as low spiritual energy allowing attack in the form of nightmare and sleep paralysis.

Concerns about having PTSD in locations where the lay understanding of the disorder generates catastrophic cognitions. If laypersons in a group know of the scientific syndrome of PTSD, then their lay understanding of "PTSD" will have important implications for PTSD severity. That understanding will produce certain catastrophic cognitions about trauma symptoms. One needs to distinguish

PTSD as a scientific syndrome (as understood by a psychologist) from PTSD as a popular syndrome (as understood by a layperson), what might be called a *scientific-syndrome PTSD* versus *popular-syndrome PTSD* (as elaborated in self-help books, commercials, the media, and conversation). If members of a cultural group have considerable catastrophic cognitions about PTSD and its symptoms, this will worsen the disorder and result in a certain course – for example, more disability, the amplification of certain symptoms like anger and poor concentration. (The lay understanding of PTSD is another "cultural syndrome," but here we give it its own category.)

Survival guilt. This may be, for example, from having witnessed others dying from starvation, torture, or murder (Resick & Schnicke, 1996). Among Cambodian refugees, who often watched relatives die from starvation and other preventable causes, survival guilt is heightened by cultural ideas about the effects of neglecting death rites and fears about the ability of the deceased to afflict the living (Hinton, Peou, Joshi, Nickerson, & Simon, 2013). That is, survival guilt often involves spiritual schemas.

Catastrophic beliefs about the bodily and mental effects of trauma. These include, for example, concerns that one's body or mind has been permanently damaged (Clark & Ehlers, 2004; Dunmore et al., 2001; Halligan et al., 2003). Often Cambodian refugees worry that trauma has caused irreparable harming of the vascular vessels of the body, predisposing to stroke and other disorders, and that it has caused a permanent weakening of the body, so that like a depleted battery, it can never be fully recharged again (Hinton et al., 2002); or as described earlier, poor concentration may be ascribed to having received a blow to the head in the past that has caused the brain to become too loose in the skull, with some patients claiming to hear it move upon turning the head. As these examples suggest, catastrophic cognitions about the long-term effects of trauma will involve "cultural syndromes" and ideas about ethnophysiology – and will relate to the local ethnopsychology. These might be called body and mind schemas that result from trauma. (These may be considered parts of the self-schema.)

Negative spiritual schemas. This refers to the meaning of the trauma and its related symptoms in respect to the local conceptualization of spirits and other supernatural forces. Cambodian patients worry about being assaulted by demons and the spirits of the deceased, especially if they consider themselves to be in a weakened spiritual or physical state; for instance, if someone died during the Pol Pot period without proper cremation rites being performed, the deceased may attack the living in nightmares or at other times. In the case of a deceased relative, trauma-related distress may play out in a bereavement idiom, in concerns about the spiritual status of the deceased (Hinton et al., 2013).

Negative self-schemas. These cause low self-esteem and other effects (Benight & Bandura, 2004; Foa et al., 1999). For many individuals, living through the Pol Pot period created a sense of helplessness and low self-efficacy as a result of being treated as a slave for many years by the Khmer Rouge. Other processes like survival guilt and an inability to work will also create negative self-schemas.

Negative world-schemas. These create a feeling of hopelessness, a lack of meaning, and a sense of injustice (Foa et al., 1999). For many individuals, living through the Pol Pot period created a deep sense of the world being an unjust place; for these individuals, the Cambodian genocide calls into question the very nature of Cambodian culture and of Buddhism itself.

Anxiety and depression. These disorders will induce somatic symptoms and increase arousal, hypervigilance, negative interpretive bias, and amygdala reactivity (Barlow, 2002), with these processes resulting from anxiety and depression worsening all the psychopathological processes outlined earlier.

Poor emotional regulation. This results from such deficits as decreased ability to distance and distract from affects as well as change affects (Cisler, Olatunji, Feldner, & Forsyth, 2010; Cloitre, Koenen, Cohen, & Han, 2002). Poor emotional regulation influences all the motion-related processes outlined earlier. Cambodians have impaired emotion regulation (e.g., of anger), and in an attempt at recovery, many patients utilize emotion-regulation techniques taught in the context of Buddhism (Nickerson & Hinton, 2011). An important area of research concerns whether local healing traditions can improve the ability to emotionally regulate.

Concluding Remarks

In this chapter we have explored the cross-cultural variation of certain anxiety disorders as defined in the *DSM* (PAD, GAD [worry], and PTSD) by using a particular analytic approach. Our approach was RDoCian, attending to dimensions (e.g., catastrophic cognitions, worry, trauma recall), combined with a network analysis framework, highlighting comorbidity in dynamic models. In particular, we emphasized cognitive-causative processes, such as catastrophic cognitions, in these models. This RDoCian comorbid approach as represented in the models can guide the analysis of panic attacks (panic disorder), GAD (worry), and trauma-related disorder (PTSD) in cross-cultural perspective. It might be called a dynamic network model of anxiety disorders.

The current chapter suggests that to examine an anxiety disorder in cross-cultural perspective, one should evaluate not only whether it can be "diagnosed" and its features found in other cultural contexts but additionally how that particular type of disorder is generated in other cultural contexts. This might be called the *cross-cultural study of psychopathological mechanisms*. Psychological theorists have put forth theories of how anxiety disorders are generated, and those theories can be tested by examining cross-cultural data. Cross-cultural research will provide insights into the validity of the *DSM* as applied to other cultures, will give insights into how the *DSM* might be revised to reflect true, basic psychopathological processes, valid for all cultures, rather than being a somewhat arbitrary set of categories; and will give insights into the exact workings of psychopathological processes in other cultural contexts.

Using an approach that examines psychopathological mechanisms in cross-cultural perspective, we illustrated the role of catastrophic cognitions in the anxiety disorders. Building on this finding, and in light of the cross-cultural evidence, we argue that it is important to investigate a group's ethnophysiology and cultural syndromes, and the related catastrophic cognitions. For instance, if a patient has a certain symptom in a panic attack, one must determine whether the patient attributes the symptom to a disorder of physiology or to a cultural syndrome, that is, examine the symptom-related ethnophyisology and cultural syndromes. As outlined in this chapter, ethnophysiologies and cultural syndromes are not just "idioms of distress" – but rather they give rise to catastrophic cognitions that play a key role in anxiety disorder, including PD, GAD, and PTSD.

In respect to comorbidity, the current review suggests that it is arbitrary to consider GAD, PD, and PTSD to be totally separate entities, or put more broadly, worry, GAD, panic attacks, PD, and PTSD. When the putative psychological mechanisms generating these disorders are carefully examined in cross-cultural context, hybrid entities are often seen to occur. For example, it might be more useful to have diagnostic category for panic attacks, with an optional qualification as to whether the attacks feature catastrophic cognitions (CC-type panic attacks), trauma associations (TA-type panic attacks), or both (CC-TA-type panic attacks). Triggers might be specified, for example, worry in the case of worry-triggered panic attacks. This is a phenomenological description that gives importance to cognitions and may help guide therapeutic approaches.

In addition, the current chapter would suggest the need for analyzing "worry episodes," what might be called "worry attacks," not just GAD (this is, in fact, a more RDoCian approach, given that "worry" is a rumination dimension), and would suggest the need to determine the worry-episode-induced symptoms (e.g., dizziness, muscle tension, cold extremities), including whether the episode some-times escalates to panic – and if so, a way to classify the panic in respect to the three types mentioned earlier (i.e., a CC-, TA-, or CC-TA-panic attack). As indicated for Cambodian refugees, GAD-type worry episodes often trigger PD-type catastrophic cognitions and PTSD-type trauma associations, which in turn increases anxiety, depression, and health concerns, so producing a vicious cycle of worsening. This model of anxiety psychopathology gives clues as to how comorbidity commonly occurs between GAD and other disorders, such as PD and PTSD, a comorbidity that is commonly observed in other cultural contexts, and this model gives clues as to how such comorbidity is perpetuated. This model of worry-related psycho-pathology can be investigated by examining its validity in other cultural contexts.

As suggested in the current review, an adequate examination of anxiety disorders in other cultures requires multiple analytic approaches. One should use the models we have presented to investigate PD, GAD, and PTSD in different cultural contexts, investigating each variable in the model for the disorder in question. For example, these models also require an investigation of the local conceptualization of symptoms of the group, determining the following:

- ethnophysiological and ethnopsychological understandings of the cause and consequences of anxiety symptoms;
- cultural syndromes to which anxiety symptoms are attributed;
- catastrophic cognitions about anxiety symptoms; and
- local ideas about how the anxiety symptoms should be treated.

The models presented here have implications beyond diagnostic considerations. Only through such investigation can adequate treatments of anxiety disorders in other cultural contexts be developed (Hinton & Good, 2009, 2016; Hinton & Patel, in press; Hinton, Rivera, Hofmann, Barlow, & Otto, 2012). It is critical to determine the local psychological mechanisms that produce the disorder in question in order to address those processes in treatment. The models identify important treatment targets in disorders. In fact, the models have guided our treatments for anxiety disorders in other cultural groups (Hinton et al., 2012; Hinton & Patel, in press). Core symptoms, like somatic symptoms and panic need to be identified and then treated, for example, by addressing local catastrophic cognitions and teaching techniques to reduce arousal and somatic distress such as applied stretching. Worry is a key process to address in many groups, leading to looping processes, each part of which may be targeted: this might be through meditation to help treat worry and other attention control strategies. In general, the models emphasize the need, when designing treatments, to analyze symptom dimensions (RDoCian approach) and the interaction of symptoms (network models). These dimensions and symptom interactions can then be targeted in a culturally sensitive way, prioritizing the targeting of key processes in causal networks.

In sum, we have presented here causal network models of anxiety disorders – for panic attacks, PD, GAD, and trauma-related disorder (PTSD) – that suggest how these anxiety disorders can be investigated in cross-cultural perspective. The models can also be used in evaluation and in designing treatment, and in investigating the cross-cultural variation in the anxiety disorders.

Notes

1. The ethnopsychology and the understanding of mental symptoms will likewise be a key issue.
2. Cambodians consider engaging in worry to be both a cause of weakness, namely, a "weakness cause," and an indicator of being weak, namely, a "weakness indicator." This dual status is true of other worry symptoms such as poor sleep and appetite. In this way, vicious cycles of worsening occur: the patient thinking that worry is causing poor sleep, and that poor sleep will weaken the body and cause more worry.
3. The trauma recall may be in the form of a nightmare that relives a trauma or the trauma recall upon awakening, from the arousal or from the content, for example, a dream of being chased evoking any trauma characterized by threat. The hypnagogic/hypnopompic hallucination may be of a trauma perpetrator or through arousal and the sense of threat recall trauma.

References

American Psychiatric Association. (2013). *Diagnostic and Statistical Manual of Mental Disorders* (5th edn). Washington, DC: American Psychiatric Association.

Barlow, D. H. (2002). *Anxiety and Its Disorders: The Nature and Treatment of Anxiety and Panic* (2nd edn). New York, NY: Guilford Press.

Beck, A. T. (1988). Cognitive approaches to panic disorder: Theory and therapy. In S. Rachman & J. Maser (eds.), *Panic: Psychological Perspectives* (pp. 33–54). Hillsdale, MI: Lawrence Erlbaum.

Benight, C. C. & Bandura, A. (2004). Social cognitive theory of posttraumatic recovery: The role of perceived self-efficacy. *Behaviour Research Therapy*, *42*(10), 1129–1148.

Borsboom, D. & Cramer, A. O. (2013). Network analysis: An integrative approach to the structure of psychopathology. *Annual Review of Clinical Psychology*, *9*, 91–121.

Bouton, M., Mineka, S., & Barlow, D. (2001). A modern learning theory perspective on the etiology of panic disorder. *Psychological Review*, 108, 4–32.

Bui, E. & Fava, M. (2017). From depression to anxiety, and back. *Acta Psychiatrica Scandinavica*, 10, *136*(4), 341–342.

Casey, B. J., Craddock, N., Cuthbert, B. N., Hyman, S. E., Lee, F. S., & Ressler, K. J. (2013). DSM-5 and RDoC: Progress in psychiatry research? *Nature Reviews: Neuroscience*, *14*(11), 810–814.

Chambless, D. L., Caputo, G. C., Bright, P., & Gallagher, R. (1984). Assessment of fear of fear in agoraphobics: The body sensations questionnaire and the agoraphobic cognitions questionnaire. *Journal of Counseling and Clinical Psychology*, 6, 1090–1097.

Cisler, J. M., Olatunji, B. O., Feldner, M. T., & Forsyth, J. P. (2010). Emotion regulation and the anxiety disorders: An integrative review. *Journal of Psychopathology and Behavioral Assessment*, *32*(1), 68–82.

Clark, D. M. (1986). A cognitive approach to panic. *Behaviour Research and Therapy, 24*, 461–470.

Clark, D. M. & Ehlers, A. (2004). Posttraumatic stress disorder: From cognitive theory to therapy. In R. L. Leahy (ed.), *Contemporary Cognitive Therapy* (pp. 141–160). New York, NY: Guilford Press.

Cloitre, M., Koenen, K. C., Cohen, L. R., & Han, H. (2002). Skills training in affective and interpersonal regulation followed by exposure: A phase-based treatment for PTSD related to childhood abuse. *Journal of Consulting and Clinical Psychology, 70*(5), 1067–1074.

Craske, M. G. (2003). *Origins of Phobias and Anxiety Disorders: Why More Women Than Men?* Amsterdam; Boston, MA: Elsevier.

Dunmore, E., Clark, D. M., & Ehlers, A. (2001). A prospective investigation of the role of cognitive factors in persistent posttraumatic stress disorder (PTSD) after physical and sexual assault. *Behaviour Research and Therapy, 39*, 1063–1084.

Foa, E. B., Ehlers, A., Clark, D. M., Tolin, D. F., & Orsillo, S. M. (1999). The Posttraumatic Cognitions Inventory (PTCI): Development and validation. *Psychological Assessment, 11*, 303–314.

Foa, E. B. & Rothbaum, B. O. (1998). *Treating the Trauma of Rape: Cognitive-Behavioral Therapy for PTSD*. New York, NY: Guilford Press.

Frewen, P. A., Schmittmann, V. D., Bringmann, L. F., & Borsboom, D. (2013). Perceived causal relations between anxiety, posttraumatic stress and depression: Extension to moderation, mediation, and network analysis. *European Journal of Psychotraumatology*, 4.

Gorman, J. M. (2004). *Fear and Anxiety: Benefits of Translational Research*. Washington, DC: American Psychiatric Association.

Halligan, S. L., Michael, T., Clark, D. M., & Ehlers, A. (2003). Posttraumatic stress disorder following assault: The role of cognitive processing, trauma memory, and appraisal. *Journal of Consulting and Clinical Psychology*, *71*, 410–431.

Hinton, D. E., Ba, P., Peou, S., & Um, K. (2000). Panic disorder among Cambodian refugees attending a psychiatric clinic: Prevalence and subtypes. *General Hospital Psychiatry*, *22*, 437–444.

Hinton, D. E., Chau, H., Nguyen, L., Nguyen, M., Pham, T., Quinn, S., et al. (2001). Panic disorder among Vietnamese refugees attending a psychiatric clinic: Prevalence and subtypes. *General Hospital Psychiatry*, *23*, 337–344.

Hinton, D. E., Chhean, D., Fama, J. M., Pollack, M. H., & McNally, R. J. (2007). Gastrointestinal-focused panic attacks among Cambodian refugees: Associated psychopathology, flashbacks, and catastrophic cognitions. *Journal of Anxiety Disorders*, *21*, 42–58.

Hinton, D. E., Chhean, D., Pich, V., Um, K., Fama, J. M., & Pollack, M. H. (2006). Neck-focused panic attacks among Cambodian refugees; A logistic and linear regression analysis. *Journal of Anxiety Disorders*, *20*, 119–138.

Hinton, D. E. & Good, B. J. (eds.). (2009). *Culture and Panic Disorder*. Palo Alto, CA: Stanford University Press.

Hinton, D. E. & Good, B. J. (eds.). (2016). *Culture and PTSD: Trauma in Historical and Global Perspective*. Philadelphia, PA: University of Pennsylvania Press.

Hinton, D. E., Hinton, A., Chhean, D., Pich, V., Loeum, J. R., & Pollack, M. H. (2009). Nightmares among Cambodian refugees: The breaching of concentric ontological security. *Culture, Medicine, and Psychiatry*, *33*, 219–265.

Hinton, D. E., Hinton, L., Tran, M., Nguyen, L., Hsia, C., & Pollack, M. H. (2006). Orthostatically induced panic attacks among Vietnamese refugees: Associated psychopathology, flashbacks, and catastrophic cognitions. *Depression and Anxiety*, *23*(2), 113–115.

Hinton, D. E., Hinton, L., Tran, M., Nguyen, M., Nguyen, L., Hsia, C., et al. (2007). Orthostatic panic attacks among Vietnamese refugees. *Transcultural Psychiatry*, *44*, 515–545.

Hinton, D. E. & Hinton, S. D. (2002). Panic disorder, somatization, and the new cross-cultural psychiatry; The seven bodies of a medical anthropology of panic. *Culture, Medicine, and Psychiatry*, 26, 155–178.

Hinton, D. E., Hinton, S. D., Um, K., Chea, A., & Sak, S. (2002). The Khmer "weak heart" syndrome: Fear of death from palpitations. *Transcultural Psychiatry*, *39*, 323–344.

Hinton, D. E., Hofmann, S. G., Orr, S. P., Pitman, R. K., Pollack, M. H., & Pole, N. (2010). A psychobiocultural model of orthostatic panic among Cambodian refugees: Flashbacks, catastrophic cognitions, and reduced orthostatic blood-pressure response. *Psychological Trauma: Theory, Research, Practice, and Policy*, *2*, 63–70.

Hinton, D. E., Hofmann, S. G., Pitman, R. K., Pollack, M. H., & Barlow, D. H. (2008). The panic attack–PTSD model: Applicability to orthostatic panic among Cambodian refugee. *Cognitive Behaviour Therapy, 27,* 101–116.

Hinton, D. E., Howes, D., & Kirmayer, L. J. (2008). Toward a medical anthropology of sensations: Definitions and research agenda. *Transcultural Psychiatry, 45*(2), 142–162.

Hinton, D. E., Hsia, C., Um, K., & Otto, M. W. (2003). Anger-associated panic attacks in Cambodian refugees with PTSD: A multiple baseline examination of clinical data. *Behaviour Research and Therapy, 41*(6), 647–654.

Hinton, D. E., Lewis-Fernández, R., Kirmayer, L. J., & Weiss, M. G. (2016). Supplementary module 1: Explanatory module. In R. Lewis-Fernandez, N. Aggarwal, L. Hinton, D. Hinton & L. J. Kirmayer (eds.), *The DSM-5 Handbook on the Cultural Formulation Interview* (pp. 53–67). Washington, DC: American Psychiatric Press.

Hinton, D. E., Nickerson, A., & Bryant, R. A. (2011). Worry, worry attacks, and PTSD among Cambodian refugees: A path analysis investigation. *Social Science and Medicine, 72,* 1817–1825.

Hinton, D. E., Park, L., Hsia, C., Hofmann, S., & Pollack, M. H. (2009). Anxiety disorder presentations in Asian populations: A review. *CNS Neuroscience and Therapeutics, 15*(3), 295–303.

Hinton, D. E., & Patel, A. (in press). Cultural adaptations of CBT. *Psychiatry Clinics.*

Hinton, D. E., Peou, S., Joshi, S., Nickerson, A., & Simon, N. (2013). Normal grief and complicated bereavement among traumatized Cambodian refugees: Cultural context and the central role of dreams of the deceased. *Culture, Medicine, and Psychiatry, 37,* 427–464.

Hinton, D. E., Pich, V., Chhean, D., & Pollack, M. H. (2005). "The ghost pushes you down": Sleep paralysis-type panic attacks in a Khmer refugee population. *Transcultural Psychiatry, 42,* 46–78.

Hinton, D. E., Pich, V., Chhean, D., Pollack, M. H., & McNally, R. J. (2005). Sleep paralysis among Cambodian refugees: Association with PTSD diagnosis and severity. *Depression and Anxiety, 22*(2), 47–51.

Hinton, D. E., Pich, V., Marques, L., Nickerson, A., & Pollack, M. H. (2010). *Khyâl* attacks: A key idiom of distress among traumatized Cambodian refugees. *Culture, Medicine and Psychiatry, 34,* 244–278.

Hinton, D. E., Rasmussen, A., Nou, L., Pollack, M. H., & Good, M. J. (2009). Anger, PTSD, and the nuclear family: A study of Cambodian refugees. *Social Science and Medicine, 69,* 1387–1394.

Hinton, D. E., Reis, R., & de Jong, J. T. (2016). A transcultural model of the centrality of "thinking a lot" in psychopathologies across the globe and the process of localization: A Cambodian refugee example. *Culture, Medicine, and Psychiatry, 40,* 570–619.

Hinton, D. E., Rivera, E., Hofmann, S. G., Barlow, D. H., & Otto, M. W. (2012). Adapting CBT for traumatized refugees and ethnic minority patients: Examples from culturally adapted CBT (CA-CBT). *Transcultural Psychiatry, 49,* 340–365.

Hinton, D. E., So, V., Pollack, M. H., Pitman, R. K., & Orr, S. P. (2004). The psychophysiology of orthostatic panic in Cambodian refugees attending a psychiatric clinic. *Journal of Psychopathology and Behavioral Assessment, 26,* 1–13.

Hinton, D. E., Um, K., & Ba, P. (2001a). *Kyol goeu* ("wind overload") part I: A cultural syndrome of orthostatic panic among Khmer refugees. *Transcultural Psychiatry 38*, 403–432.

Hinton, D. E., Um, K., & Ba, P. (2001b). *Kyol goeu* ("wind overload") part II: Prevalence, characteristics and mechanisms of *kyol goeu* and near-*kyol goeu* episodes of Khmer patients attending a psychiatric clinic. *Transcultural Psychiatry, 38* 433–460.

Hinton, D. E., Um, K., & Ba, P. (2001c). A unique panic-disorder presentation among Khmer refugees: The sore-neck syndrome. *Culture, Medicine, and Psychiatry, 25* (3), 297–316.

Hofmann, S. G., Curtiss, J., & McNally, R. J. (2016). A complex network perspective on clinical science. *Perspectives in Psychological Science, 11*(5), 597–605.

Kaiser, B., Haroz, E., Kohrt, B., Bolton, P., Bass, J., & Hinton, D. E. (2015). Thinking too much: A systematic review of a common idiom of distress. *Social Science and Medicine, 147*, 170–183.

Katon, W. (1984). Panic disorder and somatization. Review of 55 cases. *American Journal of Medicine, 77*(1), 101–106.

Khawaja, N. G. & Oei, T. P. (1998). Catastrophic cognitions in panic disorder with and without agoraphobia. *Clinical Psychology Review, 18*(3), 341–365.

Kirmayer, L. J. & Sartorius, N. (2007). Cultural models and somatic syndromes. *Psychosomatic Medicine, 69*, 832–840.

McNally, R. J. (1994). *Panic Disorder: A Critical Analysis*. New York, NY: Guilford Press.

McNally, R. J. (2012). The ontology of posttraumatic stress disorder: Natural kind, social construction, or causal system? *Clinical Psychology Science and Practice, 19*(3), 220–228.

McNally, R. J. (2016). Can network analysis transform psychopathology? *Behavior Research Therapy, 86*, 95–104.

Morris, S. E. & Cuthbert, B. N. (2012). Research Domain Criteria: Cognitive systems, neural circuits, and dimensions of behavior. *Dialogues in Clinical Neuroscience, 14*(1), 29–37.

Nickerson, A. & Hinton, D. E. (2011). Anger regulation in traumatized Cambodian refugees: The perspectives of Buddhist Monks. *Culture, Medicine, and Psychiatry, 35*, 396–416.

Noyes, R. & Hoehn-Saric, R. (1998). *The Anxiety Disorders*. Cambridge: Cambridge University Press.

Rapee, R. M., Craske, M. G., & Barlow, D. H. (1994). Assessment instrument for panic disorder that includes fear of sensation-producing activities: The Albany Panic and Phobia Questionnaire. *Anxiety, 1*(3), 114–122.

Resick, P. & Schnicke, M. (1996). *Cognitive Processing Therapy for Rape Victims*. London; New Delhi: Sage Publications.

Sanislow, C. A., Pine, D. S., Quinn, K. J., Kozak, M. J., Garvey, M. A., Heinssen, R. K., et al. (2010). Developing constructs for psychopathology research: Research domain criteria. *Journal of Abnormal Psychology, 119*(4), 631–639.

Watson, D. (2005). Rethinking the mood and anxiety disorders: A quantitative hierarchical model for *DSM-V. Journal of Abnormal Psychology, 114*(4), 522–536.

Wells, A. (2009). *Metacognitive Therapy for Anxiety and Depression*. New York, NY: Guilford.

Etiology and Phenomenology of Specific Anxiety Disorders

15 Specific Phobia

Peter J. Castagna, Marie Nebel-Schwalm,
Thompson E. Davis III, and Peter Muris

The *Diagnostic and Statistical Manual of Mental Disorders, 5th edition* (*DSM-5*) (American Psychiatric Association, 2013) outlines nearly a dozen anxiety disorders and phobias. Most of these disorders include a criterion requiring interference, or clinically significant distress, in academic, social, occupational, or other important areas of functioning. Overall, anxiety disorders have a moderate to high impact on functioning (Demyttenaere et al., 2004), and, typically, are accompanied by shyness, social withdrawal, skill deficits, maladaptive cognitions, and problematic social, parent, and sibling relations (Elizabeth et al., 2006; Ezpeleta et al., 2001; Gallagher & Cartwright-Hatton, 2008; Reijntjes, Kamphuis, Prinzie, & Telch, 2010; Rubin, 2014). Since a majority of adults with anxiety disorders struggled with anxiety at some point in childhood, it is important to have an understanding of developmental biopsychosocial factors associated with childhood anxiety as they shape and provide context for anxiety disorders that develop in later life. Developmentally, specific phobias typically have one of the earliest onsets (American Psychiatric Association, 2013), are arguably the most prevalent (Kessler, Petukhova, Sampson, Zaslavsky, & Wittchen, 2012), and are the focus of the current chapter.

The goal of the current chapter is to review the epidemiology, etiology, and phenomenology of specific phobias in both childhood and adulthood. To this end, we begin by reviewing the epidemiology of specific phobias throughout the life span. Following this, we describe the etiology outlined by a number of theoretical models. Next, we describe clinical presentations of individuals with various specific phobias, noting the course, possible differential diagnoses, and typical comorbidities. Finally, we end by integrating this information with the Research and Domain criteria (RDoC) initiative developed by the US National Institute of Mental Health (NIMH).

Specific Phobia Diagnostic Criteria

"Specific phobia" was termed "simple phobia" in the *Diagnostic and Statistical Manual of Mental Disorders, 3rd edition* (*DSM–III*) (American Psychiatric Association, 1980) and the *Diagnostic and Statistical Manual of Mental Disorders, 3rd edition revised* (*DSM–III–R*) (American Psychiatric

Association, 1987), but altered to "specific phobia" in the *Diagnostic and Statistical Manual of Mental Disorders, 4th edition* (*DSM-IV*) (American Psychiatric Association, 1994) and the *Diagnostic and Statistical Manual of Mental Disorders, 4th edition, text revision* (*DSM-IV-TR*) (American Psychiatric Association, 2000). According to the *DSM-5*, specific phobias are characterized by a marked fear or anxiety about a specific object or situation (e.g., animals, heights, blood), where, in children, the fear can be expressed by crying, tantrums, freezing, or clinging. The feared object/situation always provokes immediate fear and is actively avoided (or endured with intense fear or anxiety), and the fear is out of proportion to the actual danger posed by the specific object/situation and to the sociocultural context. The fear, anxiety, or avoidance should also show evidence of being persistent, typically lasting six months or more. As with all anxiety disorders, the symptoms must cause clinically significant distress or impairment in an important area of functioning (e.g., social, occupational, academic), and are not explained by another mental disorder. When diagnosing a specific phobia, the clinician must specify the phobic stimulus. The *DSM-5* outlines five specifiers: animal (e.g., dogs, snakes, spiders), natural environment (e.g., storms, water, heights), blood-injection -injury (BII) (e.g., needles, blood, medical procedures), situational (e.g., airplanes, cars, elevators), or other (e.g., choking, vomiting, loud noises).

The decision to create specifiers, first occurring in the *DSM-IV*, was based on findings that specific phobia subtypes differ on their etiology, age of onset, physiological reaction, and focus of apprehension (Craske & Sipsas, 1992). Moreover, factor analyses of specific phobia subtypes have found that animal and BII represent separate factors, whereas natural environment and situational subtypes tend to cluster together (Fredrickson, Annas, Fischer, & Wik, 1996; Muris, Schmidt, & Merckelbach, 1999). When multiple specific phobias are present, which occurs in approximately 75% of individuals meeting criteria (American Psychiatric Association, 2013), the clinician codes multiple specific phobias, specifying the phobic object (e.g., specific phobia, natural environment, and specific phobia, animal).

Impairment Associated with Specific Phobias

As children and adolescents continue to learn about the world, it is a normal part of development to have transitory fears (Craske, 1997; Davis & Ollendick, 2011; Ollendick, 1979). Normal fear is defined as the typical reaction to a real or imagined threat that is considered an essential and adaptive aspect of development (Morris & Kratochwill, 1983; Muris & Field, 2011). Specific phobias, in contrast, can be differentiated from normal developmental fears in that the phobic reaction is excessive and out of proportion to the demands of the situation, leads to avoidance, persists over time, and is maladaptive (Silverman & Rabian, 1994). Fears are usually described as reactions to specific stimuli that evoke escape and avoidance behaviors (Castagna, Davis, & Lilly, 2017; Davis et al., 2013; Fonseca & Perrin, 2011). In contrast, anxiety is viewed as a diffuse reaction to less specific stimuli (Barlow, 2002). Although these terms have been used interchangeably in the past, there are key differences between them.

A specific phobia in childhood can be mild, age-specific, and transitory (Ollendick, 1979); however, some of these fears can also become intense and persistent, causing distress and impairment (Muris & Merckelbach, 2000; Muris, Merckelbach, Mayer, & Prins, 2000; Spence & McCathie, 1993). As well, adolescents and young adults (i.e., 14 to 24 years old) with a specific phobia report severe impairment in their routine activities (Wittchen, Nelson, & Lachner, 1998). Further, between 9% and 32% of these phobic individuals report impairment in numerous areas of their lives (e.g., at work or school, leisure activities, and social contact). Last, Perrin, Hersen, and Kazdin (1996) noted that specific phobias have the poorest rate of recovery, when prospectively examining the course and outcome of anxiety disorders in clinically referred children. Of adults with specific phobia, only 10–12% will seek treatment (Stinson et al., 2007). They will likely have a fear for nine years on average before it develops into a specific phobia; however, adults live with their fear an average of 20 years before seeking treatment, even once it is recognized (Antony, Brown, & Barlow, 1997; Stinson et al., 2007). Overall, a specific phobia is a highly prevalent, persistent, often chronic anxiety disorder associated with serious impairment (Alonso et al., 2004; Depla, Margreet, van Balkom, & de Graaf, 2008; Goisman et al., 1998; Magee, Eaton, Wittchen, McGonagle, & Kessler, 1996; Oosterink, De Jongh, & Aartman, 2009). It may be unsurprising, then, that specific phobias present a substantial economic burden and are a serious public health problem (Alonso et al., 2004; Greenberg et al., 1999). In all, a diagnosis of specific phobia, in childhood and adulthood, is associated with intense, persistent fear that causes significant distress and impairment, often in a number of domains, which poses a serious public health problem.

Epidemiology of Specific Phobia

Epidemiological studies assess various types of prevalence rates. The lifetime prevalence is the percentage of individuals who have a particular disorder once in their life. In contrast, the annual prevalence is the proportion of individuals who experienced the disorder in the 12 months prior to the survey. Therefore, disorders of longer duration are likely to be overrepresented in annual prevalence rates compared with those of short duration. Finally, the point prevalence is the percentage of individuals with a disorder on a certain day. This section focuses on the lifetime, 12-month, and point prevalence of specific phobia, and its subtypes, as well as age of onset and important sex differences in adults and youth.

Adult Samples

An estimated 40% of the population suffers from one or more fears of a specific object or situation at some point in their lives (Curtis, Magee, Eaton, Wittchen, & Kessler,

1998; Depla et al., 2008; Oosterink, De Jongh, & Hoogstraten, 2009). Specific phobias are the most prevalent group of mental disorders, with a lifetime prevalence rate of 12.5% in adults 18 years and older, with a median age of onset of seven years (Kessler, Berglund et al., 2005). In adults aged 18 to 64, the 12-month and point prevalence have been found to be 10.1% (Kessler et al., 2012) and 9.9% (Becker et al., 2007), respectively. Finally, women appear to have higher prevalence rates of fears and specific phobias than men (e.g., 15.6% versus 8.2% collapsed across specific phobias) (Fredrikson, Annas, Fischer, & Wik, 1996; Oosterink et al., 2009).

Youth Samples Anywhere between 30% and 40% of youth report being afraid of a specific object or situation (Essau et al., 2000; Ollendick, King, & Frary, 1989). In a large sample of 10,148 adolescents aged 13 to 17 years, specific phobia was the most common disorder with a 15.8% 12-month prevalence and a 9.5% 30-day prevalence (Kessler et al., 2012). The lifetime prevalence of specific phobia in youth samples has typically been smaller, ranging between 2.3% and 3.5% (Essau et al., 2000; Kashani, Orvaschel, Rosenberg, & Reid, 1989; Wittchen et al., 1998). The rate found in clinics is much higher than that in an epidemiological setting. For example, in the Pittsburgh Clinic Sample that included 188 children and adolescents with anxiety disorders, it was found that 20% met criteria for a specific phobia (Last, Perrin, Hersen, & Kazdin, 1992).

Strauss and Last (1993) reported that the peak ages for specific phobias are at 10–11 and 12–13 years, with the mean age of onset being around 7–8 years. However, there is evidence that specific phobia subtypes differ in terms of prevalence, sex distribution, and age of onset. For example, in the natural environment, animal, blood-injury subtype and other types, the age of onset varies between 8 and 13 years (Czajkowski, Kendler, Tambs, Røysamb, & Reichborn-Kjennerud, 2011; Depla et al., 2008; Lipsitz et al., 2001), while the situational subtype appears to have a higher age of onset, typically around 14 to 15 years (Depla et al., 2008). As well, Öst (1987, 1991) reported that the age of onset for animal phobia was 7 years, blood phobia 9 years, dental phobia 12 years, and BII phobia between 7 and 9 years.

Paralleling the skewed gender distribution in adult samples, the prevalence of specific phobia typically differs between girls and boys. In the Wittchen et al. (1998) study, significantly more girls than boys met *DSM-IV* criteria for a specific phobia, with percentages of 3.3% versus 1.2%. Notably, it is unclear what drives the difference between boys and girls in the prevalence of specific phobia, though sex-role stereotyping (Sarason, Davidson, Lighthall, Waite, & Ruebush, 1960) and differences in sex hormones (Seeman, 1997) have been suggested.

Cultural, Racial, and Ethnic Considerations

Few studies address cultural differences in the prevalence of specific phobias across racial and ethnic groups within the United States; however, the research conducted has found important differences. Karno and colleagues (1989) found that prevalence rates of specific phobia were higher among Mexican-Americans when compared to Caucasian-Americans. Interestingly, rates were lower for Mexican-Americans born in Mexico, compared to those born in the United States, indicating that acculturation and factors associated with migration may play a key role. African-Americans also have been found to have higher rates of specific phobia than Caucasian-Americans, even after controlling for socioeconomic factors (Brown, Eaton, & Sussman, 1990). A recent comparison confirmed higher rates of phobias among African-Americans as compared to Caucasian-Americans (Chapman, Kertz, Zurlage, & Woodruff-Borden, 2008). These authors also found differences among specific phobia subtypes; situational phobias were endorsed more often by Caucasian-Americans, and natural environmental phobias were endorsed more often by African-Americans. Within the animal subtype, both groups endorsed spider and snake phobias, but African-Americans were more likely to also endorse stinging insects, dogs, rats, and mice. In all, research to date suggests important differences in the prevalence of specific phobia, along with their subtypes, in various racial and ethnic groups within the United States, which are likely influenced by variations in culture. Although a dearth of literature currently exists on these differences, what is known has important implications for the treatment of specific phobias.

Etiology of Specific Phobias

Fear is an emotion composed of several constructs that are influenced by one's autobiographical memories. Through numerous associative networks, emotion-relevant information contained in long-term memory is stimulated, and can cue a particular emotion (Lang, Cuthbert, & Bradley, 1998, p. 656; Salzman & Fusi, 2010). Put differently, emotion is a consolidation of properties based on sensations associated with the stimulus (e.g., physiological responses), our potential responses (e.g., approach or avoidance), and the meaning given to the stimulus or situation (e.g., harm potential), which further connect the stimulus and response units (Drobes & Lang, 1995; Foa & Kozak, 1998; Lang et al., 1998). Overall, these associative networks broadly guide our approach or avoidance of stimuli based on the information activated. Öhman (1993) posited that phobic stimuli are quickly processed by sub-cortical structures. Such information processing leads to a basic analysis of the stimulus and initiates an immediate fear response. This fear response is elicited prior to an individual's conscious awareness of the feared stimulus, which may explain a phobic person's tendency to view the fear as uncontrollable. Research on masked fear stimuli (i.e., the presentation of feared stimuli outside of one's conscious awareness) has provided support for this hypothesis (e.g., Öhman & Soares, 1994; Siegel, Anderson, & Han, 2011; Siegel & Gallagher, 2015; Siegel & Warren, 2013; Siegel & Weinberger, 2012), but the importance of the interaction between subcortical and cortical structures should not be ignored (see LeDoux & Brown, 2017; Siegel et al., 2017). So, how is this fear-relevant information learned and then associated with a specific stimulus to increase the likelihood of developing a specific phobia?

Broadly speaking, anxiety and fear can be characterized as a number of neural networks that facilitate emotional responding or changes in physiology, behavior, and cognition (i.e., the three-systems-model) (Foa & Kozak, 1986; Lang, 1979), which come together in a subjective experience of emotion (Davis & Ollendick, 2005). Pathological fear differs from typical and more normative experiences by cueing a fear network that incorporates exaggerated emotional responses that are distressing and difficult to alter (Foa & Kozak, 1986, 1998). Conceived of in this way, individuals with a specific phobia have a maladaptive response to an particular stimulus (e.g., a dog), which is likely associated with maladaptive cognitions about the feared stimulus (e.g., the dog is going to bite me), avoidance of the feared stimulus (e.g., refusing to go to the park because one might see a dog), and physiological reactions to the feared stimulus that are often interpreted as problematic (e.g., "my heart is beating so fast – something is wrong with me"). However, these responses depend upon the individual's fear network potentiation and the potentiation of the associative network. For example, some individuals may not have maladaptive interpretations of their physiological responses, or have low levels of physiological arousal in relation to the feared stimulus (e.g., Allen, Allen, Austin, Waldron, & Ollendick, 2015; Ollendick, Allen, Benoit, & Cowart, 2011). In addition, not all types of specific phobia have similar three-component (i.e., behavioral, cognitive, physiological) profiles; for instance, animal-type and BII-type phobias are both characterized by subjective distress, but individuals with animal-type specific phobia typically report fear-related distress, whereas distress associated with BII is often described as disgust and repulsion (Page, 1994). Therefore, an individual with a specific phobia is an individual with emotional difficulties rooted in a multitude of developmental, biological, environmental, and experiential factors that are dynamic and reciprocal, and that differ depending on the particular type of specific phobia (Davis, 2009). For example, an individual with a specific phobia may display maladaptive arousal (e.g., increased heart rate) when seeing a dog, have maladaptive cognitions (e.g., thinking: "that dog could kill me"), and exhibit behavioral avoidance (e.g., leaving the area where the dog is located). Often, the escape behavior is paired with an immediate reduction in fear that maintains the overall behavioral chain. Early in development, these emotional responses are observed by parents or caregivers, who often express positive, empathetic responses. These parenting behaviors can serve to further maintain the fear response. The parent or caregiver's responses are taken in by the child and further influence maladaptive emotional responding while potentially confirming distorted thinking and expectations about the feared stimulus in a reciprocal fashion (McLaughlin, Hatzenbuehler, & Hilt, 2009). In addition, the individual may be negatively reinforced for future avoidance by their history of escape behaviors, and reduced aversive physiology and cognition associated with avoidance. Overall, the behavioral chain may be associated with a sense of helplessness and uncontrollability (Mineka & Zinbarg, 2006).

Anxiety disorders, broadly, have been posited to arise through four related, reciprocal mechanisms that often work in combination: classical conditioning, modeling, negative information transfer, and a nonassociative mechanism (for reviews, see Fisak & Grills-Taquechel, 2007; Mineka & Oehlberg, 2008; Mineka & Zinbarg, 2006; Muris, Merckelbach, de Jong, & Ollendick, 2002). A specific phobia, therefore, is thought to be transmitted through associative means (e.g., learning) by directly experiencing a negative interaction with a specific stimulus, by seeing someone else have a fearful response to a specific stimulus, or by reading about the fearful characteristics of a specific stimulus (i.e., vicarious fear learning) (Mineka & Zinbarg, 2006). Nonassociative processes are important to consider as well. Specifically, some individuals can have an innate biological predisposition (e.g., genetic and/or epigenetic) to an exaggerated fear response or a lower threshold to exhibit a fear response. From these basic mechanisms, the etiology of specific phobia can be broadly understood by the interaction between associative mechanisms (i.e., classical conditioning, modeling, and/or negative information transfer) to a stimulus and nonassociative mechanisms (i.e., biological predisposition), where the associative mechanisms are necessary for the development of a specific phobia given one's innate predisposition (Marks, 2002). Unfortunately, the interaction between these four mechanisms is not well understood, and their current descriptions are overly simplified.

Over time, etiological risk factors accumulate and interact with one another. For instance, a portion of the population exhibits desynchrony, where only partial emotional responses (e.g., low arousal, but high distress) occur in response to a feared stimulus (Allen et al., 2015; Rachman & Hodgson, 1974). Etiological models of specific phobia should include current advances in developmental psychology and developmental psychopathology. One such example is research on multifinality and equifinality (Cicchetti & Rogosch, 1996). Multifinality refers to individuals with similar learning histories (e.g., being bitten by a dog) but different psychological, developmental trajectories. In contrast, equifinality is a term used to describe individuals with vastly different learning histories but who develop the same psychological, developmental trajectory (e.g., a specific phobia). For example, two children both have negative experiences with a specific stimulus (e.g., getting bitten by a dog), yet only one develops a specific phobia, or both develop different anxiety disorders.

Multifinality and equifinality contribute to etiological models by providing essential information on psychological, developmental trajectories. Moreover, psychopathology is influenced by both when a child is observed (e.g., age, developmental milestones attained, environmental context) and who is evaluating the child's behavior (e.g., the observer's perspective, demands placed on the child, orientation, and biases) (Mash & Dozois, 2003). In all, child psychopathology is a multifaceted construct, consisting of an amalgamation of child-specific and environmental factors, as well as the impressions of those around him or her. Further, a child's behavior in response to a particular stimulus may or may not be maladaptive; however, a caregiver's accommodation (e.g., allowing the child to avoid dog parks), intolerance (e.g., dismissal of their distress), or misinterpretation of normative child behaviors (e.g., all children are afraid of something) can deny a child needed help and/or contribute to the development of a specific phobia (Thompson-Hollands, Kerns, Pincus, & Comer, 2014). Conversely, as previously mentioned, a caregiver's empathic consoling following a child's distress, avoidance, and escape behavior in response to a specific stimulus can also maintain and exacerbate a child's pathological fear. Clearly, caregivers must traverse a fine line when interacting with their fearful child, paying particular attention to the information they are communicating, directly or indirectly, regarding their child's reaction to a feared stimulus.

Etiological models of specific phobias increasingly need to incorporate developmental milestones, such as the development and refinement of the fear response. Researchers have begun to integrate etiological theories with known mechanisms within a developmental psychology framework. For instance, etiological theories of specific phobias now include a discussion of genetics, temperament, and child-rearing and parenting, as well as other factors (Muris & Merckelbach, 2001; Rapee, Schniering, & Hudson, 2009), and increasingly lend themselves to discussion of possible transdiagnostic constructs, such as those outlined by the Research Domain Criteria initiative (RDoC) (see Insel et al., 2010; Insel & Cuthbert, 2009). Specific phobias can be conceptualized as a continuum where an individual's risk and resiliency factors for the development of a specific phobia are couched in how developmental and environmental factors move a child up or down the continuum from a certain innate set point (Lang, McTeague, & Bradley, 2014). Some of these influential factors are reviewed briefly next.

Genetics

Although it is clear that etiological factors (i.e., classical conditioning, modeling, and/or negative information transfer) often play a role in the development of a specific phobia, combinations of distressing experiences, such as those based on modeling and negative information, account for less than 50% of the variance in the prediction of an individual's specific phobia (Oosterink, De Jongh, & Aartman, 2009). Nonassociative pathways have been posited to account for such findings on the etiology of specific phobias (Poulton & Menzies, 2002). Nonassociative pathways emphasize that a number of fears are retrospectively attributed to no known origin other than one recalling having always been afraid. They may in part have an evolutionary origin and pertain to particular stimuli that, at one point in time, served as a challenge to the survival of humans. For example, the preparedness hypothesis (Seligman, 1971) suggests that aversive conditioning interacts with evolutionary processes to produce a specific phobia.

Genetic susceptibility is one nonassociative factor that may play a role in the development of specific phobias (see Hettema, Neale, & Kendler, 2001). The diathesis-stress model describes the combination of genetic and environmental influences (Monroe & Simons, 1991). Genetic predisposition (i.e., diathesis) interacts with environment and life events (stressors) in an effort to explain behaviors, cognitions, or physiology related to a particular disorder. According to this view, genetic vulnerability and degree of environmental stressors share an inverse relationship (Jang, 2005).

It has long been observed that there is a familial component to fears and phobias (Depla et al., 2008; Fyer et al., 1995; Hettema et al., 2001). More than 15 years ago, a meta-analysis of behavioral genetic studies on specific phobia suggested moderate heritability, with an estimated heritability ranging from 20% to 40% (Hettema et al., 2001). However, specific phobias were grouped together with the other anxiety diagnostic categories (i.e., social phobia, generalized social phobia, and agoraphobia). More recently, van Houtem and colleagues (2013) conducted a review and meta-analysis of the heritability of specific phobia subtypes and corresponding fears. Their findings suggested a wide range in heritability estimates within and among specific phobia subtypes. For example, the BII subtype had the highest heritability, ranging from 28% to 63% (M = 33%); the heritability of animal subtype specific phobia ranged from 22% to 44% (M = 32%), while heritability estimates for situational subtype specific phobia ranged from 0% to 33% (M = 25%). Finally, the heritability of a miscellaneous subtype fear was found to range from 0% to 41% (M = 25%).

Overall, the results suggest that, apart from additive genetic effects, unique environmental effects appear to explain most of the variance, whereas the influence of common environmental effects seems relatively modest. Unique environments (e.g., classical conditioning events, stressful life events, and other biopsychosocial stress factors) can have strong influences on the development of a specific phobia. Therefore, an individual's genetic profile may explain why one individual reacts with more maladaptive cognitions, misinterpretation of physiological responses, and behavioral avoidance during or following a conditioning experience than another, making him or her more vulnerable to acquire a specific phobia than others (e.g., multifinality). Notably, an individual's genetic profile is not by any means a comprehensive picture of his or her genetic vulnerability; genes must also be understood in regards to their cellular environment, where DNA methylation, histone modification, and non-coding RNA-associated gene silencing can further alter an individual's vulnerability (e.g., Szyf, McGowan, & Meaney, 2008).

Temperament

For nearly a century, children have been understood to have different temperaments. A child's temperament involves several dimensions such as emotionality, activity, and sociability (Buss & Plomin, 1984). One such temperament that encompasses several temperament dimensions is behavioral inhibition. Kagan and colleagues (Kagan, 1989; Kagan, Reznick, & Gibbons, 1989; Kagan, Reznick, & Snidman, 1988) have found that approximately 10% to 15% of children are predisposed to be fussy, irritable infants, shy, fearful toddlers, and cautious, quiet, and introverted into childhood and adolescence. Conversely, approximately 15% of youth show the reverse profile. The remainder of the population falls somewhere on the continuum between these two extremes. Kagan hypothesized that behaviorally inhibited children have heightened arousal (i.e., exaggerated amygdala and hypothalamic network responses), especially to novel stimuli where they react under such conditions with sympathetic arousal (Kagan, Reznick, & Snidman, 1987).

Biederman and colleagues (1990) examined groups of children at seven years old that had been categorized as either behaviorally inhibited or behaviorally uninhibited at 21 months of age. They found that behaviorally inhibited children, categorized nearly five years prior, had significantly higher rates of specific phobias, when compared to the children categorized as behaviorally uninhibited (31.8% versus 5.3%). Notably, when Hirshfeld and colleagues (1992) reexamined these data, they found that approximately 55% of the inhibited children and 47% of the uninhibited children maintained stable group status across the five-year period. Further, they found that the stable-inhibited had the highest rates of specific phobia (i.e., 50%), whereas only 10% of the children in the unstable-inhibited group met criteria for a specific phobia. Temperament does not occur within a vacuum, however; behavioral inhibition manifests given an individual's genetic liability and is influenced and interacts with a child's genetic profile (Smoller et al., 2003).

Parent–Child Interaction

Parents of anxious children have been described as overprotective, where they often shield their children from potentially fearful stimuli (Hudson & Rapee, 2005). More specifically, overprotective parenting and anxious childrearing have been associated with behavioral inhibition (van Brakel, Muris, Bögels, & Thomassen, 2006). Behavioral inhibition early in childhood seems to elicit overprotective and controlling parenting behavior, thereby also increasing the risk for anxiety disorders in the future. Parents of anxious children are more than twice as likely to excessively control their children's behaviors and emotions (Hudson & Rapee, 2001; Siqueland, Kendall, & Steinberg, 1996). For example, when anxious children are compared to controls, their families are described as more controlling and less supportive (Stark, Humphrey, Crook, & Lewis, 1990). In addition, Wood, McLeod, Sigman, Hwang, and Chu (2003) found anxious children had parents who were observed to be less accepting, more critical, overly controlling, and overprotective. Direct observational studies during ambiguous and stressful situations have found support for protective and insulating parenting styles as well (Barrett et al., 1996; Dadds et al., 1996; Siqueland, Kendall, & Steinberg, 1996; Whaley, Pinto, & Sigman, 1999). Interestingly, Kagan et al. (1987) reported that children who stopped being inhibited (i.e., unstable-inhibited) tend to come from families in which children were encouraged to be sociable and outgoing. Overall, the probability and stability of a specific phobia may be related to a combination of genetic influences, temperament, parental psychopathology, parenting style, and environmental factors that interact in a reciprocal manner, playing a significant role in how a child or an adult's specific phobia presents clinically.

Clinical Presentation of Specific Phobias

Specific phobias were once thought to cause low levels of impairment and distress compared to other disorders (Antony & Barlow, 2002). However, this perception is misleading. An international study that investigated health and employment productivity found that specific phobias were among the top 10 most disabling mental conditions (Alonso et al., 2004). Large samples from two nations (i.e., the United States and New Zealand) found similar rates of severe impairment associated with this disorder: 21.9% (Kessler, Chiu, Demler, & Walters, 2005) and 21.6% (Wells et al., 2006). Yet few people seek treatment for specific phobias (Magee et al., 1996), despite the fact that highly effective evidence-based treatments are available (Wolitzky-Taylor, Horowitz, Powers, & Telch, 2008).

As noted earlier, across subtypes, phobias manifest at different ages and under a variety of circumstances. Many times, individuals do not recall a specific event when the phobia began, whereas in some cases it can clearly be delineated. Although there is heterogeneity of subtypes, etiology, and severity, phobias impact the individual in similar areas of functioning (Davis, May, & Whiting, 2011; Davis & Ollendick, 2005).

Physiology

The most common physiological reaction is arousal via the sympathetic nervous system. This involves a rapid heart rate, increased respiration, and perspiration, and prepares the individual for "fight or flight" (Barlow, Chorpita, & Turovsky, 1996). However, not all subtypes show similar responses. In the subtype of BII phobia, a biphasic response has been noted where the sympathetic arousal is followed by a parasympathetic response that involves shallow breathing, a sudden drop in blood pressure, dizziness, and vasovagal syncope (i.e., fainting) (Marks, 1988; Page, 1994).

Cognitions

Cognitions include thoughts, ruminations, beliefs, mental processes, and expectations a person has about the feared stimulus. Cognitive distortions (e.g., unrealistic beliefs, negative biases) are commonly reported by individuals with a specific phobia. Catastrophic cognitions refer to an extreme, negative outcome a person can imagine with regard to the feared object or situation, and are important to assess when treating phobias. Representations of catastrophic cognitions from individuals with animal, pill swallowing, and medical procedure phobias include "The cockroach will land on me, get into my clothes and infect me" (Botella et al., 2011, p. 219); "I cannot swallow pills. If I try to swallow a pill it will get stuck; if it gets stuck, I will choke" (Davis, Reuther, & Rudy, 2013, p. 403); "The [racing] heartbeat causes me to lose control. If I have a medical procedure, I will die" (Chapman & DeLapp, 2014, p. 7).

Perceptual biases are another cognitive feature of specific phobia. They involve threat detection and attentional processes (Cisler & Koster, 2010). Perceptual biases are often measured using tasks that assess processing speed, selective attention, and parallel processing, such as an emotional Stroop task (Becker, Rinck, Margraf, & Roth, 2001; MacLeod, 1991). In an emotional Stroop task, individuals are asked to name the ink color of each word that is presented (e.g., red, green, blue, black). Perceptual bias is demonstrated when one set of words (e.g., fear-relevant) is processed at a different speed than another (e.g., non-fear-relevant). For example, fear-relevant words for a study about spider phobia included "spider," "web," "hidden," "creep," "hairy," and "insect," and non-fear-relevant words included "percentage," "potato," "month," "fork," "blanket," and "pocket" (van den Hout, Tenney, Huygens, & de Jong, 1997). Results from this study were that fear-relevant stimuli caused significantly greater delays than non-fear-relevant stimuli for individuals with a spider phobia. Also, this effect was characterized by a dose response such that individuals with more severe phobic reactions showed greater delays. Last, following treatment (i.e., one-session behavioral exposure), this perceptual bias was reduced along with rated levels of fear.

The presence of fear also distorts the accuracy of risk estimation for individuals with phobias (de Jong, 2014). For example, a person with a fear of flying may overestimate the actual risk of danger, as seen by the following: "I feel fear, thus there must be danger" (de Jong, 2014, p. 134). The distortions grow as exposure to the feared object becomes imminent. A person without any plans to travel can more accurately estimate the risk of flying, but as the day arrives to board a plane, this estimate becomes grossly distorted (Beck, 2005). The distortion of perceptions was displayed in a study on fear of heights. Individuals with and without a fear of heights were asked to walk out onto a balcony and estimate the distance to the ground (Teachman, Stefanucci, Clerkin, Cody, & Proffitt, 2008). Those with a fear of heights estimated the distance to be significantly larger (and were less accurate) than those without a fear of heights. Unlike the deficits of delayed processing and inaccurate risk assessment, other differences in perceptions show heightened abilities. Studies that measure speed of fear-relevant stimulus detection found that individuals with an animal phobia were faster at accurately detecting their feared animal than those without a phobia (Öhman, Flykt, & Esteves, 2001).

Behavior

Active avoidance of the feared stimulus or situation is a primary behavioral manifestation of specific phobias. Individuals do sometimes endure exposure, but this is done at the cost of experiencing marked levels of distress. Avoidance can cause significant functional impairment such as turning down a promotion that required frequent flying, delaying important medical procedures, and moving out of a home after seeing spiders a few days in a row (Antony & Barlow, 2002). As the number of avoided situations expands, the scope of the functional impairment tends to increase. For example, a child with a button phobia experienced progressive avoidance (Saavedra & Silverman, 2002). Following an incident when a large jar of buttons spilled on him at school, the boy began to avoid touching buttons. Because his school uniform had buttons, he could no longer dress himself on schooldays. Once he was dressed, he began to avoid touching his school uniform at all. Eventually, he avoided touching anything that his uniform touched. As a result, his schoolwork was negatively impacted due to his excessive concern and distraction with avoiding all contact with buttons.

Subjective-Affective Experience

Fear and anxiety are key affective components of specific phobias and are associated with physiological changes, phobia-related cognitions, and avoidant behavior. However, other emotional states can emerge, including disgust, embarrassment, and shame. Disgust sensitivity was found among individuals with spider and BII phobias (Sawchuk, Lohr, Tolin, Lee, & Kleinknecht, 2000) and has been shown to decline following phobia treatment. In a study that monitored disgust and fear levels for individuals with BII phobia, both fear and disgust declined, but fear had a sharper drop than disgust (Olatunji, Smits, Connelly, Willems, & Lohr, 2007). Embarrassment can also be associated with specific phobias. People with dental phobia experience embarrassment and shame related to teeth decay as a result of avoiding dental care (Moore, Brodsgaard, & Rosenberg, 2004). Feeling embarrassed was associated with inhibited smiling and laughing, hiding the mouth, turning away from others when smiling, and low self-esteem. Also, for individuals with a vomiting phobia, feeling shame at making a mess was associated with a key factor that reinforced their avoidant behaviors (Price, Veale, & Brewin, 2012).

Social Functioning

Specific phobias affect interpersonal relationships and social functioning in many ways. A person with a fear of spiders may rely on others to check the mailbox or mow the lawn. A person who fears storms may insist that their loved one stays with him/her for reassurance. A person with a fear of driving will need to rely on others to complete errands or take them places. This dependency on others can strain relationships and cause resentment. Family and friends of someone with a specific phobia may not understand the extent of the phobia and its disabling impact. They may blame the person for being manipulative, selfish, or silly when the individual is unable to carry out expected tasks and perform social roles. A woman who had a phobia of wasps was ridiculed by her husband and son. They called her "childish" and told her to "grow up" (Davidson, 2005). Reactions to individuals with specific phobias (even among medical professionals) are commonly dismissive and judgmental rather than compassionate and helpful.

Social isolation is preferred by some. "I stayed away from people because I thought they would notice" (Davidson, 2005, p. 2160). Dental phobia can lead to social avoidance due to embarrassment, poor self-esteem, feelings of inferiority, and shame about facial appearance (Moore et al., 2004). Treatment initiation is less likely the longer a person waits to seek professional help. The stigma of specific phobia places pressure on many people to keep silent and hide the fact that they have a disorder. Stigma also reinforces treatment avoidance and further deterioration of social functioning. Evidence for this was found for all subtypes of specific phobia (*OR* ranged from 2.9 for fear of storms, to 9.3 for fear of being alone) (Depla, ten Have, van Balkom, & de Graaf, 2008). Youth also experience social impairment. Parents reported greater social problems, particularly for youth with natural environment phobias (Ollendick, Raishevich, Davis, Sirbu, & Öst, 2010).

Overall, specific phobias can cause significant impairment through physiological alarm or fainting reactions, avoidant behaviors, distorted cognitions and perceptual biases, and emotional distress. Social functioning is also negatively impacted. Specific phobias can lead to job loss, social isolation, and low self-esteem. Further, stigma and misunderstanding by others reinforces the tendency to hide one's phobia and not seek treatment.

Course of Specific Phobia

Specific phobia has a long duration, and is frequently a chronic and disabling condition. Though fears from early childhood often remit without treatment (e.g., ghosts), some plateau in adolescence (e.g., insects) and others show continued increases through adolescence (e.g., dentist) (Laing, Fernyhough, Turner, & Freeston, 2009). Phobias in place by adolescence have a more chronic course. A longitudinal study found that being diagnosed with specific phobia at either 13 or 16 years of age had an increased risk for specific phobia at 22 years of age (*OR* = 3.79) (Pine, Cohen, Gurley, Brook, & Ma, 1998). Very few people seek treatment (Wolitzky-Taylor et al., 2008); however, prognosis following treatment is very good in studies using exposure-based treatment for adults (Choy, Fyer, & Lipsitz, 2007; Wolitzky-Taylor et al., 2008) and also highly effective for children and adolescents (Davis, Ollendick, & Öst, 2012; Ollendick & Davis, 2013). More is needed to remove barriers to treatment (e.g., fear, shame, and stigma) for individuals with specific phobia.

Diagnosing specific phobia can be challenging. It can be difficult to differentiate this diagnosis from other anxiety disorders, especially in individuals with comorbid conditions (cf. Davis, White, & Ollendick, 2014). In addition, normative fears (especially for children and adolescents) are an important consideration when determining whether a person meets criteria for a specific phobia diagnosis (Ollendick & Vasey, 1999). Developmentally appropriate fears can be distinguished from phobias by their scope, onset, duration, intensity, and level of interference with daily functioning (Crozier, Gillihan, & Powers, 2011).

Normative fears in infancy include loud noises and strangers (Silverman & Moreno, 2005), and early childhood is characterized by fears of monsters, which tend to diminish by 10 years of age (Laing, Fernyhough, Turner, & Freeston, 2009).

Comorbidities with Specific Phobia

Specific phobia is highly comorbid with a number of other disorders. Many factors affect comorbidity estimates such as sample characteristics (e.g., community or clinical, age of participants), design and methodology (e.g., retrospective or prospective, establishing a primary diagnosis), and measurement choice (e.g., brief surveys or structured interviews). Generally, comorbidity rates for primary diagnoses of specific phobia are lower than when specific phobia is a non-primary diagnosis (Sanderson, DiNardo, Rapee, & Barlow, 1990). Among two large community survey samples, the majority of people with specific phobia had a comorbid disorder – 62% (Kessler, Chiu, Demler, & Walters, 2005) and 83.4% (Magee et al., 1996).

An outpatient clinical sample ($n = 1,127$) found that specific phobia was associated with an increase in lifetime comorbidity for any Axis I disorder ($OR = 1.66$) and 15% of the sample with one specific phobia had another specific phobia diagnosis (Brown, Campbell, Lehman, Grisham, & Mancill, 2001). The number of comorbid specific phobias from an epidemiological survey was much larger. The majority of people (71%) with a lifetime specific phobia diagnosis had more than one phobia (Stinson et al., 2007). This was associated with greater severity, impairment, and additional comorbidities. Lifetime comorbidity rates ranged from lower rates for substance use (alcohol, drug, and nicotine ORs ranged from 2.2 to 2.5), followed by mood disorders ($OR = 3.4$), personality disorders ($OR = 4.2$), and anxiety disorders ($OR = 5.6$). The largest reported rate was for panic disorder with agoraphobia ($OR = 19.2$).

Studies that examine a different primary diagnosis with secondary specific phobia show high co-occurring rates as well. For various principal diagnoses, specific phobia comorbidity rates were 65.6% (panic disorder) (Starcevic & Bogojevic, 1997); 20% and 44% (social phobia) (Goisman et al., 1998; Iancu et al., 2006); 23% (agoraphobia without panic) (Goisman et al., 1998); 20% (agoraphobia with panic) (Goisman et al., 1998); and 19% (generalized anxiety disorder) (Goisman et al., 1998). Among those with primary major depressive disorder, animal phobias had an odds ratio of 1.56 and situation phobias had an odds ratio of 2.12. (Kendler, Neale, Kessler, Heath, & Eaves, 1993).

Link to Later Psychopathology

In a prospective study, the presence of a specific phobia in adolescence increased the risk of depression in adulthood ($OR = 1.9$); however, other anxiety disorders had higher risks for later onset of depression, namely generalized anxiety disorder, panic disorder, agoraphobia, and social phobia (Bittner et al., 2004). Comorbidity status in adolescence moderated this result. Specific phobia with a comorbid condition in adolescence had a greater association with depression in adulthood (*OR* = 5.7), but specific phobia without comorbidity in adolescence did not elevate this risk (*OR* = 1.4, 0.8–2.3) (Bittner et al., 2004). Similarly, Choy, Fyer, and Goodwin (2007) found high comorbidity among depression and specific phobia (*OR* = 1.9). They also found evidence that specific phobia is an independent contributor to depression for individuals with two or more fears, and fears of heights, animals, and/or closed spaces.

A prospective study with young women examined whether specific phobia predicted the onset of other disorders after 17 months (Trumpf, Margraf, Vriends, Meyer, & Becker, 2010). Those with a specific phobia at intake (as compared to those without specific phobia) had higher rates of any anxiety disorder (15.1% vs. 9.0%), generalized anxiety disorder (6.6% vs. 2.1%), and somatoform disorders (5.0% vs. 1.8%) at follow-up.

Comorbidities in Different Cultures

Information from various cultures can be helpful in understanding how specific phobia is experienced cross-culturally.

Among child and younger adolescent samples, a community school-based sample of Korean children and adolescents (6–17 years of age) had a prevalence rate for specific phobia of 7.9%, 28.1% of which had a comorbid diagnosis (Kim et al., 2010). Comorbidity rates for anxiety disorders were highest (*OR* = 12.48), followed by ADHD (*OR* = 2.62) and ODD (*OR* = 2.14); there were no elevated comorbid rates for elimination or tic disorders (Kim et al., 2010).

Adolescents in Germany (ages 12–17) completed measures of fears and phobias in a school-based study (Essau et al., 2000). Almost 40% reported fears, yet only 3.5% met criteria for specific phobia. Comorbidity rates were highest for anxiety disorders (47.2%), followed by depressive disorders (36.1%), somatoform disorders (33.3%), and substance use disorders (8.3%). Because the total comorbidity rate was not reported, the highest reported rate (i.e., 47.2% for anxiety disorders) may be an underestimation of total comorbidity for this sample. While these studies provide information regarding how phobias are experienced in other cultures via prevalence and comorbidity, direct cross-cultural comparisons are needed to better understand cultural variations.

In summary, comorbidity in individuals with specific phobia is the norm rather than the exception. Differences have been noted when specific phobia is a primary or non-primary diagnosis; however, regardless of primary status, high rates remain of co-occurring anxiety, mood, and somatoform disorders. Studies from various cultures provide a basis for comparison, but more research is needed. Given the high degree of overlap in the current nosology, there has been a shift in research funded by the NIMH to examine dimensions of observable behavior and neurobiological measures, as opposed to diagnostic classification, to better understand mental illness.

Research Domain Criteria (RDoC) and Specific Phobias

The *DSM-5* provides diagnostic criteria for a specific phobia based on shared symptomatology. An individual's report of symptoms at interview, as well as the clinician's evaluation of their clinical significance, determines whether these features are present. The mental health field has relied on the nosology of primarily subjective symptom clusters to guide diagnostic classification; however, some have suggested that these diagnostic groups are consensus-based subjective categories treated as discrete states of dysfunction (Hyman, 2010). The NIMH directly addressed this issue by beginning a new research program (see Insel & Cuthbert, 2009) called the Research Domain Criteria (RDoC) initiative. The RDoC is not meant to be a classification system, but rather an orientation for psychopathological research with the goal to "implement, for research purposes, a classification system based upon dimensions of observable behavior and neurobiological measures" (www.nimh.nih.gov/about/strategic-planning-reports/index.shtml). Five domains are outlined: negative valence systems, positive valence systems, cognitive systems, systems for social processes, and arousal/modulatory systems, all of which have their own constructs. Level of specificity is outlined by the units of analysis presented by the RDoC: genes, molecules, cells, circuits, physiology, behavior, and self-reports.

Of particular relevance to specific phobia are the negative valence systems, cognitive systems, and arousal/modulatory systems. More specifically, the constructs within the negative valence system of significance are the acute threat/fear and potential threat constructs; within the cognitive systems, they are the attention, perception, and cognitive control constructs; and within the arousal/modulatory systems domain, they are the arousal construct. How each domain and its relevant constructs relate to specific phobia is briefly discussed hereafter.

Negative Valence Systems

Response to acute threat/fear involves the defensive motivation system (i.e., "fight or flight") that influences behavior to protect against impending harm. This can be in response to either exteroceptive or interoceptive threats. As applied to specific phobia, it is typically conceptualized as being in response to an exteroceptive stimulus (e.g., a dog); however, interoceptive threats also have their role within specific phobia. For instance, an individual may perceive his or her physiological responses (i.e., arousal construct of the arousal/modulatory domain) to a specific stimulus as life-threatening (e.g., "My heart's beating so fast; I'm going to have a heart attack").

In contrast, potential harm is more ambiguous or uncertain than acute threat and can be thought of as anxious apprehension. Behavioral responses to potential harm can involve increased vigilance (e.g., to enhance risk assessment), typically driven by higher-order, cortical structures that are qualitatively distinct from those to acute threat/fear. In regards to specific phobia, an individual may become apprehensive about encountering their feared stimulus. For example, a mother with a fear of dogs may be nervous about needing to pick her daughter up from the park. In addition, some specific phobia subtypes may differ in the importance of these two constructs. It is likely that situational subtype-specific phobias (e.g., darkness, elevators) are well distributed across both constructs, whereas animal subtype-specific phobias more strongly reflect the acute threat/fear construct, though, as outlined earlier, the potential harm construct is also relevant.

Cognitive Systems

The attention construct refers to processes that regulate access to awareness, higher perceptual processes, and motor action. Similarly, the perception construct refers to calculations that create and transform sensory information representing the external environment. These constructs relate to specific phobia through attention biases (e.g., Roy et al., 2008), covariation bias (i.e., the tendency to overestimate the association between phobic stimuli and aversive outcomes) (Tomarken, Mineka, & Cook, 1989; Tomarken, Sutton, & Mineka, 1995), and "ex consequentia" inference (Arntz et al., 1995). "Ex consequentia" refers to a perceptual bias where individuals with specific phobia, compared to non-phobic individuals, interpret their fear responses as evidence of danger (Arntz et al., 1995). Taken together, a child or an adult with a specific phobia of spiders may automatically orient their attention toward a fear-related stimulus and overestimate the likelihood that a particular spider is dangerous (i.e., covariation bias), as well as interpret their fear symptoms as evidence that the spider is indeed dangerous (i.e., "ex consequentia").

Effortful cognitive control is defined as the regulation of other cognitive and emotion systems in an effort to produce goal-directed behavior when preexisting modes of responding are not available due to the novel context. Cognitive control, as related to specific phobia, can be characterized as difficulties regulating emotional response to a feared stimulus. For instance, an individual with a specific phobia may find it more difficult than their non-phobic counterpart to cognitively reappraise or distance themselves when feeling fearful. Research has indeed found that individuals with specific phobia display deficits in effortful cognitive control following exposure to their feared stimulus (Hermann et al., 2009).

Arousal/Modulatory Systems

Arousal is a construct characterized by a dimension of sensitivity to external and internal stimuli, which facilitates interaction with the environment according to context. Typically, sympathetic nervous system activation is indicated by high heart rate, low heart rate variability, and increased heart rate acceleration under stressful conditions. Individuals with specific phobia have been shown to have higher heart rate variability (Chalmers, Quintana, Abbott, & Kemp, 2014), startle reflex, and accelerated heart rate under stressful conditions

(Lang, McTeague, & Bradley, 2016). Of note, not all specific phobia subtypes show this trend. For example, the BII subtype demonstrates a biphasic modal physiological response, where the dramatic reduction in blood volume may result in fainting that is shown by some BII subtype-specific phobia (Kleinknecht, 1987).

In sum, the RDoC initiative was devised to orient psychopathological research, with the goal to implement a classification system grounded in dimensions of observable behavior and neurobiological measures. Although judgment on the success of such a lofty initiative is premature, it has the potential to spur novel research that is likely to transcend diagnostic categories. As applied to individuals with a specific phobia, the negative valence systems, cognitive systems, and arousal/modulatory systems are of particular relevance. More specifically, acute threat/fear, potential threat, attention, perception, cognitive control, and arousal constructs serve as important starting points to better understanding fearful behavior from the RDoC perspective, with the hope that such research will generalize across other fear-related psychopathology.

References

Allen, K. B., Allen, B., Austin, K. E., Waldron, J. C., & Ollendick, T. H. (2015). Synchrony–desynchrony in the tripartite model of fear: Predicting treatment outcome in clinically phobic children. *Behaviour Research and Therapy, 71*, 54–64.

Alonso, J., Angermeyer, M. C., Bernert, S., Bruffaerts, R., Brugha, T. S., Bryson, H., … Haro, J. M. (2004). 12-month comorbidity patterns and associated factors in Europe: Results from the European Study of the Epidemiology of Mental Disorders (ESEMeD) project. *Acta Psychiatrica Scandinavica, 109*(s420), 28–37.

American Psychiatric Association. (1980). *Diagnostic and Statistical Manual of Mental Disorders* (3rd edn). Washington, DC: American Psychiatric Association.

American Psychiatric Association. (1987). *Diagnostic and Statistical Manual of Mental Disorders* (3rd edn, revised). Washington, DC: American Psychiatric Association.

American Psychiatric Association. (1994). *Diagnostic and Statistical Manual of Mental Disorders* (4th edn). Washington, DC: American Psychiatric Association.

American Psychiatric Association. (2000). *Diagnostic and Statistical Manual of Mental Disorders* (4th edn, text revision). Washington, DC: American Psychiatric Association.

American Psychiatric Association. (2013). *Diagnostic and Statistical Manual of Mental Disorders* (5th edn). Washington, DC: American Psychiatric Association.

Antony, M. M. & Barlow, D. H. (2002). Specific phobias. In D. Barlow (ed.), *Anxiety and Its Disorders* (pp. 380–417). New York, NY: Guilford Press.

Antony, M. M., Brown, T. A., & Barlow, D. H. (1997). Heterogeneity among specific phobia types in DSM-IV. *Behaviour Research and Therapy, 35*, 1089–1100.

Arntz, A., Rauner, M., & van den Hout, M. (1995). "If I feel anxious, there must be danger": Ex-consequentia reasoning in inferring danger in anxiety disorders. *Behaviour Research and Therapy, 33*(8), 917–925.

Barlow, D. H. (2002). *Anxiety and Its Disorders: The Nature and Treatment of Anxiety and Panic* (2nd edn). New York, NY: Guilford Press.

Barlow, D. H., Chorpita, B. F., & Turovsky, J. (1996). Fear, panic, anxiety, and disorders of emotion. In D. A. Hope, (ed.), *Perspectives on Anxiety, Panic, & Fear* (pp. 251–328). Lincoln, NE: University of Nebraska Press.

Barrett, P. M., Dadds, M. R., & Rapee, R. M. (1996). Family treatment of childhood anxiety: A controlled trial. *Journal of Consulting and Clinical Psychology, 64*(2), 333–342.

Beck, A. T. (2005). Simple phobias. In A. T. Beck, G. Emery, & R. L. Greenberg (eds.), *Anxiety Disorders and Phobias: A Cognitive Perspective* (pp. 115–132). Cambridge, MA: Basic Books.

Becker, E. S., Rinck, M., Margraf, J., & Roth, W. T. (2001). The emotional Stroop effect in anxiety disorders: General emotionality or disorder specificity? *Anxiety Disorders, 15*, 147–159.

Becker, E. S., Rinck, M., Türke, V., Kause, P., Goodwin, R., Neumer, S., & Margraf, J. (2007). Epidemiology of specific phobia subtypes: Findings from the Dresden Mental Health Study. *European Psychiatry, 22*(2), 69–74.

Biederman, J., Rosenbaum, J. F., Hirshfeld, D. R., Faraone, V., Bolduc, E., Gersten, M., Meminger, S., & Reznick, S. (1990). Psychiatric correlates of behavioral inhibition in young children of parents with and without psychiatric disorders. *Archives of General Psychiatry, 47*, 21–26.

Bittner, A., Goodwin, R. D., Wittchen, H., Beesdo, K., Hofler, M., & Lieb, R. (2004). What characteristics of primary anxiety disorders predict subsequent major depressive disorder? *Journal of Clinical Psychiatry, 65*, 618–626.

Botella, C., Breton-López, J., Quero, S., Baños, R. M., García-Palacios, A., Zaragoza, I., & Alcaniz, M. (2011). Treating cockroach phobia using a serious game on a mobile phone and augmented reality exposure: A single case study. *Computers in Human Behavior, 27*, 217–227. doi: 10.1016/j.chb.2010.07.043Bracha, 2006

Brown, D. R., Eaton, W. W., & Sussman, L. (1990). Racial differences in prevalence of phobic disorders. *Journal of Nervous and Mental Disease, 178*, 434–441.

Brown, T. A., Campbell, L. A., Lehman, C. L., Grisham, J. R., & Mancill, R. B. (2001). Current and lifetime comorbidity of the DSM-IV anxiety and mood disorders in a large clinical sample. *Journal of Abnormal Psychology, 110*, 585–500. doi: 10.1037//0021-843X.110.4.585

Buss, A. & Plomin, R. (1984). *Temperament: Early Developing Personality Traits.* Hillsdale, NJ: Erlbaum.

Caspi, A., Elder, G. H., & Bem, D. J. (1988). Moving away from the world: Life-course patterns of shy children. *Developmental Psychology, 24*(6), 824–831.

Castagna, P., Davis III, T. E., & Lilly, M. (2017). The Behavioral Avoidance Task with anxious youth: A review of procedures, properties, and criticisms. *Clinical Child and Family Psychology Review, 20*(2), 162–184.

Chalmers, J. A., Quintana, D. S., Abbott, M. J., & Kemp, A. H. (2014). Anxiety disorders are associated with reduced heart rate variability: a meta-analysis. *Frontiers in Psychiatry, 5*, 80.

Chapman, L. K. & DeLapp, R. C. T. (2014). Nine session treatment of a blood-injection-injury phobia with manualized cognitive behavioral therapy: An adult case example. *Clinical Case Studies, 13*, 299–312. doi: 10.1177/1534650113509304

Chapman, L. K., Kertz, S. J., Zurlage, M. M., & Woodruff-Borden, J. (2008). A confirmatory factor analysis of specific phobia domains in African American and Caucasian American young adults. *Journal of Anxiety Disorders, 22,* 763–771. doi: 10.1016/j.janxdis.2007.08.003

Choy, Y., Fyer, A. J., & Goodwin, R. D. (2007). Specific phobia and comorbid depression: A closer look at the National Comorbidity Survey data. *Comprehensive Psychiatry, 48,* 132–136. doi: 10.1016/j.comppsych.2006.10.010

Choy, Y., Fyer, A. J., & Lipsitz, J. D. (2007). Treatment of specific phobia in adults. *Clinical Psychology Review, 27,* 266–286. doi: 10.1016/j.cpr.2006.10.002

Cicchetti, D. & Rogosch, F. A. (1996). Equifinality and multifinality in developmental psychopathology. *Development and Psychopathology, 8*(4), 597–600.

Cisler, J. M. & Koster, E. H. W. (2010). Mechanisms of attentional biases towards threat in anxiety disorders: An integrative review. *Clinical Psychology Review, 30,* 203–216. doi: 10.1016/j.cpr.2009.11.003

Connolly, J., Hallam, R. S., & Marks, I. M. (1976). Selective association of fainting with blood-injury-illness fear. *Behavior Therapy, 7*(1), 8–13.

Craske, M. G. (1997). Fear and anxiety in children and adolescents. *Bulletin of the Menninger Clinic.*

Craske, M. G. & Sipsas, A. (1992). Animal phobias versus claustrophobias: Exteroceptive versus interoceptive cues. *Behaviour Research and Therapy, 30*(6), 569–581.

Crozier, M., Gillihan, S. J., & Powers, M. B. (2011). Issues in differential diagnosis: Phobias and phobic conditions. In D. McKay & E. A. Storch (eds.), *Handbook of Child and Adolescent Anxiety Disorders* (pp. 7–22). New York, NY: Springer.

Curtis, G. C., Magee, W. J., Eaton, W. W., Wittchen, H. U., & Kessler, R. C. (1998). Specific fears and phobias: Epidemiology and classification. *British Journal of Psychiatry, 173*(3), 212–217.

Czajkowski, N., Kendler, K. S., Tambs, K., Røysamb, E., & Reichborn-Kjennerud, T. (2011). The structure of genetic and environmental risk factors for phobias in women. *Psychological Medicine, 41*(9), 1987–1995.

Dadds, M. R., Barrett, P. M., Rapee, R. M., & Ryan, S. (1996). Family process and child anxiety and aggression: An observational analysis. *Journal of Abnormal Child Psychology, 24*(6), 715–734.

Davidson, J. (2005). Contesting stigma and contested emotions: Personal experience and public perception of specific phobias. *Social Science & Medicine, 61,* 2155–2164. doi: 10.1016/j.socscimed.2005.04.030

Davis III, T. E. (2009). PTSD, anxiety, and phobias. In J. Matson, F. Andrasik, & M. Matson (eds.), *Treating Childhood Psychopathology and Developmental Disorders.* New York, NY: Springer Science and Business Media, LLC.

Davis III, T. E., May, A. C., & Whiting, S. E. (2011). Evidence-based treatment of anxiety and phobia in children and adolescents: Current status and effects on the emotional response. *Clinical Psychology Review, 31,* 592–602.

Davis III, T. E. & Ollendick, T. (2005). Empirically supported treatments for specific phobia in children: Do efficacious treatments address the components of a phobic response? *Clinical Psychology: Science and Practice, 12,* 144–160. doi: 10.1093/clipsy/bpi018

Davis III, T. E. & Ollendick,T. H. (2011). Specific phobias. In D. McKay & E. Storch (eds.), *Handbook of Child and Adolescent Anxiety Disorders* (pp. 231–244).New York, NY: Springer Science and Business Media, LLC.

Davis III, T. E., Ollendick, T. H., & Öst, L. G. (eds.). (2012). *Intensive One-Session Treatment of Specific Phobias*. New York, NY: Springer Science and Business Media, LLC.

Davis III,T. E., Reuther, E., May, A., Rudy, B., Munson, M., Jenkins, W., & Whiting, S. (2013). The Behavioral Avoidance Task using Imaginal Exposure (BATIE): A paper-and-pencil version of traditional in vivo behavioral avoidance tasks. *Psychological Assessment, 25*, 1111–1119.

Davis III, T. E., Reuther,E. T., & Rudy, B. M. (2013). One-session treatment of a specific phobia of swallowing pills: A case study. *Clinical Case Studies,*12, 399–410. doi: 10.1177/1534650113497533

Davis III, T. E., White, S. W., & Ollendick, T. H. (eds.). (2014). *Handbook of Autism and Anxiety*. New York, NY: Springer Science and Business Media, LLC.

Demyttenaere, K., Bruffaerts, R., Posada-Villa, J., Gasquet, I., Kovess, V., Lepine, J. P., . . . Chatterji, S. (2004). Prevalence, severity, and unmet need for treatment of mental disorders in the World Health Organization World Mental Health Surveys. *Journal of the American Medical Association, 291*(21), 2581–2590.

Depla, M. F., Margreet, L., van Balkom, A. J., & de Graaf, R. (2008). Specific fears and phobias in the general population: Results from the Netherlands Mental Health Survey and Incidence Study (NEMESIS). *Social Psychiatry and Psychiatric Epidemiology, 43*(3), 200–208.

Depla, M. F., ten Have, M. L., van Balkom, A. J., & de Graaf, R. (2008). Specific fears and phobias in the general population: Results from the Netherlands Mental Health Survey and Incidence Study (NEMESIS). *Social Psychiatry and Psychiatric Epidemiology, 43*(3), 200–208. doi: 10.1007/s00127-007–0291-z

Drobes, D. J. & Lang, P. J. (1995). Bioinformational theory and behavior therapy. In W. O'Donohue & L. Krasner (eds.), *Theories of Behavior Therapy: Exploring Behavior Change* (pp. 229–257). Washington, DC: American Psychological Association.

Elizabeth, J., King, N., Ollendick, T. H., Gullone, E., Tonge, B., Watson, S., & Macdermott, S. (2006). Social anxiety disorder in children and youth: A research update on etiological factors. *Counselling Psychology Quarterly, 19*, 151–163.

Essau, C. A., Conradt, J., & Petermann, F. (2000). Frequency, comorbidity, and psychosocial impairment of anxiety disorders in German adolescents. *Journal of Anxiety Disorders, 14*(3), 263–279.

Ezpeleta, L., Keeler, G., Erkanli, A., Costello, E. J., & Angold, A. (2001). Epidemiology of psychiatric disability in childhood and adolescence. *Journal of Child Psychology and Psychiatry, 42*(7), 901–914.

Fisak Jr.,B. & Grills-Taquechel, A. E. (2007). Parental modeling, reinforcement, and information transfer: Risk factors in the development of child anxiety? *Clinical Child and Family Psychology Review, 10*(3), 213–231.

Foa, E. B. & Kozak, M. J. (1986). Emotional processing of fear: Exposure to corrective information. *Psychological Bulletin, 99*, 20–35.

Foa, E. B. & Kozak, M. J. (1998). Clinical applications of bioinformational theory: Understanding anxiety and its treatment. *Behavior Therapy, 29*, 675–690.

Fonseca, A. C. & Perrin, S. (2011). The clinical phenomenology and classification of child and adolescent anxiety. In W. K. Silverman & A. P. Field (eds.), *Anxiety Disorders in Children and Adolescents* (pp. 25–56). New York, NY: Cambridge University Press.

Fredrickson, M., Annas, P., Fischer, H., & Wik, G. (1996). Gender and age differences in the prevalence of specific fears and phobias. *Behaviour Research and Therapy, 34,* 33–39.

Fyer, A. J., Mannuzza, S., Chapman, T. F., Martin, L. Y., & Klein, D. F. (1995). Specificity in familial aggregation of phobic disorders. *Archives of General Psychiatry, 52*(7), 564–573.

Gallagher, B. & Cartwright-Hatton, S. (2008).The relationship between parenting factors and trait anxiety: Mediating role of cognitive errors and metacognition. *Journal of Anxiety Disorders, 22*(4), 722–733.

Goisman, R. M., Allsworth, J., Rogers, M. P., Warshaw, M. G., Goldenberg, I., Vasile, R. G., . . . Keller, M. B. (1998). Simple phobia as a comorbid anxiety disorder. *Depression and Anxiety, 7*(3), 105–112.

Greenberg, P. E., Sisitsky, T., Kessler, R. C., Finkelstein, S. N., Berndt, E. R., Davidson, J. R., . . . Fyer, A. J. (1999). The economic burden of anxiety disorders in the 1990s. *Journal of Clinical Psychiatry, 60*(7), 427–435.

Hermann, A., Schäfer, A., Walter, B., Stark, R., Vaitl, D., & Schienle, A. (2009). Emotion regulation in spider phobia: Role of the medial prefrontal cortex. *Social Cognitive and Affective Neuroscience, 4*(3), 257–267.

Hettema, J. M., Neale, M. C., & Kendler, K. S. (2001). A review and meta-analysis of the genetic epidemiology of anxiety disorders. *American Journal of Psychiatry, 158*(10), 1568–1578.

Hirshfeld, D. R., Rosenbaum, J. F., Biederman, J., Bolduc, E. A., Faraone, S. V., Snidman, N., Reznick, J. S., & Kagan, J. (1992). Stable behavioral inhibition and its association with anxiety disorder. *Journal of the American Academy of Child and Adolescent Psychiatry, 31,* 103–111.

Hudson, J. L. & Rapee, R. M. (2001). Parent–child interactions and anxiety disorders: An observational study. *Behaviour Research and Therapy, 39*(12), 1411–1427.

Hudson, J. L. & Rapee, R. M. (2005). Parental perceptions of overprotection: Specific to anxious children or shared between siblings? *Behaviour Change, 22*(03), 185–194.

Hyman, S. E. (2010). The diagnosis of mental disorders: The problem of reification. *Annual Review of Clinical Psychology, 6,* 155–79.

Iancua, I., Levin, J., Hermesh, H., Dannon, P., Poreh, A., Ben-Yehuda, Y., . . . Kotler, M. (2006). Social phobia symptoms: Prevalence, sociodemographic correlates, and overlap with specific phobia symptoms. *Comprehensive Psychiatry, 47,* 399–405. doi: 10.1016/j.comppsych.2006.01.008

Insel, T. R. & Cuthbert, B. N. (2009). Endophenotypes: Bridging genomic complexity and disorder heterogeneity. *Biological Psychiatry, 66*(11), 988–989.

Insel, T., Cuthbert, B., Garvey, M., Heinssen, R., Pine, D. S., Quinn, K., . . . Wang, P. (2010). Research Domain Criteria (RDoC): Toward a new classification framework for research on mental disorders. *American Journal of Psychiatry, 167*(7), 748–751.

Jang, K. L. (2005). *The Behavioral Genetics of Psychopathology: A Clinical Guide.* Mahwah, NJ: Routledge Press.

de Jong, P. J. (2014). Danger-confirming reasoning and phobic beliefs. In N. Galbraith (ed.), *Aberrant Beliefs and Reasoning* (pp. 132–153). New York, NY: Psychology Press.

Kagan, J. (1989). Temperamental contributions to social behavior. *American Psychologist, 44*, 668–674.

Kagan, J., Reznick, J. S., & Gibbons, J. (1989). Inhibited and uninhibited types of children. *Child Development, 60*, 838–845.

Kagan, J., Reznick, J. S., & Snidman, N. (1987). The physiology and psychology of behavioral inhibition. *Child Development, 58*, 1459–1473.

Kagan, J., Reznick, J. S., & Snidman, N. (1988). Biological bases of childhood shyness. *Science, 240*, 167–171.

Karno, M., Golding, J. M., Burnam, M. A., Hough, R. L., Escobar, J. I., Wells, K. M., & Boyer, R. (1989). Anxiety disorders among Mexican Americans and non-Hispanic whites in Los Angeles. *Journal of Nervous and Mental Disease, 177*, 202–209.

Kashani, J. H., Orvaschel, H., Rosenberg, T. K., & Reid, J. C. (1989). Psychopathology in a community sample of children and adolescents: A developmental perspective. *Journal of the American Academy of Child & Adolescent Psychiatry, 28*(5), 701–706.

Kendler, K. S., Neale, M. C., Kessler, R. C., Heath, A. C., & Eaves, L. J. (1993). Major depression and phobias: The genetic and environmental sources of comorbidity. *Psychological Medicine, 23*, 361–371.

Kessler, R. C., Berglund, P., Demler, O., Jin, R., Merikangas, K. R., & Walters, E. E. (2005). Lifetime prevalence and age-of-onset distributions of DSM-IV disorders in the National Comorbidity Survey Replication. *Archives of General Psychiatry, 62*(6), 593–602.

Kessler, R. C., Chiu, W. T., Demler, O., & Walters, E. E. (2005). Prevalence, severity, and comorbidity of 12-month DSM-IV disorders in the National Comorbidity Survey Replication. *Archives of General Psychiatry, 62*, 617–627. doi: 10.1001/archpsyc.62.6.617.

Kessler, R. C., Petukhova, M., Sampson, N. A., Zaslavsky, A. M., & Wittchen, H. U. (2012). Twelve-month and lifetime prevalence and lifetime morbid risk of anxiety and mood disorders in the United States. *International Journal of Methods in Psychiatric Research, 21*(3), 169–184.

Kim, S., Kim, B., Cho, S., Kim, J., Shin, M., Yoo, H., & Kim, H. W. (2010). The prevalence of specific phobia and associated co-morbid features in children and adolescents. *Journal of Anxiety Disorders, 24*, 629–634. doi: 10.1016/j.anxdis.2010.04.004

Kleinknecht, R. A. (1987). Vasovagal syncope and blood/injury fear. *Behaviour Research and Therapy, 25*(3), 175–178.

Laing, S. V., Fernyhough, C., Turner, M., & Freeston, M. H. (2009). Fear, worry, and ritualistic behaviour in childhood: Developmental trends and interrelations. *Infant and Child Development, 18*, 351–366. doi: 10.1002/icd.627

Lang, P. J., Bradley, M. M., & Cuthbert, B. N. (1998). Emotion, motivation, and anxiety: Brain mechanisms and psychophysiology. *Biological Psychiatry, 44*(12), 1248–1263.

Lang, P. J., McTeague, L. M., & Bradley, M. M. (2014). Pathological anxiety and function/dysfunction in the brain's fear/defense circuitry. *Restorative Neurology and Neuroscience, 32*, 63–77.

Lang, P. J., McTeague, L. M., & Bradley, M. M. (2016). RDoC, DSM, and the reflex physiology of fear: A biodimensional analysis of the anxiety disorders spectrum. *Psychophysiology, 53*(3), 336–347.

Last, C. G., Hansen, C., & Franco, N. (1997). Anxious children in adulthood: A prospective study of adjustment. *Journal of the American Academy of Child & Adolescent Psychiatry, 36*(5), 645–652.

Last, C. G., Perrin, S., Hersen, M., & Kazdin, A. E. (1992). A prospective study of childhood anxiety disorders. *Journal of the American Academy of Child & Adolescent Psychiatry, 31*(6), 1070–1076.

LeDoux, J. E. & Brown, R. (2017). A higher-order theory of emotional consciousness. *Proceedings of the National Academy of Sciences, 114*(10), E2016–E2025.

Liddell, A. & Lyons, M. (1978). Thunderstorm phobias. *Behaviour Research and Therapy, 16*(4), 306–308.

Lipsitz, J. D., Barlow, D. H., Manuzza, S., Hofmann, S. G., & Fyer, A. J. (2002). Clinical features of four DSM-IV–specific phobia subtypes. *Journal of Nervous Mental Disease, 190*, 471–478. doi: 10.1097/01.NMD.0000022449.79274.48

Lipsitz, J. D., Fyer, A. J., Paterniti, A., & Klein, D. F. (2001). Emetophobia: Preliminary results of an Internet survey. *Depression and Anxiety, 14*(2), 149–152.

MacLeod, C. M. (1991). Half a century of research on the Stroop effect: An integrative review. *Psychological Bulletin, 109*, 163–203.

Magee, W. J., Eaton, W. W., Wittchen, H. U., McGonagle, K. A., & Kessler, R. C. (1996). Agoraphobia, simple phobia, and social phobia in the National Comorbidity Survey. *Archives of General Psychiatry, 53*(2), 159–168.

Marks, I. (1988). Blood-injury phobia: A review. *American Journal of Psychiatry, 145*(10), 1207–1213.

Marks, I. (2002). Innate and learned fears are at opposite ends of a continuum of associability. *Behaviour Research and Therapy, 40*, 165–167.

Mash, E. & Dozois, D. (2003).Child psychopathology: A developmental-systems perspective. In E. Mash & R. Barkley (eds.), *Child Psychopathology* (2nd edn) (pp. 3–71). New York, NY: Guilford Press.

McLaughlin, K. A., Hatzenbuehler, M. L., & Hilt, L. M. (2009). Emotion dysregulation as a mechanism linking peer victimization to internalizing symptoms in adolescents. *Journal of Consulting and Clinical Psychology, 77*(5), 894–904.

Mednick, L. M. & Claar, R. L. (2012). Treatment of severe blood-injection-injury phobia with the applied-tension method: Two adolescent case examples. *Clinical Case Studies, 11*, 24–34. doi: 10.1177/1534650112437405

Mineka, S. & Oehlberg, K. (2008). The relevance of recent developments in classical conditioning to understanding the etiology and maintenance of anxiety disorders. *Acta Psychologica, 127*(3), 567–580.

Mineka, S. & Zinbarg, R. (2006). A contemporary learning theory perspective on the etiology of anxiety disorders: It's not what you thought it was. *American Psychologist, 61*(1), 10–27.

Monroe, S. M. & Simons, A. D. (1991). Diathesis-stress theories in the context of life stress research: Implications for the depressive disorders. *Psychological Bulletin, 110*(3), 406–425.

Morris, R. J. & Kratochwill, T. R. (1983). *Treating Children's Fears and Phobias: A Behavioral Approach*. New York, NY: Pergamon Press.

Moore, R., Brødsgaard, I., & Rosenberg, N. (2004). The contribution of embarrassment to phobic dental anxiety: A qualitative research study. *BioMedCentral Psychiatry, 4*, 1–11. doi: 10–10.1186/1471-244X-4–10

Muris, P. & Field, A. P. (2011). The "normal" development of fear. In W. K. Silverman & A. P. Field (eds.), *Anxiety Disorders in Children and Adolescents* (2nd edn). New York, NY: Cambridge University Press.

Muris, P. & Merckelbach, H. (2000). How serious are common childhood fears? II. The parents' point of view. *Behaviour Research and Therapy, 38*, 813–818.

Muris, P. & Merckelbach, H. (2001). The etiology of childhood specific phobia: A multifactorial model. In M. W. Vasey & M. R. Dadds (eds.), *The Developmental Psychopathology of Anxiety* (pp. 355–385). New York, NY: Oxford University Press.

Muris, P., Merckelbach, H., de Jong, P. J., & Ollendick, T. H. (2002). The etiology of specific fears and phobias in children: A critique of the non-associative account. *Behaviour Research and Therapy, 40*(2), 185–195.

Muris, P., Merckelbach, H., Mayer, B., & Prins, E. (2000). How serious are common childhood fears? *Behaviour Research and Therapy, 38*, 217–228.

Muris, P., Schmidt, H., & Merckelbach, H. (1999). The structure of specific phobia symptoms among children and adolescents. *Behaviour Research and Therapy, 37*(9), 863–868.

Öhman, A. (1993). Fear and anxiety as emotional phenomena: Clinical phenomenology, evolutionary perspectives, and information processing mechanisms. In M. Lewis & J. M. Haviland (eds.), *Handbook of emotions.* New York, NY: Guilford Press.

Öhman, A., Flykt, A., & Esteves, F. (2001). Motion drives attention: Detecting the snake in the grass. *Journal of Experimental Psychology: General, 130*, 466–478. doi: 10.1037//0096–3445.130.3.466

Öhman, A. & Soares, J. J. (1994). "Unconscious anxiety": Phobic responses to masked stimuli. *Journal of Abnormal Psychology, 103*(2), 231.

Olatunji, B. O., Smits, J. A. J., Connolly, K., Willems, J., & Lohr, J. M. (2007). Examination of the decline in fear and disgust during exposure to threat-relevant stimuli in blood-injection-injury phobia. *Journal of Anxiety Disorders, 21*, 445–455. doi: 10.1016/j.janxdis.2006.05.001

Ollendick, T. H. (1979) Fear reduction techniques with children. In P. Miller & R. Eisler (eds.), *Progress in Behavioral Modification*, Vol. 8 (pp. 127–168). New York, NY: Academic Press.

Ollendick, T., Allen, B., Benoit, K., & Cowart, M. (2011). The tripartite model of fear in children with specific phobias: Assessing concordance and discordance using the behavioral approach test. *Behaviour Research and Therapy, 49*(8), 459–465.

Ollendick, T. H. & Davis, T. E. (2013). One-session treatment for specific phobias: A review of Ost's single-session exposure with children and adolescents. *Cognitive Behaviour Therapy, 42*, 275–283. doi: 10.1080/16506073.2013.773062

Ollendick, T. H., King, N. J., & Frary, R. B. (1989). Fears in children and adolescents: Reliability and generalizability across gender, age and nationality. *Behaviour Research and Therapy, 27*(1), 19–26.

Ollendick, T. H., Raishevich, N., Davis, T. E., Sirbu, C. & Öst, L. (2010). Specific phobia in youth: Phenomenology and psychological characteristics. *Behavior Therapy, 41*, 133–141. doi: 10.1016/j.beth.2009.02.002.

Ollendick, T. H. & Vasey, M. W. (1999). Developmental theory and the practice of clinical child psychology. *Journal of Clinical Child Psychology, 28*, 457–466.

Oosterink, F. M. D., de Jongh, A., & Aartman, I. H. A. (2009). Negative events and their potential risk of precipitating pathological forms of dental anxiety. *Journal of Anxiety Disorders, 23*(4), 451–457.

Oosterink, F., de Jongh, A., & Hoogstraten, J. (2009). Prevalence of dental fear and phobia relative to other fear and phobia subtypes. *European Journal of Oral Sciences, 117*(2), 135–143.

Öst, L. G. (1987). Age of onset in different phobias. *Journal of Abnormal Psychology, 96*(3), 223–230.

Öst, L. G. (1991). Acquisition of blood and injection phobia and anxiety response patterns in clinical patients. *Behaviour Research and Therapy, 29*(4), 323–332.

Öst, L. & Sterner, U. (1987). Applied tension: A specific behavioral method for treatment of blood phobia. *Behaviour Research and Therapy, 25*, 25–29.

Öst, L. G., Sterner, U., & Lindahl, I. L. (1984). Physiological responses in blood phobics. *Behaviour Research and Therapy, 22*(2), 109–117.

Page, A. C. (1994). Blood-injury phobia. *Clinical Psychology Review, 14*(5), 443–461.

Pine, D. S., Cohen, P., Gurley, D., Brook, J., & Ma, Y. (1998). The risk for early adulthood anxiety and depressive disorders in adolescents with anxiety and depressive disorders. *Archives of General Psychiatry, 55*, 56–64.

Poulton, R. & Menzies, R. G. (2002). Non-associative fear acquisition: A review of the evidence from retrospective and longitudinal research. *Behaviour Research and Therapy, 40*(2), 127–149.

Price, K., Veale, D., & Brewin, C. R. (2012). Intrusive imagery in people with a specific phobia of vomiting. *Journal of Behavior Therapy and Experimental Psychiatry, 43*, 672–678. doi: 10.1016/j.jbtep.2011.09.007

Rachman, S. & Hodgson, R. (1974). I. Synchrony and desynchrony in fear and avoidance. *Behaviour Research and Therapy, 12*(4), 311–318.

Rapee, R. M., Schniering, C. A., & Hudson, J. L. (2009). Anxiety disorders during childhood and adolescence: Origins and treatment. *Annual Review of Clinical Psychology, 5*, 311–341.

Reijntjes, A., Kamphuis, J. H., Prinzie, P., & Telch, M. J. (2010). Peer victimization and internalizing problems in children: A meta-analysis of longitudinal studies. *Child Abuse & Neglect, 34*(4), 244–252.

Roy, A. K., Vasa, R. A., Bruck, M., Mogg, K., Bradley, B. P., Sweeney, M., . . . CAMS Team. (2008). Attention bias toward threat in pediatric anxiety disorders. *Journal of the American Academy of Child & Adolescent Psychiatry, 47*(10), 1189–1196.

Rubin, K. H. (2014). The Waterloo longitudinal project: Correlates and consequences of social withdrawal from childhood to adolescence. In K. H. Rubin & J. B. Asendorpf (eds.), *Social Withdrawal, Inhibition, and Shyness in Childhood* (pp. 291–314). Hillsdale, NJ: Lawrence Erlbaum Associates.

Saavedra, L. M. & Silverman, W. K. (2002). Case study: Disgust and a specific phobia of buttons. *Journal of the American Academy of Child & Adolescent Psychiatry, 41*, 1376–1379. doi: 10.1097/00004583-200211000-00020

Salzman, C. D. & Fusi, S. (2010). Emotion, cognition, and mental state representation in amygdala and prefrontal cortex. *Annual Review of Neuroscience, 33*, 173–202.

Sanderson, W. C., DiNardo, P. A., Rapee, R. M., & Barlow, D. H. (1990). Syndrome comorbidity in patients diagnosed with a DSM-III-R anxiety disorder. *Journal of Abnormal Psychology, 99*, 308–312.

Sarason, S. B., Davidson, K. S., Lighthall, F. F., Waite, R. R., & Ruebush, B. K. (1960). *Anxiety in Elementary School Children: A Report of Research*. Hoboken, NJ: John Wiley & Sons.

Sareen, J., Chartier, M., Kjernisted, K. D., & Stein, M. B. (2001). Comorbidity of phobic disorders with alcoholism in a Canadian community sample. *Canadian Journal of Psychiatry, 46*, 733–740.

Sawchuk, C. N., Lohr, J. M., Tolin, D. F., Lee, T. C., & Kleinknecht, R. A. (2000). Disgust sensitivity and contamination fears in spider and blood-injection-injury phobias. *Behaviour Research and Therapy, 38*, 753–772.

Seeman, M. V. (1997). Psychopathology in women and men: Focus on female hormones. *American Journal of Psychiatry, 154*(12), 1641–1647.

Seligman, M. E. (1971). Phobias and preparedness. *Behavior Therapy, 2*(3), 307–320.

Siegel, P., Anderson, J. F., & Han, E. (2011). Very brief exposure II: The effects of unreportable stimuli on reducing phobic behavior. *Consciousness and Cognition, 20*(2), 181–190.

Siegel, P. & Gallagher, K. A. (2015). Delaying in vivo exposure to a tarantula with very brief exposure to phobic stimuli. *Journal of Behavior Therapy and Experimental Psychiatry, 46*, 182–188.

Siegel, P. & Warren, R. (2013). The effect of very brief exposure on experienced fear after in vivo exposure. *Cognition & Emotion, 27*(6), 1013–1022.

Siegel, P., Warren, R., Wang, Z., Yang, J., Cohen, D., Anderson, J. F., . . . Peterson, B. S. (2017). Less is more: Neural activity during very brief and clearly visible exposure to phobic stimuli. *Human Brain Mapping*.

Siegel, P. & Weinberger, J. (2012). Less is more: The effects of very brief versus clearly visible exposure. *Emotion, 12*(2), 394–402.

Silverman, W. K. & Moreno, J. (2005). Specific phobia. *Child Adolescent Psychiatric Clinics of North America, 14*, 819–843. doi: 10.1016/j.chc.2005.05.004

Silverman, W. K. & Rabian, B. (1994). Specific phobias. In T. H. Ollendick, N. J. King, & W. Yule (eds.), *International Handbook of Phobic and Anxiety Disorders in Children and Adolescents* (pp. 87–110). New York, NY: Plenum.

Siqueland, L., Kendall, P. C., & Steinberg, L. (1996). Anxiety in children: Perceived family environments and observed family interaction. *Journal of Clinical Child Psychology, 25*(2), 225–237.

Smoller, J. W., Rosenbaum, J. F., Biederman, J., Kennedy, J., Dai, D., Racette, S. R., . . . Tsuang, M. T. (2003). Association of a genetic marker at the corticotropin-releasing hormone locus with behavioral inhibition. *Biological Psychiatry, 54*(12), 1376–1381.

Spence, S. H. & McCathie, H. (1993). The stability of fears in children: A two-year prospective study. *Journal of Child Psychology and Psychiatry, 34*(4), 579–585.

Starcevic, V. & Bogojevic, G. (1997). Comorbidity of panic disorder with agoraphobia and specific phobia: Relationship with the subtypes of specific phobia. *Comprehensive Psychiatry, 38*, 315–320.

Stark, K. D., Humphrey, L. L., Crook, K., & Lewis, K. (1990). Perceived family environments of depressed and anxious children: Child's and maternal figure's perspectives. *Journal of Abnormal Child Psychology, 18*(5), 527–547.

Stinson, F. S., Dawson, D. A., Chou, S. P., Smith, S., Goldstein, R. B., Ruan, W. J., & Grant, B. F. (2007). The epidemiology of DSM-IV specific phobia in the USA: Result of the national Epidemiologic Survey on Alcohol and Related Conditions. *Psychological Medicine*, *37*, 1047–1059. doi: 10.1017/s0033291707000086

Strauss, C. C., Frame, C. L., & Forehand, R. (1987). Psychosocial impairment associated with anxiety in children. *Journal of Clinical Child Psychology*, *16*(3), 235–239.

Strauss, C. C. & Last, C. G. (1993). Social and simple phobias in children. *Journal of Anxiety Disorders*, *7*(2), 141–152.

Szyf, M., McGowan, P., & Meaney, M. (2008).The social environment and the epigenome. *Environmental and Molecular Mutagenesis*, *49*, 46–60.

Teachman, B. A., Stefanucci, J. K., Clerkin, E. M., Cody, M. W., & Proffitt, D. R. (2008). New mode of fear expression: Perceptual bias in height fear. *Emotion*, *8*, 296–301. doi: 10.1037/1528–3542.8.2.296

Thompson-Hollands, J., Kerns, C. E., Pincus, D. B., & Comer, J. S. (2014). Parental accommodation of child anxiety and related symptoms: Range, impact, and correlates. *Journal of Anxiety Disorders*, *28*(8), 765–773.

Tomarken, A. J., Mineka, S., & Cook, M. (1989). Fear-relevant selective associations and covariation bias. *Journal of Abnormal Psychology*, *98*(4), 381–394.

Tomarken, A. J., Sutton, S. K., & Mineka, S. (1995). Fear-relevant illusory correlations: What types of associations promote judgmental bias? *Journal of Abnormal Psychology*, *104*(2), 312–326.

Trumpf, J., Margraf, J., Vriends, N., Meyer, A. H., & Becker, E. S. (2010). Specific phobia predicts psychopathology in young women. *Social Psychiatry and Psychiatric Epidemiology*, *45*, 1161–1166. doi: 10.1007/s00127-009–015905

van Brakel, A. M., Muris, P., Bögels, S. M., & Thomassen, C. (2006). A multifactorial model for the etiology of anxiety in non-clinical adolescents: Main and interactive effects of behavioral inhibition, attachment and parental rearing. *Journal of Child and Family Studies*, *15*(5), 568–578.

van den Hout, M., Tenney, N., Huygens, K., & de Jong, P. (1997). Preconscious processing bias in specific phobia. *Behavior Research and Therapy*, *35*, 29–34.

van Houtem, C. M. H. H., Laine, M. L., Boomsma, D. I., Ligthart, L., van Wijk, A. J., & De Jongh, A. (2013). A review and meta-analysis of the heritability of specific phobia subtypes and corresponding fears. *Journal of Anxiety Disorders*, *27*(4), 379–388.

Wells, E. J., Browne, M. A. O., Scott, K. M., McGee, M. A., Baxter, J. & Kokaual, J. (2006). Prevalence, interference with life and severity of 12-month DSM-IV disorders in Te Rau Hinengaro: The New Zealand Mental Health Survey. *Australian and New Zealand Journal of Psychiatry*, *40*, 845–854.

Whaley, S. E., Pinto, A., & Sigman, M. (1999). Characterizing interactions between anxious mothers and their children. *Journal of Consulting and Clinical Psychology*, *67*, 826–836.

Wittchen, H. U., Nelson, C. B., & Lachner, G. (1998). Prevalence of mental disorders and psychosocial impairments in adolescents and young adults. *Psychological Medicine*, *28*(1), 109–126.

Wolitzky-Taylor, K. B., Horowitz, J. D., Powers, M. B., Telch, M. J. (2008). Psychological approaches in the treatment of specific phobias: A meta-analysis. *Clinical Psychology Review*, *28*, 1021–1037. doi: 10.1016/j.cpr.2008.02.007

Wood, J. J. (2006). Parental intrusiveness and children's separation anxiety in a clinical sample. *Child Psychiatry and Human Development*, *37*(1), 73–87.

Wood, J. J., McLeod, B. D., Sigman, M., Hwang, W. C., & Chu, B. C. (2003). Parenting and childhood anxiety: Theory, empirical findings, and future directions. *Journal of Child Psychology and Psychiatry*, *44*(1), 134–151.

Woodward, L. J. & Fergusson, D. M. (2001). Life course outcomes of young people with anxiety disorders in adolescence. *Journal of the American Academy of Child & Adolescent Psychiatry*, *40*(9), 1086–1093.

16 Panic Disorder and Agoraphobia

Bethany A. Teachman, Miranda L. Beltzer, and Alexandra J. Werntz

"He who fears something gives it power over him."

Moorish proverb

In this chapter, we provide a review of panic disorder (PD) and agoraphobia. In addition to outlining the clinical presentation of the disorders, including diagnostic features, epidemiology and typical course, differential diagnoses and comorbidity, we present a summary of the theoretical models that inform current conceptualizations of the disorders. Next, given the rise in focus on the transdiagnostic features of psychopathology, we discuss how researchers and clinicians can conceptualize PD and agoraphobia across multiple biological and behavioral levels of analysis, as put forth by the Research Domain Criteria (RDoC) framework.

Clinical Presentation

Mary is a 66-year-old African American woman with asthma coming in to talk with her primary care doctor. She is a former smoker and admits to not exercising as frequently as she would like. Over the past six months, she has gained 50 pounds, and her family members have noticed that she is not attending church or family gatherings as frequently as she was before. She told her doctor that she has had a few "anxiety attacks" over the past six months, and does not know their cause. How might we understand Mary's experience?

Panic Disorder

The American Psychiatric Association's *Diagnostic and Statistical Manual* (*DSM-5*) (2013) defines PD as the recurrence of unexpected panic attacks that have been followed for at least one month by "persistent concern or worry about additional panic attacks or their consequences," and/or "a significant maladaptive change in behavior related to the attacks" (p. 208).

Panic attacks can happen both within and outside the context of PD. Panic attacks are sudden in onset, peak within minutes, and are tied to a sense of imminent threat. Although there is the possibility of more culture-specific symptoms, at least 4 of the following 13 symptoms must be present for a *full-symptom panic attack*:

"palpitations, pounding heart, or accelerated heart rate; sweating; trembling or shaking; sensations of shortness of breath or smothering; feelings of choking; chest pain or discomfort; nausea or abdominal distress; feeling dizzy, unsteady, light-headed or faint; chills or heat sensations; parethesias (numbness or tingling sensations); derealization (feelings of unreality) or depersonalization (being detached from oneself); fearing of losing control or 'going crazy'; and fear of dying" (American Psychiatric Association, 2013, p. 208). Panic attacks can vary widely in terms of symptoms, triggers, and severity. When an attack consists of fewer than four symptoms, it is called a *limited-symptom attack. Unexpected panic attacks* feel like they happen out of nowhere, where the individual does not notice an obvious trigger or cue, whereas *expected panic attacks* occur when there is a trigger that is known as a stressor for that person (e.g., interpersonal conflict or being in a crowd). To meet diagnostic criteria for PD, panic attacks are not attributable to a medical condition or substance use and are not better explained by another mental disorder. Critically, simply having panic attacks does not constitute a diagnosis; rather, the critical element is how one changes their life due to fear of the attacks.

To receive a diagnosis of PD, a pattern of worry about the attacks and/or avoidance behaviors must be present for at least one month. Worry may center on the consequences of the attack (e.g., the panic attack is a sign of a serious medical condition or a symptom of "going crazy") or concerns about having future attacks. The individual may also engage in behaviors to avoid having panic attacks, such as stopping strenuous activity to avoid cuing bodily sensations that mimic or provoke panic symptoms, or restricting activities in places where panic attacks have previously occurred (e.g., no longer going to restaurants) or where help may not be readily available (e.g., on a hike). These worries and behaviors are extreme, interfering with daily life.

PD is also marked by catastrophic misinterpretations of bodily sensations and the assumption that panic attacks are uncontrollable, and these maladaptive cognitions predict PD severity (Casey, Oei, Newcombe, & Kenardy, 2004) and play a mediating role in the effective treatment of PD (Casey, Newcombe, & Oei, 2005). Although these cognitions are not explicitly included in diagnostic criteria, they constitute an important part of the phenomenology and treatment of PD. When panic symptoms initially arise, which can routinely occur for benign reasons such as experiencing a racing heart after climbing the stairs, an individual vulnerable to PD often thinks the symptoms are a sign of something catastrophic like a heart attack and feels they are unable to manage them.

In Mary's case, after reluctantly telling her doctor more about her "anxiety attacks," she and her doctor agreed that she has been having panic attacks. Her first panic attack was six months ago while she was at the park with her grandson. She suddenly felt out of breath and dizzy, and she could feel her heart pounding almost "out of her chest" and sweat running down her face. She reported falling down and having trouble breathing for a few minutes, until an ambulance picked her up. Mary said it was the scariest thing she had ever experienced. Now, she is scared to go to the park because it might happen again, even though she misses spending time with her grandson. She endorsed having at least two or three panic attacks a month, and sometimes she had noticed that she can predict when they will happen. Her doctor described the adaptive role of normal anxiety, and explained how panic attacks are a form of maladaptive anxiety that involve the experience of extreme fear and a rush of physiological symptoms when no objective danger is present. Her doctor told her that she likely has PD.

Epidemiology and Course

In a nationally representative cross-sectional study of panic attacks and PD across 25 lower-middle, middle-, and high-income countries, lifetime prevalence of panic attacks was 13.2% of adults, and lifetime prevalence of PD was 1.7% of adults (de Jonge et al., 2016). Fairly consistently across countries of different income levels, higher incidence of panic attacks and PD was associated with being a woman, being younger than 60 years old, lower education level, being divorced/separated/ widowed, and having a lower household income. Using *DSM-5* criteria, the median age of onset for PD is 32 years old (de Jonge et al., 2016). Among English-speaking Americans using *DSM-IV* criteria, the median age of onset for PD was 24 years old (Kessler et al., 2005), suggesting the new criteria may be associated with later onset. Without treatment, PD is chronic but can vary in severity over time (American Psychiatric Association, 2013).

Differential Diagnoses and Comorbidity

PD requires the presence of more than one full-symptom panic attack, and attacks can occur in the context of disorders other than PD; for instance, a person who only experiences or fears attacks when driving over bridges may have a phobia but not PD. Thus, other anxiety disorders should be considered if only limited-symptom panic attacks have been experienced or if attacks only arise in specific feared situations. When a panic attack is present in the context of another disorder, a diagnosis can be made with the specifier (e.g., posttraumatic stress disorder with panic attacks). Panic attacks caused by medical conditions or substances/ medications also do not meet criteria for a PD diagnosis.

Among individuals with lifetime PD, 80.4% will have another comorbid mental disorder: PD is most highly comorbid with other anxiety disorders (63.1% of individuals with lifetime PD) and mood disorders (53.7%), while substance abuse disorders (26.2% of individuals with lifetime PD) and impulse control disorders (10.4%) had lower, albeit still substantial, comorbidity rates with PD (de Jonge et al., 2016). There is also high comorbidity with medical illnesses, including respiratory illnesses such as chronic obstructive pulmonary disease and asthma, cardiovascular disease, gastrointestinal distress, and diabetes (Meuret, Kroll, & Ritz, 2017). A recent review of medical illnesses and PD suggests that not only are there risk factors that likely predict the onset of both the medical illness and PD independently – including dispositional vulnerability factors (e.g., serotonin transporter gene promoter [5TTLPR] polymorphism) and environmental and psychosocial risk factors (e.g., early life adversity or perinatal exposure to cigarette smoke) – but there also may be a bidirectional relationship between the onset of PD and medical illness (see review by Meuret et al., 2017). The overlap of panic and medical illness symptoms may also make diagnosis and treatment particularly complicated.

Mary's case highlights the complex links across problem areas that often arise when PD presents in the context of a challenging medical history. She has been struggling with asthma for years (which is one of the reasons she quit smoking), but she noted that since her first panic attack, she has been reluctant to do anything that might make her asthma worse. She hates the tight feeling in her chest during asthma attacks and now worries that they might lead to full panic attacks. And, since exercise exacerbates her respiratory symptoms, she has almost completely stopped going on walks outside. This has caused her to spend more time worrying about her medical condition and panic symptoms, which has led to an increase in depressive symptoms. She says she eats fatty snacks to feel better, but admits that this might be why she has gained so much weight. The combination of the fear of panic attacks, the weight gain, and the depression has Mary feeling trapped.

Agoraphobia

Historically, Goldstein and Chambless (1978) defined *complex agoraphobia* as a *fear of fear*, with "a tendency to misapprehend the causal antecedents of uncomfortable feelings" (p. 51). As outlined earlier, this more accurately represents the current conceptualization of PD. Agoraphobia is the fear or anxiety of being in a (typically public) space from which escape may not be possible. More specifically, to meet *DSM-5* diagnostic criteria for agoraphobia, an individual must have intense fear of two or more of the following settings or situations: public transportation, open spaces, enclosed spaces (e.g., shops, theaters), standing in a line or crowd, or being away from home alone. Thoughts that escape will not be possible in the event of embarrassing symptoms (e.g., incontinence) or a panic attack are often present. These fears are not only out of proportion to the actual danger that may accompany that situation, but they also cause behavioral (e.g., reduction of time spent out of the home) and cognitive (e.g., denial of anxious symptoms) avoidance of the situation. A pattern of extreme avoidance, sometimes even leading to a person being homebound in severe cases, is typical of the presentation. The symptoms must be present for at least six months, and if the individual has a medical condition, the fear must be excessive – over and above realistic medical concerns (e.g., if an individual has a cardiovascular condition, it may not be excessive to worry about having a heart attack).

Epidemiology and Course

Based on *DSM-IV* diagnostic criteria, the lifetime prevalence is 0.8% for agoraphobia with comorbid panic attacks (but not PD) and 1.1% for agoraphobia with PD (Kessler et al., 2006), and it is even higher for agoraphobia without history of panic attacks (~3–5% or greater; see review by Wittchen, Gloster, Beesdo-Baum, Fava, & Craske, 2010). In the Wittchen et al. (2010) review, the researchers conclude from numerous longitudinal studies that agoraphobia is just as likely to precede panic attacks as it is to follow them, though this has been debated. Wittchen and colleagues also note that age of onset estimates for agoraphobia without PD are not well established, though their review suggests that mean onset may be between 25 and 29 years, with a second high-incidence period emerging after the age of 40. Women are twice as likely as men to suffer from the disorder. Like PD, agoraphobia's course is persistent and chronic without treatment.

Differential Diagnoses and Comorbidity

Agoraphobia should be assessed independently from PD. Historically, PD and agoraphobia have been linked, with diagnoses in *DSM-IV-TR* including PD with or without agoraphobia, and agoraphobia without a history of PD (see brief review and commentary on changes in Asmundson, Taylor, & Smits, 2014). In *DSM-5*, PD is listed as a separate anxiety disorder from agoraphobia, with a note indicating that the two may be comorbid. Results from multivariate comorbidity models suggest that the current conceptualization of PD as a distinct mental disorder from agoraphobia is warranted, given the disorders loaded onto different superordinate factors when relations among a large set of disorders was examined simultaneously (Greene & Eaton, 2016).

Differential diagnosis between agoraphobia and specific phobias should take into account the specificity of the phobia. For example, if the feared situation is limited to one place, then specific phobia, situational type, should be considered. Agoraphobia requires the fear of two or more public situations. Agoraphobia is also differentiated from social anxiety disorder in that social anxiety disorder is marked by fear of negative evaluation by others, regardless of the setting. Applying these considerations to Mary's case, the doctor also asked Mary about any fears of being in public given that Mary's daughter expressed worry about her social isolation. Mary commented that in addition to avoiding the park with her grandson, she often skips church and family gatherings. When asked why she was skipping these events she used to enjoy, Mary noted she worries that she will be trapped and have a panic attack. While she also noted that having a panic attack would embarrass her because she would look like a "crazy person," her response indicated that fear of panic symptoms was the primary driver of her avoidance, so a social anxiety disorder diagnosis would not be warranted in this case.

According to *DSM-5*, agoraphobia is most commonly comorbid with other anxiety disorders, depressive disorders, posttraumatic stress disorder, and alcohol use disorder. Within a Dutch sample, among individuals with current depression, there was a 10% lifetime comorbidity with agoraphobia (without panic); among individuals with current social anxiety disorder, there was a 14% lifetime comorbidity; and among individuals with generalized anxiety disorder, there was a 13% lifetime comorbidity (Lamers et al., 2011). Notably, given the overlap in symptoms between PD and agoraphobia (e.g., avoidance of situations due to fear of panic symptoms), it is important not to "double whammy"; that is, not assign two diagnoses when one would adequately encompass the symptoms.

Theoretical models: What causes and maintains PD and agoraphobia? A large number of theories have been put forward to explain the onset and maintenance of PD and agoraphobia. In many cases, these theories are not mutually exclusive but reflect different levels of analysis (e.g., neurochemical versus behavioral) and different degrees of proximity to the disorder features (e.g., early life experiences that serve as distal risk factors for one day developing PD or agoraphobia to more proximal changes in cognitions and respiration that indicate a panic attack may be imminent). Notably, because PD and agoraphobia were generally grouped together prior to *DSM-5*, many models of etiology and maintenance are relevant to both disorders, so we discuss the theoretical models for both disorders simultaneously. This is also consistent with the RDoC approach (described later in this chapter) that emphasizes transdiagnostic vulnerabilities and recognizes the considerable overlap across anxiety problems (e.g., excessive subjective distress, threat cognitions, and avoidant behavior).

Given that many theoretical models are compatible, some researchers have attempted to develop more integrated models that reflect a broad range of early learning, biological, and psychosocial vulnerability factors along a distal-to-proximal continuum. In particular, we use McGinn, Nooner, Cohen and Leaberry's (2015) Unified Model of the Etiology of Panic as a framework to guide this review. As illustrated in Figure 16.1, the model outlines six stages of vulnerability that ultimately lead to active panic symptoms. Within each domain of vulnerability, we review key models that have advanced our understanding of the etiology and maintenance of PD and agoraphobia.

While this framework is a useful organizing heuristic, our review places greater emphasis on the role of avoidance behaviors than is evident in the figure, in part because this makes the model more applicable to agoraphobia as well as panic, and because avoidance is critical to understanding why the range of anxiety difficulties shifts from normative to pathological levels. Also, while there is some intuitive appeal to discussing vulnerability along a continuum from distal to more proximal, it would be a mistake to view the model as a linear progression. At this stage, there can be no doubt that many of the components of the model are bidirectionally related and vulnerability to disorders is rarely a simple linear process. Moreover, the figure shows the influence of biological factors at only one stage, but there are important biological influences throughout the continuum/stages. Thus, we assume that vulnerability for a given person will involve some but likely not all of these steps, and the person may experience different stages multiple times, getting caught

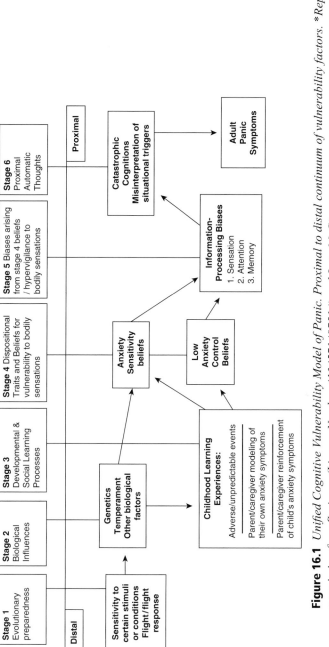

Figure 16.1 *Unified Cognitive Vulnerability Model of Panic. Proximal to distal continuum of vulnerability factors. *Reprinted with permission from Springer (License Number 4134571497514) and Lata McGinn.*

in cycles that constitute a particular vulnerability for them. For this reason, the stages are referred to as areas of vulnerability, rather than temporal stages, and a key challenge for clinicians is determining the particular subset of more proximal maintaining factors that need to be targeted for a given individual.

Vulnerability Area 1: Evolutionary Preparedness

To understand the etiology of acute panic, and the extreme anxious apprehension experienced during agoraphobia, it is essential to keep in mind that fear, anxiety, and the fight-or-flight response experienced during a panic attack are all adaptive responses (see Bouton, Mineka, & Barlow, 2001), and one would never want to eliminate these emotional reactions because they are strong and effective responses to real dangers. During the fight-or-flight response that is typically part of acute panic attacks, a series of changes are occurring in the body that prepare the organism to attack or escape during a dangerous situation (e.g., accelerating lung and heart action to enable rapid movement, with increased blood flow to muscles and greater muscle tension). These changes are thought to confer survival value because they support a temporary increase in strength and speed; for example, this is useful if a predator is actually chasing you! A different reaction occurs when a threat is more diffuse and less immediate as happens for agoraphobic individuals as they consider entering a situation in which they fear escape could be difficult; for instance, an animal may freeze when a predator is detected (but not actually attacking). This reaction is thought to help increase hypervigilance to identify threats and potentiate or prepare the body for the more active, defensive fight-or-flight response should it be needed.

Fanselow and colleagues' threat imminence model has been particularly helpful to elucidate how evolutionarily adaptive responses to predators and other threats can map onto current threat responses and associated neural systems (e.g., Fanselow & Lester, 1988; Rau & Fanselow, 2007). When a potential threat is initially detected and active threat of attack is still somewhat remote, anticipatory anxiety is elevated and characterized by more passive freezing. As described by Mobbs et al. (2009), summarizing the work of Fanselow, LeDoux, and numerous neuroscientists, "when a remote threat is confronted, specialized higher cortico-limbic regions including the ventral mPFC (vmPFC) and hippocampus gather contingency and contextual information and, via the amygdala instigate survival actions by controlling midbrain systems [e.g., ventrolateral periaqueductal gray (PAG) evoked freezing]" (p. 12235). Moving along the continuum of threat imminence, however, when active defensive reactions are required, including immediate escape and avoidance (e.g., as fight or flight is triggered during a predator attack), midbrain regions like the dorsolateral PAG becoming dominant as forebrain circuits are inhibited.

In some ways it is odd to refer to evolutionary prepared sensitivity to threat as a vulnerability factor because of its adaptive nature, but recognizing the role these alarm systems play in responding to threat is important to understanding a given individual's ultimate vulnerability to pathological panic and anxiety. As we discuss in what follows, in the context of PD or agoraphobia, these useful alarms are triggering at times they are not needed, which begs the question – what leads someone to have an overly sensitive alarm system? Each of the subsequent areas of vulnerability in the model addresses this question in a slightly different way.

Vulnerability Area 2: Biological Influences

Many different biological factors can increase vulnerability to developing PD or agoraphobia, including individual differences in genes, neuroanatomy, autonomic reactivity, neurotransmitter functioning, and respiration/hyperventilation, among others. This suggests biological influences at play from inception through to the onset and maintenance of a given panic attack (in PD) or decision to avoid entering a crowded theater (in agoraphobia). Notwithstanding, the evidence does not suggest biological determinism; having panic or other anxiety disorders run in the family, for instance, does not mean a given individual will necessarily develop a disorder.

Evidence for genetic transmission of vulnerability to PD comes from twin studies indicating that PD and agoraphobia are far more likely to occur in a monozygotic twin, relative to a dizygotic twin, of a patient with PD. Further, the first-degree relatives of patients with PD are many times more likely to develop PD than are the first-degree relatives of healthy control individuals (see reviews in Hettema, Neale, & Kendler, 2001, and Schumacher et al., 2011). While these twin and family studies provide considerable convergent evidence suggesting a genetic link, critics note that further research is needed to clarify whether monozygotic twins have more comparable environmental experiences than dizygotic twins have because of the possibility that these shared environmental experiences are the key to the heightened vulnerability. Adoption studies will be helpful in this regard. Also, many open questions remain about the extent to which the inherited vulnerability is specific to PD or is a more general vulnerability to developing an affective disorder as a function of greater neuroticism, a known transdiagnostic risk factor (see Barlow, Sauer-Zavala, Carl, Bullis, & Ellard, 2014).

An alternate approach to evaluating genetic influences is to identify actual candidate genes tied to the disorders. A recent meta-analysis examining case–control association studies to identify specific candidate genes in PD pointed to some methodological limitations of the existing literature (e.g., underpowered studies), but also identified three variants that indicated significant associations after correction for multiple testing (derived from studies with samples of European ancestry): TMEM132D rs7370927, rs11060369, and COMT rs4680 (Howe et al., 2015). The researchers called for future research with larger samples and examination of genome-wide approaches to better capture the range of genetic variation in diverse clinical samples. Taken together, it seems reasonable to conclude that there is likely a substantial genetic component to PD and agoraphobia, but the genetic contributions are complex and not yet well understood (see Asmundson et al., 2014).

At the neuroanatomical level, a number of neural structures and functions have been implicated in a *fear network* that contributes to conditioned fear responses in animals and is hypothesized to also contribute to panic and other forms of fear and anxiety in humans. Gorman's influential neuroanatomical hypothesis (Gorman, Kent, Sullivan, & Coplan, 2000; and see updates by Dresler et al., 2013) focuses on the amygdala and its connections, especially projections to the hippocampus, medial prefrontal cortex, hypothalamus, and brainstem. More broadly, the amygdala's role as part of the limbic system is seen as central to coordinating the neurotransmitters involved in fear, anxiety, and panic, while the periaqueductal gray within the midbrain system plays a central role in defensive responses, as described earlier in the threat imminence model. When the dorsolateral periaqueductal gray (dlPAG) is electrically stimulated, it produces a cascade of alertness, freezing, and then escape behaviors (aligning well with the symptom presentation in agoraphobia), while stimulation of the ventral periaqueductal gray (vPAG) can produce a range of responses similar to those seen during a panic attack (see Steimer, 2002).

Another intriguing but more controversial indicator of a biological influence on vulnerability to PD comes from responses to laboratory provocations of panic attacks. Given that it is difficult to catch a panic attack happening in natural circumstances, researchers have long relied on substance-based provocations, such as having participants breathe carbon dioxide (CO_2)-enhanced air (see Gorlin, Beadel, Roberson-Nay, & Teachman, 2014; Roberson-Nay, Beadel, Gorlin, Latendresse, & Teachman, 2015). What makes these studies interesting is that the provocations can trigger heightened physiological reactivity in most people (e.g., shortness of breath, racing heart), but only trigger panic attacks in certain individuals, especially those vulnerable to or with PD. Some researchers believe that the laboratory provocation is activating an underlying biological dysfunction, but this idea is controversial and considerable evidence suggests that psychological factors mediate the impact of the provocation (e.g., beliefs about control over the substance administration, expectancies manipulated via instructions; see Rapee, Mattick, & Murrell, 1986; Salkovskis & Clark, 1990, for examples). Thus, while there is greater likelihood of a panic attack (and sometimes more autonomic reactivity) in response to a laboratory provocation among individuals with, versus without, PD, it is not clear that this follows from a biological dysfunction.

There is also evidence that a range of neurotransmitters or neuromodulators may play a role in the etiology of PD, especially serotonin and endogenous opioids, though as with the other biological influences discussed, the data do not suggest a simple story. Graeff (2017) highlights two key hypotheses about neurochemical vulnerability to PD. The first hypothesis proposes that PD is characterized by "deficient serotonergic inhibition of neurons localized in the dorsal periaqueductal gray matter of the midbrain that organizes defensive reactions to cope with proximal threats as well as of sympathomotor control areas of the rostral ventrolateral medulla that generate neurovegetative symptoms of the panic attack" (p. 48). The second hypothesis focuses on the absence of normative endogenous opioids in panic patients that would normally buffer against panic attacks in healthy individuals. Rat models have indicated that serotonin interacts synergistically with endogenous opioids to constrain proximal defensive reactions, thereby (theoretically) inhibiting panic attacks. When this process is inhibited, the individual will be more prone to react with panic-like defense strategies. Work is ongoing to determine how well the findings from animal models translate to humans, and there is mixed evidence about when serotonin will enhance versus decrease anxiety reactions (see Steimer, 2002).

One of the most influential early biological accounts of panic vulnerability was Klein's suffocation false alarm theory of PD (Klein, 1993, and updated in Preter & Klein, 2008, 2014). The original theory proposed "that a physiologic misinterpretation by a suffocation monitor misfires an evolved suffocation alarm system. This produces sudden respiratory distress followed swiftly by a brief hyperventilation, panic, and the urge to flee" (Klein, 1993, p. 306). The expanded theory integrates the more recent evidence on the role of endogenous opioids in inhibiting panic-like reactions, described earlier. Preter and Klein argue that both sensitivity to suffocation and separation anxiety are partly controlled by endogenous opioids, leading them to suggest that an *episodic functional endogenous opioid deficit* is a cause of PD (Preter & Klein, 1998, 2014).

The suffocation false alarm theory is tied to a broader set of theories following from the observation of many similarities between the symptoms of a panic attack and hyperventilation. The broad hypothesis is that individuals who go on to develop PD are actually chronically hyperventilating and dramatically increase their breathing during periods of stress, leading to a discrepancy between oxygen inhaled and CO_2 exhaled. To compensate for the effects of hyperventilation and altered respiratory rate, the individual experiences shortness of breath, trembling, and the various symptoms associated with panic attacks. Notably, the evidence for persons who are chronic hyperventilators is mixed and this theory is unlikely to account for the variety of ways in which panic attacks are triggered for different people given evidence that forced hyperventilation only produces panic attacks in a subgroup of panic patients (see discussion in Brown, Smits, Powers, & Telch, 2003; Meuret, Ritz, Wilhelm, & Roth, 2005). Also, Klein's updated formulation suggests that the overly sensitive suffocation monitor in persons vulnerable to PD acts as a false alarm, becoming hypersensitive to even low levels of CO_2. As a result of falsely perceiving that oxygen supply is low and they are suffocating, the theory suggests, persons vulnerable to PD experience shortness of breath and start to hyperventilate to try to lower their CO_2 level. Note that this suggests hyperventilation has been proposed as both a cause of panic attacks and a consequence of the initial onset of panic. Thus, the evidence suggests CO_2 hypersensitivity is linked to panic spectrum liability among at least a subset of persons who go on to develop PD, but much remains to be determined about the sequence of these links and for whom these factors will play a prominent role in disorder vulnerability (see Roberson-Nay et al., 2015).

In summary, many different biological features contribute to vulnerability to PD and agoraphobia, with more research currently available to understand the etiology of panic attacks, relative to the apprehension and avoidance tied to agoraphobia. It should also be clear that there is not a simple story about biological dysfunction and there is not a single biological pathway that can account for the diverse ways PD and agoraphobia are expressed. Moreover, the evidence strongly suggests that any biological vulnerabilities that exist interact with the environment and a broad range of learning and other psychological processes to result in the expression of disordered behavior (Choe et al., 2013). Thus, we now consider some of the many psychological vulnerabilities that have been identified.

Vulnerability Area 3: Learning Processes

Numerous theorists have emphasized the role of learning in the etiology and maintenance of PD and agoraphobia, both in terms of early learning experiences that heighten future vulnerability and in the critical transition from an initial panic attack, which many people will experience, to developing full-blown PD, which happens to far fewer people. Thus, while McGinn's model emphasized early experiences, we think it critical to consider learning models more broadly, given their centrality to accounting for pathological anxiety.

Retrospective, correlational evidence suggests that individuals who go on to develop PD were more likely than non-anxious adults to have had caregivers that both modeled and reinforced more sick role behaviors in response to anxiety symptoms when they were children or adolescents (e.g., suggesting a child should lie down after experiencing a racing heart due to anxiety) (Ehlers, 1993). While suggestive, methodological limitations of these studies mean conclusions about causal contributions are not possible. Note this focus on early learning experiences in cognitive behavioral models is quite different from psychodynamic and psychoanalytic models that suggest fear, anxiety, and panic symptoms are triggered by symbols that are related to infantile wishes or fears, or dependency conflicts with parents (see Rudden, Milrod, Aronson, & Target, 2008). These latter models provide intriguing narratives but lack empirical support. More recent psychodynamic formulations emphasize the supposed unconscious meanings reflected by panic symptoms, especially core unconscious conflicts tied to separation and autonomy, anger, and guilt (Milrod et al., 2015).

Considering learning processes from both distal and proximal perspectives, Barlow has written extensively about the myriad of factors that interact to lead to the development of PD and agoraphobia. His integrated model (Barlow, 1988, 2002) and later updates based on a modern learning theory perspective (Bouton et al., 2001) have been highly influential and bring together many of the vulnerability areas described thus far. He and colleagues assume a biological vulnerability (likely to some extent genetically transmitted) and early learning experiences that suggest the environment is uncontrollable and unpredictable, which combine to make the individual especially reactive to stressors. As a result, the individual has an overreaction to a life stressor, responding with a false alarm as though the stressor was truly and imminently dangerous. As noted, many people will experience a false alarm, often referred to as nonclinical panic, at some point (Norton, Cox, & Malan, 1992). Critically, a subset of these individuals with heightened vulnerabilities then go on to associate the original false alarm with the heart racing, dizziness, and other somatic sensations that accompanied the feeling of anxiety and panic. This classically conditioned association results in *learned alarms*, whereby the somatic sensations become highly feared because of the possibility they could lead to another alarm (i.e., panic attack). This fear of future attacks and consequent hypervigilance for, and avoidance of, situations that might trigger anxiety or provoke anxiety-linked somatic sensations fuels the transition from a single false alarm to PD. There is considerable empirical support for many tenets of these learning accounts, including the proposition that somatic cues can become conditioned to anxiety and alarms, and that individuals with PD have an exaggerated fear response to somatic sensations.

This exaggerated sensitivity and reactivity to somatic cues is fundamental not only to conditioning accounts of panic but also to vulnerabilities at the dispositional belief, cognitive bias, and automatic thoughts levels, as we outline later in this chapter. Moreover, conditioning accounts have also been central to understanding the development and maintenance of agoraphobia, though the focus has been more on operant (versus classical) conditioning. Specifically, the avoidance and escape behaviors, which are the hallmark of agoraphobia as a person desperately seeks to evade triggering anxiety or panic, are reinforced because the avoidance temporarily reduces autonomic arousal. Thus, avoidance (falsely) appears to be effective at helping the vulnerable individual meet their goal of preventing the escalation of anxiety, but it comes at a huge cost as the avoidance generalizes to more and more contexts and the individual's life becomes narrower and more impaired.

Vulnerability Area 4: Dispositional Beliefs: Anxiety Sensitivity and Control

Strong evidence indicates that certain trait-like or dispositional beliefs heighten vulnerability for the development of anxiety disorders, especially PD. In particular, the expectancy theory of anxiety sensitivity refers to a fear of symptoms relating to anxiety based on the belief that these symptoms can have serious negative physical, social, or psychological consequences (e.g., Reiss, 1991; Reiss & McNally, 1985). For instance, a racing heart is believed to be dangerous because it could signify that a heart attack is imminent, while feeling unable to focus is frightening because it may be a sign of going "crazy," and feeling shaky is scary because it will be noticed and harshly judged by others. Often referred to as a *fear of fear*, anxiety sensitivity is a well-established marker of heightened risk for developing an anxiety disorder (see discussion in Olatunji & Wolitzky-Taylor, 2009). It appears to be particularly important to the development of PD (Ehlers, 1995; Hayward, Killen, Kraemer, & Taylor,

2000; see Teachman, 2005), though the link to panic is not unique (e.g., heightened anxiety sensitivity in a group of military recruits undergoing stressful basic training predicted more unexpected subsequent panic attacks but also more anxiety and depressive symptoms in general; Schmidt, Lerew, & Jackson, 1997).

While anxiety sensitivity is thought to reflect a trait-like belief, there is clear evidence that it can be modified. There are numerous examples of anxiety sensitivity decreasing over the course of cognitive behavior therapy (see review by Otto, Reilly-Harrington, & Taylor, 1999) and more recent evidence of change following interpretation training via cognitive bias modification (see Steinman & Teachman, 2010). Moreover, there is even evidence that reductions in anxiety sensitivity following cognitive behavior therapy for PD completely mediated the decrease in global impairment due to panic (Smits, Powers, Cho, & Telch, 2004).

Other important beliefs with empirical support indicating they are closely tied to PD include low perceived control, which is thought to confer a general psychological vulnerability (e.g., in Barlow's triple vulnerability model; see Barlow, 2002), and panic self-efficacy, which reflects a core belief about whether one can cope with panic symptoms (e.g., Casey, Oei, & Newcombe, 2005; Gallagher et al., 2013). Panic self-efficacy may even be a mechanism of change in panic symptoms following cognitive behavior therapy (e.g., Casey et al., 2005). As noted by McGinn et al. (2015), holding beliefs that anxiety symptoms are dangerous, and that one cannot cope with or control these symptoms, sets the stage for a cascade of negative cognitive biases and automatic thoughts that only serve to further heighten the fears of, and motivation to avoid, these symptoms. Suddenly, being out of breath after climbing the stairs is not simply a normal sign of being winded, but is thought to signal a serious and imminent threat.

Vulnerability Areas 5 and 6: Cognitive Biases and Automatic Thoughts

As we have outlined, the world and even one's own bodily reactions are seen as highly threatening by individuals vulnerable to PD and agoraphobia. Whether due to biological vulnerabilities, various early learning and conditioning experiences, holding a set of beliefs that suggest one is in danger, or some combination of these factors, individuals vulnerable to anxiety disorders process information in their environment in a way that reinforces their sense of danger and vulnerability. Information-processing models (e.g., Beck, Emery, & Greenberg, 1985) highlight the many ways in which anxious individuals preferentially attend to threatening cues in their environment, such as hypervigiliantly scanning for even minor bodily changes, and then assign negative interpretations to ambiguous cues, and even exhibit biases outside of conscious control, including automatic anxiety associations in memory (see general review in Teachman, Joormann, Steinman, & Gotlib, 2012, and examples specific to PD in Teachman, Marker, & Smith-Janik, 2008; Teachman, Smith-Janik, & Saporito, 2007).

The most prominent cognitive model of PD, developed by Clark (1986), focuses on a particular type of interpretation bias – the tendency to catastrophically misinterpret bodily sensations (e.g., thinking a racing heart means one might be having a heart attack). There is extensive support for the link between catastrophic misinterpretations of bodily sensations and PD, including higher rates of misinterpretations in patients with PD, as opposed to patients with other anxiety disorders or healthy control participants (e.g., Chambless & Gracely, 1989; Harvey, Richards, Dziadosz, & Swindell, 1993; McNally & Foa, 1987), and evidence for change in the misinterpretations following successful treatment (see Craske & Barlow, 2007; also see the meta-analysis by Gould, Otto, & Pollack, 1995). Moreover, there is evidence that the extent of reduction in catastrophic misinterpretations of bodily sensations predicts subsequent reductions in symptoms during cognitive behavior therapy for PD (Teachman, Marker, & Clerkin, 2010), establishing temporal precedence for changes in cognitions predicting later changes in symptoms.

This bias to assign threatening meanings to ambiguous bodily sensations can happen very rapidly and unintentionally, so the thoughts that follow from this bias (e.g., I'm going to faint/go crazy/have a heart attack/die) are often referred to as *automatic thoughts*. While there is extensive support for cognitive biases and threat-oriented automatic thoughts in PD (and to a lesser extent in agoraphobia), there are also open questions about whether these cognitive processes are necessarily present during panic attacks. Some patients with PD report not being aware of any catastrophic cognitions, and it is not unusual for a patient to experience a nocturnal panic attack, during which they wake in the midst of an attack (so they were not alert and consciously experiencing threat cognitions). To account for these experiences, cognitive models have suggested that the thoughts may occur outside of full conscious awareness, and even when a person is asleep (see review in Taylor & Asmundson, 2016). For example, just as most people wake up during the night when they need to go to the bathroom, indicating that there was some ongoing, unconscious monitoring of bodily sensations while sleeping, so too will patients with PD wake up should they detect a change in heart rate or respiration because they are so vigilant for, and fearful of, these changes (see Taylor, 2000).

As this brief review illustrates, no one simple path can account for the range of ways that PD and agoraphobia develop and are maintained. While many open questions remain about specific causal pathways for different subgroups of patients, it is clear that a complex mix of biological and psychological factors interact to produce the extreme fear, anxious apprehension, and escape and avoidance behaviors that cause so much impairment in people's lives. In recognition of the many different levels of analysis – from genes to self-reported conscious cognitions – that contribute to the emergence of psychopathology, recent efforts to classify and measure the symptoms of mental illnesses like PD and agoraphobia have shifted away from traditional, diagnostic categorical models toward more dimensional, transdiagnostic approaches. We consider how the symptoms of PD and agoraphobia can be understood in light of this new framework.

Connecting Panic Disorder and Agoraphobia Diagnoses to Research Domain Criteria

The Research Domain Criteria (RDoC) from the National Institute of Mental Health is a framework for studying and conceptualizing mental disorders along dimensions of observable behaviors and biological functions, with multiple units of analysis for each dimension (Cuthbert & Insel, 2013; Kozak & Cuthbert, 2016). Applying an RDoC lens to PD and agoraphobia can help us understand their characteristic features in a dimensional, rather than categorical, way. An RDoC conceptualization also nudges us to think about processes contributing to etiology and maintenance of these disorders that may cut across diagnostic categories.

Here, we draw largely on Hamm et al.'s (2016) RDoC conceptualization of PD with agoraphobia and also note other elements of the RDoC matrix that have been implicated in the literature on PD. The RDoC matrix is organized by units of analysis from those observable on a larger scale, including paradigms and behavior, down to genes and molecules. The broadest categorization within the matrix is by domain, with domains then broken down further into component constructs. The RDoC domains include positive and negative valence systems, cognitive systems, social processes, and arousal and regulatory systems. There are significant PD and agoraphobia symptom correspondences with multiple RDoC systems domains, including the arousal and cognitive systems (for instance, as described earlier, physiological arousal and cognitive biases are important components of anxiety and panic responses). However, we focus on the *negative valence system* given the defining role of negative affect in PD and agoraphobia, and focus in particular on two constructs nested within the negative valence system: *potential threat (anxiety)* and *acute threat (fear)*. While the general public often uses the terms *anxiety* and *fear* interchangeably, in the clinical science literature, anxiety is conceptually differentiated from fear (and panic) by the imminence and identifiability of threat; fear is a phasic response to a proximal, identifiable threat, whereas anxiety is a sustained response to an uncertain, future threat characterized by distress, apprehension, and worry (Schmitz & Grillon, 2012). The two states are also characterized by dissociable neurobiological and physiological responses (Perusini & Fanselow, 2015).

PD with agoraphobia has been conceptualized as a set of defensive responses organized along a dimension of proximity of threat, in line with the threat imminence model (Fanselow, 1994). In this conceptualization, worry about experiencing a panic attack and the biological processes accompanying this worry, including hypervigilance and potentiated startle, fall into the potential threat (anxiety) construct. These symptoms occur when a person is in a potentially threatening environment or attentive for signs of a past threat that has yet to return (e.g., in a shopping mall where they previously experienced a panic attack). Once the person has begun to notice bodily changes that they fear might indicate a panic attack, a different set of defensive responses begins, including selective attention, startle potentiation, and freezing. These may ultimately culminate in a panic attack or an attempt to escape the situation. Once the threat of a panic attack is detected, the cascade of physiological changes leading up to a panic attack or escape is defined as part of the acute threat (fear) construct. We consider each of these stages of threat in turn, and ways in which PD and agoraphobia symptoms can be measured within each unit of analysis.

Potential Threat (Anxiety)

In PD and agoraphobia, worry about future panic attacks or anxiety symptoms falls into the potential threat (anxiety) construct. As illustrated by examples from each of the RDoC units of analysis in what follows, hypervigilance for and hypersensitivity to threat, coupled with negative interpretive biases of interoceptive signals (i.e., the catastrophic misinterpretation of bodily sensation described earlier), contribute to the maintenance of PD and agoraphobia.

Paradigms unit of analysis. The NPU-threat task (Schmitz & Grillon, 2012) is an effective paradigm to illustrate the role of hypersensitivity to threat in PD. This paradigm measures fear- and anxiety-potentiated startle by using facial electromyography to measure eye blink magnitude to cues predictive of no aversive events, predictable aversive events, or unpredictable aversive events. The nature of the aversive event (e.g., electrical shock, scream, blast of air) can be modified as appropriate for the population under study. Specific to PD is the NPU respiratory threat test (NPUr), which uses breathing occlusion (a brief period of time during which breathing in or out is impossible) as the aversive event (Schroijen et al., 2016). In the NPU-threat task, fear-potentiated startle is defined as the difference in startle magnitude between cue and no cue during the predictable condition. Anxiety-potentiated startle is defined as the difference between no cue during the unpredictable condition and no cue during the no aversive events condition.

Self-report unit of analysis. Patients with PD or agoraphobia will explicitly report heightened sensitivity to potential threats, especially perceived bodily threats. As described in the section on theoretical models, the tendency to catastrophize somatic sensations and fear anxiety symptoms (i.e., anxiety sensitivity) contributes to the maintenance of anxiety about future panic attacks (in PD) and uncontrollable somatic symptoms (in agoraphobia). Anxiety sensitivity, the *fear of fear*, is typically measured with the Anxiety Sensitivity Index (ASI) (Reiss, Peterson, Gursky, & McNally, 1986; revised ASI-3, Taylor et al., 2007). The ASI-3 contains three subscales: physical, cognitive, and social concerns.

Physiology unit of analysis. Individuals with PD show elevated startle potentiation as part of their response to potential threat, that is, in a threatening context and in response to diffuse, distal threat, but the elevation is not present in response to proximal threat (Grillon, Ameli, Goddard, Woods, & Davis, 1994). On the NPU-threat task, individuals with PD have shown elevated anxiety-potentiated startle relative to healthy control participants (Grillon et al., 2008; Shankman et al., 2013).

These results suggest that PD may be characterized by elevated startle potentiation in environments where threat has happened in the past and to unpredictable aversive events, both of which reflect anxiety.

Circuits unit of analysis. Heightened responses to potential threats in PD and agoraphobia are also evident when measured at the level of neural circuits. Using structural and functional magnetic resonance imaging, anxiety sensitivity has been related to increased size and hyperactivity of the insula (Graeff & Del-Ben, 2008; Stein, Simmons, Feinstein, & Paulus, 2007) and anterior cingulate cortex (Holtz, Pané-Farré, Wendt, Lotze, & Hamm, 2012; Killgore, Britton, Price, Gold, & Rauch, 2011; Rosso et al., 2010), which are involved in ascribing negative meaning to interoceptive signals (Dillon et al., 2014). Thus, altered structure and function in the insula and anterior cingulate cortex may underlie an increased sensitivity to interoceptive signals, like rapid heartbeat, which may in turn maintain anxiety about somatic symptoms. Additionally, lesion studies have found that the amygdala is necessary for generating anticipatory anxiety to CO_2 inhalation, but not for panic attacks, suggesting that it is involved in agoraphobic situations and expected panic attacks (Johnson, Federici, & Shekhar, 2014).

Molecules unit of analysis. Focusing on the molecular level and building on the amygdala's role in response to potential threat in PD and agoraphobia, neuroimaging studies of rats suggest that sustained fear is mediated by the amygdala releasing corticotropin-releasing factor (CRF), which binds to receptors in the bed nucleus of the stria terminalis (for a review, see Davis, Walker, Miles, & Grillon, 2010). CRF is also important in startle potentiation, and excess CRF release and CRF1 receptor signaling may be implicated in PD (Risbrough & Stein, 2006).

Genes unit of analysis. Although there are still many open questions about the specific genetic contributions to PD and agoraphobia, based on genotyping studies of single-nucleotide polymorphisms (SNPs), one SNP of the corticotropin-releasing hormone receptor gene *CRHR1*, which reduces gene expression, has been found to significantly increase risk for PD in women (Weber et al., 2015). This risk allele was associated with less active avoidance on an entrapment behavioral approach task (prematurely escaping an agoraphobic situation), but with increased anxiety sensitivity (Weber et al., 2015). It was also associated with reduced expression of the *CRHR1* receptor in the forebrain and amygdala. Relatedly, carriers of the risk allele showed reduced frontal cortical activation during fear conditioning and increased amygdala activation as a response to safety signal presentation, which may reflect fear over-generalization underlying anxious apprehension (Weber et al., 2015). Another *CRHR1* SNP has also been related to risk for PD, further implicating this gene in the etiology of PD (Keck et al., 2008), perhaps through increased anxiety sensitivity and aberrant fear learning. Note, however, that the studies referenced earlier used a candidate gene approach based on systems implicated in PD, and it is not known whether these findings would emerge if a genome-wide approach were employed instead.

Acute Threat (Fear)

A series of arousal-related changes follows from detection of a threat and precedes panic attack/escape behavior (e.g., the fear response starts when a person with PD notices their rapid heartbeat, then construes it as a heart attack, and escalates their reaction until they have a panic attack). This escalation and freezing behavior can be conceptualized as falling into the acute threat (fear) construct of the RDoC matrix (Hamm et al., 2016; Perusini & Fanselow, 2015). Panic attacks and escaping from the panic-inducing situation are also discussed in what follows, even though these represent responses to an even more imminent danger.

Paradigms unit of analysis. Tasks used for measuring fear tend to expose individuals to the object of their fear; in the case of PD and agoraphobia, the fears targeted are typically either claustrophobia (particularly relevant for agoraphobia) or somatic sensations. One classic measure of fear responding is the behavioral approach task, in which individuals are exposed to the object of their fear, and the degree to which they approach or endure the threat is measured. Behavioral approach tasks may also be used to examine the fear response itself, and neural, physiological, and self-report measures can be taken before, during, and after the behavioral approach task. For individuals with PD, enclosure in a small, dark chamber for a period of time (an entrapment behavioral approach task) may be used as an exposure to target claustrophobia (Hamm et al., 2016; Öst, Johansson, & Jerremalm, 1982; Rachman & Taylor, 1993). Biological challenges that provoke bodily sensations similar to feared panic symptoms may also be used as interoceptive exposures. For example, spinning provokes dizziness, breathing CO_2-enriched air provokes hypercapnia, and breathing through a straw provokes gastrointestinal symptoms. All of these behavioral approach tasks have been used to elicit symptoms of panic, and in some cases, panic attacks, in individuals with and without a diagnosis of PD.

Self-report unit of analysis. Following biological models that posit breathing-related symptoms as triggering panic attacks, fear of suffocation is a central cognition in PD and agoraphobia for some patients (Klein, 1993). Fear of suffocation can be measured with the suffocation subscale of the Claustrophobia Questionnaire (Radomsky, Rachman, Thordarson, Mcisaac, & Teachman, 2001), and has been shown to predict response to a CO_2 challenge (Alius, Pané-Farré, Von Leupoldt, & Hamm, 2013; Mcnally & Eke, 1996; Rassovsky, Kushner, Schwarze, & Wangensteen, 2000). Elevated fear of suffocation also correlates with fear and avoidance on an entrapment behavioral approach task (Hamm et al., 2016).

Physiology unit of analysis. Several arousal-related changes accompany the dynamic fear response, and some of these responses differ based on the imminence of threat. Once a threat has been detected and attentive freezing occurs, startle is potentiated, and then when the individual responds behaviorally to the threat either with a panic attack or escape, this startle response is inhibited (see discussion in

Hamm et al., 2016). Similarly, heart rate increases prior to and during a panic attack or escape from an agoraphobic situation, suggesting that this escalation of autonomic arousal prompts the initiation of panic/escape (Hamm et al., 2016). Research on fear-potentiated startle has yielded conflicting results on the effects of PD, with some finding elevated fear-potentiated startle in individuals with PD relative to healthy control participants, and others finding no difference (Cuthbert et al., 2003; Gorka, Liu, Sarapas, & Shankman, 2015; Grillon et al., 2008; Lang & McTeague, 2009; Shankman et al., 2013). These mixed findings may be due to different types of aversive events employed in different studies (e.g., sound versus shock), and may reflect more interindividual variability in which types of stimuli elicit a fear response in PD. As an example of this variability, when confronted with an entrapment behavioral approach task, about 11% of participants refused to start the exposure, 21% terminated the exposure prior to the full 10 minutes, 36% completed the exposure while reporting medium to high levels of anxiety, and the final 32% completed the full exposure and did not report increased anxiety (Richter et al., 2012). The anxious completers showed more physiological signs of defensive reactivity (higher heart rate and skin conductance, fear-potentiated startle) compared with the non-anxious completers, indicating that the same agoraphobic situation can elicit subjective and physiological fear reactions in some individuals with PD with agoraphobia, but not others.

Circuits unit of analysis. Animal studies have shown that once a threat has been detected, attention is selectively allocated to the threat and motor freezing occurs, mediated by the projections of the amygdala to the ventral periaqueductal gray (Hamm et al., 2016). The initiation of a panic attack or other escape behavior is also driven by the dorsal periaqueductal gray (Hamm, Richter, & Pané-Farré, 2014). In studies using structural magnetic resonance imaging, PD has been associated with increased gray matter volume in the midbrain and brainstem regions (Protopopescu et al., 2006), with dorsal midbrain volume correlated with disorder severity (Fujiwara et al., 2011), further implicating the periaqueductal gray.

Molecules unit of analysis. Pharmacologic studies have implicated hyperactivity in serotonergic and noradrenergic systems in panic attacks, finding that drugs that increase activity in serotonergic and noradrenergic systems induce more panic attacks among individuals with PD than among those without PD (Johnson et al., 2014). The effectiveness of tricyclic antidepressants, selective serotonin reuptake inhibitors, and selective noradrenergic reuptake inhibitors in treating panic attacks and PD provides additional support for the role of these systems in maintaining the disorder (Johnson et al., 2014).

Genes unit of analysis. In line with the roles of the serotonergic and noradrenergic systems noted earlier, genes underlying these systems may also confer risk for PD. As noted in the earlier section on genetic components of potential threat (anxiety), these findings should be interpreted cautiously, as they are based on candidate gene, rather than genome-wide, approaches. A polymorphism in the promoter region of a gene encoding monoamine oxidase A (MAOA-uVNTR), an enzyme that metabolizes serotonin and norepinephrine, has been implicated in PD in women (Deckert et al., 1999; Maron et al., 2005; Samochowiec et al., 2004). These long allele risk variants are linked with increased gene expression. During an entrapment behavioral approach task, participants with risk variants reported more fear and had elevated heart rate, and all but one of the 34 participants who reported having a panic attack during the exposure had one of the risk variants (Hamm et al., 2016; Reif et al., 2014). This suggests this gene may confer risk though an overactive fear system and increased likelihood of panic attack. Further supporting the role of serotonin in PD, a polymorphism in the transcriptional control region of a serotonin autoreceptor gene, which functions to reduce serotonergic neurotransmission, has been related to escape behavior from an entrapment behavioral approach task in individuals with PD with agoraphobia (Straube et al., 2014), and the effect appears driven by the agoraphobia (Rothe et al., 2004).

Conclusion

PD and agoraphobia both involve worry about losing control, fear of bodily sensations, and avoidance behaviors, but also are marked by distinct diagnostic features. To receive a diagnosis of PD, a person must experience recurrent unexpected panic attacks, and their worry is particularly about future panic attacks or their consequences. Agoraphobia, on the other hand, is more related to fear or anxiety about situations from which escape might be difficult, particularly if one had a panic attack or lost control in other ways. Biological vulnerabilities may confer risk to developing PD and agoraphobia, including individual differences in genes, neuroanatomy, autonomic reactivity, neurotransmitter functioning, and respiration/hyperventilation. In addition, cognitive biases, including heightened attention to interoceptive cues and catastrophic misinterpretations of somatic sensations, increase vulnerability and maintain these disorders.

PD and agoraphobia are highly comorbid with other anxiety and mood disorders, and also with medical illnesses, suggesting transdiagnostic risk factors that may be examined from an RDoC framework. Within this framework, panic attacks and the physiological and psychological changes that precede them can be conceptualized as acute threat (fear) responses. Worries about losing control, future anxiety symptoms, and not being able to escape a situation can be thought of as potential threat (anxiety) responses, and responses to both acute and potential threats are nested within the negative valence systems domain.

Future research should incorporate newer methodologies to enhance understanding about the acquisition and maintenance of PD and agoraphobia. For instance, ambulatory monitoring of individuals with PD and agoraphobia will likely be fruitful to observe physiological and psychological changes during daily life to identify periods of hypervigilance, avoidance or escape, and naturalistic panic attacks, rather than those induced in the laboratory. Such studies may have implications for development of just-in-time interventions that can reach affected individuals when they need them most via cell phones or other portable devices. In addition, most genetic studies of PD and agoraphobia have analyzed candidate SNPs, but fewer genome-wide association studies have been conducted. Given the heterogeneity in defensive responding in PD and agoraphobia and likely varied pathways to developing these disorders, future studies should aim to associate particular genetic and neurobiological differences with patterns of defensive responding, which would likely require very large samples. To better understand transdiagnostic, dimensional processes conferring risk for PD and agoraphobia, future studies may consider recruiting participants with less "pure" PD or agoraphobia, allowing more comorbidities and subthreshold symptoms. Also inspired by the RDoC framework, taking measurements across multiple units of analysis should deepen our understanding of fear and anxiety processes, which will hopefully lead to more effective treatments to alleviate the burden of these disorders.

References

Alius, M. G., Pané-Farré, C. A., Von Leupoldt, A., & Hamm, A. O. (2013). Induction of dyspnea evokes increased anxiety and maladaptive breathing in individuals with high anxiety sensitivity and suffocation fear. *Psychophysiology*, *50*(5), 488–497. http://doi.org/10.1111/psyp.12028

American Psychiatric Association (2013). *Diagnostic and Statistical Manual of Mental Disorders* (5th edn). Arlington, VA: American Psychiatric Association.

Asmundson, G. J. G., Taylor, S., & Smits, J. A. J. (2014). Panic disorder and agoraphobia: An overview and commentary on DSM-5 changes. *Depression and Anxiety*, *31*(6), 480–486. doi: 10.1002/da.22277

Barlow, D. H. (1988, 2002). *Anxiety and Its Disorders: The Nature and Treatment of Anxiety and Panic*. New York, NY: Guilford Press.

Barlow, D. H., Sauer-Zavala, S., Carl, J. R., Bullis, J. R., & Ellard, K. K. (2014). The nature, diagnosis, and treatment of neuroticism: Back to the future. *Clinical Psychological Science*, *2*(3), 344–365.

Beck, A. T., Emery, G., & Greenberg, R. I. (1985). *Anxiety Disorders and Phobias*. New York, NY: Basic Books.

Bouton, M. E., Mineka, S., & Barlow, D. H. (2001). A modern learning theory perspective on the etiology of panic disorder. *Psychological Review*, *108*(1), 4–32.

Brown, M., Smits, J. A., Powers, M. B., & Telch, M. J. (2003). Differential sensitivity of the three ASI factors in predicting panic disorder patients' subjective and behavioral response to hyperventilation challenge. *Journal of Anxiety Disorders*, *17*(5), 583–591.

Casey, L. M., Newcombe, P. A., & Oei, T. P. (2005). Cognitive mediation of panic severity: The role of catastrophic misinterpretation of bodily sensations and panic self-efficacy. *Cognitive Therapy and Research*, *29*(2), 187–200. doi: 10.1007/s10608-005-3164-3

Casey, L. M., Oei, T. P. S., & Newcombe, P. A. (2005). Looking beyond the negatives: A time period analysis of positive cognitions, negative cognitions, and working alliance in cognitive behavior therapy for panic disorder. *Psychotherapy Research*, *15*(1–2), 55–68.

Casey, L. M., Oei, T. P., Newcombe, P. A., & Kenardy, J. (2004). The role of catastrophic misinterpretation of bodily sensations and panic self-efficacy in predicting panic severity. *Journal of Anxiety Disorders*, *18*(3), 325–340. doi: 10.1016/s0887-6185(02)00257–8

Chambless, D. L. & Gracely, E. J. (1989). Fear of fear and the anxiety disorders. *Cognitive Therapy and Research*, *13*(1), 9–20.

Choe, A. Y., Kim, B., Lee, K. S., Lee, J. E., Lee, J. Y., Choi, T. K., & Lee, S. H. (2013). Serotonergic genes (*5-HTT* and *HTR1A*) and separation life events: Gene-by-environment interaction for panic disorder. *Neuropsychobiology*, *67*(4), 192–200.

Clark, D. M. (1986). A cognitive approach to panic. *Behaviour Research and Therapy*, *24*(4), 461–470.

Craske, M. G. & Barlow, D. H. (2007). Panic disorder and agoraphobia. In D. Barlow (ed.), *Clinical Handbook of Psychological Disorders* (4th edn) (pp. 1–64). New York, NY: Guilford Press.

Cuthbert, B. N. & Insel, T. R. (2013). Toward the future of psychiatric diagnosis: The seven pillars of RDoC. *BMC Medicine*, *11*(1), 126. http://doi.org/10.1186/1741-7015-11-126

Cuthbert, B. N., Lang, P. J., Strauss, C., Drobes, D., Patrick, C. J., & Bradley, M. M. (2003). The psychophysiology of anxiety disorder: Fear memory imagery. *Psychophysiology*, *40*(3), 407–422.

Davis, M., Walker, D. L., Miles, L., & Grillon, C. (2010). Phasic vs sustained fear in rats and humans: Role of the extended amygdala in fear vs anxiety. *Neuropsychopharmacology: Official Publication of the American College of Neuropsychopharmacology*, *35*(1), 105–135. http://doi.org/10.1038/npp.2009.109

de Jonge, P., Roest, A. M., Lim, C. C. W., Florescu, S. E., Bromet, E. J., Stein, D. J., … Scott, K. M. (2016). Cross-national epidemiology of panic disorder and panic attacks in the world mental health surveys. *Depression and Anxiety*, *33*(12), 1155–1177. doi: 10.1002/da.22572

Deckert, J., Catalano, M., Syagailo, Y. V. Bosi, M., Okladnova, O., Di Bella, D., … Lesch, K. P. (1999). Excess of high activity monoamine oxidase A gene promoter alleles in female patients with panic disorder. *Human Molecular Genetics*, *8*(4), 621–624.

Dillon, D. G., Rosso, I. M., Pechtel, P., Killgore, W. D. S., Rauch, S. L., & Pizzagalli, D. A. (2014). Peril and pleasure: An RDoC-inspired examination of threat responses and reward processing in anxiety and depression. *Depression and Anxiety*, *31*(3), 233–249. http://doi.org/10.1002/da.22202.

Dresler, T., Guhn, A., Tupak, S. V., Ehlis, A. C., Herrmann, M. J., Fallgatter, A. J., … Domschke, K. (2013). Revise the revised? New dimensions of the neuroanatomical hypothesis of panic disorder. *Journal of Neural Transmission*, *120*(1), 3–29.

Ehlers, A. (1993). Somatic symptoms and panic attacks: A retrospective study of learning experiences. *Behaviour Research and Therapy*, *31*(3), 269–278.

Ehlers, A. (1995). A 1-year prospective study of panic attacks: Clinical course and factors associated with maintenance. *Journal of Abnormal Psychology*, *104*(1), 164–172.

Fanselow, M. S. (1994). Neural organization of the defensive behavior system responsible for fear. *Psychonomic Bulletin & Review*, *1*(4), 429–438. http://doi.org/10.3758/BF03210947

Fanselow, M. S. & Lester, L. S. (1988). A functional behavioristic approach to aversively motivated behavior: Predatory imminence as a determinant of the topography of defensive behavior. In R. C. Bolles & M. D. Beecher (eds.), *Evolution and Learning* (pp. 185–212). Hillsdale, NJ: Lawrence Erlbaum Associates.

Fujiwara, A., Yoshida, T., Otsuka, T., Hayano, F., Asami, T., Narita, H., . . . Hirayasu, Y. (2011). Midbrain volume increase in patients with panic disorder. *Psychiatry and Clinical Neurosciences*, *65*(4), 365–373. http://doi.org/10.1111/j.1440–1819.2011.02219.x

Gallagher, M. W., Payne, L. A., White, K. S., Shear, K. M., Woods, S. W., Gorman, J. M., & Barlow, D. H. (2013). Mechanisms of change in cognitive behavioral therapy for panic disorder: The unique effects of self-efficacy and anxiety sensitivity. *Behaviour Research and Therapy*, *51*(11), 767–777.

Goldstein, A. J. & Chambless, D. L. (1978). A reanalysis of agoraphobia. *Behavior Therapy*, *9*(1), 47–59. doi: 10.1016/S0005-7894(78)80053–7

Gorka, S. M., Liu, H., Sarapas, C., & Shankman, S. A. (2015). Time course of threat responding in panic disorder and depression. *International Journal of Psychophysiology*, *98*(1), 87–94. http://doi.org/10.1016/j.ijpsycho.2015.07.005

Gorlin, E. I., Beadel, J. R., Roberson-Nay, R., & Teachman, B. A. (2014). The self-fulfilling panic prophecy: Anxiety-related control attributions uniquely predict reactivity to a 7.5% CO_2 challenge. *Cognitive Therapy and Research*, *38*(6), 585–599.

Gorman, J. M., Kent, J. M., Sullivan, G. M., & Coplan, J. D. (2000). Neuroanatomical hypothesis of panic disorder, revised. *American Journal of Psychiatry*, *157*(4), 493–505.

Gould, R. A., Otto, M. W., & Pollack, M. H. (1995). A meta-analysis of treatment outcome for panic disorder. *Clinical Psychology Review*, *15*(8), 819–844.

Graeff, F. G. (2017). Translational approach to the pathophysiology of panic disorder: Focus on serotonin and endogenous opioids. *Neuroscience and Biobehavioral Reviews*, *76*, 48–55.

Graeff, F. G. & Del-Ben, C. M. (2008). Neurobiology of panic disorder: From animal models to brain neuroimaging. *Neuroscience and Biobehavioral Reviews*, *32*(7), 1326–1335. http://doi.org/10.1016/j.neubiorev.2008.05.017

Greene, A. L. & Eaton, N. R. (2016). Panic disorder and agoraphobia: A direct comparison of their multivariate comorbidity patterns. *Journal of Affective Disorders*, *190*, 75–83. doi: 10.1016/j.jad.2015.09.060

Grillon, C., Ameli, R., Goddard, A., Woods, S. W., & Davis, M. (1994). Baseline and fear-potentiated startle in panic disorder patients. *Biological Psychiatry*, *35*(7), 431–439.

Grillon, C., Lissek, S., Rabin, S., Mcdowell, D., Dvir, S., & Pine, D. S. (2008). Increased anxiety during anticipation of unpredictable but not predictable aversive stimuli as a psychophysiologic marker of panic disorder. *American Journal of Psychiatry*, *165*(7), 898–904. http://doi.org/10.1176/appi.ajp.2007.07101581

Hamm, A. O., Richter, J., & Pané-Farré, C. A. (2014). When the threat comes from inside the body: A neuroscience based learning perspective of the etiology of panic disorder. *Restorative Neurology and Neuroscience, 32*(1), 79–93. http://doi.org/10 .3233/RNN-139011

Hamm, A. O., Richter, J. A. N., Pané-Farré, C. A., Wittchen, H., Vossbeck-Elsebusch, A. N., Gerlach, A. L., . . . Gerdes, A. B. M. (2016). Panic disorder with agoraphobia from a behavioral neuroscience perspective: Applying the research principles formulated by the Research Domain Criteria (RDoC) initiative. *Psychophysiology, 53,* 312–322. http://doi.org/10.1111/psyp.12553

Harvey, J. M., Richards, J. C., Dziadosz, T., & Swindell, A. (1993). Misinterpretation of ambiguous stimuli in panic disorder. *Cognitive Therapy and Research, 17*(3), 235–248.

Hayward, C., Killen, J. D., Kraemer, H. C., & Taylor, C. B. (2000). Predictors of panic attacks in adolescents. *Journal of the American Academy of Child and Adolescent Psychiatry, 39*(2), 207–214.

Hettema, J. M., Neale, M. C., & Kendler, K. S. (2001). A review and meta-analysis of the genetic epidemiology of anxiety disorders. *American Journal of Psychiatry, 158* (10), 1568–1578.

Holtz, K., Pané-Farré, C. A., Wendt, J., Lotze, M., & Hamm, A. O. (2012). Brain activation during anticipation of interoceptive threat. *NeuroImage, 61*(4), 857–865. http://doi .org/10.1016/j.neuroimage.2012.03.019

Howe, A. S., Buttenschøn, H. N., Bani-Fatemi, A., Maron, E., Otowa, T., Erhardt, A., . . . Domschke, K. (2015). Candidate genes in panic disorder: Meta-analyses of 23 common variants in major anxiogenic pathways. *Molecular Psychiatry, 21*(5), 665–679.

Johnson, P. L., Federici, L. M., & Shekhar, A. (2014). Etiology, triggers and neurochemical circuits associated with unexpected, expected, and laboratory-induced panic attacks. *Neuroscience and Biobehavioral Reviews, 46,* 429–454. http://doi.org/10 .1016/j.neubiorev.2014.07.027

Keck, M. E., Kern, N., Erhardt, A., Unschuld, P. G., Ising, M., Salyakina, D., . . . Binder, E. B. (2008). Combined effects of exonic polymorphisms in *CRHR1* and *AVPR1B* genes in a case/control study for panic disorder. *American Journal of Medical Genetics, Part B: Neuropsychiatric Genetics, 147B*(7), 1196–1204. http://doi.org/10.1002/ajmg.b.30750

Kessler, R. C., Berglund, P., Demler, O., Jin, R., Merikangas, K. R., & Walters, E. E. (2005). Lifetime prevalence and age-of-onset distributions of DSM-IV disorders in the national comorbidity survey replication. *Archives of General Psychiatry, 62*(6), 593–602. doi: 10.1001/archpsyc.62.6.593

Kessler, R. C., Chiu, W. T., Jin, R., Ruscio, A. M., Shear, K., & Walters, E. E. (2006). The epidemiology of panic attacks, panic disorder, and agoraphobia in the national comorbidity survey replication. *Archives of General Psychiatry, 63*(4), 415–424. doi: 10.1001/archpsyc.63.4.415

Killgore, W. D. S., Britton, J. C., Price, L. M., Gold, A. L., & Rauch, S. L. (2011). Neural correlates of anxiety sensitivity during masked presentation of affective faces. *Depression and Anxiety, 28*(3), 243–249. http://doi.org/10.1002/da.20788

Klein, D. F. (1993). False suffocation alarms, spontaneous panics, and related conditions. An integrative hypothesis. *Archives of General Psychiatry, 50*(4), 306–317.

Kozak, M. J. & Cuthbert, B. N. (2016). The NIMH Research Domain Criteria Initiative: Background, issues, and pragmatics. *Psychophysiology*, *53*(3), 286–297. http://doi.org/10.1111/psyp.12518

Lamers, F., van Oppen, P., Comijs, H. C., Smit, J. H., Spinhoven, P., van Balkom, A. J. L. M., . . . Penninx, B. W. J. H. (2011). Comorbidity patterns of anxiety and depressive disorders in a large cohort study: The Netherlands Study of Depression and Anxiety (NESDA). *Journal of Clinical Psychiatry*, *72*(3), 341–348.

Lang, P. J. & McTeague, L. M. (2009). The anxiety disorder spectrum: Fear imagery, physiological reactivity, and differential diagnosis. *Anxiety Stress Coping*, *22*(1), 5–25. http://doi.org/10.1080/10615800802478247

Maron, E., Lang, A., Tasa, G., Liivlaid, L., Tõru, I., Must, A., . . . Shlik, J. (2005). Associations between serotonin-related gene polymorphisms and panic disorder. *International Journal of Neuropsychopharmacology*, *8*(2), 261–266. http://doi.org/10.1017/S1461145704004985

McGinn, L. K., Nooner, K. B., Cohen, J., & Leaberry, K. D. (2015). The role of early experience and cognitive vulnerability: Presenting a unified model of the etiology of panic. *Cognitive Therapy and Research*, *39*(4), 508–519.

McNally, R. J. & Eke, M. (1996). Anxiety sensitivity, suffocation fear, and breath-holding duration as predictors of response to carbon dioxide challenge. *Journal of Abnormal Psychology*, *105*(1), 146–149.

McNally, R. J. & Foa, E. B. (1987). Cognition and agoraphobia: Bias in the interpretation of threat. *Cognitive Therapy and Research*, *11*(5), 567–581.

Meuret, A. E., Kroll, J., & Ritz, T. (2017). Panic disorder comorbidity with medical conditions and treatment implications. *Annual Review of Clinical Psychology*, *13*(1), 209–240. doi: 10.1146/annurev-clinpsy-021815-093044

Meuret, A. E., Ritz, T., Wilhelm, F. H., & Roth, W. T. (2005). Voluntary hyperventilation in the treatment of panic disorder: Functions of hyperventilation, their implications for breathing training, and recommendations for standardization. *Clinical Psychology Review*, *25*(3), 285–306.

Milrod, B., Chambless, D. L., Gallop, R., Busch, F. N., Schwalberg, M., McCarthy, K. S., . . . Barber, J. P. (2015). Psychotherapies for panic disorder: A tale of two sites. *Journal of Clinical Psychiatry*, *77*(7), 927–935.

Mobbs, D., Marchant, J. L., Hassabis, D., Seymour, B., Tan, G., Gray, M., . . . Frith, C. D. (2009). From threat to fear: The neural organization of defensive fear systems in humans. *Journal of Neuroscience*, *29*(39), 12236–12243.

Norton, G. R., Cox, B. J., & Malan, J. (1992). Nonclinical panickers: A critical review. *Clinical Psychology Review*, *12*(2), 121–139.

Olatunji, B. O. & Wolitzky-Taylor, K. B. (2009). Anxiety sensitivity and the anxiety disorders: A meta-analytic review and synthesis. *Psychological Bulletin*, *135*(6), 974–999.

Öst, L.-G., Johansson, J., & Jerremalm, A. (1982). Individual response patterns and the effects of different behavioral methods in the treatment of claustrophobia. *Behaviour Research and Therapy*, *20*(5), 445–460. http://doi.org/10.1016/0005-7967(82)90066-3

Otto, M. W., Reilly-Harrington, N. A., & Taylor, S. (1999). The impact of treatment on anxiety sensitivity. In S. Taylor (ed.), *Anxiety Sensitivity: Theory, Research, and*

Treatment of the Fear of Anxiety (pp. 321–336). Mahwah, NJ: Lawrence Erlbaum Associates.

Perusini, J. N. & Fanselow, M. S. (2015). Neurobehavioral perspectives on the distinction between fear and anxiety. *Learning & Memory, 22*(9), 417–425. http://doi.org/10 .1101/lm.039180.115

Preter, M. & Klein, D. F. (1998). Panic disorder and the suffocation false alarm theory: Current state of knowledge and further implications for neurobiologic theory testing. In *The Panic Respiration Connection* (pp. 1–24). Milan: MDM Medical Media Srl.

Preter, M. & Klein, D. F. (2008). Panic, suffocation false alarms, separation anxiety and endogenous opioids. *Progress in Neuro-Psychopharmacology and Biological Psychiatry, 32*, 603–661.

Preter, M. & Klein, D. F. (2014). Lifelong opioidergic vulnerability through early life separation: A recent extension of the false suffocation alarm theory of panic disorder. *Neuroscience and Biobehavioral Reviews, 46*, 345–351.

Protopopescu, X., Pan, H., Tuescher, O., Cloitre, M., Goldstein, M., Engelien, A., . . . Silbersweig, D. (2006). Increased brainstem volume in panic disorder: A voxel-based morphometric study. *Neuroreport, 17*(4), 361–363.

Rachman, S. & Taylor, S. (1993). Analyses of claustrophobia. *Journal of Anxiety Disorders, 7*(4), 281–291. http://doi.org/https://doi.org/10.1016/0887–6185(93)90025-G

Radomsky, A. S., Rachman, S., Thordarson, D. S., Mcisaac, H. K., & Teachman, B. A. (2001). The Claustrophobia Questionnaire. *Journal of Anxiety Disorder, 15*(4), 287–297.

Rapee, R., Mattick, R., & Murrell, E. (1986). Cognitive mediation in the affective component of spontaneous panic attacks. *Journal of Behavior Therapy and Experimental Psychiatry, 17*(4), 245–253.

Rassovsky, Y., Kushner, M. G., Schwarze, N. J., & Wangensteen, O. D. (2000). Psychological and physiological predictors of response to carbon dioxide challenge in individuals with panic disorder. *Journal of Abnormal Psychology, 109*(4), 616–623.

Rau, V. & Fanselow, M. S. (2007). Neurobiological and neuroethological perspectives on fear and anxiety. In *Understanding Trauma: Integrating Biological, Clinical, and Cultural Perspectives* (pp. 27–40).

Reif, A., Richter, J., Straube, B., Höfler, M., Lueken, U., Gloster, A. T., . . . Deckert, J. (2014). MAOA and mechanisms of panic disorder revisited: From bench to molecular psychotherapy. *Molecular Psychiatry, 19*(1), 122–128. http://doi.org /10.1038/mp.2012.172

Reiss, S. (1991). Expectancy model of fear, anxiety, and panic. *Clinical Psychology Review, 11*(2), 141–153.

Reiss, S. & McNally, R. J. (1985). Expectancy model of fear. In S. Reiss and R. R. Bootzin (eds.), *Theoretical Issues in Behavior Therapy* (pp. 107–121). New York, NY: Academic Press.

Reiss, S., Peterson, R. A., Gursky, D. M., & McNally, R. J. (1986). Anxiety sensitivity, anxiety frequency and the prediction of fearfulness. *Behavior Research and Therapy, 24*(1), 1–8. http://doi.org/10.1016/0005–7967(86)90143–9

Richter, J., Hamm, A. O., Pané-Farré, C. A., Gerlach, A. L., Gloster, A. T., Wittchen, H. U., . . . Arolt, V. (2012). Dynamics of defensive reactivity in patients with panic disorder and agoraphobia: Implications for the etiology of panic disorder. *Biological Psychiatry*, *72*(6), 512–520. http://doi.org/10.1016/j .biopsych.2012.03.035

Risbrough, V. B. & Stein, M. B. (2006). Role of corticotropin releasing factor in anxiety disorders: A translational research perspective. *Hormones and Behavior*, *50*(4), 550–561.

Roberson-Nay, R., Beadel, J. R., Gorlin, E. I., Latendresse, S. J., & Teachman, B. A. (2015). Examining the latent class structure of CO2 hypersensitivity using time course trajectories of panic response systems. *Journal of Behavior Therapy and Experimental Psychiatry*, *47*, 68–76.

Rosso, I. M., Makris, N., Britton, J. C., . . . Rauch, S. L. (2010). Anxiety sensitivity correlates with two indices of right anterior insula structure in specific animal phobia. *Depression and Anxiety*, *27*(12), 1104–1110. http://doi.org/10.1002/da .20765.

Rothe, C., Gutknecht, L., Freitag, C., Tauber, R., Mo, R., Wagner, G., . . . No, M. M. (2004). Association of a functional – 1019C > G 5-HT1A receptor gene polymorphism with panic disorder with agoraphobia. *International Journal of Neuropsychopharmacology*, *7*(2), 189–192. http://doi.org/10.1017 /S1461145703004061

Rudden, M. G., Milrod, B., Aronson, A., & Target, M. (2008). Reflective functioning in panic disorder patients. *Mentalization: Theoretical Considerations, Research Findings, and Clinical Implications*, *29*, 185.

Salkovskis, P. M. & Clark, D. M. (1990). Affective responses to hyperventilation: A test of the cognitive model of panic. *Behaviour Research and Therapy*, *28*(1), 51–61.

Samochowiec, J., Hajduk, A., Samochowiec, A., Horodnicki, J., Stępień, G., Grzywacz, A., & Kucharska-Mazur, J. (2004). Association studies of *MAO-A, COMT*, and *5-HTT* genes polymorphisms in patients with anxiety disorders of the phobic spectrum. *Psychiatry Research*, *128*(1), 21–26. http://doi.org/10.1016/j.psychres.2004.05 .012

Schmidt, N. B., Lerew, D. R., & Jackson, R. J. (1997). The role of anxiety sensitivity in the pathogenesis of panic: Prospective evaluation of spontaneous panic attacks during acute stress. *Journal of Abnormal Psychology*, *106*(3), 355–364.

Schmitz, A. & Grillon, C. (2012). Assessing fear and anxiety in humans using the threat of predictable and unpredictable aversive events (the NPU-threat test). *Nature Protocols*, *7*(3), 527–532. http://doi.org/10.1038/nprot.2012.001

Schroijen, M., Fantoni, S., Rivera, C., Vervliet, B., Schruers, K., van den Bergh, O., & van Diest, I. (2016). Defensive activation to (un)predictable interoceptive threat: The NPU respiratory threat test (NPUr). *Psychophysiology*, *53*(6), 905–913. http://doi.org/10.1111/psyp.12621

Schumacher, J., Kristensen, A. S., Wendland, J. R., Nöthen, M. M., Mors, O., & McMahon, F. J. (2011). The genetics of panic disorder. *Journal of Medical Genetics*, *48*(6), 361–368.

Shankman, S. A., Nelson, B. D., Sarapas, C., Robison-Andrew, E. J., Campbell, M. L., Altman, S. E., . . . Gorka, S. M. (2013). A psychophysiological investigation of threat and reward sensitivity in individuals with panic disorder and/or major depressive disorder. *Journal of Abnormal Psychology*, *122*(2), 322–338. http://doi .org/10.1037/a0030747

Smits, J. A., Powers, M. B., Cho, Y., & Telch, M. J. (2004). Mechanism of change in cognitive-behavioral treatment of panic disorder: Evidence for the fear of fear mediational hypothesis. *Journal of Consulting and Clinical Psychology, 72*(4), 646–652.

Steimer, T. (2002). The biology of fear-and anxiety-related behaviors. *Dialogues in Clinical Neuroscience, 4*(3), 231–250.

Stein, M. B., Simmons, A. N., Feinstein, J. S., & Paulus, M. P. (2007). Increased amygdala and insula activation during emotion processing in anxiety-prone subjects. *American Journal of Psychiatry, 164*(2), 318–327.

Steinman, S. A. & Teachman, B. A. (2010). Modifying interpretations among individuals high in anxiety sensitivity. *Journal of Anxiety Disorders, 24*(1), 71–78.

Straube, B., Reif, A., Richter, J., Lueken, U., Weber, H., Arolt, V., ... Konrad, C. (2014). The functional − 1019C / G HTR1A polymorphism and mechanisms of fear. *Translational Psychiatry, 4*(12). http://doi.org/10.1038/tp.2014.130

Taylor, S. (2000). *Understanding and Treating Panic Disorder: Cognitive-Behavioural Approaches*. Chichester: John Wiley & Sons Ltd.

Taylor, S., & Asmundson, G. J. G. (2016). Panic disorder and agoraphobia. A. Carr & M. McNulty (eds.), *The Handbook of Adult Clinical Psychology: An Evidence Based Practice Approach* (pp. 467–491). London: Routledge.

Taylor, S., Zvolensky, M. J., Cox, B. J., Deacon, B., Heimberg, R. G., Ledley, D. R., ... Arrindell, W. A. (2007). Robust dimensions of anxiety sensitivity: Development and initial validation of the Anxiety Sensitivity Index – 3. *Psychological Assessment, 19*(2), 176–188. http://doi.org/10.1037/1040–3590.19.2.176

Teachman, B. A. (2005). Information processing and anxiety sensitivity: Cognitive vulnerability to panic reflected in interpretation and memory biases. *Cognitive Therapy and Research, 29*(4), 479–499.

Teachman, B. A., Joormann, J., Steinman, S. A., & Gotlib, I. H. (2012). Automaticity in anxiety disorders and major depressive disorder. *Clinical Psychology Review, 32*, 575–603.

Teachman, B. A., Marker, C. D., & Clerkin, E. M. (2010). Catastrophic misinterpretations as a predictor of symptom change during treatment for panic disorder. *Journal of Consulting and Clinical Psychology, 78*(6), 964.

Teachman, B. A., Marker, C. D., & Smith-Janik, S. B. (2008). Automatic associations and panic disorder: Trajectories of change over the course of treatment. *Journal of Consulting and Clinical Psychology, 76*, 988–1002.

Teachman, B. A., Smith-Janik, S. B., & Saporito, J. (2007). Information processing biases and panic disorder: Relationships among cognitive and symptom measures. *Behaviour Research and Therapy, 45*, 1791–1811.

Weber, H., Richter, J., Straube, B., Lueken, U., Domschke, K., Schartner, C., ... Reif, A. (2015). Allelic variation in *CRHR1* predisposes to panic disorder: Evidence for biased fear processing. *Molecular Psychiatry, 21*(6), 813–822. http://doi.org/10.1038/mp.2015.125

Wittchen, H.-U., Gloster, A. T., Beesdo-Baum, K., Fava, G. A., & Craske, M. G. (2010). Agoraphobia: A review of the diagnostic classificatory position and criteria. *Depression and Anxiety, 27*(2), 113–133. doi: 10.1002/da.20646

17 Social Anxiety Disorder

Arielle Horenstein, Rachel M. Butler,
and Richard G. Heimberg

Definition, Epidemiology, Course, and Comorbidity

Social anxiety disorder (SAD) (also known as social phobia) has been included in the *Diagnostic and Statistical Manual of Mental Disorders* (*DSM*) since the publication of the *DSM-III* (American Psychiatric Association [APA], 1980). SAD is characterized by pervasive and chronic fear of negative evaluation by others in one or more social situations. Examples of commonly feared situations include public speaking, initiating conversations, participating in work or school, speaking with authority figures, and making requests of others. Individuals with SAD fear they will do something to humiliate or embarrass themselves in these situations, which often leads to intense distress and the onset of physiological symptoms of anxiety such as perspiration, elevated heart rate, or nausea. For those with SAD, feared social situations may also elicit panic attacks (Potter et al., 2014). Due to the intensity of the associated distress, SAD generally leads to marked avoidance of social situations. Therefore, SAD is not only associated with significant distress but can also lead to significant impairments in a person's occupational, social, and romantic functioning, and overall quality of life (Acarturk et al., 2009; Aderka et al., 2012; Bruch, Fallon, & Heimberg, 2003; Schneier et al., 1994).

According to the National Comorbidity Survey Replication, approximately 12.1% of the US population will experience SAD during their lifetime, and 7.1% of the population will experience SAD in a given 12-month period (Kessler, Berglund et al., 2005; Kessler, Chiu, Demler, Merikangas, & Walters, 2005). Thus, SAD is among the most prevalent DSM disorders. More conservative reports suggest that the lifetime prevalence of SAD is about 5.0% and the 12-month prevalence is about 2.8% in the United States (Grant et al., 2005). Men and women tend to experience SAD at comparable lifetime rates (13.0% females, 11.1% males), and the onset of SAD typically occurs during adolescence or by early adulthood (Kessler, Berglund, et al., 2005). Although the average age of onset is during early adolescence, many individuals with SAD report having suffered from symptoms of social anxiety such as shyness or fear of embarrassment during childhood. Despite the distress and impairment that individuals with SAD experience, only roughly 20–35% receive treatment specifically for SAD (Grant et al., 2005; Ruscio et al., 2008), and those who do seek treatment tend to do so well after disorder onset (Grant et al., 2005). Compared to other anxiety disorders, SAD seems to be fairly chronic and less likely to remit without treatment (Yonkers, Bruce, Dyck, & Keller, 2003; Yonkers, Dyck, & Keller, 2001).

In addition to being one of the most prevalent DSM disorders, SAD is often comorbid with other mental disorders, and comorbidity is often associated with a higher degree of impairment and a more chronic course of illness. SAD is highly comorbid with other anxiety disorders such as panic disorder, agoraphobia, specific phobia, generalized anxiety disorder (GAD), posttraumatic stress disorder, and separation anxiety disorder (Ruscio et al., 2008). Comorbidity with other anxiety disorders such as GAD seems to negatively impact the likelihood of recovery and increase the chance that SAD will recur (Bruce et al., 2005). Comparably high rates of comorbidity between SAD and depression have been reported. For example, in a sample of individuals with major depressive disorder, 41% of individuals also met criteria for SAD (Brown et al., 2001). Because SAD is associated with increased risk for the development of depression, dysthymia, and bipolar disorder (Kessler, Stang, Wittchen, Stein, & Walters, 1999), it is important to consider how comorbidity with these disorders affects functioning. The co-occurrence of SAD and depression is related to greater functional impairment, more intense suicidal ideation, and increased risk of attempting suicide (Stein et al., 2001). Those with comorbid SAD and mood disorders also remain more impaired by their SAD symptoms following cognitive-behavioral treatment (Erwin, Heimberg, Juster, & Mindlin, 2002). Alcohol and substance use disorders are also highly comorbid with SAD, especially in treatment-seeking populations (Grant et al., 2004). In the majority of comorbid cases, the onset of SAD precedes the onset of alcohol use disorders, and SAD tends to be associated with more severe alcohol abuse and dependence (Schneier et al., 2010). The high rates of comorbidity with other anxiety disorders, depression, and alcohol and substance use disorders contribute to the full picture of impairment and distress experienced by individuals with SAD and have important implications for the course of illness and treatment-seeking behaviors.

Prominent Cognitive-Behavioral Models of SAD

Several influential cognitive-behavioral models of SAD have been put forth over the years (e.g., D. Clark & Wells, 1995; Hofmann, 2007; Rapee & Heimberg, 1997; Q. Wong & Rapee, 2016) that have sought to define the core cognitive and behavioral features that drive the development and maintenance of SAD. Models of SAD that we review here (and a number of others) have been previously and extensively reviewed by J. Wong, Gordon, and Heimberg (2014) and Schultz and Heimberg (2008).

The model of SAD developed by D. Clark and Wells (1995) proposed that individuals with SAD hold certain assumptions about themselves and others that lead them to evaluate social situations as dangerous or threatening. These assumptions include negative beliefs about the self (i.e., I am boring, odd, etc.), excessively high self-standards in social situations (i.e., I must *always* sound intelligent), and the belief that the risks of an imperfect social performance are high (i.e., they will lead to negative evaluation and/or rejection by others). This model significantly overlaps with another early cognitive-behavioral model developed by Rapee and Heimberg (1997), which also proposed that at the core of SAD is the assumption that, while acceptance from others is vitally important, one's own ability to meet others' expectations is low and the likelihood of negative evaluation from others is high. These kinds of core assumptions among individuals with SAD may lead to the enhanced detection of threat in social situations and to the interpretation of ambiguous social cues as signs of a poor performance or negative evaluation from others.

These models propose that when individuals with social anxiety enter or anticipate entering a social situation, they begin to process themselves as "a social object" (D. Clark & Wells, 1995), or a "mental representation of self as seen by others" is activated (Rapee & Heimberg, 1997). In both models, individuals begin to direct their attention to internal bodily cues, or physiological signs of anxiety, to help them evaluate their own performance. Rapee and Heimberg also highlight the biased use of external cues (i.e., others' facial expressions), in addition to internal cues, to evaluate social performance. As a result, individuals with social anxiety tend to equate bodily sensations of anxiety (i.e., shaking, blushing) with poor performance and are more likely to allocate attention to external cues that signal negative evaluation; for instance, during a presentation they may only pay attention to the one person in the audience who is not smiling. D. Clark and Wells (1995) and Rapee and Heimberg (1997) also propose that socially anxious individuals tend to visualize themselves from an observer's perspective, or from the point of view of others. These visualizations can often be distorted (Hackmann, Clark, & McManus, 2000; Hackmann, Surawy, & Clark, 1998). For example, a socially anxious individual may be more likely to see an image of himself in a recent social situation in which he is sweating or blushing, and these symptoms are perceived as apparent to others and as eliciting negative judgment.

Both models also propose that individuals with social anxiety may utilize certain behaviors or mental processes termed "safety behaviors" or "subtle avoidance behaviors" to prevent negative evaluation from others while not entirely avoiding a social situation. These behaviors may range from standing on the periphery of a group to memorizing what one plans to say in a conversation or presentation and, although they may reduce anxiety in the moment, they ultimately prevent socially anxious individuals from becoming fully engaged in a social interaction or situation and from coming into contact with evidence that negative evaluation from others might not occur. In addition, utilization of safety behaviors may actually increase the likelihood of performance deficits and negative evaluation from others, inadvertently leading to the opposite effect of what was originally intended.

Another component of D. Clark and Wells's initial model that is included in Heimberg, Brozovich, and Rapee's (2014) revised model is the engagement among individuals with SAD in negative cognitive processing both before and after social situations, which may serve to maintain negative images and beliefs about the self and about the outcomes of social situations. Anticipatory processing prior to the event may lead to avoidance of the situation or prime individuals to view themselves as social objects upon entering the situation. Following the interaction, an individual may review the events and outcomes of the social situation in a negatively biased manner, a practice termed *post-event processing* (Brozovich & Heimberg, 2008; D. Clark & Wells, 1995). Post-event processing also serves to maintain the negative self-image socially anxious individuals hold of themselves in social situations and increases the likelihood that future social situations will be avoided and/or viewed again in a negatively biased manner.

Another influential cognitive-behavioral model of SAD was proposed by Hofmann (2007) and has significant overlap with the Clark–Wells and Rapee–Heimberg models. A major component of SAD in Hofmann's model is the discrepancy between the perceived social standards of others and an individual's perceived ability to meet those standards. Hofmann also highlights the allocation of attention to internal and external cues to monitor and evaluate one's own social performance. In addition, Hofmann proposes that individuals with social anxiety are interested in making a particular impression, but doubt their ability to do so (see Schlenker & Leary, 1982) and have difficulty defining and setting more specific social goals and selecting strategies to achieve them. Individuals with SAD are also posited to have little perceived personal control over their emotional responses in social situations and identify themselves as having poor social skills. In combination with a high estimated social cost of poor performance, these perceptions lead to anticipation of social failures, which in turn leads to overt avoidance and/or the use of safety behaviors in social situations. As in other prominent models of SAD, individuals also engage in post-event processing, which is in turn associated with avoidance of similar situations in the future.

Another model of SAD was recently proposed by Q. Wong and Rapee (2016), with a primary aim of integrating both etiological and maintaining factors of SAD into a single model. In their model, they rely on the social-evaluation threat (SET) principle, which reflects the degree of threat value perceived by an individual in response to social-evaluative stimuli. Social-evaluative threat value exists on a continuum from low to high, and certain etiological factors, such as inherited tendencies (e.g., behavioral inhibition), early family and peer experiences, and/or stressful life events, contribute to an increase in the threat value an individual generally assigns to social-evaluative stimuli. Q. Wong and Rapee posit that the degree of a person's threat value present in their SET principle is reflected in their neurobiology and cognitive responses to social-evaluative stimuli. In addition, increased threat value leads to increased development of what Q. Wong and Rapee call primary cognitive and behavioral processes, including increased attention to self and external threats in the environment, as well as avoidance and escape of social situations. These primary cognitive and behavioral processes function as a way to improve an individual's ability to detect and eliminate social threat in the environment; however, as described in previous models, these processes also serve to maintain the threat value associated with social stimuli and can lead to the development of actual performance deficits due to repeated avoidance, increased anxiety, and reduced attentional resources during social situations. Q. Wong and Rapee suggest that, as an individual matures over time, secondary cognitive and behavioral processes develop, including anticipatory processing, post-event processing, the use of safety behaviors, and cognitive avoidance. These processes also serve to maintain the threat value of social stimuli over time by continuing to increase the detection of threat cues, preventing full exposure to social situations, and interfering with social performance. This model has significant overlap with the earlier models previously described but includes a more etiological and developmental framework to understand the processes involved in SAD.

Overall, each of these models attempts to address how and why SAD is maintained over time and, despite some noteworthy distinctions, they agree on the primary emotional, cognitive, and behavioral processes involved in the disorder. In this chapter, we provide a more detailed review of many of the components included in these models and the research supporting their role in the development and maintenance of SAD.

Social Anxiety in an RDoC Framework

The Research Domain Criteria (RDoC) initiative was launched by the National Institute of Mental Health in 2008 as a framework through which to conceptualize and conduct psychological research. Rather than studying psychological disorders categorically, RDoC focuses on dimensional constructs including observable behaviors and neurobiological indices (Insel et al., 2010), which are grouped into research domains. In this chapter, we examine both etiological and maintenance processes in SAD that occur within the following domains: Negative Valence Systems, Cognitive Systems, Positive Valence Systems, and Systems for Social Processes. Within SAD, the Negative Valence Systems domain includes the acute fears in social anxiety (i.e., evaluative fears) that are integral to the disorder. The Cognitive Systems domain encompasses biases in attention, attentional control, interpretation, and processing tendencies that may serve to maintain anxiety. Low positive affect in SAD is discussed as a component of the Positive Valence Systems domain. Finally, we examine how constructs within the Systems for Social Processes domain, such as attachment and interpersonal relationships, are involved in the experience of SAD. We also discuss important processes involved in SAD that may not be involved in one particular domain, including central behavioral processes (i.e., avoidance behavior) and emotion regulation difficulties and their role in the experience and maintenance of the disorder.

Negative Valence Systems

Fear of Negative Evaluation

As described previously, one of the core features of SAD is an extreme fear of negative evaluation (FNE) by others. FNE encompasses the fear that one's behavior in social situations will be judged poorly by others, the experience of distress when faced with possible negative evaluation, and the tendency to avoid situations in which evaluation may occur (Watson & Friend, 1969). Although FNE has long been considered central to the experience of SAD and has been used in a number of studies as a proxy for SAD (Heimberg, 1994), it was not specifically included in the SAD criteria until *DSM-5* (APA, 2013).

Studies of patients with SAD confirm that, compared to non-anxious controls, they have more extreme FNE (Weeks et al., 2005). Furthermore, FNE seems to be relatively specific to SAD. For example, in one study, participants with SAD reported significantly greater FNE than those with panic disorder (Ball, Otto, Pollack, Uccello, & Rosenbaum, 1995). Additionally, FNE relates significantly to social avoidance but not to agoraphobic avoidance (Collins, Westra, Dozois, & Stewart, 2005). Another study examining the associations between sensitivity to negative evaluation and obsessive-compulsive symptoms, worry, social anxiety, and panic found that sensitivity to negative evaluation predicted only social anxiety and worry (Kotov, Watson, Robles, & Schmidt, 2007). FNE also seems to be sensitive to the effects of treatment for SAD in that it decreases following treatment, is related to clinical functioning, and correlates with changes in depression, anxiety, and social avoidance (Collins et al., 2005; Heimberg, 1994).

Fear of Positive Evaluation

Although negative evaluation has long been considered *the* core feature of SAD, fear of positive evaluation (FPE), or fear and distress surrounding positive social judgment by others, may also be a core feature of the disorder (Weeks, Heimberg, & Rodebaugh, 2008). Some researchers explain the phenomena of FPE as a problem of "raising the bar," such that individuals with social anxiety fear that if they receive positive evaluation they will not be able to maintain the same high level of performance in the future, which will ultimately lead to negative evaluation by others (Wallace & Alden, 1995, 1997). However, this process is better conceptualized as a delayed fear of negative evaluation, and research suggests that the construct of FPE is distinct from it. Evolutionary perspectives suggest that individuals with SAD may fear that positive evaluation will lead to an increase in social status, causing others to feel threatened and react defensively, creating conflict (Gilbert, 2001, 2014). Longitudinal examination suggests that FPE and FNE are in fact distinct, trait-like constructs, and that FPE is not simply a fear of future negative evaluation (Rodebaugh, Weeks, Gordon, Langer, & Heimberg, 2012). Weeks and Howell (2012) found that, compared to fear of negative evaluation, fear of positive evaluation was significantly and uniquely related to concerns that making a positive impression would lead to social reprisal or retaliation from others. Several studies using confirmatory factor analysis support a two-factor structure over a one-factor structure for dimensions of evaluative fears, suggesting that positive and negative evaluative fears are independent (e.g., Weeks, Heimberg, & Rodebaugh, 2008). This two-factor structure of evaluative fears has been replicated in clinical samples of patients with anxiety disorders (Fergus et al., 2009) and specifically with SAD (Weeks, Heimberg, Rodebaugh, Goldin, & Gross, 2012).

In support of the central role of FPE in SAD, research has shown that social anxiety is linked to greater FPE (Weeks, Heimberg, Rodebaugh, & Norton, 2008; Weeks et al., 2012) and that FPE accounts for a comparable amount of variation in SAD symptoms as FNE (Teale Sapach, Carleton, Mulvogue, Weeks, & Heimberg, 2015). Furthermore, FPE has been associated with the perception of positive feedback as less accurate, a relationship that is mediated by the degree of discomfort experienced in receiving positive feedback (Weeks, Heimberg, Rodebaugh, & Norton, 2008). FPE seems to be related to a general suppression of positive experiences, including lower trait positive affect and less frequent positive automatic thoughts (Weeks & Howell, 2012). On the other hand, both FPE and FNE are associated with trait negative affect and negative automatic thoughts.

Fear of positive evaluation also seems to be specifically related to SAD compared to other forms of psychopathology. In a clinical sample, FPE was significantly higher in patients with SAD than in patients with other anxiety disorders (Fergus et al., 2009). Due to the high comorbidity between social anxiety and depression, researchers have examined whether FPE is more closely related to social anxiety than depression. Using structural equation modeling and hierarchical regression analyses, Wang, Hsu, Chiu, and Liang (2012) demonstrated that, whereas FNE was more strongly related to social anxiety than depression, FPE predicted only social anxiety. Weeks (2015) replicated this pattern in an independent dataset. These findings suggest that, although FNE is a factor in both social anxiety and, to a lesser degree, depression, FPE may be a distinguishing feature of social anxiety.

In both undergraduate and clinical samples, FPE has been shown to be stable across time (Rodebaugh, Weeks, et al., 2012; Weeks et al., 2012). However, a study showing that that FPE decreased significantly from pre- to post-treatment found that this effect was comparable to the changes in social anxiety symptoms over treatment (Fergus et al., 2009), suggesting that FPE may be sensitive to change over the course of treatment for SAD.

Cognitive Systems

Primary Cognitive Processes

Attentional bias toward social threat. Cognitive-behavioral models of SAD (e.g., D. Clark & Wells, 1995; Hofmann, 2007; Rapee & Heimberg, 1997; Q. Wong & Rapee, 2016) posit that individuals with social anxiety direct heightened attention to cues suggesting that they are being evaluated by others. Experimentally, attentional bias toward threat has often been investigated using dot-probe tasks that present a word or face pair (e.g., one threatening and one neutral) on the screen followed by a probe in the same location as one of the cues. Individuals with social anxiety tend to respond faster to probes replacing social threat cues than neutral cues, a phenomenon not typically seen in non-anxious controls (e.g., Mogg, Philippot, & Bradley, 2004; Pishyar, Harris, & Menzies, 2004). These findings suggest that socially anxious individuals' attention is biased toward social threat cues.

Attention bias modification, which manipulates attention away from threat stimuli, can successfully reduce social anxiety symptoms (e.g., Amir et al., 2009; Schmidt, Richey, Buckner, & Timpano, 2009). Similarly, training attention toward threat increases social anxiety during a social rejection task (Heeren, Pechard, & Philippot, 2012), suggesting that vigilant attention to threat cues may play a causal role in the development and maintenance of SAD.

The vigilance-avoidance hypothesis (Mogg & Bradley, 1998) proposes that anxious individuals are initially hypervigilant to a threat stimulus but then avert their attention away from the stimulus as a defense against that threat. By directing attention away from a potentially threatening stimulus (e.g., a facial expression), the individual is unable to further process the stimulus and make a non-threatening reappraisal of it, preventing the habituation of anxiety. Some evidence for the vigilance-avoidance hypothesis has been presented (see Bögels & Mansell, 2004, for a review). However, other research suggests that socially anxious individuals may actually have difficulty disengaging attention from social threat cues in the environment, as demonstrated by their slower response to cued targets preceded by a social threat word compared with a neutral word (e.g., Amir, Elias, Klumpp, & Przeworski, 2003). Thus, they may have trouble both attending and disattending, increasing the amount of time during which they are focused on threatening stimuli.

Attentional bias away from positive social information. SAD may also be characterized by an attentional bias away from positive social information. Taylor, Bomyea, and Amir (2010) found that shifting attention away from positive social stimuli mediated the relationship between social anxiety and state anxiety on a speech task. Additionally, by tracking eye movement during an attentional cuing task, researchers found that individuals with SAD were quicker to disengage attention from positive cues than non-anxious controls (N. Chen, Clarke, MacLeod,

& Guastella, 2012). Yu and colleagues (2014) examined this positive attention bias using a modified dot-probe task and found that, compared to a low social anxiety group, those with high social anxiety showed avoidance of positive social words when the words were presented for only 100 ms, but not when the words were presented for 500 or 1, 250 ms, suggesting that this bias may be present very early in the stream of cognition. Biased attention away from positive cues may play a causal role in the development and maintenance of social anxiety by preventing individuals from gathering information that would challenge their negative perceptions of social situations. This potentially causal role is supported by findings that training attention toward positive information decreases anxiety reactivity after a speech task (Taylor, Bomyea, & Amir, 2011).

There is also some evidence suggesting that, regardless of positive or negative valence, individuals with social anxiety are biased to direct attention away from *any* social cue. For instance, regardless of the emotion depicted by the faces, socially anxious participants responded faster in a dot-probe task to household objects than to faces (Y. Chen, Ehlers, Clark, & Mansell, 2002).

Attentional control. Individuals with SAD also seem to have difficulty with volitional control of attention. Moriya and Tanno (2008) found that social anxiety was inversely related to self-reported attentional control. On an emotional anti-saccade task, a task used to assess an individual's ability to inhibit reflexive eye movements toward stimuli, individuals with high levels of social anxiety committed more errors (i.e., looking at a peripheral stimulus rather than in the opposite direction as instructed) than individuals with moderate social anxiety, regardless of facial expression presented. These results seem to indicate that the deficits in attentional control seen among individuals with social anxiety are not specific to threatening stimuli. The results of this study held even after controlling for state and trait anxiety levels, suggesting that attentional control deficits may be related to executive functioning deficits rather than heightened anxiety levels (Wieser, Pauli, & Mühlberger, 2009).

Attentional control may also help explain individual differences in attention bias. Taylor, Cross, and Amir (2016) identified attentional control as a moderator of the association between social anxiety and difficulty disengaging attention from threat. Higher levels of social anxiety combined with poor attentional shifting, one specific domain of attentional control, was related to delayed attentional disengagement from threat cues in their study. Furthermore, attentional control deficits may partially explain diminished positive affect in social anxiety, potentially through their negative impact on social interaction and on the encoding of positive social information (Morrison & Heimberg, 2013).

Attention bias modification tasks may increase attentional control through training, regardless of whether the training is toward threat, non-threat, or no contingency. Anxiety associated with a speech task was reduced for all three contingency groups, suggesting that improving general attentional control reduces anxiety (Heeren, Mogoase, McNally, Schmitz, & Philippot, 2015; McNally, Enock, Tsai, & Tousian, 2013). Difficulties with effortful control of attention may be one primary process by which SAD develops, yet emerging research indicates that attentional control may be improved through attention bias modification tasks.

Self-focused attention. Theories of SAD suggest that threatening social stimuli or perceived danger lead individuals to turn attention inward toward the self. In fact, self-focused attention is related to higher levels of social anxiety (e.g., Grisham, King, Makkar, & Felmingham, 2015; Hope & Heimberg, 1988). During eye tracking during a video chat with an attractive male confederate, individuals with SAD were more self-focused (i.e., looked at the image of themselves more) than controls in all phases of the study (Vriends, Meral, Bargas-Avila, Stadler, & Bögels, 2017). Furthermore, individuals with social anxiety tend to report memories of threatening or high-anxiety social events from the perspective of an observer compared to non-anxious controls (Coles, Turk, & Heimberg, 2002; Coles, Turk, Heimberg, & Fresco, 2001; Wells, Clark, & Ahmad, 1998) and individuals with other anxiety disorders (Wells & Papageorgiou, 1999).

Self-focused attention also seems to be related to self-appraisal of performance in social situations. Nilsson and Lundh (2016) manipulated participants' focus of attention prior to listening to an audio recording of their own speech and found that participants who reduced self-focus evaluated their voice more positively in the first speech, an effect that generalized to the second speech. Furthermore, positive speech evaluations were associated with reductions in performance anxiety. Studies that manipulate self-focused attention before or during a speech task have also found evidence that self-focused attention leads to higher social anxiety (Bögels & Lamers, 2002; Woody & Rodriguez, 2000; Zou, Hudson, & Rapee, 2007), again suggesting that self-focused attention may play a role in the maintenance of SAD.

Interpretation bias. Interpretation bias refers to the tendency to make threatening or negative interpretations of ambiguous stimuli. Individuals with SAD tend to have a negative interpretation bias, in that they make significantly more negative interpretations of ambiguous social situations than controls, trait anxious, or dysphoric individuals (Amir, Beard, & Bower, 2005). Furthermore, they interpret positive events as threatening at a higher frequency than non-anxious controls (Alden, Taylor, Mellings, & Laposa, 2008; Laposa, Cassin, & Rector, 2010). Based on these findings, negative interpretation bias for social information seems to be particularly related to SAD.

Efforts to assess automatic interpretations using computerized tasks have sometimes demonstrated that, rather than showing a threat bias, individuals with SAD may lack the benign interpretation bias seen in non-anxious controls (Amir, Prouvost, & Kuckertz, 2012). In other words, those with SAD are slower to accept benign interpretations of neutral cues in social situations, which can maintain social anxiety by making the social interaction seem more threatening. Another line of research examining interpretation of facial expressions has garnered mixed results, with some studies finding support for enhanced negative interpretation of facial expressions in social anxiety (e.g., Joorman & Gotlib, 2006; Maoz et al., 2016) and others finding mixed (e.g., Bell et al., 2011) or no biased interpretation compared to controls (e.g., Jusyte & Shonenberg, 2014).

Interpretation bias may play a causal role in the maintenance of social anxiety. Support for this assertion comes from studies that modify interpretation bias using computerized programs similar to attention bias modification. These programs seem to decrease social anxiety in adults with high social anxiety and generalized SAD by reducing threat interpretations and increasing non-threat interpretations of cues (Amir & Taylor, 2012; Beard & Amir, 2008).

Secondary Cognitive Processes

Anticipatory processing. Anticipatory processing is intrusive, unwanted, recurrent, or ruminative thinking leading up to a social event, which often includes drawing upon memories of past social events. Examination of anticipatory processing in adults with high levels of social anxiety revealed two factors related to anticipatory processing: avoidance and preparation (Mills, Grant, Lechner, & Judah, 2013). The avoidance factor, related to escape and avoidance of social situations, seemed to be more maladaptive in that it predicted social anxiety, negative interpretations, and state anxiety. In a study by Vassilopoulos (2004), higher levels of social anxiety were associated with greater levels of anticipatory processing even after controlling for trait anxiety and depression.

Researchers have also manipulated anticipatory processing prior to a speech task. Compared to engaging in a distraction task, engaging in anticipatory processing increased anxiety in those with both high and low social anxiety and negatively affected their speech performance (Q. Wong & Moulds, 2011). Other studies have also shown that anticipatory processing is associated with increased anxiety (Vassilopoulos, 2005) and the maintenance of high levels of anxiety prior to social tasks (Hinrichsen & Clark, 2003). In alignment with cognitive-behavioral models of SAD, anticipatory processing has been shown to lead to increased reporting of conditional beliefs about social evaluation and stronger beliefs about high standards for social performance among individuals with high social anxiety (Q. Wong & Moulds, 2011). Another study showed that anticipatory processing before a speech task increased both state anxiety and the frequency of negative self-images among individuals with social anxiety compared to non-anxious individuals (Brown & Stopa, 2007). Those with high social anxiety who engaged in anticipatory processing also tended to predict poorer speech task performance than those who engaged in a distraction task prior to the speech (Vassilopoulos, 2005). Penney and Abbott (2015) investigated predictors of anticipatory processing before a speech task and found that FNE, anticipated performance appraisal, threat appraisal, state anxiety prior to the speech, and performance appraisal all accounted for significant variance in anticipatory processing. Furthermore, anticipatory processing, threat appraisal, and self-efficacy predicted participants' state anxiety during the speech.

Overall, anticipatory processing seems to play an important role in the maintenance of social anxiety by heightening state anxiety prior to and during social events and negatively impacting predictions of performance and performance ratings.

Post-event processing. Post-event processing (PEP) is a cognitive activity in which an individual repeatedly reviews his or her behavior or performance, as well as others' perceived reactions, following a social interaction. Engaging in PEP may include a detailed reconstruction of the memory of the social event and tends to be ruminative, negative, and self-focused in nature (Brozovich & Heimberg, 2008). Anticipatory and post-event processing are inherently intertwined; individuals with social anxiety often review past social interactions in order to prepare for an upcoming one, participating in processing that is both post hoc and anticipatory in nature. PEP is often seen as providing a "bridge from the socially anxious past to the socially anxious future" (Heimberg et al., 2014, p. 718).

Levels of PEP following a social task such as a speech or social interaction are higher for individuals with high social anxiety (Dannahy & Stopa, 2007; Edwards, Rapee, & Franklin, 2003). Perini, Abbott, and Rapee (2006) found that socially anxious individuals experienced more negative PEP characterized by higher frequency of negative thoughts, greater engagement with negative thoughts, less control of negative thoughts, and a greater degree of distress related to the negative thoughts compared to control participants. Although PEP has been demonstrated in other anxiety disorders (Laposa, Collimore, & Rector, 2014), it seems to be particularly related to social anxiety. For instance, Makkar and Grisham (2011) found that PEP was predicted by social anxiety over and above depression and trait anxiety. Additionally, individuals with SAD engage in more PEP after a speech task and have significantly more positive beliefs about the benefits of PEP than both anxious and non-anxious controls (Gavric, Moscovitch, Rowa, & McCabe, 2017). Despite the positive metacognitive beliefs about PEP held by individuals with SAD, the use of PEP seems to have a detrimental effect by contributing to the maintenance of social anxiety over time.

Emerging research has examined how PEP relates to factors such as self-focused attention, mental imagery, threat appraisal, self-judgments, and self-performance evaluation. Self-focused attention predicts higher levels of PEP (Helbig-Lang, von Auer, Neubauer, Murray, & Gerlach, 2016), and self-focused attention during or after a social interaction specifically leads to more negative PEP (Gaydukevych & Kocovski, 2012). PEP using mental imagery as opposed to semantic processing seems to be particularly detrimental as it raises anxiety and leads individuals to make more socially anxious interpretations of ambiguous situations (Brozovich & Heimberg, 2013). Threat appraisal, or the appraisal of the probability of receiving negative evaluation, after a speech task also predicts PEP (Penney & Abbott, 2015). PEP also appears to be related to socially anxious individuals' appraisal of their own social performance, such that greater PEP is related to more negative performance ratings (Abbott & Rapee, 2004; Rowa, Gavric, Stead, LeMoult, & McCabe,

2016). Rowa and colleagues (2016) also found that poorer perception of performance predicted more PEP, which mediated the relationship between performance ratings after the speech task and ratings five days later. Similarly, for those with social anxiety, high trait PEP predicted more negative judgments about the self a week after a social interaction (Brozovich & Heimberg, 2011). These findings each suggest that there may be a cycle of self-focused attention, threat appraisal, and self-appraisal that leads to negative post-event processing and the maintenance of anxiety by confirming a negative image of the self in social situations. PEP also seems to decrease willingness to engage in future social tasks or interactions among individuals with SAD, thus perpetuating the cycle of social anxiety by decreasing opportunities for positive social experiences (Rowa et al., 2016).

Behavioral Processes

Primary Behavioral Processes

Avoidance and escape of social situations. The behavioral processes involved in SAD are currently recognized for their negative influence on the onset and maintenance of SAD. According to Q. Wong and Rapee's (2016) recent model of SAD, the behavioral processes involved in SAD may be best conceptually divided into primary and secondary processes. According to their model, minimization of social-evaluative threat may initially be accomplished by an individual via the primary behavioral processes of avoidance and escape. First, and most naturally, individuals with severe social anxiety might find social situations so threatening that they will go to great lengths to avoid these situations altogether. Whenever possible, they may attempt to avoid situations and, when faced with these situations, attempt to escape as quickly as possible (e.g., leaving a party or excusing themselves quickly from a conversation). Although escape from anxiety-provoking situations can provide individuals with immediate relief from anxiety in the moment, it can also contribute to long-term maintenance of anxiety when the ultimate outcome of the anxiety-provoking situation is never experienced, leaving negative beliefs and assumptions about the likelihood of a poor outcome both unchallenged and unchanged.

The overall level of impairment experienced by individuals with SAD may in part be indicative of the extent to which individuals with SAD engage in primary avoidance and escape processes. Social anxiety is associated with significant functional impairment in occupational, social, and personal domains (Ruscio et al., 2008; Stein & Kean, 2000). For instance, individuals with SAD experience more missed hours of work relative to individuals without SAD (Wittchen, Feutsch, Sonntag, Müller, & Liebowitz, 2000) are more likely to fail or drop out of high school than individuals without SAD (Simon et al., 2002; Stein & Kean, 2000), and are more likely to be single and live alone compared to individuals with other anxiety disorders, such as panic disorder (Norton et al., 1996). Although many complex factors contribute to the impairment associated with SAD, overt avoidance and escape of social situations may contribute significantly to these specific occupational, academic, and relationship difficulties.

In addition to avoidance of social situations in everyday life, treatment avoidance seems to be especially common among individuals with SAD, which may in part be explained by the avoidance of the social interaction inherent to seeking psychological help, as well as a fear of being negatively evaluated by healthcare professionals. Despite the extent of the distress and impairment in functioning experienced by most individuals with SAD, epidemiological research indicates that approximately half of individuals with SAD never seek treatment and that, among those that do, it is often after 15–20 years of experiencing significant symptoms (Grant et al., 2005). In addition, in one study, social anxiety ratings completed online by individuals who visited a website about social anxiety were significantly higher – by approximately 1.5 standard deviations – than similar ratings provided by individuals seeking treatment at an anxiety clinic. Of those who visited the website, only about one-third reported having previously sought treatment for their social anxiety (Erwin, Turk, Heimberg, Fresco, & Hantula, 2004). These findings perhaps suggest that many individuals with higher levels of social anxiety may also be more likely to avoid means of information-seeking and treatment that require social interaction.

Secondary Behavioral Processes

Safety behaviors. Total avoidance or escape of social situations is not always feasible, and individuals with social anxiety may also engage in more subtle avoidance behaviors (safety behaviors), which are actions utilized to prevent or reduce the likelihood of a feared outcome (Salkovskis, 1991). D. Clark and Wells (1995) suggested broadly categorizing safety behaviors into two types: an avoidance-type, which is meant to reduce a person's participation in the social situation, and an impression-management type, which is instead meant to control the impression one is making on others. In the case of an individual with social anxiety, avoidance safety behaviors might include behaviors such as only speaking to people one knows well at a party or sitting in the back of a room in a meeting in order to minimize scrutiny, whereas impression-management safety behaviors may include excessively rehearsing what one is going to say to avoid stumbling over words during a speech or wearing a black shirt in order to decrease the visibility of sweat. Unlike avoidance and escape, Q. Wong and Rapee (2016) consider safety behaviors to be secondary behavioral processes, which are more complex behavioral processes that develop over time in an attempt to decrease the degree of exposure to social threat. As discussed previously in the chapter, each major model of SAD (D. Clark & Wells, 1995; Heimberg et al., 2014; Hofmann 2007; Q. Wong & Rapee, 2016) includes safety behaviors and identifies their central role in the maintenance of social anxiety. The broader literature on the role of safety behaviors in the onset and maintenance of SAD has been extensively reviewed (Piccirillo, Dryman, & Heimberg, 2016).

The use of safety behaviors is strongly related to fears of negative evaluation (Alden & Bieling, 1998; Okajima, Kanai, Chen, & Sakano, 2009) and fears that personal negative attributes will be exposed to others (Moscovitch, Rowa et al., 2013). Furthermore, individuals with high levels of social anxiety are more likely to utilize safety behaviors during social interactions than individuals with lower levels of social anxiety (McManus, Sacadura, & Clark, 2008; Stangier, Heidenreich, & Scherelleh-Engel, 2006). As is the case with overt avoidance, the use of safety behaviors likely reduces anxiety for an individual in the moment, but serves to maintain social anxiety over the long term by preventing the individual from fully engaging in the social experience and gathering disconfirmatory evidence regarding the feared outcome. In addition, the use of safety behaviors often leads socially anxious individuals to attribute positive outcomes of social situations to these behaviors and not to their own abilities (D. Clark, 2001; D. Clark & Wells, 1995, Heimberg et al., 2014; Wells et al., 1995). For example, an individual may believe that a speech only went well because of his excessive memorization of the material, rather than his own public speaking skill. Thus, safety behaviors can serve to maintain individuals' belief in their own low skill and ineffectiveness in handling social situations.

In an initial study conducted by Wells and colleagues (1995) to examine the potential interference of safety behaviors in the reduction of anxiety during exposures to social situations, eight individuals with SAD participated in two separate therapeutic exposures, one in which they received explicit instructions from the therapist to reduce safety behaviors and the other in which they did not. Explicit instructions to reduce safety behaviors during the exposure were associated with greater reductions in anxiety and belief in the feared outcome, as well as increased ratings of the effectiveness of the exposure compared to the ratings after the condition in which the participants were not explicitly instructed to reduce safety behaviors. Other studies have similarly found that specific instructions to reduce safety behaviors during exposures to social interaction are associated with decreased negative judgments of one's own performance and increased accuracy in reports of one's own social behavior among individuals with SAD (Taylor & Alden, 2010). Safety behaviors also seem to directly increase the experience of anxiety in social situations; for instance, when individuals with high social anxiety are instructed to use safety behaviors, they report higher levels of anxiety and lower levels of positive affect during the interaction (Langer & Rodebaugh, 2013; McManus et al., 2008).

Safety behaviors may also indirectly maintain social anxiety in the long term due to their detrimental effect on the individual's actual social performance. The use of safety behaviors is often objectively noticeable and associated with making a more negative impression on interaction partners. In one study, conversation partners rated individuals with SAD as exhibiting a higher number of safety behaviors than individuals without SAD, which were associated with overall poorer performance ratings by other objective observers (Stevens et al., 2010). Further evidence suggests that the use of safety behaviors is associated with decreased conversation-partner ratings of likability (Langer & Rodebaugh, 2013; McManus et al., 2008; Plasencia, Alden, & Taylor, 2011), topic-appropriateness (Alden & Bieling, 1998), and desire for future interaction (Plasencia et al., 2011). Safety behaviors are also related to an individual's own feelings of competence during an interaction. For instance, when instructed to use safety behaviors, individuals with social anxiety also reported believing that they appeared more anxious during the interaction and rated their own performance more poorly compared to individuals who were not instructed to use safety behaviors (Langer & Rodebaugh, 2013; McManus et al., 2008). More recent research suggests that the use of safety behaviors may be related to concerns among individuals with SAD that "showing their true selves" will lead to negative evaluation by others; despite these concerns, learning techniques to increase authenticity in an interaction by reducing the use of safety behaviors was associated with an increase in positive affect, positive perceptions of their conversation partner's response, and a greater desire for future interaction among individuals with SAD, compared to those who did not learn the same techniques (Plasencia, Taylor, & Alden, 2016). Taken together, research seems to demonstrate that safety behaviors may increase anxiety, negative perceptions of one's performance, negative evaluation by others, and interference with social performance and that reductions in safety behaviors lead to more positive outcomes.

Perhaps due to safety behaviors' association with negative perceptions of one's own performance, they have been shown to be associated with increased PEP following a social event (Kiko et al., 2012; Makkar & Grisham, 2011; Mitchell & Schmidt, 2014), which in turn may lead to increased anxiety and safety behavior use at a future event. However, safety behavior use does not always predict PEP above and beyond an individual's negative assumptions (Makkar & Grisham, 2011) or dysfunctional cognitions (Kiko et al., 2012), which seem to be some of the most powerful predictors of PEP among individuals with SAD. These findings perhaps suggest that safety behaviors contribute to engagement in other types of maladaptive thinking patterns, such as negative assumptions and dysfunctional cognitions, which in turn are associated with higher levels of PEP (Kiko et al., 2012). Others have argued that because it is often utilized as a way to identify past social mistakes and prevent those mistakes from occurring again in the future (Heimberg et al., 2014; Hofmann, 2007), PEP may itself be considered a safety behavior, insomuch as individuals believe it is a necessary process to manage future social situations effectively (Piccirillo et al., 2016).

Substance use is another common way that individuals attempt to avoid or alleviate anxiety and may be considered a safety behavior among individuals with SAD. Evidence suggests that social avoidance is associated with increased marijuana-related problems (Buckner, Heimberg, & Schmidt, 2011). Furthermore, safety behavior frequency mediated the relationship between anxiety symptom severity and cannabis problem severity (Buckner et al., 2017). These findings might suggest that substance use is a safety behavior among individuals with SAD, or at least that the propensity to engage in safety behaviors among individuals with anxiety is strongly associated with substance use.

Positive Valence Systems

Positive Affect

Positive affect is a dimension reflecting the extent to which one experiences pleasurable engagement with the environment or positive moods such as enthusiasm, interest, and joy. The tripartite model of anxiety and depression proposes that negative affect is shared by both anxiety and depression, whereas physiological hyperarousal is more characteristic of anxiety and low positive affect is more characteristic of depression (L. Clark & Watson, 1991). However, several studies have shown that social anxiety is also associated with low positive affect (Brown, Chorpita, & Barlow, 1998; Chorpita, Plummer, & Moffit, 2000; Hughes et al., 2006; Kashdan, 2007; Watson, Clark, & Carey 1988) in addition to high negative affect. In particular, social interaction anxiety has been shown to have a specific and unique relationship with hedonic deficits (Hughes et al., 2006; Kashdan, 2002) that is not attributable to other internalizing conditions that often co-occur with social anxiety, such as depression or generalized anxiety (Kashdan, 2004).

There is evidence to suggest that the relationship between social anxiety and low positive affect is partially mediated by both cognitive and attentional processes associated with SAD. For instance, low positive affect is associated with the tendency of individuals with social anxiety to engage in negative interpretation of positive social events (Alden et al., 2008). Higher levels of social anxiety are associated with cognitions related to inhibiting positive emotion (e.g., "I don't deserve to feel this good") (Eisner, Johnson, & Carver, 2009). In addition, and as discussed earlier in the chapter, lower attentional control mediates the effect of social anxiety on low positive affect (Morrison & Heimberg, 2013). It may be the case that an increased probability of interpreting events in a negative manner, combined with decreased attentional control, together contribute to a focus among individuals with SAD toward threat-relevant information and away from positive information, resulting in decreased encoding of positive information and overall diminished positive affect (Y. Chen et al., 2002; Morrison & Heimberg, 2013; Pishyar et al., 2004).

Another hypothesis for why SAD may be characterized by low positive affect is that individuals with social anxiety engage in fewer positive experiences in day-to-day life, in part due to avoidance of social interactions. In an attempt to examine the relationship between social anxiety and hedonic activity, Kashdan and Steger (2006) conducted a 21-day experience sampling study that tracked day-to-day events, social anxiety symptoms, and emotion regulation strategies. In general, individuals with social anxiety engaged in fewer positive events and experienced lower positive affect compared to non-anxious individuals. In addition, the number of positive events experienced among socially anxious individuals was lowest on days when they both experienced higher levels of social anxiety and attempted to suppress their anxiety. Other daily diaries studies have also found evidence that people with higher levels of social anxiety report fewer and less intense positive emotions across both social and nonsocial situations (e.g., Kashdan & Collins, 2010) and that lower positive affect among socially anxious individuals is associated with attempts on the part of the socially anxious individuals to suppress both positive and negative emotional experiences (Blalock, Kashdan, & Farmer, 2016; O'Toole, Jensen, & Fentz, 2014). Taken together, these studies seem to suggest that disruptions in the experience of positive emotion and the quantity of positive experiences may be in part due to emotion regulation difficulties among individuals with social anxiety.

The association between social anxiety and low positive affect may also be implicated in the anticipation of future social events among individuals with SAD. Lucock and Salkovskis (1988) found that socially anxious individuals rated the probability of future positive events much lower than non-anxious individuals. In addition, individuals with SAD tend to anticipate more frequent and intense negative emotional reactions to positive events than non-anxious individuals, despite having higher expectations for the potential of positive social events to increase their self-esteem (Gilboa-Schechtman, Franklin, & Foa, 2000). This may suggest that high expectations of positive events, combined with increased negative affect during these events, inhibits the generation of positive emotion in these situations and could possibly lead to avoidance of similar future events.

Emotion Regulation

Emotion regulation refers to the processes by which individuals attempt to influence personal emotional experiences and expression (Gross, 1998). Theoretical models have recognized the role of emotion regulation processes in contributing to the persistence of social anxiety (Heimberg et al., 2014; Hofmann, Sawyer, Fang, & Asnaani, 2012). Much of the research thus far on the role of emotion regulation in SAD has focused on two primary emotion regulation strategies – expressive suppression, defined as an attempt to hide or suppress the outward expression of an emotion, and cognitive reappraisal, an attempt to reinterpret the meaning of an emotional stimulus in order to shift one's own emotional response. Overall, individuals with SAD seem to have a poorer understanding of their own emotional experiences compared to both anxious and non-anxious individuals (Mennin, Holaway, Fresco, Moore, & Heimberg, 2007; Mennin, McLaughlin, & Flanagan, 2009; Turk, Heimberg, Luterek, Mennin, & Fresco, 2005) and have a tendency to engage in more maladaptive forms of emotion regulation, such as expressive suppression, as well as a tendency to exhibit difficulty in successfully executing more adaptive forms of emotion regulation, such as cognitive reappraisal.

Expressive suppression is commonly employed among individuals with SAD for both positive and negative emotions (e.g., Blalock et al., 2016; D'Avanzato, Joorman, Siemer, & Gotlib, 2013; Farmer & Kashdan, 2012; Werner, Goldin, Ball, Heimberg, & Gross, 2011) and often has the paradoxical effect of increasing the intensity of negative emotions, such as sadness or anxiety (Campbell-Sills, Barlow, Brown, & Hofmann, 2006; Gross, 2014; Gross & John, 2003), as well as dampening the intensity of positive emotions (Kalokerinos, Greenaway, & Denson, 2015). Indeed, individuals with SAD have reported lower self-efficacy than non-anxious individuals in the use of expressive suppression to downregulate anxiety (Werner et al., 2011). In addition, the attempt to suppress negative emotion may lead to an overall reduction in the experiences of positive emotion. As discussed previously, Kashdan and Steger (2006) found that individuals experienced less positive affect and fewer positive events on days during which they experienced high levels of social anxiety and attempted to suppress their anxiety. Expressive suppression is also associated with increased distraction and lower enjoyment during social interactions (Butler et al., 2003), poorer memory for social information (Richards & Gross, 2000), and decreased authenticity and closeness in relationships (Gross & John, 2003), all of which may decrease the potential for positive experiences gained from interpersonal contact.

Because individuals with SAD are less likely to express both positive and negative emotion, an individual with SAD may be perceived as aloof, unfriendly, or inauthentic by others and experience lower levels of social support. For instance, Butler and colleagues (2003) asked pairs of female participants to discuss their reactions to an emotional video with each other. Conversation partners of those who were given instructions to suppress their emotions reported feeling lower levels of rapport with their partners, less liking for their partners, and lower desire for future interaction compared to the conversation partners of those who were not given instructions to suppress their emotions. Other studies have also found an association between expressive suppression and lower reported social and emotional support from peers, as well as lower peer ratings of closeness to those high in expressive suppression (Gross & John, 2003). Therefore, the emotion regulation strategies that individuals with SAD employ seem to be strongly related to the type of evaluation they receive from others and may have consequences for the level of closeness and support they experience within their relationships. The tendency to be less emotionally expressive may itself be considered a safety behavior that, although intended to reduce negative evaluation from others during social interactions, often leads to the opposite of that intended effect (Heimberg et al., 2014).

Cognitive reappraisal, an emotion regulation strategy that is generally seen as more adaptive than expressive suppression, is usually associated with the successful regulation of emotions in the desired direction (i.e., downregulating negative emotion and upregulating positive emotion) (Kalokerinos et al., 2015). Cognitive reappraisal is used just as frequently by socially anxious individuals as non-anxious individuals (Farmer & Kashdan, 2012; Kashdan & Steger, 2006; Kivity & Huppert, 2016; O'Toole et al., 2014), but socially anxious individuals perceive themselves as less effective in utilizing the strategy compared to their non-anxious peers (Farmer & Kashdan, 2012; Helbig-Lang, Rusch, Rief, & Lincoln, 2015; Kivity & Huppert, 2016; Werner et al., 2011). For instance, Farmer and Kashdan (2012) found that, although cognitive reappraisal was effective in managing negative emotions associated with social events among individuals low in social anxiety, it was an ineffective strategy in managing emotion among individuals high in social anxiety. In addition to being an ineffective strategy for managing negative affect, cognitive reappraisal may be used less frequently among individuals with SAD for positive emotions (e.g., "I can prolong this positive emotion") (Blalock et al., 2016), perhaps also contributing to overall lower levels of positive affect. Individuals high in social anxiety are also less likely to utilize cognitive reappraisal in response to negative mental imagery (e.g., by mentally altering an emotionally impactful image in some way) (Moscovitch, Chiupka, & Gavric, 2013). Less frequent use of a potentially adaptive strategy for negative mental imagery may be especially important in understanding the role of poor emotion regulation in the persistence of SAD, due to the central role of negative self-imagery in the experience and maintenance of social anxiety over time (Heimberg et al., 2014).

Systems for Social Processes

Attachment

As outlined in theoretical models of SAD, mental representations of self and others may be associated with the interpretation of social situations as threatening or unpredictable among individuals with social anxiety. Per attachment theory (Bowlby 1988), underlying notions of self and others, or internal working models, are formulated over time from accumulated interpersonal interactions within caregiver, peer, and romantic relationships. Attachment theory suggests that interactions with others, and the internal working models that form as a result, serve as the basis of the mental representations used to understand ourselves and others. Attachment style, characterized in adulthood by an individual's developed internal working models, has been proposed to be associated with the experience social anxiety, as internal working models may inform how individuals view and interpret social situations (see Manning, Dickson, Palmier-Claus, Cunliffe, & Taylor, 2017, for a review).

Insecure attachment style is often conceptually divided into two types: anxious-ambivalent, characterized by negative working models of the self as undesirable or inferior, and avoidant, characterized by negative working models of others as cruel and rejecting (e.g., Ainsworth, Blehar, Waters, & Wall, 1978; Ravitz, Maunder, Hunter, Sthankiya, & Lancee, 2010). Other categorical models of insecure attachment include fearful attachment (Bartholomew, 1990), which is thought to incorporate both anxious and avoidant working models and has been found to be particularly strongly associated with social anxiety (Gajwani, Patterson, & Birchwood, 2013; van Buren &

Colley, 2002). Several studies indicate that individuals with social anxiety are more likely than non-anxious individuals to report insecure attachment (Eng, Heimberg, Hart, Schneier, & Liebowitz, 2001; Michail & Birchwood, 2014; Weisman, Aderka, Marom, Hermesh, & Gilboa-Schechtman, 2011) and that both anxious and avoidant attachment styles are associated with social anxiety (Mickelson, Kessler, & Shaver, 1997; Weisman et al., 2011). Some studies have found that avoidant attachment has stronger associations with social anxiety than anxious attachment, controlling for cognitive features such as flexibility, locus of control, and repetitive thinking, as well as other factors such as submissive behavior and social comparison (Dag & Gülüm, 2013; Gülüm & Dag, 2014; Weisman et al., 2011). Another study showed that the significant associations between both anxious and avoidant attachment styles and social anxiety disappeared after controlling for behavioral inhibition and neuroticism (Boelen, Reijntjes, & Carleton, 2014). Therefore, it is possible that insecure attachment style may not contribute to the prediction of social anxiety above and beyond other associated traits and temperamental factors.

It is also possible that insecure attachment style contributes to the experience of social anxiety indirectly. For instance, many studies have shown significant mediators of the relationship between attachment style and social anxiety, including perceived social support (Roring, 2008), cognitive flexibility and locus of control (Dag & Gülüm, 2013), and social comparison and submissive behavior (Aderka, Weisman, Shahar, & Gilboa-Schechtman, 2009). Each of these studies points to different avenues through which we can understand the relationship between attachment and social anxiety. It is important to note that these studies are cross-sectional, and that there are limited longitudinal studies to support the notion that attachment style causally or indirectly predicts social anxiety; however, there is some evidence that this may indeed be the case (Bifulco et al., 2006).

Another hypothesis to consider regarding the relationship between attachment and social anxiety is that insecure attachment may impact the quality of interpersonal relationships and reduce overall social support due to fewer contacts, decreased trust of others, and increased negative interpretation of social events, perhaps leading to reinforcement of social anxiety over time (Manning et al., 2017). One study found that avoidant attachment moderated the relationship between intranasal oxytocin administration and social behaviors among individuals with SAD during a social rejection task, such that oxytocin led to increased affiliation and cooperation with others only among those with high avoidant attachment (Fang, Hoge, Heinrichs, & Hofmann, 2014). This finding perhaps suggests that insecure attachment style is closely related to some of the social-behavioral and affiliative tendencies among individuals with SAD that, by extension, may impact the quality of their interpersonal relationships.

Relationships

Individuals with SAD consistently report significant impairment in interpersonal relationships (Aderka et al., 2012; Rodebaugh, 2009; Rodebaugh, Fernandez, &

Levinson, 2012; Schneier et al., 1994). Interpersonal impairment associated with social anxiety has been shown to extend from lower friendship quality (Rodebaugh, 2009; Rodebaugh, Fernandez, & Levinson, 2012) to less sexual communication, satisfaction, and intimacy within romantic relationships (Montesi et al., 2013; Sparrevohn & Rapee, 2009).

Although individuals with SAD tend to underestimate the quality of their interactions compared to their actual performance (Voncken & Bogels, 2008), there is evidence to suggest that social anxiety can lead to behaviors that may indeed elicit negative evaluation from others, thereby reducing the likelihood of new relationships or the quality and satisfaction gained from existing ones. For instance, individuals with social anxiety tend to initiate conversations, talk, and self-disclose less than non-anxious individuals (Pilkonis, 1977; Snell, 1989), and the length of contact and degree of personal disclosure are important factors in determining the degree of negative judgment received by others (Voncken & Dijk, 2013). Individuals with social anxiety are also more likely to engage in safety behaviors, which have similarly been shown to be associated with decreased ratings by others of likeability and desire for future contact with the individuals utilizing them (Langer & Rodebaugh, 2013; McManus et al., 2008; Plasencia et al., 2011). Therefore, it may be the case that these behavioral correlates of social anxiety do indeed impact the quality of interactions and may interfere with the formation of close or high-quality relationships among individuals with SAD.

Furthermore, social anxiety may be associated with lower satisfaction in relationships due to difficulties in pursuing desirable, rather than safer, interactions. Rodebaugh, Bielak, Vidovic, and Moscovitch (2016) asked individuals in an undergraduate and community sample to rate the extent to which they would like to interact with vignette characters of varying degrees of warmth and dominance. Individuals high in social anxiety exhibited a tendency to prefer characters based on their dominance and warmth, but to a lesser degree than individuals low in social anxiety due to a competing tendency to also prefer characters who were more similar to themselves. This finding seems to suggest that individuals with social anxiety desire interaction with warm and confident individuals, but that this desire is coupled with a competing one to interact safely with individuals who are more like them, but who perhaps have less socially desirable traits (Rodebaugh et al., 2016). The authors argue that overall, relationship pursuit tendencies among individuals high in social anxiety may lead to an increased sense of safety in interactions, but also to overall lower satisfaction in their relationships.

Concluding Remarks

Since its formal recognition in the *DSM-III*, there has been significant progress in our understanding of the nature of the many processes implicated in the etiology and/or maintenance of SAD. Research has generally supported the prominent features and processes of SAD as outlined by the influential models discussed in this chapter. In particular, we highlighted the role of fears of negative and positive evaluation, attentional bias and control, interpretation bias, anticipatory and post-event processing, overt and subtle avoidance behaviors, positive affect, emotion regulation, and attachment and interpersonal processes in the phenomenology of SAD. Continued research should aim at further validation and refinement of the models reviewed, as well as further clarification of the interactions between the multiple cognitive, behavioral, affective, and social processes involved in SAD. For instance, areas of more recent exploration – including emotion regulation difficulties and diminished positive affect among individuals with SAD – have proven to be of great importance in understanding the experience and persistence of social anxiety; further development of these newer areas of study, particularly as they interact with more well-established cognitive and behavioral processes involved in SAD, will continue to lend to the growth of a more comprehensive and nuanced understanding of the disorder.

Furthermore, continuing to conceptualize social anxiety through an RDoC framework may provide a useful context for understanding the mechanisms and domains of functioning associated with SAD. In particular, viewing the mechanisms of social anxiety as they pertain to the systems of functioning specified by the RDoC framework could clarify the overlap between social anxiety and other aspects of psychological functioning and functional impairments that also cut across these systems. In line with the goals of the RDoC approach, future research will likely seek to provide a more sophisticated picture of the multiple domains of dysfunction in SAD by utilizing multiple levels of analysis (e.g., genes, neurobiology, physiology, behavior, and self-report).

Overall, years of study have led to great strides in our conceptualization of the etiology and phenomenology of SAD. As always, more work needs to be done to refine and expand this conceptualization, and we anticipate many more important developments that will come of this continued endeavor.

References

Abbott, M. J. & Rapee, R. M. (2004). Post-event rumination and negative self-appraisal in social phobia before and after treatment. *Journal of Abnormal Psychology, 113*, 136–144. doi: 10.1037/0021-843X.113.1.136

Acarturk, C., Smit, F., de Graaf, R., van Straten, A., ten Have, M., & Cuijpers, P. (2009). Economic costs of social phobia: A population-based study. *Journal of Affective Disorders, 115*, 421–429. doi: 10.1016/j.jad.2008.10.008

Aderka, I. M., Hofmann, S. G., Nickerson, A., Hermesh, H., Gilboa-Schechtman, E., & Marom, S. (2012). Functional impairment in social anxiety disorder. *Journal of Anxiety Disorders, 26*, 393–400. doi: 10.1016/j.janxdis.2012.01.003

Aderka, I. M., Weisman, O., Shahar, G., & Gilboa-Schechtman, E. (2009). The roles of the social rank and attachment systems in social anxiety. *Personality and Individual Differences, 47*, 284–288. doi: 10.1016/j.paid.2009.03.014

Ainsworth, M. D. S., Blehar, M. C., Waters, E., & Wall, S. (1978). *Patterns of Attachment.* Hillsdale, NJ: Erlbaum.

Alden, L. E. & Bieling, P. (1998). Interpersonal consequences of the pursuit of safety. *Behaviour Research and Therapy*, *36*, 53–64. doi: 10.1016/S0005-7967(97) 00072-7

Alden, L. E., Taylor, C. T., Mellings, T. M., & Laposa, J. M. (2008). Social anxiety and the interpretation of positive social events. *Journal of Anxiety Disorders*, *22*, 577–590. doi: 10.1016/j.janxdis.2007.05.007

American Psychiatric Association (1980). *Diagnostic and Statistical Manual of Mental Disorders* (3rd edn). Washington, DC: American Psychiatric Association.

American Psychiatric Association. (2013). *Diagnostic and Statistical Manual of Mental Disorders* (5th edn). Arlington, VA: American Psychiatric Press, Inc.

Amir, N., Beard, C., & Bower, E. (2005). Interpretation bias and social anxiety. *Cognitive Therapy and Research*, *29*, 433–443. doi: 10.1007/s10608-005–2834-5

Amir, N., Beard, C., Taylor, C. T., Klumpp, H., Elias, J., Burns, M., & Chen, X. (2009). Attention training in individuals with generalized social phobia: A randomized controlled trial. *Journal of Consulting and Clinical Psychology*, *77*, 961–973. doi: 10.1037/a0016685

Amir, N., Elias, J., Klumpp, H., & Przeworski, A. (2003). Attentional bias to threat in social phobia: Facilitated processing of threat or difficulty disengaging attention from threat? *Behaviour Research and Therapy*, *41*, 1325–1335. doi: 10.1016/S0005-7967(03)00039-1

Amir, N., Prouvost, C., & Kuckertz, J. M. (2012) Lack of a benign interpretation bias in social anxiety disorder. *Cognitive Behaviour Therapy*, *41*, 119–129. doi: 10.1080/ 16506073.2012.662655

Amir, N. & Taylor, C. T. (2012). Interpretation training in individuals with generalized social anxiety disorder: A randomized controlled trial. *Journal of Consulting and Clinical Psychology*, *80*, 497–511. doi: 10.1037/a0026928

Ball, S. G., Otto, M. W., Pollack, M. H., Uccello, R., & Rosenbaum, J. F. (1995). Differentiating social phobia and panic disorder: A test of core beliefs. *Cognitive Therapy and Research*, *19*, 473–482. doi: 10.1007/BF02230413

Bartholomew, K. (1990). Avoidance of intimacy: An attachment perspective. *Journal of Social and Personal Relationships*, *7*, 147–178. doi: 10.1177/0265407590072001

Beard, C. & Amir, N. (2008). A multi-session interpretation modification program: Changes in interpretation and social anxiety symptoms. *Behaviour Research and Therapy*, *46*, 1135–1141. doi: 10.1016/j.brat.2008.05.012

Bell, C., Bourke, C., Colhoun, H., Carter, F., Frampton, C., & Porter, R. (2011). The misclassification of facial expressions in generalised social phobia. *Journal of Anxiety Disorders*, *25*, 278–283. doi: 10.1080/13546800444000254

Bifulco, A., Kwon, J., Jacobs, C., Moran, P. M., Bunn, A., & Beer, N. (2006). Adult attachment style as mediator between childhood neglect/abuse and adult depression and anxiety. *Social Psychiatry and Psychiatric Epidemiology*, *41*, 796–805. doi: 10.1007/s00127-006–0101-z

Blalock, D. V., Kashdan, T. B., & Farmer, A. S. (2016). Trait and daily emotion regulation in social anxiety disorder. *Cognitive Therapy and Research*, *40*, 416–425. doi: 10.1007/s10608-015–9739-8

Boelen, P. A., Reijntjes, A., & Carleton, R. N. (2014). Intolerance of uncertainty and adult separation anxiety. *Cognitive Behaviour Therapy*, *43*, 133–144. doi: 10.1080/16506073.2014.888755

Bögels, S. M. & Lamers, C. T. J. (2002). The causal role of self-awareness in blushing-anxious, socially-anxious and social phobic individuals. *Behaviour Research and Therapy*, *40*, 1367–1384. doi: 10.1016/S0005-7967(01)00096-1

Bögels, S. M. & Mansell, W. (2004). Attention processes in the maintenance and treatment of social phobia: Hypervigilance, avoidance and self-focused attention. *Clinical Psychology Review*, *24*, 827–856. doi: 10.1016/j.cpr.2004.06.005

Bowlby, J. (1988). Attachment, communication, and the therapeutic process. In J. Bowlby (ed.), *A Secure Base: Clinical Applications of Attachment Theory* (pp. 137–157). London: Routledge.

Brown, M. & Stopa, L. (2007). Does anticipation help or hinder performance in a subsequent speech? *Behavioural and Cognitive Psychotherapy*, *35*, 133–147. doi: 10.1017/S1352465806003481

Brown, T. A., Campbell, L. A., Lehman, C. L., Grisham, J. R., & Mancill, R. B. (2001). Current and lifetime comorbidity of the *DSM-IV* anxiety and mood disorders in a large clinical sample. *Journal of Abnormal Psychology*, *110*, 585–599. doi: 10.1037/0021-843X.110.4.585

Brown, T. A., Chorpita, B. F., & Barlow, D. H. (1998). Structural relationships among dimensions of the *DSM-IV* anxiety and mood disorders and dimensions of negative affect, positive affect, and autonomic arousal. *Journal of Abnormal Psychology*, *107*, 179–192. doi: 10.1037/0021-843X.107.2.179

Brozovich, F. & Heimberg, R. G. (2008). An analysis of post-event processing in social anxiety disorder. *Clinical Psychology Review*, *28*, 891–903. doi: 10.1016/j.cpr.2008.01.002

Brozovich, F. & Heimberg, R. G. (2011). The relationship of post-event processing to self-evaluation of performance in social anxiety. *Behavior Therapy*, *42*, 224–235. doi: 10.1016/j.beth.2010.08.005

Brozovich, F. & Heimberg, R. G. (2013). Mental imagery and post-event processing in anticipation of a speech performance among socially anxious individuals. *Behavior Therapy*, *44*, 701–716. doi: 10.1016/j.beth.2013.07.001

Bruce, S. E., Yonkers, K. A., Otto, M. W., Eisen, J. L., Weisberg, R. B., Pagano, M., . . . Keller, M. B. (2005). Influence of psychiatric comorbidity on recovery and recurrence in generalized anxiety disorder, social phobia, and panic disorder: A 12-year prospective study. *American Journal of Psychiatry*, *162*, 1179–1187. doi: 10.1176/appi.ajp.162.6.1179

Bruch, M.A., Fallon, M., & Heimberg, R.G. (2003). Social phobia and difficulties in occupational adjustment. *Journal of Counseling Psychology*, *50*, 109–117. doi: 10.1037/0022–0167.50.1.109

Buckner, J. D., Heimberg, R. G., & Schmidt, N. B. (2011). Social anxiety and marijuana-related problems: The role of social avoidance. *Addictive Behaviors*, *36*, 129–132. doi: 10.1016/j.addbeh.2010.08.015

Buckner, J. D., Zvolensky, M. J., Ecker, A. H., Jeffries, E. R., Lemke, A. W., Dean, K. E., . . . Gallagher, M. W. (2017). Anxiety and cannabis-related problem severity among dually diagnosed outpatients: The impact of false safety behaviors. *Addictive Behaviors*, *70*, 49–53. doi: 10.1016/j.addbeh.2017.02.014

Butler, E. A., Egloff, B., Wilhelm, F. H., Smith, N. C., Erickson, E. A., & Gross, J. J. (2003). The social consequences of expressive suppression. *Emotion, 3*, 48–67. doi: 10.1037/1528–3542.3.1.48

Campbell-Sills, L., Barlow, D. H., Brown, T. A., & Hofmann, S. G. (2006). Acceptability and suppression of negative emotion in anxiety and mood disorders. *Emotion, 6*, 587–595. doi: 10.1037/1528–3542.6.4.587

Chen, N. T., Clarke, P. J., MacLeod, C., & Guastella, A. J. (2012). Biased attentional processing of positive stimuli in social anxiety disorder: An eye movement study. *Cognitive Behaviour Therapy, 41*, 96–107. doi: 10.1080/16506073.2012.666562

Chen, Y. P., Ehlers, A., Clark, D. M., & Mansell, W. (2002). Patients with generalized social phobia direct their attention away from faces. *Behaviour Research and Therapy, 40*, 677–687. doi: 10.1016/S0005-7967(01)00086–9

Chorpita, B. F., Plummer, C. M., & Moffitt, C. E. (2000). Relations of tripartite dimensions of emotion to childhood anxiety and mood disorders. *Journal of Abnormal Child Psychology, 28*, 299–310. doi: 10.1023/A:1005152505888

Clark, D. M. (2001). A cognitive perspective on social phobia. In W. R. Crozier & L. E. Alden (eds.), *International Handbook of Social Anxiety: Concepts, Research and Intervention Relating to the Self and Shyness* (pp. 405–430). Chichester: Wiley.

Clark, D. M. & Wells, A. (1995). A cognitive model of social phobia. In R. G. Heimberg, M. R. Liebowitz, D. A. Hope, & F. R. Schneier (eds.), *Social Phobia: Diagnosis, Assessment, and Treatment* (pp. 69–93). New York, NY: Guilford Press.

Clark, L. A. & Watson, D. (1991). Tripartite model of anxiety and depression: Psychometric evidence and taxonomic implications. *Journal of Abnormal Psychology, 100*, 316–336. doi: 1037/0021-843X.100.3.316

Coles, M. E., Turk, C. L., & Heimberg, R. G. (2002). The role of memory perspective in social phobia: Immediate and delayed memories for role-played situations. *Behavioural and Cognitive Psychotherapy, 30*, 415–425. doi: 10.1017/S1352465802004034

Coles, M. E., Turk, C. L., Heimberg, R. G., & Fresco, D. M. (2001). Effects of varying levels of anxiety within social situations: Relationship to memory perspective and attributions in social phobia. *Behaviour Research and Therapy, 39*, 651–665. doi: 10.1016/S0005-7967(00)00035–8

Collins, K. A., Westra, H. A., Dozois, D. J., & Stewart, S. H. (2005). The validity of the brief version of the Fear of Negative Evaluation Scale. *Journal of Anxiety Disorders, 19*, 345–359. doi: 10.1016/j.janxdis.2004.02.003

Dağ, İ. G. & Gülüm, İ. V. (2013). The mediator role of cognitive features in the relationship between adult attachment patterns and psychopathology symptoms: Cognitive flexibility. *Turkish Journal of Psychiatry, 24*, 240–247.

Dannahy, L. & Stopa, L. (2007). Post-event processing in social anxiety. *Behaviour Research and Therapy, 45*, 1207–1219. doi: 10.1016/j.brat.2006.08.017

D'Avanzato, C., Joormann, J., Siemer, M., & Gotlib, I. H. (2013). Emotion regulation in depression and anxiety: Examining diagnostic specificity and stability of strategy use. *Cognitive Therapy and Research, 37*, 968–980. doi: 10.1007/s10608-013–9537-0

Edwards, S. L., Rapee, R. M., & Franklin, J. (2003). Postevent rumination and recall bias for a social performance event in high and low socially anxious individuals. *Cognitive Therapy and Research, 27*, 603–617. doi: 10.1023/A:1026395526858

Eisner, L. R., Johnson, S. L., & Carver, C. S. (2009). Positive affect regulation in anxiety disorders. *Journal of Anxiety Disorders*, *23*, 645–649. doi: 10.1016/j.janxdis.2009.02.001

Eng, W., Heimberg, R. G., Hart, T. A., Schneier, F. R., & Liebowitz, M. R. (2001). Attachment in individuals with social anxiety disorder: The relationship among adult attachment styles, social anxiety, and depression. *Emotion*, *1*, 365–380. doi: 10.1037/1528–3542.1.4.365

Erwin, B. A., Heimberg, R. G., Juster, H., & Mindlin, M. (2002). Comorbid anxiety and mood disorders among persons with social anxiety disorder. *Behaviour Research and Therapy*, *40*, 19–35. doi: 10.1016/S0005-7967(00)00114–5

Erwin, B. A., Turk, C. L., Heimberg, R. G., Fresco, D. M., & Hantula, D. A. (2004). The Internet: Home to a severe population of individuals with social anxiety disorder? *Journal of Anxiety Disorders*, *18*, 629–646. doi: 10.1016/j.janxdis.2003.08.002

Fang, A., Hoge, E. A., Heinrichs, M., & Hofmann, S. G. (2014). Attachment style moderates the effects of oxytocin on social behaviors and cognitions during social rejection applying a research domain criteria framework to social anxiety. *Clinical Psychological Science*, *2*, 740–747. doi: 10.1177/2167702614527948

Farmer, A. S. & Kashdan, T. B. (2012). Social anxiety and emotion regulation in daily life: Spillover effects on positive and negative social events. *Cognitive Behaviour Therapy*, *41*, 152–162. doi: 10.1080/16506073.2012.666561

Fergus, T. A., Valentiner, D. P., McGrath, P. B., Stephenson, K., Gier, S., & Jencius, S. (2009). The Fear of Positive Evaluation Scale: Psychometric properties in a clinical sample. *Journal of Anxiety Disorders*, *23*, 1177–1183. doi: 10.1016/j.janxdis.2009.07.024

Gajwani, R., Patterson, P., & Birchwood, M. (2013). Attachment: Developmental pathways to affective dysregulation in young people at ultra-high risk of developing psychosis. *British Journal of Clinical Psychology*, *52*, 424–437. doi: 10.1111/bjc.12027

Gavric, D., Moscovitch, D. A., Rowa, K., & McCabe, R. E. (2017). Post-event processing in social anxiety disorder: Examining the mediating roles of positive metacognitive beliefs and perceptions of performance. *Behaviour Research and Therapy*, *91*, 1–12. doi: 10.1016/j.brat.2017.01.002

Gaydukevych, D. & Kocovski, N. L. (2012). Effect of self-focused attention on post-event processing in social anxiety. *Behaviour Research and Therapy*, *50*, 47–55. doi: 10.1016/j.brat.2011.10.010

Gilbert, P. (2001). Evolution and social anxiety: The role of attraction, social competition, and social hierarchies. *Psychiatric Clinics of North America*, *24*, 723–751. doi: 10.1016/S0193-953X(05)70260–4

Gilbert, P. (2014). Evolutionary models: Practical and conceptual utility for the treatment and study of social anxiety disorder. In J. W. Weeks (ed.), *The Wiley Blackwell Handbook of Social Anxiety Disorder* (pp. 24–52). New York, NY: Wiley-Blackwell. doi: 10.1002/9781118653920.ch2

Gilboa-Schechtman, E., Franklin, M. E., & Foa, E. B. (2000). Anticipated reactions to social events: Differences among individuals with generalized social phobia, obsessive compulsive disorder, and nonanxious controls. *Cognitive Therapy and Research*, *24*, 731–746. doi: 10.1023/A:1005595513315

Grant, B. F., Hasin, D. S., Blanco, C., Stinson, F. S., Chou, S. P., Goldstein, R. B., . . . Huang, B. (2005). The epidemiology of social anxiety disorder in the United States: Results from the National Epidemiologic Survey on Alcohol and Related Conditions. *Journal of Clinical Psychiatry, 66*, 1351–1361.

Grant, B. F., Stinson, F. S., Dawson, D. A., Chou, S. P., Dufour, M. C., Compton, W., . . . Kaplan, K. (2004). Prevalence and co-occurrence of substance use disorders and independent mood and anxiety disorders: Results from the National Epidemiologic Survey on Alcohol and Related Conditions. *Archives of General Psychiatry, 61*, 807–816. doi: 10.1001/archpsyc.61.8.807

Grisham, J. R., King, B. J., Makkar, S. R., & Felmingham, K. L. (2015). The contributions of arousal and self-focused attention to avoidance in social anxiety. *Anxiety, Stress, & Coping, 28*, 303–320. doi: 10.1080/10615806.2014.968144

Gross, J. J. (1998). The emerging field of emotion regulation: An integrative review. *Review of General Psychology, 2*, 271–299. doi: 10.1037/1089–2680.2.3.271

Gross, J. J. (2014). Emotion regulation: Conceptual and empirical foundations. In J. J. Gross (ed.), *Handbook of Emotion Regulation, Second Edition* (pp. 3–22). New York, NY: Guilford Press.

Gross, J. J. & John, O. P. (2003). Individual differences in two emotion regulation processes: Implications for affect, relationships, and well-being. *Journal of Personality and Social Psychology, 85*, 348–362. doi: 10.1037/0022–3514.85.2.348

Gülüm, İ. V. & Dağ, İ. G. (2014). The mediator role of the cognitive features in the relationship between adult attachment patterns and psychopathology symptoms: The locus of control and repetitive thinking. *Turkish Journal of Psychiatry, 25*, 244–252.

Hackmann, A., Clark, D. M., & McManus, F. (2000). Recurrent images and early memories in social phobia. *Behaviour Research and Therapy, 38*, 601–610. doi: 10.1016/S0005-7967(99)00161–8

Hackmann, A., Surawy, C., & Clark, D. M. (1998). Seeing yourself through others' eyes: A study of spontaneously occurring images in social phobia. *Behavioural and Cognitive Psychotherapy, 26*, 3–12. doi: 10.1017/S1352465898000022

Heeren, A., Mogoaşe, C., McNally, R. J., Schmitz, A., & Philippot, P. (2015). Does attention bias modification improve attentional control? A double-blind randomized experiment with individuals with social anxiety disorder. *Journal of Anxiety Disorders, 29*, 35–42. doi: 10.1016/j.janxdis.2014.10.007

Heeren, A., Peschard, V., & Philippot, P. (2012). The causal role of attentional bias for threat cues in social anxiety: A test on a cyber-ostracism task. *Cognitive Therapy and Research, 36*, 512–521. doi: 10.1007/s10608-011–9394-7

Heimberg, R. G. (1994). Cognitive assessment strategies and the measurement of outcome of treatment for social phobia. *Behaviour Research and Therapy, 32*, 269–280. doi: 10.1016/0005–7967(94)90121-X

Heimberg, R.G., Brozovich, F. A., & Rapee, R. M. (2014). A cognitive-behavioral model of social anxiety disorder. In S. G. Hofmann & P. M. DiBartolo (eds.), *Social Anxiety: Clinical, Developmental, and Social Perspectives* (3rd edn) (pp. 705–728). Waltham, MA: Academic Press. doi: 10.1016/B978-0–12-394427–6.00024–8

Helbig-Lang, S., Rusch, S., Rief, W., & Lincoln, T. M. (2015). The strategy does not matter: Effects of acceptance, reappraisal, and distraction on the course of anticipatory anxiety in social anxiety disorder. *Psychology and Psychotherapy: Theory, Research and Practice*, *88*, 366–377. doi: 10.1111/papt.12053

Helbig-Lang, S., von Auer, M., Neubauer, K., Murray, E., & Gerlach, A. L. (2016). Post-event processing in social anxiety disorder after real-life social situations: An ambulatory assessment study. *Behaviour Research and Therapy*, *84*, 27–34. doi: 10.1016/j.brat.2016.07.003

Hinrichsen, H. & Clark, D. M. (2003). Anticipatory processing in social anxiety: Two pilot studies. *Journal of Behavior Therapy and Experimental Psychiatry*, 34, 205–218. doi: 10.1016/S0005-7916(03)00050-8

Hofmann, S. G. (2007). Cognitive factors that maintain social anxiety disorder: A comprehensive model and its treatment implications. *Cognitive Behaviour Therapy*, *36*, 193–209. doi: 10.1080/16506070701421313

Hofmann, S. G., Sawyer, A. T., Fang, A., & Asnaani, A. (2012). Emotion dysregulation model of mood and anxiety disorders. *Depression and Anxiety*, *29*, 409–416. doi: 10.1002/da.21888

Hope, D. A. & Heimberg, R. G. (1988). Public and private self-consciousness and social phobia. *Journal of Personality Assessment*, *52*, 626–639. doi: 10.1207/s15327752jpa5204_3

Hughes, A. A., Heimberg, R. G., Coles, M. E., Gibb, B. E., Liebowitz, M. R., & Schneier, F. R. (2006). Relations of the factors of the tripartite model of anxiety and depression to types of social anxiety. *Behaviour Research and Therapy*, *44*, 1629–1641. doi: 10.1016/j.brat.2005.10.015

Insel, T., Cuthbert, B., Garvey, M., Heinssen, R., Pine, D. S., Quinn, K., Sanislow, C., Wang, P. (2010). Research domain criteria (RDoC): Toward a new classification framework for research on mental disorders. *American Journal of Psychiatry*, *167*, 748–751. doi: 10.1176/appi.ajp.2010.09091379

Joormann, J. & Gotlib, I. H. (2006). Is this happiness I see? Biases in the identification of emotional facial expressions in depression and social phobia. *Journal of Abnormal Psychology*, *115*, 705–714. doi: 10.1037/0021-843X.115.4.705

Jusyte, A. & Schönenberg, M. (2014). Threat processing in generalized social phobia: An investigation of interpretation biases in ambiguous facial affect. *Psychiatry Research*, *217*, 100–106. doi: 10.1016/j.psychres.2013.12.031

Kalokerinos, E. K., Greenaway, K. H., & Denson, T. F. (2015). Reappraisal but not suppression downregulates the experience of positive and negative emotion. *Emotion*, *15*, 271–275. doi: 10.1037/emo0000025

Kashdan, T. B. (2002). Social anxiety dimensions, neuroticism, and the contours of positive psychological functioning. *Cognitive Therapy and Research*, *26*, 789–810. doi: 10.1023/A:1021293501345

Kashdan, T. B. (2004). The neglected relationship between social interaction anxiety and hedonic deficits: Differentiation from depressive symptoms. *Journal of Anxiety Disorders*, *18*, 719–730. doi: 10.1016/j.janxdis.2003.08.001

Kashdan, T. B. (2007). Social anxiety spectrum and diminished positive experiences: Theoretical synthesis and meta-analysis. *Clinical Psychology Review*, *27*, 348–365. doi: 10.1016/j.cpr.2006.12.003

Kashdan, T. B. & Collins, R. L. (2010). Social anxiety and the experience of positive emotion and anger in everyday life: An ecological momentary assessment approach. *Anxiety, Stress, & Coping*, *23*, 259–272. doi: 10.1080/10615800802641950

Kashdan, T. B. & Steger, M. F. (2006). Expanding the topography of social anxiety: An experience-sampling assessment of positive emotions, positive events, and emotion suppression. *Psychological Science*, *17*, 120–128.

Kessler, R. C., Berglund, P., Demler, O., Jin, R., Merikangas, K. R., & Walters, E. E. (2005). Lifetime prevalence and age-of-onset distributions of *DSM-IV* disorders in the National Comorbidity Survey Replication. *Archives of General Psychiatry*, *62*, 593–602. doi: 10.1001/archpsyc.62.6.593

Kessler, R. C., Chiu, W. T., Demler, O., Merikangas, K., & Walters, E. E. (2005). Prevalence, severity, and comorbidity of 12-month *DSM-IV* disorders in the National Comorbidity Survey Replication. *Archives of General Psychiatry*, *62*, 617–627. doi: 0.1001/archpsyc.62.6.617

Kessler, R. C., Stang, P., Wittchen, H. U., Stein, M., & Walters, E. E. (1999). Lifetime co-morbidities between social phobia and mood disorders in the US National Comorbidity Survey. *Psychological Medicine*, *29*, 555–567.

Kiko, S., Stevens, S., Mall, A. K., Steil, R., Bohus, M., & Hermann, C. (2012). Predicting post-event processing in social anxiety disorder following two prototypical social situations: State variables and dispositional determinants. *Behaviour Research and Therapy*, *50*, 617–626. doi: 10.1016/j.brat.2012.06.001

Kivity, Y. & Huppert, J. D. (2016). Does cognitive reappraisal reduce anxiety? A daily diary study of a micro-intervention with individuals with high social anxiety. *Journal of Consulting and Clinical Psychology*, *84*, 269–283. doi: 10.1037/ccp0000075

Kotov, R., Watson, D., Robles, J. P., & Schmidt, N. B. (2007). Personality traits and anxiety symptoms: The multilevel trait predictor model. *Behaviour Research and Therapy*, *45*, 1485–1503. doi: 10.1016/j.brat.2006.11.011

Langer, J. K. & Rodebaugh, T. L. (2013). Social anxiety and gaze avoidance: Averting gaze but not anxiety. *Cognitive Therapy and Research*, *37*, 1110–1120. doi: 10.1007/s10608-013-9546-z

Laposa, J. M., Cassin, S. E., & Rector, N. A. (2010). Interpretation of positive social events in social phobia: An examination of cognitive correlates and diagnostic distinction. *Journal of Anxiety Disorders*, *24*, 203–210. doi: 10.1016/j.janxdis.2009.10.009

Laposa, J. M., Collimore, K. C., & Rector, N. A. (2014). Is post-event processing a social anxiety specific or transdiagnostic cognitive process in the anxiety spectrum? *Behavioural and Cognitive Psychotherapy*, *42*, 706–717. doi: 10.1017/S135246581300074X

Lucock, M. P. & Salkovskis, P. M. (1988). Cognitive factors in social anxiety and its treatment. *Behaviour Research and Therapy*, *26*, 297–302. doi: 10.1016/0005-7967(88)90081-2

Makkar, S. R. & Grisham, J. R. (2011). The predictors and contents of post-event processing in social anxiety. *Cognitive Therapy and Research*, *35*, 118–133. doi: 10.1007/s10608-011-9357-z

Manning, R. P., Dickson, J. M., Palmier-Claus, J., Cunliffe, A., & Taylor, P. J. (2017). A systematic review of adult attachment and social anxiety. *Journal of Affective Disorders*, *211*, 44–59. doi: 10.1016/j.jad.2016.12.020

Maoz, K., Eldar, S., Stoddard, J., Pine, D. S., Leibenluft, E., & Bar-Haim, Y. (2016). Angry-happy interpretations of ambiguous faces in social anxiety disorder. *Psychiatry Research*, *241*, 122–127. doi: 10.1016/j.psychres.2016.04.100

McManus, F., Sacadura, C., & Clark, D. M. (2008). Why social anxiety persists: An experimental investigation of the role of safety behaviours as a maintaining factor. *Journal of Behavior Therapy and Experimental Psychiatry*, *39*, 147–161. doi: 10.1016/j.jbtep.2006.12.002

McNally, R. J., Enock, P. M., Tsai, C., & Tousian, M. (2013). Attention bias modification for reducing speech anxiety. *Behaviour Research and Therapy*, *51*, 882–888. doi: 10.1016/j.brat.2013.10.001

Mennin, D. S., Holaway, R. M., Fresco, D. M., Moore, M. T., & Heimberg, R. G. (2007). Delineating components of emotion and its dysregulation in anxiety and mood psychopathology. *Behavior Therapy*, *38*, 284–302. doi: 10.1016/j.beth.2006.09.001

Mennin, D. S., McLaughlin, K. A., & Flanagan, T. J. (2009). Emotion regulation deficits in generalized anxiety disorder, social anxiety disorder, and their co-occurrence. *Journal of Anxiety Disorders*, *23*, 866–871. doi: 10.1016/j.janxdis.2009.04.006

Michail, M. & Birchwood, M. (2014). Social anxiety in first-episode psychosis: The role of childhood trauma and adult attachment. *Journal of Affective Disorders*, *163*, 102–109. doi: 10.1016/j.jad.2014.03.033

Mickelson, K. D., Kessler, R. C., & Shaver, P. R. (1997). Adult attachment in a nationally representative sample. *Journal of Personality and Social Psychology*, *73*, 1092–1106. doi: 10.1037/0022–3514.73.5.1092

Mills, A. C., Grant, D. M., Lechner, W. V., & Judah, M. R. (2013). Psychometric properties of the Anticipatory Social Behaviours Questionnaire. *Journal of Psychopathology and Behavioral Assessment*, *35*, 346–355. doi: 10.1007/s10862-013–9339-4

Mitchell, M. A. & Schmidt, N. B. (2014). General in-situation safety behaviors are uniquely associated with post-event processing. *Journal of Behavior Therapy and Experimental Psychiatry*, *45*, 229–233. doi: 10.1016/j.jbtep.2013.11.001

Mogg, K. & Bradley, B. P. (1998). A cognitive-motivational analysis of anxiety. *Behaviour Research and Therapy*, *36*, 809–848. doi: 10.1016/S0005-7967(98)00063–1

Mogg, K., Philippot, P., & Bradley, B. P. (2004). Selective attention to angry faces in clinical social phobia. *Journal of Abnormal Psychology*, *113*, 160–165. doi: 10.1037/0021-843X.113.1.160

Montesi, J. L., Conner, B. T., Gordon, E. A., Fauber, R. L., Kim, K. H., & Heimberg, R. G. (2013). On the relationship among social anxiety, intimacy, sexual communication, and sexual satisfaction in young couples. *Archives of Sexual Behavior*, *42*, 81–91. doi: 10.1007/s10508-012–9929-3

Moriya, J. & Tanno, Y. (2008). Relationships between negative emotionality and attentional control in effortful control. *Personality and Individual Differences*, *44*, 1348–1355. doi: 10.1016/j.paid.2007.12.003

Morrison, A. S. & Heimberg, R. G. (2013). Attentional control mediates the effect of social anxiety on positive affect. *Journal of Anxiety Disorders*, *27*, 56–67. doi: 10.1016/j.janxdis.2012.10.002

Moscovitch, D. A., Chiupka, C. A., & Gavric, D. L. (2013). Within the mind's eye: Negative mental imagery activates different emotion regulation strategies in high versus low socially anxious individuals. *Journal of Behavior Therapy and Experimental Psychiatry*, *44*, 426–432. doi: 10.1016/j.jbtep.2013.05.002

Moscovitch, D. A., Rowa, K., Paulitzki, J. R., Ierullo, M. D., Chiang, B., Antony, M. M., & McCabe, R. E. (2013). Self-portrayal concerns and their relation to safety behaviors and negative affect in social anxiety disorder. *Behaviour Research and Therapy, 51,* 476–486. doi: 10.1016/j.brat.2013.05.002

Nilsson, J. E. C. & Lundh, L. G. (2016). Audio feedback with reduced self-focus as an intervention for social anxiety: An experimental study. *Cognitive Behaviour Therapy, 45,* 150–162. doi: 10.1080/16506073.2015.1126633

Norton, G. R., McLeod, L., Guertin, J., Hewitt, P. L., Walker, J. R., & Stein, M. B. (1996). Panic disorder or social phobia: Which is worse? *Behaviour Research and Therapy, 34,* 273–276. doi: 10.1016/0005–7967(95)00066–6

Okajima, I., Kanai, Y., Chen, J., & Sakano, Y. (2009). Effects of safety behaviour on the maintenance of anxiety and negative belief social anxiety disorder. *International Journal of Social Psychiatry, 55,* 71–81. doi: 10.1177/0020764008092191

O'Toole, M. S., Jensen, M. B., Fentz, H. N., Zachariae, R., & Hougaard, E. (2014). Emotion differentiation and emotion regulation in high and low socially anxious individuals: An experience-sampling study. *Cognitive Therapy and Research, 38,* 428–438. doi: 10.1007/s10608-014-9611-2

Penney, E. S. & Abbott, M. J. (2015). The impact of perceived standards on state anxiety, appraisal processes, and negative pre-and post-event rumination in social anxiety disorder. *Cognitive Therapy and Research, 39,* 162–177. doi: 10.1007/s10608-014–9639-3

Perini, S. J., Abbott, M. J., & Rapee, R. M. (2006). Perception of performance as a mediator in the relationship between social anxiety and negative post-event rumination. *Cognitive Therapy and Research, 30,* 645–659. doi: 10.1007/s10608-006–9023-z

Piccirillo, M. L., Dryman, M. T., & Heimberg, R. G. (2016). Safety behaviors in adults with social anxiety: Review and future directions. *Behavior Therapy, 47,* 675–687. doi: 10.1016/j.beth.2015.11.005

Pilkonis, P. A. (1977). Shyness, public and private, and its relationship to other measures of social behavior. *Journal of Personality, 45,* 585–595. doi: 10.1111/j.1467–6494.1977.tb00173.x

Pishyar, R., Harris, L. M., & Menzies, R. G. (2004). Attentional bias for words and faces in social anxiety. *Anxiety, Stress & Coping, 17,* 23–36. doi: 10.1080/10615800310001601458

Plasencia, M. L., Alden, L. E., & Taylor, C. T. (2011). Differential effects of safety behaviour subtypes in social anxiety disorder. *Behaviour Research and Therapy, 49,* 665–675. doi: 10.1016/j.brat.2011.07.005

Plasencia, M. L., Taylor, C. T., & Alden, L. E. (2016). Unmasking one's true self facilitates positive relational outcomes: Authenticity promotes social approach processes in social anxiety disorder. *Clinical Psychological Science, 4,* 1002–1014. doi: 10.1177/2167702615622204

Potter, C., Wong, J., Heimberg, R. G., Blanco, C., Liu, S., Wang, S., & Schneier, F. R. (2014). Situational panic attacks in social anxiety disorder. *Journal of Affective Disorders, 167,* 1–7. doi: 10.1016/j.jad.2014.05.044

Rapee, R. M. & Heimberg, R. G. (1997). A cognitive-behavioral model of anxiety in social phobia. *Behaviour Research and Therapy, 35,* 741–756. doi: 10.1016/S0005-7967(97)00022–3

Ravitz, P., Maunder, R., Hunter, J., Sthankiya, B., & Lancee, W. (2010). Adult attachment measures: A 25-year review. *Journal of Psychosomatic Research, 69,* 419–432. doi: 10.1016/j.jpsychores.2009.08.006

Richards, J. M. & Gross, J. J. (2000). Emotion regulation and memory: The cognitive costs of keeping one's cool. *Journal of Personality and Social Psychology*, *79*, 410–424. doi: 10.1037/0022–3514.79.3.410

Rodebaugh, T. L. (2009). Social phobia and perceived friendship quality. *Journal of Anxiety Disorders*, *23*, 872–878. doi: 10.1016/j.janxdis.2009.05.001

Rodebaugh, T. L., Bielak, T., Vidovic, V., & Moscovitch, D. A. (2016). The effects of social anxiety on interpersonal evaluations of warmth and dominance. *Journal of Anxiety Disorders*, *38*, 68–78. doi: 10.1016/j.janxdis.2016.01.002

Rodebaugh, T. L., Fernandez, K. C., & Levinson, C. A. (2012). Testing the effects of social anxiety disorder on friendship quality across gender and ethnicity. *Cognitive Behaviour Therapy*, *41*, 130–139. doi: 10.1080/16506073.2012.661451

Rodebaugh, T. L., Weeks, J. W., Gordon, E. A., Langer, J. K., & Heimberg, R. G. (2012). The longitudinal relationship between fear of positive evaluation and fear of negative evaluation. *Anxiety, Stress & Coping*, *25*, 167–182. doi: 10.1080/10615806.2011.569709

Roring, S. A., II (2008). The relationships among adult attachment style, perceived social support, and social anxiety in college students (Doctoral Dissertation). Retrieved from ProQuest Dissertations & Theses A&I (Order No. 1457137).

Rowa, K., Gavric, D., Stead, V., LeMoult, J., & McCabe, R. E. (2016). The pernicious effects of post-event processing in social anxiety disorder. *Journal of Experimental Psychopathology*, *7*, 577–587. doi: 10.5127/jep.056916

Ruscio, A. M., Brown, T. A., Chiu, W. T., Sareen, J., Stein, M. B., & Kessler, R. C. (2008). Social fears and social phobia in the USA: Results from the National Comorbidity Survey Replication. *Psychological Medicine*, *38*, 15–28. doi: 10.1017/S0033291707001699

Salkovskis, P. M. (1991). The importance of behaviour in the maintenance of anxiety and panic: A cognitive account. *Behavioural Psychotherapy*, *19*, 6–19. doi: 10.1017/S0141347300011472

Schlenker, B. R. & Leary, M. R. (1982). Social anxiety and self-presentation: A conceptualization model. *Psychological Bulletin*, *92*, 641–669. doi: 10.1037/0033–2909.92.3.641

Schmidt, N. B., Richey, J. A., Buckner, J. D., & Timpano, K. R. (2009). Attention training for generalized social anxiety disorder. *Journal of Abnormal Psychology*, *118*, 5–14. doi: 10.1037/a0013643

Schneier, F. R., Foose, T. E., Hasin, D. S., Heimberg, R. G., Liu, S. M., Grant, B. F., & Blanco, C. (2010). Social anxiety disorder and alcohol use disorder co-morbidity in the National Epidemiologic Survey on Alcohol and Related Conditions. *Psychological Medicine*, *40*, 977–988. doi: 10.1017/S0033291709991231

Schneier, F. R., Heckelman, L. R., Garfinkel, R., Campeas, R., Fallon, B. A., Gitow, A., . . . Liebowitz, M. R. (1994). Functional impairment in social phobia. *Journal of Clinical Psychiatry*, *55*, 322–331.

Schultz, L.T. & Heimberg, R.G. (2008). Attentional focus in social anxiety disorder: Potential for interactive processes. *Clinical Psychology Review*, *28*, 1206–1221. doi: 10.1016/j.cpr.2008.04.003

Simon, N. M., Otto, M. W., Korbly, N. B., Peters, P. M., Nicolaou, D. C., & Pollack, M. H. (2002). Quality of life in social anxiety disorder compared with panic disorder and the general population. *Psychiatric Services*, *53*, 714–718. doi: 10.1176/appi.ps.53.6.714

Snell, Jr., W. E. (1989). Willingness to self-disclose to female and male friends as a function of social anxiety and gender. *Personality and Social Psychology Bulletin, 15*, 113–125. doi: 10.1177/0146167289151011

Sparrevohn, R. M. & Rapee, R. M. (2009). Self-disclosure, emotional expression and intimacy within romantic relationships of people with social phobia. *Behaviour Research and Therapy, 47*, 1074–1078. doi: 10.1016/j.brat.2009.07.016

Stangier, U., Heidenreich, T., & Schermelleh-Engel, K. (2006). Safety behaviors and social performance in patients with generalized social phobia. *Journal of Cognitive Psychotherapy, 20*, 17–31. doi: 10.1891/jcop.20.1.17

Stein, M. B., Fuetsch, M., Müller, N., Höfler, M., Lieb, R., & Wittchen, H. U. (2001). Social anxiety disorder and the risk of depression: A prospective community study of adolescents and young adults. *Archives of General Psychiatry, 58*, 251–256. doi: 10.1001/archpsyc.58.3.251

Stein, M. B. & Kean, Y. M. (2000). Disability and quality of life in social phobia: Epidemiologic findings. *American Journal of Psychiatry, 157*, 1606–1613. doi: 10.1176/appi.ajp.157.10.1606

Stevens, S., Hofmann, M., Kiko, S., Mall, A. K., Steil, R., Bohus, M., & Hermann, C. (2010). What determines observer-rated social performance in individuals with social anxiety disorder? *Journal of Anxiety Disorders, 24*, 830–836. doi: 10.1016/j.janxdis.2010.06.005

Taylor, C. T. & Alden, L. E. (2010). Safety behaviors and judgmental biases in social anxiety disorder. *Behaviour Research and Therapy, 48*, 226–237. doi: 10.1016/j.brat.2009.11.005

Taylor, C. T., Bomyea, J., & Amir, N. (2010). Attentional bias away from positive social information mediates the link between social anxiety and anxiety vulnerability to a social stressor. *Journal of Anxiety Disorders, 24*, 403–408. doi: 10.1016/j.janxdis.2010.02.004

Taylor, C. T., Bomyea, J., & Amir, N. (2011). Malleability of attentional bias for positive emotional information and anxiety vulnerability. *Emotion, 11*, 127–138. doi: 10.1037/a0021301

Taylor, C. T., Cross, K., & Amir, N. (2016). Attentional control moderates the relationship between social anxiety symptoms and attentional disengagement from threatening information. *Journal of Behavior Therapy and Experimental Psychiatry, 50*, 68–76. doi: 10.1016/j.jbtep.2015.05.008

Teale Sapach, M. J., Carleton, R. N., Mulvogue, M. K., Weeks, J. W., & Heimberg, R. G. (2015). Cognitive constructs and social anxiety disorder: Beyond fearing negative evaluation. *Cognitive Behaviour Therapy, 44*, 63–73. doi: 10.1080/16506073.2014.961539

Turk, C. L., Heimberg, R. G., Luterek, J. A., Mennin, D. S., & Fresco, D. M. (2005). Emotion dysregulation in generalized anxiety disorder: A comparison with social anxiety disorder. *Cognitive Therapy and Research, 29*, 89–106. doi: 10.1007/s10608-005-1651-1

van Buren, A. & Cooley, E. L. (2002). Attachment styles, view of self and negative affect. *North American Journal of Psychology, 4*, 417–430.

Vassilopoulos, S. P. (2004). Anticipatory processing in social anxiety. *Behavioural and Cognitive Psychotherapy, 32*, 303–311. doi: 10.1017/S1352465804001377

Vassilopoulos, S. P. (2005). Anticipatory processing plays a role in maintaining social anxiety. *Anxiety, Stress, and Coping, 18*, 321–332. doi: 10.1080/10615800500258149

Voncken, M. J. & Bögels, S. M. (2008). Social performance deficits in social anxiety disorder: Reality during conversation and biased perception during speech. *Journal of Anxiety Disorders*, *22*, 1384–1392. doi: 10.1016/j.janxdis.2008.02.001

Voncken, M. J. & Dijk, K. F. L. (2013). Socially anxious individuals get a second chance after being disliked at first sight: The role of self-disclosure in the development of likeability in sequential social contact. *Cognitive Therapy and Research*, *37*, 7–17. doi: 10.1007/s10608-012–9449-4

Vriends, N., Meral, Y., Bargas-Avila, J. A., Stadler, C., & Bögels, S. M. (2017). How do I look? Self-focused attention during a video chat of women with social anxiety (disorder). *Behaviour Research and Therapy*, *92*, 77–86. doi: 10.1016/j.brat.2017.02.008

Wallace, S. T. & Alden, L. E. (1995). Social anxiety and standard setting following social success or failure. *Cognitive Therapy and Research*, *19*, 613–631. doi: 10.1007/BF02227857

Wallace, S. T. & Alden, L. E. (1997). Social phobia and positive social events: The price of success. *Journal of Abnormal Psychology*, *106*, 416. doi: 10.1037//0021-843X.106.3.416

Wang, W. T., Hsu, W. Y., Chiu, Y. C., & Liang, C. W. (2012). The hierarchical model of social interaction anxiety and depression: The critical roles of fears of evaluation. *Journal of Anxiety Disorders*, *26*, 215–224. doi: 10.1016/j.janxdis.2011.11.004

Watson, D., Clark, L. A., & Carey, G. (1988). Positive and negative affectivity and their relation to anxiety and depressive disorders. *Journal of Abnormal Psychology*, *97*, 346–353. doi: 10.1037/0021-843X.97.3.346

Watson, D. & Friend, R. (1969). Measurement of social-evaluative anxiety. *Journal of Consulting and Clinical Psychology*, *33*, 448–457. doi: 10.1037/h0027806

Weeks, J. W. (2015). Replication and extension of a hierarchical model of social anxiety and depression: Fear of positive evaluation as a key unique factor in social anxiety. *Cognitive Behaviour Therapy*, *44*, 103–116. doi: 10.1080/16506073.2014.990050

Weeks, J. W., Heimberg, R. G., Fresco, D. M., Hart, T. A., Turk, C. L., Schneier, F. R., & Liebowitz, M. R. (2005). Empirical validation and psychometric evaluation of the Brief Fear of Negative Evaluation Scale in patients with social anxiety disorder. *Psychological Assessment*, *17*, 179. doi: 10.1037/1040–3590.17.2.179

Weeks, J. W., Heimberg, R. G., & Rodebaugh, T. L. (2008). The Fear of Positive Evaluation Scale: Assessing a proposed cognitive component of social anxiety. *Journal of Anxiety Disorders*, *22*, 44–55. doi: 10.1016/j.janxdis.2007.08.002

Weeks, J. W., Heimberg, R. G., Rodebaugh, T. L., Goldin, P. R., & Gross, J. J. (2012). Psychometric evaluation of the Fear of Positive Evaluation Scale in patients with social anxiety disorder. *Psychological Assessment*, *24*, 301–312. doi: 10.1037/a0025723

Weeks, J. W., Heimberg, R. G., Rodebaugh, T. L., & Norton, P. J. (2008). Exploring the relationship between fear of positive evaluation and social anxiety. *Journal of Anxiety Disorders*, *22*, 386–400. doi: 10.1016/j.janxdis.2007.04.009

Weeks, J. W. & Howell, A. N. (2012). The bivalent fear of evaluation model of social anxiety: Further integrating findings on fears of positive and negative evaluation. *Cognitive Behaviour Therapy*, *41*, 83–95. doi: 10.1080/16506073.2012.661452

Weisman, O., Aderka, I. M., Marom, S., Hermesh, H., & Gilboa-Schechtman, E. (2011). Social rank and affiliation in social anxiety disorder. *Behaviour Research and Therapy, 49*, 399–405. doi: 10.1016/j.brat.2011.03.010

Wells, A., Clark, D. M., & Ahmad, S. (1998). How do I look with my mind's eye: Perspective taking in social phobic imagery. *Behaviour Research and Therapy, 36*, 631–634. doi: 10.1016/S0005-7967(98)00037–0

Wells, A., Clark, D. M., Salkovskis, P., Ludgate, J., Hackmann, A., & Gelder, M. (1995). Social phobia: The role of in-situation safety behaviors in maintaining anxiety and negative beliefs. *Behavior Therapy, 26*, 153–161. doi: 10.1016/S0005-7894(05)80088–7

Wells, A. & Papageorgiou, C. (1999). The observer perspective: Biased imagery in social phobia, agoraphobia, and blood/injury phobia. *Behaviour Research and Therapy, 37*, 653–658. doi: 10.1016/S0005-7967(98)00150–8

Werner, K. H., Goldin, P. R., Ball, T. M., Heimberg, R. G., & Gross, J. J. (2011). Assessing emotion regulation in social anxiety disorder: The emotion regulation interview. *Journal of Psychopathology and Behavioral Assessment, 33*, 346–354. doi: 10.1007/s10862-011–9225-x

Wieser, M. J., Pauli, P., & Mühlberger, A. (2009). Probing the attentional control theory in social anxiety: An emotional saccade task. *Cognitive, Affective, & Behavioral Neuroscience, 9*, 314–322. doi: 10.3758/CABN.9.3.314

Wittchen, H. U., Fuetsch, M., Sonntag, H., Müller, N., & Liebowitz, M. (2000). Disability and quality of life in pure and comorbid social phobia: Findings from a controlled study. *European Psychiatry, 15*, 46–58. doi: 10.1016/S0924-9338(00)00211-X

Wong, J., Gordon, E. A., & Heimberg, R. G. (2014). Cognitive-behavioral models of social anxiety disorder. In J. W. Weeks (ed.), *The Wiley-Blackwell Handbook of Social Anxiety Disorder* (pp. 3–23).New York, NY:Wiley-Blackwell. doi: 10.1002/9781118653920.ch1

Wong, Q. J. & Moulds, M. L. (2011). Impact of anticipatory processing versus distraction on multiple indices of anxiety in socially anxious individuals. *Behaviour Research and Therapy, 49*, 700–706. doi: 10.1016/j.brat.2011.07.007

Wong, Q. J. & Rapee, R. M. (2016). The aetiology and maintenance of social anxiety disorder: A synthesis of complimentary theoretical models and formulation of a new integrated model. *Journal of Affective Disorders, 203*, 84–100. doi: 10.1016/j.jad.2016.05.069

Woody, S. R. & Rodriguez, B. F. (2000). Self-focused attention and social anxiety in social phobics and normal controls. *Cognitive Therapy and Research, 24*, 473–488. doi: 10.1023/A:1005583820758

Yonkers, K. A., Bruce, S. E., Dyck, I. R., & Keller, M. B. (2003). Chronicity, relapse, and illness – course of panic disorder, social phobia, and generalized anxiety disorder: Findings in men and women from 8 years of follow-up. *Depression and Anxiety, 17*, 173–179. doi: 10.1002/da.10106

Yonkers, K. A., Dyck, I. R., & Keller, M. B. (2001). An eight-year longitudinal comparison of clinical course and characteristics of social phobia among men and women. *Psychiatric Services, 52*, 637–643. doi: 10.1176/appi.ps.52.5.637

Yu, H., Li, S., Qian, M., Yang, P., Wang, X., Lin, M., & Yao, N. (2014). Time-course of attentional bias for positive social words in individuals with high and low social anxiety. *Behavioural and Cognitive Psychotherapy*, *42*, 479–490. doi: 10.1017/ S1352465813000398

Zou, J. B., Hudson, J. L., & Rapee, R. M. (2007). The effect of attentional focus on social anxiety. *Behaviour Research and Therapy*, *45*, 2326–2333. doi: 10.1016/j .brat.2007.03.014

18 Generalized Anxiety Disorder

Ki Eun Shin, Lucas S. LaFreniere, and
Michelle G. Newman

Diagnosis and Symptoms of GAD

Generalized anxiety disorder (GAD) first appeared as a diagnostic category in the *Diagnostic and Statistical Manual of Mental Disorders* (*DSM*), third edition (American Psychiatric Association, 1980). Initially, GAD was a residual category that could be diagnosed only in the absence of other Axis I diagnoses. GAD became an independent diagnosis in the *DSM-III-R*, with some major changes in the criteria (American Psychiatric Association, 1987). Excessive worry was specified as the core symptom, and the duration requirement increased from one to six months. The diagnostic criteria were further modified in the *DSM-IV* (American Psychiatric Association, 1994), where symptoms of autonomic hyperactivity were removed, and worry was required to be difficult to control instead of unrealistic. The criteria for GAD have remained the same in subsequent versions of the *DSM* (American Psychiatric Association, 2013).

The diagnostic criteria for GAD include irritability, poor concentration, sleep difficulty, restlessness, and muscle tension, but the core symptom is excessive and uncontrollable worry. Worry is also present in other disorders, but a meta-analysis showed that GAD involves greater severity/frequency of worry than other anxiety disorders (Olatunji, Wolitzky-Taylor, Sawchuk, & Ciesielski, 2010). Worry is a perseverative negative cognition where undesirable outcomes are expected. It perpetuates itself by shifting in topic and generating feelings of anxiety, which lead to more worry (Brosschot, Gerin, & Thayer, 2006). Worry is also primarily verbal–linguistic (e.g., Borkovec & Inz, 1990). Studies suggest that worry is best conceptualized as a dimensional construct, with both normal and pathological worry on the same continuum (Olatunji, Broman-Fulks, Bergman, Green, & Zlomke, 2010; Ruscio, Borkovec, & Ruscio, 2001). GAD and non-GAD worriers are differentiated by severity of distress, impairment, and uncontrollability of worry, rather than qualitative differences (Ruscio, 2002; Ruscio & Borkovec, 2004). In addition, although GAD worriers exhibit more widespread worries over multiple domains of their life compared to controls, there is also significant overlap in their worry content (Roemer, Molina, & Borkovec, 1997). Overall, these findings indicate dimensionality in the diagnosis of GAD.

Prevalence, Course, and Comorbidity in GAD

Despite changes in the GAD diagnostic criteria over time, prevalence rates have been relatively stable (Wittchen, 2002). GAD is a fairly common disorder across the globe, with a lifetime prevalence rate of 3.7% and a one-year rate of 1.8% (Ruscio et al., 2017). In US and European samples, prevalence rates ranged from 4% to 6% for lifetime, and 2% to 4% for one year based on the *DSM-IV* criteria (Carter, Wittchen, Pfister, & Kessler, 2001; Grant et al., 2005; Kessler, Berglund et al., 2005; Ruscio et al., 2017). GAD is especially common in primary care settings, accounting for 22–50% of anxiety disorder cases (Wittchen et al., 2001). Sociodemographic risk factors for GAD include being female, low income, and being widowed/separated/divorced. In particular, females are twice as likely to develop GAD than men. GAD has two onset distributions, one early at around age 24 and another after age 24 (Rhebergen et al., 2017), with the median age of onset of 31 (Kessler, Berglund et al., 2005).

The course of GAD is chronic. Symptoms wax and wane, and few achieve full remission. Based on retrospective data, GAD symptoms persisted for a decade or longer, with mean duration of illness reaching 20 years (e.g., Yonkers, Warshaw, Massion, & Keller, 1996). In 8- and 12-year studies, about 50–60% of GAD patients remitted over time, but relapse rates were 40–45% (Bruce et al., 2005; Yonkers, Bruce, Dyck, & Keller, 2003). The relapse rates suggest symptom fluctuations over time and poor maintenance of naturalistic gains in many cases.

GAD also has high comorbidity with other disorders. Across studies, 68–93% of GAD cases had at least one other comorbid Axis I disorder concurrently (e.g., Carter et al., 2001; Hunt, Issakidis, & Andrews, 2002; Ruscio et al., 2017). In addition, an estimated 80–90% of cases developed another mental disorder in their lifetime (e.g., Wittchen, Carter, Pfister, Montgomery, & Kessler, 2000). These findings show that "pure" GAD is less common than comorbid GAD. GAD has high comorbidity with depressive disorders (e.g., major depression, dysthymia), other anxiety disorders (especially panic disorder, social anxiety disorder, and specific phobias), and somatoform disorders (e.g., Kessler, Chiu, Demler, Merikangas, & Walters, 2005; Wittchen, Zhao, Kessler, & Eaton, 1994). Comorbidity, especially with mood disorders, has predicted increased disability and poor prognosis in GAD (Grant et al., 2005; Wittchen et al., 2000). High comorbidity with other disorders has also led to questions on the validity of GAD as a stand-alone diagnosis. Some have proposed that GAD is better conceptualized as a prodrome or residual disorder. However, note that comorbidity rates in GAD are not significantly higher than in other disorders such as depression (Jacobson & Newman, 2017; Kessler, DuPont, Berglund, & Wittchen, 1999) and panic disorder (Grant et al., 2005). Also, although a minority, "pure" GAD cases have been consistently identified, supporting that GAD is an independent diagnosis.

Etiological and Maintenance Factors in GAD

Negative Valence Systems in GAD

Worry, anticipation of a future aversive outcome, is inherently linked to negative emotionality. When experimentally induced, worry increased negative affect and decreased positive affect based on self-report (Llera & Newman, 2014, 2010). It also increased both anxiety and depression, although its effect on anxiety was stronger (McLaughlin, Borkovec, & Sibrava, 2007). In these studies, higher worry has predicted lower levels of relaxation as well. Evidence supports a dimensional model of worry in that worry elicits similar types of negative affect in GAD and non-GAD cases, but individuals with GAD report greater worrying and negative affect (Llera & Newman, 2014). The effects of worry on negative emotionality are also prolonged in GAD (Llera & Newman, 2017; Newman, Jacobson, Szkodny, & Sliwinski, 2016). This shows that GAD involves worry and associated negative affect at both state and trait levels.

Worry's tendency to increase distress suggests an important question on the etiological mechanism of pathological worry: why do individuals with GAD engage in worry excessively despite its emotional costs? One view is that worry serves as a maladaptive strategy to avoid negative internal experiences (Borkovec, 1994; Dugas, Gagnon, Ladouceur, & Freeston, 1998; Roemer & Orsillo, 2002; Wells, 1995). It is posited that the verbal nature of worry inhibits accessing the imagery of a fear-provoking stimulus and dampens the initial physiological reaction to the fear stimulus. Such a reduction in initial fear activation is maladaptive because it would interfere with habituation, a process of fear reduction (Foa & Kozak, 1986). Although this avoidance model of worry has been influential, it conflicts with the accruing evidence that worry actually *heightens* negative emotions rather than mitigating them (e.g., Llera & Newman, 2010). An alternative model (contrast avoidance theory) (Newman & Llera, 2011) proposes that instead of precluding negative emotions, worry creates and sustains them to prevent a further sharp increase in negative emotions (i.e., a negative contrast). When negative emotions are already elevated, there is less room for them to increase further. Evidence from experimental (Llera & Newman, 2014, 2010), self-report (Llera & Newman, 2017), and ecologically valid data (Crouch, Lewis, Erickson, & Newman, 2017; Newman, Jacobson et al., 2016) has supported the theory. Compared to relaxation or neutral mood, worry produced greater negative emotion and physiological arousal, and subsequently, lower subjective and physiological reactivity to negative emotional stimuli (Llera & Newman, 2014). In this study, the level of negative emotion during negative emotional exposure was not different between groups, suggesting that worry reduced an upward *shift* in negative emotions, rather than negative emotions as a whole.

The function of worry also has relevance for understanding the modulation of fear and anxiety in GAD. Fear and anxiety represent responses to an aversive stimulus. Fear is a reaction to imminent, acute, and specific threats (e.g., heart racing at the sight of a snake), and anxiety is apprehension of distant, uncertain, and ambiguous harm (e.g., discomfort passing a bush where a snake was once found). Distinct brain areas appear to underlie fear and anxiety. Whereas the amygdala (especially the central nucleus) has been shown to regulate a rapid-onset, short-duration reaction to threats (fear), the bed nucleus of the stria terminalis (BNST) was involved in a more persistent stress response to sustained threats (anxiety) (Lang, Davis, & Öhman, 2000; Walker, Toufexis, & Davis, 2003). Both brain areas belong to the limbic system, and project to each other as well as areas in the hypothalamus and brainstem that mediate autonomic and behavioral responses to threats.

In the GAD literature, distinct findings emerged on amygdala activity depending on the nature of experimental tasks. Studies using emotional exposure generally found hyperactivation of the amygdala in response to fear stimuli (e.g., Monk et al., 2008) or all stimuli, including non-fear stimuli (Nitschke et al., 2009). Cue-controlled anticipation of aversive stimuli or uncertainty also increased amygdala activity (Nitschke et al., 2009) whereas worry induction attenuated it (e.g., Hoehn-Saric, Lee, McLeod, & Wong, 2005). In one study, worry induction increased amygdala activation in controls, but not in GAD patients (Andreescu et al., 2011). Interestingly, GAD patients also exhibited greater activation in BNST and weaker activation in amygdala than healthy controls when faced with high uncertainty in preventing a loss in a gambling game (Yassa, Hazlett, Stark, & Hoehn-Saric, 2012).

The neural findings appear to be consistent with the theorized function of worry in prolonging negative affect to reduce a further sharp increase in negative emotions (Newman, Llera, Erickson, Przeworski, & Castonguay, 2013). Individuals with GAD exhibited greater sensitivity to fear/threat stimuli (e.g., increased amygdala activity), which may function as an etiological factor for developing pathological worry. They may use worry to sustain anxiety in response to a potential loss/ threats (e.g., increased BNST activation) and in turn, mitigate an immediate fear response (e.g., reduced amygdala activity). In line with this prediction, GAD has been repeatedly linked to neuroticism, a personality trait of proneness to negative emotional reactivity. Genetic factors shared with neuroticism account for about a half of the genetic risk for GAD (Hettema, Neale, Myers, Prescott, & Kendler, 2006). In addition, relative to social anxiety disorder or comorbid social anxiety disorder and GAD, GAD was most strongly predicted by higher negative emotional intensity and difficulty accessing effective emotion regulation strategies (Mennin, McLaughlin, & Flanagan, 2009). Studies using Pavlovian conditioning paradigms also found that high trait worry increased fear conditionability (e.g., Joos, Vansteenwegen, & Hermans, 2012). Putting these results together, individuals with GAD exhibit heightened fear reactions to threat stimuli, and this may lead them to develop maladaptive coping strategies such as worry.

Emotion regulation deficits in GAD have been also observed at a neural level in the form of disrupted top-down regulation of fear. Interestingly, the direction of dysregulation (e.g., over- or under-regulation) has been inconsistent. A systematic review (Hilbert, Lueken, & Beesdo-Baum, 2014) indicated reduced functional connectivity between the amygdala and the prefrontal cortex (PFC), a region involved in emotion regulation in GAD. On the contrary, resting state fMRI on GAD participants revealed increased amygdalar connectivity with the executive control network (e.g., PFC), which indexes cognitive control over emotional materials (Etkin, Prater, Schatzberg, Menon, & Greicius, 2009). In another study (Makovac et al., 2016), a worry induction led to greater fronto-limbic connectivity for GAD patients, but not healthy controls. One explanation for the mixed findings is that GAD patients may continuously engage in worry to maintain an anxious state and regulate an acute fear response to specific threats (increased fronto-limbic connectivity), but this rigid adherence to worry may interfere with the flexible recruitment of cognitive resources necessary for alternative regulatory strategies (e.g., reappraisal). Consistent with this hypothesis, GAD patients showed reduced recruitment of PFC or anterior cingulate cortex (ACC) when instructed to reappraise or maintain emotional responses to negative stimuli (Ball, Ramsawh, Campbell-Sills, Paulus, & Stein, 2013) or suppress worry (Andreescu et al., 2011). There is also evidence that the fronto-limbic neural circuits may function differently between individuals with and without GAD. The basolateral and centromedial parts of the amygdala typically involve distinct circuits and functions, but showed less differentiation in GAD (e.g., Etkin et al., 2009). Due to this structural and functional abnormality, amygdalar–PFC connectivity may mediate maladaptive as well as adaptive emotion regulation processes in GAD. Some (e.g., Etkin et al., 2009) proposed such circuit-level dysfunction in frontal and limbic areas as a potential etiological and maintenance factor in GAD.

In addition, worry in and of itself may contribute to the maintenance of generalized anxiety. Existing evidence suggests that worry facilitates transformation of momentary fear into sustained anxiety. For instance, anticipation of or hypervigilance to potential threats is associated with increased BNST activity, which underlies a prolonged anxiety response (e.g., Somerville, Whalen, & Kelley, 2010). In a task involving high risk for a monetary loss, GAD participants showed BNST enhancement and amygdala suppression relative to non-anxious controls (Yassa et al., 2012). These authors noted that in GAD, the amygdala might be engaged early in response to prolonged stressors, but quickly becomes disengaged as a result of a shift to activation of BNST. Another study also found that worrying after fear conditioning increased fear responses to both a conditioned fear stimulus and an unconditioned safety stimulus, as well as impaired fear extinction later (e.g., Gazendam & Kindt, 2012). These findings suggest that worry mediates the transition from fear to anxiety at both the neural and the behavioral levels. In this regard, worry may serve as a mechanism for developing chronic anxiety problems in GAD.

One overarching theme in the reviewed findings is correspondence between neural-level processes in GAD and behavioral and cognitive mechanisms for the maintenance of worry symptoms. For instance, the behavioral principle of negative reinforcement is considered an underlying maintenance factor in GAD (e.g., Newman & Llera, 2011). Negative reinforcement occurs when a certain behavior removes an aversive experience. Because most worries rarely come true, worrying is often followed by an absence of expected negative outcomes and feelings of relief. This perceived prevention of negative outcomes would reinforce and perpetuate worry. At a neural level, activation of BNST and dampening of amygdala reactivity through worry corresponds to this mechanism of negative reinforcement. Other examples of the correspondence across levels of analysis include an association between increased amygdala activity and intolerance of uncertainty, a cognitive construct linked to GAD (Schiene, Köchel, Ebner, Reishofer, & Schäfer, 2010).

Cognitive Systems in GAD

Anxiety disorders have long been associated with information-processing biases that orient cognition toward threat (McNally, 1995). Research has elucidated these threat-selective biases for GAD, factoring cognitive vulnerabilities into the etiology and maintenance of the disorder (Mathews & MacLeod, 2005). In fact, worry is itself a cognitive process focusing on threatening future outcomes. Cognitive models of worry explain the nature of GAD by relying on 1) the influence of automatic, selective attention to certain stimuli, 2) negative interpretations of stimuli, (3) a lessened ability to control cognition to detach from worry and threat, (4) worry's interference with cognitive abilities (such as memory), and 5) disorder-maintaining beliefs. For example, a cognitive model by Hirsch and Mathews (2012) frames GAD as an interaction between involuntary processes, such as harm-expectant attention and interpretation, and voluntary processes, such as cognitive control and attempts to resolve danger. Although neuroscience has addressed these factors in GAD less than in other anxiety disorders (Etkin & Wager, 2007), most of these vulnerabilities have rich support in experimental psychology.

First, many studies show that those with GAD devote especially strong attention to signs of threat. Across an informational field there is a great array of stimuli to which one can attend. Yet those with GAD have been found to specifically select out and focus on stimuli that may suggest future harm, such as angry faces over neutral faces (Bradley, Mogg, White, Groom, & de Bono, 1999) or threat words over non-threat words (MacLeod, Mathews, & Tata, 1986). They focus on threat cues more than benign cues and do so to a greater degree than controls. One meta-analysis of 11 studies established a clear attentional bias to threat in GAD with a medium effect size (Bar-Haim, Lamy, Pergamin, Bakermans-Kranenburg, & van IJzendoorn, 2007). Those with GAD also attend more *quickly* to threat cues, as demonstrated by faster eye movements toward threatening faces than controls (Mogg, Millar, & Bradley, 2000). They may show differential focus toward fearful faces as well (Mogg, Garner, & Bradley, 2007), presumably because others' fear may signal danger indirectly. Furthermore, compared to controls, those with GAD are more distracted by threat content when trying to attend to other, non-threatening information (Mathews & MacLeod, 1985), which can be maladaptive when feelings of danger are not warranted. These attentional bias effects often occur outside the person's awareness, as shown by interference effects from subliminal presentations of negative words (Mogg, Bradley, Williams, & Mathews, 1993). Across anxiety disorders, greater attention to threat is associated with higher levels of anxiety, higher severity of threat, and lower attentional control (Mathews & MacLeod, 2005). When those with GAD are constantly attending away from signs of safety and toward information that may suggest possible harm, physiological anxiety can be maintained and worry provoked. The greater anxiety brought on by worry then only increases the tendency to seek out more threatening stimuli, perpetuating the cycle.

Recent studies on error-related negativity have also suggested that those with GAD have a greater neural response to the detection of errors. In neuroscience, error-related negativity is a component of event-related potential generated in the anterior cingulate cortex to monitor for errors in the environment. A meta-analysis of 37 studies found that among dimensions of anxiety, worry was most related with error monitoring (Moser, Moran, Schroder, Donnellan, & Yeung, 2013). More specific to GAD, those with GAD (without depression) have shown a greater error-related negativity response than controls (Weinberg, Kotov, & Proudfit, 2015), though comorbid depression may diminish this relationship. A stronger neural response to errors may facilitate anxiety by highlighting one's own mistakes, those of others working toward common goals, or errors in the environment that could insinuate potential harm.

Once a person attends to an error, threat cue, or worry, he or she may then attempt to control cognition away from the source of anxiety to regulate it. This ability falls under *cognitive control*, a broad construct capturing a variety of processes responsible for directing attention and guiding goal-directed activity. These processes include the ability to shift between task sets (shifting), to override a dominant response for a task-appropriate one (inhibition), and to maintain certain information as predominant in one's mind (working memory) (Miyake et al., 2000). Since emotion regulation requires inhibition of emotion-generating responses and shifting toward other actions and reactions, deficits in regulation likely involve deficits in cognitive control.

Research on cognitive control in GAD has unveiled several differences between its functioning in those with and without the disorder. Worry was experimentally shown to deplete attentional control ability and working memory (e.g., Leigh & Hirsch, 2011). Anxious individuals also performed less well on cognitive control tasks both when threat was present and when it was not (Bishop, 2009; MacLeod & Donnellan, 1993). Neuroscience studies showed greater engagement of brain areas responsible for the downregulation of emotion (a form of control) during worry, but also dampening in the same areas during adaptive emotion regulation as well as over-reactivity in those responsible for fear. Generally, one function of both the PFC and ACC is to inhibit the reactivity of the fear-promoting amygdala via shared circuitry (Delgado, Nearing, Ledoux, & Phelps, 2008). A systematic review of fMRI studies in GAD concluded that those with GAD showed persistent activation in the PFC and ACC during and after worry, but consistently failed to adequately activate these areas during emotion regulation tasks (Mochcovitch, da Rocha Freire, Garcia, & Nardi, 2014). In those with GAD compared to controls, lesser PFC engagement was associated with greater anxiety and functional impairment (Ball et al., 2013), the PFC was activated to a lesser degree during attempts at worry suppression (Andreescu et al., 2011), and the ACC often failed to activate in ways that could reduce amygdalar activity (Etkin, Prater, Hoeft, Menon, & Schatzberg, 2010).

More specific studies on the three functions of cognitive control – shifting, inhibition, and working memory – support these general findings. There is some evidence that those with GAD exhibit difficulties with shifting between sets of information, which may lead to the perseverative quality of worry. Once they start worrying, it is harder to switch to other thoughts. For example, those with GAD made more errors from perseverating on the Wisconsin Card Sorting Task than controls (Tempesta et al., 2013). Greater costs for switching sets in GAD has been found to be a distal risk factor for developing the disorder as well (Zainal & Newman, 2017).

Inhibition ability may also be diminished in GAD. Several researchers have theorized that since uncontrollability of worry defines the disorder and predicts severity (Hallion & Ruscio, 2013), those with GAD may have a lesser ability to inhibit processes like worry when trying to engage in task-appropriate cognition (Hallion, Tolin, Assaf, Goethe, & Diefenbach, 2017). Studies have found just that. Higher worry has been positively associated with longer response times on at least three inhibitory control tasks (e.g., Beaudreau & O'Hara, 2009), and attempts to experimentally control induced worry in GAD led to inhibition accuracy costs (Hallion, Ruscio, & Jha, 2014). GAD status also predicts worse accuracy on a task strongly requiring inhibition, the Stroop (though motor inhibition ability in GAD appears intact; Hallion et al., 2017). Worse inhibitory control has been found to predict GAD 12 years later as well (Zhang et al., 2015).

Last, working memory deficits have also been revealed in GAD, but they may only arise when distracted by anxiety. It is theorized that worry should occupy a portion of available working memory capacity, leaving less capacity for targeted tasks (Eysenck & Calvo, 1992). High worriers show more restricted working memory capacity during worry than when thinking about other topics, whereas low worriers have equal capacity during both forms of thought (Hayes, Hirsch, & Mathews, 2008). Those with GAD perform worse than controls on memory tasks when both have an anxiety-inducing distractor, but equally well with a neutral distractor (Moon & Jeong, 2015; Moon, Sundaram, Choi, & Jeong, 2016). These results suggest intrusive, worrisome thinking interferes with working memory. One study found no differences between clinical and healthy elderly samples in remembering strings of digits, questioning working memory deficits in GAD (Price & Mohlman, 2007). Even so, several studies have shown reduced ability to use working memory to incorporate new task-appropriate data into information processing ("updating") in GAD (e.g., Yang et al., 2015).

The literature regarding the effect of GAD processes on other forms of memory is more uncertain. In general, it was long thought that no clear declarative memory biases were associated with anxiety (Mathews & MacLeod, 2005). For example, studies regarding implicit memory – the effect of prior experience on later behavior without conscious attempts to remember – are mixed. Some studies on GAD find better implicit memory for threatening materials relative to controls (Mathews, Mogg, May, & Eysenck, 1989) whereas others do not (Mathews, Mogg, Kentish, & Eysenck, 1995). One more recent study sought to resolve this conflict with the use of personally relevant threat stimuli (Coles, Turk, & Heimberg, 2007). This study did find an implicit memory bias for threat words, as well as a marginally significant explicit memory bias. Explicit memory bias findings for both immediate and delayed recall are also inconsistent, though this bias has more evidence than an implicit bias. Several studies also find deficits in immediate and delayed memory in young adults with GAD (Moon, Yang, & Jeong, 2015; Tempesta et al., 2013), though some studies do not, potentially due to underpowered samples (Castaneda et al., 2011). Despite this conflict in young adult samples, studies of elderly individuals with GAD have consistently shown impaired explicit memory relative to same-age controls (e.g., Butters et al., 2011; Mantella et al., 2007), suggesting GAD may compromise memory during late-life development.

Despite a portion of studies lacking memory differences, a growing body of research is highlighting morphological and functional abnormalities in the hippocampi of those with GAD, the region largely responsible for memory. In a study by Moon et al. (2015), deficits in memory for threat words in those with GAD were associated with an overactive PFC (potentially due to anxiety-control attempts) and an underactive hippocampus relative to controls. In a fine-grained study of the hippocampus in GAD, Cha et al. (2016) found physical abnormalities in the microstructure of the hippocampus in those with the disorder. These abnormalities mediated threat-processing effects and decreased anterior hippocampal reactivity relative to controls. In summary, the most consistent findings suggest that online anxiety and worry interfere with the ability to remember in GAD, those with GAD are more at risk for worse memory performance later in life, and the form and function of the memory-related hippocampal region appears to differ between those with and without GAD.

Learning – how memories and behavioral patterns come to be formed – is a yet-nascent domain of GAD research. Thus far, this emerging body of literature seems to suggest those with GAD have difficulty learning probabilities of events, such as the likelihood of future outcomes over time. Those with GAD have highly inaccurate estimated likelihoods of event occurrence: between 85% and 91% of GAD worries do not come true (Borkovec, Hazlett-Stevens, & Diaz, 1999; LaFreniere & Newman, 2018b). Moreover, at least two computerized cognitive experiments have found that those with GAD learned the reinforcement probabilities of stimuli at a slower rate over time and with less accuracy than controls (LaFreniere & Newman, 2018a).

Those with GAD not only seem to have difficulty with probability, but also are more likely to interpret emotionally ambiguous events as threatening – an interpretation bias (Eysenck, Mogg, May, Richards, & Mathews, 1991; Hazlett-Stevens & Borkovec, 2004). For those with GAD, uncertain future events are often interpreted as threatening, adverse potential outcomes receive more attention than benign ones, and situations that are actually experienced often receive negative interpretations. A negative interpretive tendency may serve a protective function against possible harm, but it may also lead to incorrect judgments that promote anxiety. Fortunately, studies find that worriers can be taught to form benign meanings of ambiguous information, which leads to fewer negative thought intrusions and lower anxiety than for those who do not receive such training (Hayes, Hirsch, & Mathews, 2010).

The in-the-moment processes of cognition described earlier can eventually lead to enduring beliefs. Research has shown that those with GAD often form positive and negative beliefs about their worry. Those with GAD tend to believe their worry is useful; they perceive it to facilitate problem-solving, buffer shifts in negative emotion, increase a sense of control, increase motivation, prepare for challenges, make one caring or conscientious, and even ward off future catastrophes as if by magic (Hebert, Dugas, Tulloch, & Holowka, 2014; Newman & Llera, 2011). These positive worry beliefs may contribute to disorder maintenance, as those with GAD depend on worry for these functions. Yet negative beliefs about worry are also associated with GAD. Often high worriers hold beliefs that worry is uncontrollable and dangerous, which may lead them to worry about their worrying (Cartwright-Hatton & Wells, 1997). With high attention to threat, difficulty detaching from it, catastrophic predictions, and worry's cognitive interference, over time those with GAD come to believe they cannot control their minds or lives, as shown by a tendency toward bearing an external locus of control (Beekman et al., 2000).

Positive Valence Systems

The most understudied domain of GAD is its positive valence systems (Morris & Rottenberg, 2015). These functions are responsible for reactions to positive motivational stimuli, situations, and contexts, such as seeking, attaining, and savoring rewards and their promotional value for future behavior. Since GAD has been primarily conceptualized as a disorder of over-responsive negative thought and affect, the possibility that those with GAD are *under*-responsive to positive-factors has been somewhat neglected. Regarding theory, the contrast avoidance model does theorize that worry is in part propagated through positive affective contrasts. When those with GAD raise their distress level through worry and then experience a positive outcome, there is a greater spike in positive emotion than for those who do not worry, reinforcing worry itself (e.g., Kim & Newman, 2016; Newman, Jacobson et al., 2016). Furthermore, those with GAD are less likely to allow themselves to dwell on positive feelings for long, because this increases the probability that if something negative occurs, they will experience an undesirable negative emotional contrast. Basic research findings on positivity have begun to accompany this theoretical framework with studies on general positive emotion, responsiveness to reward, and reward learning (Newman, Jacobson, et al., 2016).

Naturally, people vary in how strongly they experience positive emotion from the same stimulus or event. In general, those with GAD may experience less contingent positive emotional response than healthy controls, especially during worry. When reporting about general emotional state by rating scale, there is some evidence that those with GAD experience low positive emotion, even independently of co-occurring depressive symptoms (e.g., Morris & Rottenberg, 2015; Power & Tarsia, 2007), though some studies have not revealed this result (e.g., Decker, Turk, Hess, & Murray, 2008). Controlled laboratory studies are also mixed, with some showing that compared to non-GAD persons, those with GAD report less positive emotion in response to positive stimuli (Srivastava, Sharma, & Mandal, 2003), whereas others found equal positive response to happy films between control and GAD groups (Llera & Newman, 2014). Reward response does seem to diminish during worry, though: when worry is induced, self-reported positive emotion decreases (Llera & Newman, 2010; McLaughlin et al., 2007). Studies finding low positive emotion in GAD may simply be capturing emotion during active worry processes. Bridging these two topics, Ruscio, Seitchik, Gentes, Jones, and Hallion (2011) discovered that perseverative thought (worry and rumination) predicted an attenuated positive affective response to personal success for those with GAD. Those with GAD may have less of a positive response when reward is contingent on their behavior, though it is unclear whether their generalized positivity states differ from controls overall. It appears that those with GAD do have trouble imagining positive events happening to them. Wu, Szpunar, Godovich, Schacter, and Hofmann (2015) found that those with GAD had difficulty generating and repeatedly imagining plausible, self-referential positive events – a difficulty that did not dissipate across attempts – whereas controls' difficulty did decrease after repetition.

The neuroscience literature on GAD positive response is also lacking, though some research exists. Using fMRI, one study found an attenuated response to happy and fearful facial expressions in the PFC and ACC in GAD relative to controls (Palm, Elliott, McKie, Deakin, & Anderson, 2011). This blunted reaction was especially true in response to happy faces. Also, an event-related potential study found that higher GAD symptoms predicted a lower ability to differentiate gains from losses as measured by feedback-related negativity potential (Kessel, Kujawa, Hajcak Proudfit, & Klein, 2015). Thus, gains and losses may be experienced more similarly in GAD compared to those of minimal symptoms, a phenomenon known as reduced *reward sensitivity* in the ERP literature.

Emerging research suggests those with GAD may have deficits in learning by reward, or positive reinforcement learning. DeVido et al. (2009) found that those with GAD committed a significantly greater number of errors on a reward/punishment decision-making task compared to both healthy controls and those with social phobia. Yet they did not find an interaction between operant conditioning type (reward or punishment) accuracy and group, likely because of small sample size (only 16 participants had GAD). One other yet-unpublished study on reward learning did find those with GAD to learn worse by positive reinforcement than healthy controls on a probabilistic task, especially when there was a high likelihood of reward (LaFreniere & Newman, 2018a). Due to attempts to avoid a negative contrast event, those with GAD may not attend to or extend positive experience as much as controls. By dismissing positive experience in order to keep from being vulnerable to negative shifts, those with GAD may experience a reduced reward-learning response. Note that one study found that those with GAD did *not* show differences from controls in a response bias toward a more-often rewarded stimulus when rewards were not contingent on behavior (Morris & Rottenberg, 2015), though it is difficult to interpret how this applies to behavior-contingent learning. Regardless, persons with GAD do seem to be more wary of pursuing highly rewarding experiences in the near future despite a risk in the distant future. Those with GAD learn to avoid making choices that have a high immediate gain but high long-term loss significantly faster than controls (Mueller, Nguyen, Ray, & Borkovec, 2010). Last, based on self-report, GAD has been linked to low reward dependence, or the maintenance of rewarding behavior and reduction of punishment-eliciting behavior (Beesdo, Pine, Lieb, & Wittchen, 2010). Though the aforementioned studies are a promising start, positive valence in GAD deserves much more research attention.

Arousal/Regulatory Systems in GAD

One of the most widely studied dimensions of arousal in GAD is physiological arousal regulated by the autonomic nervous system (ANS). Previous studies examined physiological indices including heart rate, respiratory sinus arrhythmia, heart rate variability, and skin conductance response. Certain indices (e.g., skin conductance response) are considered more reflective of activity in the sympathetic nervous system whereas others (e.g., high frequency-heart rate variability) are predominantly mediated by the parasympathetic nervous system (Thayer, Åhs, Fredrikson, Sollers, & Wager, 2012).

A consistent pattern emerging from the studies is physiological rigidity or reduced responding to stressors in GAD (e.g., Llera & Newman, 2010; Thayer, Friedman, & Borkovec, 1996). For instance, GAD participants exhibited higher sympathetic arousal at baseline, as shown by increased heart rate and higher skin conductance levels (e.g., Fisher, Granger, & Newman, 2010). Meta-analyses also indicated reduced heart rate variability (HRV) (indicating high stable heart rate), a physiological index of flexible emotional responding, at baseline for GAD (Chalmers, Quintana, Maree, Abbott, & Kemp, 2014) as well as for worry (Ottaviani et al., 2016). A four-day ambulatory study also found lower respiratory sinus arrhythmia in GAD patients compared to controls (Hoehn-Saric, McLeod, Funderburk, & Kowalski, 2004). This lower basal HRV is important because it has been shown to suppress phasic or state-level HRV, interfering with flexible responding to emotional stimuli (Park, Vasey, van Bavel, & Thayer, 2014). In fact, GAD has been associated with reduced physiological reactivity to stressors, demonstrated by restricted ranges of HR (Hoehn-Saric, McLeod, & Zimmerli, 1989) and lower HRV (e.g., Fisher et al., 2010). In experimental studies, induced state worry also reduced physiological responses to stressors such as fear-eliciting film clips (e.g., Llera & Newman, 2010, 2014). These findings are consistent with the view that individuals with GAD use worry to sustain a negative emotional state and arousal to dampen further reactivity to negative emotional stimuli (Newman & Llera, 2011).

Although autonomic arousal or dysregulation cuts across a range of disorders, there is some evidence for specificity in response to a physiological stressor. Only GAD and panic disorder (PD), but not social anxiety disorder or obsessive-compulsive disorder, showed steeper HR increase than controls during a hyperventilation task (Pittig, Arch, Lam, & Craske, 2013). It is of note that among anxiety disorders, both GAD and PD have been most closely linked to autonomic arousal symptoms based on diagnostic criteria. Within GAD patients, those with comorbid depression fared worse, with lower HRV at baseline as well as during relaxation and worry tasks (e.g., Hofmann, Schulz, Heering, Muench, & Bufka, 2010). In addition, a recent study (Aldao, Mennin, Linardatos, & Fresco, 2010) revealed an interesting pattern where GAD participants demonstrated lower cardiac flexibility (HRV) when employing adaptive emotion regulation strategies in response to negative-emotion film clips whereas controls showed an opposite pattern. This finding is in line with relaxation-induced anxiety (RIA), a paradoxical increase in anxiety when trying to relax, in GAD (Heide & Borkovec, 1983). Heightened arousal and reduced autonomic flexibility may underlie emotion regulation deficits in GAD and the maintenance of GAD symptoms. For instance, higher peak RIA during relaxation-focused treatment, especially in the later phase, predicted worse outcomes in GAD at post-treatment and follow-up (Newman, LaFreniere, & Jacobson, 2018).

Another important construct in the arousal/regulatory systems is sleep and wakefulness. Sleep disturbance is one of the diagnostic criteria for GAD. Not surprisingly, both epidemiological and sleep laboratory studies found a high co-occurrence of GAD and sleep difficulties (e.g., Brenes et al., 2009; Monti & Monti, 2000). A majority of GAD patients endorse sleep problems, and the GAD diagnosis increases likelihood of experiencing sleep problems by more than twice (Marcks, Weisberg, Edelen, & Keller, 2010). A review of the literature suggests that GAD is more strongly associated with difficulties with sleep maintenance than sleep initiation (Monti & Monti, 2000). Polysomnographic findings showed that GAD and high-worry groups exhibited reduced total sleep time, longer sleep onset latency, greater time spent awake, and a smaller percentage of deep (slow-wave) sleep compared to controls (e.g., Papadimitriou & Linkowski, 2005; Saletu-Zyhlarz et al., 1997). This pattern also held in children with GAD (Alfano, Reynolds, Scott, Dahl, & Mellman, 2013).

There is some preliminary evidence for bidirectional causal relationships between GAD and sleep disturbance. A prospective study in children and adolescents found that GAD and sleep problems predicted each other over the course of eight years (Shanahan, Copeland, Angold, Bondy, & Costello, 2014). Sleep disturbance in adults also predicted a greater risk for developing GAD four years later, even after controlling for neuroticism and ruminative style (Batterham, Glozier, & Christensen, 2012). Although these studies have the limitation of relying on self-report in assessing sleep, they suggest that sleep problems contribute to the occurrence of GAD. A cognitive model of insomnia (Harvey, 2002) describes a vicious cycle in which sleep difficulties and worry reinforce each other. Individuals with insomnia worry excessively about their sleep (Harvey & Greenall, 2003), which then would lead to elevated anxiety (distress, arousal) and selective attention to sleep-related threat cues. Increased anxiety and attentional bias in turn, would exacerbate worry and sleep difficulties.

Based on evidence for sleep disturbance in GAD, mutations of circadian clock genes were also proposed as a potential etiological factor. Circadian clock genes are involved in regulation of circadian rhythms and found in the suprachiasmatic nucleus of the hypothalamus. Circadian rhythms refer to endogenous oscillations in physiological and metabolic processes (e.g., hormonal secretion) and govern the sleep-wake cycle. In rats, a mutation of the clock gene led to behavioral changes indicating less fear and avoidance (Roybal et al., 2007). Antianxiety medications also altered clock gene levels in the mouse cerebellum, suggesting that the change in the clock genes may mediate medication's effect on anxiety (Akiyama et al., 1999). In humans, genetic association analysis identified specific circadian-clock-related genes associated with a predisposition to develop GAD (Sipila et al., 2010). These findings provide evidence for the role of circadian clock gene mutations in the etiology of GAD.

Systems for Social Processes in GAD

GAD has been associated with interpersonal dysfunction at multiple levels. Interpersonal concerns are one of the most common worry themes in GAD (Borkovec, 1994; Dugas et al., 1998; Roemer et al., 1997). Individuals with GAD also report greater interpersonal problems and distress than controls (e.g., Przeworski et al., 2011). Moreover, GAD is linked to lack of friends (Whisman, Sheldon, & Goering, 2000), marital conflicts and dissatisfaction (McLeod, 1994; Whisman et al., 2000), greater likelihood of separation or divorce (Hunt et al., 2002), and dysfunctional family dynamics (Ben-Noun, 1998). GAD also commonly co-occurs with social anxiety (Brown, Campbell, Lehman, Grisham, & Mancill, 2001) and personality disorders (Wittchen et al., 1994), whose core symptoms are interpersonal difficulties.

Previous studies found that interpersonal problems in GAD not only caused distress to the clients, but also affected treatment outcomes and maintenance of symptoms. Change in interpersonal distress was correlated with change in GAD symptoms over the course of treatment (e.g., Salzer, Pincus, Winkelbach, Leichsenring, & Leibing, 2011). Residual interpersonal problems at post-treatment also predicted a greater return of GAD symptoms at follow-up (Borkovec, Newman, Pincus, & Lytle, 2002). Marital tension and partner hostility (e.g., Yonkers, Dyck, Warshaw, & Keller, 2000) predicted a worse treatment outcome as well. In addition, interpersonal variables moderated treatment outcomes in GAD. Higher levels of dismissing/avoidant attachment styles predicted better outcomes in cognitive behavioral therapy (CBT) augmented with interpersonal and emotional processing therapies than CBT plus supportive listening (Newman, Castonguay, Jacobson, & Moore, 2015). In another study, patients with higher intrusiveness or dominance responded better to behavioral therapy than cognitive therapy or CBT (Newman, Jacobson, Erickson, & Fisher, 2017).

Given the prevalence and importance of interpersonal dysfunction in GAD, there have been efforts to articulate theoretical mechanisms for an etiological and maintenance role of interpersonal difficulties in GAD. For instance, the interpersonal model of GAD (Newman & Erickson, 2010) proposed insecure attachment as a developmental risk factor for GAD. Drawing on Bowlby's attachment theory (e.g., Bowlby, 1980), the model posits that individuals with GAD developed maladaptive attachment with primary caretaker figures in childhood. Insecure attachment involves a negative working model, representations of the world as a threatening place and the self as inept at eliciting help/love. These representations are predicted to elicit anxiety and maladaptive strategies such as worry and certain interpersonal behaviors (e.g., role reversal/caretaking of parents) to cope with anxiety. This pattern of anxious cognitions and behaviors may then persist into adulthood.

The research literature supports a theorized link between insecure attachment and GAD. In children and adolescents, higher GAD symptoms (Muris, Mayer, & Meesters, 2000) and worry severity (Brown & Whiteside, 2008) were associated with ambivalent and avoidant attachment. Adults with GAD also reported less maternal love, more rejection and enmeshment in childhood, and greater current anger and vulnerability toward parents than controls (Cassidy, Lichtenstein-Phelps, Sibrava, Thomas, & Borkovec, 2009; Newman, Shin, & Zuellig, 2016). Currently, there is yet no strong evidence for specificity in GAD's association with distinct types of insecure attachment. Whereas some studies found a greater association with ambivalent attachment (Muris, Meesters, van Melick, & Zwambag, 2001), others showed stronger association with avoidant attachment, especially compared to other disorders (e.g., panic disorder; Bifulco et al., 2006; Newman, Shin et al., 2016), and association with both (Brown & Whiteside, 2008). There has been limited prospective data, but in adolescents, attachment relationship quality with fathers and GAD symptoms negatively predicted each other over time (van Eijck, Branje, Hale, & Meeus, 2012). Angry-dismissive attachment in adults also predicted a greater likelihood of GAD diagnosis five years later (Bifulco et al., 2006).

Evidence is also emerging for an imbalance in the neural oxytocin system in GAD. Oxytocin is a hypothalamic neuropeptide and hormone linked to a range of social functions including the formation of attachment. In both children and adults, cerebrospinal fluid and plasma oxytocin concentration levels negatively predicted trait anxiety (Carson et al., 2015). Genetic variations in the oxytocin receptor gene also predicted increased self-reported anxiety symptoms in adults (Myers et al., 2014). In addition, oxytocin has anxiolytic effects. For instance, three weeks of daily oxytocin administration reduced anxiety in GAD patients (Feifel, MacDonald, McKinney, Heisserer, & Serrano, 2011), and the use of nasal oxytocin spray prevented negative appraisals of a social situation in high trait-anxious males (Alvares, Chen, Balleine, Hickie, & Guastella, 2012). Although preliminary, evidence suggests that the oxytocin system might be involved in the etiology and pathophysiology of GAD.

Affiliation-related dysfunction in GAD has been also observed in the form of interpersonal problems. Although GAD has been associated with various types of interpersonal problems, difficulties in the affiliative domain (e.g., being overly nurturant) appear most salient. In both US (Przeworski et al., 2011) and German samples (Salzer et al., 2008), four interpersonal subtypes of GAD were identified based on participants' self-report: intrusive, exploitable, nonassertive, and cold. A subset of participants reported problems with being cold or vindictive, but the majority of GAD samples reported problems with being overly warm or submissive (Przeworski et al., 2011; Salzer et al., 2008). Similarly, GAD analogues endorsed greater empathy (Peasley, Molina, & Borkovec, 1994) and problems with being overly accommodating, self-sacrificing, nonassertive, and intrusive compared to controls (Eng & Heimberg, 2006). A recent study also showed that when controlling for depression and social anxiety, high trait worry was associated with a prototypically affiliative interpersonal style (Erickson et al., 2016). Further supporting this specificity, only pure, but not comorbid GAD predicted higher self-reported affiliative interpersonal problems than PTSD (Uhmann, Beesdo-Baum, Becker, & Hoyer, 2010). Most importantly, increasing evidence points to the role of self-reported affiliative interpersonal problems in the maintenance of GAD symptoms. GAD clients who endorsed affiliative interpersonal problems at baseline had elevated anxiety both before and after CBT (Newman et al., 2017). Affiliative interpersonal problems also predicted worse treatment outcome in psychodynamic treatment for GAD (Crits-Christoph et al., 2004).

Affiliative problem tendencies in GAD are consistent with greater role reversal, premature caretaking of one's parents in childhood (e.g., Cassidy et al., 2009), and the belief that worry means caring in GAD (Hebert et al., 2014). However, it is crucial to note that findings on affiliative interpersonal problems are based on self-report. When the informant report was examined, discrepant findings emerged. For instance, in a daily diary study, trait worry predicted higher affiliative tendencies in self-report across clinical and undergraduate samples, but greater hostile impact on others in reports by significant others (Erickson et al., 2016). Similarly, whereas GAD participants endorsed greater affiliative interpersonal problems than controls, when participants' friends reported on participants' interpersonal problems, no such group difference appeared (Eng & Heimberg, 2006). In a first-encounter situation, trait worry also predicted a tendency toward over- or underestimating one's negative interpersonal impact on others, and within GAD participants, under-estimation predicted less self-disclosure and lower liking from confederates (Erickson & Newman, 2007b). Trait worry also predicted perceiving one's own behaviors as more friendly than as perceived by an interactant whereas state worry predicted perceiving one's behaviors as more hostile than others' perception (Shin et al., 2016). These findings indicate poor awareness of one's interpersonal impact in GAD, especially in the direction of overestimating one's affiliative impact on others.

The self-claimed affiliative tendencies might be linked to GAD patients' biased other-perception in interpersonal contexts. GAD participants showed attentional bias to social threat words (e.g., Mathews & MacLeod, 1985) and hypervigilance to threatening faces relative to neutral faces (Bradley et al., 1999). Dysfunctional social cognitions in GAD also manifest as sensitivity, mistrust, suspiciousness, and hostility toward others (Mavissakalian, Hamann, Haidar, & de Groot, 1995), and these symptoms were unique to GAD when compared with depression and panic disorder (Blashfield et al., 1994). Similarly, trait worry predicted perceiving others' behaviors as cold even when controlling for social anxiety and depression (Erickson & Newman, 2007a). In a first-encounter interaction, both trait and state worry also predicted a bias toward perceiving confederates as more hostile (Shin et al., 2016). The direction of this bias in other-perception is consistent with worry's definition (anticipating future threats). It has been suggested that in GAD, sensitivity to and perceptual bias toward interpersonal threats motivate strategic behaviors to preempt or mitigate the threats (Newman et al., 2013). For instance, individuals with GAD may engage in affiliative behaviors to appease others and elicit reciprocal affiliation. However, their behaviors may not have the intended affiliative impact on others, resulting in failure to evoke favorable reactions. This may in turn reinforce the bias toward perceiving others as hostile and increase worries about interpersonal situations.

Deficits in social cognition may underlie the bias in self- and other-perception observed in GAD, but it appears that deficits are specific to certain domains of social cognition. For instance, a recent meta-analysis (Plana, Lavoie, Battaglia, & Achim, 2014) found evidence for negative attributional style in GAD, but not emotion recognition difficulties. A mixed anxiety sample including GAD also showed intact recognition of both simple (e.g., happy) and complex (e.g., desire) facial expressions relative to healthy controls (Yoon, Kim, Kim, Lee, & Lee, 2016). GAD participants also did not demonstrate problems with producing facial emotions, with comparable facial expressivity in response to emotional film clips relative to controls (Noble, 2016). They also presented greater sad facial affect during emotional disclosure to a confederate than controls (Erickson & Newman, 2007b). There is also no evidence for impairment in Theory of Mind abilities in GAD. In fact, GAD analogues demonstrated more accurate Theory of Mind reasoning for negative signals than the norm at higher levels of state worry (Zainal & Newman, 2018). Despite the limited number of studies, the findings suggest that the bias in interpersonal perceptions in GAD might not be due to deficits in ability to perceive others' emotions or infer their internal states (e.g., intentions), but due to negative attributions of interpersonal stimuli (e.g., interpreting others' angry facial emotions as directed toward self).

In addition, although cognitive processing of facial emotions appears intact, individuals with GAD exhibit heightened emotional reaction to negative facial emotions, which may contribute to their interpersonal difficulties. When instructed to identify and elicit emotions depicted in pictures of facial expressions, GAD participants did not differ from controls in recognition of facial emotions, but reported greater sadness in response to sad facial emotions and lower happiness in response to happy facial emotions (Srivastava et al., 2003). Reactivity to negative facial emotions was also observed at a neural level. Both adolescents (McClure et al., 2007; Monk et al., 2006) and adults with GAD (Blair et al., 2008) showed increased activation in ventrolateral PFC and/or ACC in response to negative facial emotions (e.g., fearful, angry). These brain areas are involved in emotion regulation, and greater activation is considered to represent a compensatory modulation upon changes in other areas (e.g., hyper-reactivity in the amygdala) (McClure et al., 2007).

Overall, the reviewed studies provide strong support for biased social perceptions of self and other and maladaptive interpersonal behaviors in GAD. In particular, affiliation-related dysfunction has been observed at multiple levels including neurobiological processes (e.g., oxytocin), subjective perceptions, and behaviors (e.g., attachment, interpersonal problems), and has been linked to the etiology and maintenance of GAD symptoms. Negative attributional style and greater emotional reactivity to negative facial emotions may underlie maladaptive interpersonal perceptions and behaviors in GAD. One limitation of the current literature is that most previous studies used a cross-sectional correlational design. As a result, there is only preliminary evidence for the causal role of interpersonal dysfunction in GAD symptoms, and vice versa. The literature awaits replication and extension using experimental and prospective designs.

Conclusion

GAD clearly has a rich and extensive history of study. Yet the disorder and its treatment still stand to benefit from further study. We conclude with suggested avenues for future research. The most uncharted domains are that of neurobiological substrates and physiology of GAD generally, as well as positive valence systems specifically. There have been fewer neuroscientific studies on GAD than other anxiety disorders (Etkin & Wager, 2007). Given that most of the studies that do exist have focused on examining neural correlates of worry or GAD, future studies should employ appropriate research methods to test an etiological role of neural factors in GAD (e.g., Granger causality analysis) (Seth, Barrett, & Barnett, 2015). In addition, one area that needs further work is the role of worry in fear generalization. Past studies have yielded discrepant findings, with high trait worry predicting both enhanced (Dunning & Hajcak, 2015) and impaired (Grant, Judah, White, & Mills, 2015) discrimination between a conditioned stimulus and a safety stimulus after fear conditioning. Elucidating whether and when worry leads to fear generalization will help researchers to understand how GAD patients acquire pervasive worries over multiple life domains. As for positive valence systems in GAD, it is yet unclear the extent to which those with GAD show deficits in reward learning, the degree of their effort valuation (or "willingness to work") for rewards, whether studies finding low positive emotion are attributable most to active worry, and whether episodic memory underrepresents positive experience in GAD. Other domains could profit from more studies as well, such as the interpersonal realm. Future studies in this area should test causal relationships over correlational ones, enhancing our understanding of a potential bidirectional relationship between worry and interpersonal dysfunction in GAD. For instance, biased social perceptions and maladaptive interpersonal strategies may maintain worry symptoms. It has been also recently proposed that worry may contribute to affiliative interpersonal problems in GAD by eliciting strategic affiliative behaviors as a means to avoid anticipated hostile responses (Newman et al., 2013). These and many other hypotheses need further exploration in future research. GAD is a prevalent and interfering disorder with a solid foundation of research on which to expand. Such a state of affairs is ripe for both science and the improvement of the valuable treatments it supports.

References

Akiyama, M., Kirihara, T., Takahashi, S., Minami, Y., Yoshinobu, Y., Moriya, T., & Shibata, S. (1999). Modulation of *mPer1* gene expression by anxiolytic drugs in mouse cerebellum. *British Journal of Pharmacology, 128*, 1616–1622. doi: 10.1038/sj.bjp.0702957

Aldao, A., Mennin, D. S., Linardatos, E., & Fresco, D. M. (2010). Differential patterns of physical symptoms and subjective processes in generalized anxiety disorder and unipolar depression. *Journal of Anxiety Disorders, 24*, 250–259. doi: 10.1016/j.janxdis.2009.12.001

Alfano, C. A., Reynolds, K., Scott, N., Dahl, R. E., & Mellman, T. A. (2013). Polysomnographic sleep patterns of non-depressed, non-medicated children with generalized anxiety disorder. *Journal of Affective Disorders, 147*, 379–384. doi: 10.1016/j.jad.2012.08.015

Alvares, G. A., Chen, N. T., Balleine, B. W., Hickie, I. B., & Guastella, A. J. (2012). Oxytocin selectively moderates negative cognitive appraisals in high trait anxious males. *Psychoneuroendocrinology, 37*, 2022–2031. doi: 10.1016/j.psyneuen.2012.04.018

American Psychiatric Association. (1980). *Diagnostic and Statistical Manual of Mental Disorders* (3rd edn). Washington, DC: American Psychiatric Association.

American Psychiatric Association. (1987). *Diagnostic and Statistical Manual of Mental Disorders* (3rd, rev. edn). Washington, DC: American Psychiatric Association.

American Psychiatric Association. (1994). *Diagnostic and Statistical Manual of Mental Disorders* (4th edn). Washington, DC: American Psychiatric Association.

American Psychiatric Association. (2013). *Diagnostic and Statistical Manual of Mental Disorders* (5th edn). Washington, DC: American Psychiatric Association. doi: 10.1176/appi.books.9780890425596

Andreescu, C., Gross, J. J., Lenze, E., Edelman, K. D., Snyder, S., Tanase, C., & Aizenstein, H. (2011). Altered cerebral blood flow patterns associated with pathologic worry in the elderly. *Depression and Anxiety*, *28*, 202–209. doi: 10.1002/da.20799

Ball, T. M., Ramsawh, H. J., Campbell-Sills, L., Paulus, M. P., & Stein, M. B. (2013). Prefrontal dysfunction during emotion regulation in generalized anxiety and panic disorders. *Psychological Medicine*, *43*, 1475–1486. doi: 10.1017/S0033291712002383

Bar-Haim, Y., Lamy, D., Pergamin, L., Bakermans-Kranenburg, M. J., & van IJzendoorn, M. H. (2007). Threat-related attentional bias in anxious and nonanxious individuals: A meta-analytic study. *Psychological Bulletin*, 133, 1–24. doi: 10.1037/0033–2909.133.1.1

Batterham, P. J., Glozier, N., & Christensen, H. (2012). Sleep disturbance, personality and the onset of depression and anxiety: Prospective cohort study. *Australian and New Zealand Journal of Psychiatry*, *46*, 1089–1098. doi: 10.1177/0004867412457997

Beaudreau, S. A. & O'Hara, R. (2009). The association of anxiety and depressive symptoms with cognitive performance in community-dwelling older adults. *Psychology and Aging*, *24*, 507–512. doi: 10.1037/a0016035

Beekman, A. T., de Beurs, E., van Balkom, A. J., Deeg, D. J., van Dyck, R., & van Tilburg, W. (2000). Anxiety and depression in later life: Co-occurrence and communality of risk factors. *American Journal of Psychiatry*, *157*, 89–95.

Beesdo, K., Pine, D. S., Lieb, R., & Wittchen, H. U. (2010). Incidence and risk patterns of anxiety and depressive disorders and categorization of generalized anxiety disorder. *Archives of General Psychiatry*, *67*, 47–57. doi: 10.1001/archgenpsychiatry.2009.177

Ben-Noun, L. (1998). Generalized anxiety disorder in dysfunctional families. *Journal of Behavior Therapy and Experimental Psychiatry*, *29*, 115–122. doi: 10.1016/S0005-7916(98)00003–2

Bifulco, A., Kwon, J., Jacobs, C., Moran, P., Bunn, A., & Beer, N. (2006). Adult attachment style as mediator between childhood neglect/abuse and adult depression and anxiety. *Social Psychiatry and Psychiatric Epidemiology*, *41*, 796–805. doi: 10.1007/s00127-006–0101-z

Bishop, S. J. (2009). Trait anxiety and impoverished prefrontal control of attention. *Nature Neuroscience*, *12*, 92–98. doi: 10.1038/nn.2242

Blair, K., Shaywitz, J., Smith, B. W., Rhodes, R., Geraci, M., Jones, M., McCaffrey, D., Vythilingam, M., Finger, E., Mondillo, K., Jacobs, M., Charney, D. S., Blair, R. J. R., Drevets, W. C., & Pine, D. S. (2008). Response to emotional expressions in generalized social phobia and generalized anxiety disorder: Evidence for separate disorders. *American Journal of Psychiatry*, *165*, 1193–1202. doi: 10.1176/appi.ajp.2008.07071060

Blashfield, R., Noyes, R., Reich, J., Woodman, C., Cook, B. L., & Garvey, M. J. (1994). Personality disorder traits in generalized anxiety and panic disorder patients. *Comprehensive Psychiatry, 35*, 329–334. doi: 10.1016/0010-440X(94)90271-2

Borkovec, T. D. (1994). The nature, functions, and origins of worry. In G. C. L. Davey & F. Tallis (eds.), *Worrying: Perspectives on Theory, Assessment and Treatment* (pp. 5–33). Oxford: Wiley.

Borkovec, T. D., Hazlett-Stevens, H., & Diaz, M. L. (1999). The role of positive beliefs about worry in generalized anxiety disorder and its treatment. *Clinical Psychology and Psychotherapy, 6*, 126–138.

Borkovec, T. D. & Inz, J. (1990). The nature of worry in generalized anxiety disorder: A predominance of thought activity. *Behaviour Research and Therapy, 28*, 153–158. doi: 10.1016/0005–7967(90)90027-G

Borkovec, T. D., Newman, M. G., Pincus, A. L., & Lytle, R. (2002). A component analysis of cognitive-behavioral therapy for generalized anxiety disorder and the role of interpersonal problems. *Journal of Consulting and Clinical Psychology, 70*, 288–298. doi: 10.1037/0022-006X .70.2.288

Bowlby, J. (1980). *Attachment and Loss: Vol. 3. Loss*. New York, NY: Basic Books.

Bradley, B. P., Mogg, K., White, J., Groom, C., & de Bono, J. (1999). Attentional bias for emotional faces in generalized anxiety disorder. *British Journal of Clinical Psychology, 38* (Pt. 3), 267–278. doi: 10.1348/014466599162845

Brenes, G. A., Miller, M. E., Stanley, M. A., Williamson, J. D., Knudson, M., & McCall, W. V. (2009). Insomnia in older adults with generalized anxiety disorder. *American Journal of Geriatric Psychiatry, 17*, 465–472. doi: 10.1097/JGP.0b013e3181987747

Brosschot, J. F., Gerin, W., & Thayer, J. F. (2006). The perseverative cognition hypothesis: A review of worry, prolonged stress-related physiological activation, and health. *Journal of Psychosomatic Research, 60*, 113–124. doi: 10.1016/j.jpsychores.2005.06.074

Brown, A. M. & Whiteside, S. P. (2008). Relations among perceived parental rearing behaviors, attachment style, and worry in anxious children. *Journal of Anxiety Disorders, 22*, 263–272. doi: 10.1016/j.janxdis.2007.02.002

Brown, T. A., Campbell, L. A., Lehman, C. L., Grisham, J. R., & Mancill, R. B. (2001). Current and lifetime comorbidity of the *DSM-IV* anxiety and mood disorders in a large clinical sample. *Journal of Abnormal Psychology, 110*, 585–599. doi: 10.1037//0021-843X.110.4.585

Bruce, S. E., Yonkers, K. A., Otto, M. W., Eisen, J. L., Weisberg, R. B., Pagano, M., Shea, M. T., & Keller, M. B. (2005). Influence of psychiatric comorbidity on recovery and recurrence in generalized anxiety disorder, social phobia, and panic disorder: A 12-year prospective study. *American Journal of Psychiatry, 162*, 1179–1187. doi: 10.1176/appi.ajp.162.6.1179

Butters, M. A., Bhalla, R. K., Andreescu, C., Wetherell, J. L., Mantella, R., Begley, A. E., & Lenze, E. J. (2011). Changes in neuropsychological functioning following treatment for late-life generalised anxiety disorder. *British Journal of Psychiatry, 199*, 211–218. doi: 10.1192/bjp.bp.110.090217

Carson, D., Berquist, S., Trujillo, T., Garner, J., Hannah, S., Hyde, S., Sumiyoshi, R., Jackson, L., Moss, J., & Strehlow, M. (2015). Cerebrospinal fluid and plasma oxytocin concentrations are positively correlated and negatively predict anxiety in children. *Molecular Psychiatry, 20,* 1085. doi: 10.1038/mp.2014.132

Carter, R. M., Wittchen, H.-U., Pfister, H., & Kessler, R. C. (2001). One-year prevalence of subthreshold and threshold *DSM-IV* generalized anxiety disorder in a nationally representative sample. *Depression and Anxiety, 13,* 78–88. doi: 10.1002/da.1020

Cartwright-Hatton, S. & Wells, A. (1997). Beliefs about worry and intrusions: The Meta-Cognitions Questionnaire and its correlates. *Journal of Anxiety Disorders, 11,* 279–296. doi: 10.1016/S0887-6185(97)00011-X

Cassidy, J., Lichtenstein-Phelps, J., Sibrava, N. J., Thomas, C. L., & Borkovec, T. D. (2009). Generalized anxiety disorder: Connections with self-reported attachment. *Behavior Therapy, 40,* 23–38. doi: 10.1016/j.beth.2007.12.004

Castaneda, A. E., Suvisaari, J., Marttunen, M., Perala, J., Saarni, S. I., Aalto-Setala, T., Lonnqvist, J., & Tuulio-Henriksson, A. (2011). Cognitive functioning in a population-based sample of young adults with anxiety disorders. *European Psychiatry, 26,* 346–353. doi: 10.1016/j.eurpsy.2009.11.006

Cha, J., Greenberg, T., Song, I., Blair Simpson, H., Posner, J., & Mujica-Parodi, L. R. (2016). Abnormal hippocampal structure and function in clinical anxiety and comorbid depression. *Hippocampus, 26,* 545–553. doi: 10.1002/hipo.22566

Chalmers, J. A., Quintana, D. S., Maree, J., Abbott, A., & Kemp, A. H. (2014). Anxiety disorders are associated with reduced heart rate variability: A meta-analysis. *Frontiers in Psychiatry, 5,* 80. doi: 10.3389/fpsyt.2014.00080

Coles, M. E., Turk, C. L., & Heimberg, R. G. (2007). Memory bias for threat in generalized anxiety disorder: The potential importance of stimulus relevance. *Cognitive Behavioral Therapy, 36,* 65–73. doi: 10.1080/16506070601070459

Crits-Christoph, P., Gibbons, M. B. C., Losardo, D., Narducci, J., Schamberger, M., & Gallop, R. (2004). Who benefits from brief psychodynamic therapy for generalized anxiety disorder? *Canadian Journal of Psychoanalysis, 12,* 301–324.

Crouch, T. A., Lewis, J. A., Erickson, T. M., & Newman, M. G. (2017). Prospective investigation of the contrast avoidance model of generalized anxiety and worry. *Behavior Therapy, 48,* 544–556. doi: 10.1016/j.beth.2016.10.001

Decker, M. L., Turk, C. L., Hess, B., & Murray, C. E. (2008). Emotion regulation among individuals classified with and without generalized anxiety disorder. *Journal of Anxiety Disorders, 22,* 485–494. doi: 10.1016/j.janxdis.2007.04.002

Delgado, M. R., Nearing, K. I., Ledoux, J. E., & Phelps, E. A. (2008). Neural circuitry underlying the regulation of conditioned fear and its relation to extinction. *Neuron, 59,* 829–838. doi: 10.1016/j.neuron.2008.06.029

DeVido, J., Jones, M., Geraci, M., Hollon, N., Blair, R. J., Pine, D. S., & Blair, K. (2009). Stimulus-reinforcement-based decision making and anxiety: Impairment in generalized anxiety disorder (GAD) but not in generalized social phobia (GSP). *Psychological Medicine, 39,* 1153–1161. doi: 10.1017/S003329170800487X

Dugas, M. J., Gagnon, F., Ladouceur, R., & Freeston, M. H. (1998). Generalized anxiety disorder: A preliminary test of a conceptual model. *Behaviour Research and Therapy, 36,* 215–226. doi: 10.1016/S0005-7967(97)00070-3

Dunning, J. P. & Hajcak, G. (2015). Gradients of fear potentiated startle during generalization, extinction, and extinction recall – and their relations with worry. *Behavior Therapy, 46,* 640–651. doi: 10.1016/j.beth.2015.06.005

Eng, W. & Heimberg, R. G. (2006). Interpersonal correlates of generalized anxiety disorder: Self versus other perception. *Journal of Anxiety Disorders*, *20*, 380–387. doi: 10.1016/j.janxdis.2005.02.005

Erickson, T. M., Newman, M. G., Siebert, E. C., Carlile, J. A., Scarsella, G. M., & Abelson, J. L. (2016). Does worrying mean caring too much? Interpersonal prototypicality of dimensional worry controlling for social anxiety and depressive symptoms. *Behavior Therapy*, *47*, 14–28. doi: 10.1016/j.beth.2015.08.003

Erickson, T. M. & Newman, M. G. (2007a) *Predicting cross-situational dysregulation of social behavior: Differential effects of worry, social anxiety, and depressive symptoms*. Paper presented at the 27th Annual Meeting of the Anxiety Disorders Association of America, St. Louis, MO.

Erickson, T. M. & Newman, M. G. (2007b). Interpersonal and emotional processes in generalized anxiety disorder analogues during social interaction tasks. *Behavior Therapy*, *38*, 364–377. doi: 10.1016/j.beth.2006.10.005

Etkin, A., Prater, K. E., Hoeft, F., Menon, V., & Schatzberg, A. F. (2010). Failure of anterior cingulate activation and connectivity with the amygdala during implicit regulation of emotional processing in generalized anxiety disorder. *American Journal of Psychiatry*, *167*, 545–554. doi: 10.1176/appi.ajp.2009.09070931

Etkin, A., Prater, K. E., Schatzberg, A. F., Menon, V., & Greicius, M. D. (2009). Disrupted amygdalar subregion functional connectivity and evidence of a compensatory network in generalized anxiety disorder. *Archives of General Psychiatry*, *66*, 1361–1372. doi: 10.1001/archgenpsychiatry.2009.104

Etkin, A. & Wager, T. D. (2007). Functional neuroimaging of anxiety: A meta-analysis of emotional processing in PTSD, social anxiety disorder, and specific phobia. *American Journal of Psychiatry*, *164*, 1476–1488. doi: 10.1176/appi.ajp.2007.07030504

Eysenck, M. W. & Calvo, M. G. (1992). Anxiety and performance: The processing efficiency theory. *Cognition and Emotion*, *6*, 404–434.

Eysenck, M. W., Mogg, K., May, J., Richards, A., & Mathews, A. (1991). Bias in interpretation of ambiguous sentences related to threat in anxiety. *Journal of Abnormal Psychology*, *100*, 144–150. doi: 10.1037/0021-843X.100.2.144

Feifel, D., MacDonald, K., McKinney, R., Heisserer, N., & Serrano, V. (2011). A randomized, placebo-controlled investigation of intranasal oxytocin in patients with anxiety. *Neuropsychopharmacology*, *36*, S324–S449. doi: 10.1038/npp.2011.293

Fisher, A. J., Granger, D. A., & Newman, M. G. (2010). Sympathetic arousal moderates self-reported physiological arousal symptoms at baseline and physiological flexibility in response to a stressor in generalized anxiety disorder. *Biological Psychology*, *83*, 191–200. doi: 10.1016/j.biopsycho.2009.12.007

Foa, E. B. & Kozak, M. J. (1986). Emotional processing of fear: Exposure to corrective information. *Psychological Bulletin*, *99*, 20–35. doi: 10.1037/0033-2909.99.1.20

Gazendam, F. J. & Kindt, M. (2012). Worrying affects associative fear learning: A startle fear conditioning study. *PLoS ONE*, *7*, e34882. doi: 10.1371/journal.pone.0034882

Grant, B. F., Hasin, D. S., Stinson, F. S., Dawson, D. A., June Ruan, W., Goldstein, R. B., Smith, S. M., Saha, T. D., & Huang, B. (2005). Prevalence, correlates, co-morbidity, and comparative disability of *DSM-IV* generalized anxiety disorder in the USA: Results from the National Epidemiologic Survey on Alcohol and Related Conditions. *Psychological Medicine, 35*, 1747–1759. doi: 10.1017/S0033291705006069

Grant, D. M., Judah, M. R., White, E. J., & Mills, A. C. (2015). Worry and discrimination of threat and safety cues: An event-related potential investigation. *Behavior Therapy, 46*, 652–660. doi: 10.1016/j.beth.2014.09.015

Hallion, L. S. & Ruscio, A. M. (2013). Should uncontrollable worry be removed from the definition of GAD? A test of incremental validity. *Journal of Abnormal Psychology, 122*, 369–375. doi: 10.1037/a0031731

Hallion, L. S., Ruscio, A. M., & Jha, A. P. (2014). Fractionating the role of executive control in control over worry: A preliminary investigation. *Behavior Research and Therapy, 54*, 1–6. doi: 10.1016/j.brat.2013.12.002

Hallion, L. S., Tolin, D. F., Assaf, M., Goethe, J., & Diefenbach, G. J. (2017). Cognitive control in generalized anxiety disorder: Relation of inhibition impairments to worry and anxiety severity. *Cognitive Therapy and Research, 41*, 610–618. doi: 10.1007/s10608-017-9832-2

Harvey, A. G. (2002). A cognitive model of insomnia. *Behaviour Research and Therapy, 40*, 869–893. doi: 10.1016/S0005-7967(01)00061-4

Harvey, A. G. & Greenall, E. (2003). Catastrophic worry in primary insomnia. *Journal of Behavior Therapy and Experimental Psychiatry, 34*, 11–23. doi: 10.1016/S0005-7916(03)00003-X

Hayes, S., Hirsch, C., & Mathews, A. (2008). Restriction of working memory capacity during worry. *Journal of Abnormal Psychology, 117*, 712–717. doi: 10.1037/a0012908

Hayes, S., Hirsch, C. R., & Mathews, A. (2010). Facilitating a benign attentional bias reduces negative thought intrusions. *Journal of Abnormal Psychology, 119*, 235–240. doi: 10.1037/a0018264

Hazlett-Stevens, H. & Borkovec, T. D. (2004). Interpretive cues and ambiguity in generalized anxiety disorder. *Behaviour Research and Therapy, 42*, 881–892. doi: 10.1016/S0005-7967(03)00204-3

Hebert, E. A., Dugas, M. J., Tulloch, T. G., & Holowka, D. W. (2014). Positive beliefs about worry: A psychometric evaluation of the Why Worry-II. *Personality and Individual Differences, 56*, 3–8. doi: 10.1016/j.paid.2013.08.009

Heide, F. J. & Borkovec, T. D. (1983). Relaxation-induced anxiety: Paradoxical anxiety enhancement due to relaxation training. *Journal of Consulting and Clinical Psychology, 51*, 171–182. doi: 10.1037/0022-006X.51.2.171

Hettema, J. M., Neale, M. C., Myers, J. M., Prescott, C. A., & Kendler, K. S. (2006). A population-based twin study of the relationship between neuroticism and internalizing disorders. *American Journal of Psychiatry, 163*, 857–864. doi: 10.1176/appi.ajp.163.5.857

Hilbert, K., Lueken, U., & Beesdo-Baum, K. (2014). Neural structures, functioning and connectivity in generalized anxiety disorder and interaction with neuroendocrine systems: A systematic review. *Journal of Affective Disorders, 158*, 114–126. doi: 10.1016/j.jad.2014.01.022

Hirsch, C. R. & Mathews, A. (2012). A cognitive model of pathological worry. *Behaviour Research and Therapy, 50*, 636–646. doi: 10.1016/j.brat.2012.06.007

Hoehn-Saric, R., Lee, J. S., McLeod, D. R., & Wong, D. F. (2005). Effect of worry on regional cerebral blood flow in nonanxious subjects. *Psychiatry Research: Neuroimaging, 140*, 259–269. doi: 10.1016/j.pscychresns.2005.05.013

Hoehn-Saric, R., McLeod, D. R., Funderburk, F., & Kowalski, P. (2004). Somatic symptoms and physiologic responses in generalized anxiety disorder and panic disorder: An ambulatory monitor study. *Archives of General Psychiatry, 61*, 913–921. doi: 10.1001/archpsyc.61.9.913

Hoehn-Saric, R., McLeod, D. R., & Zimmerli, W. D. (1989). Somatic manifestations in women with generalized anxiety disorder: Psychophysiological responses to psychological stress. *Archives of General Psychiatry, 46*, 1113–1119. doi: 10.1001/archpsyc.1989.01810120055009

Hofmann, S. G., Schulz, S. M., Heering, S., Muench, F., & Bufka, L. F. (2010). Psychophysiological correlates of generalized anxiety disorder with or without comorbid depression. *International Journal of Psychophysiology, 78*, 35–41. doi: 10.1016/j.ijpsycho.2009.12.016

Hunt, C., Issakidis, C., & Andrews, G. (2002). *DSM-IV* generalized anxiety disorder in the Australian National Survey of Mental Health and Well-Being. *Psychological Medicine, 32*, 649–659. doi: 10.1017}S0033291702005512

Jacobson, N. C., & Newman, M. G. (2017). Anxiety and depression as bidirectional risk factors for one another: A meta-analysis of longitudinal studies. *Psychological Bulletin, 143*, 1155–1200. doi:10.1037/bul0000111

Joos, E., Vansteenwegen, D., & Hermans, D. (2012). Worry as a predictor of fear acquisition in a nonclinical sample. *Behavior Modification, 36*, 723–750. doi: 10.1177/0145445512446477

Kessel, E. M., Kujawa, A., Hajcak Proudfit, G., & Klein, D. N. (2015). Neural reactivity to monetary rewards and losses differentiates social from generalized anxiety in children. *Journal of Child Psychology and Psychiatry, 56*, 792–800. doi: 10.1111/jcpp.12355

Kessler, R. C., Berglund, P., Demler, O., Jin, R., Merikangas, K. R., & Walters, E. E. (2005). Lifetime prevalence and age-of-onset distributions of *DSM-IV* disorders in the National Comorbidity Survey Replication. *Archives of General Psychiatry, 62*, 593–602. doi: 10.1001/archpsyc.62.6.593

Kessler, R. C., Chiu, W. T., Demler, O., Merikangas, K. R., & Walters, E. E. (2005). Prevalence, severity, and comorbidity of 12-month *DSM-IV* disorders in the National Comorbidity Survey Replication. *Archives of General Psychiatry, 62*, 617–627. doi: 10.1001/archpsyc.62.6.617

Kessler, R. C., DuPont, R. L., Berglund, P., & Wittchen, H. U. (1999). Impairment in pure and comorbid generalized anxiety disorder and major depression at 12 months in two national surveys. *American Journal of Psychiatry, 156*, 1915–1923.

Kim, H. & Newman, M. G. (2016) *Emotional contrast avoidance in generalized anxiety disorder and major depressive disorder: A comparison between the perseveration processes of worry and rumination*. Paper presented at the 50th Annual Meeting of the Association for Behavioral and Cognitive Therapies, New York, NY.

LaFreniere, L. S. & Newman, M. G. (2018a). *Probabilistic learning by positive and negative reinforcement in generalized anxiety disorder*. Manuscript submitted for publication.

LaFreniere, L. S. & Newman, M. G. (2018b). *Exposing worry's deceit: Percentage of untrue worries in generalized anxiety disorder treatment.* Manuscript submitted for publication.

Lang, P. J., Davis, M., & Öhman, A. (2000). Fear and anxiety: Animal models and human cognitive psychophysiology. *Journal of Affective Disorders, 61,* 137–159. doi: 10.1016/S0165-0327(00)00343-8

Leigh, E. & Hirsch, C. R. (2011). Worry in imagery and verbal form: Effect on residual working memory capacity. *Behavior Research and Therapy, 49,* 99–105. doi: 10.1016/j.brat.2010.11.005

Llera, S. J. & Newman, M. G. (2010). Effects of worry on physiological and subjective reactivity to emotional stimuli in generalized anxiety disorder and nonanxious control participants. *Emotion, 10,* 640–650. doi: 10.1037/a0019351

Llera, S. J. & Newman, M. G. (2014). Rethinking the role of worry in generalized anxiety disorder: Evidence supporting a model of emotional contrast avoidance. *Behavior Therapy, 45,* 283–299. doi: 10.1016/j.beth.2013.12.011.

Llera, S. J. & Newman, M. G. (2017). Development and validation of two measures of emotional contrast avoidance: The Contrast Avoidance Questionnaires. *Journal of Anxiety Disorders, 49,* 114–127. doi: 10.1016/j.janxdis.2017.04.008

MacLeod, C. & Donnellan, A. M. (1993). Individual differences in anxiety and the restriction of working memory capacity. *Personality and Individual Differences, 15,* 163–173. doi: 10.1016/0191–8869(93)90023-V

MacLeod, C., Mathews, A., & Tata, P. (1986). Attentional bias in emotional disorders. *Journal of Abnormal Psychology, 95,* 15–20. doi: 10.1037/0021-843X.95.1.15

Makovac, E., Meeten, F., Watson, D. R., Herman, A., Garfinkel, S. N., D. Critchley, H., & Ottaviani, C. (2016). Alterations in amygdala-prefrontal functional connectivity account for excessive worry and autonomic dysregulation in generalized anxiety disorder. *Biological Psychiatry, 80,* 786–795. doi: 10.1016/j.biopsych.2015.10.013

Mantella, R. C., Butters, M. A., Dew, M. A., Mulsant, B. H., Begley, A. E., Tracey, B., Shear, M. K., Reynolds, C. F., 3rd, & Lenze, E. J. (2007). Cognitive impairment in late-life generalized anxiety disorder. *American Journal of Geriatric Psychiatry, 15,* 673–679. doi: 10.1097/JGP.0b013e31803111f2

Marcks, B. A., Weisberg, R. B., Edelen, M. O., & Keller, M. B. (2010). The relationship between sleep disturbance and the course of anxiety disorders in primary care patients. *Psychiatry Research, 178,* 487–492. doi: 10.1016/j.psychres.2009.07.004

Mathews, A. & MacLeod, C. (1985). Selective processing of threat cues in anxiety states. *Behaviour Research and Therapy, 23,* 563–569. doi: 10.1016/0005–7967(85)90104–4

Mathews, A., & MacLeod, C. (2005). Cognitive vulnerability to emotional disorders. *Annual Review of Clinical Psychology, 1,* 167–195. doi: 10.1146/annurev. clinpsy.1.102803.143916

Mathews, A., Mogg, K., Kentish, J., & Eysenck, M. (1995). Effect of psychological treatment on cognitive bias in generalized anxiety disorder. *Behaviour and Research Therapy, 33,* 293–303. doi: 10.1016/0005–7967(94)E0022-B

Mathews, A., Mogg, K., May, J., & Eysenck, M. (1989). Implicit and explicit memory bias in anxiety. *Journal of Abnormal Psychology, 98,* 236–240. doi: 10.1037//0021-843x.98.3.236

Mavissakalian, M. R., Hamann, M. S., Haidar, S. A., & de Groot, C. M. (1995). Correlates of *DSM-III* personality disorder in generalized anxiety disorder. *Journal of Anxiety Disorders, 9,* 103–115. doi: 10.1016/0887–6185(94)00034–4

McClure, E. B., Monk, C. S., Nelson, E. E., Parrish, J. M., Adler, A., Blair, R. J. R., Fromm, S., Charney, D. S., Leibenluft, E., Ernst, M., & Pine, D. S. (2007). Abnormal attention modulation of fear circuit function in pediatric generalized anxiety disorder. *Archives of General Psychiatry, 64,* 97–106. doi: 10.1001/archpsyc.64.1.97

McLaughlin, K. A., Borkovec, T. D., & Sibrava, N. J. (2007). The effects of worry and rumination on affect states and cognitive activity. *Behavior Therapy, 38,* 23–38. doi: 10.1016/j.beth.2006.03.003

McLeod, J. D. (1994). Anxiety disorders and marital quality. *Journal of Abnormal Psychology, 103,* 767–776. doi: 10.1037/0021-843X.103.4.767

McNally, R. J. (1995). Automaticity and the anxiety disorders. *Behaviour Research and Therapy, 33,* 747–754. doi: 10.1016/0005–7967(95)00015-P

Mennin, D. S., McLaughlin, K. A., & Flanagan, T. J. (2009). Emotion regulation deficits in generalized anxiety disorder, social anxiety disorder, and their co-occurrence. *Journal of Anxiety Disorders, 23,* 866–871. doi: 10.1016/j.janxdis.2009.04.006

Miyake, A., Friedman, N. P., Emerson, M. J., Witzki, A. H., Howerter, A., & Wager, T. D. (2000). The unity and diversity of executive functions and their contributions to complex "frontal lobe" tasks: A latent variable analysis. *Cognitive Psychology, 41,* 49–100. doi: 10.1006/cogp.1999.0734

Mochcovitch, M. D., da Rocha Freire, R. C., Garcia, R. F., & Nardi, A. E. (2014). A systematic review of fMRI studies in generalized anxiety disorder: Evaluating its neural and cognitive basis. *Journal of Affective Disorders, 167,* 336–342. doi: 10.1016/j.jad.2014.06.041

Mogg, K., Bradley, B. P., Williams, R., & Mathews, A. (1993). Subliminal processing of emotional information in anxiety and depression. *Journal of Abnormal Psychology, 102,* 304–311. doi: 10.1037/0021-843X.102.2.304

Mogg, K., Garner, M., & Bradley, B. P. (2007). Anxiety and orienting of gaze to angry and fearful faces. *Biological Psychology, 76,* 163–169. doi: 10.1016/j.biopsycho.2007.07.005

Mogg, K., Millar, N., & Bradley, B. P. (2000). Biases in eye movements to threatening facial expressions in generalized anxiety disorder and depressive disorder. *Journal of Abnormal Psychology, 109,* 695–704. doi: 10.1037/0021-843X.109.4.695

Monk, C. S., Nelson, E. E., McClure, E. B., Mogg, K., Bradley, B. P., Leibenluft, E., Blair, R. J. R., Chen, G., Charney, D. S., Ernst, M., & Pine, D. S. (2006). Ventrolateral prefrontal cortex activation and attentional bias in response to angry faces in adolescents with generalized anxiety disorder. *American Journal of Psychiatry, 163,* 1091–1097. doi: 10.1176/appi.ajp.163.6.1091

Monk, C. S., Telzer, E. H., Mogg, K., Bradley, B. P., Mai, X., Louro, H. M. C., Chen, G., McClure-Tone, E. B., Ernst, M., & Pine, D. S. (2008). Amygdala and ventrolateral prefrontal cortex activation to masked angry faces in children and adolescents with generalized anxiety disorder. *Archives of General Psychiatry, 65,* 568–576. doi: 10.1001/archpsyc.65.5.568

Monti, J. M. & Monti, D. (2000). Sleep disturbance in generalized anxiety disorder and its treatment. *Sleep Medicine Reviews, 4,* 263–276. doi: 10.1053/smrv.1999.0096

Moon, C. M. & Jeong, G. W. (2015). Functional neuroanatomy on the working memory under emotional distraction in patients with generalized anxiety disorder. *Psychiatry and Clinical Neuroscience*, *69*, 609–619. doi: 10.1111/pcn.12295

Moon, C. M., Sundaram, T., Choi, N. G., & Jeong, G. W. (2016). Working memory dysfunction associated with brain functional deficits and cellular metabolic changes in patients with generalized anxiety disorder. *Psychiatry Research*, *254*, 137–144. doi: 10.1016/j.pscychresns.2016.06.013

Moon, C. M., Yang, J. C., & Jeong, G. W. (2015). Explicit verbal memory impairments associated with brain functional deficits and morphological alterations in patients with generalized anxiety disorder. *Journal of Affective Disorders*, *186*, 328–336. doi: 10.1016/j.jad.2015.07.038

Morris, B. H. & Rottenberg, J. (2015). Heightened reward learning under stress in generalized anxiety disorder: A predictor of depression resistance? *Journal of Abnormal Psychology*, *124*, 115–127. doi: 10.1037/a0036934

Moser, J. S., Moran, T. P., Schroder, H. S., Donnellan, M. B., & Yeung, N. (2013). On the relationship between anxiety and error monitoring: A meta-analysis and conceptual framework. *Frontiers in Human Neuroscience*, *7*, 466. doi: 10.3389/fnhum.2013.00466

Mueller, E. M., Nguyen, J., Ray, W. J., & Borkovec, T. D. (2010). Future-oriented decision-making in generalized anxiety disorder is evident across different versions of the Iowa Gambling Task. *Journal of Behavior Therapy and Experimental Psychiatry*, *41*, 165–171. doi: 10.1016/j.jbtep.2009.12.002

Muris, P., Mayer, B., & Meesters, C. (2000). Self-reported attachment style, anxiety, and depression in children. *Social Behavior and Personality*, *28*, 157–162. doi: 10.2224/sbp.2000.28.2.157

Muris, P., Meesters, C., van Melick, M., & Zwambag, L. (2001). Self-reported attachment style, attachment quality, and symptoms of anxiety and depression in young adolescents. *Personality and Individual Differences*, *30*, 809–818. doi: 10.1016/s0191-8869(00)00074-x

Myers, A. J., Williams, L., Gatt, J. M., McAuley-Clark, E. Z., Dobson-Stone, C., Schofield, P. R., & Nemeroff, C. B. (2014). Variation in the oxytocin receptor gene is associated with increased risk for anxiety, stress and depression in individuals with a history of exposure to early life stress. *Journal of Psychiatric Research*, *59*, 93–100. doi: 10.1016/j.jpsychires.2014.08.021

Newman, M. G., Castonguay, L. G., Jacobson, N. C., & Moore, G. A. (2015). Adult attachment as a moderator of treatment outcome for generalized anxiety disorder: Comparison between cognitive-behavioral therapy (CBT) plus supportive listening and CBT plus interpersonal and emotional processing therapy. *Journal of Consulting and Clinical Psychology*, *83*, 915. doi: 10.1037/a0039359

Newman, M. G. & Erickson, T. M. (2010). Generalized anxiety disorder. In J. G. Beck (ed.), *Interpersonal Processes in the Anxiety Disorders: Implications for Understanding Psychopathology and Treatment* (pp. 235–259). Washington, DC: American Psychological Association. doi: 10.1037/12084–009

Newman, M. G., Jacobson, N. C., Erickson, T. M., & Fisher, A. J. (2017). Interpersonal problems predict differential response to cognitive versus behavioral treatment in a randomized controlled trial. *Behavior Therapy*, *48*, 56–68. doi: 10.1016/j.beth.2016.05.005

Newman, M. G., Jacobson, N. C., Zainal, N. H., Shin, K., Szkodny, L. E., & Sliwinski, M. J. (2018). The effects of worry in daily life: An ecological momentary assessment study supporting the tenets of the contrast avoidance model. *Manuscript submitted for publication.*

Newman, M. G., LaFreniere, L. S., & Jacobson, N. C. (2018). Relaxation-induced anxiety: Effects of peak and trajectories of change on treatment outcome for generalized anxiety disorder. *Psychotherapy Research, 28,* 616–629. doi: 10.1080/10503307.2016.1253891

Newman, M. G. & Llera, S. J. (2011). A novel theory of experiential avoidance in generalized anxiety disorder: A review and synthesis of research supporting a contrast avoidance model of worry. *Clinical Psychology Review, 31,* 371–382. doi: 10.1016/j.cpr.2011.01.008

Newman, M. G., Llera, S. J., Erickson, T. M., Przeworski, A., & Castonguay, L. G. (2013). Worry and generalized anxiety disorder: A review and theoretical synthesis of research on nature, etiology, and treatment. *Annual Review of Clinical Psychology, 9,* 275–297. doi: 10.1146/annurev-clinpsy-050212–185544

Newman, M. G., Shin, K. E., & Zuellig, A. R. (2016). Developmental risk factors in generalized anxiety disorder and panic disorder. *Journal of Affective Disorders, 206,* 94–102. doi: 10.1016/j.jad.2016.07.008

Nitschke, J. B., Sarinopoulos, I., Oathes, D. J., Johnstone, T., Whalen, P. J., Davidson, R. J., & Kalin, N. H. (2009). Anticipatory activation in the amygdala and anterior cingulate in generalized anxiety disorder and prediction of treatment response. *American Journal of Psychiatry, 166,* 302–310. doi: 10.1176/appi.ajp.2008.07101682

Noble, L. (2016). Facial Expressions in Generalized Anxiety Disorder (Master's thesis). The City University of New York. Retrieved from http://academicworks.cuny.edu/hc_sas_etds/80/

Olatunji, B. O., Broman-Fulks, J. J., Bergman, S. M., Green, B. A., & Zlomke, K. R. (2010). A taxometric investigation of the latent structure of worry: Dimensionality and associations with depression, anxiety, and stress. *Behavior Therapy, 41,* 212–228. doi: 10.1016/j.beth.2009.03.001

Olatunji, B. O., Wolitzky-Taylor, K. B., Sawchuk, C. N., & Ciesielski, B. G. (2010). Worry and the anxiety disorders: A meta-analytic synthesis of specificity to GAD. *Applied and Preventive Psychology, 14,* 1–24. doi: 10.1016/j.appsy.2011.03.001

Ottaviani, C., Thayer, J. F., Verkuil, B., Lonigro, A., Medea, B., Couyoumdjian, A., & Brosschot, J. F. (2016). *Physiological Concomitants of Perseverative Cognition: A Systematic Review and Meta-Analysis.* Washington, DC: American Psychological Association.

Palm, M. E., Elliott, R., McKie, S., Deakin, J. F., & Anderson, I. M. (2011). Attenuated responses to emotional expressions in women with generalized anxiety disorder. *Psychological Medicine, 41,* 1009–1018. doi: 10.1017/S0033291710001455

Papadimitriou, G. N. & Linkowski, P. (2005). Sleep disturbance in anxiety disorders. *International Review of Psychiatry, 17,* 229–236. doi: 10.1080/09540260500104524

Park, G., Vasey, M. W., van Bavel, J. J., & Thayer, J. F. (2014). When tonic cardiac vagal tone predicts changes in phasic vagal tone: The role of fear and perceptual load. *Psychophysiology, 51,* 419–426. doi: 10.1111/psyp.12186

Peasley, C. E., Molina, S., & Borkovec, T. D. (1994, November). *Empathy in generalized anxiety disorder*. Proceedings of the 28th annual meeting of the Association for Advancement of Behavior Therapy, San Diego, CA.

Pittig, A., Arch, J. J., Lam, C. W., & Craske, M. G. (2013). Heart rate and heart rate variability in panic, social anxiety, obsessive-compulsive, and generalized anxiety disorders at baseline and in response to relaxation and hyperventilation. *International Journal of Psychophysiology, 87*, 19–27. doi: 10.1016/j.ijpsycho.2012.10.012

Plana, I., Lavoie, M. A., Battaglia, M., & Achim, A. M. (2014). A meta-analysis and scoping review of social cognition performance in social phobia, posttraumatic stress disorder and other anxiety disorders. *Journal of Anxiety Disorders, 28*, 169–177. doi: 10.1016/j.janxdis.2013.09.005

Power, M. J. & Tarsia, M. (2007). Basic and complex emotions in depression and anxiety. *Clinical Psychology and Psychotherapy, 14*, 19–31. doi: 10.1002/cpp.515

Price, R. B. & Mohlman, J. (2007). Inhibitory control and symptom severity in late life generalized anxiety disorder. *Behavior Research and Therapy, 45*, 2628–2639. doi: 10.1016/j.brat.2007.06.007

Przeworski, A., Newman, M. G., Pincus, A. L., Kasoff, M. B., Yamasaki, A. S., Castonguay, L. G., & Berlin, K. S. (2011). Interpersonal pathoplasticity in individuals with generalized anxiety disorder. *Journal of Abnormal Psychology, 120*, 286–298. doi: 10.1037/a0023334

Rhebergen, D., Aderka, I. M., van der Steenstraten, I. M., van Balkom, A., van Oppen, P., Stek, M. L., Comijs, H. C., & Batelaan, N. M. (2017). Admixture analysis of age of onset in generalized anxiety disorder. *Journal of Anxiety Disorders, 50*, 47–51. doi: 10.1016/j.janxdis.2017.05.003

Roemer, L., Molina, S., & Borkovec, T. D. (1997). An investigation of worry content among generally anxious individuals. *Journal of Nervous and Mental Disease, 185*, 314–319. doi: 10.1097/00005053–199705000-00005

Roemer, L. & Orsillo, S. M. (2002). Expanding our conceptualization of and treatment for generalized anxiety disorder: Integrating mindfulness/acceptance-based approaches with existing cognitive-behavioral models. *Clinical Psychology: Science and Practice, 9*, 54–68. doi: 10.1093/clipsy/9.1.54

Roybal, K., Theobold, D., Graham, A., DiNieri, J. A., Russo, S. J., Krishnan, V., Chakravarty, S., Peevey, J., Oehrlein, N., & Birnbaum, S. (2007). Mania-like behavior induced by disruption of CLOCK. *Proceedings of the National Academy of Sciences, 104*, 6406–6411. doi: 10.1073/pnas.0609625104

Ruscio, A. M. (2002). Delimiting the boundaries of generalized anxiety disorder: Differentiating high worriers with and without GAD. *Journal of Anxiety Disorders, 16*, 377–400. doi: 10.1016/S0887-6185(02)00130–5

Ruscio, A. M. & Borkovec, T. D. (2004). Experience and appraisal of worry among high worriers with and without generalized anxiety disorder. *Behaviour Research and Therapy, 42*, 1469–1482. doi: 10.1016/j.brat.2003.10.007

Ruscio, A. M., Borkovec, T. D., & Ruscio, J. (2001). A taxometric investigation of the latent structure of worry. *Journal of Abnormal Psychology, 110*, 413–422. doi: 10.1037/0021-843X.110.3.413

Ruscio, A. M., Hallion, L. S., Lim, C. C. W., Aguilar-Gaxiola, S., Al-Hamzawi, A., Alonso, J., Andrade, L. H., Borges, G., Bromet, E. J., Bunting, B., Caldas de

Almeida, J. M., Demyttenaere, K., Florescu, S., de Girolamo, G., Gureje, O., Haro, J. M., He, Y., Hinkov, H., Hu, C., de Jonge, P., Karam, E. G., Lee, S., Lepine, J. P., Levinson, D., Mneimneh, Z., Navarro-Mateu, F., Posada-Villa, J., Slade, T., Stein, D. J., Torres, Y., Uda, H., Wojtyniak, B., Kessler, R. C., Chatterji, S., & Scott, K. M. (2017). Cross-sectional comparison of the epidemiology of *DSM-5* generalized anxiety disorder across the globe. *JAMA Psychiatry*, *74*, 465–475. doi: 10.1001/jamapsychiatry.2017.0056

Ruscio, A. M., Seitchik, A. E., Gentes, E. L., Jones, J. D., & Hallion, L. S. (2011). Perseverative thought: A robust predictor of response to emotional challenge in generalized anxiety disorder and major depressive disorder. *Behavior Research and Therapy*, *49*, 867–874. doi: 10.1016/j.brat.2011.10.001

Saletu-Zyhlarz, G., Saletu, B., Anderer, P., Brandstätter, N., Frey, R., Gruber, G., Klosch, G., Mandl, M., Grunberger, J., & Linzmayer, L. (1997). Nonorganic insomnia in generalized anxiety disorder. 1. Controlled studies on sleep, awakening and daytime vigilance utilizing polysomnography and EEG mapping. *Neuropsychobiology*, *36*, 117–129. doi: 10.1159/000119373

Salzer, S., Pincus, A. L., Hoyer, J., Kreische, R., Leichsenring, F., & Leibing, E. (2008). Interpersonal subtypes within generalized anxiety disorder. *Journal of Personality Assessment*, *90*, 292–299. doi: 10.1080/00223890701885076

Salzer, S., Pincus, A. L., Winkelbach, C., Leichsenring, F., & Leibing, E. (2011). Interpersonal subtypes and change of interpersonal problems in the treatment of patients with generalized anxiety disorder: A pilot study. *Psychotherapy: Theory, Research, Practice, Training*, *48*, 304–310. doi: 10.1037/a0022013

Schienle, A., Köchel, A., Ebner, F., Reishofer, G., & Schäfer, A. (2010). Neural correlates of intolerance of uncertainty. *Neuroscience Letters*, *479*, 272–276. doi: 10.1016/j.neulet.2010.05.078

Seth, A. K., Barrett, A. B., & Barnett, L. (2015). Granger causality analysis in neuroscience and neuroimaging. *Journal of Neuroscience*, *35*, 3293–3297. doi: 10.1523/JNEUROSCI.4399–14.2015

Shanahan, L., Copeland, W. E., Angold, A., Bondy, C. L., & Costello, E. J. (2014). Sleep problems predict and are predicted by generalized anxiety/depression and oppositional defiant disorder. *Journal of the American Academy of Child and Adolescent Psychiatry*, *53*, 550–558. doi: 10.1016/j.jaac.2013.12.029

Shin, K., Newman, M. G., Hammaker, S., Fabinyi, C., Sheintoch, M., Kilbert, R., Purnell, J., & Choi, J. (2016) *Effects of Trait and Induced Worry on Interpersonal Perceptions and Behaviors*. Paper presented at the 2016 Association for Behavioral and Cognitive Therapies Annual Convention, New York, NY.

Sipila, T., Kananen, L., Greco, D., Donner, J., Silander, K., Terwilliger, J. D., Auvinen, P., Peltonen, L., Lonnqvist, J., Pirkola, S., Partonen, T., & Hovatta, I. (2010). An association analysis of circadian genes in anxiety disorders. *Biological Psychiatry*, *67*, 1163–1170. doi: 10.1016/j.biopsych.2009.12.011

Somerville, L. H., Whalen, P. J., & Kelley, W. M. (2010). Human bed nucleus of the stria terminalis indexes hypervigilant threat monitoring. *Biological Psychiatry*, *68*, 416–424. doi: 10.1016/j.biopsych.2010.04.002

Srivastava, S., Sharma, H. O., & Mandal, M. K. (2003). Mood induction with facial expressions of emotion in patients with generalized anxiety disorder. *Depression & Anxiety*, *18*, 144–148. doi: 10.1002/da.10128

Tempesta, D., Mazza, M., Serroni, N., Moschetta, F. S., Di Giannantonio, M., Ferrara, M., & De Berardis, D. (2013). Neuropsychological functioning in young subjects with generalized anxiety disorder with and without pharmacotherapy. *Progress in Neuropsychopharmacology and Biological Psychiatry*, *45*, 236–241. doi: 10.1016/j.pnpbp.2013.06.006

Thayer, J. F., Åhs, F., Fredrikson, M., Sollers, J. J., & Wager, T. D. (2012). A meta-analysis of heart rate variability and neuroimaging studies: Implications for heart rate variability as a marker of stress and health. *Neuroscience & Biobehavioral Reviews*, *36*, 747–756. doi: 10.1016/j.neubiorev.2011.11.009

Thayer, J. F., Friedman, B. H., & Borkovec, T. D. (1996). Autonomic characteristics of generalized anxiety disorder and worry. *Biological Psychiatry*, *39*, 255–266. doi: 10.1016/0006-3223(95)00136-0

Uhmann, S., Beesdo-Baum, K., Becker, E. S., & Hoyer, J. (2010). Specificity of interpersonal problems in generalized anxiety disorder versus other anxiety disorders and depression. *Journal of Nervous and Mental Disease*, *198*, 846–851. doi: 10.1097/NMD.0b013e3181f98063

van Eijck, F. E., Branje, S. J., Hale, W. W., & Meeus, W. H. (2012). Longitudinal associations between perceived parent–adolescent attachment relationship quality and generalized anxiety disorder symptoms in adolescence. *Journal of Abnormal Child Psychology*, *40*, 871–883. doi: 10.1007/s10802-012-9613-z

Walker, D. L., Toufexis, D. J., & Davis, M. (2003). Role of the bed nucleus of the stria terminalis versus the amygdala in fear, stress, and anxiety. *European Journal of Pharmacology*, *463*, 199–216. doi: 10.1016/S0014-2999(03)01282-2

Weinberg, A., Kotov, R., & Proudfit, G. H. (2015). Neural indicators of error processing in generalized anxiety disorder, obsessive-compulsive disorder, and major depressive disorder. *Journal of Abnormal Psychology*, *124*, 172–185. doi: 10.1037/abn0000019

Wells, A. (1995). Meta-cognition and worry: A cognitive model of generalized anxiety disorder. *Behavioural and Cognitive Psychotherapy*, *23*, 301–320. doi: 10.1017/S1352465800015836

Whisman, M. A., Sheldon, C. T., & Goering, P. (2000). Psychiatric disorders and dissatisfaction with social relationships: Does type of relationship matter? *Journal of Abnormal Psychology*, *109*, 803–808. doi: 10.1037/0021-843X.109.4.803

Wittchen, H. U. (2002). Generalized anxiety disorder: Prevalence, burden, and cost to society. *Depression and Anxiety*, *16*, 162–171. doi: 10.1002/da.10065

Wittchen, H. U., Carter, R. M., Pfister, H., Montgomery, S. A., & Kessler, R. C. (2000). Disabilities and quality of life in pure and comorbid generalized anxiety disorder and major depression in a national survey. *International Clinical Psychopharmacology*, *15*, 319–328. doi: 10.1097/00004850-200015060-00002

Wittchen, H. U., Krause, P., Hoyer, J., Beesdo, K., Jacobi, F., Hofler, M., & Winter, S. (2001). Prevalence and correlates of generalized anxiety disorders in primary care. *Fortschritte der Medizin Originalien*, *119* Suppl. (1), 17–25.

Wittchen, H. U., Zhao, S., Kessler, R. C., & Eaton, W. W. (1994). *DSM-III-R* generalized anxiety disorder in the National Comorbidity Survey. *Archives of General Psychiatry*, *51*, 355–364. doi: 10.1001/archpsyc.1994.03950050015002

Wu, J. Q., Szpunar, K. K., Godovich, S. A., Schacter, D. L., & Hofmann, S. G. (2015). Episodic future thinking in generalized anxiety disorder. *Journal of Anxiety Disorders*, *36*, 1–8. doi: 10.1016/j.janxdis.2015.09.005

Yang, Y., Zhang, X., Zhu, Y., Dai, Y., Liu, T., & Wang, Y. (2015). Cognitive impairment in generalized anxiety disorder revealed by event-related potential N270. *Neuropsychiatric Disease and Treatment*, *11*, 1405–1411. doi: 10.2147/NDT.S84666

Yassa, M. A., Hazlett, R. L., Stark, C. E., & Hoehn-Saric, R. (2012). Functional MRI of the amygdala and bed nucleus of the stria terminalis during conditions of uncertainty in generalized anxiety disorder. *Journal of Psychiatric Research*, *46*, 1045–1052. doi: 10.1016/j.jpsychires.2012.04.013

Yonkers, K. A., Bruce, S. E., Dyck, I. R., & Keller, M. B. (2003). Chronicity, relapse, and illness-course of panic disorder, social phobia, and generalized anxiety disorder: Findings in men and women from 8 years of follow-up. *Depression and Anxiety*, *17*, 173–179. doi: 10.1002/da.10106

Yonkers, K. A., Dyck, I. R., Warshaw, M., & Keller, M. B. (2000). Factors predicting the clinical course of generalised anxiety disorder. *British Journal of Psychiatry*, *176*, 544–549. doi: 10.1192/bjp.176.6.544

Yonkers, K. A., Warshaw, M. G., Massion, A. O., & Keller, M. B. (1996). Phenomenology and course of generalised anxiety disorder. *British Journal of Psychiatry*, *168*, 308–313. doi: 10.1192/bjp.168.3.308

Yoon, S., Kim, H., S., Kim, J.-I., Lee, S., & Lee, S.-H. (2016). Reading simple and complex facial expressions in patients with major depressive disorder and anxiety disorders. *Psychiatry and Clinical Neurosciences*, *70*, 151–158. doi: 10.1111/pcn.12369

Zainal, N. H., & Newman, M. G. (2018). Worry amplifies theory-of-mind reasoning for negatively valenced social stimuli in generalized anxiety disorder. *Journal of Affective Disorders, 227*, 824–833. doi:10.1016/j.jad.2017.11.084

Zainal, N. H., & Newman, M. G. (2017). Executive function and other cognitive deficits are distal risk factors of generalized anxiety disorder 9 years later. *Psychological Medicine*, 1–9. doi:10.1017/S0033291717003579

Zhang, X., Norton, J., Carriere, I., Ritchie, K., Chaudieu, I., & Ancelin, M. L. (2015). Risk factors for late-onset generalized anxiety disorder: Results from a 12-year prospective cohort (the ESPRIT study). *Translational Psychiatry*, *5*, e536. doi: 10.1038/tp.2015.31

19 Separation Anxiety Disorder

Andrew R. Eisen and Kristin L. Toffey

Major advances have occurred in the conceptualization, assessment, and treatment of separation anxiety and related problems. For instance, separation anxiety disorder (SAD) is no longer solely a childhood phenomenon. If left untreated, separation anxiety may linger into adulthood or serve as a general risk factor for the development of generalized anxiety, panic, or depressive symptoms. In fact, the assessment, classification, and treatment of adult separation anxiety disorder (ASAD) is emerging as an important area of investigation.

This chapter begins with a review of the prevalence, epidemiology, classification, comorbidity, and developmental course of SAD across the life span. We then discuss how dimensional models, transdiagnostic mechanisms, and the National Institute of Mental Health's (NIMH) Research Domain Criteria (RDoC) inform our latest thinking regarding the etiology and maintenance of SAD. This chapter concludes with a comprehensive assessment section and the most recent evidence-based treatment approaches for SAD.

Prevalence and Epidemiology of Separation Anxiety Disorder

Separation anxiety disorder is the most frequently diagnosed childhood anxiety disorder (Boyd, Gullone, Kostanski, Ollendick, & Shek, 2000). Separation anxiety accounts for approximately half of the treatment-related referrals for anxiety disorders (Cartwright-Hatton, McNicol, & Doubleday, 2006). Prevalence estimates of anxiety disorders in early-aged, preschool children range from 0.3% to 6.5% (Carpenter et al., 2016; Franz et al., 2013). However, less than 15% of children presenting with anxiety disorders actually receive mental health services (Carpenter et al., 2016). This is due in part to a lack of affordable treatment options and a paucity of psychometrically sound tools for identifying and treating early-aged children (Carpenter et al., 2016).

The average age of onset for SAD is typically around seven years old (Kessler, Petukhova, Sampson, Zaslavsky, & Wittchen, 2012). When examining prevalence estimates across the life span, the median age of onset was in the late teens for high/upper-middle-income countries, and in the mid-20s for low/lower-middle-income countries (Silove et al., 2015). Regarding gender, however, lifetime prevalence estimates are significantly higher for females as compared to males (5.6% vs. 4.0%) (Silove et al., 2015). In fact, studies have demonstrated that lifetime prevalence for SAD is twice as high for females as compared to males (e.g., Kessler et al., 2012).

Naturally, prevalence estimates for SAD in clinical settings are quite robust. As many as 49% of children and 46% of adults seeking clinic services meet criteria for SAD (Hammerness et al., 2008; Manicavasagar et al., 2010).

For example, Silove, Marnane, Wagner, Manicavasagar, and Rees (2010) examined the prevalence of ASAD in anxiety clinics. Adult separation anxiety disorder accounted for 23% of all diagnoses assigned at the clinic. Key predictors of ASAD included retrospective reports of childhood adversities and the occurrence of traumatic events (Silove et al., 2015).

The symptom presentation in SAD differs with developmental stage and age. Younger children (ages 5–8) are more likely to report a higher frequency of nightmares and distress upon separation from caregivers as compared to older children (ages 9–12) (Allen, Lavallee, Herren, Ruhe, & Schneider, 2010). In addition, younger children are less likely to identify specific threats related to their separation anxiety. Older children, on the other hand, tend to endorse cognitive factors and specific fears of certain events (Hanna, Fischer, & Fluent, 2006). Finally, adolescents tend to endorse a higher frequency of intense somatic symptoms (e.g., panic) as compared to younger children (Allen et al., 2010).

The clinical presentation of SAD in adulthood is similar to adolescence regarding separation-related somatic complaints (Manicavasagar et al., 2010). However, adults experience separation-related fears about partners rather than caregivers (Manicavasagar et al., 2010). In addition, ASAD is associated with greater functional impairment. For example, Pini et al. (2005) examined the prevalence of SAD in an adult outpatient sample presenting with mood and anxiety disorders. A diagnosis of ASAD (20.7%) was associated with severe functional impairment in both work and social relationships.

Classification

The fifth edition of the *Diagnostic and Statistical Manual of Mental Disorders* (*DSM-5*) (American Psychiatric Association [APA], 2013) characterizes SAD as "developmentally inappropriate and excessive fear or anxiety concerning separation from those to whom the individual is attached." In order to meet *DSM-5* criteria for SAD, at least three of the following eight criteria must be evident:

(1) Recurrent excessive distress when anticipating or experiencing separation from home or from major attachment figures.
(2) Persistent and excessive worry about losing major attachment figures or about possible harm to them, such as illness, injury, disasters, or death.
(3) Persistent and excessive worry about experiencing an untoward event.

(4) Persistent reluctance or refusal to go out, away from home, to school, to work, or elsewhere because of fear of separation.

(5) Persistent and excessive fear of or reluctance about being alone or without major attachment figures at home or in other settings.

(6) Persistent reluctance or refusal to sleep away from home or to go to sleep without being near a major attachment figure.

(7) Repeated nightmares involving the theme of separation.

(8) Repeated complaints of physical symptoms when separation from major attachment figures occurs or is anticipated (APA, 2013).

DSM-5 also states that fear, anxiety, and/ or avoidance is persistent, lasting at least four weeks in children and adolescents, and typically, six months or more in adults. Last, symptom presentation must cause clinically significant distress or functional impairment in one or more domains (i.e., social, occupational, academic), and the disturbance is not better explained by another mental disorder (APA, 2013).

The revisions of SAD in *DSM-5* took place in both the classification of the disorder and diagnostic criteria (Carmassi, Gesi, Massimetti, Shear, & Dell'Osso, 2015). For example, *DSM-5* recognizes SAD as an anxiety disorder. In regards to the diagnostic criteria, *DSM-IV-TR* (APA, 2000) solely acknowledged the onset of SAD in childhood (i.e., onset of SAD must have occurred before the age of 18), whereas *DSM-5* acknowledges the presence and onset of SAD across the life span (i.e., no age of onset is specified).

Separation anxiety disorder is classified differently in the 10th edition of the *International Classification of Diseases* (*ICD-10*) (World Health Organization [WHO], 2016). Similar to the *DSM-IV-TR*, the *ICD-10-CM* classifies SAD as "Separation anxiety disorder of childhood." While the specific indicator of SAD is the same in *DSM-5* and *ICD-10*, they differ in criteria related to age of onset, symptom duration, and impairment.

For example, *ICD-10* states that age of onset is before the age of six, whereas no age of onset is specified in *DSM-5*. Similar to *DSM-5, ICD-10* states that duration of symptoms is at least four weeks. However, *ICD-10* does not include the symptom duration specified for adults. In addition, *ICD-10* criteria state that there is an absence of generalized anxiety disorder (GAD) of childhood, whereas GAD can be a comorbid diagnosis with SAD in the *DSM-5*.

Diagnostic Comorbidity

Comorbidity is often the rule, not the exception, among individuals with SAD (Kearney, Sims, Pursell, & Tillotson, 2003; Kendall, Brady, & Verduin, 2001; Shear, Jin, Ruscio, Walters, & Kessler, 2006; Silove et al., 2015). Youths with anxiety disorders rarely present for treatment with symptoms of a single psychological disorder. According to the World Mental Health surveys, lifetime SAD is comorbid with as many as 13 other disorders (Silove et al., 2015). In one such study, 79% of children with SAD had at least one comorbid disorder, and 54% had two or more comorbid disorders (Kendall et al., 2001).

In general, SAD is frequently comorbid with other anxiety disorders (Shear et al., 2006). Specifically, SAD is comorbid with generalized anxiety disorder (GAD) (17% to 25%), social phobia (SP) (33.4%), and obsessive-compulsive disorder (OCD) (4.3% to 17%) (Mroczkowski et al., 2011; Shear et al., 2006). These findings are not surprising given that GAD and OCD are both associated with worry and somatic complaints (Eisen et al., 2011).

For example, GAD co-occurs with SAD approximately one-third of the time (Kendall et al., 2001). Obsessive-compulsive disorder is comorbid with SAD as much as 24–34% of the time (Geller, Biederman, Griffin, Jones, & Lefkowitz, 1996). Comorbid OCD and SAD are associated with an earlier onset of panic disorder (Goodwin, Lipsitz, Chapman, Manuzza, & Fyer, 2001).

High rates of comorbidity also occur between SAD and panic disorder (PD), especially at the symptom level. For example, comorbid separation anxiety co-occurred in youths with panic attacks as much as 73% of the time (Masi, Favilla, Mucci, & Millepiedi, 2000). The link between childhood separation anxiety and adult panic has been well documented (Battaglia et al., 2016; Lewinsohn, Holm-DeNoma, Small, Seeley, & Joiner, 2008). However, studies have also failed to support this relationship (e.g., Aschenbrand, Kendall, & Webb, 2003). Thus, additional research is necessary to clarify the precise relationship between child-hood SAD and adult PD.

In addition to co-occurring with other anxiety disorders, SAD is also comorbid with major depressive disorder (MDD). For example, approximately 26.3% to 37% of youths with SAD also met diagnostic criteria for MDD (Burstein et al., 2012; Shear et al., 2006). Co-occurring depression may emerge when SAD becomes debilitating and/or interferes with at least two domains of functioning (e.g., school, social, or family) (Cummings, Caporino, & Kendall, 2014).

Separation anxiety disorder also co-occurs with externalizing disorders (Hammerness et al., 2008). For example, SAD co-occurs with attention-deficit hyperactivity disorder (ADHD) (21.3% to 22.0%), oppositional-defiant disorder (ODD) (12.0% to 19.6%), and conduct disorder (CD) (21.4%) (Shear et al., 2006; Verduin & Kendall, 2003).

Finally, SAD also co-occurs with various behavioral problems such as temper tantrums, screaming, school refusal, and homesickness, especially when separation is inevitable (Eisen & Schaefer, 2005). Regarding adults, 88.5% of individuals with ASAD often have at least one other co-occurring psychiatric disorder (Shear et al., 2006).

Developmental Course

The onset of separation anxiety symptoms can present as acute or insidious (Eisen et al., 2011). Initially, separation anxiety may occur in anticipation of harm to the child and/or attachment figure, life stressors, or relatively innocuous events such as a nightmare or stomachache. Maintenance of separation-related symptoms often stems from parental accommodation (Eisen, Raleigh, & Neuhoff, 2008).

For example, when a parent allows a child to miss school or an extracurricular activity, presumably for "feeling sick," such avoidance strengthens the child's separation-related fears. Parental accommodation may also occur in the form of overprotection (Eisen & Engler, 2006). (See section "Etiology and Maintenance of SAD" for a more in-depth discussion.)

Separation anxiety symptoms can be chronic in nature, but generally undergo alternating periods of waxing and waning (Eisen, Pincus, Hashim, Cheron, & Santucci, 2008). Younger children (ages 5–8) report a higher frequency of night-mares and distress upon separation from caregivers as compared to older children (ages 9–12). Adolescents endorse a higher frequency of somatic symptoms as compared to younger children (Allen et al., 2010). Overall, most youth experiencing SAD recover from symptoms over time. However, separation-anxious symptoms may linger into adulthood or serve as a general risk factor for the development of co-occurring anxiety, panic, or depressive symptoms (Brückl et al., 2007; Lewinsohn et al., 2008).

Etiology and Maintenance of Separation Anxiety Disorder

Anxiety disorders are developed and maintained due to an interplay of genetic, cognitive, and environmental factors (Battaglia et al., 2016; Eisen et al., 2008; Feigon, Waldman, Levy, & Hay, 1997; Goldsmith & Gottesman, 1981). Twin and mother–child studies have examined biological factors associated with the development of SAD. The majority of evidence supports the hypothesis that child anxiety is accounted for by genetic as well as shared and non-shared environmental factors (Silberg et al., 2015).

Biological Vulnerability

Twin studies suggest that genetics accounts for about 30% of the variance, shared environments account for 20% of the variance (i.e., those factors within the family system and neighborhood), and non-shared/ individual environmental factors account for the remaining 50% of the variance in childhood anxiety (Drake & Ginsburg, 2012).

Silberg and colleagues (2015) examined the shared genetic and environmental influences on early temperament and psychopathology in Hispanic twins. In general, findings revealed additive genetic factors accounted for 28% of the variance in SAD. More specifically, a single genetic pattern was associated with a difficult temperament, SAD, ODD, and ADHD. In addition, behavioral inhibition demonstrated to be a risk factor for SAD and ODD through both genetic and environmental pathways. These findings support the hypothesis that ODD and

SAD may stem from the shared transdiagnostic mechanism of emotion regulation (Cunningham & Ollendick, 2010).

Neurobiological Dimensions

The RDoC (Insel et al., 2010) is an initiative developed by the NIMH. In general, the RDoC aims to construct a scientific understanding of psychopathology in terms of individual differences in well-defined constructs related to neurobiology and behavior across the life span. More specifically, the RDoC aims to link variations in mental health to variations in broad domains of functioning that cut across disorders as defined within current nosological systems (e.g., *DSM-5* and *ICD-10*) (De Los Reyes & Aldao, 2015). Given the promising utility of RDoC, we discuss its potential application to the development and maintenance of SAD.

Presently, RDoC describes five neurobiological dimensions that relate to symptom expressions of one or more existing mental disorder categories. These domains include negative valence systems, positive valence systems, cognition systems, social processes systems, and arousal/ regulatory systems. The neurobehavioral dimension that has most relevance and applicability for understanding internalizing disorders in general, and SAD in particular, is the negative valence systems (Moser, Durbin, Patrick, & Schmidt, 2015).

The negative valence systems includes constructs responsible for reactions to aversive situations or context, such as fear, anxiety, and loss. Within the negative valence systems domain, defensive reactivity is a construct that describes the emotional state of fear as it relates to reactivity of the brain's defensive motivational system, which functions to prime action in the presence of threat cues (Moser et al., 2015). Defensive reactivity has been assessed using constructs such as negative emotionality (i.e., assessing the distress-proneness related to fears) and behavioral inhibition.

Regarding SAD, defensive reactivity occurs in the distress and emotional state of fear as expressed by youth during separation from caregivers. What underlies separation anxiety is a fear of potential harm to the self (e.g., abandoned, kidnapped) and/or harm to the caregiver (e.g., accident, illness). As the intensity and frequency of separation-related worries spiral, youths engage in avoidance and/or safety-seeking behaviors (Eisen et al., 2008). The RDoC model highlights the degree to which a child's type of defensive reactivity can serve as a maintenance process in SAD. Behavioral and neuropsychological assessments of defensive reactivity have the potential to provide greater diagnostic clarity, thus better informing our intervention approaches (Weinberg et al., 2016).

Transdiagnostic Mechanisms

In line with the RDoC initiative, a transdiagnostic framework provides a similar approach to assessment and translational research for child psychopathology. A transdiagnostic framework has three defining elements: first, an examination of the similarities and differences among distinct psychological disorders; second, a utilization of basic biopsychosocial mechanisms for comparing and contrasting disorders; third, assessment and treatment approaches targeting the core and underlying mechanisms of disorders. Overall, these three elements, singly or in combination, generating the most efficient and efficacious interventions (Chu, Temkin, & Toffey, 2016).

A recent review of transdiagnostic mechanisms in youth described five processes with growing support in the field. These processes are stress and coping, cognitive biases, behavioral avoidance, rumination, and peer relations (Chu et al., 2016). Each of these mechanisms is outlined within the five domains of RDoC. Given the remarkable overlap between the two frameworks, future studies should explore the feasibility of integrating and/or merging the two approaches for advancing the assessment and treatment of psychological disorders in youth.

While studies have shown genetic, biological, and/or temperamental vulnerability associated with SAD, environmental factors appear to have a strong influence as well (Vasey & Dadds, 2001). In fact, environmental factors, especially related to one's family, may influence SAD more than any other anxiety-related disorder in childhood.

Parental Attachment

Numerous studies support the relationship between parental anxious attachment style and childhood psychopathology, including anxiety, depression, and externalizing problems (Westen, Nakash, Thomas, & Bradley, 2006). Low parental warmth and emotional neglect appear to be antecedents to childhood anxiety.

For example, Eapen et al. (2014) examined the association between early maternal attachment experiences, SAD, and oxytocin plasma levels during pregnancy and the early postpartum period. On the one hand, under the best of circumstances, a mother's secure attachment style with low separation anxiety elicits oxytocin release that assists in stress regulation and promotion of positive attachment patterns and parent–child bonding.

The results of the study, however, demonstrated that maternal anxious attachment style coupled with high separation anxiety led to maternal rumination, distress, and anxiety. Future longitudinal studies need to explore how oxytocin effects parental attachment from pregnancy through early childhood.

Parental Accommodation and Intrusiveness

Parental accommodation and intrusiveness are considered risk factors for the development and/or maintenance of childhood SAD (Eisen & Schaefer, 2005; Wood, 2006). Parental accommodation is a form of overprotection in which parents may restrict a child's participation in potentially anxiety-provoking situations. Examples include, assisting the child to avoid feared stimuli, changing family routine or activities to minimize demands, and giving excessive reassurance to allay worries (Lebowitz, Panza, Su, & Bloch, 2012; Thompson-Hollands, Kerns, Pincus, & Comer, 2014). Separation-related behaviors that prompt the likelihood of parental accommodation include frequent check-ins, school refusal in order to stay near the caregiver, and co-sleeping. Ultimately, these behaviors affect family routine and activities, leading to impairment in parental work, romantic, and social lives, as well as parental time spent with other siblings.

While the parents of anxious youth believe that accommodating behaviors results in a decrease of distress for the child, in the long term, these behaviors often maintain and/or intensify a child's avoidance through negative reinforcement (Ginsburg, Siqueland, Masia-Warner, & Hedtke, 2004). When excessive restrictions occur, a child's SAD may adversely affect school performance, peer relations/ extracurricular activities, and family life (see Eisen & Engler, 2006; Eisen & Schaefer, 2005).

There is increasing evidence for parental accommodation as a phenomenon that occurs with many anxiety-related and other childhood disorders (Cooper-Vince, Pincus, & Comer, 2014). For example, Lebowitz et al. (2013) examined parental accommodation and its relation with childhood anxiety disorders. Results revealed that GAD and SAD had the strongest associations within the scope of parental accommodation interference with family functioning.

Parental intrusiveness, on the other hand, involves a parent's disproportionate regulation of a child's emotions, behaviors, and autonomous decision-making. Examples include excessive parental participation and control in a child's daily activities, such as morning and bedtime routines. Doing so hinders a child's independence and mastery of developmentally appropriate behaviors and activities (Wood, 2006).

Like parental accommodation, parental intrusiveness is intended to reduce childhood distress. However, it encourages dependence, reduced confidence, and a lack of mastery of everyday activities in all domains of a child's life (Eisen & Schaefer, 2005). Thus, it is imperative for clinicians to assess parenting behaviors when formulating treatment plans for youths with separation anxiety. Parental accommodation and/or intrusiveness can easily fuel a child's fear of rejection and separation (Schimmenti & Bifulco, 2015).

It is evident that numerous, well-established etiological and maintenance factors are associated with SAD. Eisen and colleagues (Eisen & Engler, 2006; Eisen et al., 2008) developed a framework for the assessment and treatment of childhood anxiety disorders in general and SAD in particular. Their conceptual model highlights the relationship between core symptom dimensions and specific anxiety disorders, in which seeking safety is the primary mechanism in the development and maintenance of the disorder As such, we provide an overview of this model in the subsequent section.

A Dimensional Conceptualization of Separation Anxiety Disorder

A number of symptom dimensions are associated with anxiety disorders in children and adolescents. These include a fear of physical illness (FPI), worry about calamitous events (WCE), phobic avoidance (PA), and safety-seeking behaviors (SSB) (see Eisen & Schaefer, 2005; Eisen et al., 2008).

Somatic complaints are common in youth with anxiety disorders and typically occur in anticipation of anxiety-provoking situations (Crawley et al., 2014). Most youth can handle the occasional discomfort associated with a headache or stomachache. Rather, the fear of serious consequences emanating from these uncomfortable physical sensations is most debilitating. Youth are often terrified of choking, vomiting, or catching a serious illness. This FPI is common across anxiety disorders, most notably panic disorder (Hajinlian et al., 2003).

Similarly, worry is also ubiquitous in clinical and normative samples. Approximately 60% of typically developing youths report experiencing some separation-related worries about harm to self or others (Muris, Merckelbach, Meesters, & van den Brand, 2002). Common childhood worries include personal health and safety, family, friends, school, and athletic performance. The content of these worries tends to highlight the possibility of calamitous events (WCE) to self, others, and/or the environment (e.g., being kidnapped, natural disasters, terrorism). As the intensity and frequency of worry increases, anxious youth tend to engage in PA and/or SSB via safety signals (Eisen et al., 2008). Safety signals are persons, places, objects, and actions that assist youth to feel more secure in anticipation of and/or during anxiety-provoking events (Eisen & Schaefer, 2005; Eisen et al., 2008). While safety signals may help a child or adolescent be more functional, they may limit one's ability to develop coping skills (see Eisen & Schaefer, 2005) and can interfere with habituation during in vivo exposures (Barlow, 2002).

Seeking Safety in SAD

A child with excessive fears of being alone (FBA) is likely to avoid places in the home environment in which a caregiver is not present. The child may refuse to be alone somewhere in the house (e.g., bedroom, finished basement, bathroom) and/or sleep alone at night. A child with a fear of being abandoned (FAB) may refuse to attend school or other settings in which the caregiver or other safe person is not proximal (Krajniak, Anderson, & Eisen, 2016). A fear of abandonment is the most predictive symptom dimension of SAD and is associated with serious consequences such as school refusal and social isolation (Eisen et al., 2011).

Seeking safety is likely to occur when exposure to separation-related events is inevitable. For example, a child with FAB may agree to stay in a situation that requires separation from the caregiver (e.g., school, extracurricular activities, play dates) if a safe person is accessible. The role of this safety signal may be fulfilled by an individual known to the child (e.g., caregiver, nurse, teacher) that could help prevent a personal disaster. Similarly, a child who fears being alone somewhere (due to FPI) will seek safety by shadowing an adult that agrees to stay close by, just in case physical illness becomes a reality.

SAD Subtypes

In order to further individualize the symptom dimensions for case conceptualization and treatment planning, Eisen and colleagues developed four subtypes of separation anxiety: "Follower," "Visitor," "Misfortune Teller," and "Timekeeper" (see Eisen & Engler, 2006).

The first two subtypes capture the FBA dimension of separation anxiety. The Follower refers to a child with a fear of being alone during the day, typically somewhere in the house. In this case, the child's fear is maintained by FPI. If avoidance is not possible, the child will seek safety in the form of a "medical monitor" (i.e., someone who is designated to stay proximal in case illness occurs). The Visitor is afraid to be alone at night (i.e., sleeping in their bed independently). This fear is maintained by WCE. The primary calamitous worry is an intruder breaking into the house during the night. If the child is unable to avoid sleeping in their bed alone, the safety-seeking behavior is the designation of a "security guard" (i.e., someone who remains vigilant throughout the night for signs of intruders).

The third and fourth subtypes capture the FAB dimension of separation anxiety. In the case of the Misfortune Teller, a child's FAB is maintained by FPI. In order to reduce the physical distress, the safety-seeking behavior is the designation of an adult to fulfill the role of a "lifeguard" (i.e., someone who can remain proximal in the case of illness occurring). Finally, the Timekeeper's FAB is maintained by WCE. The Timekeeper's key worry involves the primary caregiver's whereabouts and safety. The safety-seeking behavior that is triggered is a "parental bodyguard." The child must be informed of the caregiver's whereabouts at all times and/or an agreement for the caregiver to remain proximal.

This dimensional model allows for the facilitation of individualized assessment, conceptualization, and treatment planning for separation anxiety and related anxiety disorders. Clinicians can utilize the framework to better understand and treat various clinical presentations of anxiety disorders such as SAD, PD, GAD, OCD, and posttraumatic disorder (PTSD). More importantly, the heart of the model addresses subthreshold symptoms with significant functional impairment. Once core symptom dimensions and SSB are identified, the goal is to eliminate maladaptive behaviors and replace them with evidence-based coping strategies. (For a full explication of the model and step-by-step treatment guidelines, please see Eisen, 2008; Eisen & Engler, 2006; Eisen et al., 2008; Eisen & Schaefer, 2005.)

Relationship to Specific Disorders

For purposes of differential diagnosis, we discuss how our dimensional model clarifies distinctions between SAD and other anxiety disorders in children and adolescents.

SAD vs. PD

While panic attacks have been observed in children, there is skepticism as to whether their experience resembles PD as observed in adolescents and adults (Kearney & Silverman, 1992; Kossowsky et al., 2013). For example, a child with SAD may experience a panic attack that is maintained by FPI. The intensity of fear and/or physical discomfort may also approximate adult panic (see Eisen & Schaefer, 2005). However, panic in children is limited to one or two somatic complaints. In addition, characteristic cognitive symptoms such as "losing control" or "going crazy" in adult PD may not yet be evident in children with panic (Nelles & Barlow, 1988). From a developmental perspective, this finding is not surprising. Most importantly, panic observed in children is likely triggered by situational cues rather than being unexpected or "out of the blue."

Although both panic and separation anxiety may be maintained by FPI, PD is associated with heightened anxiety sensitivity (Kearney, Sims, Pursell, & Tillotson, 2003). Children with elevated anxiety sensitivity are not only distressed by bodily sensations, but more importantly, worried about the consequences of these physical sensations. For this reason, the Child Anxiety Sensitivity Index (CASI) (Silverman, Fleisig, Rabian, & Peterson, 1991) can be a useful tool for distinguishing PD from more general somatic complaints.

Both SAD and PD may be maintained by FPI and/or WCE (Eisen et al., 2008). However, phobic avoidance for SAD often revolves around fears of being alone and/or being abandoned. Panic disorder, however, more likely resembles abandonment fears (i.e., afraid to venture away from home) unless, of course, nocturnal panic attacks are present. The most critical distinction is that SAD is largely about having access to safe persons, whereas youths with PD are likely to have broader safety needs that encompass persons, places, objects, or actions (see Eisen & Schaefer, 2005, for a full explication).

SAD vs. PTSD

Due to the overlap of symptoms, trauma may be mistaken for separation-related fears that are irrational or stem from insecure parent–child attachments. For instance, children with both SAD and PTSD frequently experience anxiety in the form of excessive worry, somatic complaints, and/or panic attacks, fears of being alone, especially sleeping alone, social withdrawal, and school refusal behavior (e.g., Yule, 2001).

As a first step, it is essential to determine whether a child or close family member actually has experienced or is continuing to experience trauma-related exposure (Eisen et al., 2008). Sometimes the trauma may remain unknown, for instance, if a child is fearful of potential repercussions stemming from sexual abuse. Most importantly, a child or adolescent must respond with intense fear, helplessness, or horror (APA, 2000). Despite these distinctions, differential diagnosis may still be challenging, given that there are often multiple forms of exposure intermixed with features of PTSD, SAD, and/or depression (see Eisen et al., 2008). Therefore, it is important to understand the signs and symptoms that are unique to PTSD.

Unlike SAD, trauma-related symptoms are more likely to be varied, severe, and frequently result in serious disruptions to daily functioning. In addition, trauma is more likely to be associated with self-destructive behaviors (Johnson, 1998; Kiser, Heston, Millsap, & Pruitt, 1991) sexual problems (Dubowitz, Black, Harrington, & Verschoore, 1993), confusion, impaired sense of trust, disruptive relationships, substance abuse, and suicidal behavior (Tufts New England Medical Center, Division of Child and Adolescent Psychiatry, 1984).

Children with PTSD may not experience FPI, but are more likely to have strong levels of generalized physiological arousal and be hypervigilant to associations of the traumatic event. In addition, phobic avoidance is likely to be strong and more generalized than one would expect from SAD. Worry about calamitous events may also be severe and cued by associations. Finally, seeking safety for youths with PTSD is common and occurs in the form of safe persons and places.

GAD, OCD, and SAD

Symptoms of generalized worry are often excessive and varied in domains of content, challenging to control, and associated with a presence of somatic complaints (Eisen et al., 2008). Obsessions, on the other hand, are intrusive and bizarre. For example, the content of obsessions may include thoughts or images of having serious diseases or getting rabies from accidentally stepping in animal feces. Youth with OCD will go to great lengths to avoid these distressing thoughts or images. For example, a child with a fear of getting rabies from accidentally stepping on animal feces might repeatedly check the soles of their shoes, leave their shoes outside of their home, refuse to play outside, and/or have ritualized bathing methods when showering and washing hands.

Generalized worries and obsessions tend to follow a developmental trajectory. For instance, worrisome thoughts do not become prominent until at least eight years of age (Muris et al., 2002). As age increases, worry typically becomes more pervasive and severe and is often accompanied by depression during adolescence. Typical age of onset for GAD is around 10–14 years (Albano, Chorpita, & Barlow, 1996). Obsessive thoughts are rare in young children, and when OCD develops early (5–8), rituals typically develop in response to feeling uncomfortable or from overwhelming urges (Piacentini & Graae, 1997).

Seeking safety in OCD is frequent and intense and is triggered by obsessive thoughts, images, or impulses. Given the more innocuous nature of GAD-related worries, youths typically only seek safety (e.g., needing excessive reassurance from parents) at the height of their worries. Although separation anxiety-related worries can be obsessive, youths with SAD more typically seek safety in anticipation of being alone and/or abandoned. Thinking about, worry, and/or obsessing about these situations triggers WCE and FPI.

Assessment Approaches for Separation Anxiety Disorder

Separation anxiety disorder requires a comprehensive and ongoing assessment. The assessment process begins with an initial consultation and intake, and should be continued throughout the course of treatment. The clinical presentation and formulation of SAD varies greatly on an individual basis. Factors that may differ from child to child include functional impairment, comorbidity, symptom presentation, and maintaining factors.

When assessing SAD, it is essential to obtain a detailed psychosocial history, especially developmental and family histories. Semi-structured clinical interviews have tremendous utility for evaluating SAD and related internalizing and externalizing disorders. Empirically supported measures should be administered to assess symptom dimensions as reported by multiple informants (i.e., self, parent, and teacher), since discrepancies among informants is the norm (Evans, Thirlwall, Cooper, & Creswell, 2017; Villabø, Oerbeck, Skirbekk, Hansen, & Kristensen, 2016).

Consultation with Caregivers

The initial step in the assessment of SAD begins with an informal information-gathering interview with the child's primary caregivers. Detailed questions related to a child's history in areas of developmental, family, academic, social, and emotional functioning should then be addressed. The overarching goal is to formulate a treatment plan that identifies core symptom dimensions, SSB, and maintaining factors (Eisen & Schaefer, 2005).

Diagnostic Interviews

Structured clinical interviews provide mental health professionals with a framework for the sequence of questioning about the onset, severity, and frequency of symptoms, as well as the functional impairment associated with psychological disorders. The Anxiety Disorders Interview Schedule for DSM-IV, Child and Parent Version (ADIS-IV-C/P) (Silverman & Albano, 1996) is the most commonly used semi-structured clinical interview to assess SAD and related internalizing and externalizing disorders. The ADIS-IV-C/P has excellent psychometric properties for diagnosing anxiety disorders in youth (Silverman Saavedra & Pina, 2001; Wood, Pacentini, Bergman, McCracken, & Barrios, 2002). The ADIS-IV-C/P provides separate child and parent interviews.

The Schedule for Affective Disorders and Schizophrenia for School Age Children, Present and Lifetime Version (K-SADS-PL) (Kaufman et al., 1997) and the Diagnostic Interview Schedule for Children, Version IV (DISC-IV) (Shaffer, Fisher, Lucas, Dulcan, & Schwab-Stone, 2000) are often used to assess child psychopathology more broadly. Both the K-SADS-PL and the DISC-IV are semi-structured interviews used to assess the nature of past and current psychological disorders in accordance with *DSM-IV* criteria. The psychometric properties of the K-SADS-PL have supported the convergent validity of commonly co-occurring psychological disorders such as anxiety, depression, and ADHD (Ambrosini, 2000; Kaufman et al., 1997). Most recently, evidence supports the convergent and divergent validity of K-SADS-PL for the diagnoses of SAD, social and specific phobias (Villabø et al., 2016).

Child Self-Report Measures

Child self-report measures are an important part of the assessment process. These measures afford children and adolescents an opportunity to endorse symptoms in a written and independent format. Self-report measures are useful for obtaining information about separation anxiety and related problems and should be part of a comprehensive assessment. In the following section, we discuss the key child self-report measures utilized in the assessment of separation anxiety and related problems.

Separation Anxiety Assessment Scale – Child and Parent Versions (SAAS-C/P) (Eisen, Hahn, Hajinlian, Winder, & Pincus, 2005; Eisen & Schaefer, 2005) is a 34-item self-report measure that assesses specific dimensions of childhood separation anxiety and related symptoms. The SAAS-C provides a conceptual framework that permits individualized case formulation and treatment planning for SAD (see Eisen & Schaefer, 2005, to obtain a copy of the scale and permission for use).

The SAAS-C captures the four key symptom dimensions of our conceptual model. These include FBA (e.g., "How often are you afraid to sleep alone at night?"), FAB (e.g., "How often are you afraid to go on a play date at a new friend's house?"), FPI (e.g., "How often are you afraid to go to school if you feel sick?"), and WCE (e.g., "How often do you worry that bad things will happen to you?"). The SAAS-C also contains a nine-item safety signal index that assesses a child's dependence on safe persons, places, objects, and actions (e.g., "How often do you need your mom or dad to stay with you when you go on a play date?"). Evidence supports the psychometric properties of the SAAS-C/P, including its factor structure, validity, reliability, and clinical utility. (Hahn, Hajinlian, Eisen, Winder, & Pincus, 2003; Hajinlian et al., 2003; Hajinlian, Mesnik, & Eisen, 2005).

The Child Behavior Checklist (CBCL) (Achenbach, 1991), is a 118-item, self-report measure used to assess childhood anxiety-related symptoms, as well as broad behaviors, problems, and competencies for youth between the ages of 6 and 18. The CBCL includes internalizing and externalizing factors as well as eight subscales. Two of the eight subscales were designed to target anxiety problems (i.e., the Internalizing syndrome scale [CBCL-INT] and the Anxious/Depressed [CBCL-A/D] scale). Both scales are empirically supported, and have solid psychometric properties (Achenbach, 1991).

The Multidimensional Anxiety Scale for Children (MASC) (March, Parker, Sullivan, Stallings, & Conners, 1997) is a 39-item, four-factor, self-report measure developed to assess a broad range of anxiety symptoms. The four factors are physical symptoms, harm avoidance, social anxiety, and separation anxiety/ panic. In addition, the MASC includes the following subscales: Tense/Restless, Somatic/Autonomic, Total Physical Symptoms, Perfectionism, Anxious Coping, Total Harm Avoidance, Humiliation/Rejection, Performance Fears, Total Social Anxiety, Separation/ Panic, and Total MASC score. The MASC has excellent psychometric properties (March et al., 1997).

The Spence Children's Anxiety Scale (SCAS) (Spence, 1997) is a 44-item, six-subscale, structured, self-report measure designed to assess symptoms of childhood anxiety as reported by both parent and child. The SCAS measures a broad range of anxiety symptoms, provides information about childhood anxiety and related disorders, and includes a specific subscale to assess separation anxiety symptoms. The SCAS subscales include separation anxiety, social anxiety, panic/agoraphobia, generalized anxiety, obsessions/compulsions, and physical injury fears. The six-subscale structure of the SCAS has been confirmed by a factor analysis (Spence, 1997). The SCAS possesses excellent psychometric properties (Muris, Merckelbach, Ollendick, King, & Bogie, 2002; Muris, Schmidt, & Merckelbach, 2000).

The Screen for Child Anxiety Related Emotional Disorders-Revised (SCARED-R) (Muris, Merckelbach, Schmidt, & Tierney, 1999) is a 66-item, self-report measure to assess child anxiety. The items on the SCARED-R assess for *DSM-IV* anxiety disorders in youth. Eight-items specifically assess for SAD. The SCARED-R possesses solid psychometric properties for most scales (Muris, Dreessen, Bogels, Weckx, & van Melick, 2004).

The Revised Children's Manifest Anxiety Scale (RCMAS) (Reynolds & Richman, 1978) is a 37-item self-report scale that possesses strong psychometric properties, and contains four subscales: Worry/Oversensitivity, Physiological, Concentration, and Lying. The RCMAS includes a number of separation-related items such as "It is hard for me to get to sleep at night," "Often I feel sick to my stomach," "I wake up scared some of the time," "I worry when I go to bed at night," and "I often worry about something bad happening to me." Elevated scores on the RCMAS are useful for identifying a differential diagnosis between GAD and SAD (Eisen et al., 2008).

The Child Anxiety Sensitivity Index (CASI) (Silverman et al., 1991) is an 18-item self-report measure that assesses how aversive children view their physical sensations. Sample items include, "It scares me when I feel like I'm going to throw up." The CASI has excellent psychometric properties (e.g., Rabian, Peterson, Richters, & Jensen, 1993). Elevated scores are predictive of PD (Kearney et al., 1997).

The State-Trait Anxiety Inventory for Children (STAIC) (Spielberger, 1973) consists of two 20-item scales that measure state (variable) and trait (stable or chronic) anxiety. Both scales possess strong psychometric properties (Spielberger, 1973) and contain relevant items for assessing separation anxiety, for example, "I worry about school" and "I worry about my parents." Similar to the RCMAS, the STAIC's elevated trait anxiety scores can be useful for distinguishing SAD from GAD (Eisen et al., 2011).

Parent Report Measures

Given the potential differences and contradictions between child and parent reports, it is important to administer measures from both perspectives. To date, the majority of separation-related measures previously discussed also include complementary parent versions. Other notable parent report measures for assessing child separation anxiety and related problems include the Separation Anxiety Avoidance Inventory – Parent Version (SAAI–P) (Schneider & In-Albon, 2005) and the Revised Child Anxiety and Depression Scale – Parent Version (RCADS-P) (Ebesutani et al., 2010).

Special Populations

Recently, an interest in separation anxiety in early-aged children and adults has emerged (Ehrenreich, Santucci, & Weiner, 2008). Early identification and treatment of early-aged children is critical given the link between untreated separation anxiety and the development of later psychopathology (e.g., Aschenbrand, Kendall, & Webb, 2003).

Assessment of Preschool-Aged Children

The Preschool Age Psychiatric Assessment (PAPA) (Egger et al., 2006) is a clinical interview designed to assess childhood psychopathology as well as risk and protective factors in early-aged children between the ages of two and five. Evidence supports the psychometric properties of the PAPA (Egger et al., 2006).

Recently, Carpenter et al. (2016) investigated the use of PAPA with the application of a machine-learning tool to better identify children at risk for an anxiety disorder. Results revealed an accuracy rate of more than 96% for the identification of GAD and SAD. The PAPA is a promising instrument to identify at-risk preschool-aged children.

Assessment of Adults

A few measures are available for assessing adult separation anxiety, now that *DSM-5* includes adult SAD. These measures include the Separation Anxiety Symptom Inventory (SASI) (Silove et al., 1993), the Adult Separation Anxiety Structured

Interview (ASA-SI) (Manicavasagar, Silove, & Curtis, 1997), the Adult Separation Anxiety-27 (ASA-27) (Manicavasagar, Silove, Wagner, & Drobny, 2003), and the Screen for Adult Anxiety Related Disorders (SCAARED) (Angulo et al., 2017). The SCAARED is the newest scale for the assessment of anxiety disorders in adults that is based on *DSM-5* criteria and includes a separation anxiety factor. Future research is necessary to examine the nature and treatment of SAD in adults and its relation to early-aged anxiety in children.

Evidence-Based Treatment Methods for SAD

Cognitive behavioral therapy (CBT) is considered a gold standard and an empirically supported treatment method for childhood anxiety (Hollon & Beck, 2013; Ishikawa, Okajima, Matsuoka, & Sakano, 2007). Individual and group formats are effective forms of therapy in this population (Ishikawa et al., 2007). Specialized treatment programs for youths with separation anxiety are beginning to emerge. These innovative programs include parent training/ family-based approaches.

Parent Training

Eisen, Raleigh, and Neuhoff (2008) developed a 10-week integrated cognitive-behavioral parent-training program for children and adolescents with SAD. The program guided parents in the implementation of cognitive-behavioral strategies with their children.

During the first two sessions, parents were educated about the characteristics of separation anxiety in children. The third through sixth sessions encompassed skill-building exercises to help parents implement progressive muscle relaxation cognitive therapy techniques with their children. Sessions seven through nine were devoted to practicing exposure-based techniques. The final session emphasized relapse prevention exercises and the need for consistency and continual practice. Weekly homework assignments helped reinforce information addressed in sessions.

The parent-training program initially examined six families of parents and children 7–10 years of age using a multiple baseline design. Results revealed that parent training yielded impressive improvements in parenting abilities, parental anxiety and stress, and perceived severity of a child's separation anxiety symptoms. These parental changes led to significant alleviation of children's SAD symptoms, including reductions in somatic complaints. In fact, five of the six child participants did not meet criteria for SAD following the program, which was maintained at six-month follow-up (Eisen, Raleigh, et al., 2008).

Camp CARD (Center for Anxiety and Related Disorders), an intensive, one-week group cognitive-behavioral intervention, was developed for children aged 8–11 with a principal diagnosis of SAD (Santucci, Ehrenreich, Trosper, Bennett, &

Pincus, 2009). This one-week program was examined in a pilot study with five children.

Camp CARD's approach utilized evidence-based CBT methods (e.g., psycho-education, identification and management of somatic symptoms, cognitive restructuring, problem-solving skills, and relapse prevention), in addition to incorporating separation and social context components that are frequently avoided among children with SAD.

Throughout the program, parental presence gradually lessened, with the final session implemented in a sleepover format. Results revealed that all five participants' separation anxiety symptoms diminished significantly at the conclusion of treatment. None of the participants met SAD criteria, which was maintained at two-month follow-up.

Schneider, Blatter-Meunier, Herren, and Adornetto (2011) developed a CBT approach designed for children and adolescents with SAD. Their treatment method included sixteen 50-minute sessions of separation anxiety-specific interventions such as parent training and classical cognitive-behavioral methodologies over 12 weeks.

The first four weeks consisted of psycho-education with the child independently, followed by four weekly individual sessions with the parent. The next eight weeks consisted of weekly sessions, each split into one part with the parent and child and the second with the parent only.

Results of a random assignment efficacy study of 43 children, aged five to seven with a primary SAD diagnosis revealed promising results. Approximately 76% of the children in the SAD treatment group no longer met the *DSM-IV* criteria at follow-up, compared to about 14% in the wait-list control group (Schneider et al., 2011).

Family-Based Treatment

Family-based treatment (FBT) emphasizes the importance of family interactions in the onset and maintenance of anxiety symptoms (Krajniak, Anderson, & Eisen, 2016). Parent–child interaction therapy (PCIT) is one such treatment, and attempts to reshape problematic behaviors by modifying interactions between the parent–child dyad, promoting secure attachment, and improving family function. During structured play therapy sessions, parents receive training that emphasizes positive attention, problem-solving, and effective communication. The emphasis is on reshaping parent behaviors rather than engaging the child.

Pincus, Eyberg, and Choate (2005) modified their PCIT protocol for conduct-disordered youth and applied to 10 children, aged four to eight with primary diagnoses of SAD. Although preliminary, the results were quite promising. Please see Eisen et al. (2008) for a full explication of using PCIT to treat youths with separation anxiety and related externalizing problems.

Attachment-based family therapy (ABFT) encourages child autonomy and separation from parents by changing parenting behaviors, such as overprotection and communication style between parent and child (Siqueland, Rynn, & Diamond, 2005).

In a preliminary investigation, Siqueland et al. (2005) compared ABFT to traditional CBT for adolescents aged 12–17 years. Eleven adolescents with primary diagnoses of GAD, SAD, or social phobia and their families were randomly assigned to either ABFT/CBT or CBT treatment. The CBT condition consisted of relaxation training, cognitive restructuring, and exposure-based assignments. The first eight sessions of the ABFT/CBT condition involved traditional CBT components. The remaining eight sessions revolved around a family's beliefs, behaviors, and interactions, and the development of a flexible attachment style between parent and child.

Treatment promoted open communication in families and facilitated opportunities for the adolescents to express themselves and develop strong self-identities. At post-treatment, four of six adolescents in the CBT group no longer met diagnostic criteria for an anxiety disorder compared to two of five in the ABFT/CBT group. At six-month follow-up, none of the participants in the CBT group met diagnostic criteria compared to four of five in the ABFT/CBT group. Despite the limited sample size, ABFT shows promise and warrants further investigation as a potential treatment for separation-anxious youth.

References

Achenbach, T. M. (1991). *Manual for the Child Behavior Checklist/4–18 and 1991 Profile.* Burlington, VT: University of Vermont Department of Psychiatry.

Albano, A. M., Chorpita, B. F., & Barlow, D. H. (1996). Childhood anxiety disorders. In E. J. Mash & R. A. Barkley (eds.), *Child Psychopathology* (pp. 196–241). New York, NY: Guilford Press.

Allen, J. L., Lavallee, K. L., Herren, C., Ruhe, K., & Schneider, S. (2010). *DSM-IV* criteria for childhood separation anxiety disorder: Informant, age and sex differences. *Journal of Anxiety Disorders, 24,* 946–952.

Ambrosini, P. J. (2000). Historical development and present status of the Schedule for Affective Disorders and Schizophrenia for School-Age Children (K-SADS). *Journal of the American Academy of Child and Adolescent Psychiatry, 39,* 49–58.

American Psychiatric Association. (2013). *Diagnostic and Statistical Manual of Mental Disorders* (5th edn). Arlington, VA: American Psychiatric Publishing.

American Psychiatric Association. (2000). *Diagnostic and Statistical Manual of Mental Disorders* (4th edn, text rev.). Washington, DC: American Psychiatric Association.

Angulo, M., Rooks, B. T., Gill, M. K., Goldstein, T. R., Sakolsky, D. J., Goldstein, B. I., Monk, K. R., Hickey, M. B., Diler, R. S., Hafeman, D. M., Merranko, J. A., Axelson, D., & Birmaher, B. B. (2017). Psychometrics for the screen for adult anxiety-related disorders (SCAARED): A new scale for the assessment of *DSM-5* anxiety disorders. *Psychiatry Research, 253,* 84–90.

Aschenbrand, S. G., Kendall, P. C., & Webb, A. (2003). Is childhood separation anxiety disorder a predictor of adult panic disorder and agoraphobia? A seven-year longitudinal study. *Journal of the American Academy of Child & Adolescent Psychiatry, 42*(12), 1478–1485.

Barlow, D. H. (2002). *Anxiety and Its Disorders: The Nature and Treatment of Anxiety and Panic* (2nd edn). New York, NY: Guilford Press.

Battaglia, M., Touchette, É., Garon-Carrier, G., Dionne, G., Côté, S. M., Vitaro, F., ... Boivin, M. (2016). Distinct trajectories of separation anxiety in the preschool years: Persistence at school entry and early-life associated factors. *Journal of Child Psychology and Psychiatry, 57*(1), 39–46.

Birmaher, B., Khetarpal, S., Brent, D., Cully, M., Balach, L., Kaufman, J., & Neer, S. M. (1997). The Screen for Child Anxiety Related Emotional Disorders (SCARED): Scale construction and psychometric characteristics. *Journal of the American Academy of Child and Adolescent Psychiatry 36*, 545–553.

Boyd, C. P., Gullone, E., Kostanski, M., Ollendick, T. H., & Shek, D. T. (2000). Prevalence of anxiety and depression in Australian adolescents: Comparisons with worldwide data. *Journal of Genetic Psychology, 61*, 479–492.

Brückl, T. M., Wittchen, H. U., Hofler, M., Pfister, H., Schneider, S., & Lieb, R. (2007). Childhood separation anxiety and the risk of subsequent psychopathology: Results from a community study. *Psychotherapy and Psychosomatics 76*, 47–56.

Burstein, M., Georgiades, K., Lamers, F., Swanson, S. A., Cui, L., He, J. P., ... Merikangas, K. R. (2012). Empirically derived subtypes of lifetime anxiety disorders: Developmental and clinical correlates in US adolescents. *Journal of Consulting and Clinical Psychology 80*, 102.

Carmassi, C., Gesi, C., Massimetti, E., Shear, M. K., & Dell'Osso, L. (2015). Separation anxiety disorder in the *DSM-5* era. *Journal of Psychopathology, 21*, 365–371.

Carpenter, K. L., Sprechmann, P., Calderbank, R., Sapiro, G., & Egger, H. L. (2016). Quantifying risk for anxiety disorders in preschool children: A machine learning approach. *PloS One, 11*(11), e0165524.

Cartwright-Hatton, S., McNichol, K., & Doubleday, F. (2006). Anxiety in a neglected population: Prevalence of anxiety disorders in pre-adolescent children. *Clinical Psychology Review, 7*, 817–833.

Chorpita, B. F., Brown, T. A., & Barlow, D. H. (2016). Perceived control as a mediator of family environment. *Behavior Therapy, 47*(5), 622–632.

Chu, B., Temkin, A., & Toffey, K. (2016). Transdiagnostic mechanisms and treatments for children and adolescents: An emerging field. Oxford Handbooks Online.

Cooper-Vince, C. E., Emmert-Aronson, B. O., Pincus, D. B., & Comer, J. S. (2014). The diagnostic utility of separation anxiety disorder symptoms: An item response theory analysis. *Journal of Abnormal Child Psychology, 42*(3), 417.

Crawley, S. A., Caporino, N. E., Birmaher, B., Ginsburg, G., Piacentini, J., Albano, A. M., ... McCracken, J. (2014). Somatic complaints in anxious youth. *Child Psychiatry and Human Development, 45*(4), 398.

Cummings, C. M., Caporino, N. E., & Kendall, P. C. (2014). Comorbidity of anxiety and depression in children and adolescents: 20 years after. *Psychological Bulletin, 140* (3), 816.

Cunningham, N. R. & Ollendick, T. H. (2010).Comorbidity of anxiety and conduct problems in children: Implications for clinical research and practice. *Journal of Clinical Child and Family Psychology Review, 13*, 333–347.

De Los Reyes, A. & Aldao, A. (2015).Introduction to the special issue: Toward implementing physiological measures in clinical child and adolescent assessments. *Journal of Clinical Child & Adolescent Psychology, 44*(2), 221–237.

Drake, K. L. & Ginsburg, G. S. (2012).Family factors in the development, treatment, and prevention of childhood anxiety disorders. *Clinical Child and Family Psychology Review, 15*(2), 144–162.

Dubowitz, H., Black, M., Harrington, D., & Verschoore, A. (1993). A follow-up study of behavior problems associated with child sexual abuse. *Child Abuse and Neglect, 17*, 743–754.

Eapen, V., Dadds, M., Barnett, B., Kohlhoff, J., Khan, F., Radom, N., & Silove, D. M. (2014). Separation anxiety, attachment and inter-personal representations: Disentangling the role of oxytocin in the perinatal period. *PLoS One, 9*(9), e107745.

Ebesutani, C., Bernstein, A., Nakamura, B. J., Chorpita, B. F., & Weisz, J. R. (2010). A psychometric analysis of the Revised Child Anxiety and Depression Scale – Parent Version in a clinical sample. *Journal of Abnormal Child Psychology 38*, 249–260.

Egger, H. L., Erkanli, A., Keeler, G., Potts, E., Walter, B. K., & Angold, A. (2006).Test-retest reliability of the preschool age psychiatric assessment (PAPA). *Journal of the American Academy of Child and Adolescent Psychiatry, 45*, 538–549.

Ehrenreich, J. T., Santucci, L. C., & Weiner, C. L. (2008). Separation anxiety disorder in youth: Phenomenology, assessment, and treatment. *Psicologia conductual, 16*(3), 389.

Eisen, A. R. & Engler, L. B. (2006). *Helping Your Child Overcome Separation Anxiety or School Refusal: A Step-by-Step Guide for Parents*. Oakland, CA: New Harbinger Publications.

Eisen, A. R., Hahn, L., Hajinlian, J., Winder, B., & Pincus, D. B. (2005). Separation Anxiety Assessment Scales-Child and Parent versions. See Eisen and Schaefer (2005) for copies of the scale and permission for use.

Eisen, A. R., Pincus, D. B., Hashim, R., Cheron, D., & Santucci, L. (2008). Seeking safety. In A. R. Eisen (ed.), *Treating Childhood Behavioral and Emotional Problems: A Step-by-Step Evidence-Based Approach* (pp. 1–52). New York, NY: Guilford Press.

Eisen, A. R., Raleigh, H., & Neuhoff, C. C. (2008). The unique impact of parent training for separation anxiety disorder in children. *Behavior Therapy 39*, 195–206.

Eisen, A. R. & Schaefer, C. E. (2005). *Separation Anxiety in Children and Adolescents: An Individualized Approach to Assessment and Treatment*. New York, NY: Guilford Press.

Eisen, A. R., Sussman, J. M., Schmidt, T. Mason, L. Hausler, L. A., & Hashim, R. (2011). Separation anxiety disorder. In D. McKay & E. A. Storch (ed.), *Handbook of Child and Adolescent Anxiety Disorders, Part 4* (pp. 245–259). New York, NY: Springer Science + Business Media.

Evans, R., Thirlwall, K., Cooper, P., & Creswell, C. (2017). Using symptom and interference questionnaires to identify recovery among children with anxiety disorders. *Psychological Assessment, 29*(7), 835.

Feigon, S. A., Waldman, I. D., Levy, F., & Hay, D. A. (1997) Genetic and environmental influences on various anxiety disorder symptoms in children. *Behavior Genetics, 27*, 588–589.

Franz, L., Angold, A., Copeland, W., Costello, E. J., Towe-Goodman, N., & Egger, H. (2013). Preschool anxiety disorders in pediatric primary care: Prevalence and comorbidity. *Journal of the American Academy of Child and Adolescent Psychiatry, 52*, 1294–1303.

Geller, D., Biederman, J., Griffin, S., Jones, J., & Lefkowitz, T. (1996). Comorbidity of juvenile obsessive-compulsive disorder in children and adolescents: Phenomenology and family history. *Journal of the American Academy of Child and Adolescent Psychiatry, 35*, 1637–1646.

Ginsburg, G. S., Siqueland, L., Masia-Warner, C., & Hedtke, K. A. (2004). Anxiety disorders in children: Family matters. *Cognitive and Behavioral Practice, 11*, 1.

Goldsmith H. & Gottesman, I. (1981). Origins of variation in behavioral style: A longitudinal study of temperament in young twins. *Child Development, 52*, 91–103.

Goodwin, R., Lipsitz, J. D., Chapman, T. F., Manuzza, S., & Fyer, A. J. (2001).Obsessive-compulsive disorder and separation anxiety comorbidity in early onset panic disorder. *Psychological Medicine, 31*, 1307–1310.

Hahn, L., Hajinlian, J., Eisen, A. R., Winder, B., & Pincus, D. B. (2003). Measuring the Dimensions of Separation Anxiety and Early Panic in Children and Adolescents: The Separation Anxiety Assessment Scale. In A. R. Eisen (Chair) *Recent Advances in the Treatment of Separation Anxiety and Panic in Children and Adolescents*. Paper Presented at the 37th annual convention, AABT, Boston, MA (November).

Hajinlian, J., Hahn, L. G., Eisen, A. R., Zilli-Richardson, L., Reddy, L. A., Winder, B., & Pincus, D. (2003, November). *The phenomenon of separation anxiety across* DSM-IV *internalizing and externalizing disorders*. Poster session presented at the 37th annual convention of the Association for the Advancement of Behavior Therapy, Boston, MA.

Hajinlian, J., Mesnik, J., & Eisen, A. R. (2005, November). *Separation anxiety symptom dimensions and* DSM-IV *anxiety disorders: Correlates, comorbidity, and clinical utility*. Poster presented at the 39th annual convention of the Association for behavioral and cognitive therapies, Washington, DC.

Hammerness, P., Harpold, T., Petty, C., Menard, C., Zar-Kessler, C., & Biederman, J. (2008). Characterizing non-OCD anxiety disorders in psychiatrically referred children and adolescents. *Journal of Affective Disorders 105*, 213–219.

Hanna, G., Fischer, D., & Fluent, T. (2006). Separation anxiety disorder and school refusal in children and adolescents. *Pediatrics in Review 27*, 56–63.

Hollon, S. D. & Beck, A. T. (2013). Cognitive and cognitive-behavioral therapies. In M. J. Lambert (ed.), *Bergin and Garfield's Handbook of Psychotherapy and Behavior Change* (6th edn) (pp. 393–442). New York, NY: Wiley.

Insel, T., Cuthbert, B., Garvey, M., Heinssen, R., Pine, D. S., Quinn, K., Sanislow, C., & Wang, P. (2010).Research Domain Criteria (RDoC): Toward a new classification framework For research on mental disorders. *American Journal of Psychiatry, 7*, 748–751.

Ishikawa, S., Okajima, I., Matsuoka, H., & Sakano, Y. (2007). Cognitive-behavioural therapy for anxiety in children and adolescents: A meta-analysis. *Child and Adolescent Mental Health, 12*, 164–172.

Johnson, T.C. (1998). Understanding children's sexual behaviors–what's natural and healthy? South Pasadena, CA: Author

Kaufman, J., Birmaher, B., Brent, D., Rao, U., et al. (1997). Schedule for Affective Disorders and Schizophrenia for School-Age Children – Present and Lifetime Version (K-SADS-PL): Initial reliability and validity data. *Journal of the American Academy of Child and Adolescent Psychiatry, 36*, 980–988.

Kearney, C. A., Albano, A. M., Eisen, A. R., Allan, W. D., & Barlow, D. H. (1997). The phenomenology of panic disorder in youngsters: An empirical study of a clinical sample. *Journal of Anxiety Disorders*, *11*, 49–62.

Kearney, C. A. & Silverman, W. K. (1992). Let's not push the panic button: A critical analysis of panic and panic disorder in adolescents. *Clinical Psychology Review*, *12*, 293–305.

Kearney, C. A., Sims, K. E., Pursell, C. R., & Tillotson, C. A. (2003). Separation anxiety disorder in young children: A longitudinal and family analysis. *Journal of Clinical Child and Adolescent Psychiatry*, *32*, 593–598.

Kendall, P. C., Brady, E. U., & Verduin, T. L. (2001). Comorbidity in childhood anxiety disorders and treatment outcome. *Journal of the American Academy of Child and Adolescent Psychiatry*, *40*, 787–794.

Kessler, R., Petukhova, M., Sampson, N., Zaslavsky, A., & Wittchen, H. (2012). Twelve-month and lifetime prevalence and lifetime morbid risk of anxiety and mood disorders in the United States. *International Journal of Methods in Psychiatric Research*, *21*, 169–184.

Kiser, L. J., Heston, J., Millsap, P.A., & Pruitt, D. B. (1991). Physical and sexual abuse in childhood: Relationship with posttraumatic stress disorder. *Journal of the American Academy of Child and Adolescent Psychiatry*, *30*, 776–783.

Kossowsky, J., Pfaltz, M., Schneider, S., Taeymans, J., Locher, C., & Gaab, J. (2013). The separation anxiety hypothesis of panic disorder revisited: A meta-analysis. *American Journal of Psychiatry*, *170*, 768–781.

Krajniak, M. I., Anderson, K., & Eisen, A. R. (2016). Separation anxiety. In H. S. Friedman (ed.), *Encyclopedia of Mental Health* (2nd edn, Vol. 4) (pp. 128–132). Waltham, MA: Academic Press.

Lebowitz, E. R., Panza, K. E., Su, J., & Bloch, M. H. (2012). Family accommodation in obsessive-compulsive disorder. *Expert Review of Neurotherapeutics*, *12*, 229–238.

Lebowitz, E. R., Woolston, J., Bar-Haim, Y., Calvocoressi, L., Dauser, C., Warnick, E., . . . Vitulano, L. A. (2013). Family accommodation in pediatric anxiety disorders. *Depression and Anxiety*, *30*(1), 47–54.

Lewinsohn, P. M., Holm-DeNoma, J. M., Small, J. W., Seely, J. R., & Joiner, T. E. (2008). Separation anxiety disorder in childhood as a risk factor for future mental illness. *Journal of the American Academy of Child and Adolescent Psychiatry*, *47*, 548–555.

Manicavasagar, V., Marnane, C., Pini, S., Abelli, M., Rees, S., Eapen, V., & Silove, D. (2010). Adult separation anxiety disorder: A disorder comes of age. *Current Psychiatry Reports*, *12*, 290–297.

Manicavasagar, V., Silove, D., & Curtis, J. (1997). Separation anxiety in adulthood: A phenomenological investigation. *Comprehensive Psychiatry*, *38*, 274–282.

Manicavasagar, V., Silove, D., Wagner, R., & Drobny, J. (2003). A self-report questionnaire for measuring separation anxiety in adulthood. *Comprehensive Psychiatry*, *44*, 146–153.

March, J. S., Parker, J., Sullivan, K., Stallings, P., & Conners, K. (1997). The multidimensional anxiety scale for children (MASC): Factor structure, reliability, and validity. *Journal of the American Academy of Child and Adolescent Psychiatry*, *36*, 554–565.

Masi, G., Favilla, L., Mucci, M., & Millepiedi, S. (2000). Panic disorder in clinically referred children and adolescents. *Child Psychiatry and Human Development*, *31*, 139–151.

Moser, J. S., Durbin, C. E., Patrick, C. J., & Schmidt, N. B. (2015).Combining neural and behavioral indicators in the assessment of internalizing psychopathology in children and adolescents. *Journal of Clinical Child & Adolescent Psychology*, *44*(2), 329–340.

Mroczkowski, M., Goes, F., Riddle, M., Grados, M., Greenberg, B., ... Samuels, J. (2011). Separation anxiety disorder in OCD. *Depression and Anxiety*, *28*, 256–262.

Muris, P., Dreessen, L., Bogels, S., Weckx, M., & van Melick, M. (2004). A questionnaire for screening a broad range of *DSM*-defined anxiety disorder symptoms in clinically referred children and adolescents. *Journal of Child Psychology and Psychiatry*, *45*(4), 813–820.

Muris, P., Merckelbach, H., Meesters, C., & van den Brand, K. (2002). Cognitive development and worry in normal children. *Cognitive Therapy and Research*, *26*, 775–785.

Muris, P., Merckelbach, H., Ollendick, T. H., King, N., & Bogie, N. (2002).Three traditional and three new childhood anxiety questionnaires: Reliability and validity in a normal Adolescent sample. *Behaviour Research and Therapy*, *40*, 753–772.

Muris, P., Merckelbach, H., Schimdt, H., & Tierney, S. (1999).Disgust sensitivity, trait anxiety, and anxiety disorders symptoms in normal children. *Behaviour Research and Therapy*, *37*, 953–961.

Muris, P., Schimdt, H., & Merckelbach, H. (2000). Correlations among two self-report questionnaires for measuring *DSM*-defined anxiety disorder symptoms in children. The Screen for Child Anxiety Related Emotional Disorders and the Spence children's anxiety scale. *Personality and Individual Differences*, *28*, 333–346.

Nelles, W. B. & Barlow, D. H. (1988). Do children panic? *Clinical Psychology Review*, *8*, 359–372.

Piacentini, J. & Graae, F. (1997). Childhood OCD. In E. Hollander & D. Stein (eds.), *Obsessive-Compulsive Disorder: Diagnosis, Etiology, and Treatment* (pp. 23–46). New York, NY: Marcel Dekker.

Pincus, D. B., Eyberg, S. M., & Choate, M. L. (2005). Adapting parent–child interaction therapy for young children with separation anxiety disorder. *Education and Treatment of Children*, *28*, 163–181.

Pini, S., Abelli, M., Mauri, M., Muti, M., Iazzetta, P., Banti, S., & Cassano, G. B. (2005). Clinical correlates and significance of separation anxiety in patients with bipolar disorder. *Bipolar Disorders*, *7*(4), 370–376.

Rabian, B., Peterson, R. A., Richters, J., & Jensen, P.S. (1993). Anxiety sensitivity among anxious children. *Journal of Clinical Child Psychology*, *22*, 441–446.

Reynolds, C. R. & Richmond, B. O. (1978). What I think and feel: A revised measure of children's manifest anxiety. *Journal of Abnormal Child Psychology*, *6*, 271–280.

Santucci, L. C., Ehrenreich, J. T., Trosper, S. E., Bennett, S. M., & Pincus, D. B. (2009). Development and preliminary evaluation of a one-week summer treatment program for separation anxiety disorder. *Cognitive and Behavioral Practice 16*, 317–331.

Schimmenti, A. & Bifulco, A. (2015).Linking lack of care in childhood to anxiety disorders in emerging adulthood: The role of attachment styles. *Child and Adolescent Mental Health*, *20*(1),41–48.

Schneider, S., Blatter-Meunier, J., Herren, C., Adornetto, C., In-Albon, T., & Lavallee, K. (2011). Disorder-specific cognitive-behavioral treatment for separation anxiety disorder in young children: A randomized waitlist-controlled trial. *Psychotherapy and Psychosomatics*, *80*, 206–215.

Schneider, S., Blatter-Meunier, J., Herren, C., In-Albon, T., Adornetto, C., Meyer, A., & Lavallee, K. L. (2013). The efficacy of a family-based cognitive-behavioral treatment for separation anxiety disorder in children aged 8–13: A randomized comparison with a general anxiety program. *Journal of Consulting and Clinical Psychology*, *81*(5), 932.

Schneider, S. & In-Albon, T. (2005). Separation Anxiety Avoidance Inventory, child and parent versions. Unpublished Manuscript. University of Basel.

Shaffer, D., Fischer, P., Lucas, C. P., Duncan, M. R., & Schwab-Stone, M. E. (2000).NIMH diagnostic interview schedule for children. *Journal of the American Academy of Child and Adolescent Psychiatry*, *39*, 28–38.

Shear, K., Jin, R., Ruscio, A., Walters, E., & Kessler, R. (2006). Prevalence and correlates of estimated *DSM-IV* child and adult separation anxiety disorder in the National Comorbidity Survey Replication. *American Journal of Psychiatry*, *163*, 1074–1083.

Silberg, J. L., Gillespie, N., Moore, A. A., Eaves, L. J., Bates, J., Aggen, S., . . . Canino, G. (2015). Shared genetic and environmental influences on early temperament and preschool psychiatric disorders in Hispanic twins. *Twin Research and Human Genetics*, *18*(2), 171–178.

Silove, D., Alonso, J., Bromet, E., Gruber, M., Sampson, N., Scott, K., . . . de Jonge, P. (2015). Pediatric-onset and adult-onset separation anxiety disorder across countries in the World Mental Health Survey. *American Journal of Psychiatry*, *172*(7), 647–656.

Silove, D., Manicavasagar, V., O'Connell, D., Blaszczynski, A., Wagner, R., & Henry, J. (1993). The development of the Separation Anxiety Symptom Inventory (SASI). *Australian and New Zealand Journal of Psychiatry*, 27, 477–488.

Silove, D. M., Marnane, C. L., Wagner, R., Manicavasagar, V. L., & Rees, S. (2010). The prevalence and correlates of adult separation anxiety disorder in an anxiety clinic. *BMC Psychiatry*, *10*(1), 21.

Silverman, W. K. & Albano, A. M. (1996). *Anxiety Disorders Interview Schedule for DSM-IV – Child and Parent Versions*. San Antonio, TX: Psychological Corporation.

Silverman, W. K., Fleisig, W., Rabian, B., & Peterson, R. A. (1991). The child anxiety sensitivity index. *Journal of Clinical Child Psychology*, 20, 162–168.

Silverman W. K., Saavedra, L. M., & Pina, A. A. (2001) Test-retest reliability of anxiety symptoms and diagnoses with the Anxiety Disorders Interview Schedule for *DSM-IV*: Child and Parent Versions. *Journal of the American Academy of Child and Adolescent Psychiatry*, *40*, 937–944.

Siqueland, L., Rynn, M., & Diamond, G. S. (2005). Cognitive behavioral and attachment-based family therapy for anxious adolescents: Phase I and II studies. *Journal of Anxiety Disorders*, *19*, 361–381.

Spence, S. H. (1997). The Spence children's anxiety scale (SCAS). Structure of anxiety symptoms in children. *Journal of Abnormal Psychology*, *106*, 280–297.

Spielberger, C. D. (1973). *Manual for the State-Trait Anxiety Inventory for Children*. Palo Alto, CA: Consulting Psychologists Press.

Thompson-Hollands, J., Kerns, C. E., Pincus, D. B., & Comer, J. S. (2014). Parental accommodation of child anxiety and related symptoms: Range, impact, and correlates. *Journal of anxiety disorders*, *28*(8), 765–773.

Tufts' New England Medical Center, Division of Child Psychiatry. (1984). *Sexually Exploited Children: Service and Research Project*. Final report for the Office of Juvenile Justice and Delinquency Prevention. Washington, DC: US Department of Justice.

Vasey, M. W. & Dadds, M. R. (2001). An introduction to the developmental psychopathology of anxiety. In M. W. Vasey & M. R. Dadds (ed.), *The Developmental Psychopathology of Anxiety*. New York, NY: Oxford University Press.

Verduin, T. L. & Kendall, P. C. (2003). Differential occurrence of comorbidity within childhood anxiety disorders. *Journal of Clinical Child and Adolescent Psychology 32*, 290–295.

Villabø, M. A., Oerbeck, B., Skirbekk, B., Hansen, B. H., & Kristensen, H. (2016). Convergent and divergent validity of K-SADS-PL anxiety and attention deficit hyperactivity disorder diagnoses in a clinical sample of school-aged children. *Nordic Journal of Psychiatry*, *70*(5), 358–364.

Weinberg, A., Meyer, A., Hale-Rude, E., Perlman, G., Kotov, R., Klein, D. N., & Hajcak, G. (2016). Error-related negativity (ERN) and sustained threat: Conceptual framework and empirical evaluation in an adolescent sample. *Psychophysiology*, *53*(3), 372–385.

Westen, D., Nakash, O., Thomas, C., & Bradley, R. (2006). Clinical assessment of attachment patterns and personality disorder in adolescents and adults. *Journal of Consulting and Clinical Psychology*, *74*, 1065–1085.

Wood, J. J. (2006). Parental intrusiveness and children's separation anxiety in a clinical sample. *Child Psychiatry & Human Development*, *37*, 73–87.

Wood, J. J., Piacentini, J.C., Bergman, R.L., McCracken J., & Barrios V. (2002). Concurrent validity of the anxiety disorders section of the Anxiety Disorders Interview Schedule for *DSM-IV*: Child and Parent Versions. *Journal of Clinical Child and Adolescent Psychology*, *31*, 335–342.

World Health Organization. (2016). *The ICD-10 Classification of Mental and Behavioural disorders: Clinical Descriptions and Diagnostic Guidelines*. Geneva: World Health Organization.

Yule, W. (2001). Posttraumatic stress disorder in the general population and in children. *Journal of Clinical Psychiatry*, *62*, 23–28.

20 Selective Mutism

Christopher A. Kearney, Andrew Gerthoffer, Amanda Howard, and Rachele Diliberto

Selective mutism is a persistent and debilitating psychiatric disorder in which a child fails to speak in situations where speaking is expected. Children with selective mutism often speak well in familiar situations, such as at home, but rarely speak at school or in other public settings. The disorder must interfere with educational or occupational achievement or social communication, and must last at least one month, excluding the first month of school. A diagnosis of selective mutism does not generally apply to youths with a communication disorder such as stuttering or a fluency disorder, though comorbidity can occur. The diagnosis also does not generally apply to youths, such as new immigrants, who lack comfort or knowledge with the primary language spoken in public situations. If language skills are adequate in this scenario, however, a diagnosis of selective mutism may apply. The disorder does not occur exclusively among those with autism spectrum disorder or a psychotic disorder.

Selective mutism is listed as an anxiety disorder in the *Diagnostic and Statistical Manual of Mental Disorders* (fifth edition) (*DSM-5*) (American Psychiatric Association, 2013). However, selective mutism is the only *DSM-5* anxiety disorder that does not reference fear or anxiety in its diagnostic criteria. In addition, the *DSM-5* lists many associated features that support a diagnosis of selective mutism. These associated features include temperamental characteristics such as shyness and negativism, anxiety-based characteristics such as fear of social embarrassment and compulsivity, social problems such as isolation and withdrawal, and oppositional characteristics such as temper tantrums. Selective mutism is listed as a disorder of social functioning with onset specific to childhood and adolescence in the *International Classification of Diseases, Tenth Revision, Clinical Modification* (*ICD-10-CM*) (American Medical Association, 2018).

Epidemiology

Prevalence rates for selective mutism vary in the literature because researchers utilize different classification systems, assessment measures, settings, and samples. The overall prevalence of selective mutism is considered rare, however, perhaps ranging from 0.03% to 1.90% (Bergman, Piacentini, & McCracken, 2002; Chavira, Stein, Bailey, & Stein, 2004; Kumpulainen, Rasanen, Raaska, & Samppi,

1998; Sharp, Sherman, & Gross, 2007). Prevalence rates for selective mutism among immigrant children may be somewhat higher and reportedly range from 2.2% to 28.0% (Elizur & Perednik, 2003; Steinhausen & Juzi, 1996). Prevalence rates for selective mutism among children with speech and language delays or difficulties may also be higher than in the general population (Manassis et al., 2003).

Age of onset for selective mutism ranges from 2.7 to 6.5 years, though formal diagnosis is more common at age 5–8 years as a child enters school and is increasingly expected to speak to others outside of the home and perform various academic tasks that require speech (Cunningham, McHolm, Boyle, & Patel, 2004; Ford, Sladeczek, Carlson, & Kratochwill, 1998; Kristensen, 2000; Sharp et al., 2007; Steinhausen & Juzi, 1996). Selective mutism may occur in females more than males in clinical samples, with a common gender ratio of 2:1, but the gender ratio is more comparable in community- and school-based samples (Bergman et al., 2002; Elizur & Perednik, 2003; Karakaya et al., 2008; Kumpulainen et al., 1998; Muris & Ollendick, 2015). Wong (2010) noted that reported gender differences may be due to small sample sizes and the relatively rare nature of the disorder. Males with selective mutism may have slightly higher rates of oppositional defiant disorder than females (Alyanak et al., 2013).

Course

Children with selective mutism likely have various outcomes, though few formal longitudinal studies exist with standardized assessments and robust sample sizes. Selective mutism is generally viewed as a persistent disorder with a fair to poor outcome (Hua & Major, 2016). Adolescents with selective mutism displayed substantial rates of agoraphobia without panic disorder (27%) in one study (Gensthaler et al., 2016a). Adults diagnosed as children often continue to experience deficient speaking behaviors, residual social phobia, and other anxiety disorders (Steinhausen & Juzi, 1996). These adults may show deficits in social communication as well as mood or other emotional disorders that result in social withdrawal and economic impairments, including higher unemployment rates (Remschmidt, Poller, Herpertz-Dahlmann, Hennighausen, & Gutenbrunner, 2001).

Other individuals with selective mutism demonstrate improvement with time. Complete remission was reported in 39% of participants in one longitudinal study, with an additional 29% displaying "remarkable improvement" (Remschmidt et al., 2001). Steinhausen and colleagues (2006) followed 33 individuals with selective mutism into young adulthood and found their symptoms to have slightly (18.2%), markedly (24.2%), or totally (57.6%) improved. Intensity of selective mutism symptoms tended to gradually decline (54.5%), remain the same (42.4%), or fluctuate (3.0%) over time. More than half (57.6%) displayed another mental disorder in adulthood, most commonly a phobic (42.4%) or substance use (15.2%) disorder. A more expanded context of selective mutism symptoms, such as number of situations where speaking did not occur, best predicted poorer outcome. The course of selective mutism may be substantially impacted, however, by evolving and personalized interventions that intensively target frequency and audibility of speech among young children with the disorder (later intervention section).

Clinical Presentations

Children with selective mutism display a wide range of symptoms and behaviors in various settings. Children with selective mutism most commonly withhold speech in school settings, toward both peers and teachers, which can interfere with academic and social development (Bergman, Keller, Piacentini, & Bergman, 2008; Cunningham et al., 2004). Children may withhold speech in other public settings as well, such as restaurants, markets, parks, and social events (Scott & Beidel, 2011). Many display low volume and frequency of speech and less spontaneity of speech (Ford et al., 1998).

In many of these settings, children with selective mutism sometimes rely on alternative forms of communication, or compensatory behaviors. Examples include facial expressions, monosyllabic utterances, nodding, gesturing, pulling, pushing, pointing, writing, or grunting (Conn & Coyne, 2014; Omdal & Galloway, 2007; Shriver, Segool, & Gortmarker, 2011). Other children with selective mutism offer little in the way of nonverbal communication, however, and may avoid eye contact and many other expressions (Krolian, 1998). These behaviors could relate to different internalizing and externalizing behavior problems that are summarized next.

Internalizing behaviors. Children with selective mutism are often described in clinical settings as anxious, submissive, dependent, depressed, shy, timid, reticent, inhibited, fearful, withdrawn, and compulsive. Children with selective mutism often freeze when spoken to, blush, avoid eye contact, cling to parents, and resist separation (Kopp & Gilberg, 1997; Kristensen, 1997; Steinhausen & Juzi, 1996; Yeganeh, Beidel, Turner, Pina, & Silverman, 2003). Most children with selective mutism meet criteria for an additional anxiety disorder, which can include specific phobia, generalized anxiety disorder, and separation anxiety disorder (Manassis et al., 2003; Nowakowski et al., 2011; Oerbeck, Stein, Wentzel-Larsen, Langsrud, & Kristensen, 2014). Others may display symptoms of depression (Alyanak et al., 2013). The most common comorbid internalizing disorder in this population, however, is social anxiety.

Social anxiety is considered a hallmark symptom of most children with selective mutism. Many children with selective mutism avoid or withdraw from social situations and display fear and timidity in these situations (Ford et al., 1998). Children with selective mutism often express fears of social embarrassment and judgment as well as physical symptoms of social anxiety (Standart & Le Couteur, 2003; Yeganeh et al., 2003). Several researchers have reported very high rates of comorbidity of social anxiety disorder and selective mutism in their samples (Chavira, Shipon-Blum, Cohan, & Stein, 2007; Oerbeck et al., 2014; Vecchio & Kearney, 2005). Children with selective mutism also display elevated anxiety and social phobia symptoms compared to control children (Bergman et al., 2002; Cunningham, McHolm, & Boyle, 2006; Elizur & Perednik, 2003; Kristensen, 2000). In addition, clinicians and observers tend to endorse more severe social anxiety symptoms in children with selective mutism compared to those with social anxiety (Yeganeh, Beidel, & Turner, 2006). Selective mutism has thus been proposed by some as an extreme manifestation or developmental variant of social phobia (Bergman et al., 2002; Black & Uhde, 1995; Dummit et al., 1997; Silveira, Jainer, England, & Bates, 2004).

Other data, however, call into question the particularly severe nature of social anxiety among children with selective mutism. Some researchers have found little difference in social anxiety, internalizing symptoms, and comorbid disorders across children with selective mutism and children with social phobia or other anxiety disorders (Levin-Decanini, Connolly, Simpson, Suarez, & Jacob, 2013; Vecchio & Kearney, 2005; Young, Bunnel, & Beidel, 2012). Others note that children with selective mutism differ little from those with social phobia on peer interaction tasks or self-report measures of general fear and social and trait anxiety (Yeganeh et al., 2003, 2006). Children with selective mutism have also reported lower fear of negative evaluation and lower physiological, separation, and social anxiety than children with social phobia in other studies (Manassis et al., 2003; Melfsen, Walitza, & Warnke, 2006; Young et al., 2012). Clinical behavioral profiles (later section) reveal nuanced and substantial symptom heterogeneity among children with selective mutism and may help to explain some of these discrepant findings.

Externalizing behaviors. Children with selective mutism are sometimes described in clinical settings as having various externalizing behaviors as well. Some children with selective mutism have been depicted as stubborn, controlling, aggressive, disobedient, negative, suspicious, manipulative, sulky, and demanding (Andersson & Thomsen, 1998; Kristensen, 2001; Vasilyeva, 2013; Yanof, 1996). Children with selective mutism may also display temper tantrums, lack flexibility, and be difficult to please (Kumpulainen et al., 1998; Steinhausen & Juzi, 1996).

Oppositional behaviors occur among some children with selective mutism as well, including school refusal, testing authority, and lying (Omdal & Galloway, 2007). Ford and colleagues (1998) found that parents of children with past or current selective mutism reported toileting problems, strong-willed behavior, refusal to talk, sullenness, irritability, argumentativeness, school disobedience, whining, and temper tantrums. Negativism, defiance, and oppositional behavior have been reported in up to 90% of children with selective mutism (Krohn et al., 1992). Formal oppositional defiant disorder has been found in 6.8–29.0% of children with selective mutism (Arie et al., 2007; Yeganeh et al., 2006).

Others have found few externalizing behavior problems among children with selective mutism, however, or attribute the problems to anxiety-based reactions. Parent ratings of externalizing behavior problems are often in the normative range

(Steinhausen & Juzi, 1996; Yeganeh et al., 2003). Cunningham and colleagues (2006) did not find a greater incidence of parent- or teacher-reported oppositional defiant disorder symptoms in children with selective mutism compared to controls. Vecchio and Kearney (2005) found no difference in parent-reported oppositional defiant disorder symptoms among children with selective mutism, anxiety disorders, or no disorder. Externalizing behavior problems could represent defiance or a refusal to speak or participate in certain situations. The problems could also represent misinterpretation of severe social anxiety as oppositionality by others, a desire to avoid anxiety-provoking social situations or obligations, or attention-seeking behavior (Skedgell, Fornander, & Kearney, 2017).

Social Problems

Children with selective mutism often do not initiate or maintain friendships or speak with other children, which can cause long-term problems with social functioning and peer interactions (Sharkey & McNicholas, 2008). Peer rejection, teasing, and preference for younger playmates may occur (Giddan, Ross, Sechler, & Becker, 1997; Zelenko & Shaw, 2000). Kumpulainen and colleagues (1998), using teacher report, found that 16% of children with selective mutism were rejected in class, 13% were rejected during classroom breaks, and 5% were bullied. Diliberto and Kearney (2016) found parent-reported social problems to be associated with both anxious and oppositional behavioral profiles in youth with selective mutism.

Socially deficient behaviors among children with selective mutism include withdrawal, clinging to adults, low voice volume, poor eye contact, and crying, among others (Standart & Le Couteur, 2003; Wong, 2010). Cunningham and colleagues (2004) found that parents rated their children with selective mutism lower on social responsibility, cooperation, control, and assertion than controls. Teachers rated children with selective mutism lower on social assertion than controls. Children with selective mutism often did not initiate conversations or invite peers to play in the classroom. Similarly, Carbone and colleagues (2010) revealed, via parent report, that children with selective mutism had lower social responsibility than mixed anxiety and control groups. The selective mutism group was also lower in social assertion and social control than controls.

Others have found, however, that victimization and bullying are not necessarily more common to children with selective mutism and that many of these children believe themselves to be accepted and liked by their peers (Ale, Mann, Menzel, Storch, & Lewin, 2013; Cunningham et al., 2004, 2006). Youth with selective mutism may engage in social situations without speaking, and many do make appropriate social responses such as smiling and participate in games and other group activities at recess and social gatherings (Dow, Sonies, Scheib, Moss, & Leonard, 1995; Kearney, 2010). Those with selective mutism often communicate effectively using body language, facial expressions, and gestures, sometimes with peer assistance (Omdal & Galloway, 2008). Cunningham and colleagues (2006) reported that youth with selective mutism had nonverbal social cooperation scores comparable to control children. In addition, Cunningham and colleagues (2004) reported that the number of organizations enrolled in outside of school, including sports and clubs, did not differ between selective mutism and control groups.

Temperament. Children with selective mutism are often reported to have behaviorally inhibited and shy temperaments (Muris, Hendriks, & Bot, 2016; Young et al., 2012). Gensthaler and colleagues (2016b) examined retrospective accounts of behavioral inhibition in infants for youth with current selective mutism or social anxiety. Youth with selective mutism had higher infant behavioral inhibition scores than youth with social anxiety. Children with selective mutism often display elevated scores on self-report measures of social anxiety and shyness (Carbone et al., 2010; Dummit et al., 1997; Steinhausen & Juzi, 1996). Earlier speculation in the literature was that selective mutism represented a particularly severe and speech-based form of behavioral inhibition (Anstendig, 1999; Black & Uhde, 1995).

Behavioral inhibition and shyness in children with selective mutism may have more nuanced characteristics, however. Kristensen and Torgersen (2002) found that children with selective mutism with speech and language delays displayed elevated shyness and lower sociability than controls. However, maternal reports revealed that children with selective mutism with speech and language delays were more sociable and less emotional than children with selective mutism without speech problems. Children with selective mutism without language problems were rated as more shy and emotional and less active and social than control children. In addition, Diliberto and Kearney (2016) reported that shyness was associated with children with selective mutism with an anxious profile but not with those with an oppositional profile.

Other temperamental characteristics have also been found among children with selective mutism. Examples include less adaptability to transition and change and lowered activity (Ford et al., 1998; Mulligan, Hale, & Shipon-Blum, 2015; Shriver et al., 2011). In addition, children with selective mutism are sometimes described with features of negative emotionality or heightened, adverse responses to distressing situations (Marakovitz, Wagmiller, Mian, Briggs-Gowan, & Carter, 2011; Vasilyeva, 2013). Conversely, however, depression or dysphoric mood have been noted in some studies of children with selective mutism (Cunningham et al., 2006; Kopp & Gillberg, 1997).

Communication and Developmental Problems

A *DSM-5* diagnosis of selective mutism has caveats with respect to communication and developmental disorders, but both sets of problems are common to this population. Up to two-thirds of children with selective mutism may have a developmental disorder or delay, including motor and elimination delays, and as many as 30–50% may have aspects of a communication disorder (Arie et al., 2007; Kristensen, 2000; Steinhausen et al., 2006). Mulligan and colleagues (2015) reported that diagnoses of speech and language disorders tended to be more common among children who had selective mutism and sensory and anxiety problems.

Speech and language deficits are a key clinical aspect of many children with selective mutism. Problems often occur in receptive language, discrimination of speech sounds, detailed narratives, phonological awareness, and grammar (Klein, Armstrong, & Shipon-Blum, 2013; Manassis et al., 2003, 2007; McInnes, Fung, Manassis, Fiksenbaum, & Tannock, 2004). Some have speculated that selective mutism is a neurodevelopmental disorder marked partly by deficits in auditory efferent feedback pathways that can affect speech and language (later biological section) (Henkin & Bar-Haim, 2015; Muchnik et al., 2013).

Behavioral Profiles

Researchers have begun to explore empirically based clinical behavioral profiles among children with selective mutism given the substantial symptom heterogeneity characteristic of this population. These profile studies were partly based on earlier works that purportedly identified children with selective mutism as anxious or oppositional (Ford et al., 1998). Cohan and colleagues (2008) utilized caregivers of youth aged 5–12 years with selective mutism to evaluate their child's communication delays, social and behavior problems, functional impairments, internalizing and externalizing symptoms, and expressive and receptive language abilities. Latent profile analyses supported a three-class solution: anxious-mildly oppositional, anxious-communication delayed, and exclusively anxious.

The anxious-mildly oppositional group, comprising 44.6% of the sample, was characterized by borderline clinical scores for behavior problems and syntax and clinically significant social anxiety scores. Behavior problems were largely home-based and consistent with stubborn or controlling behavior in anxiety-provoking situations, and less consistent with widespread rule-breaking and aggression. The anxious-communication delayed group, comprising 43.1% of the sample, was characterized by poor receptive language abilities and syntax as well as clinically significant social anxiety. This group demonstrated greater selective mutism symptom severity and behavior problems than the exclusively anxious group and was the most impaired. The exclusively anxious group, comprising 12.3% of the sample, was characterized by less anxiety and better expressive and receptive language abilities than the anxious-communication delayed group. The findings suggested that clinically significant anxiety is likely present in children with selective mutism but that other factors, such as oppositionality and speech and language problems, also play a role.

Diliberto and Kearney (2016) examined parent ratings of internalizing and externalizing behavior problems among youth with selective mutism in a clinical setting. Commonly endorsed items from the Child Behavior Checklist (Achenbach & Rescorla, 2001) were subjected to an exploratory and then confirmatory factor analysis and revealed two distinct factors of anxious and oppositional behaviors.

The anxious factor was characterized by a desire to be alone rather than with others, social withdrawal, nervousness, not eating well, sudden changes in mood, and fearfulness/anxiety. Scores from the anxious factor were related to other measures of social problems, social anxiety disorder symptoms, and aggressive behaviors, the latter more linked to argumentativeness than physical aggression. The oppositional factor was characterized by argumentativeness, temper tantrums, whining, stubbornness, and demands for attention. Scores from the oppositional factor were related to other measures of aggressive behaviors and oppositional defiant disorder symptoms and inversely to social anxiety disorder symptoms.

Mulligan and colleagues (2015) conducted a cluster analysis of responses from the Selective Mutism Comprehensive Diagnostic Questionnaire, a clinician-administered measure of selective mutism symptoms. Five subtypes were identified. Global mutism was the largest subtype (50.0% of the sample) and was characterized by less impairment, including less academic impairment, and a 2:1 female-to-male ratio. Low-functioning mutism (16.2% of the sample) was characterized by more substantial academic problems, sensory and executive problems, special education placement, family psychopathology, and an even gender ratio.

Sensory/pathology mutism (15.5% of the sample) was characterized by more frequent diagnoses of sensory integration disorder, oppositional behavior and lability, bilingualism, separation anxiety problems, and motor skill delays. An even gender ratio was reported for this subtype, which was described as the most impaired and perhaps the most difficult to treat. Anxiety/language mutism (10.6% of the sample) was characterized by more frequent comorbid anxiety disorder diagnoses, environmental stress exposure, speech impediments, and diagnoses of speech and language disorders. The female-to-male ratio was 2:1 for this subtype. Finally, emotional/behavioral mutism (7.7% of the sample) was characterized by few academic problems despite substantial executive functioning difficulties and oppositional and labile behavior. The female-to-male ratio was 10:1 for this subtype.

The authors of these empirically derived clinical profiles of selective mutism concluded generally that selective mutism is a multifaceted and heterogeneous problem, findings that support the extensive historical descriptions of this population. The findings have important implications for conceptualizing selective mutism as more than simply an anxiety disorder. In addition, the profiles have clear implications for assessment and for assigning personalized treatment, a point that is explored in greater depth in the later clinical sections.

Family Factors

Several parent and family characteristics have been found to be associated with selective mutism in children. Parents of children with selective mutism are often reported to be anxious and depressed (Chavira et al., 2007; Steinhausen et al., 2006). A history of mutism and taciturn personality traits has been reported in some parents as well, though this is not necessarily common to this population and may be more evident among parents of children with selective mutism but without a communication disorder (Kristensen & Torgersen, 2001; Remschmidt et al., 2001). Symptoms of selective mutism tend to be more common in other family members as well compared to controls (Black & Uhde, 1995; Kristensen, 2000).

Parent–child relationships have also been examined in this population. Edison and colleagues (2011) examined structured, verbally demanding as well as free-play situations to observe parent–child interactions. Parents of children with selective mutism granted more autonomy in free play than structured contexts. However, these parents granted less autonomy in both contexts than parents of children with and without anxiety. Greater child anxiety was associated with greater control, less autonomy and child-initiated speaking, and younger child age. Families of youth with selective mutism have also been described as enmeshed, conflictual, overdependent, and less socially active than controls (Vecchio & Kearney, 2005; Yeganeh et al., 2006). Youth with selective mutism may also argue and display temper tantrums with parents (Diliberto & Kearney, 2016; Kumpulainen et al., 1998; Steinhausen & Juzi, 1996).

Theoretical Perspectives of Selective Mutism

Various perspectives exist regarding the development and maintenance of selective mutism. These perspectives are based on several risk factors for this population and can be sorted generally into biological, behavioral, and family systems categories. These perspectives are described next, followed by a brief discussion of a developmental psychopathology model.

Biological

Researchers from a biological perspective posit that selective mutism is a neuro-developmental disorder that may have some genetic and temperamental basis. Little genetic data are available with respect to selective mutism, though case studies of monozygotic and dizygotic twins provide preliminary support for concordance (Gray, Jordan, Ziegler, & Livingston, 2002; Segal, 2003). Stein and colleagues (2011) found a polymorphism (*rs2710102*) on the gene *CNTNAP2* (on chromosome 7) to be associated with social anxiety and selective mutism. This variation has been noted as well in studies of delayed language among children with autism. The authors noted, however, that strict replication of this finding, as well as large-scale genetic studies of selective mutism, is still needed.

Selective mutism or reserved speech have also been found at a higher rate in parents of children with selective mutism than the general population, and reticence, introversion, and shyness are common personality characteristics as well (Kristensen & Torgersen, 2001, 2002; Remschmidt et al., 2001). As mentioned, behavioral inhibition and use of fewer words is also a frequent early characteristic of many of these children (Muris et al., 2016). Parents of children with selective mutism also display elevated rates of social anxiety and avoidant personality disorders, suggesting some possible heritability (Chavira et al., 2007).

Children with selective mutism may also have impaired ability to process incoming auditory signals (Bar-Haim et al., 2004). Children with selective mutism with abnormal auditory efferent activity are impaired when asked to process auditory input during vocalization (Arie et al., 2007). Speech may be avoided because speaking while processing incoming stimuli is overly difficult. Children with selective mutism may also have difficulty shifting behavioral states to engage with others and are thus inhibited when asked to respond verbally and behaviorally. Heilman and colleagues (2012) asked children with selective mutism to engage in a social interaction and physical exercise task and examined their vagal response. Children with selective mutism had difficulty shifting between these two tasks and had a "sluggish" vagal break, which was marked by a reduced cardiac vagal tone and a dampened heart rate. In addition, children with selective mutism have demonstrated lower heart rate, blood pressure, and skin conductance than youth with social anxiety disorder during a social interaction activity (Young et al., 2012).

Behavioral

Researchers from a behavioral perspective posit that selective mutism is a disorder impacted heavily by operant factors that maintain failure or refusal to speak, which can vary across children and settings (Ale et al., 2013). Operant factors may involve negative reinforcement, or termination of an aversive stimulus. Some children with selective mutism may decline to speak to reduce anxiety in a given situation, to avoid displaying inefficient or underdeveloped speaking skills, or to avoid aversive directives from others (Casey, 2012; Schum, 2006). Other operant factors may involve positive reinforcement. Some children with selective mutism may decline to speak to increase social or sensory (physical) feedback or attention from others (Kearney & Vecchio, 2006). Other children with selective mutism may decline to speak due to a combination of operant factors as well, suggesting the need for a functional assessment-based intervention plan for this population (Kern, Starosta, Cook, Bambara, & Gresham, 2007).

A behavioral perspective of selective mutism may also include associative learning responses, especially those involving trauma and stress. Andersson and Thomsen (1998) reported that one-third of their sample of children with selective mutism experienced a traumatic or stressful event during the time they were learning to speak. Mulligan and colleagues (2015) reported that 28.2% of their sample of youth with selective mutism experienced some trauma. Some children may learn that not speaking is an effective way to cope with a stressful or traumatic event such as parental maltreatment or peer-based bullying (Wong, 2010).

Family Systems

Researchers from a family systems perspective posit that selective mutism may result from faulty relationships (Anstendig, 1999; Steinhausen & Adamek, 1997). Families with children with selective mutism may be marked by limited communication, overcontrolling but ambivalent parents, enmeshment, and overdependence (Krysanski, 2003; Yeganeh et al., 2006; Zelenko & Shaw, 2000). Marital problems are common to this population as well, and some parents inadvertently reinforce their child's mutism by attending to, or compensating for, the child's lack of speech (Remschmidt et al., 2001). Immigrant status has been identified as a risk factor for a selective mutism diagnosis as well, though familiarity with a culture's dominant language must be considered (Elizur & Perednik, 2003; Toppelberg, Tabors, Coggins, Lum, & Burger, 2005).

Developmental Psychopathology

The etiology of selective mutism likely involves interplay among several biological, temperamental, behavioral, and family factors, implying that a developmental psychopathology perspective is best for understanding this population. Pertinent risk factors could also reflect Research Domain Criteria (RDoC) constructs such as acute or potential threat, reward valuation, expectancies, language, social communication, understanding mental states, and arousal. A constellation of risk factors may interact in different ways for different children, along various pathways, that help produce a concluding selective mutism result (Muris & Ollendick, 2015). The idea of multiple pathways toward a disorder, or equifinality, is a key aspect of a developmental psychopathology perspective and one that applies well to the heterogeneous symptoms and behaviors that comprise selective mutism.

Pathways toward selective mutism could reflect those evident for children with anxiety disorders, children with oppositional problems, and children with communication deficiencies, for example (Cohan, Price, & Stein, 2006). An anxiety-based pathway could involve early genetic and behavioral inhibition predispositions as well as later environmental factors such as distress in interpersonal interactions and social avoidance. An oppositional pathway could involve key operant factors, parent responses, and family dynamics that help produce coercive interactions, poor relationship quality, and noncompliance. A communication deficiency pathway could involve neurodevelopmental deficits in speech, language, or learning that preclude a child's ability to function quickly and effectively in social-academic exchanges. A combination of risk factors could interact as well to form a blend of these pathways that still leads to selective mutism.

A developmental psychopathology perspective of selective mutism, including the notion of multiple pathways, implies as well that a diverse set of assessment and intervention strategies are needed for this population (Viana, Beidel, & Rabian, 2009). In addition, a developmental psychopathology perspective suggests that failure to achieve a particular developmental benchmark impedes a child's ability to master subsequent benchmarks. A child who does not speak publicly during preschool years, for example, is likely to have substantial problems with social and academic tasks in early grades that require extensive verbalization. This process denotes the need for research into prevention and early intervention with this population.

Assessment

The assessment of selective mutism generally focuses on evaluating the parameters and function of a child's failure or refusal to speak. Children with selective mutism often demonstrate social anxiety, mild oppositional problems, and/or communication problems, so assessment is often concentrated on these constructs as well. Assessment for this population typically includes interviews, questionnaires, behavioral observations, and formal testing and review of records.

Interviews for this population may be more fruitful if conducted with parents, teachers, and relevant others, though children with selective mutism may respond nonverbally to yes-no or other simple questions. The Anxiety Disorders Interview Schedule: Child and Parent Versions is a semi-structured interview that contains a specific section for selective mutism that mirrors diagnostic criteria (Silverman & Albano, 1996; *DSM-5* edition in development). In addition, the Functional Diagnostic Protocol covers conditions under which selective mutism occurs and what reinforcers maintain mutism over time (Schill, Kratochwill, & Gardner, 1996). The Selective Mutism Comprehensive Diagnostic Questionnaire, mentioned earlier, is a clinician-administered instrument that focuses on settings in which selective mutism occurs as well as frequency, severity, and pervasiveness of symptoms (Mulligan et al., 2015).

Unstructured interviews may also be used to gather information about a child's diagnostic status regarding selective mutism, interference with academic or social functioning, specific settings in which a child fails to speak or is reluctant to speak, range of speaking behavior (e.g., mouthing, whispering, low-volume speech) in each setting, compensatory behaviors, functions that maintain mutism, contextual factors that impact mutism, and how parents and teachers and others respond to a child's mutism (Kearney, 2010).

Questionnaires for this population include the Selective Mutism Questionnaire to assess a child's willingness to speak to others in school, home/family, and public/social situations (Bergman et al., 2008). Degree of interference or distress associated with a child's mutism are assessed by other items. The measure has strong psychometric properties (Letamendi et al., 2008). A related instrument, the School Speech Questionnaire, is a short measure completed by the teacher regarding school-based speaking behavior in different situations. In addition, the Rating Scale for Elective Mutism is a measure of clinical and contextual factors surrounding failure to speak (Facon, Sahiri, & Rivière, 2008). Other researchers focus on parent and teacher daily recordings of number of words spoken, mouthed, or whispered that day across several situations as well as to whom the child spoke and the audibility of the child's speech (Vecchio & Kearney, 2009). Many other questionnaires are relevant to selective mutism as well, particularly self-report measures of social and other forms of anxiety and parent/teacher checklists for internalizing and externalizing behavior problems (Fisak, Oliveros, & Ehrenreich, 2006).

Behavioral observations of a child with selective mutism are sometimes used to gather information about the depth of a child's failure to speak in various situations, with whom a child will interact in public situations, how others respond to a child's mutism, communication problems, compensatory behaviors, and language differences (Toppelberg et al., 2005). Audio or video recordings from parents may be useful in this regard as well (Jackson, Allen, Boothe, Nava, & Coates, 2005). School-based observations may focus on peer–child and teacher–child interactions, avoided situations, and performance in various academic tasks (Mitchell & Kratochwill, 2013).

Observations can also be used to evaluate whether a child's failure to speak is due to (1) a desire to decrease anxiety, (2) a desire to increase social or sensory (physical) feedback from others, (3) a desire to avoid aversive directives from others, and/or (4) inefficient or underdeveloped speaking skills (Kearney, 2010). Contextual variables that impact selective mutism could be detected as well, including problematic family communications, parental shyness, school-based threats, and whether English or another language is primarily spoken in the home (Hua & Major, 2016).

Intellectual/achievement and speech/language assessment for youths with selective mutism is sometimes necessary, and may need to concentrate on nonverbal tasks. Examples include performance subscales on standardized intelligence tests and neuropsychological or receptive language subscales or tests that allow for nonverbal responses (Fung, Manassis, Kenny, & Fiksenbaum, 2002). Speech and language assessment may involve the use of written narratives (McInnes et al., 2004). Extant attendance, academic, and other school-based records and teacher interviews may be useful as well to determine whether selective mutism has resulted in additional problems (Martinez et al., 2015).

Intervention

Intervention for selective mutism is generally designed to increase a child's audible and frequent speech in public situations and to reduce nonverbal compensatory behaviors and distress. The most common and empirically supported treatments for selective mutism are behavioral in nature. Exposure-based practices are a core feature of these treatments and involve increasing frequency and audibility of speech in various settings on a graduated basis. Selective mutism is a heterogeneous disorder, however, so exposure-based practices are often combined with stimulus fading, self-modeling, shaping and prompting, social skills and language-based training, and parent-based contingency management and family therapy (all discussed in what follows). Pharmacotherapy in the form of selective serotonin reuptake inhibitors (SSRIs) may serve as a useful adjunct to exposure-based practices to reduce social anxiety and inhibiting behavior, though large-scale studies remain needed (Manassis, Oerbeck, & Overgaard, 2016; Wong, 2010).

Exposure-based practices involve having a child practice saying words in increasingly difficult or anxiety-provoking situations, which are often listed on a hierarchy (Bergman et al., 2013). Such practice may begin in a child's home and later progress to a clinician's office, various community settings, and school-based settings such as classrooms. Exposure-based practices can also involve hierarchies of audibility that range from mouthing words to whispering to barely audible speech to low-volume speech to full-volume speech (Oerbeck et al., 2014).

Exposure-based practices are often combined with stimulus fading, which involves systematically increasing the difficulty of an exposure by fading in new stimuli such as peers or teachers (Beare, Torgerson, & Creviston, 2008). Such practices may also include self-modeling, or audiotaping or videotaping a child as he speaks clearly and well in a comfortable situation such as home. Self-modeling is specifically designed to reward appropriate speech and increase self-efficacy (Kehle, Bray, Byer-Alcorace, Theodore, & Kovac, 2012). In addition, shaping refers to reinforcing successive approximations of audible and frequent speech. These approximations may include initial vocalizations, verbalizations, formal speech, and increased audibility and duration of speech (Zakszeski & DuPaul, 2017).

Exposure-based practices may be combined as well with social skills training given that many of these children have arrested interpersonal skills and abilities to develop friends. An emphasis may be placed on establishing and maintaining eye contact, starting and maintaining conversations effectively, and initiating friendships (Klein, Armstrong, Skira, & Gordon, 2017). In addition, social skills training may be extended to social-academic tasks such as asking or answering a question in class, responding to instructions, giving oral presentations, or participating in specialized classes (Fisak et al., 2006).

Exposure-based practices have been combined with other interventions as well, including language and phonics training (Kearney, 2010) and somatic management practices to control physical aspects of anxiety (Lang et al., 2016). Such practices must be tailored to the developmental level and bilingual nature of children in this population (Christon et al., 2012; Jacob, Suveg, & Shaffer, 2013; Vecchio & Kearney, 2007). In addition, because school settings often involve the most intransigent situations regarding selective mutism, consulting with school officials and conducting classroom-based exposures are often crucial for this population (Cleave, 2009).

Parent-based contingency management is sometimes used to support exposure-based practices as well. This approach involves establishing rewards and disincentives for a child's behavior, with a particular focus on appropriate and audible speech in public settings and natural situations (Busse & Downey, 2011). Parents are also encouraged to replicate exposures completed during a therapy session, reward gradual increases in speech audibility and frequency, and reduce compensatory behaviors such as pointing or gesturing (Vecchio & Kearney, 2009). Family accommodation of selective mutism behaviors, such as speaking or answering for a child, is also targeted (Reuther, Davis, Moree, & Matson, 2011).

Other interventions for selective mutism include family therapy, group therapy, Internet-based approaches, and Tier 1 prevention strategies. Family therapy for selective mutism focuses on educating family members about the disorder, exploring family communications that impact a child's mutism, and addressing enmeshed or overcontrolling parent–child relationships (Monzo, Micotti, & Rashid, 2015; Sloan, 2007). Other researchers have focused on group therapy (Sharkey, McNicholas, Barry, Begley, & Ahern, 2008; Skedgell et al., 2017) to help parents and children gather support to manage speech in public settings via exposure-based practices, anxiety reduction skills, and contingency management.

An Internet-based approach may also be useful for children reluctant to see a therapist in his or her office. This approach has been used to focus on providing psychoeducation about selective mutism, recognizing symptoms of anxiety, using specific social skills, and practicing anxiety management techniques (Bunnell & Beidel, 2013; Fung et al., 2002). Others have advocated for a Tier 1, school-based approach to help prevent symptoms of selective mutism in young children. Such an approach could involve communications to, and trainings with, parents to identify potential anxiety and speaking problems, early identification of mutism behaviors, preparation of preschoolers for kindergarten, and schoolwide oral communication programs. The latter could include maintaining expectancies for speaking, providing ample opportunities and sufficient time for children to respond to others, and minimizing reinforcement of any inappropriate nonverbal communication strategies (Busse & Downey, 2011; Keen, Fonseca, & Wintgens, 2008).

Conclusion

Selective mutism is a potentially debilitating and chronic disorder and one that has proven to be multifaceted, heterogeneous, and complex. The conceptualization of selective mutism has come full circle historically to better represent the various risk factors and potential pathways that characterize this population. Research is still needed on a personalized approach to assessment and intervention for children with selective mutism. In addition, clinical and other efforts to help prevent selective mutism and subsequent problems in social-academic functioning, especially in preschool and in the early grades, must be developed. Widespread information-based strategies to better educate parents and school officials regarding selective mutism, and how the problem interferes with development, are highly recommended as well.

References

Achenbach, T. M., & Rescorla, L. A. (2001). *Manual for ASEBA School-Age Forms & Profiles*. Burlington, VT: University of Vermont, Research Center for Children, Youth, & Families.

Ale, C. M., Mann, A., Menzel, J., Storch, E. A., & Lewin, A. B. (2013). Two cases of early childhood selective mutism: Variations and treatment complexities. *Clinical Case Studies*, *12*, 278–290. doi: 10.1177/1534650113482358

Alyanak, B., Kilincaslan, A., Harmanci, H. S., Demirkaya, S. K., Yurtbay, T., & Vehid, H. E. (2013). Parental adjustment, parenting attitudes and emotional and behavioral problems in children with selective mutism. *Journal of Anxiety Disorders*, *27*, 9–15. doi: 10.1016/j.janxdis.2012.10.001

American Medical Association. (2018). *ICD-10-CM 2018: The Complete Official Codebook*. Atlanta, GA: American Medical Association.

American Psychiatric Association. (2013). *Diagnostic and Statistical Manual for Mental Disorders, 5th Edition (DSM-5)*. Washington, DC: American Psychiatric Association.

Andersson, C. B. & Thomsen, P. H. (1998). Electively mute children: An analysis of 37 Danish cases. *Nordic Journal of Psychiatry*, *52*, 231–238. doi: 10.1080/08039489850139157

Anstendig, K. (1999). Is selective mutism an anxiety disorder? Rethinking its *DSM-IV* classification. *Journal Anxiety Disorders*, *13*, 417–434. doi: 10.1016/S0887-6185(99)00012–2

Arie, M., Henkin, Y., Lamy, D., Tetin-Schneidere, S., Apter, A., Sadeh, A., & Bar-Haim, Y. (2007). Reduced auditory processing capacity during vocalization in children with selective mutism. *Biological Psychiatry*, *61*, 419–421. doi: 10.1016/j.biopsych.2006.02.020

Bar-Haim, Y., Henkin, Y., Ari-Even-Roth, D., Tetin-Schneider, S., Hildesheimer, M., & Muchnik, C. (2004). Reduced auditory efferent activity in childhood selective mutism. *Biological Psychiatry*, *55*, 1061–1068. doi: 10.1016/j.biopsych.2004.02.021

Beare, P., Torgerson, C., & Creviston, C. (2008). Increasing verbal behavior of a student who is selectively mute. *Journal of Emotional and Behavioral Disorders*, *16*, 248–255. doi: 10.1177/1063426608317356

Bergman, R. L., Gonzalez, A., Piacentini, J., & Keller, M. L. (2013). Integrated behavior therapy for selective mutism: A randomized controlled pilot study. *Behaviour Research and Therapy*, *51*, 680–689. doi: 10.1016/j.brat.2013.07.003

Bergman, R. L., Keller, M. L., Piacentini, J., & Bergman, A. J. (2008). The development and psychometric properties of the selective mutism questionnaire. *Journal of Clinical Child and Adolescent Psychology*, *37*, 456–464. doi: 10.1080/15374410801955805

Bergman, R. L., Piacentini, J., & McCracken, J. (2002). Prevalence and description of selective mutism in a school-based sample. *Journal of the American Academy of Child and Adolescent Psychiatry 41*, 938–946. doi: 10.1097/00004583–200208000-00012

Black, B. & Uhde, T. (1995). Psychiatric characteristics of children with selective mutism: A pilot study. *Journal of the American Academy of Child and Adolescent Psychiatry 34*, 847–855. doi: 10.1097/00004583–199507000-00007

Bunnell, B. E. & Beidel, D. C. (2013). Incorporating technology into the treatment of a 17-year-old female with selective mutism. *Clinical Case Studies*, *12*, 291–306. doi: 10.1177/1534650113483357

Busse, R. T. & Downey, J. (2011). Selective mutism: A three-tiered approach to prevention and intervention. *Contemporary School Psychology*, *15*, 53–63.

Carbone, D., Schmidt, L. A., Cunningham, C. E., McHolm, A. E., Edison, S., St. Pierre, J., & Boyle, M. H. (2010). Behavioral and socioemotional functioning in children with selective mutism: A comparison with anxious and typically developing children across multiple informants. *Journal of Abnormal Child Psychology*, *38*, 1057–1067. doi: 10.1007/s10802-010–9425-y

Casey, L. B. (2012). Promoting speech in selective mutism: Experimental analysis, differential reinforcement, and stimulus fading. *Journal of Speech and Language Pathology-Applied Behavior Analysis*, *5*, 65–72.

Chavira, D. A., Shipon-Blum, E., Cohan, S., & Stein, M. B. (2007). Selective mutism and social anxiety disorder: All in the family? *Journal of the American Academy of Child and Adolescent Psychiatry*, *46*, 1464–1472. doi: 10.1097/chi.0b013e318149366a

Chavira, D. A., Stein, M. B., Bailey, K., & Stein, M. T. (2004). Comorbidity of generalized social anxiety disorder and depression in a pediatric primary care sample. *Journal of Affective Disorders*, *80*, 163–171. doi: 10.1016/S0165-0327(03)00103–4

Christon, L. M., Robinson, E. M., Arnold, C. C., Lund, H. G., Vrana, S. R., & Southam-Gerow, M. A. (2012). Modular cognitive-behavioral treatment of an adolescent female with selective mutism and social phobia: A case study. *Clinical Case Studies*, *11*, 474–491. doi: 10.1177/1534650112463956

Cleave, H. (2009). Too anxious to speak? The implications of current research into selective mutism for educational psychology practice. *Educational Psychology in Practice*, *25*, 233–246. doi: 10.1080/02667360903151791

Cohan, S. L., Chavira, D. A., Shipon-Blum, E., Hitchcock, C., Roesch, S. C., & Stein, M. B. (2008). Refining the classification of children with selective mutism: A latent profile analysis. *Journal of Clinical Child and Adolescent Psychology*, *37*, 770–784. doi: 10.1080/15374410802359759

Cohan, S. L., Price, J. M., & Stein, M. B. (2006). Suffering in silence: Why a developmental psychopathology perspective on selective mutism is needed. *Journal of Developmental and Behavioral Pediatrics*, *27*, 341–355. doi: 10.1097/00004703–200608000-00011

Conn, B. M. & Coyne, L. W. (2014). Selective mutism in early childhood: Assessment and treatment of an African American preschool boy. *Clinical Case Studies*, *13*, 487–500. doi: 10.1177/1534650114522912

Cunningham, C. E., McHolm, A. E., & Boyle, M. H. (2006). Social phobia, anxiety, oppositional behavior, social skills, and self-concept in children with specific selective mutism, generalized selective mutism, and community controls. *European Child and Adolescent Psychiatry*, *15*, 245–255. doi: 10.1007/s00787-006–0529-4

Cunningham, C. E., McHolm, A., Boyle, M. H., & Patel, S. (2004). Behavioral and emotional adjustment, family functioning, academic performance, and social relationships in children with selective mutism. *Journal of Child Psychology and Psychiatry and Applied Disciplines*, *45*, 1363–1372. doi: 10.1111/j.1469–7610.2004.00327.x

Diliberto, R. A. & Kearney, C. A. (2016). Anxiety and oppositional behavior profiles among youth with selective mutism. *Journal of Communication Disorders*, *59*, 16–23. doi: 10.1016/j.jcomdis.2015.11.001

Dow, S. P., Sonies, B. C., Scheib, D., Moss, S. E., & Leonard, H. L. (1995). Practical guidelines for the assessment and treatment of selective mutism. *Journal of the American Academy of Child and Adolescent Psychiatry*, *34*, 836–846. doi: 10.1097/00004583-199507000-00006

Dummit, III, E. S., Klein, R. G., Tancer, N. K., Asche, B., Martin, J., & Fairbanks, J. A. (1997). Systematic assessment of 50 children with selective mutism. *Journal of the American Academy of Child and Adolescent Psychiatry*, *36*, 653–660. doi: 10.1097/00004583-199705000-00016

Edison, S. C., Evans, M., McHolm, A. E., Cunningham, C. E., Nowakowski, M. E., Boyle, M., & Schmidt, L. A. (2011). An investigation of control among parents of selectively mute, anxious, and nonanxious children. *Child Psychiatry and Human Development*, *42*, 270–290. doi: 10.1007/s10578-010-0214-1

Ekornås, B., Lundervold, A. J., Tjus, T., & Heimann, M. (2010a). Anxiety disorders in 8–11-year-old children: Motor skill performance and self-perception of competence. *Scandinavian Journal of Psychology*, 51, 271–277.

Ekornås, B., Lundervold, A. J., Tjus, T., & Heimann, M., Linköpings universitet, Institutionen för beteendevetenskap och lärande,... Filosofiska fakulteten. (2010). Anxiety disorders in 8–11-year-old children: Motor skill performance and self-perception of competence. *Scandinavian Journal of Psychology*, 51(3), 271. doi: 10.1111/j.1467-9450.2009.00763.x

Elizur, Y. & Perednik, R. (2003). Prevalence and description of selective mutism in immigrant and native families: A controlled study. *Journal of the American Academy of Child and Adolescent Psychiatry*, *4*, 1451–1459. doi: 10.1097/00004583-200312000-00012

Facon, B., Sahiri, S., & Rivière, V. (2008). A controlled single-case treatment of severe long-term selective mutism in a child with mental retardation. *Behavior Therapy*, *39*, 313–321. doi: 10.1016/j.beth.2007.09.004

Fisak. Jr., B. J., Oliveros, A., & Ehrenreich, J. T. (2006). Assessment and behavioral treatment of selective mutism. *Clinical Case Studies*, *5*, 382–402. doi: 10.1177/1534650104269029

Ford, M. A., Sladeczek, I. E., Carlson, J., & Kratochwill, T. R. (1998). Selective mutism: Phenomenological characteristics. *School Psychology Quarterly*, *13*, 192–227. doi: 10.1037/h0088982

Fung, D. S., Manassis, K., Kenny, A., & Fiksenbaum, L. (2002). Web-based CBT for selective mutism. *Journal of the American Academy of Child and Adolescent Psychiatry*, *41*, 112–113. doi: 10.1097/00004583-200202000-00003

Gensthaler, A., Khalaf, S., Ligges, M., Kaess, M., Freitag, C. M., & Schwenck, C. (2016b). Selective mutism and temperament: The silence and behavioral inhibition to the unfamiliar. *European Child & Adolescent Psychiatry*, *25*, 1113–1120. doi: 10.1007/s00787-016-0835-4

Gensthaler, A., Maichrowitz, V., Kaess, M., Ligges, M., Freitag, C. M., & Schwenck, C. (2016a). Selective mutism: The fraternal twin of childhood social phobia. *Psychopathology*, *49*, 95–107. doi: 10.1159/000444882

Giddan, J. J., Ross, G. J., Sechler, L. L., & Becker, B. R. (1997). Selective mutism in elementary school: Multidisciplinary interventions. *Language, Speech, and Hearing Services in Schools, 28*, 127–133. doi: 10.1044/0161-1461.2802.127

Gray, R. M., Jordan, C. M., Ziegler, R. S., & Livingston, R. B. (2002). Two sets of twins with selective mutism: Neuropsychological findings. *Child Neuropsychology, 8*, 41–51. doi: 10.1076/chin.8.1.41.8717

Heilman, K. J., Connolly, S. D., Padilla, W. O., Wrzosek, M. I., Graczyk, P. A., & Porges, S. W. (2012). Sluggish vagal break reactivity to physical exercise challenge in children with selective mutism. *Development and Psychopathology, 24*, 241–250. doi: 10.1017/S0954579411000800

Henkin, Y. & Bar-Haim, Y. (2015). An auditory-neuroscience perspective on the development of selective mutism. *Developmental Cognitive Neuroscience, 12*, 86–93. doi: 10.1016/j.dcn.2015.01.002

Hua, A. & Major, N. (2016). Selective mutism. *Current Opinion in Pediatrics, 28*, 114–120. doi: 10.1097/MOP.0000000000000300

Jackson, M. F., Allen, R. S., Boothe, A. B., Nava, M. L., & Coates, A. (2005). Innovative analyses and interventions in the treatment of selective mutism. *Clinical Case Studies, 4*, 81–112. doi: 10.1177/1534650103259676

Jacob, M. L., Suveg, C., & Shaffer, A. (2013). Developmentally sensitive behavioral treatment of a 4-year-old, Korean girl with selective mutism. *Clinical Case Studies, 12*, 335–347. doi: 10.1177/1534650113492997

Karakaya, I., Şişmanlar, Ş. G., Öç, Ö. Y., Memik, N. Ç., Coşkun, A., Ağaoğlu, B., & Yavuz, C. I. (2008). Selective mutism: A school-based cross-sectional study from Turkey. *European Child and Adolescent Psychiatry, 17*, 114–117. doi: 10.1007/s00787-007-0644-x

Kearney, C. A. (2010). *Helping Children with Selective Mutism and Their Parents: A Guide for School-Based Professionals*. New York, NY: Oxford.

Kearney, C. A. & Vecchio, J. (2006). Functional analysis and treatment of selective mutism in children. *Journal of Speech and Language Pathology–Applied Behavior Analysis, 1*, 141–148.

Keen, D. V., Fonseca, S., & Wintgens, A. (2008). Selective mutism: A consensus based care pathway of good practice. *Archives of Disease in Childhood, 93*, 838–844. doi: 10.1136/adc.2007.129437

Kehle, T. J., Bray, M. A., Byer-Alcorace, G. F., Theodore, L. A., & Kovac, L. M. (2012). Augmented self-modeling as an intervention for selective mutism. *Psychology in the Schools, 49*, 93–103. doi: 10.1002/pits.21589

Kern, L., Starosta, K. M., Cook, C. R., Bambara, L. M., & Gresham, F. R. (2007). Functional assessment-based intervention for selective mutism. *Behavioral Disorders, 32*, 94–108.

Klein, E. R., Armstrong, S. L., & Shipon-Blum, E. (2013). Assessing spoken language competence in children with selective mutism: Using parents as test presenters. *Communication Disorders Quarterly, 34*, 184–195. doi: 10.1177/1525740112455053

Klein, E. R., Armstrong, S. L., Skira, K., & Gordon, J. (2017). Social Communication Anxiety Treatment (S-CAT) for children and families with selective mutism: A pilot study. *Clinical Child Psychology and Psychiatry, 22*, 90–108. doi: 10.1177/1359104516633497

Kopp, S. & Gillberg, C. (1997). Selective mutism: A population-based study: A research note. *Journal of Child Psychology and Psychiatry and Applied Disciplines, 38*, 257–262. doi: 10.1111/j.1469–7610.1997.tb01859.x

Kristensen, H. (1997). Elective mutism associated with developmental disorder/delay: Two case studies. *European Child and Adolescent Psychiatry, 6*, 234–239. doi: 10.1007/s007870050035.

Kristensen, H. (2000). Selective mutism and comorbidity with developmental disorder/delay, anxiety disorder, and elimination disorder. *Journal of the American Academy of Child and Adolescent Psychiatry, 39*, 249–256. doi: 10.1097/00004583–200002000–00026.

Kristensen, H. (2001). Multiple informants' report of emotional and behavioural problems in a nation-wide sample of selective mute children and controls. *European Child and Adolescent Psychiatry, 10*, 135–142. doi: 10.1007/s007870170037.

Kristensen, H. & Torgersen, S. (2001). MCMI-II personality traits and symptom traits in parents of children with selective mutism: A case-control study. *Journal of Abnormal Psychology, 110*, 648–652. doi: 10.1037/0021-843X.110.4.648

Kristensen, H. & Torgersen, S. (2002). A case-control study of EAS child and parental temperaments in selectively mute children with and without a co-morbid communication disorder. *Nordic Journal of Psychiatry, 56*, 347–353. doi: 10.1080/080394802760322114

Krohn, D. D., Weckstein, S. M., & Wright H. L. (1992). A study of the effectiveness of a specific treatment for elective mutism. *Journal of the American Academy of Child and Adolescent Psychiatry 31*, 711–718. doi: 10.1097/00004583–199207000–00020

Krolian, E. (1998). "Speech is silver but silence is golden": Day hospital treatment of two electively mute children. *Clinical Social Work Journal, 16*, 355–377. doi: 10.1007/BF00755146

Krysanski, V. L. (2003). A brief review of selective mutism literature. *Journal of Psychology, 137*, 29–40. doi: 10.1080/00223980309600597

Kumpulainen, K., Rasanen, R., Raaska, H., & Samppi, V. (1998). Selective mutism among second-graders in an elementary school. *European Child and Adolescent Psychiatry 7*, 24–29. doi: 10.1007/s007870050041

Lang, C., Nir, Z., Gothelf, A., Domachevsky, S., Ginton, L., Kushnir, J., & Gothelf, D. (2016). The outcome of children with selective mutism following cognitive behavioral intervention: A follow-up study. *European Journal of Pediatrics, 175*, 481–487. doi: 10.1007/s00431-015–2651-0

Letamendi, A. M., Chavira, D. A., Hitchcock, C. A., Roesch, S. C., Shipon-Blum, E., & Stein, M. B. (2008). Selective Mutism Questionnaire: Measurement structure and validity. *Journal of the American Academy of Child and Adolescent Psychiatry, 47*, 1197–1204. doi: 10.1097/CHI.0b013e3181825a7b

Levin-Decanini, T., Connolly, S. D., Simpson, D., Suarez, L., & Jacob, S. (2013). Comparison of behavioral profiles for anxiety-related comorbidities including ADHD and selective mutism in children: Behavioral profiles of children with anxiety. *Depression and Anxiety, 30*, 857–864. doi: 10.1002/da.22094

Manassis, K., Fung, D., Tannock, R., Sloman, L., Fiksenbaum, L., & McInnes, A. (2003). Characterizing selective mutism: Is it more than social anxiety? *Depression and Anxiety, 18*, 153–161. doi: 10.1002/da.10125.

Manassis, K., Oerbeck, B., & Overgaard, K. R. (2016). The use of medication in selective mutism: A systematic review. *European Child and Adolescent Psychiatry, 25*, 571–578. doi: 10.1007/s00787-015–0794-1

Manassis, K., Tannock, R., Garland, E. J., Minde, K., McInnes, A., & Clark, S. (2007). The sounds of silence: Language, cognition and anxiety in selective mutism. *Journal of the American Academy of Child and Adolescent Psychiatry, 46*, 1187–1195. doi: 10.1097/CHI.0b013e318076b7ab

Marakovitz, S. E., Wagmiller, R. L., Mian, N. D., Briggs-Gowan, M. J., & Carter, A. S. (2011). Lost toy? Monsters under the bed? Contributions of temperament and family factors to early internalizing problems in boys and girls. *Journal of Clinical Child and Adolescent Psychology, 40*, 233–244. doi: 10.1080/15374416.2011.546036

Martinez, Y. J., Tannock, R., Manassis, K., Garland, E. J., Clark, S., & McInnes, A. (2015). The teachers' role in the assessment of selective mutism and anxiety disorders. *Canadian Journal of School Psychology, 30*, 83–101. doi: 10.1177/0829573514566377

McInnes, A., Fung, D., Manassis, K., Fiksenbaum, L., & Tannock, R. (2004). Narrative skills in children with selective mutism: An exploratory study. *American Journal of Speech-Language Pathology, 13*, 304–315. doi: 10.1044/1058–0360(2004/031)

Melfsen, S., Walitza, S., & Warnke, A. (2006). The extent of social anxiety in combination with mental disorders. *European Child and Adolescent Psychiatry, 15*, 111–117. doi: 10.1007/s00787-006–0510-2

Mitchell, A. D. & Kratochwill, T. R. (2013). Treatment of selective mutism: Applications in the clinic and school through conjoint consultation. *Journal of Educational and Psychological Consultation, 23*, 36–62. doi: 10.1080/10474412.2013.757151

Monzo, M. P., Micotti, S., & Rashid, S. (2015). The mutism of the mind: Child and family therapists at work with children and families suffering with selective mutism. *Journal of Child Psychotherapy, 41*, 22–40. doi: 10.1080/0075417X.2015.1005385

Muchnik, C., Ari-Even Roth, D., Hildesheimer, M., Arie, M., Bar-Haim, Y., & Henkin, Y. (2013). Abnormalities in auditory efferent activities in children with selective mutism. *Audiology and Neurotology, 18*, 353–361. doi: 10.1159/000354160

Mulligan, C. A., Hale, J. B., & Shipon-Blum, E. (2015). Selective mutism: Identification of subtypes and implications for treatment. *Journal of Education and Human Development, 4*, 79–96. doi: 10.15640/jehd.v4n1a9

Muris, P., Hendriks, E., & Bot, S. (2016). Children of few words: Relations among selective mutism, behavioral inhibition, and (social) anxiety symptoms in 3-to 6-year-olds. *Child Psychiatry and Human Development, 47*, 94–101. doi: 10.1007/s10578-015–0547-x

Muris, P. & Ollendick, T. H. (2015). Children who are anxious in silence: A review on selective mutism, the new anxiety disorder in *DSM-5*. *Clinical Child and Family Psychology Review, 18*, 151–169. doi: 10.1007/s10567-015–0181-y

Nowakowski, M. E., Tasker, S. L., Cunningham, C. E., McHolm, A. E., Edison, S., Pierre, J. S., … Schmidt, L. A. (2011). Joint attention in parent–child dyads involving children with selective mutism: A comparison between anxious and typically developing children. *Child Psychiatry and Human Development, 42*, 78–92. doi: 10.1007/s10578-010–0208-z

Oerbeck, B., Stein, M. B., Wentzel-Larsen, T., Langsrud, O., & Kristensen, H. (2014). A randomized controlled trial of a home and school-based intervention for selective mutism: Defocused communication and behavioural techniques. *Child and Adolescent Mental Health*, *19*, 192–198. doi: 0.1111/camh.12045

Omdal, H. & Galloway, D. (2007). Interviews with selectively mute children. *Emotional and Behavioural Difficulties*, *12*, 205–214. doi: 10.1080/13632750701489956

Omdal, H. & Galloway, D. (2008). Could selective mutism be re-conceptualised as a specific phobia of expressive speech? An exploratory post-hoc study. *Child and Adolescent Mental Health*, *13*, 74–81. doi: 10.1111/j.1475–3588.2007.00454.x

Remschmidt, H., Poller, M., Herpertz-Dahlmann, B., Hennighausen, K., & Gutenbrunner, C. (2001). A follow-up study of 45 patients with elective mutism. *European Archives of Psychiatry and Clinical Neuroscience*, *251*, 284–296. doi: 10.1007/PL00007547

Reuther, E. T., Davis, T. E., Moree, B. N., & Matson, J. L. (2011). Treating selective mutism using modular CBT for child anxiety: A case study. *Journal of Clinical Child and Adolescent Psychology*, *40*, 156–163. doi: 10.1080/15374416.2011.533415

Schill, M. T., Kratochwill, T. R., & Gardner, W. I. (1996). An assessment protocol for selective mutism: Analogue assessment using parents as facilitators. *Journal of School Psychology*, *34*, 1–21. doi: 10.1016/0022–4405(95)00023–2

Schum, R. L. (2006). Clinical perspectives on the treatment of selective mutism. *Journal of Speech and Language Pathology–Applied Behavior Analysis*, *1*, 149–163.

Scott, S. & Beidel, D.C. (2011). Selective mutism: An update and suggestions for future research. *Current Psychiatry Reports*, *13*, 251–257. doi: 10.1007/s11920-011–0201-7

Segal, N. L. (2003). "Two" quiet: Monozygotic female twins with selective mutism. *Clinical Child Psychology and Psychiatry*, *8*, 473–488. doi: 10.1177/13591045030084005

Sharkey, L. & McNicholas, F. (2008). "More than 100 years of silence," elective mutism: A review of the literature. *European Child and Adolescent Psychiatry*, *17*, 255–263. doi: 10.1007/s00787-007–0658-4

Sharkey, L., McNicholas, F., Barry, E., Begley, M., & Ahern, S. (2008). Group therapy for selective mutism: A parents' and children's treatment group. *Journal of Behavior Therapy and Experimental Psychiatry*, *39*, 538–545. doi: 10.1016/j.jbtep.2007.12.002

Sharp, W. G., Sherman, C., & Gross, A. M. (2007). Selective mutism and anxiety: A review of the current conceptualization of the disorder. *Journal of Anxiety Disorders*, *21*, 568–579. doi: 10.1016/j.janxdis.2006.07.002

Shriver, M. D., Segool, N., & Gortmarker, V. (2011). Behavior observations for linking assessment to treatment for selective mutism. *Education and Treatment of Children*, *34*, 389–410. doi: 10.1353/etc.2011.0023

Silveira, R., Jainer, A. K., England, T., & Bates, G. (2004). Fluoxetine treatment of selective mutism in pervasive developmental disorder. *International Journal of Psychiatry in Clinical Practice*, *8*, 179–180. doi: 10.1080/13651500410006143

Silverman, W. K. & Albano, A. M. (1996). *The Anxiety Disorders Interview Schedule for Children for DSM-IV, Child and Parent Versions*. San Antonio, TX: Psychological Corporation.

Skedgell, K. K., Fornander, M., & Kearney, C. A. (2017). Personalized individual and group therapy for multifaceted selective mutism. *Clinical Case Studies*, *16*, 166–181. doi: 10.1177/1534650116685619

Sloan, T. L. (2007). Family therapy with selectively mute children: A case study. *Journal of Marital and Family Therapy, 33*, 94–105. doi: 10.1111/j.1752–0606.2007.00008.x

Standart, S. & Le Couteur, A. (2003). The quiet child: A literature review of selective mutism. *Child and Adolescent Mental Health, 8*, 154–160. doi: 10.1111/1475–3588.00065

Stein, M. B., Yang, B. Z., Chavira, D. A., Hitchcock, C. A., Sung, S. C., Shipon-Blum, E., & Gelernter, J. (2011). A common genetic variant in the neurexin superfamily member CNTNAP2 is associated with increased risk for selective mutism and social anxiety-related traits. *Biological Psychiatry, 69*, 825–831. doi: 10.1016/j.biopsych.2010.11.008

Steinhausen, H. C. & Adamek, R. (1997). The family history of children with elective mutism: A research report. *European Child and Adolescent Psychiatry, 6*, 107–111. doi: 10.1007/s007870050015

Steinhausen, H. C. & Juzi, C. (1996). Elective mutism: An analysis of 100 cases. *Journal of the American Academy of Child and Adolescent Psychiatry, 35*, 606–614. doi: 10.1097/00004583–199605000-00015

Steinhausen, H. C., Wachter, M., Laimböck, K., & Metzke, C. W. (2006). A long-term outcome study of selective mutism in childhood. *Journal of Child Psychology and Psychiatry and Applied Disciplines, 47*, 751–756. doi: 10.1111/j.1469–7610.2005.01560.x

Toppelberg, C. O., Tabors, P., Coggins, A., Lum, K., & Burger, C. (2005). Differential diagnosis of selective mutism in bilingual children. *Journal of the American Academy of Child and Adolescent Psychiatry, 44*, 592–595. doi: 10.1097/01.chi.0000157549.87078.f8

Vasilyeva, N. (2013). Significant factors in the development of elective mutism: A single case study of a 5 year-old girl. *British Journal of Psychotherapy, 29*, 373–388. doi: 10.1111/bjp.12036

Vecchio, J. L. & Kearney, C. A. (2005). Selective mutism in children: Comparison to youths with and without anxiety disorders. *Journal of Psychopathology and Behavioral Assessment, 27*, 31–37. doi: 10.1007/s10862-005–3263-1

Vecchio, J. L. & Kearney, C. A. (2007). Assessment and treatment of a Hispanic youth with selective mutism. *Clinical Case Studies, 6*, 34–43. doi: 10.1177/1534650106290393

Vecchio, J. L. & Kearney, C. A. (2009). Treating youths with selective mutism with an alternating design of exposure-based practice and contingency management. *Behavior Therapy, 40*, 380–392. doi: 10.1016/j.beth.2008.10.005

Viana, A. G., Beidel, D. C., & Rabian, B. (2009). Selective mutism: A review and integration of the last 15 years. *Clinical Psychology Review, 29*, 57–67. doi: 10.1016/j.cpr.2008.09.009

Wong, P. (2010). Selective mutism: A review of etiology, comorbidities, and treatment. *Psychiatry, 7*, 23–31.

Yanof, J. (1996). Language, communication, and transference in child analysis. II. Is child analysis really analysis? *Journal of the American Psychoanalytic Association, 44*, 79–100. doi: 10.1177/000306519604400105

Yeganeh, R., Beidel, D. C., & Turner, S. M. (2006). Selective mutism: More than social anxiety? *Depression and Anxiety, 23*, 117–123. doi: 10.1002/da.20139

Yeganeh, R., Beidel, D. C., Turner, S. M., Pina, A. A., & Silverman, W. K. (2003). Clinical distinctions between selective mutism and social phobia: An investigation of childhood psychopathology. *Journal of the American Academy of Child and Adolescent Psychiatry, 42*, 1069–1075. doi: 10.1097/01.CHI.0000070262.24125.2

Young, B. J., Bunnel, B. E., & Beidel, D. C. (2012), Evaluations of children with selective mutism and social phobia: A comparison of psychological and psychophysiological arousal. *Behavior Modification, 36*, 525–544. doi: 10.1177/0145445512443980

Zakszeski, B. N. & DuPaul, G. J. (2017). Reinforce, shape, expose, and fade: A review of treatments for selective mutism (2005–2015). *School Mental Health, 9*, 1–15. doi: 10.1007/s12310-016–9198-8

Zelenko, M. & Shaw, R. (2000). Case study: Selective mutism in an immigrant child. *Clinical Child Psychology and Psychiatry, 5*, 555–562. doi: 10.1177/1359104500005004009

Etiology and Phenomenology of Specific OCD Spectrum Disorders

21 Obsessive-Compulsive and Related Disorders

Lillian Reuman and Jonathan S. Abramowitz

Obsessive-compulsive disorder (OCD) is among the most devastating psychological conditions. Its symptoms often interfere with work or school, interpersonal relationships, and activities of daily living (e.g., watching television, childcare). OCD is a complex and highly heterogeneous syndrome, and numerous conceptual approaches have been proposed in an attempt to understand its psychopathology. In this chapter we address the nature of OCD and a number of conditions presumed to be associated with it. We also describe the major theoretical models proposed to explain the development and maintenance of OCD. We present a discussion of the strengths and limitations of each perspective as supported by the available empirical literature.

Phenomenology

The hallmark signs of OCD include obsessions and compulsions (defined in what follows), which are time-consuming, associated with distress, and interfere with work or school, interpersonal relationships, and activities of daily living (e.g., running errands). Further, the psychopathology of obsessions and compulsions is complex, as affected individuals struggle with ubiquitous unwanted thoughts, doubts, and urges that, while seemingly senseless, are perceived as signs of danger and threat. Moreover, obsessions and compulsions are heterogeneous and occur across theme-based symptom dimensions. This highly variable presentation can perplex clinicians and complicate treatment. In order to address and clarify this nuanced psychological condition, this section describes the phenomenology of obsessions and compulsions. The section will also address the extent to which obsessions and compulsions are related to so-called "obsessive-compulsive and related disorders" (OCRDs).

Obsessions

Obsessions refer to intrusive, persistent private occurrences (i.e., thoughts, images, doubts, and ideas) that the person experiences as unwanted or senseless (American Psychiatric Association [APA], 2013). These thoughts are often experienced as repugnant, and they provoke anxiety or guilt. Although highly person-specific, obsessions can be organized into themes such as contamination (e.g., concerns about germs), responsibility for causing or not preventing harm, taboo thoughts (about sex, violence, and blasphemy), and the need for order and symmetry. Unlike other types of repetitive thoughts that are often described as "obsessive" (e.g., adoration for one's new car or attachment to one's hobby), clinical obsessions are experienced as *unwanted* or *uncontrollable* in that they "invade" and persist in one's consciousness. They often seem to occur spontaneously at what seems like the most inconvenient times (e.g., a thought about harm while spending time with one's newborn baby), or are triggered by something in the environment (e.g., the sight of a cross provokes blasphemous thoughts). Further, obsessions are not in line with the person's self-image (i.e., ego-dystonic); that is, a mother who has thoughts about harming her newborn views herself as a good mother and maintains that she would never want to act upon her thoughts. Finally, obsessions are *resisted*. Individuals intently attempt to "deal with," neutralize, or avoid their unwanted internal experiences. The motivation to resist is activated by the fear that if action is not taken, negative consequences will ensue.

Compulsions

Compulsions are urges to engage in behaviors, such as overt or mental rituals, that reduce or remove distress associated with obsessions. Rituals, which are functionally related to obsessions, typically belong to the following categories: decontamination (washing/cleaning), checking (e.g., ensuring that the door is locked or the stove is off, repeatedly asking someone for assurances), repeating routine activities (e.g., turning a light switch off and on), ordering and arranging, and mental rituals (e.g., repeating a mantra to neutralize a blasphemous thought). These behaviors are often performed according to self-prescribed rules. They are usually recognized (at least to some extent) as senseless and excessive (although, as we discuss later in this chapter, insight into the senselessness of these symptoms varies from person to person, and even within an individual over time). In contrast to involuntary repetitive behaviors such as tics, rituals are deliberate. Finally, compulsive behaviors have a specific function: they are performed to reduce distress. This function stands in contrast to *impulsive* behaviors (e.g., hair-pulling or skin-picking), which are carried out because they produce pleasure, distraction, or gratification (APA, 2013).

Avoidance

Avoidance behavior is another strategy commonly deployed in response to obsessions, usually to prevent unwanted thoughts, negative outcomes, uncertainty, and compulsive urges. Avoidance is intended to prevent exposure to situations that would provoke obsessional anxiety and necessitate compulsive rituals. For example, one woman avoided pencils because they evoked obsessional thoughts of stabbing others in the eye. Other patients engage in avoidance so that they do not have to carry out time-consuming or embarrassing rituals. For example, one client avoided driving past cemeteries so that he would not have to engage in extensive praying rituals that were triggered by thoughts and images of the dead. Ultimately, avoidance is problematic, as it does not provide an opportunity for the individual to come into contact with the feared situation and learn that the feared outcomes are unlikely to materialize.

Symptom Dimensions

Although there are grounds for conceptualizing OCD as a homogeneous disorder, research has identified reliable and valid symptom dimensions comprised of both obsessions and compulsions (Abramowitz et al., 2010; McKay et al., 2004). These dimensions include: (a) contamination (contamination obsessions and decontamination rituals), (b) responsibility for harm and mistakes (aggressive obsessions and checking rituals), (c) incompleteness (obsessions about order or exactness and arranging rituals), and (d) unacceptable violent, sexual, or blasphemous thoughts with mental rituals. Specifically, obsessions about responsibility for harm and mistakes are associated with checking rituals that serve to provide reassurance; obsessions about incompleteness and the need for symmetry and exactness occur along with ordering, arranging, and counting rituals; contamination obsessions that feature the sense of tactile or mental contamination or disgust co-occur with washing and cleaning rituals; and religious, sexual, and violent obsessions often trigger mental rituals, efforts to neutralize and suppress unwanted thoughts, and other forms of checking and reassurance-seeking behaviors.

Ego Dystonia

Ego dystonicity refers to the degree to which someone's obsessions are inconsistent with the ways in which he or she views him/herself with respect to ideals and morals (Clark, 2004). Given that obsessions occur outside the context of one's value system, they are perceived as a threat to one's self. Not surprisingly, the nature of obsessive concerns can lead individuals to question their character and engage in rituals to neutralize or counteract their unwelcome beliefs. Ego dystonicity is most apparent in the responsibility for harm and unacceptable thoughts symptom dimensions, as obsessional thoughts about stabbing someone or hitting someone with their car run counter to moral codes. Further, sexual obsessions (i.e., thoughts about molesting another person) or obsessions related to vulnerable victims (i.e., young children or elderly parents) (Berman, Wheaton, & Abramowitz, 2012) may elicit increased guilt and distress and cause individuals to fret about "latent sexual and aggressive desires" (Clark, 2004, p. 29). Ego dystonicity also arises among meticulous individuals with OCD who may be troubled by the obsessive doubt related to making a mistake, which could be considered intolerable and out of line with one's standards. This quality of ego dystonicity among obsessive beliefs also separates obsessions and compulsions in the context of OCD from other repetitive behaviors such as hair-pulling, which may produce pleasure.

Insight

As previously alluded to, the insight an individual has into the senselessness of his or her obsessions and compulsions varies widely. While some clients recognize the irrationality of their OCD symptoms (e.g., "I realize the probability of hitting someone while driving to work is very low, but I just can't take the chance"), others hold a firm conviction that these intrusive thoughts and behaviors are rational. Insight may shift over time and can vary according to different symptom domains. For example, a client might recognize that her obsessive thoughts about bad luck from the number 13 are senseless and simultaneously have poor insight into the irrationality of her religious obsessions.

The *Diagnostic and Statistical Manual – Fifth Edition* (*DSM-5*) (APA, 2013) criteria for OCD include the specifiers "good or fair insight," "poor insight," and "absent insight" to denote the degree to which the person views his or her obsessional fears and compulsive behavior as reasonable. Although many individuals with OCD recognize – to some degree – that their obsessions and compulsions are senseless and/or extreme, studies suggest that 4% of patients are convinced that their symptoms are realistic (i.e., poor or absent insight) (Foa & Kozak, 1995). Individuals with poor insight lack self-awareness regarding their obsessions and compulsions. Individuals with delusional conviction believe that their obsessions are realistic and reasonable (Eisen et al., 2001). Poorer insight appears to be associated with religious obsessions, fears of mistakes, and aggressive obsessional impulses (Tolin, Abramowitz, Kozak, & Foa, 2001).

Certainty

Intolerance of uncertainty (IU) refers to "beliefs about the necessity of being certain, about the capacity to cope with unpredictable change, and about adequate functioning in situations which are inherently ambiguous" (Obsessive Compulsive Cognitions Working Group [OCCWG], 1997, p. 678). IU is an important domain of dysfunctional cognition associated with OCD (OCCWG, 1997), as individuals with OCD often report pathological doubt – and an intolerance of uncertainty – with regard to feared objects, situations, and beliefs (e.g., "I need to know for certain that I have not sinned"). Individuals with a greater intolerance of uncertainty characteristically find uncertainty stressful and upsetting, believe that uncertainty should be avoided at all costs, and experience impairment in uncertain or ambiguous situations (Buhr & Dugas, 2002). Although this uncertainty may be most visible and applicable in certain overt rituals (e.g., checking behaviors within the responsibility for harm symptom domain), it is present across OCD symptom dimensions. This doubt may be due to impairments in memory and or diminished confidence in one's memory (e.g., Foa, Amir, Gershuny, Molnar, & Kozak, 1997);

relatedly, rituals may stem from a heightened desire for certainty (i.e., intolerance of uncertainty) and memory vividness.

Prevalence and Course of OCD

The lifetime prevalence estimates of OCD are between 0.7% and 2.9% (e.g., Kessler et al., 2005), with slightly higher prevalence rates among females than among males (Bogetto, Venturello, Albert, Maina, & Ravizza, 1999). The disorder typically begins by age 25 but can onset at any age; childhood or adolescence onset is common. Average age of onset, however, is slightly earlier in males (about 21 years) than in females (22 to 24 years) (Rasmussen & Eisen, 1992). The course of OCD is chronic with a low rate of spontaneous remission. Left untreated, symptoms fluctuate and are often exacerbated during periods of increased life stress. Although effective treatments exist, full recovery is often the exception rather than the rule.

Interpersonal Aspects of OCD

OCD often occurs in an interpersonal context and negatively impacts the sufferer's relationships (e.g., marriages). In turn, dysfunctional relationship patterns can promote the maintenance of OCD symptoms such that a vicious cycle continues. In an attempt to demonstrate care and concern for an affected individual, a partner or spouse might inadvertently behave in ways that maintain OCD symptoms by helping with compulsive rituals and avoidance behavior (i.e., *symptom accommodation*). Conversely, arguments about the seeming illogic of one's OCD symptoms may also create relationship distress and conflict, which further exacerbate the anxiety and obsessional symptoms.

Symptom accommodation. Accommodation occurs when a friend or relative participates in the loved one's rituals, facilitates avoidance strategies, assumes daily responsibilities for the sufferer, or helps to resolve problems that have resulted from the patient's obsessional fears and compulsive urges. Accommodation can occur at the request (or demand) of the affected individual, who intentionally solicits help for controlling his or her anxiety. In other instances, loved ones voluntarily accommodate because they wish to empathize with their suffering partners or prevent their loved one from becoming highly anxious. Conceptually, accommodation by a relative or close friend perpetuates OCD symptoms by the same mechanism as avoidance and compulsive rituals. For instance, consider a woman with obsessional fears of accidentally hitting a pedestrian while driving who requests that her husband drive the couple's children to school each day. By engaging in this behavior (i.e., by accommodating his wife's OCD symptoms), he prevents his wife from learning that her feared consequences are unlikely to materialize. Furthermore, she misses the opportunity to learn that she could manage the temporary anxiety that accompanies her repugnant obsessions.

Relationship conflict. Relationship stress and conflict play an important role in the maintenance of OCD. Families in which one member suffers from OCD often report problems with interdependency, unassertiveness, and avoidant communication patterns that foster stress and conflict. This is likely a bidirectional relationship, as OCD symptoms and relationship distress influence each other. For example, a husband's contentious relationship with his wife might contribute to overall anxiety and uncertainty that feeds into his obsessional doubting. His excessive checking, reassurance seeking, and overly cautious actions could also precipitate frequent disagreements. In particular, poor problem-solving skills, hostility, and criticism might increase distress and contribute to OCD.

Obsessive-Compulsive Related Disorders (OCRDs)

Once classified as an anxiety disorder, within the most recent edition of the *DSM*, OCD has been moved to become the hallmark condition within a new grouping of disorders: the OCRDs. These conditions are grouped together on the basis of "shared compulsive behavior and failures in behavioral inhibition" (Fineberg et al., 2011, p. 21). This novel DSM category includes: (a) two disorders making their debut in *DSM-5* (hoarding disorder and skin-picking [excoriation] disorder), (b) a former somatoform disorder, body dysmorphic disorder (BDD), and (c) hair-pulling disorder (formerly known as trichotillomania and classified as an impulse control disorder). The notion of OCRDs was initially conceived on the basis of overlaps in overt symptom presentation (e.g., repetitive thinking and behavior patterns) (Hollander, Kwon, Stein, & Broatch, 1996). Proponents maintain that the repetitive thinking or behavior patterns of these disorders fall along a continuum of failure in behavior inhibition (i.e., the inability to cease one's actions) with compulsive and impulsive behaviors at opposite ends of the spectrum (Fineberg et al., 2011). At one end of the continuum are compulsive disorders such as OCD and BDD; impulse control problems (e.g., skin-picking and hair-pulling, which are characterized by pleasurable consequences) fall at the other end of the continuum. Essentially, the unifying factor among the OCRDs is the presence of repetitive behaviors that the person seemingly cannot stop performing. By emphasizing the presence of repetitive behaviors (compulsive, body-focused, impulsive, or otherwise) as a criterion for the OCRD class, this approach overlooks other essential (and arguably more fundamental) features of OCD (e.g., fear) and putatively related conditions. Other authors (e.g., Abramowitz & Jacoby, 2015) have criticized the grouping of these disorders on the basis of important differences in phenomenology among the various conditions, as we critically examine next.

Hair-pulling disorder. The *DSM-5* includes five criteria for hair-pulling disorder; the first two are: (a) recurrent hair-pulling resulting in hair loss and (b) repeated attempts to stop the hair-pulling. Considering these two criteria in isolation among patients who repetitively pull their hair suggests that shared features with OCD exist; however, a more careful examination suggests that hair-pulling is phenomenologically distinct from OCD. Although OCD and hair-pulling disorder both involve repetitive behavior, the intrusive anxiety-evoking obsessional thoughts that occur in OCD are not present in trichotillomania. Obsessional fear motivates rituals in OCD, yet research indicates that feelings of general tension, depression, anger, boredom, frustration, indecision, or fatigue precipitate urges to pull hair (Christenson et al., 1993). Studies also suggest that hair-pulling in trichotillomania, unlike rituals in OCD, leads to pleasurable feelings (e.g., Schreiber, Odlaug, & Grant, 2011).

Skin-picking. With nearly identical criteria to hair-pulling disorder, skin-picking disorder (i.e., excoriation disorder) does not involve obsessional thoughts, and repetitive skin-picking functions differently than do compulsive rituals in OCD. Clinically significant skin-picking may be triggered by an array of antecedents (e.g., general stress, apprehension, boredom, tiredness) (e.g., Arnold, Auchenbach, & McElroy, 2001), and emotion regulation difficulties (i.e., emotional reactivity) have been shown to predict skin-picking (Snorrason et al., 2010). Skin picking can also be triggered by the feel (e.g., a bump or unevenness) or look (e.g., a blemish or discoloration) of the skin. In contrast to deliberate, anxiety-reducing compulsive behavior in OCD, episodes of skin-picking often begin outside of the person's awareness (i.e., they are unfocused) and become more focused after a period of time (e.g., Keuthen et al., 2000).

Body dysmorphic disorder. Unlike the aforementioned conditions (skin-picking and hair-pulling), BDD symptoms do appear to overlap in important ways with OCD symptoms. Two main criteria for BDD include: a) a preoccupation with one or more perceived defects or flaws in one's physical appearance (i.e., a belief that one looks ugly or deformed), and b) excessive repetitive behaviors (e.g., checking one's appearance) or mental acts (e.g., comparing oneself to others) performed to relieve distress associated with the preoccupation. Research and clinical observations suggest genuine similarities in how these repetitive symptoms are experienced and how they function to maintain the disorders. In particular, appearance-related worries in BDD are experienced as intrusive, unwanted, and anxiety provoking. BDD rituals function to reduce anxiety and are not experienced as pleasurable (Phillips et al., 2010). Moreover, research shows that the excessive checking and comparing behaviors contribute to maintaining the appearance-related preoccupations in much the same way that compulsive rituals maintain obsessional fears in OCD (Phillips et al., 2010).

Hoarding disorder. The *DSM-5* describes hoarding disorder as characterized by excessive acquisition and difficulty discarding or parting with possessions – even those of limited value – due to an intense perceived need to save such items and distress associated with discarding them. As a result, large numbers of possessions accumulate and clutter the person's living areas to the extent that it may become difficult to use the living space for its intended purposes. Hoarding is actually observed in a number of *DSM* conditions, including depression, anorexia nervosa, schizophrenia, and dementia (e.g., Abramowitz et al., 2008, Frankenburg,

1984, Luchins et al., 1992), and the text of the *DSM-5* does not make clear why it is included as an OCRD. For several decades, however, hoarding was considered a symptom of OCD (e.g., Coles et al., 2003). Yet hoarding symptoms differ markedly from those of OCD. First, although hoarding involves recurring thoughts of acquiring and maintaining possessions, these thoughts are not experienced as fear-provoking in the same way that OCD obsessions are, and they are not particularly intrusive or unwanted (Rachman et al., 2009; Wheaton et al., 2011). Moreover, excessive acquiring and saving does not result in an escape from obsessional anxiety in the way that washing or checking in OCD does, and thus cannot be conceptualized as "compulsive" or "ritualistic" in the OCD sense.

OCD and Research Domain Criteria (RDoC)

Recognized as the predominant approach to date for classifying psychopathology, the *DSM-5* offers descriptive criteria for diagnosing OCD; however, it is not without criticism. Among the many critiques are the high rates of diagnostic comorbidity (i.e., overlapping symptoms *across* disorders) on the one hand and heterogeneity (i.e., wide variations) *within* categories of disorders on the other hand. Accordingly, some researchers have developed alternative classification systems to address these challenges. One such system is the Research Domain Criteria (RDoC), put forth by the National Institute for Mental Health (NIMH). RDoC represents an attempt to examine "underlying [transdiagnostic] neurobiological systems" based on the premise that many mental disorders fall along dimensions (e.g., cognition, mood) and are marked by traits that exist along a continuum ranging from normal to severe (NIMH, 2008). Although this is a newer framework and additional research is warranted to determine its validity, three specific RDoC domains (i.e., systems) are directly applicable to the context of OCD: First, the *negative valence domain* entails constructs that include fear, distress, and aggression. Within OCD, systems related to acute and potential threat/fear are of particular interest. Second, the *positive valence system* includes constructs such as reward seeking and learning, decision-making, and habit formation. Given preliminary evidence of aberrant reward processing in OCD (e.g., Nielen, Den Boer, & Smid, 2009), further research is necessary to explore this construct. Last, the domain of cognition aims to break down complex cognitive functions in order to understand simpler components. Of relevance in the context of OCD are constructs such as working memory and fear conditioning, which we discuss within the next section of this chapter.

Etiology and Maintenance

Models Based on Conditioning and Learning Theory

Throughout the 20th century, conditioning models based on learning theory formed the basis of clinicians' and researchers' understanding of OCD and other fear-based problems. A predominant model was Mowrer's (1960) two-factor theory, which proposed that obsessional fears were acquired by classical conditioning and maintained by operant conditioning (i.e., reinforcement). For example, an obsessional fear of molesting one's young niece could arise from an incident in which the person had an aversive experience (the unconditioned stimulus, which could include the physiological experience of anxiety or fear itself) in the presence of their niece (the conditioned stimulus), leading to a classically conditioned fear. Negative reinforcement then maintains the obsessional fear. That is, avoiding or escaping from distress (e.g., by avoiding one's niece) or engaging in compulsive rituals (e.g., by "neutralizing" the unwanted thoughts with a mantra such as "I am a good person") serves to reduce anxiety and prevent the disconfirmation of feared consequences.

Conditioning models, however, have some limitations. First, many individuals with OCD do not recall conditioning experiences in the context of their obsession that would have led to the development of obsessional fear. Second, behavioral models have difficulty explaining the emergence, persistence, and content of repugnant sexual, religious, and violent obsessions (e.g., obsessional images of Jesus-related fellatio). Third, this model fails to explain why the themes and content of obsessions and compulsions may shift for an individual over time. With these limitations in mind, theorists shifted to consider the role that cognitive processes play in the development and persistence of OCD.

General Cognitive Deficit Models

Research regarding cognitive deficits in OCD has taken two directions. The first main area of research focuses on dysfunctions or deficits in cognitive processing, which may have neurobiological or neuropsychological origins. The idea that individuals with OCD suffer from cognitive processing deficits is intuitively appealing. For example, it seems plausible that those with checking rituals have a memory problem and can't recall whether they completed an action, such as locking the door. Alternately, individuals could have a deficit in their ability to accurately recall whether they *actually* turned off the oven or merely *imagined* doing so (i.e., a *reality monitoring* deficit). Research findings, however, provide little support for these types of memory problems in OCD (Abramovitch, Abramowitz, & Mittelman, 2013). In fact, rather than memory deficits, the most consistent finding in the literature has been that individuals with OCD have less *confidence* in their own memory than do individuals without OCD (e.g., Foa, Amir, Gershuny, Molnar, & Kozak, 1997; McNally & Kohlbeck, 1993; Woods, Vevea, Chambless, & Bayen, 2002).

Research has also examined whether the intrusive, repetitious, and seemingly uncontrollable quality of obsessional thoughts is the result of deficits in cognitive inhibition – the inability to stop thinking about something. Research in this domain posits that individuals with OCD are less able than neurotypical (healthy) individuals to forget or dismiss thoughts about senseless mental stimuli. For example, when given tests of recall and recognition, individuals with OCD have more difficulty forgetting negative material (and material related to their OCD concerns) relative to positive and neutral material than healthy control subjects who do not show this bias (e.g., Tolin, Hamlin, & Foa, 2002).

Poor cognitive inhibition might explain the high *frequency* of obsessional thoughts, yet the idea that OCD arises from general cognitive deficits has not added to our understanding of or ability to treat the problem. It seems likely that apparent memory and processing deficits are better accounted for by *cognitive biases* in which obsessional anxiety leads to preferential processing of threat-relevant stimuli. For example, individuals who possess a biased perception that they are responsible for negative events or outcomes may have reduced confidence in their memory, leading to compulsive checking. Checking rituals may function as a way of reducing doubts that have arisen because of mistaken beliefs about one's memory and ability to manage uncertainty and pathological overestimates of responsibility for harm. These types of mistaken beliefs are the focus of the cognitive specificity hypothesis of OCD, as described next.

Cognitive Specificity Models

The cognitive specificity approach to OCD proposes that obsessions and compulsions arise from particular types of maladaptive interpretations (i.e., dysfunctional beliefs). Such models are based on Beck's (1976) cognitive specificity hypothesis, which posits that each type of psychopathology is associated with a distinct type or pattern of dysfunctional beliefs. Depression, for example, is said to arise from overly negative beliefs about oneself, the world, and the future (e.g., "I'm a loser"). Panic disorder is thought to be associated with catastrophic misinterpretations of the physical sensations that accompany normal responses to anxiety (i.e., fight/flight; "When my heart races, I think I'm having a heart attack"). With respect to OCD, specific dysfunctional beliefs have been theoretically linked to particular symptom domains. For example, beliefs about inflated personal responsibility have been conceptually linked to obsessions about harm and mistakes and checking compulsions (Salkovskis, 1985). Further, beliefs about the over-importance of one's intrusive thoughts (e.g., "Immoral thoughts mean I'm an immoral person") have been linked to violent, sexual, and religious obsessions (e.g., Frost & Steketee, 2002).

Given the heterogeneity of OCD symptoms, a number of similar approaches have built upon Beck's cognitive model. Among these models is Salkovskis's (1985, 1989) cognitive approach. This approach starts with the finding that most people experience unwanted intrusive thoughts (i.e., thoughts, images, and impulses that intrude into consciousness) (e.g., Rachman & de Silva, 1978). Such "normal" or "nonclinical" unwanted thoughts tend to be less frequent, less distressing, and shorter in duration than "clinically significant" obsessions that are characteristic of individuals with OCD (Rachman & de Silva, 1978; Salkovskis & Harrison, 1984). Clinical and nonclinical obsessions, however, share similar thematic content such as violence, contamination, sex, and doubts (Rachman & de Silva, 1978). Thus, a comprehensive model of OCD must delineate why many individuals experience intrusive thoughts, yet only a small percentage of people experience frequent, distressing, and persistent clinical obsessions.

Salkovskis suggests that intrusive thoughts reflect the person's current concerns and are triggered by internal or external cues that remind the person of his or her concerns. For example, intrusive thoughts about accidentally hitting pedestrians with an automobile may be triggered by driving past people walking on the side of the road. Salkovskis asserts that nonclinical intrusive thoughts only take on additional meaning (i.e., escalate into obsessions) when they are *appraised* to be threatening and related to one's personal responsibility, e.g., the intrusive image of pushing a stranger in front of an oncoming train. Although upsetting, most people experiencing such an intrusion would not regard it as personally meaningful or as having harm-related implications (i.e., it would be considered, and subsequently dismissed, as "mental noise"). Such an intrusion might develop into a clinical obsession, however, if the person appraises it as indicating that he or she has the responsibility for causing or preventing the accompanying disastrous consequences, e.g., if the person made an appraisal such as the following: "Thinking about pushing a stranger in front of an oncoming train means that I'm a dangerous and immoral citizen who must take extra care to ensure that I don't lose control." Such interpretations evoke distress and motivate the individual to try to suppress or remove the unwanted intrusion (e.g., by replacing it with a "good" thought), and to attempt to prevent the content of the intrusion from actually occurring (e.g., by avoiding subway platforms). Thus, compulsive rituals are cast in this model as efforts to remove intrusions and to prevent any perceived harmful consequences.

The question remains: why do some, but not all, people interpret and appraise intrusive thoughts in terms of harm and responsibility? Beck (1976) proposed that one's experiences form the basic assumptions we hold about ourselves and the world, including beliefs about personal responsibility and about the significance of unwanted thoughts (e.g., the core belief that all our thoughts are significant). Such beliefs may be acquired from a strict moral or religious upbringing or from other experiences that teach the person extreme or rigid codes of conduct and responsibility (Salkovskis, Shafran, Rachman, & Freeston, 1999).

Why doesn't a person with OCD recognize these thoughts as senseless and dismiss them? Salkovskis proposed that rituals develop and persist as coping strategies for obsessional thoughts for two reasons. First, compulsive rituals are reinforced by the immediate (albeit temporary) reduction in obsessional distress that they often produce (i.e., negative reinforcement, as in the conditioning model). Second, they maintain obsessions by preventing the person from learning that his or her beliefs and appraisals are unrealistic and unlikely to materialize. That is, when a person ritualizes, s/he fails to learn that obsessional thoughts and situations aren't dangerous, Instead, s/he continues to believe that a catastrophe would have occurred had s/he not performed the ritual. Other theorists (e.g.,

Rachman, 2003) have similarly proposed that compulsive rituals increase the frequency and repetitiveness of obsessions by serving as reminders of intrusions (i.e., retrieval cues), thereby triggering their reoccurrence. For example, compulsive reassurance seeking can remind the person of his or her obsessional doubts. Therefore, attempts to distract one's self from obsessional thoughts can paradoxically *increase* the frequency of these thoughts and images. Rituals can also strengthen one's perceived responsibility. For example, when the feared consequences of thinking a violent thought do not occur after performing a mental ritual, it strengthens the perception of personal responsibility (i.e., that the person is solely responsible for removing the potential threat and must continue to prevent it from happening in the future).

In summary, the cognitive model of OCD proposes that obsessions and compulsions develop when a person habitually interprets normal intrusive thoughts as posing a threat for which he or she is personally responsible. This leads to distress and attempts to remove the intrusion to alleviate discomfort and prevent the feared consequences. But this response paradoxically increases the frequency of intrusions. Thus, the intrusions become persistent and distressing, and they escalate into clinical obsessions. Compulsive rituals maintain the obsessions and prevent the person from evaluating the accuracy of his or her interpretations. Avoidance is analogous to compulsive rituals in that avoidance functions as a strategy for reducing anxiety. Avoidance and rituals differ in that avoidance is a passive anxiety reduction strategy and ritual use is an active strategy.

Salkovskis's model emphasizes the role of responsibility appraisals of intrusive thoughts. Other authors, however, have developed additional cognitive models by expanding on the types of dysfunctional beliefs and appraisals that contribute to OCD. Although these cognitive models differ in some ways, they are more similar than they are different. Most of the differences between these models relate to the emphasis that they give to certain types of dysfunctional beliefs. Rachman (1998), for example, focuses on beliefs concerning the significance of intrusive thoughts (e.g., "If I think an immoral thought, it means I'm an immoral person"). Thus, for Rachman, obsessions arise when the person misinterprets the intrusive thought as implying that he or she is "bad, mad, or dangerous." *Thought-action fusion* (TAF) is an important concept in this model (Shafran, Thordarson, & Rachman, 1996). Thought-action fusion refers to the notion that one's unwanted thoughts will inevitably be translated into actions (i.e., likelihood TAF) (e.g., "I might cause my father to have a car accident just by thinking about it") or that thoughts are the moral equivalent of actions (i.e., moral TAF) (e.g., "Thinking about pushing a stranger in front of an oncoming train is just as bad as actually doing it"). The most comprehensive contemporary cognitive model of OCD was developed collaboratively by members of the OCCWG (Frost & Steketee, 2002). The OCCWG model accounts for the heterogeneity of OCD symptoms by proposing that particular beliefs (or patterns of beliefs) are important for specific types of OCD symptoms.

Implications of cognitive specificity models. The cognitive-behavioral approach to OCD provides a logical and consistent account of symptoms that assumes intact learning (conditioning) processes and normally functioning (albeit biased and maladaptive) cognitive processes. Further, hypothesized maladaptive beliefs and appraisals are viewed as "errors." Additionally, avoidance and compulsive behaviors to reduce perceived threat could be considered adaptive if harm were likely; however, OCD clients' obsessive fears and rituals are maladaptive because they are out of proportion to the actual threat of the situation. Therefore, avoidance and compulsive rituals are not only irrational, but also are highly problematic since they perpetuate a vicious cycle of misappraisals and distress.

The model also has implications for the treatment for OCD symptoms. Specifically, treatment based on this model must accomplish two things: (a) the correction of maladaptive beliefs and appraisals that lead to obsessional fear and (b) the termination of avoidance and compulsive rituals that prevent the correction of maladaptive beliefs and extinction of anxiety. In short, the task of cognitive behavior therapy (CBT) for OCD is to foster an evaluation of obsessional stimuli as nonthreatening and therefore not demanding of further action. Patients must come to understand their problem not in terms of the risk of feared consequences, but in terms of how they are thinking and behaving in response to stimuli that objectively pose a low risk of harm (e.g., Abramowitz & Jacoby, 2015).

Empirical status. Data from three lines of evidence – self-report questionnaire research, laboratory experiments, and longitudinal studies support the cognitive specificity approach to OCD. Results from questionnaire studies consistently reveal that people with OCD are more likely than those without OCD to overestimate the likelihood of harm and interpret intrusive thoughts as meaningful, threatening, or in terms of responsibility for harm (e.g., Abramowitz, Whiteside, Lynam, & Kalsy, 2003; Freeston, Ladouceur, Gagnon, & Thibodeau, 1993; OCCWG, 2003; Salkovskis et al., 2000; Shafran et al., 1996). Although such studies suggest a relationship between OCD and cognitive variables, these correlational data do not address whether cognitive biases play a causal role in the onset of obsessive-compulsive symptoms. Results from experimentally controlled studies must be examined for evidence of causal directionality.

Several laboratory experiments have addressed the effects of interpretations of intrusive thoughts on OCD symptoms (Ladouceur et al., 1995; Lopatka & Rachman, 1995; Rassin, Merckelbach, Muris, & Spaan, 1999). For example, Rassin and colleagues (1999) connected 45 participants to equipment that, participants were told, would monitor their thoughts for 15 minutes. To induce dysfunctional appraisals, participants who had been randomly assigned to the experimental condition were told that thinking the word "apple" would automatically result in a mild electric shock to another person (a confederate of the experimenter) whom they had met earlier. Participants were also informed that by pressing a certain button immediately after having an "apple" thought, they could prevent the shock – this was intended to simulate a compulsive ritual. At the same time a group of subjects in the control group were told only that the electrical equipment would merely monitor their thoughts. Results indicated that during the 15-minute monitoring period, the experimental group reported more intrusive "apple" thoughts, more guilt, greater subjective discomfort, and more intense resistance to thoughts about apples compared to the control group. Moreover, there was a strong association between the number of reported "apple" thoughts and the number of button presses. Data suggest that intrusive thoughts and compulsive behaviors can indeed be evoked by experimentally manipulating participants' beliefs about the significance and harmfulness of intrusive thoughts.

Although the results from this experiment suggest that beliefs can cause OCD symptoms in a *laboratory* setting, it does not necessarily generalize to the development of OCD in naturalistic settings. Thus, longitudinal studies in which individuals are assessed for cognitive variables and then followed up after some critical event are apt to be particularly informative. Pregnancy and the postpartum period represent periods of increased vulnerability to OCD onset; therefore, this period provides prime opportunity to examine hypotheses about potential cognitive determinants of OCD. To examine this question, researchers (Abramowitz, Khandher, Nelson, Deacon, & Rygwall, 2006) administered measures of OCD-related dysfunctional beliefs to first-time expecting parents (mothers- and fathers-to-be) during the third trimester of pregnancy. Between two and three months after childbirth, these new parents were again contacted and assessed for the presence and intensity of unwanted intrusive thoughts about their newborn. Not surprisingly, 75% of these new parents reported unwanted infant-related thoughts ("nonclinical obsessions") (e.g., an image of dropping the child down the stairs or off the balcony). Moreover, after controlling for baseline levels of obsessive-compulsive symptoms and trait anxiety, the strength of OCD-related dysfunctional beliefs pre-child birth was a significant predictor of obsessive-compulsive symptom intensity in the postpartum period. These data support the cognitive-behavioral model and suggest that the tendency to overestimate the chances of harm and significance of intrusive thoughts is a risk factor for the development of more severe obsessive-compulsive symptoms.

Despite the fact that dysfunctional beliefs (as posited by cognitive models) do appear to have a causal association with obsessive-compulsive symptoms, existing cognitive models of OCD may not fully explain obsessive-compulsive symptoms. Other factors are likely involved in determining the onset of obsessive-compulsive problems. Additionally, a small group of individuals with OCD do not show the types of dysfunctional beliefs thought to be tied to OCD onset (Taylor et al., 2006). Generally, cognitive specificity models hold some validity yet require additional research and modification. Future models should include additional etiologically relevant variables (e.g., disgust) (Cisler, Brady, Olatunji, & Lohr, 2010), and limitations of the model should be more clearly defined.

Neurobiological Models of OCD

Serotonin hypothesis. Serotonin is a monoamine neurotransmitter purported to play a role in the regulation of mood, appetite, and sleep. The serotonin hypothesis, originally proposed in the context of depression, suggests that obsessions and compulsions arise from abnormalities in this neurotransmitter system, specifically a hypersensitivity of the postsynaptic serotonergic receptors (Zohar & Insel, 1987). Three lines of evidence are cited to support the serotonin hypothesis: medication outcome studies, biological marker studies, and biological challenge studies in which OCD symptoms are evoked using serotonin agonists and antagonists. The pharmacotherapy literature has been fairly consistent in showing that selective serotonin reuptake inhibitor (SSRI) medications (e.g., fluoxetine), which are thought to manipulate available levels of this neurotransmitter, are more effective than placebo and medications with other presumed mechanisms of action (e.g., imipramine) in reducing OCD symptoms. In contrast, studies of biological markers – such as blood and cerebrospinal fluid levels of serotonin metabolites – have provided inconclusive results regarding a relationship between serotonin and OCD (e.g., Insel, Mueller, Alterman, Linnoila, & Murphy, 1985). Similarly, results from studies using the pharmacological challenge paradigm are largely incompatible with the serotonin hypothesis (Hollander et al., 1992).

    Structural models. Structural models of OCD hypothesize that this problem is caused by neuroanatomical and functional abnormalities in particular areas of the brain, specifically the orbitofrontal-subcortical circuits, which are thought to connect brain regions involved in processing information with those involved in the initiation of behavioral responses. The classical conceptualization of this circuitry consists of a direct and an indirect pathway. The direct pathway projects from the cerebral cortex to the striatum to the internal segment of the globus pallidus/substantia nigra, pars reticulata complex, then to the thalamus and back to the cortex. The indirect pathway is similar, but projects from the striatum to the external segment of the globus pallidus to the subthalamic nucleus before returning to the common pathway. Overactivity of the direct circuit is thought to give rise to OCD symptoms.

    Structural models of OCD are derived from neuroimaging studies in which activity levels in specific brain areas are compared between people with and without the condition. Investigations using positron emission tomography (PET) have found that increased glucose utilization in the orbitofrontal cortex (OFC), caudate, thalamus, prefrontal cortex, and anterior cingulate is correlated with the presence of OCD (i.e., greater in patients compared to non-patients) (e.g., Baxter et al., 1988). Studies using single photon emission computed tomography (SPECT) have reported decreased blood flow to the OFC, caudate, various areas of the cortex, and thalamus in OCD patients compared to non-patients (for a review, see Whiteside, Port, & Abramowitz, 2004). Finally, studies comparing individuals with OCD to healthy controls using magnetic resonance spectroscopy (MRS) have reported decreased levels of various markers of neuronal viability in the left and right striatum and in the medial thalamus (e.g., Fitzgerald, Moore, Paulson, Stewart, & Rosenberg, 2000). Although findings vary, a meta-analysis of 10 PET and SPECT studies revealed that individuals with OCD display more activity in the orbital gyrus and the head of the caudate nucleus in comparison to healthy controls (Whiteside et al., 2004).

Genetic contributions. Although some findings suggest that OCD symptoms are heritable, with "likely common genetic influences of modest effect" (Nestadt, Grados, & Samuels, 2010), there is no evidence of specific genes that influence OCD symptoms (Stewart et al., 2013). Extant research also suggests that individuals with OCD are more likely to have first-degree relatives who suffer from the same disorder than are healthy controls who do not have OCD (e.g., Hettema, Neale, & Kendler, 2001), although this does not rule out environmental factors. Further, twin studies suggest that obsessive-compulsive symptoms are heritable (van Grootheest, Cath, Beekman, & Boomsma, 2005). No heritable sex differences have been found; however, familiarity may be stronger in childhood-onset OCD than in cases characterized by later development (Rosario-Campos et al., 2005).

Evaluation and empirical status of biological models. Despite several decades of research to elucidate biological factors in OCD, the overall evidence that specific biological variables play a role in the etiology of OCD is weak. In fact, a large international study group has reached the consensus that there are no biological or genetic markers of OCD (Bandelow et al., 2016, 2017). Moreover, there has been little research on the biological factors associated with other OCRDs. This scientific reality notwithstanding, there are numerous conceptual and theoretical limitations of biological models of OCD. First, no explanation has been offered for how neurotransmitter, neuroanatomical, or genetic abnormalities might translate into OCD symptoms as opposed to the symptoms of other disorders (e.g., why does hypersensitivity of postsynaptic receptors cause obsessional thoughts or compulsive rituals as opposed to social anxiety or panic attacks?). In addition, biological models are unable to explain (a) the fact that OCD symptoms are generally constrained to the particular themes discussed earlier, and (b) why someone would experience one type of obsession (e.g., contamination), but not another (e.g., sexual).

A third problem with biological models is their logical basis. The strongest evidence for the serotonin hypothesis of OCD, for example, is the apparent superiority of serotonergic medication over other sorts of pharmacotherapies. Yet since the serotonin hypothesis *originated from* the findings of preferential efficacy of serotonergic medication over nonserotonergic antidepressants (e.g., imipramine), the assertion that the effectiveness of these medications supports the serotonin hypothesis is circular. Further still, there is a logical fallacy in deriving etiological models from treatment results. Indeed, such *post hoc ergo proper hoc* (i.e., *after this therefore because of this*) reasoning is logically flawed (e.g., the sun rises after the rooster crows, therefore the crowing rooster causes the sun to rise). Evidence from controlled studies of differences in serotonergic functioning between individuals with and without OCD, which *could* be used to indicate problems with serotonergic functioning, however, are especially inconsistent; thus there is actually little convincing evidence that OCD is caused by an abnormally functioning serotonin system.

A final limitation with biological models is that they are based on correlational studies, which cannot address (a) whether true abnormalities exist, and (b) whether the observed relationships are causal. That is, all neuroimaging studies comparing OCD patients to control participants simply show associations between OCD symptoms and brain structure or function. They do not reveal whether any differences in the brain predate the development of OCD, or whether it is something about having OCD that causes changes in the brain. Moreover, most neuroimaging studies compare OCD patients with non-patients, rather than with individuals with other psychiatric diagnoses. Accordingly, the literature cannot determine whether any findings with respect to the brain are specific to individuals with OCD, or generally characteristic of those with various sorts of psychopathology. All of this is not to say that biology does not play a role in the development of OCD – it almost certainly does. Yet it is likely that these factors are general (e.g., vulnerability to anxiety or neuroticism, or perhaps to the various factors outlined by the RDoC formulation) as opposed to being specific to obsessions and compulsions. Moreover, it is likely that any biological factors interact with environmental influences to dictate the vastly heterogeneous and person-specific expression of OCD (and OCRD) symptoms.

References

Abramovitch, A., Abramowitz, J. S., & Mittelman, A. (2013). The neuropsychology of adult obsessive-compulsive disorder: A meta-analysis. *Clinical Psychology Review, 33,* 1163–1171.

Abramowitz, J. S., Deacon, B. J., Olatunji, B. O., Wheaton, M. G., Berman, N. C., Losardo, D., . . . Björgvinsson, T. (2010). Assessment of obsessive-compulsive symptom dimensions: Development and evaluation of the Dimensional Obsessive-Compulsive Scale. *Psychological Assessment, 22,* 180–198.

Abramowitz, J. S. & Jacoby, R. J. (2015). Obsessive-compulsive and related disorders: A critical review of the new diagnostic class. *Annual Review of Clinical Psychology, 11,* 165–186. https://doi.org/10.1146/annurev-clinpsy-032813–153713

Abramowitz, J. S., Khandker, M., Nelson, C. A., Deacon, B. J., & Rygwall, R. (2006). The role of cognitive factors in the pathogenesis of obsessive-compulsive symptoms: A prospective study. *Behaviour Research and Therapy, 44,* 1361–1374.

Abramowitz, J. S., Wheaton, M. G., & Storch, E. A. (2008). The status of hoarding as a symptom of obsessive-compulsive disorder *Behaviour Research and Therapy, 46*(9), 1026–1033.

Abramowitz, J. S., Whiteside, S., Lynam, D., & Kalsy, S. (2003). Is thought-action fusion specific to obsessive-compulsive disorder?: A mediating role of negative affect. *Behaviour Research and Therapy, 41,* 1069–1079.

American Psychiatric Association (APA). (2013). *Diagnostic and Statistical Manual of Mental Disorders* (5th edn). Washington, DC: American Psychiatric Association.

Arnold, L. M., Auchenbach, M. B., & McElroy, S. L. (2001). Psychogenic excoriation. *CNS Drugs*, *15*, 351–359.

Bandelow, B., Baldwin, D., Abelli, M., Altamura, C., Dell'Osso, B., Domschke, K., ... Riederer, P. (2016). Biological markers for anxiety disorders, OCD and PTSD – a consensus statement. Part I: Neuroimaging and genetics. *World Journal of Biological Psychiatry*, *17*(5), 321–365.

Bandelow, B., Baldwin, D., Abelli, M., Bolea-Alamanac, B., Bourin, M., Chamberlain, S. R., ... Riederer, P. (2017). Biological markers for anxiety disorders, OCD and PTSD: A consensus statement. Part II: Neurochemistry, neurophysiology and neurocognition. *World Journal of Biological Psychiatry*, *18*(3), 162–214.

Baxter, L. R., Schwartz, J. M., Mazziotta, J. C., Phelps, M. E., & Pahl, J. J. (1988). Cerebral glucose metabolic rates in nondepressed patients with obsessive-compulsive disorder. *American Journal of Psychiatry*, *145*, 1560–1563.

Beck, A. T. (1976). *Cognitive Therapy and the Emotional Disorders*. New York, NY: International Universities Press.

Berman, N. C., Wheaton, M. G., & Abramowitz, J. S. (2012). The "Arnold Schwarzenegger Effect": Is strength of the "victim" related to misinterpretations of harm intrusions? *Behaviour Research and Therapy*, 50, 761–766.

Bogetto, F., Venturello, S., Albert, U., Maina, G., & Ravizza, L. (1999). Gender-related clinical differences in obsessive-compulsive disorder. *European Psychiatry*, *14*, 434–441.

Buhr, K. & Dugas, M. J. (2002). The intolerance of uncertainty scale: Psychometric properties of the English version. *Behaviour Research and Therapy*, *40*, 931–945.

Christenson, G. A., Ristvedt, S. L., & Mackenzie, T. B. (1993). Identification of trichotillomania cue profiles. *Behaviour Research and Therapy*, *31*, 315–320.

Cisler, J. M., Brady, R. E., Olatunji, B. O., & Lohr, J. M. (2010). Disgust and obsessive beliefs in contamination-related OCD. *Cognitive Therapy and Research*, *34*(5), 439–448.

Clark, D. A. (2004). *Cognitive-Behavioral Therapy for OCD*. New York, NY: Guilford Press.

Coles, M. E., Frost, R. O., Heimberg, R. G., & Rhéaume, J. (2003). "Not just right experiences": perfectionism, obsessive-compulsive features and general psychopathology. *Behaviour Research and Therapy*, *41*, 681–700.

Eisen, J. L., Rasmussen, S. A., Phillips, K. A., Price, L. H., Davidson, J., Lydiard, R. B., Ninan, P., & Piggott, T. (2001). Insight and treatment outcome in obsessive-compulsive disorder. *Comprehensive Psychiatry*, *42*, 494–497.

Fineberg, N. A., Saxena, S., Zohar, J., & Craig, K. J. (2007). Obsessive-compulsive disorder: Boundary issues. *CNS Spectrums*, *12*, 359–375.

Fineberg, N. A., Saxena, S., Zohar, J., & Craig, K. J. (2011). Obsessive-compulsive disorder: Boundary issues. In *Obsessive Compulsive Spectrum Disorders: Refining the Research Agenda for* DSM-V, ed. E. Hollander, J. Zohar, P. J. Sirovatka, & D. A. Regier (pp. 1–32). Washington, DC: American Psychiatric Association.

Fitzgerald, K. D., Moore, G. J., Paulson, L. A., Stewart, C. M., & Rosenberg, D. R. (2000). Proton spectroscopic imaging of the thalamus in treatment-naive pediatric obsessive-compulsive disorder. *Biological Psychiatry*, *47*, 174–182.

Foa, E. B., Amir, N., Gershuny, B., Molnar, C., & Kozak, M. J. (1997). Implicit and explicit memory in obsessive-compulsive disorder. *Journal of Anxiety Disorders, 11*, 119–129.

Foa, E. B. & Kozak, M. J. (1995). *DSM-IV* field trial: Obsessive-compulsive disorder. *American Journal of Psychiatry, 152*, 90–96.

Frankenburg, F. R. (1984). Hoarding in anorexia nervosa. *British Journal of Medical Psychology, 57*(1), 57–60.

Freeston, M. H., Ladouceur, R., Gagnon, F., & Thibodeau, N. (1993). Beliefs about obsessional thoughts. *Journal of Psychopathology and Behavioral Assessment, 15*, 1–21.

Frost, R. O. & Steketee, G. (eds.). (2002). *Cognitive Approaches to Obsessions and Compulsions: Theory, Assessment, and Treatment*. New York, NY: Elsevier.

Hettema, J. M., Neale, M. C., & Kendler, K. S. (2001). A review and meta-analysis of the genetic epidemiology of anxiety disorders. *American Journal of Psychiatry, 158*, 1568–1578.

Hollander, E., DeCaria, C. M., Nitescu, A., Gully, R., Suckow, R. F., Cooper, T. B., ... Liebowitz, M. R. (1992). Serotonergic function in obsessive-compulsive disorder: Behavioral and neuroendocrine responses to oral m-chlorophenylpiperazine and fenfluramine in patients and healthy volunteers. *Archives of General Psychiatry, 49*, 21–28.

Hollander, E., Kwon, J. H., Stein, D. J., & Broatch, J. (1996). Obsessive-compulsive and spectrum disorders: Overview and quality of life issues. *Journal of Clinical Psychiatry, 57*, 3–6.

Insel, T. R., Mueller, E. A., Alterman, I., Linnoila, M., & Murphy, D. L. (1985). Obsessive-compulsive disorder and serotonin: Is there a connection? *Biological Psychiatry, 20*, 1174–1188.

Kessler, R. C., Berglund, P., Demler, O., Jin, R., Merikangas, K. R., & Walters, E. E. (2005). Lifetime prevalence and age-of-onset distributions of *DSM-IV* disorders in the National Comorbidity Survey Replication. *Archives of General Psychiatry, 62*, 593–602.

Keuthen, N. J., Deckersbach, T., Wilhelm, S., Hale, E., Fraim, C., Baer, L., ... Jenike, M. A. (2000). Repetitive skin-picking in a student population and comparison with a sample of self-injurious skin-pickers. *Psychosomatics, 41*, 210–215.

Ladouceur, R., Rhéaume, J., Freeston, M. H., Aublet, F., Jean, K., Lachance, S., ... de Pokomandy-Morin, K. (1995). Experimental manipulations of responsibility: An analogue test for models of obsessive-compulsive disorder. *Behaviour Research and Therapy, 33*, 937–946.

Lopatka, C. & Rachman, S. (1995). Perceived responsibility and compulsive checking: An experimental analysis. *Behaviour Research and Therapy, 33*, 673–684.

Luchins, D. J., Goldman, M. B., Lieb, M., & Hanrahan, P. (1992). Repetitive behaviors in chronically institutionalized schizophrenic patients. *Schizophrenia Research, 8*(2), 119–123.

McKay, D., Abramowitz, J. S., Calamari, J. E., Kyrios, M., Radomsky, A., Sookman, D., ... Wilhelm, S. (2004). A critical evaluation of obsessive-compulsive disorder subtypes: Symptoms versus mechanisms. *Clinical Psychology Review, 24*, 283–313.

McNally, R. J. & Kohlbeck, P. A. (1993). Reality monitoring in obsessive-compulsive disorder. *Behaviour Research and Therapy, 31*, 249–253.

Mowrer, O. (1960). *Learning Theory and Behavior.* Hoboken, NJ: Wiley and Sons.

National Institute of Mental Health. (2008). The National Institute of Mental Health strategic plan (NIH Publication No. 08–6368). Retrieved from www.nimh.nih .gov/about/strategic-planning-reports/index.shtml

Nestadt, G., Grados, M., & Samuels, J. F. (2010). Genetics of OCD. *Psychiatric Clinics of North America, 33,* 141–158.

Nielen, M. M., Den Boer, J. A., & Smid, H. (2009). Patients with obsessive-compulsive disorder are impaired in associative learning based on external feedback. *Psychological Medicine, 39,* 1519–1526.

Obsessive Compulsive Cognitions Working Group. (1997). Cognitive assessment of obsessive-compulsive disorder. *Behaviour Research and Therapy, 35,* 667–681.

Obsessive Compulsive Cognitions Working Group. (2003). Psychometric validation of the obsessive beliefs questionnaire and the interpretation of intrusions inventory: Part I. *Behaviour Research and Therapy, 41,* 863–878.

Phillips, K. A., Wilhelm, S., Koran, L. M., Didie, E. R., Fallon, B. A., Feusner, J., & Stein, D. J. (2010). Body dysmorphic disorder: Some key issues for *DSM-V. Depression and Anxiety, 27,* 573–591.

Rachman, S. (1998). A cognitive theory of obsessions: Elaborations. *Behaviour Research and Therapy, 36,* 385–401.

Rachman, S. (2003). *The Treatment of Obsessions.* New York, NY: Oxford University Press.

Rachman, S. & de Silva, P. (1978). Abnormal and normal obsessions. *Behaviour Research and Therapy, 16,* 233–248.

Rachman, S., Elliott, C. M., Shafran, R., & Radomsky, A. S. (2009). Separating hoarding from OCD. *Behaviour Research and Therapy, 47*(6), 520–522.

Rasmussen, S. A. & Eisen, J. L. (1992). The epidemiology and clinical features of obsessive compulsive disorder. *Psychiatric Clinics of North America, 15,* 743–758.

Rassin, E., Merckelbach, H., Muris, P., & Spaan, V. (1999). Thought-action fusion as a causal factor in the development of intrusions. *Behaviour Research and Therapy, 37,* 231–237.

Rosario-Campos, M. C., Leckman, J. F., Curi, M., Quatrano, S., Katsovitch, L., Miguel, E. C., & Pauls, D. L. (2005). A family study of early-onset obsessive-compulsive disorder. *American Journal of Medical Genetics Part B: Neuropsychiatric Genetics, 136,* 92–97.

Salkovskis, P. M. (1985). Obsessional-compulsive problems: A cognitive-behavioural analysis. *Behaviour Research and Therapy, 23,* 571–583.

Salkovskis, P. M. (1989). Cognitive-behavioural factors and the persistence of intrusive thoughts in obsessional problems. *Behaviour Research and Therapy, 27,* 677–682.

Salkovskis, P. M. & Harrison, J. (1984). Abnormal and normal obsessions: A replication. *Behaviour Research and Therapy, 22,* 549–552.

Salkovskis, P., Shafran, R., Rachman, S., & Freeston, M. H. (1999). Multiple pathways to inflated responsibility beliefs in obsessional problems: Possible origins and implications for therapy and research. *Behaviour Research and Therapy, 37,* 1055–1072.

Salkovskis, P. M., Wroe, A. L., Gledhill, A., Morrison, N., Forrester, E., Richards, C., . . . Thorpe, S. (2000). Responsibility attitudes and interpretations are characteristic of obsessive compulsive disorder. *Behaviour Research and Therapy, 38,* 347–372.

Schreiber, L., Odlaug, B. L., & Grant, J. E. (2011). Impulse control disorders: Updated review of clinical characteristics and pharmacological management. *Frontiers in Psychiatry, 2*, 1–11.

Shafran, R., Thordarson, D. S., & Rachman, S. (1996). Thought-action fusion in obsessive compulsive disorder. *Journal of Anxiety Disorders, 10*, 379–391.

Snorrason, Í., Smári, J., & Ólafsson, R. P. (2010). Emotion regulation in pathological skin picking: Findings from a non-treatment seeking sample. *Journal of Behavior Therapy and Experimental Psychiatry, 41*, 238–245.

Stewart, S. E., Yu, D., Scharf, J. M., Neale, B. M., Fagerness, J. A., Mathews, C. A., ... Pauls, D. L. (2013). Genome-wide association study of obsessive-compulsive disorder. *Molecular Psychiatry, 18*, 788–798.

Taylor, S., Abramowitz, J. S., McKay, D., Calamari, J. C., Sookman, D., Kyrios, M., Wilhelm, S., & Carmin, C. (2006). Do dysfunctional beliefs play a role in all types of obsessive-compulsive disorder? *Journal of Anxiety Disorders, 20*, 85–97.

Tolin, D. F., Abramowitz, J. S., Kozak, M. J., & Foa, E. B. (2001). Fixity of belief, perceptual aberration, and magical ideation in obsessive-compulsive disorder. *Journal of Anxiety Disorders, 15*, 501–510.

Tolin, D. F., Hamlin, C., & Foa, E. B. (2002). Directed forgetting in obsessive-compulsive disorder: Replication and extension. *Behaviour Research and Therapy, 40*, 793–803.

van Grootheest, D. S., Cath, D. C., Beekman, A. T., & Boomsma, D. I. (2005). Twin studies on obsessive-compulsive disorder: A review. *Twin Research and Human Genetics, 8*, 450–458.

Wheaton, M. G., Abramowitz, J. S., Fabricant, L. E., Berman, N. C., & Franklin, J. C. (2011). Is hoarding a symptom of obsessive-compulsive disorder? *International Journal of Cognitive Therapy, 4*(3), 225–238.

Whiteside, S. P., Port, J. D., & Abramowitz, J. S. (2004). A meta-analysis of functional neuroimaging in obsessive-compulsive disorder. *Psychiatry Research: Neuroimaging, 132*, 69–79.

Woods, C. M., Vevea, J. L., Chambless, D. L., & Bayen, U. J. (2002). Are compulsive checkers impaired in memory? A meta-analytic review. *Clinical Psychology: Science and Practice, 9*, 353–366.

Zohar, J. & Insel, T. R. (1987). Obsessive-compulsive disorder: Psychobiological approaches to diagnosis, treatment, and pathophysiology. *Biological Psychiatry, 22*, 667–687.

22 Body Dysmorphic Disorder

Emma Baldock and David Veale

Defining Body Dysmorphic Disorder

Body dysmorphic disorder (BDD) refers to a distressing and disabling preoccupation with a perceived defect in one's normal appearance. It has a typical onset in adolescent years, it tends to persist if left untreated, and it has a high burden of morbidity and mortality associated with it (Angelakis, Gooding, & Panagioti, 2016; Bjornsson et al., 2013; Phillips, Menard, Fay, & Weisberg, 2005; Phillips, Pagano, Menard, & Stout, 2006). The 11th edition of the *International Classification of Diseases* from the World Health Organization will contain a separate diagnosis of BDD in the group of Obsessive Compulsive and Related Disorders (Toh, Castle, & Rossell, 2017b; Veale & Matsunaga, 2014). In *ICD-10* it was classified within Somatoform Disorders and without a distinct entry of its own. The proposed diagnostic features of BDD in *ICD-11* are to include the following. First, a preoccupation with a perceived defect or flaw in appearance, or with ugliness in general, which is either unnoticeable or only slightly noticeable to others. Second, excessive self-consciousness, and third, coping behaviors that are either forms of verification (for example, mirror-checking), or attempts to camouflage or alter the perceived defect, or attempts to avoid situations or internal thoughts and images that increase distress (Veale & Matsunaga, 2014).

ICD-11 will also advise on how to differentiate BDD from other disorders, including eating disorders, social anxiety disorder, obsessive-compulsive disorder, and adjustment disorder. Body image disturbance is shared by BDD and the eating disorders, but in eating disorders the preoccupation with body image and the associated behaviors are predominantly about being too fat or overweight and trying to achieve a low weight. Body dysmorphic disorder shares with social anxiety disorder the fear of negative evaluation by others, but in BDD the fear is driven by appearance-related concerns rather than aspects of social performance such as saying something stupid or looking anxious. BDD may present very similarly to OCD in terms of obsessions and compulsions, but in BDD these are all focused on appearance. If appearance is objectively disfigured, for example through injury, then BDD cannot be diagnosed and a diagnosis of adjustment disorder may be considered instead (Veale & Matsunaga, 2014).

The prevalence of BDD has been difficult to study because of under recognition of the disorder. Nevertheless, a cluster of prevalence studies now exist. Veale, Gledhill, Christodoulou, and Hodsoll (2016) provide weighted prevalence estimates of BDD in a range of different settings. They report a weighted prevalence of 1.9% of adults in the community, compared with 0.3% for anorexia nervosa and 0.5% for schizophrenia; a weighted prevalence of 3.3% in students, 7.4% in psychiatric inpatient settings, 5.8% in psychiatric outpatient settings, 11.3% in dermatological settings, 13.2% in general cosmetic settings, and 20% in rhinoplasty clinics. In terms of limitations they note a high heterogeneity of results among studies in cosmetic surgery settings; small numbers in psychiatric settings; the restriction of community studies to Europe and the United States; and the inclusion of only one adolescent study. Möllmann, Dietel, Hunger, and Buhlmann (2017) used self-report measures to assess for BDD based on *DSM-5* criteria in 308 German participants aged between 15 and 21. Eleven (3.6%) met criteria for BDD. Schneider, Mond, Turner, and Hudson (2017) calculated the prevalence of 'probable' and 'subthreshold' BDD using self-report measures in a group of 3,149 Australian high school students. They reported that 3.4% met their criteria for subthreshold BDD, and 1.7% met their criteria for probable BDD.

Phenomenology of BDD

Tom Cash's elaboration of the concept of body image provides an excellent starting point for an account of the phenomenology of BDD. In his editorial for the first issue of the journal *Body Image*, Cash (2004) reflects on his own corpus of research, which was already extensive by this time, and that, while initially focused on what he calls the 'outside view' of human appearance, had shifted to what he calls the 'inside view' of human appearance. As he articulates in the editorial, whereas the 'outside view' concerns what we look like 'on the outside', or the objective or social reality of appearance (how we appear to others, or how others 'see' us), the 'inside view', which is 'body image', concerns the individual's own subjective experience of their appearance. 'Body image', he writes, 'refers to the multifaceted psychological experience of embodiment, especially but not exclusively one's physical appearance' (p. 1). 'It encompasses one's body-related self-perceptions and self-attitudes, including thoughts, beliefs, feelings, and behaviors' (pp. 1–2). To what Cash has already made explicit here we can add as particularly pertinent to BDD early memories that have informed the shaping of body image; visual images of how one looks; imagery in other sensory domains, especially the tactile and somatosensory domains; and also the concept of the more elusive 'felt sense' of how one appears to others.

Having a body image or images (Cash likes to use the term in the plural to emphasize the multiplicity of the individual's experience of embodiment) is part and parcel of being human. As we expound the phenomenology of BDD, we therefore want to articulate what characterizes an individual's body image or body images in BDD in particular and how this differs from emotionally healthy forms of body image.

People with BDD are distressed by their appearance when others do not perceive any problem. Buhlmann, Etcoff, and Wilhelm (2008) studied this discrepancy between self and other evaluations of attractiveness more formally in a study of 19 people with BDD, 21 with OCD and 21 healthy controls. As predicted, the BDD group rated their own attractiveness significantly lower than independent evaluators for the study did. While underrating their own attractiveness they also gave higher attractiveness ratings to photographs of 'attractive' others than the healthy controls and participants with OCD did. Jansen, Smeets, Martijn, and Nederkoorn (2006) studied this discrepancy between self and other evaluations of attractiveness in people with an eating disorder and healthy controls. The healthy controls in her study rated their own attractiveness much more positively than individual evaluators did, while those with eating disorders failed to show this positive bias. People with BDD also rate themselves unfavorably relative to their own standards: Veale, Kinderman, Riley, and Lambrou (2003) reported significant discrepancies in how 107 BDD patients thought they looked (their 'self-actual' appearance) compared both with their 'self-ideal' appearance (how they wanted to appear in an ideal world) and their 'self-should' appearance (how they thought they should look from a moral or aesthetic perspective).

Other research indicates distinct differences between people with BDD and healthy controls in the form and quality of the imagery that is experienced as part of their body image. Osman, Cooper, Hackmann, and Veale (2004) used a semi-structured interview to study this in 18 participants with BDD and 18 healthy controls. Participants were asked to recall a recent time when they had felt anxious about their appearance and then to report any images or impressions they had experienced at the time, of the way they looked or the way others might see them. They were asked about all sensory modalities, for example whether they could see or smell anything in their image or impression. They were also asked whether they noticed any sensations inside their body in connection with their image or impression, and how negative and vivid the image or impression was. They were also asked to rate the perspective from which they viewed their image or impression. While almost all participants reported images and impressions in connection with their memory, the quality and form of the imagery was quite different between groups. Imagery in the BDD group was significantly more negative and vivid and it was experienced without exception from an 'observer perspective' (as if through an external observer's eyes) whereas for all the healthy controls the images were experienced from a 'field perspective' (through the individual's eyes). In addition, it was distinctive of the images in the BDD group that specific facial and bodily features (e.g., a person's nose) took up a large proportion of the image as a whole. Osman et al. (2004) also found that 15 of the 18 BDD participants in her study (and only 2 of the control participants) identified a particular memory associated with their image of themselves. All the memories were of appearance-related teasing or bullying at school or self-consciousness around appearance changes in adolescence, and the participants' median age at the time of the remembered event was 11 years old.

Body image encompasses beliefs about the self in connection with appearance and it was another distinctive feature of the BDD group in the study by Osman et al. (2004) that participants made negative self-judgments as a result of their negative images of how they looked and that these negative judgments related not only to their appearance, e.g., 'unattractive' and 'ugly', but also to their self as a whole, e.g., 'inferior' and 'worthless' (Cooper & Osman, 2007). This indicates that people with BDD may hold appearance as an 'idealized value' – that is a value that has developed into overriding importance in defining the self and self-worth (Veale, 2002). For example, one of the patients who completed a survey of 50 BDD patients conducted by Veale et al. (1996) said: 'If my appearance is defective then I am worthless or helpless and I will end up alone and isolated'; and in the words of a patient from a clinical treatment paper by Geremia and Neziroglu (2001): 'How I feel about myself as a person is usually related to how I feel about the way I look.' Healthy cognitive processing of the self is characterized by multiplicity and flexibility. For example, an individual may find self-definition and self-worth through a range of roles as a father, a husband, a scientist, a saxophonist and so on. Conversely, in BDD appearance may assume such importance that regardless of other aspects of the self an individual may feel worthless as a result of how they feel they look.

Questionnaire studies and implicit association studies have also yielded results consistent with this idea that people with BDD place greater importance on their appearance than others do. For example, Phillips et al. (2005) report on a study evaluating 98 people with BDD on the Body Dysmorphic Disorder Examination Scale. One of the items in this scale assesses the importance of perceived appearance defects in terms of their influence on the individual's evaluation of themselves as a person as compared to other characteristics. The mean score for this group of patients was high (4.5 out of 6). Buhlmann, Teachman, Naumann, Fehlinger, and Rief (2009) used an implicit association test to probe the same phenomenon and found that relative to healthy controls (n = 20), BDD participants (n = 21) had lower implicit self-esteem and a stronger implicit association between attractive and competent, although there was no difference between groups in associations between attractive and important. Buhlmann, Teachman, and Kathmann (2011) refined the design of this earlier study by using an implicit measure that is less amenable to conscious control and found that BDD participants (n = 36) did show a stronger association between attractive and important compared with individuals with a dermatologic condition (n = 36) and healthy controls (n = 36). The BDD participants also endorsed stronger beliefs that attractiveness is important on the explicit questionnaire measure used.

Body image also encompasses the emotional experiences connected to an individual's view of how they look. Anxiety, self-disgust, and shame are commonly reported in BDD, and shame may be particularly prominent (Veale & Gilbert, 2014). One study found significantly higher levels of implicit shame associations in a clinically diagnosed BDD group compared with groups with obsessive-compulsive disorder, social anxiety disorder, and healthy controls (Clerkin, Bethany, Teachman, & Smith, 2014). Weingarden, Renshaw, Davidson, and Wilhelm (2017) recruited 184 people with BDD through the Internet in a questionnaire study and found that body shame in particular was more strongly associated with BDD phenomenology whereas general shame was more strongly associated with adverse psychosocial outcomes.

The behavioral dimension of body image encompasses everything an individual does as a consequence of how they think and feel about how they look. For the individual with BDD all such behaviors are focused on managing the threat of being negatively judged and rejected on the basis of appearance ('safety-seeking behaviors', Salkovskis [1991]), and managing the intense negative emotions that are experienced in connection with appearance. In brief, people with BDD are constantly in a threat mode in connection with their body image (Veale & Gilbert, 2014). Veale and Neziroglu (2010) propose that this threat mode is related to the aversive conditioning of body image to aversive past memories that have not been emotionally processed. Therefore the individual remains oriented to old threats and interprets and reacts to current situations in these terms. An individual's overall organization in response to threat encompasses attentional, cognitive, and perceptual biases as well as overt behavioral responses, and we discuss these here under the broad category of safety-seeking behaviors.

Veale and Neziroglu (2010) categorize safety-seeking behaviors in BDD into three types according to their function. First, there are behaviors whose function it is to assess and monitor the level of appearance-related threat. Second, there are behaviors whose function it is to correct appearance. Third, there are behaviors whose function it is to avoid the scrutiny of appearance. Threat-assessment behaviors include checking appearance in the mirror and by touch, seeking reassurance from others about appearance, comparing their appearance with others, especially in terms of their disliked features, and especially in relation to attractive others (Anson, Veale, & Miles, 2015), and worrying about appearance. Threat assessment also includes attentional processes of vigilance for negative reactions in others, a bias for perceiving anger in the faces of others (e.g., Toh, Castle, & Rossell, 2015), selective attention for disliked features (Grocholewski, Kliem, & Heinrichs, 2012, and Greenberg, Reuman, Hartmann, Kasarskis, & Wilhelm, 2014) and for favorable features in others (Anson et al., 2015), and a focus on one's own appearance-related thoughts and feelings (Windheim, Veale, & Anson, 2011). Alteration behaviors include cosmetic surgery itself, as well as planning and deliberating over cosmetic surgery and conducting mental cosmetic surgery. Avoidance of scrutiny behaviors include the gross avoidance of people as well as more subtle forms of avoidance such as the use of make-up and the avoidance of bright lights.

While healthy controls also engage in many of these behaviors, including checking appearance in the mirror and comparing appearance to others, the constant orientation to threat is distinctive to the BDD group. People with BDD therefore engage in these behaviors far more frequently than healthy controls do and also in different forms and with different functions. Anson et al. (2015) has studied comparing in more detail in a standardized questionnaire study with a group of 35 people with BDD and 45 healthy controls. The BDD patients reported significantly higher levels of comparing than the controls, and their comparisons were mainly focused on their disliked features and comparing these with favorable versions of the same feature in others, whereas comparisons in controls were mainly focused on appearance as a whole. Mirror use in BDD is characterized by a greater frequency and duration of sessions and by an effort to achieve particular internal states such as feeling right about how one looks (Baldock & Veale, 2017; Veale & Riley, 2001). The orientation to threat, and the use of mirrors to manage this threat, leads to differences in the typical form of mirror use, such as standing far closer than healthy controls tend to stand (Veale & Riley, 2001; Windheim et al., 2011).

Veale's concept of 'the self as an aesthetic object' (see Baldock, Anson, & Veale, 2012) provides a neat conceptual summary of the main components of the phenomenology of BDD that we have summarized here. First, the individual's view of how they look is dominated by their disliked features rather than their appearance as a whole. Second, the individual's view of themselves as a person is dominated by their appearance rather than their many various attributes and ways of being. Third, the individual has a negative experience of how they look (hypothesized to be based on aversive conditioning and linked to aversive memories) and anticipates being criticized and rejected as a person on this basis. Finally, they therefore adopt a threat mode that is characterized by, among other things, intense self-consciousness and an experience of themselves as if seen through the judging eyes of others (the observer perspective). Attention is both self-focused and characterized by vigilance for signs of negative judgment and rejection in others; behaviors are oriented to assessing the level of threat (e.g., checking in the mirror to see how bad one looks), trying to alter the level of threat by altering appearance (e.g., redoing hair until it feels right), and subtle or gross avoidance of threat (e.g., staying in or meeting people but remaining in dimly lit parts of the room in an effort to conceal perceived appearance flaws). These behaviors (including the way in which attention is deployed) all prolong and exacerbate the individual's experience of themselves as an (unacceptable) aesthetic object.

Etiology of BDD

In this part of the chapter our aim is to present a summary of current understanding concerning the etiology of BDD. By etiology we refer both to the acquisition or development of the disorder and also to the maintenance of the disorder. When we discuss maintenance factors we assume a manipulability theory of causation (e.g., Woodward, 2003). Manipulability theories of causation regard causes as devices for manipulating effects. Therefore, in the simplest and broadest sense, something is a maintaining factor for BDD if reducing it or taking it away leads to symptom relief and if introducing it or increasing it leads to symptom exacerbation. For example, selective attention to disliked aspects of a person's appearance is a maintenance factor for BDD if intervening to increase or reduce this selective attention leads to related increases or reductions in appearance-related distress.

When we discuss the acquisition or development of the disorder, as opposed to its maintenance, we do not assume any particular theory of causation but we pay attention to the following concepts. First, the distinction between necessary versus non-necessary causes and between sufficient and non-sufficient causes; and second, different levels of explanation for disorder, including the neurobiological, the behavioral and cognitive, and the evolutionary and sociocultural. Something is a necessary cause of BDD if without it the BDD syndrome would not emerge. Something is a sufficient cause of BDD if its presence always leads to the emergence of the BDD syndrome.

We note that the major theoretical models of BDD appeal to multiple causes and levels of explanation, both in their treatment of maintenance factors and acquisition or development factors. No model assumes that any single factor is either a necessary or sufficient cause in the acquisition of the disorder. It is consistent with this that a single factor might contribute to the accumulated risk of developing BDD on its own, or it may only contribute to accumulated risk in combination with one or more other factors. Given the absence of necessary and sufficient single risk factors or causes here, and that these factors are therefore not always linked with disorder – and indeed may sometimes be advantageous in certain contexts (e.g., the neuropsychological trait of a detail-focused processing style) – we take the decision not to use terms such as *dysfunction* or *pathogenic* to refer to these factors and to preserve these disorder-related terms for the syndrome itself.

Overview of the Models and What They Emphasize

We review two families of theoretical models of BDD in this chapter: the neurobiological (for a model based on a systematic review of the literature, see Grace, Labuschagne, Kaplan, & Rossell, 2017) and the cognitive behavioral (Phillips et al., 2005; Veale & Neziroglu, 2010; Wilhelm, Phillips, & Steketee, 2013). These models are complementary rather than mutually exclusive. As noted earlier, they each appeal to multiple levels of explanation but vary in the level of explanation they emphasize and in how much they emphasize acquisition versus maintenance factors.

Cognitive-behavioral models assume a diathesis-stress model in which a biological vulnerability combines with a certain sort of learning history and certain environmental stressors to produce the BDD syndrome. Their main emphasis in terms of theoretical elaboration and empirical testing is on causal maintenance factors. Behavioral models hypothesize that the maintenance of the disorder centers on the conditioned fear of appearance and that negative reinforcement processes (avoidance and the subsequent short-term reduction in negative affect) maintain this fear association. Cognitive models hypothesize that the maintenance of the disorder centers on appearance-related threat appraisals along with accompanying biases in attention, perception, and interpretation, and avoidance and safety behaviors that function to manage the perceived threat but that paradoxically serve to maintain it. While the emphasis of these models is on causal maintenance factors they do also provide accounts of how appearance-related threat may be formed, particularly through social learning and conditioning processes.

Neurobiological models do not place the same emphasis as cognitive-behavioral models do on causal maintenance factors and they may not always make the distinction between causes relating to acquisition versus maintenance. They hypothesize a role for genetic vulnerabilities in the acquisition of BDD, and a role for aspects of neuropsychology, neuroanatomy, and neurochemistry in either the acquisition or maintenance of the disorder. The neuropsychology literature is very well developed relative to studies of neuroanatomy and function, hence we focus on neuropsychological aspects after a review of genetic studies.

Neurobiological Models

Genetic factors. Norton and Paulus (2017) review genetic studies in the anxiety disorders. These consist of family concordance studies, genetic epidemiological studies, and linkage and candidate gene-association studies. The authors note that early familial concordance studies suggested that there may be a genetic transmission of disorder-specific risk. Richter, Tharmalingam, and Burroughs (2004) reported that 6–10% of first-degree family members have BDD. Phillips et al. (2005) reported on a sample of 200 with a BDD diagnosis and found that 20% had at least one first-degree relative with BDD, and that 5.8% of all first-degree relatives had BDD.

Genetic epidemiological studies have the advantage over concordance studies of allowing for the disentangling of familial, shared environmental, and genetic variability. Monzani et al. (2012) used twin modeling methods (n = 3,544) and a self-report measure of dysmorphic concern and concluded that genetic factors accounted for approximately 44% of the variance, with non-shared environmental factors and measurement error accounting for the rest. However, this does not mean that the genetic factors were specific to BDD. Indeed, in their review of genetic epidemiological studies as a whole, Norton and Pauls (2017) conclude that there is little or no evidence for a diagnosis-specific genetic influence on anxiety disorders. Rather, 'the evidence suggests genetic transmission of any anxiety or depressive disorder ... with developmental and learning factors being largely responsible for determining the manifestation of specific disorders.' They also note that much of the nonspecific genetic influence appears to be common with the personality trait of neuroticism.

Linkage studies are designed to relate gene functionality to their chromosomal location. Richter et al. (2004) carried out the first gene association study in BDD and found an association between the γ-aminobutyric acid (*GABA A-Y2*) gene and comorbid BDD-OCD but not OCD alone. They also reported a trend association with the serotonin transporter polymorphism (*5-HTTPRL*) short allele. Phillips et al. (2015) recruited a sample of 50 individuals with a BDD diagnosis and 38 healthy controls and, like Richter et al. (2004), found an association for the *GABA A-Y2* gene, although this association did not survive correction for multiple testing. The AA allele of the *GABA A-Y2* gene was more frequent in the BDD group than in controls. They, like Richter, found a trend association for the *5-HTTPRL* gene, with the s/s allele occurring more frequently in BDD subjects than in controls. They did not find an association for the *HTR1B* gene, which has previously been implicated in OCD. Phillips et al. (2015) were restricted by a small sample size. Clearly further studies with more power are needed before any conclusions can be drawn concerning the presence or otherwise of consistently observed candidate genes that raise the risk for BDD in particular. Even then, such a discovery looks unlikely: Norton and Paulus (2017) conclude that few chromosomal loci have been consistently identified as potential genetic targets either for anxiety disorders generally or for specific anxiety diagnoses. The search for robust candidate genes is likely to be more fruitful if it is directed at simpler phenotypes that are associated with, but not defining of, the disorder, such as neuroticism or aspects of visual processing.

Neuropsychology

Neurobiological phenotypes offer some promise as targets for future genetic studies. One of the most developed areas of research here in connection with BDD is aligned with the visual perception aspect of cognitive systems within the Research Domain Criteria (RDoC) framework proposed by the National Institute for Mental Health (NIMH). Beilharz, Castle, Grace, and Rossell (2017) have published a systematic review of visual processing studies in BDD. They highlight the main difference in people with BDD over healthy controls to be 'a dominance of detailed local processing over global processing and associated changes in brain activation in visual regions'. Much of the work in this area has been carried out by Feusner and colleagues, as reflected in the reviews by Beilharz et al. (2017) and Grace et al. (2017). One of the findings leading to this conclusion of a dominance of local processing is that people with BDD have shown a reduced face inversion effect with an associated reduction in activity in the occipital regions (Feusner et al., 2010). Similarly, Toh et al. (2017) found that people with BDD showed reduced face and object inversion effects relative to an OCD group and healthy control group, and this was accounted for by those with BDD being more accurate in identifying inverted Mooney faces and objects. The face and object inversion effect refers to the finding that healthy controls are slower at processing details of the face or object when it is upside down compared with when it is the right way up. Feusner, Yaryura-Tobias, and Saxena (2008) have interpreted the reduced face and object inversion effect in BDD to mean that configural or global processing of stimuli is weaker in BDD. However, Silverstein et al. (2015) found that a group of BDD patients performed as well as healthy controls and OCD patients on a perceptual organization task that taps into global processing. Hence this may be less a deficit in global processing and more a preference for, or a particular strength in, detail-focused processing. This might be advantageous in some contexts (e.g., doing editorial work) and a liability in other contexts (e.g., coping with appearance-related teasing). Interestingly, this same detail-focused neuropsychological profile has been observed in people with autistic spectrum disorders (ASD) (Happe & Frith, 2006), and Vasudeva and Hollander (2017) reflect on this shared profile in a report on two case studies of patients with both ASD and BDD. The same profile has also been observed in people currently ill with, and recovered from, anorexia nervosa (Lopez, Tchanturia, Stahl, Booth, and Holliday, 2008). Parallel studies in currently ill and recovered BDD patients would be informative, as would samples defined as 'at risk' for BDD (e.g., with subclinical presentations). Blum, Redden, and Grant (2017) used a group of this kind, although numbers were very small (n = 5) compared with 82 controls. They did not probe local versus global processing but they found evidence of executive functioning impairment in this at-risk group.

Neuro-Anatomy and Functional Neuro-Anatomy

Grace et al. (2017) present a systematic review and a theoretical model of the neurobiology of BDD on the basis of 19 studies that fulfilled their inclusion criteria. They identify the temporal gyrus, limbic system, and prefrontal cortex as important regions in BDD in which abnormalities may drive disordered visual perception (including excessive attention to detail) and emotional arousal in BDD. They note in the limitations section that the studies reviewed had small sample sizes of less than 20 and that there is substantial overlap of participants between the studies. They conclude that the underlying neuropathophysiology of BDD remains largely untested and unknown.

Cognitive-Behavioral Models

In this part of the chapter we focus on the causal maintenance of BDD as understood within cognitive-behavioral models of the disorder. Candidate causal maintenance factors may or may not be implicated in the acquisition of the disorder. The key is whether manipulating these factors leads to predictable changes in BDD symptomatology and, most importantly, whether reducing them or eliminating them leads to symptom relief.

Attentional processes in the causal maintenance of BDD. In this first section, we focus on attentional processes in people with BDD within the context of a cognitive-behavioral framework. We ask the following questions: first, once the syndrome is in place – that is, the criteria for BDD are met and the experience of intense appearance-related threat is triggered – where do people with BDD direct their attention? Second, is it possible to manipulate attentional processes in order to achieve symptom relief?

Cognitive-behavioral models hypothesize a range of attentional biases in BDD and conceptualize these in relation to appearance-related threat. Threat monitoring and threat management strategies therefore kick in, including a range of attentional processes: selective attention to perceived flaws in their appearance (over and above their appearance as a whole), selective attention to perceived attractive features in others (especially of the same feature that they dislike in themselves), selective attention to signs of appearance-related criticism or rejection by others, and selective attention to internal appearance-related stimuli (thoughts, images, sensations, emotions) with reduced attention to external stimuli (their conversation partner, the task at hand, the wider environment).

Two eye-tracking studies have demonstrated an attentional bias for their disliked features in people with BDD (Greenberg et al., 2014; Grocholewski et al., 2012). In these same studies, healthy control participants showed the opposite pattern of giving more attention to the features they liked in themselves. Kollei, Horndasch, Erim, and Martin (2017) reported a slightly different pattern in another eye-tracking study. In this study, BDD participants gave equal attention to attractive and unattractive features in their own face, but focused less attention on their attractive parts than healthy controls did. Compared with healthy controls they focused more attention on attractive features in the attractive other faces. Hence there is evidence for a bias not only toward their own unattractive features but also toward *attractive* features in other people. Toh et al. (2017) used an emotional Stroop task and eye-tracking methodology and found significant Stroop interference for BDD-negative words relative to healthy controls and an OCD group. Eye-tracking was only mildly anomalous in clinical groups with evidence of some avoidance of certain disorder-relevant words.

We are not aware of any eye-tracking studies that have examined comparing processes in BDD. However, Anson et al. (2015) studied comparing using a questionnaire methodology and found that participants with BDD (n = 35) compared their disliked features with the parallel feature in others, and that comparing was more frequent when targets for comparison were more attractive. Selective attention to others specifically for signs of appearance-related criticism is addressed in the next paragraph in the context of studies on emotion perception and interpretation biases.

Self-focused attention has been very little studied in BDD. Windheim et al. (2011) included self-focused attention as a key variable in their experimental study of the effects of looking in the mirror for short and long durations in participants with BDD and healthy controls. Self-focused attention increased comparably for both groups as a result of mirror-gazing, but was significantly elevated at the baseline in the BDD group compared with the healthy control group.

There are treatment interventions that manipulate attentional processes within cognitive-behavioral therapies for BDD. Typically, a combination of perceptual mirror retraining, mindfulness, and attention training are used in order to broaden out attention from perceived flaws to the body as a whole, and from the self and appearance-related stimuli to other people, other aspects of the external environment (e.g., the task at hand), and non-appearance-related stimuli. Perceptual mirror retraining (e.g., Veale & Neziroglu, 2010, pp. 317–319) involves teaching participants to describe their entire body in neutral nonjudgmental language while looking in the mirror. Mindfulness and attention training take various different forms but are geared toward skilling participants in shifting their attention away from disorder-related targets (e.g., perceived flaws, attractive others, and signs of hostility in others) and onto non-disorder-related targets (e.g., what their conversation partner is saying, or the feel of the wind against their face as they walk along the street) (see, e.g., Veale & Neziroglu, 2010).

There have been at least five randomized controlled trials of cognitive behavioral therapy for BDD, with reasonable treatment outcomes, in which some form of perceptual retraining and attention training has been included among the treatment components (Greenberg, Mothi, & Wilhelm, 2016; Mataix-Cols et al., 2015; Veale et al., 1996, 2014; Wilhelm et al., 2014). However, interventions targeting selective attention have not been studied in isolation from other core treatment components such as exposure. Hence their role as causal maintenance factors in BDD is yet to be substantiated.

Processes of interpretation and emotion perception in the causal maintenance of BDD. In this next section, we focus on processes of interpretation and emotion perception in people with BDD. We ask the following questions: first, once the syndrome is in place, what is observed in terms of how people with BDD perceive emotions in others and in how they interpret the thoughts and emotions of others in appearance-related scenarios? Second, is it possible to manipulate these perceptual and interpretative processes in order to achieve symptom relief?

Along with attentional biases, cognitive-behavioral models also hypothesize a range of interpretation and emotion perception biases in BDD. Again, these are conceptualized in terms of efforts to monitor and manage appearance-related threat and include a readiness to interpret the facial expressions and intent of others in terms of negative evaluation and rejection.

Toh et al. (2015) studied emotion perception using the Eckman pictures and an eye tracker in 21 participants with BDD, 19 with OCD, and 21 healthy controls. The BDD participants were poorer at identifying the correct emotion in the faces and they showed an angry recognition bias. They also displayed an unusual scanning profile characterized by both enhanced staring and extensive scanning. The authors suggest that this unusual scanning profile may relate to selective attention to, and avoidance of, the feature in the faces that corresponded to the patient's own perceived flaw. In this case, the emotion perception deficit may be secondary to attentional processes and might be most effectively corrected, as the authors suggest, through perceptual retraining in which patients are taught to focus on the whole rather than on their disliked features.

An angry recognition bias in participants with BDD has also been found in other studies. Buhlmann, McNally, Etcoff, Tuschen-Caffier, and Wilhelm (2004) found no differences between BDD, OCD and healthy control groups in a face discrimination task, but poorer emotion recognition in BDD participants, including a bias for misinterpreting faces as angry. Jefferies et al. (2012) found BDD participants (n = 12) superior at recognizing inverted faces compared with healthy controls (n = 16) but less good at recognizing both anger and fear. Buhlmann, Etcoff, and Wilhelm (2006) reported that BDD participants (n = 18) showed a bias for misinterpreting faces as contemptuous or angry but only in association with *self*-referent scenarios, and not in association with *other*-reference scenarios. This is consistent with the hypothesis that people with BDD have a readiness to perceive hostility in others that is related to their perception of appearance-related threat (and therefore self-related threat). Buhlmann, Winter, and Kathmann (2013) reported comparable emotion recognition performance on a 'reading the mind in the eyes task' in BDD participants and healthy controls and Buhlmann, Gleiss, Rupf, Zschenderlein, and Kathmann (2011) found no group differences between BDD participants and controls in general emotion recognition but less accuracy in BDD participants in identifying neutral expressions.

Several studies have reported on negative interpretation biases in participants with BDD. Buhlmann, McNally, Wilhelm, and Florin (2002) compared a BDD group, an OCD group, and a healthy control group for their choice of interpretations for ambiguous body-related, social, and general scenarios. The BDD participants were unique in showing a negative interpretative bias for body-related and social scenarios. Clerkin and Teachman (2009) reported that appearance-related cognitive biases predicted distress and avoidance related to mirror-gazing in participants who were either high (n = 32) or low (n = 31) in BDD symptoms. Buhlmann, Wacker, and Dziobek (2015) built on previous studies by using video scenarios and inviting participants to consider the emotions, thoughts, and intentions of individuals in these scenarios. They found that participants with BDD and SAD were less good than OCD participants were at reading other people's mental states, but there were no group differences in reading other people's emotions.

To our knowledge two studies thus far report on efforts to modify interpretative biases in BDD and to study the impact on measures of emotional vulnerability and symptomatology. In Summers and Cougle (2016) participants were 40 people with BDD as diagnosed by a face-to-face interview. There was random assignment to placebo training or training that targeted social evaluation and appearance-related interpretation biases. Interpretation bias modification (IBM) training successfully reduced threat interpretations of ambiguous scenarios and those with high pretreatment BDD symptoms experienced reductions in BDD symptoms post training. This supports the notion of interpretation biases as causal maintenance factors in BDD. In Premo, Sarfan, and Clerkin (2016), participants were 86 people with elevated BDD symptoms. Interpretation bias training was successful: negative BDD-relevant interpretations were reduced in participants who completed the positive training condition. However, there was no significant effect of the training on BDD-related distress and avoidance as assessed by a mirror stressor task.

Safety seeking and compulsive behaviors as causal maintenance factors. Cognitive-behavioral models hypothesize that safety-seeking, avoidance, and compulsive behaviors maintain appearance-related threat appraisals and anxiety in BDD. The main supporting evidence we have for this is indirect evidence from the positive results of cognitive behavioral therapy as assessed in randomized controlled trials (see Beilharz et al., 2017; Harrison et al., 2016, for reviews). Cognitive behavioral therapy for BDD includes without exception some aspects of reversing avoidance and dropping safety-seeking and compulsive behaviors. However, few studies have isolated specific treatment components. The exception are one or two studies of Exposure and Response Prevention (ERP) alone. Gorbis (2004) reports on a study of seven participants given 15 ERP sessions involving distorted mirrors. Five out of seven showed a 75–80% symptom reduction and had no further plastic surgery over a subsequent five-year period. Clearly these numbers are small and the study was not controlled. Khemlani-Patel and Neziroglu (2011) randomly allocated five participants to cognitive therapy with ERP and five to ERP only, delivered in 24 90-minute sessions over eight weeks. Both groups showed equivalent improvement in symptoms, leading to the conclusion that cognitive therapy did not enhance ERP. Neither group showed any change in appearance dissatisfaction.

Life experience and learning history in the development of BDD. In this section, we consider the acquisition of BDD from the perspective of cognitive-behavioral models. To set this in the broader context, Norton and Paulus (2017) conclude that candidate factors currently identified for the acquisition of anxiety disorders are not specific to one anxiety disorder over another. So where does this leave us in terms of the acquisition of BDD in particular? Well, against the background of these risk factors for *any* anxiety disorder, cognitive-behavioral models hypothesize that conditioning and learning processes hook onto the particularities of an individual's history to determine the shaping of one particular anxiety disorder over another. The 'particularities of an individual's history' include a much greater level of granularity or specificity than is captured by the factors such as neuroticism that have been reviewed by Norton and Paulus (2017). We start to move here to considering details such as the experience of being called fat, or the experience of being repeatedly praised for looking beautiful. In the case of the acquisition of BDD the task is to describe the kind of learning histories that can lead an individual both to place great importance on their appearance and to develop negative appraisals of their appearance that are discrepant with how others see them.

Cognitive-behavioral models hypothesize that appearance may become specially valuable and important to the individual, even before they have developed negative beliefs about how they look, through the processes of conditioning and social learning. For example, how an individual looks (conditioned stimulus) may have elicited praise and other forms of desirable attention from others (unconditioned stimulus). This experience may lead the individual to associate their appearance with positive forms of attention and to associate their self-worth with their appearance. As well as direct learning of this kind, vicarious learning occurs. For example, an individual may observe other people being praised for how they look; they may also observe other people making a lot of comments about their own and other people's appearance (whether positive, neutral, or negative); and they may also be taught explicitly that attractive people are more likely to succeed and therefore, implicitly, that being unattractive is something to fear. Neziroglu (2004) reports from her clinical experience that many of her patients with BDD were positively or intermittently reinforced for their appearance. The only empirical study that reports on this that we were able to identify is the study by Weingarden, Curley, Renshaw, and Wilhelm (2017) in which 165 adults with BDD were asked whether they remembered a specific experience or event that may be the origin of their appearance concerns. Sixty-two adults reported a triggering event, and 25 of these events involved what the authors describe as 'experiences that instilled cultural or societal messages about the importance of beauty'.

With this learning about the importance of appearance in place, conditioning processes are also hypothesized to account for the development of negative appearance-related beliefs in the individual. In brief, it is hypothesized that an unconditioned stimulus such as teasing (an interpersonal example) or the perception of a bump on the skin (an intrapersonal example) elicits an unconditioned response, which is typically disgust, shame, or anxiety. Anything associated with the teasing (e.g., an aspect of appearance that the teasing centers on) or that is similar or related to the bump (e.g., other unevenness on the skin) can become conditioned stimuli that elicit the same response of disgust, shame, or anxiety (the conditioned response). Whatever is associated with the original conditioned stimulus may not relate directly to appearance. For example, if someone experiences teasing (unconditioned stimulus) about their trousers (conditioned stimulus) and feels shame (unconditioned response), their legs may become a conditioned stimulus for shame by association with their trousers. Or if someone has an injury (unconditioned stimulus) to their arm (conditioned stimulus) and feels fear and disgust (unconditioned response), their healed arm and even their unaffected arm may both become conditioned stimuli for fear and disgust by association.

Cognitive-behavioral models of BDD hypothesize that exposure to stressful life events is a risk factor for the development of negative appearance-related beliefs through the kinds of conditioning processes described earlier. Stressful life events that have been studied as potential risk factors include appearance-related and general teasing and bullying, physical, sexual, and emotional abuse, and changes in physical appearance and physical stigmata such as acne or eczema. Stressful life events can be chronic (e.g., repeated bullying or abuse) or singular and acute (e.g., a single negative appearance-related comment). Stressful life events may singly contribute to the aggregation of risk for developing BDD or they may only add to that risk in combination with other individual or environmental factors. Researchers have recognized the importance of trying to capture not just the objective burden of life stress in individuals who go on to develop BDD (e.g., how does this compare with clinical and nonclinical controls?) but also recall and reporting processes (e.g., do people with BDD differ in their recall or reporting of stressful life events?).

A handful of studies using retrospective self-report methodologies with adult participants reporting on historical experiences have found higher rates of teasing and bullying experiences (including, but not exclusively, appearance-related) in people with BDD compared to healthy controls (Buhlmann, Cook, Fama, & Wilhelm, 2007; Buhlmann, Marques, & Wilhelm, 2012); and also higher rates of abuse, compared to healthy controls (Buhlmann et al., 2012; Veale et al., 2015), clinical controls (Neziroglu, Khemlani-Patel, & Yaryura-Tobias, 2006; Veale, 2015), and published norms (Didie et al., 2006). Other retrospective self-report studies have shown correlations between severity of childhood bullying and BDD symptom severity in nonclinical samples (Boyda & Shevlin, 2011; Menees, Grieve, Mienaltowski, & Pope, 2013; Webb, Zimmer-Gembeck, & Mastro, 2016; Wolke & Sapouna, 2008). These studies do not permit the disentangling of the objective aspect of the burden of life stress in terms of frequency and intensity from the subjective aspects of recall and reporting.

Building on these studies, Webb et al. (2016) made some progress toward disentangling objective event burden from subjective recall factors by introducing peer ratings and by seeking reports on very recent history and current perceptions as opposed to more distant histories. They took self-report measures at two time points separated by one year, on symptoms relevant to BDD and current perception of peer acceptance in 367 Australian students, along with their reports on who was popular and victimized in their class, and how much they liked their classmates. The results supported both the stress-exposure model (adverse social experiences increased BDD-like symptoms) and the stress-generation hypothesis (BDD-like symptoms exacerbated low perceptions of peer-acceptance). Participants were not assessed for BDD, hence this study assumes that BDD-like symptoms are on a continuum with the full disorder.

Weingarden et al. (2017) built on the existing literature by providing a patient-centered 'bottom-up' approach in which they probed a clinical sample for links in their own minds between adverse events and their BDD with the question 'do you remember a specific experience or event that may be the origin of your appearance concerns?' For participants who answered 'yes', they then provided an open text field for participants to describe the event. Participants were 165 adults recruited through the Internet and diagnosed using the Body Dysmorphic Disorder Questionnaire (BDD-Q). Of all the participants, 37.6% explicitly attributed their appearance concerns to a specific triggering event. They also found that the most frequently described events involved teasing and bullying incidents of which 96% concerned physical appearance, followed by situations that emphasized social or cultural messages of beauty. Abuse experiences were infrequently described overall. Furthermore, most events were ongoing incidents that recurred over time rather than being single events and they were mostly interpersonal in nature.

Miller and Brock (2017) conducted a meta-analysis to study trauma (as distinct from stressful life events) in relationship to obsessive-compulsive spectrum symptoms (including BDD). Four of the 24 studies that met inclusion criteria concerned BDD in particular. A significant overall effect size was reported, indicating that exposure to past trauma is associate with a higher severity of obsessive-compulsive spectrum symptoms.

Targeting emotional memories as a causal maintenance factor. Veale and Neziroglu (2010) propose that historical aversive conditioning to body image continues to maintain appearance-related threat and anxiety in the present and that re-scripting aversive memories that relate to present concerns may reduce the experience of appearance-related in the present. Willson et al. (2016) use a multiple-baseline single-case experimental design to test imagery re-scripting as an isolated intervention with six individuals with BDD. Four out of the six participants showed significant symptomatic improvement after the intervention.

Conclusions

We have sought to summarize the existing literature on the phenomenology and the etiology of BDD, both in terms of acquisition and maintenance of the disorder. Many of the neurobiological and cognitive models are complementary (e.g., detail-focused processing within neurobiological models and selective attention to flaws within cognitive models). Many of the studies reviewed here are small and have heterogeneous populations. The findings may therefore depend on who has been recruited for a particular study. Many of the findings are not specific to BDD and may be found in other mental disorders, suggesting transdiagnostic processes. This opens up the possibility of transdiagnostic interventions that may be adapted for different disorders.

References

Angelakis, I., Gooding, P. A., & Panagioti, M. (2016). Suicidality in BDD: A systematic review with meta-analysis. *Clinical Psychology Review, 49*, 55–66.

Anson, M., Veale, D., & Miles, S (2015). Appearance comparison in individuals with body dysmorphic disorder and controls. *Body Image, 15*, 132–140.

Baldock, E., Anson, M., & Veale, D. (2012). The stopping criteria for mirror-gazing in body dysmorphic disorder. *British Journal of Clinical Psychology, 51*, 323–344.

Baldock, E. & Veale, D. (2017). The Self as an Aesthetic Object: Body Image, Beliefs about the Self, and Shame in a Cognitive-Behavioural Model of Body Dysmorphic Disorder. In Body Dysmorphic Disorder: Advances in Research and Clinical Practice. Edited by Dr Katharine A. Phillips.

Beilharz, F., Castle, D. J., Grace. S., & Rossell, S. L. (2017). A systematic review of visual processing and associated treatments in BDD. *Acta Psychiatrica Scandinavia*, *136*, 16–36.

Bjornsson, A. S., Didie, E. R., Grant, J. E., Menard, W., Stalker, E., & Phillips, K. A. (2013). Age at onset and clinical correlates in body dysmorphic disorder. *Comprehensive Psychiatry*, *54*, 893–903.

Blum, A. W., Redden, S. A., & Grant, J. E. (2017) Neurocognitive functioning in young adults with subclinical BDD. *Psychiatric Quarterly*. doi: 10.1007/s11126-017-9510-2.

Boyda, D. & Shevlin, M. (2011). Childhood victimisation as a predictor of muscle dysmorphia in adult male bodybuilders. *Irish Journal of Psychology*, *32*, 105–115.

Buhlmann, U., Cook, L. M., Fama, J. M., & Wilhelm, S. (2007). Perceived teasing experiences in BDD. *Body Image*, *4*(4), 381–385.

Buhlmann, U., Etcoff, N. L., & Wilhelm, S. (2006). Emotion recognition bias for contempt and anger in BDD. *Journal of Psychiatric Research*, *40*, 105–111.

Buhlmann, U., Etcoff, N. L., & Wilhelm, S. (2008). Facial attractiveness ratings and perfectionism in body dysmorphic disorder and obsessive-compulsive disorder. *Journal of Anxiety Disorders*, *22*(3), 540–547.

Buhlmann, U., Gleiss, M. J., Rupf, L., Zschenderlein, K., & Kathmann, N.(2011). Modifying emotion recognition deficits in BDD: An experimental investigation. *Depression and Anxiety*, *28*, 924–931.

Buhlmann, U., Marques, L. M., & Wilhelm, S. (2012). Traumatic experiences in individuals with body dysmorphic disorder. *Journal of Nervous and Mental Disease*, *200*, 95–98.

Buhlmann, U., McNally, R. J., Etcoff, N. L., Tuschen-Caffier, B., & Wilhelm, S. (2004). Emotion recognition deficits in body dysmorphic disorder. *Journal of Psychiatric Research*, *38*, 201–206.

Buhlmann, U., McNally, R. J., Wilhelm, S., & Florin, I. (2002). Selective processing of emotional information in BDD. *Journal of Anxiety Disorders*, *16*, 289–298.

Buhlmann, U., Teachman, B. A., & Kathmann, N. (2011). Evaluating implicit attractiveness beliefs in body dysmorphic disorder using the Go/No-go Association Task. *Journal of Behaviour Therapy and Experimental Psychiatry*, *42*, 192–197.

Buhlmann, U., Teachman, B. A., Naumann, E., Fehlinger, T., & Rief, W. (2009). The meaning of beauty: Implicit and explicit self-esteem and attractiveness beliefs in body dysmorphic disorder. *Journal of Anxiety Disorders*, *23*, 694–702.

Buhlmann, U., Wacker, R., & Dziobek, I. (2015). Inferring other people's states of mind: Comparison across social anxiety, body dysmorphic, and obsessive-compulsive disorders. *Journal of Anxiety Disorders*, *34*, 107–113.

Buhlmann, U., Wilhelm, S., Glaesmer, H., Mewes, R., Brähler, E., & Rief, W. (2011). Perceived appearance-related teasing in body dysmorphic Disorder: A population-based survey. *International Journal of Cognitive Therapy*, *4*(4), 342–348.

Buhlmann, U., Winter, A., & Kathmann, N. (2013). Emotion recognition in BDD: Application of the Reading the Mind in the Eyes task. *Body Image*, *10*, 247–250.

Cash, T. (2004). Body image: Past, present, and future. *Body Image*, *1*, 1–5.

Clerkin, E. M., Bethany, A., Teachman, A. R., & Smith, A. R. (2014). Specificity of implicit-shame associations: Comparison across body dysmorphic, obsessive-compulsive, and social anxiety disorders. *Clinical Psychological Science*, *2*(5), 560–575.

Clerkin, E. M. & Teachman, A. R. (2009). Automatic and strategic measures of mirror gazing among individuals with body dysmorphic disorder symptoms. *Journal of Nervous & Mental Disease, 197*(8), 589–598.

Cooper, M. & Osman, S. (2007). Metacognition in body dysmorphic disorder: A preliminary exploration. *Journal of Cognitive Psychotherapy, 21*(2), 148–155.

Didie, E., Tortolani, C. C., Pope, C. G., Menard, W., Fay, C., & Phillips, K. A. (2006). Childhood abuse and neglect in body dysmorphic disorder. *Child Abuse & Neglect, 30*, 1105–1115.

Feusner, J. D., Moller, H., Altstein, L., Sugar, C., Bookheimer, S., Yoon, J., & Hembacher, E. (2010). Inverted face processing in body dysmorphic disorder. *Journal of Psychiatric Research, 44*(15), 1088–1094.

Feusner, J. D., Yaryura-Tobias, J., & Saxena, J. (2008). The pathophysiology of body dysmorphic disorder. *Body Image, 5*, 3–12.

Geremia, J. & Neziroglu, F. (2001). Cognitive therapy in the treatment of body dysmorphic disorder. *Clinical Psychology & Psychotherapy, 8*, 243–251.

Gorbis, E. (2004). Crooked mirrors: The externalization of self-image in BDD. *Behavior Therapy, 27*, 74–76.

Grace, S. A., Labuschagne, I., Kaplan, R. A., & Rossell, S. L. (2017). The neurobiology of body dysmorphic disorder: A systematic review and theoretical model. *Neuroscience and Biobehavioural Reviews, 83*, 83–96.

Greenberg, J. L., Mothi, S. S., & Wilhelm, S. (2016). CBT for adolescent BDD: A pilot study. *Behavior Therapy, 47*, 213–224.

Greenberg, J. L., Reuman, L., Hartmann, A. S., Kasarskis, I., & Wilhelm, S. (2014). Visual hot spots: An eye tracking study of attention bias in BDD. *Psychiatry Research, 57*, 125–132.

Grocholewski, A., Kliem, S., & Heinrichs, N. (2012). Selective attention to imagined facial ugliness is specific to body dysmorphic disorder. *Body Image, 9*, 261–269.

Happe, F. & Frith, U. (2006). The weak coherence account: Detail-focused cognitive style in autism spectrum disorders. *Journal of Autism and Developmental Disorders, 36*, 5–25.

Harrison, A., Fernández de la Cruz, L., Enander, J., Radua, J., & Mataix-Cols, D. (2016). Cognitive-behavioral therapy for body dysmorphic disorder: A systematic review and meta-analysis of randomized controlled trials. *Clinical Psychology Review, 48*(4), 3–51.

Jansen, A., Smeets, T., Martijn, C., & Nederkoorn, C. (2006). I see what you see: The lack of a self-serving body-image bias in eating disorders. *British Journal of Clinical Psychology, 45*, 123–135.

Jefferies, K., Laws, K. R., & Fineberg, N. (2012). Superior face recognition in BDD. *Journal of Obsessive Compulsive and Related Disorders, 1*, 175–179.

Jefferies-Sewell, K., Chamberlain, S. R., Fineberg, N. A., & Laws, K. R. Cognitive dysfunction in body dysmorphic disorder: New implications for nosological systems and neurobiological models. *CNS Spectrums, 22*(1), 51–60.

Khemlani-Patel, J., & Neziroglu, F. (2011). CBT for BDD: A comparative investigation. *International Journal of Cognitive Therapy, 4*, 363–380.

Kollei, I., Horndasch, S., Erim, Y., & Martin, A. (2017). Visual selective attention in body dysmorphic disorder, bulimia nervosa and healthy controls. *Journal of Psychosomatic Research, 92*, 26–33.

Lopez, C., Tchanturia, K., Stahl, D., Booth, R., & Holliday, J. (2008). An examination of the concept of central coherence in women with anorexia nervosa. *International Journal of Eating Disorders*, *41*, 143–152.

Mataix-Cols, D., Fernández de la Cruz, L., Isomura, K., Anson, M., Turner, C., Monzani, B., Cadman, J., Bowyer, L., Heyman, I., Veale, D., & Krebs, G. (2015). A pilot randomized controlled trial of cognitive-behavioral therapy for adolescents with body dysmorphic disorder. *Journal of the American Academy of Child and Adolescent Psychiatry*, *54*, 895–904.

Menees, L., Grieve, F. G., Mienaltowski, A., & Pope, J. (2013). Critical comments about the body and muscle dysmorphia symptoms in collegiate men. *International Journal of Men's Health*, *12*, 17–28.

Miller, M. L. & Brock, R. L. (2017). The effect of trauma on the severity of obsessive-compulsive spectrum symptoms: A meta-analysis. *Journal of Anxiety Disorders*, *47*, 29–44.

Möllmann, A., Dietel, F. A., Hunger, A., & Buhlmann, U. (2017). Prevalence of body dysmorphic disorder and associated features in German adolescents: A self-report survey.

Monzani, B., Rijsdijk, F., Iervolino, A. C., Anson, M., Cherkas, L., & Mataix-Cols, D. (2012). Evidence for a genetic overlap between body dysmorphic concerns and obsessive-compulsive symptoms in an adult female community twin sample. *American Journal of Medical Genetics Part B: Neuropsychiatric Genetics*, *159B*, 376–382.

Neziroglu, F. (2004). A behavioral model for BDD. *Psychiatric Annals*, *34*, 915–920.

Neziroglu, F., Khemlani-Patel, S., & Yaryura-Tobias, J. A. (2006). Rates of abuse in body dysmorphic disorder and obsessive-compulsive disorder. *Body Image*, *3*, 189–193.

Norton, P. J. & Paulus, D. J. (2017). Transdiagnostic models of anxiety disorder: Theoretical and empirical underpinnings. *Clinical Psychology Review*, *56*, 122–137.

Osman, S., Cooper., M., Hackmann, M., & Veale, D. (2004). Spontaneously occurring images and early memories in people with body dysmorphic disorder. *Memory*, *12*, 428–436.

Phillips, K. A. (2005). *The Broken Mirror: Understanding and Treating Body Dysmorphic Disorder*. New York, NY: Oxford University Press.

Phillips. K. A., Menard, W., Fay, C., & Weisberg, R. (2005). Demographic characteristics, phenomenology, comorbidity etc. *Psychosomatics*, *46*, 317–325.

Phillips, K. A., Pagano, M. E., Menard, W., & Stout, R. L. (2006). A 12-month follow-up study of the course of body dysmorphic disorder. *American Journal of Psychiatry*, *163*, 907–912.

Phillips, K. A., Zai, G., & King, N. A. (2015). A prelim candidate gene study in BDD. *Journal of Obsessive Compulsive and Related Disorders*, *6*, 72–76.

Premo, J. E., Sarfan, L. D., & Clerkin, E. M. (2016). Training interpretation biases among individuals with body dysmorphic disorder symptoms. *Body Image*, *16*, 54–62.

Richter, M. A., Tharmalingam, S., & Burroughs, E. (2004). A preliminary genetics investigation of BDD and OCD. *Neuropsychopharmacology*, 29 (suppl. 1), S200.

Salkovskis, P. M. (1991). The importance of behaviour in the maintenance of anxiety and panic: A cognitive account. *Behavioural Psychotherapy*, *19*, 6–19.

Schneider, S. C., Mond, J., Turner, C. M., & Hudson, J. L. (2017). Subthreshold BDD in adolescents: Prevalence and impact. *Psychiatry Research*, *251*, 125–130.

Silverstein, S., Elliott, C. M., Feusner, J. D., Keane, B. P., Mikkilineni, D., Hansen, N., Hartmann, A., & Wilhelm, S. (2015). Comparison of visual perception organization in schizophrenia and body dysmorphic disorder. *Psychiatry Research*, 426–433.

Summers, B. J. & Cougle, J. R. (2016). Modifying interpretation biases in body dysmorphic disorder: Evaluation of a brief computerized treatment. *Behaviour Research and Therapy*, *87*, 117–127.

Toh, W. L., Castle, D. J., & Rossell, S. J. (2015). Facial affect recognition in body dysmorphic disorder versus obsessive-compulsive disorder: An eye-tracking study. *Journal of Anxiety Disorders*, *35*, 49–59.

Toh, W. L., Castle, D. J., & Rossell, S. L. (2017a). Attentional biases in BDD: Eye-tracking using the emotional Stroop task. *Comprehensive Psychiatry*, *74*, 151–161.

Toh, W. L., Castle, D. J., & Rossell, S. J. (2017b). Characterisation of BDD versus OCD: In light of current DSM-5 nosology. *Journal of OC and R Disorders*, *12*, 117–126.

Toh, W. L., Castle, D. J., & Rossell, S. L. (2017c). Face and object perception in BDD versus OCD: The Mooney Faces Task. *Journal of the International Neuropsychological Society*, *22*, 1–10.

Toh, W. L., Castle, D. J., & Rossell, S. L. (2017d). How individuals with BDD process their own face: A quantitative and qualitative investigation based on eye-tracking paradigm. *Cognitive Neuropsychiatry*, *22*(3), 213–232.

Vasudeva, S. B. & Hollander, E. (2017). BDD in patients with ASD: A reflection of increased local processing and self-focus. *American Journal of Psychiatry*, *174*(4), 313–316.

Veale, D. (2002). Over-valued ideas: A conceptual analysis. *Behaviour Research and Therapy*, *40*, 383–400.

Veale, D., Anson, M., Miles, S., Pieta, M., Costa, A., & Ellison, N. (2014). Efficacy of cognitive behaviour therapy CBT versus anxiety management for BDD: An RCT. *Psychotherapy and Psychosomatics*, *83*, 341–353.

Veale, D., Boocock, A., Gournay, K., Dryden, W., Shah, F., Willson, R., & Walburn, J. (1996). Body dysmorphic disorder: A survey of 50 cases. *British Journal of Psychiatry*, *169*, 196–201.

Veale, D., & Gilbert, P. (2014) Body dysmorphic disorder: The functional and evolutionary context and a compassionate mind. *Journal of Obsessive Compulsive and Related Disorders*, *3*, 150–160.

Veale, D., Gledhill, L., Christodoulou, P., & Hodsoll, J. (2016). Body dysmorphic disorder in different settings: A systematic review and estimated weighted prevalence. *Body Image*, *18*, 168–186.

Veale, D., Kinderman, P., Riley, S., & Lambrou, C. (2003) Self-discrepancy in body dysmorphic disorder. *British Journal of Clinical Psychology*, *42*, 157–169.

Veale, D. & Matsunaga, H. (2014) Body dysmorphic disorder and olfactory reference disorder: Proposals for ICD11. *Revista Brasileira de Psiquiatria: RBP Psychiatry*, 36, Suppl. 1, 14–20.

Veale, D., Miles, S., Read, J., Troglia, A., Carmona, L., Fiorito, C., Wells, H., Wylie, K., & Muir, G. (2015). Environmental and physical risk factors for men to develop body dysmorphic disorder concerning penis size compared to men anxious about their penis size and men with no concerns: A cohort study. *Journal of Obsessive-Compulsive and Related Disorders*, *6*, 49–58.

Veale, D. & Neziroglu, F. (2010). *Body Dysmorphic Disorder: A Treatment Manual*. Chichester: Wiley.

Veale, D. & Riley, S. (2001). Mirror, mirror on the wall, who is the ugliest of them all? The psychopathology of mirror gazing in body dysmorphic sisorder. *Behaviour Research and Therapy*, *39*, 1381–1393.

Webb, H. J., Zimmer-Gembeck, M. J., & Mastro, S. (2016). Stress exposure and generation: A conjoint longitudinal model of body dysmorphic symptoms, peer acceptance, popularity, and victimization. *Body Image*, *18*, 14–18.

Weingarden, H., Curley, E. E., Renshaw, K. D., & Wilhelm, S. (2017). Patient-identified events implicated in the development of body dysmorphic disorder. *Body Image*, *21*, 19–25.

Weingarden, H., Renshaw, K. D., Davidson, E., & Wilhelm, S. (2017). Relative relationships of general shame and body shame with body dysmorphic phenomenology and psychosocial outcomes. *Journal of Obsessive-Compulsive and Related Disorders*, *14*, 1–6.

Weingarden, H., Renshaw, K. D., Wilhelm, S., Tangney, J. P., & DiMauro, J. (2016). Anxiety and shame as risk factors for depression, suicidality, and functional impairment in body dysmorphic disorder and obsessive compulsive disorder. *Journal of Nervous and Mental Disease*, *204*, 832–839.

Wilhelm, S., Phillips, K. A., Didie, E., Buhlmann, U., Greenberg, J. L., Fama, J. M., Keshaviah, A., & Steketee, G. (2014) Modular cognitive-behavioral therapy for body dysmorphic disorder: A randomized controlled trial. *Behavior Therapy*, *45*, 314–327.

Wilhelm, S., Phillips, K., & Steketee G. (2013). *Cognitive-Behavioural Therapy for Body Dysmorphic Disorder: A Treatment Manual*. New York, NY: Guildford Press.

Willson, R., Veale, D., & Freeston, M. (2016). Imagery rescripting in body dysmorphic disorder: A single case experimental design. *Behavior Therapy*, *47*(2), 248–261.

Windheim, K., Veale, D., & Anson, M. (2011). Mirror gazing in body dysmorphic disorder and healthy controls: Effects of duration of gazing. *Behaviour Therapy and Research*, *49*, 555–564.

Wolke, D. & Sapouna, M. (2008). Big men feeling small: Childhood bullying experience, muscle dysmorphia and other mental health problems in bodybuilders. *Psychology of Sport and Exercise*, *9*, 595–604.

Woodward, J. (2003). *Making Things Happen: A Theory of Causal Explanation*. Oxford: Oxford University Press.

23 Hoarding Disorder

Kristen S. Springer, Blaise L. Worden,
and David F. Tolin

According to the *Diagnostic and Statistical Manual of Mental Disorders* (*DSM-5*) (American Psychiatric Association, 2013), hoarding disorder (HD) is characterized by a persistent difficulty discarding or parting with belongings (regardless of value). The difficulty discarding is typically associated with strong beliefs regarding sentimental attachment, aversion to wastefulness, and/or perceiving the objects may be needed in the future, resulting in significant emotional distress when attempting to discard, with significant indecisiveness. The functional consequence of this saving behavior is clutter in living spaces that prevents those spaces from being used as intended. Similar to most *DSM-5* diagnoses, diagnosis of HD is only made in the presence of significant functional impairment (e.g., financial, legal, social) and/or emotional distress, and only when symptoms are not better accounted for by a medical disorder (e.g., brain injury) or other psychological disorder (e.g., major depression, psychotic disorder). Associated specifiers of HD include limited insight into the severity of the problem, as well as excessive acquisition of items that may not be needed or that the individual cannot comfortably afford.

In this chapter, we review potential mechanisms of the etiology and maintenance of HD according to the National Institute of Mental Health's Research Domain Criteria (RDoC) (Cuthbert, 2014; Insel et al., 2010). The RDoC model integrates multiple dimensions and levels of analysis to determine basic building blocks of psychopathology, which may be transdiagnostic. The RDoC model is designed to be comprehensively inclusive of all forms of pathology, and certainly not all of these constructs have been examined in HD or are relevant to HD. Therefore, we present and summarize research relevant to the RDoC model as it pertains to HD (see Table 23.1), organizing these by the following larger dimensions outlined in the RDoC matrix:

Negative valence systems. Negative valence as defined by the RDoC model includes responses to aversive situations or context, such as fear, anxiety, or loss. Subdomains of the negative valence system include acute threat ("fear"), potential threat ("anxiety"), sustained threat, loss, and frustrative non-reward.

Positive valence systems. The positive valence domain refers to responses to positive motivational situations or contexts, such as reward-seeking, consumption, and reward/habit learning. Subdomains of the positive valence system include

Table 23.1 *Research Domain Criteria (RDoC)-related findings in hoarding*

System	Level of Analysis						
	Genes	Molecules	Cells	Circuits	Physiology	Behavior	Self-report
Negative Valence	• $COMT\ Val^{158}Met$ polymorphism • $BDNF\ Val^{66}Met$ polymorphism			• VMPFC activation when discarding • OFC activation when discarding • ACC and insula activation when discarding	• Heightened ERN for possession-related decisions	• Avoidance of discarding • Avoidance of emotional distress	• Fear of decision-making • Fear of losing possessions • Baseline depressed mood • Elicited sadness • Anxiety and sadness when discarding • Impulsivity (urgency and lack of perseverance)
Positive Valence	• $COMT\ Val^{158}Met$ polymorphism			• NAcc activation when acquiring		• Excessive acquiring • Lower risk aversion • Impaired reward learning • Intertemporal discounting of objects	• Emotional attachment to objects • Positive affect when acquiring

Table 23.1 (cont.)

System	Genes	Molecules	Cells	Circuits	Physiology	Behavior	Self-report
				Level of Analysis			
Cognitive Systems				• Diminished baseline ACC activation • Diminished ACC and insula activation during control tasks • Lower MFG activity during go/no-go	• Diminished ERN • Diminished SCR fluctuations during reward learning	• Diminished attention • Poor memory encoding strategies • Diminished cognitive flexibility • Impaired categorization ability • Diminished response inhibition	• Inattention • Memory impairment and poor memory confidence • Impulsivity (attentional, motoric)

approach motivation, responsiveness to reward attainment, reward learning, and habit.

Cognitive systems. The cognitive systems domain includes various information-processing and neurocognitive functions. Subdomains include attention, declarative memory, working memory, and cognitive control.

These RDoC dimensions can be examined across several units of analysis. Those units of analysis that have been examined in HD research and will be discussed within each of the dimensional headings include *genes, circuits, physiology, behavior*, and *self-report*. Last, it is important to note that some areas (e.g., impulsivity) do not always fit neatly into one construct of the RDoC matrix since there can be considerable overlap. Therefore, in this chapter, topics are discussed in the one area of the matrix where the authors believe it most appropriately applies.

The Negative Valence System in Hoarding Disorder

Evidence from several levels of analysis suggests that HD is characterized by abnormal negative affective responses, particularly in the context of making discarding decisions.

Negative valence and self-report. Based on self-report data from individuals with HD, discarding, sorting, and decision-making are frequently accompanied by significant anxiety, fear, sadness, and/or guilt. Anxious responses appear related to exaggerated fears about potential consequences of discarding. For example, on the Saving Cognitions Inventory (SCI), which measures hoarding-related attitudes and beliefs, those with HD significantly endorsed a variety of fears related to their possessions: losing their belongings if not kept in sight, fears of their belongings being moved or discarded, and fears of losing memories or important information associated with their possessions (Steketee, Frost, & Kyrios, 2003). Compared to clinical and healthy control participants, participants with HD reported greater anxiety and sadness while sorting personal possessions in the laboratory (Grisham, Norberg, Williams, Certoma, & Kadib, 2010) and while making discarding decisions about possessions (Tolin et al., 2012). Exaggerated beliefs about potential consequences of discarding likely heighten the perceived potential for a decision that may be regretted in the future, contributing to broader aversion to decision-making. Excessive acquiring behaviors may also be motivated in large part as a way to mitigate negative emotions. Individuals with HD reported feared consequences of not acquiring that were similar to those related to discarding, such as: losing out on important information, acquiring to avoid things going to waste, or acquiring to escape or alleviate negative emotions (Frost, Steketee, Tolin, Sinopoli, & Ruby, 2015).

Fear related to decision-making may go beyond decisions related to possessions: on the Fears about Decision Making subscale of the Frost Indecisiveness Scale (Frost & Gross, 1993; Frost & Shows, 1993), participants with HD report greater fear of decision-making in general than do healthy controls (Frost, Tolin, Steketee, & Oh, 2011).

In addition to anxiety, negative valence in HD is also likely to include feelings such as sadness or loss. In a sample of participants with OCD, those with significant hoarding symptoms scored significantly higher on the Beck Depression Inventory (BDI) (Beck, Ward, Mendelson, Mock, & Erbaugh, 1961) than did those without hoarding symptoms (Wheaton, Timpano, Lasalle-Ricci, & Murphy, 2008). HD commonly co-occurs with other disorders characterized by negative affectivity such as major depressive disorder (51%), generalized anxiety disorder (24%), and social anxiety disorder (24%) (Frost, Steketee, & Tolin, 2011). It remains unclear whether these elevated scores are due to comorbid depressive disorder, vs. a central feature of HD. However, one study (Timpano, Shaw, Cougle, & Fitch, 2014) examined undergraduate volunteers undergoing a negative mood induction unrelated to possessions; they found that HD symptoms were significantly correlated with the degree of elicited sadness and guilt, even after controlling for baseline levels of depression. Therefore, it may be that hoarding is related to increased emotional reactivity, at least for negative emotions such as sadness and guilt.

The impact of negative emotions in HD may be compounded by poor tolerance of those emotions. Several studies using unselected undergraduates have found a relationship between scores on hoarding symptom questionnaires and measures of distress tolerance (e.g., Norberg, Keyan, & Grisham, 2015; Phung, Moulding, Taylor, & Nedeljkovic, 2015; Timpano et al., 2014). Among undergraduate volunteers, hoarding symptoms correlate significantly with self-reported urgency (e.g., "I have trouble controlling my impulses") as well as lack of perseverance (e.g., "I tend to give up easily") (Timpano et al., 2013; Timpano et al., 2014). Individuals with HD exhibit higher levels of self-reported urgency than do those with mixed anxiety disorders, though group differences were strongly confounded with age (Rasmussen, Brown, Steketee, & Barlow, 2013).

Negative valence and behavior. One of the defining behavioral features of HD is avoidance of discarding possessions due to perceived need to save them, resulting in emotional distress when considering discarding (American Psychiatric Association, 2013). This emotional distress criterion has been confirmed in laboratory research, in which the degree of self-reported anxiety and sadness was significantly negatively correlated with the number of possessions discarded (Tolin et al., 2012). Furthermore, HD may be characterized by a globally avoidant coping style: on the Brief COPE (Carver, 1997), a self-report measure of emotional and behavioral coping strategies, behavioral disengagement (i.e., use of overt avoidance as a coping strategy) significantly correlated with HD severity as well as with anxiety and depression in individuals with HD (Ayers, Castriotta, Dozier, Espejo, & Porter, 2014).

Negative valence and genes. The fear of decision-making found in participants with HD may represent a heritable endophenotypic marker; clinically unaffected relatives of individuals with HD tend to report greater fear of decision-making than do individuals without a family history of HD (Frost, Tolin, et al., 2011; Samuels et al., 2007). Two heritable polymorphisms, in particular, may be associated with negative valence systems that contribute to vulnerability to develop HD. The first is the $Val^{158}Met$ polymorphism of the *catechol-O-methyltransferase* (*COMT*) gene, of which the *met/met* genotype was significantly more common among OCD patients with hoarding symptoms (39%) than among OCD patients without hoarding symptoms (21%) and healthy control participants (16%) (Lochner et al., 2005). *COMT* degrades dopamine and other catecholamines in the prefrontal cortex (PFC). The $Val^{158}Met$ polymorphism reduces the activity of *COMT*, resulting in higher extracellular dopamine in the PFC (J. Chen et al., 2004). Individuals with this polymorphism tend to show higher levels of neuroticism and anxiety (Montag, Jurkiewicz, & Reuter, 2012), as well as greater sensory and affective responses to pain (Zubieta et al., 2003), than do those without the polymorphism. Individuals with this polymorphism have also been shown to exhibit greater PFC activation while viewing sad faces (Lelli-Chiesa et al., 2011) as well as increased early posterior negativity (EPN) while viewing negative pictures, compared to individuals without the polymorphism (Herrmann et al., 2009), suggesting that the polymorphism may confer vulnerability to exaggerated negative affective reactions.

Another genetic factor of interest in HD is the $Val^{66}Met$ polymorphism of the *brain-derived neurotropic factor* (*BDNF*) gene, of which the *val/val* genotype was elevated in hoarding-related OCD patients with (83%) and without (72%) obesity, compared to obese (70%) and normal weight non-OCD controls (60%) (Timpano, Schmidt, Wheaton, Wendland, & Murphy, 2011). The *BDNF* gene controls the production of BDNF, which promotes neuroplasticity; the *val/val* genotype reduces the amount of available BDNF (Lang, Hellweg, Sander, & Gallinat, 2009). Individuals with the *val/val* genotype exhibit greater self-reported, endocrine, and cardiovascular reactivity to stressors (Alexander et al., 2010), as well as higher levels of trait anxiety (Lang et al., 2005) and neuroticism (Sen et al., 2003). There may be a gene–environment interaction, in which individuals with the *val/val* genotype of the $Val^{66}Met$ polymorphism are particularly sensitive to early negative life events, developing emotion-focused coping strategies and diminished perceived control, creating a vulnerability to affective disturbance (Caldwell et al., 2013).

Negative valence and circuits. Negative valence systems are also reflected in research using functional magnetic resonance imaging (fMRI) in HD. Specifically, hoarding is associated with greater activity in neural regions that are associated with processing of negative emotional material, and efforts to regulate negative emotions under conditions of symptom provocation. In OCD patients with significant hoarding symptoms, imaginal discarding elicited significantly greater activation in the bilateral anterior ventromedial prefrontal cortex (VMPFC) compared to OCD patients without hoarding symptoms and healthy control participants (An et al., 2009); in a similar study, the degree of self-reported hoarding-related distress among patients with OCD correlated significantly with the degree of activation in the left precentral gyrus and right orbitofrontal cortex (OFC) (Mataix-

Cols et al., 2004). Thus, at least in individuals with OCD, hoarding symptoms are associated with hyperactivity in brain regions that are associated with the processing of negative emotion during imagined discarding.

Two studies of patients with primary HD examined neural response to actual decisions about whether to keep or discard possessions. In the first study (Tolin, Kiehl, Worhunsky, Book, & Maltby, 2009), compared to healthy controls, HD patients exhibited excessive hemodynamic activity in the lateral OFC and parahippocampal gyrus, regions that are associated with the experience of punishment (Kringelbach, 2005), heightened emotional engagement in affective decision-making (Northoff et al., 2006), and the processing of unpleasant emotions (Lane et al., 1997). Among HD participants, decisions to keep possessions (vs. items that did not belong to the participant) were associated with greater activity in a number of emotion-processing regions including the superior and middle temporal gyrus, medial frontal gyrus (MFG), and anterior cingulate cortex (ACC) than were decisions to discard personal possessions. In a second study, Tolin et al. (2012) attempted to separate the decision-making process from the act of discarding in order to examine neural processes during both. They found that compared to OCD patients and healthy controls, when making decisions about personal possessions (vs. control items), HD patients exhibited greater activity in ACC and anterior insula. This pattern is broadly consistent with activation of the salience network, an interaction of brain regions that is implicated in acute anxious reactions (Paulus & Stein, 2006). The degree of activation in these regions correlated significantly not only with HD severity, but also with self-ratings of indecisiveness and "not just right" feelings among participants with HD (Tolin et al., 2012). The central finding, therefore, is that individuals with HD show reacting with heightened salience activity during discarding decisions that corresponds to self-reported negative emotion.

The Positive Valence System in Hoarding Disorder

Although not as well studied as negative valence, positive valence certainly plays a significant role in HD. Positive valence, as it relates to HD, is more likely reflected in excessive acquisition, comfort-in-objects, and other appetitive behaviors. The remarkably high level of compulsive buying (61%), as well as elevated rates of impulse control disorders such as kleptomania (10%), pathological gambling (6%), and trichotillomania (5%) in HD patients, compared to individuals with non-hoarding OCD (Frost, Steketee et al., 2011), suggest an overlap in approach-, reward-, and habit-related systems.

Positive valence and self-report. In HD, saving is often motivated by strong feelings of attachment to objects. In one study (Frost, Hartl, Christian, & Williams, 1995), scores on a measure of hoarding severity significantly correlated with endorsement of items such as "When I get upset, I turn to my possessions for comfort" and "My life would not feel complete if I were not surrounded by my possessions." Similarly, patients with HD gave stronger endorsements to statements suggestive of emotional attachment (e.g., "I love some of my belongings the way I love some people"; "This possession provides me with emotional comfort") than did patients with OCD or healthy control participants (Steketee et al., 2003).

The acquiring behavior common in HD may also be associated with positive valence systems. Compulsive buying is not a distinct *DSM-5* diagnosis; however, compulsive acquiring behavior is present in nearly two-thirds of individuals with HD and it is reasonable to expect some shared positive valence mechanisms. Individuals with compulsive buying report immediate euphoria and excitement upon acquiring, though negative valence processes such as guilt may follow later (Miltenberger et al., 2003). Compulsive buyers are also more likely to endorse statements such as "Buying things makes me happy" and "Shopping is fun" than are individuals without compulsive buying tendencies (Koran, Faber, Aboujaoude, Large, & Serpe, 2006). Similarly, when asked to identify their reasons for acquiring, individuals with HD endorse positive emotions as motivators (acquiring things because they are emotionally significant) and aesthetic reasons (acquiring things because they are beautiful or aesthetically pleasing) more than do patients with OCD and healthy control participants (Frost et al., 2015).

Positive valence and behavior. Excessive acquisition behaviors are likely to be more often present than not in HD (Frost, Tolin, Steketee, Fitch, & Selbo-Bruns, 2009). As mentioned earlier, these appetitive acquisition behaviors are likely motivated, at least in part, by positive emotions.

Positive valence in HD may be also characterized by some maladaptive approach behaviors consistent with facets of impulsivity. Gambling-style tasks, derived from behavioral economics, show that individuals with HD exhibit less risk aversion than do healthy controls (Aranovich, Cavagnaro, Pitt, Myung, & Mathews, 2017). Furthermore, individuals with higher hoarding symptoms exhibit intertemporal discounting for material goods, tending to choose immediate small rewards rather than a larger reward after a time delay. However, these effects appear less evident with monetary rewards, suggesting that this aspect of impulsivity may be limited to possessions rather than a general trait of impulsivity (Vickers, Preston, Gonzalez, & Angott, 2016).

Positive valence and circuits. To date, there has been little examination of positive valence neurocircuitry in HD. However, one fMRI study, in which healthy participants made decisions about whether to acquire hypothetical items, showed that the degree of clutter, beliefs about why items should be kept, and emotional attachment to objects correlated significantly with activation in the bilateral nucleus accumbens (NAcc) (Wang, Seidler, Hall, & Preston, 2012). The NAcc is implicated in reward motivation, including normative purchasing behavior (Knutson, Rick, Wimmer, Prelec, & Loewenstein, 2007), suggesting an enhanced desirability of objects.

The Cognitive System in Hoarding Disorder

HD appears to be characterized by impairments in cognitive systems. There appear to be particular deficits in some areas of executive functioning, such as attention, organization, and problem-solving. Consistent with this are high rates of co-occurring attention-deficit/hyperactivity disorder (ADHD), which tends to have substantial overlap with these executive functioning issues. In one large study (Sheppard et al., 2010), 28% of HD patients, compared to 3% of OCD patients, met *DSM-IV-TR* diagnostic criteria for the inattentive subtype of ADHD (Frost, Steketee et al., 2011). Among OCD patients, those with hoarding symptoms had a risk of ADHD almost 10 times higher than those without hoarding symptoms.

In addition, hoarding behaviors have been noted in cognitively impaired individuals such as those with frontotemporal dementia (Hwang, Tsai, Yang, Liu, & Lirng, 1998; Nakaaki et al., 2007) and associated with acute insult to frontal regions of the brain (Anderson, Damasio, & Damasio, 2005; Eslinger & Damasio, 1985; Volle, Beato, Levy, & Dubois, 2002). These studies of neurological insult or injury suggest that the frontal lobe, which is often characterized as the seat of executive functions (Diamond, 2013; Takeuchi et al., 2013) is likely key to the development of HD pathology.

The cognitive system and self-report. Individuals with HD often endorse significant problems of attention. In one study, 75% of participants with HD scored at least one standard deviation above the normative mean for age- and gender-matched community controls on an self-report inattention scale (Frost, Steketee et al., 2011). In a group of HD patients, OCD patients, and healthy controls, ADHD inattentive symptoms, but not OCD symptoms, predicted the severity of hoarding symptoms when controlling for age and general distress (Tolin & Villavicencio, 2011). Memory concerns are also frequently reported by individuals with HD. Compared to healthy controls, HD participants report lower confidence in their memory, contributing to a desire to keep their belongings in sight (Hartl et al., 2004) and to save possessions in order to preserve memories or information that they feel may be referenced in the future (Steketee et al., 2003). Curiously, however, the self-reported memory deficits in HD may not comport with actual performance on neuropsychological tests, suggesting that individuals with HD may underestimate their actual cognitive function (Moshier et al., 2016).

Impulsivity, described previously in the Negative Valence and Positive Valence sections, also overlaps with the construct of cognitive control. Undergraduate volunteers with high hoarding symptoms report greater attentional (e.g., "I don't pay attention") and motor (e.g., "I act on the spur of the moment") impulsivity (Timpano et al., 2013). Related, students with higher hoarding symptoms endorse lower levels of behavioral self-control than do those with lower hoarding symptoms, even after controlling for depression and anxiety (Timpano & Schmidt, 2013).

The cognitive system and behavior. Although results on neuropsychological measures have been mixed (Grisham, Brown, Savage, Steketee, & Barlow, 2007; Park et al., 2016), there is reasonable support for an association between HD and deficits in some cognitive systems. Specifically, although different tests have yielded different results, research suggests problems in sustained attention, memory, cognitive flexibility, categorization, and cognitive control (Grisham & Baldwin, 2015; Woody, Kellman-McFarlane, & Welsted, 2014). On the Continuous Performance Test (CPT), a measure of sustained attention, individuals with HD have slower response times than do both nonclinical controls (Tolin, Villavicencio, Umbach, & Kurtz, 2011) and clinical controls (Grisham et al., 2007), even when controlling for co-occurring depression; the severity of these attentional impairments correlates with hoarding symptom severity (Raines, Timpano, & Schmidt, 2014).

Working memory appears broadly intact in individuals with HD (e.g., Grisham et al., 2010; Mackin, Arean, Delucchi, & Mathews, 2011; Mackin et al., 2016; McMillan, Rees, & Pestell, 2013). However, two studies (Ayers et al., 2013; Dozier, Wetherell, Twamley, Schiehser, & Ayers, 2016) showed that older individuals with HD had significant impairment on the Wechsler Adult Intelligence Scale (WAIS) (Wechsler, 2008) digit span and letter-number sequencing, which reflect working memory and attention. In one, older individuals with HD performed more poorly than did healthy age-matched controls (Ayers et al., 2013), although task performance did not correlate with hoarding severity. In the other, age was predictive of impaired task performance (Dozier et al., 2016). Delayed recall has largely been found to be intact in HD (e.g., Dinn, Sisman, & Aycicegi-Dinn, 2013; Moshier et al., 2016; Sumner, Noack, Filoteo, Maddox, & Saxena, 2016), although in one study (Mackin et al., 2016), individuals with HD performed markedly worse than did nonclinical controls on a measure of visuospatial delayed recall (Brief Visuospatial Memory Task) (Benedict, 1997). Some preliminary evidence suggests that these apparent memory impairments of HD patients on this visuospatial task may be due to inefficient organization and encoding of the stimuli rather than retrieval (Hartl et al., 2004; Sumner et al., 2016).

HD may be characterized by diminished cognitive flexibility. Among older adults with HD, 18% showed at least mild perseverative errors on the Wisconsin Card Sort Task (WCST) (Heaton, Chelune, Talley, Kay, & Curtiss, 1993), and 12% were classified as having mild or worse impairment on the category-switching task of the Delis-Kaplan Executive Functioning Scale (D-KEFS) (Delis, Kaplan, & Kramer, 2001). WCST perseverative errors were predictive of hoarding severity (Ayers, Dozier, Wetherell, Twamley, & Schiehser, 2016). This diminished cognitive flexibility is further supported by eye-tracking research showing that nonclinical individuals with high hoarding symptoms had more difficulty disengaging from distracting photographic stimuli than did those with low reported hoarding symptoms (Carbonella & Timpano, 2016).

Difficulties with categorization are also likely to be present in HD. Two studies (Grisham et al., 2010; Wincze, Steketee, & Frost, 2007) have demonstrated that when categorizing possessions, individuals with HD take longer to categorize and create more categories than do nonclinical controls (i.e., their categories are under-inclusive). Similarly, on a neuropsychological task of categorization unrelated to personal possessions (the D-KEFS sorting test), individuals with HD performed significantly worse than did nonclinical controls (Mackin et al., 2016) and a small sample of age-matched controls with depression (Mackin et al., 2011). Among older individuals with HD, these differences were quite pronounced, with 67% showing impaired categorization ability, vs. 13% of the depressed-only sample (Mackin et al., 2011).

Finally, some studies have examined impulsivity, as conceptualized as inhibition of a pre-potent response. In one study, individuals with HD made more errors of commission than did healthy controls and mixed clinical controls on the Continuous Performance Test, a finding consistent with impaired behavioral inhibition (Grisham et al., 2007). In another study, individuals with HD (along with a separate sample of individuals with both OCD and HD) made more commission errors than did nonclinical controls on the Stop Signal Task (Morein-Zamir et al., 2014). However, others have failed to replicate this finding (e.g., Blom et al., 2011; Hough et al., 2016; Rasmussen et al., 2013; Tolin, Witt, & Stevens, 2014).

The cognitive system and physiology. Electroencephalography (EEG) research has focused on error-related negativity (ERN), a response that occurs 80–150 msec after errors are committed during various tasks, even when the person is not explicitly aware of making the error (Nieuwenhuis, Ridderinkhof, Blom, Band, & Kok, 2001). A small number of studies have examined ERN, a measure of cortical electrical activity, in which higher amplitudes are associated with successful detection of error commission. Individuals with HD had significantly lower ERN amplitudes during a test of response inhibition (flanker task) than did healthy control participants and those with OCD (Mathews et al., 2016). Similarly, among participants with OCD, high lifetime scores on the symmetry/hoarding dimension of the Yale-Brown Obsessive-Compulsive Scale (Y-BOCS) (Goodman et al., 1989) symptom checklist were associated at a trend level with reduced ERN during a flanker task (Riesel, Kathmann, & Endrass, 2014). A study of undergraduate students failed to replicate the relationship between decreased ERN and hoarding symptoms, and found, conversely, that hoarding symptoms were predictive of *greater* ERN in response to possession-related decisions (Baldwin, Whitford, & Grisham, 2016). Hoarding, therefore, may be associated with a general tendency toward diminished error monitoring, though during possession decisions, error monitoring may become hypersensitive.

This tendency toward diminished error reactivity (outside possession-related stimuli) is echoed in peripheral physiology. In one study (Lawrence et al., 2006) that used a gambling task, OCD patients with hoarding symptoms also exhibited less fluctuation in skin conductance response (SCR) across the trial types (i.e., win vs. loss) than did OCD participants without hoarding symptoms, suggesting diminished capacity to integrate reward and non-reward into decision-making.

Indeed, the degree of skin conductance fluctuation was significantly associated with overall performance, and the under-responsive pattern observed in OCD patients with HD was not unlike that seen among individuals with pathological gambling (Goudriaan, Oosterlaan, de Beurs, & van den Brink, 2006) and substance use disorders (Sawyer, Poey, Ruiz, Marinkovic, & Oscar-Berman, 2015).

The cognitive system and circuits. In a resting-state PET study, OCD patients with hoarding symptoms showed significantly less glucose metabolism in the ACC than did those without hoarding symptoms (Saxena et al., 2004). This finding was echoed in an fMRI study (Tolin et al., 2012), in which individuals with HD or OCD and healthy control participants made decisions about whether to discard their own possessions or control items that did not belong to them. During control-item decisions, participants with HD were characterized by relative hypoactivity in both ACC and insula, suggesting under-engagement of the salience network. Attenuated salience activation suggests that individuals with HD often fail to engage brain regions necessary for attending to routine information and assigning relative importance.

Further circuit-level evidence of diminished cognitive control is shown in an fMRI study of individuals with HD or OCD completing a go/no-go task. During correct rejection trials (indicating successful response inhibition), participants with HD showed lower activity in the middle frontal gyrus (Tolin et al., 2014), a region associated with executive function (see Alvarez & Emory, 2006, for review) and information-gathering during go/no-go (Talati & Hirsch, 2005). Here again, the overall impression is one of under-engagement of cognitive control systems.

Conclusions

HD was recognized as a distinct *DSM-5* diagnosis only four years ago. Research on the mechanisms of HD is still in its early stages as systematic research on hoarding has only been conducted on a substantial scale within the past decade (Pertusa et al., 2010; Steketee & Frost, 2003). The RDoC matrix provides a useful way to categorize what is known thus far and where the major gaps in our in our knowledge lie. To date, research on hoarding and HD has largely focused on three domains: Negative Valence, Positive Valence, and Cognitive Systems. Taken together, these studies suggest a biphasic process in HD, in which distinct mechanisms are active at rest and under provocation conditions.

Admittedly, much of the extant research does not map neatly on to the RDoC constructs, as many laboratory tasks and measures tap multiple domains (e.g., Negative Valence and Cognitive Systems simultaneously). Future research should further isolate specific mechanisms of the disorder. Nevertheless, the available literature, superimposed on the RDoC matrix to the extent possible, can help clarify several important elements of HD, namely, difficulty discarding, excessive acquiring, and disorganization.

Saving behavior, the first diagnostic criterion of HD, appears to be associated with negative affective experience, avoidant coping, and cognitive and neural abnormalities related to decision-making about possessions. At the circuit level of analysis, when individuals with HD must make a decision about whether to keep or discard a possession, the salience network becomes hyperactive (Tolin et al., 2012). This may either lead to, or be a result of, excessive attachment to objects, including hypersentimentality, fears of losing or forgetting possessions, and fears of losing memories of people or events. Furthermore, frontal regions, including the OFC (Tolin et al., 2009) and VMPFC (An et al., 2009) are similarly over-engaged, suggesting impaired decision-making and difficulty with emotion regulation. Physiologically, during decisions about possessions, ERN is amplified (Baldwin et al., 2016), suggesting a heightened vigilance for, or perception of, errors in decision-making or a feeling that one's decisions are "not just right" (Tolin et al., 2012). At the self-report level of analysis, these phenomena are experienced in the form of acute feelings of anxiety (Frost, Tolin et al., 2011; Grisham et al., 2010) or sadness (Tolin et al., 2012) when sorting, affective reactions to which those with hoarding symptoms are already likely to be particularly prone as evidenced by mood induction research (Timpano et al., 2014). Behaviorally, categorizing possessions becomes difficult, with impaired ability to group like items together (Grisham et al., 2010; Wincze et al., 2007). It is perhaps not surprising that sorting, decision-making, and discarding are perceived as aversive and are therefore typically avoided. As is the case in many forms of psychopathology marked by behavioral avoidance as a coping strategy, we would predict that this behavior likely only serves to maintain or exacerbate discomfort in the long run.

Genetic factors, including the *COMT Val^{158}Met* and *BDNF Val^{66}Met* polymorphisms, may predispose individuals to these negative affective and behavioral reactions (Lochner et al., 2005; Timpano et al., 2011). These genetic factors may interact with stressful or traumatic events throughout the life span; hoarding is associated with a greater frequency of lifetime traumatic and highly distressing events than is OCD (Cromer, Schmidt, & Murphy, 2007), particularly physical and sexual aggression and having belongings taken by force (Hartl, Duffany, Allen, Steketee, & Frost, 2005; Landau et al., 2011; Samuels et al., 2008). Furthermore, hoarding severity is positively associated with the number of traumatic events that occurred prior to the onset of HD (Przeworski, Cain, & Dunbeck, 2014).

Acquiring, though not a diagnostic criterion for HD, is a strongly associated feature. At the circuit level, items that could potentially be acquired appear to activate the NAcc (Wang et al., 2012), which may heighten the perceived desirability of the items. Impulsivity, as evidenced by self-reported urgency (Timpano et al., 2013), intertemporal discounting (Vickers et al., 2016), and potentially diminished response inhibition (Grisham et al., 2007; Morein-Zamir et al., 2014), suggests difficulty recruiting cognitive control processes necessary for delaying immediate gratification by acquiring possessions. Acquiring behaviors may result in a quick but temporary sense of positive affect (Miltenberger et al., 2003) and are thereby reinforced, yet we would predict that the accumulation of clutter further exacerbates longer-term negative affect and avoidant coping strategies.

The clutter found in the homes of individuals with HD results not only from acquiring and saving behaviors, but also from an inability to employ effective organizational strategies. At the self-report level of analysis, individuals with HD report high levels of inattention (Frost, Steketee et al., 2011), associated with lack of task perseverance (Timpano et al., 2013). They further exhibit high rates of co-occurring depression (Frost, Steketee et al., 2011), which further complicates effective functioning. Those with depression and inattention report more severe hoarding symptoms and associated impairment (Hall, Tolin, Frost, & Steketee, 2013). At the circuit level of analysis, individuals with HD show baseline hypoactivity in salience network regions including the ACC (Saxena et al., 2004; Tolin et al., 2012) and insula (Tolin et al., 2012). During more complex (but still hoarding-unrelated) tasks, they may also under-engage the executive control of the MFG (Tolin et al., 2014). This under-engagement of salience and top-down processing regions is echoed in the physiology-level findings of diminished ERN during error-prone tasks (Mathews et al., 2016; Riesel et al., 2014) and reduced SCR fluctuations during reward-based learning (Lawrence et al., 2006). The under-engagement might further explain the problems of insight and motivation often seen in HD (see Worden, DiLoreto, & Tolin, 2014, for review). We suggest that many individuals with HD may sometimes fail to recognize the severity of their behavior, to be acutely distressed by the presence of clutter and squalor, or to perceive a need for behavioral change because of the under-engagement of cognitive control systems, which contributes not only to hoarding symptoms but to depression and inattention as well.

As evidenced by Table 23.1, much within the RDoC Negative Valence, Positive Valence, and Cognitive Systems domains remains to be examined in HD. The molecular level of analysis has not been used; molecules such as cortisol, which is one of the most widely used biomarkers of hypothalamic-pituitary-adrenal (HPA) axis activity and is elevated in disorders characterized by negative valence, might be a useful target. Cellular analysis has not been addressed; dopaminergic cells might be used to evaluate reward learning abnormalities (Positive Valence), whereas GABAergic and other cells might be examined in the context of Negative Valence. The physiology (both peripheral and central) of positive affect, particularly under acquisition provocation, has not been studied in HD. The peripheral physiology of Negative Valence in HD (e.g., eye-blink startle, skin conductance, heart rate) would help distinguish among the subdomain(s) (e.g., acute threat, potential threat, sustained threat, loss, and frustrative non-reward).

Other RDoC domains worth considering in HD include Social Processes, which include Affiliation and Attachment, Social Communication, Perception and Understanding of Self, and Perception and Understanding of Others. Individuals with HD report comparatively extreme emotional attachment to objects (Grisham et al., 2009; Nedelisky & Steele, 2009), often anthropomorphizing these possessions, report more conflictual relationships with caregivers during development (D. Chen et al., 2017), and are often relatively socially isolated (Medard & Kellett, 2014). Furthermore, among student volunteers, a weak but significant relationship was found between HD symptoms and autistic traits (Xu, Fu, Wang, & Zhang, 2015), making this an intriguing candidate for further study of constructs such as perception of others' emotional states. Additionally, Arousal and Regulatory Systems, which include Arousal, Circadian Rhythms, and Sleep-Wakefulness, is understudied in HD. In one study of individuals with HD, self-reported sleep difficulties were associated with greater acquiring and difficulty discarding (Raines, Portero, Unruh, Short, & Schmidt, 2015), though the causality is not clear.

Finally, as research accumulates evidence of potential mechanisms of HD, it will be important to understand which of these mechanisms are complications of HD (e.g., resulting from illness chronicity or subsequent psychosocial stressors) versus those that represent endophenotypes or heritable traits that correlate with vulnerability to develop the condition (Gottesman & Gould, 2003). It has been established that HD is highly heritable, with genetic factors accounting for 36–54% of illness risk (Iervolino et al., 2009; Iervolino, Rijsdijk, Cherkas, Fullana, & Mataix-Cols, 2011; Mathews, Delucchi, Cath, Willemsen, & Boomsma, 2014). Identification of endophenotypic markers would likely result in a narrower range of target mechanisms (Glahn et al., 2014) and new innovations in preventative and ameliorative treatments (Hasler, Drevets, Gould, Gottesman, & Manji, 2006) as has been the case in other complex disorders such as schizophrenia (Braff, Freedman, Schork, & Gottesman, 2007; Calkins et al., 2007; Gur et al., 2007), bipolar disorder (Ahearn et al., 2002; Lenox, Gould, & Manji, 2002), and Alzheimer's disease (Kurz, Riemenschneider, Drzezga, & Lautenschlager, 2002; Neugroschl & Davis, 2002).

References

Ahearn, E. P., Speer, M. C., Chen, Y. T., Steffens, D. C., Cassidy, F., Van Meter, S., . . . Krishnan, K. R. (2002). Investigation of *Notch3* as a candidate gene for bipolar disorder using brain hyperintensities as an endophenotype. *American Journal of Medical Genetics*, *114*(6), 652–658. doi: 10.1002/ajmg.10512

Alexander, N., Osinsky, R., Schmitz, A., Mueller, E., Kuepper, Y., & Hennig, J. (2010). The *BDNF Val66Met* polymorphism affects HPA-axis reactivity to acute stress. *Psychoneuroendocrinology*, *35*(6), 949–953. doi: 10.1016/j.psyneuen.2009.12.008

Alvarez, J. A. & Emory, E. (2006). Executive function and the frontal lobes: A meta-analytic review. *Neuropsychology Review*, *16*(1), 17–42. doi: 10.1007/s11065-006–9002-x

American Psychiatric Association. (2013). *Diagnostic and Statistical Manual of Mental Disorders* (5th edn). Washington, DC: American Psychiatric Association.

An, S. K., Mataix-Cols, D., Lawrence, N. S., Wooderson, S., Giampietro, V., Speckens, A., . . . Phillips, M. L. (2009). To discard or not to discard: The neural basis of hoarding symptoms in obsessive-compulsive disorder. *Molecular Psychiatry*, *14*(3), 318–331. doi: 4002129 [pii] 10.1038/sj.mp.4002129

Anderson, S. W., Damasio, H., & Damasio, A. R. (2005). A neural basis for collecting behaviour in humans. *Brain*, *128*(Pt. 1), 201–212.

Aranovich, G. J., Cavagnaro, D. R., Pitt, M. A., Myung, J. I., & Mathews, C. A. (2017). A model-based analysis of decision making under risk in obsessive-compulsive and hoarding disorders. *Journal of Psychiatric Research*, *90*, 126–132.

Ayers, C. R., Castriotta, N., Dozier, M. E., Espejo, E. P., & Porter, B. (2014). Behavioral and experiential avoidance in patients with hoarding disorder. *Journal of Behavior Therapy and Experimental Psychiatry*, *45*(3), 408–414. doi: 10.1016/j.jbtep.2014.04.005

Ayers, C. R., Dozier, M. E., Wetherell, J. L., Twamley, E. W., & Schiehser, D. M. (2016). Executive functioning in participants over age of 50 with hoarding disorder. *American Journal of Geriatric Psychiatry*, *24*(5), 342–349. doi: 10.1016/j.jagp.2015.10.009

Ayers, C. R., Wetherell, J. L., Schiehser, D., Almklov, E., Golshan, S., & Saxena, S. (2013). Executive functioning in older adults with hoarding disorder. *International Journal of Geriatric Psychiatry*, *28*(11), 1175–1181. doi: 10.1002/gps.3940

Baldwin, P. A., Whitford, T. J., & Grisham, J. R. (2016). The relationship between hoarding symptoms, intolerance of uncertainty, and error-related negativity. *Journal of Psychopathology and Behavioral Assessment*, 1–9.

Beck, A. T., Ward, C. H., Mendelson, M., Mock, J., & Erbaugh, J. (1961). An inventory for measuring depression. *Archives of General Psychiatry*, *4*, 53–63.

Benedict, R. H. (1997). *Brief Visuospatial Memory Test-Revised*. Germany: Psychological Assessment Resources, Inc.

Blom, R. M., Samuels, J. F., Grados, M. A., Chen, Y., Bienvenu, O. J., Riddle, M. A., . . . Nestadt, G. (2011). Cognitive functioning in compulsive hoarding. *Journal of Anxiety Disorders*, *25*(8), 1139–1144. doi: 10.1016/j.janxdis.2011.08.005

Braff, D. L., Freedman, R., Schork, N. J., & Gottesman, I. I. (2007). Deconstructing schizophrenia: An overview of the use of endophenotypes in order to understand a complex disorder. *Schizophrenia Bulletin*, *33*(1), 21–32. doi: 10.1093/schbul/sbl049

Caldwell, W., McInnis, O. A., McQuaid, R. J., Liu, G., Stead, J. D., Anisman, H., & Hayley, S. (2013). The role of the *Val66Met* polymorphism of the brain derived neurotrophic factor gene in coping strategies relevant to depressive symptoms. *PLoS One*, *8*(6), e65547. doi: 10.1371/journal.pone.0065547

Calkins, M. E., Dobie, D. J., Cadenhead, K. S., Olincy, A., Freedman, R., Green, M. F., . . . Braff, D. L. (2007). The Consortium on the Genetics of Endophenotypes in Schizophrenia: Model recruitment, assessment, and endophenotyping methods for a multisite collaboration. *Schizophrenia Bulletin*, *33*(1), 33–48. doi: 10.1093/schbul/sbl044

Carbonella, J. Y. & Timpano, K. R. (2016). Examining the link between hoarding symptoms and cognitive flexibility deficits. *Behavior Therapy*, *47*(2), 262–273. doi: 10.1016/j.beth.2015.11.003

Carver, C. S. (1997). You want to measure coping but your protocol's too long: Consider the brief COPE. *International Journal of Behavioral Medicine*, *4*(1), 92–100. doi: 10.1207/s15327558ijbm0401_6

Chen, D., Bienvenu, O. J., Krasnow, J., Wang, Y., Grados, M. A., Cullen, B., . . . Samuels, J. (2017). Parental bonding and hoarding in obsessive-compulsive disorder. *Comprehensive Psychiatry*, *73*, 43–52. doi: 10.1016/j.comppsych.2016.11.004

Chen, J., Lipska, B. K., Halim, N., Ma, Q. D., Matsumoto, M., Melhem, S., . . . Weinberger, D. R. (2004). Functional analysis of genetic variation in catechol-O-methyltransferase (COMT): Effects on mRNA, protein, and enzyme activity in postmortem human brain. *American Journal of Human Genetics, 75*(5), 807–821. doi: 10.1086/425589

Cromer, K. R., Schmidt, N. B., & Murphy, D. L. (2007). Do traumatic events influence the clinical expression of compulsive hoarding? *Behaviour Research and Therapy, 45*(11), 2581–2592.

Cuthbert, B. N. (2014). The RDoC framework: Facilitating transition from ICD/DSM to dimensional approaches that integrate neuroscience and psychopathology. *World Psychiatry, 13*(1), 28–35. doi: 10.1002/wps.20087

Delis, D. C., Kaplan, E., & Kramer, J. H. (2001). *Delis-Kaplan Executive Function System (D-KEFS)*. San Antonio, TX: Harcourt Assessment.

Diamond, A. (2013). Executive functions. *Annual Review of Psychology, 64*, 135–168. doi: 10.1146/annurev-psych-113011-143750

Dinn, W. M., Sisman, S., & Aycicegi-Dinn, A. (2013). Neurocognitive and clinical correlates of compulsive hoarding. *Procedia: Social and Behavioral Sciences, 82*, 355–359.

Dozier, M. E., Wetherell, J. L., Twamley, E. W., Schiehser, D. M., & Ayers, C. R. (2016). The relationship between age and neurocognitive and daily functioning in adults with hoarding disorder. *International Journal of Geriatric Psychiatry, 31*(12), 1329–1336. doi: 10.1002/gps.4438

Eslinger, P. J. & Damasio, A. R. (1985). Severe disturbance of higher cognition after bilateral frontal lobe ablation: Patient EVR. *Neurology, 35*, 1731–1741.

Frost, R. O. & Gross, R. (1993). The hoarding of possessions. *Behaviour Research and Therapy, 31*, 367–382. doi: 10.1016/0005-7967(93)90094-B

Frost, R. O., Hartl, T., Christian, R., & Williams, N. (1995). The value of possessions in compulsive hoarding: Patterns of use and attachment. *Behaviour Research and Therapy, 33*, 897–902.

Frost, R. O. & Shows, D. L. (1993). The nature and measurement of compulsive indecisiveness. *Behaviour Research and Therapy, 31*(7), 683–692.

Frost, R. O., Steketee, G., & Tolin, D. F. (2011). Comorbidity in hoarding disorder. *Depression and Anxiety, 28*(10), 876–884. doi: 10.1002/da.20861

Frost, R. O., Steketee, G., Tolin, D. F., Sinopoli, N., & Ruby, D. (2015). Motives for acquiring and saving in hoarding disorder, OCD, and community controls. *Journal of Obsessive-Compulsive and Related Disorders, 4*, 54–59.

Frost, R. O., Tolin, D. F., & Maltby, N. (2010). Insight-related challenges in the treatment of hoarding. *Cognitive and Behavioral Practice, 17*, 404–413.

Frost, R. O., Tolin, D. F., Steketee, G., Fitch, K. E., & Selbo-Bruns, A. (2009). Excessive acquisition in hoarding. *Journal of Anxiety Disorders, 23*(5), 632–639.

Frost, R. O., Tolin, D. F., Steketee, G., & Oh, M. (2011). Indecisiveness and hoarding. *International Journal of Cognitive Therapy, 4*, 253–262.

Glahn, D. C., Knowles, E. E., McKay, D. R., Sprooten, E., Raventos, H., Blangero, J., . . . Almasy, L. (2014). Arguments for the sake of endophenotypes: Examining common misconceptions about the use of endophenotypes in psychiatric genetics. *American Journal of Medical Genetics B Neuropsychiatric Genetics, 165B*(2), 122–130. doi: 10.1002/ajmg.b.32221

Goodman, W. K., Price, L. H., Rasmussen, S. A., Mazure, C., Fleischmann, R. L., Hill, C. L., ... Charney, D. S. (1989). The Yale-Brown Obsessive Compulsive Scale. I. Development, use, and reliability. *Archives of General Psychiatry, 46*(11), 1006–1011. doi: 10.1001/archpsyc.1989.01810110048007

Gottesman, I. I. & Gould, T. D. (2003). The endophenotype concept in psychiatry: Etymology and strategic intentions. *American Journal of Psychiatry, 160*(4), 636–645. doi: 10.1176/appi.ajp.160.4.636

Goudriaan, A. E., Oosterlaan, J., de Beurs, E., & van den Brink, W. (2006). Psychophysiological determinants and concomitants of deficient decision making in pathological gamblers. *Drug and Alcohol Dependence, 84*(3), 231–239. doi: 10.1016/j.drugalcdep.2006.02.007

Grisham, J. R. & Baldwin, P. A. (2015). Neuropsychological and neurophysiological insights into hoarding disorder. *Neuropsychiatric Disease and Treatment, 11*, 951–962. doi: 10.2147/NDT.S62084

Grisham, J. R., Brown, T. A., Savage, C. R., Steketee, G., & Barlow, D. H. (2007). Neuropsychological impairment associated with compulsive hoarding. *Behavior Research and Therapy, 45*, 1471–1483.

Grisham, J. R., Frost, R. O., Steketee, G., Kim, H. J., Tarkoff, A., & Hood, S. (2009). Formation of attachment to possessions in compulsive hoarding. *Journal of Anxiety Disorders, 23*(3), 357–361. doi: 10.1016/j.janxdis.2008.12.006

Grisham, J. R., Norberg, M. M., Williams, A. D., Certoma, S. P., & Kadib, R. (2010). Categorization and cognitive deficits in compulsive hoarding. *Behavior Research and Therapy, 48*(9), 866–872. doi: 10.1016/j.brat.2010.05.011

Gur, R. E., Calkins, M. E., Gur, R. C., Horan, W. P., Nuechterlein, K. H., Seidman, L. J., & Stone, W. S. (2007). The Consortium on the Genetics of Schizophrenia: Neurocognitive endophenotypes. *Schizophrenia Bulletin, 33*(1), 49–68. doi: 10.1093/schbul/sbl055

Hall, B. J., Tolin, D. F., Frost, R. O., & Steketee, G. (2013). An exploration of comorbid symptoms and clinical correlates of clinically significant hoarding symptoms. *Depression and Anxiety, 30*(1), 67–76.

Hartl, T. L., Duffany, S. R., Allen, G. J., Steketee, G., & Frost, R. O. (2005). Relationships among compulsive hoarding, trauma, and attention-deficit/hyperactivity disorder. *Behavior Research and Therapy, 43*(2), 269–276. doi: S0005-7967(04)00053-1

Hartl, T. L., Frost, R. O., Allen, G. J., Deckersbach, T., Steketee, G., Duffany, S. R., & Savage, C. R. (2004). Actual and perceived memory deficits in individuals with compulsive hoarding. *Depression and Anxiety, 20*(2), 59–69. doi: 10.1002/da.20010

Hasler, G., Drevets, W. C., Gould, T. D., Gottesman, I. I., & Manji, H. K. (2006). Toward constructing an endophenotype strategy for bipolar disorders. *Biological Psychiatry, 60*(2), 93–105. doi: 10.1016/j.biopsych.2005.11.006

Heaton, R. H., Chelune, G. J., Talley, J. L., Kay, G. G., & Curtiss, G. (1993). *Wisconsin Card Sorting Test Manual: Revised and Expanded*. Lutz, FL: Psychological Assessment Resources.

Herrmann, M. J., Wurflein, H., Schreppel, T., Koehler, S., Muhlberger, A., Reif, A. ... Fallgatter, A. J. (2009). *Catechol-O-methyltransferase Val158Met* genotype affects neural correlates of aversive stimuli processing. *Cognitive, Affective, & Behavioral Neuroscience, 9*(2), 168–172. doi: 10.3758/CABN.9.2.168

Hough, C. M., Luks, T. L., Lai, K., Vigil, O., Guillory, S., Nongpiur, A., . . . Mathews, C. A. (2016). Comparison of brain activation patterns during executive function tasks in hoarding disorder and non-hoarding OCD. *Psychiatry Research*, *255*, 50–59. doi: 10.1016/j.pscychresns.2016.07.007

Hwang, J. P., Tsai, S. J., Yang, C. H., Liu, K. M., & Lirng, J. F. (1998). Hoarding behavior in dementia. A preliminary report. *American Journal of Geriatric Psychiatry*, *6*, 285–289.

Iervolino, A. C., Perroud, N., Fullana, M. A., Guipponi, M., Cherkas, L., Collier, D. A., & Mataix-Cols, D. (2009). Prevalence and heritability of compulsive hoarding: A twin study. *American Journal of Psychiatry*, *166*(10), 1156–1161. doi: appi. ajp.2009.08121789

Iervolino, A. C., Rijsdijk, F. V., Cherkas, L., Fullana, M. A., & Mataix-Cols, D. (2011). A multivariate twin study of obsessive-compulsive symptom dimensions. *Archives of General Psychiatry*, *68*(6), 637–644. doi: 10.1001/archgenpsychiatry.2011.54

Insel, T., Cuthbert, B., Garvey, M., Heinssen, R., Pine, D. S., Quinn, K., . . . Wang, P. (2010). Research domain criteria (RDoC): toward a new classification framework for research on mental disorders. *American Journal of Psychiatry*, *167*(7), 748–751. doi: 10.1176/appi.ajp.2010.09091379

Knutson, B., Rick, S., Wimmer, G. E., Prelec, D., & Loewenstein, G. (2007). Neural predictors of purchases. *Neuron*, *53*(1), 147–156. doi: S0896-6273(06)00904-4

Koran, L. M., Faber, R. J., Aboujaoude, E., Large, M. D., & Serpe, R. T. (2006). Estimated prevalence of compulsive buying behavior in the United States. *American Journal of Psychiatry*, *163*(10), 1806–1812.

Kringelbach, M. L. (2005). The human orbitofrontal cortex: Linking reward to hedonic experience. *Nature Reviews Neuroscience*, *6*(9), 691–702.

Kurz, A., Riemenschneider, M., Drzezga, A., & Lautenschlager, N. (2002). The role of biological markers in the early and differential diagnosis of Alzheimer's disease. *Journal of Neural Transmission. Supplementum*, (62), 127–133.

Landau, D., Iervolino, A. C., Pertusa, A., Santo, S., Singh, S., & Mataix-Cols, D. (2011). Stressful life events and material deprivation in hoarding disorder. *Journal of Anxiety Disorders*, *25*(2), 192–202. doi: S0887-6185(10)00184-2

Lane, R. D., Reiman, E. M., Bradley, M. M., Lang, P. J., Ahern, G. L., Davidson, R. J., & Schwartz, G. E. (1997). Neuroanatomical correlates of pleasant and unpleasant emotion. *Neuropsychologia*, *35*(11), 1437–1444.

Lang, U. E., Hellweg, R., Kalus, P., Bajbouj, M., Lenzen, K. P., Sander, T., . . . Gallinat, J. (2005). Association of a functional *BDNF* polymorphism and anxiety-related personality traits. *Psychopharmacology*, *180*(1), 95–99. doi: 10.1007/s00213-004-2137-7

Lang, U. E., Hellweg, R., Sander, T., & Gallinat, J. (2009). The Met allele of the *BDNF Val66Met* polymorphism is associated with increased BDNF serum concentrations. *Molecular Psychiatry*, *14*(2), 120–122. doi: 10.1038/mp.2008.80

Lawrence, N. S., Wooderson, S., Mataix-Cols, D., David, R., Speckens, A., & Phillips, M. L. (2006). Decision making and set shifting impairments are associated with distinct symptom dimensions in obsessive-compulsive disorder. *Neuropsychology*, *20*(4), 409–419.

Lelli-Chiesa, G., Kempton, M. J., Jogia, J., Tatarelli, R., Girardi, P., Powell, J., . . . Frangou, S. (2011). The impact of the *Val158Met catechol-O-methyltransferase* genotype on neural correlates of sad facial affect processing in patients with bipolar disorder and their relatives. *Psychological Medicine*, *41*(4), 779–788. doi: 10.1017/S0033291710001431

Lenox, R. H., Gould, T. D., & Manji, H. K. (2002). Endophenotypes in bipolar disorder. *American Journal of Medical Genetics*, *114*(4), 391–406. doi: 10.1002/ajmg.10360

Lochner, C., Kinnear, C. J., Hemmings, S. M., Seller, C., Niehaus, D. J., Knowles, J. A., . . . Stein, D. J. (2005). Hoarding in obsessive-compulsive disorder: Clinical and genetic correlates. *Journal of Clinical Psychiatry*, *66*, 1155–1160.

Mackin, R. S., Arean, P. A., Delucchi, K. L., & Mathews, C. A. (2011). Cognitive functioning in individuals with severe compulsive hoarding behaviors and late life depression. *International Journal of Geriatric Psychiatry*, *26*(3), 314–321. doi: 10.1002/gps.2531

Mackin, R. S., Vigil, O., Insel, P., Kivowitz, A., Kupferman, E., Hough, C. M., . . . Mathews, C. A. (2016). Patterns of clinically significant cognitive impairment in hoarding disorder. *Depression and Anxiety*, *33*(3), 211–218. doi: 10.1002/da.22439

Mataix-Cols, D., Wooderson, S., Lawrence, N., Brammer, M. J., Speckens, A., & Phillips, M. L. (2004). Distinct neural correlates of washing, checking, and hoarding symptom dimensions in obsessive-compulsive disorder. *Archives of General Psychiatry*, *61*(6), 564–576.

Mathews, C. A., Delucchi, K., Cath, D. C., Willemsen, G., & Boomsma, D. I. (2014). Partitioning the etiology of hoarding and obsessive-compulsive symptoms. *Psychological Medicine*, *44*(13), 2867–2876. doi: 10.1017/S0033291714000269

Mathews, C. A., Perez, V. B., Roach, B. J., Fekri, S., Vigil, O., Kupferman, E., & Mathalon, D. H. (2016). Error-related brain activity dissociates hoarding disorder from obsessive-compulsive disorder. *Psychological Medicine*, *46*(2), 367–379. doi: 10.1017/S0033291715001889

McMillan, S. G., Rees, C. S., & Pestell, C. (2013). An investigation of executive functioning, attention and working memory in compulsive hoarding. *Behavioral Cognitive Psychotherapy*, *41*(5), 610–625. doi: 10.1017/S1352465812000835

Medard, E. & Kellett, S. (2014). The role of adult attachment and social support in hoarding disorder. *Behavioral Cognitive Psychotherapy*, *42*(5), 629–633. doi: 10.1017/S1352465813000659

Miltenberger, R. G., Redlin, J., Crosby, R., Stickney, M., Mitchell, J., Wonderlich, S., . . . Smyth, J. (2003). Direct and retrospective assessment of factors contributing to compulsive buying. *Journal of Behavior Therapy and Experimental Psychiatry*, 34(1), 1–9.

Montag, C., Jurkiewicz, M., & Reuter, M. (2012). The role of the *catechol-O-methyltransferase* (*COMT*) gene in personality and related psychopathological disorders. *CNS Neurological Disorders Drug Targets*, *11*(3), 236–250.

Morein-Zamir, S., Papmeyer, M., Pertusa, A., Chamberlain, S. R., Fineberg, N. A., Sahakian, B. J., . . . Robbins, T. W. (2014). The profile of executive function in OCD hoarders and hoarding disorder. *Psychiatry Research*, *215*(3), 659–667. doi: 10.1016/j.psychres.2013.12.026

Moshier, S. J., Wootton, B. M., Bragdon, L. B., Tolin, D. F., Davis, E., DiMauro, J., & Diefenbach, G. J. (2016). The relationship between self-reported and objective neuropsychological impairments in patients with hoarding disorder. *Journal of Obsessive-Compulsive and Related Disorders*, *9*, 9–15.

Nakaaki, S., Murata, Y., Sato, J., Shinagawa, Y., Hongo, J., Tatsumi, H., . . . Furukawa, T. A. (2007). Impairment of decision-making cognition in a case of frontotemporal lobar degeneration (FTLD) presenting with pathologic gambling and hoarding as the initial symptoms. *Cognitive Behavioral Neurology*, *20*(2), 121–125.

Nedelisky, A. & Steele, M. (2009). Attachment to people and to objects in obsessive-compulsive disorder: An exploratory comparison of hoarders and non-hoarders. *Attachment & Human Development, 11*(4), 365–383. doi: 10.1080/14616730903016987

Neugroschl, J. & Davis, K. L. (2002). Biological markers in Alzheimer disease. *American Journal of Geriatric Psychiatry, 10*(6), 660–677.

Nieuwenhuis, S., Ridderinkhof, K. R., Blom, J., Band, G. P., & Kok, A. (2001). Error-related brain potentials are differentially related to awareness of response errors: Evidence from an antisaccade task. *Psychophysiology, 38*(5), 752–760.

Norberg, M. M., Keyan, D., & Grisham, J. R. (2015). Mood influences the relationship between distress intolerance and discarding. *Journal of Obsessive-Compulsive and Related Disorders, 6*, 77–82.

Northoff, G., Grimm, S., Boeker, H., Schmidt, C., Bermpohl, F., Heinzel, A., . . . Boesiger, P. (2006). Affective judgment and beneficial decision making: Ventromedial prefrontal activity correlates with performance in the Iowa Gambling Task. *Human Brain Mapping, 27*(7), 572–587.

Park, J. M., Samuels, J. F., Grados, M. A., Riddle, M. A., Bienvenu, O. J., Goes, F. S., . . . Geller, D. A. (2016). ADHD and executive functioning deficits in OCD youths who hoard. *Journal of Psychiatric Research, 82*, 141–148. doi: 10.1016/j.jpsychires.2016.07.024

Paulus, M. P. & Stein, M. B. (2006). An insular view of anxiety. *Biological Psychiatry, 60*(4), 383–387. doi: S0006-3223(06)00476–8 [pii] 10.1016/j.biopsych.2006.03.042

Pertusa, A., Frost, R. O., Fullana, M. A., Samuels, J., Steketee, G., Tolin, D., . . . Mataix-Cols, D. (2010). Refining the diagnostic boundaries of compulsive hoarding: A critical review. *Clinical Psychology Review, 30*(4), 371–386. doi: S0272-7358(10) 00020–6 [pii]10.1016/j.cpr.2010.01.007

Phung, P. J., Moulding, R., Taylor, J. K., & Nedeljkovic, M. (2015). Emotional regulation, attachment to possessions and hoarding symptoms. *Scandinavian Journal of Psychology, 56*(5), 573–581. doi: 10.1111/sjop.12239

Przeworski, A., Cain, N., & Dunbeck, K. (2014). Traumatic life events in individuals with hoarding symptoms, obsessive-compulsive symptoms, and comorbid obsessive-compulsive and hoarding symptoms. *Journal of Obsessive-Compulsive and Related Disorders, 3*(1), 52–59.

Raines, A. M., Portero, A. K., Unruh, A. S., Short, N. A., & Schmidt, N. B. (2015). An initial investigation of the relationship between insomnia and hoarding. *Journal of Clinical Psychology, 71*(7), 707–714. doi: 10.1002/jclp.22161

Raines, A. M., Timpano, K. R., & Schmidt, N. B. (2014). Effects of clutter on information processing deficits in individuals with hoarding disorder. *Journal of Affective Disorders, 166*, 30–35. doi: 10.1016/j.jad.2014.04.074

Rasmussen, J., Brown, T. A., Steketee, G., & Barlow, D. H. (2013). Impulsivity in hoarding. *Journal of Obsessive-Compulsive and Related Disorders, 2*, 183–191.

Riesel, A., Kathmann, N., & Endrass, T. (2014). Overactive performance monitoring in obsessive-compulsive disorder is independent of symptom expression. *European Archives of Psychiatry and Clinical Neuroscience, 264*(8), 707–717.

Samuels, J. F., Bienvenu, O. J., Grados, M. A., Cullen, B., Riddle, M. A., Liang, K. Y., . . . Nestadt, G. (2008). Prevalence and correlates of hoarding behavior in a community-based sample. *Behavior Research and Therapy, 46*(7), 836–844.

Samuels, J. F., Bienvenu, O. J., Pinto, A., Fyer, A. J., McCracken, J. T., Rauch, S. L., . . . Nestadt, G. (2007). Hoarding in obsessive-compulsive disorder: Results from the OCD Collaborative Genetics Study. *Behaviour Research and Therapy*, *45*, 673–686. doi: 10.1016/j.brat.2006.05.008

Sawyer, K. S., Poey, A., Ruiz, S. M., Marinkovic, K., & Oscar-Berman, M. (2015). Measures of skin conductance and heart rate in alcoholic men and women during memory performance. *PeerJ*, *3*, e941.

Saxena, S., Brody, A. L., Maidment, K. M., Smith, E. C., Zohrabi, N., Katz, E., . . . Baxter, L. R., Jr. (2004). Cerebral glucose metabolism in obsessive-compulsive hoarding. *American Journal of Psychiatry*, *161*(6), 1038–1048.

Sen, S., Nesse, R. M., Stoltenberg, S. F., Li, S., Gleiberman, L., Chakravarti, A., . . . Burmeister, M. (2003). A BDNF coding variant is associated with the NEO personality inventory domain neuroticism, a risk factor for depression. *Neuropsychopharmacology*, *28*(2), 397–401. doi: 10.1038/sj.npp.1300053

Sheppard, B., Chavira, D., Azzam, A., Grados, M. A., Umana, P., Garrido, H., & Mathews, C. A. (2010). ADHD prevalence and association with hoarding behaviors in childhood-onset OCD. *Depression and Anxiety*, *27*(7), 667–674. doi: 10.1002/da.20691

Steketee, G. & Frost, R. O. (2003). Compulsive hoarding: Current status of the research. *Clinical Psychology Review*, *23*, 905–927.

Steketee, G., Frost, R. O., & Kyrios, M. (2003). Cognitive aspects of compulsive hoarding. *Cognitive Therapy and Research*, *27*, 463–479.

Sumner, J. M., Noack, C. G., Filoteo, J. V., Maddox, W. T., & Saxena, S. (2016). Neurocognitive performance in unmedicated patients with hoarding disorder. *Neuropsychology*, *30*(2), 157–168. doi: 10.1037/neu0000234

Takeuchi, H., Taki, Y., Sassa, Y., Hashizume, H., Sekiguchi, A., Fukushima, A., & Kawashima, R. (2013). Brain structures associated with executive functions during everyday events in a non-clinical sample. *Brain Structure and Function*, *218*(4), 1017–1032. doi: 10.1007/s00429-012-0444-z

Talati, A. & Hirsch, J. (2005). Functional specialization within the medial frontal gyrus for perceptual go/no-go decisions based on "what," "when," and "where" related information: An fMRI study. *Journal of Cognitive Neuroscience*, *17*(7), 981–993. doi: 10.1162/0898929054475226

Timpano, K. R., Rasmussen, J., Exner, C., Rief, W., Schmidt, N. B., & Wilhelm, S. (2013). Hoarding and the multi-faceted construct of impulsivity: A cross-cultural investigation. *Journal of Psychiatric Research*, *47*(3), 363–370. doi: 10.1016/j.jpsychires.2012.10.017

Timpano, K. R., & Schmidt, N. B. (2013). The relationship between self-control deficits and hoarding: A multimethod investigation across three samples. *Journal of Abnormal Psychology*, *122*(1), 13–25. doi: 10.1037/a0029760

Timpano, K. R., Schmidt, N. B., Wheaton, M. G., Wendland, J. R., & Murphy, D. L. (2011). Consideration of the *BDNF* gene in relation to two phenotypes: Hoarding and obesity. *Journal of Abnormal Psychology*, *120*(3), 700–707. doi: 10.1037/a0024159

Timpano, K. R., Shaw, A. M., Cougle, J. R., & Fitch, K. E. (2014). A multifaceted assessment of emotional tolerance and intensity in hoarding. *Behavior Therapy*, *45*(5), 690–699. doi: 10.1016/j.beth.2014.04.002

Tolin, D. F., Frost, R. O., & Steketee, G. (2007). An open trial of cognitive-behavioral therapy for compulsive hoarding. *Behavior Research and Therapy*, *45*, 1461–1470.

Tolin, D. F., Kiehl, K. A., Worhunsky, P., Book, G. A., & Maltby, N. (2009). An exploratory study of the neural mechanisms of decision making in compulsive hoarding. *Psychological Medicine, 39*(2), 325–336. doi: 10.1017/S0033291708003371

Tolin, D. F., Stevens, M. C., Villavicencio, A. L., Norberg, M. M., Calhoun, V. D., Frost, R. O., . . . Pearlson, G. D. (2012). Neural mechanisms of decision making in hoarding disorder. *Archives of General Psychiatry, 69*(8), 832–841. doi: 10.1001/archgenpsychiatry.2011.1980

Tolin, D. F. & Villavicencio, A. (2011). Inattention, but not OCD, predicts the core features of hoarding disorder. *Behaviour Research and Therapy, 49*(2), 120–125. doi: S0005-7967(10)00249-4 [pii] 10.1016/j.brat.2010.12.002

Tolin, D. F., Villavicencio, A., Umbach, A., & Kurtz, M. M. (2011). Neuropsychological functioning in hoarding disorder. *Psychiatry Research, 189*(3), 413–418. doi: S0165-1781(11)00502-6 [pii] 10.1016/j.psychres.2011.06.022

Tolin, D. F., Witt, S. T., & Stevens, M. C. (2014). Hoarding disorder and obsessive-compulsive disorder show different patterns of neural activity during response inhibition. *Psychiatry Research, 221*, 142–148.

Vickers, B. D., Preston, S. D., Gonzalez, R., & Angott, A. M. (2016). Hoarders only discount consumables and are more patient for money. *Frontiers in Behavioral Neuroscience, 10*.

Volle, E., Beato, R., Levy, R., & Dubois, B. (2002). Forced collectionism after orbitofrontal damage. *Neurology, 58*(3), 488–490.

Wang, J. M., Seidler, R. D., Hall, J. L., & Preston, S. D. (2012). The neural bases of acquisitiveness: Decisions to acquire and discard everyday goods differ across frames, items, and individuals. *Neuropsychologia, 50*(5), 939–948. doi: S0028-3932(12)00059-0 [pii] 10.1016/j.neuropsychologia.2012.01.033

Wechsler, D. (2008). *Wechsler Adult Intelligence Scale, Fourth Edition*. San Antonio, TX: Pearson.

Wheaton, M., Timpano, K. R., Lasalle-Ricci, V. H., & Murphy, D. (2008). Characterizing the hoarding phenotype in individuals with OCD: Associations with comorbidity, severity and gender. *Journal of Anxiety Disorders, 22*(2), 243–252.

Wincze, J. P., Steketee, G., & Frost, R. O. (2007). Categorization in compulsive hoarding. *Behavior Research and Therapy, 45*(1), 63–72. doi: 10.1016/j.brat.2006.01.012

Woody, S. R., Kellman-McFarlane, K., & Welsted, A. (2014). Review of cognitive performance in hoarding disorder. *Clinical Psychology Review, 34*(4), 324–336. doi: 10.1016/j.cpr.2014.04.002

Worden, B. L., DiLoreto, J., & Tolin, D. F. (2014). Insight and motivation. In R. O. Frost & G. Steketee (eds.), *The Oxford Handbook of Hoarding and Acquiring*. New York, NY: Oxford University Press.

Xu, W., Fu, Z., Wang, J., & Zhang, Y. (2015). Relationship between autistic traits and hoarding in a large non-clinical Chinese sample: Mediating effect of anxiety and depression. *Psychological Reports, 116*(1), 23–32. doi: 10.2466/15.PR0.116k17w0

Zubieta, J. K., Heitzeg, M. M., Smith, Y. R., Bueller, J. A., Xu, K., Xu, Y., . . . Goldman, D. (2003). *COMT val158met* genotype affects mu-opioid neurotransmitter responses to a pain stressor. *Science, 299*(5610), 1240–1243. doi: 10.1126/science.1078546

24 Body-Focused Repetitive Behavior Disorders

Dan J. Stein and Christine Lochner

Hair-pulling, skin-picking, and other body-focused repetitive behaviors (BFRBs) have been described in the medical literature since the time of Hippocrates. However, disorders such as trichotillomania and skin-picking have been recognized in psychiatric classification systems only relatively recently. Research on the phenomenology and psychobiology of trichotillomania was given significant impetus by the hypothesis that hair-pulling had features in common with the compulsions of obsessive-compulsive disorder (OCD), and so would respond more robustly to serotonergic agents than to noradrenergic drugs. This chapter describes the results of such work, outlining the pros and cons of classifying body-focused repetitive behavior disorders (BFRBDs) as obsessive-compulsive and related conditions, and considering the extent to which modern cognitive-affective neuroscience, including constructs from the Research Domain Criteria (RDoC) framework, are useful in understanding BFRBs and BFRBDs.

Phenomenology

Trichotillomania

Diagnostic classification and criteria. Hippocrates noted the presence of plucking of the hair in the context of depression, and hair-pulling has long been described in a range of nonmedical texts, including the Bible (Stein, Christenson, & Hollander, 1999). In the 19th century, French physician Hallopeau coined the term *trichotillomania* (from the Latin *trich* = hair, and *tillo* = pull), to describe patients with repetitive hair-pulling. Another important early description in the medical literature comprised a large case series of patients with trichobezoar; many individuals with trichotillomania swallow their hair, and this may in turn lead to complications such as gastrointestinal obstruction (Bouwer & Stein, 1998).

Researchers at the National Institute of Mental Health (NIMH) in the United States made the key observation in the 1980s that patients with OCD responded more robustly to clomipramine, a serotonergic antidepressant, than to desipramine, a noradrenergic medication. Patients with hair-pulling wondered whether they had a form of OCD, and would respond to clomipramine. Early data suggested that trichotillomania, like OCD, indeed responded more robustly to clomipramine than to desipramine (Swedo et al., 1989). A serotonergic hypothesis of obsessive-compulsive and related disorders, although somewhat simplistic, led to a range of useful research on these conditions (Stein, 2000).

In 1987, the revised third edition of the *DSM* included trichotillomania (TTM) as an impulse control disorder not elsewhere classified. The diagnostic criteria for this condition reflected this rubric: in addition to having repetitive hair-pulling, individuals needed to experience tension prior to hair-pulling or when attempting to resist hair-pulling, and pleasure, gratification, or relief after the hair-pulling. Additional diagnostic criteria included the clinical criterion (individuals needed to experience clinical distress or impairment associated with the hair-pulling) and a hierarchy criterion (hair-pulling not better explained by another mental or general medical disorder).

Empirical investigation indicated, however, that not all patients with chronic hair-pulling symptoms in fact describe rising tension or pleasure, gratification or relief associated with hair-pulling (Lochner et al., 2011; Stein, Grant, et al., 2010). Furthermore, there were no significant sociodemographic or clinical differences between individuals who did and did not meet these two criteria. *DSM-5* therefore deleted these criteria, replacing them with a criterion that emphasizes that patients attempted to decrease the hair-pulling (American Psychiatric Association, 2013).

Clinical features and comorbidity. A number of additional features of TTM, not included in the diagnostic criteria, are worth noting. First, hair may be pulled from any part of the body, although it is most commonly pulled from the scalp. Hair-pulling may be patterned in key ways; patients may seek out particular hairs, may play with the hair in specific ways, and may mouth, chew, or swallow hair once it is pulled. States of hyperarousal (e.g., anxiety) and hypoarousal (e.g., boredom) may trigger hair-pulling (Christenson et al., 1993). Some patients pull from inanimate objects (e.g., carpets), some from pets, and some from other people. Hair-pulling may be done in a more focused way (i.e., in response to a specific urge) or more automatically (e.g., without a great deal of awareness); the Milwaukee Inventory for Subtypes of Trichotillomania scale can assess these (Keuthen et al., 2015).

Second, hair-pulling typically starts at around puberty, and is much more common in females (Stein, Grant, et al., 2010). While some babies pull out their hair, there is little work on such individuals, and the vast majority appear to resolve during development. Adult patients very commonly note onset around or after the time of puberty (Flessner et al., 2010). A limited number of survey studies suggest that TTM has a 12-month prevalence of 1–2%, with a ratio of 10 females to 1 male (du Toit, van Kradenburg, Niehaus, & Stein, 2001). Hair-pulling may endure for many years, sometimes with variation in picking sites, and sometimes with a waxing and waning course. In women, hair-pulling may alter with hormonal changes (e.g., menstruation, perimenopause).

Third, considerable impairment and morbidity are associated with TTM. The Trichotillomania Impact Project (TIP) emphasized that patients not only carry a range of negative feelings related to their hair-pulling (e.g., shame, low self-esteem), they also spend considerable time on hair-pulling or on camouflaging bald spots, and symptoms interfere with several areas of life (e.g., avoidance of social and interpersonal relationships, academic and occupational impairment) (Woods et al., 2006). A range of medical sequelae may also present (e.g., blepharitis). In some cases, there is serious morbidity; trichobezoars, for example, can have fatal consequences in humans.

Fourth, a range of comorbid conditions may be present in patients with TTM. The most common comorbidity is with skin-picking disorder (SPD) and other BFRBDs (Stein et al., 2008). Cognitive obsessive-compulsive and related disorders, such as OCD, body dysmorphic disorder (BDD), and hoarding disorder (HD), are also more common in TTM than in the general population (Stein, Grant et al., 2010). A range of mood and anxiety disorders may also be present in patients with TTM (Woods et al., 2006). First-degree relatives of individuals with TTM are at increased risk for TTM as well as other obsessive-compulsive and related disorders (Bienvenu et al., 2012).

Skin-Picking Disorder

Diagnostic classification and criteria. The term *neurotic excoriation* was coined by Erasmus Wilson in 1875 and described by dermatologists in the 19th century. French dermatologist Brocq used the term *acne excoriee* to describe skin-picking in young patients with acne. A range of other terms have since been used in the literature, including *dermatillomania, skin-picking disorder*, and *excoriation disorder* (Grant et al., 2012; Snorrason, Stein, & Woods, 2013). There are pros and cons of using different terms; for example the term *dermatillomania* parallels that of *trichotillomania* and has some continuity with the medical literature, but, on the other hand, the suffix "mania" seems inappropriate in the context of this condition. *DSM-5* attempted a compromise solution, using the term *excoriation disorder* (consistent with an older literature), as well as *skin-picking disorder* (consistent with the wish for a descriptive nomenclature).

In *DSM-5*, there was a relatively high bar for adding a new disorder to the nosology. Criteria were proposed for the definition of a mental disorder, and guidelines were provided for the sort of evidence required to establish a new condition (Stein, Phillips et al., 2010). The DSM-5 Scientific Review Committee (Kendler, 2013) accepted skin-picking disorder as a new condition, on the basis of a range of evidence provided to them. Importantly, consumer advocacy groups provided strong support for the addition of this category (Stein & Phillips, 2013). By the time of *ICD-11* discussions, it was already accepted that SPD would be included, and there was more of a focus on whether TTM and SPD should be classified together (Grant & Stein, 2014). Given similarities in symptomatology and clinical features (Lochner et al., 2005; Snorrason, Belleau, & Woods, 2012), the decision was made to have these fall under the parent category of BFRBDs.

Clinical features and comorbidity. A number of additional features of SPD, not included in the diagnostic criteria, are worth noting. Skin may be picked from any part of the body, although patients may prefer to pick from more readily accessible sites, or from sites that are relatively easy to hide. Skin-picking may be patterned in key ways; patients may search for skin irregularities, may manipulate scabs in a particular way, and may mouth, chew, or swallow scabs once they are pulled. While most individuals pick with their nails, skin may be picked with tweezers or a range of other implements. States of hyperarousal (e.g., anxiety) and hypoarousal (e.g., boredom) may trigger skin-picking. Skin-picking may be done in a more focused way (i.e., in response to a specific urge) or more automatically (e. g., without a great deal of awareness); the Milwaukee Inventory for Dimensions of Adult Skin-Picking scale can assess these (Walther, Flessner, et al., 2009).

Skin-picking may begin around puberty or somewhat later in adolescence or early adulthood (Grant et al., 2012). The disorder often begins with a dermatological condition, such as eczema or acne. A limited number of survey studies suggest that SPD has a lifetime prevalence of 1–2%, and three-quarters of individuals with SPD are female. SPD may persist for many years, sometimes with a waxing and waning course.

The Skin-Picking Impact Project demonstrated the significant impairment associated with SPD (Tucker, Woods, Flessner, Franklin, & Franklin, 2011). Individuals with SPD may have negative feelings related to their skin-picking (e.g., shame, low self-esteem); they also spend considerable time on skin-picking or on camouflaging bald spots, and symptoms may interfere with several areas of life (e.g., avoidance of social and interpersonal relationships, academic and occupational impairment). Skin-picking may lead to infection, scarring, and other dermatological consequences. In some cases, such sequelae can be very serious indeed, with life-threatening complications.

Patients with SPD may suffer from a broad range of comorbid conditions. The most common comorbid condition is other BFRBDs, including TTM (Snorrason, Ricketts et al., 2012). OCD and cognitive obsessive-compulsive and related disorders are also more common in patients with SPD (in body dysmorphic disorder, SPD may either be a comorbid condition, or skin-picking may be secondary to the BDD; i.e., an attempt to improve appearance) (Grant, Menard, & Phillips, 2006). Patients may also have a range of mood and anxiety conditions. First-degree relatives of individuals with SPD are at increased risk for SPD, as well as other obsessive-compulsive and related disorders (Bienvenu et al., 2012).

Other Body-Focused Repetitive Behaviors

A range of other BFRBs have been described, including cheek-biting, lip-chewing, nose-picking, and nail-biting (Jefferson & Thompson, 1995; Sarkhel, Praharaj, & Aktar, 2011; Stein & Hollander, 1992). While they have generally received less study than TTM and SPD, they can be highly prevalent, and associated with significant morbidity (Halteh, Scher, & Lipner, 2017; Rieder & Tosti, 2016).

From a phenomenological perspective they seem to have a great deal in common with SPD and TTM, although further comparative work is needed in order to reach definitive conclusions. From a nosological perspective, one relevant consideration is the differential diagnosis of BFRBDs from stereotypic movement disorder and from non-suicidal self-injury.

Stereotypic movement disorder (SMD) is classified in the *DSM-5* section on neurodevelopmental disorders. It is characterized by repetitive, seemingly driven, and apparently purposeless motor behavior such as hand-waving in children, and includes self-injurious behaviors such as head-banging (Stein & Christenson, 1998; Stein & Woods, 2014). SMD typically has very early onset, while BFRBs typically begin somewhat later. For example, skin-picking in Prader-Willi syndrome may be diagnosed with a stereotypic movement disorder, rather than with SPD. Similarly, severe self-mutilation may be seen in a number of neurogenetic disorders, and the appropriate diagnosis would be SMD. Nevertheless, there is a good deal of overlap between TTM, SPD, and SMD (Stein, Bouwer, & Niehaus, 1997; Stein, Grant et al., 2010; Stein & Woods, 2014).

According to *DSM-5*, non-suicidal self-injury is characterized by repetitive intentional self-inflicted damage to the surface of the body. Such self-injurious behaviors are likely to induce bleeding, bruising, or pain (e.g., cutting, burning, stabbing, hitting, excessive rubbing), with the expectation that the injury will not lead to severe physical harm (i.e., there is no suicidal intent). Self-injurious non-suicidal behavior is often triggered by negative emotional states, and may respond to specific pharmacotherapies, for example, selective serotonin reuptake inhibitors (SSRIs), and to particular forms of psychotherapy (McKay & Andover, 2012; Schiavone & Links, 2013). Whether this entity is distinct from existing notions of BFRBDs therefore remains unclear.

Summary

From a phenomenological perspective, there are some similarities across OCD and related disorders but also significant differences between the various conditions that make up this chapter of the *DSM-5* and *ICD-11*. A broad notion of "compulsivity" emphasizes the extent to which there are similarities, including repetitive behavior (Fineberg et al., 2014). At the same time there are clinically important distinctions, for example, patients with TTM and SPD do not have obsessions. It is notable that analysis of latent factors in twin studies of patients with OCD and related disorders indicates that a single latent factor cuts across these conditions, while a second factor loads exclusively on TTM and SPD (Monzani, Rijsdijk, Harris, & Mataix-Cols, 2014). Furthermore, TTM and SPD are largely influenced by the same genetic factor.

DSM-5 has focused primarily on issues of diagnostic validity; the decision to include obsessive-compulsive and related disorders as a separate category was influenced by a range of findings pointing to common psychobiological mechanisms across these disorders (Ferrão, Miguel, & Stein, 2009; Phillips et al., 2010;

Stein et al., 2007). At the same time, there are important psychobiological distinctions. *ICD-11* focused a great deal on issues of clinical utility; from a public health perspective, for example, it is important to screen for these often overlooked conditions, and similar evaluation and assessment tools are used across these disorders (Grant & Stein, 2014; Stein, Fontenelle, & Reed, 2014; Stein et al., 2016). At the same time, given differences in underlying psychobiological mechanisms, different treatments for these conditions are required. In the next section, we address psychobiological and genetic issues in more detail.

Cognitive-Affective Neuroscience

Cognitive-Affective Systems

Body-focused repetitive behaviors can be conceptualized as relatively simple stereotypies or habits, in contradistinction to more complex perseverative behaviors such as compulsions (Ridley, 1994; Stein, Chamberlain, & Fineberg, 2006). Despite this phenomenological homogeneity, habits may have a fairly complex psychobiology. Here we emphasize three aspects of the psychobiology of habitual behaviors, consistent with an A-B-C model of habit disorders.

First, habits may be worse at times of stress, or in response to aversive cues. Patients with TTM, for example, appear to have psychological inflexibility; they have difficulty in resisting maladaptive behaviors that are triggered by aversive cognitions and emotions (Houghton et al., 2014). Furthermore, patients with BFRBs have negative affective states (i.e., anxiety, tension or boredom) prior to hair-pulling or skin-picking (Snorrason, Smari, & Olafsson, 2010). Thus, there is an affective (A) component to habitual behavior, with emotion regulation difficulties possibly playing a key role in these conditions (Roberts, O'Connor, & Belanger, 2013). Work on the RDoC negative valence system (Insel et al., 2010) may well be relevant in this context.

Second, habits may reflect the presence of an altered reward process, which ensures initiation and maintenance of the habitual behavior. Notably, the Skin Picking Reward scale has measures of how strongly skin-picking is "liked" (with pleasurable feelings during skin-picking or "wanted" (with motivation to seek this reward). The Wanting scale is associated with picking urges, greater cue reactivity, and more picking-related routines/habits (Snorrason, Olafsson, Nedeljkovic, Castle, & Rossell, 2015). Thus, there is a component of behavioral addiction (B) that seems relevant to understanding habitual BFRBs such as hair-pulling and skin-picking. Work on the RDoC construct of positive valence systems appears relevant here.

Third, habits may reflect an impairment in control (C). There is some phenomenological and neuropsychological evidence for this; for example, there is evidence of increased impulsivity, as assessed by a range of different measures, in different BFRBs (Leppink et al., 2016; Stein et al., 1995) and deficits in inhibitory control have been demonstrated on neuropsychological testing in some studies (Fineberg et al., 2014). In a recent systematic review of the neuropsychology of TTM, Slikboer and colleagues note the small sample sizes and the lack of replication in the field, and emphasize the need for further work on response inhibition in BFRBRs (Slikboer, Reser, Nedeljkovic, Castle, & Rossell, 2017). RDoC work on the cognitive system and executive functions seems relevant to understanding this aspect of habitual behavior.

Neural Circuitry

Consistent with this understanding of the cognitive-affective neuroscience of habits, brain-imaging studies have found a range of abnormalities in patients with TTM and SPD. In particular, brain-imaging studies of TTM and SPD have provided some support for the involvement of (1) cortical-striatal circuitry, including findings of differences in cingulate and putamen volume (i.e., neurocircuitry involved in motor generation and suppression); (2) amygdala (i.e., neurocircuitry involved in responding to affective stimuli); and (3) nucleus accumbens (i.e., neurocircuitry involved in reward processing) (Slikboer et al., 2017). Such findings therefore provide some support for the A-B-C model of habit disorders outlined earlier.

Neuroimaging studies of BFRBs are, however, at an early stage. Study samples have been small, investigations have typically been exploratory in nature, and the entire literature comprises fewer than 15 studies at this point in time (Slikboer et al., 2017). Thus, due caution must be taken in reaching premature conclusions, and much further investigation is needed, along the lines of ongoing collaborative work in OCD (Boedhoe et al., 2017). Nevertheless, individual studies have revealed a number of useful pathways for future investigation. For example, Odlaug and colleagues demonstrated functional under-activation of frontal, cingulate, and dorsal striatal regions during an executive planning task in SPD (Odlaug, Hampshire, Chamberlain, & Grant, 2016).

Animal studies have further supported the role of cortico-striatal-thalamic-cortical loops in obsessive-compulsive spectrum disorders (d'Angelo et al., 2014). Grooming and habit-related behaviors, for example, are mediated by fronto-striatal circuitry, and regions such as the basal ganglia therefore provide key targets for intervention in these conditions (Burguière, Monteiro, Mallet, Feng, & Graybiel, 2015; Everitt & Robbins, 2016). Optogenetic methods can now be employed to target such behavior; for example, repeated cortex (OFC)-ventromedial striatum (VMS) stimulation generated a progressive increase in grooming (Ahmari et al., 2013). Notably, animal studies have shed light on how exposure to stressors alters corticostrial circuitry and leads to a bias in habitual behavioral strategies as well as altered reward processing (Dias-Ferreira et al., 2009; Martin, Spicer, Lewis, Gluck, & Cork, 1991; Matthews & Robbins, 2003).

Genes and Environment

Twin studies of TTM suggest relatively high heritability (Novak, Keuthen, Stewart, & Pauls, 2009). A handful of candidate gene studies have been undertaken, and suggest that variants in serotonergic genes may be relevant (Flessner, Knopik, & McGreary, 2012). However, to our knowledge no well-powered genome-wide association studies have yet been undertaken for the BFRBs. Work on the genetic architecture of OCD and Tourette's disorder suggests that multiple genes, many of which may have a relatively small effect, likely play a role in BFRBDs (Davis et al., 2013). Preliminary evidence that glutamatergic variants may play an important role in OCD seems highly relevant to BFRBDs, given the role of the glutamate system in a range of systems including inhibitory control, and given the possible efficacy of glutamatergic agents in BFRBDs (Kariuki-Nyuthe et al., 2014; Stewart et al., 2013).

Animal studies have suggested that a range of molecular pathways may be involved in mediating repetitive behaviors and BFRBs (Hoppe, Ipser, Lochner, Thomas, & Stein, 2010; Langen, Kas, Staal, van Engeland, & Durston, 2011). Early influential work suggested, for example, that the *Hoxb8* gene might play a key role in grooming (Greer & Capecchi, 2002). Animal models of *SAPAP3* have shed light on the role of striatal circuits in grooming (Burguière, Monteiro, Feng, & Graybiel, 2013), although human findings on associations of *SAPAP3* genetic variants with obsessive-compulsive and related disorders have been inconsistent (Flessner et al., 2012). A good deal of work has been undertaken on the dopamine system in habits as well as in stress, reward, and executive functioning (Thierry, Tassin, Blanc, & Glowinski, 1976), and it is noteworthy that dopamine-blocking agents may decrease stereotypies and BFRBs in humans (Lochner, Roos, & Stein, 2017; Rothbart et al., 2013). The opioid system may play a key role in self-injurious behavior (Rapp & Vollmer, 2005). Environmental manipulations (e.g., deprivation vs. enrichment) influence stereotypies and grooming in animals and humans (Lochner et al., 2002; Marais et al., 2006; Mejido et al., 2009), consistent with a range of work on behavioral interventions for BFRBDs.

Summary

RDoC has been suggested as a key approach to understanding the psychobiology of mental disorders (Insel et al., 2010). A number of points deserve emphasis. First, the idea that we need to dissect out the neurobiology of symptoms that cut dimensionally across categorical psychiatric disorders is not a new one (Cloninger, 1986; Stein et al., 1995; van Praag et al., 1990). Second, the notion that such dimensions' constructs will be any less complex or heterogeneous than existing psychiatric categories is far from clear at this stage. Third, we need to be humble about current views of the neuronal circuits that are now central to RDoC constructs; these may ultimately prove to be gross over-simplifications (Stein, 2014).

One key reason for studying BFRBs is their apparent homogeneity. Whereas schizophrenia, for example, undoubtedly comprises a broad range of different conditions and diverse mechanisms, BFRBs often appear similar across different individuals, and may be accounted for by a discrete number of psychobiological pathways. Furthermore, the close analogy between grooming behaviors in animals and BFRBs in humans is highly consistent with the emphasis in RDoC on translational models. BFRBs therefore provide a useful test case to determine whether an RDoC-like approach is useful in shedding additional light on the psychobiology of BFRBDs, and ultimately in improving treatment outcomes.

Conclusion

Body-focused repetitive behaviors are a clinically important phenomenon given their high prevalence and morbidity. They have fortunately received more attention over the past several decades, and their inclusion in a new chapter of the nosology may lead to greater clinical awareness, and so ultimately to improved diagnosis and management. Nevertheless, it is important to emphasize that the obsessive-compulsive and related disorders differ in important ways, and that each requires its own approach to assessment and treatment. Fortunately, there have been important advances in both the pharmacotherapy and psychotherapy of BFRBs in recent years, as well as significant advances in consumer advocacy.

From a psychobiological perspective, the relative homogeneity of the BFRBs and BFRBDs, and their apparently close analogy with animal grooming behaviors, provides hope that psychobiological investigations informed by an RDoC-like approach will be useful. At the same time, these phenomena are complex, and much remains to be learned about the range of mechanisms that underlie them; it is unlikely that any new meta-perspective on translational research will provide a quick fix. Fortunately, consumer advocates are committed to funding ongoing work in this area, and hopefully such research will ultimately yield returns in terms of better health outcomes.

References

Ahmari, S. E., Spellman, T., Douglass, N. L., Kheirbek, M. A., Simpson, H. B., Deisseroth, K., ... Hen, R. (2013). Repeated cortico-striatal stimulation generates persistent OCD-like behavior. *Science*, *340*(6137), 1234–1239.

American Psychiatric Association. (2013). *Diagnostic and Statistical Manual of Mental Disorders* (5th edn). Arlington, VA: American Psychiatric Association.

Bienvenu, O. J., Samuels, J. F., Wuyek, L. A., Liang, K. Y., Wang, Y., Grados, M. A., ... Fyer, A. J. (2012). Is obsessive-compulsive disorder an anxiety disorder, and what, if any, are spectrum conditions? A family study perspectives. *Psychological Medicine*, *42*(1), 1–13.

Boedhoe, P. S., Schmaal, L., Abe, Y., Ameis, S. H., Arnold, P. D., Batistuzzo, M. C., . . . Brem, S. (2016). Distinct subcortical volume alterations in pediatric and adult OCD: A worldwide meta-and mega-analysis. *American Journal of Psychiatry, 174* (1), 60–69.

Bouwer, C. & Stein, D. J. (1998). Trichobezoars in trichotillomania: Case report and literature overview. *Psychosomatic Medicine, 60*(5), 658–660.

Burguière, E., Monteiro, P., Feng, G., & Graybiel, A. M. (2013). Optogenetic stimulation of lateral orbitofronto-striatal pathway suppresses compulsive behaviors. *Science, 340*(6137), 1243–1246.

Burguière, E., Monteiro, P., Mallet, L., Feng, G., & Graybiel, A. M. (2015). Striatal circuits, habits, and implications for obsessive-compulsive disorder. *Current Opinion in Neurobiology, 30*, 59–65.

Christenson, G. A., Ristvedt, S. L., & Mackenzie, T. B. (1993). Identification of trichotillomania cue profiles. *Behaviour Research and Therapy, 31*(3), 315–320.

Cloninger, C. R. (1986). A unified biosocial theory of personality and its role in the development of anxiety states. *Psychiatric Developments, 3*(2), 167–226.

d'Angelo, L. S. C., Eagle, D. M., Grant, J. E., Fineberg, N. A., Robbins, T. W., & Chamberlain, S. R. (2014). Animal models of obsessive-compulsive spectrum disorders. *CNS Spectrums, 19*(1), 28–49.

Davis, L. K., Yu, D., Keenan, C. L., Gamazon, E. R., Konkashbaev, A. I., Derks, E. M., . . . Barr, C. L. (2013). Partitioning the heritability of Tourette syndrome and obsessive compulsive disorder reveals differences in genetic architecture. *PLoS Genetics, 9*(10), e1003864.

Dias-Ferreira, E., Sousa, J. C., Melo, I., Morgado, P., Mesquita, A. R., Cerqueira, J. J., . . . Sousa, N. (2009). Chronic stress causes frontostriatal reorganization and affects decision-making. *Science, 325*(5940), 621–625.

du Toit, P. L., van Kradenburg, J., Niehaus, D. J. H., & Stein, D. J. (2001). Characteristics and phenomenology of hair-pulling: An exploration of subtypes. *Comprehensive Psychiatry, 42*(3), 247–256.

Everitt, B. J. & Robbins, T. W. (2016). Drug addiction: Updating actions to habits to compulsions ten years on. *Annual Review of Psychology, 67*, 23–50.

Ferrão, Y. A., Miguel, E., & Stein, D. J. (2009). Tourette's syndrome, trichotillomania, and obsessive-compulsive disorder: How closely are they related?. *Psychiatry Research, 170*(1), 32–42.

Fineberg, N. A., Chamberlain, S. R., Goudriaan, A. E., Stein, D. J., Vanderschuren, L. J., Gillan, C. M., . . . Denys, D. (2014). New developments in human neurocognition: Clinical, genetic, and brain imaging correlates of impulsivity and compulsivity. *CNS Spectrums, 19*(1), 69–89.

Flessner, C. A., Knopik, V. S., & McGeary, J. (2012). Hair pulling disorder (trichotillomania): Genes, neurobiology, and a model for understanding impulsivity and compulsivity. *Psychiatry Research, 199*(3), 151–158.

Flessner, C. A., Lochner, C., Stein, D. J., Woods, D. W., Franklin, M. E., & Keuthen, N. J. (2010). Age of onset of trichotillomania symptoms: Investigating clinical correlates. *Journal of Nervous and Mental Disease, 198*(12), 896–900.

Grant, J. E., Menard, W., & Phillips, K. A. (2006). Pathological skin picking in individuals with body dysmorphic disorder. *General Hospital Psychiatry, 28*(6), 487–493.

Grant, J. E., Odlaug, B. L., Chamberlain, S. R., Keuthen, N. J., Lochner, C., & Stein, D. J. (2012). Skin picking disorder. *American Journal of Psychiatry*, *169*(11), 1143–1149.

Grant, J. E. & Stein, D. J. (2014). Body-focused repetitive behavior disorders in *ICD-11*. *Revista brasileira de psiquiatria*, *36*, 59–64.

Greer, J. M. & Capecchi, M. R. (2002). *Hoxb8* is required for normal grooming behavior in mice. *Neuron*, *33*(1), 23–34.

Halteh, P., Scher, R. K., & Lipner, S. R. (2017). Onychophagia: A nail-biting conundrum for physicians. *Journal of Dermatological Treatment*, *28*(2), 166–172.

Hoppe, L. J., Ipser, J., Lochner, C., Thomas, K. G. F., & Stein, D. J. (2010). Should there be a category: "Grooming disorders?" In A. V. Kalueff, J. L. LaPorte, & C. L. Bergner (eds.), *Neurobiology of Grooming Behavior* (pp. 226–251). New York, NY: Cambridge University Press.

Houghton, D. C., Compton, S. N., Twohig, M. P., Saunders, S. M., Franklin, M. E., Neal-Barnett, A. M., . . . Woods, D. W. (2014). Measuring the role of psychological inflexibility in Trichotillomania. *Psychiatry Research*, *220*(1), 356–361.

Insel, T., Cuthbert, B., Garvey, M., Heinssen, R., Pine, D. S., Quinn, K., . . . Wang, P. (2010). Research domain criteria (RDoC): Toward a new classification framework for research on mental disorders. *American Journal of Psychiatry*, *167*(7), 748–751.

Jefferson, J. W. & Thompson, T. D. (1995). Rhinotillexomania: Psychiatric disorder or habit? *Journal of Clinical Psychiatry*, *56*(2), 56–59.

Kariuki-Nyuthe, C., Gomez-Mancilla, B., & Stein, D. J. (2014). Obsessive compulsive disorder and the glutamatergic system. *Current Opinion in Psychiatry*, *27*(1), 32–37.

Kendler, K. S. (2013). A history of the DSM-5 Scientific Review Committee. *Psychological Medicine*, *43*(9), 1793–1800.

Keuthen, N. J., Tung, E. S., Woods, D. W., Franklin, M. E., Altenburger, E. M., Pauls, D. L., & Flessner, C. A. (2015). Replication study of the Milwaukee inventory for subtypes of trichotillomania–adult version in a clinically characterized sample. *Behavior Modification*, *39*(4), 580–599.

Langen, M., Kas, M. J., Staal, W. G., van Engeland, H., & Durston, S. (2011). The neurobiology of repetitive behavior: of mice . . .. *Neuroscience & Biobehavioral Reviews*, *35*(3), 345–355.

Leppink, E. W., Redden, S. A., & Grant, J. E. (2016). Impulsivity in body-focused repetitive behavior disorders: Disparate clinical associations between three distinct measures. *International Journal of Psychiatry in Clinical Practice*, *20*(1), 24–31.

Lochner, C., du Toit, P. L., Zungu-Dirwayi, N., Marais, A., van Kradenburg, J., Seedat, S., . . . & Stein, D. J. (2002). Childhood trauma in obsessive-compulsive disorder, trichotillomania, and controls. *Depression and Anxiety*, *15*(2), 66–68.

Lochner, C., Roos, A., & Stein, D. J. (2017). Excoriation (skin-picking) disorder: A systematic review of treatment options. *Neuropsychiatric Disease and Treatment*, *13*, 1867.

Lochner, C., Seedat, S., du Toit, P. L., Nel, D. G., Niehaus, D. J., Sandler, R., & Stein, D. J. (2005). Obsessive-compulsive disorder and trichotillomania: A phenomenological comparison. *BMC Psychiatry*, *5*(1), 2.

Lochner, C., Stein, D. J., Woods, D., Pauls, D. L., Franklin, M. E., Loerke, E. H., & Keuthen, N. J. (2011). The validity of DSM-IV-TR criteria B and C of hair-pulling disorder (trichotillomania): Evidence from a clinical study. *Psychiatry Research*, *189*(2), 276–280.

Marais, L., Daniels, W., Brand, L., Viljoen, F., Hugo, C., & Stein, D. J. (2006). Psychopharmacology of maternal separation anxiety in vervet monkeys. *Metabolic Brain Disease, 21*(2–3), 191–200.

Martin, L. J., Spicer, D. M., Lewis, M. H., Gluck, J. P., & Cork, L. C. (1991). Social deprivation of infant rhesus monkeys alters the chemoarchitecture of the brain: I. Subcortical regions. *Journal of Neuroscience, 11*(11), 3344–3358.

Matthews, K. & Robbins, T. W. (2003). Early experience as a determinant of adult behavioural responses to reward: The effects of repeated maternal separation in the rat. *Neuroscience & Biobehavioral Reviews, 27*(1–2), 45–55.

McKay, D. & Andover, M. (2012). Should nonsuicidal self-injury be a putative obsessive-compulsive-related condition? A critical appraisal. *Behavior Modification, 36*(1), 3–17.

Mejido, D. C., Dick, E. J., Jr., Williams, P. C., Sharp, R. M., Andrade, M. C., DiCarlo, C. D., & Hubbard, G. B. (2009). Trichobezoars in baboons. *Journal of Medical Primatology, 38*(5), 302–309.

Monzani, B., Rijsdijk, F., Harris, J., & Mataix-Cols, D. (2014). The structure of genetic and environmental risk factors for dimensional representations of *DSM-5* obsessive-compulsive spectrum disorders. *Journal of American Medicine Psychiatry, 71*(2), 182–189.

Novak, C. E., Keuthen, N. J., Stewart, S. E., & Pauls, D. L. (2009). A twin concordance study of trichotillomania. *American Journal of Medical Genetics Part B: Neuropsychiatric Genetics, 150B*(7), 944–949.

Odlaug, B. L., Hampshire, A., Chamberlain, S. R., & Grant, J. E. (2016). Abnormal brain activation in excoriation (skin-picking) disorder: Evidence from an executive planning fMRI study. *British Journal of Psychiatry, 208*(2), 168–174.

Phillips, K. A., Stein, D. J., Rauch, S. L., Hollander, E., Fallon, B. A., Barsky, A., ... Leckman, J. (2010). Should an obsessive-compulsive spectrum grouping of disorders be included in *DSM-V*? *Depression and Anxiety, 27*(6), 528–555.

Rapp, J. T. & Vollmer, T. R. (2005). Stereotypy II: A review of neurobiological interpretations and suggestions for an integration with behavioral methods. *Research in Developmental Disabilities, 26*(6), 548–564.

Ridley, R. M. (1994). The psychology of perserverative and stereotyped behaviour. *Progress in Neurobiology, 44*(2), 221–231.

Rieder, E. A. & Tosti, A. (2016). Onychotillomania: An underrecognized disorder. *Journal of the American Academy of Dermatology, 75*(6), 1245–1250.

Roberts, S., O'Connor, K., & Belanger, C. (2013). Emotion regulation and other psychological models for body-focused repetitive behaviors. *Clinical Psychology Review 33*(6), 745–762.

Rothbart, R., Amos, T., Siegfried, N., Ipser, J. C., Fineberg, N., Chamberlain, S. R., & Stein, D. J. (2013). Pharmacotherapy for trichotillomania. *The Cochrane Database of Systematic Reviews*, 11 CD007662.

Sarkhel, S., Praharaj, S. K., & Akhtar, S. (2011). Cheek-biting disorder: Another stereotypic movement disorder? *Journal of Anxiety Disorders, 25*(8), 1085–1086.

Schiavone, F. L. & Links, P. S. (2013). Common elements for the psychotherapeutic management of patients with self injurious behavior. *Child Abuse and Neglect, 37*(2–3), 133–138.

Slikboer, R., Reser, M. P., Nedeljkovic, M., Castle, D. J., & Rossell, S. L. (2017). Systematic review of published primary studies of neuropsychology and neuroimaging in trichotillomania. *Journal of the International Neuropsychological Society, 24*(2), 1–18.

Snorrason, I., Belleau, E. L., & Woods, D. W. (2012). How related are hair pulling disorder (trichotillomania) and skin picking disorder? A review of evidence for comorbidity, similarities and shared etiology. *Clinical Psychology Review, 32*(7), 618–629.

Snorrason, I., Olafsson, R. P., Houghton, D. C., Woods, D. W., & Lee, H. J. (2015). "Wanting" and "liking" skin picking: A validation of the Skin Picking Reward Scale. *Journal of Behavioral Addictions, 4*(4), 250–262.

Snorrason, I., Ricketts, E. J., Flessner, C. A., Franklin, M. E., Stein, D. J., & Woods, D. W. (2012). Skin picking disorder is associated with other body-focused repetitive behaviors: Findings from an Internet study. *Annals of Clinical Psychiatry, 24*(4), 292–299.

Snorrason, I., Smari, J., & Olafsson, R. P. (2010). Emotion regulation in pathological skin picking: Findings from a non-treatment seeking sample. *Journal of Behavior Therapy and Experimental Psychiatry, 41*(3), 238–245.

Snorrason, I., Stein, D. J., & Woods, D. W. (2013). Classification of excoriation (skin picking) disorder: Current status and future directions. *Acta Psychiatrica Scandinavica, 128*(5), 406–407.

Stein, D. J. (2000). Neurobiology of the obsessive-compulsive spectrum disorders. *Biological Psychiatry, 47*(4), 296–304.

Stein, D. J. (2014). An integrative approach to psychiatric diagnosis and research. *World Psychiatry, 13*(1), 51–53.

Stein, D. J., Bouwer, C., & Niehaus, D. J. (1997). Stereotypic movement disorder. *Journal of Clinical Psychiatry, 58*(4), 177–178.

Stein, D. J., Chamberlain, S. R., & Fineberg, N. (2006). An A-B-C model of habit disorders: Hair-pulling, skin-picking, and other stereotypic conditions. *CNS Spectrums, 11*(11), 824–827.

Stein, D. & Christenson, G. (1998). Stereotypic movement disorder: A neglected problem. *Psychiatric Annals, 28*(6), 304.

Stein, D. J., Christenson, G. A., & Hollander, E. (1999). *Trichotillomania*. Washington, DC: American Psychiatric Press.

Stein, D. J., Flessner, C. A., Franklin, M., Keuthen, N. J., Lochner, C., & Woods, D. W. (2008). Is trichotillomania a stereotypic movement disorder? An analysis of body-focused repetitive behaviors in people with hair-pulling. *Annals of Clinical Psychiatry, 20*(4), 194–198.

Stein, D. J., Fontenelle, L. F., & Reed, G. M. (2014). Obsessive-compulsive and related disorders in *ICD-11*. *Revista Brasileira de Psiquiatria, 36*(1), 1–2.

Stein, D. J., Garner, J. P., Keuthen, N. J., Franklin, M. E., Walkup, J. T., & Woods, D. W. (2007). Trichotillomania, stereotypic movement disorder, and related disorders. *Current Psychiatry Reports, 9*(4), 301–302.

Stein, D. J., Grant, J. E., Franklin, M. E., Keuthen, N., Lochner, C., Singer, H. S., & Woods, D. W. (2010). Trichotillomania (hair pulling disorder), skin picking disorder, and stereotypic movement disorder: Toward *DSM-V*. *Depression and Anxiety, 27*(6), 611–626.

Stein, D. J. & Hollander, E. (1992). Dermatology and conditions related to obsessive-compulsive disorder. *Journal of the American Academy of Dermatology*, *26*(2), 237–242.

Stein, D. J., Kogan, C. S., Atmaca, M., Fineberg, N. A., Fontenelle, L. F., Grant, J. E., . . . Reed, G. M. (2016). The classification of Obsessive-Compulsive and Related Disorders in the *ICD-11*. *Journal of Affective Disorders*, *190*, 663–674.

Stein, D. J., Mullen, L., Islam, M. N., Cohen, L., DeCaria, C. M., & Hollander, E. (1995). Compulsive and impulsive symptomatology in trichotillomania. *Psychopathology*, *28*(4), 208–213.

Stein, D. J. & Phillips, K. A. (2013). Patient advocacy and DSM-5. *BMC Medicine*, *11*, 133.

Stein, D. J., Phillips, K. A., Bolton, D., Fulford, K. W., Sadler, J. Z., & Kendler, K. S. (2010). What is a mental/psychiatric disorder? From *DSM-IV* to *DSM-V*. *Psychological Medicine*, *40*(11), 1759–1765.

Stein, D. J. & Woods, D. W. (2014). Stereotyped movement disorder in *ICD-11*. *Revista Brasileira de Psiquiatria*, *36*(1), 65–68.

Stewart, S. E., Yu, D., Scharf, J. M., Neale, B. M., Fagerness, J. A., Mathews, C. A., . . . Pauls, D. L. (2013). Genome-wide association study of obsessive-compulsive disorder. *Molecular Psychiatry*, *18*(7), 788–798.

Swedo, S. E., Leonard, H. L., Rapoport, J. L., Lenane, M. C., Goldberger, E. L., & Cheslow, D. L. (1989). A double-blind comparison of clomipramine and desipramine in the treatment of trichotillomania (hair pulling). *New England Journal of Medicine*, *321*(8), 497–501.

Thierry, A. M., Tassin, J. P., Blanc, G., & J. Glowinski (1976). Selective activation of mesocortical DA system by stress. *Nature*, *263*(5574), 242–244.

Tucker, B. T., Woods, D. W., Flessner, C. A., Franklin, S. A., & Franklin, M. E. (2011). The Skin Picking Impact Project: Phenomenology, interference, and treatment utilization of pathological skin picking in a population-based sample. *Journal of Anxiety Disorders*, *25*(1), 88–95.

van Praag, H. M., Asnis, G. M., Kahn, R. S., Brown, S. L., Korn, M., Friedman, J. M., & Wetzler, S. (1990). Nosological tunnel vision in biological psychiatry: A plea for a functional psychopathology. *Annals of the New York Academy of Sciences*, *600*, 501–510.

Walther, M. R., Flessner, C. A., Conelea, C. A., & Woods, D. W. (2009). The Milwaukee Inventory for the Dimensions of Adult Skin Picking (MIDAS): Initial development and psychometric properties. *Journal of Behavior Therapy and Experimental Psychiatry*, *40*, 127–135.

Woods, D. W., Flessner, C. A., Franklin, M. E., Keuthen, N. J., Goodwin, R. D., Stein, D. J., & Walther, M. R. (2006). The Trichotillomania Impact Project (TIP): Exploring phenomenology, functional impairment, and treatment utilization. *Journal of Clinical Psychiatry*, *67*(12), 1877–1888.

Etiology and Phenomenology of Specific Trauma- and Stressor-Related Disorders

25 Acute Stress Disorder

Joshua C. Morganstein, Suzanne Yang,
Gary H. Wynn, David M. Benedek,
and Robert J. Ursano

Acute stress disorder (ASD) as defined by the *Diagnostic and Statistical Manual of Mental Disorders*, fifth edition (*DSM-5*) is a mental condition that can develop shortly after exposure to a traumatic event.

ASD shares many features with posttraumatic stress disorder (PTSD) (see Chapter 26, this volume), but most notably differs in timing with symptoms during the 3–30-day window after exposure. The section of this chapter on *Phenomenology* describes the range of psychological and behavioral responses to traumatic events. The symptoms are organized into categories including intrusion, negative mood, dissociation, avoidance, and arousal. Many of these symptoms are identical to those in the criteria for PTSD. Other mental disorders (e.g., depression, substance abuse), stress reactions, and distress-related behavioral changes not meeting criteria for a diagnosable disorder can occur in the timeframe for ASD. Therefore, the differential diagnosis, comorbidities, and other clinical features associated with ASD are also reviewed.

The section of this chapter on *Etiology* begins with a review of findings in ASD epidemiological studies with a focus on the idea that many individuals exposed to trauma do not develop ASD and followed by describing groups that may be at greater risk for ASD. The section then discusses the neurobiology of responses by reviewing the evolving knowledge base on underlying mechanisms. Abnormalities in brain functions associated with the development of ASD or PTSD as well as protective factors are described. The value of examining symptoms and biological functioning using dimensional constructs is then explored through conceptual frameworks such as the Research Domain Criteria (RDoC) and emerging psychobiological evidence. ASD, as a time-limited constellation of symptoms with implications for longer-term outcomes, is particularly suited to a dimensional approach, as the clinical presentation may change over the post-trauma period from weeks to months. Certain symptoms or sets of symptoms may have more substantial impact on functioning during this time than the categorically defined syndrome. Changes in diagnostic criteria introduced in the *DSM-5* reflect the notion that early on following trauma exposure, symptoms and clinical presentation may be in flux, impacting certain brain functions and not others, prior to development of a stable clinical syndrome such as PTSD. The ability to intervene with individualized treatments in acute stress may be enhanced by examining selected aspects of ASD that are personalized and particularly impactful for specific individuals or subgroups.

Clinical Phenomenology

Definitions of Traumatic Events

Scholars in medicine, psychology, and other fields liberally use the terms *trauma* and *traumatized* to describe a broad range of life events including injuries, distressing events, extreme stressors, and adversity. Moreover, there is a tendency to blur the boundary between an event and reactions to the event. From a diagnostic and research perspective, it is useful to define a number of terms.

Trauma, derived from the Greek word meaning "wound," in its most simple definition is a physical or mental injury. Diagnostic criteria for ASD, as well as PTSD, describe *traumatic events* as "[e]xposure to actual or threatened death, serious injury or sexual violence" through direct experience, witnessing, learning that a close friend or family member experienced a violent or accidental event, or repeated or extreme exposure to aversive details (American Psychiatric Association, 2013). *Traumatic stress* refers to the broad continuum of responses seen after a traumatic event including distress reactions, health risk behaviors, and a number of psychiatric disorders. *Acute stress* refers to the responses in the immediate aftermath of a traumatic event.

Four types of trauma exposure are included in the criteria according to *DSM-5*. For ASD as well as PTSD, these include (i) direct experience, (ii) witnessing the trauma occur to others, (iii) learning that the trauma occurred to a close family member or friend, or (iv) repeated or extreme aversive exposure to the details of the traumatic event. Traumatic events can include motor vehicle and other accidents, sexual or physical assault, natural disasters, or mass violence, as well as serious medical events, such as acute myocardial infarction or severely complicated childbirth. These definitions of trauma exposure in *DSM-5* represent a substantial change in the diagnostic criteria compared to those in *DSM-IV-TR*, which required "an event or events that involved actual or threatened death or serious injury, or a threat to the physical integrity of self or others" (American Psychiatric Association, 2000). Additionally, in *DSM-5*, ASD, like PTSD, no longer requires an individual respond to an event with intense fear, helplessness, or horror as was required in *DSM-IV-TR* (American Psychiatric Association, 2000).

Oftentimes, the circumstances surrounding a traumatic event involve other types of adversities and stressors, such as property damage, financial stress, and disruption of work, social relationships, and access to services. These may themselves result in psychological disequilibrium both distinct from and related to responses directly tied to a traumatic event. Thus, assessment of the precise relationship between presenting symptoms and the traumatic event, as distinguished from other contextual stressors, is crucial to establishing or ruling out a diagnosis of ASD.

Individual Reactions to Traumatic Events

Literature on the psychological impact of traumatic events comes largely from studies of war, accidents, and disaster events. Traumatic events, including combat-related traumatic exposures, vary in circumstances and characteristics. Characteristics such as the accidental versus intentional nature of injuries may influence the psychological response and rates of ASD and PTSD (J. Y. Stein, Wilmot, & Solomon, 2016).

Overall, most individuals exposed to traumatic events respond with little to no adverse psychological effects. These individuals promptly and effectively resume their social and occupational activities (a phenomenon of resilience). Some may even experience an increased sense of competence, self-efficacy, and a belief in their abilities to manage future stressors, often termed *posttraumatic growth*. Some individuals, however, will experience a range of adverse psychological and behavioral effects including distress reactions, health risk behaviors, and psychiatric disorders (see Figure 25.1). Overall these responses can be viewed as a continuum of responses from normal to pathological.

Specific characteristics or circumstances of traumatic events may amplify or mitigate traumatic stress responses. Duration and intensity of exposure are the most consistent factors predicting adverse outcomes in populations exposed to traumatic events. When compared to natural disasters, traumatic events involving intentional human action such as sexual assault tend to result in the most severe psychological and behavioral effects as well as functional impairment (Norris et al., 2002). Events characterized by significant uncertainty as to the extent of immediate risk and lasting effects of exposure, such as infectious disease outbreaks and nuclear

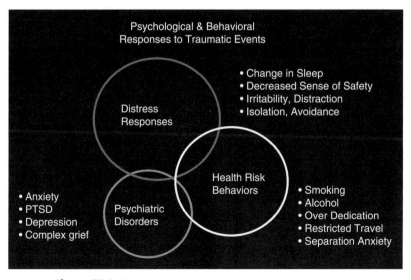

Figure 25.1 *Psychological and behavioral responses to traumatic events*

accidents, tend to be associated with more severe psychological impact and high rates of somatic symptoms. Much research over decades has tried to distinguish the clinical sequelae of different types of traumatic events (Benjet et al., 2016; J. Y. Stein et al., 2016).

Immediately following a traumatic event, distress reactions often predominate. Individuals may feel a sense of fear, vulnerability, and anger. Demoralization and a loss of hope may also occur. Individuals may experience insomnia, irritability, and feelings of distractibility (Rundell & Ursano, 1996). Some individuals will focus on physical symptoms in lieu of psychological distress and present to health care settings for general medical care. Somatic symptoms such as headache, dizziness, nausea, fatigue, and weakness are common in the aftermath of a traumatic event, even in the absence of an identifiable physical disorder (Ford, 1997). Traumatic events are also often associated with physical injury and pain, such as following sexual assault (McLean et al., 2012). Many individuals seeking care will present to primary care providers or emergency settings. An awareness of distress reactions as a frequent consequence of traumatic events is important for primary care and emergency providers to consider as part of the differential diagnosis of these symptoms.

Health-risky behaviors are also known to increase following traumatic events. Increased consumption of alcohol, caffeine, or tobacco is a common coping mechanism and may represent a form of self-medication for symptoms related to psychological distress (Tucker, Pfefferbaum, Nitiema, Wendling, & Brown, 2016). Reduced involvement in social activities and isolation may result in decreased utilization of support networks (Rubin, Brewin, Greenberg, Simpson, & Wessely, 2005). Individuals with trauma exposure are at increased risk for suicidal ideation and behavior, particularly in association with sexual and interpersonal violence (D. J. Stein et al., 2010) or with onset of an acute mental disorder (Mahendraraj, Durgan, & Chamberlain, 2016). In a cohort study of individuals seen in a psychiatric treatment setting, individuals with an ICD code for acute stress reaction (ASR) (see later in this chapter) had an elevated rate of all-cause mortality and suicide over a 16-year period (Gradus et al., 2010, 2015). Following traumatic events, interpersonal violence may increase as the distress of family and community members escalates (Harville, Taylor, Tesfai, Xu, & Buekens, 2011).

In some individuals, symptoms may persist and progress to psychiatric disorders following the exposure. The most widely studied of these disorders is PTSD (Ursano et al., 2010). ASD has received substantially less scientific inquiry. Many studies suggest that approximately 10% of those exposed to a traumatic event will develop ASD. However, many more individuals will experience milder or fewer symptoms, which can nevertheless persist and impair functioning over time (Goldmann & Galea, 2014). Although less is known regarding the evolution of ASD symptoms in relation to trauma type, studies of the course of PTSD have shown that symptomatology varies. Those who experience trauma as the result of intentional acts typically display increasing symptoms over time (see Figure 25.2).

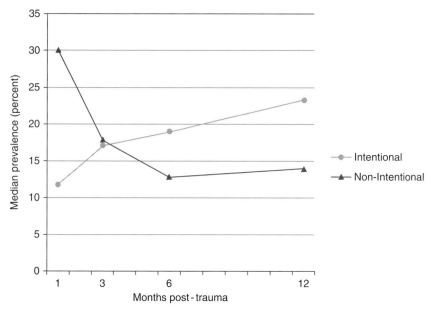

Figure 25.2 *Prevalence of PTSD over time in intentional versus non-intentional trauma. NOTE: Median prevalence of PTSD in* DSM-5 *experiencing categories of intentional and non-intentional trauma (N = 14 and 21 studies, respectively) (Santiago et al., 2013)*

Core Clinical Features

Acute Stress Reaction in the International Classification of Diseases (ICD)

The *International Classification of Diseases* (*ICD*), currently in its 10th version, is established by the World Health Organization for use in reporting medical conditions in a variety of international settings. A code for "acute stress reaction" was present since 1975 in *ICD-9* and is currently described in *ICD-10* as follows:

> A transient disorder that develops in an individual without any other apparent mental disorder in response to exceptional physical and mental stress and that usually subsides within hours or days. Individual vulnerability and coping capacity play a role in the occurrence and severity of acute stress reactions. The symptoms show a typically mixed and changing picture and include an initial state of "daze" with some constriction of the field of consciousness and narrowing of attention, inability to comprehend stimuli, and disorientation. This state may be followed either by further withdrawal from the surrounding situation (to the extent of a dissociative stupor), or by agitation and over-activity (flight reaction or fugue). Autonomic signs of panic anxiety (tachycardia, sweating, flushing) are commonly present. The symptoms usually appear within minutes of the impact of the stressful stimulus or event, and disappear within two to three days (often within hours). Partial or complete amnesia for the episode may be present. If the symptoms persist, a change in diagnosis should be considered.

Isserlin (2008) remarks that ASR was intended as a descriptor for the individual's current state, whereas ASD was designed for use in predicting prognosis. ASD did not effectively detect future PTSD cases, however, as many individuals who developed PTSD did not initially meet criteria for ASD. ASR, on the other hand, was present in nearly all future PTSD cases. Thus, although short-lived by definition, ASR often did not resolve.

The *ICD-11* revision proposes a new definition that will categorize ASR as a normative condition rather than as a disorder, though it could still be a valid focus of treatment (Maercker et al., 2013). The use of *DSM-5* ASD in the United States may in part be driven by the need for a diagnosis in US medical care in order to obtain reimbursement for treatment (Maercker et al., 2013). Notably, the *ICD* definition of PTSD allows for diagnosis within the first month, and therefore ASD would overlap with PTSD if it were to be included in the *ICD-11*. PTSD, in the draft *ICD-11*, is included in "Disorders specifically associated with stress," the symptoms of which "must persist for at least several weeks," while ASR is categorized separately among "Factors associated with harmful or traumatic events."

The proposed definition of ASR in *ICD-11* thus emphasizes the broad nature of initial symptoms and the expected normative nature of the reaction:

> Acute stress reaction refers to the development of transient emotional, somatic, cognitive, or behavioural symptoms as a result of exposure to an event or situation (either short- or long-lasting) of an extremely threatening or horrific nature (e.g., natural or human-made disasters, combat, serious accidents, sexual violence, assault). Symptoms may include autonomic signs of anxiety (e.g., tachycardia, sweating, flushing), being in a daze, confusion, sadness, anxiety, anger, despair, overactivity, inactivity, social withdrawal, or stupor. The response to the stressor is considered to be normal given the severity of the stressor, and usually begins to subside within a few days after the event or following removal from the threatening situation. (World Health Organization, 2017)

This proposed definition contrasts with the *DSM-5* definition of ASD, which adheres to a structured, categorical framework with specified criteria.

DSM-5 Symptom Criteria for ASD

During the first 48–72 hours after a traumatic event, some individuals may be very anxious, depressed, agitated, or angry. Others may appear minimally affected, or emotionally flat as a result of injury, personal loss, pain, or dissociative phenomena (Shalev, 2002). In *DSM-5*, ASD symptoms must have persisted for at least three days following a traumatic event. These symptoms can persist up to 30 days under the ASD criteria, but beyond 30 days would necessitate another diagnosis such as PTSD.

Table 25.1 compares the *DSM-IV* and *DSM-5* criteria for ASD. The *DSM-5* identifies five categories by which ASD symptoms are clustered, including: (1) intrusion symptoms (such as recurrent, involuntary, and distressing memories,

Table 25.1 *Comparison of DSM-IV and DSM-5 criteria for acute stress disorder*

DSM-IV-TR diagnostic criteria for acute stress disorder (*DSM-IV-TR* code 308.3)	*DSM-5* diagnostic criteria for acute stress disorder (*DSM-5* code 308.3)

A. The person has been exposed to a traumatic event in which both of the following were present:
  1. The person experienced, witnessed, or was confronted with an event or events that involved actual or threatened death or serious injury, or a threat to the physical integrity of self or others.
  2. The person's response involved intense fear, helplessness, or horror.
 	
B. Either while experiencing or after experiencing the distressing event, the individual has three (or more) of the following dissociative symptoms:
  1. a subjective sense of numbing, detachment, or absence of emotional responsiveness
  2. a reduction in awareness of his or her surroundings (e.g., "being in a daze")
  3. derealization
  4. depersonalization
  5. dissociative amnesia (i.e., inability to recall an important aspect of the trauma).
 	
C. The traumatic event is persistently reexperienced in at least one of the following ways: recurrent images, thoughts, dreams, illusions, flashback episodes, or a sense of reliving the experience; or distress on exposure to reminders of the traumatic event.
	A. Exposure to actual or threatened death, serious injury, or sexual violence in one (or more) of the following ways:
	  1. Directly experiencing the traumatic event(s).
	  2. Witnessing, in person, the event(s) as it occurred to others.
	  3. Learning that the traumatic event(s) occurred to a close family member or close friend. Note: In cases of actual or threatened death of a family member or friend, the event(s) must have been violent or accidental.
	  4. Experiencing repeated or extreme exposure to aversive details of the traumatic event(s) (e.g., first responders collecting human remains; police officers repeatedly exposed to details of child abuse).
	  Note: Criterion A4 does not apply to exposure through electronic media, television, movies, or pictures, unless this exposure is work related.
	
	B. Presence of nine (or more) of the following symptoms from any of the five categories of intrusion, negative mood, dissociation, avoidance, and arousal, beginning or worsening after the traumatic event(s) occurred:
	  Intrusion Symptoms
	  1. Recurrent, involuntary, and intrusive distressing memories of the traumatic event(s). Note: In children, repetitive play may occur in which themes or aspects of the traumatic event(s) are expressed.

2. Recurrent distressing dreams in which the content and/or effect of the dream are related to the event(s). Note: In children, there may be frightening dreams without recognizable content.

3. Dissociative reactions (e.g., flashbacks) in which the individual feels or acts as if the traumatic event(s) were recurring. (Such reactions may occur on a continuum, with the most extreme expression being a complete loss of awareness of present surroundings.) Note: In children, trauma-specific reenactment may occur in play.

4. Intense or prolonged psychological distress or marked physiological reactions in response to internal or external cues that symbolize or resemble an aspect of the traumatic event(s).
   Negative Mood

5. Persistent inability to experience positive emotions (e.g., inability to experience happiness, satisfaction, or loving feelings).
   Dissociative Symptoms

6. An altered sense of the reality of one's surroundings or oneself (e.g., seeing oneself from another person's perspective, being in a daze, time slowing).

7. Inability to remember an important aspect of the traumatic event(s) (typically due to dissociative amnesia and not to other factors such as head injury, alcohol, or drugs).
   Avoidance Symptoms

8. Efforts to avoid distressing memories, thoughts, or feelings about or closely associated with the traumatic event(s).

9. Efforts to avoid external reminders (people, places, conversations, activities, objects, situations) that arouse distressing memories, thoughts, or feelings about or closely associated with the traumatic event(s).
   Arousal Symptoms

D. Marked avoidance of stimuli that arouse recollections of the trauma (e.g., thoughts, feelings, conversations, activities, places, people).

E. Marked symptoms of anxiety or increased arousal (e.g., difficulty sleeping, irritability, poor concentration, hypervigilance, exaggerated startle response, motor restlessness).

F. The disturbance causes clinically significant distress or impairment in social, occupational, or other important areas of functioning or impairs the individual's ability to pursue some necessary task such as obtaining necessary assistance or mobilizing personal resources by telling family members about the traumatic experience.

G. The disturbance lasts for a minimum of two days and a maximum of four weeks and occurs within four weeks of the traumatic event.

H. The disturbance is not due to the direct physiological effects of a substance (e.g., a drug of abuse, a medication) or a general medical condition, is not better accounted for by Brief Psychotic Disorder, and is not merely an exacerbation of a preexisting Axis I or Axis II disorder.

10. Sleep disturbance (e.g., difficulty falling or staying asleep, restless sleep).
11. Irritable behavior and angry outbursts (with little or no provocation), typically expressed as verbal or physical aggression toward people or objects.
12. Hypervigilance.
13. Problems with concentration.
14. Exaggerated startle response.

C. Duration of the disturbance (symptoms in Criterion B) is three days to one month after trauma exposure.
   Note: Symptoms typically begin immediately after the trauma, but persistence for at least three days and up to a month is needed to meet disorder criteria.

D. The disturbance causes clinically significant distress or impairment in social, occupational, or other important areas of functioning.

E. The disturbance is not attributable to the physiological effects of a substance (e.g., medication or alcohol) or another medical condition (e.g., mild traumatic brain injury) and is not better explained by brief psychotic disorder.

recurrent distressing dreams, dissociative reactions, or distress or reactivity to trauma cues); (2) negative mood (persistent inability to experience positive emotions); (3) dissociative symptoms (altered sense of reality of surroundings or self, inability to remember important aspects of the event); (4) avoidance symptoms (such as avoidance of distressing memories, thoughts, or feelings about the trauma, or avoidance of external reminders of the trauma); (5) arousal symptoms (such as irritability, hypervigilance, exaggerated startle, problems with concentration, or sleep disturbance).

Early clinical evidence suggested that ASD was a good predictor of the development of PTSD. However, the failure of more rigorous research to demonstrate this predictive relationship was part of the impetus for reformulating the diagnosis in *DSM-5*. A meta-analysis of the relationship between *DSM-IV* ASD and PTSD concluded that while the majority of individuals with a diagnosis of ASD subsequently develop PTSD or another psychiatric disorder, most people who eventually experience a psychiatric disorder did not display ASD (Bryant et al., 2015).

Research has thus clarified the heterogeneity of acute stress responses. A perceived overemphasis on dissociation and on the predictive value of *DSM-IV* ASD led to significant changes in *DSM-5* criteria (Bryant, 2011). The intended emphasis is now on utility of the diagnosis for clinical identification of severity of the acute stress response rather than on prognosis or prediction. The *DSM-5* definition of ASD now requires 9 out of 14 possible symptoms without regard to particular symptom clusters. Importantly, the presence of dissociation is no longer required for the diagnosis. Although a unidimensional model may not optimally represent the latent structure of ASD symptoms (Armour & Elklit, 2013), removal of the clusters allows for broader detection of clinically significant syndromes that warrant attention. In a recent study, network analysis showed that associations within the reexperiencing symptom cluster and among symptom clusters were strengthened over time (Bryant et al., 2017), suggesting that early presentations of post-traumatic symptoms are malleable and in flux.

The emphasis on dissociation in *DSM-IV* ASD proved not to be an effective indicator of future development of PTSD. Nevertheless, other symptoms or clusters of symptoms may be useful for prognosis and for targeting treatments to prevent the further development of psychiatric disorders following trauma exposure. A number of studies have examined ways to parse the ASD syndrome into subtypes. Studies have varied as to whether a three-factor or four-factor model best describes the clusters of ASD (Armour & Elklit, 2013; Hansen, Lasgaard, & Elklit, 2013). Efforts to examine whether there is a dissociative subtype of ASD resulted in the finding of a possible intrusion subtype, associated with peri-traumatic panic symptoms and somatization at one week after the trauma exposure (Armour & Hansen, 2015). Features present in ASD may correspond to subgroups of PTSD; for instance, negative cognitions of self and neuroticism (along with highly symptomatic ASD) were predictive of highly symptomatic PTSD (Hansen, Hyland, & Armour, 2016).

Although the current *DSM-5* criteria are based on the number of symptoms without clustering, studies have suggested that subgroups divided by the extent of arousal symptoms may be more effective in predicting the later onset of PTSD (Shevlin, Hyland, & Elklit, 2014). More refined approaches using dimensional constructs and intermediate phenotypes may be salient to the long-term prediction of clinically significant impairment.

Other Posttraumatic Syndromes

The differential diagnosis of symptoms associated with ASD encompasses a broad set of diagnoses, ranging from physical and psychiatric disorders to normative, expected responses to extremely stressful events. Table 25.2 highlights disorders to consider during the first 30 days following trauma. People exposed to disasters, for instance, are at increased risk for depression (Miguel-Tobal et al., 2006), generalized anxiety disorder, panic disorder, increased substance use (North et al., 1999), and other conditions. Individuals with prior trauma, either in childhood or adulthood, may be more susceptible to react to new traumatic stressors.

For a single discrete traumatic event, ASD can be readily distinguished from PTSD based on the time interval since the event. For less discrete (process traumas) or recurring traumas as might be experienced in cases of child abuse, domestic violence, multiple combat exposures, or a series of natural disasters (e.g., during hurricane season in certain locations), the distinction between ASD and PTSD may be less clear. No convention or consensus exists regarding the diagnosis of symptom episodes lasting less than one month but recurring in the course of trauma exposures repeated over months to years. However, such symptom presentations may be better conceptualized for the purposes of treatment as PTSD with acute exacerbations rather than recurrent ASD.

Major Depressive Disorder

A substantial proportion of trauma-exposed individuals develop symptoms consistent with major depressive disorder (MDD) (Tang, Liu, Liu, Xue, & Zhang, 2014). Mood disorders may occur independently from trauma- and stressor-related disorders, but they are also an established risk factor for the development of PTSD in newly exposed individuals (Bromet, Sonnega, & Kessler, 1998). In a study of 9/11 World Trade Center disaster workers, 15% had probable ASD, 26% had probable depression, and 10% had both (Biggs et al., 2010). Symptoms of depression such as insomnia, poor concentration, and decreased interest in formerly enjoyable activities are also present in diagnostic criteria for ASD. The restricted affect that accompanies emotional numbing in ASD may resemble the diminished affect of depression. Due to high rates of comorbid depression in individuals with ASD, the relationship of depressive symptoms and trauma exposure needs to be better understood. The *DSM-5* permits the diagnosis of both MDD and ASD when full symptom criteria for both

Table 25.2 *Differential diagnosis in the first month following exposure to a traumatic event*

Diagnosis	Symptomatic criteria	Functional criteria	Time course	Acute care considerations
Acute stress disorder (ASD)	A. Exposure to actual or threatened death, serious injury, or sexual violence B. Presence of nine or more symptoms from any of the five categories of intrusion, negative mood, dissociation, avoidance, and arousal	Symptoms are associated with clinically significant distress or impairments in social, occupational, or other important areas of functioning.	Duration of the disturbance is three days to one month.	Not all injured patients with immediate distress will experience symptoms meeting full criteria.
Major depressive episode	Five or more of the following symptoms: depressed mood, diminished interest in pleasurable activities, weight loss or gain, insomnia or hypersomnia, agitation or retardation, fatigue or energy loss, feelings of worthlessness, poor concentration, and suicidal ideation	Symptoms cause clinically significant distress or impairment in social, occupational, or other important areas of functioning.	Symptoms must be present for two weeks.	Major depressive episode can be diagnosed in conjunction with ASD. Injured trauma survivors frequently present with multiple symptoms of a depressive episode early on (i.e., before two weeks after the traumatic injury).

Adjustment disorder	A. Development of emotional or behavioral symptoms in response to an identifiable stressor. Symptoms can include depression, anxiety, conduct disturbance, or other emotional disturbance. B. The symptoms or behaviors are clinically significant as evidenced by marked distress.	Emotional or behavioral symptoms are associated with marked impairment in social, occupational, or other important areas of functioning or are out of proportion to the severity of the stressor.	Onset occurs within three months of the stressor(s). Symptoms persist for no longer than six months after the stressor or its consequences have ended.	*DSM-5* suggests that the adjustment disorder diagnosis be used for patients who develop a symptom pattern that is not entirely consistent with the criteria for ASD. Nonspecific symptomatic requirements make adjustment disorder a useful diagnosis for the many patients who experience posttraumatic behavioral and emotional disturbances that include symptoms that do not fit into other diagnostic rubrics (e.g., patients who present with marked somatic symptom amplification) or do not meet the diagnostic thresholds for ASD.
Brief Psychotic Disorder	(A) Presence of one (or more) of the following symptoms. At least one of these must be (1), (2), or (3):	After one month, eventual full return to premorbid level of functioning	Duration of an episode of the disturbance is at least one day but less than one month.	*DSM-5* specifies that "[t]he disturbance is not better explained by major depressive or bipolar disorder with psychotic features or another

(1) Delusions.
(2) Hallucinations.
(3) Disorganized   speech (e.g., frequent derailment or incoherence).
(4) Grossly   disorganized or catatonic behavior.
    Note: Do not include a symptom if it is a culturally sanctioned response.

psychotic disorder such as schizophrenia or catatonia, and is not attributable to the physiological effects of a substance (e.g., a drug of abuse, a medication) or another medical condition." Specifiers include "with marked stressor(s)": "If symptoms occur in response to events that, singly or together, would be markedly stressful to almost anyone in similar circumstances in the individual's culture." The latter syndrome has been described as a "brief reactive psychosis."

are present. Given the two-week duration of symptoms required for a diagnosis of MDD, the onset of the disorder may occur within the same time frame as ASD.

Adjustment Disorder

In *DSM-5*, adjustment disorder is included among the trauma- and stressor-related disorders. As noted earlier, individuals exposed to events that meet trauma exposure criteria for ASD often experience transient symptoms that differ from a syndromal diagnosis of ASD in duration, level of distress, or functional impairment associated with the symptoms (O'Donnell et al., 2016). To the extent that symptoms persist, result in dysfunction or distress, and yet do not meet full criteria for ASD, a diagnosis of adjustment disorder may be assigned to describe the clinical syndrome arising from trauma exposure and requiring intervention.

Psychotic and Dissociative Disorders

Occasionally, individuals respond to traumatic events with symptoms that involve a loss of reality testing or dissociation. The *DSM-5* allows for a diagnosis of brief psychotic disorder with the specifier "with marked stressor(s)" to indicate that symptoms such as delusions, hallucinations, and disorganized speech occur for one day to one month "in response to events that, singly or together, would be markedly stressful to almost anyone in similar circumstances in the individual's culture." This specifier is broad but able to cover traumatic events. In addition, derealization, depersonalization, and other dissociative symptoms that do not meet criteria for ASD may occur in the initial days and weeks following the traumatic event.

Other Clinical Considerations

Features of personality disorders and symptoms associated with ASD (e.g., impulsivity, irritability, difficulty with affect modulation, dissociative phenomena, and comorbid substance abuse) may overlap. Therefore, an ASD diagnosis may be "masked" by predominant symptoms of a personality disorder. A thorough clinical evaluation to clarify the onset and duration of symptoms, and whether the individual recently experienced a traumatic stressor will typically differentiate ASD from a personality disorder. Due to the time course, confusion between chronic PTSD symptoms and personality disorder is more common. A history of childhood trauma in adults with personality disorders is common and also predisposes for adult PTSD. Regardless, personality disorders should be considered in the diagnosis of symptomatic persons in the aftermath of trauma as comorbid illness that may influence the individual's response to treatment and other interventions.

A number of additional clinically relevant issues may be associated with ASD. These include somatic complaints, shame, impaired modulation of affect, survivor guilt, difficulties in interpersonal relationships, changes in behavior, or concern regarding moral themes arising from the event. Given the limited time frame of

ASD, the extent of comorbidity with major psychiatric disorders has not been well characterized. ASD often occurs in contexts that may involve severe physical injury (vehicular accidents, violent crime). Somatic complaints without clear etiology are common phenomena among persons with histories of traumatic exposure, including those with ASD or PTSD (Salmon & Calderbank, 1996). However, persistent somatic concerns in the absence of identifiable pathology may also suggest the presence of a somatoform disorder. Finally, trauma-exposed populations may engage in altered patterns of substance use (alcohol, tobacco, or illicit substances) (Ulibarri, Ulloa, & Salazar, 2015; Vlahov et al., 2002) with or without comorbid ASD (Biggs et al., 2010).

Grief is a common phenomenon following traumatic events. Many investigators and clinicians will consider such a diagnosis in the aftermath of trauma, based on persistent, intense grief, intrusive recollections or images of the death, preoccupation with the loss, and avoidance of reminders. The *DSM-5* does not currently recognize a "grief" disorder, due largely to lack of consensus and ongoing research into criteria that most effectively identify a grief-related disorder. However, a recent study found that criteria for *complicated grief*, more so than criteria for *prolonged grief disorder* or *persistent complex bereavement disorder*, accurately identified symptoms of grief that were clinically impairing (Cozza et al., 2016). While the proposed symptoms overlap with those of ASD, PTSD, and MDD, persons may experience grief symptoms without meeting full criteria for any one of these disorders. If preoccupation with the suddenness, violence, or catastrophic aspects of the loss interferes with the normal bereavement process, the syndrome may represent a different (and pathological) bereavement process. "Traumatic grief" is another proposed diagnostic entity distinguished from complicated grief, by additional distress related to cognitive reenactment of the death or loss, terror, and avoidance of reminders (Prigerson et al., 1999). ASD is unlikely to be confused with complicated or traumatic grief given that the former is time-limited and the latter require symptoms to be present over an extended period of time. However, bereavement and grief-related syndromes should be considered as a potential focus of treatment in persons who have experienced a traumatic loss.

As previously discussed, most individuals who experience traumatic events will demonstrate resilience, i.e., limited or no adverse psychological effects, maintaining their prior level of functioning (deRoon-Cassini, Mancini, Rusch, & Bonanno, 2010). In some instances, resilience may be difficult to distinguish from avoidance of seeking help. Limited seeking of mental health care has been observed in the aftermath of trauma, with notable disparities in service utilization based on sex, race, education, and socioeconomic status.

Thus, additional clinical features or associated conditions not accounted for in the formal diagnostic criteria may contribute greatly to the total burden of social and occupational dysfunction or impairment resulting from these disorders.

Etiology

The presence of specific symptoms or associated clinical features in a given individual may inform overall prognosis. Research that aligns these symptoms/features with dimensional constructs and underlying biology will help refine these predictors of prognosis. At the very least, such an approach may help to target future interventions for specific symptoms causing dysfunction in a given patient. In what follows, we explore the prospect of using dimensional approaches by examining the heterogeneity of reactions to trauma of different types, and by identifying some of the known risk factors for developing PTSD. These elements may serve as a starting point for outlining differences among individuals and for more precise targeting of symptoms that are strongly related to the individual's distress and dysfunction.

Epidemiology and Risk Factors

Multiple epidemiologic studies have revealed that traumatic exposures are very common in the general population. The National Comorbidity Survey (Kessler, Sonnega, Bromet, Hughes, & Nelson, 1995), using the *DSM-IV* definition in a nationally representative sample ($n = 5,877$), reported a lifetime history of at least one traumatic event in 60.7% of men and 51.2% of women, with many individuals (25–50%) experiencing two or more such traumas. Other community-based samples have reported similar or even greater incidence rates (43–92% of men and 37–87% of women) for at least one traumatic exposure (Norris, 1992; M. B. Stein, Walker, Hazen, & Forde, 1997). Worldwide traumatic event data from the World Mental Health Survey Consortium reported 70.4% of survey participants experienced at least one traumatic event and 30.5% experienced four or more distinct traumatic events (Benjet et al., 2016).

The most common types of trauma reported worldwide were accidents and injuries (36.3%); unexpected death of a loved one (31.4%); witnessing someone seriously injured, death, or a dead body (23.7%); being mugged (14.5%); and life-threatening automobile accidents (14.0%) (Benjet et al., 2016). In a large US sample of older adults, the most common types of lifetime trauma reported were unexpected death of a loved one (66.5%), illness or accident of a loved one (39.8%), abortion/stillbirth (35.8%), motor vehicle accident (22.6%), and personal life-threatening illness (22.3%) (Ogle, Rubin, & Siegler, 2014). Based on a systematic review, worldwide rates of female victims of non-partner sexual violence for 2010 were estimated to be 7.2% across geographical regions (range 3.3–21%) (Abrahams et al., 2014). Specific epidemiologic data regarding the percentage of individuals who report exposure as a result of deliberate terrorist attacks are lacking, but such exposure would be represented as a subset of those who reported witnessing someone seriously injured, death, or a dead body. Unrepresented in these surveys are persons whose traumatic exposures were limited to hearing repeated details of others who experienced significant trauma. Safety workers and first responders working in the immediate aftermath of critical incidents and clinicians working with trauma victims are among those for whom the diagnosis of ASD should be considered within the definitions in *DSM-5*.

The lifetime rates of ASD are unclear. As with the studies of traumatic exposure, estimates vary with the diagnostic criteria applied (e.g., *DSM-IV* versus *DSM-5*), the sample studied, the nature of the trauma exposure, and the assessment procedure used (e.g., telephone survey versus face-to-face interview) (Brewin, Andrews, & Valentine, 2000). Generally, the point prevalence of ASD after acute traumatic exposure has been estimated at 5–20% (Bryant, Creamer, O'Donnell, Silove, & McFarlane, 2012; Bryant & Harvey, 2000).

Still, the relatively low rate of ASD following trauma exposure illustrates the point that while exposure is necessary for the development of ASD, many other factors play a role. One major reason for this differentiation is that not all traumatic events are equally associated with the development of ASD or PTSD. In fact, some of the most commonly experienced traumatic events are least likely to be associated with PTSD. In the National Comorbidity Study, lifetime prevalence of being in a natural disaster or fire, and witnessing someone being badly injured or killed ranged from 14% to 36% (depending on specific event and gender) (Kessler et al., 1995). The prevalence of these exposures was greater than the prevalence of being raped (less than 1% for men and approximately 9% for women). However, the prevalence of PTSD related to rape was 46% for men and 65% for women. In another study, the rate of ASD related to rape was 69% in a mostly female sample of individuals presenting to a hospital (Armour & Elklit, 2013).

In comparison, 4% of individuals developed ASD following an urban bombing/terrorist attack (Holman, Garfin, & Silver, 2014), as did 10% among Danish bank employees who were exposed to robbery (Armour & Hansen, 2015). Among earthquake survivors randomly sampled from multiple affected regions, 15% developed ASD (Yuan et al., 2013), while only 5% among those presenting for mental health treatment following an earthquake had ASD (Roncone et al., 2013).

Nevertheless, reactions to traumatic events, even those most strongly associated with the development of ASD (such as rape), are often transient and may resolve within weeks after the event. One study of rape victims evaluated weekly for the presence of PTSD symptoms found that while 94% met full symptom (but not duration) criteria 12 days after the assault, only 64% met criteria one month after the assault. By three months that number fell to 47% (Rothbaum, Foa, Murdock, & Walsh, 1992). Longitudinal studies of New York City residents in close proximity to the 9/11 terrorist attacks demonstrated a decline in PTSD from the 7.5% initially reported to 1.7% by five months and 0.6% by six to nine months after the attacks (Galea, Boscarino, Resnick, & Vlahov, 2003; Galea, Vlahov et al., 2003). Thus, the majority of persons exposed to traumatic events who experience posttraumatic symptoms will recover without intervention.

Risk factors for developing ASD include history of a mental disorder, history of a prior trauma, childhood trauma, and female gender (American Psychiatric Association, 2013). In addition, negative affectivity (neuroticism), avoidant coping style, and disordered attachment (American Psychiatric Association, 2013; Cardeña & Carlson, 2011) have been associated with ASD. Perceptions at the time of the event or shortly thereafter are also related to risk for ASD. For instance, perceived severity or a catastrophic appraisal of the traumatic event, including exaggerated belief regarding future harm, guilt, or hopelessness, have been predictive of ASD (American Psychiatric Association, 2013). Perceived helplessness or life threat and perceived safety after the event may predict ASD symptom levels (Hansen & Elklit, 2011). ASD severity has also been associated with trait anxiety, suicide risk, and negative appraisals of the event (Suliman, Troeman, Stein, & Seedat, 2013). Symptoms that may constitute common predictors for both ASD and PTSD include peri-traumatic panic, anxiety sensitivity, and negative cognitions regarding self (Hansen, Armour, Wittmann, Elklit, & Shevlin, 2014).

Neurobiology

Stress can modify an individual's learning, emotional and cognitive processing, and memory through physiological changes involving altered perceptions and modification of responses to future events. These alterations can be adaptive in the short term when experienced under moderate and manageable increases in stress. Under severe or sustained conditions of stress, however, the detrimental impact on brain structure and function can be substantial. These conditions can induce significant changes to brain structures at both the gross and microscopic levels. These changes can result in altered synaptic transmission due to continued trauma exposure or due to sustained acute symptoms long after the traumatic situation has subsided.

Recent advances in molecular biology, psychophysiology, and neuroimaging have led to a greater understanding of the consequences of severe or sustained stress, but a great deal remains to be learned. The relationships connecting genetics, epigenetic expression, development, environmental factors, and posttraumatic neural activity leading up to the onset of ASD and PTSD are currently beyond our understanding. Scientific advances, however, have provided considerable insight into normative (adaptive) and pathological responses to extreme stressors and the processes related to the development of intrusive memories – which appear to drive the biological mechanisms and behavioral responses to such stressors in disease progression (Reiser et al., 2014). In this sense, fear memory and fear extinction have served as constructs for understanding the onset and sustainment of ASD and PTSD, though other mechanisms likely also play an important role. Fear may be modulated and modified by cortical circuits that support conscious experience such as the association cortex involved in cognitive processes (LeDoux & Pine, 2016).

Until recently, research has focused on characterizing the neurobiology of stress-related disorders according to categorical diagnoses defined in the *DSM-IV* or *DSM-5*. As the knowledge base advances, substantial heterogeneity noted in trauma-exposed populations has led to newer conceptualizations of psychopathology, which may prove effective in parsing subtypes. Although specific identification of biologically homogeneous subtypes has yet to be achieved, a review of the traumatic stress response and biological markers will help to describe the complexity of neurobiological changes in trauma- and stressor-related disorders.

Traumatic Stress Response

Trauma exposure results in both immediate and long-term endocrine changes that affect metabolism and neurophysiology. As part of a phylogenetically conserved response, the sympathetic nervous system is rapidly activated by the perception of danger and threat. Rapid sympathetic activation directly signals the adrenal medulla to increase output of epinephrine and norepinephrine. These neurotransmitters act to increase heart rate, blood pressure, energy metabolism, and skin conductance characteristic of the "fight-or-flight" response. Acting also through higher cognitive centers within the brain, noradrenergic activity results in heightened attention and vigilance also characteristic of the stress response (see Figure 25.3). Freezing or dissociation represent alternative responses when fight or flight is unfeasible (Deppermann, Storchak, Fallgatter, & Ehlis, 2014). The stress response is a normal reaction, but it can become dysregulated and lead to chronic, sustained physiological changes.

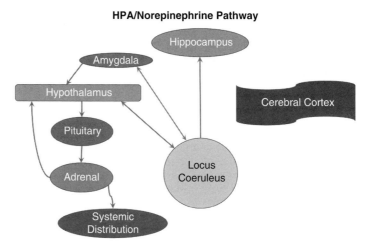

Figure 25.3 *Noradrenergic circuitry in the traumatic stress response. Acute response: "fight or flight," fear, conditioning, memory consolidation, ASD/ PTSD; associated symptoms: hypervigilance, arousal, fear, startle, flashbacks, intrusive recollections*

The circuitry described earlier in this chapter is central to arousal, memory formation, and learning, and is important to conceptualizations of traumatic stress as a failure of extinction learning (Fitzgerald, Seemann, & Maren, 2014). While certain cognitive aspects of such memories appear to be stored in the hippocampus, emotions associated with particular life experiences appear to be stored in the amygdala (Janak & Tye, 2015). Processing or integrating emotional and semantic (factual) aspects of experience involves communication between these brainstem structures and the neocortex (e.g., the association areas of the frontal cortex). Thinking, talking, or dreaming about past experience involves the transfer of information from the hippocampus and amygdala into the left neocortex (Solomon & Heide, 2005).

The understanding of the meaning of the event as a past (but no longer imminent) threat such that "fight or flight" is no longer reactivated is the process of extinction learning. Hence, pathological responses to trauma may be conceptualized as a failure of higher cortical structures such as the vmPFC, via noradrenergic communication, to inhibit limbic brainstem structures such as the amygdala and insula.

Longer-term central nervous system (CNS) alterations appear to arise from sustained activity of the aforementioned acute responses. Noradrenergic cell bodies in the locus coeruleus (LC) project to the medial prefrontal cortex (MPFC) through extensive branching. The MPFC consists of the orbitofrontal cortex, anterior cingulate, subcallosal gyrus, and prefrontal areas. Noradrenergic communication between the MPFC and other limbic structures (e.g., amygdala, hippocampus) mediate memory and learning in response to stressful or frightening stimuli. Since norepinephrine (NE) is also important in attention, memory, and arousal, it has been suggested that altered functioning of noradrenergic neurons may be particularly implicated in hyperarousal and reexperiencing symptoms in PTSD (Southwick et al., 1999). These symptoms and dysregulated norepinephrine neurotransmission are part of a dysfunctional pathway that develops as part of PTSD (see Figure 25.4).

This neural circuitry model emphasizes the central role of noradrenergic hyperactivity on arousal, memory, fear response, fear conditioning, and therefore posttraumatic symptom development. Serotonergic projections from the raphe nuclei, in addition to having a modulatory influence on the LC, communicate directly with limbic and cortical structures important to the "fight-or-flight" response and may therefore have both a direct and an indirect role in the development of symptoms related to heightened arousal, irritability, and aggression (Nisenbaum & Abercrombie, 1993). Additionally, the inhibitory and excitatory influences of γ-aminobutyric acid (GABA) and glutamate on these systems also play an important role in regulating neuronal activity. Others systems such as those involving excitatory NMDA receptors and endocannabinoid receptors have been shown to have a role in the traumatic stress response.

In contrast to the rapid sympathetic response, a delayed response that contributes to chronic stress response involves release of hormones from the adrenal cortex,

Serotonin Pathways

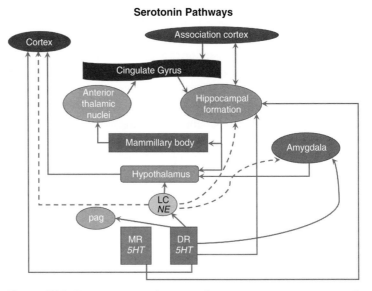

Figure 25.4 *Serotonergic pathways in the traumatic stress response. Acute response: "fight or flight," rage, attenuation of fear, ASD/PTSD; associated symptoms: aggression/violence, anger, impulsivity, anxiety, depression*

based on signaling from the hypothalamus. Via the hypothalamus, adrenergic stimulus activates the hypothalamic-pituitary-adrenal (HPA) axis, leading to increased levels of cortisol and stimulation of glucocorticoid receptors involved in memory consolidation (Deppermann et al., 2014).

Noradrenergic and serotonergic neurotransmission and alterations in HPA axis function are the most well-established traumatic stress response mechanisms (Hendrickson & Raskind, 2016; Otis, Werner, & Mueller, 2015; Pietrzak et al., 2013; Southwick et al., 1999). The search for biological markers has therefore focused on these neurobiological systems.

Biomarkers of Traumatic Stress

Using categorical diagnoses, principally in individuals with PTSD, a number of molecular markers have been examined for their relationship to mechanisms of traumatic stress response. Biological markers identified in earlier investigations included low cortisol in the acute aftermath of traumatic exposure and elevated resting heart rate (Delahanty, Raimonde, & Spoonster, 2000; Shalev et al., 1998). More recent studies have focused effort on identification of genetic markers.

Brain-derived neurotrophic factor (BDNF) is involved in synaptic plasticity, dendritic spine density, and memory formation (Andero, Choi, & Ressler, 2014; Bennett & Lagopoulos, 2014). Chronic stress is associated with an increase in

BDNF in the basal lateral amygdala and decreases in the hippocampus (Bennett & Lagopoulos, 2014). BDNF is modulated by glucocorticoids and mineralocorticoids, both implicated in traumatic stress reactions (Bennett & Lagopoulos, 2014). In a 2008 case report, serum BDNF levels were elevated in one ASD and one PTSD patient, and both demonstrated decrease in BDNF with effective treatment (Hauck et al., 2009). In a study of traffic accident survivors evaluated on average 10 days after exposure and at six months, plasma BDNF levels and *Val66Met* genotyping were not associated with either ASD or PTSD, but increased plasma BDNF was associated with higher lifetime trauma exposures (van den Heuvel, Suliman, Malan-Muller, Hemmings, & Seedat, 2016).

Although there may be specific effects of BDNF in trauma- and stressor-related disorders, BDNF is also involved in phobia and panic disorder (Andero et al., 2014) and other CNS disorders, including Alzheimer disease, Huntington disease, depression, schizophrenia, and substance abuse (Benarroch, 2015). BDNF involvement in multiple disorders suggests that its role in trauma- and stressor-related disorders involves shared pathways that could be better elucidated through studies that include multiple diagnostic groups. Along similar lines, FK506 binding protein 51 (FKBP5) is a heat shock protein involved in regulating glucocorticoid receptors (Zannas & Binder, 2014), whose variants are implicated in several psychiatric disorders, including PTSD (Gillespie, Phifer, Bradley, & Ressler, 2009).

Perhaps more specific to the HPA axis stress response in trauma, the pituitary adenylate cyclase activating polypeptide (PACAP) has been implicated in PTSD. PACAP and its receptors have been found in both autonomic stress and HPA pathways (Hammack & May, 2015). Elevated levels have been correlated with PTSD symptoms in female but not male subjects (Hammack & May, 2015).

A calcium-binding protein associated with both depression and PTSD and regulated by glucocorticoids, p11, has been overexpressed in individuals with PTSD, whereas it is decreased in other psychiatric disorders such as depression (Zhang et al., 2011). mRNA expression was found to be decreased in PTSD and elevated in MDD, bipolar disorder, and schizophrenia, suggesting that p11 could function as a biomarker specific to traumatic stress disorders (Su et al., 2009).

Epigenetic regulation of genes implicated in PTSD (e.g., through DNA methylation) is an area of promise for detection of stress-related alterations (Klengel, Pape, Binder, & Mehta, 2014). Studies to date have predominantly used animal models and peripheral blood samples in humans. Zannas et al. (2015) recommend that, given the specificity of epigenetic changes, studies in human postmortem brain tissue are critical to pursue. They further note that the use of phenomenological criteria and categorical diagnoses to define PTSD may limit signal detection, and recommend using endophenotypes and dimensional phenotypes for case definition. Presently, public sector and private research institutions are engaged in case identification (through record review and third-party interview) of PTSD brain tissue from decedents who have already donated their brains for such studies (Mighdoll et al., 2017). In addition, the Uniformed Services University (USU) and the Veterans Affairs National Center for Posttraumatic Stress Disorder

(NCPTSD) have established the VA Biorepository Brain Bank and initiated enrollment of potential donors consenting to longitudinal follow-up to allow for such dimensional characterization of their PTSD symptoms prior to death and tissue donation for genetic and epigenetic studies(Friedman et al., in press).

One approach to the identification of genetic markers has been to examine shared heritability across related disorders in studies that include, for instance, PTSD, MDD, and anxiety disorders (Smoller, 2016). Transdiagnostic exploration of genes by environment effects may lead to characterization of common biological underpinnings that are otherwise difficult to discern using a categorical diagnosis (Montalvo-Ortiz, Gelernter, Hudziak, & Kaufman, 2016). Another approach extends this logic further, examining core constructs in a population that includes nonclinical, subthreshold, and clinical samples. As discussed in what follows, a goal of this approach is to identify intermediate phenotypes that underpin the more complex syndromally defined phenotypes in categorical disorders.

Using Dimensional Constructs to Understand Acute Stress Disorder

The variability of human response to traumatic events means that individuals may develop significant symptoms and distress without meeting full diagnostic criteria for ASD or PTSD (Zlotnick, Franklin, & Zimmerman, 2002). That such persons may nonetheless be significantly impaired raises questions about the current symptom threshold criteria. For instance, subthreshold symptoms of PTSD may be associated with hopelessness, suicidal ideation, aggression, and low quality of life (Gellis, Mavandadi, & Oslin, 2010; Jakupcak et al., 2007; Jakupcak et al., 2011; Zlotnick et al., 2002). Randomized controlled trials of medication and therapy have focused on reducing readily identifiable core symptoms – since these symptoms most readily lend themselves to quantification with severity scales. And yet changes in belief systems, view of self, ability to trust others, and related changes in social and occupational functioning may affect patients' lives to a far greater extent than easily recognized symptoms that comprise a categorical diagnosis. The extent to which these additional features represent disabling aspects of the disorder, and the extent to which they can be targeted by available treatments are questions for further research to answer. Additional constructs related to traumatic stress that are well characterized in relation to underlying neurobiology may yield new diagnostic subcategories or refined criteria to guide mechanistic and therapeutic investigations.

Mapping RDoC Constructs to ASD

Categorical diagnoses and clinical phenomenology may be limited in their ability to detect underlying biological processes and to parse heterogeneity within a population of individuals exposed to traumatic events. Conceptualizing psycho-pathology on a continuum with normal brain functioning may allow for more nuanced observations of how symptoms and biological changes are correlated. Examining ASD as part of a broader spectrum of early responses to traumatic events may reveal patterns of change in basic brain functions.

One recent approach toward a possible revision in nosology is to consider whether psychobiological constructs are involved across diagnostic categories such that disorders fundamentally share common mechanisms. The *DSM-5* revision included cross-cutting measures as a way to characterize these com-monalities in clinical phenomenology (Narrow et al., 2013). The National Institute of Mental Health's Research Domain Criteria (RDoC) program extends this logic further into basic biology, and has been one of the main drivers of recent changes in the conceptualization of psychopathology (Kozak & Cuthbert, 2016).

Drawing upon methods and concepts from experimental psychology and clinical neuroscience, the RDoC proposes a set of dimensional constructs that are inclusive of both normal and pathological brain functioning, as repre-sented through a range of clinical and neurobiological measurements (Kozak & Cuthbert, 2016). This approach seeks to examine continuous distributions in symptom measures (e.g., clinical rating instruments) and related biological constructs measured in a variety of ways (e.g., molecular markers, psycho-physiology, neuroimaging). Individuals with different scores on a given clin-ical measure can be identified and compared on these biological measurements. Combining clinical and psychobiological data in this way may lead to identification of biologically homogeneous subtypes. A theoreti-cal assumption of such an approach is that a given latent construct can be represented via multiple types of data.

The RDoC Matrix is a living document that is periodically updated. It is organized into systems that include constructs and sub-constructs and proposes different types or levels of data as "units of analysis" (e.g., genes, circuits, behavior, self-report). As the RDoC Matrix becomes further populated, methods of analysis to identify patterns across and within *DSM* diagnostic categories are expected to maximize the value of the information for characterization of the heterogeneity inherent in many clinical disorders.

In addition to attempting to situate *DSM-5* disorders within the RDoC Matrix to examine transdiagnostic commonalities, it is perhaps also useful to select con-structs and findings from the RDoC that map onto existing symptom criteria for ASD. This could reveal gaps that need to be addressed, as has recently been proposed for PTSD (Schmidt & Vermetten, 2017). Schmidt and Vermetten devel-oped a map of PTSD pathopsychobiology within the RDoC framework, which serves as a useful tool for further examining ASD as well (see Table 25.3). This effort resulted in the identification of additional constructs that are not yet included in the RDoC and that merit further emphasis in PTSD research. Schmidt and Vermetten remark that:

Table 25.3 *Integration of findings on PTSD pathopsychobiology in the RDoC framework (Schmidt & Vermetten, 2017)*

Construct	Negative valence systems	Positive valence systems	Cognitive systems	Arousal
Self-reports	Fear to be confronted with trauma-related cues, anxiety	Appetite ↓, interest ↓ libido↓ Feeling to feel nothing (numbing)	Deficits in: memory, attention, concentration. Attention and memory bias to threat	Nervousness, sleeping, problems
Behaviors	Anxious avoidance that can transform into generalized avoidance	Anhedonia (only partial overlap with emotional numbering)	Concentration and memory deficits, reduced school+work performance	Nervousness, sleeping problems, jumpiness
Physiology	Fear conditioning, fear extinction, attention to threat stimuli, impaired neuroendocrine release of hormones	Reward functioning, memory	Explicit memory pathway: temporal and diencephalic neural network. Implicit memory pathway: right occipital cortex	Startle response↑SNS activity↑
Neural circuits	BLA + mPFC promote fear conditioning Fear extinction: HC→+ILC→+BLA □ CA PTSD: mPFC fails to inhibit AMY. HC has impaired safety signaling	Anhedonia: mesocorticolimbic reward pathway (VTA→BLA, the mPFC + NA) Motivation: dopamine consumption: opioid + GABA receptors	AMY activity ↑, insular activity ↑, HC ↑↓ (depending on type of cue), attention bias: AMY, dorsal ACC, insula, (vmPFC)	Locus coeruleus (LC)-norepinephrine arousal system (in particular LC →AMY circuit)
Cells	BLA: inhibitory interneurons CA: output neurons	Dopaminergic, gabaergic + opioidergic neurons	Various cell types. Further studies needed!	Adrenergic neurons
Molecules	D-cycloserine, L-DOPA, yohimbine	SSRIs, oxytocin Numbing: ?	HAT inhibitors HDAC inhibitors	Adrenoreceptor-blockers such as prazosin, propranolol
Genes	*BDNF val66val, COMTval 158met, 5-HTTLPR*	DAT	Picture recognition: methylation of GR promoter, fear ext./cons.: variety of epigenetic mechanisms	Deletion variant of α2B adrenergic receptor, polymorphism inβ2-adrenergic receptor (ADRB2)

BLA basolateral amygdala, *CA* central amygdala, *mPFC* medical prefrontal cortex, *ILC* infralimbic cortex, *HC* hippocampus, *SNS* sympathetic nervous system, *BDNF* brain-derived neurotrophic factor, *COMT* catechol-O-methyltransferase, *5-HTTLPR* serotonin transporter gene, *SSRIs* serotonin reuptake inhibitors, *DAT* dopamine transporter, *SNS* sympathetic nervous system, *AMY* amygdala, *ACC* anterior cingulate cortex, *VTA* ventral tegmental area, *NA* nucleus accumbens, *GR* glucocorticoid receptor. Symbols: →, influence; →+, activation; □, inhibition, ↓, reduction; ↑, increase. Note that the domain "social processes" is not reviewed here.

> [T]he RDoC system is unquestionably useful for PTSD research. However, there are some facets of PTSD pathobiology that do not easily fit into the proposed RDoC research domains, in particular PTSD-associated impairments in emotion processing and dissociative symptoms.

They therefore propose two new domains, "stress and emotion regulation" and "maintenance of consciousness." Although further refinement may be needed to operationalize these domains and clarify their relationship to existing RDoC constructs, the identification of research needs is equally applicable to ASD. Reorganization of posttraumatic syndromes using dimensional constructs could lead to identification of more precise treatment targets that are valid for symptoms across diagnoses rather than constellations of symptoms as represented in categorically defined *DSM-5* disorders.

Approaches using the RDoC framework are diverse and complex. On the one hand, the inclusion of multiple diagnostic categories within one study may allow for measurement of constructs across different types of psychopathology. On the other hand, studies including subthreshold conditions and nonclinical populations exposed to trauma may improve signal detection by including a broader range of post-trauma manifestations and corresponding variations in brain function. ASD as a time-limited constellation of symptoms is only one of several posttraumatic syndromes. Comparisons of ASD either with other disorders such as MDD or adjustment disorder may reveal patterns of early change in the neurobiological response to trauma exposure. The recent alignment of ASD criteria with PTSD, however, may encourage investigators to examine the continuum of posttraumatic responses over time, from the initial weeks to months after the traumatic event.

Clinical Dimensions

Efforts to parse trauma-related disorders have resulted in theoretical models that distinguish symptoms involving an altered state of consciousness from symptoms that are more characteristic of a waking state (e.g., flashbacks versus intrusive memories) (Lanius, 2015). Although the model has been discussed for PTSD (Frewen & Lanius, 2014) in light of the existence of a dissociative subtype, it has yet to be explored in ASD.

Other models may be more applicable to ASD subtypes, and these in turn may illuminate aspects of PTSD. One possibility is an intrusion subtype of ASD. Efforts to identify other ASD subtypes have noted that individuals with ASD with high levels of avoidance and dissociation also are more highly symptomatic (Hansen, Armour, Wang, Elklit, & Bryant, 2015). In one study, ASD subjects were directed in an experiment task to remember or forget aversive, neutral, or positive words. ASD subjects had directed forgetting for trauma-related and neutral words but not positive words immediately after the trauma, while non-trauma-exposed individuals demonstrated forgetting of all word types. This phenomenon suggests trait-like preferential encoding of positive words in individuals with ASD (Moulds & Bryant, 2008). Related, studies of thought suppression in ASD have suggested that the ability to suppress is a function of cognitive load. In one study, ASD subjects were randomized to no-load or load conditions. The group assigned to cognitive load demonstrated lower suppression of memories, increased priming responses to trauma-related words, and higher level of intrusion during a "think anything" phase (Nixon & Rackebrandt, 2016). There was no difference in attentional bias or effect of working memory between the two groups. ASD subjects have also demonstrated a deficit in associative memory in relation to emotionally neutral stimuli (Guez et al., 2013). Individuals with ASD have a decreased ability to inhibit inappropriate responses and an increased impairment in cognitive appraisals (Abolghasemi, Bakhshian, & Narimani, 2013). Whether these dimensions detected in ASD samples are related to brain functions that can be observed in subthreshold conditions or those exposed to trauma but asymptomatic has yet to be determined.

Neuroimaging

As previously noted, given the short time frame for ASD, there are many logistical challenges to conducting research, particularly studies that involve complex instrumentation such as neuroimaging. Few studies of ASD have therefore examined structural and functional brain imaging characteristics. In a small prospective study, firefighters who went on to develop ASD after trauma exposure demonstrated increased activation compared to baseline in the amygdala, dorsolateral prefrontal, and orbitofrontal regions on fMRI, suggesting acute alterations in fear processing (Reynaud et al., 2015). In another study, which examined subjects an average of 17 days after trauma exposure, individuals with ASD had increased midline cortical activation in the precuneus, cuneus, post-central gyrus, and pre-supplementary motor areas in response to trauma-related pictures, suggesting that ASD is associated with emotional salience processing (Cwik, Sartory, Schürholt, Knuppertz, & Seitz, 2014). A study assessing ASD clinical ratings as well as neuroimaging at two to four months after trauma exposure showed that peri-traumatic dissociation was associated with PTSD and activation of the right occipital lobe on fMRI (Daniels et al., 2012). In another study among individuals with ASD who did not go on to develop PTSD, structural MRI showed no changes from baseline in the hippocampus or amygdala (Szabo, Kelemen, Levy-Gigi, & Keri, 2015), suggesting that PTSD-related changes may occur later in the evolution of illness. Given the availability of task-based neuroimaging paradigms for the RDoC construct of acute threat, methods are readily available to examine the immediate and short-term effects of ASD. A recent theoretical model of bihemispheric autonomic functioning that specifically references the RDoC framework posits transient lateralization of brain functions and has been proposed to explain traumatic stress-related symptoms as alterations in autonomic processes (Lee, Gerdes, Tegeler, Shaltout, & Tegeler, 2014).

Psychophysiology

As a set of methods, psychophysiology is a broad category that encompasses many different types of measurement, ranging from physiological reactivity to script-driven imagery (Bauer et al., 2013) to EEG, EMG, and ERP. The RDoC framework is particularly suited to the examination of psychophysiological data (Shankman & Gorka, 2015). As transdiagnostic commonalities emerge and are confirmed through further study, the relationship of RDOC constructs and categorically defined clinical phenomena will need to be clarified. In addition, state versus trait-based constructs that are related to brain dysfunction will need to be distinguished. Integration of the different units of analysis, some of which are more directly related to the clinical presentation than others, will require new methodological solutions due to differences in scale, as mentioned previously. Validation of measurements in large-scale studies and mechanisms for data sharing are continued challenges (Patrick & Hajcak, 2016; Zoellner & Foa, 2016).

The study of startle reactivity is of particular relevance to trauma- and stressor-related disorders. Exaggerated startle response is a clinical criterion for ASD and PTSD, thus making this symptom one of particular interest to study from a psychophysiology perspective. Examination of P300 amplitude and skin conductance in response to auditory tones revealed that ASD subjects had higher reactivity than persons with PTSD and either traumatized or non-traumatized controls (Felmingham, Rennie, Gordon, & Bryant, 2012). Impaired inhibition of fear response on potentiated startle has been examined in PTSD, with possible use of reactivity as a differentiator of subtypes (McTeague et al., 2010). Heightened magnitude of the startle response on electromyography (eye blink) within four weeks following trauma exposure was associated with pre-trauma physiologic reactivity (Guthrie & Bryant, 2005). In another study including ASD subjects, fear-potentiated startle measures indicated impairment in fear learning (i.e., fear inhibition to safety cues) (Jovanovic et al., 2013).

Although the use of psychophysiological measurements such as skin conductance, heart rate variability, potentiated startle, and EEG in posttraumatic psychopathology is not itself new, the inclusion of this set of measures in more broadly defined study populations and the use of new ways of combining data to explore shared dimensions of trauma-related mental disorders may lead to improved detection of biologically homogeneous functions.

Conclusion

Exposure to traumatic events initiates a complex biological, psychological, and social system that determines the individual's response. Social scientists, historians, and psychiatrists discussed the impact of traumatic experience on individuals and populations for centuries before the diagnosis of ASD was specifically defined. Our definitions have subsequently been updated in light of new data as well as in accordance with the various purposes that a diagnosis may serve. Scientific investigation has begun to elucidate the psychobiological mechanisms underlying a wide range of human responses to traumatic events. The inherent challenges in designing and conducting rigorous studies in the immediate aftermath of trauma is one reason the literature on ASD is more limited than the body of knowledge on PTSD. Future research should seek to more effectively parse the heterogeneity in populations exposed to trauma by identifying individual and group-specific risk factors or vulnerabilities and their relationship to underlying neurobiology. Identification of at-risk groups as well as factors impacting treatment response or adherence may advance evidence-based approaches to the recognition and management of ASD in the aftermath of trauma. Given that criteria for ASD and PTSD have become more closely aligned in *DSM-5*, the opportunity exists to examine these posttraumatic syndromes together on a temporal continuum, to improve our understanding of the factors that determine how and when post-traumatic symptoms evolve or resolve over time.

References

Abolghasemi, A., Bakhshian, F., & Narimani, M. (2013). Response inhibition and cognitive appraisal in clients with acute stress disorder and posttraumatic stress disorder. *Iranian Journal of Psychiatry*, *8*(3), 124–130.

Abrahams, N., Devries, K., Watts, C., Pallitto, C., Petzold, M., Shamu, S., & García-Moreno, C. (2014). Worldwide prevalence of non-partner sexual violence: A systematic review. *Lancet*, *383*(9929), 1648–1654.

American Psychiatric Association. (2000). *Diagnostic and Statistical Manual of Mental Disorders* (4th edn). Washington, DC: American Psychiatric Association.

American Psychiatric Association. (2013). *Diagnostic and Statistical Manual of Mental Disorders* (5th edn). Arlington, VA:American Psychiatric Association.

Andero, R., Choi, D. C., & Ressler, K. J. (2014). BDNF-TrkB receptor regulation of distributed adult neural plasticity, memory formation, and psychiatric disorders. *Progress in Molecular Biology and Translational Science*, *122*, 169–192.

Armour, C. & Elklit, A. (2013). The latent structure of acute stress disorder: A posttraumatic stress disorder approach. *Psychological Trauma*, *5*(1), 18–25.

Armour, C. & Hansen, M. (2015). Assessing *DSM-5* latent subtypes of acute stress disorder: Dissociative or intrusive? *Psychiatry Research*, *225*(3), 476–483.

Bauer, M. R., Ruef, A. M., Pineles, S. L., Japuntich, S. J., Macklin, M. L., Lasko, N. B., & Orr, S. P. (2013). Psychophysiological assessment of PTSD: A potential research domain criteria construct. *Psychological Assessment*, *25*(3), 1037–1043.

Benarroch, E. E. (2015). Brain-derived neurotrophic factor: Regulation, effects, and potential clinical relevance. *Neurology*, *84*(16), 1693–1704.

Benjet, C., Bromet, E., Karam, E. G., Kessler, R. C., Mclaughlin, K. A., Ruscio, A. M., . . . Koenen, K. C. (2016). The epidemiology of traumatic event exposure worldwide: Results from the World Mental Health Survey Consortium. *Psychological Medicine*, *46*(2), 327–343.

Bennett, M. & Lagopoulos, J. (2014). Stress and trauma: BDNF control of dendritic-spine formation and regression. *Progress in Neurobiology*, *112*, 80–99.

Biggs, Q. M., Fullerton, C. S., Reeves, J. J., Grieger, T. A., Reissman, D., & Ursano, R. J. (2010). Acute stress disorder, depression, and tobacco use in disaster workers following 9/11. *American Journal of Orthopsychiatry*, *80*(4), 586–592.

Brewin, C. R., Andrews, B., & Valentine, J. D. (2000). Meta-analysis of risk factors for posttraumatic stress disorder in trauma-exposed adults. *Journal of Consulting and Clinical Psychology*, *68*(5), 748–766.

Bromet, E., Sonnega, A., & Kessler, R. C. (1998). Risk factors for *DSM-III-R* posttraumatic stress disorder: Findings from the National Comorbidity Survey. *American Journal of Epidemiology*, *147*(4), 353–361.

Bryant, R. A. (2011). Acute stress disorder as a predictor of posttraumatic stress disorder: A systematic review. *Journal of Clinical Psychiatry*, *72*(2), 233–239.

Bryant, R. A., Creamer, M., O'Donnell, M., Forbes, D., Mcfarlane, A. C., Silove, D., & Hadzi-Pavlovic, D. (2017). Acute and chronic posttraumatic stress symptoms in the emergence of posttraumatic stress disorder. *JAMA Psychiatry*, *74*(2), 135–142.

Bryant, R. A., Creamer, M., O'Donnell, M., Silove, D., & Mcfarlane, A. C. (2012). The capacity of acute stress disorder to predict posttraumatic psychiatric disorders. *Journal of Psychiatric Research*, *46*(2), 168–173.

Bryant, R. A., Creamer, M., O'Donnell, M., Silove, D., Mcfarlane, A. C., & Forbes, D. (2014). A comparison of the capacity of *DSM-IV* and *DSM-5* acute stress disorder definitions to predict posttraumatic stress disorder and related disorders. *Journal of Clinical Psychiatry*, *76*(4), 391–397.

Bryant, R. A. & Harvey, A. G. (2000). *Acute Stress Disorder: A Handbook of Theory, Assessment, and Treatment*. Washington, DC: American Psychological Association.

Cardeña, E. & Carlson, E. (2011). Acute stress disorder revisited. *Annual Review of Clinical Psychology*, *7*(1), 245–267.

Cozza, S. J., Fisher, J. E., Mauro, C., Zhou, J., Ortiz, C. D., Skritskaya, N., . . . Shear, M. K. (2016). Performance of *DSM-5* persistent complex bereavement disorder criteria in a community sample of bereaved military family members. *American Journal of Psychiatry*, *173*(9), 919–929.

Cwik, J. C., Sartory, G., Schürholt, B., Knuppertz, H., & Seitz, R. J. (2014). Posterior midline activation during symptom provocation in acute stress disorder: An fMRI study. *Frontiers in Psychiatry*, 5(49).

Daniels, J. K., Coupland, N. J., Hegadoren, K. M., Rowe, B. H., Densmore, M., Neufeld, R. W., & Lanius, R. A. (2012). Neural and behavioral correlates of peritraumatic dissociation in an acutely traumatized sample. *Journal of Clinical Psychiatry*, *73*(4), 420–426.

Delahanty, D. L., Raimonde, A., & Spoonster, E. (2000). Initial posttraumatic urinary cortisol levels predict subsequent PTSD symptoms in motor vehicle accident victims. *Biological Psychiatry*, *48*(9), 940–947.

Deppermann, S., Storchak, H., Fallgatter, A., & Ehlis, A. (2014). Stress-induced neuroplasticity: (Mal)adaptation to adverse life events in patients with PTSD – A critical overview. *Neuroscience*, *283*, 166–177.

deRoon-Cassini, T. A., Mancini, A. D., Rusch, M. D., & Bonanno, G. A. (2010). Psychopathology and resilience following traumatic injury: A latent growth mixture model analysis. *Rehabilitation Psychology*, *55*(1), 1–11.

Felmingham, K. L., Rennie, C., Gordon, E., & Bryant, R. A. (2012). Autonomic and cortical reactivity in acute and chronic posttraumatic stress. *Biological Psychology*, *90*(3), 224–227.

Fitzgerald, P. J., Seemann, J. R., & Maren, S. (2014). Can fear extinction be enhanced? A review of pharmacological and behavioral findings. *Brain Research Bulletin*, *105*, 46–60.

Ford, C. V. (1997). Somatic symptoms, somatization, and traumatic stress: An overview. *Nordic Journal of Psychiatry*, *51*(1), 5–13.

Frewen, P. A. & Lanius, R. A. (2014). Trauma-related altered states of consciousness: Exploring the 4-D model. *Journal of Trauma & Dissociation*, *15*(4), 436–456.

Friedman, M. J., Huber, B. R., Brady, C. B., Ursano, R. J., Benedek, D. M., Kowall, N. W., ...The Traumatic Stress Brain Research Group. (in press). The Department of Veterans Affairs Biorepository Brain Bank: A national resource for research on Posttraumatic Stress Disorder. *Current Psychiatric Reports*.

Galea, S., Boscarino, J., Resnick, H., & Vlahov, D. (2003). Mental health in New York City after the September 11th terrorist attacks: Results from two population surveys. In R. W. Mandersheid & M. J. Henderson (eds.), *Mental Health, United States, 2002*. Washington, DC: US Government Printing Office.

Galea, S., Vlahov, D., Resick, H., Ahern, J., Susser, E., Gold, J., ... Kilpatrick, D. (2003). Trends of probable posttraumatic stress disorder in New York City after the September 11 terrorist attacks. *American Journal of Epidemiology*, *158*(6), 514–524.

Gellis, L. A., Mavandadi, S., & Oslin, D. W. (2010). Functional quality of life in full versus partial posttraumatic stress disorder among veterans returning from Iraq and Afghanistan. *The Primary Care Companion to The Journal of Clinical Psychiatry*, 12(3).

Gillespie, C. F., Phifer, J., Bradley, B., & Ressler, K. J. (2009). Risk and resilience: Genetic and environmental influences on development of the stress response. *Depression and Anxiety*, *26*(11), 984–992.

Goldmann, E. & Galea, S. (2014). Mental health consequences of disasters. *Annual Review of Public Health*, *35*, 169–183.

Gradus, J. L., Antonsen, S., Svensson, E., Lash, T. L., Resick, P. A., & Hansen, J. G. (2015). Trauma, comorbidity, and mortality following diagnoses of severe stress and adjustment disorders: A nationwide cohort study. *American Journal of Epidemiology*, *182*(5), 451–458.

Gradus, J. L., Qin, P., Lincoln, A. K., Miller, M., Lawler, E., Sorensen, H. T., & Lash, T. L. (2010). Acute stress reaction and completed suicide. *International Journal of Epidemiology*, *39*(6), 1478–1484.

Guez, J., Cohen, J., Naveh-Benjamin, M., Shiber, A., Yankovsky, Y., Saar, R., & Shalev, H. (2013). Associative memory impairment in acute stress disorder: Characteristics and time course. *Psychiatry Research*, *209*(3), 479–484.

Guthrie, R. M. & Bryant, R. A. (2005). Auditory startle response in firefighters before and after trauma exposure. *American Journal of Psychiatry*, *162*(2), 283–290.

Hammack, S. E. & May, V. (2015). Pituitary adenylate cyclase activating polypeptide in stress-related disorders: Data convergence from animal and human studies. *Biological Psychiatry*, *78*(3), 167–177.

Hansen, M., Armour, C., Wang, L., Elklit, A., & Bryant, R. A. (2015). Assessing possible *DSM-5* ASD subtypes in a sample of victims meeting caseness for *DSM-5* ASD based on self-report following multiple forms of traumatic exposure. *Journal of Anxiety Disorders*, *31*, 84–89.

Hansen, M., Armour, C., Wittmann, L., Elklit, A., & Shevlin, M. (2014). Is there a common pathway to developing ASD and PTSD symptoms? *Journal of Anxiety Disorders*, *28*(8), 865–872.

Hansen, M. & Elklit, A. (2011). Predictors of acute stress disorder in response to bank robbery. *European Journal of Psychotraumatology*, *2*.

Hansen, M., Hyland, P., & Armour, C. (2016). Does highly symptomatic class membership in the acute phase predict highly symptomatic classification in victims 6 months after traumatic exposure? *Journal of Anxiety Disorders*, *40*, 44–51.

Hansen, M., Lasgaard, M., & Elklit, A. (2013). The latent factor structure of acute stress disorder following bank robbery: Testing alternative models in light of the pending *DSM-5*. *British Journal of Clinical Psychology*, *52*(1), 82–91.

Harville, E. W., Taylor, C. A., Tesfai, H., Xu, X., & Buekens, P. (2011). Experience of Hurricane Katrina and reported intimate partner violence. *Journal of Interpersonal Violence*, *26*(4), 833–845.

Hauck, S., Gomes, F., Silveira Junior Ede, M., Almeida, E., Possa, M., & Ceitlin, L. H. (2009). Serum levels of brain-derived neurotrophic factor in acute and posttraumatic stress disorder: A case report study. *Revista Brasileira De Psiquiatria*, *31*(1), 48–51.

Hendrickson, R. C. & Raskind, M. A. (2016). Noradrenergic dysregulation in the pathophysiology of PTSD. *Experimental Neurology*, *284*(Pt B), 181–195.

Holman, E. A., Garfin, D. R., & Silver, R. C. (2014). Media's role in broadcasting acute stress following the Boston Marathon bombings. *Proceedings of the National Academy of Sciences of the United States of America*, *111*(1), 93–98.

Isserlin, L., Zerach, G., & Solomon, Z. (2008). Acute stress responses: A review and synthesis of ASD, ASR, and CSR. *American Journal of Orthopsychiatry*, *78*(4), 423–429.

Jakupcak, M., Conybeare, D., Phelps, L., Hunt, S., Holmes, H. A., Felker, B., . . . McFall, M. E. (2007). Anger, hostility, and aggression among Iraq and Afghanistan War veterans reporting PTSD and subthreshold PTSD. *Journal of Trauma Stress*, *20*(6), 945–954.

Jakupcak, M., Hoerster, K. D., Varra, A., Vannoy, S., Felker, B., & Hunt, S. (2011). Hopelessness and suicidal ideation in Iraq and Afghanistan War veterans reporting subthreshold and threshold posttraumatic stress disorder. *Journal of Nervous and Mental Disease*, *199*(4), 272–275.

Janak, P. H. & Tye, K. M. (2015). From circuits to behaviour in the amygdala. *Nature*, *517*(7534), 284–292.

Jovanovic, T., Sakoman, A. J., Kozaric-Kovacic, D., Mestrovic, A. H., Duncan, E. J., Davis, M., & Norrholm, S. D. (2013). Acute stress disorder versus chronic posttraumatic stress disorder: Inhibition of fear as a function of time since trauma. *Depression and Anxiety*, *30*(3), 217–224.

Kessler, R. C., Sonnega, A., Bromet, E., Hughes, M., & Nelson, C. B. (1995). Posttraumatic stress disorder in the National Comorbidity Survey. *Archives of General Psychiatry*, *52*(12), 1048–1060.

Klengel, T., Pape, J., Binder, E. B., & Mehta, D. (2014). The role of DNA methylation in stress-related psychiatric disorders. *Neuropharmacology*, *80*, 115–132.

Kozak, M. J. & Cuthbert, B. N. (2016). The NIMH Research Domain Criteria Initiative: Background, issues, and pragmatics. *Psychophysiology*, *53*(3), 286–297.

Lanius, R. A. (2015). Trauma-related dissociation and altered states of consciousness: A call for clinical, treatment, and neuroscience research. *European Journal of Psychotraumatology*, *6*, 27905.

LeDoux, J. E. & Pine, D. S. (2016). Using neuroscience to help understand fear and anxiety: A two-system framework. *American Journal of Psychiatry*, *173*(11), 1083–1093.

Lee, S. W., Gerdes, L., Tegeler, C. L., Shaltout, H. A., & Tegeler, C. H. (2014). A bihemispheric autonomic model for traumatic stress effects on health and behavior. *Frontiers in Psychology*, *5*, 843.

Maercker, A., Brewin, C. R., Bryant, R. A., Cloitre, M., van Ommeren, M., Jones, L. M., . . . Reed, G. M. (2013). Diagnosis and classification of disorders specifically associated with stress: Proposals for *ICD-11*. *World Psychiatry*, *12*(3), 198–206.

Mahendraraj, K., Durgan, D. M., & Chamberlain, R. S. (2016). Acute mental disorders and short and long term morbidity in patients with third degree flame burn: A population-based outcome study of 96,451 patients from the Nationwide Inpatient Sample (NIS) database (2001–2011). *Burns*, *42*(8), 1766–1773.

McLean, S. A., Soward, A. C., Ballina, L. E., Rossi, C., Rotolo, S., Wheeler, R., . . . Liberzon, I. (2012). Acute severe pain is a common consequence of sexual assault. *Journal of Pain*, *13*(8), 736–741.

McTeague, L. M., Lang, P. J., Laplante, M. C., Cuthbert, B. N., Shumen, J. R., & Bradley, M. M. (2010). Aversive imagery in posttraumatic stress disorder: Trauma recurrence, comorbidity, and physiological reactivity. *Biological Psychiatry*, *67*(4), 346–356.

Mighdoll, M. I., Deep-Soboslay, A., Bharadwaj, R. A., Cotoia, J. A., Benedek, D. M., Hyde, T. M., & Kleinman, J. E. (2017). Implementation and clinical characteristics of a posttraumatic stress disorder brain collection. *Journal of Neuroscience Research*.

Miguel-Tobal, J. J., Cano-Vindel, A., Gonzalez-Ordi, H., Iruarrizaga, I., Rudenstine, S., Vlahov, D., & Galea, S. (2006). PTSD and depression after the Madrid March 11 train bombings. *Journal of Traumatic Stress*, *19*(1), 69–80.

Montalvo-Ortiz, J. L., Gelernter, J., Hudziak, J., & Kaufman, J. (2016). RDoC and translational perspectives on the genetics of trauma-related psychiatric disorders. *American Journal of Medical Genetics Part B: Neuropsychiatric Genetics*, *171b*(1), 81–91.

Moulds, M. L. & Bryant, R. A. (2008). Avoidant encoding in acute stress disorder: A prospective study. *Depression and Anxiety*, *25*(12), E195–198.

Narrow, W. E., Clarke, D. E., Kuramoto, S. J., Kraemer, H. C., Kupfer, D. J., Greiner, L., & Regier, D. A. (2013). *DSM-5* field trials in the United States and Canada, Part III: Development and reliability testing of a cross-cutting symptom assessment for *DSM-5*. *American Journal of Psychiatry*, *170*(1), 71–82.

Nisenbaum, L. K. & Abercrombie, E. D. (1993). Presynaptic alterations associated with enhancement of evoked release and synthesis of norepinephrine in hippocampus of chronically cold-stressed rats. *Brain Research*, *608*(2), 280–287.

Nixon, R. D. & Rackebrandt, J. (2016). Cognitive load undermines thought suppression in acute stress disorder. *Behavioral Therapy*, *47*(3), 388–403.

Norris, F. H. (1992). Epidemiology of trauma: Frequency and impact of different potentially traumatic events on different demographic groups. *Journal of Consulting and Clinical Psychology*, *60*(3), 409–418.

Norris, F. H., Friedman, M. J., Watson, P. J., Byrne, C. M., Diaz, E., & Kaniasty, K. (2002). 60,000 disaster victims speak: Part I. An empirical review of the empirical literature, 1981–2001. *Psychiatry, 65*(3), 207–239.

North, C. S., Nixon, S. J., Shariat, S., Mallonee, S., McMillen, J. C., Spitznagel, E. L., & Smith, E. M. (1999). Psychiatric disorders among survivors of the Oklahoma City bombing. *Journal of the American Medical Association, 282*(8), 755–762.

O'Donnell, M. L., Alkemade, N., Creamer, M., McFarlane, A. C., Silove, D., Bryant, R. A., . . . Forbes, D. (2016). A longitudinal study of adjustment disorder after trauma exposure. *American Journal of Psychiatry, 173*(12), 1231–1238. doi: 10.1176/appi. ajp.2016.16010071

Ogle, C. M., Rubin, D. C., & Siegler, I. C. (2014). Cumulative exposure to traumatic events in older adults. *Aging & Mental Health, 18*(3), 316–325. doi: 10.1080/ 13607863.2013.832730

Otis, J. M., Werner, C. T., & Mueller, D. (2015). Noradrenergic regulation of fear and drug-associated memory reconsolidation. *Neuropsychopharmacology, 40*(4), 793–803. doi: 10.1038/npp.2014.243

Patrick, C. J. & Hajcak, G. (2016). RDoC: Translating promise into progress. *Psychophysiology, 53*(3), 415–424. doi: 10.1111/psyp.12612

Pietrzak, R. H., Gallezot, J. D., Ding, Y. S., Henry, S., Potenza, M. N., Southwick, S. M., . . . Neumeister, A. (2013). Association of posttraumatic stress disorder with reduced in vivo norepinephrine transporter availability in the locus coeruleus. *Journal of the American Medical Association Psychiatry, 70*(11), 1199–1205. doi: 10.1001/ jamapsychiatry.2013.399

Prigerson, H. G., Shear, M. K., Jacobs, S. C., Reynolds, C. F., 3rd, Maciejewski, P. K., Davidson, J. R., . . . Zisook, S. (1999). Consensus criteria for traumatic grief. A preliminary empirical test. *British Journal of Psychiatry, 174*, 67–73. doi: 10.1192/bjp.174.1.67

Reiser, E. M., Weiss, E. M., Schulter, G., Holmes, E. A., Fink, A., & Papousek, I. (2014). Prefrontal-posterior coupling while observing the suffering of other people, and the development of intrusive memories. *Psychophysiology, 51*(6), 546–555. doi: 10.1111/psyp.12197

Reynaud, E., Guedj, E., Trousselard, M., El Khoury-Malhame, M., Zendjidjian, X., Fakra, E., . . . Khalfa, S. (2015). Acute stress disorder modifies cerebral activity of amygdala and prefrontal cortex. *Cognitive Neuroscience, 6*(1), 39–43. doi: 10.1080/17588928.2014.996212

Roncone, R., Giusti, L., Mazza, M., Bianchini, V., Ussorio, D., Pollice, R., & Casacchia, M. (2013). Persistent fear of aftershocks, impairment of working memory, and acute stress disorder predict posttraumatic stress disorder: 6-month follow-up of help seekers following the L'Aquila earthquake. *Springerplus, 2*, 636. doi: 10.1186/ 2193–1801-2–636

Rothbaum, B. O., Foa, E. B., Murdock, T., & Walsh, W. (1992). A prospective examination of posttraumatic stress disorder in rape victims. *Journal of Traumatic Stress, 5*, 455–475. doi: 10.1002/jts.2490050309

Rubin, G. J., Brewin, C. R., Greenberg, N., Simpson, J., & Wessely, S. (2005). Psychological and behavioural reactions to the bombings in London on 7 July 2005: Cross sectional survey of a representative sample of Londoners. *British Medical Journal, 331*(7517), 606. doi: 10.1136/bmj.38583.728484.3A

Rundell, J. F. & Ursano, R. J. (1996). Psychiatric responses to trauma. In R. J. Ursano & A. E. Norwood (eds.), *Emotional Aftermath of the Persian Gulf War Veterans, Communities, and Nations* (pp. 43–81). Washington, DC: American Psychiatric Press.

Salmon, P. & Calderbank, S. (1996). The relationship of childhood physical and sexual abuse to adult illness behavior. *Journal of Psychosomatic Research, 40*(3), 329–336. doi: 10.1016/0022–3999(95)00580–3

Santiago, P. N., Ursano, R. J., Gray, C. L., Pynoos, R. S., Spiegel, D., Lewis-Fernandez, R., . . . Fullerton, C. S. (2013). A systematic review of PTSD prevalence and trajectories in *DSM-5* defined trauma exposed populations: Intentional and non-intentional traumatic events. *Public Library of Science One, 8*(4), e59236. doi: 10.1371/journal. pone.0059236

Schmidt, U. & Vermetten, E. (2017). Integrating NIMH Research Domain Criteria (RDoC) into PTSD research. *Current Topics in Behavioral Neuroscience.* 1–23. doi: 10.1007/7854_2017_1

Shalev, A. Y. (2002). Acute stress reactions in adults. *Biological Psychiatry, 51*(7), 532–543. doi: 10.1016/S0006-3223(02)01335–5

Shalev, A. Y., Sahar, T., Freedman, S., Peri, T., Glick, N., Brandes, D., . . . Pitman, R. K. (1998). A prospective study of heart rate response following trauma and the subsequent development of posttraumatic stress disorder. *Archives of General Psychiatry, 55*(6), 553–559. doi: 10.1001/archpsyc.55.6.553

Shankman, S. A. & Gorka, S. M. (2015). Psychopathology research in the RDoC era: Unanswered questions and the importance of the psychophysiological unit of analysis. *International Journal of Psychophysiology, 98*(2 Pt 2), 330–337. doi: 10.1016/j.ijpsycho.2015.01.001

Shevlin, M., Hyland, P., & Elklit, A. (2014). Different profiles of acute stress disorder differentially predict posttraumatic stress disorder in a large sample of female victims of sexual trauma. *Psychological Assessment, 26*(4), 1155–1161. doi: 10.1037/a0037272

Smoller, J. W. (2016). The genetics of stress-related disorders: PTSD, depression, and anxiety disorders. *Neuropsychopharmacology, 41*(1), 297–319. doi: 10.1038/ npp.2015.266

Solomon, E. P. & Heide, K. M. (2005). The biology of trauma: Implications for treatment. *Journal of Interpersonal Violence, 20*(1), 51–60. doi: 10.1177/0886260504268119

Southwick, S. M., Bremner, J. D., Rasmusson, A., Morgan, C. A., 3rd, Arnsten, A., & Charney, D. S. (1999). Role of norepinephrine in the pathophysiology and treatment of posttraumatic stress disorder. *Biological Psychiatry, 46*(9), 1192–1204. doi: 10.1016/S0006-3223(99)00219-X

Stein, D. J., Chiu, W. T., Hwang, I., Kessler, R. C., Sampson, N., Alonso, J., . . . Nock, M. K. (2010). Cross-national analysis of the associations between traumatic events and suicidal behavior: Findings from the WHO World Mental Health Surveys. *Public Library of Science One, 5*(5), e10574. doi: 10.1371/journal.pone.0010574

Stein, J. Y., Wilmot, D. V., & Solomon, Z. (2016). Does one size fit all? Nosological, clinical, and scientific implications of variations in PTSD Criterion A. *Journal of Anxiety Disorders, 43*, 106–117. doi: 10.1016/j.janxdis.2016.07.001

Stein, M. B., Walker, J. R., Hazen, A. L., & Forde, D. R. (1997). Full and partial posttraumatic stress disorder: findings from a community survey. *American Journal of Psychiatry, 154*(8), 1114–1119. doi: 10.1176/ajp.154.8.1114

Su, T. P., Zhang, L., Chung, M. Y., Chen, Y. S., Bi, Y. M., Chou, Y. H., . . . Ursano, R. (2009). Levels of the potential biomarker p11 in peripheral blood cells distinguish patients with PTSD from those with other major psychiatric disorders. *Journal of Psychiatric Research*, *43*(13), 1078–1085. doi: 10.1016/j.jpsychires.2009.03.010

Suliman, S., Troeman, Z., Stein, D. J., & Seedat, S. (2013). Predictors of acute stress disorder severity. *Journal of Affective Disorders*, *149*(1–3), 277–281. doi: 10.1016/j.jad.2013.01.041

Szabo, C., Kelemen, O., Levy-Gigi, E., & Keri, S. (2015). Acute response to psychological trauma and subsequent recovery: No changes in brain structure. *Psychiatry Research*, *231*(3), 269–272. doi: 10.1016/j.pscychresns.2015.01.005

Tang, B., Liu, X., Liu, Y., Xue, C., & Zhang, L. (2014). A meta-analysis of risk factors for depression in adults and children after natural disasters. *BioMed Central Public Health*, *14*, 623. doi: 10.1186/1471–2458-14–623

Tucker, P., Pfefferbaum, B., Nitiema, P., Wendling, T. L., & Brown, S. (2016). Intensely exposed Oklahoma City terrorism survivors: Long-term mental health and health needs and posttraumatic growth. *Journal of Nervous and Mental Disease*, *204*(3), 203–209. doi: 10.1097/NMD.0000000000000456

Ulibarri, M. D., Ulloa, E. C., & Salazar, M. (2015). Associations between mental health, substance use, and sexual abuse experiences among Latinas. *Journal of Child Sexual Abuse*, *24*(1), 35–54. doi: 10.1080/10538712.2015.976303

Ursano, R. J., Goldenberg, M., Zhang, L., Carlton, J., Fullerton, C. S., Li, H., . . . Benedek, D. (2010). Posttraumatic stress disorder and traumatic stress: From bench to bedside, from war to disaster. *Annals of the New York Academy of Sciences*, *1208*, 72–81. doi: 10.1111/j.1749–6632.2010.05721.x

van den Heuvel, L., Suliman, S., Malan-Muller, S., Hemmings, S., & Seedat, S. (2016). Brain-derived neurotrophic factor *Val66met* polymorphism and plasma levels in road traffic accident survivors. *Anxiety, Stress, & Coping*, *29*(6), 616–629. doi: 10.1080/10615806.2016.1163545

Vlahov, D., Galea, S., Resick, H., Ahern, J., Boscarino, J. A., Bucuvalas, M., . . . Kilpatrick, D. (2002). Increased use of cigarettes, alcohol, and marijuana among Manhattan, New York, residents after the September 11th terrorist attacks. *American Journal of Epidemiology*, *155*(11), 988–996.

World Health Organization. (2017). *The ICD-11 Classification of Mental and Behavioural Disorders: Clinical Descriptions and Diagnostic Guidelines (beta version)*. Geneva: World Health Organization.

Yuan, K. C., Ruo Yao, Z., Zhen Yu, S., Xu Dong, Z., Jian Zhong, Y., Edwards, J. G., & Edwards, G. D. (2013). Prevalence and predictors of stress disorders following two earthquakes. *International Journal of Social Psychiatry*, *59*(6), 525–530. doi: 10.1177/0020764012453233

Zannas, A. S. & Binder, E. B. (2014). Gene–environment interactions at the *FKBP5* locus: sensitive periods, mechanisms and pleiotropism. *Genes, Brain and Behavior*, *13* (1), 25–37. doi: 10.1111/gbb.12104

Zannas, A. S., Provencal, N., & Binder, E. B. (2015). Epigenetics of posttraumatic stress disorder: Current evidence, challenges, and future directions. *Biological Psychiatry*, *78*(5), 327–335. doi: 10.1016/j.biopsych.2015.04.003

Zhang, L., Li, H., Hu, X., Li, X. X., Smerin, S., & Ursano, R. (2011). Glucocorticoid-induced p11 over-expression and chromatin remodeling: A novel molecular mechanism of traumatic stress? *Medical Hypotheses*, *76*(6), 774–777. doi: 10.1016/j.mehy.2011.02.015

Zlotnick, C., Franklin, C. L., & Zimmerman, M. (2002). Does "subthreshold" posttraumatic stress disorder have any clinical relevance? *Comprehensive Psychiatry*, *43*(6), 413–419. doi: 10.1053/comp.2002.35900

Zoellner, L. A. & Foa, E. B. (2016). Applying Research Domain Criteria (RDoC) to the study of fear and anxiety: A critical comment. *Psychophysiology*, *53*(3), 332–335. doi: 10.1111/psyp.12588

26 Posttraumatic Stress Disorder

Katherine Buchholz, Zoe Feingold,
and Tara E. Galovski

Etiology and Phenomenology of Posttraumatic Stress Disorder

Exposure to trauma is not uncommon. Epidemiological studies estimate that approximately 50–90% of the US population is exposed to at least one traumatic event in their lifetime (Breslau et al., 1998; Kessler, 2000; Kilpatrick et al., 2013). In the recent National Stressful Events Survey (Kilpatrick et al., 2013), 90% of the 2,953 adults in the sample had been exposed to at least one traumatic event with the most common trauma being physical or sexual assault (53%), death of a close family member or friend due to violence/accident/disaster (52%), and natural disaster (51%). Trauma exposure in less-developed countries is likely greater with global prevalence rates of at least one traumatic exposure across the lifetime estimated in 70% of the population and 31% experiencing four or more traumatic events (Benjet et al., 2016).

While rates of trauma exposure are high, only a minority of trauma-exposed people experience chronic trauma-related distress (e.g., Bonanno, 2005; Kessler, Sonnega, Bromet, Hughes, & Nelson, 1995; Kilpatrick et al., 2013). The most prevalent psychological consequence to exposure of trauma is posttraumatic stress disorder (PTSD). Lifetime risk for PTSD in US population-based samples (including those not reporting a traumatic event) has consistently been documented at 7–9% (Breslau & Davis, 1992; Breslau, Davis, Andreski, & Peterson, 1991; Kessler et al., 1995; Kilpatrick et al., 2013). Although PTSD was not formally recognized as a mental health disorder until its inclusion in the third edition of the *Diagnostic and Statistical Manual of Mental Disorders* (*DSM-III*) (American Psychological Association, 1980) in 1980, descriptive accounts of symptoms we now associate with PTSD can be recognized throughout history. In 1896, Kreapelin described the "fright neuroses" (*schreckneurose*) he observed in survivors of serious accidents and injuries (Jablensky, 1985). Likewise, physicians and military psychiatrists have documented changes in soldiers' behavior and mental health upon returning from war throughout history, describing reactions as "gross stress reactions" and "war neuroses" (Shephard, 2001). With the advent of the women's movement and efforts by the National Organization for Women in the early 1970s to increase attention to and legislation around the sexual and physical assault of women, recognition of posttraumatic reactions secondary to interpersonal assaults proliferated, resulting in increased awareness, legislation, and research (Friedman, Resnick, & Keane, 2014). Throughout these historic accounts and with some variability, the core features of trauma-related distress are consistent: chronic, persistent, and intrusive reactions to stimuli reminiscent of the trauma, subsequent significant avoidance of trauma reminders, and an elevated level of perceived threat and hyperarousal.

Classification and Diagnosis of PTSD

The common, core, clinically observed symptoms in these and other historic accounts of trauma reactions were used as the basis for the inclusion of PTSD in the *DSM-III*. Since that time the *DSM* has provided the diagnostic criteria most commonly used for diagnosing PTSD in the United States. Revisions to the diagnostic criteria have occurred with each iteration of the *DSM*, and although most classifications of psychiatric disorders remained relatively intact in the recent revision of the *DSM* from editions IV to 5, the conceptualization of the trauma and stress-related mental disorders changed substantially (see Friedman, Kilpatrick, Schnurr, & Weathers, 2016, and Hoge et al., 2016, for a discussion on the pros and cons of these recent changes). Marking a departure from the previous version of the *DSM-IV* (American Psychiatric Association, 1994), the *DSM-5* removed PTSD and acute stress disorder (ASD) from the Anxiety Disorder spectrum to a newly developed spectrum titled "Trauma and Stressor-Related Disorders" (American Psychiatric Association, 2013). Disorders that explicitly link symptomatology to exposure to an external, traumatic, or stressful event are included in this new spectrum (PTSD, ASD, reactive attachment disorder [RAD], disinhibited social engagement disorder [DSED], and adjustment disorders). This recategorization of mental disorders attests to the unique nature of symptomatology distinctly associated with a clear etiological event (McNally, 2003). The *DSM* currently has defined this etiological event in PTSD and ASD (Criterion A trauma) as "exposure to actual or threatened death, serious injury or sexual violation," and a criterion A trauma includes situations in which an individual (1) directly experiences the traumatic event; (2) learns that the traumatic event occurred to a close family member or friend; or (3) experiences first-hand repeated or extreme exposure to aversive details of the traumatic event. Events or experiences that are considered criterion A traumas include rape or sexual assaults, combat exposure, motor vehicle accidents, and natural disasters among many other experiences.

Notably, the *DSM-5* (American Psychological Association, 2013) also includes substantial changes to the specific diagnostic criteria of PTSD – likely due to the proliferation of research on psychological and psychobiological mediators and moderators involved in the process of integrating trauma-related information over the past two decades. Specifically, the *DSM-5* has increased the 17 symptoms of PTSD to 20 categorized into four clusters: reexperiencing, avoidance, alterations in mood or cognitions, and hyperarousal. Reexperiencing symptoms focus on ways a person relives their experience of the traumatic event (American Psychiatric Association, 2013). These symptoms include intrusive thoughts, nightmares, reliving the event (e.g., flashbacks), emotional distress in response to traumatic reminders, and physical reactivity in response to traumatic reminders. Out of these five symptoms, a person must endorse at least one. Avoidance is a hallmark symptom of PTSD, and some theories suggest that avoidance symptoms contribute to the maintenance of the disorder (Brewin & Holmes, 2003; Foa & Kozak, 1986). The two symptoms in this category include cognitive avoidance in which a person attempts to avoid thoughts or feelings surrounding the trauma and experiential avoidance in which a person avoids external reminders of the trauma such as people, activities, or places that remind them of the event. Criteria are met for the avoidance cluster if at least one of two symptoms is present.

The third symptom cluster, negative alterations in mood and cognitions, was added to the diagnostic criteria in the *DSM-5*. Symptoms in this cluster include an inability to recall important aspects of the traumatic event (formerly in the avoidance cluster), persistent negative beliefs and expectations regarding the self and the world, excessive blame directed at oneself or others, persistent negative emotions or mood, decreased interest in activities (also formerly in the avoidance cluster), feeling detached from others (formerly an avoidance symptom), and difficulty experiencing positive emotions. To meet criteria in this category, at least two of the seven symptoms must be present. The last symptom cluster is alterations in arousal and reactivity. These symptoms include irritable or aggressive behavior, reckless behavior, hypervigilance, heightened startle response, difficulties concentrating, and sleep problems. To meet the criteria for the hyperarousal symptom cluster, at least two of the six symptoms must be present.

The required number of symptoms from each cluster must be met for a full diagnosis. Additionally, symptoms must have been present for at least one month, and they must cause significant distress or functional impairment. The *DSM-5* diagnosis of PTSD also includes two specifiers to describe significant symptoms of dissociation that can accompany PTSD. These two specifiers are: depersonalization (individual experiences high levels of feeling as if he or she is an outside observer of or detached from him or herself) and derealization (experience of unreality, distance, or distortion). One final specifier, delayed expression, is used if full diagnostic criteria are met only after six months following the traumatic event.

The increase in symptoms in the *DSM-5* version of PTSD diagnostic criteria stands in marked contrast to the World Health Organization's *International Classification of Diseases*, 11th Revision (*ICD-11*), the most commonly utilized diagnostic manual outside of the United States. The *ICD-11* (scheduled to be released in 2018) includes only six symptoms in the diagnosis of PTSD: intrusive memories (in the form of thoughts, flashbacks, or nightmares); intense emotional distress; avoidance of thoughts or memories of the trauma, avoidance of activities, situations, or people that remind one of the trauma; persistent perceptions of heightened threat; hypervigilance or exaggerated startle response (for discussion on *DSM-5* vs. *ICD 11*, see Brewin, 2013; Friedman, 2013; Kilpatrick, 2013; Maercker & Perkonigg, 2013).

Prevalence of PTSD

Despite high rates of trauma exposure, lifetime risk for PTSD in US general population samples (including those not reporting a traumatic event) has consistently been documented between 7% and 9% (Breslau & Davis, 1992; Breslau et al., 1991; Kessler et al., 1995; Kilpatrick et al., 2013). It is noteworthy that the majority of individuals who experience a traumatic event do not go on to develop PTSD (e.g., Kessler et al., 1995; Kilpatrick et al., 2013). Conditional risk for PTSD, or the rate at which those exposed to a qualifying traumatic stressor subsequently develop PTSD, hovers at or below 15% in nationally representative surveys in the United States, Mexico, and Australia (Creamer, Burgess, & McFarlane, 2001; Kessler et al., 1995; Kilpatrick et al., 2013; Norris et al., 2003).

Certain traumatic experiences are statistically more likely to lead to the onset of PTSD than others. Crime victimization, or direct exposure to physical and/or sexual violence, has consistently been demonstrated as the category of trauma most highly correlated with subsequent development of PTSD (e.g., Breslau et al., 1998; Kilpatrick et al., 2013; Resnick, Kilpatrick, Dansky, Saunders, & Best, 1993). In multiple large-scale studies, the experience of rape or sexual assault resulted in the highest likelihood of developing PTSD compared to all other traumatic experiences, including physical abuse, witnessing death/violence, experiencing a disaster or life-threatening accident (Breslau et al., 1998; Kilpatrick et al., 2013; Norris et al., 2003). In Kessler and colleagues' (1995) nationally representative study of adults in the United States, 19% of the sample was found to have experienced a life-threatening accident, but only 8% of those who experienced such a trauma met criteria for PTSD based on the event. By comparison, 55% of respondents who experienced rape met criteria for PTSD attributable to that event. Direct exposure to nonsexual violence has also been associated with high conditional risk for PTSD, though at significantly higher rates in women than men. Results from the national comorbidity survey (NCS) showed that 22% of men and 49% of women exposed to physical abuse met criteria for PTSD (Kessler et al., 1995). Resnick and colleagues' (1993) study of women across the United States found that 39% of participants exposed to physical assault had developed PTSD. The percentage of women exposed to physical violence who met criteria for PTSD (13.1%) in Norris and colleagues' (2003) study of civilians across four cities in Mexico was much higher than the percentage of men who developed PTSD attributable to physical violence (3.6%).

Military Populations

Given the heightened risk of exposure to trauma through the course of military service during wartime, PTSD is often associated with veterans and combat trauma, and research supports this association. Hoge and colleagues (2004) found that 95% of Army and Marine veterans of Operation Enduring Freedom (OEF) and

Operation Iraqi Freedom (OIF) reported having been shot at, and 89% reported receiving incoming artillery, rocket, or mortar fire. Seventy-six percent reported seeing ill or injured civilians that they were unable to help, 95% had seen dead bodies or human remains, and 87% had known someone killed or seriously injured (Hoge et al., 2004). In a large-scale, nationally representative study of male and female OEF/OIF veterans accessing Veterans Association (VA) health services, 13% were found to have a diagnosis of PTSD (Seal, Bertenthal, Miner, Sen, & Marmar, 2007). Though there is limited research capturing Vietnam veterans' exposure to traumas during service, results from the National Vietnam Veterans Readjustment Study (NVVRS), have found estimates of lifetime PTSD among male combat veterans of the Vietnam era as high as 31%, with a rate of 26% found in female Vietnam veterans (Weiss et al., 1992).

PTSD around the World

Documentation of trauma exposure in nationally representative samples outside of the United States has been limited. Using the Australian National Survey of Mental Health and Well-Being, Creamer, Burgess, and McFarlane (2001) reported a 57% rate of trauma exposure in a nationally representative Australian sample of 10,641 adult participants. Similar to findings in the United States, the majority of participants reporting any traumatic event had experienced more than one event throughout his or her lifetime. Most commonly, traumatic events included witnessing someone being badly injured or killed (27%), being involved in a life-threatening accident (21%), or experiencing a natural disaster (16%). A community survey of roughly 1,000 adults in a Midwestern Canadian city reported a lifetime rate of exposure to trauma of 78% (Stein, Walker, Hazen, & Forde, 1997). Norris and colleagues (2003) surveyed 2,509 adults from four cities in Mexico, reporting 76% of the sample with exposure to at least one traumatic event. Most frequently reported events included loss of a loved one due to homicide, suicide, or accident (38%), witnessing someone being injured or killed (35%), life-threatening accident (32%), and physical assault (20%).

Based on nationally representative data from the World Health Organization (WHO) World Mental Health (WHM) Survey Initiative (Kessler & Ustun, 2008), lifetime prevalence of PTSD outside of the United States ranges from less than 1% in China to 8.8% in Northern Ireland (Koenen et al., 2017). In this study, the lifetime prevalence of PTSD in the United States was 6.9% with only two countries (Australia and Northern Ireland) reporting a greater lifetime prevalence. These survey results suggest that lifetime prevalence of PTSD is higher in the United States compared to many other countries. Additional studies, however, have shown prevalence rates of lifetime PTSD that are more comparable to results found in US general population studies. Norris and colleagues (2003) reported a lifetime PTSD prevalence rate of 11% in a sample from four Mexican cities. In a study of roughly 3,000 adults from four post-conflict countries, lifetime rates of PTSD were reported as high as 37% (Algeria), 28% (Cambodia), 16% (Ethiopia), and 18% (Gaza) (de Jong et al., 2001).

Development of PTSD

The development of mental health outcomes (including PTSD) secondary to traumatic events has most often been tracked following single, discrete events such as a disaster, mass casualty, or terrorist attack (e.g., Gruebner, Lowe et al., 2016; Gruebner, Sykora et al., 2016), within specific populations such as combat veterans (Berntsen et al., 2012) and first responders (Marchand, Nadeau, Beaulieu-Prévost, Boyer, & Martin, 2015), or within study samples defined by their trauma type such as rape survivors (Rothbaum, Foa, Riggs, Murdock, & Walsh, 1992), following serious injury (Osenbach et al., 2014) and within war refugee populations (Hobfoll et al., 2009). The preponderance of the research has focused on the pathological response to trauma exposure with most attention paid to the development and maintenance of posttraumatic stress and, to a lesser extent, depression (Hobfoll et al., 2009). Recently, studies conducted following mass casualty exposure or terrorism (Bonanno, 2005; Bonanno, Rennicke, & Dekel, 2005; Hobfoll et al., 2009), and natural disaster (reviewed in Norris & Stevens, 2007) consistently show that the majority of individuals exposed to trauma do not report pathological distress, or are *resistant* and never develop clinical levels of symptoms. Further, survivors of trauma may be classified as *recovered*, a trajectory marked by initial increased symptomatology that decreases naturally over time (Bonanno, 2005; Norris, Stevens, Pfefferbaum, Wyche, & Pfefferbaum, 2008). A third trajectory, termed the *chronic distress* trajectory (Hobfoll et al., 2009), includes individuals who report elevated symptoms following the traumatic event with little or no improvement over a reasonable amount of time. Finally, a fourth trajectory, also described by Hobfoll et al. (2009) and termed *delayed distress*, describes a group with low levels of distress in the immediate aftermath of the event, but with increasing symptomatology over time. Understanding trajectories of resistance, recovery, and distress in the aftermath of a traumatic event is critical in the development of a roadmap for understanding both the development of PTSD and successful adaptation following adversity, stress, and disturbance (Norris & Stevens, 2007).

Mental health trajectories following trauma exposure vary depending on a host of variables including the type and number of exposures, situational variables such as the chronicity of the event and extent of ongoing exposure, losses and injuries suffered, perceived and actual support, and a host of individual and contextual variables during and following the event (Dohrenwend, Turner, Turse, Lewis-Fernandez, & Yager, 2008; Gapen et al., 2011; Goldmann et al., 2011; Hobfoll et al., 2009; Osenbach et al., 2014; Yehuda & Bierer, 2009). Further, trauma variables and contextual features may interact with one another and additional risk factors to determine initial mental health outcomes and fluctuations in those outcomes over time (Brewin, Andrews, & Valentine, 2000; Roberts, Gilman, Breslau, Breslau, & Koenen, 2011; Schumm, Briggs-Phillips, & Hobfoll, 2006).

Research on mental health trajectories following trauma exposure highlights that many individuals experience natural recovery following trauma exposure. Although the majority of people may experience initial elevated levels of post-traumatic stress and depression secondary to trauma exposure, in the majority of people these symptoms decrease over time. Therefore, trauma does not inevitably lead to PTSD. Rather PTSD occurs when natural recovery is impeded or blocked, and symptoms become consistent and chronic. Because of this, PTSD is often conceptualized as a disorder of non-recovery (Resick, Monson, & Chard, 2007).

Theoretical Models of PTSD

Historical Theories of Trauma

Multiple theories have emerged to explain the acquisition and maintenance of PTSD symptoms in people who have experienced a traumatic event. Contemporary psychological theories of PTSD have developed from early psychologists and theorists dating back to the late 19th century (Monson, Friedman, & La Bash, 2007; Resick, 2001). These early theories provided a foundation for how clinicians and researchers currently conceptualize and treat PTSD. Psychoanalysts of the late 1800s often studied and treated people with a history of trauma. In his early work, Sigmund Freud posited that hysteria was an effect of early childhood sexual abuse (Freud & Breuer, 1895), and influenced which defense mechanisms were utilized. His recognition that early childhood trauma could affect psychological development and contribute to mental health outcomes was not well accepted, leading Freud to reverse his views. A contemporary of Freud, Pierre Janet, also studied the effect of trauma on people. His work focused on mental schemes. Janet suggested that people formed mental schemes based on their past experience, and that these schemes influenced people's interactions with the world. He suggested that people who experienced traumatic events had difficulty integrating their fear-laden memory into their existing schemes and personal narrative (Janet, Paul, & Paul, 1925).

In the early 1900s, behaviorism emerged in the field of psychology as an alternative to psychoanalytic approaches that tended to focus on internal thoughts and the subconscious. In contrast to psychoanalysts, behaviorists focused primarily on observable behavior. Classical (Pavlov & Thompson, 1902) and operant conditioning (Skinner, 1945) demonstrated how behaviors could be learned or conditioned. Acquisition of fear through conditioning procedures set the foundation for many theoretical models of PTSD. In his seminal study, Pavlov demonstrated associative learning with dogs. Using dogs' natural reaction to food (salivating), Pavlov paired the sound of a ringing bell with the presentation of food. Eventually, the dogs would begin to salivate at the ring of the bell prior to the presentation of food, demonstrating a conditioned response (salivating) to a once neutral stimulus. He also found that this new conditioned response (salivating at the sound of the bell) could be extinguished by ringing the bell repeatedly without the presentation of food, resulting in an un-pairing of the bell and food. While classical conditioning focused on associative learning through pairing of unconditioned stimulus with neutral stimulus, operant conditioning focused on shaping new behavior through manipulating consequences of the operant stimulus. In other words, through operant conditioning, target behaviors, "operants," could be increased or decreased based on the experienced consequence (negative or positive reinforcement and punishment).

The classic case of Little Albert (Watson & Rayner, 1920) is an example of how classical and operant conditioning are related to the development and maintenance of fear. In this study, classical conditioning was used to elicit a fear response in Little Albert to a white rat. To do this, Watson presented Albert with a white rat and played a loud, frightening noise. The noise was frightening to Albert (unconditioned response). Albert associated the neutral stimulus (white rat) with the unconditioned stimulus (the scary noise) and became fearful (conditioned or learned response) of the rat (now the conditioned stimulus). This fear then generalized to other stimuli such as a Santa mask, a dog, and a rabbit. Whenever he was presented with the rat, Albert would run away, leading to the persistence of his fear despite the fact that the loud sound was no longer paired with the rat. This maintenance of fear can be explained by operant conditioning in which Albert's avoidance served as a negative reinforcer of his fear such that fleeing from the scary stimulus alleviated his fear. This avoidance strategy prevented the fear response from extinguishing.

Through combining the principles of both classical and operant conditioning, Orval Hobart Mowrer developed his two-factor theory (Mowrer, 1947, 1960) to explain conditioned fears. As applied to PTSD, Mowrer's theory suggests classical conditioning underlies the initial posttraumatic response (Kilpatrick, Veronen, & Resick, 1979). Through this process, fear is associated with future presentations of previously neutral stimuli that were present at the time of the trauma. For example, someone who is physically assaulted after leaving a chocolate store may experience a fear response when they see a chocolate store in the future. Or a person who is fired upon in a combat situation may later experience fear when a car backfires or during loud thunder. The previously innocuous stimuli (chocolate store, car, thunder) are conditioned stimuli and generate reactions similar (conditioned responses) to those experienced during the actual traumatic event. The second part of Mowrer's two-factor theory suggests that operant conditioning is responsible for the maintenance of PTSD symptoms. Just as Little Albert's avoidance negatively reinforced his fear of the rat, in people with PTSD avoidance of trauma reminders (both internal and external) serves as a negative reinforcer maintaining fear in relation to the traumatic event.

The 1960s brought about the cognitive revolution in the field of psychology. While behaviorism focused primarily on observable behavior with less attention to cognitions (termed *private events*) due to the inability to observe and measure internal events with the same methodology that one observes overt behaviors, psychologists of the mid-20th century turned their focus to just that. Relevant to later cognitive theories of PTSD is the construct of schemas (Monson et al., 2007). The construct of schemas was introduced by Frederic Bartlett. Bartlett (1932) proposed that people developed schemas based on their past experiences, cultural beliefs, and general knowledge. These schemas are then used to understand and retain new information about themselves and the world.

The concept of schemas was further explored by developmental psychologist Jean Piaget. Piaget introduced the cognitive processes of assimilation and accommodation (Piaget, 1965). Using schema theory, Piaget suggested that as people take in new information and experiences, they attempt to incorporate this new information into their mental framework. If new information matches existing schemas, people will naturally integrate this information into their existing framework (assimilation). However, if the new information is discordant with their existing schemas, people will adjust their beliefs in order to accommodate the new information (accommodation). The processes of assimilation and accommodation allow people to confirm their existing beliefs and adapt their beliefs to fit new experiences and knowledge. Schema theory and the cognitive processes of assimilation and accommodation set the foundation for Horowitz, who applied similar concepts to the experience of trauma. Horowitz described a concept he called "completion tendency" in which people have a psychological need to integrate discordant information with their existing beliefs (Horowitz, 1986). Until this integration is complete, trauma information remains active in people's memories.

Contemporary Theoretical Models of PTSD

Contemporary theories on PTSD grew out of the work of the earlier theorists. These theories have been developed and refined over time, and many of these contemporary theories have informed clinical treatment protocols.

Emotional processing theory. Emotional processing theory was developed from Lang's bioinformational theory of fear (1977, 1979). Drawing from aspects of both behavioral and cognitive theories, Lang's bioinformational theory stated that fear is stored in memory structures that contain three types of information: the feared stimulus, the associated behavioral responses (e.g., increased heart rate, leaving the situation, sweating), and the meaning of the feared stimulus and behavioral responses. Lang suggested that these large, diffuse fear structures are activated when something in the environment matches something stored in the structures. Therefore, these fear structures remained stored, and outside of awareness, until an environmental trigger activates the structure and brings it into awareness, leading to the behavioral response. For example, the sound of a firework in the distance may activate a fear structure containing a memory of combat with a behavioral response of taking cover or leaving a situation and a meaning component of "I am in danger."

Foa and Kozak (1986) built upon the bioinformational theory in their development of emotional processing theory. They posited that pathological fear structures, such as those associated with PTSD, demonstrated impairment in the ability to process fear. It was thought that these pathological fear structures included extreme or exaggerated response elements and were more difficult to alter or change. Additionally, it was suggested that these pathological fear structures included associations that were based on an altered perception of the actual traumatic event. When applied directly to PTSD, emotional processing theory suggests that the meaning elements of pathological fear structures include cognitive distortions such as "the world is a dangerous place" and "I am incompetent" (Rauch & Foa, 2006).

These pathological fear structures are continually activated by environmental stimuli and are maintained through avoidance. To modify the fear structure, Foa and Kozak (1986) proposed that the fear structure must be activated and new information that contradicts information in the existing fear structure must be presented. When the new information is integrated into the activated fear structure, an emotional change occurs. Therefore, avoidance is a main factor in the maintenance of PTSD symptoms. Avoidance of trauma reminders prevents people with PTSD from acquiring contradictory new information to challenge or alter their existing fear structure.

Emotional processing theory has informed prolonged exposure (PE), one of the evidenced-based treatments for PTSD (Foa, 2011; Foa, Hembree, & Rothbaum, 2007; Rauch & Foa, 2006). Exposure – presentation of the feared stimulus in a safe environment – is perceived as an active mechanism of change in PE. Through exposure people are able to break the cycle of trauma-related avoidance. By approaching trauma reminders and memories through in vivo and imaginal exposure, people activate their trauma-related fear structure and are able to integrate new information into their existing fear structures to process their experience of trauma.

Social cognitive theory. Social cognitive theory of PTSD integrates aspects of information-processing theories and schema theories (Hollon & Garber, 1988; Janoff-Bulman, 1992; McCann & Pearlman, 1990; Resick, 2001). Social cognitive theory states PTSD develops due to a failure to accurately integrate a trauma memory within a person's belief structure or personal schemas. How people interpret their experience of the traumatic event, and how that interpretation is connected to their emotional response, is central to social cognitive theory. The theory posits that in the aftermath of trauma, people attempt to reconcile their experience with their belief structure or personal schemas through assimilation (changing the memory of the trauma to fit into their belief structure), accommodation (adjusting their belief structure to fit the trauma memory), and over-accommodation (broadly and rigidly changing the belief structure to fit the trauma memory) (Hollon & Garber, 1988; Resick & Schnicke, 1992).

In the natural recovery process, individuals who experience traumatic events utilize the process of accommodation to effectively integrate their trauma into their belief structure. However, people who develop PTSD following trauma exposure are unable effectively to integrate their traumatic experience with their core schemas. The discrepancy between their experience and belief structure impedes the natural recovery process and underlies the symptoms of PTSD (Hollon & Garber, 1988; Resick & Schnicke, 1992). Assimilation and over-accommodation disrupt adaptive processing of the trauma memory and contribute to the maintenance of PTSD symptoms. Therefore, it is necessary for people with PTSD to examine and assess the accuracy of their interpretations of traumatic experiences in order to adaptively integrate the trauma information into their existing belief structure.

Social cognitive theory has informed cognitive processing therapy (CPT), another evidenced-based therapy for PTSD (Resick, 2001; Resick et al., 2007; Resick & Schnicke, 1992). CPT takes into account preexisting negative belief systems by observing that trauma information is not always schema discrepant, but can also align with prior beliefs – essentially providing evidence for those preexisting negative beliefs and, ultimately, contributing to PTSD (Resick, 2001; Resick et al., 2007). The goal of CPT is to help people identify, examine, and challenge inaccurate trauma-related cognitions (termed *stuck points* in CPT) such as those that had been assimilated or over-accommodated, to help a person more accurately process the trauma information, come to different and more adaptive conclusions, and reduce associated distress. Challenging and restructuring dysfunctional or unhelpful cognitions allows a person to accurately assess their experience of trauma and process both natural (e.g., fear, sadness) and manufactured (e.g., self-blame, guilt) emotions stemming from the trauma.

Dual representation theory. In contrast to these theories, the dual representation theory of PTSD posits that two separate memory systems simultaneously encode the traumatic experience (Brewin, Dalgleish, & Joseph, 1996; Brewin & Holmes, 2003). The first of these two systems is the "verbally accessible memory" (VAM) system. Trauma memories in the VAM system are accessible. They can be intentionally retrieved and communicated to others just as any other autobiographical memory. VAM trauma memories, however, are limited to information that has been consciously processed before, during, and after the trauma. The second memory system is the "situationally accessible memory" (SAM) system. SAM memories include trauma information that is not verbally accessible such as sensory information or bodily responses that were not consciously recorded during the trauma. Generally, trauma information in the SAM system is difficult to communicate to others and is recalled through exposure to reminders instead of intentional recall.

The dual representation theory suggests two different pathological processes (Brewin & Holmes, 2003). While the VAM is associated with PTSD symptoms of altered cognitions and negative emotions due to cognitive distortions, the SAM system underlies reexperiencing symptoms such as flashbacks. Therefore, to treat PTSD according to this theory, it is necessary to address both the negative appraisals of the VAM system and more automatic processes of the SAM system. Symptom reduction is achieved through both cognitive restructuring (that engages the VAM system) and exposure (that engages the SAM system).

Emerging Models

The contemporary theories discussed earlier have led to effective treatments for people with PTSD, and have informed research over time. However, these theories focus solely on PTSD and offer limited explanations for the high rates of co-occurrence of other mental health disorders such as major depression, generalized anxiety disorder, and substance use disorders with PTSD. Research has consistently found that more than 50% of people with PTSD have a comorbid mental health concern (Kessler et al., 1995; Pietrzak, Goldstein, Southwick, & Grant, 2011). One report using data from the National Epidemiologic Survey on Alcohol and Related Conditions (NESARC) (Pietrzak et al., 2011) found that among people with PTSD 62% have a comorbid mood disorder, 59% have a comorbid anxiety disorder, and 46% have a comorbid substance use disorder. Kessler and colleagues (1995) found that more than 40% of people with PTSD met criteria for three or more mental health disorders.

Multiple explanations have been proposed to account for co-occurrence of PTSD and other mental health disorders (see Brown & Barlow, 2002, 2009). One possible explanation is that many mental health disorders have overlapping symptom criteria (e.g., PTSD and depression both include symptoms related to restricted affect, persistent negative moods, and sleep problems). A second potential explanation is that the presence of one mental health disorder may make it more likely that a person will develop another disorder. Research has found that preexisting psychological disorders (prior to trauma exposure) such as depression and substance use increase risk for developing PTSD, and other disorders are commonly developed secondary to PTSD. For example, a person with PTSD may develop a substance use disorder through increasing their substance use to avoid thinking about their trauma. Still another possible explanation is that core vulnerabilities underlie the development of multiple disorders, meaning that disorders across diagnostic categories may develop from the same core factors. This final explanation is the basis for a transdiagnostic model or approach to mental health (Barlow, Sauer-Zavala, Carl, Bullis, & Ellard, 2014; Brown & Barlow, 2009). The transdiagnostic approach focuses on core vulnerabilities or factors that underlie multiple mental health disorders and accounts for co-occurrence of multiple disorders. This model shifts conceptualizations away from the discrete diagnostic categories and instead focuses on latent dimensional features such as negative affect or preoccupation with autonomic arousal (Barlow et al., 2014). Therefore, treatments are less focused on targeting symptoms or mechanisms specific to a single disorder, and instead are created to address the underlying transdiagnostic factor in order to facilitate overall improvement in mental health (Barlow, Allen, & Choate, 2004; Gutner, Galovski, Bovin, & Schnurr, 2016).

Another dimensional approach is the National Institute of Mental Health's (NIMH) Research Diagnostic Criteria (RDoC) initiative. RDoC contrasts with the formal categorical approaches evident in the *DSM* and *ICD* diagnostic criteria for mental disorders that rely on observable symptoms rather than pathophysiology.

Burgeoning research in the fields of clinical neuroscience and genetics has furthered our understanding of the etiology of posttraumatic stress and related mental disorders. Increased attention on the pathophysiology underlying mental disorders represents a more dimensional approach to understanding the etiology of mental disorders, which, in turn, increases the likelihood that common mechanisms of dysfunction will be identified. The RDoC initiative adopted by the NIMH recognizes the need for a cohesive framework for ongoing research that relies on pathophysiology (with an emphasis on neuroscience and genomics) to inform diagnostic classification strategies. The basic premise of the RDoC framework assumes that mental illness is best understood as disorders of "brain function and structure" – a departure from the nosology evident in the *DSM* and *ICD* classification systems (Insel & Lieberman, 2013). The ultimate goal of the RDoC framework is to propel the development of more targeted and precise intervention methods and strategies – ultimately improving clinical outcomes (Insel et al., 2010). The extent to which the biosignatures necessary for the success of this goal will be identified in a particularly heterogeneous disorder such as PTSD (Young, 2014) is yet to be determined.

The RDoC initiative has identified five domains: negative valance systems, positive valence systems, cognitive systems, social processes, and arousal and regulatory systems. Researchers have yet to fully create a conceptualization of PTSD based in the RDoC domains; however, research on the negative valance system that includes the constructs of acute threat (fear) and potential threat (anxiety) indicates impairments in these systems in people with PTSD (Bauer et al., 2013; Pineles et al., 2013).

Conclusion

The majority of people are exposed to at least one traumatic event during their lifetime, and a substantial minority will experience significant trauma-related distress in the form of PTSD. PTSD is a chronic disorder that includes symptoms of reliving the traumatic event, avoiding internal and external trauma reminders, negative alterations in mood and cognitions, and hyperarousal. While the psychological effects of trauma exposure have been documented throughout history, PTSD was not formally identified as a mental health disorder until its inclusion in the *DSM-III*. Since that time, the diagnosis has been revised multiple times with the most recent iteration of the *DSM* moving PTSD from the Anxiety Disorders to a new classification of Trauma and Stressor-Related Disorders.

Theories of PTSD have developed from both behavioral and cognitive traditions. Emotional processing theory, social cognitive theory, and the dual representation model are contemporary theories developed to explain the etiology and maintenance of PTSD symptoms.

While emotional processing theory posits that pathological fear structures containing information on the trauma memory, behavioral responses, and meaning components underlie PTSD symptoms, social cognitive theory states that PTSD is the result of a discrepancy between people's belief system and their experience of trauma. While emotional processing theory views avoidance of trauma reminders as the main contributing factor to the maintenance of PTSD symptoms, social cognitive theory suggests that assimilation (changing the trauma memory to fit one's belief structure) and over-accommodation (rigidly changing one's beliefs to fit the trauma memory) maintain PTSD symptoms and prevent natural recovery from occurring. The dual representation theory attempts to combine components of both emotional processing and social cognitive theories by suggesting that two separate memory systems encode trauma memories. The VAM system is verbally accessible and contains pieces of the memory that can be intentionally recalled while the SAM system stores aspects of the trauma memory that have not been consciously processed. Processing of the memory in both systems is needed for symptom reduction to occur.

Finally, with increased recognition of comorbidity across disorders and the increased interest in investigations of neurobiological mechanisms or biomarkers of psychological disorders, new dimensional approaches have emerged. Researchers have moved toward examining transdiagnostic factors defined as core vulnerabilities that span multiple disorders and provide an explanation for high rates of comorbid disorders. Similarly, the NIMH has introduced the RDoC initiative to examine dimensional constructs across diagnostic categories to better understand what core mechanisms may contribute to pathological processes across categorical diagnoses.

References

American Psychiatric Association. (1980). *Diagnostic and Statistical Manual, 3rd Edition (DSM-III)*. Washington, DC: American Psychiatric Association.

American Psychiatric Association. (1994). *Diagnostic and Statistical Manual of Mental Disorders* (4th edn). Washington, DC: American Psychiatric Association.

American Psychiatric Association. (2013). *Diagnostic and Statistical Manual of Mental Disorders: DSM-5*. Washington, DC: American Psychiatric Association.

Barlow, D. H., Allen, L. B., & Choate, M. L. (2004). Toward a unified treatment for emotional disorders. *Behavior Therapy, 35*(2), 205–230. https://doi.org/10.1016/S0005-7894(04)80036-4

Barlow, D. H., Sauer-Zavala, S., Carl, J. R., Bullis, J. R., & Ellard, K. K. (2014). The nature, diagnosis, and treatment of neuroticism: Back to the future. *Clinical Psychological Science, 2*(3), 344–365.

Bartlett, F. C. (1932). *Remembering: An Experimental and Social Study*. Cambridge: Cambridge University Press. Retrieved from www.citeulike.org/group/9538/article/4434739.

Bauer, M. R., Ruef, A. M., Pineles, S. L., Japuntich, S. J., Macklin, M. L., Lasko, N. B., & Orr, S. P. (2013). Psychophysiological assessment of PTSD: A potential Research Domain Criteria construct. *Psychological Assessment, 25*(3), 1037.

Benjet, C., Bromet, E., Karam, E. G., Kessler, R. C., McLaughlin, K. A., Ruscio, A. M., . . . others. (2016). The epidemiology of traumatic event exposure worldwide: Results from the World Mental Health Survey Consortium. *Psychological Medicine*, *46* (2), 327–343.

Berntsen, D., Johannessen, K. B., Thomsen, Y. D., Bertelsen, M., Hoyle, R. H., & Rubin, D. C. (2012). Peace and war: Trajectories of posttraumatic stress disorder symptoms before, during, and after military deployment in Afghanistan. *Psychological Science*, *23*(12), 1557–1565.

Bonanno, G. A. (2005). Resilience in the face of potential trauma. *Current Directions in Psychological Science*, *14*(3), 135–138. https://doi.org/10.1111/j.0963–7214 .2005.00347.x

Bonanno, G. A., Rennicke, C., & Dekel, S. (2005). Self-enhancement among high-exposure survivors of the September 11th terrorist attack: Resilience or social maladjustment? *Journal of Personality and Social Psychology*, *88*(6), 984–998. https://doi.org/10.1037/0022–3514.88.6.984

Breslau, N. & Davis, G. C. (1992). Posttraumatic stress disorder in an urban population of young adults: Risk factors for chronicity. *American Journal of Psychiatry*, *149*(5), 671–675. https://doi.org/10.1176/ajp.149.5.671

Breslau, N., Davis, G. C., Andreski, P., & Peterson, E. (1991). Traumatic events and posttraumatic stress disorder in an urban population of young adults. *Archives of General Psychiatry*, *48*(3), 216–222. https://doi.org/10.1001/archpsyc.1991 .01810270028003

Breslau, N., Kessler, R. C., Chilcoat, H. D., Schultz, L. R., Davis, G. C., & Andreski, P. (1998). Trauma and posttraumatic stress disorder in the community: The 1996 Detroit Area Survey of Trauma. *Archives of General Psychiatry*, *55*(7), 626–632.

Brewin, C. R. (2013). "I wouldn't start from here": An alternative perspective on PTSD from the *ICD-11*: Comment on Friedman (2013). *Journal of Traumatic Stress, 26* (5), 557–559. https://doi.org/10.1002/jts.21843

Brewin, C. R., Andrews, B., & Valentine, J. D. (2000). Meta-analysis of risk factors for posttraumatic stress disorder in trauma-exposed adults. *Journal of Consulting and Clinical Psychology*, *68*(5), 748–766. https://doi.org/10.1037/0022-006X.68.5.748

Brewin, C. R., Dalgleish, T., & Joseph, S. (1996). A dual representation theory of posttraumatic stress disorder. *Psychological Review*, *103*(4), 670.

Brewin, C. R. & Holmes, E. A. (2003). Psychological theories of posttraumatic stress disorder. *Clinical Psychology Review*, *23*(3), 339–376.

Brown, T. A. & Barlow, D. H. (2002). Classification of anxiety and mood disorders. *Anxiety and Its Disorders: The Nature and Treatment of Anxiety and Panic*, *2*, 292–327.

Brown, T. A. & Barlow, D. H. (2009). A proposal for a dimensional classification system based on the shared features of the *DSM-IV* anxiety and mood disorders: Implications for assessment and treatment. *Psychological Assessment*, *21*(3), 256.

Creamer, M., Burgess, P., & McFarlane, A. C. (2001). Post-traumatic stress disorder: Findings from the Australian National Survey of Mental Health and Well-Being. *Psychological Medicine*, *31*(7), 1237–1247. https://doi.org/10.1017 /S0033291701004287

de Jong, J. T., Komproe, I. H., van Ommeren, M., El Masri, M., Araya, M., Khaled, N., . . . Somasundaram, D. (2001). Lifetime events and posttraumatic stress disorder in 4 postconflict settings. *JAMA*, *286*(5), 555–562.

Dohrenwend, B. P., Turner, J. B., Turse, N. A., Lewis-Fernandez, R., & Yager, T. J. (2008). War-related posttraumatic stress disorder in black, Hispanic, and majority white Vietnam veterans: The roles of exposure and vulnerability. *Journal of Traumatic Stress, 21*(2), 133–141. https://doi.org/10.1002/jts.20327

Foa, E. B. (2011). Prolonged exposure therapy: Past, present, and future. *Depression and Anxiety, 28*(12), 1043–1047. https://doi.org/10.1002/da.20907

Foa, E. B., Hembree, E. A., & Rothbaum, B. O. (2007). *Prolonged Exposure Therapy for PTSD*. New York, NY: Oxford University Press.

Foa, E. B. & Kozak, M. J. (1986). Emotional processing of fear: Exposure to corrective information. *Psychological Bulletin, 99*(1), 20–35.

Freud, S. & Breuer, J. (1895). *Studies on Hysteria,* vol. 2. *The Standard Edition of the Complete Psychological Works of Sigmund Freud, 1953–86*. London.

Friedman, M. J. (2013). PTSD in the *DSM-5*: Reply to Brewin (2013), Kilpatrick (2013), and Maercker and Perkonigg (2013). *Journal of Traumatic Stress, 26*(5), 567–569. https://doi.org/10.1002/jts.21847

Friedman, M. J., Kilpatrick, D. G., Schnurr, P. P., & Weathers, F. W. (2016). Correcting misconceptions about the diagnostic criteria for posttraumatic stress disorder in *DSM-5*. *JAMA Psychiatry, 73*(7), 753–754. https://doi.org/10.1001/jamapsychia try.2016.0745

Friedman, M. J., Resick, P. A., & Keane, T. M. (2014). PTSD from DSM-III to DSM-5: Progress and challenges. *Handbook of PTSD: Science and Practice*, 3–20.

Gapen, M., Cross, D., Ortigo, K., Graham, A., Johnson, E., Evces, M., ... Bradley, B. (2011). Perceived neighborhood disorder, community cohesion, and PTSD symptoms among low-income African Americans in an urban health setting. *American Journal of Orthopsychiatry, 81*(1), 31–37. https://doi.org/10.1111/j.1939–0025 .2010.01069.x

Goldmann, E., Aiello, A., Uddin, M., Delva, J., Koenen, K., Gant, L. M., & Galea, S. (2011). Pervasive exposure to violence and posttraumatic stress disorder in a predominantly African American urban community: The Detroit neighborhood health study. *Journal of Traumatic Stress, 24*(6), 747–751. https://doi.org/10.1002 /jts.20705

Gruebner, O., Lowe, S. R., Tracy, M., Cerdá, M., Joshi, S., Norris, F. H., & Galea, S. (2016). The geography of mental health and general wellness in Galveston Bay after Hurricane Ike: A spatial epidemiologic study with longitudinal data. *Disaster Medicine and Public Health Preparedness, 10*(2), 261–273.

Gruebner, O., Sykora, M., Lowe, S. R., Shankardass, K., Trinquart, L., Jackson, T., ... Galea, S. (2016). Mental health surveillance after the terrorist attacks in Paris. *Lancet, 387*(10034), 2195–2196.

Gutner, C. A., Galovski, T., Bovin, M. J., & Schnurr, P. P. (2016). Emergence of transdiagnostic treatments for PTSD and posttraumatic distress. *Current Psychiatry Reports, 18*(10), 95.

Hobfoll, S. E., Palmieri, P. A., Johnson, R. J., Canetti-Nisim, D., Hall, B. J., & Galea, S. (2009). Trajectories of resilience, resistance, and distress during ongoing terrorism: The case of Jews and Arabs in Israel. *Journal of Consulting and Clinical Psychology, 77*(1), 138.

Hoge, C. W., Castro, C. A., Messer, S. C., McGurk, D., Cotting, D. I., & Koffman, R. L. (2004). Combat duty in Iraq and Afghanistan, mental health problems, and barriers to care. *New England Journal of Medicine, 351*(1), 13–22. https://doi.org /10.1056/NEJMoa040603

Hoge, C. W., Yehuda, R., Castro, C. A., McFarlane, A. C., Vermetten, E., Jetly, R., . . . others. (2016). Unintended consequences of changing the definition of posttraumatic stress disorder in *DSM-5*: Critique and call for action. *JAMA Psychiatry, 73*(7), 750–752.

Hollon, S. D. & Garber, J. (1988). Cognitive therapy. In L. Y. Abramson (ed.), *Social Cognition and Clinical Psychology: A Synthesis* (pp. 204–253). New York, NY: Guilford Press.

Horowitz, M. J. (1986). Stress-response syndromes: A review of posttraumatic and adjustment disorders. *Psychiatric Services, 37*(3), 241–249.

Insel, T. R., Cuthbert, B., Garvey, M., Heinssen, R., Pine, D. S., Quinn, K., . . . Wang, P. (2010). *Research Domain Criteria (RDoC): Toward a New Classification Framework for Research on Mental Disorders.* Washington, DC: American Psychiatric Association. Retrieved from http://ajp.psychiatryonline.org.proxy.lib .umich.edu/doi/full/10.1176/appi.ajp.2010.09091379.

Insel, T. R. & Lieberman, J. A. (2013). *DSM-5* and *RDoC*: Shared Interests. National Institute of Mental Health.

Jablensky, A. (1985). Approaches to the definition and classification of anxiety and related disorders in European psychiatry. In A. H. Tuma & J. D. Maser (eds.), *Anxiety and the Anxiety Disorders* (p. 737). Hillsdale, NJ: Lawrence Erlbaum Associates.

Janet, P. M. F., Paul, E. T., & Paul, C. T. (1925). *Psychological Healing.* 2 vols. Retrieved from http://psycnet.apa.org/psycinfo/1925–10456-000.

Janoff-Bulman, R. (1992). *Shattered Assumptions: Towards a New Psychology of Trauma.* New York, NY: Free Press.

Kessler, R. C. (2000). Posttraumatic stress disorder: The burden to the individual and to society. *Journal of Clinical Psychiatry.* Retrieved from http://psycnet.apa.org .proxy.lib.umich.edu/psycinfo/2000–15312-001.

Kessler, R. C., Sonnega, A., Bromet, E., Hughes, M., & Nelson, C. B. (1995). Posttraumatic stress disorder in the national comorbidity survey. *Archives of General Psychiatry, 52,* 1048–1060.

Kessler, R. C. & Ustun, T. B. (2008). The WHO Mental Health Surveys. *Global Perspectives on the Epidemiology of Mental Disorders.* Retrieved from www.uade.inpsiquiatria .edu.mx/pagina_contenidos/Articulos%20Jorge/2008/The%20Mexican% 20National%20Comorbidity%20Survey%3B%20overview%20and%20results.pdf.

Kilpatrick, D. G. (2013). The *DSM-5* got PTSD right: Comment on Friedman (2013). *Journal of Traumatic Stress, 26*(5), 563–566. https://doi.org/10.1002/jts.21844

Kilpatrick, D. G., Resnick, H. S., Milanak, M. E., Miller, M. W., Keyes, K. M., & Friedman, M. J. (2013). National estimates of exposure to traumatic events and PTSD prevalence using *DSM-IV* and *DSM-5* criteria. *Journal of Traumatic Stress, 26,* 537–547. https://doi.org/10.1002/jts.21848

Kilpatrick, D. G., Veronen, L. J., & Resick, P. A. (1979). The aftermath of rape: Recent empirical findings. *American Journal of Orthopsychiatry, 49*(4), 658.

Koenen, K. C., Ratanatharathorn, A., Ng, L., McLaughlin, K. A., Bromet, E. J., Stein, D. J., . . . Kessler, R. C. (2017). Posttraumatic stress disorder in the World Mental Health Surveys. *Psychological Medicine,* 1–15. https://doi.org/10.1017 /S0033291717000708

Lang, P. J. (1977). Imagery in therapy: An information processing analysis of fear. *Behavior Therapy*, *8*(5), 862–886.

Lang, P. J. (1979). A bio-informational theory of emotional imagery. *Psychophysiology*, *16*(6), 495–512.

Maercker, A. & Perkonigg, A. (2013). Applying an international perspective in defining PTSD and related disorders: Comment on Friedman (2013). *Journal of Traumatic Stress*, *26*(5), 560–562. https://doi.org/10.1002/jts.21852

Marchand, A., Nadeau, C., Beaulieu-Prévost, D., Boyer, R., & Martin, M. (2015). Predictors of posttraumatic stress disorder among police officers: A prospective study. *Psychological Trauma: Theory, Research, Practice, and Policy*, *7*(3), 212–221. https://doi.org/10.1037/a0038780

McCann, I. L. & Pearlman, L. A. (1990). Vicarious traumatization: A framework for understanding the psychological effects of working with victims. *Journal of Traumatic Stress*, *3*(1), 131–149.

McCann, I. L., Sakheim, D. K., & Abrahamson, D. J. (1988). Trauma and victimization: A model of psychological adaptation. *Counseling Psychologist*, *16*, 531–594.

McNally, R. J. (2003). Progress and controversy in the study of posttraumatic stress disorder. *Annual Review of Psychology*, *54*(1), 229–252. https://doi.org/10.1146/annurev.psych.54.101601.145112

Monson, C. M., Friedman, M. J., & La Bash, H. A. (2007). A psychological history of PTSD. In M. J. Friedman, T. M. Keane, & P. A. Resnick (eds.), *Handbook of PTSD: Science and Practice* (pp. 37–52). New York, NY: Guildford Press.

Mowrer, O. (1947). On the dual nature of learning: A re-interpretation of "conditioning" and" problem-solving." *Harvard Educational Review*. Retrieved from http://psycnet.apa.org/psycinfo/1950–03076-001.

Mowrer, O. (1960). *Learning Theory and Behavior*. Retrieved from http://doi.apa.org/index.cfm?fa=search.exportFormat&uid=2005–06665-000&recType=psycinfo&singlerecord=1&searchresultpage=true

Norris, F. H., Murphy, A. D., Baker, C. K., Perilla, J. L., Rodriguez, F. G., & Rodriguez, J. de J. G. (2003). Epidemiology of trauma and posttraumatic stress disorder in Mexico. *Journal of Abnormal Psychology*, *112*(4), 646–656. https://doi.org/10.1037/0021-843X.112.4.646

Norris, F. H. & Stevens, S. P. (2007). Community resilience and the principles of mass trauma intervention. *Psychiatry*, *70*(4), 320–328. https://doi.org/10.1521/psyc.2007.70.4.320

Norris, F. H., Stevens, S. P., Pfefferbaum, B., Wyche, K. F., & Pfefferbaum, R. L. (2008). Community resilience as a metaphor, theory, set of capacities, and strategy for disaster readiness. *American Journal of Community Psychology*, *41*(1–2), 127–150. https://doi.org/10.1007/s10464-007-9156-6

Osenbach, J. E., Lewis, C., Rosenfeld, B., Russo, J., Ingraham, L. M., Peterson, R., . . . Zatzick, D. F. (2014). Exploring the longitudinal trajectories of posttraumatic stress disorder in injured trauma survivors. *Psychiatry: Interpersonal and Biological Processes*, *77*(4), 386–397.

Pavlov, I. P. & Thompson, W. H. (1902). *The Work of the Digestive Glands*. Charles Griffin. Retrieved from https://books.google.com/books?hl=en &id=21YXAQAAMAAJ&oi=fnd&pg=PA1&dq=pavlov+1902+&ots=hvnYAwGWOV&sig=_saayhBxgw0V4oIi0xOzNSP0HbU.

Piaget, J. (1965). The stages of the intellectual development of the child. *Educational Psychology in Context: Readings for Future Teachers*, 98–106.

Pietrzak, R. H., Goldstein, R. B., Southwick, S. M., & Grant, B. F. (2011). Prevalence and Axis I comorbidity of full and partial posttraumatic stress disorder in the United States: Results from Wave 2 of the National Epidemiologic Survey on Alcohol and Related Conditions. *Journal of Anxiety Disorders*, *25*(3), 456–465. https://doi.org/10.1016/j.janxdis.2010.11.010

Pineles, S. L., Suvak, M. K., Liverant, G. I., Gregor, K., Wisco, B. E., Pitman, R. K., & Orr, S. P. (2013). Psychophysiologic reactivity, subjective distress, and their associations with PTSD diagnosis. *Journal of Abnormal Psychology*, *122*(3), 635.

Rauch, S. & Foa, E. B. (2006). Emotional processing theory (EPT) and exposure therapy for PTSD. *Journal of Contemporary Psychotherapy*, *36*(2), 61–65. https://doi.org/10.1007/s10879-006-9008-y

Resick, P. A. (2001). *Stress and Trauma* (1st edn). East Sussex:Psychology Press.

Resick, P. A., Monson, C. M., & Chard, K. M. (2007). *Cognitive Processing Therapy: Veteran/Military Manual*. Washington, DC: Veterans Administration.

Resick, P. A. & Schnicke, M. K. (1992). Cognitive processing therapy for sexual assault victims. *Journal of Consulting and Clinical Psychology*, *60*(5), 748–756.

Resnick, H. S., Kilpatrick, D. G., Dansky, B. S., Saunders, B. E., & Best, C. L. (1993). Prevalence of civilian trauma and posttraumatic stress disorder in a representative national sample of women. *Journal of Consulting and Clinical Psychology*, *61*(6), 984–991.

Roberts, A. L., Gilman, S. E., Breslau, J., Breslau, N., & Koenen, K. C. (2011). Race/ethnic differences in exposure to traumatic events, development of post-traumatic stress disorder, and treatment-seeking for post-traumatic stress disorder in the United States. *Psychological Medicine*, *41*(1), 71–83. https://doi.org/10.1017/S0033291710000401

Rothbaum, B. O., Foa, E. B., Riggs, D. S., Murdock, T., & Walsh, W. (1992). A prospective examination of post-traumatic stress disorder in rape victims. *Journal of Traumatic Stress*, *5*, 455–475.

Schumm, J. A., Briggs-Phillips, M., & Hobfoll, S. E. (2006). Cumulative interpersonal traumas and social support as risk and resiliency factors in predicting PTSD and depression among inner-city women. *Journal of Traumatic Stress*, *19*(6), 825–836. https://doi.org/10.1002/jts.20159

Seal, K. H., Bertenthal, D., Miner, C. R., Sen, S., & Marmar, C. (2007). Bringing the war back home: Mental health disorders among 103,788 US veterans returning from Iraq and Afghanistan seen at Department of Veterans Affairs facilities. *Archives of Internal Medicine*, *167*(5), 476–482. https://doi.org/10.1001/archinte.167.5.476

Shephard, B. (2001). *A War of Nerves: Soldiers and Psychiatrists in the Twentieth Century*. Cambridge, MA: Harvard University Press.

Skinner, B. F. (1945). The operational analysis of psychological terms. *Psychological Review*, *52*(5), 270.

Stein, M. B., Walker, J. R., Hazen, A. L., & Forde, D. R. (1997). Full and partial posttraumatic stress disorder: Findings from a community survey. *American Journal of Psychiatry*, *154*(8), 1114–1119.

Watson, J. B. & Rayner, R. (1920). Conditioned emotional reactions. *Journal of Experimental Psychology*, *3*(1), 1.

Weiss, D. S., Marmar, C. R., Schlenger, W. E., Fairbank, J. A., Kathleen Jordan, B., Hough, R. L., & Kulka, R. A. (1992). The prevalence of lifetime and partial post-traumatic stress disorder in Vietnam theater veterans. *Journal of Traumatic Stress*, *5*(3), 365–376. https://doi.org/10.1002/jts.2490050304

Yehuda, R. & Bierer, L. M. (2009). The relevance of epigenetics to PTSD: Implications for the *DSM-V*. *Journal of Traumatic Stress*, *22*(5), 427–434. https://doi.org/10.1002/jts.20448

Young, G. (2014). PTSD, endophenotypes, the RDoC, and the *DSM-5*. *Psychological Injury and Law*, *7*(1), 75–91.

27 Reactive Attachment Disorder

Kimberly Renk

Making a diagnosis of reactive attachment disorder often has proven difficult. This difficulty has been due to confusion among the actual diagnostic criteria outlined in the *Diagnostic and Statistical Manual of Mental Disorders (DSM)*, the usage of the general label of "attachment disorder" in clinical and research contexts, and difficulties that young children can manifest in the context of insecure attachment patterns in parent–young child interactions (Woolgar & Scott, 2014). In fact, disorders of attachment are actually quite rare when diagnostic criteria are applied appropriately (Zeanah, Chesher, Boris, & the AACAP Committee on Quality Issues, 2016). Instead, Allen (2016) suggested that practitioners often (erroneously) diagnose reactive attachment disorder when young children have experienced significant disruptions in their early caregiving followed by subsequent behavioral issues, rather than ensuring that these young children actually meet the criteria described in the *DSM*. Even if such a diagnosis is made, there is no guarantee that young children with such a diagnosis will receive an evidence-based intervention that will improve their symptom profile and their connections to available caregivers (Boris, 2003; Boris & Renk, 2017). Given these issues, some even have argued that reactive attachment disorder should be removed from the *DSM* completely (Allen, 2016).

Although the diagnostic categories of reactive attachment disorder and the newer disinhibited social engagement disorder may be difficult for clinicians to use, even when clinicians are working with high-risk young children (e.g., young children who have been adopted, are in foster care, and/or have been maltreated) (Boris et al., 2004), disorders of attachment may be of some utility for children who have spent their early lives in institutional settings. In fact, many of the findings of most importance for understanding reactive attachment disorder have been discussed in the context of children who have spent their early lives in such institutional settings (Allen, 2016), and the symptom presentations of these children have informed changes in the diagnostic criteria for reactive attachment disorder over time (Zeanah & Gleason, 2015). Most research has examined reactive attachment disorder in young children between the ages of one and five years (Zeanah et al., 2016), making knowledge of young children an important context for understanding the symptoms associated with this disorder.

Certainly, symptoms of reactive attachment disorder tend to occur in conjunction with the experience of abuse and/or neglect but do not develop in every instance of abuse and/or neglect. In fact, reactive attachment disorder appears to be quite rare. For example, although 19–40% of children who were maltreated and in foster care may have exhibited signs of reactive attachment disorder (as defined by the *DSM-IV*) (American Psychiatric Association [APA], 1994) in some studies (Lehmann, Havik, Havik, & Heiervang, 2013; Zeanah et al., 2004), other studies suggested that only 4.1% of four-and-a-half-year-old children in an institutional setting demonstrated the emotionally withdrawn/inhibited subtype of reactive attachment disorder (Gleason et al., 2011). The symptoms of reactive attachment disorder also appear to improve reliably over time after young children are removed from institutional settings (Leiden Conference, 2012), making diagnosis complicated. In contrast, in the general population, the prevalence of reactive attachment disorder has been estimated to be 1.4% in children, with comorbidities noted for attention-deficit/hyperactivity disorder, posttraumatic stress disorder, and autism spectrum disorder (Minnis et al., 2013; Pritchett et al., 2013).

As is discussed in this chapter, disruptions in the early caregiving that children receive have been identified as a main etiology of reactive attachment disorder. Nonetheless, examining some of the neurobiological changes that can occur when early caregiving is disrupted may be helpful for furthering our understanding of this disorder and its consequent sequelae. A current framework for shaping this discussion may be the Research Domain Criteria (RDoC) framework outlined by the National Institute of Mental Health (NIMH) (Insel et al., 2010). The RDoC are based in part on the view that psychological disorders are neurodevelopmental in nature and emphasize a focus on developmental processes themselves. In particular, these processes interact with environmental and social factors (Cuthbert, 2014). In other words, the RDoC seek to reconsider psychological symptoms in a framework of transdiagnostic constructs reflecting core mechanisms of these symptoms (Cuthbert & Kozak, 2013). Clearly, relationships between clusters of clinical symptoms and dysregulated neurobiological systems are complex, with disorders involving many different disrupted mechanistic factors (Sanislow et al., 2010). Nonetheless, the RDoC allow for the incorporation of integrative neuroscience research into the understanding of current diagnostic categories (NIMH, 2008).

The RDoC approach could be particularly applicable to further understanding reactive attachment disorder and disinhibited social engagement disorder, as the RDoC appear to be consistent with the theory of intersubjectivity (i.e., the process whereby an infant's brain development is supported by the intuitive responses of parents or caregivers) (Trevarthen & Aitkin, 2001). In fact, the theory of intersubjectivity has been suggested as a valuable framework for understanding reactive attachment disorder (Minnis, Marwick, Arthur, & McLaughlin, 2006). According to Minnis and colleagues (2006), intersubjectivity can be concordant (e.g., when a young child and his or her caregiver are attuned to each other) or discordant (e.g., when interactions prompt the experience of distress or discomfort). Relationships that are characterized by too much discordance can be detrimental to development (Murray, Kempton, Woolgar, & Hooper, 1993), can negatively impact social understanding (Trevarthen, 1998), and (of particular relevance to this chapter) can have implications for important brain functions and social functioning (Trevarthen & Aitkin, 2001).

From the RDoC perspective, Kaufman and colleagues (2015) also argue that studying children who were maltreated can be advantageous for furthering the objectives of the RDoC project, as such children often do not respond to standard interventions, are relatively homogeneous in the sense that they all experience psychological symptoms associated with stress-related mechanisms, and can be compared to animal models as part of translational research. The RDoC approach also may foster better delivery of future interventions, as integration of clinical and experimental findings from multiple approaches, the identification of valid and reliable phenotypes for psychiatric disorders (Stanislow et al., 2010), and an improved understanding of genetic risk may lead to a more tailored combination of interventions (Cuthbert, 2014). Such an approach may have particular relevance to disorders of attachment. For example, one study in Connecticut suggested that children who were involved with protective services for abuse and/or neglect issues composed about 65% of psychiatric hospital admissions in that location prior to providers being trauma-informed but about 30% of psychiatric hospital admissions after providers became trauma-informed (Schaefer, 2007, as cited in Kaufman et al., 2015). Clearly, understanding the factors underlying disorders of attachment and becoming more trauma-informed when etiological factors include abuse and/or neglect issues could lead to more effective approaches to intervention.

Given these issues, this chapter briefly outlines the history of reactive attachment disorder as well as the current diagnostic criteria for reactive attachment disorder and the newer disinhibited social disengagement disorder. This chapter then discusses potential etiological mechanisms for these disorders, both in terms of an attachment-related understanding of such mechanisms and with the RDoC domains in mind. Finally, the implications of these etiological mechanisms are reviewed in closing for the assessment and intervention services that are provided to children with reactive attachment disorder and disinhibited social disengagement disorder.

History of Reactive Attachment Disorder

As already noted, much of the earliest work examining disorders of attachment in young children was completed with children who spent their early years in institutional settings and with those who had been abused and/or neglected (e.g., Goldfarb, 1945; Provence & Lipton, 1962; Tizard & Hodges, 1978). In conjunction with this early work, two major types of affectional disorders were described in very young institutionalized children. These disorders included an emotionally withdrawn presentation (i.e., those who exhibited little social responsiveness, little positive affect, and a lack of comfort seeking when distressed) and a socially indiscriminant presentation (i.e., those who engaged in comfort seeking with non-select adults) (Tizard & Rees, 1975).

Consistent with this early research, the *DSM-III* (APA, 1980) included the first "attachment" disorder, which was labeled "Reactive Attachment Disorder of Infancy." The essential features of this disorder included signs of poor emotional development (e.g., a lack of age-appropriate social responsiveness) and poor physical development (e.g., failure to thrive). These symptoms had to be manifested prior to eight months of age in conjunction with a lack of adequate caregiving, although the *DSM-III* described some symptoms that could occur starting at approximately two months of age (APA, 1980). Given these criteria, however, criticisms arose readily from attachment researchers, as many noted that young children do not exhibit attachment behaviors with a discriminated caregiver until approximately six months of age (Allen, 2016; Rutter & Shaffer, 1980). As a result, the diagnosis of reactive attachment disorder was not useful for describing problematic attachment between young children and their caregivers and only could be used to account for young children having reactions to problems in their caregiving. Further, Chatoor, Ganiban, Colin, Plummer, and Harmon (1998) noted that young children who exhibited failure to thrive could have varying patterns of attachment with caregivers, suggesting that only a minority would meet criteria for reactive attachment disorder. As a result, the description of reactive attachment disorder provided in *DSM-III* was less than helpful in understanding what could go wrong with attachment between young children and their caregivers.

Although "Reactive Attachment Disorder of Infancy or Early Childhood" still was present in the *DSM-III-R*, the essential feature of this diagnostic category then was described as "markedly disturbed social relatedness in most contexts" (APA, 1987, p. 91). This feature could (again) manifest with a social inhibition presentation (i.e., with the young child showing little to no interest in caregivers) or an indiscriminate sociability presentation (i.e., with the young child showing a lack of selective attachments while having diffuse attachments along with a lack of appropriate boundaries). According to the *DSM-III-R*, however, symptoms had to be present by the time the child was five years of age. These symptoms again were attributed to "grossly pathogenic care that preceded the onset of the disturbance" (APA, 1987, p. 91). Similar to criticisms of this diagnosis in *DSM-III*, many researchers (e.g., Richters & Volkmar, 1994; Zeanah & Boris, 2000) indicated that this diagnostic description was not compatible with attachment theory and instead could only describe problematic social behavior (Allen, 2016). Even among these consistent criticisms, diagnostic criteria for "Reactive Attachment Disorder" remained relatively unchanged across *DSM-IV* (APA, 1994) and *DSM-IV-TR* (APA, 2000).

Distinguishing Reactive Attachment Disorder and Disinhibited Social Engagement Disorder

Clearly, the criticisms of the reactive attachment disorder diagnostic criteria provided in the early editions of the *DSM* were noteworthy. New research regarding the symptom profiles accompanying reactive attachment disorder was considered with the construction of the fifth edition of the *DSM* (*DSM-5*) (APA, 2013), however. This more recent line of research focused on the distinctness of the two subtypes that had been described historically for reactive attachment disorder. For example, Gleason and colleagues (2011) suggested that each of the two different subtypes of reactive attachment disorder demonstrated acceptable internal consistency and criterion validity. The withdrawn/inhibited subtype of reactive attachment disorder was associated significantly with caregiving and attachment security as well as with symptoms of depression (Gleason et al., 2011). In contrast, the indiscriminately social/disinhibited subtype of reactive attachment disorder was not associated with caregiver quality but was associated with activity/impulsivity, inhibitory control, and attention-deficit/hyperactivity disorder (Gleason et al., 2011). Similarly, other research suggested that the disinhibited subtype of reactive attachment disorder was related with more internalizing and externalizing behavior problems (Jonkman et al., 2014) and may be better construed as a neurodevelopmental disorder (rather than a dysfunction of normal attachment processes) (Rutter et al., 2009). Given findings such as these, the two different subtypes of reactive attachment disorder were noted to differ in their phenomenology, course, correlates, and other factors (Zeanah & Gleason, 2010, 2015). Thus, Gleason and colleagues (2011) and others (Jonkman et al., 2014) concluded that descriptions for two distinct syndromes were warranted.

By making a distinction between the two subtypes of reactive attachment disorder, the different manifestations that young children's emotional and behavioral functioning could take when the attachment between those young children and their primary caregiver(s) was underdeveloped or disrupted could be better described. The use of two different diagnostic categories also would address the common problem with heterogeneity within diagnostic categories that is recognized with the RDoC. That is, when diagnostic criteria are not optimally helpful, different individuals may be classified into the same category, even if they exhibit differences in the number or nature of symptoms (Sanislow et al., 2010). Clearly, heterogeneity was evident across the two subtypes of reactive attachment disorder, likely adding to the confusion that has surrounded this disorder historically.

Current DSM-5 Reactive Attachment Disorder Criteria

Consistent with the aforementioned research, the *DSM-5* (the most current edition of the *DSM*) (APA, 2013) outlines diagnostic criteria for reactive attachment disorder and a new and separate disorder, disinhibited social engagement disorder. Both disorders are categorized in the "Trauma- and Stressor-Related Disorders" section of *DSM-5* (APA, 2013), having been moved from the "Disorders Usually First Diagnosed in Infancy, Childhood, or Adolescence" section of prior *DSM*s. Although some researchers have suggested that these disorders should be considered as disorders of nonattachment (Zeanah & Boris, 2000), the move to the "Trauma- and Stressor-Related Disorders" section of *DSM-5* acknowledges the role that factors outside of the individual can play in the development of the symptom profile described for these disorders.

In the *DSM-5*, a diagnosis of reactive attachment disorder can be assigned to a young child when he or she has experienced "a consistent pattern of inhibited, emotionally withdrawn behavior" toward caregivers (APA, 2013, p. 265). In other words, young children who are diagnosed with reactive attachment disorder do not seek out comfort from or respond to comfort provided by a caregiver when they are distressed. That is, these young children do not seek out their caregivers to be a safe haven for them (Renk & Boris, 2017) and do not show a preferential attachment to an attachment figure (Zeanah et al., 2016). To meet *DSM-5* diagnostic criteria, this pattern of behavior must be evident prior to the child reaching five years of age. In addition to exhibiting this pattern of interaction behavior, the young child must demonstrate "persistent social and emotional disturbance," including minimal socioemotional responsiveness to others, limited positive affect, and/or irritability, sadness, or fearfulness when such a reaction would not be warranted in interactions with others (APA, 2013, p. 265). Thus, signs of social unresponsiveness and emotion regulation difficulties are evident (Zeanah et al., 2016). Based on the diagnostic criteria provided, the *DSM-5* suggested that young children who exhibit this profile of symptoms also have experienced insufficient care, as evidenced by social neglect or deprivation, repeated changes in their primary caregiver, or rearing in a setting that offered limited opportunities to form stable attachments. Generally, the *DSM* suggested that this experience of insufficient care can be presumed to be responsible for the manifested symptom profile (APA, 2013).

In contrast, the *DSM*-5 diagnosis of disinhibited social engagement disorder is meant to describe young children who exhibit a pattern of behavior where they "actively approach and interact with unfamiliar adults" with reduced or absent reticence, overly familiar behavior, a lack of secure base behavior (i.e., they fail to check back with their primary caregiver), and/or a willingness to go off with unfamiliar adults (APA, 2013, p. 268). That is, these young children do not exhibit selectivity in their attachment behaviors and do not seek out any one individual as their safe haven (Boris & Renk, 2017), as they do not hesitate to approach and interact with unfamiliar adults (Zeanah et al., 2015). The young child should have a developmental age of at least nine months to receive this diagnosis. Again, the *DSM-5* suggested that young children who exhibit this profile of interaction behaviors have experienced insufficient care, as evidenced by social neglect or deprivation, repeated changes in primary caregivers, or rearing in a setting that offered limited opportunities to form stable attachments. In other words, the *DSM-5* suggested that this experience can be presumed to be responsible for the manifested symptom profile (APA, 2013). Thus, both reactive attachment disorder and disinhibited social engagement disorder are described as having the same underlying causal factors, although these causal factors result in different manifestations of symptoms in each disorder.

Social Neglect as the Main Etiology of Reactive Attachment Disorder and Disinhibited Social Engagement Disorder

As just noted, the *DSM-5* (APA, 2013) describes both reactive attachment disorder and disinhibited social engagement disorder as resulting from serious social neglect, although not every young child who experiences serious social neglect will develop one of these disorders. In fact, the degree of adversity experienced has been related to the severity of symptoms manifested (Zeanah, Smyke, Koga, & Carlson, 2005), with the lack of attachment to a preferred caregiver being rare when young children are exposed to reasonably responsive caregiving environments (Zeanah et al., 2015). For example, it is estimated that 10% of severely neglected children meet criteria for reactive attachment disorder and that 20% of such children meet criteria for disinhibited social engagement disorder (APA, 2013). In conjunction with findings such as these, a newly updated practice parameter for reactive attachment disorder and disinhibited social engagement disorder suggested that children who have been in institutional settings or in foster care should be screened for disorders of attachment (Zeanah et al., 2016), particularly given their greater risk for pathogenic care and related symptoms.

With regard to both disorders, social neglect generally would be anticipated starting in the first months of children's lives, with the prognosis for each child depending on the quality of the caregiving environment following the social neglect that the child experiences. With regard to reactive attachment disorder, clinical features of the disorder have been described as manifesting similarly between nine months and five years of age. Although the *DSM-5* notes uncertainty as to whether symptoms of reactive attachment disorder can occur past this age range (APA, 2013), other research has suggested that symptoms of this disorder can occur in school-age children and adolescents who were in institutional settings in their early years and who were maltreated (Elovainio et al., 2015). Nonetheless, symptoms of this disorder can diminish significantly when children are removed from institutional care and/or are placed in foster care (Smyke et al., 2012), suggesting a main path for remediation through appropriate and responsive caregiving from caregivers who may become preferred over time and experience.

With regard to disinhibited social engagement disorder, neglect occurring after two years of age may not prompt a clinical manifestation of symptoms related to this disorder to occur. Nonetheless, the *DSM-5* (APA, 2013) suggested that this disorder can persist at least into middle childhood, moving from indiscriminate social behavior in toddlerhood to attention-seeking in preschoolers to verbal and physical overfamiliarity in middle childhood to overfamiliarity with peers in adolescence. In other words, symptoms can be stable over time if social neglect persists (APA, 2013). Given the experience of social neglect, other developmental delays (e.g., cognitive and language delays, stereotypies, and malnutrition) also may occur with both disorders (APA, 2013), although different comorbidities may be likely across them (as noted earlier).

Using Attachment Theory to Further Understanding of Reactive Attachment Disorder and Disinhibited Social Engagement Disorder

Beyond considering just social neglect as the main etiology proposed by the *DSM-5* (APA, 2013) for reactive attachment disorder and disinhibited social engagement disorder, there also should be evidence that the attachment system has failed and that the young child has not formed a discriminated attachment to a particular caregiver (Prior & Glaser, 2006). Such determinations would require the consideration of attachment theory as conceptualized initially by Bowlby (1980). Bowlby (1980) described attachment as an evolutionarily driven, transactional process that develops over the course of a predictable timeline. In fact, infants are believed to be biologically predisposed to attach to their caregivers, as these caregivers provide protection (Cassidy, 2008), help infants learn to regulate themselves, and shape infants' brain development through early interactions (Landers & Sullivan, 2012).

Although infants do not show clear preferences for particular caregivers in the first six months of life, infants begin to demonstrate preferred and discriminated attachments between seven and nine months of age. At this age, infants begin to show tendencies to seek comfort and nurturance from their caregivers, to exhibit stranger anxiety, and to protest separation from their caregivers (Boris & Renk, 2017). The strategies that infants develop to maintain proximity to their caregivers are derived from their perceptions of their caregivers' availability and what maximizes that availability (Zilberstein, 2014). As such, the degree of synchrony and mutual responsiveness that is shown in infant–caregiver interactions tends to predict infants' later attachment security with their caregivers (Beebe et al., 2010). In other words, attachment patterns develop in the context of repeated infant–caregiver interactions as infants explore their environment and then seek proximity from their caregivers for comfort and support over time. These attachment patterns have been studied and categorized using observational paradigms, such as the Strange Situation (Ainsworth, Blehar, Waters, & Wall, 1978). The Strange Situation is an interactional paradigm that activates young children's attachment system by exposing young children to free play, introduction to an unfamiliar adult, and separations and reunions with their caregiver during a short period of time in a controlled environment. See Boris and Renk (2017) for a depiction of the types of interaction episodes included in the Strange Situation and Zeanah, and colleagues (2016) for an alternate observation paradigm that could be useful.

Using the Strange Situation, seminal studies of attachment patterns suggested that young children may develop secure or insecure attachment patterns (Ainsworth et al., 1978). Those young children who develop a secure attachment to their caregivers seek out their caregivers when they are distressed, anticipating that their caregivers will provide comfort in a warm and efficient manner. Further, when these young children are separated from their caregivers, they become distressed but can be comforted quickly when reunified with their caregivers (Boris & Renk, 2017). Such patterns of behavior are likely achieved in conjunction with caregivers demonstrating responsiveness, and sensitivity to their infants' signals, showing attunement as they verbalize their infants' feelings and conveying awareness and receptivity through their behaviors (Tronick, Als, & Adamson, 1979).

Those young children who develop an insecure attachment can demonstrate their insecurity in a variety of ways. When young children have developed an insecure-ambivalent attachment pattern, they become distressed with separation from their caregivers but are calmed less quickly and efficiently than those with a secure attachment. When young children have developed an insecure-avoidant attachment pattern, they tend to not signal their caregivers when they are distressed, even after being separated and reunified with their caregivers (Boris & Renk, 2017). Such attachment patterns likely develop in conjunction with caregivers being either intermittently responsive to their infants' cues or emotionally unavailable (Ainsworth et al., 1978).

Finally, when young children have developed a disorganized attachment pattern, they do not demonstrate coherent strategies for managing their interactions or their separation from and reunification with their caregivers. Instead, they may appear uncertain about the responses that they will receive from their caregivers (Boris & Renk, 2017) and may even appear fearful (Main & Solomon, 1986). Such attachment patterns likely develop when caregivers have shown that they cannot provide comfort to their infants, particularly when they withdraw emotionally, respond in ways that induce fear, or engage in contradictory or confusing behaviors (Lyons-Ruth & Jacobvitz, 2008). Such caregiver behaviors may be particularly evident in cases where abuse and/or neglect have been identified. Overall, interactions that occur in the context of these attachment patterns can impact brain development as well as the development of the limbic and autonomic nervous systems (Schore, 2001).

Bowlby (1988) also suggested that these attachment patterns become reinforced and internalized as generalized internal working models of relationships, or mental representations that generalize across relationship experiences (Stern, 1985). These internal working models form the foundation of young children's understanding of relational patterns and strategies to get their attachment needs met and shape their expectations of and approaches to the self and others (Zilberstein, 2014). Children who have been attached securely to their caregivers exhibit more flexibility in updating these internal working models as they acquire new information about the world and their interactions with other individuals, whereas children who have been attached insecurely to their caregivers tend to be more rigid and less able to make changes in their internal working models (Liotti, 2004). Research also has suggested that there are important connections between the capacity to reflect on the mental states of others (i.e., mentalization) and attachment security. Attachment security, in turn, has been related to better emotional regulation, better recognition of emotions in other individuals, and greater appreciation of how emotions may influence behavior (Fonagy, Gergely, & Target, 2009; Thompson, 2009). In contrast, attachment insecurity and/or disorganization has been related to difficulties in the process of reflecting on the mental states of others (Boris & Renk, 2017).

Attachment disorganization also has been related to the social risk factors with which young children must contend, such as when parents are unavailable to attend to their young children's security needs because of their own psychological symptoms, substance misuse, and trauma or loss. These social risk factors lead back to connections among early deprivation and profound impacts on young children's development, as demonstrated by the aforementioned research on young children who have spent their early years in institutional settings or who have experienced abuse and/or neglect (Zeanah & Boris, 2000). Overall, beyond considering social neglect, young children's attachment behaviors in the context of their interactions with their primary caregivers can provide important information about the presence of disorders of attachment. Such knowledge could further facilitate the identification of key attachment indicators for reactive attachment disorder and disinhibited social engagement disorder.

Using the RDoC to Add to Our Understanding of Reactive Attachment Disorder and Disinhibited Social Engagement Disorder

No clear linkage between neurobiological factors and reactive attachment disorder or disinhibited social engagement disorder has been established according to the *DSM-5* (APA, 2013). Nonetheless, the RDoC may prove helpful in furthering our understanding of such connections, as these criteria are meant to facilitate the diagnosis, prevention, and treatment of psychological disorders using psychobiological indicators (Kozak & Cuthbert, 2016). In particular, the intent of the RDoC is to define basic dimensions of functioning that can be studied across multiple units of analysis (e.g., genes, neural circuits, behaviors) (Hershenberg & Goldfried, 2015). In support of using the RDoC for disorders such as reactive attachment disorder and disinhibited social engagement disorder, developmental psychopathology frameworks integrate biological and psychological vulnerabilities that interact with environmental factors (Cicchetti, 2008; Hershenberg & Goldfried, 2015).

Given the manner in which attachment develops between young children and their caregivers, psychological vulnerabilities and environmental factors already have been shown to be important in the understanding of attachment behaviors in general and disorders of attachment in particular. Gaining further information about biological vulnerabilities could add to our understanding of underlying neurobiological underpinnings for these disorders as well. Although such information generally has not been examined in young children who have been diagnosed with reactive attachment disorder or disinhibited social engagement disorder, research examining the neurobiological underpinnings of specific symptoms that could be related to these disorders and other social risk factors may be a helpful starting point. This information is discussed here in the context of the RDoC domains that have been defined thus far. Certainly, it will be evident that some of the RDoC domains are more relevant and have received more attention than others.

Negative Valence Systems

The *Negative Valence Systems* domain of the RDoC includes response to acute threat (fear), response to potential harm (anxiety), response to sustained threat, frustrative non-reward, and loss (NIMH Research Domain Criteria, 2011). Certainly, this domain may have particular relevance to reactive attachment disorder and disinhibited social engagement disorder given the disruptions that occur in the attachment relationships of young children who are assigned these diagnoses and the reactions that they may experience as a result. Research has suggested that several brain areas may be important for understanding responses related to this RDoC domain, with the amygdala, ventromedial prefrontal cortex, and hippocampus being key structures in the fear circuit (Hartley & Phelps, 2010). Further, the hypothalamic-pituitary-adrenal (HPA) axis can experience changes in response to stress (Charney, Grillon, & Bremner, 1998). For example, some studies have suggested that a lack of caregiver sensitivity and positive regard are associated with a suppression of the HPA axis (Johnson & Gunnar, 2011). The medial prefrontal cortex also may play a role in the differential impact that acute versus chronic stress can have (Maier et al., 2009). Thus, attachment may impact stress-regulating biological systems, and social connections may modulate fear reactivity in the brain (Charuvastra & Cloitre, 2008).

The experience of early social neglect that is described as necessary for reactive attachment disorder and disinhibited social engagement disorder should be considered closely in the context of this RDoC domain. For example, early adversity has been related to alterations in brain structure (i.e., both for grey matter and for white matter; Hart & Rubia, 2012). Many of these neuroanatomical alterations appear to be related and to impact the manner in which individuals regulate stress responses to emotional stimuli (Teicher & Samson, 2013). As an example, Shimada and colleagues (2015) found that children with reactive attachment disorder showed reduced grey matter volume in the left primary visual cortex when compared to children who were typically developing, with internalizing problems being a significant predictor of this reduced grey matter volume for those in the reactive attachment disorder group. This finding appeared particularly important as the visual cortex is part of the neurocircuit that regulates stress responses to visual images (Teicher & Samson, 2013), with the visual cortex conveying emotional signals to and receiving feedback from the amygdala (Adolphs, 2004). Shimada and colleagues (2015) suggested that, based on their findings, individuals who have reactive attachment disorder may have difficulty processing positive emotional visual images, as the left hemisphere is specialized for positive emotions (Silberman & Weingartner, 1986). If this finding were to have clinical or attachment implications, it could be the case that such a neurological deficit could contribute to an exacerbation of reactive attachment disorder symptoms and/or attachment difficulties over time.

Other research also suggested that childhood maltreatment early in life can be associated with long-term dysfunction in the regulation of cortisol, a hormone released in response to stress (Hunter et al., 2011). For example, Dozier and colleagues (2008) described alterations in the production of salivary cortisol in toddlers who had been maltreated and who were in foster care. These alterations appeared to be remediated when environments improved (Dozier et al., 2006) and were not noted in children who had been adopted (Kočovská et al., 2013). Such findings speak to the importance of remediating the environment in which children develop and of providing reasonably responsive caregivers. As already noted, reactive attachment disorder symptoms can diminish over time when such caregivers are provided (e.g., Smyke et al., 2012).

Newer research also is considering epigenetics (i.e., functionally relevant genome modifications that do not involve DNA nucleotide sequence changes) (Zhang & Meaney, 2010) in the context of stress reactions. Epigenetic mechanisms may mediate the alterations in stress-reactivity and structural and functional changes in the brain that are associated with early adversity (McGowan et al., 2009; Zhang & Meaney, 2010). For example, rat models of neglect (defined as decreased pup licking and grooming and arched-back nursing by mothers) suggested that such rat behaviors resulted in increased DNA methylation of the glucocorticoid receptor gene promoter in the hippocampus of offspring. Increased DNA methylation often has been related to gene silencing. These differences occurred early in life, could be reversed with cross-fostering, and could persist into adulthood (Weaver et al., 2004). Certainly, this domain would be particularly relevant to further understanding the consequences of the pathogenic care that young children would have received to meet criteria for reactive attachment disorder and disinhibited social engagement disorder. Further research in this domain also may have exciting implications for furthering our understanding of active neurobiological mechanisms in these disorders.

Positive Valence Systems

The *Positive Valence Systems* domain of RDoC includes reward seeking, learning, and habit formation (Stanislow et al., 2010). Research has suggested that the mesolimbic dopamine system plays a role in incentive motivation and reward, with connections to addiction-related behaviors and to depressive symptoms, such as anhedonia and lack of energy (Nestler et al., 2002), as well as to temperament characteristics, such as extraversion and surgency (Depue & Collins, 1999). Certainly, such connections may be most relevant to understanding the consequences of the social risk factors that may be present in caregivers who exhibit psychological symptoms, misuse substances, or have experienced trauma or loss. Further, when infants have been abused or neglected, brain connections that provide healthy adaptation, learning, and positive emotions do not develop properly and may retract or be eliminated (Vela, 2014).

Initial research examining neural reward processing in children with different disorders suggested that children with reactive attachment disorder showed decreased activity in the caudate, putamen, and thalamus during high and low monetary reward conditions (when compared to children with attention-deficit/hyperactivity disorder and children who were developing typically). These findings suggested a significant decrease in reward sensitivity and significant dopaminergic dysfunction in children with reactive attachment disorder (Mizuno et al., 2015; Takiguchi et al., 2015). The activity of the putamen further was related to the severity of the co-occurring posttraumatic stress and dissociative symptoms these children exhibited (Mizuno et al., 2015). Such findings may be consistent with studies suggesting that gene by environment predictors demonstrate pleiotropy, where one gene can impact multiple seemingly unrelated phenotypes (Montalvo-Ortiz, Gelernter, Hudziak, & Kaufman, 2016). Given such findings, the Positive Valence System may have important indirect implications for understanding the etiology of reactive attachment disorder and disinhibited social engagement disorder.

Arousal and Regulatory Systems

The *Arousal and Regulatory Systems* domain of RDoC includes arousal, sleep wakefulness, and circadian rhythms (Smith Stover & Keeshin, in press). Overall, these systems are important for the maintenance of homeostasis, with a number of brain areas implicated in this process. For example, glutamatergic and cholinergic reticular systems are important for arousal as well as for sleep and wakefulness (Stanislow et al., 2010). With early childhood maltreatment and subsequent disruptions in attachment, the developing brain and related neurobiological systems can be impacted greatly. For example, the maturation of stress-regulating systems can be vulnerable to relational trauma, as these systems are experience dependent (Rinaman, Levitt, & Card, 2000). Further, damage to the hippocampus and related neural networks can impact impulse control and self-regulation of behavior (Fitzgerald, Wong, & Zucker, 2013). More work needs to be done regarding this domain, however, to determine its utility in understanding the etiology and symptomatology of reactive attachment disorder and disinhibited social engagement disorder.

Cognitive Processes

The *Cognitive Processes* domain of the RDoC is relatively broad, with complex connections to other constructs (e.g., affect) (Stanislow et al., 2010), but still is impacted when children are mistreated. For example, problems with attention, memory, and impulse control can occur in the context of trauma-related psychiatric disorders and are associated with changes in the executive control circuit that is related to a variety of other brain systems (Kaufman & Weder, 2010). When infants have been abused or neglected, their brains establish and consolidate the connections that they need for survival. Unfortunately, these connections may not be adaptive or flexible enough to respond to typical environmental demands and learning when these infants find themselves in more appropriate contexts later in their lives. With the establishment of these connections, the expression of negative emotions also tends to be promoted. Such connections also can become maladaptive when a child is put in a more caring and nurturing environment (e.g., through adoption) (Vela, 2014). Such findings suggest that the early experiences of children who have been abused and/or neglected may have long-term implications for their functioning in this domain.

This domain also could be considered in the context of the mentalization concept discussed earlier (i.e., the ability to recognize mental states in oneself and in others, including reflection on the thoughts, emotions, desires, and needs of oneself and others) (Fitzgerald et al., 2013). As part of this concept, mental representations involve the encoding of autobiographical memories about oneself, others, and relationships, with this encoding process starting around the second and third years of life (Howe & Courage, 1997). These memories merge into a coherent narrative based on familial and cultural experiences (Atran, Medin, & Rose, 2005), with this narrative being influenced by early relationship disorders and trauma (Conway & Pleydell-Pearce, 2000). For example, stress responses can increase glucosteroid release, which can have a negative effect on the hippocampus and the medial temporal lobe, both of which are involved with memory and stress regulation (Markowitsch et al., 1997). Such mental representations also may carry through to adulthood and impact parenting, particularly as familiar events like parenting are related to the internal working models developed for self and relationships (Fitzgerald et al., 2013; Verschuren, Marcven, & Schoefs, 1996). Although mental representations may have long-term implications for parenting based on individuals' own upbringing, more work needs to be done to fully identify and understand the neurobiological underpinnings of such representations.

Social Processes

The *Social Processes* domain of the RDoC contains four constructs: affiliation and attachment, social communication, understanding of self, and understanding of other (Smith Stover & Keeshin, in press). In conjunction with these constructs, the RDoC recognize the critical roles of development, environment, and the evolution of psychopathology over time (Garvey, Avenevoli, & Anderson, 2016), although they do not specifically include these components in the RDoC matrix (Smith Stover & Keeshin, in press). Nonetheless, this domain has particular importance for the understanding of reactive attachment disorder and disinhibited social engagement disorder, given its close connection to caregiver functioning, attachment behaviors, and young children's interactions with caregivers.

With regard to affiliation and attachment, new neurobiological findings may have important implications for our understanding of parents' behaviors, allowing us to better inform parenting interventions (Renk et al., 2016). Early research in this area began with the examination of animal models, such as the prairie vole (i.e., a species that exhibits strong pair bonding and alloparental behavior), with the role of oxytocin and vasopressin systems identified as important for bonding behaviors (Pitkow et al., 2001). The role of oxytocin now is being examined in intervention trials with human caregivers with variable success (Feldman, Weller, Zagoory-Sharon, & Levine, 2007). Dopamine also is being examined closely, as it is involved in reward and motivation pathways that are central to misuse of substances but also to parent–child interactions (Edelman & Tononi, 1995). Again, studies of prairie voles suggested that their amphetamine abuse impaired pair bonding and partner preferences through oxytocin-mediated mechanism, with oxytocin and dopamine systems mediating the relationship between substance misuse and pair bonding (Young, Liu, Gobrogge, Wang, & Wang, 2014). Clearly, there are likely important neurobiological mechanisms for understanding parenting behaviors in this domain, although more work is needed to fully understand the direct impact of such mechanisms.

With particular relevance to the development of attachment behaviors, the amygdala, septal nuclei, and anterior cingulate gyrus develop synaptic connections rapidly during the first year of life (Vela, 2014). For both animals and humans, damage to the amygdala results in impairments in the danger detection system (e.g., Bauman et al., 2004a, 2004b) and inappropriate responses to ambiguous social cues (Buchanan, Tranel, & Adolphs, 2009), as may be active for those young children who are diagnosed with disinhibited social engagement disorder. Further, the development of the septal nuclei and anterior cingulate gyrus enables human infants to develop stable, selective attachment that can be strengthened through positive reinforcement and caring caregiver–infant interactions and that becomes more discriminating as infants reach approximately 7–8 months of age. As infants reach 9–12 months of age, they develop protective fear and separation anxiety, achievements that prevent indiscriminate social seeking from occurring (Vela,

2014). Affiliation and attachment can be important for resilience as well as for the development of various symptoms (Smith Stover & Keeshin, in press). For example, exposure to childhood maltreatment (consistent with the idea of pathogenic care noted in the aforementioned criteria) has been related to insecure attachment in general (Baer & Martinez, 2006) and to the development of reactive attachment disorder in particular (Stafford, Zeanah, & Scheeringa, 2003).

With regard to understanding of self and others, Smith Stover and Keeshin (in press) noted that emotional awareness (or the capacity to be aware of and describe one's own emotions and those of others) (Frijda, 2007) may be relevant. Early trauma may impact right brain development, the part of the brain that processes social-emotional information and that potentially stores internal working models of attachment relationships (Schore, 1994, 2000, 2001). More work is needed to connect these findings to those of the Cognitive Processes RDoC domain discussed earlier.

Working Memory Processes

With regard to the *Working Memory Processes* domain of the RDoC, the hippocampus is important in the storage and consolidation of information into long-term memory (Vela, 2014). Along with the medial hypothalamus and the septal nuclei, the hippocampus prevents extreme arousal and maintains quiet alertness (Vela, 2014). The hippocampus also works with the amygdala, with the hippocampus being important for the organizing of episodic memory and the amygdala being important for the mediating of emotional memory (Lewis, 2005) as well as storing emotional aspects and personal reactions to events (Joseph, 1996). Such connections may have important implications for the consolidation of internal working models discussed earlier.

Bringing All Mechanisms Together for Reactive Attachment Disorder and Disinhibited Social Engagement Disorder

Although the diagnostic categories of reactive attachment disorder and the newer disinhibited social engagement disorder have proven difficult for clinicians to understand and use effectively (e.g., Boris et al., 2004), disorders of attachment may be of particular utility when describing children who have spent their early lives in institutional settings and/or who have been abused or neglected. Although seminal attachment theory clearly has shaped our understanding of attachment patterns that could be relevant to better understanding reactive attachment disorder and now disinhibited social engagement disorder, the RDoC have the potential to shape new ways of conceptualizing and operationalizing clinical problems (Patrick & Hajcak, 2016b) relevant to these disorders as well. Understanding these potentially interactive etiologies could carry us past the simple underlying etiology of social neglect noted in the *DSM* for these disorders.

Given that the RDoC can potentially inform our understanding of risk and resilience (Shankman & Gorka, 2015), application of these criteria to reactive attachment disorder and disinhibited social engagement disorder seems to be a good fit, particularly if future work proceeds with a consideration of the interaction of environmental influences and core biobehavioral measures across the different developmental stages of particularly high-risk young children. Certainly, further refinement of the diagnoses of reactive attachment disorder and disinhibited social engagement disorder will likely benefit from addressing some of the challenges posed by the RDoC criteria, which include refining and developing approaches to multilevel construct conceptualization (Macnamara & Phan, 2016). For example, Patrick and Hajcak (2016a) suggested that particular symptoms could be examined more broadly and quantified continuously using *DSM* criteria counts but that this work should be done in the context of several types of data that could be evaluated as complementary symptom indicators. As prescribed by the newly revised practice parameter for reactive attachment disorder and disinhibited social engagement disorder (Zeanah et al., 2016), an assessment process may start with a simple inquiry about whether a young child who is at risk has demonstrated any type of attachment behaviors and whether that young child is reticent with strangers. Such information would provide the foundation for further examination, particularly if that young child also has a history of institutional care, foster care, or adoption and/or accompanying deprivation. Answers to such questions then would lead to a more formal assessment, if such an assessment was deemed to be warranted. Such an assessment should include several psychological and neurological indicators as well as explicit observation (hopefully with a structured paradigm) of the young child's pattern of attachment behaviors with his or her primary caregivers. Careful differential diagnosis with an eye toward the presence of comorbid disorders also should be completed (Zeanah et al., 2016).

Prescriptions for preventive interventions for psychopathology in the context of the RDoC also have been suggested (Zalta & Shankman, 2016). Such interventions may have the potential to address the risk and resilience mechanisms that may determine whether young children would develop reactive attachment disorder or disinhibited social engagement disorder, particularly when considered in the context of selective-indicated interventions (i.e., those interventions that serve high-risk groups based on both external-contextual and internal-RDoC constructs) (Zalta & Shankman, 2016). For example, animal models using the prairie vole already have suggested that positive social support may be an important factor in promoting resilience in offspring who were maltreated (Cohen, Liberzon, & Matar, 2014), with paraventricular nucleus oxytocin being a critical neurobiological mechanism by which social support can alleviate the negative effects of stress (Smith & Wang, 2014). Human research also has suggested that the clinical benefits of cognitive behavioral therapy can be mediated by adaptive changes in brain circuits that control emotion regulation in anxiety disorders (e.g., Goldin et al., 2013). Such findings may lend themselves to interventions for young children diagnosed with reactive attachment disorder or disinhibited social engagement disorder, as these young children will likely require intensive, long-term intervention (Vela, 2014). Certainly, prescriptions for approaches to intervention have been suggested for these disorders. In particular, the safety of these young children's current placements should be ensured so that re-traumatization does not occur and so that appropriate, responsive, and emotionally responsive attachment figures can be provided (Zeanah et al., 2016). If needed, evidence-based interventions known to address attachment behaviors (e.g., via Circle of Security-Parenting) (Powell, Cooper, Hoffman, & Marvin, 2013) and related trauma (e.g., via Child-Parent Psychotherapy) (Lieberman & van Horn, 2009) also could be made available. In conjunction with these targeted interventions, comorbid disorders also should be addressed, and interventions demonstrated to be harmful (e.g., "compression holding," "rebirthing therapy") should be avoided (Zeanah et al., 2016). By building a strong etiological understanding including the consideration of social risk, attachment behaviors, and neurobiological mechanisms, appropriate interventions for young children with these diagnoses can be provided in the most informed fashion, allowing them to achieve their most optimal functioning.

References

Adolphs, R. (2004). Emotional vision. *Nature Neuroscience*, *7*, 1167–1168.

Ainsworth, M. D. S., Blehar, M. C., Waters, E., & Wall, S. (1978). *Patterns of Attachment: A Psychological Study of the Strange Situation*. New York, NY: Wiley.

Allen, B. (2016). A RADical idea: A call to eliminate "attachment disorder" and "attachment therapy" from the clinical lexicon. *Evidence-Based Practice in Child and Adolescent Mental Health*, *1*, 60–71.

American Psychiatric Association (APA). (1980). *Diagnostic and Statistical Manual of Mental Disorders-Third Edition (DSM-III)*. Washington, DC: American Psychiatric Association.

American Psychiatric Association (APA). (1987). *Diagnostic and Statistical Manual of Mental Disorders-Third Edition-Revised (DSM-III-R)*. Washington, DC: American Psychiatric Association.

American Psychiatric Association (APA). (1994). *Diagnostic and Statistical Manual of Mental Disorders-Fourth Edition (DSM-IV)*. Washington, DC: American Psychiatric Association.

American Psychiatric Association (APA). (2000). *Diagnostic and Statistical Manual of Mental Disorders-Fourth Edition-Text Revision (DSM-IV-TR)*. Washington, DC: American Psychiatric Association.

American Psychiatric Association (APA). (2013). *Diagnostic and Statistical Manual of Mental Disorders-Fifth Edition (DSM-5)*. Washington, DC: American Psychiatric Association.

Atran, S., Medin, D. L., & Ross, N. O. (2005). The cultural mind: Environmental decision making and cultural modeling within and across populations. *Psychological Review, 112*, 744–776.

Baer, J. C. & Martinez, C. D. (2006). Child maltreatment and insecure attachment: A meta-analysis. *Journal of Reproductive and Infant Psychology, 24*, 187–197.

Bauman, M. D., Lavenex, P., Mason, W. A., Capitanio, J. P., & Amaral, D. G (2004a). The development of mother–infant interactions after neonatal amygdala lesions in rhesus monkeys. *Journal of Neuroscience, 24*, 711–721.

Bauman, M. D., Lavenex, P., Mason, W. A., Capitanio, J. P., & Amaral, D. G. (2004b). The development of social behavior following amygdala lesions in rhesus monkeys. *Journal of Cognitive Neuroscience, 16*, 1388–1411.

Beebe, B., Jaffe, J., Markese, S., Buck, K., Chen, H., Cohen, P., Bahrick, L., Andrews, H., & Feldstein, S. (2010). The origins of 12-month attachment: A microanalysis of 4-month mother–infant interaction. *Attachment and Human Development, 12*, 3–141.

Boris, N. W. (2003). Attachment, aggression and holding: A cautionary tale. *Attachment and Human Development, 5*, 245–247.

Boris, N. W., Hinshaw-Fuselier, S. S., Smyke, A., Scheeringa, M. S., Heller, S. S., & Zeanah, C. H. (2004). Comparing criteria for attachment disorders: Establishing reliability and validity in high-risk samples. *Journal of the American Academy of Child and Adolescent Psychiatry, 43*, 68–577.

Boris, N. W. & Renk, K. (2017). Beyond reactive attachment disorder: How might attachment research inform child psychiatry practice? *Child and Adolescent Psychiatric Clinics of North America, 26*, 455–476.

Bowlby, J. (1980). By ethology out of psycho-analysis: An experiment in interbreeding. *Animal Behavior, 28*, 649–656.

Bowlby, J. (1988). *A Secure Base*. New York, NY: Basic Books.

Buchanan, T. W., Tranel, D., & Adolphs, R. (2009). The human amygdala in human function. In P. J. Whalen & E. A. Phelps (eds.), *The Human Amygdala* (pp. 289–318). New York, NY: Guilford Press.

Cassidy, J. (2008). The nature of the child's ties. In J. Cassidy & P. R. Shaver (eds.), *Handbook of Attachment: Theory, Research and Clinical Applications* (2nd edn (pp. 3–22). New York, NY: Guilford Press.

Charney, D., Grillon, C., & Bremner, J. D. (1998). The neurobiological basis of anxiety and fear: Circuits, mechanisms, and neurochemical interactions (Part I). *Neuroscientist, 4*, 35–44.

Charuvastra, A. & Cloitre, M. (2008). Social bonds and posttraumatic stress disorder. *Annual Review of Psychology, 59*, 301–328.

Chatoor, I., Ganiban, J., Colin, V., Plummer, N., & Harmon, R. J. (1998). Attachment and feeding problems: A reexamination of nonorganic failure to thrive and attachment insecurity. *Journal of the American Academy of Child and Adolescent Psychiatry, 37*, 1217–1224.

Cichetti, D. (2008). A multiple-levels-of-analysis perspective on research in developmental psychopathology. In T. P. Beauchaine & S. P. Hinshaw (eds.), *Child and Adolescent Psychopathology* (pp. 27–57). Hoboken, NJ: Wiley.

Cohen, H., Liberzon, I., & Matar, M. A. (2014). Translational implications of oxytocin-mediated social buffering following immobilization stress in female prairie voles. *Biological Psychiatry, 76*, 268–269.

Conway, M. A. & Pleydell-Pearce, C. (2000). The construction of autobiographical memories in the self-memory system. *Psychological Review, 107*, 261–288.

Cuthbert, B. N. (2014). Research domain criteria: Toward future psychiatric nosology. *Asian Journal of Psychiatry, 7*, 4–5.

Cuthbert, B. N. & Kozak, M. J. (2013). Constructing constructs for psychopathology: The NIMH research domain criteria. *Journal of Abnormal Psychology, 122*, 928–937.

Depue, R. A. & Collins, P. F. (1999). Neurobiology of the structure of personality: Dopamine, facilitation of incentive motivation, and extraversion. *Behavioral and Brain Sciences, 22*, 491–517.

Dozier, M., Manni, M., Gordon, M., Peloso, E., Gunnar, M., Stovall-Mc, K., Eldreth, D., & Levine, S. (2006). Foster children's diurnal production of cortisol: An exploratory study. *Child Maltreatment, 11*, 189–197.

Dozier, M., Peloso, E., Lewis, E., Laurenceau, J., & Levine, S. (2008). Effects of an attachment-based intervention on the cortisol production of infants and toddlers in foster care. *Development and Psychopathology, 20*, 845–859.

Edelman, G. M. & Tononi, G. (1995). Neural Darwinism: The brain as a selectional system. In J. Cornwell (ed.), *Nature's Imagination: The Frontiers of Scientific Vision* (pp. 78–100). New York, NY: Oxford University Press.

Elovainio, M., Raaska, H., Sinkkonen, J., Mäkipää, S., & Lapinieimu, H. (2015). Associations between attachment-related symptoms and later psychological problems among international adoptees: Results from the FinAdo study. *Scandinavian Journal of Psychology, 56*, 53–61.

Feldman, R., Weller, A., Zagoory-Sharon, O., & Levine, A. (2007). Evidence for a neuroendocrinological foundation of human affiliation: Plasma oxytocin levels across pregnancy and the postpartum period predict mother–infant bonding. *Psychological Science, 18*, 965–970.

Fitzgerald, H. E., Wong, M. M., & Zucker, R. A. (2013). Early origins of alcohol use and abuse: Mental representations, relationships, and the challenge of assessing the risk-resilience continuum very early in the life of the child. In N. E. Suchman, M. Pajulo, & L. C. Mayes (eds.), *Parenting and Substance Abuse: Developmental Approaches to Intervention*. New York, NY: Oxford University Press.

Fonagy, P., Gergely, G., & Target, M. (2009). Psychoanalytic constructs and attachment theory and research. In J. Cassidy & P. R. Shaver (eds.), *Handbook of Attachment: Theory, Research and Clinical Applications* (2nd edn) (pp. 783–810). New York, NY: Guilford Press.

Frijda, N. H. (2007). *The Laws of Emotion*. Hillsdale, NJ: Lawrence Erlbaum Associates, Publishers.

Garvey, M., Avenevoli, S., & Anderson, K. (2016). The National Institute of Mental Health Research Domain Criteria and clinical research in child and adolescent psychiatry. *Journal of the American Academy of Child and Adolescent Psychiatry, 55*, 93–98.

Gleason, M. M., Fox, N. A., Drury, S., Smyke, A., Egger, H. I., Nelson, III, C. A., Gregas, M. C., & Zeanah, C. H. (2011). Validity of evidence-derived criteria for reactive attachment disorder: Indiscriminately social/disinhibited and emotionally withdrawn/inhibited types. *Journal of the American Academy of Child and Adolescent Psychiatry, 50*, 216–231.

Goldfarb, W. (1945). The effects of psychological deprivation in infancy. *American Journal of Psychiatry, 102,* 18–33.

Goldin, P. R., Ziv, M., Jazaieri, H., Hahn, K., Heimberg, R., & Gross, J. J. (2013). Impact of cognitive behavioral therapy for social anxiety disorder on the neural dynamics of cognitive reappraisal of negative self-beliefs: Randomized clinical trial. *JAMA Psychiatry, 70,* 1048–1056.

Hart, H. & Rubia, K. (2012). Neuroimaging of child abuse: A critical review. *Frontiers of Human Neuroscience, 6,* 52.

Hartley, C. A. & Phelps, E. A. (2010). Changing fear: The neurocircuitry of emotion regulation. *Neuropsychopharmacology, 35,* 136–146.

Hershenberg, R. & Goldfried, M. R. (2015). Implications of the RDoC for the research and practice of psychotherapy. *Behavior Therapy, 46,* 156–165.

Howe, M. L. & Courage, M. L. (1997). The emergence and early development of autobiographical memory. *Psychological Review, 104,* 499–523.

Hunter, L., Minnis, H., & Wilson, P. (2011). Altered stress responses in children exposed to early adversity: A systematic review of salivary cortisol studies. *Stress, 14,* 614–626.

Insel, T. R., Cuthbert, B., Garvey, M., Heinssen, R., Pine, D. S., Quinn, K., & Wang, P. (2010). Research domain criteria (RDoC): Toward a new classification framework for research on mental disorders. *American Journal of Psychiatry, 167,* 748–751.

Johnson, D. & Gunnar, M. (2011). Growth failure in institutionalized children. *Monographs of the Society for Research in Child Development, 76,* 92–126.

Jonkman, C. S., Oosterman, M., Schuenger, C., Bolle, E. A., Boer, F., & Lindauer, R. J. L. (2014). Disturbances in attachment: Inhibited and disinhibited symptoms in foster children. *Child and Adolescent Psychiatry and Mental Health, 8,* 21.

Joseph, R. (1996). *Neuropsychiatry, Neuropsychology and Clinical Neuroscience: Emotion Cognition, Language, Memory, Brain Damage, and Abnormal Behavior* (2nd edn). Baltimore, MD: Williams & Wilkins.

Kaufman, J., Gelernter, J., Hudziak, J., Tyrka, A. R., & Coplan, J. D. (2015). The research domain criteria (RDoC) project and studies of risk and resilience in maltreated children. *Journal of the American Academy of Child and Adolescent Psychiatry, 54,* 617–625.

Kaufman, J. & Weder, N. (2010). Neurobiology of early life stress: Evolving concepts. In A. Martin, L. Scahill, & C. J. Kratochvil (eds.), *Pediatric Psychopharmacology* (2nd edn). New York, NY: Oxford University Press.

Kočovská, E., Wilson, P., Young, D., Wallace, A. M., Gorski, C., Follan, M., Smillie, M., Puckering, C., Barnes, J., Gillberg, C., & Minnis, H. (2013). Cortisol secretion in children with symptoms of reactive attachment disorder. *Psychiatry Research, 209,* 74–77.

Kozak, M. J. & Cuthbert, B. N. (2016). The NIMH Research Domain Criteria Initiative: Background, issues, and pragmatics. *Psychophysiology, 53,* 286–297.

Landers, M S. & Sullivan, R. M. (2012). The development and neurobiology of infant attachment and fear. *Developmental Neuroscience, 34,* 101–114.

Lehmann, S., Havik, O. E., Havik, T., & Heiervang, E. R. (2013). Mental disorders in foster children: A study of prevalence, comorbidity, and risk factors. *Child and Adolescent Psychiatry and Mental Health, 7,* 39.

Leiden Conference on the Development and Care of Children without Permanent Parents. (2012). The development and care of institutionally reared children. *Child Development Perspectives*, *6*, 174–180.

Lewis, M. D. (2005). Self-organizing individual differences in brain development. *Developmental Review*, *25*, 252–277.

Lieberman, A. F. & van Horn, P. (2009). Child-parent psychotherapy: A developmental approach to mental health treatment in infancy and early childhood. In C. J. Zeanah (eds.), *Handbook of Infant Mental Health* (3rd edn) (pp. 439–449). New York, NY: Guilford Press.

Liotti, G. (2004). Trauma, dissociation, and disorganized attachment: Three strands of a single braid. *Psychotherapy: Theory, Research, Practice, Training*, *41*, 472–486.

Lyons-Ruth, K. & Jacobvitz, D. (2008). Attachment disorganization, genetic factors, parenting contexts and developmental transformation from infancy to adulthood. In J. Cassidy & P. Shaver (eds.), *Handbook of Attachment: Theory, Research and Clinical Applications* (2nd edn) (pp. 666–697). New York, NY: Guilford Press.

Macnamara, A. & Phan, K. L. (2016). Psychobiological operationalization of RDoC constructs: Methodological and conceptual opportunities and challenges. *Psychophysiology*, *53*, 406–409.

Maier, S. F., Amat, J., Baratta, M. V., Bland, S. T., Christianson, J. C., Thompson, B., . . . Watkins, L. R. (2009). The role of the medial prefrontal cortex in mediating resistance and vulnerability to the impact of adverse events. In C. M. Pariante, R. M. Nesse, D. Nutt, & L. Wolpert (eds.), *Understanding Depression: A Translational Approach* (pp. 157–171). Oxford: Oxford University Press.

Main, M. & Solomon, J. (1986). Discovery of an insecure-disorganized/disoriented attachment pattern. *Affective Development in Infancy* (pp. 95–124). Westport, CT: Ablex Publishing.

Markowitsch, H. J., Thiel, A., Kessler, J., von Stockhausen, H. M., & Heiss, W. D. (1997). Ecphorizing semi-conscious episodic information via the right temporal polar cortex: A PET study. *Neurocase*, *3*, 445–449.

McGowan, P. O., Sasaki, A., D'Alessio, A. C., Dymov, S., Labonté, B., Szyf, M., Turecki, G., & Meaney, M. J. (2009). Epigenetic regulation of the glucocorticoid receptor in human brain associates with childhood abuse. *Nature Neuroscience*, *12*, 342–348.

Minnis, H., Macmillan, S., Pritchett, R., Young, D., Wallace, B., Butcher, J., Sim, F., Baynham, K., Davidson, C., & Gillberg, C. (2013). Prevalence of reactive attachment disorder in a deprived population. *British Journal of Psychiatry*, *202*, 342–346.

Minnis, H., Marwick, H., Arthur, J., & McLaughlin, A. (2006). Reactive attachment disorder: A theoretical model beyond attachment. *European Child and Adolescent Psychiatry*, *15*, 336–342.

Mizuno, K., Takiguchi, S., Yamazaki, M., Asano, M., Kato, S., Kuriyama, K., Watanabe, Y., Sadato, N., & Tomoda, A. (2015). Impaired neural reward processing in children and adolescents with reactive attachment disorder: A pilot study. *Asian Journal of Psychiatry*, *17*, 89–93.

Montalvo-Ortiz, J. L., Gelernter, J., Hudziak, J., & Kaufman, J. (2016). RDoC and translational perspectives on the genetics of trauma-related psychiatric disorders. *American Journal of Medical Genetics, Part B, 171B*, 81–91.

Murray, I., Kempton, C., Woolgar, M., & Hooper, R. (1993). Depressed mothers' speech to their infants and its relation to infant gender and cognitive development. *Journal of Child Psychology and Psychiatry, 34*, 1083–1101.

National Institute of Mental Health (NIMH). (2008). *The National Institute of Mental Health strategic plan* (NIH Publication No. 08–6368). Retrieved from www .nimh.nih.gov/about/strategic-planning-reports/index.shtml.

Nestler, E. J., Barrot, M., DiLeone, R. J., Eisch, A. J., Gold, S. J., & Monteggia, L. M. (2002). Neurobiology of depression. *Neuron, 34*, 13–25.

Patrick, C. J. & Hajcak, G. (2016a). RDoC: Translating promise into progress. *Psychophysiology, 53*, 415–424.

Patrick, C. J. & Hajcak, G. (2016b). Reshaping clinical science: Introduction to the special issues on psychophysiology and the NIMH Research Domain Criteria (RDoC) initiative. *Psychophysiology*, 53, 281–285.

Pitkow, L. J., Sharer, C. A., Ren, X., Insel, T. R., Terwilliger, E. F., & Young, L. J. (2001). Facilitation of affiliation and pair-bond formation by vasopressin receptor gene transfer into the ventral forebrain of a monogamous vole. *Journal of Neuroscience, 21*, 7392–7396.

Powell, B., Cooper, G., Hoffman, K., & Marvin, R. S. (2013). *The Circle of Security Intervention: Enhancing Attachment in Early Parent–Child Relationships.* New York, NY: Guilford Press.

Prior, V. & Glaser, D. (2006). *Understanding Attachment and Attachment Disorders: Theory, Evidence and Practice.* London: Jessica Kingsley.

Pritchett, R., Pritchett, J., Marshall, E., Davidson, C., & Minnis, H. (2013). Reactive attachment disorder in the general population: A hidden ESSENCE disorder. *Scientific World Journal, 2013*, Article ID 818157.

Provence, S. & Lipton, R. C. (1962). *Infants in Institutions.* New York, NY: International Publisher Press.

Renk, K., Boris, N. W., Kolomeyer, E., Lowell, A., Puff, J., Cunningham, A., Khan, M., & McSwiggan, M. (2016). The state of evidence-based parenting interventions for parents who are substance-involved. *Pediatric Research-Nature, 79*, 177–183.

Richters, M. M. & Volkmar, F. R. (1994). Reactive attachment disorder of infancy or early childhood. *Journal of the American Academy of Child and Adolescent Psychiatry, 33*, 328–332.

Rinaman, L., Levitt, P., & Card, J. P. (2000). Progressive postnatal assembly of limbic-autonomic circuits revealed by central transneuronal transport of pseudorabies virus. *Journal of Neuroscience, 20*, 2731–2741.

Rutter, M., Kreppner, J., & Sonuga-Burke, E. (2009). Emanuel Miller Lecture: Attachment insecurity, disinhibited attachment, and attachment disorders: Where do research findings leave the concepts? *Journal of Child Psychology and Psychiatry and Allied Discipline, 50*, 529–543.

Rutter, M. & Shaffer, D. (1980). *DSM-III*: A step forward or back in terms of the classification of child psychiatric disorders? *Journal of the American Academy of Child Psychiatry, 19*, 371–394.

Sanislow, C. A., Pine, D. S., Quinn, K. J., Kozak, M. J., Garvey, M. A., Heinssen, R. K., Wang, P. S., & Cuthbert, B. N. (2010). Developing constructs for psychopathology research: Research domain criteria. *Journal of Abnormal Psychology, 119*, 631–639.

Schaefer, M. (2007). *Public Sector Behavioral Health for Children and Families: Aligning Systems and Incentives*. New Haven, CT: Zigler Center in Child Development and Social Policy Colloquium Series

Schore, A. N. (1994). *Affect Regulation and the Origin of the Self: The Neurobiology of Emotional Development*. New York, NY: Psychology Press and Routledge.

Schore, A. N. (2000). Attachment and the regulation of the right brain. *Attachment & Human Development*, *2*, 23–47.

Schore, A. N. (2001). The effects of early relational trauma on right brain development, affect regulation, and infant mental health. *Infant Mental Health Journal*, *22*, 201–269.

Shankman, S. A. & Gorka, S. M. (2015). Psychopathology research in the RDoC era: Unanswered questions and the importance of the psychophysiological unit of analysis. *International Journal of Psychophysiology*, 98 (2, Part 2), 330–337.

Shimada, K., Takiguchi, S., Mizushima, S., Fujisawa, T. X., Saito, D. N., Kosaka, H., Okazawa, H., & Tomoda, A. (2015). Reduced visual cortex grey matter volume in children and adolescents with reactive attachment disorder. *NeuroImage: Clinical*, *9*, 13–19.

Silberman, E. K. & Weingartner, H. (1986). Hemispheric lateralization of function related to emotion. *Brain Cognition*, *5*, 322–353.

Smith, A. S. & Wang, Z. (2014). Hypothalamic oxytocin mediates social buffering of the stress response. *Biological Psychiatry*, *76*, 281–288.

Smith Stover, C. & Keeshin, B. (In press). Research domain criteria and the study of trauma in children: Implications for assessment and treatment research. *Clinical Psychology Review.*

Smyke, A. T., Zeanah, C. H., Gleason, M. M., Drury, S. S., Fox, N. A., Nelson, C. A., & Guthri, D. (2012). A randomized controlled trial comparing foster care and institutional care for children with signs of reactive attachment disorder. *American Journal of Psychiatry*, *169*, 508–514.

Stafford, B., Zeanah, C. H., & Scheeringa, M. (2003). Exploring psychopathology in the early childhood: PTSD and attachment disorders in DC: 0–3 and *DSM-IV. Infant Mental Health Journal*, *24*, 398–409.

Stern, D. N. (1985). *The Interpersonal World of the Infant*. New York, NY: Basic Books.

Takiguchi, S., Fujisawa, T. X., Mizushima, S., Saito, D. N., Okamoto, Y., Shimada, K., Koizumi, M., Kumazaki, H., Jung, M., Kosaka, H., Hiratani, M., Ohshima, Y., Teicher, M. H., & Tomoda, A. (2015). Ventral striatum dysfunction in children and adolescents with reactive attachment disorder: Functional MRI study. *BJPsych Open*, *1*, 121–128.

Teicher, M. H. & Samson, J. A. (2013). Childhood maltreatment and psychopathology: A case for ecophenotypic variants as clinically and neurobiologically distinct subtypes. *American Journal of Psychiatry*, *170*, 1114–1133.

Thompson, R. (2009). Early attachment and later development: Familiar questions, new answers. In J. Cassidy & P. R. Shaver (eds.), *Handbook of Attachment: Theory, Research and Clinical Applications* (2nd edn) (pp. 348–365). New York, NY: Guilford Press.

Tizard, B. & Hodges, J. (1978). The effect of early institutional rearing on the development of eight year old children. *Journal of Child Psychology and Psychiatry*, *19*, 99–118.

Tizard, B. & Rees, J. (1975). The effect of early institutional rearing on the behavior problems and affectional relationships of four-year-old children. *Journal of Child Psychology and Psychiatry*, *16*, 61–73.

Trevarthen, C. (1998). The concept and foundations of infant intersubjectivity. In S. Braten (ed.), *Intersubjective Communication and Emotion in Early Ontogeny* (pp. 15–46). Cambridge: Cambridge University Press.

Trevarthen, C. & Aitkin, K. J. (2001). Infant intersubjectivity research, theory, and clinical applications. *Journal of Child Psychology and Psychiatry*, *42*, 3–48.

Tronick, E., Als, H., & Adamson, L. (1979). Structure of early face-to-face communicative interactions. In M. Bullowa (ed.), *Before Speech: The Beginning of Interpersonal Communication* (pp. 349–372). Cambridge: Cambridge University Press.

Vela, R. M. (2014). The effect of severe stress on early brain development, attachment, and emotions: A psychoanatomical formulation. *Psychiatric Clinics of North America*, *37*, 519–534.

Verschuren, K., Marcven, A., & Schoefs, V. (1996). The internal working model of the self: Attachment and competence in five-year-olds. *Child Development*, *67*, 2493–2511.

Weaver, I. C., Cervoni, N., Champagne, F. A., D'Alessio, A. C., Sharma, S., Seckl, J. R., & Meaney, M. J. (2004). Epigenetic programming by maternal behavior. *Nature Neuroscience*, *7*, 847–854.

Woolgar, M. & Scott, S. (2014). The negative consequences of over-diagnosing attachment disorders in adopted children: The importance of comprehensive formulations. *Clinical Child Psychology and Psychiatry*, *19*, 355–366.

Young, K. A., Liu, Y., Gobrogge, K. I., Wang, H., & Wang, Z. (2014). Oxytocin reverse amphetamine-induced deficits in social bonding: Evidence for an interaction with nucleus accumbens dopamine. *Journal of Neuroscience*, *34*, 8499–8506.

Zalta, A. K. & Shankman, S. A. (2016). Conducting psychopathology prevention research in the RDoC era. *Clinical Psychology: Science and Practice*, *23*, 94–104.

Zeanah, C. H. & Boris, N. W. (2000). Disturbances and disorders of attachment in early childhood. In C. H. Zeanah (ed.), *Handbook of Infant Mental Health* (2nd edn) (pp. 353–368). New York, NY: Guilford Press.

Zeanah, C. H., Chesher, T., Boris, N. W., & the AACAP Committee on Quality Issues. (2016). Practice parameter for the assessment and treatment of children and adolescents with reactive attachment disorder and disinhibited social engagement disorder. *Journal of the American Academy of Child and Adolescent Psychiatry*, *55*, 990–1003.

Zeanah, C. H. & Gleason, M. M. (2010). *Reactive Attachment Disorder: A Review for* DSM-5. Washington, DC: American Psychiatric Association.

Zeanah, C. H. & Gleason, M. M. (2015). Annual research review: Attachment disorders in early childhood: Clinical presentation, causes, correlates, and treatment. *Journal of Child Psychology and Psychiatry*, *56*, 207–222.

Zeanah, C. H., Scheeringa, M., Boris, N. W., Heller, S. S., Smyke, A. T., & Trapani, J. (2004). Reactive attachment disorder in maltreated toddlers. *Child Abuse and Neglect*, *28*, 877–888.

Zeanah, C. H., Smyke, A. T., Koga, S. F., & Carlson, E. (2005). Attachment in institutionalized and community children in Romania. *Child Development, 76*, 1015–1028.

Zhang, T. Y. & Meaney, M. J. (2010). Epigenetics and the environmental regulation of the genome and its function. *Annual Review of Psychology, 61*, 439–466.

Zilberstein, K. (2014). The use and limitations of attachment theory in child psychotherapy. *Psychotherapy, 51*, 93–103.

Treatment and Prevention of Anxiety and Related Disorders

28 Anxiety Disorders

Joseph K. Carpenter, Kristina Conroy, and Stefan G. Hofmann

Anxiety disorders are highly prevalent and result in a substantial negative impact on quality of life, psychosocial functioning, and physical health (Comer et al., 2011; Hendriks et al., 2016). At some point in their lives, most individuals affected by an anxiety disorder will come into contact with a treatment provider as a result of their condition (Wang, Angermeyer, et al., 2007). As a result, understanding the most effective methods for treating anxiety disorders is paramount. This chapter first provides an overview of the different forms of treatment for anxiety disorders, including traditional cognitive behavioral therapy, acceptance and mindfulness-based treatments, relaxation, pharmacotherapy, and psychodynamic therapy, as well as the evidence for the efficacy of each treatment. Next, this chapter reviews the various treatment components that make up evidence-based treatments for anxiety disorders, with an emphasis on the treatment targets and interventions with transdiagnostic relevance. These treatment components include psychoeducation, exposure, cognitive restructuring, mindfulness, and relaxation. The chapter concludes by highlighting important future directions for reducing the enormous burden to society caused by anxiety disorders.

Cognitive Behavioral Therapy

Cognitive behavioral therapy (CBT) is considered the gold standard of treatment for adult anxiety disorders (NICE, 2011). CBT consists of a class of scientifically informed interventions that view emotional disorders as persisting due to dysfunctional beliefs and maladaptive behavioral patterns (Hofmann, Asmundson, & Beck, 2013). In the case of anxiety disorders specifically, these unhelpful beliefs are related to overestimating the likelihood of negative outcomes, and a perceived inability to cope with anxiety-inducing situations. Such perceptions result in patterns of behavioral and cognitive avoidance, which often become habit and reinforce maladaptive beliefs about threat. Treatment with CBT addresses maladaptive cognitions through *cognitive restructuring*, which involves identifying automatic thinking patterns and developing more useful or realistic alternative interpretations. Behavioral factors contributing to the maintenance of anxiety, on other hand, are targeted by the use of *exposure* exercises, which involve systematically confronting anxiety-inducing situations in order to learn that feared outcomes are unlikely to occur. More detailed descriptions of these and other common CBT techniques used in CBT are provided later in the chapter.

Evidence for the efficacy of CBT comes from a number of clinical trials that have shown CBT to be associated with a reduction in anxiety symptoms (Butler et al., 2006; Hofmann, Asnaani, Vonk, Sawyer, & Fang, 2012). Specifically, meta-analyses have shown CBT to result in superior outcomes compared to various control conditions for social anxiety disorder (SAD) (Mayo-Wilston et al., 2014), generalized anxiety disorder (GAD) (Cuijpers et al., 2014), panic disorder (PD) (Pompoli et al., 2016), and specific phobias (Wolitzky-Taylor, Horowitz, Powers, & Telch, 2008), as well as other fear-based disorders like obsessive-compulsive disorder (OCD) (Olatunji et al., 2013) and posttraumatic stress disorder (PTSD) (Bisson et al., 2013). Recent meta-analyses have also examined the effect of CBT across multiple types of anxiety disorders, and demonstrated superiority in comparison to waitlist controls (Bandelow et al., 2015) and treatment as usual (Watts et al., 2015). To date, perhaps the most rigorous evaluation of the efficacy of CBT comes from a meta-analysis by Hofmann and Smits (2008), which compared the effect of CBT to psychological or pharmacological placebo in 27 randomized controlled trials (RCTs) of CBT for SAD, PTSD, PD, acute stress disorder, OCD, and GAD. Using placebo-controlled trials in this instance is important for understanding the specific effect of CBT (as opposed to treatment generally), as such a comparison condition better controls for the effects of patient expectations and the therapeutic relationship on treatment outcome. Findings revealed CBT interventions to be superior to psychological and pharmacological placebo conditions, with controlled effect sizes for continuous measures of anxiety symptoms in the medium to large range. Furthermore, patients completing CBT were more than four times more likely to be treatment responders than those completing placebo treatment. A recent extension and update of this study essentially replicated these findings (Carpenter et al., 2018).

Given the high rates of comorbidity with depression among anxious populations (Goldberg, Krueger, Andrews, & Hobbs, 2009; Kaufman & Charney, 2000), depressive symptoms are often evaluated as outcome measures in CBT treatment studies for anxiety disorders. Cuijpers and colleagues (2016) conducted a meta-analysis on 46 clinical trials of CBT for anxiety disorders and found that CBT was associated with moderate to large effects on symptoms of depression. The effect sizes were comparable to direct treatment for major depressive disorder (MDD). Researchers have also examined the effects of CBT for anxiety disorders on other symptoms not directly targeted in treatment, such as quality of life. Hofmann, Wu, and Boettcher (2014) conducted a meta-analysis examining the effect of CBT for anxiety disorders on self-reported quality of life, which captures outcomes such as patients' subjective view of their life circumstances, overall mental and physical health, social and family relationships, and functioning at work and at home. Pooling together the results from 44 studies, CBT significantly outperformed control conditions, with a controlled effect size in the moderate range.

One of the most frequently noted criticisms of the extant literature on CBT is the generalizability of CBT trials (e.g., Westen & Morrison, 2001). Specifically, critics question whether the effects of CBT delivered by expert therapists in highly controlled clinical trials extend to treatment delivered by community providers with more complex and diverse patients seen in routine clinical practice. In response to such a critique, Hans and Hiller (2013) conducted a meta-analysis of nonrandomized effectiveness studies for adult anxiety disorders and found that CBT was widely effective in routine clinical settings; both disorder-specific symptoms as well as general anxiety and depression showed improvement at the conclusion of treatment as well as at 12-month follow-up visits. Notably, however, 63% of the studies included were conducted with completer-only samples and 30% of studies did not report participant dropout rates. Similarly, only a minority (24%) of the placebo-controlled RCTs in Hofmann and Smits (2008) used intent-to-treat analyses. This represents an important limitation of CBT, as studies with completer-only samples are at risk of producing inflated effect sizes due to the possibility of nonresponding patients who systematically discontinued treatment prior to completion.

In addition, not all patients respond favorably to CBT, with response rates estimated at 60–70% (Loerinc et al., 2015), and more data on long-term outcomes are needed (Hans & Hiller, 2013). Furthermore, on average approximately 27% of CBT patients in routine clinical practice drop out before the conclusion of their treatment (van Ingen, Freiheit, & Vye, 2009). Nonetheless, extant literature shows that response rates for CBT are higher and dropout rates are no different than comparison treatments (Hofmann & Smits, 2008). In addition, the evidence base supporting the efficacy of CBT far outpaces that of any other treatment approach, thus making it the treatment of choice for anxiety disorders.

Treatment formats in CBT. Although CBT was originally developed as an individual, face-to-face therapy, it has also been successfully delivered in group settings, through computerized programs, and in self-help formats. Having a variety of formats through which CBT can be delivered is important because access to a particular form of treatment may be limited by geographic or financial barriers, and because individual preferences and feelings of stigma may make one form more desirable over another for individuals considering treatment. Patient preference as well as levels of disorder severity should be taken into consideration as therapists consider variations of CBT that best suit patients' needs.

Group CBT. Group therapy has the potential to yield benefits such as normalizing symptomology, providing patients with the opportunity to give and receive support from others, and allowing the influence of successful behavior from group members who are doing well to spread to other members of the group (Wersebe, Sijbrandij, & Cuijpers, 2013). Additionally, group treatments are more time- and cost-effective. The most obvious beneficiaries of group CBT are socially anxious patients, as the group format provides a unique opportunity to encounter feared settings and become more comfortable with social interaction during therapy.

However, research on group CBT presents mixed results across disorders. Studies have shown group CBT to be effective compared to waitlist or placebo for SAD and OCD (Marchand et al., 2009; Mörtberg et al., 2006; Wersebe et al., 2013), and comparable to individual CBT for PD (Jónsson et al., 2011). A significant number of studies have also shown that group CBT is less effective than individual CBT for GAD and SAD (Covin et al., 2008; Hedman et al., 2013; Mayo-Wilson et al., 2014; Stangier et al., 2003), likely because therapists cannot provide the same attention to address patients' individual issues. It is also important to note that group and individual CBT can be used together; patients may benefit from beginning treatment in a group format and then progressing into individual therapy to allow for increased therapist guidance and individualized exercises (Hofmann et al., 2013).

Computerized CBT. Computer-based CBT (cCBT) for anxiety disorders has received a recent surge of exploration, as it has the potential to increase accessibility of treatment and reduce costs. A recent meta-analysis of RCTs comparing cCBT to wait-list, in-person CBT, and Internet control for the treatment of anxiety disorders found cCBT superior to wait-list and equivalent to in-person CBT (Adelman, Panza, Bartley, Bontempo, & Bloch, 2014). An important issue with cCBT, however, is whether some level of remote therapist support is necessary. A meta-analysis by Spek and colleagues (2007) found that interventions that included therapist support yielded a large effect size, whereas those that did not yielded only a small effect size (Spek et al., 2007). In contrast to this finding, however, is a study by Berger and colleagues (2011) that compared three arms of Internet-based treatment for SAD with varying levels of therapist support. The study found no significant difference between groups. Also of note, the age of participants has the potential to moderate the effect of cCBT such that older adults may benefit less from digital intervention due to generational differences in comfort with technology (Barak et al., 2008; Grist & Cavanaugh, 2013). The implementation of cCBT is relatively new, and more research is necessary to evaluate the impact of therapist support and other potential moderators of treatment success.

"Third Wave" Therapies

Over the past three decades, researchers have expanded upon CBT for anxiety disorders to include mindfulness and acceptance-based treatments. Some refer to this class of therapy as the "third wave" of CBT, as such treatment approaches focus not just on the content of one's thoughts but also on one's *relationship* to them (Hayes, 2004). Accordingly, third wave therapies rely on treatment strategies such as mindfulness, acceptance, cognitive defusion, experiential learning, and contextual change motivated by the focus on clients' values and life goals (Hayes, 2004). The most popular adaptations of this approach are acceptance and commitment therapy (ACT) and mindfulness-based therapies (mindfulness-based cognitive therapy [MBCT] and mindfulness-based stress reduction [MBSR]). Of note, some have argued against the notion of these treatments forming a "new wave," citing that ACT and mindfulness-based therapies are more similar to than different from traditional CBT (Hofmann, 2008a; Hofmann & Asmundson, 2008). Nonetheless, such authors acknowledge that these treatment approaches have brought about meaningful changes and advancements in the treatment of anxiety (Hayes & Hofmann, 2017). Brief overviews and supporting evidences of these therapeutic approaches are provided in what follows.

Acceptance and commitment therapy (ACT). ACT is based on the notion that the goal of treatment is not to decrease anxiety, but rather to promote psychological flexibility and enable patients to live in accordance with their values, regardless of their subjective anxiety (Hayes, Pistorello, & Levin, 2012). Accordingly, ACT does not attempt to identify and correct cognitive distortions or directly regulate physiological sensations like traditional CBT. It instead employs an acceptance-based approach using techniques such as mindfulness, cognitive defusion, and self-as-context to change a patient's relationship with anxiety (Hayes, Luoma, Bond, Masuda, & Lillis, 2006). For instance, a common ACT technique involves responding to anxious thoughts or feelings by saying "I am having the thought/feeling of anxiety," in order to create distance from the lived experience of anxiety. ACT still relies on exposure techniques, but exposure is viewed as an opportunity to practice behaving in accordance with one's goals or values, rather than an exercise designed to reduce anxiety.

A number of meta-analyses of RCTs have shown ACT to be superior to control conditions (Hayes et al., 2006; Powers, Vörding, & Emmelkamp, 2009), and some indicate that ACT is as effective as established treatments (Bluett, Homan, Morrison, Levin, & Twohig, 2014). In one of the few direct comparisons of ACT and traditional CBT, Arch and colleagues (2012) found the two treatments to be equally efficacious for a sample of patients with mixed anxiety disorders, including PD with or without agoraphobia, specific phobia, SAD, and GAD. However, findings did indicate greater improvements in quality of life in the CBT condition, while ACT led to superior outcomes on measures of psychological flexibility. In addition, CBT was found to be superior to ACT among patients with moderate levels of anxiety sensitivity, whereas ACT outperformed CBT among patients with comorbid mood disorders (Wolitzky-Taylor, Arch, Rosenfield, & Craske, 2012). Although existing research does not suggest differential efficacy between ACT and traditional CBT for anxiety disorders, the potential to personalize treatment based on individual characteristics is a promising future direction for research and practice. Additionally, some researchers have suggested that the integration of ACT techniques in CBT protocols (Bluett et al., 2014) holds particular promise.

Mindfulness-based therapies. Another group of therapies that emerged as part of the "third wave" is rooted in the ancient Buddhist practice of mindfulness. Mindfulness refers to the process of adopting a nonjudgmental awareness of present experience, including one's sensations, thoughts, bodily states, consciousness, and environment (Kabat-Zinn, 2003). MBCT (Segal, Williams, & Teasdale, 2002) and MBSR (Kabat-Zinn, 1982) integrate mindfulness practices with elements of traditional CBT, and are based on the idea that taking a more accepting and less judgmental stance toward one's negative emotions can lessen their hold on day-to-day experiences.

A number of studies have shown that MBTs result in moderate reductions in anxiety symptoms associated with medical illnesses or other psychiatric disorders (Hofmann, Sawyer, Witt, & Oh, 2010). A growing number of clinical trials have also looked directly at MBTs for individuals with anxiety disorders. Two trials showed that a meditation-based stress reduction program (Lee et al., 2007) and MBCT (Kim et al., 2009) for patients with GAD and PD led to greater reductions in anxiety symptoms than an anxiety education control condition. A later study demonstrated MBSR to lead to significant reductions in anxiety symptoms among patients with GAD. However, MBSR was not significantly different from a stress management education condition (Hoge et al., 2013). Another treatment study indicated that MBSR benefited patients with SAD, but was not as effective as group CBT (Koszycki, Benger, Shlik, & Bradwejn, 2007). Lastly, a study on veterans with mixed anxiety disorders showed equivalent outcomes of MBSR and CBT on principal disorder severity at post-treatment and follow-up (Arch, Ayers et al., 2013). However, CBT outperformed MBSR on anxious arousal outcomes, while MBSR led to greater reductions in worry and comorbid emotional disorders than traditional CBT. In an interesting parallel with the moderator analysis of ACT vs. CBT by Wolitzky-Taylor and colleagues (2012), MBSR outperformed CBT among those with moderate to severe depressive symptoms (Arch & Ayers, 2013). Taken together, the results of MBTs for the treatment of anxiety are encouraging, though studies showing equivalent outcomes to active controls (Hoge et al., 2013) or inferior outcomes to CBT (Koszycki et al., 2007) suggest further investigation and treatment development may be warranted.

Other Treatment Approaches

Pharmacotherapy. Psychopharmacological approaches have been widely employed in the treatment of adult anxiety disorders. Based on research examining efficacy, side-effects, and the frequency of harmful interactions with other medications, the World Federation of Societies of Biological Psychiatry reported selective serotonin reuptake inhibitors (SSRIs) as the first-line pharmacological treatment for anxiety disorders. Other medications recommended for the treatment of anxiety include serotonin-noradrenaline reuptake inhibitors (SNRIs), tricyclic antidepressants (TCAs), benzodiazepines, monoamine oxidase inhibitors (MAOIs), and the calcium channel modulator pregabalin (Bandelow et al., 2008). Of note, clinical guidelines warn that benzodiazepines should be used sparingly and with significant caution, as tolerance and dependence can arise as a result of the immediate and temporary anxiety relief they provide (NICE, 2014).

Regarding all medication classes, research has shown that a significant number of patients do not respond to psychopharmacological interventions or do not experience complete remission of symptoms (Farach et al., 2012; Pollack, Otto et al., 2008). For instance, between one-third and one-half of patients treated with an antidepressant for anxiety experience a relapse of symptoms (Pollack et al., 2008). Researchers attribute the problem to the limited amount of long-term efficacy combined with the increasing number of drug classes available to treat anxiety disorders. Furthermore, clinicians often change medication, combine medication, or alter dosing without evidence-based guidance (Farach et al., 2012). Therefore, future research is necessary to inform optimal selection and sequencing of existing treatments.

Several studies have directly compared the effects of pharmacological treatment to CBT for anxiety disorders, finding superiority of CBT (Roshanaei-Moghaddam et al., 2011) or equality of efficacy (Bandelow et al., 2008). Cuijpers and colleagues (2013) conducted a meta-analysis of direct comparisons between antidepressants and psychotherapy for the treatment of depressive and anxiety disorders, finding little to no difference between psychotherapies and pharmacotherapies, with the exception of TCAs and nondirective supportive counseling, which were less efficacious than comparative treatments (SSRIs, monoamine oxidase inhibitors, CBT, interpersonal psychotherapy, problem-solving therapy, psychodynamic psychotherapy, and others). In addition, Bandelow and colleagues (2015) conducted a meta-analysis on all psychopharmacological treatments that had demonstrated efficacy in an RCT and were licensed in at least one country, and compared their effects to placebo and available psychological treatments for the treatment of PD, GAD, and SAD. SSRIs, SNRIs, and pregabalin yielded the largest effect sizes among the medications, while individual CBT yielded the largest effect size among the psychological treatments. On the whole, pharmacotherapy had higher effect sizes than psychological therapies when grouped together, and symptom improvement occurred faster with psychopharmacological treatments. However, note that symptom improvement has been shown to be maintained after the termination of CBT, whereas symptoms often return after the termination of medication (Otto, Smits, & Reese, 2005).

Pharmacotherapy in combination with psychotherapy has produced mixed results in the literature (Farach et al., 2012; Otto, Smits, & Reese, 2005). With the exception of PD and GAD, studies on combined pharmacological and psychological treatments have not shown superiority of combined treatment to either treatment alone (Bandelow et al., 2008; Cuijpers et al., 2014; Hofmann, Sawyer, Korte, & Smits, 2009). When pursuing a combination of treatment, one must also consider the potential increase in time and resources required of patients.

Cognitive enhancers. Aside from the psychopharmacological medications described earlier, a number of recent studies have explored the use of medications referred to as cognitive enhancers, which target the learning processes thought to be central to effective psychotherapy for anxiety disorders. Of these medications D-cycloserine (DCS), a partial agonist at the glycine recognition site of the glutamatergic NMDA receptor, has received the most attention for its potential to enhance extinction learning processes in the context of exposure therapy (Hofmann, 2014). Meta-analytic research has shown DCS to accelerate the effect of exposure therapy compared to placebo (Mataix-Cols et al., 2017; Rodrigues et al., 2014), but not all studies have resulted in positive effects (e.g., Hofmann et al., 2013). Hofmann's (2014) review of the clinical studies concluded that inconsistencies in the literature are largely accounted for by failure to consider both dosing and dose timing of DCS. For instance, studies have shown that patients' level of fear at the end of their exposure exercise predicts the overall effect of DCS administration (Smits et al., 2013a; Smits et al., 2013b). DCS augmented the effect of exposure sessions when self-reported fear levels at the end of the exposure were low, whereas it had the opposite effect if end fear levels were high. More research is under way to investigate whether selective administration of DCS following exposures with low end fear levels can maximize the benefits of the medication (Hofmann et al., 2015).

Psychodynamic therapy. Psychodynamic therapy is also widely practiced for the treatment of anxiety disorders. Varying significantly from the cognitive-behavioral orientation, the psychodynamic approach attempts to uncover patients' unconscious processes through fostering insight into the origins of one's emotions, thoughts, and conflicts within current relationships (Gabbard, 2004). In order to achieve this understanding, emphasis is placed on the way in which patients' conflicts play out in the patient–therapist relationship. A growing number of clinical trials have investigated the efficacy of psychodynamic therapy for PD and SAD, some of which have compared psychodynamic therapy to CBT. For PD, the two treatments were found to be equivalent in a randomized controlled trial by Leichsenring and colleagues (2009), and in an effectiveness study by Beutel and colleagues (2013). However, these results are of questionable validity given some significant methodological limitations (Hofmann, 2016a, 2016b), as described later in this chapter. More recently, panic-focused psychodynamic psychotherapy was compared with CBT and applied relaxation (AR) (Milrod et al., 2015). Results were complicated by site differences, such that no differences between treatments were seen in reductions in panic symptoms at one site, whereas another site showed greater effects of CBT. For SAD, psychodynamic treatment was found to be superior to a credible placebo control in one randomized trial (Knijnik, Kapczinski, Chachamovich, Margis, & Eizirik, 2004). In another study comparing psychodynamic therapy with CBT, the two treatments led to equivalent response rates, but CBT was associated with higher rates of remission and greater reductions on measures of social phobia and interpersonal problems (Leichsenring et al., 2013).

While these results suggest that psychodynamic therapy may be an efficacious treatment for SAD and PD, such an approach does not consistently produce equivalent results to CBT. Furthermore, the empirical and theoretical basis of psychodynamic therapy has been criticized. In reviewing a meta-analysis that suggested psychodynamic treatment was as efficacious as other established treatments (Leichsenring et al., 2015), Hofmann (2016a) found substantial risk of bias in a large number of the studies included. Furthermore, research validating the conceptual basis and proposed mechanisms of change in psychodynamic therapy is lacking (Hofmann, 2016b), which is an important aspect of establishing an evidence-based treatment.

Applied relaxation. Applied relaxation (AR) is another long-standing technique that was first used to treat PD and phobias and was later applied treat GAD (Hayes-Skelton, Roemer, Orsillo, & Borkovec, 2013). AR aims to teach patients how to decrease muscle tension through relaxation in order to counteract high levels of anxiety (Öst, 1987). Early studies with PD patients compared AR to cognitive therapy, wait-list, and active controls, and found AR as or more effective than controls (Öst, 1988) and equivalent to cognitive therapy (Öst & Westling, 1995; Öst, Westling, & Hellström, 1993) in reducing symptoms up to 15 months after termination of treatment. However, another study found that CBT was superior to AR in reducing panic frequency and symptom severity (Arntz & van den Hout, 1996). For GAD, AR has been found to be comparable to CBT (Dugas et al., 2010) as either a stand-alone treatment or in combination with cognitive therapy. Dugas and colleagues (2010) compared a 12-week protocol of AR alone to CBT and found equivalence of efficacy in the short term (12 weeks) and long term (6-, 12-, and 24-month follow-ups) on five out of six outcomes. However, CBT produced significantly greater symptom improvement immediately after treatment termination. Other trials (Hayes-Skelton, Roemer, & Orsillo, 2013; Hoyer et al., 2009; Wells et al., 2010) have elucidated AR's optimal benefit for GAD in combination with other evidence-based treatment. Therefore, AR is no longer commonly employed as a stand-alone treatment, but rather as a helpful additive to CBT.

Treatment Components

While anxiety can manifest in a wide variety of symptoms across different disorders, the basic components of evidence-based treatments tend to be quite similar regardless of the specific clinical presentation. This is appropriate, given the research showing that anxiety disorders have a number of shared underlying mechanisms, including neuroticism (Barlow, Sauer-Zavala, Carl, Bullis, & Ellard, 2014), intolerance of uncertainty (McEvoy & Mahoney, 2012), anxiety sensitivity (Boswell et al., 2013), distress tolerance (Leyro, Zvolensky, & Bernstein), perfectionism (Egan, Wade & Shafran, 2011), and experiential avoidance (Chawla & Ostafin, 2007), among others. The components of anxiety treatments thus tend to target one or more of these shared mechanisms, with potential adjustments in the delivery of such treatments components based on an individual's clinical presentation. The next section of this chapter reviews the procedures involved in such treatment components, the theoretical and empirical basis for their use, and issues related to maximizing their effectiveness.

Psychoeducation

Treatment for anxiety normally begins with at least one to two sessions of psychoeducation about the nature of anxiety, including how it develops, how it is maintained, and how it is effectively treated. Although the details covered by these early sessions may vary, in one form or another, patients are typically introduced to the idea that anxiety consists of thoughts, physical sensations, and behaviors (or behavioral urges) that occur in response to anticipated danger or other negative consequences. Patients are taught that anxiety is not inherently problematic, but rather it is a universally experienced emotion that serves the essential function of helping to prepare us for potential threats. Individuals with anxiety disorders, however, have an overly sensitive alarm system that causes them to respond to potentially threatening situations in an exaggerated manner. Patients learn that such exaggerated threat responses become particularly problematic when they lead to patterns of avoidance behavior, one of the most prominent factors in maintaining anxiety (Krypotos, Effting, Kindt, & Beckers, 2015). Patients are encouraged to see that despite the temporary relief resulting from avoidance, such behavior reinforces the notion that danger is present in the first place, and prevents them from developing more realistic appraisals about the likelihood of their feared consequences actually occurring.

Presenting psychoeducational material in this way serves several important functions. First, breaking anxiety down in to its constituent parts (thoughts, physical sensations, behaviors) provides patients the language to understand and describe their experience of anxiety, and helps them see how the different components of anxiety reinforce one another (e.g., anxious thinking becomes more intense when one's heart is racing). Daily self-monitoring of anxiety, which is typically assigned as homework during psychoeducation sessions, can help to bolster a patient's awareness of his or her emotions from this perspective. Second, teaching patients that anxiety serves an adaptive function normalizes the experience of anxiety and helps patients more accurately understand the nature of their problem: feeling anxiety is not inherently bad, but problems arise as a result of attempts to avoid anxiety-inducing situations. Third, discussing the way in which avoidance maintains anxiety helps establish a credible rationale for conducting exposures, a treatment component for which patient buy-in and expectation of success are particularly important (Price & Anderson, 2012; Taylor, 2003).

Little research has been conducted on the specific impact of psychoeducation on symptom change in anxiety, or on issues like how much psychoeducation is necessary or what material needs to be covered. However, treatments consisting purely of psychoeducation have been shown to have small effects on symptom improvements in psychological distress (Donker, Griffiths, Cuijpers, & Christensen, 2009), and some evidence suggests that the administration of a psychoeducation module within a larger treatment can lead to changes in beliefs about emotions and other treatment-relevant skills (Sauer-Zavala et al., 2017). Furthermore, a substantial portion of patients receiving anxiety treatment sees meaningful symptom improvements in the first two to four sessions, before additional treatment ingredients have been introduced (Crits-Cristoph et al., 2001; Westra, Dozois, & Marcus, 2007). Such findings lend credence to the idea that psychoeducation can have an impact on symptoms by itself.

Exposure

Exposure techniques consist of patients deliberately and repeatedly confronting feared situations while refraining from engaging in avoidance behaviors. These techniques are an essential part of most anxiety treatments, and have been widely demonstrated to be effective even in the absence of other treatment components (Ougrin, 2011). Such success comes from the numerous underlying mechanisms of anxiety disorders that exposure targets. For one, successful exposure exercises cause changes in patients' exaggerated beliefs about the possibility of threat by teaching them that their feared consequences are unlikely to occur. For instance, a socially anxious patient might think that he or she will stumble over his or her words and sound completely incoherent when giving a presentation in front of a group. By actually giving the presentation, the patient can learn that his or her speech is much more fluent and coherent than he or she expected, a realization that is often assisted by the use of confederate feedback or videotape review. Patients may also have expectations about the persistence of anxiety in such an exposure situation, believing that their anxiety will only decline if they leave the situation. Through exposure patients can learn that if they persist in the situation for long enough, for instance giving a presentation for 10–15 minutes rather than getting it over as quickly as possible, their anxiety goes down and their expectations about the persistence of heightened anxiety are disconfirmed.

Exposures can also target biased beliefs about the cost of potential negative events by creating a situation in which the feared situation actually occurs. This can be an important element of treatment because even if a patient comes to realize that the probability of a negative outcome is low, his or her anxiety may be maintained if the consequences of that negative event are perceived as disastrous (Foa, Huppert, & Cahill, 2006). For instance, the thought of giving a stumbling and incoherent speech may seem unacceptable to a socially anxious patient, and therefore will cause the patient to become highly anxious even though he or she has never given the type of speech he or she is afraid of. The negative consequences of such an occurrence, however, could be tested through a social mishap exposure in which the patient intentionally stumbles over his or her words and says things that do not make sense (Fang, Sawyer, Asnaani, & Hofmann, 2013). The patient may feel as if they appeared completely incompetent and ridiculous, but through feedback from audience members can learn that stumbling over words made them look less ridiculous than they thought. Or even more powerfully, the patient might get no feedback from the audience, and instead reflect on the long-term significance of the anxiety or other negative consequences they are experiencing in the moment. A therapist might ask, for instance, "Do you think the audience members will be thinking about how you made an incoherent speech later tonight?" or "How much will you care about your speech a week, month or year from now?" Concretely considering such possibilities after the exposure, as well as reflecting back at a later time point on how much they continue to be concerned about their behavior during the exposure, can help patients realize that their concerns are exaggerated, leading to a long-term reduction in anxiety.

Another important outcome of exposure exercises is that patients have the opportunity to learn that they can function in the context of high levels of anxiety. The socially anxious patient might feel as if he or she won't be able to speak properly on account of anxiety, or a patient with a driving phobia might feel like he or she is incapable of competently driving a car because of panic symptoms. These concerns are almost always exaggerated, however, and the experience of realizing this tends to leads to a greater sense of self-efficacy regarding one's ability to cope with intense anxiety (Fentz et al., 2013). This process of learning to cope with strong anxiety symptoms is also assisted through instructing patients to focus their attention on the task at hand during an exposure (e.g., driving), rather than on the internal experience of anxiety, as such an attentional shift can reduce the intensity and interference of anxiety symptoms (Mörtberg, Hoffart, Boecking, & Clark, 2015; Wells & Papageorgiou, 1998).

Variants of exposure. While exposure is frequently conducted by having patients confront feared situational stimuli in vivo, several variants of exposure provide clinicians more flexibility in the types of fears that can be effectively targeted. One such variation is interoceptive exposure, which involves intentionally eliciting the physical symptoms associated with an anxiety response such as shortness of breath, a racing heart, or dizziness. For many patients, such interoceptive sensations have become associated with negative emotional experiences because of the strong physical sensations that occur during periods of anxiety, and therefore become feared stimuli in their own right (Barlow, 1988). Similar to situational exposure, repeated confrontation of such fears without avoidance provides the opportunity for patients to learn that such physical sensations are not in fact dangerous. While originally developed to treat the sensitivity to physical anxiety symptoms present in PD, a growing understanding that anxiety sensitivity is present transdiagnostically has led to greater utilization of interoceptive exposure in the treatment of a variety of anxiety disorders (Boettcher, Brake, & Barlow, 2016). Interoceptive exposures can also be used in combination with situational exposures (e.g., hyperventilating before delivering a speech) in order to optimize the feared consequences an exposure can test. Common techniques used for interoceptive exposure include running in place or up stairs, straw-breathing, spinning in a circle, muscle tensing, and head-shaking. Of note, significant intra-individual variability is seen in the distress resulting from different procedures (Lee et al., 2006), so clinicians may need to try a number of different techniques before identifying an effective exposure.

Another variant of exposure involves playing out a feared situation in one's imagination, a procedure that is useful when the feared situation is something that is difficult or unethical to actually create. Such imaginal exposure is used frequently to retell the narrative of a trauma in PTSD, and also can be utilized to play out a feared catastrophic scenario about the future in OCD and GAD. The rationale behind such a technique is that in imagination patients are able to confront fearful thoughts and accompanying physical sensations that tend to be avoided through cognitive strategies like worry or through overt avoidance behavior. After repeated exposure to such imagined worst-case scenarios, patients' emotional distress tends to decline as they realize that such emotions by themselves cannot do any real harm, and/or by seeing they could cope with the feared scenario better than they originally thought (Hoyer & Beesdo-Baum, 2012). For instance, an individual who has intense worry about the status of his or her relationship would vividly imagine a scene in which his or her significant other breaks off the relationship. Through repeated imagination of this scene, the accompanying emotions would tend to decline as the individual realizes the scene is just an image and is not actually harmful, and that he or she could cope with such an occurrence even though it would be difficult.

Maximizing the effects of exposure. While exposure has been practiced as a treatment for anxiety disorders for at least 50 years (e.g., Wolpe, 1968), recent research has illuminated a number of insights about the mechanisms of exposure that can help maximize its efficacy. One issue that has garnered significant attention in the literature is the extent to which reduction in fear levels during exposure matters for subsequent improvement in anxiety symptoms. While habituation to a feared situation during the course of an exposure can appear to suggest therapeutic learning, there is limited evidence demonstrating that fear reduction during exposures is a meaningful predictor of treatment outcome (Asnaani, McLean, & Foa, 2016; Craske et al., 2008). Research has shown that extinction learning, the purported mechanism of exposure therapy, does not rely on processes of habituation, but rather leads to the formation of a new safety memory that overrides the original fear response (Bouton, 2002). This means that exposures ought to be designed in ways that maximize the formation of this new safety memory, as well as a patient's ability to retrieve this memory in future situations (Craske, Treanor, Conway, Zbozinek, & Vervliet, 2014).

One of the primary ways in which such inhibitory learning can be facilitated is through maximizing violations of patient's expectations. Hofmann (2008b) argues that even though exposure is a behavioral technique, its effects are cognitively mediated by changes in one's beliefs about the likelihood and cost of harm. Thus having patients explicitly describe their expectations about what will happen when they confront their feared situation is helpful for highlighting the extent to which such expectations are inaccurate. The learning that occurs from having such expectations violated will then be reinforced if upon completion of the exposure, patients review the discrepancy between their predicted outcomes and what actually occurred (Rescorla & Wagner, 1972). Exposures can also be designed to continue until patients no longer believe that their feared outcome will occur. Deacon and colleagues (2013) demonstrated this in a treatment study for PD in which patients persisted with repeated interoceptive exposures consisting of hyperventilation until they rated that there was less than a 5% chance that their most feared outcome (e.g., "I will run out of air" or "I will pass out") would occur. Results showed that such an intensive form of interoceptive exposure was more effective in reducing panic symptoms than treatment using a prespecified (lower) number of exposures, and that these effects were accounted for by greater reductions in negative outcome expectancies and fear tolerance. Such a result highlights the benefits of focusing on expectancy violation as a means of changing beliefs and forming safety memories during exposure.

In addition to expectancy violations, therapists need to create exposure exercises with substantial variability in the situations and contexts used in order to enhance the strength and retrievability of the safety memories formed during exposure. As mentioned previously, extinction learning inhibits rather than eliminates fear memories, meaning that fear is highly susceptible to renewal when patients are presented with a slightly different stimulus than previously encountered during an exposure (Vervliet, Vansteenwegen, Baeyens, Hermans, & Eelen, 2005), or the same feared situation but in a different context (Mineka, Mystkowski, Hladek, & Rodriguez, 1999). Accordingly, varying the location of exposure training has been shown to lead to reduced anxiety symptoms at long-term follow-up (Vansteenwegen, Vervliet, Hermans, Thewissen, & Eelen, 2007) and reduced renewal of fear during exposure in a novel context (Bandarian-Balooch, Neumann, & Boschen, 2015; Shiban, Pauli, & Mühlberger, 2013) compared to exposure training in the same location. In addition, using varying exposure stimuli has been shown to eliminate return of fear in response to the presentation of novel feared stimuli (Rowe & Craske, 1998). Interestingly, greater variability in minute-to-minute subjective fear during an exposure task has also been shown to predict superior treatment outcomes (Culver, Stoyanova, & Craske, 2012; Kircanski et al., 2012), suggesting that emotional state can also serve as a context with which safety becomes associated. Together these results show that varying the features of exposures throughout the course of treatment is important to ensure that safety learning is not just associated with the specific experience of a successful exposure, but can generalize across situations.

Safety behaviors in exposure. Another important issue in the administration of effective exposure therapy is the elimination of safety behaviors, or actions meant to minimize, prevent, or avoid feared outcomes in an anxiety-inducing situation. For instance, a patient with PD and agoraphobia may be willing to enter a crowd, but only if accompanied by a close partner whose presence will diminish the patient's anxiety response. As reviewed in Blakey and Abramowitz (2016), safety behaviors can interfere with exposure therapy in a number of ways, as well as generally maintain clinical levels of anxiety. For one, safety behaviors can lead to misattributions of safety, as patients associate the absence of an expected aversive outcome to the presence of the safety signal (e.g., a partner in a crowd), instead of learning that such a situation is not actually as dangerous as originally believed (Salkovskis, 1991). Relatedly, safety behaviors disrupt therapeutic information processing by suggesting that safe situations are in fact dangerous (Gangemi, Mancini, & van den Hout, 2012; van den Hout et al., 2014), and by increasing attentional resources toward threatening stimuli (Stewart, Westra, Thompson, & Conrad, 2000) and away from disconfirmatory information (Sloan & Telch, 2002). Furthermore, the use of safety behaviors during exposure may reinforce the notion that anxiety is intolerable and something to be minimized. This is contraindicated given that one of the mechanisms theorized to be responsible for improvement from exposure is greater distress tolerance (Craske et al., 2008).

Despite the strong theoretical rationale for the deleterious effects of safety behaviors, there is mixed evidence on the extent to which the use of safety behaviors negatively impacts treatment outcome. In fact, some research suggests that permitting the use of safety behaviors can increase the acceptability of exposure therapy (Levy, Senn, & Radomsky, 2014; Milosevic & Radomsky, 2013) and enable greater approach behavior during the course of exposure (Goetz & Lee, 2015; Levy & Radomsky, 2014). Furthermore, a meta-analysis of 20 studies by Meulders, van Daele, Volders, and Vlaeyen (2016) found only a borderline significant ($p = 0.08$) advantage of self-reported fear after exposure without safety behaviors compared to baseline behavior, and no significant advantage of baseline exposure behavior compared to exposure in which participants were explicitly instructed to engage in safety behaviors. Of note, the authors point out that because safety behaviors tend to reduce exposure-related distress, post-intervention fear levels may not capture the negative impact of safety behaviors on therapeutic learning as well as follow-up assessments, and data on follow-up symptom outcomes in the studies in the meta-analysis were lacking.

Nonetheless, a separate meta-analysis by Podină, Koster, Philippot, Dethier, and David (2013) showed that distraction during exposure, which can be conceptualized as a safety behavior, led to superior effects on behavioral approach tasks at both post-intervention and follow-up assessments points when compared to attention-focused exposure. This finding also extended to self-reported distress ratings among studies with multiple exposure sessions, and that used interactive distractions (i.e., patient–therapist communication about non-fear-related topics). Regarding the results of both Podina et al. (2013) and Meulders et al. (2016), it should be noted that safety behaviors might have been found to be helpful or at least not harmful because they enhanced self-efficacy or a patient's ability to meet goals for an exposure, but could still have harmful effects if symptom reduction is attributed to the use of the safety behavior. Furthermore, the gradual elimination of safety behaviors can also lead to an enhanced self-efficacy, while also fostering greater therapeutic learning through continued expectancy violations. Accordingly, a sizable number of studies have shown that the gradual elimination of safety behaviors (in contrast to strict prevention) leads to enhanced outcomes compared to continued safety behavior use (see Telch & Lancaster, 2012). Clinically, it is typically recommended (e.g., Blakey & Abramowitz, 2016; Telch & Lancaster, 2012) that therapists carefully monitor safety behaviors, permit them early in treatment only to the extent to which it is necessary to facilitate treatment acceptability, enable greater approach to feared situations and foster self-efficacy, and then work with patients to fade such behaviors as treatment progresses.

Cognitive Restructuring

Cognitive restructuring is a core technique of anxiety treatment that consists of identifying unhelpful thinking patterns and developing more realistic alternative ways of viewing situations. The technique is typically introduced by demonstrating how almost all situations are somewhat ambiguous, with a variety of plausible interpretations that can be made based off whatever information is present. For instance, if a patient notices that a friend walks by him or her without acknowledgment, this could be interpreted as happening because the friend simply did not notice the patient, or as an intentional slight because they do not like him or her. Patients are encouraged to see how these different interpretations can lead to substantially different emotional reactions, and how it is not the event itself but one's appraisal of it that leads to anxiety or other negative emotions. In the prior example, interpreting the friend's lack of acknowledgment as a slight might lead a patient to feel anxious about the status of the friendship, whereas a neutral interpretation about the friend's intentions might not lead to an emotional reaction at all. Patients are also taught that individuals tend to develop patterns of interpretation based on their affective state, past experiences, and core beliefs about themselves and the outside world. Someone who has a high degree of interpersonal sensitivity and frequently worries about social rejection, for example, would readily appraise the ambiguous situation as indicative of rejection.

Bringing these patterns of interpretation to awareness is the first step toward cognitive restructuring, and is often assisted by the identification of certain "thinking traps," or errors in logical reasoning that lead to unrealistic or unhelpful interpretations. As discussed previously, for anxiety patients these thinking traps tend to be related to either an overestimation of the likelihood of danger or the cost of danger. To help combat such thinking traps, therapists engage in Socratic questioning that guides a patient's awareness toward alternative information they are not considering in making their evaluation of danger (Beck & Emery, 1985). For instance, to combat a patient's anxiety that something terrible has happened to his wife after she did not answer a phone call, the therapist might explore with the patient what evidence there is that something terrible has happened, what the probability of such an occurrence actually is, and whether the negative prediction the patient is making is driven by his intense emotions rather than the facts. Such questioning can also be used to combat cost overestimation. For example, with a patient who is intensely anxious about being late, a therapist might explore what concretely is likely to happen as a result of being late, would she be able to be cope with such an outcome, and whether she has been late in the past and whether it was as bad as she feared. The ultimate goal is for patients to be able to engage in such cognitive restructuring processes independently, allowing them to be more flexible in their interpretation of anxiety-inducing situations.

Experimental evidence has shown cognitive restructuring to lead to an immediate reduction of anxiety responses (Hofmann, Heering, Sawyer, & Asnaani, 2009), even for conditioned fears (Shurick et al., 2012). Furthermore, therapies using cognitive restructuring techniques without explicit use of exposure exercises have been shown to be highly efficacious, and generally lead to equivalent outcomes as exposure-based therapy (Ougrin, 2011). In spite of such evidence, some question whether the inclusion of cognitive techniques in the treatment of anxiety is necessary, citing evidence that addition of cognitive restructuring to exposure techniques does not improve treatment outcome beyond standard exposure therapy (Longmore & Worrell, 2007). In addition, some argue that engaging in cognitive restructuring to combat probability or cost overestimation prior to or during exposure actually takes away from the effects of exposure because it reduces expectancy violations (Craske et al., 2014).

Despite these critiques, cognitive techniques clearly have an important place in anxiety treatment. For one, using cognitive restructuring after an exposure exercise can be effective in combating any negative interpretations of exposure outcomes that patients may have (Hofmann & Otto, 2008). For instance, patients with social anxiety often ruminate after a social interaction on mistakes they might have made or the way they were perceived, even when such an interaction is framed as an exposure. In response, a therapist might help the patient reframe what happened by asking him or her how likely it is that the person the patient interacted with is still thinking about the interaction, and how much the patient will care about the way he or she acted a day, a week, or even a year later. By helping a patient reframe the outcome in this way, cognitive restructuring can help to reinforce or enhance the discrepancy between a patient's expectations and reality, rather than reducing expectancy violations. This may be particularly important given the evidence that some individuals with anxiety disorders demonstrate deficits in extinction learning, which can be overcome by the use of cognitive reappraisal strategies (Blechert et al., 2015).

Another important use of cognitive restructuring in the treatment of anxiety can be to address metacognitions. Metacognitive processes involve the appraisal and monitoring of one's thinking, as well as attempt's to control mental activity. Maladaptive metacognitive beliefs have been implicated in the development and maintenance of anxiety disorders, particularly GAD (Wells, 2000). These beliefs often present as beliefs that worry or anxiety is uncontrollable and harmful. Paradoxically, patients also often believe that the experience of anxiety is necessary as a means of preparation for potentially negative events. To combat such harmful metacognitive beliefs, cognitive restructuring techniques can be used to highlight instances of the patient's experience in which he or she was able to control anxiety, for example, or to evaluate counterevidence for beliefs about the positive impact of worry (Wells, 2007). Of note, such a cognitive approach often does include what are referred to as behavioral experiments, in which patients "test out" their beliefs in the form of exposures or other behavioral exercises, effectively representing a blend of behavioral and cognitive techniques. Numerous studies have demonstrated the efficacy of targeting meta-cognitive beliefs in the treatment of anxiety disorders (Normann, Emmerik, & Morina, 2014).

Mindfulness

Mindfulness has become an increasingly common strategy for addressing anxiety, often in conjunction with other treatment components. Mindfulness training begins by teaching patients how to direct their attention to the present moment rather than thinking about the past or future, since past- and future-oriented thinking often leads to worry or rumination among individuals prone to anxiety (Roemer & Orsillo, 2002). The breath is often used as an anchor for present moment awareness, as it is always present, but any observable sensation (e.g., a sight, sound, or physical sensation) can be attended to as a way of reorienting to the present. Typically therapists will guide patients through brief meditations in which patients are given an opportunity to focus on particular sensations like the breath, one's body, a piece of music, or even food (e.g., the raisin exercise, in which patients mindfully observe the sensations associated with eating a raisin).

In addition to present moment awareness, mindfulness training involves teaching patients to develop an attitude of acceptance and nonjudgment. Such an attitude is important because judging situations or experiences (e.g., anxiety) as unwanted or unacceptable can exacerbate their negative impact and lead to maladaptive attempts to control one's emotions. This is often demonstrated by the white bear experiment, in which patients are asked to think of anything except a white bear for 30 seconds. Inevitably, this leads to frequent thoughts about a white bear, and this is used as an example of how attempts to suppress anxious thoughts or feelings can actually make them worse. In order to help foster an attitude of nonjudgment, patients are taught to simply describe things they notice, including thoughts or sensations related to anxiety. If they notice judgments, the idea is to simply notice that they are judging and label it as such (e.g., "I am having the thought that this situation is unpleasant and notice an urge to escape"). Typically the practice of present moment awareness and nonjudgment starts with more benign, non-emotional situations to help patients master the technique, before applying it to situations in which stronger emotions are present. As patients build more proficiency with this skill, they begin to realize how an attitude of acceptance can actually decrease the intensity of anxiety and increase their ability to engage in goal-directed action.

Research on acceptance and mindfulness in experimental settings has consistently demonstrated that such techniques are effective in helping to regulate emotions (Kohl, Rief, & Glombiewski, 2012), and effects are as strong as cognitive reappraisal (Hofmann et al., 2009). Furthermore, improvements in mindfulness skills during treatment have been shown to account for improvement in symptoms of anxiety and other psychological symptoms (Visted, Vøllestad, Nielsen, & Nielsen, 2014). While research on the mechanisms through which mindfulness has its effects is still emerging, empirical evidence and theoretical work suggest that processes of attention regulation, reappraisal, exposure, change in self-perspective, and self-compassion each play a role (Hölzel et al., 2011). Of note, the processes understood to underlie mindfulness have been referred to using a wide variety of terms, including *decentering, metacognitive awareness, cognitive distancing, re-perceiving*, and *cognitive defusion*, among others (Bernstein et al., 2015). Further work is needed to clarify the extent to which these processes are distinct, and the exact role they play in reducing symptoms of anxiety.

Relaxation

Relaxation is not typically considered a core element of evidence-based anxiety treatments. This is because emphasizing relaxation as a primary way to combat anxiety can send the message to patients that anxiety sensations are dangerous and need to be avoided or controlled, which is at odds with the cognitive and behavioral principles central to effective treatment. Nonetheless, relaxation techniques can serve a purpose as an easily taught and used coping tool for experiences of high distress. For instance, high levels of distress are known to interfere with the cognitive regulation of emotion (Raio, Orederu, & Palazzolo, 2013), and thus the use of a brief relaxation technique can help downregulate a person's anxiety enough that they may be able to more effectively reappraise an anxiety-inducing situation.

One of the most common and easily implemented relaxation techniques is breathing retraining. Typically when individuals are anxious, they take short, quick breaths akin to hyperventilation that exacerbate the anxiety response by signaling a sympathetic nervous system response. In breathing retraining, patients are taught to take slow, full breaths, filling their diaphragm with air so that their body reaches a more balanced level of oxygen and carbon dioxide, thereby triggering a relaxation response (Hazlett-Stevens & Craske, 2009). A related technique mentioned previously as part of applied relaxation treatments is progressive muscle relaxation (PMR). In PMR, patients engage in diaphragmatic breathing while simultaneously tensing (during inhalation) and then relaxing (during exhalation) distinct muscle groups. This process of intentionally tensing and then relaxing muscles is meant to highlight the contrast between tension and relaxation for patients, leading to an enhanced relaxation response. Finally, mental imagery can be an effective relaxation technique. Patients imagine a scene in which they feel totally and completely relaxed, and vividly try to imagine as many sensory details as possible so that they can be present in the scene more fully. As patients continue practicing such an imagery exercise, they tend to become more skilled at fully immersing themselves in the scene, and imagining the scene can quickly produce a sensation of relaxation.

Transdiagnostic Approaches

Given the substantial amount of comorbidity across anxiety disorders and other forms of psychopathology (Brown & Barlow, 2009), developing treatments that can target shared underlying processes across diagnostic categories is highly important. Fortunately, the treatment components reviewed in this chapter are applicable to any variety of anxiety disorder(s), as well as many other emotional disorders. Based on these treatment components and our growing understanding of the shared mechanisms of anxiety disorders, a number of formalized transdiagnostic treatments have been developed and empirically tested in the past decade. For instance, Barlow and colleagues (2010) developed the Unified Protocol, which consists of four core modules designed to target core aspects of emotional disorders: increasing emotional awareness, facilitating flexibility in appraisals, identifying and preventing behavioral and emotional avoidance, and situational and interoceptive exposure to emotion cues.

Evidence for such transdiagnostic approaches has been steadily emerging. Both the Unified Protocol (Barlow et al., 2017) and another group transdiagnostic treatment tested by Norton and Barrera (2012) have shown equivalent efficacy for a mixed anxiety disorders sample to gold-standard single-diagnosis protocols. This is important because transdiagnostic treatments are argued to be useful from an efficiency standpoint, such that therapists seeing patients with a wide variety of presentations only need to learn a single protocol (Wilamowska et al., 2010). With evidence suggesting that a transdiagnostic protocol is equally effective to matching patients with a single diagnosis treatment, such efficiency can be achieved without sacrificing efficacy.

In addition to broad-based transdiagnostic treatments, a number of interventions designed to target a specific facet underlying anxiety disorders have been tested in recent years. For instance, different mechanism-specific treatments have been shown to work effectively on reducing anxiety sensitivity (Keough & Schmidt,

2012; Olthuis, Watt, Mackinnon, & Stewart, 2014), distress tolerance (Macatee & Cougle, 2015), perfectionism (Rozental et al., 2017), and intolerance of uncertainty (Oglesby, Allan, & Schmidt, 2017). Such treatments are particularly important because they present the opportunity to personalize treatment based on particular facets underlying an individual's anxiety, rather than a diagnosis based purely on symptom presentation. Also of note, several of these interventions (Macatee & Cougle, 2015; Olthuis et al., 2014) were delivered remotely through the telephone or a computer program, which has important implications for dissemination and increasing access to treatment.

Conclusions and Future Directions

While anxiety is a highly prevalent and debilitating disorder, work over the past several decades has led to a number of treatments that can effectively decrease anxiety symptoms, as well as lead to improvements in other areas like depression and quality of life. First and foremost of these is CBT, a scientifically grounded intervention consisting of exposure and cognitive restructuring techniques that help patients more effectively respond to their anxiety. Building upon traditional CBT, the field has seen the development of mindfulness- and acceptance-based treatments that provide additional tools for patients and alternative approaches for therapists treating anxiety disorders. While the quantity of evidence supporting such approaches has not reached that of traditional CBT, they have nonetheless moved the field forward. Of particular promise is the potential for matching patients to a particular treatment that is likely to be most effective for address their specific presentation.

Although CBT is effective, there is certainly room for improvement in both response and retention rates. Two promising directions for addressing this need for improvement are personalized medicine and the development of treatments that target underlying mechanisms of anxiety disorders rather than broad symptom presentations. We anticipate that the field will continue moving away from techniques for specific DSM-defined syndromes, and toward empirically supported process-based therapies that focus on relevant treatment mechanisms linked to theory (Hayes & Hofmann, 2017; Hofmann & Hayes, 2018). The approach of the National Institute of Mental Health's Research Domain Criteria (RDoC), which is a framework for understanding mental disorders rooted in dysfunctional brain circuitry, brought about a much-needed discussion about the limits and problems of the existing *DSM* classification system. However, we do not believe that including biological aspects will be sufficient or necessary to develop an improved psychiatric classification system. Instead, we believe that the time is ripe to move beyond a simplistic latent disease model toward a system that takes an evidence-based and person-centered approach to linking treatment techniques to underlying processes related to mental and behavioral health.

Beyond maximizing the efficacy of anxiety treatment, two additional areas of work need to be addressed to reduce the impact that anxiety disorders have on the population. The first is prevention. Treating an anxiety disorder that has already developed is likely to be much more cost- and time-intensive than providing individuals with the tools to more effectively deal with their emotions before an anxiety disorder develops. Research on prevention programs for anxiety disorders has been growing, particularly with children and adolescents, but effect sizes for measures of anxiety symptoms compared to control conditions tend to be small, and results from long-term follow-up show more variable efficacy (Fisak, Richard, & Mann, 2011). Generally research and development of depression prevention programs has outpaced targeted anxiety prevention, and few studies have examined the effect of such prevention programs on incidence rates of anxiety disorders after a long-term follow-up period (Stockings et al., 2016). Nonetheless, some progress has been made. A recent study by Topper, Watkins, Ehmmelkamp, and Ehring (2017) tested a six-week cognitive behavioral prevention training in both an online and group format for adolescents and young adults with high levels of repetitive negative thinking. Results showed that one year after the study, the training was associated with either an 18.0% (group intervention) or 16.0% (online intervention) prevalence of GAD, compared to 42.2% for a wait-list control. Further high-quality studies targeting other processes underlying anxiety are needed to continue the advancement of prevention efforts.

A second important area in need of further research is the dissemination of evidence-based treatments for anxiety disorders. In spite of the strong evidence base for CBT, most individuals seeking treatment for anxiety in community settings receive medication or non-CBT psychotherapy (Wolitzky-Taylor, Zimmerman, Arch, De Guzman, & Lagmasino, 2015), severely limiting the benefit that can be achieved. The barriers to effectively disseminating and implementing evidence-based treatments are substantial, and include factors such as a lack of training opportunities for practitioners, skeptical attitudes about randomized controlled trials and psychotherapy research generally, organizational and economic concerns, and a lack of attention to practitioner concerns in dissemination efforts (Gunter & Whittal, 2010). Specific to anxiety disorders, many therapists have reservations about delivering exposure therapy, which leads them to not use such techniques at all, or to deliver them suboptimally (Deacon et al., 2013). Research examining ways to overcome such barriers and disseminate evidence-based treatments for anxiety disorders has been conducted (e.g., Harned et al., 2014), but more work is needed if we hope to continue increasing the ability for individuals with anxiety to access effective treatments and attain wellness.

References

Adelman, C. B., Panza, K. E., Bartley, C. A., Bontempo, A., & Bloch, M. H. (2014). A meta-analysis of computerized cognitive-behavioral therapy for the treatment of *DSM-5* anxiety disorders. *Journal of Clinical Psychiatry, 75*, 695–704.

Arch, J. J. & Ayers, C. R. (2013). Which treatment worked better for whom? Moderators of group cognitive behavioral therapy versus adapted mindfulness based stress reduction for anxiety disorders. *Behaviour Research and Therapy*, *51*, 4–442.

Arch, J. J., Ayers, C. R., Baker, A., Almklov, E., Dean, D. J., & Craske, M. G. (2013). Randomized clinical trial of adapted mindfulness-based stress reduction versus group cognitive behavioral therapy for heterogeneous anxiety disorders. *Behaviour Research and Therapy*, *51*, 185–196.

Arch, J. J., Eifert, G. H., Davies, C., Vilardaga, J. C. P., Rose, R. D., & Craske, M. G. (2012). Randomized clinical trial of cognitive behavioral therapy (CBT) versus acceptance and commitment therapy (ACT) for mixed anxiety disorders. *Journal of Consulting and Clinical Psychology*, *80*, 750–765.

Arntz, A. & van den Hout, M. (1996). Psychological treatments of panic disorder without agoraphobia: Cognitive therapy versus applied relaxation. *Behaviour Research and Therapy*, *34*, 113–121.

Asnaani, A., McLean, C. P., & Foa, E. B. (2016). Updating Watson & Marks (1971): How has our understanding of the mechanisms of extinction learning evolved and where is our field going next? *Behavior Therapy*, *47*, 654–668.

Bandarian-Balooch, S., Neumann, D. L., & Boschen, M. J. (2015). Exposure treatment in multiple contexts attenuates return of fear via renewal in high spider fearful individuals. *Journal of Behavior Therapy and Experimental Psychiatry*, *47*, 138–144.

Bandelow, B., Reitt, M., Röver, C., Michaelis, S., Görlich, Y., & Wedekind, D. (2015). Efficacy of treatments for anxiety disorders: A meta-analysis. *International Clinical Psychopharmacology*, *30*, 183–192.

Bandelow, B., Zohar, J., Hollander, E., Kasper, S., Möller, H. J., WFSBP Task Force on Treatment Guidelines for Anxiety, Obsessive Compulsive and Post-Traumatic Stress Disorders . . . Vega, J. (2008). World Federation of Societies of Biological Psychiatry (WFSBP) guidelines for the pharmacological treatment of anxiety, obsessive-compulsive and post-traumatic stress disorders – first revision. *World Journal of Biological Psychiatry*, *9*, 248–312.

Barak, A., Hen, L., Boniel-Nissim, M., & Shapira, N. A. (2008). A comprehensive review and a meta-analysis of the effectiveness of internet-based psychotherapeutic interventions. *Journal of Technology in Human Services*, *26*, 109–160.

Barlow, D. H. (1988). *Anxiety and Its disorders: The Nature and Treatment of Anxiety and Panic*. New York, NY: Guilford Press.

Barlow, D. H., Farchione, T. J., Bullis, J. R., Gallagher, M. W., Murray-Latin, H., Sauer-Zavala, S. E., . . . Cassiello-Robbins, C. (2017). The Unified Protocol for Transdiagnostic Treatment of Emotional Disorders compared with diagnosis-specific protocols for anxiety disorders: A randomized clinical trial. *JAMA Psychiatry*. Published online August 2, 2017. doi: 10.1001/jamapsychiatry.2017.2164

Barlow, D. H., Farchione, T. J., Fairholme, C. P., Ellard, K. K., Boisseau, C. L., Allen, L. B., & May, J. T. E. (2010). *Unified Protocol for Transdiagnostic Treatment of Emotional Disorders: Therapist Guide*. Oxford: Oxford University Press.

Barlow, D. H., Sauer-Zavala, S., Carl, J. R., Bullis, J. R., & Ellard, K. K. (2014). The nature, diagnosis, and treatment of neuroticism: Back to the future. *Clinical Psychological Science*, *2*, 344–365.

Beck, A. T. & Emery, G. (1985). *Anxiety Disorders and Phobias: A Cognitive Perspective*. New York, NY: Basic Books.

Berger, T., Caspar, F., Richardson, R., Kneubühler, B., Sutter, D., & Andersson, G. (2011). Internet-based treatment of social phobia: A randomized controlled trial comparing unguided with two types of guided self-help. *Behaviour Research and Therapy*, *49*, 158–169.

Bernstein, A., Hadash, Y., Lichtash, Y., Tanay, G., Shepherd, K., & Fresco, D. M. (2015). Decentering and related constructs: A critical review and metacognitive processes model. *Perspectives on Psychological Science*, *10*, 599–617.

Beutel, M. E., Scheurich, V., Knebel, A., Michal, M., Wiltink, J., Graf-Morgenstern, M., & Subic-Wrana, C. (2013). Implementing panic-focused psychodynamic psychotherapy into clinical practice. *Canadian Journal of Psychiatry/La Revue Canadienne De Psychiatrie*, *58*, 326–334.

Bisson, J. I., Roberts, N. P., Andrew, M., Cooper, R., & Lewis, C. (2013). Psychological therapies for chronic post-traumatic stress disorder (PTSD) in adults. *Cochrane Library*.

Blakey, S. M. & Abramowitz, J. S. (2016). The effects of safety behaviors during exposure therapy for anxiety: Critical analysis from an inhibitory learning perspective. *Clinical Psychology Review*, *49*, 1–15.

Blechert, J., Wilhelm, F. H., Williams, H., Braams, B. R., Jou, J., & Gross, J. J. (2015). Reappraisal facilitates extinction in healthy and socially anxious individuals. *Journal of Behavior Therapy and Experimental Psychiatry*, *46*, 141–150.

Bluett, E. J., Homan, K. J., Morrison, K. L., Levin, M. E., & Twohig, M. P. (2014). Acceptance and commitment therapy for anxiety and OCD spectrum disorders: An empirical review. *Journal of Anxiety Disorders*, *28*, 612–624.

Boettcher, H., Brake, C. A., & Barlow, D. H. (2016). Origins and outlook of interoceptive exposure. *Journal of Behavior Therapy and Experimental Psychiatry*, *53*, 41–51.

Boswell, J. F., Farchione, T. J., Sauer-Zavala, S., Murray, H. W., Fortune, M. R., & Barlow, D. H. (2013). Anxiety sensitivity and interoceptive exposure: A transdiagnostic construct and change strategy. *Behavior Therapy*, *44*, 417–431.

Bouton, M. E. (2002). Context, ambiguity, and unlearning: Sources of relapse after behavioral extinction. *Biological Psychiatry*, *52*, 976–986.

Brown, T. A. & Barlow, D. H. (2009). A proposal for a dimensional classification system based on the shared features of the *DSM-IV* anxiety and mood disorders: Implications for assessment and treatment. *Psychological Assessment*, *21*, 256–271.

Butler, A. C., Chapman, J. E., Forman, E. M., & Beck, A. T. (2006). The empirical status of cognitive-behavioral therapy: A review of meta-analyses. *Clinical Psychology Review*, *26*, 17–31.

Carpenter, J. K., Andrews, L. A., Witcraft, S. M., Powers, M. B., Smits J. A., & Hofmann, S. G. (2018). Cognitive behavioral therapy for anxiety and related disorders: A meta-analysis of randomized placebo-controlled trials. *Depression and Anxiety*, *35*, 502–514.

Chawla, N. & Ostafin, B. (2007). Experiential avoidance as a functional dimensional approach to psychopathology: An empirical review. *Journal of Clinical Psychology*, *63*, 871–890.

Comer, J. S., Blanco, C., Hasin, D. S., Liu, S. M., Grant, B. F., Turner, J. B., & Olfson, M. (2011). Health-related quality of life across the anxiety disorders. *Journal of Clinical Psychiatry*, *72*, 43–50.

Covin, R., Ouimet, A. J., Seeds, P. M., & Dozois, D. J. (2008). A meta-analysis of CBT for pathological worry among clients with GAD. *Journal of Anxiety Disorders*, *22*, 108–116.

Craske, M. G., Kircanski, K., Zelikowsky, M., Mystkowski, J., Chowdhury, N., & Baker, A. (2008). Optimizing inhibitory learning during exposure therapy. *Behaviour Research and Therapy*, *46*, 5–27.

Craske, M. G., Treanor, M., Conway, C. C., Zbozinek, T., & Vervliet, B. (2014). Maximizing exposure therapy: An inhibitory learning approach. *Behaviour Research and Therapy*, 58, 10–23.

Crits-Christoph, P., Connolly, M. B., Gallop, R., Barber, J. P., Tu, X., Gladis, M., et al. (2001). Early improvement during manual-guided cognitive and dynamic psychotherapies predicts 16-week remission status. *Journal of Psychotherapy Practice and Research*, 10, 145–154.

Cuijpers, P., Berking, M., Andersson, G., Quigley, L., Kleiboer, A., & Dobson, K. S. (2013). A meta-analysis of cognitive-behavioural therapy for adult depression, alone and in comparison with other treatments. *Canadian Journal of Psychiatry*, *58*, 376–385.

Cuijpers, P., Cristea, I. A., Weitz, E., Gentili, C., & Berking, M. (2016). The effects of cognitive and behavioural therapies for anxiety disorders on depression: A meta-analysis. *Psychological Medicine*, *46*, 3451–3462.

Cuijpers, P., Sijbrandij, M., Koole, S., Huibers, M., Berking, M., & Andersson, G. (2014). Psychological treatment of generalized anxiety disorder: A meta-analysis. *Clinical Psychology Review*, *34*, 130–140.

Culver, N. C., Stoyanova, M., & Craske, M. G. (2012). Emotional variability and sustained arousal during exposure. *Journal of Behavior Therapy and Experimental Psychiatry*, *43*, 787–793.

Deacon, B. J., Farrell, N. R., Kemp, J. J., Dixon, L. J., Sy, J. T., Zhang, A. R., & McGrath, P. B.(2013). Assessing therapist reservations about exposure therapy for anxiety disorders: The Therapist Beliefs about Exposure Scale. *Journal of Anxiety Disorders*, *27*(8), 772–780.

Deacon, B., Kemp, J. J., Dixon, L. J., Sy, J. T., Farrell, N. R., & Zhang, A. R. (2013). Maximizing the efficacy of interoceptive exposure by optimizing inhibitory learning: A randomized controlled trial. *Behaviour Research and Therapy*, *51*, 588–596.

Donker, T., Griffiths, K. M., Cuijpers, P., & Christensen, H. (2009). Psychoeducation for depression, anxiety and psychological distress: a meta-analysis. *BMC Medicine*, *7*, 79.

Dugas, M. J., Brillon, P., Savard, P., Turcotte, J., Gaudet, A., Ladouceur, R., … Gervais, N. J. (2010). A randomized clinical trial of cognitive-behavioral therapy and applied relaxation for adults with generalized anxiety disorder. *Behavior Therapy*, *41*, 46–58.

Egan, S. J., Wade, T. D., & Shafran, R. (2011). Perfectionism as a transdiagnostic process: A clinical review. *Clinical Psychology Review*, *31*, 203–212.

Fang, A., Sawyer, A. T., Asnaani, A., & Hofmann, S. G. (2013). Social mishap exposures for social anxiety disorder: An important treatment ingredient. *Cognitive and Behavioral Practice*, *20*, 213–220.

Farach, F. J., Pruitt, L. D., Jun, J. J., Jerud, A. B., Zoellner, L. A., & Roy-Byrne, P. P. (2012). Pharmacological treatment of anxiety disorders: Current treatments and future directions. *Journal of Anxiety Disorders*, *26*, 833–843.

Fentz, H. N., Hoffart, A., Jensen, M. B., Arendt, M., O'Toole, M. S., Rosenberg, N. K., & Hougaard, E. (2013). Mechanisms of change in cognitive behaviour therapy for panic disorder: The role of panic self-efficacy and catastrophic misinterpretations. *Behaviour Research and Therapy, 51*, 579–587.

Fisak, B. J., Richard, D., & Mann, A. (2011). The prevention of child and adolescent anxiety: A meta-analytic review. *Prevention Science, 12*, 255–268.

Foa, E. B., Huppert, J. D., & Cahill, S. P. (2006). Emotional processing theory: An update. In B. O. Rothbaum (ed.), *Pathological Anxiety: Emotional Processing in Etiology and Treatment* (pp. 3–24). New York, NY: Guilford Press.

Gabbard, G. O. (2004). *Long-Term Psychodynamic Psychotherapy: A Basic Text.* Washington, DC: American Psychiatric Publishing.

Gangemi, A., Mancini, F., & van den Hout, M. (2012). Behavior as information: "If I avoid, then there must be danger." *Journal of Behavior Therapy and Experimental Psychiatry, 43*, 1032–1038.

Goetz, A. R. & Lee, H. (2015). The effects of preventive and restorative safety behaviors on a single-session of exposure therapy for contamination fear. *Journal of Behavior Therapy and Experimental Psychiatry, 46*, 151–157.

Goldberg, D. P., Krueger, R. F., Andrews, G., & Hobbs, M. J. (2009). Emotional disorders: Cluster 4 of the proposed meta-structure for *DSM-V* and *ICD-11*. *Psychological Medicine, 39*, 2043–2059.

Grist, R. & Cavanagh, K. (2013). Computerised cognitive behavioural therapy for common mental health disorders, what works, for whom under what circumstances? A systematic review and meta-analysis. *Journal of Contemporary Psychotherapy, 43*, 243–251.

Gunter, R. W. & Whittal, M. L. (2010). Dissemination of cognitive-behavioral treatments for anxiety disorders: Overcoming barriers and improving patient access. *Clinical Psychology Review, 30*, 194–202.

Hans, E. & Hiller, W. (2013). A meta-analysis of nonrandomized effectiveness studies on outpatient cognitive behavioral therapy for adult anxiety disorders. *Clinical Psychology Review, 33*, 954–964.

Harned, M. S., Dimeff, L. A., Woodcock, E. A., Kelly, T., Zavertnik, J., Contreras, I., & Danner, S. M. (2014). Exposing clinicians to exposure: A randomized controlled dissemination trial of exposure therapy for anxiety disorders. *Behavior Therapy, 45*, 731–744.

Hayes, S. C. (2004). Acceptance and commitment therapy, relational frame theory, and the third wave of behavioral and cognitive therapies. *Behavior Therapy, 35*, 638–665.

Hayes, S. C. & Hofmann, S. G. (eds.) (2017). *Process-Based CBT: The Science and Core Clinical Competencies of Cognitive Behavioral Therapy.* Oakland, CA: New Harbinger Publications.

Hayes, S. C. & Hofmann, S. G. (2017). The third wave of cognitive behavioral therapy and the rise of process-based care. *World Psychiatry, 16*, 245–246.

Hayes, S. C., Luoma, J. B., Bond, F. W., Masuda, A., & Lillis, J. (2006). Acceptance and commitment therapy: Model, processes and outcomes. *Behaviour Research and Therapy, 44*, 1–25.

Hayes, S. C., Pistorello, J., & Levin, M. E. (2012). Acceptance and commitment therapy as a unified model of behavior change. *Counseling Psychologist, 40*, 976–1002.

Hayes-Skelton, S. A., Roemer, L., & Orsillo, S. M. (2013). A randomized clinical trial comparing an acceptance-based behavior therapy to applied relaxation for generalized anxiety disorder. *Journal of Consulting and Clinical Psychology, 81*, 761.

Hayes-Skelton, S. A., Roemer, L., Orsillo, S. M., & Borkovec, T. D. (2013). A contemporary view of applied relaxation for generalized anxiety disorder. *Cognitive Behaviour Therapy, 42*, 292–302.

Hazlett-Stevens, H. & Craske, M. G. (2009). Breathing retraining and diaphragmatic breathing techniques. In W. T. O'Donohue & J. E. Fisher (eds.), *General Principles and Empirically Supported Techniques of Cognitive Behavior Therapy* (pp. 167–172). Hoboken, NJ: John Wiley & Sons Inc.

Hedman, E., Mörtberg, E., Hesser, H., Clark, D. M., Lekander, M., Andersson, E., & Ljótsson, B. (2013). Mediators in psychological treatment of social anxiety disorder: Individual cognitive therapy compared to cognitive behavioral group therapy. *Behaviour Research and Therapy, 51*, 696–705.

Hendriks, S. M., Spijker, J., Licht, C. M., Hardeveld, F., de Graaf, R., Batelaan, N. M., . . . Beekman, A. T. (2016). Long-term disability in anxiety disorders. *BMC Psychiatry, 16*, 248.

Hofmann, S. G. (2008a). Acceptance and commitment therapy: New wave or morita therapy? *Clinical Psychology: Science and Practice, 15*, 280–285.

Hofmann, S. G. (2008b). Cognitive processes during fear acquisition and extinction in animals and humans: Implications for exposure therapy of anxiety disorders. *Clinical Psychology Review, 28*, 199–210.

Hofmann, S. G. (2014). D-cycloserine for treating anxiety disorders: Making good exposures better and bad exposures worse. *Depression and Anxiety, 31*, 175.

Hofmann, S. G. (2016a, January 22). Psychodynamic therapy meets evidence-based medicine: A systematic review using updated criteria. Retrieved from www.ncbi.nlm.nih.gov/pubmed/26303562/#comments.

Hofmann, S. G. (2016b). Psychodynamic therapy: A poorly defined concept with questionable evidence. *Evidence-Based Mental Health, 19*, 63.

Hofmann, S. G. & Asmundson, G. J. (2008). Acceptance and mindfulness-based therapy: New wave or old hat? *Clinical Psychology Review, 28*, 1–16.

Hofmann, S. G., Asmundson, G. J., & Beck, A. T. (2013). The science of cognitive therapy. *Behavior Therapy, 44*, 199–212.

Hofmann, S. G., Asnaani, A., Vonk, I. J., Sawyer, A. T., & Fang, A. (2012). The efficacy of cognitive behavioral therapy: A review of meta-analyses. *Cognitive Therapy and Research, 36*, 427–440.

Hofmann, S. G., Carpenter, J. K., Otto, M. W., Rosenfield, D., Smits, J. A., & Pollack, M. H. (2015). Dose timing of d-cycloserine to augment cognitive behavioral therapy for social anxiety: Study design and rationale. *Contemporary Clinical Trials, 43*, 223–230.

Hofmann, S. G., & Hayes, S. C. (2018). The future of intervention science: Process-based therapy. *Clinical Psychological Science*. Advance online publication. https://doi.org/10.1002/da.22728.

Hofmann, S. G., Heering, S., Sawyer, A. T., & Asnaani, A. (2009). How to handle anxiety: The effects of reappraisal, acceptance, and suppression strategies on anxious arousal. *Behaviour Research and Therapy, 47*, 389–394.

Hofmann, S. G. & Otto, M. W. (2008). *Cognitive-Behavior Therapy for Social Anxiety Disorder: Evidence-Based and Disorder-Specific Treatment Techniques.* New York, NY: Routledge/Taylor & Francis Group.

Hofmann, S. G., Sawyer, A. T., Korte, K. J., & Smits, J. A. (2009). Is it beneficial to add pharmacotherapy to cognitive-behavioral therapy when treating anxiety disorders? A meta-analytic review. *International Journal of Cognitive Therapy*, *2*, 160–175.

Hofmann, S. G., Sawyer, A. T., Witt, A. A., & Oh, D. (2010). The effect of mindfulness-based therapy on anxiety and depression: A meta-analytic review. *Journal of Consulting and Clinical Psychology*, *78*, 169.

Hofmann, S. G. & Smits, J. A. (2008). Cognitive-behavioral therapy for adult anxiety disorders: A meta-analysis of randomized placebo-controlled trials. *Journal of Clinical Psychiatry*, *69*, 621–632.

Hofmann, S. G., Smits, J. J., Rosenfield, D., Simon, N., Otto, M. W., Meuret, A. E., … Pollack, M. H. (2013). D-cycloserine as an augmentation strategy with cognitive-behavioral therapy for social anxiety disorder. *American Journal of Psychiatry*, *170*, 751–758.

Hofmann, S. G., Wu, J. Q., & Boettcher, H. (2014). Effect of cognitive-behavioral therapy for anxiety disorders on quality of life: A meta-analysis. *Journal of Consulting and Clinical Psychology*, *82*, 1228–1228.

Hoge, E. A., Bui, E., Marques, L., Metcalf, C. A., Morris, L. K., Robinaugh, D. J., … Simon, N. M. (2013). Randomized controlled trial of mindfulness meditation for generalized anxiety disorder: Effects on anxiety and stress reactivity. *Journal of Clinical Psychiatry*, *74*, 786.

Hölzel, B. K., Lazar, S. W., Gard, T., Schuman-Olivier, Z., Vago, D. R., & Ott, U. (2011). How does mindfulness meditation work? Proposing mechanisms of action from a conceptual and neural perspective. *Perspectives on Psychological Science*, *6*, 537–559.

Hoyer, J., Beesdo, K., Gloster, A. T., Runge, J., Höfler, M., & Becker, E. S. (2009). Worry exposure versus applied relaxation in the treatment of generalized anxiety disorder. *Psychotherapy and Psychosomatics*, *78*, 106–115.

Hoyer, J. & Beesdo-Baum, K. (2012). Prolonged imaginal exposure based on worry scenarios. In P. Neudeck & H. Wittchen (eds.), *Exposure Therapy: Rethinking the Model – Refining the Method* (pp. 245–260). New York, NY: Springer Science + Business Media.

Jónsson, H., Hougaard, E., & Bennedsen, B. E. (2011). Randomized comparative study of group versus individual cognitive behavioural therapy for obsessive compulsive disorder. *Acta Psychiatrica Scandinavica*, *123*, 387–397.

Kabat-Zinn, J. (1982). An outpatient program in behavioral medicine for chronic pain patients based on the practice of mindfulness meditation: Theoretical considerations and preliminary results. *General Hospital Psychiatry*, *4*, 33–47.

Kabat-Zinn, J. (2003). Mindfulness-based interventions in context: Past, present, and future. *Clinical Psychology: Science and Practice*, *10*, 144–156.

Kaufman, J. & Charney, D. (2000). Comorbidity of mood and anxiety disorders. *Depression and Anxiety*, *12*, 69–76.

Keough, M. E. & Schmidt, N. B. (2012). Refinement of a brief anxiety sensitivity reduction intervention. *Journal of Consulting and Clinical Psychology*, *80*, 766–772.

Kim, Y. W., Lee, S. H., Choi, T. K., Suh, S. Y., Kim, B., Kim, C. M., . . . Song, S. K. (2009). Effectiveness of mindfulness-based cognitive therapy as an adjuvant to pharmacotherapy in patients with panic disorder or generalized anxiety disorder. *Depression and Anxiety, 26*, 601–606.

Kircanski, K., Mortazavi, A., Castriotta, N., Baker, A. S., Mystkowski, J. L., Yi, R., Craske., M. G. (2012). Challenges to the traditional exposure paradigm: Variability in exposure therapy for contamination fears. *Journal of Behavior Therapy and Experimental Psychiatry, 43*, 745–751.

Knijnik, D. Z., Kapczinski, F., Chachamovich, E., Margis, R., & Eizirik, C. L. (2004). Psicoterapia psicodinâmica em grupo para fobia social generalizada [Psychodynamic group treatment for generalized social phobia]. *Revista Brasileira De Psiquiatria, 26*, 77–81.

Kohl, A., Rief, W., & Glombiewski, J. A. (2012). How effective are acceptance strategies? A meta-analytic review of experimental results. *Journal of Behavior Therapy and Experimental Psychiatry, 43*, 988–1001.

Koszycki, D., Benger, M., Shlik, J., & Bradwejn, J. (2007). Randomized trial of a meditation-based stress reduction program and cognitive behavior therapy in generalized social anxiety disorder. *Behaviour Research and Therapy, 45*, 2518–2526.

Krypotos, A. M., Effting, M., Kindt, M., & Beckers, T. (2015). Avoidance learning: A review of theoretical models and recent developments. *Frontiers in Behavioral Neuroscience, 9*,189.

Lee, S. H., Ahn, S. C., Lee, Y. J., Choi, T. K., Yook, K. H., & Suh, S. Y. (2007). Effectiveness of a meditation-based stress management program as an adjunct to pharmacotherapy in patients with anxiety disorder. *Journal of Psychosomatic Research, 62*, 189–195.

Lee, K., Noda, Y., Nakano, Y., Ogawa, S., Kinoshita, Y., Funayama, T., & Furukawa, T. A. (2006). Interoceptive hypersensitivity and interoceptive exposure in patients with panic disorder: specificity and effectiveness. *BMC Psychiatry, 6*, 32.

Leichsenring, F., Luyten, P., Hilsenroth, M. J., Abbass, A., Barber, J. P., . . . Steinert, C. (2015). Psychodynamic therapy meets evidence-based medicine: A systematic review using updated criteria. *Lancet Psychiatry, 2*, 648–660.

Leichsenring, F., Salzer, S., Beutel, M. E., Herpertz, S., Hiller, W., Hoyer, J., . . . Leibing, E. (2013). Psychodynamic therapy and cognitive-behavioral therapy in social anxiety disorder: A multicenter randomized controlled trial. *American Journal of Psychiatry, 170*, 759–767.

Leichsenring, F., Salzer, S., Jaeger, U., Kächele, H., Kreische, R., Leweke, F., . . . Leibing, E. (2009). Short-term psychodynamic psychotherapy and cognitive-behavioral therapy in generalized anxiety disorder: A randomized, controlled trial. *American Journal of Psychiatry, 166*, 875–881.

Levy, H. & Radomsky, A. S. (2014). Safety behaviour enhances the acceptability of exposure. *Cognitive Behaviour Therapy, 43*, 83–92.

Levy, H. C., Senn, J. M., & Radomsky, A. S. (2014). Further support for the acceptability enhancing roles of safety behavior and a cognitive rationale in cognitive behavioral therapy for anxiety disorders. *Journal of Cognitive Psychotherapy, 28*, 303–316.

Lewis, A. J., Dennerstein, M., & Gibbs, P. M. (2008). Short-term psychodynamic psychotherapy: Review of recent process and outcome studies. *Australian and New Zealand Journal of Psychiatry, 42*, 445–455.

Loerinc, A. G., Meuret, A. E., Twohig, M. P., Rosenfield, D., Bluett, E. J., & Craske, M. G. (2015). Response rates for CBT for anxiety disorders: Need for standardized criteria. *Clinical Psychology Review*, *42*, 72–82.

Longmore, R. J. & Worrell, M. (2007). Do we need to challenge thoughts in cognitive behavior therapy?. *Clinical Psychology Review*, *27*, 173–187.

Macatee, R. J. & Cougle, J. R. (2015). Development and evaluation of a computerized intervention for low distress tolerance and its effect on performance on a neutralization task. *Journal of Behavior Therapy and Experimental Psychiatry*, *48*, 33–39.

Marchand, A., Roberge, P., Primiano, S., & Germain, V. (2009). A randomized, controlled clinical trial of standard, group and brief cognitive-behavioral therapy for panic disorder with agoraphobia: A two-year follow-up. *Journal of Anxiety Disorders*, *23*, 1139–1147.

Mataix-Cols, D., Fernández de la Cruz, L., Monzani, B., Rosenfield, D., Andersson, E., Pé`rez-Vigil, A., ... Rück, C. (2017). D-cycloserine augmentation of exposure-based cognitive-behavior therapy for anxiety, obsessive-compulsive, and posttraumatic stress disorders: Systematic review and meta-analysis of individual participant data. *JAMA Psychiatry*, *74*, 501–510.

Mayo-Wilson, E., Dias, S., Mavranezouli, I., Kew, K., Clark, D. M., Ades, A. E., & Pilling, S. (2014). Psychological and pharmacological interventions for social anxiety disorder in adults: A systematic review and network meta-analysis. *Lancet Psychiatry*, *1*, 368–376.

McEvoy, P. M. & Mahoney, A. E. (2012). To be sure, to be sure: Intolerance of uncertainty mediates symptoms of various anxiety disorders and depression. *Behavior Therapy*, *43*, 533–545.

Meulders, A., Van Daele, T., Volders, S., & Vlaeyen, J. W. (2016). The use of safety-seeking behavior in exposure-based treatments for fear and anxiety: Benefit or burden? A meta-analytic review. *Clinical Psychology Review*, *45*, 144–156.

Milosevic, I. & Radomsky, A. S. (2013). Incorporating the judicious use of safety behavior into exposure-based treatments for anxiety disorders: A study of treatment acceptability. *Journal of Cognitive Psychotherapy: An International Quarterly*, *27*, 155–174.

Milrod, B., Chambless, D. L., Gallop, R., Busch, F. N., Schwalberg, M., McCarthy, K. S., Gross, C., Sharpless, B. A., Leon, A. C., & Barber, J. P. (2015). Psychotherapies for panic disorder: A tale of two sites. *Journal of Clinical Psychiatry*.

Mineka, S., Mystkowski, J. L., Hladek, D., & Rodriguez, B. I. (1999). The effects of changing contexts on return of fear following exposure therapy for spider fear. *Journal of Consulting and Clinical Psychology*, *67*, 599–604.

Mörtberg, E., Hoffart, A., Boecking, B., & Clark, D. M. (2015). Shifting the focus of one's attention mediates improvement in cognitive therapy for social anxiety disorder. *Behavioural and Cognitive Psychotherapy*, *43*, 63.

Mörtberg, E., Karlsson, A., Fyring, C., & Sundin, Ö. (2006). Intensive cognitive-behavioral group treatment (CBGT) of social phobia: A randomized controlled study. *Journal of Anxiety Disorders*, *20*, 646–660.

National Institute for Health and Clinical Excellence (2011). Anxiety: Management of anxiety (panic disorder, with or without agoraphobia, and generalised anxiety disorder) in adults in primary, secondary and community care. Retrieved from www.nice.org.uk.

National Institute for Health and Clinical Excellence (2014). Anxiety disorders: Quality statement 3 – Pharmacological treatment. Retrieved from www.nice.org.uk.

Normann, N., Emmerik, A. A., & Morina, N. (2014). The efficacy of metacognitive therapy for anxiety and depression: A meta-analytic review. *Depression and Anxiety*, *31*, 402–411.

Norton, P. J. & Barrera, T. L. (2012). Transdiagnostic versus diagnosis-specific CBT for anxiety disorders: A preliminary randomized controlled noninferiority trial. *Depression and Anxiety*, *29*, 874–882.

Oglesby, M. E., Allan, N. P., & Schmidt, N. B. (2017). Randomized control trial investigating the efficacy of a computer-based intolerance of uncertainty intervention. *Behaviour Research and Therapy*, *95*, 50–57.

Olatunji, B. O., Davis, M. L., Powers, M. B., & Smits, J. A. (2013). Cognitive-behavioral therapy for obsessive-compulsive disorder: A meta-analysis of treatment outcome and moderators. *Journal of Psychiatric Research*, *47*, 33–41.

Olthuis, J. V., Watt, M. C., Mackinnon, S. P., & Stewart, S. H. (2014). Telephone-delivered cognitive behavioral therapy for high anxiety sensitivity: A randomized controlled trial. *Journal of Consulting and Clinical Psychology*, *82*, 1005–1022.

Öst, L. G. (1987). Applied relaxation: Description of a coping technique and review of controlled studies. *Behaviour Research and Therapy*, *25*, 397–409.

Öst, L. G. (1988). Applied relaxation vs progressive relaxation in the treatment of panic disorder. *Behaviour Research and Therapy*, *26*, 13–22.

Öst, L. G., & Westling, B. E. (1995). Applied relaxation vs cognitive behavior therapy in the treatment of panic disorder. *Behaviour Research and Therapy*, *33*, 145–158.

Öst, L. G., Westling, B. E., & Hellström, K. (1993). Applied relaxation, exposure in vivo and cognitive methods in the treatment of panic disorder with agoraphobia. *Behaviour Research and Therapy*, *31*, 383–394.

Otto, M. W., Smits, J. A., & Reese, H. E. (2005). Combined psychotherapy and pharmacotherapy for mood and anxiety disorders in adults: Review and analysis. *Clinical Psychology: Science and Practice*, *12*, 72–86.

Ougrin, D. (2011). Efficacy of exposure versus cognitive therapy in anxiety disorders: Systematic review and meta-analysis. *BMC Psychiatry*, *11*, 200.

Podină, I. R., Koster, E. H., Philippot, P., Dethier, V., & David, D. O. (2013). Optimal attentional focus during exposure in specific phobia: A meta-analysis. *Clinical Psychology Review*, *33*, 1172–1183.

Pollack, M. H., Otto, M. W., Roy-Byrne, P. P., Coplan, J. D., Rothbaum, B. O., Simon, N. M., & Gorman, J. M. (2008). Novel treatment approaches for refractory anxiety disorders. *Depression and Anxiety*, *25*, 467–476.

Pompoli, A., Furukawa, T. A., Imai, H., Tajika, A., Efthimiou, O., & Salanti, G. (2016). Psychological therapies for panic disorder with or without agoraphobia in adults: A network meta-analysis. *The Cochrane Library*.

Powers, M. B., Vörding, M. B. Z. V. S., & Emmelkamp, P. M. (2009). Acceptance and commitment therapy: A meta-analytic review. *Psychotherapy and Psychosomatics*, *78*(2), 73–80.

Price, M. & Anderson, P. L. (2012). Outcome expectancy as a predictor of treatment response in cognitive behavioral therapy for public speaking fears within social anxiety disorder. *Psychotherapy*, *49*, 173–179.

Raio, C. M., Orederu, T. A., Palazzolo, L., Shurick, A. A., & Phelps, E. A. (2013). Cognitive emotion regulation fails the stress test. *Proceedings of the National Academy of Sciences*, *110*, 15139–15144.

Rescorla, R. A. & Wagner, A. R. (1972). A theory of Pavlovian conditioning: Variations in the effectiveness of reinforcement and non-reinforcement. In A. H. Prokasy (ed.), *Classical Conditioning II: Current Research and Theory* (pp. 64–99). New York, NY: Appleton-Century-Croft.

Rodrigues, H., Figueira, I., Lopes, A., Gonçalves, R., Mendlowicz, M. V., Coutinho, E. S. F., & Ventura, P. (2014). Does D-cycloserine enhance exposure therapy for anxiety disorders in humans? A meta-analysis. *PloS One*, *9*, e93519.

Roemer, L. & Orsillo, S. M. (2002). Expanding our conceptualization of and treatment for generalized anxiety disorder: Integrating mindfulness/acceptance-based approaches with existing cognitive-behavioral models. *Clinical Psychology: Science and Practice*, *9*, 54–68.

Roshanaei-Moghaddam, B., Pauly, M. C., Atkins, D. C., Baldwin, S. A., Stein, M. B., & Roy-Byrne, P. (2011). Relative effects of CBT and pharmacotherapy in depression versus anxiety: Is medication somewhat better for depression, and CBT somewhat better for anxiety?. *Depression and Anxiety*, *28*, 560–567.

Rowe, M. K. & Craske, M. G. (1998). Effects of varied-stimulus exposure training on fear reduction and return of fear. *Behaviour Research and Therapy*, *36*, 719–734.

Rozental, A., Shafran, R., Wade, T., Egan, S., Nordgren, L. B., Carlbring, P., . . . Trosell, L. (2017). A randomized controlled trial of Internet-Based Cognitive Behavior Therapy for perfectionism including an investigation of outcome predictors. *Behaviour Research and Therapy*.

Salkovskis, P. M. (1991). The importance of behaviour in the maintenance of anxiety and panic: A cognitive account. *Behavioural Psychotherapy*, 19, 6–19.

Sauer-Zavala, S., Cassiello-Robbins, C., Conklin, L. R., Bullis, J. R., Thompson-Hollands, J., & Kennedy, K. A. (2017). Isolating the unique effects of the unified protocol treatment modules using single case experimental design. *Behavior Modification*, *41*, 286–307.

Segal, Z. V., Williams, J. M. G., & Teasdale, J. D. (2002). *Mindfulness-Based Cognitive Therapy for Depression: A New Approach to Preventing Relapse*. New York, NY: Guilford Press.

Shurick, A. A., Hamilton, J. R., Harris, L. T., Roy, A. K., Gross, J. J., & Phelps, E. A. (2012). Durable effects of cognitive restructuring on conditioned fear. *Emotion*, *12*, 1393–1397.

Shiban, Y., Pauli, P., & Mühlberger, A. (2013). Effect of multiple context exposure on renewal in spider phobia. *Behaviour Research and Therapy*, *51*, 68–74.

Sloan, T. & Telch, M. J. (2002). The effects of safety-seeking behavior and guided threat reappraisal on fear reduction during exposure: An experimental investigation. *Behaviour Research and Therapy*, *40*, 235–251.

Smits, J. A., Rosenfield, D., Otto, M. W., Marques, L., Davis, M. L., Meuret, A. E., . . . Hofmann, S. G. (2013). D-cycloserine enhancement of exposure therapy for social anxiety disorder depends on the success of exposure sessions. *Journal of Psychiatric Research*, *47*, 1455–1461.

Smits, J. A., Rosenfield, D., Otto, M. W., Powers, M. B., Hofmann, S. G., Telch, M. J., . . . Tart, C. D. (2013). D-cycloserine enhancement of fear extinction is specific to successful exposure sessions: Evidence from the treatment of height phobia. *Biological Psychiatry*, *73*, 1054–1058.

Spek, V., Cuijpers, P. I. M., Nyklíček, I., Riper, H., Keyzer, J., & Pop, V. (2007).Internet-based cognitive behaviour therapy for symptoms of depression and anxiety: A meta-analysis. *Psychological Medicine*, *37*, 319–328.

Stangier, U., Heidenreich, T., Peitz, M., Lauterbach, W., & Clark, D. M. (2003). Cognitive therapy for social phobia: Individual versus group treatment. *Behaviour Research and Therapy*, *41*, 991–1007.

Stewart, S. H., Westra, H. A., Thompson, C. E., & Conrad, B. E. (2000). Effects of naturalistic benzodiazepine use on selective attention to threat cues among anxiety disorder patients. *Cognitive Therapy and Research*, *24*, 67–85.

Stockings, E. A., Degenhardt, L., Dobbins, T., Lee, Y. Y., Erskine, H. E., Whiteford, H. A., & Patton, G. (2016). Preventing depression and anxiety in young people: A review of the joint efficacy of universal, selective and indicated prevention. *Psychological Medicine*, *46*, 11–26.

Taylor, S. (2003). Outcome predictors for three PTSD treatments: Exposure therapy, EMDR, and relaxation training. *Journal of Cognitive Psychotherapy*, *17*, 149–162.

Telch, M. J. & Lancaster, C. L. (2012). Is there room for safety behaviors in exposure therapy for anxiety disorders?. In P. Neudeck & H. Wittchen (eds.), *Exposure Therapy: Rethinking the Model – Refining the Method* (pp. 313–334). New York, NY: Springer Science.

Topper, M., Emmelkamp, P. M., Watkins, E., & Ehring, T. (2017). Prevention of anxiety disorders and depression by targeting excessive worry and rumination in adolescents and young adults: A randomized controlled trial. *Behaviour Research and Therapy*, *90*, 123–136.

van den Hout, M., Gangemi, A., Mancini, F., Engelhard, I. M., Rijkeboer, M. M., van Dams, M., & Klugkist, I. (2014). Behavior as information about threat in anxiety disorders: A comparison of patients with anxiety disorders and non-anxious controls. *Journal of Behavior Therapy and Experimental Psychiatry*, *45*, 489–495.

van Ingen, D. J., Freiheit, S. R., & Vye, C. S. (2009). From the lab to the clinic: Effectiveness of cognitive behavioral treatments for anxiety disorders. *Professional Psychology: Research and Practice*, *40*, 69–74.

Vansteenwegen, D., Vervliet, B., Hermans, D., Thewissen, R., & Eelen, P. (2007). Verbal, behavioural and physiological assessment of the generalization of exposure-based fear reduction in a spider-anxious population. *Behaviour Research and Therapy*, *45*, 291–300.

Vervliet, B., Vansteenwegen, D., Baeyens, F., Hermans, D., & Eelen, P. (2005). Return of fear in a human differential conditioning paradigm caused by a stimulus change after extinction. *Behaviour Research and Therapy*, *43*, 357–371.

Visted, E., Vøllestad, J., Nielsen, M. B., & Nielsen, G. H. (2014). The impact of group-based mindfulness training on self-reported mindfulness: A systematic review and meta-analysis. *Mindfulness*, *6*, 501–522.

Wang, P. S., Aguilar-Gaxiola, S., Alonso, J., Angermeyer, M. C., Borges, G., Bromet, E. J., . . . Haro, J. M. (2007). Use of mental health services for anxiety, mood, and substance disorders in 17 countries in the WHO world mental health surveys. *Lancet*, *370*, 841–850.

Wang, P. S., Angermeyer, M., Borges, G., Bruffaerts, R., Chiu, W. T., De Girolamo, G., . . . Kessler, R. C. (2007). Delay and failure in treatment seeking after first onset of mental disorders in the World Health Organization's World Mental Health Survey Initiative. *World Psychiatry*, *6*, 177–185.

Watts, S. E., Turnell, A., Kladnitski, N., Newby, J. M., & Andrews, G. (2015). Treatment-as-usual (TAU) is anything but usual: A meta-analysis of CBT versus TAU for anxiety and depression. *Journal of Affective Disorders*, *175*, 152–167.

Wells, A. (2000). *Emotional Disorders and Metacognition: Innovative Cognitive Therapy.* New York, NY: John Wiley & Sons Ltd.

Wells, A. (2007). Cognition about cognition: Metacognitive therapy and change in generalized anxiety disorder and social phobia. *Cognitive and Behavioral Practice*, *14*, 18–25.

Wells, A. & Papageorgiou, C. (1998). Social phobia: Effects of external attention on anxiety, negative beliefs, and perspective taking. *Behavior Therapy*, *29*, 357–370.

Wells, A., Welford, M., King, P., Papageorgiou, C., Wisely, J., & Mendel, E. (2010). A pilot randomized trial of metacognitive therapy vs applied relaxation in the treatment of adults with generalized anxiety disorder. *Behaviour Research and Therapy*, *48*, 429–434.

Wersebe, H., Sijbrandij, M., & Cuijpers, P. (2013). Psychological group-treatments of social anxiety disorder: A meta-analysis. *Plos One*, *8*, e79034.

Westen, D. & Morrison, K. (2001). A multidimensional meta-analysis of treatments for depression, panic, and generalized anxiety disorder: An empirical examination of the status of empirically supported therapies. *Journal of Consulting and Clinical Psychology*, *69*, 875–899.

Westra, H. A., Dozois, D. J., & Marcus, M. (2007). Expectancy, homework compliance, and initial change in cognitive-behavioral therapy for anxiety. *Journal of Consulting and Clinical Psychology*, *75*, 363–373.

Wilamowska, Z. A., Thompson-Hollands, J., Fairholme, C. P., Ellard, K. K., Farchione, T. J., & Barlow, D. H. (2010). Conceptual background, development, and preliminary data from the unified protocol for transdiagnostic treatment of emotional disorders. *Depression and Anxiety*, *27*, 882–890.

Wolitzky-Taylor, K. B., Arch, J. J., Rosenfield, D., & Craske, M. G. (2012). Moderators and non-specific predictors of treatment outcome for anxiety disorders: A comparison of cognitive behavioral therapy to acceptance and commitment therapy. *Journal of Consulting and Clinical Psychology*, *80*, 786–799.

Wolitzky-Taylor, K. B., Horowitz, J. D., Powers, M. B., & Telch, M. J. (2008). Psychological approaches in the treatment of specific phobias: A meta-analysis. *Clinical Psychology Review*, *28*, 1021–1037.

Wolitzky-Taylor, K., Zimmermann, M., Arch, J. J., De Guzman, E., & Lagomasino, I. (2015). Has evidence-based psychosocial treatment for anxiety disorders permeated usual care in community mental health settings? *Behaviour Research and Therapy*, *72*, 9–17.

Wolpe, J. (1968). Psychotherapy by reciprocal inhibition. *Integrative Physiological and Behavioral Science*, *3*, 234–240.

29 OCD Spectrum Disorders

Martin E. Franklin, Simone Budzyn, and Holly Freeman

Introduction

In this chapter, we describe the category of disorders now known in *DSM-5* as "OCD and Related Conditions (OCRDs)," then summarize the treatment outcome literature with respect to each of the included disorders in turn. There is considerable debate in the field now about the utility of the *DSM* classification system, as those with opposing views have recently emphasized cross-cutting concepts and variables applicable to multiple mental health conditions that may better reflect the neurobiological and psychological mechanisms that underlie psychopathology. This view is perhaps best explicated in discussions of the Research Domain Criteria (RDoC), which was emphasized at the National Institute of Mental Health (NIMH) in the past decade (Clark, Cuthbert, Lewis-Fernandez, Narrow, & Reed, 2017; Kozak & Cuthbert, 2016). In particular, the use of dimensional measures to capture variation rather than categorical or diagnostic measures may provide greater traction for discovery of brain-behavior associations and for characterization of their developmental time courses and functional significance (Casey, Oliveri, & Insel, 2014). With this shift came a movement toward developing a biologically based taxonomy to guide translational and intervention research (Insel et al., 2010) which, because resources are finite, came at the expense of funding randomized controlled trials (RCTs) for the treatment of *DSM*-diagnosed clinical disorders (Hershenberg & Goldfried, 2015). Whether this shift proves to be a scientific advance remains to be seen, but suffice it to say for now that new RCTs examining the relative and combined efficacy of candidate treatments for the OCRDs will likely be few and far between as a result. In obsessive-compulsive disorder (OCD) in particular, the adult literature includes findings from many RCTs; less has been published on youth, but a substantive literature supports the efficacy of cognitive behavioral therapy (CBT), pharmacotherapy with selective serotonin reuptake inhibitors (SSRIs), and their combination (Franklin et al., 2015). However, the literature on the other OCRDs is sparse, and thus the absence of funding for efficacy studies will leave us all having to interpolate across the empirical gaps when it comes to selecting treatments and informing patients of the rationale for our choices. We acknowledge as much in the following review of OCRDs, but also offer what we can in the way of empirical evidence for the various treatments that have been put forth.

The aforementioned biological approach certainly has its virulent critics as well (e.g., Deacon, 2013), who posit that the biomedical model of mental disorders has not yielded the pharmacotherapy innovation promised and, at the same time, has neglected psychotherapy process work, inhibited cognitive and behavioral treatment innovation and dissemination, and widened the divide among scientists and practitioners. A common thread in our own thinking about this model is, even if the neural pathways of illness could be better mapped and understood, how long will it take for such work to directly influence clinical care? Identifying that the source of the premonitory urge in Tourette syndrome is a specific signal emanating from the series of brain structures known as the basal ganglia, which are implicated in Parkinson's disease, would certainly be interesting, and the research explicating that process thoroughly would be a candidate for high-end medical journals. At the same time, how and when does mapping of this, or any other neural pathway for that matter, lead to changes in pharmacotherapy or even psychotherapy for those who suffer from the condition being studied? In the spirit of this book's overarching intent, we attempt to address some of the relevant issues on both sides of these arguments as we discuss OCD and the related disorders.

Another issue that is apparent in the literature is that the fields of adult and child psychopathology and treatment are too often viewed as separate entities, when in fact the majority of mental health conditions are seen across the developmental spectrum. Some conditions appear to be most commonly observed in youth, such as attention-deficit disorders, whereas others, such as mood disorders, are more common in adults. What is clear enough by now, though, is that development affects expression of the symptoms of these disorders, and this is certainly true of OCRDs. For example, as in adults, OCD in youth is characterized by obsessions and compulsions, but the kinds of things that children might worry about, their level of insight as to the senselessness of these symptoms, their capacity to introspect and report on their internal states, their degree of knowledge about realistic vs. unrealistic fears, etc., all affect how we understand the complex interplay among symptoms and, by extension, how we might work effectively to help our younger patients understand core concepts and apply them in the service of reducing and eliminating the compulsions that maintain fear and discomfort. We attempt in our review of the treatment literature to bridge the gap between what has been done in adult vs. child and adolescent samples, and to speculate as to how research across the developmental spectrum may enhance our understanding of each of the OCRDs and promote treatment development efforts tailored to the challenges that people face as they move from childhood to adulthood (e.g., Peters et al., 2016).

OCD and Related Disorders

The *DSM-5* (American Psychiatric Association, 2013) included a new diagnostic category called Obsessive-Compulsive and Related Disorders (OCRDs) which includes (1) obsessive-compulsive disorder (OCD); (2) body dysmorphic disorder (BDD); (3) hoarding disorder; (4) trichotillomania (TTM) (hair-pulling disorder); and (5) excoriation (skin-picking) disorder. For each of these conditions, differentiating the disorder from subclinical symptoms requires assessment of a number of factors, including the individual's level of distress and functional impairment. The key features of the *DSM-5* OCRDs are listed in what follows:

OCD: Characterized by the presence of unwanted or intrusive thoughts, images, or urges, as well as repetitive behaviors or mental acts the person feels driven to perform in response to the obsession or according to rigid rules.

BDD: Characterized by cognitive symptoms such as perceived defects or flaws in physical appearance, as well as associated repetitive behaviors or mental acts.

Hoarding Disorder: Persistent difficulty discarding or parting with possessions, regardless of their actual value; the difficulty substantially compromises the intended use of the physical spaces in which the possessions are housed.

TTM: Recurrent pulling out of one's own hair, resulting in hair loss; repeated attempts to decrease or stop hair-pulling.

Excoriation Disorder: Recurrent skin-picking resulting in skin lesions; repeated attempts to decrease or stop skin-picking.

OCD itself was previously classified as an anxiety disorder, whereas the other OCRDs that existed in the *DSM-IV*, BDD and TTM, came from the categories of somatoform disorders and impulse control disorders, respectively. The decision to group them together was in part based on evidence of an underlying relationship between two or more disorders, which could be indicated by frequency of co-occurrence; symptom similarity; onset, presentation, and progression of disorders; environmental risk factors; neural substrates and biomarkers; and treatment response. Several of the aforementioned factors still strike us as aspirational rather than data driven (e.g., neural substrates, biomarkers), and are clearly reflective of the kind of biological reductionism that currently permeates if not dominates the field. The function of the repetitive behaviors in the maintenance of illness did not appear to play a key role in the reclassification system, which allowed strange bedfellows such as OCD, which is driven largely by negative reinforcement (e.g., washing compulsions designed to reduce the likelihood of becoming ill), to wind up in the same category as TTM, which appears to be driven largely by positive reinforcement (e.g., pulling out a hair and playing with the root in response to boredom). These caveats notwithstanding, the *DSM-5* does provide us with some topics for spirited debate if not for experimental study, such as the role of cross-cutting variables in the phenomenology of disorders housed under this seemingly broad umbrella (e.g., impulse control deficits, cognitive biases).

Of greatest curiosity in the repackaging of OCD and associated conditions was the continued separation of OCD and tic disorders in the *DSM-5*: these conditions certainly meet several of the criteria listed earlier as justifying inclusion in the OCRD category for the other disorders, such as a very high rate of co-occurrence (e.g., Hirschtritt, Pauls, Dion, Grados, & Illman, 2015). Indeed, OCD itself was deemed sufficiently intertwined with tic symptoms that a new specifier, tic-related OCD, is now included in the *DSM-5* for the purpose of "identifying individuals with a current or past comorbid tic disorder, because this comorbidity may have important clinical implications." Nevertheless, tic disorders remained outside the OCD awning, classified instead under "Neurodevelopmental Disorders." The reasons for this are myriad, long debated, and not entirely based in the objectivity of science, although one of our most preeminent philosophers of science, Thomas Kuhn, noted that "the algorithms of individuals ... to select a theory ... are all ultimately different by virtue of the subjective considerations with which each must complete the objective criteria before any computation can be done" (Kuhn, 1977, p. 109). In other words, science is a human endeavor that is influenced by the subjective, and in this case the subjective is influenced by the difficult fight that took place over many years to have Tourette syndrome included under a neurological umbrella as far as classification goes. The other OCRDs also have their biological substrates, i.e., nobody is saying that these conditions do not involve underlying neurobiological processes, but those arguing that Tourette syndrome should not be shifted under the OCRDs label made that decision with the pragmatic considerations of losing status as a neurological disorder fully in mind (see Roessner, Hoekstra, & Rothenberger, 2011).

Treatment Outcome Literature for the OC Spectrum Conditions

OCD. Effective treatments for OCD in adults include medication and CBT. In terms of pharmacotherapy, serotonin reuptake inhibitors (SRIs) are the only medications approved by the US Food and Drug Administration for OCD. The SRIs include clomipramine (CMI), a tricyclic antidepressant with strong serotonin reuptake inhibition, and the SSRIs (fluoxetine, fluvoxamine, paroxetine, sertraline, citalopram, escitalopram). Depending on the study and the definition of response, 14% to 65% of patients respond to an adequate SRI trial. However, most SRI responders continue to have clinically significant symptoms that affect functioning and quality of life.

Two types of CBT for OCD have been studied in RCTs most frequently: exposure plus response prevention (ERP) and cognitive therapy (CT). Studies suggest that both treatments are effective in reducing OCD symptoms (e.g., Cottraux et al., 2001; Whittal et al., 2005), although results from a meta-analytic review indicate that CTs that included exposure were superior to those that did not (Abramowitz et al., 2002). American Psychiatric Association practice guidelines for OCD recommend ERP as a first-line treatment for OCD, with CT a secondary option (Koran et al., 2007). ERP teaches patients new strategies to cope with obsessions and compulsions (Foa, Yadin, & Lichner, 2012). Specifically, patients are taught to confront situations that elicit obsessional distress ("exposure," e.g., sitting on the floor, where they feel contaminated by germs) and to refrain from performing compulsions ("response prevention," e.g., excessive washing and cleaning). The mechanisms by which ERP's effects are realized have been the subject of much debate, but the prevailing view continues to involve a blend of cognitive and behavioral factors: exposure provides an opportunity for patients to have their fear-relevant beliefs disconfirmed by their own experience, thus providing what Foa and Kozak (1986) referred to as corrective information. Exposures should therefore be tailored to address the patient's feared beliefs in order to maximize the contrast between what was believed initially and what can be gathered via experience, and should be provided in multiple contexts to promote new learning. There is a subset of OCD patients, however, those with "Not Just Right" OCD or disgust- or discomfort-driven compulsions, for whom this more cognitive conceptualization may not match ideally; when treating these patients, emphasis is often put on learning how to tolerate discomfort and function better in the presence of the relevant stimuli rather than on habituation or cognitive change per se (Arch & Abramowitz, 2015).

ERP has been found superior to a host of control treatments, including placebo medication, relaxation, and anxiety management (for a review, see Olatunji, Rosenfield, et al., 2013). Foa and Kozak's (1996) review of 12 treatment studies involving a total of 330 patients found that 83% of patients who completed EX/RP therapy were classified as responding favorably to treatment. In 12 studies reporting long-term follow-up of a total of 376 patients, 76% were considered to have successfully maintained their gains. CBT programs comprised of cognitive and exposure techniques have been found efficacious for OCD when delivered individually or in group formats (e.g., Anderson & Reese, 2007).

Only one RCT to date has examined the efficacy of EMDR for OCD. This study found that 12 weeks of EMDR was superior to citalopram at post-treatment (Nazari, Momeni, Jariani, & Tarrahi, 2011). The study used a low dose (20 mg) of citalopram that is lower than the recommended dose for OCD and did not include a follow-up assessment. Thus, additional research is needed to evaluate the efficacy of EMDR for OCD. Acceptance and commitment therapy (ACT), a form of behavior therapy, has also been found efficacious in the treatment of OCD relative to a relaxation control condition (Twohig et al., 2010); dropout from both conditions was low, and post-treatment gains made in both conditions were maintained to follow-up. The absence of formal exposure in the ACT protocol raises questions about whether ACT may be an alternative treatment option for those who reject exposure-based interventions.

RCTs examining the efficacy of combined treatment in OCD (e.g., Marks et al., 1988) generally suggest that combined treatment is not superior to ERP alone. For example, in a trial comparing 12 weeks of intensive EX/RP with and without CMI or placebo, ERP was superior to placebo, not significantly different from CMI+EX/RP, and superior to CMI at reducing OCD symptoms (Foa et al., 2005). Similarly, cognitive coping therapy plus pharmacotherapy was found superior to pharmacotherapy alone (Ma et al., 2013). A recent meta-analysis of 468 patients with OCD found that pharmacotherapy combined with CBT was superior to pharmacotherapy alone, but that combined therapy was not superior to CBT alone (Huang, Li, Han, Xiong, & Ma, 2013).

As is true of most other pediatric internalizing disorders, the CBT outcome literature in pediatric OCD began with age-downward extension of protocols found efficacious with adults, then publication of single case studies, case series, and open clinical trials involving these protocols. March and Mulle's manual (1998) served as the study protocol for the Pediatric OCD Treatment Study (POTS I) (POTS Team, 2004) and POTS II (Franklin et al., 2011), as well as several other published studies; a more specifically tailored manual for young children with OCD was derived from the POTS manual as well (Freeman et al., 2008, 2014). The open trials conducted in the 1990s revealed remarkably similar and encouraging findings across settings and cultures: at post-treatment, the majority to the vast majority of patients were responders, with clinically meaningful and statistically significant symptom reductions reported. This pilot work set the stage for randomized studies evaluating the efficacy of CBT, which collectively provide further support for the efficacy of CBT.

CBT involving ERP has garnered enough research support in the last two decades to be considered an empirically supported treatment, with randomized studies from around the world attesting to its efficacy relative to various comparison conditions (e.g., pill placebo in POTS I, relaxation in Piacentini et al., 2011) and to active pharmacotherapy (for recent reviews, see Franklin et al., 2015; Freeman et al., 2014). The effects appear to be both robust and durable, with follow-up studies indicating that the effects of treatment last for up to nine months after treatment has ended (e.g., Barrett et al., 2004, 2005; Franklin et al., 1998). Intensive treatment regimens are effective, although weekly treatment for approximately 12–14 weeks appears to be sufficient for most patients (Franklin et al., 1998; Storch et al., 2007). With respect to making clinical judgments about whether a more intensive form of CBT is needed for a given patient, it may well be the case that symptom severity, comorbidity, readiness for change, and case complexity (e.g., family problems) dictate whether a more intensive approach is needed; however, the literature examining the predictive value of such factors is limited. What is also evident from the literature is that the treatment of very young children requires a family-based approach; indeed, a multisite RCT supported the use of family-based ERP over family-based relaxation (Freeman et al., 2014), in terms of reducing OCD symptoms but also OCD-related impairment.

Building on a small initial comparison of pharmacotherapy versus ERP (de Haan et al., 1998), on the extensive adult OCD literature (e.g., Marks et al., 1988), and on a much larger multisite, randomized, placebo-controlled trial establishing the efficacy of sertraline in pediatric OCD (March et al., 1998), POTS I (Pediatric OCD Treatment Study Team, 2004) was the first multisite, randomized, controlled trial to directly compare the efficacy of an established medication (sertraline) (SER), CBT, and their combination (COMB) to a control condition, pill placebo (PBO). A total of 112 volunteers between the ages of 7–17 inclusive with a primary

DSM-IV diagnosis of OCD entered the trial. Findings indicated a significant advantage for all three active treatments – COMB, CBT, and SER – over PBO. In terms of comparisons of the active treatments on Children's Yale-Brown Obsessive-Compulsive Scale (CY-BOCS) continuous outcomes, COMB was found superior to both CBT and to SER, which did not differ from one another. A significant site effect was also detected in POTS I, which indicated that CBT alone at Penn was clearly superior to CBT at Duke, whereas the reverse was true for SER alone, although not as robustly so. Notably, no site-by-treatment interactions were found for COMB or for PBO, suggesting that the effects of combined treatment are less vulnerable to site-specific influences.

As noted earlier, even trials using adequate medication doses and durations were still leaving the great majority of patients with clinically significant residual symptoms, and thus the chances for remission or excellent response are lower with medication alone. These observations led the POTS team to design a next-phase research trial to address the issue of treatment augmentation (adding an additional treatment to a current treatment) as well as treatment transportability (developing a treatment in a research setting specifically for use in community clinical settings). This study was known as the POTS II trial (Franklin et al., 2011), which examined the relative efficacy of: (1) medication management (MM) provided by a study psychiatrist (MM only); (2) MM plus OCD-specific CBT as delivered by a study psychologist (MM+CBT); and (3) MM plus instructions in CBT (MM+I-CBT) delivered by the study psychiatrist assigned to provide MM. The acute treatment phase lasted for 12 weeks; notably, CBT in the MM+CBT condition followed the 14 hour-long sessions protocol used in POTS I (March & Mulle, 1998), whereas I-CBT in the MM+I-CBT condition involved only seven brief sessions and did not include in-session exposure. This design decision was made to test the efficacy of a treatment that, if found efficacious, could be readily incorporated into the pharmacotherapy clinics where youth with OCD receive care. POTS II's findings indicated that MM+CBT was superior to MM alone and to MM +I-CBT, which, contrary to study hypotheses, failed to separate statistically from one another (69% response for MM+CBT versus 34% for MM+I-CBT and 30% for MM alone, where response was defined as a 30% reduction in baseline CY-BOCS score). POTS II provided further evidence for the efficacy of combined treatment, in this case administered sequentially rather than simultaneously, and also high-lighted the potential need for using the "full dose" of CBT in order to achieve optimal outcomes.

Another large, multisite study examined the augmentative effects of DCS in pediatric OCD (Storch et al., 2016), and found that DCS did not augment the efficacy of CBT, in large part because of a floor effect: ERP alone was highly efficacious, thus making it difficult to identify an augmentative effect for DCS. At this point, the study team suggested that future research identify specific character-istics of youth who may benefit from DCS augmentation; although not examined as yet, it is likely the predictors of partial response to the full regimen or slower reductions in symptoms by mid-treatment would be likely candidates to pursue.

Both alone and in combination with SRIs, CBT provides a viable treatment alternative to SSRIs alone (Ivarsson et al., 2015), although the paucity of trained CBT therapists continues to make it difficult in some regions to heed the expert consensus guidelines recommendations (e.g., AACAP) to start with CBT alone or with COMB.

Dissemination of CBT for pediatric OCD thus remains a pressing challenge to the field, although research supporting a "supervision of supervisors" model is promising (e.g., Valderhaug et al., 2007). Data suggest that this model can yield impressive results that are comparable to those achieved in the academic medical settings that developed the CBT protocol use with children and adolescents (e.g., Farrell et al., 2010; Torp et al., 2015).

BDD. Of all the conditions classified under OCRDs, BDD may most closely resemble OCD both in terms of form but also function: intrusive thoughts abound, and give rise to urges to engage in repetitive behaviors to reduce the likelihood of feared consequences (e.g., checking repeatedly to make sure physical flaws cannot be detected); more passive forms of avoidance also play a prominent role in BDD, such as refusing to go out in daylight. Comorbidity is the norm, with depression and other anxiety disorders being the most common co-occurring disorders (Gunstad & Phillips, 2003). One difference between OCD and BDD is that the continuum of insight is shifted in the latter condition: less than 5% of OCD patients have poor or no insight (e.g., Foa et al., 1995), whereas approximately one-third of BDD patients lack insight into the senselessness of their symptoms (Phillips et al., 2006). Poor insight is a known prognostic indicator of attenuated outcome (Foa et al., 1999), and the putative mechanism by which these effects are realized may well be reduced via between-session homework compliance (e.g., Simpson et al., 2011): individuals with OCD who are convinced that their feared consequences will result if they do not engage in compulsions will typically not complete exposures, and will not reduce associated avoidance behaviors. Thus, clinical methods to address poor insight in particular are sorely needed in OCD and BDD alike.

As is the case with OCD, treatment for BDD also typically involves CBT that focuses on ERP, as well as SSRIs. In a recent review and meta-analysis of CBT for BDD, Harrison and colleagues (2016) identified seven RCTs that included 299 patients, from which they determined that CBT was superior to various placebo conditions in reducing BDD symptoms and depression while also improving insight, and that gains were maintained for up to four months post-treatment. All but one of the seven randomized trials tested face-to-face treatments, whereas one examined an Internet-based delivery, which may have particular appeal for patients whose symptoms and associated avoidance are so severe as to preclude their inclusion in clinic-based interventions. All but one of the trials reviewed were conducted with adults (Mataix-Cols et al., 2015); as is the case with OCD, BDD onset typically occurs by adolescence, which highlights the importance of additional research and attention involving teens with BDD. The authors also noted that the effect sizes were comparable to those reported in recent meta-analyses for OCD (e.g., Olatunji, Davis, Powers, & Smits, 2013), which runs counter to clinical wisdom suggesting that BDD is necessarily difficult to treat.

A follow-up study conducted with the sample who participated in the lone adolescent BDD RCT provided additional information regarding the durability of outcomes with this population (Krebs et al., 2016). Thirty adolescents participated in the initial trial, and all of those who received CBT participated in the 12-month naturalistic follow-up study, regardless of whether they had been allocated to CBT initially or had first completed the control treatment, which involved receiving written psychoeducational materials and weekly telephone monitoring. Participants remained significantly improved on BDD and secondary outcome measures at 12-month follow-up; however, the majority remained at least somewhat symptomatic, which led the investigators to recommend treatment development to focus on enhancing efficacy as well as longer-term monitoring of symptoms.

In contrast to the extensive literature in OCD, researchers have done little in examining the efficacy of pharmacotherapy for BDD. In the only double-blind, placebo-controlled trial available to date, fluoxetine was found more efficacious than pill placebo (Phillips, Albertini, & Rasmussen, 2002); treatment response was neither universal nor complete, and the broader literature on OCRDs makes clear that relapse upon medication discontinuation is the norm. In a double-blind, placebo-controlled trial examining pharmacotherapy relapse prevention, Phillips and colleagues (2016) randomized 100 adults with BDD to receive open-label escitalopram; responders were then randomized to double-blind continuation treatment of active medication versus switching to placebo for six months. The Phase 1 outcomes were encouraging, in that 67% of treated patients met criteria for treatment response; time to relapse was significantly longer with escitalopram compared with placebo crossover treatment, with 18% and 40% relapse rates over the six-month length of Phase II. Randomized controlled trials examining the relative and combined efficacy of CBT and pharmacotherapy have yet to be conducted, however, and would significantly advance the field with respect to how best to optimize outcomes in BDD.

Hoarding Disorder. Originally classified as a subtype of OCD, hoarding disorder has now been given its own designation under the OCRDs. The rationale for moving hoarding disorder out of the OCD diagnostic category has been presented in detail elsewhere (e.g., Wheaton et al., 2011); suffice it to say here that research on its basic phenomenology, associated disorders, and attenuated response to ERP (e.g., Abramowitz et al., 2003) contributed to the creation of the new category. Frost and Hartl (1996) and Steketee and Frost (2003) identified specific problems in hoarders that included: (1) a host of information-processing deficits; (2) maladaptive beliefs about and attachment to possessions; and (3) maladaptive emotional responses and behavioral patterns including avoidance. Executive functioning deficits and specific ADHD symptoms are evident in high rates in this population, which may help explain how possessions can take over the spaces into which they were allocated. One patient we treated years back, when asked about a veritable mountain of printed matter on her dining room table, was asked to categorize the material in front of us; her response, which was simply, "Stuff from last year," made immediately clear how deficits in organizational ability and avoidance collectively yielded the accumulation. Discarding the material without building a new infrastructure for managing incoming material would clearly be insufficient to help this patient declutter and maintain a more functional living space; clinical observations such as these spawned efforts to tailor CBT to better meet the needs of those suffering from hoarding disorder.

Treatment development efforts made in the wake of research indicating that hoarding did not respond especially favorably to ERP resulted in new conceptual approaches to the condition. In particular, a greater emphasis was placed in treatment on motivational interviewing techniques, while graded exposure to non-acquiring, training in sorting and discarding, cognitive restructuring of hoarding-specific thoughts, and organizational training were also included (Steketee & Frost, 2014). A recent meta-analysis of treatment outcome for CBT-based approaches, informed by improved understanding of the cognitive and behavioral mechanisms underlying hoarding, yielded large effect sizes for such interventions (Tolin, Frost, Steketee, & Muroff, 2015). These treatment effects appear to be most robust for the symptoms involving difficulty discarding; smaller but still significant effects were seen for clutter and acquiring. From this same meta-analysis, which included data from 10 trials, it also appeared that female gender, younger age, a greater number of CBT sessions, and a greater number of home visits were associated with better clinical outcomes. Across all the studies, patients in general remained in the clinical range at post-treatment, which indicates that further treatment development may well be needed.

Another recently published literature review in hoarding disorder identified substantive problems with the methodological quality of the studies conducted thus far, and their collective outcome indicated that CBT; medications including SSRIs, venlafaxine, and extended-release methylphenidate; cognitive remediation; and multi-component interventions for relatives yielded statistically significant improvements in hoarding symptoms, although these reductions were generally modest and many participants remained in the clinical range after treatment (Thompson, Fernández de la Cruz, Mataix-Cols, & Onwumere, 2017). High drop-out rates were also noted across the various studies and treatments, thus patient retention strategies may also need to be developed.

With respect to hoarding in youth, much less has been done with respect to treatment development and efficacy testing, though scholars have conducted some research on clinical symptoms. A large sample of youth with OCD was recruited, and the factor structure of the CY-BOCS was examined, with hoarding loading with symmetry and associated with both depression and anxiety (Højgaard et al., 2017). Storch and colleagues found, in youth ages 7–17 with OCD, that those who endorsed hoarding symptoms had a higher frequency of panic disorder, somatic complaints, and internalizing and externalizing comorbidity. Frank and colleagues

(2014) examined hoarding symptoms in a sample of youth ages 10 or younger with OCD, and found that, when compared to youth who did not endorse hoarding symptoms ($n = 35$), those included in the hoarding group ($n = 33$) had an earlier onset of any symptoms, a higher proportion of comorbid ADHD symptoms, and a higher likelihood of a provisional anxiety diagnosis. The ADHD and executive functioning findings appear consistently across the developmental spectrum, and likely require remediation in addition to focusing on addressing discarding and acquisition as well.

TTM. A wide variety of treatments have been attempted clinically to alleviate TTM symptoms in adults, adolescents, and children, including cognitive and behavioral therapies, supportive counseling, support groups, hypnosis, medications, and combined approaches (Woods et al., 2006). The scientific literature supporting the efficacy of these approaches, however, is not well developed, with fewer than 20 RCTs available to guide treatment choice and implementation. Most of the available randomized treatment outcome studies have examined behavioral therapies or medications, and their collective findings have been somewhat mixed, especially with respect to the efficacy of medication. Further, only one of these randomized trials was conducted with a pediatric sample (Franklin et al., 2011a), despite clear evidence that onset during childhood or adolescence is the norm. Recent reviews (e.g., Franklin et al., 2011d; Woods & Houghton, 2014) have highlighted several key points: (1) cognitive-behavioral treatments are associated with relatively large effect sizes in adults following acute treatment, although relapse appears to be a problem; (2) SSRIs generally do not appear to be efficacious in reducing hair-pulling symptoms per se; (3) several compounds that appear to affect other neurotransmitter systems hold some promise for the treatment of TTM; (4) combined treatments with behavioral therapy plus medication may also prove useful; and (5) the absence of evidence from RCTs conducted with pediatric samples hinders treatment development and treatment planning for perhaps the most vulnerable population of TTM sufferers.

Behavioral interventions for TTM (e.g., Franklin et al., 2011a) have generally included three core elements: (1) awareness training, wherein techniques (e.g., self-monitoring) are implemented to improve the patient's awareness of pulling and, better yet, the patient's awareness of the urge that precedes pulling; (2) stimulus control, which includes a variety of methods that serve as "speed bumps" to reduce the likelihood that pulling behavior begins; and (3) competing response training, where patients are taught, at the earliest sign of pulling or of the urge to pull, to engage in a behavior that is physically incompatible with pulling for a brief period of time until the urge subsides. These core methods were developed and tested initially by Azrin and Nunn (1973), and comprise the main elements of contemporary behavioral treatment, although some habit reversal training protocols have also included other techniques (e.g., relaxation training, cognitive strategies to address dysfunctional thoughts that precipitate pulling).

Expert opinion (Flessner et al., 2010) is convergent with the treatment outcome literature in supporting the use of cognitive-behavioral treatments that include habit reversal training as the first-line option in TTM. It is also generally accepted now that SSRIs, though potentially useful to address comorbid symptoms of anxiety and depression, are not considered first-line treatments for pulling per se. One study did support the efficacy of an SSRI in combination with behavioral therapy over behavioral therapy and medication alone (Dougherty et al., 2006); replication of these findings is needed. New developments in pharmacotherapy discussed later in this chapter open the possibility for examining the relative and combined efficacy of these novel approaches in concert with behavior therapy as well. Whether these treatments should be started simultaneously or delivered sequentially – for example, pre-medication with an agent of established efficacy followed by behavioral intervention when pulling urges are lowered by medication effects – also needs to be examined using randomized designs.

Behavior therapy, though efficacious, is not without its limitations, the most alarming of which is the observation that relapse following treatment is common (e.g., Lerner et al., 1998). Treatment development work is already under way in several labs to examine whether behavior therapy involving habit reversal training can be augmented by methods designed specifically to address negative emotions. There is also hope that the research tools developed to examine pulling styles more specifically will aid clinical researchers in providing more targeted behavioral interventions that can be tailored to individual pulling profiles.

Recent developments in pharmacotherapy offer encouragement that therapies that modulate neurotransmitter systems other than serotonin will prove helpful in reducing pulling behavior and pulling urges. Bloch and colleagues' (2007) thorough review of the treatment outcome literature highlights the fact that the SSRIs offer little in the way of clinical benefit above and beyond what can be expected from pill placebo. Clomipramine, a tricyclic antidepressant with serotonergic and other properties, appears to be more efficacious than placebo, but its unfavorable side effect profile renders it a second-line treatment.

Perhaps the most important development in pharmacotherapy for TTM involves the use of the glutamate modulator NAC, which was found superior to pill placebo in an RCT for adults with TTM (Grant et al., 2009). Treatment response rates for the NAC condition were not only clearly superior to the control condition, but they also yielded rates that were comparable to those observed in CBT trials with adults. Further, the side effect profile was quite favorable, which may well make this compound the most promising recent development in the field. Notably, NAC is not an FDA-regulated product, so it is readily available in health food stores. Comparability of products containing NAC from manufacturer to manufacturer, however, is unknown.

Excoriation Disorder. Just as OCD and BDD share considerable overlap in terms of both form and function of repetitive behaviors, excoriation disorder shares many roots with TTM, most specifically the engagement in the repetitive behavior in response to urges that are typically experienced at the site of said behavior. Positive reinforcement is often reported in response to engaging in the behavior in the moment, even if negative affect is experienced later in response to the resulting damage. Neither condition appears to be heavily mediated by cognition, i.e., thoughts associated with anxiety per se; when skin-picking is associated with fear-based reasoning such as needing to get a contaminant out of the skin, a diagnosis of OCD might be more appropriate. Skin-picking may be done using the fingernails or implements such as needles, pins, or tweezers; not surprisingly, when implements are used, the associated scarring and skin infections are more common (Selles, McGuire, Small, & Storch, 2016). Again like TTM, excoriation disorder is associated with a host of comorbid conditions, as well as shame and guilt about having engaged in the behavior; skin-picking too can take place in a focused manner as well as more automatically at times, and the affective function of each type of skin-picking may vary.

Treatment for skin-picking has closely mirrored what is done with TTM, most specifically involving the use of behavioral interventions that include habit reversal training, which essentially comes down to engaging in a competing behavior instead of the target behavior when urges occur. A handful of available randomized trials attest to the efficacy of behavioral interventions; in a recent meta-analysis (Selles et al., 2016), CBT involving habit reversal therapy was found to yield a moderate effect size that holds out promise for individuals suffering from this condition. A host of pharmacotherapy options have been examined, all in small trials, and the results of these studies suggest efficacy for SSRIs and lamotrigine, a glutamate modulator that has been used elsewhere as a mood stabilizer and an anticonvulsant. Findings here too have yielded moderate to large effects, although the formal examination of combined treatment strategies has yet to be done.

Very little data are available to elucidate the presentation, phenomenology, associated psychopathology and comorbidity, and treatment response in youth, again despite the fact that many if not most patients with excoriation disorder begin picking in childhood or adolescence. Clearly more work needs to be done in order to provide guidance regarding the etiology, developmental course, and patterns of associated comorbid conditions over the course of childhood into adolescence. One might surmise that the functional similarity to TTM will help in the interim, and it likely will, but more information is still sorely needed.

Conclusion

Every iteration of the *Diagnostic and Statistical Manual of Mental Disorders* has generated controversy, and *DSM-5* has certainly been no exception. A cogent and detailed analysis by Abramowitz and Jacoby (2015) duly noted a number of inconsistencies within the OCRDs, and our own critical comments in this chapter raise questions as to whether the final selection of which disorders to include and which to exclude has indeed carved nature at its joints. The grouping together of these disorders appears to be justified in part by the presence of repetitive behaviors, but the reasons for these repetitive behaviors, i.e., their function, gets short shrift; moreover, many other disorders involving repetitive behaviors (e.g., anorexia nervosa, gambling addiction) do not get classified as OCRDs. They also review the data on family patterns, neurobiological factors, neurotransmission, treatment response, and brain structure and function, and conclude that in each of these areas also the scientific case for grouping these disorders together has not been met. The false perception of equivalence among these disorders could result in clinicians conceptualizing and treating these conditions in a similar fashion (Abramowitz & Jacoby, 2015); in particular, the absence of fear-based cognitions driving repetitive behaviors in TTM and excoriation disorder would lead to trying to force a round peg into a square hole in terms of behavioral intervention, and this may well be at the expense of patients.

These critiques notwithstanding, there may be no ideal way to create or modify a complex document that purports to accurately represent current scientific knowledge and clinical consensus regarding conditions that involve a great deal of overlap among symptoms. Further, one must consider the human element that went into the selection process, which may widen the gap between objectivity and the end product. Sir Alex Issigonis, a 20th-century car maker, noted as much within his own field when he proclaimed, likely in a fit of frustration about having to compromise his own vision on a car design: "A camel is a horse that was created by a committee." The OCRDs include conditions that have some overlapping formal if not functional similarity, and include disorders that tend to co-occur at higher than the base rates seen in the population. Its utility may well be seen down the road when researchers begin the process of accruing samples of individuals across all the OCRDs and examining some of the variables that may be involved more or less in particular disorders, such as impulsivity, fixed belief, and response inhibition deficits. Machine learning methodologies are being brought to bear to help make the most of large datasets; some interesting work of this sort has begun already in OCD, which in and of itself is a heterogeneous condition in which some theoretical constructs such as fear might be more or less associated with the core psychopathology (e.g., Askland et al., 2015; Insiesta, Stahl, & McGuffin, 2016). Funding for such endeavors will likely take place under RDoC-related initiatives, and the outcomes of such studies may elucidate whether the OCRDs are indeed first and second cousins whose underlying biology can improve our understanding of each of these conditions and thereby promote treatment development, or whether they are simply strangers on a train.

Assumptions about shared biology in the OCRDs and the causal assumptions inherent in biological reductionism (e.g., the patient is engaging in compulsions because of a chemical imbalance) bring us closer to some fundamental controversies in the field, most notably the tendency to assert causality when only correlational data are available. Some of the core physiological research in support of a biological explanation for OCD, such as Baxter and colleagues' seminal neuroimaging studies (see Baxter, 1994), suffers from a lack of clarity regarding whether the observed biological findings in patients diagnosed with OCD, when compared to controls, are the cause of OCD or simply a downstream consequence of having the illness. A recent novelty book put together by a mathematically oriented writer, *Spurious Correlations* (Vigen, 2015), provides many humorous examples of variables that are highly correlated yet clearly without establishment of a causal arrow. For example, over a 10-year period, there is a 0.95 correlation between the number of people who drowned after falling out of a fishing boat and the marriage rate in the state of Kentucky; similarly, there is a 0.80 correlation between the number of letters in the winning word at the Scripps National Spelling Bee and the number of people killed by venomous spiders. In the end, it will be enormously important for scientists who conduct this biological research to be highly skeptical of their own conclusions and to take other possible explanations of the pathways to these illnesses seriously, lest we wind up with a stagnant pool of myriad biological findings that cannot be coherently linked to one another or lead us as a field to the development of testable hypotheses that will elucidate the path forward to improved understanding and empirically informed treatment development efforts in the OCRDs. Despite 20 years of substantive progress, treatment response for all of these conditions, whether present in adults or youth, remains neither universal nor complete. Thus, finding ways to improve outcomes continues to be a major clinical research priority.

References

Abramowitz, J. S., Franklin, M. E., Schwartz, S. A., & Furr, J. M. (2003). Symptom presentation and outcome of cognitive-behavioral therapy for obsessive-compulsive disorder. *Journal of Consulting and Clinical Psychology, 71*(6), 1049–1057.

Abramowitz, J. S. & Jacoby, R. J. (2015). Obsessive-compulsive and related disorders: A critical review of the new diagnostic class. *Annual Review of Clinical Psychology, 11*, 165–186.

Abramowitz, J. S., Franklin, M. E., & Foa, E. B. (2002). Empirical status of cognitive behavioral therapy for obsessive compulsive disorder: A meta-analytic review. *Romanian Journal of Cognitive and Behavioral Therapy, 2*, 89–104.

Abramowitz, J. S., Whiteside, S. P., & Deacon, R. J. (2005). The effectiveness of treatment for pediatric obsessive-compulsive disorder: A meta-analysis. *Behavior Therapy, 36*, 55–63.

American Psychiatric Association. (2013). *Diagnostic and Statistical Manual of Mental Disorders* (5th edn). Washington, DC: American Psychiatric Association.

Anderson, R. A. & Rees, C. S. (2007). Group versus individual cognitive behavioural treatment for obsessive-compulsive disorder: A controlled trial. *Behaviour Research and Therapy, 45*(1), 123–137.

Arch, J. J. & Abramowitz, J. S. (2015). Exposure therapy for obsessive-compulsive disorder: An optimizing inhibitory learning approach. *Journal of Obsessive-Compulsive and Related Disorders, 6*, 174–182.

Askland, K. D., Garnaat, S., Sibrava, N. J., Boisseau, C. L., Strong, D., Mancebo, M., Greenberg, B., Rasmussen, S., & Eisen, J. (2015). Prediction of remission in obsessive compulsive disorder using a novel machine learning strategy. *International Journal of Methods in Psychiatry Research, 24*(2), 156–169.

Azrin, N. H. & Nunn, R. G. (1973). Habit-reversal: A method of eliminating nervous habits and tics. *Behaviour Research and Therapy, 11*, 619–628.

Barrett, P.M., Farrell, L. J., Dadds, M., & Boulter, N. (2005). Cognitive-behavioral family treatment of childhood obsessive-compulsive disorder: Long-term follow-up and predictors of outcome. *Journal of the American Academy of Child & Adolescent Psychiatry, 44*, 1005–1014.

Barrett, P., Healy-Farrell, L., & March, J. S. (2004). Cognitive-behavioral family treatment of childhood obsessive-compulsive disorder: A controlled trial. *Journal of the American Academy of Child and Adolescent Psychiatry, 43*(1), 46–62.

Baxter, L. (1994). Positron emission tomography studies of cerebral glucose metabolism in obsessive-compulsive disorder. *Journal of Clinical Psychiatry, 55* (Suppl.), 54–59.

Bloch, M. H., Landeros-Weisenberger, A. L., Dombrowski P., Kelmendi, B., Wegner, R., Nudel, J., Pittenger, C., Leckman, J. F., & Coric, V. (2007). Systematic review: Pharmacological and behavioral treatment for trichotillomania. *Biological Psychiatry, 62*, 839–846.

Casey, B. J., Oliveri, M. E., & Insel, T. (2014). A neurodevelopmental perspective on the research domain criteria (RDoC) framework. *Biological Psychiatry, 76*(5), 350–353.

Clark, L. A., Cuthbert, B., Lewis-Fernández, R., Narrow, W. E., & Reed, G. M. (2017). Three approaches to understanding and classifying mental disorder: *ICD-11, DSM-5*, and the National Institute of Mental Health's Research Domain Criteria (RDoC). *Psychological Science in the Public Interest, 18*(2), 72–145.

Cottraux, J., Note, I., Nan Yao, S., Lafont, S., Note, B., Mollard, E., … Dartigues, J. F. (2001). A randomized controlled trial of cognitive therapy versus intensive behavior therapy in obsessive-compulsive disorder. *Psychotherapy and Psychosomatics 70*, 288–297.

Deacon, B. J. (2013). The biomedical model of mental disorder: A critical analysis of its validity, utility, and effects on psychotherapy research. *Clinical Psychology Review, 33*(7), 846–861.

de Haan, E., Hoodgum, K. A. L., Buitelaar, J. K., & Keijsers, G. (1998). Behavior therapy versus clomipramine in obsessive-compulsive disorders in children and adolescents. *Journal of the American Academy of Child & Adolescent Psychiatry, 37*, 1022–1029.

DeVeaugh-Geiss, J., Moroz, G., Biederman, J., Cantwell, D. P., Fontaine, R., Greist, J. H., … Landau, P. (1992). Clomipramine hydrochloride in childhood and adolescent obsessive-compulsive disorder: A multicenter trial. *Journal of the American Academy of Child and Adolescent Psychiatry, 31*, 45–49.

Dougherty, D. D., Loh, R., Jenike, M. A., & Keuthen, N. J. (2006).Single modality versus dual modality treatment for trichotillomania: Sertraline, behavioral therapy, or both? *Journal of Clinical Psychiatry, 67*, 1086–1092.

Farrell, L. J., Schlup, B., & Boshcen, M. J. (2010). Cognitive-behavioral treatment of childhood obsessive-compulsive disorder in community-based clinical practice:

Clinical significance and benchmarking against efficacy. *Behaviour Research & Therapy*, *48*, 409–417.

Flessner, C. A., Penzel, F., Trichotillomania Learning Center–Scientific Advisory Board, & Keuthen, N. J. (2010). Current treatment practices for children and adults with trichotillomania: Consensus among experts. *Cognitive and Behavioral Practice*, *17*, 290–300.

Foa, E. B., Abramowitz, J. S., Franklin, M. E., & Kozak, M. J. (1999). Feared consequences, fixity of belief, and treatment outcome in patients with obsessive-compulsive disorder. *Behavior Therapy*, *30*(4), 717–724.

Foa, E. B. & Kozak, M. J. (1986). Emotional processing of fear: Exposure to corrective information. *Psychological Bulletin*, *99*(1), 20–35.

Foa, E. B. & Kozak, M. J. (1995). *DSM-IV* field trial: Obsessive-compulsive disorder. *American Journal of Psychiatry*, *152*(1), 90–96.

Foa, E. B. & Kozak, M. J. (1996). Psychological treatment for obsessive-compulsive disorder. In M. R. Mavissakalian & R. F. Prien (eds.), *Long-Term Treatments of Anxiety Disorders* (pp. 285–309). Arlington, VA: American Psychiatric Association.

Foa, E. B., Kozak, M. J., Goodman, W. K., Hollander, E., Jenike, M. A., & Rasmussen, S. A. (1995). "*DSM-IV* field trial: Obsessive-compulsive disorder": Correction. *American Journal of Psychiatry*, *152*(4), 654.

Foa, E. B., Liebowitz, M. R., Kozak, M. J., Davies, S., Campeas, R., Franklin, M. E., … Tu, X. (2005). Randomized, placebo-controlled trial of exposure and ritual prevention, clomipramine, and their combination in the treatment of obsessive-compulsive disorder. *American Journal of Psychiatry*, *162*(1), 151–161.

Foa, E. B., Yadin, E., & Lichner, T. K. (2012). *Exposure and Response (Ritual) Prevention for Obsessive-Compulsive Disorder: Therapist Guide* (2nd edn). New York, NY: Oxford University Press.

Frank, H., Stewart, E., Walther, M., Benito, K., Freeman, J., Conelea, C., & Garcia, A. (2014). Hoarding behavior among young children with obsessive-compulsive disorder. *Journal of Obsessive-Compulsive and Related Disorders*, *3*(1), 6–11.

Franklin, M. E., Edson, A. L., Ledley, D. A., & Cahill, S. P. (2011). Behavior therapy for pediatric trichotillomania: A randomized controlled trial. *Journal of the American Academy of Child & Adolescent Psychiatry*, *50*(8), 763–771.

Franklin, M. E. & Foa, E. B. (2011). Treatment of obsessive compulsive disorder. *Annual Review of Clinical Psychology*, *7*, 229–243.

Franklin, M. E., Kozak, M. J., Cashman, L. A., Coles, M. E., Rheingold, A. A., & Foa, E. B. (1998). Cognitive-behavioral treatment of pediatric obsessive-compulsive disorder: An open clinical trial. *Journal of the American Academy of Child & Adolescent Psychiatry*, *37*(4), 412–419.

Franklin, M. E., Kratz, H. E., Freeman, J. B., Ivarsson, T., Heyman, I., Sookman, D., … March, J. (2015). Cognitive-behavioral therapy for pediatric obsessive-compulsive disorder: Empirical review and clinical recommendations. *Psychiatry Research*, *227*(1), 78–92.

Franklin, M. E., Sapyta, J., Freeman, J. B., Khanna, M., Compton, S., Almirall, D., … March, J. S. (2011). Cognitive behavior therapy augmentation of pharmacotherapy in pediatric obsessive compulsive disorder: The pediatric OCD treatment study II randomized controlled trial. *Journal of the American Medical Association*, *306*, 1224–1232.

Franklin, M. E., Zagrabbe, K., & Benavides, K. L. (2011). Trichotillomania and its treatment: A review and recommendations. *Expert Review of Neurotherapeutics, 11*(8), 1165–1174.

Freeman, J. B., Garcia, A. M., Coyne, L., Ale, C., Przeworski, A., Himle, M., … Leonard, H. L. (2008). Early childhood OCD: Preliminary findings from a family-based cognitive-behavioral approach. *Journal of the American Academy of Child and Adolescent Psychiatry, 47*, 593–602.

Freeman, J., Sapyta, J., Garcia, A., Compton, S., Khanna, M., Flessner, C., … Franklin, M. (2014). Family-based treatment of early childhood obsessive-compulsive disorder: The pediatric obsessive-compulsive disorder treatment study for young children (POTS Jr.): A randomized clinical trial. *JAMA Psychiatry, 71*(6): 689–698.

Frost, R. O. & Hartl, T. L. (1996). A cognitive-behavioral model of compulsive hoarding. *Behaviour Research and Therapy, 34*(4), 341–350.

Frost, R. O., Steketee, G., & Williams, L. (2002). Compulsive buying, compulsive hoarding, and obsessive-compulsive disorder. *Behavior Therapy, 33*(2), 201–214.

Garcia, A. M., Sapyta, J. J., Moore, P. S., Freeman, J. B., Franklin, M. E., March, J. S., & Foa, E. B. (2010). Predictors and moderators of treatment outcome in the pediatric obsessive compulsive treatment study (POTS I). *Journal of the American Academy of Child and Adolescent Psychiatry, 49*(10), 1024–1033.

Grant, J. E., Odlaug, B. L., & Kim, S. W. (2009). *N*-acetylcysteine, a glutamate modulator, in the treatment of trichotillomania. *Archives of General Psychiatry, 66*, 756–763.

Gunstad, J. & Phillips, K. A. (2003). Axis I comorbidity in body dysmorphic disorder. *Comprehensive Psychiatry, 44*(4), 270–276.

Harrison, A., Fernández de la Cruz, L. Enander, J., Radua, J., & Mataix-Cols, D. (2016). Cognitive-behavioral therapy for body dysmorphic disorder: A systematic review and meta-analysis of randomized controlled trials. *Clinical Psychology Review, 48*, 43–51.

Hershenberg, R. & Goldfried, M. R. (2015). Implications of RDoC for the research and practice of psychotherapy. *Behavior Therapy, 46*(2), 156–165.

Hirschtritt, M. E., Pauls, D. L., Dion, Y., Grados, M. A., Illmann, C., King, R. A., … Mathews, C. A. (2015). Lifetime prevalence, age of risk, and genetic relationships of comorbid psychiatric disorders in Tourette syndrome. *JAMA Psychiatry, 72*(4),325–333.

Kozak, M. J. & Cuthbert, B. N. (2016). The NIMH research domain criteria initiative: Background, issues, and pragmatics. *Psychophysiology, 53*(3), 286–297.

Højgaard, D. R. M. A., Mortensen, E. L., Ivarsson, T., Hybel, K., Skarphedinsson, G., Nissen, J. B., … Thomsen, P. H. (2017). Structure and clinical correlates of obsessive-compulsive symptoms in a large sample of children and adolescents: A factor analytic study across five nations. *European Child & Adolescent Psychiatry, 26*(3), 281–291.

Huang, F., Li, Z., Han, H., Xiong, H., & Ma, Y. (2013). Cognitive behavioral therapy combined with pharmacotherapy for obsessive compulsive disorder: A meta-analysis. *Chinese Mental Health Journal, 27*(9), 643–649.

Iniesta, R., Stahl, D., & McGuffin, P. (2016). Machine learning, statistical learning, and the future of biological research in psychiatry. *Psychological Medicine, 46*, 2455–2465.

Insel, T. R., Cuthbert, B. N., Garvey, M. A., Heinssen, R. K., Pine, D. S., Quinn, K. J., Sanislow, C., & Wang, P. S. (2010). Research domain criteria (RDoC): Toward a new classification framework for research on mental disorders. *American Journal of Psychiatry*, *167*, 748–751.

Ivarsson, T., Skarphedinsson, G., Kornør, H., Axelsdottir, B., Biedilæ, S., Heyman, I., … March, J. (2015). The place of and evidence for serotonin reuptake inhibitors (SRIs) for obsessive compulsive disorder (OCD) in children and adolescents: Views based on a systematic review and meta-analysis. *Psychiatry Research*, *227*(1), 93–103.

Koran, L. M., Hanna, G. L., Hollander, E., Nestadt, G., & Simpson, H. B. (2007). American Psychiatric Association practice guidelines for the treatment of patients with obsessive-compulsive disorder. *American Journal of Psychiatry*, *164*(7 Suppl.), 5–53.

Kozak, M. J. & Cuthbert, B. N. (2016). The NIMH research domain criteria initiative: Background, issues, and pragmatics. *Psychophysiology*, *53*(3), 286–297.

Krebs, G., Fernández de la Cruz, L., Monzani, B., Bowyer, L., Anson, M., Cadman, J., … Mataix-Cols, D. (2017). Long-term outcomes of cognitive-behavioral therapy for adolescent body dysmorphic disorder. *Behavior Therapy*, *48*(4), 462–473.

Kuhn, T. S. (1977). *The Essential Tension: Selected Studies in Tradition and Change.* Chicago, IL: Chicago University Press.

Lerner, J., Franklin, M. E., Meadows, E. A., Hembree, E., & Foa, E. B. (1998).Effectiveness of a cognitive-behavioral treatment program for trichotillomania: An uncontrolled evaluation. *Behavior Therapy*, *29*, 157–171.

Ma, J. D., Wang, C. H., Li, H. F., Zhang, X. L., Zhang, Y. L., Hou, Y. H., Liu, X. H., & Hu, X. Z. (2013). Article I. Cognitive-coping therapy for obsessive-compulsive disorder: A randomized controlled trial. *Journal of Psychiatry Research*, *47*(11), 1785–1790.

March, J. & Mulle, K. (1998). *OCD in Children and Adolescents: A Cognitive-Behavioral Treatment Manual.* New York, NY: Guilford Press.

Marks, I. M., Lelliott, P. T., Basoglu, M., Noshiravani, H., et al. (1988). Clomipramine, self-exposure, and therapist-aided exposure for obsessive-compulsive rituals. *British Journal of Psychiatry*, *152*, 522–534.

Mataix-Cols, D., Fernández de la Cruz, L., Isomura, K., Anson, M., Turner, C., Monzani, B., … Krebs, G. (2015). A pilot randomized controlled trial of cognitive-behavioral therapy for adolescents with body dysmorphic disorder. *Journal of the American Academy of Child & Adolescent Psychiatry*, *54*(11), 895–904.

Nazari, H., Momeni, N., Jariani, M., & Tarrahi, M. J. (2011). Comparison of eye movement desensitization and reprocessing with citalopram in treatment of obsessive-compulsive disorder. *International Journal of Psychiatry in Clinical Practice*, *15*(4), 270–274.

Olatunji, B. O., Davis, M. L., Powers, M. B., & Smits, J. A. J. (2013). Cognitive-behavioral therapy for obsessive-compulsive disorder: A meta-analysis of treatment outcome and moderators. *Journal of Psychiatric Research*, *47*(1), 33–41.

Olatunji, B. O., Rosenfield, D., Tart, C. D., Cottraux, J., Powers, M. B., & Smits, J. A. J. (2013). Behavioral versus cognitive treatment of obsessive-compulsive disorder: An examination of outcome and mediators of change. *Journal of Consulting and Clinical Psychology*, *81*(3), 415–428.

Pediatric OCD Treatment Study Team. (2004). Cognitive-behavioral therapy, sertraline, and their combination for children and adolescents with obsessive-compulsive disorder: The pediatric OCD treatment study (POTS) randomized controlled trial. *Journal of the American Medical Association, 292*(16), 1969–1976.

Peters, A. T., Jacobs, R. H., Feldhaus, C., Henry, D. B., Albano, A. M., Langenecker, S. A., … Curry, J. F. (2016). Trajectories of functioning into emerging adulthood following treatment for adolescent depression. *Journal of Adolescent Health, 58*(3), 253–259.

Phillips, K. A., Albertini, R. S., & Rasmussen, S. A. (2002). A randomized placebo-controlled trial of fluoxetine in body dysmorphic disorder. *Archives of General Psychiatry, 59*(4), 381–388.

Phillips, K. A., Keshaviah, A., Dougherty, D. D., Stout, R. L., Menard, W., & Wilhelm, S. (2016). Pharmacotherapy relapse prevention in body dysmorphic disorder: A double-blind, placebo-controlled trial. *American Journal of Psychiatry, 173*(9), 887–895.

Phillips, K. A., Menard, W., Pagano, M., Fay, C., & Stout, R. (2006). Delusional versus nondelusional body dysmorphic disorder: Clinical features and course of illness. *Journal of Psychiatric Research, 40*(2), 95–104.

Phillips, K. A., Stein, D. J., Rauch, S. L., Hollander, E., Fallon, B. A., Barsky, A., … Leckman, J. (2010). Should an obsessive-compulsive spectrum grouping of disorders be included in *DSM-V*? *Depression and Anxiety, 27*(6), 528–555.

Piacentini, J., Bergman, R. L., Chang, S., Landley, A., Peris, T., Wood, J. J., & McCracken, J. (2011). Controlled comparison of family cognitive behavioral therapy and psychoeducation/relaxation training for child obsessive-compulsive disorder. *Journal of the American Academy of Child & Adolescent Psychiatry, 50*(11), 1149–1161.

Roessner, V., Hoekstra, P. J., & Rothenberger, A. (2011). Tourette's disorder and other tic disorders in *DSM-5*: A comment. *European Child & Adolescent Psychiatry, 20*(2), 71–74.

Selles, R. R., McGuire, J. F., Small, B. J., & Storch, E. A. (2016). A systematic review and meta-analysis of psychiatric treatments for excoriation (skin-picking) disorder. *General Hospital Psychiatry, 41*, 29–37.

Simpson, H. B., Foa, E. B., Liebowitz, M. R., Huppert, J. D., Cahill, S., Maher, M. J., … Campeas, R. (2013). Cognitive-behavioral therapy vs risperidone for augmenting serotonin reuptake inhibitors in obsessive-compulsive disorder: A randomized clinical trial. *JAMA Psychiatry, 70*(11), 1190–1198.

Simpson, H., Foa, E., Liebowitz, M., Ledley, D., Huppert, J., Cahill, S., … Franklin, M. (2008). A randomized, controlled trial of cognitive-behavioral therapy for augmenting pharmacotherapy in obsessive-compulsive disorder. *American Journal of Psychiatry, 65*, 621–630.

Simpson, H. B., Maher, M. J., Wang, Y., Bao, Y., Foa, E. B., & Franklin, M. (2011). Patient adherence predicts outcome from cognitive behavioral therapy in obsessive-compulsive disorder. *Journal of Consulting and Clinical Psychology, 79*(2), 247–252.

Steketee, G. & Frost, R. O. (2014). *Treatment for Hoarding Disorder: Therapist Guide* (2nd edn). New York, NY: Oxford University Press.

Storch, E. A., Geffken, G. R., Merlo, L. J., Mann, G., Duke, D., Munson, M., … Goodman, W. K. (2007). Family-based cognitive-behavioral therapy for pediatric obsessive-compulsive disorder: Comparison of intensive and weekly approaches. *Journal of the American Academy of Child and Adolescent Psychiatry, 46*(4), 469–478.

Storch, E. A., Wilhelm, S., Sprich, S., Henin, A., Micco, J., Small, B. J., … Geller, D. A. (2016). Efficacy of augmentation of cognitive behavior therapy with weight-adjusted D-cycloserine vs placebo in pediatric obsessive-compulsive disorder: A randomized clinical trial. *JAMA Psychiatry*, *73*(8), 779–788.

Thompson, C., Fernández de la Cruz, L., Mataix-Cols, D., & Onwumere, J. (2017). A systematic review and quality assessment of psychological, pharmacological, and family-based interventions for hoarding disorder. *Asian Journal of Psychiatry*, *27*, 53–66.

Tolin, D. F., Frost, R. O., Steketee, G., & Muroff, J. (2015). Cognitive behavioral therapy for hoarding disorder: A meta-analysis. *Depression and Anxiety*, *32*(3), 158–166.

Torp, N. C., Dahl, K., Skarphedinsson, G., Thomson, P. H., Valderhaug, R., Weidle, B., … Ivarsson, T. (2015). Effectiveness of cognitive behavior treatment for pediatric obsessive compulsive disorder: Acute outcomes from the Nordic Long-Term OCD Treatment Study (NordLOTS). *Behaviour Research and Therapy*, *64*, 15–23.

Twohig, M. P., Hayes, S. C., Plumb, J. C., Pruitt, L. D., Collins, A. B., Hazlett-Stevens, H., & Woidneck, M. R. (2010). A randomized clinical trial of acceptance and commitment therapy versus progressive relaxation training for obsessive-compulsive disorder. *Journal of Consulting and Clinical Psychology*, *78*(5), 705–716.

Valderhaug, R., Larsson, B., Götestam, K. G., & Piacentini, J. (2007). An open clinical trial of cognitive-behaviour therapy in children and adolescents with obsessive-compulsive disorder administered in regular outpatient clinics. *Behaviour Research and Therapy*, *45*(3), 577–589.

Wheaton, M. G., Abramowitz, J. S., Fabricant, L. E., Berman, N. C., & Franklin, J. C. (2011). Is hoarding a symptom of obsessive-compulsive disorder? *International Journal of Cognitive Therapy*, *4*(3), 225–238.

Whittal, M. L., Thordarson, D. S., & McLean, P. D. (2005). Treatment of obsessive-compulsive disorder: Cognitive behavior therapy vs. exposure and response prevention. *Behaviour Research and Therapy*, *42*(12), 1559–1576.

Woods, D. W., Flessner, C. A., Franklin, M. E., Wetterneck, C. T., Walther, M., Anderson, E., & Cardona, D .(2006). Understanding and treating trichotillomania: What we know and what we don't know. *Psychiatric Clinics of North America*, *29*, 487–501.

Woods, D. W. & Houghton, D. C. (2014). Diagnosis, evaluation, and management of trichotillomania. *Psychiatric Clinics of North America*, *37*(3), 301–317.

30 Trauma- and Stressor-Related Disorders

Andrew M. Sherrill and Sheila A. M. Rauch

Introduction

The menu of interventions for posttraumatic stress disorder (PTSD) is expansive and diverse. Much like a restaurant patron investigating a dense and comprehensive list of entrées, the trauma clinician faces a blessing and a curse. The blessing is many effective options. The possibility of satisfying every restaurant patron seems to increase with greater numbers of entrées. However, what if the restaurant has one or two "can't miss" dishes that far exceed the quality of the other options? The curse of the expansive menu is that you might overlook the best choice in favor of what is familiar and safe or, on the other hand, exotic and novel. The first objective of this chapter is to help orient trauma clinicians to the best options on the menu as determined by the empirical literature.

More than 30 years of research now provide clear support for a few leading "entrées." The two psychotherapies with the most consistent empirical and theoretical support are prolonged exposure (PE) (Foa, Hembree, & Rothbaum, 2007) and cognitive processing therapy (CPT) (Resick, Monson, & Chard, 2017), which are described in detail in what follows. However, despite near-universal recommendation of these interventions by professional associations and government bodies, clinicians often fail to offer them to their patients with PTSD. While the reasons for this are many, clinicians often cite a sense that patients may not accept these interventions or that they believe patients may not be ready or able to do them (Cook, Dinnen, Simiola, Thompson, & Schnurr, 2014). Fortunately, treatment receptivity and suitability are empirical questions and, as this chapter reviews, the data suggest the use of PE and CPT in diverse contexts and populations and with few contraindications. How can we improve utilization rates of PE and CPT? The second objective of this chapter is to orient trauma researchers and policy makers to consume and participate in the emerging field of implementation science to improve the availability of first-line PTSD treatments.

Emergence of Evidence-Based Practices

Assessment

Although this chapter focuses on interventions, it is critical to acknowledge that evidence-based practice begins with evidence-based assessment, not the simple pairing of a manual to a diagnosis (Hunsley & Mash, 2005). Evidence-based assessment requires clinicians, clinic managers, and policy makers to integrate clinical expertise with patient preferences and systematically collected data using psychometrically sound methods. An evidence-based approach also necessitates continuous reassessment of patients during treatment and programs as a whole, followed by making necessary adjustments. Guidelines for evidence-based assessment are beyond the scope of this chapter. However, any trauma clinician should become familiar with gold-standard assessment tools for trauma-related pathology, which are outlined in Chapter 13 of this volume. Moreover, given that evidence-based assessment includes multicultural sensitivity and responsiveness, trauma clinicians should become familiar with cultural considerations in anxiety-, trauma-, and stressor-related disorders, which are outlined in Chapter 14 of this volume.

Diagnostic classification systems are an essential component in evidence-based assessment. However, a list of symptoms does not inform a clinician's understanding of how a condition developed or can be treated, which is often the desired outcome of an evidence-based assessment. In *DSM-5* (American Psychiatric Association [APA], 2013), PTSD and its often-preceding condition called acute stress disorder (ASD) are not grouped in the "Anxiety Disorders" section and no longer emphasize peri-traumatic reactions, as was done previously in *DSM-IV-TR* (APA, 2000). These changes should not affect how PTSD is conceptualized by evidence-based interventions and their theoretical frameworks (e.g., PE and emotional processing theory) (Foa & Kozak, 1986). The underlying processes of PTSD (e.g., physiology, neurobiology, information processing, and learning) are indeed consistent with anxiety disorders (Zoellner, Pruitt, Farach, & Jun, 2014). Moreover, peri-traumatic reactions such as dissociation and fear can explain long-term, anxiety-based reactions to trauma content (Bovin & Marx, 2011).

PTSD and ASD are now placed into a new section called "Trauma- and Stressor-Related Disorders," along with adjustment disorders and two childhood disorders called reactive attachment disorder and disinhibited social engagement disorder. This new section emphasizes static environmental histories (e.g., exposure to traumatic events), not malleable anxiety processes (e.g., conditioned fear responses and maladaptive avoidance strategies). Unlike PTSD, little is known about how to treat reactive attachment disorder or disinhibited social engagement disorder. It is unknown if insights related to PTSD will generalize to these conditions or vice versa. Therefore, the utility of the Trauma- and Stressor-Related Disorders section in *DSM-5* is unclear and additional research is needed to determine what unites these diagnoses beyond historic exposure to trauma.

Thankfully, evidence-based assessment is not driven by *DSM-5* but rather uses *DSM-5* as a potentially helpful tool. To use this tool appropriately, trauma clinicians must pay particular attention to differential diagnosis. Distress and dysphoria are features of many emotional disorders including PTSD, major depressive disorder (MDD), and generalized anxiety disorder (GAD), which explains high comorbidity rates. Differential diagnosis requires strong clinical interviewing skills to determine if distress and dysphoria are secondary effects of fear-based processes of reexperiencing and avoidance, which are the core features of PTSD (Zoellner et al., 2014). This distinction often hinges on symptom onset (e.g., before or after trauma) and conducting brief functional analyses (e.g., avoiding pleasurable activities and social settings due to trauma reminders rather than fear of embarrassment or entrapment). False positives for PTSD can result when patients present with GAD or MDD and happen to have a trauma history, which not only results in ineffective treatment planning but can also inappropriately create negative impressions in patients and clinicians about the treatability of PTSD. Decades of research indicates that PTSD and related disorders such as GAD and MDD are treatable conditions, though only accurate assessment can ensure patients are offered appropriate evidence-based interventions.

Psychotherapy

As stated earlier, the menu of psychotherapy options for PTSD is expansive, which has benefits and drawbacks with respect to (a) providing adequate care and (b) implementing evidence-based practices. Over the past two decades, many researchers have synthesized the clinical trial literature using systematic reviews and meta-analyses (Bisson, Roberts, Andrew, Cooper, & Lewis, 2013; Cusack et al., 2016; Ehlers et al., 2010; Foa & Meadows, 1997; Harvey, Bryant, & Tarrier, 2003; Roberts et al., 2015). A pessimistic view of the variety of treatments is that it indicates the field is not close to consensus with respect to how to conceptualize and treat PTSD. However, the majority of reviews indicate the treatments with the strongest empirical and theoretical support focus on maladaptive trauma-related memories, emotions, thoughts, and behaviors and share many overlapping strategies. These treatments are broadly referred to as "trauma-focused psychotherapies" (TFPs) and can be grouped by their primary active ingredient: exposure therapy (e.g., PE) and cognitive therapy (e.g., CPT).

This chapter prioritizes discussion of treatments that are supported by high-quality clinical trials. The quality of a given study is determined by the degree of adherence to the following best practices in PTSD treatment research: clearly defined target symptoms, valid measurement, randomization blindness among all staff and especially outcome assessors (plus confirmation of blindness), assessor training, manualized treatment protocols, unbiased assignment to treatment conditions, treatment and assessment fidelity assessments and corrections, and patient engagement in protocol-specific tasks (Foa & Meadows, 1997; Harvey et al., 2003). Several promising and innovative treatments are not reviewed in this chapter due to not meeting all of these high standards of investigation in the peer-reviewed literature. Additionally, several treatments that, at best, have been shown to outperform non-treatment controls will not be discussed. For many years, PTSD has proven to be a treatable condition. We now need to know the best treatments for particular patients, complaints, and settings.

Psychotherapy with strong efficacy support. In general, meta-analyses and systematic reviews support TFPs (Bisson et al., 2013; Cusack et al., 2016; Lee et al., 2016; Watts et al., 2013). However, TFPs are not equally effective, nor do they address the same problems equally for all the same patients. Simply focusing on trauma-related processes does not indicate that empirical support for similar therapies "carry over." Unfortunately, the vaguely defined category of TFPs has interfered with appropriate interpretations of the literature (Benish, Imel, & Wampold, 2008; Ehlers et al., 2010). Therefore, we create a distinction between TFPs emphasizing primarily either exposure therapy or cognitive therapy. Within each of these categories, we articulate which specific protocols have the strongest empirical support.

Exposure therapy. Exposure therapy for PTSD has received the most attention in clinical trials, especially PE (Foa et al., 2007). PE is based on emotional processing theory (Foa & Kozak, 1986), which conceptualizes PTSD as a pathological manifestation of a fear structure for "escaping danger" that includes representations for fear stimuli, fear responses, and meaning associated with the stimuli and responses. This fear structure is maintained by unhelpful avoidance and thoughts. In order to change the fear structure, PE asks patients to approach distressing trauma-related stimuli and memories until patients experience reduced levels of distress (in general and when encountering traumatic content) and understand that they can handle trauma-related distress without avoidance or use of unhelpful coping strategies.

The standard PE protocol requires 10–15 90-minute sessions (Foa et al., 2007) that almost exclusively emphasize preparing for, conducting, and processing imaginal exposure and *in vivo* exposure. Imaginal exposure involves repeatedly revisiting the index trauma(s) by closing one's eyes while using the present tense to describe all actions, sensations, thoughts, and emotions that occurred. On rare occasions, patients may opt to facilitate this process using paper and pen (i.e., written exposure). *In vivo* exposure involves systematic and gradual engagement in an increasingly challenging hierarchy of safe trauma reminders as well as conditions habitually avoided or tolerated with great distress. When indicated and available, each exposure modality can be facilitated by virtual reality technology. All exposure practices, especially imaginal exposures, are processed with the clinician in order to refine helpful perspectives and thoughts. PE also has components of psychoeducation and stress management (breathing retraining) that facilitate engagement but are not considered active ingredients. PE is flexible in that some components can be delivered in groups (e.g., psychoeducation, stress management, and *in vivo* exposure) and session frequency can adjust to different settings (once per week, twice per week, or daily).

The empirical support for PE is strong. Large treatment effects are consistently demonstrated for PTSD and secondary outcomes (e.g., depression, anxiety, and quality of life) across trauma types (e.g., combat vs. rape) and regardless of time since trauma (Powers et al., 2010). Further, recent studies have demonstrated that patients benefit despite carrying multiple comorbidities such as dissociation, borderline personality disorder, psychosis, substance use disorders, and major depression (e.g., van Minnen, Harned, Zoellner, & Mills, 2012). Despite these encouraging findings, many trauma clinicians do not recommend PE due to concerns that comorbidities, low motivation, and low cognitive functioning may interfere with treatment adherence (Cook, Dinnen, Simiola et al., 2014). Myths that PTSD patients are too fragile for PE, or that PE is insufficient and ungeneralizable to the real world, have long been documented and refuted (Feeny, Hembree, & Zoellner, 2003). These non-empirically based beliefs likely contribute to low rates of PE use, even among those who have received training (Rosen et al., 2016). For this reason, this chapter strongly emphasizes the need to use implementation science to facilitate the accessibility and quality of PE treatment in nonacademic contexts.

In addition to PE, several trauma-focused exposure therapies have sufficient evidence to demonstrate effectiveness, even if their literature base is small in comparison to PE. Treatments that use learning theories as a basis for their frameworks include narrative exposure therapy (NET) (Ertl, Pfeiffer, Schauer, Elbert, & Neuner, 2011; Stenmark, Catani, Neuner, Elbert, & Holen, 2013), written exposure therapy (WET) (Resick et al., 2008; Sloan, Marx, Bovin, Feinstein, & Gallagher, 2012), and reconsolidation of traumatic memories (RTM) (Gray & Bourke, 2015). Other therapies use exposure practices, though the mechanism of change is unclear and the evidence base much less (brief eclectic psychotherapy, Gersons, Carlier, Lamberts, & van der Kolk, 2000; eye movement desensitization and reprocessing [EMDR], Shapiro, 1995). Theory suggests that these treatments may operate through similar mechanisms of action as PE (Rauch & Liberzon, 2016). However, research to illuminate the specific mechanisms underlying each individual protocol is extremely costly and difficult.

EMDR is a TFP that is occasionally categorized as an exposure therapy and other times given its own category, outside the umbrella of cognitive behavioral therapies. The standard EMDR protocol (Shapiro, 1995) involves exposing patients to specific trauma-related images and thoughts while inducing a dual attention task, namely saccadic eye movements. The patient then attends to current thoughts, sensations, and physical reactions related to the trauma. During this process, the clinician identifies useful moments to cue thought-stopping and the development and acceptance of positive thoughts related to the trauma.

Findings largely indicate that EMDR is similarly efficacious as PE (e.g., Rothbaum, Astin, & Marsteller, 2005), with some evidence that PE is more effective in reducing the hallmark PTSD symptoms of reexperiencing and avoidance (Taylor et al., 2003). However, the mechanisms involved in EMDR are unclear – this remains an area ripe for research not just within EMDR but also the larger field of cognitive science. The dual attention task is not used in any other treatment for any other disorder and it first emerged from anecdotal experience of its original developer, not basic research. Several hypotheses for the mechanism underlying dual attention tasks have been explored including respondent conditioning (i.e., memory paired with lower arousal resulting from eye movements), mindfulness-like distancing and free association, orientating to trauma content without avoidance, enhancing retrieval of episodic memory by increasing interhemispheric interaction, and reducing vividness of trauma content due to taxing working memory (Gunter & Bodner, 2009; Jeffries & Davis, 2013). Dismantling studies demonstrate that neither the dual attention tasks (e.g., eye movements) nor cognitive elements contribute to outcome (Cahill, Carrigan, & Frueh, 1999; Cusack & Spates, 1999). The most parsimonious and scientifically conservative view is that EMDR is an imaginal exposure therapy that may benefit from a dual attention task that modulates the tolerability of exposures.

Surely, no psychotherapy has a perfect explanation or evidence for its mechanism of action. The empirical status of treatment mechanisms has become increasingly important and yet still understudied (Kazdin, 2007; Rauch & Liberzon, 2016). In the end, we may find that many treatments may operate through similar processes; however, clinical scientists and evidence-based clinicians have given greater attention to treatments with demonstrable mechanisms. Efforts to identify mechanisms of change is not mere explanation; rather, mechanism research promises to improve conceptual frameworks and intervention strategies. When mechanisms are ambiguous, it is difficult for patients, clinicians, and researchers to monitor treatment gains and refine approaches. Compared to other treatments for PTSD and other anxiety-based disorders, exposure therapy is supported strongly by theory, whether viewed from the perspective of emotional processing theory (Rauch & Foa, 2006) or inhibitory learning (Craske et al., 2008). Since multiple mechanisms are at work on PE, a provider may use continuous feedback of changes in trauma-related cognitions in therapy to monitor progress. Additionally, the provider may use within- and between-session galvanic skin response during exposures to provide feedback on extinction processes in treatment. However, the field has yet to solidly demonstrate and replicate many of the purported causal mechanisms. Rather than invest more resources in developing and studying the effectiveness of arguably redundant therapies, a prudent approach to move the field forward would be to prioritize research that seeks to understand how effective treatments such as PE work (Rauch & Liberzon, 2016) and then build on what we learn.

Cognitive therapy. TFPs primarily emphasizing cognitive restructuring have garnered empirical support as well. Consistent with classical cognitive therapy (Beck, 1976), this treatment is based on the assumption that appraisals of events determine emotions and behaviors. Therefore, the central therapeutic technique of cognitive therapy is developing the skills of identifying unhelpful trauma-related thoughts, challenging these thoughts, and then developing and accepting helpful thoughts.

The most studied cognitive therapy for PTSD is CPT (Resick et al., 2017). In this treatment, traumatic events are theorized to weaken previously held positive beliefs about oneself, the world, and the future or strengthen previously held negative beliefs about oneself, the world, and the future. CPT uses social cognitive theory to categorize two types of problematic thoughts: assimilation and over-accommodation. Assimilated thoughts involve interpreting the trauma in such a way that it helps the person make sense of the trauma given previously held beliefs (e.g., "Since only bad things happen to bad people, I must be bad"). Over-accommodated thoughts involve changing previously held beliefs in order to make sense of the trauma (e.g., "I now know that all men are dangerous"). CPT anticipates that most patients with PTSD will have problematic over-accommodated thoughts within the themes of safety, trust, control, esteem, and intimacy. The goal of cognitive restructuring in CPT is to help the patient develop and accept balanced accommodations such as "Sometimes bad things happen to good people," or "There are dangerous men in the world but most men do not assault women."

Originally, CPT included a written account of the traumatic event that the patient would read between sessions until habituation. The most recent iteration of the CPT protocol uses the written account as an option depending on patient preference (Resick et al., 2017). This change was motivated by a dismantling study that found CPT was just as effective without the written account in reducing PTSD and depression symptom severity (Resick et al., 2008). Further, other forms of trauma-focused cognitive therapy have demonstrated efficacy without exposure-based tasks (Ehlers, Clark, Hackmann, McManus, & Fennell, 2005). Even if cognitive therapy is sufficient as a stand-alone treatment for PTSD symptoms, clinicians may find it useful to use written accounts to facilitate habituation for patients reexperiencing during treatment procedures and to help the patient and clinician identify assimilated beliefs.

Much like exposure therapy, an important benefit of cognitive therapy is its flexibility. Preliminary support has been found for cognitive therapy for PTSD within the context of couples therapy (Monson et al., 2012), group therapy (Resick et al., 2017), and parent-child therapy (Cary & McMillen, 2012). Some preliminary evidence suggests it can be effective in as little as two sessions (Jung & Steil, 2013). However, much like exposure therapy, there is little research demonstrating causal roles in purported mechanisms of cognitive therapies for PTSD (Rauch & Liberzon, 2016). Cognitive therapies have been packaged in a wide variety of protocols and, surely, additional creative repackaging of cognitive therapies is in development. Again, a prudent approach to move the field forward would be to understand how CPT, as the most studied and used cognitive therapy, achieves its therapeutic effects.

Psychotherapy with limited efficacy support. Although there is strong evidence in support of trauma-focused exposure therapy and cognitive therapy for PTSD, it is important to acknowledge that there have not been major advances since the 1980s, when treatments for anxiety (exposure therapy) and depression (cognitive therapy) were repackaged for the treatment of PTSD (Resick, Monson, Gutner, & Maslej, 2014). These treatments receive the vast amount of resources for development, research, and implementation. Other treatments are available that do not focus on trauma-related memories and appraisals (hereafter labeled "non-TFPs") but rather emphasize coping and interpersonal skills. Several of these treatments have been shown to outperform waitlists and are occasionally not worse than established treatments like PE or CPT, though the quality of these trials varies substantially (Bisson et al., 2013; Cusack et al., 2016). Non-TFPs with some empirical support have targeted the following mechanisms of change: anxiety management (stress inoculation training; Foa et al., 1999; Meichenbaum & Deffenbacher, 1988), emotion regulation (skills training in affective and interpersonal regulation; Cloitre, Koenen, Cohen, & Han, 2002), problem-solving current stressors (present-centered therapy; Foa et al., 1999; Suris, Link-Malcolm, Chard, Ahn, & North, 2013), and healthy interpersonal relationships (interpersonal therapy; Markowitz et al., 2015).

These non-TFPs are designed specifically for PTSD but they target dysphoria and distress, which might be secondary to fear-based pathology related to trauma content (Zoellner et al., 2014). A common response to treating the heterogeneity of PTSD phenomenology is to provide phase-based treatment that targets dysphoria and distress prior to targeting maladaptive responses and appraisals to trauma content (e.g., Cloitre et al., 2002). However, more complexity in treatments (i.e., more components) has not resulted in greater effectiveness but rather higher dropout rates (Hembree et al., 2003), which may be a by-product of experiencing a greater delay from active components in the amelioration of PTSD. Mechanism research for TFPs and non-TFPs will likely add clarity to why treatments that focus on trauma-related memories and thoughts tend to be more efficacious. These insights may facilitate decisions of when to offer non-TFPs.

Psychotherapy with insufficient efficacy support. Several interventions are used frequently despite evidence of non-effectiveness, even when evidence-based TFPs are available. Overall, the most used intervention is probably unstructured supportive therapy. All evidence-based TFPs require clinicians to have strong "common factors" such as therapeutic alliance, positive regard, empathy, and genuineness. Simply put, all modalities need skilled clinicians. Further, it is reasonable to suspect that some clinicians are more effective than others using the same TFP protocol. Therapist factors matter. However, nonspecific skills and attributes in trauma clinicians should be viewed as necessary but insufficient. The use of psychoeducation also seems to be necessary but insufficient. Understanding one's diagnosis and how treatment will address symptoms is not an active treatment but it can facilitate the perceived relevance of the treatment and the patient's adherence to treatment.

In addition to unstructured supportive therapy and psychoeducation, other approaches have been used frequently despite not being subjected to clinical trials using contemporary standards. These approaches include relaxation (Marks et al., 1998; Taylor et al., 2003) as well as hypnosis and psychodynamic therapy (Brom, Kleber, & Defares, 1989). Some therapists identify as eclectic or integrative and use these relatively unsupported treatments with components of evidence-based treatments. However, no empirical evidence supports an eclectic strategy (Cusack et al., 2016). Even adding two apparently effective strategies does not appear to have an additive effect (e.g., adding cognitive restructuring to exposure treatment) (Foa et al., 2005; Marks et al., 1998).

No evidence suggests iatrogenic effects of treatments such as supportive counseling, psychoeducation, relaxation training, hypnosis, and psychodynamic therapy when used as stand-alone or eclectic treatments. However, their continued use is a barrier to the implementation of evidence-based care. Sources of this barrier vary widely but often include inaccurate clinician beliefs, underdeveloped clinician skills, and clinic constraints such as high caseloads, limited patient contact (frequency and duration of sessions), and prioritization of groups and transdiagnostic treatment protocols. This chapter provides a review of how implementation science seeks to better understand and overcome these barriers.

Pharmacotherapy

Many medications have been tested in the treatment of PTSD and associated features. However, this chapter only reviews those with supportive evidence and minimal side effects and those with contraindicating evidence. A comprehensive review is beyond the scope of this chapter (see Hoskins et al., 2015; Lee et al., 2016; Watts et al., 2013). Moreover, although non-pharmacologic biological treatments have received increased attention (e.g., electroconvulsive therapy, vagal nerve stimulation, and transcranial magnetic stimulation), these innovative approaches are not reviewed because their evidence base is underdeveloped in comparison to psychotherapies and pharmacotherapies.

Medications with strong efficacy support. To date, the medications with the most support are one serotonin-norepinephrine reuptake inhibitor (SNRI) called venlafaxine (*Effexor*) and three selective serotonin reuptake inhibitors (SSRIs) called sertraline (*Zoloft*), paroxetine (*Paxil*), and fluoxetine (*Prozac*) (Hoskins et al., 2015; Lee et al., 2016; Watts et al., 2013). However, the effect sizes for these medications are smaller than TFPs. In addition, unlike psychotherapy, these interventions have several side effects (SNRIs: increased blood pressure and withdrawal symptoms; SSRIs: sexual dysfunction, increased sweating, potential for increased suicidal thoughts, gastrointestinal upset, and fatigue).

Due to the small-to-moderate effect sizes of these medications, identifying benefits and side effects requires large clinical trials. Unfortunately, large trials that do not demonstrate significant effects are often not published. For example, an alpha-1 blocker called prazosin (*Minipress*), which has traditionally been prescribed to treat high blood pressure but now also is prescribed to treat trauma nightmares (Lee et al., 2016), was recently subjected to its first large trial and found to not outperform placebo (Cooperative Studies Program #563: Prazosin and Combat Trauma, 2016). This trial has not yet been published despite its implications. Is the prescriber-observed effect of prazosin purely placebo? It is difficult to identify the contribution of placebo effects to any given medication. However, better understanding placebo effects in PTSD psychopharmacotherapy is an area ripe for future research. Prazosin is one medication likely to benefit from placebo processes because it is described as non-psychiatric (e.g., "blood pressure medication") and induces physiological effects that are safe and internally observable.

Medications with potential iatrogenic effects. Evidence indicates that benzodiazepines are contraindicated medications for PTSD, especially alprazolam (*Xanax*) and clonazepam (*Klonopin*). However, benzodiazepines have widespread use as a primary agent or an as-needed medication despite no evidence of effectiveness. In fact, benzodiazepines may have iatrogenic effects on PTSD, aggression, depression, and substance use (Guina, Rossetter, DeRhodes, Nahhas, & Welton, 2015). Yet prescriptions and refills continue. Why? Individuals often seek medication when they experience acute reexperiencing symptoms that can be misdiagnosed as non-cued panic attacks, for which benzodiazepines are often prescribed. Unfortunately, benzodiazepines are often difficult to discontinue due to withdrawal effects. As the saying goes, these medications are "easier to prescribe than discontinue." Benzodiazepines are typically very effective in reducing short-term distress, which may initially be seen as a desirable effect for prescribers and patients. However, no evidence suggests these medications reduce long-term distress or facilitate healthy behaviors. In fact, their ability to dampen strong anxiety reactions is so robust that it has been shown to interfere with exposure-based psychotherapy, which requires physiological reactivity in order for exposure mechanisms to operate (Rothbaum et al., 2014).

Medication versus psychotherapy. Little research has compared TFPs to first-line medications, though TFPs consistently demonstrate larger effect sizes than medications (Lee et al., 2016; Watts et al., 2013). In addition to effect size, there are other reasons to view TFPs as preferable to medications. First, effects of TFPs last longer than medications, which are typically only effective for as long as they are used. Second, side effects are more likely with medications. Third, when asked, patients prefer psychotherapy to medications (Simiola, Neilson, Thompson, & Cook, 2015). Fourth, patients are not more likely to drop out or refuse psychotherapy than medications, despite the significantly greater time commitment (Swift, Greenberg, Tompkins, & Parkin, 2017). Of course, medications can be prescribed simultaneously with TFPs. Conventional wisdom is that medications in combination with psychotherapy is the best option. However, this perspective is not consistently supported (Popiel, Zawadzki, Pragłowska, & Teichman, 2015; Rothbaum et al., 2006; Schneier et al., 2012; Simon et al., 2008). Clearly, more research is needed on combined therapies given that many patients are recommended both.

Complementary and Integrative Health Treatments

Interest in complementary and integrative health modalities for trauma- and stressor-related disorders has increased. These approaches view health and well-being as determined by interdependent connections between the body, mind, spirit, and community (Boon, Verhoef, O'Hara, Findlay, & Majid, 2004). Several approaches are now supported by clinical trials (Wahbeh, Senders, Neuendorf, & Cayton, 2014), though none of these treatments has been directly compared against evidence-based TFPs and often allow patients to engage in other treatments during trial participation. They should therefore be viewed as complementary, not as alternatives. Four popular treatments are reviewed: mindfulness meditation, acupuncture, yoga, and recreation.

Mindfulness is the process of intentionally attending to internal and external events in the present moment and without judgment (Kabat-Zinn, 1990). Mindfulness meditation practices have reached ubiquity in diagnostically diverse health centers and among non-patients seeking to improve quality of life (Pickert, 2014). Mindfulness is often used as a component of evidence-based cognitive-behavioral therapies for a range of emotional disorders (e.g., acceptance and commitment therapy) (Lang et al., 2016). In these cases, mindfulness is used to facilitate cognitive-behavioral processes and, therefore, not considered a complementary or integrative health approach. In other cases, however, mindfulness is used as a stand-alone active ingredient, such as mindfulness-based stress reduction (MBSR) (Kabat-Zinn, Lipworth, Burney & Sellers, 1987; Polusny et al., 2015).

Reviews of clinical trials have found MBSR and similar interventions reduce PTSD symptoms, though the methodological rigor of these studies is not strong and the size of symptom change does not approach that seen with PE or CPT (Banks, Newman, & Saleem, 2015). Unfortunately, given the many mindfulness options for PTSD treatment, all with different techniques and "dosages" of practice time, research and development resources have been spread thin. In the largest trial to date, Polusny et al. (2015) found group-delivered MBSR (vs. active control) resulted in a small effect in symptom severity reduction. However, conclusions are tempered because groups were not equivalent (MBSR nearly doubled the session time of the control) and pretreatment severity was higher in MBSR, meaning the observed effect might reflect pretreatment group differences, not the actual impact of MBSR. Additional trials using non-inferiority designs are needed that compare mindfulness to TFPs and, if possible, match session time and homework demands. Following efficacy evidence in the treatment of PTSD, mechanism research should explore if present-moment contact and nonjudgmental observation may facilitate natural recovery of PTSD via indirect exposure to trauma content (internal and external) while fostering behavioral activation and physiological regulation. One additional area to explore empirically is the use of mindfulness interventions to complement evidence-based psychotherapy and pharmacotherapy in order to foster engagement, adherence, and relapse prevention.

Acupuncture has demonstrated effectiveness in comparison to control conditions in reducing PTSD symptoms (Engel et al., 2014; Hollifield, Sinclair-Lian, Warner, & Hammerschlag, 2007) and has an additive effective when used as adjunct to cognitive behavioral therapy (Zhang, Bin, Xie, Xu, & Jiong, 2011). Additionally, the emotional freedom technique (EFT) (Church et al., 2013; Karatzias et al., 2011) is a treatment in development for PTSD derived from acupuncture (tapping acupuncture points rather than using needles). While this emerging evidence for acupuncture and related treatments is encouraging, one difficulty is that placebo effects are difficult to assess and rule out. Further, the mechanisms of action with respect to PTSD symptom reduction are currently unknown. Therefore, although acupuncture does not appear to be harmful, little is known about how it might benefit individuals with PTSD.

Yoga, similar to mindfulness, is a traditionally Eastern practice now immensely popular in Western culture including health care centers. Also similar to mindfulness, there are different types of yoga. Most secular yoga practices involve physical postures, controlled breathing, and present-moment contact. Yoga may help treat PTSD through a variety of behavioral and physiological mechanisms (Wells, Lang, Schmalzl, Groessl, & Strauss, 2016) including learning to regulate the autonomic nervous system (Streeter, Gerbarg, Saper, Ciraulo, & Brown, 2012). Despite yoga's popularity, however, the evidence is still in its infancy and would benefit from randomized trials of PTSD-specific protocols using contemporary methodological standards (Wells et al., 2016).

Last, recreation and physical exercise have become popular approaches to complement evidence-based practices. This approach has involved a vast variety of activities such as hiking, hunting, fishing, surfing, horse riding, swimming with sharks, and dog ownership. For those preferring creative activities, trauma clinicians have also incorporated art modalities such as painting, poetry, music, and dance. This wide range of available options is desirable for patients who prefer a nonverbal approach to improving mental health. Generally, the intended mechanism of these activities is to facilitate some combination of relaxation, exposure, cognitive restructuring, and interpersonal communication. However, in PTSD, if not implemented with these mechanisms in mind, these activities can also function as avoidance of trauma content. Further, while many of these recreational activities are free, some are quite costly and provided through organizations without reference to whether they actually show improved function. Importantly, research on these approaches to date does not meet the methodological rigors established by trials of TFPs and pharmacotherapies (Johnson, Lahad, & Gray, 2009; Rosenbaum et al., 2015). Although it is important to consider patient preference, treatment decisions must also be based on evidence with providers helping patients to approach those treatments most likely to result in robust and stable improvements in functioning.

Prevention

Unique among *DSM-5* diagnoses, trauma- and stressor-related disorders have known start points (i.e., the traumatic event). Since posttraumatic reactions are not conceptualized as pathological for the few weeks after the index trauma, there is a real opportunity to prevent a syndrome from developing. One of the first and most widely used preventative approaches is critical incident stress debriefing (CISD) or "brief psychological debriefing," which involves providing immediate group-based opportunities for trauma-exposed individuals to discuss their trauma experience and receive psychoeducation and social support (Mitchell, 1983). Clinical trials show that CISD does not reduce the likelihood of developing PTSD or other psychiatric symptoms when compared to control conditions and may even result in iatrogenic effects (Rose, Bisson, Churchill, & Wessely, 2002). Other studies have also found universal prevention strategies ineffective in reducing PTSD following trauma. The failure of universal prevention protocols led clinical researchers to consider targeted interventions for individuals most likely to develop PTSD. To date, the most successful prevention efforts have (a) used strict inclusion criteria to identify at-risk trauma survivors and (b) employed protocols modeled from evidence-based TFPs. The success of these prevention efforts underscores the clinical utility of evidence-based theory, such as the critical roles of avoidance and unhelpful thoughts in the development and maintenance of PTSD symptoms.

Immediate intervention TFPs (i.e., within several days of trauma) have demonstrated preliminary support, especially protocols emphasizing exposure (Kearns, Ressler, Zatzick, & Rothbaum, 2012). Recently, Rothbaum and colleagues (2012) found a modified version of PE (three weekly 60-minute sessions with all PE components condensed) outperformed an assessment-only condition with respect to PTSD symptoms severity at three-month follow-up. This immediate intervention was especially effective for rape victims. To be included in this trial, adult patients needed to be sober and alert, desire immediate treatment, be able to recall the event, and not experience severe physical pain. Future research can explore if these are necessary conditions for a successful outcome. Additionally, future research should explore why immediate intervention PE seems to be more effective than CISD, which also includes revisiting the traumatic experience. A critical difference between these approaches is that immediate intervention PE provides opportunities for habituation and emotional processing within a one-to-one context. These elements may be essential to the recovery process.

In addition to immediate intervention of high-risk patients, another prevention strategy is to treat those who exhibit ASD within the first month of trauma exposure. The most effective treatments for ASD are TFPs as compared to supportive counseling or non-treatment controls (Forneris et al., 2013; Kliem & Kröger,

2013). These treatments typically last four to six sessions and include a combination of psychoeducation, imaginal and *in vivo* exposure, cognitive restructuring, and anxiety management. Recently, Nixon and colleagues (2016) found a modified version of CPT (six weekly 90-minutes sessions with all CPT components condensed) outperformed treatment as usual (combination of supportive counseling, psychoeducation, problem-solving, mindfulness, and values-based techniques) at 12-month follow-up. Participants were crisis center patients who experienced sexual assault within the past month and met criteria for ASD. Exclusion criteria included uncontrolled psychosis, substance dependence, cognitive impairment, significant suicide risk, and ongoing trauma. Similar to immediate intervention PE, research needs to determine if these variables or others should be used to identify candidates for preventative TFP. Further, the beneficial focus on trauma appraisals over other non-TFP strategies (e.g., supportive counseling and mindfulness) suggests that adaptively modifying assimilation and over-accommodation may be essential to the recovery process and, thus, should be examined further.

Preventing any disorder is an exciting possibility from a public health perspective. Research to date suggests PTSD may be preventable, though the field is far from disseminating best practices. The very real possibility that iatrogenic effects may occur for some interventions warrants caution among researchers and clinicians who are faced with demands to intervene immediately. The possibility for immediate use of pharmacotherapy is intuitively appealing. One could imagine widespread dispensing of prophylactic medications to soldiers after battles and civilians after natural disasters and terrorist attacks. Several clinical trials have examined a range of medications administered immediately after trauma (e.g., temazepam, gabapentin, escitalopram, and propranolol) without efficacy. Indeed, hydrocortisone is the only medication that has shown real promise in well-conducted prevention trials (Delahanty et al., 2013; Zohar et al., 2011). Given that natural recovery is the normative response to trauma (Bonanno & Mancini, 2012; Rothbaum, Foa, Riggs, Murdock, & Walsh, 1992), consistent evidence of efficacy in well-conducted clinical research is needed prior to recommending any form of supposed preventive medication.

In particular, the possibility of limited-use prophylactic medications would be a paradigm shift that warrants extreme caution. The generalizability of any successful clinical trial must be closely scrutinized, as unlike most viruses and bacterium, trauma is an inconsistent environmental pathogen. Many endogenous and exogenous factors occur before, during, and after the trauma that determine symptom trajectory (Bonanno & Mancini, 2012; Bovin & Marx, 2011). Vigilant attention within clinical research is needed with respect to dosage, administration timing, and identification of those most likely to benefit. Predictors of trauma-related pathology, including biomarkers that can be assessed quickly in emergency departments and crisis centers, promise to produce important insights with respect to prevention. Unfortunately, the current etiology literature, outlined in Chapters 25 and 26, has not yet translated into clinical assessment tools that can identify individuals likely to respond to prevention interventions.

In sum, the excitement surrounding the possibility of preventative interventions has not produced effective clinical applications beyond the insight that it is safe and feasible to individually deliver evidence-based TFPs after trauma exposure, either immediately (Rothbaum et al., 2016) or after meeting criteria for ASD (Nixon et al., 2016). However, it is difficult to predict who will benefit from a preventative intervention. Given that most trauma survivors naturally recover from immediate symptoms of PTSD, deciding who benefits from a preventative intervention is taking a shot in the dark. Thus, a major emphasis for clinical researchers is to develop effective assessment strategies to identify patients most like to receive benefit.

Summation of Current Clinical Literature

Following evidence-based assessment and confirmation of PTSD diagnosis and other relevant biopsychosocial factors, clinicians face an expansive menu of treatment options. To date, the empirical evidence strongly favors TFP, especially PE and CPT. These treatments can be delivered safely as soon as a patient exhibits ASD or PTSD or several decades after the index trauma. There are few contraindications for these treatments. PE and CPT have flexibility in how they can be implemented, though no evidence supports the "eclectic use" of protocol components. The most promising medications are SSRIs and one SNRI, though their effectiveness appears to be weaker than evidence-based TFPs. If TFPs are not available, or informed patients decline TFPs, there are several non-TFP interventions that are better than no treatment. There is no compelling evidence to suggest that patients benefit from non-TFPs prior to starting TFPs. Last, complementary or integrative health treatments are not strongly supported by clinical trials, though most have few drawbacks besides the possibility of delaying effective treatment. Altogether, the past 30 years of clinical research is encouraging; however, most individuals suffering from PTSD have not profited from this research. The next section of this chapter outlines how implementation science can transport best practices from the ivory tower to the clinical trenches.

Implementation of Evidence-Based Practices

The development of evidence-based practices is practically meaningless if they are not actually used. Our best PTSD treatments (PE and CPT) are buried within an expansive menu and their description is less appetizing or exciting than other choices (e.g., swimming with sharks). In the United States, 8% of adults will meet diagnostic criteria for PTSD during their lifetime; that is, tens of millions (Kilpatrick et al., 2013). However, only a small minority will receive first-line treatments, even in PTSD specialty clinics (e.g., 6% of patients) (Shiner et al., 2013). Challenges to the implementation of evidence-base practices in the mental health field are widely documented (Sobell, 1996). In this chapter, specific considerations with respect to PTSD treatment are discussed. First, we review insights from implementation science and a useful conceptual framework to understand the current state of TFP implementation. Second, we review successes and challenges of the largest ever TFP implementation effort, the US Veterans Health Administration's (VHA) rollouts of PE and CPT. Third, we review current intervention innovations that may improve implementation such as challenging traditional outpatient paradigms, using 21st-century technological advances, and better leveraging mechanisms of action.

Implementation Science

In the 1990s, there was strong concern in the mental health field regarding the gap between clinical science and clinicians (Sobell, 1996). By that time, evidence-based practices had begun to emerge but we did not know if or how clinicians would adopt an empirical approach to their clinical work. The scientist–clinician gap remains concerning (Shiner et al., 2013). However, for the past two decades, implementation science has emerged into an essential discipline within the mental health field that promises to bridge the gap between the ivory tower and the clinical trenches (Stirman, Gutner, Langdon, & Graham, 2016). We outline the major findings of implementation science in the mental health field and PTSD interventions specifically. These findings can help explain how to most effectively approach implementation from the perspectives of not just treatment developers but also funding bodies, agencies, clinics, and clinicians.

Implementation science emerged, in part, from the realization that best practices do not effectively spread through health care networks passively, trickling down from the ivory tower via peer-reviewed publications. Best practices have also not spread through dissemination alone, such as distribution of ideas and materials to targeted audiences by clinical scientists willing to provide workshops and webinars. Rather, successful implementation requires the use of a set of strategies at multiple levels to integrate best practices into specific settings and, at times, change aspects of how settings operate (Stirman et al., 2016). A useful tool to understand existing implementation strategies across health services is the Consolidated Framework for Implementation Research (CFIR), which provides implementation science with a taxonomy, terminologies, and definitions (Damschroder et al., 2009). CFIR allows for implementation science in one field to translate to another. The most up-to-date list of CFIR constructs and corresponding empirical support can be found on this wiki-based website: cfirguide.org (CFIR Research Team, 2014). From the CFIR perspective, implementation strategies are parsed into five levels. These first four levels are the primary concern of administrators and supervisors: process (e.g., how implementation is actually enacted), outer context (e.g., mandates and funding), inner context (e.g., clinic culture and leadership), and characteristics of the clinician (e.g., attributes and attitudes). The fifth level is the primary concern of treatment developers: characteristics of the intervention itself (e.g., compatibility and trialability). Insights from implementation science are discussed with respect to each of these five levels.

First, process implementation strategies are the "blueprints" for how strategies at all five levels are enacted – the cycle of planning, engaging, executing, and evaluating (Damschroder et al., 2009). In actual practice, these stages in the process cycle are often unfinished and not sequential. Implementation efforts that are ultimately successful often anticipate that several iterations of incomplete cycles will be required to reach implementation goals. Unfortunately, this level of implementation has been the most difficult to define and measure. Implementation at the process level ranges from explicit micromanaging to implicit grassroots change. To date, the most comprehensive implementation blueprint for PTSD has been the VHA's current rollouts of PE and CPT (Karlin & Cross, 2014; Karlin et al., 2010). In the next section, these rollouts are discussed as a case example of successes and challenges at the process level of implementation.

Second, outer context implementation strategies are those used in the domains of provider- and consumer-driven advocacy, legislation, and mechanisms for funding and reimbursement (Damschroder et al., 2009). Recently, the public's access to evidence-based health care (e.g., the Patient Protection and Affordable Care Act) has been a hotly debated topic among providers, consumers, business leaders, and politicians. However, influence at the sociopolitical level with respect to implementing specific interventions has been understudied and most knowledge is based on qualitative studies. Taking from business models, long-term cost-effectiveness at the outer context level is often viewed as a key driving force for implementing best practices. For example, mathematical simulations can put a dollar sign on societal "costs" and estimate how quickly access to an evidence-based practice will "pay for itself" (e.g., two years for PTSD and depression in US service members) (Kilmer, Eibner, Ringel, & Pacula, 2011). Government agencies and insurers often reimburse best practices at higher rates, contract with agencies that provide best practices, and invest resources into agencies in order to initiate best practices. As a means to address the increasing costs associated with the increasing numbers of PTSD-diagnosed service members returning from conflicts in Iraq and Afghanistan, the VHA mandated that all of its medical centers offer PE and CPT (Karlin & Cross, 2014). While this mandate has effectively facilitated allocation of resources, it should not be viewed as a sufficient strategy to sustain implementation (Raghavan, Bright, & Shadoin, 2008). Implementation science indicates that policy makers should develop meaningful partnerships with providers and consumers. Implementation is shaped by the perspectives, priorities, and knowledge of those directly delivering and receiving the intervention (Stirman et al., 2016).

Third, inner context implementation strategies are those used in the local settings in which the intervention is used (Damschroder et al., 2009). There is strong evidence that the inner context highly influences implementation in mental health (Stirman et al., 2016). For example, in a study of 38 VA residential PTSD programs, the use of PE and CPT was positively correlated to variables demarcating a supportive inner context including having adequate time for TFPs, sufficient number of TFP-trained providers, availability for TFP consultation, and expectations that TFPs will be used (Cook, Dinnen, Thompson et al., 2015). Qualitative findings from the same sample indicate implementation is especially likely if leadership actively supports use of PE and CPT (e.g., participating in the provision of treatment) (Cook, Dinnen, Coyne, et al., 2015). Local settings vary widely with regard to "readiness for change" as determined by the setting's ability to change (e.g., adequate resources and capacity), willingness to change (e.g., supportive leadership and culture), and perceived importance of change (e.g., relevance and prioritization). Assessment of inner context variables can result in changes to implementation strategies (e.g., establishing a cross-setting learning collaborative if internal resources are insufficient) or changes to inner context variables to better support implementation (e.g., improving leadership or culture via training in evidence-based practice).

Fourth, clinician characteristic implementation strategies are those that aim to refine malleable attributes and skills of providers or modify implementation efforts to accommodate static characteristics such as demographics and graduate degree (Damschroder et al., 2009). Most frequently, mental health practices are disseminated through workshops and webinars with varying degrees of experiential learning. However, an increasingly popular clinician-level implementation strategy in mental health is in-person or online didactic training and follow-up consultation, which is then rewarded by certification if fidelity benchmarks are observed. The first hurdle is often clinicians' attitudes about treatments – they practice only what they believe they can do with success. For example, CPT implementation in VA medical centers is more likely if the clinician views CPT as more effective than other treatments and compatible with the clinician's skillset and perspective (Cook, Dinnen, Coyne, et al., 2015). Fortunately, comprehensive training models can enhance clinician expectancies for TFPs (Ruzek et al., 2016). Beyond improving attitudes, evidence suggests training with built-in consultation enhances behavioral skill development in PTSD clinicians (Ruzek et al., 2014). However, training and follow-up consultation often do not help the clinician reach fidelity ratings expected in clinical trials (Sholomskas et al., 2005). Therefore, effective consultation and supervision techniques have emerged and warrant the attention of trainers (e.g., role-playing and modeling are more effective than discussion) (Bearman et al., 2013). Other ways of improving clinician skills following supervision and consultation are matching trainee characteristics to certain training strategies, providing training incentives, and monitoring fidelity (Stirman et al., 2016).

Fifth, intervention characteristic implementation strategies are those that refine aspects of the intervention to better fit the context and clinician (Damschroder et al., 2009). Treatment developers may cringe at the idea of protocol modification. However, evidence suggests this happens regularly already in PE and CPT (Cook, Dinnen, Thompson, Simiola, & Schnurr, 2014). Clinics occasionally change the protocol's scripted content and eliminate components (e.g., using *in vivo* exposure but not imaginal exposure in PE). Even clinicians well trained and supportive of specific protocols are likely to make fidelity-inconsistent modifications (Stirman et al., 2015). Rather than ignore this reality, treatment developers can join clinics' attempts to deviate effectively from standardized protocols. One possibility is that some protocol elements might be sufficiently robust to allow a certain margin of error while remaining effective. Meta-analytic evidence suggests neither protocol fidelity nor competence predicts patient outcomes (Webb, DeRubeis, & Barber, 2010). Much attention in PTSD implementation efforts is given to improve clinician skills (Rosen et al., 2016); however, other factors can highly influential such as the fit between the setting, patient, and protocol. Therefore, it would behoove treatment developers to identify essential elements (i.e., mechanisms of action) and investigate potential modifications to suggest as options. The developers of CPT have taken this approach with respect to making the written trauma account optional in the latest manual (Resick et al., 2017) based on a dismantling study demonstrating that the account was not needed to achieve effectiveness (Resick et al., 2008). Some have called for the availability of transdiagnostic protocols using modules that can be applied based on case conceptualization; however, as reviewed earlier, the intervention literature strongly recommends disorder-specific protocols for PTSD, namely TFPs.

Last, in addition to these five levels, CFIR emphasizes that implementation efforts should maintain awareness that strategies at each of these levels interact in complex ways (Damschroder et al., 2009). Variables at one level can enhance or diminish the influence of a strategy at another level (Stirman et al., 2016). Therefore, when assessing implementation outcomes, it is important to assess and solicit feedback at multiple levels. For example, when evaluating the success of the VHA PE rollout, low utilization after training may reflect clinician characteristics (e.g., negative attitudes); however, when inner context is also considered (e.g., clinic prioritization for group treatment), the impact of intervention characteristics may become apparent (e.g., developers can investigate if *in vivo* exposure can be delivered in groups).

Implementation Case Example: VHA Rollouts

Starting in 2006, the VHA rollouts of PE and CPT have been unprecedented implementation efforts in terms of scale and system change (Karlin et al., 2010). While not necessarily set up to start with CFIR in mind, the current efforts employ implementation strategies at all levels specified by CFIR (Karlin & Cross, 2010). Therefore, lessons learned from these rollouts can potentially guide implementation efforts in other systems of various sizes, training programs, and independent clinicians.

Starting at the outer context level, there are reasons for optimism (Rosen et al., 2016). The VHA has a network of experts and centralized resources and policies. In addition, due to ongoing conflicts in Iraq and Afghanistan, PTSD treatment is in the consciousness of the public and has been prioritized by governing bodies and funding mechanisms. At the inner context level, the VHA made the following investments: funding travel for training, protecting consultation time, permitting

90-minute sessions for individual PE and group CPT, implementing progress note templates to monitor fidelity, supporting a mentorship program for clinic managers, and authorizing a new position charged with coordinating evidence-based practice at each medical center. The clinician-level implementation strategy includes training models designed by each treatment's developer (Edna Foa and Patricia Resick for PE and CPT, respectively), which require completion of two cases delivered faithfully while participating in weekly case consultation with experts. At the intervention level, the selected protocols have strong effectiveness evidence, are compatible with other cognitive behavioral therapies used by VHA clinicians, and can be scaled via training a subset of clinicians to become trainers themselves (i.e., "second-generation trainers"). This section reviews insights from the VHA rollouts of PE and CPT, particularly with regard to the CFIR levels of process, outer context, inner context, and clinician characteristics. For more than 10 years since the start of the rollouts, the PE and CPT protocols have remained largely unchanged. Barriers to implementation have revealed a need to use innovative perspectives to refine intervention-level implementation strategies, which are reviewed in the next section.

What have been the successes of the PE and CPT rollouts? As of 2016, 1,865 VHA clinicians have completed PE training and 2,685 have completed CPT training (Rosen et al., 2016). Training typically improves attitudes toward these treatments and motivation for implementation (Ruzek et al., 2016). Intent-to-treat analyses have shown that patients treated by newly trained VHA clinicians in both PE and CPT have exhibited PTSD symptom reduction at similar rates to that of veteran-specific clinical trials (Chard et al., 2012; Eftekhari et al., 2013). Moreover, rollout participants' prior clinical training and degree had little impact on effectiveness (Eftekhari et al., 2015). Thus, the robustness of these interventions does not seem to be diminished by the clinician's lack of expertise or prior experiences. Even more promising is that second-generation trainers have proven as effective as the rollouts' initial trainers with respect to their trainees' patient outcomes (Karlin et al., 2010). Together, these findings suggest that the rollouts are effective, scalable, and sustainable.

What have been the challenges of the PE and CPT rollouts? Simply put, trained clinicians are not using these treatments as much as anticipated. Despite successful completion of PE and CPT training, rollout participants generally use these interventions for only several cases at a time or even less frequently (Rosen et al., 2016; Ruzek et al., 2016). Low implementation rates are even found in some PTSD specialty clinics (Finley et al., 2015; Shiner et al., 2013). Indeed, some VA clinicians have rejected the top-down mandate to provide these interventions despite evidence of efficacy.

Implementing PE and CPT is not just a matter of clinician training; clinics must prioritize these treatments (Rosen et al., 2016). Use of PE and CPT within the VHA is largely driven by the extent to which the clinic is sufficiently staffed (Finley et al., 2015) and dedicates time and resources for these treatments (Cook, Dinnen, Thompson, et al., 2015). Technically, these protocols are now available at all VA medical centers; however, many clinics still do not have a sufficient number of PE- or CPT-trained clinicians (Hamblen et al., 2015) or adequate clinic flow to allow patients to access them without significant obstacles, such as multiple intake assessments. VHA clinicians often have large caseloads and, if they are trained in PE or CPT, they must collaborate with clinic managers to determine if a short-term investment of weekly TFP will ultimately lead to a smaller caseload due to successful treatment completion and subsequent discharge from the clinic. Often, clinicians will reserve a limited number of weekly TFP slots and need to use the majority of the remaining slots for case management. Some settings are further restricted because these treatments do not fit with the clinic's structure (e.g., limited availability of individual, weekly slots of 60 or 90 minutes) and culture (e.g., preference for psychodynamics or attitudes that PTSD is manageable but not treatable) (Hamblen et al., 2015; Rosen et al., 2016).

At the clinician level, one of the most critical implementation barriers is vague and unsystematic assessments of patient "readiness" for TFPs (Cook et al., 2014; Hamblen et al., 2015). Low readiness is typically operationalized as clinician-inferred low motivation and comorbid conditions such as personality disorders, substance abuse, and low cognitive functioning stemming from traumatic brain injury (Cook et al., 2014). However, what may appear as low motivation for TFPs may actually be the normal avoidance that is part of PTSD. Accordingly, both PE and CPT include psychoeducation and motivational strategies to increase motivation for treatment as a part of the standard clinical protocols. Furthermore, while some comorbid features may indeed interfere with treatment (e.g., unmanaged psychosis and mania), recent trials have demonstrated TFPs can be effective for a wide range of clinical presentations including severe mental illness and low levels of cognitive functioning (Chard et al., 2011; Grubaugh et al., 2016; van Minnen et al., 2012; Wolf, Lunney, & Schnurr, 2016). Efforts to enhance access to these effective treatments to populations with complex presentations should be improved.

Last, in addition to context- and clinician-level implementation barriers, the process level of VHA rollouts (i.e., blueprints) is currently between cycles of evaluation and planning. Many clinicians are trained in PE and CPT, though the application to patient care is unclear. In addition to low utilization rates, measuring procedure drift after training has been elusive. However, post-training fidelity is more likely to occur if initial consultation is highly directive and individualized and if trainees sustain contact with consultants (Watts et al., 2014). Other ideas to enhance fidelity are peer consultation, booster training, and using clinical progress note templates with session checklists (Rosen et al., 2016). The future of the rollouts is difficult to anticipate. However, no new treatment modalities have demonstrated superior outcomes to PE and CPT since the start of the rollouts. Any future change in implementation of PE and CPT with VHA will likely reflect innovations in how the mechanisms of action in PE and CPT are delivered, which are reviewed next.

Intervention Innovations

In addition to strategies to enhance "implementation readiness" in the clinician, the clinician's setting, and the larger sociopolitical context, the intervention itself can have inherent barriers that require innovative solutions (Damschroder et al., 2009). Therefore, incremental improvements in the efficacy and utility of a mental health intervention is often a necessary step in the implementation process (Stirman et al., 2016). Two strategies promise to improve our implementation of first-line treatments. First, clinical scientists can develop and test innovative ways of packaging and delivering interventions to fit patients, clinicians, and their surrounding contexts. Some work on this is under way with specific modifications for use of PE and CPT in intensive outpatient programs, primary care, and other more specific practice settings. Second, clinical scientists can identify effective treatment mechanisms of action and use this knowledge to refine treatment delivery.

Innovation in TFP packaging. Psychotherapy was originally developed for affluent and educated adults of Western cultures who had time to attend weekly, in-person, individual sessions with expertly trained professionals over the course of months or years. This history has influenced how most psychotherapy protocols proscribe treatment delivery in the 21st century. Unfortunately, most people who would benefit from treatment do not fit into this mold and agencies cannot meet this demand. Thus, contemporary clinical scientists have challenged historical paradigms to improve patient receptivity and retention, speed of recovery, and overall impact. In recent years, researchers have developed and empirically tested innovative ways to package and deliver the active ingredients of TFPs (Rauch & Rothbaum, 2016). Specifically, TFPs have been examined within groups, primary care, massed formats, and high-tech platforms such as virtual reality and the Internet.

TFPs in groups. One of the first attempts to improve implementation was to offer treatments in groups rather than individually. Groups relieve burden from understaffed clinics and provide unique therapeutic factors (e.g., peer support, observational learning, and opportunities to practice interpersonal skills immediately). Unfortunately, the effectiveness of groups compared to individual treatment is an understudied area within the PTSD intervention literature. It is known that PTSD group therapy, on average, is better than nothing (Bisson et al., 2013; Sloan et al., 2013; Smith et al., 2015). However, there is evidence that the group format may diminish the effect of TFPs (Resick et al., 2015, 2017). In fact, no specific modality of group therapy for PTSD has demonstrated superiority (Sloan et al., 2013). These findings provide little guidance with respect to treatment planning and suggest that individual TFP may be the most effective strategy, which clinics will have to weigh against the financial and staffing burden of treating patients one at a time.

TFPs in primary care. An alternate strategy to increase access to effective PTSD treatment is to move the effective elements of the PTSD intervention to settings that patients prefer. An illustrative example of this approach is the modification of PE for delivery by primary care mental health providers, which uses only four to six 30-minute sessions and guided practices at home. Pilot studies and a recently completed randomized controlled trial in military service members support the efficacy of this intervention with significant reductions in PTSD and roughly a 40% remission rate at post-treatment (Cigrang et al., 2011, 2015). The PE in primary care protocol uses written exposure exercises tailored to include processing items the patient then reviews and processes in session with the clinician. In addition, *in vivo* exercises are conducted (only a few given the short duration of treatment) with the expectation of continued independent work. In addition to the intervention, primary care PE clinicians have a facilitated referral to PTSD specialty clinics for those who do not remit at post-treatment. This will allow access to a larger population of patients with some receiving an adequate dose for response while the remainder can be facilitated into the higher level of care.

TFPs in massed format. An alternative to weekly outpatient sessions is massed treatment delivery, for example, using a daily intensive outpatient format to deliver a full cognitive-behavioral protocol over the course of two or three weeks. Massed sessions in the treatment of depression and anxiety have resulted in quicker rates of improvement (and equal overall reduction) when compared to conventional weekly delivery (Cuijpers, Huibers, Ebert, Koole, & Andersson, 2013; Storch et al., 2008). For PTSD, the main benefits of massing sessions are to increase support and reduce opportunities to avoid tasks between sessions or dropout altogether. Massed sessions may also make TFP more available for patients unable to attend weekly sessions due to education, employment, deployments, and family responsibilities. Consistent with this perspective, fewer days between sessions has been shown to predict better outcomes in TFPs (Gutner, Suvak, Sloan, & Resick, 2016). For these reasons, clinical researchers have explored doing imaginal and *in vivo* exposure therapy every day for two or three weeks (Blount, Cigrang, Foa, Ford, & Peterson, 2014). An ongoing open trial is investigating the effectiveness of a massed PE protocol that includes individually delivered imaginal exposure and group-delivered psychoeducation, breathing retraining, and *in vivo* exposure (e.g., Rauch et al., 2017). In addition to increasing access to TFPs, the quick patient turnaround in massed formats may facilitate implementation by promoting rapid clinician training, program evaluation, and feedback integration, while also preventing a build-up of a non-active caseload.

TRPs in high-tech platforms. Sitting face to face might seem important to the psychotherapy process. However, that might be just because it has always been done that way. Recent advances in information technology platforms and public adoption of these platforms gives reason to challenge this assumption, especially for the sake of improving implementation when face-to-face psychotherapy is not optimal.

First, delivering TFP via videoconferencing promises to expand access while not diminishing effectiveness (Maieritsch et al., 2016; Morland et al., 2015; Yuen et al., 2015). Many patients with PTSD have difficulty physically attending sessions for a myriad of reasons (ambulation difficulties, lack of transportation, rural setting, transient lifestyle, and stigma). However, many patients have access to smartphones and computers with videoconferencing applications that allow them to bring the therapist into their context. This technology may also have unique advantages to in-person treatment. For example, through videoconferencing, therapist-assisted *in vivo* exposures can occur anywhere within the geographic coverage of the patient's mobile provider and with the use of wearable devices (or simply placing a smartphone's video camera in one's front pocket).

Second, cognitive-behavioral treatments for PTSD delivered through automated online systems have shown promising effects (Kuester, Niemeyer, & Knaevelsrud, 2016). In the Internet age, the public has moved beyond simple online tasks like reading the news and watching videos to more complicated tasks like engaging in complex online communities and workplaces. Automated Internet-based therapies promise to increase access even more than videoconferencing because the presence of a clinician is not always needed. An intriguing possibility is that some patients may prefer to use automated systems. Consumers have not yet had the option of psychotherapy without psychotherapists.

Last, mounting evidence indicates the use of virtual reality technology is a highly valuable tool to facilitate exposure therapy for PTSD (Gonçalves, Pedrozo, Coutinho, Figueira, & Ventura, 2012). Virtual reality exposure therapy for PTSD began in the 1990s (Rothbaum et al., 1999) but only now is equipment affordable for widespread implementation in PTSD clinics. Most available software includes multimodal environments (e.g., sounds, sights, smells, and vibrations in the ground), such as driving on a bumpy highway in Iraq with burning roadside debris. These sensorial and interactive attributes enhance immersion and thus facilitate emotional engagement during exposures. This process eliminates avoidance and gives the clinician the ability to control the delivery of stress-provoking stimuli on a gradual rate based on the patient's needs. Some *in vivo* exposures are infeasible (e.g., landing an aircraft) or uncontrollable (e.g., garbage near road) but can be repeated many times within virtual environments. There are some limitations such as insufficiently realistic stimuli, limited ability to personalize content, and inability to use naturalistic ambulation or dialog. However, these limitations are likely temporary in nature, as technological advances in the coming years promise to develop hardware and software (e.g., biofeedback and artificial intelligence) that further increase immersion and stimuli specificity.

Innovations in leveraging mechanisms of action. This chapter's emphasis on implementation can be viewed as a testament to the encouraging (albeit under-utilized) developments in PTSD treatment research. However, there is no reason to stall innovation while clinicians "catch up" to the state of the current science. There is plenty of room for improvement to improve our best clinical tools (Rauch &

Liberzon, 2016). In addition to the innovative approaches described earlier, one strategy to improve TFPs is to identify the mechanisms by which they work and then, using this knowledge, reorganize these protocols to better target the mechanism (Kazdin, 2007; Rauch & Liberzon, 2016). Unfortunately, our empirical knowledge of "which" treatments work far exceeds our knowledge of "how" treatments work.

Perhaps psychology cannot sufficiently explain how psychological interventions work. Perhaps psychological constructs are too broad and, at times, epiphenomenological. If so, mechanism research may benefit from an innovative approach in which psychopathology is viewed in terms of transdiagnostic systems of functioning and described using constructs and methodologies from multiple disciplines (e.g., psychology, neuroscience, and genetics). It will be especially illuminating to understand how these systems of functioning are impacted by various interventions, namely those we know work (i.e., PE and CPT). What can non-psychological research tell us about what gets "turned off or on" in psychological interventions?

In 2008, the US National Institute of Mental Health (NIMH) initiated the Research Domain Criteria (RDoC) project (Cuthbert, 2014). The purpose of RDoC is to focus research and organize findings on dimensions of functioning (from health to pathology) at various units of analyses (from genes to neural circuits to observable behavior, all equally weighted). Ideally, this strategy will develop a psychopathology classification system based on the integration of neuroscientific and behavioral indices. This is an intentional departure from research constrained by the problematic categories of *DSM-5* and other diagnostic manuals that are primarily based on descriptive phenomenology (Cuthbert, 2014). Currently, RDoC specifies five domains: Negative Valence Systems (e.g., fear), Positive Valence Systems (e.g., reward learning), Cognitive Systems (e.g., attention), Systems of Social Processes (e.g., perceptions of self), and Arousal and Regulatory Systems (e.g., arousal).

Recently, Schmidt and Vermetten (2017) have synthesized findings on PTSD pathopsychobiology into the RDoC framework. Their review indicates that our understanding of trauma- and stressor-related pathology has been constrained by the PTSD construct, which is only phenomenologically defined and suffers from considerable heterogeneity (Zoellner et al., 2014). They acknowledge that despite decades of research using *DSM*, robust biomarkers and medications have yet to emerge in routine clinical practice. Their assessment of the literature from the RDoC perspective indicates that the development of trauma- and stressor-related pathology is most related to fear processing, reward functioning, explicit and implicit memory pathways, and the sympathetic nervous system. They advocate for the RDoC as an alternative to understanding trauma- and stressor-related pathology because it reveals several areas of needed research that can produce clinical insights. For example, they emphasize that amygdala over-activation seems to play a role in all RDoC domains within trauma-exposed samples, yet further research is still needed to identify the nature of the amygdala's role in each domain. They also claim RDoC does not sufficiently capture other areas of pathology in trauma-exposed samples such as emotion regulation and dissociation. Psychologists have studied these areas for many years and, if added to RDoC as new domains, the field's understanding may profit from investigation by non-psychologists such as geneticists and biologists.

The RDoC framework has already fostered innovative studies that can advance PTSD intervention research. For example, to help elucidate the mechanisms by which PE improves symptoms of comorbid PTSD and substance use disorder, Zambrano-Vazquez et al. (2017) found that changes in self-reported RDoC domain functioning (Negative Valence Systems, Arousal and Regulatory Systems, and Cognitive Systems) explained post-treatment trauma-elicited distress and alcohol craving. This study motivates future research to better understand shared vulnerabilities of seemingly disparate diagnoses and refine our models for how treatment mechanisms work. An example of a shared vulnerability within the RDoC Negative Valence Systems is the psychophysiological index termed "fear load" (Norrholm et al., 2015). Fear load is a high level of fear-potentiated startle reflex (assessed with electromyography recordings of orbicularis oculi) during the early phase of an extinction condition. Evidence suggests fear load is significantly related to trauma intrusions and physiological reactions to trauma memories (Norrholm et al., 2011, 2015). Researchers are now investigating if fear load may be a common intermediate phenotype underlying PTSD and other fear-related disorders such as specific and social phobias. If so, fear load assessments (e.g., the acoustic startle paradigm) can be used as a biological marker of transdiagnostic symptom severity and predictor of efficacy in extinction-related treatment (e.g., PE).

RDoC has been criticized as emphasizing neurobiological dysfunction in psychopathology while minimizing the roles of psychological and social variables (Hershenberg & Goldfried, 2015). Zoellner and Foa (2016) argue higher-order psychological constructs should be central in RDoC due to their potential to synthesize diverse multidisciplinary findings, especially neurobiological constructs that account for little variance in mental health difficulties. Existing psychosocial theories of PTSD might be inherently imperfect due to problems with our current nosology; however, these theories have been necessary for the development of evidence-based practices (Gillihan, Cahill, & Foa, 2014). One can assume that TFPs achieve their effects through changes in one or more of RDoC's domains of functioning. For example, understanding how the mechanisms through which imaginal exposure of trauma memories works can illuminate the nature of the Negative Valence Systems and potential interactions with Cognitive Systems and Arousal and Regulation Systems. Therefore, better understanding treatment mechanisms in TFPs can be fully consistent with the purpose of the RDoC framework, so long as the NIMH continues to fund RDoC-informed clinical trials conducted by clinical psychologists. In psychopathology, it is important to neither split meaningful constructs into meaningless constructs nor meaninglessly lump together meaningfully different units. As such, the success of RDoC with respect to improving interventions will hinge on its ability to prioritize multidisciplinary research. A fruitful area of RDoC research will be to identify mechanisms of action in TFPs and explore innovative methods to leverage these mechanisms to achieve superior outcomes than those resulting from current TFP protocols.

Summary

The expansive menu of options for the treatment and prevention of trauma- and stressor-related disorders has proven a blessing and a curse. Providers and patients are happy to have choices – but they unwittingly overlook the best ones. Science has allowed the best interventions to emerge from the rich collection of ideas and health traditions. However, widespread enactment of best practices has yet to come to fruition. This chapter digests 30 years of clinical research to help orient clinicians to the most effective treatments, namely PE and CPT. However, improving clinician awareness of the intervention literature is just one strategy of many needed for successful implementation. Researchers and policy makers who support evidence-based health care need to use implementation science to improve the probability that people suffering after trauma exposure gain access to high-quality treatment. Rather than using only top-down mandates, the field can help clinicians adopt best practices through consistent training and support for effective use of interventions that result in improved function. Moreover, we can make our best practices better through understanding mechanisms and how to make treatments more efficient and effective. Treatment developers will benefit from collaborating with non-psychology researchers and innovators in the area of information technology. The menu of options is confusing and intimidating. The time has come to show off our best entrées and dare to make them even better.

References

American Psychiatric Association. (2000). *Diagnostic and Statistical Manual of Mental Disorders* (4th edn, text revision) *(DSM-IV-TR)*. Arlington, VA: American Psychiatric Publishing.

American Psychiatric Association. (2013). *Diagnostic and Statistical Manual of Mental Disorders* (5th edn) *(DSM-5)*. Arlington, VA: American Psychiatric Publishing.

Banks, K., Newman, E., & Saleem, J. (2015). An overview of the research on mindfulness based interventions for treating symptoms of post-traumatic stress disorder: A systematic review. *Journal of Clinical Psychology, 71*(10), 935–963.

Bearman, S. K., Weisz, J. R., Chorpita, B. F., Hoagwood, K., Ward, A., Ugueto, A. M., . . . Research Network on Youth Mental Health. (2013). More practice, less preach? The role of supervision processes and therapist characteristics in EBP implementation. *Administration and Policy in Mental Health and Mental Health Services Research, 40*(6), 518–529.

Beck, A. T. (1976). *Cognitive Therapy and the Emotional Disorders*. Madison, WI: International Universities Press.

Benish, S. G., Imel, Z. E., & Wampold, B. E. (2008). The relative efficacy of bona fide psychotherapies for treating post-traumatic stress disorder: A meta-analysis of direct comparisons. *Clinical Psychology Review*, *28*(5), 746–758.

Bisson, J. I., Roberts, N. P., Andrew, M., Cooper, R., & Lewis, C. (2013). Psychological therapies for chronic post-traumatic stress disorder (PTSD) in adults. *Cochrane Database of Systematic Reviews*, *12*, CD00338.

Blount, T. H., Cigrang, J. A., Foa, E. B., Ford, H. L., & Peterson, A. L. (2014). Intensive outpatient prolonged exposure for combat-related PTSD: A case study. *Cognitive and Behavioral Practice*, *21*(1), 89–96.

Bonanno, G. A. & Mancini, A. D. (2012). Beyond resilience and PTSD: Mapping the heterogeneity of responses to potential trauma. *Psychological Trauma: Theory, Research, Practice, and Policy*, *4*(1), 74–83.

Boon, H., Verhoef, M., O'Hara, D., Findlay, B., & Majid, N. (2004). Integrative healthcare: Arriving at a working definition. *Alternative Therapies in Health and Medicine*, *10*(5), 48–56.

Bovin, M. J. & Marx, B. P. (2011). The importance of the peritraumatic experience in defining traumatic stress. *Psychological Bulletin*, *137*(1), 47–67.

Brom, D., Kleber, R. J., & Defares, P. B. (1989). Brief psychotherapy for posttraumatic stress disorders. *Journal of Consulting and Clinical Psychology*, *57*(5), 607–612.

Cahill, S. P., Carrigan, M. H., & Frueh, B. C. (1999). Does EMDR work? And if so, why? A critical review of controlled outcome and dismantling research. *Journal of Anxiety Disorders*, *13*(1), 5–33.

Cary, C. E. & McMillen, J. C. (2012). The data behind the dissemination: A systematic review of trauma-focused cognitive behavioral therapy for use with children and youth. *Children and Youth Services Review*, *34*(4), 748–757.

CFIR Research Team (2014, October). CFIR Technical Assistance Website. Ann Arbor, MI: Center for Clinical Management Research. Available at: http://cfirguide.org/index.html. Accessed May 15, 2017.

Church, D., Hawk, C., Brooks, A. J., Toukolehto, O., Wren, M., Dinter, I., & Stein, P. (2013). Psychological trauma symptom improvement in veterans using emotional freedom techniques: A randomized controlled trial. *Journal of Nervous and Mental Disease*, *201*(2), 153–160.

Cigrang, J. A., Rauch, S. A., Avila, L. L., Bryan, C. J., Goodie, J. L., Hryshko-Mullen, A., ... Consortium, t. S. S. (2011). Treatment of active-duty military with PTSD in primary care: Early findings. *Psychological Services*, *8*(2), 104–113.

Cigrang, J. A., Rauch, S. A. M., Mintz, J., Brundige, A., Avila, L. L., Bryan, C. J., ... Peterson, A. L. (2015). Treatment of active duty military with PTSD in primary care: A follow-up report. *Journal of Anxiety Disorders*, *36*, 110–114.

Cloitre, M., Koenen, K. C., Cohen, L. R., & Han, H. (2002). Skills training in affective and interpersonal regulation followed by exposure: A phase-based treatment for PTSD related to childhood abuse. *Journal of Consulting and Clinical Psychology*, *70*(5), 1067–1-74.

Cook, J. M., Dinnen, S., Coyne, J. C., Thompson, R., Simiola, V., Ruzek, J., & Schnurr, P. P. (2015). Evaluation of an implementation model: A national investigation of VA residential programs. *Administration and Policy in Mental Health and Mental Health Services Research*, *42*(2), 147–156.

Cook, J. M., Dinnen, S., Simiola, V., Thompson, R., & Schnurr, P. P. (2014). VA residential provider perceptions of dissuading factors to the use of two evidence-based PTSD treatments. *Professional Psychology Research and Practice*, *45*, 136–142.

Cook, J. M., Dinnen, S., Thompson, R., Ruzek, J., Coyne, J. C., & Schnurr, P. P. (2015). A quantitative test of an implementation framework in 38 VA residential PTSD programs. *Administration and Policy in Mental Health and Mental Health Services Research*, *42*(4), 462–473.

Cook, J. M., Dinnen, S., Thompson, R., Simiola, V., & Schnurr, P. P. (2014). Changes in implementation of two evidence-based psychotherapies for PTSD in VA residential treatment programs: A national investigation. *Journal of Traumatic Stress*, *27* (2), 137–143.

Cooperative Studies Program #563: Prazosin and Combat Trauma (2016). Retrieved from http://clinicaltrials.gov (Identification No. NCT00532493)

Craske, M. G., Kircanski, K., Zelikowsky, M., Mystkowski, J., Chowdhury, N., & Baker, A. (2008). Optimizing inhibitory learning during exposure therapy. *Behaviour Research and Therapy*, *46*(1), 5–27.

Cuijpers, P., Huibers, M., Ebert, D. D., Koole, S. L., & Andersson, G. (2013). How much psychotherapy is needed to treat depression? A metaregression analysis. *Journal of Affective Disorders*, *149*(1), 1–13.

Cusack, K., Jonas, D. E., Forneris, C. A., Wines, C., Sonis, J., Middleton, J. C., . . . Weil, A. (2016). Psychological treatments for adults with posttraumatic stress disorder: A systematic review and meta-analysis. *Clinical Psychology Review*, *43*, 128–141.

Cusack, K. & Spates, C. R. (1999). The cognitive dismantling of eye movement desensitization and reprocessing (EMDR) treatment of posttraumatic stress disorder (PTSD). *Journal of Anxiety Disorders*, *13*(1), 87–99.

Cuthbert, B. N. (2014). The RDoC framework: Facilitating transition from ICD/DSM to dimensional approaches that integrate neuroscience and psychopathology. *World Psychiatry*, *13*(1), 28–35.

Damschroder, L. J., Aron, D. C., Keith, R. E., Kirsh, S. R., Alexander, J. A., & Lowery, J. C. (2009). Fostering implementation of health services research findings into practice: A consolidated framework for advancing implementation science. *Implementation Science*, *4*(1), 50.

Delahanty, D. L., Gabert-Quillen, C., Ostrowski, S. A., Nugent, N. R., Fischer, B., Morris, A., . . . Fallon, W. (2013). The efficacy of initial hydrocortisone administration at preventing posttraumatic distress in adult trauma patients: A randomized trial. *CNS Spectrums*, *18*(2), 103–111.

Eftekhari, A., Crowley, J., Garvert, D. W., Ruzek, J. I., Karlin, B. E., & Rosen, C. S. (2015). Training of clinicians in exposure therapy: Clinician correlates of outcomes. *Journal of Traumatic Stress*, *28*, 65–68.

Eftekhari, A., Ruzek, J. I., Crowley, J., Rosen, C. S., Greenbaum, M. A., & Karlin, B. E. (2013). Effectiveness of national implementation of prolonged exposure therapy in VA care. *JAMA Psychiatry*, *70*, 949–955.

Ehlers, A., Bisson, J., Clark, D. M., Creamer, M., Pilling, S., Richards, D., . . . Yule, W. (2010). Do all psychological treatments really work the same in posttraumatic stress disorder? *Clinical Psychology Review*, *30*(2), 269–276.

Ehlers, A., Clark, D. M., Hackmann, A., McManus, F., & Fennell, M. (2005). Cognitive therapy for post-traumatic stress disorder: Development and evaluation. *Behaviour Research and Therapy*, *43*(4), 413–431.

Engel, C. C., Cordova, E. H., Benedek, D. M., Liu, X., Gore, K. L., Goertz, C., . . . Ursano, R. J. (2014). Randomized effectiveness trial of a brief course of acupuncture for posttraumatic stress disorder. *Medical Care*, *52*, S57–S64.

Ertl, V., Pfeiffer, A., Schauer, E., Elbert, T., & Neuner, F. (2011). Community-implemented trauma therapy for former child soldiers in northern Uganda: A randomized controlled trial. *JAMA*, *306*(5), 503–512.

Feeny, N. C., Hembree, E. A., & Zoellner, L. A. (2003). Myths regarding exposure therapy for PTSD. *Cognitive and Behavioral Practice*, *10*(1), 85–90.

Finley, E. P., Garcia, H. A., Ketchum, N. S., McGeary, D. D., McGeary, C. A., Stirman, S. W., & Peterson, A. L. (2015). Utilization of evidence-based psychotherapies in Veterans Affairs posttraumatic stress disorder outpatient clinics. *Psychological Services*, *12*(1), 73–82.

Foa, E. B., Dancu, C. V., Hembree, E. A., Jaycox, L. H., Meadows, E. A., & Street, G. P. (1999). A comparison of exposure therapy, stress inoculation training, and their combination for reducing posttraumatic stress disorder in female assault victims. *Journal of Consulting and Clinical Psychology*, *67*(2), 194–200.

Foa, E. B., Hembree, E. A., Cahill, S. P., Rauch, S. A., Riggs, D. S., Feeny, N. C., & Yadin, E. (2005). Randomized trial of prolonged exposure for posttraumatic stress disorder with and without cognitive restructuring: Outcome at academic and community clinics. *Journal of Consulting and Clinical Psychology*, *73*(5), 953–964.

Foa, E. B., Hembree, E. A., & Rothbaum, B. O. (2007). *Prolonged Exposure Therapy for PTSD: Emotional Processing of Traumatic Experiences: Therapist Guide*. Oxford: Oxford University Press.

Foa, E. B. & Kozak, M. J. (1986). Emotional processing of fear: Exposure to corrective information. *Psychological Bulletin*, *99*(1), 20–35.

Foa, E. B. & Meadows, E. A. (1997). Psychosocial treatments for posttraumatic stress disorder: A critical review. *Annual Review of Psychology*, *48*(1), 449–480.

Forneris, C. A., Gartlehner, G., Brownley, K. A., Gaynes, B. N., Sonis, J., Coker-Schwimmer, E., . . . Lohr, K. N. (2013). Interventions to prevent posttraumatic stress disorder: A systematic review. *American Journal of Preventive Medicine*, *44*(6), 635–650.

Fortney, J. C., Pyne, J. M., Kimbrell, T. A., Hudson, T. J., Robinson, D. E., Schneider, R., . . . Schnurr, P. P. (2015). Telemedicine-based collaborative care for posttraumatic stress disorder: A randomized clinical trial. *JAMA Psychiatry*, *72*(1), 58–67.

Gersons, B. P., Carlier, I. V., Lamberts, R. D., & van der Kolk, B. A. (2000). Randomized clinical trial of brief eclectic psychotherapy for police officers with post-traumatic stress disorder. *Journal of Traumatic Stress*, *13*(2), 333–347.

Gillihan, S., Cahill, S., & Foa, E. (2014). Psychological theories of PTSD. In M. J. Friedman, T. M. Keane, & P. A. Resick (eds.), *Handbook of PTSD: Science and Practice* (pp. 166–184). New York, NY: Guilford Press.

Gonçalves, R., Pedrozo, A. L., Coutinho, E. S. F., Figueira, I., & Ventura, P. (2012). Efficacy of virtual reality exposure therapy in the treatment of PTSD: A systematic review. *PloS ONE*, *7*(12), e48469.

Gray, R. M. & Bourke, F. (2015). Remediation of intrusive symptoms of PTSD in fewer than five sessions: A 30-person pre-pilot study of the RTM Protocol. *Journal of Military, Veteran and Family Health*, *1*(2), 13–20.

Grubaugh, A. L., Clapp, J. D., Frueh, B. C., Tuerk, P. W., Knapp, R. G., & Egede, L. E. (2016). Open trial of exposure therapy for PTSD among patients with severe and persistent mental illness. *Behaviour Research and Therapy*, *78*, 1–12.

Guina, J., Rossetter, S. R., DeRhodes, B. J., Nahhas, R. W., & Welton, R. S. (2015). Benzodiazepines for PTSD: A systematic review and meta-analysis. *Journal of Psychiatric Practice*, *21*(4), 281–303.

Gunter, R. W. & Bodner, G. E. (2009). EMDR works . . . but how? Recent progress in the search for treatment mechanisms. *Journal of EMDR Practice and Research*, *3*(3), 161–168.

Gutner, C. A., Suvak, M. K., Sloan, D. M., & Resick, P. A. (2016). Does timing matter? Examining the impact of session timing on outcome. *Journal of Consulting and Clinical Psychology*, *84*(12), 1108–1115.

Hamblen, J. L., Bernardy, N. C., Sherrieb, K., Norris, F. H., Cook, J. M., Louis, C. A., & Schnurr, P. P. (2015). VA PTSD clinic director perspectives: How readiness guides provision of evidence-based PTSD treatment. *Professional Psychology: Research and Practice*, *46*, 90–96.

Harvey, A. G., Bryant, R. A., & Tarrier, N. (2003). Cognitive behaviour therapy for posttraumatic stress disorder. *Clinical Psychology Review*, *23*(3), 501–522.

Hembree, E. A., Foa, E. B., Dorfan, N. M., Street, G. P., Kowalski, J., & Tu, X. (2003). Do patients drop out prematurely from exposure therapy for PTSD? *Journal of Traumatic Stress*, *16*(6), 555–562.

Hershenberg, R. & Goldfried, M. R. (2015). Implications of RDoC for the research and practice of psychotherapy. *Behavior Therapy*, *46*(2), 156–165.

Hollifield, M., Sinclair-Lian, N., Warner, T. D., & Hammerschlag, R. (2007). Acupuncture for posttraumatic stress disorder: A randomized controlled pilot trial. *Journal of Nervous and Mental Disease*, *195*(6), 504–513.

Hoskins, M., Pearce, J., Bethell, A., Dankova, L., Barbui, C., Tol, W. A., . . . Bisson, J. I. (2015). Pharmacotherapy for post-traumatic stress disorder: Systematic review and meta-analysis. *British Journal of Psychiatry*, *206*(2), 93–100.

Hunsley, J. & Mash, E. J. (2005). Introduction to the special section on developing guidelines for the evidence-based assessment (EBA) of adult disorders. *Psychological Assessment*, *17*(3), 251–255.

Jeffries, F. W. & Davis, P. (2013). What is the role of eye movements in eye movement desensitization and reprocessing (EMDR) for post-traumatic stress disorder (PTSD)? A review. *Behavioural and Cognitive Psychotherapy*, *41*(3), 290–300.

Johnson, D. R., Lahad, M., & Gray, A. (2009). Creative therapies for adults. In E. B. Foa, T. M. Keane, M. J. Friedman, & J. A. Cohen (eds.), *Effective Treatments for PTSD* (pp. 479–490). New York, NY: Guilford Press.

Jung, K. & Steil, R. (2013). A randomized controlled trial on cognitive restructuring and imagery modification to reduce the feeling of being contaminated in adult survivors of childhood sexual abuse suffering from posttraumatic stress disorder. *Psychotherapy and Psychosomatics*, *82*(4), 213–220.

Kabat-Zinn, J. (1990). *Full Catastrophe Living: Using the Wisdom of Your Body and Mind to Face Stress, Pain, and Illness*. New York, NY: Dell Publishing.

Kabat-Zinn, J., Lipworth, L., Burney, R., & Sellers, W. (1987). Four-year follow-up of a meditation-based program for the self-regulation of chronic pain: Treatment outcomes and compliance. *Clinical Journal of Pain*, *2*, 159–173.

Karatzias, T., Power, K., Brown, K., McGoldrick, T., Begum, M., Young, J., Loughran, P., Chouliara, Z., & Adam, S. (2011). A controlled comparison of the effectiveness and efficiency of two psychological therapies for posttraumatic stress disorder. *Journal of Nervous and Mental Disease*, *199*(6), 372–378.

Karlin, B. E. & Cross, G. (2014). From the laboratory to the therapy room: National dissemination and implementation of evidence-based psychotherapies in the US Department of Veterans Affairs Health Care System. *American Psychologist*, *69*(1), 19–33.

Karlin, B. E., Ruzek, J. I., Chard, K. M., Eftekhari, A., Monson, C. M., Hembree, E. A., . . . Foa, E. B. (2010). Dissemination of evidence-based psychological treatments for posttraumatic stress disorder in the Veterans Health Administration. *Journal of Traumatic Stress*, *23*(6), 663–673.

Kazdin, A. E. (2007). Mediators and mechanisms of change in psychotherapy research. *Annual Review of Clinical Psychology*, *3*, 1–27.

Kearns, M. C., Ressler, K. J., Zatzick, D., & Rothbaum, B. O. (2012). Early interventions for PTSD: A review. *Depression and Anxiety*, *29*(10), 833–842.

Kilmer, B., Eibner, C., Ringel, J. S., & Pacula, R. L. (2011). Invisible wounds, visible savings? Using microsimulation to estimate the costs and savings associated with providing evidence-based treatment for PTSD and depression to veterans of Operation Enduring Freedom and Operation Iraqi Freedom. *Psychological Trauma: Theory, Research, Practice, and Policy*, *3*(2), 201–211.

Kilpatrick, D. G., Resnick, H. S., Milanak, M. E., Miller, M. W., Keyes, K. M., & Friedman, M. J. (2013). National estimates of exposure to traumatic events and PTSD prevalence using *DSM-IV* and *DSM-5* criteria. *Journal of Traumatic Stress*, *26*(5), 537–547.

Kip, K. E., Rosenzweig, L., Hernandez, D. F., Shuman, A., Sullivan, K. L., Long, C. J., . . . Sahebzamani, F. M. (2013). Randomized controlled trial of accelerated resolution therapy (ART) for symptoms of combat-related post-traumatic stress disorder (PTSD). *Military Medicine*, *178*(12), 1298–1309.

Kliem, S. & Kröger, C. (2013). Prevention of chronic PTSD with early cognitive behavioral therapy: A meta-analysis using mixed-effects modeling. *Behaviour Research and Therapy*, *51*(11), 753–761.

Kuester, A., Niemeyer, H., & Knaevelsrud, C. (2016). Internet-based interventions for posttraumatic stress: A meta-analysis of randomized controlled trials. *Clinical Psychology Review*, *43*, 1–16.

Lang, A. J., Schnurr, P. P., Jain, S., He, F., Walser, R. D., Bolton, E., . . . Strauss, J. (2016). Randomized controlled trial of acceptance and commitment therapy for distress and impairment in OEF/OIF/OND veterans. *Psychological Trauma: Theory, Research, Practice and Policy*, Advance Online Publication.

Lee, D. J., Schnitzlein, C. W., Wolf, J. P., Vythilingam, M., Rasmusson, A. M., & Hoge, C. W. (2016). Psychotherapy versus pharmacotherapy for posttraumatic stress disorder: Systemic review and meta-analyses to determine first-line treatments. *Depression and Anxiety*, *33*, 792–806.

Maieritsch, K. P., Smith, T. L., Hessinger, J. D., Ahearn, E. P., Eickhoff, J. C., & Zhao, Q. (2016). Randomized controlled equivalence trial comparing videoconference and in person delivery of cognitive processing therapy for PTSD. *Journal of Telemedicine and Telecare*, *22*(4), 238–243.

Markowitz, J. C., Petkova, E., Biyanova, T., Ding, K., Suh, E. J., & Neria, Y. (2015). Exploring personality diagnosis stability following acute psychotherapy for chronic posttraumatic stress disorder. *Depression and Anxiety*, *32*(12), 919–926.

Marks, I., Lovell, K., Noshirvani, H., Livanou, M., & Thrasher, S. (1998). Treatment of posttraumatic stress disorder by exposure and/or cognitive restructuring: A controlled study. *Archives of General Psychiatry*, *55*(4), 317–325.

Meichenbaum, D. H. & Deffenbacher, J. L. (1988). Stress inoculation training. *Counseling Psychologist*, *16*(1), 69–90.

Mitchell, J. T. (1983). When disaster strikes: The critical incident stress debriefing process. *Journal of Emergency Medical Services*, *8*, 36–39.

Monson, C. M., Fredman, S. J., Macdonald, A., Pukay-Martin, N. D., Resick, P. A., & Schnurr, P. P. (2012). Effect of cognitive-behavioral couple therapy for PTSD: A randomized controlled trial. *JAMA*, *308*(7), 700–709.

Morland, L. A., Mackintosh, M. A., Rosen, C. S., Willis, E., Resick, P., Chard, K., & Frueh, B. C. (2015). Telemedicine versus in-person delivery of cognitive processing therapy for women with posttraumatic stress disorder: A randomized non-inferiority trial. *Depression and Anxiety*, *32*(11), 811–820.

Nixon, R. D. V., Best., T., Wilksch, S. R., & Angelakis, S. (2016). Cognitive processing therapy for the treatment of acute stress disorder following sexual assault: A randomised effectiveness study. *Behavior Change*, *33*(4), 232–250.

Norrholm, S. D., Glover, E. M., Stevens, J. S., Fani, N., Galatzer-Levy, I. R., Bradley, B., . . . Jovanovic, T. (2015). Fear load: The psychophysiological over-expression of fear as an intermediate phenotype associated with trauma reactions. *International Journal of Psychophysiology*, *98*(2), 270–275.

Norrholm, S. D., Jovanovic, T., Olin, I. W., Sands, L. A., Bradley, B., & Ressler, K. J. (2011). Fear extinction in traumatized civilians with posttraumatic stress disorder: Relation to symptom severity. *Biological Psychiatry*, *69*(6), 556–563.

Pickert, K. (2014). The mindful revolution. *New York Times*, 23, 40–49.

Polusny, M. A., Erbes, C. R., Thuras, P., Moran, A., Lamberty, G. J., Collins, R. C., . . . Lim, K. O. (2015). Mindfulness-based stress reduction for posttraumatic stress disorder among veterans: A randomized clinical trial. *JAMA*, *314*(5), 456–465.

Popiel, A., Zawadzki, B., Pragłowska, E., & Teichman, Y. (2015). Prolonged exposure, paroxetine and the combination in the treatment of PTSD following a motor vehicle accident. A randomized clinical trial – the "TRAKT" study. *Journal of Behavior Therapy and Experimental Psychiatry*, *48*, 17–26.

Powers, M. B., Halpern, J. M., Ferenschak, M. P., Gillihan, S. J., & Foa, E. B. (2010). A meta-analytic review of prolonged exposure for posttraumatic stress disorder. *Clinical Psychology Review*, *30*(6), 635–641.

Raghavan, R., Bright, C. L., & Shadoin, A. L. (2008). Toward a policy ecology of implementation of evidence-based practices in public mental health settings. *Implementation Science*, *3*(1), 26.

Rauch, S. A. M. & Foa, E. (2006). Emotional processing theory (EPT) and exposure therapy for PTSD. *Journal of Contemporary Psychotherapy*, *36*(2), 61.

Rauch, S. A. M. & Liberzon, I. (2016). Mechanisms of action in psychotherapy. In I. Liberzon & K. Ressler (eds.), *Neurobiology of PTSD: From Brain to Mind* (pp. 353–372). New York, NY: Oxford University Press.

Rauch, S. A. M., Post, L., Yasinski, C. W., Sherrill, A. M., Maples-Keller, J. L., ... Rothbaum, B. O. (2017, April). Healing the invisible wounds of war: Emory Healthcare Veterans Program intensive outpatient program for PTSD. In D. Yusko (Chair), *From the lab to the world: Is it possible to do prolonged exposure for PTSD in "real clinics?"* Symposium conducted at the annual conference for the Anxiety and Depression Association of American in San Francisco, CA.

Rauch, S. A. M. & Rothbaum, B. O. (2016). Innovations in exposure therapy for PTSD treatment. *Practice Innovations*, *1*(3), 189–196.

Resick, P. A., Galovski, T. E., Uhlmansiek, M. O. B., Scher, C. D., Clum, G. A., & Young-Xu, Y. (2008). A randomized clinical trial to dismantle components of cognitive processing therapy for posttraumatic stress disorder in female victims of interpersonal violence. *Journal of Consulting and Clinical Psychology*, *76*(2), 243–258.

Resick, P. A., Monson, C. M., & Chard, K. M. (2017). *Cognitive Processing Therapy for PTSD: A Comprehensive Manual*. New York, NY: Guilford Press.

Resick, P. A., Monson, C. M., Gutner, C. A., & Maslej, M. M. (2014). Psychosocial treatments for adults with PTSD. In M. J. Friedman, T. M. Keane, & P. A. Resick (eds.), *Handbook of PTSD: Science and Practice* (pp. 419–436). New York, NY: Guilford Press.

Resick, P. A., Wachen, J. S., Dondanville, K. A., Pruiksma, K. E., Yarvis, J. S., Peterson, A. L., ... STRONG STAR Consortium (2017). Effect of group vs individual cognitive processing therapy in active-duty military seeking treatment for posttraumatic stress disorder: A randomized clinical trial. *JAMA Psychiatry*, *74* (1), 28–36.

Resick, P. A., Wachen, J. S., Mintz, J., Young-McCaughan, S., Roache, J. D., Borah, A. M., ... Peterson, A. L. (2015). A randomized clinical trial of group cognitive processing therapy compared with group present-centered therapy for PTSD among active duty military personnel. *Journal of Consulting and Clinical Psychology*, *83*(6), 1058–1068.

Roberts, N. P., Roberts, P. A., Jones, N., & Bisson, J. I. (2015). Psychological interventions for post-traumatic stress disorder and comorbid substance use disorder: A systematic review and meta-analysis. *Clinical Psychology Review*, *38*, 25–38.

Rose, S. C., Bisson, J., Churchill, R., & Wessely, S. (2002). Psychological debriefing for preventing posttraumatic stress disorder (PTSD). *Cochrane Database of Systematic Reviews*, *2*, CD000560.

Rosen, C. S., Matthieu, M. M., Stirman, S. W., Cook, J. M., Landes, S., Bernardy, N. C., ... Hamblen, J. L. (2016). A review of studies on the system-wide implementation of evidence-based psychotherapies for posttraumatic stress disorder in the Veterans Health Administration. *Administration and Policy in Mental Health and Mental Health Services Research*, *43*(6), 957–977.

Rosenbaum, S., Vancampfort, D., Steel, Z., Newby, J., Ward, P. B., & Stubbs, B. (2015). Physical activity in the treatment of post-traumatic stress disorder: A systematic review and meta-analysis. *Psychiatry Research*, *230*(2), 130–136.

Rothbaum, B. O., Astin, M. C., & Marsteller, F. (2005). Prolonged exposure versus eye movement desensitization and reprocessing (EMDR) for PTSD rape victims. *Journal of Traumatic Stress*, *18*(6), 607–616.

Rothbaum, B. O., Cahill, S. P., Foa, E. B., Davidson, J. R., Compton, J., Connor, K. M., . . . Hahn, C. G. (2006). Augmentation of sertraline with prolonged exposure in the treatment of post-traumatic stress disorder. *Journal of Traumatic Stress*, *19*(5), 625–638.

Rothbaum, B. O., Foa, E. B., Riggs, D. S., Murdock, T., & Walsh, W. (1992). A prospective examination of posttraumatic stress disorder in rape victims. *Journal of Traumatic Stress*, *5*(3), 455–475.

Rothbaum, B. O., Hodges, L., Alarcon, R., Ready, D., Shahar, F., Graap, K., . . . Baltzell, D. (1999). Virtual reality exposure therapy for PTSD Vietnam veterans: A case study. *Journal of Traumatic Stress*, *12*(2), 263–271.

Rothbaum, B. O., Kearns, M. C., Price, M., Malcoun, E., Davis, M., Ressler, K. J., . . . Houry, D. (2012). Early intervention may prevent the development of posttraumatic stress disorder: A randomized pilot civilian study with modified prolonged exposure. *Biological Psychiatry*, *72*(11), 957–963.

Rothbaum, B. O., Price, M., Jovanovic, T., Norrholm, S. D., Gerardi, M., Dunlop, B., . . . Ressler, K. J. (2014). A randomized, double-blind evaluation of D-cycloserine or alprazolam combined with virtual reality exposure therapy for posttraumatic stress disorder in Iraq and Afghanistan War veterans. *American Journal of Psychiatry*, *171*(6), 640–648.

Ruzek, J. I., Eftekhari, A., Rosen, C. S., Crowley, J. J., Kuhn, E., Foa, E. B., . . . Karlin, B. E. (2016). Effects of a comprehensive training program on clinician beliefs about and intention to use prolonged exposure therapy for PTSD. *Psychological Trauma: Theory, Research, Practice, and Policy*, *8*(3), 348–355.

Ruzek, J. I., Rosen, R. C., Garvert, D. W., Smith, L. D., Sears, K. C., Marceau, L., . . . Stoddard, A. M. (2014). Online self-administered training of PTSD treatment providers in cognitive-behavioral intervention skills: Results of a randomized controlled trial. *Journal of Traumatic Stress*, *27*(6), 703–711.

Schmidt, U. & Vermetten, E. (2017). Integrating NIMH research domain criteria (RDoC) into PTSD research. In M. Geyer, B. Ellenbroek, & C. Marsden (eds.), *Current Topics in Behavioral Neuroscience* (pp. 1–23). Berlin: Springer.

Schneier, F. R., Neria, Y., Pavlicova, M., Hembree, E., Suh, E. J., Amsel, L., & Marshall, R. D. (2012). Combined prolonged exposure therapy and paroxetine for PTSD related to the World Trade Center attack: A randomized controlled trial. *American Journal of Psychiatry*, *169*(1), 80–88.

Shapiro, F. (1995). *Eye Movement Desensitization and Reprocessing: Basic Principles, Protocols, and Procedures*. New York, NY: Guilford Press.

Shiner, B., D'Avolio, L. W., Nguyen, T. M., Zayed, M. H., Young-Xu, Y., Desai, R. A., & Watts, B. V. (2013). Measuring use of evidence-based psychotherapy for posttraumatic stress disorder. *Administration and Policy in Mental Health and Mental Health Services Research*, *40*, 311–318.

Sholomskas, D. E., Syracuse-Siewert, G., Rounsaville, B. J., Ball, S. A., Nuro, K. F., & Carroll, K. M. (2005). We don't train in vain: A dissemination trial of three strategies of training clinicians in cognitive-behavioral therapy. *Journal of Consulting and Clinical Psychology*, *73*(1), 106–115.

Simiola, V., Neilson, E. C., Thompson, R., & Cook, J. M. (2015). Preferences for trauma treatment: A systematic review of the empirical literature. *Psychological Trauma: Theory, Research, Practice, and Policy, 7*(6), 516–524.

Simon, N. M., Connor, K. M., Lang, A. J., Rauch, S., Krulewicz, S., LeBeau, R. T., ... Pollack, M. H. (2008). Paroxetine CR augmentation for posttraumatic stress disorder refractory to prolonged exposure therapy. *Journal of Clinical Psychiatry, 69*(3), 400–405.

Sloan, D. M., Feinstein, B. A., Gallagher, M. W., Beck, J. G., & Keane, T. M. (2013). Efficacy of group treatment for posttraumatic stress disorder symptoms: A meta-analysis. *Psychological Trauma: Theory, Research, Practice, and Policy, 5*(2), 176–183.

Sloan, D. M., Marx, B. P., Bovin, M. J., Feinstein, B. A., & Gallagher, M. W. (2012). Written exposure as an intervention for PTSD: A randomized clinical trial with motor vehicle accident survivors. *Behaviour Research and Therapy, 50*(10), 627–635.

Smith, E. R., Porter, K. E., Messina, M. G., Beyer, J. A., Defever, M. E., Foa, E. B., & Rauch, S. A. M. (2015). Prolonged Exposure for PTSD in a Veteran group: A pilot effectiveness study. *Journal of Anxiety Disorders, 30*, 23–27.

Sobell, L. C. (1996). Bridging the gap between scientist and practitioners: The challenge before us. *Behaviour Therapy, 27*, 291–320.

Stenmark, H., Catani, C., Neuner, F., Elbert, T., & Holen, A. (2013). Treating PTSD in refugees and asylum seekers within the general health care system. A randomized controlled multicenter study. *Behavior Research and Therapy. 51*(10), 641–647.

Stirman, S. W., Gutner, C., Crits-Christoph, P., Edmunds, J., Evans, A. C., & Beidas, R. S. (2015). Relationships between clinician-level attributes and fidelity-consistent and fidelity-inconsistent modifications to an evidence-based psychotherapy. *Implementation Science, 10*(1), 115.

Stirman, S. W., Gutner, C. A., Langdon, K., & Graham, J. R. (2016). Bridging the gap between research and practice in mental health service settings: An overview of developments in implementation theory and research. *Behavior Therapy, 47*, 920–936.

Storch, E. A., Merlo, L. J., Lehmkuhl, H., Geffken, G. R., Jacob, M., Ricketts, E., ... Goodman, W. K. (2008). Cognitive-behavioral therapy for obsessive-compulsive disorder: A non-randomized comparison of intensive and weekly approaches. *Journal of Anxiety Disorders, 22*(7), 1146–1158.

Streeter, C. C., Gerbarg, P. L., Saper, R. B., Ciraulo, D. A., & Brown, R. P. (2012). Effects of yoga on the autonomic nervous system, gamma-aminobutyric-acid, and allostasis in epilepsy, depression, and post-traumatic stress disorder. *Medical Hypotheses, 78*(5), 571–579.

Suris, A., Link-Malcolm, J., Chard, K., Ahn, C., & North, C. (2013). A randomized clinical trial of cognitive processing therapy for veterans with PTSD related to military sexual trauma. *Journal of Traumatic Stress, 26*(1), 28–37.

Swift, J. K., Greenberg, R. P., Tompkins, K. A., & Parkin, S. R. (2017). Treatment refusal and premature termination in psychotherapy, pharmacotherapy, and their combination: A meta-analysis of head-to-head comparisons. *Psychotherapy, 54*, 47–57.

Taylor, S., Thordarson, D. S., Maxfield, L., Fedoroff, I. C., Lovell, K., & Ogrodniczuk, J. (2003). Comparative efficacy, speed, and adverse effects of three PTSD treatments: Exposure therapy, EMDR, and relaxation training. *Journal of Consulting and Clinical Psychology, 71*(2), 330–338.

van Minnen, A., Harned, M. S., Zoellner, L., & Mills, K. (2012). Examining potential contraindications for prolonged exposure therapy for PTSD. *European Journal of Psychotraumatology, 3*, 245–247. doi: 10.3402/ejpt.v3i0.18805

Wahbeh, H., Senders, A., Neuendorf, R., & Cayton, J. (2014). Complementary and alternative medicine for posttraumatic stress disorder symptoms: A systematic review. *Journal of Evidence-Based Complementary and Alternative Medicine, 19*(3), 161–175.

Watts, B. V., Schnurr, P. P., Mayo, L., Young-Xu, Y., Weeks, W. B., & Friedman, M. J. (2013). Meta-analysis of the efficacy of treatments for posttraumatic stress disorder. *Journal of Clinical Psychiatry, 74*(6), 541–550.

Watts, B. V., Shiner, B., Zubkoff, L., Carpenter-Song, E., Ronconi, J. M., & Coldwell, C. M. (2014). Implementation of evidence-based psychotherapies for posttraumatic stress disorder in VA specialty clinics. *Psychiatric Services, 65*, 648–653.

Webb, C. A., DeRubeis, R. J., & Barber, J. P. (2010). Therapist adherence/competence and treatment outcome. *Journal of Consulting and Clinical Psychology, 78*(2), 200–211.

Wells, S. Y., Lang, A. J., Schmalzl, L., Groessl, E. J., & Strauss, J. L. (2016). Yoga as an intervention for PTSD: A theoretical rationale and review of the literature. *Current Treatment Options in Psychiatry, 3*(1), 60–72.

Wolf, E. J., Lunney, C. A., & Schnurr, P. P. (2016). The influence of the dissociative subtype of posttraumatic stress disorder on treatment efficacy in female veterans and active duty service members. *Journal of Consulting and Clinical Psychology, 84*(1), 95–100.

Yehuda, R. & Hoge, C. W. (2016). The meaning of evidence-based treatments for veterans with posttraumatic stress disorder. *JAMA Psychiatry, 73*(5), 433–434.

Yuen, E. K., Gros, D. F., Price, M., Zeigler, S., Tuerk, P. W., Foa, E. B., & Acierno, R. (2015). Randomized controlled trial of home-based telehealth versus in-person prolonged exposure for combat-related PTSD in veterans: Preliminary results. *Journal of Clinical Psychology, 71*(6), 500–512.

Zambrano-Vazquez, L., Levy, H. C., Belleau, E. L., Dworkin, E. R., Howard, S. K., Pittenger, S. L., . . . Coffey, S. F. (2017). Using the research domain criteria framework to track domains of change in comorbid PTSD and SUD. *Psychological Trauma: Theory, Research, Practice and Policy*, Advance Online Publication.

Zandberg, L. J., Rosenfield, D., McLean, C. P., Powers, M. B., Asnaani, A., & Foa, E. B. (2016). Concurrent treatment of posttraumatic stress disorder and alcohol dependence: Predictors and moderators of outcome. *Journal of Consulting and Clinical Psychology, 84*(1), 43–56.

Zhang, Y., Bin, F. E. N. G., Xie, J. P., Xu, F. Z., & Jiong, C. H. E. N. (2011). Clinical study on treatment of the earthquake-caused post-traumatic stress disorder by cognitive-behavior therapy and acupoint stimulation. *Journal of Traditional Chinese Medicine, 31*(1), 60–63.

Zoellner, L. A. & Foa, E. B. (2016). Applying Research Domain Criteria (RDoC) to the study of fear and anxiety: A critical comment. *Psychophysiology, 53*(3), 332–335.

Zoellner, L. A., Pruitt, L. D., Farach, F. J., & Jun, J. J. (2014). Understanding heterogeneity in PTSD: Fear, dysphoria, and distress. *Depression and Anxiety, 31*(2), 97–106.

Zohar, J., Yahalom, H., Kozlovsky, N., Cwikel-Hamzany, S., Matar, M. A., Kaplan, Z., . . . Cohen, H. (2011). High dose hydrocortisone immediately after trauma may alter the trajectory of PTSD: Interplay between clinical and animal studies. *European Neuropsychopharmacology, 21*(11), 796–809.

Index